THE ENCYCLOPEDIA OF AMERICAN TELEVISION

BROADCAST PROGRAMMING POST WORLD WAR II TO 2000

THE ENCYCLOPEDIA OF AMERICAN TELEVISION

BROADCAST PROGRAMMING
POST WORLD WAR II TO 2000

RON LACKMANN

☑®
Facts On File, Inc.

The Encyclopedia of American Television

Copyright © 2003 by Ron Lackmann

Facts On File, Inc.
132 West 31st Street
New York NY 10001

Library of Congress Cataloging-in-Publication Data
Lackmann, Ronald W.
The encyclopedia of American television Broadcast Programming
Post World War II to 2000 / Ron Lackmann.
p. cm.
Includes bibliographical references and index.
ISBN 0-8160-4554-2 (alk. paper)
1. Television broadcasting—United States—Encyclopedias. I. Title: Encyclopedia of
American television Broadcast Programming World War II to 2000. II. Title.
PN1992.18 .L33 2001
791.45′0973′03—dc21
2001056856

Facts On File books are available at special discounts when purchased in bulk quantities for
businesses, associations, institutions, sales promotions. Please call our Special Sales
Department in New York at (212) 967-8800 or (800) 322-8755.

You can find Facts On File on the World Wide Web at http://www.factsonfile.com

Text design by Joan M. Toro
Cover design by Nora Wertz

Printed in the United States of America

VB Hermitage 10 9 8 7 6 5 4 3 2

This book is printed on acid-free paper.

*For the television viewers of the future . . .
especially Jennifer, Nichole, and Michael Pereira,
Elizabeth English, and Étoile Gelman*

CONTENTS

INTRODUCTION

It was the spring of 1939, and the World's Fair had just opened at Flushing Meadows, Queens, a borough of New York City. I was just five years old, and we lived in Woodhaven, not very far from Flushing Meadows, which made for many family outings to that magical site. And it was a world of wonder for all of us: My parents were dazzled by Billy Rose's Aquacade, featuring Eleanor Holm, a pretty, young 1932 Olympics swimming champion; my sister, Joyce, could have watched a Sonja Henie marionette perform to "The Skater's Waltz" forever; and I was fascinated by my tour of the Midget Village, a place where no full-sized grownups were admitted. Only children could enter, and in charge were the Singer Midgets, the tiniest adults I'd ever seen—some even smaller than I was. They were the "little people," some of whom had appeared in the film *The Wizard of Oz,* and the way they exercised the same authority as full-grown adults both amazed and terrified me. But the thing that excited my interest the most among that myriad of marvels was the exhibition in the Radio Corporation of America (RCA) building. There was this large box, which for some reason reminded me of a big radio, except that it had this small screen that showed pictures, in black and white, that exactly coordinated with the words that were being broadcast. A radio with pictures? Astounding!

Well, astounding to me. At that point, radio was probably the most important diversion of my young life, my favorite toy, and I couldn't believe it would one day come complete with pictures. But all the grownups in my life seemed sure that this was the future of home entertainment. Everything we heard on radio, they predicated, would soon be seen as well on this newfangled gadget they were calling television. As it turned out, "soon" would be interrupted for some time by World War II, and the notion of radio with pictures became a kind of back-burner idea.

True, there was some prewar activity. In 1940, there were approximately 10,000 television receivers in the New York metropolitan area, with programming emanating from WNBT, the first TV station to offer any kind of information or entertainment. WNBT was part of RCA, and many of those early sets belonged to the company's employees. Programs were not very varied, consisting mostly of newsreels, travelogues, animated cartoons, and some variety and puppet shows, and the offerings were somewhat sporadic. There was no all-day (or all-night) programming as there is today. For many hours there was nothing on that small screen. The only hints that television might turn out to be different from radio in those earliest years were cooking-demonstration and dance-lesson shows. But if 10,000 sets sounds like a large number, neither I nor anyone I knew had a television set, nor did anyone talk much about it after 1941.

It was after the war's end, in 1945, that television sets were produced and sold to the public at large. The first set to appear in my neighborhood was a DuMont, with a tiny, postcard-size screen. The man who owned it had signed up for one during the war and was among the first hundred to receive one that year. The programming was not so different from those early offerings—not very varied, frequently primitive, and with many hours between offerings. All the same, we were fascinated by it all, and would pile into the neighbor's house on any pretext, but mostly when there was something special showing. Once, I remember, one of the few stations operating decided to broadcast the Barnum and Bailey Circus that had just come to New York for its annual show. All the kids in the neighborhood pushed their way into that house. Then there was a championship boxing match—Joe Louis versus I can't remember who. But I do remember that so many people showed up to see it that the folks who owned the TV, not to mention the house, were practically shoved out onto the street.

In the few short years that followed those early offerings, TV made remarkable advances. Four networks ruled the airwaves: NBC, CBS, ABC, and DuMont, which went out of business by the mid-1950s, unable to compete with the big three. As sets became more available, families began figuring out ways to get one of their own. It took my mother and father five years after World War II's end to save enough money to purchase one. The set was definitely a formidable piece of furniture—a large cabinet with a smallish TV screen—that occupied a prominent place in the living room. There we would spend hours watching anything on the screen, including preprogram test patterns that appeared when there was nothing on, which, in the early 1950s, was a good part of the day. We even watched people talking about subjects that would have totally bored us on radio. However, more and more people bought television sets, creating a huge audience.

As those audiences grew, so did programming. Variety shows hosted by big stars featured guests who were often more celebrated than the stars themselves. Drama anthologies (self-contained plays) often introduced new actors and playwrights whose fame would spread beyond the small screen. Philco-Goodyear Television Playhouse, for example, presented a play called *Marty,* which was soon turned into an Academy Award–winning film that made its author, Paddy Chayefsky, a literary star. Actors such as Paul Newman and Charlton Heston appeared in our living rooms in both original and adapted-for-TV dramas long before they became movie superstars. Established superstars in every area of life began appearing in our living rooms in burgeoning variety—classical and popular music shows, situation comedies, series adventures of every description: hospital, detective, western, you name it. Some shows seemed transferred straight from their radio formats—with visuals, of course. "So that's what they look like," we marveled as we saw the faces behind the familiar voices for the first time. Indeed, programming expanded to fill not just the day, but most of the night. Late-night showings of old movies played opposite a combination of comedy/talk/variety programming that extended the TV schedule into the wee hours of the morning.

By decade's end, TV executives and purveyors of goods to sell realized that they had never seen an audience in such numbers before. One fairly successful show could generate millions of viewers at any given moment—a veritable miracle for advertisers. So powerful had this relatively new medium become that it threatened to put all other advertising venues out of business. It is credited with putting two very popular weekly publications—*Life* and *Look*—out of business. Indeed, these two magazines were considered mainstays by the public, with very large, loyal circulations. However, with their many color illustrations, they were expensive to produce, and only hefty advertising revenues could make the cover price low enough for the average reader. With more and more ad-

vertisers opting for TV, the two magazines gave up. (*Life* later came back by doing periodic special editions.)

At this point, it was pretty much feared that this ever-growing monster would devour all other forms of communication. Movies were failing at the box office, and it seemed obvious that TV was replacing radio as America's (and not too much later, the world's) favorite home entertainment and source of information. Both media survived by ultimately turning into something else or doing things TV couldn't do except at great cost. Television, with its voracious appetite and hours to fill, had to produce programs quickly, without compromising profits. Films could take their time and cover subjects still taboo on the small screen, with better production values and more sophistication. What's more, they could sell rights to show some of those films on television at a later date. Radio turned to nonvisual offerings—music stations, all-news networks, the antics of screwy disk and shock jocks, personal advice from pop psychologists, spiritual advice from religious leaders, and commentaries on politics, current events, and the human condition. Successful magazines did likewise, convincing advertisers that they each had a specific audience made up of people who actually bought specific products.

None of this, of course, detracted from television in any way. There was always something new it had to contribute. In the 1960s, we saw not a photograph of an assassination, but the act itself in motion. We saw a man not just land on the moon, but walk step-by-step on its surface. The horrors of war appeared in full motion (TV replaced newsreels in theaters forever, and if you want to see one of these leftovers from another age, the only place might be on—you guessed it—television) and changed the way we thought about the world. Our lives were informed as never before by this medium—sometimes for good and sometimes for ill.

In the 61 years from the time my parents took us to see the first television sets at the 1939 New York World's Fair until the millennium, it would be not quite right to say the medium never faltered. Some reports told us fewer and fewer people were watching. But television, taking its cue from the media that survived, continued to change. Even before the millennium, both programming and broadcasting stations had become numerous and diverse. Cable stations have become firmly established, and even today give the big networks (CBS, NBC, ABC, and relative newcomer Fox) a lot more than a run for their money. All told, cable watchers outnumber audiences of established networks.

Television may have more impact on world culture—at least free-world culture—than any other medium in history for disseminating information and entertainment, and shaping opinion. Revolutions may have declared all men equal, but television allows them all—country bumpkins and city slickers, rich and poor, literate and illiterate, smart and dumb, citizens natural and naturalized, people of various color and creeds,—to see the same things at the same time. No longer do city folk get to see the latest news before country people; no longer do the literate get to see the news before the illiterate. Drama, no matter how high- or low-brow, is available to all, and we all laugh together at whatever seems funny. Some people complain that it homogenizes us, and to the lowest common denominator, while others think it closes some of the gaps among people, putting all of us simultaneously in touch with the world at large, eradicating the differences that separate us from one another. But for all its detractors (and there are many), and all its watchers (there are vastly more), television has dominated our home lives for the entire second half of the 20th century. Perhaps only radio comes close as an instant distributor of ideas, information, and entertainment.

As mentioned earlier, radio was one of the biggest and most important influences of my childhood. I never forgot it, and I wanted to share its importance and those wonderful memories with those who also remembered and those who'd missed out on the magic that was radio way back when. That is how I came to write *The Encyclopedia of American Radio,* published by Facts On File. Upon completion of that undertaking, it occurred to me that a similar volume, describing the history of television in the 20th century might also be in order for those who want to remember, those much younger who want to know what they missed, and those who want to analyze where in our daily lives we went wrong or right—in short, students of popular culture.

Once I started on this project, however, I began to realize the vast scope of the project. While radio had dominated the world and domestic scene for some 25 years, television has been around for more than half a century and still counting. In addition, much more historical information is available about TV than there had ever been about radio. It seemed an unimportant popular diversion, its offerings one-time-only, throwaway stuff. Apparently, the broadcasting powers-that-be realized their mistake as interest in radio grew, and were determined not to do the same with TV. With so much information available, it becomes necessary to manage the facts—to determine what's most important to readers—to define what needs to be included in the book and where less consequential knowledge can be found should someone absolutely have to know it. In other words . . .

HOW TO USE THIS BOOK

Criteria for Inclusion

The cut-off date for material that is included in this book is the end of the year 2000. The programs and stars that entered the limelight on network television after 2000 will have to earn their own publication. However, when appropriate, current information has been provided for active series and programs canceled in 2001 or 2002.

The reader will note that programs produced for cable television networks are not to be found in this book. Such popular shows as *The Sopranos, Sex and the City, South Park,* and *Beavis and Butt-head,* have not, therefore, been included. The number of cable networks and

the multitude of programs they offer would have made their inclusion impractical in a one-volume encyclopedia. Only programs originally produced by or for the national broadcast TV networks (CBS, NBC, ABC, Fox, WB) and syndicated shows that were seen on these networks between 1947 and 2000 have been included in this volume.

Series must have lasted at least one season (that's generally 26 episodes, plus reruns, extending to a full year, by TV standards) to be included. If by some remote chance your favorite show was *Platypus Man* (on air for five months) or *Planet of the Apes* (air life four months), you won't find them here. (I will tell you later where you can find them, however.) There are, of course, certain TV events so important, whether they were a particularly significant episode of a successful or failed series, or an individual offering, they appear in this book. The miniseries *Roots,* for example, or such individual specials as *Carol Burnett and Julie Andrews at Carnegie Hall* and *Death of a Salesman* with Dustin Hoffman, are included. Generally, popularity with the public, or a unique and/or significant contribution to society are grounds for inclusion, such as the downfall of Senator Joseph McCarthy in the 1950s.

Personalities selected for inclusion were determined not only by the popularity of their shows, but also by nationally recognized awards received, interest given them by books, fan magazines, popularity polls, and again, by any contribution to or impact on society (think Leonard Bernstein). Internet surveys, indicating what people considered most memorable about their TV experiences, also entered into compiling the list.

Prime Sources of Information

Much of the information in this book came primarily from three sources: the A. C. Nielsen Company (now Nielsen Media Research) survey of top-rated shows, the National Academy of Television Arts and Sciences annual Emmy Awards, and such periodicals as *TV Guide* and *Radio/TV Mirror,* publications concerned with the medium and careful to document whatever is happening. Other books on aspects of TV were also endlessly helpful and are included in the bibliography. In one of those magazines or books I discovered *Platypus Man,* among other odd facts and minutiae relating to this subject, all too numerous to include in this volume, but available to you via the same sources.

Order of Appearance

All entries are listed alphabetically, using a word-by-word system. For example, *The Bionic Woman* (listed *Bionic Woman, The*) would come before David Birney (listed Birney, David). As indicated, articles such as *The* and *A* follow the significant words in the title.

Cross References

The last names of personalities who have separate entries in this book, apart from the shows in which they appeared, will always be set in small capitals, simply to let you know that there is more information about them elsewhere in this book. James GARNER's last name will appear this way in, for instance, the *Maverick* or *Rockford Files* entries because he has an entry of his own. *MAVERICK* and *THE ROCKFORD FILES*, on the other hand, will also be appear like this because information about them appears in Garner's entry as well as in their own.

Airtimes

Most airtimes are based on Eastern Standard Time, obtained primarily from East Coast magazines and newspapers.

Dates (Birth and Death)

Sources stating either birth or death dates of performers are not always accurate, and tend to vary, sometimes because actors tend to lie about their age, making themselves younger, and sometimes, sadly, a star falls off into obscurity and nobody is quite aware of when he or she died. I tried to go with the most reliable sources, someone closest to the subject, or chose the earliest birthdate, since the desire to be "younger" seemed fairly universal. Dates in genuine doubt are preceded by the letter "c" for "circa." An asterisk indicates no dates could be found for either birth, death, or appearance on air. A "D" indicates a personality has definitely died, but exactly when is unknown.

Show Titles

Show titles often changed as some programs' popularity increased. For instance, *You'll Never Get Rich,* starring Phil Silvers, ultimately became *The Phil Silvers Show* as the star's popularity soared even beyond the limits of the program. In listing such a program, I chose the title that lasted longest and for which it was best known. My judgment was based on how viewers best remembered said shows, and in some cases what fan magazines called them.

Names of Performers

Performers are listed by their professional names, unless their birth names are the same as the names by which we know them. If birth names differ, they appear in parentheses immediately following the professional name, e.g., Rock Hudson (Roy Harold Scherer, Jr.).

ACKNOWLEDGMENTS

A book as comprehensive as *The Encyclopedia of 20th-Century American Television* cannot be written without extensive assistance and support. I would especially like to thank the Columbia Broadcasting System, the National Broadcasting Company, the American Broadcasting Company, the Public Broadcasting System, Home Box Office, the Sesame Workshop (formerly the Children's Workshop), Jo Laverde of Nielsen Media Research, Howard Mandelbaum of Photofest, the Fox Television Network, the American Academy of Television Arts and Sciences, and the Library of Congress, all generous fonts of knowledge. Many collectors and friends also helped in the preparation of this book, and I would like to thank David Davies, Barbara Gelman, Cassandra Danz, Jay Hickerson, and James English for their assistance, support, and encouragement.

ENTRIES
A TO Z

ABBOTT, BUD (WILLIAM ALEXANDER ABBOTT 1895–1974)

Stage, screen, radio, and television comedian Bud Abbott, of the Abbott and COSTELLO comedy team, was born in Asbury Park, New Jersey. Abbott dropped out of school in 1909 when he was 13 years old and got odd jobs touring with various carnivals. Abbott had always been good with figures and found employment as a treasurer and manager at various theaters around the country. Eventually he began to work as a straight man for such popular vaudeville comedians as Harry Evanson and Harry Steepe. In 1931, Abbott filled in as straight man with a comic named Lou Costello, while he was working as a cashier at a theater in Brooklyn, New York. The two men formed an immediate bond and thereafter worked together as a comedy team, with Lou as the comic and Bud as the straight man, in various burlesque and vaudeville theaters throughout the United States. The team's big break came when they were discovered by popular radio singer KATE SMITH, who gave the team their first national exposure on her weekly variety show. The team was an instant success and soon earned their own radio show and starring roles in films such as *One Night in the Tropics* (1940), *Buck Privates* (1941) and *Abbott and Costello in the Navy* (1942). The last two films costarred the popular Andrews Sisters and made them internationally known. The films *Abbott and Costello Meet Frankenstein* (1948) and *Abbott and Costello Meet Captain Kidd* (1952), and others produced at the Universal Studios in Hollywood, followed and were very successful at the box office. Abbott and Costello made their television debut in 1950 on *The COLGATE COMEDY HOUR* variety program, which they continued to host from 1951 until 1954. In 1952, the team also became the stars of one of the first situation comedy series presented on television, *The ABBOTT AND COSTELLO SHOW*. By 1957, the team had decided to go their separate ways. For a while, Abbott attempted to recapture his popularity by forming a partnership with comedian Candy Candido, but the public wanted only Abbott with Costello and the new team failed to attract an audience. In 1966, Abbott provided his own voice for a television cartoon series, *The Abbott and Costello Show*. Bud Abbott died in relative obscurity in 1974, even though he had been one of show business's most familiar and popular performers.

ABBOTT AND COSTELLO SHOW, THE

| 1952–1953 | Syndicated series | Various times and stations |

Stage and screen comedians Bud ABBOTT and Lou COSTELLO brought their routines to television in a half-hour situation comedy series that was first released in fall 1952 and has remained on the air for over 50 years in constant reruns, even though though only 52 episodes were ever produced. Abbott and Costello were among the first big-name Hollywood stars to make the foray into television at a time when most performers believed that appearing on television meant an actor's career must be either just starting or beginning to decline. *The Abbott and Costello Show*, which was produced by Alex Gottlieb and Pat Costello (Lou's brother), revived many of the comedy team's most successful skits, such as the celebrated "Who's on First" baseball and "Moving Candle" routines, that had made them famous on radio and in films. Costarring with Abbott and Costello on the show was blond screen beauty Hillary Brooke, who played herself. Hillary's sophisticated demeanor and classy English accent made her a perfect foil for the team's zany, low-comic style. Also appearing as regulars on the show were the tall, full-figured actress Joan

Bud Abbott and Lou Costello (Author's collection)

Shawlee, the short, bald comedian Bobby Barber, Joe Kirk (as Mr. Bacciagalupe), Gordon Jones (as Mike the cop), Joe Besser (as Stinky), and comedians Sid Fields and Milt Bronson. Many of these regulars left the show after the 26th episode when *The Abbott and Costello Show* began to film more organized, better constructed situation comedies, after exhausting most of their usual vaudeville sketch material. In 1967, an animated cartoon version of *The Abbott and Costello Show* appeared on television, with Abbott providing his own voice. Unfortunately, Costello had passed away seven years before the cartoon series was released.

ABC AFTER SCHOOL/WEEKEND SPECIALS

1972–   ABC   Various times

This irregularly scheduled series of 60-minute plays, films, and documentaries is produced by ABC for younger viewers in the television audience. It centers on such subjects as race relations, child abuse, drugs, violence in schools, loss of a loved one, school bullies, academic problems, and sex, and usually features young actors as central characters. Among the various shows seen on this series over the years were *Me and Dad's New Wife,* with Kristy McNichol; *The Secret Life of T. K. Dearing,* with Jodie Foster; *Mighty Moose and the Quarterback Kid,* with Brandon Cruz; "Stoned," with Scott Baio; *Cyrano,* an ani-

mated cartoon with the voice of José Ferrer as Cyrano; *Santiago, America,* with Ruben Figueroa; *The Woman Who Willed a Miracle,* with Cloris Leachman; *Just a Regular Kid: An AIDS Story,* with Christian Hoff; *All That Glitters,* with Marc Price; *It's Only Rock and Roll,* with Carole King and Davy Jones; *Shades of a Single Protein: A Look at Race,* narrated by Oprah Winfrey; *Bonnie Raitt Has Something to Talk About,* an interview with singer Bonnie Raitt by Whoopi Goldberg, and many other outstanding presentations.

ACADEMY AWARDS CEREMONIES ON TELEVISION

Each year, one of television's most anticipated special events is the telecast of the annual Academy Awards ceremonies, presented in March. The "Oscars," as the awards are commonly called, are statuettes awarded to nominees in such categories as film acting, directing, writing, cinematography, costume and set design, screen writing, etc. Members of the Academy of Motion Picture Arts and Sciences present approximately two dozen awards at these ceremonies, including the Best Film of the Year Award. The winners are chosen by secret ballots cast by members of the Academy (actors vote for actors, directors for directors, etc., and all vote for the "Best Film of the Year"). The first Academy Awards ceremony took place in 1929 and the Best Film Award went to *Wings.* The first televised Academy Award show, however, did not take place until 1952. For years, the Academy had turned down requests from the networks to televise the annual Academy Awards ceremony, which had been heard on radio believing it would only help the competition (TV), by encouraging people to stay away from theaters showing films and instead to stay home to watch TV. Shortly before the 1952 25th annual award show, four of the major studios (Warner Brothers, Republic, Columbia, and Universal-International), which had already begun investing heavily in television production, refused to come up with their share of the expenses for the extravaganza. NBC–RCA quickly responded by offering the Academy $100,000 to make up for the lost revenue and won the right to broadcast the ceremonies on both radio and television. The first televised Academy Awards ceremony was hosted by actor/comedian Bob HOPE, who, for many years before on radio and many years after on TV, repeated his Oscar-hosting chores. The 1952 television show had both West and East Coast hookups, since many of the nominees were in New York, not in Hollywood. The East Coast proceedings were hosted by Conrad Nagel. By 1955, television had become so firmly established that the Academy had begun to nominate plays and performers that had first attracted the public's attention on TV. Ernest BORGNINE won an Oscar in 1955 as Best Actor for his performance in *Marty,* which had first been seen as a teleplay on *The PHILCO–GOODYEAR TELEVISION PLAYHOUSE* dramatic anthology series several years earlier. Also nominated for a Best Actor Award that year was James Dean for his work in *East of Eden.* Dean had begun his career, and first became noticed, as a TV actor. Over the years, in addition to Bob

Hope, who holds the record as the Academy Awards ceremonies' most frequent MC, the show has also been hosted by such popular performers as Richard Pryor, Billy Crystal, Whoopi Goldberg, and David Letterman, among others. Memorable televised incidents that have taken place during the live ceremonies have been such firsts as a naked man running across the stage, or "streaking," upstaging presenter David Niven during the 1973 live ceremony; the refusal of the Best Actor Award for his work in *The Godfather* by actor Marlon Brando, who had a Native American friend, Sacheen Littlefeather (actress Maria Cruz), announce his decision not to accept the award because he said he disapproved of the way the film industry depicted Native Americans in motion pictures and on television; and the absence of Best Actor Award nominee George C. Scott at the 1970 ceremonies, because Scott had declined the nomination, saying he thought awards were meaningless since no performance or accomplishment could be judged "better" than any other nominee, unless all things were equal. The Academy decided to give the Best Actor Award to Mr. Scott anyway, in spite of his protests.

Each year, the number of people who watch the annual Academy Awards ceremony on television steadily increases. It is estimated that more than 1 billion people worldwide watched the ceremonies on television in March 2001. The diverse motion pictures, set all over the world, that won Best Film awards in the 1980s and 1990s, when the number of viewers increased most dramatically, included: *Ordinary People* (1980), which was set in the United States, *Chariots of Fire* (1981), set in England, *Gandhi* (1982), set in India, *Terms of Endearment* (1983), set in the United States, *Amadeus* (1984), set in Austria and Germany, *Out of Africa* (1985), set in Kenya, *Platoon* (1986), set in Vietnam, *The Last Emperor* (1987), set in China, *Rain Man* (1988), set in the United States, *Driving Miss Daisy* (1989), set in Atlanta, Georgia, *Dances with Wolves* (1990), set in the developing American West, *The Silence of the Lambs* (1991), set in the United States, *Unforgiven* (1992) set in the 19th century American West, *Schindler's List* (1993), set in Poland during World War II, *Braveheart* (1995), set in 18th century Scotland, *The English Patient* (1996), mainly set in Africa, *Titanic* (1997), set on a transatlantic ocean liner at the beginning of the 20th century, *Shakespeare in Love* (1998), set in Elizabethan England, and *American Beauty* (1999), set in contemporary America. In 2000, the film *Gladiator* and its star, Russell Crowe, won Academy Awards, and Julia Roberts won the Best Actress award for her work in *Erin Brockovich*. *Gladiator*, set in ancient Rome, and *Erin Brockovich*, set in California, were more reminiscent of films that won Oscars in the years prior to 1980.

ADAM-12

Sept. 1968–Sept. 1969	NBC	Sat. 7:30–8 P.M.	
Sept. 1969–Jan. 1971	NBC	Sat. 8:30–9 P.M.	
Jan. 1971–Sept. 1971	NBC	Thurs. 9:30–10 P.M.	
Sept. 1971–Jan. 1974	NBC	Wed. 8–8:30 P.M.	
Jan. 1974–Aug. 1975	NBC	Tues. 8–8:30 P.M.	

For three years, from 1970 to 1973, this police/crime drama series was among the top-20 rated shows on television, according to A. C. Nielsen Company audience polls. The series, which was created by DRAGNET star and producer/director Jack WEBB, was produced by Tom Williams. It starred Martin Milner and Kent McCord as Los Angeles police officers Pete Malloy and Jim Reed, who patrolled various neighborhoods in L.A. in their police car, depending heavily upon radio communications to track down the bad guys (thus the title, *Adam-12* which was a radio identification code). On each telecast, the team responded to several calls during the one hour the show was aired, and there were several, rather than just one, storylines each week. William Boyett played the team's commanding officer, Sgt. MacDonald, and Gary Crosby (singer/actor Bing CROSBY's eldest son) was featured as Officer Wells. Fred Stromsoe played Officer Woods. In 1989, a syndicated version of the series called *The New Adam-12*, which starred Pete Parros and Ethan Wayne, was aired, but it did not prove as popular as the original series, and after 52 episodes it departed the airwaves.

ADAMS, DON (DONALD JAMES YARMY 1923–)

A native of New York City, actor/comedian Don Adams was the son of Irish–Hungarian immigrant parents. Adams, who is perhaps best known as agent Maxwell Smart on the GET SMART TV series (1965–1970), served in the U.S. Marines in World War II and contracted malaria during the Guadalcanal campaign. After his discharge from the marines, Adams, who was always making people laugh with his amusing antics, decided to become a stand-up comic. Adams's TV career began when he appeared on the TED MACK ORIGINAL AMATEUR HOUR. He guest-starred on the THE PERRY COMO SHOW (1948), *The Bill Dana Show* (1963), and was the voice of Tennessee Tuxedo on the *Tennessee Tuxedo and His Tales* TV cartoon series in 1963, before getting the role of Smart on the *Get Smart* series (1965–1970) and becoming a major television star. By the time *Get Smart* ended production, Adams had won three Emmy Awards for playing Maxwell Smart. He then provided the voice of *Underdog* (1964) and appeared on *The Partners* (1971), *Don Adams' Screen Test* (1974), *Check It Out* (1985), and *Pepper Ann* (1997) series, none of which became as popular as the *Get Smart* program. Adams did make memorable guest appearances, however, on such TV series as The ANDY WILLIAMS SHOW, *Wait Till Your Father Gets Home*, LOVE BOAT, and EMPTY NEST, and also appeared in such films as *The Nude Bomb* in 1980 (as Maxwell Smart) and *Back to the Beach* in 1987. He provided the voice of Inspector Gadget for the 1983 cartoon series. In 1997, he voiced Gadget Boy in *Gadget Boy's Adventures in History*, another cartoon series, and in 1999, he was the voice of "Brain" in the film *Inspector Gadget*.

The Addams Family: standing are Ted Cassidy and John Astin, seated are Lisa Loring, Carolyn Jones, and Ken Weatherwax. (Author's collection)

ADDAMS FAMILY, THE

Sept. 1964–Sept. 1966   ABC   Fri. 8:30–9 P.M.

Popular cartoons drawn by artist Charles Addams that were regularly featured in *The New Yorker* magazine during the 1940s and 50s became the unlikely subject of a popular TV series in the mid-1960s. Few people believed that a situation comedy series based on the bizarre Addams' cartoons could possibly be a success on television, even though Addams's cartoons were very funny. The characters who appeared in these cartoons were, after all, a family of ghouls. They lived in a big, Gothic, spooky mansion, complete with cobwebs, grotesque Victorian furniture, and lots of ghostly atmosphere. This family was totally unlike any other television family of the time, such as the Andersons of FATHER KNOWS BEST and the Nelsons of *The* ADVENTURES OF OZZIE AND HARRIET. The Addams family (named after the artist) featured the lovely, but somber, Morticia Addams, played by veteran film actress Carolyn Jones, who always dressed in a long black gown and had hair as long and black as her dress, and her husband, Gomez Addams, played by John Astin, who was good-natured, but had strange, sinister-looking eyes and a leering countenance. Morticia and Gomez had two children, Pugsley, played by Ken Weatherwax, a pudgy boy with a dim look on his face, and Tuesday, played by Lisa Loring, a weird young girl. Also residing in the Addams's

home were Uncle Fester Frump, played by Jackie Coogan, a bald hunchback; Grandmama Addams, played by Blossom Rock, who resembled a witch; Cousin Itt, a moving mound of hair; and the family servant, Lurch, played by Ted Cassidy, a very tall, Frankenstein-like character who always responded to the family's call with the question, "You rang?" The Addamses had a pet, a dismembered hand that was kept in a box. The family called it "Thing." People who visited the Addams's house were always terrified by what they saw, but viewers found the show highly amusing and kept it on the air for two years. An animated version of the series appeared in 1973, and this TV show was a Saturday morning children's favorite for two years. Another cartoon series resurfaced in 1992 and was on the air for five years. Two of the actors from the original series, Jackie Coogan and Ted Cassidy, provided their voices for the cartoon series. There were two successful feature films released in the 1990s based on the series and starring Anjelica Huston and Raul Julia as Morticia and Gomez Addams.

ADVENTURES IN PARADISE

Oct. 1959–Sept. 1961   ABC   Mon. 9:30–10:30 P.M.
Oct. 1961–Apr. 1961   ABC   Sun. 10–11 P.M.

From the moment tall, dark, and handsome actor Gardner McKay appeared on television in this weekly adventure series, females all over the United States knew that they were going to enjoy just looking at him, as much as their husbands and boyfriends would enjoy the show's fast-paced action. McKay played Adam Troy, the captain of a freelance schooner that sailed the South Pacific seeking adventure, cargo, passengers, and a bit of romance. Troy was a Korean War veteran who had decided to buy a schooner when the war ended. He named his boat the *Tiki*. Troy sailed between Hong Kong and the South Sea Islands. Initially, Troy's partner was a Chinese–American named Oliver Lee, played by Weaver Levy. In 1960, Troy hired a first mate named Clay Baker, played by James Holden, and the following year, he hired a burly sailor named Chris Parker, played by Guy Stockwell. Also appearing on the series at various times were Henry Slate as Bulldog Lovey, Linda Lawson as Renee, and Sondi Sodsai as Sondi. The series was created by novelist James A. Michener. When *Adventures in Paradise* was canceled after two years on the air, McKay decided to retire from acting and concentrate on becoming a writer, following in the footsteps of his idol, James A. Michener.

ADVENTURES OF OZZIE AND HARRIET, THE

Oct. 1952–June 1956   ABC   Fri. 8–8:30 P.M.
Oct. 1956–Sept. 1958   ABC   Wed. 9–9:30 P.M.
Sept. 1958–Sept. 1961   ABC   Wed. 8:30–9 P.M.
Sept. 1961–Sept. 1963   ABC   Thurs. 7–8 P.M.
Sept. 1963–Jan. 1966   ABC   Wed. 7:30–8 P.M.
Jan. 1966–Sept. 1966   ABC   Sat. 7:30–8 P.M.

First heard in 1944 on the CBS radio network *The Adventures of Ozzie and Harriet* was one of a few situation comedy series that made a successful transition from radio to television. The already successful stars of the show, Ozzie and Harriet NELSON, became even bigger successes on television than they had been on radio and in films. Ozzie Nelson had been a successful bandleader before he became a radio and TV star, and his wife, Harriet, had been a popular vocalist and film actress before she joined her husband as the star of *The Adventures of Ozzie and Harriet* on radio and television. The Nelsons were the parents of two sons, David and Ricky (Eric), and Ozzie and Harriet used their real-life family experiences as the basis for most of the show's scripts, which usually depicted the funny little things that happen in the lives of "typical" American parents who have two sons to raise. Ozzie was a good-natured, but often confused father and husband who, although always loving, sometimes got things wrong. Harriet, on the other hand, was a patient, right-on-target mother who simply employed good common sense to manage her husband, her sons, and her domestic affairs. David, Ozzie and Harriet's older son, was a serious and conscientious boy who was determined to do "the right thing." Ricky, on the other hand, was mischievous, experimental, and funny. During the show's early radio days, the Nelson sons were played by actors,

but in 1949, when their real-life sons grew old enough to express an interest in show business, their parents put them to work playing themselves. Most of the show's action took place at 822 Sycamore Street in the fictional town of Hillsdale. The Nelsons' television house was an exact replica of the family's actual home in Hollywood. As the Nelson boys grew up, *The Adventures of Ozzie and Harriet,* which had primarily centered on Ozzie and Harriet in its earliest years, began to feature David and Ricky, who had turned into handsome young teens. By this time, Ricky had become interested in rock and roll music (both Nelson boys, following their parents' lead, were musical) and became the show's major attraction in the 1960s. Ricky often performed his hit rock and roll songs on the program. *The Adventures of Ozzie and Harriet* was one of the longest-running domestic comedy series in television history, and people literally watched the Nelson boys grow up. Appearing with Ozzie, Harriet, David, and Ricky Nelson on the series were regulars Don DeFore as the Nelson's next-door neighbor "Thorny" Thornberry, Parley Baer as Darby, Lyle Talbot as Joe Randolph, Mary Jane Croft as Clara Randolph, and Jack Wagner, Constance Harper, Gordon Jones, Skip Young, Kristin Harmon (Ricky's wife), June Blair, Joe Flynn, Frank Cady, James Stacy, and others. *The Adventures of Ozzie and Harriet* was produced and directed by Ozzie Nelson, who was also the show's head writer.

ADVENTURES OF RIN TIN TIN, THE

   Oct. 1954–Aug. 1959   ABC   Fri. 7:30–8 P.M.

In 1954, former silent screen canine character Rin Tin Tin was resurrected and became the star of a weekly, half-hour children's adventure series that was set in the late 1800s at an army outpost out west. Rin Tin Tin, like his silent screen ancestor, was a magnificent German shepherd dog who was the heroic mascot of a boy who had been orphaned during an Indian raid and lived at the fort under the care of the soldiers. The show was filled with action, Indian massacres, gunfights, and horseback-riding chases. The boy, Rusty, was played by child actor Lee Aaker. Also featured in prominent roles were James Brown as Lt. Rip Masters, Joe Sawyer as Sgt. Biff O'Hara, and Rand Brooks as Cpl. Boone. Three different German shepherd dogs were actually used to portray Rin Tin Tin during the series run. Two of these dogs were actual descendants of the silent screen dog star. Reruns of the series were shown as a Saturday morning offering and began to appear on television shortly after the program stopped production in 1959.

ADVENTURES OF ROBIN HOOD, THE

   Sept. 1955–Sept. 1958   CBS   Mon. 7:30–8 P.M.

The Adventures of Ozzie and Harriet: (sitting, left to right) David Nelson and Harriet Nelson; (standing, left to right) Ricky Nelson and Ozzie Nelson (Author's collection)

This show was the first hit television series shown in the United States that was produced and filmed entirely in

Great Britain. Mainly an action/adventure series, *The Adventures of Robin Hood* was produced for the younger TV audience. The familiar story of Robin Hood and his Merry Men, a band of outlaws who robbed from the rich and gave to the poor, unfolded in weekly, half-hour episodes. The character of Robin Hood was played by handsome English actor Richard GREENE, who was well known to the moviegoing public for his many screen appearances. Greene was appropriately dashing and athletic-looking, although most of his stunts were actually performed by doubles. The series was set in England's Sherwood Forest, as was the original legend, and featured English actors in key roles. Bernadette O'Farrell and Patricia Driscoll played the lovely Maid Marian at different times; Ian Hunter was Sir Richard; Paul Eddington, and then John Dearth, played Will Scarlett. Archie Duncan and Rufus Cruikshank played Little John; Alexander Gauge played Friar Tuck; Donald Pleasance was Prince John, and Alan Wheatley was the evil Sheriff of Nottingham. The series-opening theme song became as familiar as the series itself and began

> Robin Hood, Robin Hood riding through the glen
> Robin Hood, Robin with his band of men
> Feared by bad, loved by the good
> Robin Hood, Robin Hood, Robin Hood!

In 1967, an animated Robin Hood series appeared on television, titled *Rocket Robin Hood*. In 1975, a prime-time comedy spoof, *When Things Were Rotten*, which featured Robin Hood and his Merry Men as central characters, made its TV debut. Neither of these shows was a success.

ADVENTURES OF WILD BILL HICKOK, THE
(see *Wild Bill Hickok*)

AIRWOLF

Jan. 1984–Apr. 1984	CBS	Sat. 9–10 P.M.
Aug. 1984–Jan. 1985	CBS	Sat. 8–9 P.M.
Jan. 1985–July 1985	CBS	Sat. 9–10 P.M.
July 1985–Mar. 1986	CBS	Sat. 8–9 P.M.
May 1986–June 1986	CBS	Sat. 9–10 P.M.
June 1986–July 1986	CBS	Wed. 9–10 P.M.

The first episode of this program was seen on January 22, 1984, when the CBS network aired a pilot to test audience reaction to their new series. The audience responded favorably to the exciting action/adventure program that starred a good-looking young actor named Jan-Michael Vincent as Stringfellow Hawke, a helicopter pilot. The aircraft Hawke, flew was the Airwolf, an advanced, high-tech attack helicopter of the future that could fly faster than a jet, travel around the world with ease, and blast anything that needed blasting with its enormous firing power. Hawke, in addition to piloting helicopters, was also an excellent cello player and a recluse, when he was

recruited by the U.S. government to recapture the Airwolf superhelicopter, which had been given to the enemy government of Libya by its demented creator/designer. Hawke recaptured the helicopter but refused to return it to the United States and its agency "The Firm" until they promised to find his brother, a soldier listed as "missing in action" in Vietnam. Hawke flew missions in the supercraft for private clients for the right price. Appearing on the show with Vincent as regulars were Alex Cord as Michael Archangel, a government go-between; Ernest BORGNINE as Hawke's former copilot and friend, Dominic Santini; Deborah Pratt (the wife of the series creator, Donald Bellisario); and Jean Bruce Scott.

ALAN YOUNG SHOW, THE

Apr. 1950–Mar. 1952	CBS	Thurs. 9–9:30 P.M.
Feb. 1953–June 1953	CBS	Sun. 9:30–10 P.M.

In 1950, when network television was still in its infancy and radio ruled supreme as America's favorite home entertainment medium, a young Canadian comedian named Alan YOUNG was recruited by the CBS network to appear on a new, half-hour weekly television series. *TV Guide* magazine declared the young comedian "the Charlie Chaplin of television," and other entertainment critics also applauded his intelligent and gentle humor. On the show, Young played a good-natured, even-tempered, gentle character who usually ended up becoming involved in one funny predicament after another in the show's variety sketches. At the beginning of each show, Young always performed a short monologue, which was followed by songs by various vocalists and two skits. Appearing on the show regularly with Young was actress Dawn Addams, who usually played his girlfriend. Gradually, the format of the show changed from comedy/variety to situation comedy. In spite of Young's formidable talents as an actor/comedian, *The Alan Young Show* was canceled, as CBS, like the two other major television networks, endlessly searched for new programs to satisfy their ever-increasing television viewing audiences.

ALBERT, EDDIE (EDWARD ALBERT HEIMBERGER 1908–)
After graduating from the University of Minnesota, Eddie Albert, who was born in Rock Island, Illinois, joined the circus and became a trapeze artist before deciding to try acting. Albert easily found work on radio and was heard on numerous radio shows that originated in Chicago. In 1938, Albert made his screen debut in the film *Brother Rat* and thereafter never stopped working in films, on the stage, and on television. His early screen credits included appearances in such films as *On Your Toes* (1939), *Four Wives* (1939), and *An Angel from Texas* (1940). During World War II, Albert served in the U.S. Navy and was an active participant in the battle of Tarawa (Nov. 1943), one of the bloodiest battles of the war. When the war ended, the actor returned to civilian life and resumed his acting

career. In 1953, Albert became the host of his first television series, *The Eddie Albert Show,* while continuing his stage and film career, appearing in the hit musical comedy *Bloomer Girl* on Broadway and in such popular films as *Oklahoma!* (1955), *Teahouse of the August Moon* (1956), *The Young Doctors* (1961), and *The Longest Day* (1962). In 1965, Albert made a guest appearance as a character named Olive Wendell Douglas on the PETTICOAT JUNCTION series and became a semiregular on the show. That same year, because of the popularity of the *Petticoat Junction* characters, Albert and his *Petticoat Junction* TV wife, Eva Gabor, were given a spin-off series of their own, GREEN ACRES. The series was a success. When *Green Acres* ended its original TV run in 1971, Albert continued his film work and appeared in such blockbuster hits as *The Concorde: Airport '79.* He also continued to appear as a guest star on such television series as SIMON AND SIMON, COLUMBO, MURDER, SHE WROTE, THIRTYSOMETHING, and in 1993, when he was 85 years old, played Jack Boland on the GENERAL HOSPITAL TV soap opera. He reunited with Gabor for a 1990 TV reunion movie, *Return to Green Acres.*

ALCOA PRESENTS
(see *One Step Beyond*)

ALDA, ALAN (ALPHONSO D'ABRUZZO JR. 1936–)

The son of film and stage actor Robert Alda, Alan Alda became one of television's best-known performers when he starred on the extremely popular and eventually legendary *M*A*S*H* TV series. Alan was born in New York City and had polio when he was a young child. While studying at Fordham University in New York, he decided he wanted to become an actor like his father, and after appearing in several off-Broadway plays, he made his television acting debut on a series called *Secret File, USA* in 1955. Supporting roles in such films as *Paper Lion* (1968), *Jenny* (1969), *The Mephisto Waltz* (1971), and guest-starring roles on such television series as *The* PHIL SILVERS SHOW (1955), ROUTE 66 (1960), and *The* NURSES (1962) eventually led to his being cast as Captain Benjamin Franklin "Hawkeye" Pierce on *M*A*S*H,* although he was not the producer's first choice for the role. He did not sign his contract to appear on the series until six hours before the pilot began filming. Based on a hit film of the 1960s, *M*A*S*H* went on to receive numerous awards and accolades. Alda, who remained with the series until it ended its original run in 1983 after 11 years on the air, directed and produced several episodes of the show, including the *M*A*S*H Goodbye and Farewell* final show, a feature-length TV film that was perhaps the most-viewed television program of all time. Alda's acting career continued in full swing after *M*A*S*H,* and in addition to starring in such films as *Same Time, Next Year* (1978), *California Suite* (1978), and *The Seduction of Joe Tynan* (1979) while *M*A*S*H*

was still on the air. After the series ended, he appeared in *Sweet Liberty* (1986), which he also directed, *Betsy's Wedding* (1990), Woody Allen's *Manhattan Murder Mystery* (1993), and other films, as well as numerous TV guest-starring roles on such series as ER, and *The Four Seasons* (1984). Alda is the only person to win an Emmy for acting, writing, and directing.

ALDRICH FAMILY, THE

Oct. 1949–June 1951	NBC	Sun. 7:30–8 P.M.
Sept. 1951–May 1953	NBC	Fri. 9:30–10 P.M.

Before it became a successful situation comedy series on television, *The Aldrich Family,* which was based on the hit Broadway play *What a Life* by Clifford Goldsmith, was a long-running (1939–1953) and popular radio program. In the early post–World War II years, television borrowed heavily from radio and transferred, sometimes intact, many hit shows from radio to TV. While the radio version of *The Aldrich Family* was on the air for 14 years, the TV series, which ran concurrently with the radio show, lasted only three and a half years. The series centered on a typical, middle-class American family, the Aldriches, but mainly focused on the adolescent problems of Mr. and Mrs. Aldrich's teenaged son, Henry. The series was set in the fictional town Centerville, and the family lived on Elm Street. In the short time the series was televised, no fewer than five actors played Henry Aldrich (Robert Casey, Richard Tyler, Henry Girard, Kenneth Nelson, and Bobby Ellis), three actresses played Henry's sister, Mary (Charita Bauer, Mary Malone, and June Dayton), and three actresses played Henry's mother, Alice (Lois Wilson, Nancy Carroll, Barbara Robbins). This was, obviously, very confusing to regular viewers of the show. One actor, House Jameson, played Henry's father, Sam, a role Jameson had also played on radio. Henry's best friend, Homer Brown, was also played by the same actor who played the role on radio, Jackie Kelk. Lois Wilson, who at one time played Henry's mother, was also seen as his Aunt Harriet when she wasn't playing Mrs. Aldrich. Henry's girlfriend, Kathleen, was played by Marcia Henderson. Each television program began with the introduction that had become famous on radio. Henry's mother would call, "Hen-reee . . . Henry Aldrich!" and Henry's squeaky adolescent voice would call back, "Coming, Mother!"

ALFRED HITCHCOCK PRESENTS (ALSO CALLED THE ALFRED HITCHCOCK HOUR)

Oct. 1955–Sept. 1960	CBS	Sun. 9:30–10 P.M.
Sep. 1960–Sept. 1962	NBC	Tues. 8:30–9 P.M.
Sept. 1962–Dec. 1962	CBS	Thurs. 10–11 P.M.
Jan. 1963–Sept. 1963	CBS	Fri. 9:30–10:30 P.M.
Sept. 1963–Sept. 1964	CBS	Fri. 10–11 P.M.
Oct. 1964–Sept. 1965	NBC	Mon. 10–11 P.M.
Sept. 1985–Jul. 1986	NBC	Sun. 8:30–9 P.M.

Alfred HITCHCOCK, one of Hollywood's most successful suspense/mystery film directors, took his formidable talents to television in 1960 with a half-hour, weekly series that presented stories that ended with typical Hitchcock surprise endings and often gave the impression that evil had triumphed. Hitchcock, who had directed such classic films as *The 39 Steps* (1935), *Rear Window* (1954), *North by Northwest* (1959), and *The Man Who Knew Too Much* (1934 and 1956), did not actually direct all the weekly TV shows (he directed only 20 of the several hundred stories presented on the TV show). He did, however, supervise the entire production and acted as the series' weekly host. Hitchcock's silhouetted profile was seen at the beginning of each show and became the series trademark. The camera then panned back until Hitchcock began the show by saying "Good evening" to the viewing audience and proceeded to introduce the week's story. From 1957 to 1958 many of the *Alfred Hitchcock Presents* stories were directed by Robert Altman, who later became famous as the original director of the film *M*A*S*H* that eventually became a hit TV series. Numerous guest stars appeared on the show each week, including such luminaries as Barbara Bel Geddes, Claude Rains, Gena Rowlands, Brian Keith, Cloris LEACHMAN, Steve MCQUEEN, Joanne Woodward, Peter Lorre, Dick VAN DYKE, Robert Redford, Judy Canova, and Peter Fonda, among others. In 1985, five years after Hitchcock died, "Hitch," as he was called, was resurrected from the dead, when a new *Alfred Hitchcock Presents* series was produced. Some brand-new stories and some from the old series were filmed. Hitchcock's original black-and-white introductions and closing comments were colorized for the new series, and his dialogue was rerecorded digitally to make it seem as if Hitch were actually introducing the brand-new weekly series. This certainly would have amused Hitchcock, who was known to have had a wonderful sense of humor and loved to play practical jokes on people. The *Alfred Hitchcock Presents* series' memorable theme music was Gounod's *Funeral March of a Marionette*.

ALICE

Aug. 1976	CBS	Mon. 9:30–10 P.M.
Sept. 1976–Oct. 1976	CBS	Wed. 9:30–10 P.M.
Nov. 1976–Sept. 1977	CBS	Sat. 9:30–10 P.M.
Oct. 1977–Oct. 1978	CBS	Sun. 9:30–10 P.M.
Oct. 1978–Feb. 1979	CBS	Sun. 8:30–9 P.M.
Mar. 1979–Sept. 1982	CBS	Sun. 9–9:30 P.M.
Oct. 1982–Nov. 1982	CBS	Wed. 9–9:30 P.M.
Mar. 1983–Apr. 1983	CBS	Mon. 9–9:30 P.M.
Apr. 1983–May 1983	CBS	Sun. 9–9:30 P.M.
June 1983–Jan. 1984	CBS	Sun. 8–8:30 P.M.
Jan. 1984–Dec. 1984	CBS	Sun. 9:30–10 P.M.
Jan. 1985–Mar. 1985	CBS	Tues. 8:30–9 P.M.
June 1985–July 1985	CBS	Tues. 8:30–9 P.M.

For nine years, devoted fans of *Alice* valiantly tried to keep track of the days and times their favorite TV situation comedy series was on the air, as CBS, in an attempt to find the perfect slot for the show, kept changing the day and time the show was aired. *Alice*, based on the hit film *Alice Doesn't Live Here Anymore* (1975), centered on a "modern" widow's attempt to find independence as she leaves her home and sets off for unknown places, determined to become a singer. When singing jobs prove elusive, Alice supports herself and her young son by becoming a waitress at Mel's Diner in Phoenix, Arizona. Linda LAVIN played the single mother, Alice Hyatt. Her son, Tommy, was played by Phillip McKeon. Vic Tayback played the role of Mel Sharples, the beefy, usually cranky owner of the diner (a role he had created in the original film). Polly HOLLIDAY played Florence Jean "Flo" Castleberry, a brassy, man-hungry waitress who worked at Mel's Diner with Alice. Beth Rowland played another waitress at the diner, the timid, scatterbrained Vera. Also featured in the cast in the role of Henry Beesmeyer, a regular customer at Mel's Diner, was Marvin Kaplan. Flo became one of the most popular characters on the show, and Polly Holliday was offered a TV series of her own called *Flo* and left the cast of *Alice* after four seasons. She was replaced by Diane Ladd as a waitress named Diane Dupree, who was another salty, spirited blonde. Interestingly, Ladd had played the role of Flo Castleberry in the original feature film. In 1981, Celia Weston replaced Ladd as waitress Jolene Hunnicutt. In the final, 202nd, episode of *Alice*, Alice finally realized her lifelong ambition to become a singer, and Mel sold his, by then famous, diner. *Alice's* theme song, "There's a New Girl in Town," sung by Linda Lavin at the beginning of each show, was written by Alan and Marilyn Bergman and David Shire.

ALL IN THE FAMILY

Jan. 1971–July 1971	CBS	Tues. 9:30–10 P.M.
Sept. 1971–Sept. 1975	CBS	Sat. 8–9 P.M.
Sept. 1975–Sept. 1976	CBS	Mon. 9–9:30 P.M.
Sept. 1976–Oct. 1976	CBS	Wed. 9–9:30 P.M.
Nov. 1976–Sept. 1977	CBS	Sat. 9–9:30 P.M.
Oct. 1977–Oct. 1978	CBS	Sun. 9–9:30 P.M.
Oct. 1978–Mar. 1983	CBS	Sun. 8–8:30 P.M.
Mar. 1983–May 1983	CBS	Mon. 8–8:30 P.M.
May 1983	CBS	Sun. 8–8:30 P.M.
June 1983	CBS	Mon. 9:30–10 P.M.
June 1983–Sept. 1983	CBS	Wed. 8–8:30 P.M.

No other series on television has had more impact on American culture than *All in the Family*. Based on a popular British television show, *Till Death Do Us Part*, created by Johnny Speight and first seen in Great Britain in 1968, *All in the Family's* American success was made possible thanks to film and TV producer Norman LEAR and his partner, Alan "Bud" Yorkin, who bought the American TV rights to the series from Speight. They were convinced that Speight had a good idea with his story about a working-class, British blue-collar bigot, his dithery wife, and their liberal daughter and perennial-student son-in-law, who lived with the couple in their lower middle-class home. By the time the situation comedy *All in the Family* made its debut on American television, however, Lear and Yorkin were not at all sure the public would accept such a radical program on their home screens. The series was concerned with such taboo-for-that-time subjects as bigotry and prejudice, politics, birth control, homosexuality, feminism, menopause, and wife-swapping. Their doubts were unfounded. Because of their concerns, however, Lear and Yorkin began the first few shows with a disclaimer that stated, "The program you are about to see is *All in the Family*. It seeks to throw a humorous spotlight on our frailties, prejudices, and concerns. By making them a source of laughter we hope to show . . . in a matter of fashion . . . just how absurd they are." The producers needn't have bothered with the disclaimer, because the public certainly understood the "joke," and the show was an immediate success. The main character on *All in the Family* was the patriarch of the Bunker family, Archie Bunker, a middle-aged, white, Anglo-Saxon Protestant male. Bunker had never been to college and was suspicious of anyone who had. He was a right-wing conservative and worked as a loading dock foreman at the Prendergast Tool and Die Company. Bunker and his family lived in a row house at 704 Hauser Street in Corona, a working-class neighborhood in the borough of Queens in New York City. Archie Bunker was an unqualified bigot who used such insulting terms as "spic" for Hispanics, "spades" and "jungle bunnies" for African Americans, "chinks" for Chinese people, and "hebes" and "kikes" for Jews. Expressions such as "You know how *those* people are . . ." "Stifle yourself," and "Dingbat" (a name he often used when referring to his wife, Edith) became well known to millions of the show's ever-growing number of fans). Archie's wife was a homemaker who, although a bit flakey and not particularly well educated, was a loving, kindhearted woman who exhibited an unusual amount of common sense, considering the man to whom she was married, and showed great compassion for others. The Bunkers' daughter, Gloria, was a liberal, rebellious young woman of the 1970s who could, at times, seem childish. Gloria was an admirer of the free-spirited hippies of the previous decade. Her husband, Michael "Mike" Stivic, was a liberal, progressive, if naive, penniless young college student when the series first went on the air. Archie thought he was not the right man for his "little girl," Gloria. Archie always referred to Mike Stivic as "Meathead" whenever he was confronted with his son-in-law's liberal views.

Veteran character actors Carroll O'CONNOR and Jean STAPLETON, who had been active on the stage and in films, played Archie and Edith Bunker. Sally Struthers and Rob Reiner (the son of talented actor, producer, and director Carl Reiner) played Gloria and Michael Stivic. Over the years, an interesting assortment of characters drifted on and off the series as regulars or semiregulars. Some of these characters ended up on weekly spin-off series of their own. Among the more notable were the Bunkers' African-American neighbors, George and Louise Jefferson, and their son, Lionel, played by Sherman HEMSLEY, Isobel SAN-

All in the Family: (sitting, left to right) Jean Stapleton (Edith Bunker), Jason Draeger (Joey Stivic), Carroll O'Connor (Archie Bunker); (standing, left to right) Rob Reiner (Mike Stivic) and Sally Struthers (Gloria Stivic) (Author's collection)

FORD, and Michael Evans respectively. The Jeffersons departed *All in the Family* in 1975 for a series of their own that was almost as successful as the show they left. Edith Bunker's cousin, Maude, an outspoken, liberal, well-educated woman, who was played by veteran character actress Bea ARTHUR, made an appearance on *All in the Family* in 1971, and proved so popular with the viewing public that she too was given her own spin-off series, MAUDE. When the Jeffersons departed Queens for their "uptown apartment" in Manhattan, their house was occupied by a white couple, Irene and Frank Lorenzo, played by former film star Betty Garrett and Vincent Gardenia. Gardenia remained on the show for one year, Garrett for three years. At the end of the 1977–1978 season, both Sally Struthers and Rob Reiner decided that after seven years on the show, it was time to move on, and so Michael Stivic, Gloria, and their young son, Joey Stivic (played first by Jason Draeger and then by Cory Miller) left Queens to live at a distant university where Mike had finally found a job.

One year later, in 1980, Jean Stapleton decided that she had had enough of playing Edith Bunker, and the producers had no other choice but to kill off the lovable character, since no other actress would possibly be accepted by viewers in the role. Edith's departure from the series met with an enormous number of letters sent to CBS from viewers protesting her demise, but the series continued to limp along without her for two more years with Archie as its main character. The season before Edith died, Archie had quit his job at Prendergast Tool and Die and bought his favorite hangout, Kelsey's Bar, and went into business for himself. Kelsey's had previously been owned by Tommy Kelsey, played by Brendon Dillon, and then by Bob Hastings. Edith made occasional appearances on the show the season before she left Archie a widower. When Gloria and Michael left Queens for greener pastures, Edith and Archie were alone in their house for a while, but soon a distant preadolescent niece of Edith's, Stephanie Mills, played by Danielle Brisebois, was dumped on their doorstep by low-life relations, and the Bunkers became the girl's foster parents. Martin Balsam played Archie's business partner, Murray Klein, a Jewish man. Considering Archie's bigoted past, that was certainly a big step for Archie Bunker. Also joining the cast at this time was comedienne Anne Meara as Veronica Rooney, a bar's chef, and Abraham Alvarez as José, the cook.

The show's opening theme song, "Those Were the Days," sung by Archie and Edith, was composed by Lee Adams and Charles Strouse. As the show began, Archie and Edith were seated at a piano that Edith was playing, and they sang:

By the way Glenn Miller played
Songs that made the "Hit Parade"
Folks like us, we had it made.
Those were the days!

The closing music for the show, "Remembering You," was written by Roger Kellaway.

All in the Family was the first situation comedy series videotaped in front of a live studio audience, which became a common practice thereafter. Previous shows were filmed.

ALL MY CHILDREN

Jan. 1970–present   ABC   Various times during
the daytime

All My Children one of television's most popular daytime serial dramas, was the creation of prolific soap opera writer Agnes Nixon, who was also responsible for such daytime hit series as SEARCH FOR TOMORROW, ANOTHER WORLD, and ONE LIFE TO LIVE. *All My Children* was the top-rated daytime serial drama series in 1978 and 1979, and was a close second for the following decade, surpassed only be the enormously popular GENERAL HOSPITAL series. Set in the fictional town of Pine Valley, not far from New York City, the series originally centered on two families: the Tylers and the Martins. Ten years after the series made its debut, the Martin family had become history but reappeared years later. The Tyler family, on the other hand, became the show's primary set of characters. Hugh Franklin played Dr. Charles Tyler, the patriarch of the family, and veteran film actress Ruth Warrick was his socially self-conscious wife, Phoebe. They remained the series' principal players for

Susan Lucci of *All My Children* (Author's collection)

many years. Warrick continued to play her role, in perhaps a less prominent capacity, through recent years.

During the program's early years, the focus was also on the Tylers' two children: a daughter, Ann, played successively by Dianna De Vegh, Joanna Mills, and Judith Barcroft; and a son, Lincoln, played by Peter White. Ann eventually had a nervous breakdown and was committed to a mental institution. The character returned three years later with a new actress, Gwyn Gillis, playing the role. Lincoln married a woman named Amy, played by Rosemary Prinz, who left him when rumor of her having an illegitimate child spread around Pine Valley. Prinz remained on the show and became one of *All My Children's* principal players. Without question, the most popular actress to appear on *All My Children*, however, is the infamous femme fatale, Erica Kane, played by Susan Lucci. Erica Kane became the woman viewers loved to hate—a self-centered, ambitious woman who, during the course of the show, was married no less than 11 times to eight different men in 24 years. The Kane character, and Susan Lucci, have become daytime serial legends to legions of viewers. Another of the show's popular, long-running regulars is actor David Canary, who plays twins, Adam and Stuart Chandler. By 1991, five of the original cast members were still on the show, Warrick and Lucci, and Mary Fickett, Frances Heflin, and Ray MacDonnell.

Over the years, hundreds of performers have played regular running roles on the series. They include such familiar names as Karen Gorney, Anne Meara, Ann Flood, Kelly Rippa, and Lauren Holly. Actress/comedienne Carol BURNETT made a guest appearance on the serial drama in 1976 playing a hospital patient, and she returned to the series as a regular character for several episodes in 1983. Screen legend Elizabeth Taylor, who was also a devoted fan of the series, played a walk-on role on the show, as she had done before on the *General Hospital* series. In 1995, *All My Children* celebrated its 25th year on television with a week of special episodes that commemorated its successful, audience-pleasing past as one of TV's most popular daytime drama series.

ALL STAR REVUE

| Oct. 1950–July 1951 | NBC | Wed. 8–9 P.M. |
| Sept. 1951–Apr. 1953 | NBC | Sat. 8–9 P.M. |

Comedy variety programs were popular during television's first decade of prominence in the late 1940s–early 1950s. One popular program that used this format was NBC's *All Star Revue*, which starred a rotating roster of big-name show business stars as weekly hosts. Such well-known entertainers as comedians Ed WYNN, Danny THOMAS, Martha RAYE, Olsen and Johnson, Jack CARSON, Jimmy DURANTE, Victor Borge, Bob HOPE, the Ritz Brothers, and bandleader Spike Jones and his City Slickers, ventriloquist Paul Winchell and his dummy, Jerry Mahoney, toastmaster George Jessel, and actress Tallulah Bankhead took turns hosting the series. They introduced comedy sketches, comedians, classical and pop singers, and a wide variety of other performers on this weekly, hour-long program. Also appearing as the stars of special programs on this series were ice-skating star Sonja Henie, singer Perry COMO, and comedian Ben Blue.

ALLEN, GRACIE (GRACE ETHEL CECILE ROSALIE ALLEN 1902–1964)

Comedienne Gracie Allen, the wife and performing partner of George BURNS, was born in San Francisco, California. While she was still a child, Gracie made her performing debut, appearing on stage with her father, who was a song-and-dance man named Edward Allen. When she was 14 years old, Gracie quit school and joined her sister singing and dancing in the Larry Reilly theatrical touring company. In 1922, Gracie decided that her show business career was going nowhere and left the act to become a secretary. That same year, a friend invited Gracie to see a show at a theater in New Jersey, where she was living at the time. The two went backstage after the show, and Gracie met a young comedian named George Burns, who was performing in an act with his partner, Bill Lorraine. Gracie and George formed an immediate friendship. Shortly after, George convinced Gracie to become his partner in a new comedy act in which he was to be the funny man and she would be the straight "man" who asked him the questions that led to the jokes. The team soon discovered that Gracie's questions, delivered in her high-pitched, somewhat dim comic voice,

got more laughs than George's punch lines. Wisely, George decided that Gracie should be the comic of the act, and he would be the straight man. It was a formula that proved successful for the team for almost 30 years and eventually made them stars. After three years of touring together and playing numerous second-rate vaudeville theaters, George and Gracie realized that they were in love, and married in 1926. While performing in England, the comedy team attracted a considerable amount of attention, especially when they appeared on a popular English radio show. When they returned to the United States, they discovered that word had spread of their overseas success and they were offered a weekly radio show. The program *The Burns and Allen Show,* was an immediate hit. Starring roles in films followed, and the couple continued to star in their popular weekly radio show until 1950, when the program left the air. George and Gracie had already begun appearing on a new television show, *The GEORGE BURNS AND GRACIE ALLEN SHOW,* which became one of early television's most popular weekly offerings. In 1958, because of ill health, Gracie decided to retire. The talented and well-loved comedienne died of cancer six years later, in 1964.

ALLEN, STEVE (STEPHEN VALENTINE PATRICK WILLIAM ALLEN 1921–2000)

The multitalented performer, composer, writer, and television talk show host Steve Allen was born into a show

Steve Allen (Author's collection)

business family in New York City. His mother was a well-known actress named Belle Montrose. In his early twenties, Allen went to work for the Columbia Broadcasting System. In 1950, when he was 29 years old, Allen appeared in an episode of DANGER, was a regular panelist on the popular WHAT'S MY LINE television show, hosted the *Songs for Sale* quiz program, and was the star of a weekly variety show, *The STEVE ALLEN SHOW*. Throughout the 1950s, Allen continued to be one of the most popular entertainers on television and hosted the *Talent Patrol* show (1953), *The TONIGHT SHOW* (1953) as that long-running program's first host, and starred on another *Steve Allen Show* variety series (1956). In 1955, Allen even found time to star in a full-length feature film, *The Benny Goodman Story*. The 1960s proved to be equally busy for the gifted performer, and he appeared in the film *College Confidential*, moderated the TV panel show *I'VE GOT A SECRET* from 1964 to 1973, appeared in the series *That Was the Week That Was* (1964), and starred on television in *The Steve Allen Comedy Hour* (1967). Throughout the 1970s, '80s, and '90s, Allen, in addition to numerous guest appearances on such TV productions as *The LOVE BOAT* (1977), *ST. ELSEWHERE* (1982), and *HOMICIDE: LIFE ON THE STREETS* (1993), produced, directed, and starred in the critically acclaimed *Meeting of the Minds* series that was seen on the PBS network (1977). This series also costarred his talented actress wife, Jayne Meadows. In 1987, Steve played himself on a BOLD AND THE BEAUTIFUL daytime serial episode and was lauded on the *Steve Allen's 75th Birthday Celebration* show (1998). As if his performing career did not keep him busy enough, Allen kept steadily busy writing over 50 mystery novels, books on comedy and religion, and composing numerous hit songs such as "This Could Be the Start of Something Big" and "Impossible," which became American standards. He was such a dedicated composer of songs that the *Guinness Book of World Records* listed him as "the most prolific composer of modern times," with over 4,000 songs to his credit. Steve Allen, who died in 2000, was named to the TV Hall of Fame in 1986.

ALLEN, TIM (TIMOTHY ALLEN DICK 1953–)

One of 10 children in his family, comedian Tim Allen was born in Denver, Colorado. After attending Western Michigan University for a time, Allen quit college, and decided that he wanted to pursue a career as a stand-up comic. In 1978, Allen was arrested for attempted drug dealing and was sentenced to 28 months in jail. Upon his release from prison, Allen began to pursue his stand-up comedy career in earnest. After many years of relative obscurity, appearing in comedy clubs all across the country, Allen finally got his big break when his stand-up act began to attract the attention of television producers. His big break came when he was offered a TV situation comedy series of his own, HOME IMPROVEMENT, in 1991. The show was based upon his handyman comedy routines and was an enormous success. This led to starring roles in such blockbuster films as

Tim Allen (Author's collection)

The Santa Clause (1994), *Toy Story* (Voice-1995), *Jungle 2 Jungle* (1997), *For Richer or Poorer* (1997), *Toy Story 2* (Voice-1999), and *Galaxy Quest* (1999). Because of the popularity of his TV series and films, in a short 10 years Allen's salary rose from $50,000 for *Toy Story* in 1995 to $5,000,000 for *Toy Story 2* in 1999. He was also paid an astounding $1,250,000 per episode for each appearance on *Home Improvement* during the 1999 season.

ALLEY, KIRSTIE (1955–)

Born and raised in Wichita, Kansas, Kirstie Alley attended Southeast High School in that city and was a good student and a member of the cheering squad. Alley went to Hollywood soon after she graduated from high school, determined to become an actress. Her first television exposure occurred in 1973, when she appeared as a contestant on the MATCH GAME '73 show. Her good looks eventually led to her being cast in an episode of LOVE BOAT in 1977. This was followed by good roles in the films *One More Chance* (1981) and *Star Trek II: The Wrath of Khan* (1982) and a running role on the TV series *Masquerade* (1983). An important role in the very successful *North and South* TV miniseries led to her being cast as a regular on the hit series CHEERS as Rebecca Howe, the uptight manager of the Boston bar, a role that made her a star. Leading roles in such films as *Summer School* (1987), *Look Who's Talking*

(1989), *The Last Don* (a 1997 TV miniseries), *Drop Dead Gorgeous* (1999) and many others followed. In 1997, Alley became the star of the situation comedy series *VERONICA'S CLOSET*, playing Veronica "Ronnie" Chase, which was very successful. She was married to actor Parker Stevenson in 1983, but they divorced in 1997. The couple had two children from that union. Kirstie is a devoted member of the Church of Scientology and diligently works on behalf of that organization.

ALLISON, FRAN (FRANCES ALLISON 1907–1989)

One of television's earliest stars, Fran Allison is the "Fran" who talked to Burr TILLSTROM's puppets Kukla and Ollie on the memorable *KUKLA, FRAN AND OLLIE* program. Born in La Port City, Iowa, Allison was well known to American women as Aunt Fanny, a popular character on the early morning *Don McNeill's Breakfast Club* radio show, which was on the air continuously for 35 years from 1933 to 1968. The actress also played the role of the Clara on the *Clara, Lu and Em* daytime serial, which was one of radio's earliest soap operas. It was because of her TV appearances with the Kuklapolitan Players on the *Kukla, Fran and Ollie* show, however, that Allison become one of the most recognized faces in the United States. The enormously successful series was watched by millions of children and adults each day from 1947 until the mid-1960s. Allison was also the hostess of the TV series *Quiz Kids* in 1949, as well as the hostess of the *Down You Go* quiz show in 1951. In 1957, the actress appeared as the Blue-Haired Fairy in a TV adaptation of *Pinocchio*. Throughout the 1960s, NBC produced several *Kukla, Fran and Ollie* specials, and in 1971 the PBS network revived the series for a short time. Fran's retirement ended the program's long and well-appreciated TV run.

ALLY MCBEAL

Sept. 1997–2002   Fox   Mon. 9–10 P.M.

The 1990s was the decade during which networks owned by TV companies other than the three broadcasting giants, CBS, NBC, and ABC, such as the Fox Network and HBO (Home Box Office) finally began to present and produce prime-time shows that often surpassed the popularity of the three major network's offerings. Because Fox, HBO, and other cable stations were not as restricted by the Federal Communications Commission (FCC) codes that kept major network shows from being as candid as they might have liked about such subjects as sex, homosexuality, drugs, ambitious business practices, and politics, these shows began to attract ever-increasing audiences, and gradually began to change TV viewing habits. One such show was *Ally McBeal*, an hour-long quirky comedy shown on the Fox network. The series was about a young, attractive Boston lawyer who works at the Cage/Fish & Associates firm. Ally was played by Calista Flockhart. Despite her confidence in the courtroom, Ally McBeal is unusually neu-

rotic about her personal life. The subject matter of the series hit home with millions of under-40 young professionals all across the United States, and soon everyone was talking about the weekly episodes of the show. Many women apparently identified with McBeal and her social and professional problems.

In addition to Ally, other regular characters on the series included Ally's assistant, the brassy, outspoken Elaine Bassell, played by Jane Krakowski; Ally's childhood friend and former lover, Billy Alan Thomas, played by Gil Bellows, and his wife, the beautiful attorney Georgia, played by Courtney Thorne-Smith, whom Ally wanted to hate, but instead became her best friend; Renee Raddick, the deputy district attorney and Ally's roommate, played by Lisa Nicole Carson, who constantly gave Ally advice on how to deal with men; the "shark," Richard Fish, played by Greg Germann, who was money mad and hired Ally; and John "The Biscuit" Cage, played by Peter MacNicol, the strange senior partner at Ally's firm. Also appearing on the series at times were Dyan Cannon, Lucy Liu, Eric and Steven Cohen, Brooke Burns, Portia de Rossi, Jesse L. Martin, and Tracey Ullman. Singer Vonda Shepard was heard singing songs that emphasize certain aspects of the show's story line. Shepard also sang the series theme song, "Searching My Soul." In the first few years *Ally McBeal* was on the air it surprised everyone in the industry by winning several coveted Emmy Awards, but its popularity quickly waned, leading to its cancellation.

AMEN

Sept. 1986–Apr. 1987	NBC	Sat. 9:30–10 P.M.
Jan. 1988–Sept. 1988	NBC	Sat. 9:30–10 P.M.
Oct. 1988–July 1989	NBC	Sat. 8:30–9 P.M.
Aug. 1989	NBC	Sat. 8–9:30 P.M.
Sept. 1989–July 1990	NBC	Sat. 8:30–9 P.M.
Aug. 1990	NBC	Sat. 8–8:30 P.M.
Dec. 1990–July 1991	NBC	Sat. 8–8:30 P.M.

A Saturday evening offering on NBC-TV for over five years, the *Amen* situation comedy series had an African-American church, the First Community Church of Philadelphia, as its setting, and revolved around the church's deacon, Ernest Frye, played by Sherman HEMSLEY, who had formerly appeared on the *ALL IN THE FAMILY* and *JEFFERSONS* series. The series also starred Clifton Davis as the church's pastor, Rev. Reuben Gregory. Also appearing in major roles were Anna Marie Horsford as Thelma Frye, Ernest's awkward daughter who was pitifully in love with the handsome Rev. Gregory; Barbara Montgomery as Casietta Hetebrink and Roz Ryan as Amelia Hetebrink; Jester Hairston as Rolly Forbes; and Franklin Seales as Lorenzo Hollingsworth, and Rosetta LeNoier as Leola Forbes. *Amen* was the first television series that used a religious setting. Clifton Davis, who played Rev. Gregory, was an actual ordained minister, as well as an actor. While the series was being aired, Davis was the assistant pastor at the Loma Linda, California,

Seventh-Day Adventist Church. The entire time this series was on prime-time TV, it had a large and loyal number of viewers and it is still popular in reruns.

AMERICAN BANDSTAND

Aug. 1957–	ABC/Syndicated	Various times
Sept. 1987	series	and stations

Before the ABC television network began to telecast *American Bandstand* to the entire country in 1957, it was a local TV show in Philadelphia, and was seen as early as 1952 with Bob Horn as its host. A studio dance program for teens, the show took advantage of teens' desire to be seen by their peers dancing to pop music and on display on the new medium that was sweeping the country, television. As rock and roll music began to replace pop and swing music, the lindy hop and slow dancing, which had been the standard dance steps throughout the United States for two decades, began to give way to wild new dances that were more suited to the new beat. It was also an opportunity for teens to show others just how different they could be, as they jumped and twisted to the new rock and roll rhythms. In 1956, a Philadelphia disc jockey named Dick CLARK took over as *American Bandstand's* host. Clark's youthful good looks, personality, and enthusiasm for the new music was just what the show needed to propel it into the national spotlight. In 1957, ABC began to offer the show to a national audience. *American Bandstand* became a sensation among America's teens, who tuned in faithfully to watch their favorite "regulars" perform on the studio dance floor. As time went by, viewers got to see their favorite rock and roll performers making guest appearances on the program. Among the notable rock and rollers who were seen on the show were The Supremes, Tom and Jerry (later known as Simon and Garfunkel), Herman's Hermits, Frankie Avalon, Chubby Checker, Fabian, Lesley Gore, Connie Francis, and James Darren, among others. (Only rock and roll legends Elvis Presley and Ricky NELSON never appeared on the popular show.) The show was telecast each weekday afternoon, when, for the most part, the "irritating sound of rock and roll music" would not disturb adults. In 1963, *American Bandstand*, with Dick Clark still firmly in charge, was aired on Saturday afternoons, gaining an even larger audience, and in 1964, the entire production moved from Philadelphia to Los Angeles, where it remained until it eventually left the air in 1987. Dick Clark became a major television personality and formed the Dick Clark Productions company, which promoted music concerts and produced other TV productions such as *Where the Action Is* and *It's Happening*. In 1987, Dick Clark and the ABC network decided to go their separate ways, and *American Bandstand* became a syndicated show, sold to various independent TV stations and seen at different times around the country. By the time the U.S. Cable network began telecasting the show in the late 1980s, David Hirsch was the program's host.

AMERICA'S FUNNIEST HOME VIDEOS

Jan. 1990–Feb. 1993	ABC	Sun. 8–8:30 P.M.
Mar. 1993–May 1993	ABC	Sun. 7–7:30 P.M.
May 1993–Sept. 1993	ABC	Sun. 8–8:30 P.M.
Sept. 1993–Dec. 1994	ABC	Sun. 7–7:30 P.M.
Jan. 1995–Jan. 1996	ABC	Sun. 7–8 P.M.
Jan. 1996–July 1996	ABC	Sun. 7:30–8 P.M.
July 1996–Dec. 1996	ABC	Sun. 7–8 P.M.
Jan. 1997	ABC	Sun. 8–9 P.M.
Feb. 1997	ABC	Sun. 7–8 P.M.
Mar. 1997	ABC	Sun. 8–9 P.M.
Apr. 1997–May 1997	ABC	Sun. 7–8 P.M.
May 1997–Sep. 1997	ABC	Sun. 8–9 P.M.
Jan. 1998–July 1998	ABC	Mon. 8–9 P.M.
July 1998–Dec. 1998	ABC	Sat. 8–9 P.M.
Mar. 1999–Apr. 1999	ABC	Thurs. 8–9 P.M.
May 1999	ABC	Sat. 8–8:30 P.M.

First presented as a television special in November 1989, this show elicited an audience reaction that was so enthusiastic that the ABC network decided to turn it into a weekly series. *America's Funniest Home Videos* took full advantage of the handheld video camera, or camcorder, craze that was sweeping the country and featured clips from tapes sent in by viewers of comic accidents, childishly foolish acts, and things as base as whistling belly buttons, grooms dropping brides as they carried them over the threshold, portable toilets being blown away to reveal occupants sitting on the commode, men endlessly dazed in pain as they are "inadvertently" struck with a blow to the groin, and numerous other tasteless visual jokes and supposedly humorous incidents. Needless to say, newspaper, magazine, and television critics were not amused by these antics and usually considered the show too low even to comment on. From 1990 to 1997, *America's Funniest Home Videos* was hosted by comedian Bob Saget. In 1998, Daisy Fuentes and John Fugelsang hosted the program. While the show was on the air, the times it was aired constantly changed. Two spin-off series, the equally tasteless *America's Funniest People* (1990–1994), and the gentler *America's Greatest Pets* (1998–1999) followed.

AMOS 'N' ANDY

June 1951–June 1953	CBS	Thurs. 8:30–9 P.M.

For over 30 years, from 1929 to 1960, the *Amos 'N' Andy* radio show was one of America's favorite programs. For two years in the 1950s, *Amos 'N' Andy* could also be seen on television as a situation comedy series. Created by and starring Freeman Gosden and Charles Correll, two white men who played the parts of African Americans, Amos and Andy, on radio and in several films in the 1930s, the television version of the program featured Black actors. Alvin Childress was Amos and Spencer Williams, Jr., was Andy. On the TV series, the part of George "The Kingfish" Stevens, who regardless of the show's title, was the series' central character on both radio and television, was played by Tim Moore. (On radio, Freeman Gosden had played "The Kingfish," in addition to playing Amos.) Amos and Andy owned the Fresh Air Taxi Company (their single cab "fleet" had no roof and thus the company's name) and lived in Harlem in New York City. "Kingfish" Stevens was Amos's and Andy's friend. He was also a rather crafty con man who was always trying to make an easy buck. Kingfish always used his convincing verbal talents, although his speech was cluttered with mispronunciations, to convince people to do things that would somehow benefit him. The Kingfish's often frustrated wife, Sapphire, was constantly berating him for his shiftless ways. Sapphire was played by Ernestine Wade, who had also played the role on the radio series. Other regular characters who appeared on the series were Lawyer Algonquin J. Calhoun, played by Johnny Lee, the slow-moving slow-talking Lightnin', played by Horace Stewart (aka Nick O'Demus), Sapphire's overbearing mother, played by Amanda Randolph, and Andy's girlfriend, Madame Queen, played by Lillian Randolph. The television series was produced by Gosden and Correll. Its familiar theme music was "Angel's Serenade" by Gaetano Braga. Even though the show was enjoyed by millions of viewers, it was suddenly dropped from the CBS roster when critics began to claim that it depicted American blacks in an unflattering light, much to the disappointment of fans of the show both white and black.

Gillian Anderson (Author's collection)

Amos 'N' Andy: (sitting, left to right) Spencer Williams, Jr. (Andy) and Alvin Childress (Amos); (standing) George "The Kingfish" Stevens (Author's collection)

ANDERSON, GILLIAN (GILLIAN LEIGH ANDERSON 1968–)

Actress Gillian Anderson, who was born and raised in Chicago, Illinois, first began acting when she was in high school. After graduating from high school, Gillian attended the national theater program at Cornell University in New York State and went on to study drama at the Goodman Theater School at DePaul University in Chicago. Anderson's first major role was in the film *The Turning* in 1992. The following year, she was cast as Special Agent Dana Katherine Scully in the television series *The X-FILES*. The series became an enormous success and soon Anderson was seen starring in such films as *Mononoke Hime* (1997), *The X-Files* (1998), *The Mighty* (1998), *Playing by Heart* (1998), and *The House of Mirth* (2000). The actress also made guest appearances in *Class of '96* (1993), *The Jon Stewart Show* (1993), *The SIMPSONS* (voice, as Dana Scully, 1999), and *FRASIER* (1993). Anderson won several Emmy Awards for her portrayal of Dana Scully on *The X-Files*. According to the actress, she is "more spontaneous" than the character she played on the hit TV series. In 1997, Gillian Anderson was chosen by *People* magazine as one of the "50 Most Beautiful People in the World."

ANDERSON, HARRY (1952–)

Upon completing his education, Harry Anderson, who was born in Newport, Rhode Island, decided he wanted to pursue a career as a magician. Unfortunately, jobs for magicians were few and far between, so Harry began to take acting classes and worked in several summer stock and off-Broadway plays before traveling to Hollywood to break into television and films. The first acting job that brought him into the spotlight was the role of "Harry the Hat" Gittis, which he played on several episodes of CHEERS in 1982 and 1983. He also appeared in supporting roles in the films *The Escape Artist* (1982) and *The Best of the Big Laff Off* (1983). In 1983, he landed his first regular role on a TV series as Judge Harold "Harry" T. Stone on NIGHT COURT, which became a long-running hit. This led to good roles in such made-for-television and feature films as *She's Having a Baby* (1988), *The Absent-Minded Professor* (1988), and *It* (1990). Guest appearances on such TV series as *The JOHN LARROQUETTE SHOW* (1993) and *LOIS & CLARK* (1993) and starring roles on *DAVE'S WORLD* (1993), which was moderately successful, and *The Science of Magic* (1997), which did not do so well, followed.

ANDY GRIFFITH SHOW, THE

Oct. 1960–July 1963	CBS	Mon. 9:30–10 P.M.
Sept. 1963–Sept. 1964	CBS	Mon. 9:30–10 P.M.
Sept. 1964–June 1965	CBS	Mon. 8:30–9 P.M.
Sept. 1965–Sept. 1968	CBS	Mon. 9–9:30 P.M.

Before Andy GRIFFITH starred on a weekly TV situation comedy series in 1960, he was a critically acclaimed actor who had played the role of Will Stockdale in *No Time for Sergeants* on the stage (1955) and in film (1958). Griffith was nominated for an Academy Award as Best Actor for playing Stockdale. He had already been heralded for his performance in his film debut, *A Face in the Crowd* (1957), directed by Elia Kazan, for which he had also been nominated for an Academy Award. Griffith's television series was a simple, but charming project by comparison to his earlier films. The show starred Griffith as Sheriff Andy Taylor, a widower who lived with his young son, Opie Taylor, played by child actor Ron HOWARD, and his housekeeper/aunt, Bea Taylor, better known as Aunt Bea, played by veteran character actress Frances Bavier. The Taylors lived in the small southern town of Mayberry in North Carolina, where most crimes were only minor events, and people lived comparatively simple, quiet lives. Mishaps in Mayberry usually took place at picnics, during feeble attempts to form a town band, when occasional misbehavior by a drunk disturbed the peace and quiet of the town, or when some household catastrophe occurred. For the most part, that was about as bad as things ever got in Mayberry, unless con men and ruffians visited the town to upset things. Sheriff Andy's deputy was his cousin, Barney Fife, expertly played by actor Don KNOTTS, who was inept, hypertense, and certainly more confident than his abilities would seem to indicate. Barney provided most of the laughs on the show and became its chief asset for many years. Also providing a generous amount of comedy during the show's early years was a lovable, naive country bumpkin named Gomer Pyle, who was the town's gas station attendant. The role was played by Jim NABORS, who went on to star in a spin-off series GOMER PYLE in 1964.

Other memorable characters who appeared on the show were Andy's girlfriend, Ellie Walker, played by Elinor Donahue, who had been one of the stars of FATHER KNOWS BEST; town gossip Clara Edward, played by Hope Summers; Goober Pyle, who took over for Gomer when he left the series, played by George Lindsey; the town barber Floyd Lawson, played by character actor Howard McNear; and Mayor Stoner, played by Parley Baer. Also, Ken Berry appeared as Sam Jones, Betty Lynn as Thelma Lou, Hal Smith as Chris Campbell, Jack Burns as Warren Ferguson, Paul Hartman as Emmett Clark, and Burt Mustin as Jud Crowley, In 1968, Don Knotts departed the show for films, and Andy Griffith thought the series had run long enough and was becoming stale, and he quit. Ken Berry became the lead of a new series, MAYBERRY, R.F.D., which tried to continue the Griffith show's tradition. *Mayberry, R.F.D.* ran for three years with Frances Bavier, George Lindsey, Paul Hartman, and Jack Dodson repeating their Griffith show roles, but the series, without Andy Griffith and Don Knotts, did not have the staying power of the original series and was canceled in 1971.

ANDY WILLIAMS SHOW, THE

July 1958–Sept. 1958	ABC	Thurs. 9–9:30 P.M.
July 1959–Sept. 1959	CBS	Tues. 10–11 P.M.
Sept. 1962–June 1963	NBC	Thurs. 10–11 P.M.
Sept. 1963–May 1964	NBC	Tues. 10–11 P.M.
Oct. 1964–May 1966	NBC	Mon. 9–10 P.M.
Sept. 1966–May 1967	NBC	Sun. 10–11 P.M.
Sept. 1969–July 1971	NBC	Sat. 7:30–8:30 P.M.

Pop singer Andy WILLIAMS, whose smooth, romantic rendition of "Moon River" helped to make him one of the entertainment world's most popular performers, had his first successful *Andy Williams Show* on television in 1958. It was a summer replacement on the ABC network. Williams had appeared with singer June Valli on a 15-minute, Tuesday and Thursday musical program the year before on NBC. It was called *The Andy Williams–June Valli Show* and was aired for only one month. After a second season as a summer replacement on ABC, Williams was offered an hour-long, weekly variety/music show of his own on CBS in 1962. One year later, the one-hour show moved from CBS to NBC, where it remained until 1967. Two years later, *The Andy Williams Show* resurfaced on NBC, where it remained for three more years. Each week, celebrated stars of stage, screen, and television made guest appearances on the show, including such luminaries as Dick VAN DYKE, The Lennon Sisters, Jonathan WINTERS, the husband and wife singing team of Steve Lawrence and Eydie Gorme, comedians Irwin Corey and Charlie Callas, among others. Regulars on the show included Mort Lindsey and his orchestra, the Dick Williams Singers, the Peter Gennaro Dancers, the Goodtime Singers, and Randy Sparks and the New Christy Minstrels. But of all the talented people who appeared on *The Andy Williams Show,* it was a close harmony singing group of adolescent and preadolescent boys, the Osmond Brothers, who became the program's most popular attractions. The Osmonds were weekly favorites on the show from 1962 until 1971. In 1976, Williams hosted a half-hour syndicated show called *Andy,* which, although popular with his numerous fans, did not attract the same kind of attention as did his earlier television efforts, and was canceled after one year.

ANN SOTHERN SHOW, THE

Oct. 1958–July 1960	CBS	Mon. 9:30–10 P.M.
Oct. 1960–Dec. 1960	CBS	Thurs. 9:30–10 P.M.
Dec. 1960–Mar. 1961	CBS	Thurs. 7:30–8 P.M.
July 1961–Sept. 1962	CBS	Mon. 9:30–10 P.M.

Ann SOTHERN, an important film actress in the 1930s and '40s, was one of the first Hollywood stars to have a popular situation comedy series on television. *PRIVATE SECRETARY* was on the air from 1953 until 1957. In 1958, Sothern decided to change the format of her series and changed its name to *The ANN SOTHERN SHOW.* On her new show, Ann played an entirely different character. Private secretary Susie McNamara became Katy O'Connor, an assistant manager at the plush Bartley House Hotel in New York City. *The Ann Sothern Show* featured longtime Hollywood character actor Ernest Truex as Katy's boss, Jason Macauley (1958–1959); Ann Tyrell as Katy's roommate and best friend, Olive Smith; Jack Mullaney as Johnny Wallace; Jacques Scott as Paul Martine; Reta Shaw as Flora Macauley, the boss's wife; Don Porter as James Devery, Katy's love interest; Louis Nye as Dr. Delbert Gray; Ken Berry as Woody; and Jesse White as Oscar Pudney. Both Don Porter and Ann Tyrell had previously appeared with Sothern on the *Private Secretary* series. Although Sothern, and the show, were popular with many viewers, *The Ann Sothern Show* ran for only two years. Most people considered the series a continuation of *Private Secretary,* even though the settings and characters' names were different; and after watching Ann playing what they felt was the same role, they began to lose interest in the format after nine years and *The Ann Sothern Show* was canceled.

ANNIE OAKLEY

Apr. 1953–	Syndicated	Various stations
Dec. 1956	series	and times

A gun-toting, pigtailed Annie Oakley, who was an actual American Wild West character starring with the Buffalo Bill Cody Wild West Show in the late 1800s to the early 1900s, became the main character of a 30-minute television adventure series directed toward younger viewers. Mostly fiction, this series did not draw very heavily upon actual facts about the real Annie Oakley. Like Oakley,

however, Gail DAVIS, the actress who played Annie, was a sharpshooter and an excellent horseback rider. Davis had appeared in many western film serials before becoming Annie Oakley on television. On the series, Annie's friend and silent suitor was lawman Deputy Sheriff Lofty Craig, played by Brad Johnson. Jimmy Hughes played Annie's younger brother, Tagg Oakley, When the *Annie Oakley* series left the air, Gail Davis continued to appear in short films and with Gene AUTRY's traveling rodeo show billed as "Annie Oakley," and she later became a show business celebrities' manager. In all, 81 episodes of the *Annie Oakley* series were filmed, and they can still be seen in reruns on occasion.

ANOTHER WORLD

May, 1964–1999	NBC	Various times during the daytime

One of several daytime serial dramas created by Irna Phillips for television, *Another World* was the first soap opera to expand from a half-hour, five days a week, to a full hour, five days a week. It was also the first serial drama to engender a spin-off series, *SOMERSET* in 1970, and a second spin-off series, *TEXAS,* in 1980. During the 1970s, *Another World,* which was owned by the Procter and Gamble Company, was the second-highest rated daytime serial drama on television for most of that decade. Set in the fictional town of Bay City, the series' original opening stated that *Another World* depicted "the world of events we live in and the world of feelings and dreams that we strive for." During the show's early years, the series centered on accountant Jim Matthews, played by Hugh Marlowe, his wife, Mary, played by Virginia Dwyer, and their three children: their eldest daughter, Pat, played successively by Susan Trustman and then Beverly Penberthy; their son, Dr. Russ Matthews, played by Joey Trent, Sam Groom, Bob Hover, and David Bailey; and their youngest daughter, Alice, played by Jacquelyn Courtney, Susan Harney, Wesley Ann Pfenning, Vana Tribbey, Linda Borgeson, then Jacquelyn Courtney once again. Sara Cunningham, Audra Lindley, Nancy Wickwire, and Irene Dailey played the Matthews' widowed sister-in-law, Liz Matthews. Also in the cast in those early years were Joe Gallison as Liz's son, lawyer Bill Matthews (who drowned in 1968); Lisa Chapman as Liz's daughter, Janet; and Fran Sharon, Roni Dengel, Lisa Cameron, and Lynn Milgrim as Liz's daughter, Susan. As on most soap operas, these characters gradually faded from view as others began to replace them as the central focuses in the ever-changing story lines. In the years that followed, many other actors who became audience favorites appeared on the series, including Constance Ford as Ada David Downs Hobson (Ford played the role from 1967 until shortly before her death in 1993); Ann Wedgeworth as Lohoma Vane; Victoria Wyndham, as Ada's daughter, Rachel; George Reinholt and then David Canary as Stephen Frame; Victoria Thompson and then Christine Jones as the evil Janice Frame; Judith Barcroft and then Susan Sullivan as Lenore Moore Curtin; former film star Ann Sheridan as Catherine Corning; Donald Madden as Dr. Kurt Landis; Charles Durning and then Dolph Sweet as Lt. Gil McGowen (who married Ada); and many others.

ANSARA, MICHAEL (1922–)

Although he is perhaps best known for playing Native Americans such as Cochise on the hit television series *BROKEN ARROW* (1956–1960) Michael Ansara is actually of Syrian descent. Born in a small town in Syria, Ansara immigrated to the United States with his parents and settled in New England. Ten years later, the family moved to California, where Michael attended Los Angeles City College, hoping to become a doctor. While there, he discovered the drama department and abandoned his medical studies to major in theater studies, and appeared in college plays. He then studied and performed at the Pasadena Playhouse with such later-to-be-famous classmates as Charles BRONSON, Carolyn JONES, and Aaron SPELLING. In 1944, Ansara won a small role in the film *Action in Arabia*. This led to appearances on such television shows as *The LONE RANGER*, *Family Theatre*, *ALFRED HITCHCOCK PRESENTS*, and *The ADVENTURES OF RIN TIN TIN*, and numerous films including *Desert Hawk* (1950), *My Favorite Spy* (1951), *Brave Warrior* (1952), *Serpent of the Nile* (1953), *Julius Caesar* (1953), *The Lawless Breed* (1952), *The Egyptian* (1954), *Sign of the Pagan* (1955), *Abbott and Costello Meet the Mummy* (1955), and *The Lone Ranger* (1956), usually playing foreign exotics or Native Americans, because of his dark, swarthy good looks. In 1956, Ansara won the role of Cochise on the *Broken Arrow* television series and became a star. When *Broken Arrow* left the air, Ansara continued to appear in films and TV shows and eventually had another regular role on the *BUCK ROGERS IN THE 25TH CENTURY* series in 1979. The busy actor was constantly working throughout the 1980s and '90s. At present Ansara is retired, but occasionally performs voice roles for cartoons. Most notably, he is the voice of Mr. Freeze on *The New Batman/Superman Adventures* (1997), and he performed the same task for *Batman Beyond: The Movie* (1999), also as the voice of Dr. Victor Fries/Mr. Freeze.

ANTIQUES ROADSHOW

| 1996–present | PBS | Tues. & Sat. 8–9 & 7–8 P.M. |

One of PBS's top-rated programs, with almost 15 million viewers tuning in each week, *Antiques Roadshow* has a simple formula for success: Members of the public are invited to bring antiques and collectibles to an *Antiques Roadshow* event, held in various cities all around the United States and Canada, and have them evaluated by professional antiques dealers from such prestigious auction houses as Christie's, William Doyle Galleries, Skinner, and Sotheby's, as well as independent appraisers and deal-

ers from across the nation. Chris Jurrel was the show's host for four seasons, but in 2000, Dan Elias took over the hosting assignment. Among the evaluators most frequently seen are Caroline Ashleigh, Noel Barrett, Frank H. Boos, John A. Buxton, Gordon S. Converse, Nicholas Dawes, Leila Dunbar, Ken Farmer, J. Michael Flanigan, Ruth Franchi, Kathleen Guzman, Leigh and Leslie Keno, Tim Luke, David McCarron, Wayne Pratt, David Rago, and Jonathan Smellenburg. *Antiques Roadshow* is produced for PBS by WGBH in Boston, Massachusetts.

ARDEN, EVE (EUNICE QUEDENS 1908–1990)

Eve Arden was an actress who enjoyed impressive longevity and success in films, radio, television, and on the stage. Arden was born in Mill Valley, California. Her sophisticated looks and droll delivery made her a wonderful best friend and second female lead in countless films throughout the 1930s and '40s. Arden had quit school when she was 16 years old to join an acting company. In the 1930s, she attracted the attention of Hollywood producers while she was performing a skit in the *Ziegfeld Follies* on Broadway. A major break for the actress occurred in 1937, when she won an important supporting role in the film *Stage Door*, which starred Katharine Hepburn and Ginger Rogers. Eve subsequently played significant roles in such films as *Having Wonderful Time* (1938), *No, No Nanette* (1940), *Ziegfeld Girl* (1941), *Cover Girl* (1944), *Mildred Pierce* (1945), *The Voice of the Turtle* (1947), and *One Touch of Venus* (1948), as well as numerous other films. In 1948, Arden was first heard as the love-starved English teacher Connie Brooks on the *OUR MISS BROOKS* radio show. The show was an immediate success and became one of the CBS radio network's most popular programs. In 1952, the series became a hit on television as well, and in 1955, Arden also starred in a feature-length film, *Our Miss Brooks*. Two other TV series followed, *The Eve Arden Show* (1957) and *The MOTHERS-IN-LAW*, neither of which equaled the success of *Our Miss Brooks*. Eve Arden continued to act in films. In 1959, she appeared in the very successful *Anatomy of a Murder*, playing the important supporting role of Maida, and in 1960, she was featured in another important film, *The Dark at the Top of the Stairs*. From the early 1950s until 1985 (her last major TV appearance was on *Amazing Stories*), Arden appeared as a guest star on such memorable TV programs as *I LOVE LUCY*, *The MAN FROM U.N.C.L.E.*, *BEWITCHED*, *MAUDE*, *ELLERY QUEEN*, and *B. J. AND THE BEAR*. Rarely taking a hiatus from her film and television work, toward the end of her career Arden appeared in the films *Grease* in 1978 and *Grease 2* in 1982, and played the stepmother in the TV special *Cinderella* in 1984. Failing health forced the actress into retirement, and in 1990, she suffered a massive heart attack and died.

ARNAZ, DESI (DESIDERIO ALBERTO ARNAZ Y DE ACHA III 1917–1986)

Before Desi Arnaz became a television star and a TV mogul with his *I LOVE LUCY* series, he was a band singer and musician. He was born in Santiago, Cuba, and his father was that city's mayor. In 1933, the Batista revolution in Cuba led to the senior Arnaz's arrest and jailing. The Arnaz family, which was quite wealthy, was stripped of its power, money, and property. When Desi's father was released from prison, the family fled Cuba and settled in Miami, Florida, where Desi's first job was cleaning canary cages. Desi, who had always aspired to be a professional musician, formed a small Latino band and was discovered by famous Latino bandleader Xavier Cugat, who hired him to perform with his band. Desi eventually decided to form another band and was almost single-handedly responsible for the conga craze that swept the United States in the late 1930s. In 1940, Desi won a role in the Broadway revue *Too Many Girls,* and his good looks and talent attracted the attention of Hollywood producers, who signed him to a contract to appear in films. In his first film, Arnaz repeated his stage performance in *Too Many Girls.* Unmemorable roles in such films as *Father Takes a Wife* (1941) and *Holiday In Havana* (1949) did little to advance his film career, but he did have success as a nightclub performer in the United States and Cuba. In 1951, Desi and his film actress wife, Lucille BALL, decided to try television and developed a situation comedy series about a Cuban-American bandleader and his wacky, trouble-prone wife, whom they called Lucy and Ricky Ricardo. The series was an enormous success, and eventually it became a television classic. They formed the Desilu Company and not only took over the production of *I Love Lucy,* but also developed and sometimes starred in other projects, including several films and the *Lucy–Desi Comedy Hour* (1957) and the *Westinghouse Desilu Playhouse* (1958). Lucy and Desi became one of Hollywood's richest couples. After divorcing Lucy when the *I Love Lucy* series had run its course and apparently taken its toll on their relationship, Desi continued to work as an actor and performer on TV and in film, and appeared in such productions as *The* MOTHERS-IN-LAW, *The* VIRGINIAN, IRONSIDE, and in the film *The Escape Artist* (1982). In 1986, Desi, a heavy smoker most of his life, died of lung cancer.

ARNESS, JAMES (JAMES AURNESS 1923–)

James Arness, whom most people best remember as Marshal Matt Dillon of Dodge City on the long-running, classic western television series GUNSMOKE, was born in Minneapolis, Minnesota. Arness, whose brother Peter GRAVES also became an actor, served in the U.S. military during World War II and was wounded in action in Italy. After the war, he decided to pursue his dream of becoming an actor and went to Hollywood to break into films. His tall, rugged, good looks won him a role in the film *The Farmer's Daughter* (1947), as one of Loretta YOUNG's farm-boy brothers. (Loretta received an Academy Award for her effort in this film.) Arness appeared in numerous films such as *Battleground* (1949), *Sierra* (1950), *The Thing from Another World* (1951), *Horizons West* (1952), *Hondo* (1953), and *Them!* (1954) before being

cast in the Dillon role on *Gunsmoke* in 1955. At six feet seven inches, Arness was the tallest actor to ever play a leading role in films or on television. *Gunsmoke* had been a successful series on radio, before it was seen on television, and it became an instant success, running concurrently on both mediums (with William Conrad playing the Dillon role on radio). The radio series ended its run in 1961. The television show continued to run for another 14 years, becoming the longest-running series on television, until it was canceled in 1975 after 20 years on the air. Arness continued to appear in occasional films such as *The First Traveling Saleslady* (1956) and *Gun the Man Down* (1956) while starring on *Gunsmoke.* In 1977, Arness appeared in the TV miniseries *How the West Was Won.* Several years after *Gunsmoke* left the air, James Arness came out of semiretirement to star in a made-for-television movie, *Red River,* and he also starred in several subsequent *Gunsmoke* movies on television in 1990, 1992, 1993, and 1994.

ARSENIO HALL SHOW, THE

Jan. 1989–	Syndicated	Various times
Sept. 1994	series	and stations

In 1989, comedian Arsenio Hall became the first African-American performer to host a successful late-night talk show on television, fulfilling one of his lifelong dreams. Hall admitted that as a teenager he would perform a stand-up routine in front of the mirror in his bedroom. When he completed his education, he started performing as a stand-up comic. After several regular appearances on various short-lived television variety shows, such as *The 1/2 Hour Comedy Hour, Motown Revue,* and *Thicke of the Night,* Hall took over Joan Rivers's hosting chores on the Fox networks' late-night talk show in 1987. The show's ratings improved, but the show was canceled. Arsenio Hall began to work in films and starred with his friend Eddie Murphy in the successful *Coming to America* (1988), which was produced by Paramount Pictures. Paramount, pleased with his performance in the film, signed Hall to host an hour-long talk show, *The Arsenio Hall Show,* which was a syndicated hit in the 1988–1989 season. The show proved more popular with younger audiences than rival talk shows like NBC's TONIGHT SHOW with Johnny CARSON and CBS's ill-fated *Pat Sajak Show.* The guests on Arsenio's show differed from guests seen on the other evening talk shows, and many soul and rap music acts were featured. Hall even managed to snare presidential candidate Bill Clinton as a guest during the 1992 campaign. In June 1990, *TV Guide* magazine named Arsenio Hall "TV Person of the Year." Unfortunately, when the competition between Jay LENO on NBC's TONIGHT SHOW and David LETTERMAN who became the star of CBS's LATE SHOW began to attract increasingly more attention and larger audiences, Arsenio Hall's syndicated show, which was on the air at the same time in many cities, began to lose viewers. *The Arsenio Hall Show* suspended production in 1994 and ended on a rather unpleasant note, with Hall angrily telling his bosses to "kiss [his] black ass." This certainly did not endear him to network officials, and, as of this date, his career as a TV talk show host is in limbo. Hall did, however, land a starring role in *Martial Law* in late 1998.

ARTHUR, BEA (BERNICE FRANKEL 1923–)

A native New Yorker, Bea Arthur began her acting career in that city, appearing in such successful off-Broadway plays as *The Threepenny Opera* and *Ulysses in Nightown.* Arthur made her television debut as a regular on the *Caesar's Hour* (Sid CAESAR) variety show in 1956. In 1964, the actress made her first major Broadway appearance as Yente the Matchmaker in the musical comedy *Fiddler on the Roof,* and in 1966, Arthur appeared on Broadway once again in the major role of Vera Charles in the musical *Mame,* which starred Angela LANSBURY in the title role. Arthur won a Tony Award as Best Supporting Actress in a Musical for her efforts. Arthur attracted a good deal of attention in the hit comedy film *Lovers and Other Strangers* in 1970, playing Bea Vecchio, an Italian mother used to getting what she wanted. In 1971, the actress appeared as Edith Bunker's liberal activist cousin, Maude, on the very successful ALL IN THE FAMILY TV series. The exchanges between Archie Bunker, the bigot, and the left-leaning Maude, became one of the most talked about TV events of the 1970–1971 season, and Arthur became so popular she was offered a spin-off series of her own, MAUDE, which made its debut in 1972. The show was an immediate hit and had a healthy six-year run. While she was appearing as Maude, Arthur also managed to find time to repeat her performance as Vera Charles in the film version of *Mame,* which starred Lucille BALL as Mame. In 1983, the actress starred in a TV situation comedy series, *Amanda's,* that was not successful, but in 1985, another TV series in which she starred, GOLDEN GIRLS, was a television success. For three years, the show was rated among the top-10 TV series in the United States, won numerous awards for Arthur and her costars Betty WHITE, Rue McCLANAHAN, and Estelle GETTY, and had a seven-year run. Bea Arthur also made appearances on several hit TV shows, including STAR TREK, *The* MARY TYLER MOORE SHOW, EMPTY NEST, ELLEN, and *Beggars and Choosers,* among others. Constantly sought after as a character actress, Bea Arthur appeared in the film *For Better or For Worse* (1996) and *Enemies of Laughter* (2000).

ARTHUR GODFREY AND HIS FRIENDS (AKA THE ARTHUR GODFREY SHOW)

Jan. 1949–June 1957	CBS	Wed. 8–9 P.M.
Sept. 1958–Apr. 1959	CBS	Tues. 9–9:30 P.M.

One of the most popular stars on radio throughout the 1940s, Arthur GODFREY's arrival on television in 1949 became one of the most talked about events in the United States, even though very few Americans had television receivers in their homes. Most people were convinced Godfrey's down to earth, chatty delivery was a natural for the new medium, and they were right. An hour-long, weekly variety show, *Arthur Godfrey and His Friends* featured several members of his radio show cast (the radio show continued to run each weekday in the morning hours) such as the singing group The Chordettes (Virginia Osborn, Carol Hagedorn, Dorothy Schwartz, and Janet Ertell), announcer Tony Marvin, pop singers Janette Davis and Bill Lawrence, the Mariners quartet (Jim Lewis, Tom Lockard, Nat Dickerson, and Martin Karl), Archie Blyer and His Orchestra, tenor Frank Parker, and soprano Marion Marlowe, and many new "friends," including Hawaiian singer Haleloke, singer/heartthrob Julius LaRosa, Lu Ann Simms, the McGuire Sisters (Christine, Dorothy, and Phyllis), Irish singer Carmel Quinn, and singer Pat Boone, who went on to become a film star after two successful years on the show from 1955 to 1957. Godfrey, who was the undisputed star of the show, chatted with his "friends" before he introduced the musical selection they were going to perform, talked about things that disturbed or pleased him (his love of piloting his own airplane, playing his ukulele, Hawaii, his farm in Virginia, etc., were often mentioned). Musical numbers on the evening variety show became increasingly more elaborate, and cast members, dressed in various costumes, performed in front of beautiful sets. Although most of the shows were telecast from New York City, as time went on and the show continued to remain popular, weekly themes such as "The Christmas Show," "Spring Is Here," "The Visit to Hawaii," etc., were presented, and the entire cast often traveled to various exotic locales. On one occasion the cast did an entire show from a battleship. (Godfrey had been in the U.S. Navy when he was a young man.)

Entertainment columnist Ben Gross, who wrote for the New York *Daily News,* summed up "the old redhead" Godfrey's appeal this way: "It is his friendliness, his good cheer, his small town mischievousness and his kindly philosophy . . . or maybe it's his magnetism, his personal attractiveness" that made him a success. Godfrey's "good cheer," "kindly philosophy," and "friendliness," were certainly tarnished when his obviously inflated ego and nastiness became increasingly apparent to viewers. Eventually, Godfrey fired his popular singer Julius LaRosa, announcing to a live audience, that it was "Julie's ([LaRosa's]) swan song." The singer's "sin" was that he had begun to complain about the ballet lessons Godfrey was expecting his cast to take, even though their increasingly busy recording schedules and show rehearsals did not allow them much time for such extra training. Godfrey had apparently begun to feel that he was invincible, since the CBS network had given him total autonomy regarding his show and cast and usually gave in to his every whim, because of his enormous popularity. Increasingly, his on-the-air feuds with such people as columnist/TV panelist Dorothy Kilgallen, whom he called "a liar," Ed Sullivan, whom he labeled "a dope," and newspaperman John Crosby, whom Godfrey called "a fatuous ass," did nothing to endear him to the press, other celebrities, or the public, and his popularity began to fade. Eventually, by the late 1950s, Godfrey, who had wielded so much power and was so loved by the public during television's first major decade, saw his popularity diminish to the point where, by the time he died in 1983, he had been all but forgotten by the television industry and many of his former fans.

ARTHUR GODFREY'S TALENT SCOUTS

Dec. 1948–July 1958	CBS	Mon. 8:30–9 P.M.

Memorably sponsored by Lipton tea and Lipton soups (most early television shows had just one sponsor who picked up the show's entire production cost), *Arthur Godfrey's Talent Scouts* has often been confused with TED MACK'S ORIGINAL AMATEUR HOUR. The two shows were actually very different. *Ted Mack's Original Amateur Hour* usually presented untried talent and often included unusual acts such as spoon players, whistlers, and yodelers. *Arthur Godfrey's Talent Scouts* featured professional and semiprofessional performers who were looking for their first big break in show business. Before each act performed, the show's host, Arthur GODFREY, would interview "talent scouts" who had "discovered" the performers and brought them to the attention of the show's producers. These talent scouts were usually family members or friends of the performers, or people who had heard them perform somewhere and thought them worthy of being featured on the *Talent Scouts* show. After preshow tryouts, acts were selected that would give viewers the greatest variety of performances on a single program. Godfrey's cozy chats with the scouts, and his reaction to the performers after they had finished their act, could often mean the difference between who was judged "best act of the evening," as determined by an audience applause meter at the end of the show. Many of the ARTHUR GODFREY AND HIS FRIENDS regulars, such as Carmel Quinn, the Chordettes, Pat Boone, and the McGuire Sisters were first seen by Godfrey on the *Talent Scouts* show. Other later-to-be-famous entertainers who got their first major exposure on the show include Rosemary Clooney, Tony Bennett, Connie Francis (who played an accordion), Steve Lawrence, Al Martino, Roy Clark, Leslie Uggams, and Patsy Cline. *Talent Scouts* was the number-one-rated show on television in the 1951–1952 season. In 1952–1953, *Talent Scouts* and *Arthur Godfrey and His Friends* were the number-two-rated shows, with *I LOVE LUCY* ranking first.

ARTHUR MURRAY DANCE PARTY, THE

July 1950– Sept. 1950	ABC	Thurs. 9–9:30 P.M.
Oct. 1950– Jan. 1951	DUMONT	Sun. 9–10 P.M.
Jan. 1951– Mar. 1951	DUMONT	Sun. 9–9:30 P.M.
Apr. 1951– June 1951	ABC	Mon. 9–9:30 P.M.
Sept. 1951– Dec. 1951	ABC	Wed. 9–9:30 P.M.
Jan. 1952– May 1952	ABC	Sun. 9–9:30 P.M.
July 1952– Aug. 1952	CBS	Fri. 8–8:30 P.M.
Oct. 1952– Apr. 1953	DUMONT	Sun. 10–10:30 P.M.
June 1953– Oct. 1953	CBS	Sun. 9:30–10 P.M.
Oct. 1953– Apr. 1954	NBC	Mon. 7:30–7:45 P.M.
June 1954– Sept. 1954	NBC	Tues. 8:30–9 P.M.
June 1955– Sept. 1955	NBC	Tues. 8:30–9 P.M.
Apr. 1956– Sept. 1956	CBS	Thurs. 10–10:30 P.M.
Apr. 1957– June 1957	NBC	Tues. 8–8:30 P.M.
July 1957– Sept. 1957	NBC	Mon. 9:30–10 P.M.
Sept. 1958– Sept. 1959	NBC	Mon. 10–10:30 P.M.
Sept. 1959– June 1960	NBC	Tues. 9–9:30 P.M.
June 1960– Sept. 1960	NBC	Tues. 9:30–10 P.M.

For 10 years, as it moved from time slot to to time slot and station to station, *The Arthur Murray Dance Party* (sometimes called *The Arthur Murray Show* and *The Arthur Murray Party*) continued to generate a loyal viewing audience who remained faithful to the program the entire time it was on the air. Hosted by dance school owners Arthur MURRAY and his wife, Kathryn, the entire show centered on social dancing and encouraged people to learn to dance. In the program's early years, each show featured a mystery dance segment when viewers could win free dance instruction at an Arthur Murray Studio by sending in a postcard correctly identifying the dance steps being shown. The show's setting was a dance party, and in between dancing, Kathryn would chat with the Arthur Murray Dancers, who were instructors at the Murrays' school, and sometimes a special guest star appeared on the show. Arthur, who always looked as if he thought he was somewhere else, usually remained silent and just smiled. When he did say something, it was usually short and sweet. Kathryn was the show's real star and did most of the talking on the program. Arthur did, however, occasionally dance with Kathryn and other dancers, and displayed remarkable dexterity and grace considering his age (he was in his late fifties and early sixties at the time of the shows). At the end of each show, Kathryn always said, "See you next time. Till then, put a little fun in your life. Try dancing!" For many of the years it was televised, *The Arthur Murray Dance Party* was a summer replacement series.

AS THE WORLD TURNS

1956–present	CBS	Various times

For over 45 years, *As the World Turns,* which like ANOTHER WORLD was another of Irna Phillips's daytime serial drama creations, has been one of television's most popular shows. From 1959 to 1979, the series was daytime TV's highest-rated soap opera, and for a brief time, a spin-off series, *Our Private World,* turned up on the CBS network, but failed to attract an audience and was canceled after a short time. In 1974, *As the World Turns,* which had been a half-hour show for most of its early years, became a full hour, five-day-a-week program, and many new characters were introduced to fill up the added half hour. Set in the fictional midwestern town of Oakdale, the series originally centered on two families living in that town, the Hugheses and Lowells. Although the Lowells have long since been dropped from the story line, the Hugheses continue to dominate most of the series' episodes, and several of the Hughes family's original characters have been seen on the show since its debut in 1956. Don MacLaughlin was the patriarch of the Hughes family, lawyer Chris Hughes, and Helen Wagner played his wife, Nancy. MacLaughlin remained with the series for 30 years until his death, and Wagner played Nancy until 1981, when she left the show, but then returned to the series shortly before MacLaughlin's death and is still the matriarch of the Hughes clan to this day. Hal Studer, Richard Holland, Jim Noble, Peter Brandon, Martin West, and Conrad Fawkes played Chris and Nancy's son, Don Hughes, at different times; Rosemary Prinz (a very popular early performer on the series) and then Phoebe Brandon played their daughter, Penny Hughes; and Bobby Alford, Ronnie Welsh, and finally Don Hastings (who plays the same role currently) played Bob Hughes, who became a doctor. Grandpa Hughes was played by Santos Ortega and then William Lee, until the character died in 1968. The Lowell family consisted of Jim Lowell, who died in 1957, played by Les Damon; his wife, Claire, played successively by Anne Burr, Gertrude Warner, Nancy Wickwire, Jone Allison, and Barbara Berjer; Jim's father, Judge Lowell, played by William Johnstone; and Jim and Claire's daughter, Ellen, played by Wendy Drew and then Patricia Bruder, who remained on the show for over 40 years. The Lowells eventually faded from the show, except for Ellen, who married her former father-in-law, the widower Dr. David Stewart, played by Henderson Forsythe, who had previously adopted Ellen and his son's illegitimate child. The child, a son who literally grew up on the series, was played over the years by Paul O'Keefe, Doug Chapin, Jess Rowland, John Colenback, and John Reilly. Dr. Stewart's son by his previous marriage, Paul Stewart, was played by Alan Howard, Edmund Gaynes,

Steve Mines, Michael Hawkins, Garson DeBramanino, Marco St. John, and Dean Santoro. Most of these characters, with the exception of Chris and Nancy Hughes, David and Ellen Stewart, and Bob Hughes, met with early deaths or had more fortunate departures from Oakdale.

In 1960, a character first appeared on the show who for the next 25 years dominated the series story line—Lisa Miller, played by actress Eileen Fulton. Much hated, self-serving, yet lovely and even charmingly villainous, Lisa became the character viewers loved to hate as she plotted to destroy marriages and manipulate people. From the first day she arrived in Oakdale, Lisa's main target romantically was the Hughes son, Bob, whom she considered a good catch, since his family were among Oakdale's leading citizens. The couple did eventually marry, and Lisa had a son, Tom, but she was soon having affairs with other men and eventually left town in disgrace, only to return and carry on with a series of lovers who also became her husbands. Over the years, Lisa has mellowed and even managed to join the Hughes clan as a reasonably respectable citizen of Oakdale and a successful businesswoman who owned a newspaper and a popular restaurant, the Mona Lisa.

In the 1970s and '80s, new characters began to dominate the daily episodes. Among the most popular were the villainous James Stenbeck, played by Anthony Herrara; Barbara Ryan, played by Donna Wandry for a short time and then by Colleen Zank; Dr. John Dixon, played by Larry Bryggman; Kim Reynolds, played by Kathryn Hays; the rich and powerful Lucinda Walsh, played by Elizabeth Hubbard; and Iva Snyder, played by Lisa Brown, who still makes occasional appearance. In recent years, major additions to the cast who have remained with the show have included Lucy Deakins, Heather Rattray, and Martha Byrne as Lily Snyder/Walsh; Kathleen Widdoes as Emma Snyder; Jon Hensley as Holden Snyder; Jennifer Ashe as Meg Snyder; Michael Swan as Duncan McKechnie; and Benjamin Henrickson as Detective Hal Munson.

As the World Turns was the number-one rated soap opera on television for many years throughout the late 1950s, the 1960s, and the 1970s. By the 1980s, however, the series' popularity had diminished. In the late 1990s, the program once again began to draw viewers. This was mainly due to an infusion of new characters and actors on the series, including the reintroduction of arch villain James Stenbeck, played, for the most part, by Anthony Herrera; Craig Montgomery, played by Hunt Block; Emily Stewart (a character that had previously been played by several other actresses) with Menighan Hensley playing Emily; Dr. Ben Harris, played by Peter Parros, Molly Conlon, played by Lesli Kay; and Carly Tenny, played by Maura West. In 2001, actress Martha Byrne, who played the sweet and wholesome Lili Snyder on the series, took on the role of her own twin sister, Rose DeAngelo. Rose had never appeared or even been mentioned on the series before. The twin sisters had been adopted at birth by different people, and neither Rose nor Lili knew she had a twin until a chance meeting at a New Jersey adult entertainment club. In time, Rose surpassed Lili in popularity with fans of the show. Ellen Walsh has been the director of *As the World Turns* since 2000.

ASNER, EDWARD (1929–)

Best known as the character Lou Grant from his appearances on *The MARY TYLER MOORE SHOW* and *LOU GRANT*, Ed Asner, who was born in Kansas City, Kansas, has had a long and distinguished career as an actor. Asner appeared on such memorable television series as *NAKED CITY* in 1958, *ROUTE 66* in 1960, *The UNTOUCHABLES* in 1959, *ALFRED HITCHCOCK PRESENTS* in 1962, *The VIRGINIAN* in 1962, *The FUGITIVE* in 1963, *The NAME OF THE GAME* in 1968, *MISSION IMPOSSIBLE* in 1966, to name just a few, before he was cast as Lou Grant on the highly successful situation comedy series *The Mary Tyler Moore Show* in 1970. In 1977, Asner repeated his Lou Grant role on a new, entirely different adventure series bearing the Moore show character's name, *Lou Grant*. Although Asner later starred in several less-than-successful TV series, including *The Bronx Zoo* (1987), *Captain Planet and the Planeteers* (1990—voice), *The Trials of Rosie O'Neill* (1990), *Fish Police* (1992—voice), *Thunder Alley* (1994), *Spider Man* (1993—voice), *Bruno the Kid* (1996—voice), *Ask Harriet* (1998), *The Closer* (1998), and *Max Steel* (2000—voice), he has remained constantly in demand as a character actor and guest-starred in hundreds of TV series and made-for-TV films, and such successful feature films as *Fort Apache, the Bronx* (1981), *Yes, Virginia, There Is a Santa Claus* (1991—TV), *Gypsy* (with Bette Midler, 1993), and *The Perfect Game* (2000).

ASTAIRE, FRED (FREDERICK AUSTERLITZ JR. 1899–1987)

The son of immigrant parents from Austria who settled in Omaha, Nebraska, where he was born, Fred Astaire began his show business career at the tender age of five, dancing with his sister, Adele, in vaudeville and later on Broadway in such stage successes as *Lady Be Good* (1924), *Funny Face* (1927), *The Band Wagon* (1931), and *The Gay Divorcée* (1934). When Adele decided to retire from show business in 1932, Fred traveled to Hollywood, hoping to become a film star. The RKO Studios decided to take a chance on the gifted, but not particularly handsome Astaire, and signed him to a contract. He was summarily loaned out to the MGM Studios to appear in their musical film *Dancing Lady* (1933). Although his performance in that film received good reviews, it was Astaire's first role at RKO in *Flying Down to Rio* (1933), dancing with actress Ginger Rogers for the first time, that made him an "overnight" film star. Subsequent costarring appearances with Rogers in such blockbuster films as *The Gay Divorcee* (1934), *Top Hat* (1935), *Swing Time* (1936), *Shall We Dance?* (1937), and *The Story of Vernon and Irene Castle* (1939), and others, eventually made Fred Astaire and Ginger Rogers Hollywood legends. By the 1940s, Rogers and Astaire decided to go their separate ways. Ginger subse-

quently won an Academy Award as Best Actress for her performance in *Kitty Foyle*, as Astaire continued to star in musicals such as *You Were Never Lovelier* (1942) with Rita Hayworth and *Holiday Inn* (1942) with Bing CROSBY. At MGM, Astaire starred in popular films including *Ziegfeld Follies* (1946), *Easter Parade* (1948), which costarred Judy GARLAND, *The Barkleys of Broadway* (1949), with his former dance partner Ginger Rogers, and *Three Little Words* (1950). Other successful musical films included *Funny Face* (1957) and *Silk Stockings* (1957). As early as 1948, Fred Astaire had made guest appearances on such television shows as Ed SULLIVAN's *TOAST OF THE TOWN* program and had also appeared on *The GENERAL ELECTRIC THEATER* in 1954. In 1958, Astaire appeared in his first television special, *An Evening with Fred Astaire,* dancing with a new partner, Barrie Chase, to music provided by the Jonah Jones Quartet. The special was so well received that *Another Evening with Fred Astaire* was presented the following year, which was equally successful. In 1959, Astaire made his dramatic acting debut in the antiwar film *On the Beach*, and in 1962, Astaire became the host and sometimes star on the *Alcoa Premiere* dramatic anthology series. Astaire joined the cast of the TV series *IT TAKES A THIEF*, playing Robert WAGNER's father, Alistair Mundy, in 1968 and remained with the show until 1970. An impressive dramatic performance in the successful film *The Towering Inferno* in 1974 led to more supporting roles as a character actor on TV and in films. Astaire continued working in films and on television until shortly before his death in 1987.

A-TEAM, THE

Jan. 1983	NBC	Sun. 10–11 P.M.
Feb. 1983–Aug. 1986	NBC	Tues. 8–9 P.M.
Aug. 1986–Dec. 1986	NBC	Fri. 8–9 P.M.
Dec. 1986–Apr. 1987	NBC	Tues. 8–9 P.M.
May 1987–Jun. 1987	NBC	Sun. 7–8 P.M.

This action/adventure series did not take itself too seriously, even though there were violent scenes on display. The A-Team was a crack group of four former military men who had been in the service during the Vietnam War and became mercenaries after being discharged. The military was in constant pursuit of the team, whom they suspected were profiting from funds stolen from the Bank of Hanoi. The A-Team worked for anyone who had the price to pay them for planning and executing an assignment that required their military expertise. Even though the U.S. military was determined to arrest the A-Team and bring them to justice, they always skillfully managed to avoid being apprehended. George Peppard played Captain John "Hannibal" Smith, the team's leader, a cigar-smoking master of disguises and the brains of the outfit. The muscle man of the group was an African American named Sgt. Bosco "B. A." Barracus, played by an actor named Mr. T. (real name Laurence Tureaud), who in spite of his gruff exterior was somewhat of dandy who sported numerous gold chains around his neck and gem encrusted rings, as well as a Mohawk haircut. B. A. became one of the show's most popular characters. Dirk Benedict played Templeton Peck, nicknamed "Face" because of his good looks. Face was an expert impersonator/actor who could always be depended upon to successfully infiltrate whatever enemy the team was pitted against. Dwight Schultz played the wildest and most amusing member of the team, H. M. "Howlin' Mad" Murdock. A running gag on the show was B. A. Barracus's fear of being in an airplane, especially when it was being flown by Howlin' Mad, who enjoyed watching B. A. squirm. In fall 1987, the U.S. military finally apprehended the A-Team and forced them to become government agents. The interesting music for the series was composed by Mike Post and Peter Carpenter. A total of 128 episodes of the show were produced, which can still be seen in reruns.

AUTRY, GENE (ORVON GENE AUTRY 1907–1998)

One of America's most popular entertainers throughout the 1930s and '40s, cowboy star Gene Autry was born in the country near Tioga, Texas. Autry was one of the first cowboy stars to realize that television was going to be an important medium, and in 1950, he starred on a weekly TV series, *The GENE AUTRY SHOW* (aka *Melody Ranch*). Before he became an actor, Gene Autry worked as a laborer with the St. Louis and San Francisco Railroad in Oklahoma and then became a telegrapher. Always a good singer, Gene began singing professionally on a local radio station in 1928, and later, he made his film debut in *In Old Santa Fe* (1934), which starred Ken Maynard, and he appeared in a 13-episode serial, The *Phantom Empire*. One year later, Autry signed a contract with Republic Pictures and made hundreds of western "B," or second-feature, films from the 1930s to the 1950s. These films were extremely popular, and had such titles as *Melody Trail, Singing Cowboy, Boots and Saddles, Colorado Sunset, Wagon Team,* and *Winning of the West*. During World War II, Autry was an officer with the Air Transport Com-

mand, and after the war, he returned to film acting. Always a good businessman, Autry formed the Flying A company in the late 1940s and produced his own television series, *The Gene Autry Show,* as well as such popular children's adventure series as *ANNIE OAKLEY* and *The Adventures of Champion*. By the early 1960s, Gene Autry had become one of the wealthiest men in Hollywood and owned real estate, radio stations, hotels, and the California Angels baseball team, which he bought in 1983. In addition to being a successful performer and businessman, Gene Autry also composed over 200 songs during his long and productive life. He died at the age of 91 in Los Angeles.

AVENGERS, THE

Mar. 1966–July 1966	ABC	Mon. 10–11 P.M.
July 1966–Sept. 1966	ABC	Thurs. 10–11 P.M.
June 1967–Sept. 1967	ABC	Fri. 10–11 P.M.
Jan. 1968–Sept. 1968	ABC	Wed. 7:30–8:30 P.M.
Sept. 1968–Sept. 1969	ABC	Mon. 7:30–8:30 P.M.

Five years before being exported to the United States, *The Avengers* television series was a major hit in Great Britain. An amusing, light adventure/spy drama, *The Avengers* starred Patrick Macnee as secret agent John Steed. On the British series, actress Honor Blackman appeared as Mcnee's costar, but when the series made its American debut, Diana Rigg was Steed's female partner, Emma Peel. When Rigg decided to leave the series in 1968 to pursue a career on the stage in Britain, she was replaced by Linda Thorson as Steed's new assistant, Tara King. "Mother," the team's government contact, was played by Patrick Newell. The spy duo used all sorts of clever methods to complete their missions, usually employing somewhat improbable technical devices to outwit their various enemies. Fifty-one episodes of the original series were filmed. In 1978, *The New Avengers* series was released, but it was not a success and lasted for just one season.

B

BAA BAA BLACK SHEEP (AKA THE BLACK SHEEP SQUADRON)

Sept. 1976–Aug. 1977	NBC	Tues. 9–10 P.M.
Dec. 1977–Mar. 1978	NBC	Wed. 9–10 P.M.
Mar. 1978–Apr. 1978	NBC	Thurs. 9–10 P.M.
July 1978	NBC	Wed. 9–10 P.M.
Aug. 1978–Sept. 1978	NBC	Fri. 8–9 P.M.

Robert CONRAD starred as fighter pilot Major Gregory "Pappy" Boyington, in this action/adventure series set during World War II. Boyington's Squadron 214 was a group of misfits who flew missions in the South Pacific and were all on the verge of being court-martialed by the Marine Corps. Boyington had received the "Pappy" nickname because his age, 35, made him the oldest member of the squadron. Appearing with Conrad as members of the squadron were Dana Elcar as his commanding officer, Col. Lard; James Whitmore, Jr., as Capt. James W. Gutterman; Dirk Blocker as Lt. Jerry Bragg; Robert Ginty as Lt. T. J. Wiley; John LARROQUETTE as Lt. Bob Anderson; W. K. Stratton as Lt. Lawrence Casey; and Simon Oakland, Joey Aresco, Jeff MacKay, Larry Manetti, Red West, Steve Richmond, Byron Chang, Katherine Cannon, Jeb Adams, Denise DuBarry, Kathy McCullen, Briane Leary, and Nancy Conrad (Robert's daughter). The story was based on the real Major Boyington's wartime adventures.

BABYLON 5

1992–1997	Syndicated	Various times and days

The popular science fiction series *Babylon 5* took place in the year A.D. 2258, 10 years after an interplanetary Earth-Minbari war ended, although alien Centauris and Narns, who were archenemies, were on the verge of starting a new interplanetary war. Weekly episodes of the series were set on a vast space station called *Babylon 5*, where 250,000 beings from all over the universe lived and worked together. The space station was large enough to accommodate many diverse neighborhoods, including affluent areas for well-to-do inhabitants and slums for less fortunate beings who lived on the station. Aliens, whose needs were different from the human and other humanlike beings, lived in specially designed locations on the space station that mimicked their home planets' particular environment. A neutral space station, *Babylon 5* was a place where representatives from different planets gathered at a United Nations–like headquarters to discuss disputes and negotiate trade agreements. In addition to the regular inhabitants and diplomats who were on the space station, many space wanderers, hustlers, and criminals, as well as business entrepreneurs, visited the station. Commander Jeffrey Sinclair, played by Michael O'Hare, was the senior military officer on *Babylon 5* when the series first aired, but he was replaced by Commander John Sheridan, played by Bruce Boxleitner, at the beginning the series' third season. Also regularly featured on the series were Lt. Commander Susan Ivanova, played by Claudia Christian, Security Chief Michael Garibaldi, played by Jerry Doyle, Dr. Stephen Franklin, played by Richard Biggs, Andrea Thompson as Talia Winters, Peter Jurasik as Londo Mollari, Mira Furlan as Delenn, Bill Mumy as Lennier, and Andreas Katsulas as G'kar, Julia Caitlin Brown, Mary Kay Adams, Ardwright Chamberlain, Robert Rusler, Jeff Conaway, Jason Carter, Patricia Tallman, Walter Koenig, Wortham Krimmer, Wayne Alexander, Tracy Scoggins, Ed Wasser, Marjorie Monaghan, Denise Gentille, Joshua Cox, Robin Atkin Downes, Kim Strauss, and Thomas MacGreevy. To many TV science fiction fans, *Babylon 5* is a series that rivaled the various STAR TREK series. In all, 110 episodes of *Babylon 5* were filmed over a five-year period.

BACHELOR FATHER

Sept. 1957–June 1959	CBS	Sun. 7:30–8 P.M.
June 1959–Sept. 1961	NBC	Thurs. 9–9:30 P.M.
Oct. 1961–Sept. 1962	ABC	Tues. 8–8:30 P.M.

John FORSYTHE played a successful, debonair Hollywood lawyer and notorious ladies' man named Bentley Gregg in this series. Gregg had become the guardian of his teenage niece, Kitty, played by Noreen Corcoran, when her parents were killed in an automobile accident. The comedy mainly stemmed from the problems the ill-prepared bachelor father, Gregg, encountered while attempting to raise his spirited niece. Sammee Tong played Gregg's amusing houseboy, Peter Tong, on the series. Also appearing in regular roles were Jimmy Boyd as Kitty's boyfriend, Howard Meecham; Joan Vohs as Elaine; Bernadette Withers as Kitty's best friend, Ginger; Del Moore and Evelyn Scott as Cal and Adalaide Mitchell; Victor Sen Yung as Peter's cousin, Charlie; Aron Kinaid as Kitty's second boyfriend, Warren Dawson, who became the love of her life; and at different times, Alice Backus, Shirley Mitchell, Sue Ann Langdon, Jeanne Bal, and Sally Mansfield as Bentley Gregg's various pretty secretaries.

BACKUS, JIM (JAMES GILMORE BACKUS 1913–1989)

An actor whose distinctive voice and face became well known to millions of people as the nearsighted Mr. Magoo in numerous TV cartoons and films, and as the very rich, marooned Thurston Howell III on the popular TV series GILLIGAN'S ISLAND, Jim Backus was born and raised in Cleveland, Ohio. One of his grade school teachers in Cleveland was Margaret Hamilton, who later became famous as the Wicked Witch in *The Wizard of Oz*. After completing grade school, Backus attended Kentucky Military. When he graduated from that institution, he traveled to New York to study at the American Academy of Dramatic Arts, determined to pursue his dream of becoming an actor. His first show business jobs were on radio working as an announcer and actor. He was a regular performer on such radio programs as *The Danny Kaye Show, The Chase and Sanborn Hour with Edgar Bergen and Charlie McCarthy,* and *The Mel Blanc Show* throughout the late 1930s and 1940s. As early as 1949, Backus was a regular performer on television and appeared on the series *Hollywood House*. In 1952, Backus was comedienne Joan Davis's costar on the successful I MARRIED JOAN TV series. Also a busy character actor in films, Backus was featured in such successful motion pictures as *I'll See You in My Dreams* (1951), *Pat and Mike* (1952) with Katharine Hepburn and Spencer Tracy, *Androcles and the Lion* (1953), *Rebel Without a Cause* (1955), playing James Dean's father, and *It's a Mad, Mad, Mad, Mad, Mad World* (1963). A versatile actor who convincingly appeared in both comedies and dramas, Backus was also frequently seen as a guest star on TV series such as *The UNTOUCHABLES, MAVERICK, I SPY, I DREAM OF JEANNIE, The BRADY BUNCH, CHICO AND THE MAN, GUNSMOKE, POLICE STORY,* and *FANTASY ISLAND,* among others. Constantly in demand as the voice of many cartoon characters in animated. TV series and films, Jim Backus remained busy until his death in 1989.

BAIO, SCOTT (SCOTT VINCENT JAMES BAIO 1961–)

From the moment Scott Baio joined the cast of the hit series HAPPY DAYS in 1977, playing Charles "Chachi" Arcola, the actor was one of the show's favorite performers. Chachi was Arthur "Fonzie" Fonzarelli's (played by Henry WINKLER) tough young cousin from New York. Baio continued to appear on *Happy Days* until 1984, but also appeared on the series *Blansky's Beauties* in 1977, which was on the air for only four months, and in 1978, as one of the stars of *Who's Watching the Kids*. In 1982, Baio appeared as Chachi on the series JOANIE LOVES CHACHI, which costarred fellow *Happy Days* performer Erin Moran, who played Joanie Cunningham. Born in New York City, Baio had been a child actor, and a year before he joined the cast of *Happy Days* had starred in the 1976 film *Bugsy Malone* with Jodie Foster. Baio's next TV series, CHARLES IN CHARGE, made its debut in 1984, but ran for just one year, as did his next series, *Baby Talk* (1991). In 1994, Baio became a regular on the DIAGNOSIS MURDER series and remained with that show for two years. Major roles in such films as *Shakedown, USA* (1979), *Foxes* (1980), *I Love New York* (1988), *Bar Hopping* (1999), and *Very Mean Men* (2000), and guest-starring appearances on such TV series as *The LOVE BOAT, The Fall Guy* (1981–1986), FULL HOUSE, *The NANNY,* and VERONICA'S CLOSET kept the actor busy when he was not working on a television series of his own.

BALL, LUCILLE (LUCILLE DESIREE BALL 1911–1989)

No other comedienne appearing on television has become as legendary a figure as Lucille Ball. She is, without question, the most revered female performer who ever appeared on television, and millions of her devoted fans still watch reruns of her enormously popular I LOVE LUCY series regularly, even though the show made its debut in 1951. Lucille Ball was born in Jamestown, New York. Her father died when she was five years old, and because her mother had to go to work to support her children, Lucille and her younger brother were raised by their grandparents. Leaving high school before she graduated, Lucille, who was always a pretty girl, went to New York City, determined to become an actress. She studied acting at the American Academy of Dramatic Arts, where one of her classmates was Bette Davis. According to Ball, even then, Davis got all the best roles and garnered the best reviews for her performances in school plays. When she finished her studies at the academy in 1933, acting roles proved elusive, so Lucille went to work as a model for Hattie Carnegie. In 1934, Ball finally landed her first major film job, in *Roman Scandals*. The pretty Miss Ball was noticed by a film scout from the RKO Studios and was offered a contract at that studio. Increas-

Lucille Ball and Desi Arnaz (Author's collection)

ingly larger roles in such films as *Top Hat* (1935), *Stage Door* (1937), *Too Many Girls* (1940) followed. During the filming of *Too Many Girls*, Lucille met and fell in love with a young Cuban performer named Desi ARNAZ, who was also appearing in the film. They dated and eventually married. Lucy left RKO and was given a contract to appear in films at the MGM Studios, where she was seen in such film musicals as *DuBarry Was a Lady* (1942) and *Best Foot Forward* (1943) and was nicknamed "Technicolor Tessie" because of her brick-red hair and peaches-and-cream complexion. In 1948, Ball became the star of a weekly situation comedy series on radio called *My Favorite Husband*, playing the wacky, trouble-prone wife of a straitlaced banker, while garnering critical acclaim for her performance in the film *Sorrowful Jones* (1949). *My Favorite Husband* was a very successful radio show, and in the early 1950s, CBS asked Lucille to repeat her role on a television series. Ball had only one request before she would agree to appear on the new television series: that her husband, Desi Arnaz, be her costar. CBS was concerned that the public might not accept the idea of a young American woman being married to a Cuban husband, but they agreed. The show, *I Love Lucy,* was an immediate success and ran for six years, never ranking lower than third in the Nielsen ratings (it was number one in four of those years) and winning more than 200 awards, including five Emmys. A shrewd businessman, Desi initially reserved all rights to these shows, which had been kinescoped and filmed, under the couple's Desilu Company

name. He eventually sold the rights to CBS for millions of dollars, bought the couple a production studio of their own, and Lucy and Desi became millionaires. By 1957, 179 episodes of *I Love Lucy* had been made but Lucy and Desi's marriage was in trouble, even though their company was flourishing. In the 1960s, in addition to the new *Lucy–Desi Comedy Hour* (1962–67), the Desilu Company also produced such TV hits as MISSION IMPOSSIBLE and STAR TREK. Lucy and Desi were divorced in 1960, but Lucille continued to star on their company's shows and was seen on *The* LUCY SHOW from 1962 to 1968 and *Here's Lucy* from 1968 to 1974, which were also successful. Deciding she wished to expand her performing horizons, Lucille appeared on Broadway in the musical comedy *Wildcat* (1961) and was the star of several films, including *Mame* (1974), *The Facts of Life* (1961), and *Critic's Choice* (1963), the last two costarring comedian Bob HOPE. When Lucille Ball died of cancer at the age of 75 in 1986, the syndicated *I Love Lucy* shows she had made with Desi Arnaz 45 years earlier were still being enjoyed by millions of viewers in over 80 countries throughout the world.

BANACEK

Sept. 1972–Dec. 1973	NBC	Wed. 8:30–10 P.M.
Jan. 1974–Sept. 1974	NBC	Tues. 8:30–10 P.M.

At a time when Polish jokes were all the rage in the United States, NBC decided it was time to introduce a Polish–American hero to the American public in the person of a clever, cool, handsome private eye of Polish–American descent named Thomas Banacek. George Peppard, who played Banacek, had enjoyed a reasonably successful career in films prior to becoming the star of this TV series. The Banacek character specialized in collecting rewards from insurance companies for recouping stolen property. He was good enough at what he did to live in the exclusive Beacon Hill section of Boston and to have a chauffeur named Jay. Jay, played by Ralph Manza, and bookstore owner Felix Mulholland, played by Murray Matheson, were his best friends and often helped in solving his cases. A semiregular on the series was a character named Carlie Kirkland, an insurance investigator, played by Christine Belford, who had a romantic attachment to Banacek. The Polish–American Congress of the United States was so pleased with the show's positive Polish/American stand, that it gave the series an award.

BARAGREY, JOHN (1918–1975)

During television's earliest days, following World War II, live dramatic anthology series were among the medium's most popular offerings, and such programs as STUDIO ONE, The GOODYEAR PLAYHOUSE, The KRAFT SUSPENSE THEATRE, OMNIBUS, PLAYHOUSE 90, and The PHILCO TELEVISION PLAYHOUSE were favorites with viewers. Adaptations of such classic works of literature as *Wuthering Heights,*

Pride and Prejudice, and *Camille* were presented regularly. Experienced actors who could remember pages of dialogue and were able to perform in a full-hour, live show with usually less than a week to rehearse were needed to fill the demands of numerous dramatic anthology shows that had begun to appear on television in the late 1940s and early 1950s. One tall, good-looking, classically trained actor, John Baragrey, easily filled the bill and starred in hundreds of early TV dramas. John Baragrey was born in 1918 in Haleyville, Alabama. After years of relative anonymity appearing onstage, Baragrey suddenly became one of the country's most famous faces at the age of 31, when he starred in countless drama series. Among the programs Baragrey appeared on regularly were *The Philco Television Playhouse* (in *Pride and Prejudice,* 1949, *Sense and Sensibility,* 1950, *Symbol: Jefferson Davis,* 1951, and others), *The Goodyear Playhouse* (in *Four Meeting,* 1952), *The UNITED STATES STEEL HOUR* (*Hedda Gabler,* 1954), and numerous ALFRED HITCHCOCK PRESENTS dramas. He also appeared in such films as *The Saxon Charm* (1948), *The Loves of Carmen* (1948), *Tall Man Riding* (1955), and *The Fugitive Kind* (1959) and had regular roles on such daytime TV serials as *The SECRET STORM* (1962–1964) and *DARK SHADOWS* (1966).

BARETTA

Jan. 1975–Mar. 1975	ABC	Fri. 10–11 P.M.
Apr. 1975–July 1975	ABC	Wed. 10–11 P.M.
Sept. 1975–Aug. 1977	ABC	Wed. 9–10 P.M.
Aug. 1977–Jan. 1978	ABC	Wed. 10–11 P.M.
Feb. 1978–June 1978	ABC	Thurs. 10–11 P.M.

The leading character on this series, Tony Baretta, played by Robert Blake, was a somewhat unconventional policeman. Baretta was a streetwise former punk who lived a decidedly different lifestyle. His home was a seedy room in a run-down hotel, where he lived with his a pet bird, a white cockatoo named Fred. The orphaned son of poor Italian immigrant parents, Baretta always dressed in a white T-shirt, jeans, and usually wore a cap, pulled jauntily down over his eyes. He knew the the city's mean streets and was easily able to infiltrate the mob and the vicious motorcycle gangs that preyed on the innocents of the city. Appearing as regulars on the show were Tom Ewell as Baretta's often drunk, older friend, Billy Truman, Dana Elcar as Baretta's boss, Inspector Shiller (later, Edward Gregory took over Shiller's job playing Inspector Hal Brubaker), Michael D. Roberts as Rooster, and Chino Williams as Fats. This gritty, uncompromising series offered viewers a lot of fast-paced action and was often criticized by reviewers for being too violent. The series' executive producer was Bernard L. Kowalski.

BARKER, BOB (ROBERT WILLIAM BARKER 1923–)

It's hard to imagine daytime television without quiz master Bob Barker on home screens. Barker, who was born in Darrington, Washington, entered broadcasting shortly after finishing his education and first came into national prominence when he replaced Ralph Edwards as the host of TRUTH OR CONSEQUENCES in 1966. Barker remained on *Truth or Consequences* until 1974, after he had already taken on *The PRICE IS RIGHT* hosting chores. In between, Barker had also hosted the *Dream Girl* (1966) and *The Family Game* (1967) TV series. *The Price Is Right* returned to television in 1972 in two different versions, after a seven-year hiatus. The show had been a popular television favorite from 1953 to 1963, with Bill CULLEN as its host. First called *The New Price Is Right,* this series originally starred Dennis James in a syndicated version and Barker as NBC's network host. Barker's show was an instant success, but James's show faded into oblivion. In 1975, *The Price Is Right* became the first daytime quiz program to expand to a full hour. For a short time, the show was an evening program as well. From 1974 until 1979, Barker was a semiregular panelist on the MATCH GAME '74 through '79 series. On occasion, Bob Barker made guest appearances in such films as *Happy Gilmore* (1996) and on the television series *The NANNY, Something So Right* (1996), and *Martial Law* (1998).

BARNABY JONES

Jan. 1973–June 1974	CBS	Sun. 9:30–10:30 P.M.
July 1974–Sept. 1974	CBS	Sat. 10–11 P.M.
Sept. 1974–Aug. 1975	CBS	Tues. 10–11 P.M.
Sept. 1975–Nov. 1975	CBS	Fri. 10–11 P.M.
Dec. 1975–Nov. 1979	CBS	Thurs. 10–11 P.M.
Dec. 1979–Sept. 1980	CBS	Thurs. 9–10 P.M.

When retired private detective Barnaby Jones's son, Hal, who had taken over his P.I. business, was killed, the old detective came out of retirement to assist the police in tracking down his son's killer. Hal's widow, Betty, went to work for her father-in-law, and when Hal's killer was apprehended, Barnaby decided to reopen his sleuthing business. The role of Barnaby Jones was played by veteran film and TV actor Buddy EBSEN, who had previously starred in the long-running TV series *The BEVERLY HILLBILLIES.* His new role surprised many viewers who had come to think of him primarily as a comedian. Betty was played by actress Lee Merriweather. Also appearing on the show in regular roles were Mark Shera as Barnaby's assistant Jedediah Romano (J. R.) Jones, Barnaby's young cousin, and Vince Howard as police Lt. Joe Taylor and then John Carter as Lt. John Biddle. The executive producer of the series was Quinn Martin, who was at the helm of numerous successful TV series. By the time *Barnaby Jones* left the air in 1980, after seven years, 177 episodes had been filmed.

BARNEY MILLER

Jan. 1975–Dec. 1976	ABC	Thurs. 8–8:30 P.M.
Dec. 1976–Mar. 1982	ABC	Thurs. 9–9:30 P.M.

| Mar. 1982–Apr. 1982 | ABC | Fri. 8:30–9 P.M. |
| Apr. 1982–Sept. 1982 | ABC | Thurs. 9–9:30 P.M. |

A police precinct house in New York City's Greenwich Village was the setting for this situation comedy series that depicted the more humorous aspects of a New York City policeman's job. Capt. Barney Miller, played by Hal LINDEN, was the central character on the series. The varied assortment of police officers under his command included the "close to retirement" Det. Phil Fish, played by Abe VIGODA; the somewhat dense Det. Stanley Wojohowicz, nicknamed "Wojo," played by Maxwell Gail; the fast-talking Det. Sgt. Chano Amenguale, played by Gregory Sierra; the slow-talking but inciteful Det. Nick Yemana, played by Jack Soo; and the clever Det. Ron Harris, played by Ron Glass (who, in the show's last season finally became the published author of a book, *Blood on the Badge*). *Barney Miller* made its television debut as part of an ABC summer replacement series, *Just for Laughs*, in 1974. Audience reaction to the show was so favorable that a regular weekly series became part of the ABC roster the following

season. Initially, Capt. Miller's wife and children and his home life were regularly featured on the series, but as life at the police precinct became more popular, Miller's family all but faded from view. Elizabeth Miller, Barney's wife, was played by Abby Dalton and then Barbara Barrie, and their children, Rachel and David, were played by Anne Wyndham and Michael Tessler. Also appearing on the series from time to time were Florence Stanley as Fish's wife, Bernice, Linda Lavin as Dr. Janet Wentworth, James Gregory as Inspector Frank Luger, Ron Carey as Officer Carl Levitt, June Gable as Det. Baptista, George Murdock as Lt. Scanlon, and Steve Landesberg as Lt. Arthur Dietrich. By the time the series left prime-time TV, 170 episodes had been completed.

BARRIS, CHUCK (1929–   )

Few people who ever saw Chuck Barris host the outrageous *GONG SHOW* variety program on television could ever forget him. A small, awkward man with sleepy eyes and a constant grin, Barris was an unlikely TV star. Born

The cast of *Barney Miller:* (left to right) Ron Glass, Max Gail, Abe Vigoda, Hal Linden, Jack Soo, and James Gregory (Author's collection)

in Philadelphia, Chuck Barris was, before he became a TV personality, a composer and producer. In 1965 he was the executive producer of *The DATING GAME* and in 1966 he produced *The NEWLYWED GAME*, which were both successful TV game shows. In 1976, when he was auditioning talent to host a new comedy variety show that was to feature generally untalented and unconventional performers, *The Gong Show,* someone suggested that he would be the perfect host for the show, because of his laid-back, almost "stoned"-looking appearance. When everyone agreed that he was perfect for the job, Barris unwillingly became a TV performer. The show was very successful, and in 1980, Barris produced and starred in *The Gong Show Movie.* In 1978, Barris produced the *$1.98 Beauty Show* and in 1979, the *Three's a Crowd* TV series. Chuck Barris was last seen playing "Irwin" in the film *Hugo Pool* in 1997.

BARRY, GENE (EUGENE KLASS 1921–)

Born in New York City, Gene Barry decided he wanted to be an actor while he was attending college, but his big break did not come until 1948, when he was 27 years old and appeared on the *Hollywood Screen Test* television show. His good looks and competent acting won him roles on such early TV series as SUSPENSE (1949), *LUX VIDEO THEATER* (1950), *LETTER TO LORETTA* (1954), *Fireside Theatre* (1955), *The MILLIONAIRE* (1955), *The Ford Television Theatre* (1956), *ALFRED HITCHCOCK PRESENTS* (1955), and many other popular shows. Barry's first regular role on a television series came in 1955, when he appeared on the successful situation comedy *OUR MISS BROOKS,* playing a character named Gene Talbot from 1955 until 1956. Roles in such films as *Soldier of Fortune* (1955), *Back from Eternity* (1956), and *Hong Kong Confidential* (1958), led to his first starring role on a TV western series, *BAT MASTERSON,* which had a healthy three year run. In 1963, Barry starred in a second hit TV series, *BURKE'S LAW,* playing secret agent Capt. Amos Burke. Numerous film roles and guest-starring appearances on such hit TV series as CHARLIE'S ANGELS, FANTASY ISLAND, *The TWILIGHT ZONE,* and *MURDER, SHE WROTE* kept Barry busy as a successful character actor throughout the 1970s, '80s, and '90s. In 1994, Barry revived his Amos Burke character in a new *Burke's Law* series, which aired for only four months.

BARRY, JACK (1918–1984)

During television's early years, Jack Barry was one of TV's most successful quiz masters, but when he was implicated in the quiz show scandals of the 1950s, he temporarily became a pariah in the industry. While he was hosting the popular TWENTY-ONE (1956), *High Low* (1957), and *Concentration* (1958) quiz shows, it was discovered that contestants were being given the answers to questions to heighten the tension on the shows and to make viewers more engrossed in the program each week. The scandal

interrupted Barry's career, and for a while he found it difficult to find work on television.

Born in New York, Barry entered radio shortly after finishing his schooling and was one of television's earliest hosts in the late 1940s to early 1950s. Barry hosted the popular children's panel show *Juvenile Jury* in 1947. He went on to host the WINKY DINK AND YOU children's series in 1953, *The Big Surprise* in 1955, and then *Twenty-One* in 1956. By 1969, Barry's reputation had recovered sufficiently from the quiz-show scandal for him to host a new show, *The Generation Gap,* which was not a success. In 1971, Barry hosted *The REEL GAME* series and then the successful *The Joker's Wild* from 1972 to 1984 and *BREAK THE BANK* in 1976. In 1984, his new show, *Play the Percentages,* began production, but Barry died from a heart attack while jogging in New York's Central Park with the show on the air for just a few months. Bill CULLEN took over his hosting chores.

BAT MASTERSON

Oct. 1958–Sept. 1959	NBC	Wed. 9:30–10 P.M.
Oct. 1959–Sept. 1960	NBC	Thurs. 8–8:30 P.M.
Sept. 1960–Sept. 1961	NBC	Thurs. 8:30–9 P.M.

In the late 1950s to early 1960s, western adventure series were extremely popular on television, and many were among the top-20 shows according to the Nielsen ratings. One popular western series was *Bat Masterson,* which starred Gene BARRY in the title role. Masterson was somewhat of a dandy, who sported a derby hat, carried a gold-topped cane, and dressed in the height of late-1800s fashion. A former lawman, Masterson roamed the Old West using his charm and intelligence to outwit outlaws and other wrongdoers, and to help people who were accused of crimes they didn't commit. Based on the life of the actual western hero, Bat Masterson, who was known to be quite an individualist, many of the episodes on this series recalled Bat Masterson's real-life adventures. The series was produced by Andy White and Frank Pitman.

BATMAN

July. 1966–Aug. 1967	ABC	Wed/Thurs. 7:30–8 P.M.
Sept. 1967–Mar. 1968	ABC	Thurs. 7:30–8 P.M.

Although it was on the air for only two years, the *Batman* adventure series created quite a stir. Until its novelty wore off, *Batman* was one of the most talked about series on television, and millions of adults, as well as children, tuned in weekly. Based on Bob Kane's popular comic book character, Batman, even though it was a "live" action series and not an animated cartoon, the show employed many cartoon features such as large, brightly colored letters that appeared above the actor's heads and read "BAM!" and "BOP!" and "BANG!" when they were fighting. Many of the shots on the show actually resembled cartoon drawings. Adam WEST starred as Bruce Wayne, who became the Batman character. Burt Ward played his young assistant, Dick Grayson, who joined Batman in his escapades as Robin. Alan Napier was Wayne's butler, Alfred Pennyworth; Madge Blake played Wayne's aunt Harriet Cooper; Neil Hamilton played Police Commissioner Gordon; Stafford Repp played Chief O'Hara; and Yvonne Craig played Barbara Gordon, the commissioner's daughter, who became Batgirl when she joined Wayne and Grayson in their crime-fighting adventures. Wayne was a rich man who had inherited his parents' fortune when they were killed by a mugger. He built a complex crime lab, disguised himself by wearing a mask and a bat costume, complete with a bat-wing cape, and battled evil forces, never revealing his true identity. One of the series' major attractions was having the audience guess who would be playing the episode's nasty villain each week. Celebrated film and TV actors vied to guest-star on the series as one of its bad guys. Some of the notables who appeared on the series playing wild, exaggerated evil-doing characters were Burgess Meredith as The Penguin; Cesar Romero as The Joker; Frank Gorshin and then John Astin as The Riddler; Vincent Price as Egghead; Victor Buono as King Tut; and Julie Newmar, Lee Ann Meriweather, and Eartha Kitt, at various times, as the wicked Catwoman. Years after the original series left the air, an animated cartoon series called *Batman, The Animated Series* surfaced in 1992. Kevin Conroy provided the voice of Batman/Wayne. It remained on the air for one year. The popular *Batman* theme music was composed by Neal Hefti. In all, 120 episodes of the series were filmed and can still be seen on occasion in reruns.

BATTLESTAR GALACTICA

Sept. 1978–Apr. 1979	ABC	Sun. 8–9 P.M.
June. 1979–Aug. 1979	ABC	Sat. 8–9 P.M.
Jan. 1980–Aug. 1980	ABC	Sun. 7–8 P.M.

In 1978, one of television's most publicized new programs was *Battlestar Galactica,* an expensively produced science fiction series that attempted to capitalize on the unexpected success of *Star Wars. Battlestar Galactica* proved to be so much like *Star Wars* that the film's producers sued the company producing *Galactica* for attempting to "steal" their film. The man who created the wonderful special effects for *Battlestar Galactica* was John Dykstra, who had indeed produced the special effects for *Star Wars.* The show was reported to have cost $1 million per episode. Most of the action on the TV series was set aboard the space ship *Galactica,* which was the only surviving craft of a fleet of space ships that had been surprised in an attack by the villainous Cylons. Lorne GREENE, formerly seen on BONANZA, played the Galactica's Commander Adama. Robert Hatch played his second in charge, Capt. Apollo; Dirk Benedict played Lt. Starbuck; and Herb Jefferson, Jr., played Lt. Boomer. Also appearing as regulars on the series were Maren Jensen, Tony Swarz, Noah Hathaway, and Terry Carter. Appearing on occasion were John Colicos as Count Baltar, Laurette Spang as Cassiopeia, Anne Lockhart as Sheba, and Kent McCord, Barry Van Dyke, Robyn Douglas, Robbie Risk, Patrick Stuart, Allan Miller, and Richard Lynch. In spite of its big budget, large cast, and fabulous special effects, the series failed to remain on the air longer than one and a half years. Before the last season ended, *Battlestar Galactica* had become an early Sunday evening children's adventure series retitled *Galactica 1980.* Only actor Lorne Greene remained on the show from the original cast.

BAYWATCH

Sept. 1989– Aug. 1990	NBC	Fri. 8–9 P.M.
Sept. 1991– May 2001	Syndicated series	Various stations and times

The most successful failure that ever appeared on American television, *Baywatch* is a series that critics, network programmers, and executives, as well as comedians who made it the butt of their jokes, could not force off the air for a decade. The show was set at Malibu Beach in Southern California, and most TV critics thought the series was a totally insignificant entertainment and that it had nothing

Burt Ward as Robin (left) and Adam West as Batman (Author's collection)

to recommend it but a lot of bare-chested, handsome young men and numerous scantily clad women frolicking on the beach where they worked as lifeguards. Millions of fans disagreed, and when NBC canceled the show after one season, the series' producers filmed new episodes and placed them in syndication. In spite of the lack of network support, the series became a national and then an international sensation, and until 2001 *Baywatch* was one of the most popular television series in the world. David HASSEL-HOFF, who later became one of the producers of the series and one of show business's richest men, played the show's central character, Mitch Buchanan, a lieutenant in charge of the Los Angeles County lifeguards at Malibu Beach. Shawn Weatherly and Parker Stevenson played lifeguards Jill Riley and Craig Pomeroy, who were prominent characters in the early episodes of the show. Over the years, a bevy of beautiful actresses and handsome actors appeared on the show, increasing audience viewing and eventually making the show the most-watched TV series in the world. Among the more prominent members of the regular cast over the years were Billy Warlock, Erika Eleniak, Peter Phelps, Holly Gallagher, Brandon Call, Jeremy Jackson, Pamela Bach, Alexandra Paul, Pamela Anderson (Lee), Susan Anton, Nicole Eggert, Yasmine Bleeth, and Gena Lee Nolin. The series was filmed mainly at the Will Rogers State Park in Los Angeles. In 1994, the estimated worldwide audience enjoyed by *Baywatch* was said to have been over 1 billion. From a series that was considered destined for failure, *Baywatch* became one of television's legendary series.

BEANY AND CECIL

Jan. 1962–Jan. 1963	ABC	Various days and times
Jan. 1963–Sept. 1965	ABC	Sat. 11:30 A.M.– 12 P.M.
Sept. 1965–Dec. 1965	ABC	Sun. 10:30–11 A.M.
Jan. 1966–Jan. 1967	ABC	Sun. 10–10:30 A.M.
Jan. 1967–Sept. 1967	ABC	Sun. 9:30–10 A.M.
Sept. 1988–Dec. 1988	ABC	Sat. 9–9:30 A.M.

On this animated cartoon series, which was based on the Emmy Award–winning puppet series originally aired in the early 1950s, *Time for Beany,* the *Beany and Cecil* show featured a character named Beany, a boy with a constant smile on his face, and a lovable sea serpent named Cecil, who was always seasick. Both the original show and the *Beany and Cecil* series were created and produced by Bob Clampett. Beany and Cecil sailed the seven seas on the good ship *Leakin' Lena,* with Captain Horatio K. Huffenpuff, Beany's uncle, at the helm. During the series' run, Beany met such unforgettable characters as Thunderbolt, the Wonder Colt; the Incredible Three-headed Threep; Pop Gunn, the western explorer; Tearalong, the Dotted Lion; Billy the Squid; Careless, the Mexican Hairless; and the villainously evil Dishonest John. Stan Freberg provided the voices for Cecil and Dishonest John, and

Daws Butler was the voice of Beany and also the voice of Uncle Captain during the series' most successful years. *Beany and Cecil* was revived in 1988, but only three months of programs were completed.

BEAT THE CLOCK

Mar. 1950	CBS	Thurs. 9:45– 10:30 P.M.
Apr. 1950–Sept. 1950	CBS	Sat. 8–9 P.M.
Sept. 1950–Mar. 1951	CBS	Fri. 10:30–11 P.M.
Mar. 1951–Sept. 1956	CBS	Sat. 7:30–8 P.M.
Sept. 1956–Feb. 1957	CBS	Sat. 7–7:30 P.M.
Feb. 1957–Sept. 1957	CBS	Fri. 7:30–8 P.M.
Oct. 1957–Feb. 1958	CBS	Sun. 6–6:30 P.M.

One of several quiz and game shows produced by the celebrated Mark GOODSON and Bill TODMAN, *Beat the Clock* began as a radio show with Bud COLLYER as its host. Collyer continued hosting the program when the series moved to television in March 1950. Contestants chosen from the studio audience had to perform various stunts before time ran out on them (usually 60 seconds). Typical stunts were throwing the most custard pies in a spouse's face, lowering a frankfurter tied to the end of a fishing line and trying to snap the largest number of mousetraps shut, and recovering marshmallows embedded in a bowl of Jell-O by using only one's mouth. Assisting Collyer during the show's first five years on the air was a beautiful young model/actress named ROXANNE (Arlen), who was the Vanna WHITE of her day. Roxanne received as many fan letters as any star at CBS at the time. In 1955, Beverly Bentley replaced Roxanne as Collyer's assistant when Roxanne left the series to try her luck as film actress (she met with little success). *Beat the Clock* remained an audience favorite for eight years and was seen on both evening and daytime versions.

BEULAH

Oct. 1950–Sept. 1953	ABC	Tues. 7:30–8 P.M.

The popular radio series *Beulah,* which had been on the air for nine years, became one of television's earliest situation comedies in 1950. Ethel Waters, and then Louise Beavers, starred as the good-natured, lovable, African-American domestic named Beulah, who worked for the Henderson family. Her boss, Harry Henderson, was played by William Post, Jr., and then by David Bruce; his wife, Alice, was played by Ginger Jones and then Jane Frazee; and their son, Donnie, was played by Clifford Sales and then Stuffy Singer. Butterfly McQueen and then Ruby Dandridge, played Beulah's friend and fellow domestic, Oriole, and Bud Harris, Dooley Wilson, and finally Ernest Whitman played Beulah's boyfriend, Bill Jackson. The Academy Award–winning actress Hattie McDaniel, who played Mammy in the film *Gone With the Wind* and played the Beulah role on radio, was announced as Ethel Waters's replacement for the second season of *Beulah,* but illness forced McDaniel to withdraw and the role went to Louise Beavers.

BEAUTY AND THE BEAST

Sept. 1987	CBS	Fri. 10–11 P.M.
Oct. 1987–Sept. 1988	CBS	Fri. 8–9 P.M.
Nov. 1988–Aug. 1989	CBS	Fri. 8–9 P.M.
Dec. 1989–Jan. 1990	CBS	Wed. 8–9 P.M.
June 1990–Aug. 1990	CBS	Sat. 9–10 P.M.

Beauty and the Beast was certainly one of television's most improbable series. A fantasy/romance, it was set in New York City and involved a young lawyer, Assistant District Attorney Catherine Chandler (the "Beauty" of the show's title), who, after she was attacked by muggers in Central Park, was left to die. Vincent, a powerful but gentle half man/half beast (the "Beast" of the show's title), who lives with other rejects and misfits deep beneath the city in a maze of tunnels and caverns and comes up only at night, rescues Catherine and takes her to his underground home to recover. By the time she has recuperated, Catherine and Vincent have fallen in love, but Catherine returns to the city aboveground and resumes her career. A strong psychic bond has developed between the two, however, and Vincent returns to the city numerous times to come to Catherine's aid whenever she is in trouble, sometimes riding on the top of subway cars to get around the city and to avoid being seen by the public. The inhabitants of Vincent's underground home include "Father," played by Roy Dotrice, whose real name was Jacob Wells, who was the leader of the underworld community. The role of Catherine was played by Linda Hamilton, and Vincent was played by Ron Perlman. Also appearing on the series was Ren Woods, Jay Acavone, Jason Allen, Cory Danziger, David Greenlee, Ellen Geer, Zachary Rosencrantz, Ritch Brinkley, Jo Anderson, Stephen McHattie, Edward Albert, and Lewis Smith. During the final season, Catherine was killed. Before she died, she gave birth to Vincent's son. Vincent was trapped by the head of a criminal empire, but escaped and took his son back to the safety of the underground home. Never a top-rated show, *Beauty and the Beast* acquired a cult following while it was on the air, even though it was only the 55th-rated show in its second season.

BEN CASEY

Oct. 1961–Sept. 1963	ABC	Mon. 10–11 P.M.
Sept. 1963–Sept. 1964	ABC	Wed. 9–10 P.M.
Sept. 1964–Mar. 1966	ABC	Mon. 10–11 P.M.

In the early 1960s, numerous TV shows used hospitals as their setting. One of the most popular medical shows on the air at this time was *Ben Casey.* "Man, woman, birth, death, infinity," a voice stated dramatically at the beginning of each show. The series became ABC's most-viewed TV program shortly after its debut, and actor Vince

Vince Edwards as Dr. Ben Casey and Sam Jaffe as Dr. Zorba (Author's collection)

EDWARDS, who played the handsome and heroic Dr. Casey, became an instant TV star. Produced by Bing Crosby Productions (singer Bing CROSBY had discovered Edwards), *Ben Casey* took place at County General Hospital. Casey's mentor was Dr. David Zorba, the chief of neurosurgery, an aged medical genius played by veteran film character actor Sam JAFFE. Also appearing on the series were Bettye Ackerman (Jaffe's much younger real-life actress wife) as Dr. Maggie Graham, Harry Landers as Dr. Ted Hoffman, Nick Dennis as Nick Kanavaros, Jeanne Bates as Nurse Willis, Stella Stevens as Jane Hancock, Ben Piazza as Dr. Mike Rogers, former screen star Franchot Tone as Dr. Daniel Niles Freeland, Jim McMullen as Dr. Terry McDaniel, and Marlyn Mason as Sally Welden. The series was created by James Moser, who was also responsible for the hit TV series MEDIC.

BENADERET, BEA (BEATRICE BENADERET 1906–1968)

Before she became one of television's best-known performers playing Kate Bradley on *PETTICOAT JUNCTION,* actress Bea Benaderet was George BURNS and Gracie ALLEN's neighbor and friend, Blanche Morton, on *The GEORGE BURNS AND GRACIE ALLEN SHOW.* An enormously talented performer, Benaderet was a successful radio actress before she appeared on television and was heard on such popular radio shows as *The Jack Benny Program, A Date with Judy, Fibber McGee and Molly, The Adventures of Ozzie* and Harriet, The Lux Radio Theater, The Great Gilder-sleeve, and hundreds of other programs. Born in New York City, Bea made her radio-acting debut when she was 12 years old and never stopped working thereafter. In addition to her busy radio and television career, Benaderet also provided the voices for hundreds of cartoon characters, including characters in the Bugs Bunny and Flintstones films. Bea's first major television appearances came on several episodes of I LOVE LUCY in 1951. Benaderet appeared regularly on numerous episodes of The BEVERLY HILLBILLIES throughout 1962 and 1963, playing the Clampett family's country cousin Pearl Bodine. The show's producers were so pleased with audience reaction to her performance that Benaderet was given a series of her own, playing a similar character, this time called Kate Bradley. She made guest appearances as Kate Bradley on the GREEN ACRES series in 1965 and 1966, which was a spin-off of her Petticoat Junction show. Kate Bradley was the mother of three lovely, buxom daughters; thus the series' setting "Hooterville." Petticoat Junction remained popular with viewers until Benaderet's untimely death from lung cancer in 1968. The series continued for two more seasons, but it had lost its punch without her. Petticoat Junction had been, for the five years Benaderet was its star, one of CBS's most popular programs, although it was never a favorite of TV critics.

BENDIX, WILLIAM (1906–1964)

When he took over the role of Chester A. Riley from Jackie GLEASON on the LIFE OF RILEY TV series in 1954, William Bendix was playing a role he had previously played on radio for six years. Bendix was, at the time, one of Hollywood's most successful character actors. Born in Manhattan, New York City, Bendix made his film debut in 1911, when he was five years old. His father, a musician, got him a small role in a silent film that starred Lillian Walker at the Vitagraph Studios in Brooklyn, where the elder Bendix was working as a handyman. Bendix did not appear in films again until 31 years later. In 1922, when he was 15 years old, Bendix was a batboy for the New York Yankees baseball team. After appearing on Broadway, most notably as the cop in On Borrowed Time (1939), Bendix moved to Hollywood, where he played major supporting roles in such classic films as Who Done It? (1942), The Glass Key (1942, starring Alan Ladd, with whom Bendix appeared in numerous films throughout the 1940s), Woman of the Year (1942), Guadalcanal Diary (1943), China (1943), The Hairy Ape (1944), Lifeboat (1944), A Bell for Adano (1945), The Blue Dahlia (1946), Calcutta (1947), The Babe Ruth Story (1948, as Babe Ruth), A Connecticut Yankee in King Arthur's Court (1949), and Macao (1952), before playing Riley on the Life of Riley TV series. When the show left the airwaves, Bendix continued to work in films and starred on another, less successful television series, The Overland Trail, in 1960. The actor also made guest appearances on such notable TV series as LIGHTS OUT, The PHILCO TELEVISION PLAYHOUSE, WAGON TRAIN, MISTER ED, and BURKE'S LAW.

The stocky, broken-nosed, large-jawed actor with the tough New York accent died at the age of 58 of malnutrition and subsequent pneumonia.

BENNY, JACK (BENJAMIN KUBELSKY 1894–1974)

For over 25 years, comedian Jack Benny was one of radio's most successful performers. Benny was one of the few entertainers who made a smooth transition from radio to television in 1950. For several years, Benny's simultaneous radio and television programs were both highly rated shows according to audience polls. For the most part, The JACK BENNY PROGRAM simply continued presenting the same type of entertainment that his radio show had offered, and many of the same cast members that had made his weekly radio program a success appeared on it. Jack Benny was born in Waukegan, Illinois, and dropped out of high school to play the violin in vaudeville. He discovered his talent for comedy when he was in the U.S. Navy in 1918, and performed for an audience of fellow sailors who laughed at his off-the-cuff remarks. Benny decided to combine his violin playing with comedy, and by the 1920s, he had become a successful performer in vaudeville. Benny subsequently appeared in several films, including The Song Writers' Revue (1929) and The Hollywood Revue of 1929, both very early "talking" motion pictures. The comedian became an overnight sensation, however, when he was heard on his first radio program in 1932. In addition to his weekly radio show, which remained one of radio's popular programs throughout the 1930s and 1940s, Benny starred in several successful film comedies during those decades, such as Broadway Melody of 1936, The Big Broadcast of 1937, Artists and Models (1937), Buck Benny Rides Again (1940), Charley's Aunt (1941), To Be or Not to Be (1942), George Washington Slept Here (1942), and the critically panned, but legendary, The Horn Blows at Midnight (1945). Benny appeared on his Jack Benny Show throughout the 1950s, and well into the 1960s, when he began to appear on TV specials, rather than having a weekly show. In addition to his own weekly TV program, Benny also hosted the SHOWER OF STARS TV series in 1954 and made numerous guest appearances on such shows as Here's Lucy, GENERAL ELECTRIC THEATER, The MILTON BERLE SHOW, The ANDY WILLIAMS SHOW, The JACKIE GLEASON SHOW, and ROWAN AND MARTIN'S LAUGH-IN. Benny's last film appearance was in the star-studded comedy It's a Mad, Mad, Mad, Mad World in 1963, playing a cameo role. One of show business's most beloved performers, Benny, who was usually depicted as a miserly, vain, self-centered skinflint on radio, television, and in films, was, in reality, according to his show business friends and his family, a modest and generous man who was totally without ego.

BENSON

| Sept. 1979–July 1980 | ABC | Thurs. 8:30–9 P.M. |
| Aug. 1980–Mar. 1983 | ABC | Fri. 8–8:30 P.M. |

Mar. 1983–Apr. 1983	ABC	Thurs. 8–87:30 P.M.
May 1983–Mar. 1985	ABC	Fri. 8–8:30 P.M.
Mar. 1985–Sept. 1985	ABC	Fri. 9–9:30 P.M.
Oct. 1985–Jan. 1986	ABC	Fri. 9–9:30 P.M.
Jan. 1986–Aug. 1986	ABC	Sat. 8:30–9 P.M.

Robert GUILLAUME originally played the part of the butler, Benson DuBois, on the SOAP television series. His sarcastic, droll characterization proved so popular with viewers that Guillaume was given a spin-off series of his own, *Benson,* created by Susan Harris. Benson worked in a governor's mansion as a household executive on Governor James Gatling's staff. The governor was played by James Noble. Benson's major nemesis on the show was the governor's Teutonic housekeeper, Gretchen Kraus, played by Inga Swenson. Other regular characters on the series included Marcy Hill, as the governor's secretary, played by Caroline McWilliams; Katie Gatling, as the governor's precocious daughter, played by Missy Gold; and Taylor, the governor's aide, played by Lewis J. Stadlen. In 1980, two new characters were added to the series, Clayton Endicott, the governor's obnoxious-but-funny chief of staff, played by Rene Auberjonois, and Pete Downey, the governor's press secretary, played by Ethan Phillips. Jerry SEINFELD and Ted DANSON (later of CHEERS fame) also appeared on the show on occasion. The series ended with Benson deciding to run for governor himself. In the last episode, Gatling and Benson were seen watching the election returns on television, but no winner was announced.

BERG, GERTRUDE (GERTRUDE EDELSTEIN 1899–1966)

In 1929, a program was heard for the first time that went on to become one of radio's, and later television's, legendary series. It was called *The GOLDBERGS,* and it was written by and starred an actress/writer named Gertrude Berg, who played Molly Goldberg, a lovable, motherly Jewish lady who was a kind, compassionate parent and neighbor and a good friend to anyone in need. The series was a combination domestic comedy and soap opera, and when it moved from radio to television in 1949, it was an instant success. Gertrude Berg was born in New York City and was 30 years old when she sold her idea for a weekly series about a Jewish mother and her family to the National Broadcasting Company. The program became one of that network's longest-running radio series, remaining on the air from 1929 until 1950, with various breaks in between. The television series ran for an impressive five years. In addition to her appearances on *The Goldbergs,* Berg also wrote and appeared on Broadway in her play *Molly and Me* and also starred in *A Majority of One.* Berg made notable guest appearances on such television shows as *The UNITED STATES STEEL HOUR* (in *Morning Star,* 1954; *Six O'Clock Call,* 1955; and *Trouble-in-Law,* 1959); and *The Alcoa Hour* (in *Paris and Mrs. Perlman,* 1956). A second TV series, *The GERTRUDE BERG SHOW,* which made its debut in 1961, with Berg playing a character named Sarah Green,

did not prove as successful as *The Goldbergs* and was canceled after a season.

BERGEN, CANDICE (CANDICE PATRICIA BERGEN 1946–)

The daughter of radio and film ventriloquist Edgar Bergen, Candice Bergen, who was born in Beverly Hills, California, grew up in the shadow of her father's dummy, Charlie McCarthy. Candice once said that Charlie McCarthy had "a bigger bedroom and more clothes" when she was child than she did. She also said that she felt as if Charlie were a second brother. Although her father was a good-looking man, Candice's beauty was definitely inherited from her mother, a former model, Frances Westerman. After graduating from Beverly Hills High School, Candice attended the University of Pennsylvania for one year, where she majored in history and creative writing. As a baby, Candice had appeared in the film *Unusual Occupations* in 1949, but she did not appear in films again until 1966, when she played Lakey Eastlake in *The Group* and Shirley Eckert in *The Sand Pebbles.* Her acting ability took Hollywood by surprise, and soon the beautiful young woman was appearing in such important films as *Carnal Knowledge* (1971), *The Wind and the Lion* (1975), *Oliver's Story* (1978), and *Gandhi* (1982). In 1988, Bergen became the star of the weekly TV situation comedy series *MURPHY BROWN,* which became a top-rated show and was on the air for 10 years. When *Murphy Brown's* run ended, Candice, who had became a widow when her husband, Louis Malle, died, decided to retire temporarily and concentrate on raising her daughter, Chloe. In 2002, Bergen hosted a talk show on cable TV's Oxygen Channel.

BERLE, MILTON (MENDEL BERLINGER 1908–2002)

Comedian Milton Berle was television's first major star. Berle first starred on TV on *The TEXACO STAR THEATER* variety show in 1948. Everyone who had a television set in 1948 was soon talking about the wild and comic antics of the comedian they began to call "Uncle Miltie," and who later became known as "Mr. Television." Actually, Berle's appearance on *The Texaco Star Theater* (1948–1953) was not the first time he had been seen on television. In 1928, when he was 20 years old, Berle had participated in an experimental telecast that originated from New York City. Unfortunately, not many people had television receivers at that time to witness his TV debut. The son of Sarah and Moses Berlinger, Milton Berle became a professional actor when, at the age of six, he appeared in an episode of the classic silent film serial, *The Perils of Pauline.* That same year, Berle was also seen in the silent film *Tillie's Punctured Romance.* As a teenage, Berle performed in vaudeville, and was featured in the silent films *Birthright* (1920) and *The Mark of Zorro* (1920). Hollywood rediscovered Berle in the early 1930s, and he began to appear in the "talking" films *Hollywood Hobbies* (1934), *Sun Valley Serenade* (1941), *Margin for*

Milton Berle (Author's collection)

(1988), and *The Best of the Rest of Milton Berle's Private Joke File* (1993).

BERNSTEIN, LEONARD (LOUIS BERNSTEIN 1918–1990)

Composer/conductor Leonard Bernstein became an unexpected television personality when his *Young People's Concerts* lectures catapulted him into the spotlight in the 1950s. An attractive man with distinguished graying hair and a pleasant on-camera personality, Bernstein was one of the foremost/conductor composers in the world, but he became even more famous because of these and subsequent television appearances. Leonard Bernstein was born in Lawrence, Massachusetts. He studied musical composition with Walter Piston at Harvard University, and then in 1939 he entered the Curtis Institute of Music in Philadelphia, where he studied conducting, orchestration, and piano. In 1943, Bernstein was appointed assistant conductor of the New York Philharmonic, and from 1945 until 1947, Bernstein conducted the New York City Center Orchestra. In 1958, he was appointed chief conductor of the New York Philharmonic. By this time, Leonard Bernstein was already well known as the composer of the ballet *Fancy Free* (1944), the musical comedy *On the Town* (1949), the musical comedy *Wonderful Town* (1953), the light opera musical *Candide* (1956), and the musical *West Side Story* (1957). Bernstein's most memorable television appearances also included the critically acclaimed *Bernstein on Beethoven: A Celebration in Vienna* in 1970; *Bernstein/Beethoven*, a TV miniseries in 1982, *Candide* in 1989, and posthumously, *A Place of Dreams: Carnegie Hall at 100* in 1991, and *Leonard Bernstein: "The Rite of Spring" in Rehearsal* (1996). A heavy smoker, Leonard Bernstein died at the age of 72 of a heart attack caused by progressive lung failure.

BERTINELLI, VALERIE (VALERIE ANNE BERTINELLI 1960–)

Actress Valerie Bertinelli, who is best known for playing Barbara Cooper on Norman Lear's ONE DAY AT A TIME TV series, was born in Wilmington, Delaware. When her father, an executive with the General Motors Company, was transferred from Wilmington to Van Nuys, California, Valerie's mother decided to enroll her daughter, who had always expressed an interest in becoming an actress, at the Tami Lynn School of Arts. In 1975, Valerie auditioned for, and won, the Barbara Cooper role on *One Day at a Time*. The series was a hit and had a healthy nine-year run. Valerie starred in several made-for-TV films during and after appearing on *One Day at a Time*, including *Young Love, First Love* (1979), *The Promise of Love* (1980), and *I Was a Mail Order Bride* (1982). She also made guest appearances on such TV series as *The HARDY BOYS MYSTERIES* in 1978. When *One Day at a Time* ended its run, Bertinelli starred on two less-than-successful TV series: *Sydney* (1990) and *Café Americain* (1993). In 1997, Valerie appeared in the TV miniseries *Night Sins* as FBI Agent Megan O'Malley, her most popular character

Error (1943), and others, playing major comic supporting roles. Berle did not become a major star, however, until he hosted *The Texaco Star Theater* television show in 1948. In 1953, Berle hosted *The Buick-Berle Show*. Both of Berle's shows were also called *The MILTON BERLE SHOW*. By this time, Berle had perfected his rapid-fire, broad comic style. While the comedian was appearing on *The Texaco Star Theater*, he had his first major film role as the star of *Always Leave Them Laughing* (1949). After a five-year hiatus, the comedian made a much-publicized return to television in 1958 as the star of *The Milton Berle Show*. The show failed to attract a large audience. Throughout the 1960s, '70s, '80s, and '90s, Milton Berle continued to appear in such films as *Let's Make Love* (1960), *It's a Mad, Mad, Mad, Mad, Mad World* (1963), *The Legend of Valentino* (1975), *The Muppet Movie* (1979), *Broadway Danny Rose* (1984), and *Pee-wee's Big Adventure* (1985), and in 1966, he attempted another TV comeback, appearing on a third *Milton Berle Show*. Once again, his TV show was not a success. In 1967, Berle became a semiregular on *The JACKIE GLEASON SHOW* (1967–1970). Milton Berle wrote three books about his life in show business: *Milton Berle: An Autobiography* (1974), *B. S., I Love You* since she played Barbara Cooper on *One Day at a Time*. Valerie is married to rock star Eddie Van Halen, and they have a son named Wolfgang.

BEVERLY HILLBILLIES, THE

Sept. 1962–Sept. 1964	CBS	Wed. 9–9:30 P.M.
Sept. 1964–Sept. 1968	CBS	Wed. 8:30–9 P.M.
Sept. 1968–Sept. 1969	CBS	Wed. 9–9:30 P.M.
Sept. 1969–Sept. 1970	CBS	Wed. 8:30–9 P.M.
Sept. 1970–Sept. 1971	CBS	Tues. 7:30–8 P.M.

Everyone's desire to come into sudden wealth could be vicariously experienced each week, when viewers watched CBS's situation comedy series *The Beverly Hillbillies*. The show was greeted with negative reviews from TV critics when it made its debut in 1962. Nine years later, these same critics were scratching their heads, wondering how such a silly, simple-minded slapstick comedy could possibly have lasted that long. The series, developed by the president of the CBS network, James. T. Aubrey, revolved around the Clampetts, a hillbilly family that lived in the Ozark Mountains. The Clampetts resided in a ramshackle mountain shack and wore raggedy clothes. On the first episode, the Clampetts had just struck it rich when oil suddenly sprouted up from the ground in their front yard. John Brewster of the OK Oil Company gave the family $25 million for the oil-drilling rights on their property, and the Clampetts decided to move to a "better Beverly Hills" in California. Their money was deposited in the Drysdale Commerce Bank in Beverly Hills, and Milburn Drysdale, the bank's president, decided the Clampetts were too naive to handle such a large sum of money themselves, so he moved them into the mansion next to his, in order to keep an eye on them. The comedy on the show revolved around the Clampetts' various encounters with people who were usually far more sophisticated and worldly than they were.

The cast of the show included veteran film actor Buddy EBSEN, as the patriarch of the Clampett family, Jed Clampett; Irene Ryan as Granny Daisy Moses; Donna Douglas as Elly Mae Clampett, Jed's beautiful daughter; and Max Baer, Jr., as Jethro Bodine, Jed's L'il Abner–like, beefy nephew. The ever-exasperated Banker Drysdale was played by Raymond Bailey. Drysdale's somewhat uptight, brittle assistant at the bank, Jane Hathaway, was played by Nancy Culp, who became one of the viewers' favorite characters. Over the years, numerous hilarious characters made appearances on the series, including Pearl Bodine, Jethro's mother, played by Bea Benaderet; Mrs. Margaret Drysdale, played by Harriet MacGibbon; John and Edythe Brewster, played by Frank Wilcox and Lisa Seagram; Jasper DePew, played by Phil Gordon; Marie, the maid, played by Sirry Steffan; Sonny Drysdale, played by Louis Nye; Janet Trego, played by Sharon Tate; Homer Cratchit, played by Percy Helton; Elverna Bradshaw, played by Elvia Allman; and Shiffy Shafer, played by Phil Silvers. In 1981, CBS produced a TV film, *The Return of*

the *Beverly Hillbillies*, with Ebsen, Douglas, Baer, and Kulp reprising their original roles. Irene Ryan had passed away by that time. *The Beverly Hillbillies'* Nielsen ratings have never been equaled by any other TV series. A total of 274 episodes of the original program were filmed.

BEVERLY HILLS 90210

Oct. 1990–Aug. 1992	FOX	Thurs. 9–10 P.M.
Jul. 1992–May 1997	FOX	Wed. 8–9 P.M.
Jun. 1997–Aug. 1997	FOX	Tues. 8–9 P.M.
Sep. 1997–2000	FOX	Wed. 8–9 P.M.

The surprise hit series of the 1990 television season was *Beverly Hills 90210*, which was produced by the prolific television and film producer Aaron SPELLING. *Beverly Hills 90210* was an hour-long dramatic series that originally centered on two 16-year-old twins, a boy and a girl, whose family had moved to Beverly Hills from Minnesota when their father, an accountant, was transferred to Southern California. The twins' attempts to fit in with their new, much more sophisticated crowd of friends at West Beverly High led to numerous problems. Immediately popular with teenagers all across the United States, and later with viewers all over the world, *Beverly Hills*

The cast of *Beverly Hills, 90210*: (clockwise from top) Ian Ziering (Steve Sanders), Tori Spelling (Donna Martin), Brian Austin Green (David Silver), Shannen Doherty (Brenda Walsh), Luke Perry (Dylan McKay), Jennie Garth (Kelly Taylor), Jason Priestly (Brandon Walsh), and Gabriele Carteris (Andrea Zuckerman) (Author's collection)

90210 dealt with such sensitive subjects as premarital sex, alcohol and drug addiction, and many other subjects of concern to teens. Jason Priestly played Brandon Walsh, and Shannen Doherty played his twin sister, Brenda. Carol Potter and James Eckhouse played the twins' parents, Cindy and Jim Walsh. Among the other original regular characters who became popular with viewers and often became the focus of weekly episodes were Kelly Taylor, the daughter of a recovering alcoholic mother, played by Jennie Garth; Steve Sanders, the adopted son of a television star, played by Ian Ziering; Andrea Zuckerman-Vasguez, the brainy editor of the school newspaper, played by Gabrielle Carteris; David Silver, played by Brian Austin Green; the ever-sullen Dylan McKay, played by Luke Perry; the dyslexic Donna Martin, played by Tori Spelling (Aaron Spelling's daughter); and Scott Scanlon, who was killed in a shooting accident, played by Douglas Emerson. As the series continued to be popular, many new performers joined the cast, and several of the show's cast members went on to appear in other TV shows and films.

BEWITCHED

Sep. 1964–Jan. 1967	ABC	Thurs. 9–9:30 P.M.
Jan. 1967–Sept. 1969	ABC	Thurs. 8:30–9 P.M.
Sept. 1969–Jan. 1972	ABC	Wed. 8–8:30 P.M.
Jan. 1972–July 1972	ABC	Sat. 8–8:30 P.M.

Bewitched: (sitting) Dick Sargent (Darrin) and Kasey Rogers (Louise Tate); (standing) Elizabeth Montgomery (Samantha) (Author's collection)

Not all witches are ugly crones, as the TV situation comedy series *Bewitched,* created by Sol Saks and produced by William Asher, proved. *Bewitched* starred Elizabeth MONTGOMERY as a beautiful, reluctant young witch named Samantha Stephens. Samantha's desire to abandon the supernatural skills she had inherited from her witch mother, Endora, and her warlock father, Maurice, both of whom thoroughly enjoyed being witches, and her attempt to live a normal life as an ordinary suburban wife, and later mother, was the basis of this show's comedy. Samantha and her mere mortal husband, Darrin, an account executive at a New York advertising agency, played by Dick York (1964–1969), and then by Dick Sargent (1969–1972), were married on the first episode of the series. As Darrin gradually became aware that his wife was a witch, things began to change. At first, Samantha refrained from using her witch's talents, which she could summon up simply by twitching her nose. As time and various domestic and marital problems surfaced, Samantha began to rely on her supernatural powers more and more. Samantha's mother, played by actress Agnes Moorehead, regularly appeared out of nowhere to cause whatever mischief she could, since she disapproved of Samantha's marriage to Darrin. Other witches and warlocks such as Samantha's father, Maurice, played by Maurice Evans; her dithery and forgetful Aunt Clara, played by Marion Lorne; her Uncle Arthur, played by Paul Lynde; and Esmerelda, played by Alice Ghostley, also made regular unannounced visits to the Stephens' home. Samantha and Darrin's next-door neighbor, Gladys Cravitz, played by Alice Pearce and then (when Pearce died) Sandra Gould, was driven wacky as she regularly began to see odd things happening in the house next door. Her husband, Abner, played by George Tobias, never saw anything and thought his wife was losing her mind. Another popular character was the heavy-set Dr. Bombay, played by Bernard Fox. In 1965, the Stephens's first child, a girl the couple named Tabitha, who inherited her mother's supernatural powers, was born. Tabitha was played by three sets of twins over the years, Heidi and Laura Gentry, Tamar and Julie Young, and Diane and Erin Murphy. The Stephens later had a nonwitch son, Adam, also played by twins, David and Greg Lawrence. After 252 episodes, the show quietly departed the airwaves, looking a bit tired after eight years on the air.

BIG TOP

July. 1950–Sept. 1950	CBS	Sat. 7–8 P.M.
Sept. 1950–Jan. 1951	CBS	Sat. 6:30–7:30 P.M.
Jan. 1951–June 1958	CBS	Sat. 12–1 P.M.

A popular, early attraction on television, *Big Top* presented circus acts and starred Jack Sterling as the ringmaster/host of the show and Ed McMahon (later of *The TONIGHT SHOW*) and Chris Keegan as clowns. Dan Lurie was a strongman who assisted the ringmaster on the show. Six acts, such as trapeze artists, animal tamers and their wild animals, and wire walkers, were seen each week. The series originated from Convention Hall in Camden, New Jersey. After just six months on the air as a prime-time attraction, *Big Top* became a Saturday afternoon show and remained on the air for seven more years.

BIG VALLEY

Sept. 1965–July. 1966	ABC	Wed. 9–10 P.M.
July. 1966–May 1969	ABC	Mon. 10–11 P.M.

Hoping to duplicate its rival NBC's success with BONANZA, ABC launched a weekly ranch family adventure/drama series of their own, *Big Valley*, in 1965. *Bonanza* centered on the patriarch/owner of an enormous ranch in Nevada and his three sons. *Big Valley* featured a strong-willed, independent widow who with her four children owned the 30,000-acre Barkley Ranch in California's San Joaquin Valley. Screen star Barbara STANWYCK played the family matriarch, Victoria Barkley. Richard Long played her lawyer son, Jarrod; Peter Breck played her always brawling son, Nick; Lee MAJORS played her rugged adopted son, Heath (who was her late husband's illegitimate offspring); and Linda Evans played her beautiful, willful daughter, Audra. In the early episodes of the series, another son, Eugene, played by Charles Briles, was also seen on the show, but he was gradually written off the series. Napolean Whiting played Silas, the Barkley's loyal retainer. The Barkleys were a feisty group who were determined to hold on to their sprawling spread of land no matter what the cost. They constantly battled crooked bankers, murderers, outlaws, and even Mexican revolutionaries to hold on to what was theirs. After four years, *Big Valley* finally gave up trying to compete with *Bonanza* (which, by that time, had already been on the air for 10 years and continued for another 4 years after that) and suspended production.

BILL COSBY SHOW, THE

Sept. 1969–May 1971	NBC	Sun. 8:30–9 P.M.
June. 1971–Aug. 1971	NBC	Tues. 7:30–8 P.M.

THE NEW BILL COSBY SHOW:
Sept. 1972–May 1973	CBS	Mon. 10–11 P.M.

THE COSBY SHOW:
Sept. 1984–June 1992	NBC	Thurs. 8–8:30 P.M.
July 1992–Sept. 1992	NBC	Thurs. 8:30–9 P.M.

The Bill Cosby Show has had several incarnations over the years. After his success on the *I SPY* adventure series in the 1960s, comedian Bill COSBY starred on a weekly situation comedy series, *The Bill Cosby Show*, playing a high school physical education teacher and coach named Chet Kincaid in a lower-middle-class neighborhood in Los Angeles. Lillian Randolph, and then Beah Richards, played his mother, Rose; Lee Weaver played his brother, Brian; and Olga James played his sister-in-law, Verna.

Sid McCoy played the principal of his school, Mr. Langford; and Joyce Bulifant played a fellow educator, guidance counselor Marsha Peterson. When *The Bill Cosby Show* ended its run, Cosby starred on a comedy/variety show called *The New Bill Cosby Show*. Cosby was the show's weekly host, and regular performers on the series included Lola Falana, Foster Brooks, the Quincy Jones Orchestra, Ronny Graham, and others. Two regular weekly sketches were featured on each show: "The Wife of the Week" and the very funny "The Dude," with Cosby playing a character so cool nothing ever seemed to bother him. It was, however, the next show that starred Bill Cosby, *The Cosby Show*, which made its TV debut in 1984, that really catapulted the comedian/actor into superstardom. On this situation comedy series, Cosby played Dr. Heathcliff (Cliff) Huxtable, a successful obstetrician. Cliff's wife, Clair, was an attorney, and the couple lived with their four children in a New York City brownstone. The Huxtable children were Sondra, who was a student at Princeton University when the show first went on the air, played by Sabrina Le Beauf; Denise, was a teen who usually said "no problem" whether there was a problem or not, played by Lisa Bonet; Theodore (Theo), a "too cool for comfort" teen, played by Malcolm-Jamal Warner; Vanessa, an overactive girl, played by Tempestt Bledsoe; and the baby of the family, Rudy, a mischievous but lovable little girl, played by Keshia Knight Pulliam. Cliff and Claire Huxtable were intelligent, sensitive parents who brought up their children with a firm hand, good common sense, and lots of love. They were the parents everyone wished they had had when they were growing up. *The Cosby Show* was the number one program on the air in the mid-1980s. The series was revived in the late 1990s and, as of this writing, continues to be the favorite show of many TV viewers.

BING CROSBY SHOW, THE

Sept. 1964–June. 1965	ABC	Mon. 9:30–10 P.M.

Although he starred in several TV specials in the 1960s and 1970s, including the highly rated *Bing Crosby in Dublin* (1965), the celebrated radio, film, and recording star of the 1930s, '40s, and '50s, Bing CROSBY had a regular series on the air for only one year, from 1964 to 1965. Crosby's half-hour show was a situation comedy series on which Bing played a former singer named Bing Collins, who had abandoned the hectic world of show business to go to work as an electrical engineer. The character soon discovered that his "normal life" was as hectic as show business, because unpredictable domestic situations kept cropping up as Collins and his wife, Ellie, played by Beverly GARLAND, tried to raise their two energetic teenage daughters, Janice and Joyce, played by Carol Faylen and Diane Sherry. Familiar Hollywood character actor Frank McHugh played the Collins's live-in handyman, Willie Walters. Each week, Bing somehow always managed to sing a song or two on the show. *The Bing Crosby Show* was produced by Steven Gethers for Bing Crosby Productions.

BIONIC WOMAN, THE

Jan. 1976–May 1977	ABC	Wed. 8–9 P.M.
Sept. 1977–Mar. 1978	NBC	Sat. 8–9 P.M.
May 1978–Sept. 1978	NBC	Sat. 8–9 P.M.

A spin-off of the popular SIX MILLION DOLLAR MAN series, *The Bionic Woman* starred Lindsay Wagner as Jaime Somers, a young woman who, after being injured in a skydiving accident, was fitted with bionic legs, a bionic right arm, and a bionic right ear that gave her supernatural physical abilities. Jaime had been a schoolteacher before her accident but used her amazing new physical abilities to fight various bad guys as an OSI (Office of Scientific Investigation) operative after her operation. Among the regular cast members seen with Wagner on the series were Richard Anderson as Oscar Goldman, her OSI boss; Martin E. Brooks as Dr. Rudy Wells; Ford Rainey as Jim Elgin; and veteran film actress Martha Scott as Helen Elgin. When *The Bionic Woman* made the switch from ABC to NBC in 1977, a new character, a bionic German shepherd named Max, became Jaime's partner and joined her in her adventures. During the series last year on TV, bizarre science fiction stories surfaced, and Jaime even had encounters with visitors from outer space.

BIRNEY, DAVID (1939–)

David Birney, who was born in Washington, D.C., entered show business after graduating from Dartmouth College and receiving a B.A. degree in English. He then attended U.C.L.A., where he earned a master's degree in theater. Birney's first important acting assignment on television, after appearing on the stage, was on an episode of *The F.B.I.* series in 1965. Regular roles on such daytime serials as *Love Is a Many Splendored Thing* (1967) and *A World Apart* (1970) led to a starring role on the BRIDGET LOVES BERNIE (1972) situation comedy series. *Bridget Loves Bernie* was about a young Jewish man who married an Irish–American Catholic girl. His next starring role was on the TV series SERPICO (1976), about an undercover cop. Birney then appeared on ST. ELSEWHERE (1982), playing Dr. Ben Samuels, who worked in a large metropolitan hospital. His last regular role on a continuing series was on *Glitter* (1984). Many starring roles in made-for-TV miniseries—*The Adams Chronicles* (1976), *Testimony of Two Men* (1977), *Master of the Game* (1984), *Secrets* (1992), and others—have made Birney one of television's busiest actors.

BIXBY, BILL (WILFRED BAILEY BIXBY 1934–1993)

Bill Bixby said he knew he wanted to be an actor when he was still in grade school in San Francisco, California,

where he was born. As soon as he finished his schooling, he began to pursue his dream and soon won acting jobs with several experimental theater groups. In 1960, Bixby made his first major television appearance on an episode of *The* ANDY GRIFFITH SHOW, and in 1961, he became a regular on *The Joey Bishop Show* (1961–1965). A starring role on the popular MY FAVORITE MARTIAN series in 1963 led to a second leading role on what became one of television's most fondly remembered series, *The* COURTSHIP OF EDDIE'S FATHER, in 1969. This lighthearted, sensitive series was about a young single father raising his son after his wife's death. It was a critical success and had a loyal, if not large, following, but it did not remain on the air long. Guest-starring appearances on such TV series as *The* TWILIGHT ZONE (1963), THAT GIRL (1966), COMBAT! (1966), IT TAKES A THIEF (1968), NIGHT GALLERY (1972), *The* STREETS OF SAN FRANCISCO (1974, 1976), and starring roles on the series *The Magician* (1973), MASQUERADE PARTY (as a regular panelist 1974), *Once Upon a Classic* (1976), *The* INCREDIBLE HULK (1978), for which he is perhaps best remembered, and *Goodnight Beantown* (1983) followed in quick succession. Bixby also directed episodes of such TV series as *Barbary Coast* (1975), *The Incredible Hulk* (1978), *Mr. Merlin* (1981), *Ferris Bueller* (1990), and BLOSSOM (1991). Bixby died at the age of 59 of cancer.

B. J. AND THE BEAR

Feb. 1979–Mar. 1980	NBC	Sat. 9–10 P.M.
Mar. 1980–Aug. 1980	NBC	Sat. 8–9 P.M.
Mar. 1981–Apr. 1981	NBC	Tues. 9–10 P.M.
Apr. 1981–Aug. 1981	NBC	Sat. 9–10 P.M.

The "B. J." in the title of this amusing adventure series was an independent trucker named Billy Joe (B. J.) McCoy, played by Greg Evigan, and the "bear" was his pet chimpanzee, whom B. J. called Bear. The two had numerous adventures together riding the roads of the United States in B. J.'s truck. Featured on the series when it first went on the air was a character named Sheriff Lobo, who was McCoy's major nemesis. Lobo was played by veteran character actor Claude Akins, who left to show after a few months to star in a spin-off series of his own, the short-lived *Misadventures of Sheriff Lobo*. The show also featured Slim Pickens as Sgt. Beauregarde Wiley; Richard Deacon as Sheriff Masters (who replaced Lobo); Conchata Ferrell as Wilhelmina Johnson, nicknamed "the Fox"; Janet Louise Johnson as B. J.'s female friend, Tommy; and Joshua Shelley as Bullets, who owned the Country Comfort Truck Stop. By the time the series left the air in 1981, all the above characters had been written off the series, and B. J. had moved to California with his chimp and expanded his trucking company. His new nemesis was Capt. Rutherford T. Grant, played by Murray Hamilton, the corrupt chief of the Special Crimes Action Team, who owned a trucking company and did everything he could to eliminate competition. B. J. hired a bevy of beautiful women as his drivers, played by twins Candi and Randi Brough, Shelia DeWindt, Barbara Horan, Judy Landers, Linda McCullough, and Sherilyn Wolter. The executive producers of the series were Glen A. Larson and Michael Sloan.

BLAKE, ROBERT (MICHAEL JAMES VIJENCIO GUBITOSI 1933–)

When he was five years old, Robert Blake, then known as Mickey Gubitosi, won a featured role in the MGM *Our Gang* film series. Born in Nutley, New Jersey, the young actor had just the right toughness and cuteness to become one of the series' major players. In 1940, Gubitosi changed his name to Bobby Blake, although he continued to use his birth name when appearing in the *Our Gang* films for three more years. As Bobby Blake, the child star attracted considerable attention playing a Native American boy, Little Beaver, on the *Red Ryder* western film serial. As Blake grew older, acting jobs became harder to find, and he had to work at odd jobs in order to support himself. Although he played impressive roles in such films as *Pork Chop Hill* in 1959 and *Town Without Pity* in 1961, it wasn't until he was cast as one of the young murderers in the film *In Cold Blood* in 1967 that his adult acting career really began to take off. Blake had been a regular on *The Richard Boone Show* in 1963, but in 1975, he became the star of his own TV series, BARETTA, which was a huge success. Although his next series *Hell Town* (1985) was not a success and was canceled after only three months, Blake continued to appear in numerous films and made guest-starring appearances on various television shows. Blake's wife was murdered in 2001, and in 2002 he was accused of the murder.

BLOCKER, DAN (DAN DAVIS BLOCKER 1928–1972)

Before he became world famous as "Hoss" Cartwright on the long-running TV western series BONANZA in 1959, Dan Blocker played supporting roles on such westerns as GUNSMOKE (1955), *Colt .45* (1957), RESTLESS GUN (1957), *The* ZANE GREY THEATER (1958), *The* RIFLEMAN (1958), and was a regular on the *Cimarron City* (1958) series. A real son of the West, Blocker was born in Bowie County, Texas. The 6-foot, 4-inch, muscular Blocker had even worked on a ranch as a young man. In addition to his many TV appearances, Blocker was also featured in such films as *The Young Captives* (1959), *The Errand Boy* (1961), *Come Blow Your Horn* (1963), and *The Cockeyed Cowboys of Calico County* (1970). In 1972, Dan Blocker died at the age of 44, after undergoing heart surgery.

BLONDIE

Jan. 1957–Sept. 1957	NBC	Fri. 8–8:30 P.M.
Sept. 1968–Jan. 1969	CBS	Thurs. 7:30–9 P.M.

Even though Chic Young's comic strip characters, Blondie and Dagwood Bumstead and their children, Cookie and Alexander, had been enormously successful in a series of films, two attempts to turn *Blondie* into a TV situation comedy series failed. The first attempt starred Arthur Lake as Dagwood (he had played Dagwood in the film series) and Pamela Britton as Blondie. Anne Barnes and Stuffy Singer played Cookie and Alexander. Florenz Ames was Dagwood's boss, Mr. Dithers; and Elvia Allman his wife, Cora Dithers. Blondie and Dagwood's next-door neighbor, Herb Woodley, was played by Hal Peary. A second attempt to turn *Blondie* into a television series occurred 10 years later. Will HUTCHINS and Patricia Harty played Dagwood and Blondie, Jim BACKUS and Henny Rackus played Mr. and Mrs. Dithers, and Pamelyn Ferdin and Peter Robbins played Cookie and Alexander. Even Dagwood's familiar and funny blunders at work and at home, his famous oversized Dagwood sandwich, and the Bumsteads' lovable and comic dog, Daisy, and her pups, could not turn either of these TV series into hits, and they were both canceled after less than one full season on the air.

BLOSSOM

Jan. 1991–June. 1991	NBC	Mon. 8:30–9 P.M.
Aug. 1991–Mar. 1995	NBC	Mon. 8:30–9 P.M.
May 1995–June 1996	NBC	Mon. 8:30–9 P.M.

A 13-year-old girl was the central character of this situation comedy series that starred Mayim Bialik as Blossom Russo. *Blossom* was first aired to test audiences reaction to it on July 5, 1990, and it proved successful enough for NBC to give it a weekly time slot, midyear, during their 1991 season. Each week's episode was seen through the eyes of the main character, Blossom, an intelligent and mature young woman. Viewers saw all the familiar early-adolescent problems that TV characters of Blossom's age usually encounter. Blossom lived with her divorced father, Nick, a studio musician, played by Ted Wass, and her two brothers, Anthony, a recovering substance abuser, played by Michael Stoyanov, and Joey, a good-looking teenage Romeo, played by Joey Lawrence. Blossom's best friend, a kooky and quirky girl named Six LeMuere, was played by Jenna Von Oy. For the show's second season, a new regular character, Grandpa Russo, played by Barnard Hughes, joined the series. The most popular character on the show was, without question, Blossom's brother, Joey, and actor Joey Lawrence became a teen idol to millions of adoring young female fans, undoubtedly keeping the series on the air longer than had he not been on it.

BOB CUMMINGS SHOW, THE (AKA *LOVE THAT BOB*)

Jan. 1955–Sept. 1955	NBC	Sun. 10:30–11 P.M.
July 1957–Sept. 1957	CBS	Thurs. 8–8:30 P.M.
Sept. 1957–Sept. 1959	NBC	Tues. 9:30–10 P.M.

Motion picture actor Robert CUMMINGS entered television in 1955, when his film career had started to slip. His TV series, *The Bob Cummings Show* (later called *Love That Bob* in syndication) featured the clean-cut Cummings as professional photographer, Bob Collins, who had a dream job photographing beautiful models all day long. Bob lived with his widowed sister, Margaret MacDonald, played by Rosemary DeCamp, and his nephew Chuck, played by Dwayne HICKMAN, who was always trying to make time with the gorgeous girls his uncle photographed and dated. One of the most popular characters on the show was Charmaine "Schultzy" Schultz, played by Ann B. DAVIS. The lovable Schultzy worked at Bob's photography studio as his assistant and had a mad crush on her boss. Also appearing on the show regularly were Nancy Kulp as Pamela Livingston, Lyle Talbot as Paul Fonda, and King Donovan as Harvey Helm. Among the bevy of beauties who were featured on the series at different times were Lisa Gaye, Diane Jergens, Mary Lawrence, Gloria Marshall, Joi Lansing, Carol Henning, and Miss Sweden of 1956, Ingrid Goude.

BOB NEWHART SHOW, THE

Sept. 1972–Oct. 1976	CBS	Sat. 9:30–10 P.M.
Nov. 1976–Sept. 1976	CBS	Sat. 8:30–9 P.M.
Sept. 1977–Apr. 1978	CBS	Sat. 8–8:30 P.M.
June 1978–Aug. 1978	CBS	Sat. 8–8:30 P.M.

Comedian Bob NEWHART originally hosted a comedy/variety program called *The Bob Newhart Show* from 1961 until 1962, but it was his situation comedy series, also called *The Bob Newhart Show* in 1972, that remained on the air for six years, for which Newhart is most fondly remembered. On this series, Newhart played a successful psychologist, Robert (Bob) Hartley. Hartley lived in a high-rise apartment in Chicago with his elementary schoolteacher wife, Emily, played by Suzanne PLESHETTE. The Hartleys' neighbor, Howard Borden, a divorced airline pilot, played by Bill Daley; his office receptionist, Carol Kester Bondurant (whom Hartley shared with a dentist), played by Marcia Wallace; and the dentist, Jerry Robinson, played by Peter Bonerz, provided much of the show's comedy, with Newhart usually playing a benumbed, owl-eyed straight man to their wisecracks. Also appearing on the series as regular characters at times were Penny MARSHALL, Larry Gelman, Patricia Smith, Florida Friebus, Renee Lippin, John Fiedler, Noam Pitlick, Lucien Scott, and Oliver Clark. Some of the series' funniest episodes occurred when Hartley was conducting his group therapy sessions and his patients interacted with one another in highly amusing ways that usually had Bob squirming uncomfortably.

BOLD AND THE BEAUTIFUL, THE

Mar. 1987–present	CBS	Various times Mon. through Fri.

One of the few daytime serial dramas that is not a full-hour weekday program, the half-hour *Bold and the Beautiful* is one of television's most popular soap operas. Using the glamorous fashion industry as its background, *The Bold and the Beautiful* centers on two very different families, both of whom have garment businesses, the upscale Forresters and the less sophisticated Spectras, who are always competing with the Forresters for top fashion honors. Originally, the series focused on the Forrester and Logan families, but the Logans, except for Brooke Logan, eventually faded from the spotlight. Over the years, Brooke has been married to the Forresters' eldest son, Ridge, as well as to his father, Eric, and has also been romantically involved with the Forresters' youngest son, Thorne. Eventually, the Spectra family's popularity with viewers increased and they became the Forresters' major antagonists. The Forresters, Eric and his on-and-off and then on-again wife, Stephanie, are played by John McCook and Susan Flannery. Clayton Norcross and then Jeff Trachta played Thorne, and Ronn Moss plays Ridge. The seductress Brooke Logan is played by Katherine Kelly Lang. The Spectra family includes the full-figured, brassy Sally Spectra, played by Darlene Conley, and her sweet, sometimes alcoholic, and recently deceased, daughter, Macy, who married Thorne, was played by Bobbie Eakes. Another popular performer is the beautiful Hunter Tylo, who plays Ridge's wife, the mother of his twins, Dr. Taylor Hayes. At one time, Lesley Woods played Grandma Logan and Joanna Johnson played Thorne's first wife, Caroline, but they eventually departed from the series. Schae Harrison continues to appear regularly as Sally Spectra's somewhat common but lovely receptionist, Darla.

BONANZA

Sept. 1959–Sept. 1961	NBC	Sat. 7:30–8:30 P.M.
Sept. 1961–Sept. 1972	NBC	Sun. 9–10 P.M.
May 1972–Aug. 1972	NBC	Tues. 7:30–8:30 P.M.
Sept. 1972–June 1973	NBC	Tues. 8–9 P.M.

For 13 years, the western series *Bonanza* was one of America's, and indeed the world's, most popular shows. The major characters on *Bonanza* were the Cartwrights, Ben Cartwright, a widower, and his three sons Adam, Eric, nicknamed "Hoss," and "Little Joe." The Cartwrights were prosperous ranchers who owned a 1,000-square-mile spread called The Ponderosa located near Virginia City, Nevada, which was the site of the famous Comstock Silver Lode. Ben Cartwright's three sons each had a different mother and all three women had died shortly after giving birth to their sons, leaving Ben to raise the boys alone. Adam, Ben's eldest son, was a serious, studious man and, like his father, was strong and steady. Adam was born in New England and his mother's name was Elizabeth. Hoss, Ben's middle son, was a burley-but-gentle bear of a man, whose mother was a Scandinavian immigrant named Ingrid. Little Joe, the youngest of Ben's sons, was spirited,

Bonanza: (left to right) Lorne Greene (Ben Cartwright), Pernell Roberts (Adam), Dan Blocker (Hoss), and Michael Landon (Little Joe) (Author's collection)

impulsive, and romantic. His mother was a woman named Marie, whom Ben had met and married while he was visiting New Orleans. She died by falling off a horse when Little Joe was still an infant. All Ben's sons had admirable qualities inherited from their father, who ruled his little empire with a strong, firm hand, but remained totally devoted to his three sons.

The role of Ben Cartwright was played by Lorne GREENE. Adam was played by Pernell Roberts, Hoss by Ban Blocker, and Little Joe by Michael LANDON. Other regulars on the series were Victor Sun Yung as the Cartwrights' faithful servant, Hop Sing; Ray Teal as Sheriff Roy Coffee; David Canary as Candy; Lou Fritzel as Dusty Rhodes; Mitch Vogel as Jamie Hunter; Tim Matheson as Griff King; and Bing Russell as Deputy Clem Foster. In 1965, Pernell Roberts decided it was time to move on to more important things and left the series. It was Dan Blocker's sudden death in 1972 that was one of the major reasons producers decided, after 14 years, that it

was time to end *Bonanza's* long and successful run. In 1988, a made-for-TV film, *Bonanza: The Next Generation*, was presented, which its producers hoped would lead to a new *Bonanza* TV series. None of the original performers appeared in the series, but Michael Landon's son, Michael Landon, Jr., and Dan Blocker's son, Dirk Blocker, were featured in the cast. The series never materialized, but two subsequent *Bonanza* made-for-TV films were made that had little, if any, residual results. The *Bonanza*-based show *The Ponderosa* appeared on cable in 2001.

BOND, WARD (WARDELL BOND 1903 OR 1905–1960)

One of Hollywood's most familiar faces, character actor Ward Bond appeared in hundreds of films throughout the 1930s, '40s, and '50s before he became a television star playing Major Seth Adams on the successful TV series *WAGON TRAIN* in 1957. The burly, gruff-voiced Bond was born in either Colorado or Nebraska, according to which source one reads. While attending the University of Southern California, where he was on the football team, a teammate, who became Bond's best friend and one of Hollywood's biggest stars, John Wayne, suggested Bond might make some money by working as an extra in films, which he did. Before long, Bond began to get small roles in films and became a close friend of film director John Ford. Roles in such classic films as *Dead End* (1937), *Drums Along the Mohawk* (1939), *Gone With the Wind* (1939), *The Grapes of Wrath* (1940), *Tobacco Road* (1941), *It's a Wonderful Life* (1946), *The Searchers* (1956), and *Rio Bravo* (1959), and hundreds of other films, made Bond one of filmdom's most successful character actors. Bond died while attending a football game in Dallas, Texas. His hit TV series, *Wagon Train,* was still in production.

BOONE, RICHARD (RICHARD ALLEN BOONE 1917–1981)

Before Richard Boone became famous for playing Paladin on the HAVE GUN WILL TRAVEL television series, he was a college student and a professional boxer and also worked in an oil fields before joining the U.S. Navy during World War II. When the war ended, Boone used the G.I. Bill to study acting at the Actor's Studio in New York City. He was determined to become an actor. Boone made his Broadway debut in a production of the classic Greek drama *Medea* and also appeared on several television dramatic anthology series in the late 1940s and early 1950s. On a 1948 *Actor's Studio* TV production, Boone was featured in a play called *You're Breaking My Heart,* and one year later he was seen in a theatrical production of *The Front Page.* In 1950, 20th Century Fox Studios signed Boone to a contract. He made his motion picture debut in *The Halls of Montezuma* that same year. Subsequently, he appeared in *The Robe* (1953), playing Pontius Pilate, and *Vicki* (1953). Boone's first regular role on a television series was as Dr. Styner on the critically successful, but not particularly popular TV show, MEDIC in 1954. His next series, HAVE GUN WILL TRAVEL, a western adventure series made its debut in 1957. Boone starred as a refined gun-for-hire named Palladin, who had high moral values. *Have Gun Will Travel* remained an audience favorite for six years. When it was canceled, Boone starred in another series, *The Richard Boone Show* (1963), which was on the air for only one season. His next TV series was *Hec Ramsey* (1972), which aired for two years. Boone's film career continued, and he was featured in such motion pictures as *Rio Conchos* (1964), *Hombre* (1967), *The Kremlin Letter* (1970), *The Shootist* (1976), and *The Bushido Blade* (his last film, 1979).

BOOTH, SHIRLEY (MARJORY FORD 1898–1992)

During her long and distinguished career as an actress, Shirley Booth was a leading lady on Broadway, appearing in such plays as *My Sister Eileen, The Matchmaker, Summertime, A Tree Grows in Brooklyn,* and *Come Back, Little Sheba;* a radio performer who was heard on such popular shows as *Duffy's Tavern* and *The Theater Guild on the Air;* and an Academy Award–winning film actress for her performance in *Come Back, Little Sheba* (1952). Booth is, however, probably best remembered for playing a lovable, down-to-earth domestic on the television situation comedy series HAZEL, for which she won several Emmy Awards. The actress also starred on the less successful TV series *A Touch of Grace* in 1973. As her distinctive voice and accent would indicate, Booth was born in New York City, and she went on the stage when she was a young woman. In addition to appearing on *Hazel* and *A Touch of Grace,* Booth also made several notable guest appearances on such television series as *The* UNITED STATES STEEL HOUR and *The* ANDY WILLIAMS SHOW.

BORGNINE, ERNEST (ERMES EFFRON BORGNINO 1917–)

Born in Hamden, Connecticut, Ernest Borgnine spent 10 years in the U.S. Navy after he finished secondary school. After his discharge from the navy, Borgnine decided that he wanted to become an actor and went to New York. One of his first acting jobs was on the children's adventure serial CAPTAIN VIDEO in 1949. After appearing on such TV anthology series as *The Ford Television Theatre,* ZANE GREY THEATER, The FIRESIDE THEATRE (1952), and GENERAL ELECTRIC THEATER in the early 1950s, Borgnine went to Hollywood, where he soon became a popular character actor, mainly playing villains in such films as *From Here to Eternity* (1953) and *Johnny Guitar* (1954). In 1955, Borgnine surprised the motion picture industry with his marvelous performance as Marty Pilletti in *Marty,* which won him a Best Actor Academy Award. *Marty* had been a TV play that starred Rod Steiger, before it became a motion picture. Borgnine's first regular television role was on the MCHALE'S NAVY series in 1962, playing Lt. Cmdr. Quinton McHale. The show was a success and ran for four years. Borgnine later appeared as the leading character on the AIR WOLF series in 1984, and then the less successful *The Single Guy* (1995) and *All Dogs Go to Heaven* (1996). He also made numerous guest appearances on such TV series as MURDER, SHE WROTE, HOME IMPROVEMENT, and JAG.

BOSLEY, TOM (THOMAS EDWARD BOSLEY 1927–)

Best known as Richie Cunningham's father on the successful HAPPY DAYS television series, actor Tom Bosley was born in Chicago, Illinois. As a young man, Bosley went to New York to pursue a career as an actor, determined to appear on Broadway. In 1958, he got his wish when he starred in the musical comedy *Fiorello!* and won a Tony Award for his performance in that play. Traveling west to Hollywood not long after after *Fiorello!* ended its Broadway run, Bosley soon appeared on such popular TV series as NAKED CITY, MISSION IMPOSSIBLE, MAUDE, *Kolchak: The Night Stalker, Wait Till Your Father Gets Home,* and *The STREETS OF SAN FRANCISCO.* After *Happy Days,* Bosley became a regular on the MURDER, SHE WROTE series, playing Jessica Fletcher's hometown sheriff; Amos Tupper. He later starred on the FATHER DOWLING MYSTERIES series in 1989 and was featured on the *Port Charles* daytime TV serial drama in 1999.

BOSOM BUDDIES

Nov. 1980–Sept. 1981	ABC	Thurs. 8:30–9 P.M.
Oct. 1981	ABC	Thurs. 9–9:30 P.M.
Nov. 1981–Jan. 1982	ABC	Fri. 8:30–9 P.M.
Feb. 1982–Mar. 1982	ABC	Thurs. 8:30–9 P.M.
May 1982–June 1982	ABC	Thurs. 8:30–9 P.M.
July 1984–Sept. 1984	ABC	NBC 9–9:30 P.M.

Bosom Buddies was a TV situation comedy series that viewers kept insisting be brought back when TV executives decided to take it off the air. The series had a large and loyal following, though its ratings never placed it among television's top-rated programs. From the moment *Bosom Buddies'* theme song, "My Life," sung by Billy Joel, was heard until the end of each episode, fans were delighted with everything they saw and heard on the series, giving it a cultlike following. The stars of the show were two engaging young actors, Tom Hanks (who later became one of Hollywood's biggest film stars) and Peter Scolari. They played two friends named Kip Wilson and Henry Desmond, who worked as underpaid lackeys at a New York City advertising agency. Kip was an aspiring artist and Henry a would-be novelist. When their cheap New York apartment is demolished, the two young men, in desperation, disguise themselves as women, Buffy and Hildegarde, and move into the inexpensive Susan B. Anthony Hotel for Women. Not only do they get cheap rent, they also come in contact with a bevy of beautiful women. Actress Holland Taylor played the boys' aggressive boss, Ruth Dunbar, at the agency, and Wendie Jo Spencer played Amy Cassidy, a resident at the Women's Hotel and the only woman who knew that Buffy and Hildegarde were actually Kip and Henry. Donna Dixon and Thelma Hopkins played Sonny and Isabelle, two beautiful residents at the women's hotel, and Lucille Benson played Lilly Sinclair, the hotel's formidable manager, who was always on the verge of discovering Buffy and Hildegarde's real identities.

BOURBON STREET BEAT

Oct. 1959–Sept. 1960   ABC   Mon. 8:30–9:30 P.M.

Bourbon Street Beat was one of TV's first hour-long detective series, and it garnered considerable attention from the press and public when it first was aired on ABC in 1959. The series was canceled after its first season, but two of the show's characters, Rex Randolph and Kenny Madison, later appeared on two new TV series, *77 SUNSET STRIP* and *SURFSIDE 6.* Set in New Orleans, *Bourbon Street Beat* starred Richard Long as Rex Randolph and Andrew Duggan as Cal Calhoun, who operated the "Randolph and Calhoun, Special Services" private detective agency. Arlene Howell played their receptionist, Melodie Lee Mercer, and Van Williams was their young assistant, Kenny Madison. Eddie Cole played "The Baron," a piano player at their favorite Bourbon Street bar. In their desire to make their series look authentic, ABC bought an actual New Orleans restaurant, The Absinthe House, placed the Randolph and Calhoun offices above it, and filmed many of the show's location shots there.

BOXLEITNER, BRUCE (1950–)

Tall and handsome Bruce Boxleitner, who was born in Elgin, Illinois, decided to become an actor when he was in college. After several years of playing small roles in regional theater productions and on several TV series such as BARETTA, HAWAII FIVE-0, GUNSMOKE, and *The MARY TYLER MOORE SHOW,* Boxleitner won the role of "The Scarecrow," Lee Stetson, in the relatively successful TV series *The SCARECROW AND MRS. KING* in 1983. He subsequently starred in the TV miniseries *North and South* in 1985, *Till We Meet Again* (aka *Judith Krantz's Till We Meet Again*) in 1989, the syndicated TNT network science fiction series BABYLON 5 from 1994 until 1998, and the made-for-TV film *Freefall* in 1999. Boxleitner married TV actress Melissa Gilbert in 1995.

BOY MEETS WORLD

Sept. 1993–Mar. 1995	ABC	Fri. 8:30–9 P.M.
May 1995–Sept. 1996	ABC	Fri. 8:30–9 P.M.
Sept. 1996–Oct. 1996	ABC	Fri. 9:30–10 P.M.
Oct. 1996–May 1998	ABC	Fri. 8:30–9 P.M.
May 1998–Sept. 1998	ABC	Fri. 9–9:30 P.M.
Sept. 1998–July 1999	ABC	Fri. 8:30–9 P.M.
July 1999	ABC	Fri. 9:30–10 P.M.

Ben Savage, the brother of Fred SAVAGE of *The WONDER YEARS* series, was only 11 years when his series *Boy Meets World* first went on the air in 1993, and was a young man of 17 when the last episode of the show was aired. On the series, Ben played the role of Cory Matthews, and the show was seen through his eyes. Cory was in a constant state of preadolescent, and later adolescent, confusion. His young life was certainly complicated by the fact that his stuffy teacher, George Feeney, played by William Daniels, lived in the house next door to him, and kept an ever-watchful eye on the boy. Cory's father, Alan Matthews, who managed a supermarket, and his housewife mother, Amy Matthews, who were played by William "Rusty" Russ and Betsy Randle respectively, did what they could to understand and guide their adolescent son, but were often too busy, or were too confused by his strange-to-them actions. Cory's siblings certainly didn't do much to help him cope with the always confusing world that seemed to be all around him. His older brother, Eric, played by Will Friedle, and his younger sister, Morgan, played by Lily Nicksay, had enough trouble dealing with their own problems to be of much help to their brother. Only his friend Shawn Turner, played by Rider Strong, seemed to understand Cory, since he shared many of the same problems that Cory was experiencing. Cory's classmates, the nerd Minkus, played by Lee Norris, and Topanga, played by Danielle Fishel, also had enough problems of their own to be of much help to Cory. During the series second season, Cory and his friends had somehow managed to get through elementary school and found themselves in middle school, where Cory's social and academic problems seemed to loom even larger than they had in the lower grades. Things got worse when Cory encountered the school bully, Harley Kiner, played by Danny McNulty, who seemed to have a grudge against Cory and all his friends. Middle school eventually gave way to high school during the six years the show was televised. When *Boy Meets World* left the air in 1999, Cory was still struggling to make it through his adolescence the best way he could, with the least amount of trouble.

BOYD, WILLIAM (1895–1972)

World famous as "Hopalong Cassidy," film and television western star William Boyd was born in Cambridge, Ohio. Bill's father was a day laborer, and when Bill was seven years old, his parents moved to Tulsa, Oklahoma, where he spent most of his childhood and early adolescence. Bill was in his teens when both of his parents died. He quit school and went to work as a grocery clerk, and then as a surveyor and an oil field worker. In 1919, Boyd decided to move to Hollywood to look for work in the budding new motion picture business. He got a job as an extra in the Cecil B. De Mille film *Why Change Your Wife?* (1920). Bill did everything he could to attract De Mille's attention by wearing fancy clothes and putting himself in the great director's line of vision at any opportunity. Boyd's good looks eventually did catch De Mille's eye, and with the director's help, he appeared in five films a year from 1920 until 1926. Eventually, Boyd was given a leading romantic role in De Mille's *The Volga Boatman* (1926). This film made Boyd a matinee idol to female filmgoers.

Boyd continued to star in films, and in 1935 he was cast in a role that would change his life forever. The film was a western called *Hop-Along Cassidy,* so called because the hero originally walked with a limp caused by a bullet wound to his leg. Boyd changed the somewhat seedy character, who had had appeared in a series of adventure novels, and made the character heroic and as pure as the driven snow. Hopalong never drank, swore, chewed tobacco, rarely kissed a girl, and always let the bad guy draw his gun first. The character became immensely popular with filmgoers, especially young viewers who usually saw the films at Saturday afternoon movie matinees. By 1943, Boyd had made 54 Hopalong Cassidy films for producer Harry Sherman, and Boyd bought the rights to the character and made 12 more films himself. In 1948, Boyd sold his ranch and bought the rights to all the Hopalong Cassidy films he had made over the years. The actor was a smart enough businessman to market the character effectively and sold hundreds of products using the Hopalong Cassidy character, making 100 percent profit from the sale of Hopalong Cassidy records, comic books, and radio shows. An enormously popular television series that showed the old Hopalong Cassidy films made its debut in 1949. It remained on the air until 1952. The show was then sold in syndication and has been seen on television, at various times, ever since. Bill Boyd, the poor boy from Tulsa, died one of the richest men in Hollywood in 1972, at the age of 74.

BRADY BUNCH, THE

Sept. 1969–Sept. 1970	ABC	Fri. 8–8:30 P.M.
Sept. 1970–Sept. 1971	ABC	Fri. 7:30–8 P.M.
Sept. 1971–Aug. 1974	ABC	Fri. 8–8:30 P.M.

Even though the original *Brady Bunch* series was on the air for only five seasons, the characters continued to appear on television periodically for the next 25 years in various new formats such as *The Brady Bunch Hour* (a variety show) in 1977, *The Brady Brides* in 1981, and *The Bradys* (a dramatic series) in 1990. An old-fashioned, 1950s-style situation comedy about how much fun it is to live in a house with a large family, *The Brady Bunch* centered on Carol and Mike Brady, played by Florence HENDERSON and Robert Reed, who were both widowed, had met and fell in love, and were married and made their two families one. Carol had three daughters from her first marriage, and Mike, an architect, had three sons, which made for some interesting and amusing domestic complications. The family lived in a comfortable four-bedroom house in the Los Angeles suburbs. In addition to Carol and Mike, the family consisted of Carol's daughters Marcia, Jan, and Cindy, played by Maureen McCormick, Eve Plumb, and Susan Olsen, and Mike's sons, Greg, Peter, and Bobby, played by Barry Williams, Christopher Knight, and Mike Lookinland. Also living in the house with the family was their trusted housekeeper/cook, Alice Nelson, played by Ann B. DAVIS, who kept the family on an even keel, and the Bradys' dog, Tiger. The Brady children's ages, when the original series made its debut, were seven to 14 years, and the characters, as well as the actors who played the parts, literally grew up in front of viewers' eyes. In 1972, an animated version of the show, *The Brady Kids,* surfaced as a Saturday morning program and was on the air for two years.

BREAK THE BANK

Oct. 1948–Sept. 1949	ABC	Fri. 9–9:30 P.M.
Oct. 1949–Jan. 1952	NBC	Wed. 10–10:30 P.M.
Jan. 1952–Feb. 1953	CBS	Sun. 9:30–10 P.M.
June 1953–Sept. 1953	NBC	Tues. 8:30–9 P.M.
Jan. 1954–Oct. 1955	ABC	Sun. 10–10:30 P.M.
Oct. 1955–June 1956	ABC	Wed. 9:30–10 P.M.
Oct. 1956–Jan. 1957	NBC	Tues. 10:30–11 P.M.

Originally heard on radio in 1945, *Break the Bank* was one of television's first popular quiz shows, making its TV debut in 1949. While on television, *Break the Bank* constantly switched from one station to another, and by the time it left the air in 1957 it had appeared on all three major networks, NBC, CBS, and ABC. The radio and early TV versions of *Break the Bank* were hosted by veteran radio announcer/quizmaster Bert PARKS. Bill CULLEN took over the hosting job in 1953. Bud COLLYER hosted a daytime version of the program in 1953. Contestants were drawn from the studio audience and were asked a series of difficult questions, after they had chosen a particular category. They won increasingly larger sums of money for each question they answered correctly and eventually were asked the question that could "break the bank," which was the cumulative amount of money left over when previous contestants had failed to answer the tough last question. The "Bank" could be worth as much as $10,000, an enormous amount of money in the early 1950s. In order to sustain viewers' interest in the show, *Break the Bank* later featured a "Wish Bowl Couple." There were contestants who were selected after having a postcard they sent in to the producers picked out of a fish bowl. In 1956, once again in order to keep their viewers watching the show, the program was renamed *Break the $250,000 Bank* and offered an even larger prize. Recognized experts were invited to be contestants on the show and answer questions to win the huge jackpot. None of the experts, however, ever managed to win the top prize. In 1976, NBC tried to revive the series with Tom Kennedy as its host, but it was not successful. A syndicated version of *Break the Bank,* hosted by Jack BARRY, also surfaced in 1976 and then again in 1985, with Gene RAYBURN as quizmaster. None of these later versions of *Break the Bank* enjoyed the success or longevity of the original series.

BRENNAN, WALTER (WALTER ANDREW BRENNAN 1894–1974)

Perhaps the most successfully employed character actor in films, Walter Brennan was one of Hollywood's most honored performers. Brennan won three Academy Awards as Best Supporting Actor, and for over 50 years he steadily worked in films and on TV, and became one of the world's most familiar faces. Walter Brennan was born in Swampscott, Massachusetts. While in school, Brennan began performing in school plays and decided he wanted to pursue a career as an actor when he graduated. While working at various odd jobs, such as a bank clerk

and lumberjack, Brennan auditioned and eventually began to get jobs on the vaudeville stage and then toured in several musical comedies. In 1917, as World War I was being fought in Europe, Brennan joined the military. After the war, Brennan went to Guatemala, where he raised pineapples; then he decided to go to Hollywood, where he sold real estate, still intent on becoming an actor. Extra jobs in several films eventually led to small, and then larger roles. By 1927, Bernnan worked steadily as an actor. A role in *Come and Get It* in 1936 won him his first Academy Award as Best Supporting Actor. Brennan could play any sort of role, from sophisticated businessman and slick con artist, to country bumpkin and drunk, which made him highly sought after by Hollywood directors and producers. The wide variety of films Brennan appeared in included *The Bride of Frankenstein* (1935), *Sergeant York* (1941), *Meet John Doe* (1941), *To Have and Have Not* (1944), *My Darling Clementine* (1946), and *Scudda Hoo! Scudda Hay!* (1948), to name just a few. In the 1950s, Brennan decided to try television. His first TV series, THE REAL McCOYS (1957–1963) made him even more famous than he already was. He later starred on the TV series *The Tycoon* (1964–1965) and *To Rome With Love* (1970–71). Brennan's last major film appearance was in *Smoke in the Wind* in 1971. He died of emphysema in 1974.

BRIDGES, LLOYD (LLOYD VERNET BRIDGES, JR. 1913–1998)

The father of two celebrated actors, Jeff and Beau Bridges, Lloyd Bridges became world famous as the star of the successful syndicated action/adventure television series SEA HUNT (1958–1961). Even though only 156 episodes of *Sea Hunt* were filmed, the series has been continuously aired for over 40 years. Born in San Leandro, California, in 1913, where his father owned a hotel, the senior Bridges attended the University of California–Los Angeles, and majored in pre-law. He soon abandoned his plans to become a lawyer, much to the disappointment of his father, and became involved with the college's drama department. Bridges met the woman who was to be his wife for the next 50 years, Dorothy Simpson, while they were both acting in a production of the play *March Hares* at U.C.L.A. Determined to pursue careers as actors, Lloyd and Dorothy left college and went to New York, where Lloyd found work in off-Broadway and Broadway plays and produced, directed, and acted in productions at a theater called "Green Mansions" in the Catskill Mountains. In 1936, Lloyd and Dorothy went to Hollywood to appear in films, and in 1941 Lloyd signed a contract with Columbia Pictures. He soon became one of Hollywood's busiest supporting players. In 1942 alone, Bridges appeared in an impressive 20 films. Among the classic motion pictures Bridges was seen in during the 1940s and 1950s were *Sahara* (1943), *Home of the Brave* (1949), and *High Noon* (1952). After *Sea Hunt,* Bridges had major roles in such celebrated TV miniseries as ROOTS (1977) and *North and South* (1986). He also appeared in the hit films *Airplane!* (1980) and *Hot Shots!* (1991). Bridges continued to work until shortly before his death at the age of 85.

BRIDGET LOVES BERNIE

Sept. 1972–Sept. 1973   CBS   Sat. 8:30–9 P.M.

In the early 1970s, several ethnic comedies made their television debuts, including ALL IN THE FAMILY and SAN- FORD AND SON. Another ethnic-oriented series was *Bridget Loves Bernie*. This series was on the air for only one year, but it is fondly remembered. *Bridget Loves Bernie* was about a young Jewish man, Bernie Steinberg, played by David BIRNEY, and his Irish–American Catholic wife, Bridget Fitzgerald, played by Meredith Baxter, and the problems they faced as a married couple coming from two entirely different ethnic backgrounds. Bernie was a struggling young writer, and Bridget was the daughter of wealthy parents; therefore, they not only had to face the problems that went along with being from two different cultures, they also had to adjust to two different lifestyles. Complicating things were Bernie's mother and father, Sam and Sophie Steinberg, played by Harold J. Stone and Bibi Osterwald, and Bridget's parents, Amy and Walt Fitzgerald, played by Audra Lindley and David Doyle. Bernie's Uncle Max Plotnick, played by Ned Glass, Bridget's uncle, Father Mike Fitzgerald, played by Robert Sampson, and the Fitzgeralds' butler, Charles, played by Ivor Barry, often tried to mediate family squab- bles. One year after the series left the air, David Birney and Meredith Baxter became a real-life married couple, but they later divorced.

BRINKLEY, DAVID (1920–   )

Newscaster David Brinkley, who was born in Wilming- ton, North Carolina, became one of the United States's most familiar faces when he began coanchoring *The Huntley-Brinkley Report* television news program, which also featured Chet HUNTLEY, in 1956. Brinkley had previ- ously worked as a journalist writing news stories for The *Wilmington* (NC) *Star-News,* before becoming a radio and television newsman. After completing his studies at the University of North Carolina and Vanderbilt Univer- sity, Brinkley joined the Army, and in 1943, he joined the NBC radio news team. Shortly after World War II ended, he began reporting the news on television and then became the coanchor of *The Huntley-Brinkley Report,* which became one of television's most-watched news shows. Brinkley hosted *The Challenge of Ideas* in 1961 and, when Chet Huntley retired in 1970, *The NBC Nightly News.* In 1981, David Brinkley left NBC and went to ABC, where he hosted the *This Week with David Brinkley* news program. Brinkley retired in 1996. Brink- ley was the author of two books about his news reporting experiences, *Washington Goes to War* (1988) and *Every- one Is Entitled to My Opinion* (1996).

BROADWAY OPEN HOUSE

May 1950–May 1951 NBC   Mon.-Fri. 11–12 P.M.
May 1951–Aug. 1951 NBC Tues.–Thurs. 11–12 P.M.

Television's first informal late-night talk/variety show, *Broadway Open House,* was the brainchild of NBC vice president Sylvester "Pat" Weaver, who later developed the TONIGHT SHOW, DING DONG SCHOOL, HOME, and *The Wide Wide World* programs. *Broadway Open House* was a combination talk, variety, song, and sketches show, and was hosted by two veteran comedians, Jerry LESTER (three days a week on Mondays, Wednesdays, and Fridays) and Morey Amsterdam (Tuesdays and Thursdays). Appearing as regulars on the series were announcer Wayne Howell; a tall, buxom blonde named DAGMAR (whose real name was Virginia Ruth Egnor); accordionist Milton Delugg and his quartet; singers Andy Roberts, Richard Hayes, Jane Harvey, and David Street; the Melolarks and Honey- dreamers singing groups; the voluptuous actress Barbara Nichols; and announcer Frank Gallop, among others. Dagmar became one of the show's major attractions and performed in many hilarious skits with Lester, always playing it wide-eyed and innocent, despite her sexy, full- figured appearance and her double-entendre delivery. Amsterdam decided to leave the series after only five months on the air. Lester decided to leave as well in 1951, from all reports, jealous of the attention Dagmar was receiving from the press and public. (The blonde Barbara Nichols had been added to divert attention from Dag- mar.) He was replaced by comedian Jack E. Leonard, but without Jerry, and in spite of the fact that Dagmar remained on the show, *Broadway Open House* was can- celed shortly after Lester's departure.

BROKAW, TOM (THOMAS JOHN BROKAW 1940–   )

Born in Webster, North Dakota, Tom Brokaw became a TV journalist shortly after graduating from college, and appeared on local news programs. He became NBC's White House correspondent in 1973, after losing the NBC TODAY SHOW hosting job. He eventually did get the early morning *Today* show assignment, and was on that series from 1976 until 1981 with Jane Pauley as his cohost. In 1982, Brokaw became the anchorman of the NBC *Nightly News* program. In addition to his anchorman duties, Brokaw also hosted the investigative prime-time news show *Exposé* in 1991, and the DATELINE NBC series, first seen in 1992.

BROKEN ARROW

Sept. 1956–Sept. 1958   ABC   Tues. 9–9:30 P.M.
Apr. 1960–Sept. 1960   ABC   Sun. 7–7:30 P.M.

Indian Agent Tom Jefford, played by actor John Lupton, and Indian Chief Cochise, played by Michael ANSARA, joined forces to fight the bad guys on this half-hour western adventure series. The two worked so closely together that they eventually became blood brothers.

The show, which made Michael Ansara a TV star, was adapted from an adventure novel, *Blood Brother*, by Elliott Arnold. When the series was canceled after two years, the public demanded it return to the airwaves and, after a two-year absence, ABC obliged and began to play repeats of earlier shows. Michael Ansara, in spite of the series having made him nationally known, did not feel the Cochise character presented Native Americans in a very flattering light. In a *TV Guide* interview, Ansara said, "Cochise could do one of two things . . . stand with his arms folded, looking noble; or stand with arms at his sides, looking noble."

BRONSON, CHARLES (CHARLES BUCHINSKY 1921–)

Charles Bronson, who is best known for his work in films, first came to the attention of the American public as the star of a weekly TV adventure series, MAN WITH A CAMERA, in 1958. Prior to, and shortly after appearances on, *Man with a Camera*, Bronson was seen on many TV series, such as RAWHIDE, BIG VALLEY, BONANZA, ALFRED HITCHCOCK PRESENTS, and *Laramie* (1959–1963), and in the films *You're in the Navy Now* (1951), *Machine Gun Kelly* (1958), *The Magnificent Seven* (1960), *The Great Escape* (1963), and *The Dirty Dozen* (1967), playing major roles. It wasn't until Bronson moved to France in 1968 and began to make films there that he became internationally known for starring in such blockbuster films as *Once Upon a Time in the West* (1969). Born to a working-class family in Ehrenfield, Pennsylvania, Bronson went to Hollywood shortly after he graduated from high school, hoping to become a star. With his *Death Wish* films, Bronson did indeed fulfill his dream of becoming a Hollywood star. The uncompromising, man-of-action character he usually portrayed was also seen in the made-for-TV films *Raid on Entebbe* (1977) and *Family of Cops* (1995).

BROOKLYN BRIDGE

Sept. 1991–Oct. 1991	CBS	Fri. 8:30–9 P.M.
Oct. 1991	CBS	Fri. 8–8:30 P.M.
Nov. 1991–Dec. 1991	CBS	Wed. 8–8:30 P.M.
Dec. 1991–June 1992	CBS	Wed. 8:30–9 P.M.
Sept. 1992–Oct. 1992	CBS	Sat. 8:30–9 P.M.
Oct. 1992–Nov. 1992	CBS	Sat. 8–8:30 P.M.
Apr. 1993	CBS	Sat. 9:30–10 P.M.
July 1993–Aug. 1993	CBS	Fri. 8:30–9 P.M.

If ever there was a television network that did everything in its power to keep a series on the air, it was CBS—and the series was *Brooklyn Bridge*. A charming domestic comedy about a lower middle-class Jewish family living in Brooklyn in the 1950s, *Brooklyn Bridge* had every element needed to make it a success. It was sentimental, well written, well acted, and made important observations about family values and loyalties. For some reason, however, the public never made *Brooklyn Bridge* the hit show

the CBS network executives hoped it would be. The central character on the series was a 14-year-old boy named Alan Silver, played by Danny Gerard. Alan lived in a Brooklyn apartment with his postal employee father and his working mother, George and Phyllis Silver, played by Peter Friedman and Amy Aquino, and his younger brother, Nathaniel, played by Matthew Louis Siegel. Living in another apartment in the same building as the Silvers were Alan's maternal grandparents, Sophie and Jules Berger, played by Marion Ross and Louis Zorich. They were always available to give good, sensible advice to their grandsons and address any wrongdoing that they felt members of the family may have been guilty of. Actress Jennie Lewis played Alan's Irish American "crush," Katie Monahan, and Adam LaVorgna, Jake Jundef, and Aeryk Egan played Alan's friends, Nicholas, Benny, and Warren respectively. Also appearing on the series from time to time were Alan Blumenfeld as Uncle Willie, Carol Kane as Aunt Sylvia, Murray Rubin as Uncle Buddy, and Armin Shimerman as Cousin Bernie. *Brooklyn Bridge* was created by Gary David Goldberg and based on Goldberg's own boyhood experiences growing up in Brooklyn in the 1950s. Goldberg had previously created the popular FAMILY TIES series.

BROSNAN, PIERCE (PIERCE BRENDAN BROSNAN 1953–)

Before he became an internationally known film actor, Pierce Brosnan was a television star in the United States and appeared in the highly successful *Mannions of America* miniseries in 1981, and the REMINGTON STEELE action/adventure series in 1982. A handsome, charming Irishman, Brosnan was born in Navan, County Meath, Ireland. His family moved to England when he was a boy, but Pierce's father abandoned his family, leaving his mother to raise her children alone. Brosnan began playing small roles in such films as the *The Mirror Crack'd* (1980) and *The Long Good Friday* (1980) before winning the important role in *The Manions of America* and then *Remington Steele*. Leading roles in many films and TV miniseries including *Nancy Astor* (1984), *Noble House* (1988), *Around the World in Eighty Days* (1989), and *Mrs. Doubtfire* (1993) followed. In 1995, Brosnan was cast as the most famous secret agent of all time, James Bond, in the film *GoldenEye*. He subsequently played Bond in *Tomorrow Never Dies* (1997) and *The World Is Not Enough* (1999) and also starred in *The Thomas Crown Affair* (1999), *Blood and Champagne* (2001), *The Tailor of Panama* (2001), and many other films.

BUCK ROGERS IN THE 25TH CENTURY

Sept. 1979–July. 1980	NBC	Thurs. 8–9 P.M.
Aug. 1980–Sept. 1980	NBC	Sat. 8–9 P.M.
June 1981–Apr. 1981	NBC	Thurs. 8–9 P.M.

NBC had high hopes for its expensive new science fiction series, *Buck Rogers in The 25th Century*, when the show made its TV debut in 1980. The series did not prove to be as successful as NBC had hoped, and remained on the air for only two seasons. The ABC network had aired a less lavish version of the program 30 years earlier, simply called *Buck Rogers,* which starred Ken Dibbs and then Robert Pastene as Buck, and Lou Prentis as his spacecraft copilot, Wilma Deering. The updated NBC series featured Gil Gerard as Col. Buck Rogers and Erin Gray as Col. Wilma Deering. Veteran radio and cartoon voice actor Mel Blanc was heard as the voice of the robot Twiki. Tim O'Connor played Dr. Huer; Eric Server was the voice of Dr. Theopolis; Pamela Hensley played the evil Princess Ardala; Henry Silva and then Michael ANSARA played Kane; Thom Christopher played Hawk; and veteran character actor Wilfred Hyde-White played Dr. Goodfellow. Although the series did manage to attract a larger-than-average audience of younger viewers, it failed to warrant its production cost and *Buck Rogers in the 25th Century* became history in April 1981.

BUFFY THE VAMPIRE SLAYER

Mar. 1997–Jan. 1998	WB/FOX	Mon. 9–10 P.M.
Jul. 1997–Aug. 1997	WB/FOX	Sun. 8–9 P.M.
Jan. 1998	WB/FOX	Tues. 8–9 P.M.
Jun. 1998–Sep. 1998	WB/FOX	Mon. 9–10 P.M.
May 1998–present	WB/FOX	Wed. 8–9 P.M.

Based on a 1992 film of the same name that starred Kristy Swanson, Donald Sutherland, and Luke Perry, *Buffy the Vampire Slayer* made its debut as a television series in 1997. A quirky adventure/horror/drama series, the TV version starred Sarah Michelle Gellar as Buffy, a 16-year-old high school student chosen against her will to spend her life battling vampires. The series featured Nicholas Brendon as her best friend, Alexander "Xander" Harris, and Alyson Hannigan as Willow Rosenberg, Emma Caulfield as Anya Enerson (1998), James Masters as Spike/William the Bloody (1997–98, 1999–present), Anthony Head as Rupert Giles (1997–2001), Charisma Carpenter as Cordelia Chase (1997–99), David Boreanaz as Angel/Angelus (1997–99), Seth Green as Daniel "Oz" Osbourne (1997–99), Michelle Trachtenberg as Dawn Summers (2000–present), Marc Blucas as Riley Finn (1999–2000), and Amber Benson as Tara Naclay (1999–2000).

According to the show's writers, "In every generation there is a chosen one . . . she alone will stand against the vampires, the demons and the forces of darkness. She is the slayer." The reluctant Buffy wished someone else had been chosen for this arduous task and tries to be as normal a teenager as possible, but she knows that she cannot escape her destiny. When the series began, Buffy had just moved to the town of Sunnydale, only to learn that the troubles she had encountered at her previous home in Los Angeles were child's play compared to what she encountered in Sunnydale. Buffy had a bad reputation at her old school in L.A.,

having burned down the high school gym, which she knew was inhabited by vampires. Fortunately, in Sunnydale, Buffy finds she is not alone in her quest to save the world. She has the help of several friends who call themselves "the Scooby Gang." Together Buffy and her friends finish high school and go on to college, where they continue to fight the demon vampires, survive one horrific encounter after another, and grow up knowing that life can indeed be a living hell.

BURKE'S LAW

Sept. 1963–Sept. 1964	ABC	Fri. 8:30–9:30 P.M.
Sept. 1964–Sept. 1965	ABC	Wed. 9:30–10:30 P.M.
Sept. 1965–Jan. 1966	ABC	Wed. 10–11 P.M.
Jan. 1994–Sept. 1994	CBS	Fri. 9–10 P.M.
May 1995–Aug. 1995	CBS	Wed. 8–9 P.M.

In 1963, Gene BARRY starred in a detective series, *Burke's Law,* playing a role not unlike the popular western character he had previously played on television, Bat Masterson. Although *Burke's Law* was set in modern-day Los Angeles and not the Wild West, Police Capt. Amos Burke was, like Masterson, somewhat of a dandy. Unlike Masterson, though, Burke was a millionaire. He lived in a mansion and was witty and elegant, yet tough when the situation called for it. Regular characters on the series were Det. Tim Tilson, played by Gary Conway; Det. Sgt. Les Hart, played by Regis Toomey; Burke's loyal chauffeur, Henry, played by Leon Lontoc; Sgt. Ames, played by Eileen O'Neill; and a character simply known as "the Man," played by Carl Benton Reid. Thirty years after the series was originally aired, *Burke's Law* resurfaced in 1994, as a new series with Gene Barry recreating his Amos Burke role. Burke had become the Chief of the Homicide Dept. for the L.A.P.D. He was joined in his crime-solving adventures by a son he had sired sometime in the years between the series' original airing and the new program's debut. The son, Peter, played by Peter Barton, had inherited his father's good looks, charm, and penchant for being a detective. The original series had featured many well-known guest stars, including Annette FUNICELLO and Sir Cedric Hardwicke, and the new series followed suit. Such luminaries as George Segal, Polly Bergen, Carol Channing, Buddy EBSEN, Milton BERLE, and Eva GABOR made guest appearances on the series. In spite of its star power, the new *Burke's Law* proved to be less interesting than the original series, and it was canceled after one and a half years on the air. The original series remained popular with viewers for three years.

BURNETT, CAROL (CAROL CREIGHTON BURNETT 1933–)

Mention "television comediennes" and the two names that most frequently come to people's minds are Lucille BALL and Carol Burnett. For decades, Carol Burnett was one of show business's leading lights, and her weekly variety show, in the late 1960s and early 1970s, was for 11 years one of America's favorite programs. Burnett was born in San Antonio, Texas, to alcoholic parents who depended upon welfare for their income. Her parents were divorced in the late 1930s and Carol went to live with her maternal grandmother, Mabel Eudora White, in Hollywood, California. When Carol graduated from Hollywood High School in 1951, she won a scholarship to the University of California, where she majored in journalism. While in college, she became interested in performing, and with her student/actor boyfriend, Don Saroyan, quit school and went to New York to break into show business. Carol worked as a hat check girl, but in less than a year she had become a regular on the *The Paul Winchell and Jerry Mahoney Show* (1950–54). This led to another regular role on the short-lived *Stanley* situation comedy series that starred comedian Buddy Hackett. In 1956 and 1957, Burnett began to make a name for herself performing in various New York City nightclubs, and her rendition of a song called "I Made a Fool of Myself Over John Foster Dulles," which she performed on NBC's *TONIGHT* and Ed Sullivan's *TOAST OF THE TOWN* on CBS,

Carol Burnett (Author's collection)

made her an overnight sensation. While she was a regular on the successful *GARRY MOORE SHOW* in 1959, she won an Emmy and starred in her first Broadway musical, *Once Upon a Mattress*. Burnett won a second Emmy for her TV special, *Julie and Carol at Carnegie Hall*, which costarred Broadway actress Julie Andrews, in 1962. In the mid-1960s, Burnett starred in the less-than-successful series *The Entertainers* 1964–1965, and on Broadway in the ill-fated musical comedy *Fade Out, Fade In* in 1964. Burnett's luck changed when her weekly variety show on CBS, *The CAROL BURNETT SHOW*, made its debut in 1967. The hour-long series, produced by her second husband, Joe Hamilton, was an enormous success and made Burnett a TV legend. *The Carol Burnett Show* won an unprecedented 22 Emmy Awards, during its 11-year run. When it was canceled in 1979, Carol began to concentrate on her acting career and appeared in such memorable films as *A Wedding* (1978), directed by Robert Altman, and the made-for-TV film *Friendly Fire* (1979). Burnett continued to appear on TV as well, and starred in numerous specials, as well as the short-lived *CAROL & COMPANY* (1990), and a new *Carol Burnett Show* in 1991, neither of which was successful. In recent years, in addition to playing the role of Jamie Buckman's mother on the *MAD ABOUT YOU* series, and winning another Emmy in 1997, Burnett also starred in the Broadway comedy *Moon Over Buffalo* (1995) and received a Tony Award nomination for her performance in that play. In 1999, Burnett starred in a musical revue, *Putting It Together*, which featured the songs of composer/lyricist Stephen Sondheim.

BURNS AND ALLEN

(see *George Burns and Gracie Allen Show, The*)

BURNS, GEORGE (NATHAN BIRNBAUM 1896–1996)

When comedian George Burns was born in New York City at the end of the 19th century, automobiles, airplanes, motion pictures, radio, and television were not available. When he died, at the age of 100, the world of entertainment and indeed the world itself, had undergone radical changes. The son of poor, immigrant Jewish parents, George attended P.S. 22, but left school after the fourth grade to get a job to help his family economically. When he was 13 years old, George, who always loved singing, became a performer on the vaudeville stage. In addition to singing, Burns also performed as a skater and a comic. Eventually, he teamed up with comedian Billy Lorraine as Lorraine's straight man. While performing in New Jersey with Lorraine, he met a pretty young girl named Gracie ALLEN, who had been a vaudeville performer herself, but who had quit the profession since her career didn't seem to be going anywhere. Burns and Allen decided to team up and form their own comedy act with George as the comedian and Gracie as the straight (wo)man. Gracie's straight woman proved to be funnier than George, so they switched places. The team of Burns and Allen became favorites with vaudeville audiences, and when they played London, England, and were heard on a radio program, they became highly sought after. By this time, Burns and Allen had fallen in love and were married. The news of their success on English radio led to a radio program of their own in the United States, and their broadcasts were on immediate success. This led to starring roles in films such as *The Big Broadcast* (1932), *The Big Broadcast of 1936*, and *Honolulu* (1939). In 1950 George and Gracie transferred their successful radio show to television, and the weekly TV situation comedy series also became an audience favorite, remaining on the air from 1950 until 1958. Gracie's health had begun to fail in the late 1950s, and she died after a long illness in 1964. George continued performing, and for a short time appeared with actress Carol Channing in a Las Vegas comedy act. Audiences found it hard to accept George without Gracie, but Burns continued to appear as a guest star on such TV programs as HERE'S LUCY, The MUPPETS, ELLERY QUEEN, and ALICE. In 1975, Burns scored a major triumph as an actor in the film *The Sunshine Boys*, (winning the Best Actor Oscar) and became an even bigger star than he already was when he starred in the films *Oh, God!* (1977, as God) and *Oh, God! You Devil* (1984). His last film was *Radioland Murders* in 1994. George Burns's formula for success was simple: "Fall in love with what you do for a living. I don't care what it is. It works."

BURR, RAYMOND (RAYMOND WILLIAM STACY BURR 1917–1993)

Raymond Burr, best known as television's Perry Mason and Ironside, was born in New Westminster, British Columbia, Canada. When he was a child, Burr's father, who was a trade agent and moved his family frequently, took his wife and children to live in China. His parents were divorced soon after they returned to Canada, and his mother moved Raymond and his siblings to Vallejo, California, where she raised him with her mother's help. When he was in his late teens, Raymond left school and took various jobs to help his mother and grandmother support the family. Some of the jobs Burr held were a ranch hand in Roswell, New Mexico, a deputy sheriff, and a photo salesman. He even sang in a nightclub for a time. During World War II, Burr served in the U.S. Navy and was wounded in action during the Battle of Okinawa. When he was discharged from the navy, Burr went to Hollywood to try to break into films, and in 1940, he made his film acting debut in *Earl of Puddlestone*. He subsequently appeared in over 90 films, including such classics as *Walk a Crooked Mile* (1948), *A Place in the Sun* (1951), and *Rear Window* (1954), among others. In 1957, Burr became the star of the PERRY MASON TV series, which became one of television's longest-running and most popular programs (1957–1966). One year after *Perry Mason* left the airwaves, Burr starred in a new series, IRONSIDE (1967–1975), which proved to be as big a success as *Perry Mason*. When *Ironside* ended its TV run, Burr continued to appear in films, but returned to the airwaves in a series of over 25 made-for-TV *Perry Mason* feature-length films that were first seen in 1985 *(Perry Mason Returns)* and ended in 1993 *(Perry Mason: The Case of the Killer Kiss)*, the year Burr died of cancer.

BUTTONS, RED (AARON CHWATT 1919–)

New York–born comedian Red Buttons was the son of working-class parents. Buttons quit school and worked at several odd jobs before he decided to become a comedian. After playing the burlesque circuit for several years, in 1944 he got a role in a feature film that starred the Andrews Sisters, *Winged Victory*. He then played small supporting roles in the films *13 Rue Madeleine* (1946) and *Footlight Varieties* (1951). In 1952, Buttons was signed to star on a new television comedy series that was to be called The RED BUTTONS SHOW. It was an enormous hit and became one of CBS most successful variety programs. Due to the show's popularity, the comedian appeared on the cover of *Time* magazine during the show's first season. By the end of the show's second season, however, the series had become a bit tired and CBS decided to cancel the show. NBC picked up the series for its third season, but after one year, they also decided to drop it from their weekly schedule of programs. After the cancellation of his show, Button's career remained in limbo for several years, but in 1957, he was cast in the film *Sayonara*. His acting in *Sayonara* won him critical acclaim and an Academy Award as Best Supporting Actor. Button's career never faltered again, and he has been steadily employed ever since winning the Oscar. First-caliber performances in such films as *The Longest Day* (1962), *Stagecoach* (1966), *The Poseidon Adventure* (1972), *Leave 'Em Laughing* (1981), and *Alice in Wonderland* (1985, as the White Rabbit) followed. In 1987, Buttons returned to television as a regular on the KNOTS LANDING series. He also guest-starred on many of TV's most successful series, including The ANDY WILLIAMS SHOW, LITTLE HOUSE ON THE PRAIRIE, FANTASY ISLAND, The COSBY SHOW, ROSEANNE, ER, and FAMILY LAW. Buttons continues to be one of Hollywood's most sought-after character actors.

BYINGTON, SPRING (1893–1971)

Although she was one of Hollywood's busiest character actresses for over 30 years, Spring Byington did not become a star until she was 61 years old and appeared on the popular DECEMBER BRIDE situation comedy series in 1954. Born in Colorado Springs, Colorado, to parents who were actors, Spring took it for granted that she would follow in their footsteps. After touring in vaudeville and the legitimate theater for several years, Spring appeared in her first film, *Papa's Slay Ride* in 1931. Her next important film role was in the classic *Little Women* (1933) playing Katharine Hepburn's and Joan Bennett's mother, Marmee, even though she wasn't much older than the film's stars. Hundreds of supporting roles in such films as *Mutiny on the Bounty* (1935), *Ah,*

Wilderness! (1935), *Dodsworth* (1936), *The Charge of the Light Brigade* (1936), *The Adventures of Tom Sawyer* (1938), *You Can't Take It With You* (1938), *The Blue Bird* (1940), *Meet John Doe* (1941), *Heaven Can Wait* (1943), *The Enchanted Cottage* (1945), *B. F.'s Daughter* (1948), and many others, followed. Byington's last role was as Daisy Cooper on the *Laramie* western TV series, which she played from 1961 to 1963.

BYRNES, EDD (EDWARD BREITENBERGER 1933–)

In 1958, Edd "Kookie" Byrnes had the "fifteen minutes of fame" pop artist Andy Warhol said most people would one day have. As one of the young stars of *77 SUNSET STRIP*, Edd, who played "hepcat" Gerald Lloyd "Kookie" Kookson III, suddenly found himself thrust into the teen idol spotlight. Fan magazines clamored to interview him, manufacturers of various products vied for his endorsements, and young female fans squealed with delight wherever he made a public appearance. As soon as *77 Sunset Strip* was canceled, Edd Byrnes faded back into the obscurity from whence he came. Before he won the Kookie role on *77 Sunset Strip,* Edd, who was born and raised in New York City, played minor roles in such films as *Reform School Girl* (1957) and *Marjorie Morningstar* (1958). When *77 Sunset Strip* became just a memory, Byrnes's career failed to go anywhere and, except for a regular role on the short-lived TV series *Where the Action Is* and a brief comeback in the film *Grease* in 1978, Byrnes's acting career consisted of playing minor supporting roles in several less than memorable films. He did, however, make guest appearances on such successful series as ALFRED HITCHCOCK PRESENTS, *The* LOVE BOAT, CHIPS, MURDER, SHE WROTE, and MARRIED . . . WITH CHILDREN. Byrnes's last major appearance came on the TV series *Shake, Rattle and Roll: An American Love Story,* in 1999.

C

CAESAR, SID (SIDNEY CAESAR 1922–)

Comedian Sid Caesar, who was born to a working-class family in Yonkers, New York, began his show business career as a musician, playing the saxophone and clarinet with the Sid Fields band in the late 1930s. During World War II, Caesar served in the U.S. Coast Guard and made his stage debut as a comedian/MC in a service show called *Tars and Spars* in 1945. He subsequently appeared in the filmed version of that show. Caesar's comedic talents attracted the attention of television executives at NBC, who offered him a regular spot on their new television comedy/variety series *The Admiral Broadway Revue* in 1949. Sid's performances on *The Admiral Broadway Revue* encouraged NBC to make Caesar the star on an ambitious, new 90-minute comedy/variety series they called YOUR SHOW OF SHOWS in 1950. This became one of television's most successful and memorable early programs. Caesar's wonderful pantomime, his skill with various accents, his double-talk routines, and his appearances in sketches with his costar, comedienne Imogene COCA, made him one of America's first major TV stars. Caesar was voted the "Best Comedian in the United States" in a poll conducted by Motion Picture Daily in 1951 and 1952. He also won a "Best Comedy Team" award with Imogene Coca from that same publication in 1953 and the Sylvania Award in 1958 for his work on television in general. In 1954, Caesar decided it was time to leave *Your Show of Shows* to star on a new series, *Caesar's Hour* (1954–1957), which was followed by his *Sid Caesar Invites You* (1958) and *The Sid Caesar Show* (1963). After appearing in the star-studded film comedy *It's a Mad, Mad, Mad, Mad, Mad World* in 1963, Sid Caesar's career went into a decline, mainly due to alcohol and pill abuse and an inflated ego. After recovering from his addictions, Caesar was seen in several motion pictures such as *Silent Movie* (1976) and *The Cheap Detective* (1978), playing supporting roles, but he never achieved the success or adulation he had enjoyed on his early television shows. Glimpses of the wonderful comic performer were certainly in evidence, however, in the films *Grease* (1978) *and Grease II* (1982) and on a MAD ABOUT YOU TV series episode in 1997, in which he played Paul Reiser's hilarious Uncle Harold.

CAGNEY & LACEY

Mar. 1982–Apr. 1982	CBS	Thurs. 9–10 P.M.
Oct. 1982–Sept. 1983	CBS	Mon. 10–11 P.M.
Mar. 1984–Dec. 1987	CBS	Mon. 10–11 P.M.
Jan. 1988–Apr. 1988	CBS	Tues. 10–11 P.M.
Apr. 1988–June 1988	CBS	Mon. 10–11 P.M.
June 1988–Aug. 1988	CBS	Thurs. 10–11 P.M.

Cagney & Lacey was the first adventure/crime series on television to feature two woman as central characters, police officers Chris Cagney, originally played by Meg Foster, who left the series after one year, and then by Susan Gless, and Mary Beth Lacey, played by Tyne Daly. If these police detectives had been males, the series would have been a rather conventional program, but with the two women as its major characters, the series became a novel attraction. Cagney was single and spontaneous and Lacey, who was married and a mother, was solid, down to earth, and practical. The combination worked, and the series placed among the Nielsen ratings top-10-rated TV shows during the 1983–1984 season. Gless and Daly won six consecutive Emmy Awards as Best Actresses in a series for their performances on *Cagney & Lacey*. Appearing in regular supporting roles on the series were Al Waxman as Lt. Bert Samuels Carl Lumbly as Det. Mark Petrie, Martin

Kove as Det. Victor Isbecki, and Sidney Clute as Det. Paul LaGuardia. John Karlen played Mary Beth's loving and patient husband, Harvey, and Tony LaTorre and Troy Slaten played Mary Beth and Harvey's sons, Harvey Junior and Michael. When CBS announced that they had decided to cancel *Cagney & Lacey* after its 1982–1983 season, the public outcry was such that CBS had second thoughts. The show returned for the 1983–1984 season, received its highest ratings that spring, and remained on the air for another four years, finally retiring from the airwaves in 1988. In 1994 and 1995, Susan Gless and Tyne Daly reprised their *Cagney & Lacey* roles and starred in two feature-length, made-for-TV films, *Cagney & Lacey: The Return* and *Cagney & Lacey: Together Again.*

CALUCCI'S DEPARTMENT

Sept. 1973–Dec. 1973   CBS   Fri. 8–8:30 P.M.

Although on television for only three months, the *Calucci's Department* situation comedy series, which starred James Coco as Joe Calucci, a supervisor at the New York State Unemployment Office, is, for some reason, one of many viewers' most fondly remembered shows, perhaps because the various supporting characters on the series depicted every ethnic and racial group in the United States and humorously satirized the foolish, bureaucratic nonsense so prevalent in Civil Service offices. Appearing on the series with Coco were Candy Azzara, Jose Perez, Jack Fletcher, Peggy Pope, Bill Lazarus, Bernard Wexler, and Rosetta LeNoire. *Calucci's Department* was created by the husband and wife team of Renee Taylor and Joe Bologna, who had written the successful play and film *Lovers and Other Strangers,* and wrote and starred in the film *Made for Each Other* (1971). Taylor made several guest-starring appearances on the show.

CAMERON, KIRK (KIRK THOMAS CAMERON 1970–   )

Before he became a teen star on the popular GROWING PAINS situation comedy series in 1985, Kirk Cameron was a child actor who was seen on the TV shows *Bret Maverick* (1981) and FULL HOUSE (1988), and was a regular on the *Two Marriages* (1983) series. The son of show business parents, Kirk was born in Panorama City, California. As Michael "Mike" Aaron Seaver on *Growing Pains,* which was first aired in 1985 and remained one of television's most popular shows for the next seven years, Cameron received more fan mail than any other performer on an ABC show for four of its seasons, and his show was among the top-20 programs on television, according to the Nielsen ratings. Cameron became the star of a second TV series, *Kirk,* in 1995, that failed to attract the attention *Growing Pains* had enjoyed. The actor also appeared in several films such as *The Best of Times* (1986), *Like Father, Like Son* (1987), *The Secrets of Back to the Future Trilogy* (1990), *Little Piece of Heaven* (TV 1991), *Star Struck* (TV 1994), *You Lucky Dog* (1998), and *Left Behind* (2000).

Kirk Cameron (Author's collection)

CANDID CAMERA

Aug. 1948–Sept. 1948	ABC	Sun. 8–8:30 P.M.
Oct. 1948	ABC	Wed. 8:30–8:45 P.M.
Nov. 1948–Dec. 1948	ABC	Fri. 8–8:30 P.M.
May 1949–July 1949	NBC	Sun. 7:30–8 P.M.
July 1949–Aug. 1949	NBC	Thurs. 9–9:30 P.M.
Sept. 1949–Sept. 1950	CBS	Mon. 9–9:30 P.M.
June 1953	NBC	Tues. 9:30–10 P.M.
July 1953	NBC	Wed. 10–10:30 P.M.
Oct. 1960–Sept. 1967	CBS	Sun. 10–10:30 P.M.
July 1990–Aug. 1990	CBS	Fri. 8:30–9 P.M.
Feb. 1998–present	CBS	Fri. 8:30–9 P.M.

Originally a radio show called *Candid Microphone,* the *Candid Camera* television series premiered in 1948. The premise of the show was simple: Plant a hidden microphone, and later a TV camera, somewhere people couldn't see it, set up a situation that would evoke a surprised, shocked, or funny reaction from an unsuspecting participant, and broadcast or telecast what you record or film for listeners or viewers to enjoy. The format was successful enough that, with various breaks in between, *Candid Camera* has been seen from 1948 until the present. The creator of this show was Allen FUNT, who also acted as the program's host, first on the *Candid Microphone* and then the *Candid Camera* series, until illness forced him to turn the hosting chores over to comedian Dom DELUISE during 1991–1992, and then to his son, Peter Funt. Funt had come up with the idea for *Candid Microphone* when he was in the military during World War II and had hidden a microphone to record servicemen's gripes, which were then broadcast by the Armed Forces Radio Network for his fellow servicemen to enjoy. Funt had several cohosts on the series, including Arthur GODFREY, 1960–1961; Durwood Kirby, 1961–1966; Bess Myerson, 1966–1967; Phyllis George, 1974–1976; Jo Ann Pflug, 1976–1977; John Bartholmew Tucker, 1977–1978; Peter Funt, 1990; and Suzanne SOMERS, 1998 to the present. Celebrities who enticed or fooled people into reacting to the various pranks, included singer Dorothy Collins and actress/author Fanny Flagg. *Candid Camera* was revived, first by NBC and CBS, and then as a syndicated show, with as many as seven to 15 years in between various series. For a time in 1955, *Candid Camera* was a segment on *The GARRY MOORE SHOW*. The latest version of this series, *Then and Now*, presents previously seen *Candid Camera* stunts as well as newly filmed segments of the same stunts.

CANNON

Sept. 1971–Sept. 1972	CBS	Tues. 9:30–10:30 P.M.
Sept. 1972–Sept. 1973	CBS	Wed. 10–11 P.M.
Sept. 1973–July 1976	CBS	Wed. 9–10 P.M.
July 1976–Sep. 1976	CBS	Sun. 10–11 P.M.

The middle-aged, heavyset actor William Conrad was an unlikely hero for a television adventure show, but that was exactly what he became when he starred on the *Cannon* series. Conrad's voice was already familiar to millions of fans as Sheriff Matt Dillon on the radio version of *GUNSMOKE*, in the late 1950s to early 1960s. Conrad was the sole regular performer on the series, playing the part of a former police detective turned private eye, Frank Cannon. The series was produced by Quinn-Martin, and during its successful five-year TV run 124 episodes were filmed. In 1980, Frank Cannon resurfaced in a made-for-TV movie titled *The Return of Frank Cannon*, with Conrad recreating his P.I. role.

CAPTAIN KANGAROO (AKA WAKE UP THE CAPTAIN)

CAPTAIN KANGAROO

Oct. 1955–Jan. 1956	CBS	Mon.–Fri. 8–9 A.M.
Jan. 1956–Sept. 1964	CBS	Mon.–Sat. 8–9 A.M.
Sept. 1964–Sept. 1965	CBS	Mon.–Fri. 8–9 A.M.
Sept. 1965–Sept. 1968	CBS	Mon.–Sat. 8–9 A.M.
Sept. 1968–Sept. 1981	CBS	Mon.–Fri. 8–9 A.M.

WAKE UP THE CAPTAIN

Sept. 1981–Jan. 1982	CBS	Mon.–Fri. 7–7:30 A.M.
Jan. 1982–Sept. 1982	CBS	Mon.–Fri. 6:30–7 A.M.

Sept. 1982–Sept. 1984	CBS	Sat. 7–8 A.M., Sun. 8–9 A.M.
Sept. 1984–Dec. 1984		Sat. 7–7:30 A.M., Sun. 8–8:30 A.M.

Television's longest-running early morning children's series, *Captain Kangaroo* was a favorite with young viewers for over 30 years. Long before *SESAME STREET* and *Barney* took on the morning baby-sitting chores for busy moms, *Captain Kangaroo* filled the job. Captain Kangaroo, a gentle, middle-aged man, got his name from a jacket he wore with large pockets that contained all sorts of wonderful things he showed children during the course of the show. The Captain was played the entire time the series was on the air by Bob KEESHAN, who had previously played Clarabell the Clown on the popular *HOWDY DOODY* children's TV show. *Captain Kangaroo* did not change over 30 years, and retained a calming, peaceful atmosphere that seemed to have a tranquilizing effect on active little preschoolers. Among the characters who regularly visited the Captain over the years were the puppets Mr. Moose, Bunny Rabbit, Miss Frog, Mr. Whispers, Ward Bird, and the live character Dennis, the Captain's bumbling assistant, who were all played by Cosmo Allegretti. The popular Mr. Green Jeans was played by Hugh "Lumpy" Brannum. *Captain Kangaroo* also frequently featured cartoons. One of the more popular cartoon seri-

Bob Keeshan as Captain Kangaroo (Author's collection)

als seen on the show was "The Adventures of Tom Terrific." Tom was a boy who could change himself into anything he wanted to be, and his companion was Mighty Manfred the Wonder Dog. Over the years, many celebrities made guest appearances on the series, including Imogene COCA, Pearl Bailey, Alan Arkin, Carol Channing, Eli Wallach, magician Doug Henning, and ballet dancer Edward Villela. Bob Keeshan became increasingly aware of the effect TV commercials were having on young viewers, and refused to allow any of the characters on *Captain Kangaroo* to promote commercial products. In 1991 and 1992, edited excerpts from the original series, combined with some new material, were made available to public television stations, which PBS readily bought. *Captain Kangaroo* had indeed been years ahead of the later PBS children's shows.

CAPTAIN MIDNIGHT (AKA *JET JACKSON, FLYING COMMANDO*)
Sept. 1954–May 1956   CBS   Sat. 11–11:30 A.M.

Captain Midnight is perhaps one of the best remembered children's action adventure television shows from the 1950s. First heard as a popular radio serial in the 1940s, *Captain Midnight* made its television debut in 1954 with Richard Webb starring as the crime-fighting pilot who flew exciting missions for his Secret Squadron. Captain Midnight, whose real name was Captain Albright, had been a brave and daring flying ace during World War I, according to the radio show, who returned to his home base precisely at midnight after flying a particulary dangerous mission, which is how he got his name. The captain's somewhat dim-witted assistant, Ichabod Mudd (nicknamed "Ikky"), played by Sid Melton, and a somewhat eccentric scientist who worked for the Secret Squadron, Aristotle Jones (called Tut), played by Olan Soulé, were regular characters on the series. When reruns of the series went into syndication, the original sponsor of the program, Ovaltine, which owned all rights to the name "Captain Midnight," refused to allow the name to be used, so the series was renamed *Jet Jackson, Flying Commando*. All references to Captain Midnight were deleted, and the name "Jet Jackson" was dubbed onto the original episodes, which confused and upset many loyal listeners and viewers of the series.

CAPTAIN VIDEO AND HIS VIDEO RANGERS

June 1949–Aug. 1949	DuMont	Mon./Tues./Thurs./Fri. 7–7:30 P.M.
Aug. 1949–Sept. 1953	DuMont	Mon.–Fri. 7–7:30 P.M.
Sept. 1953–Apr. 1955	DuMont	Mon.–Fri. 7–7:15 P.M.
Also		
Feb. 1950–Sept. 1950	DuMont	Sat. 7:30–8 P.M.
Sept. 1950–Nov. 1950	DuMont	Sat. 7–7:30 P.M.

Perhaps no other children's television adventure/science fiction series evokes more nostalgia than *Captain Video and His Video Rangers*. To people who remember seeing the show, few TV series ever involved them more than the *Captain Video Show,* in spite of being an early TV show with primitive sets, exaggerated acting, somewhat silly plots, and a very limited budget. *Captain Video and His Video Rangers* originally starred Richard Coogan as Captain Video, a scientific genius who invented such wondrous devices as the Remote Tele-Carrier, the Cosmic Vibrator, the Opticon Scillometer, and the Astra-Viewer, and led his Video Rangers, a squadron of loyal young agents who fought terrestrial and extraterrestrial bad guys, during the twenty-second century. Coogan left the series soon after it went on the air and was replaced by Al HODGE, who played the role for the next seven years. The Video Ranger, the captain's loyal teenage assistant, was played by Don Hastings, who later went to star in the long-running AS THE WORLD TURNS daytime serial. Also appearing on the series regularly were Hal Conklin as the Captain's archenemy, Dr. Pauli, and the Rangers' robot, Tobor, which is "robot" spelled backward. Various other characters on the series were played by such later-to-befamous actors as Jack KLUGMAN, Tony RANDALL, and Ernest BORGNINE. In 1956, several years after the original series made its debut, Al Hodge hosted the syndicated *Captain Video and His Cartoon Raiders* series. *Captain Video* and *His Video Rangers* was the inspiration for many TV space shows that followed, such as ROCKY JONES, SPACE RANGER; SPACE PATROL; and TOM CORBETT, SPACE CADET.

CAR 54, WHERE ARE YOU?
Sept. 1961–Sept. 1963   NBC   Sun. 8:30–9 P.M.

Police officers Gunther Toody and Francis Muldoon, of New York's 52nd Police Precinct in the Bronx, were the oddest partners who ever drove a patrol car. Toody, who was played by Joe E. Ross, was short, stocky, talkative, and somewhat dim-witted, while Muldoon, played by Fred Gwynne, was a tall, thin, quiet, and straitlaced fellow. Together, Toody and Muldoon were a strange couple who always seemed to come across more funny incidents than crimes during their police patrols. Created and produced by Nat Hiken (who was responsible for Phil Silvers's YOU'LL NEVER GET RICH series), *Car 54, Where Are You?* featured one of the most amusing and talented supporting casts on television. Al Lewis and Charlotte Rae played Officer Leo Schnauser and his wife, Sylvia, who became two of the show's most popular characters. Also featured on the show at various times were Beatrice Pons as Toody's wife, Lucille, Paul Reed as Capt. Martin Block, Albert Henderson as Officer O'Hara, Nipsey Russell as Officer Anderson, Jerome Guardino as Officer Antonnucci, Duke Farley as Officer Riley, Shelley Burton as Officer Murdock, Joe Warren as Officer Steinmetz, Bruce Kirby as Officer Kissel, Hank Garrett as Officer Ed

Joe E. Ross (Toody) and Fred Gwynne (Muldoon) of *Car 54, Where are You?* (Author's collection)

Nicholson, Jim Gormley as Officer Nelson, and Frederick O'Neill as Officer Wallace. Gwynne and Lewis were later reunited memorably in *The MUNSTERS.*

CAREY, DREW (DREW ALLISON CAREY 1958–)

Comedian Drew Carey's rise to fame and fortune was meteoric. After appearing on the STAR SEARCH television talent show in 1988, Drew, in seven years, went from being a relatively obscure stand-up comic to becoming a supporting player on such TV series as *The TORKELSONS,* COACH, ELLEN, *The George Carlin Show* (1994–1995), LOIS & CLARK, and *The Good Life* (1994), and eventually to a starring role on his own TV series, *The DREW CAREY SHOW* in 1995. Carey was born in Cleveland, Ohio. His father died when he was eight years old, and Carey suffered from severe depression for many years as a result, even attempting suicide several times. Drew joined the Marine Corps, and after being discharged decided to pursue a career as a comedian. When he was offered his own TV show in 1995, Carey was sure it would not be a success, and he was surprised when it became one of the most popular programs on the air in one season. In addition to *The Drew Carey Show,* Drew also hosts the *Whose Line Is It Anyway?* improvisational comedy series and starred in the made-for-TV film *Gepetto* in 2000, playing the title role.

CARNEY, ART (ARTHUR WILLIAM MATTHEW CARNEY 1918–)

Before Art Carney played Ed Norton on Jackie GLEASON's original *HONEYMOONERS* sketches on the *Cavalcade of Stars* show in 1949 as well as appearing on other TV comedy/variety shows, he was a busy radio actor on such programs as *Casey, Crime Photographer, Gangbusters,* and *The Henry Morgan Show.* Born in Mount Vernon, New York, Carney worked as a straight man in vaudeville for performers such as Fred Allen, Edgar Bergen, and Bert Lahr. During World War II, Carney was in the U.S. Army and fought and was wounded in action during the Battle of Normandy in 1944. When he was discharged from the army, Carney went back to work as an actor and appeared on Broadway, radio, and on such early television shows as the *Morey Amsterdam Show.* It was Carney's performance as the sewer worker Ed Norton on the *The HONEYMOONERS* sketches, however, that had made him known to viewers. The actor repeated the role of Norton on *The JACKIE GLEASON SHOW* from 1952 to 1957, which made him, along with Gleason, one of television's most popular and beloved comedians. When *The HONEYMOONERS* was discontinued, Carney appeared on Broadway in the original production of *The Odd Couple* in 1960, and on the THIS WAS THE WEEK THAT WAS TV series (1964). He subsequently starred in the film *The Yellow Rolls-Royce* in 1965, and in 1966, rejoined Jackie Gleason on a new JACKIE GLEASON SHOW. In 1974, Carney won an Academy Award as Best Actor for his portrayal of Harry in the film *Harry and Tonto.* Constantly busy as an actor throughout the 1950s, 1960s, 1970s, and 1980s, Art Carney appeared in many films, on TV specials, and in the short-lived series *Lanigan's Rabbi* in 1977, as well as guest-starring on such series as SUSPENSE, PLAYHOUSE 90, ALFRED HITCHCOCK PRESENTS, *The ANDY WILLIAMS SHOW,* BATMAN, ALICE, and FAME. Carney's last major film appearance was in *Last Action Hero* in 1993. At present, Art Carney is retired.

CAROL & COMPANY

Mar. 1990–Apr. 1990	NBC	Sat. 9:30–10 P.M.
Apr. 1990–June 1990	NBC	Sat. 10–10:30 P.M.
Aug. 1990–Mar. 1991	NBC	Sat. 10–10:30 P.M.
Mar. 1991–May 1991	NBC	Sat. 10–11 P.M.
July 1991	NBC	Sat. 10:30–11 P.M.

In 1990, comedienne Carol BURNETT, who was the star of one of TV's most popular comedy/variety shows in the 1970s, returned to television in another comedy series, *Carol & Company* in 1990. The show featured weekly "playlets" about people in unusual situations. These playlets were performed by Carol and a supporting cast that included Terry Kiser, Meagan Fay, Richard Kind, Anita Barone, Jeremy Piven, and Peter Krause. The show failed after one year. Early in 1991, in an attempt to keep the show on the air, NBC had retitled the series *The CAROL BURNETT SHOW,* but the die had already been cast, and *Carol & Company* was canceled after just one season on the air.

CAROL BURNETT SHOW, THE

Sept. 1967–May 1971	CBS	Mon. 10–11 P.M.
Sept. 1971–Nov. 1972	CBS	Wed. 8–9 P.M.
Dec. 1972–Dec. 1977	CBS	Sat. 10–11 P.M.
Dec. 1977–Mar. 1978	CBS	Sun. 10–11 P.M.
June 1978–Aug. 1978	CBS	Wed. 8–9 P.M.
Aug. 1979–Sept. 1979	ABC	Sat. 8–9 P.M.

One of television's funniest and best-remembered comedy/variety shows, *The Carol Burnett Show* starred comedienne Carol BURNETT and a cast of gifted regulars that included Harvey KORMAN, Lyle Waggoner, Vicki LAWRENCE, Tim CONWAY, the Ernest Flatt Dancers, the Harry Zimmerman and then the Peter Matz Orchestras, as well as the wonderful costumes of Bob Mackie. Week after week, for 12 years, Carol and her cast entertained viewers with songs and hilarious comedy sketches. Guest stars such as singers Steve Lawrence and his wife, Eydie Gorme, Dick VAN DYKE, who was on the show in 1977, Kenneth Mars, and Craig Richard Nelson, who were regulars in 1979, and Ken Berry appeared on the series regularly. Carol's poignant tramplike cleaning lady routines, her parodies of such classic films as *Gone With the Wind* ("Went With the Breeze"), and *Sunset Boulevard*, and such daytime serials as *AS THE WORLD TURNS* ("As the Stomach Turns"), as well as sketches that featured Burnett and Korman as a typical TV situation comedy husband and wife team, the dysfunctional Harper family (which became a spin-off series, *MAMA'S FAMILY*, that starred Vicki Lawrence), with Carol playing Eunice, a woman who could never win the approval of her mother, or fulfill her overly ambitious aspirations, and skits with Carol playing a "dumb blond" secretary (Mrs. Wiggins) to Tim Conway's always exasperated Scandinavian boss (Mr. Tudball), kept viewers tuning in to the partylike show regularly. Each week, Carol ended her shows with her theme song, "It's Time to Say Goodbye," and when Burnett sang that song on the last *Carol Burnett Show* on September 8, 1979, millions of viewers could not believe their favorite weekly comedy/variety show and star were about to become part of television history.

CAROLINE IN THE CITY

Sept. 1995–July 1996	NBC	Thurs. 9:30–10 P.M.
Aug. 1996–June 1997	NBC	Tues. 9:30–10 P.M.
July 1997–June 1998	NBC	Mon. 9–9:30 P.M.
June 1998–July 1998	NBC	Mon. 8:30–9 P.M.
Sept. 1998–Nov. 1998	NBC	Mon. 9–9:30 P.M.
Dec. 1998–Jan. 1999	NBC	Mon. 8:30–9 P.M.
Mar. 1999–May 1999	NBC	Mon. 8:30–9 P.M.

On this situation comedy series, which was set in New York City, cartoonist Caroline Duffy, played by Lea Thompson, had found success with her autobiographical comic strip "Caroline in the City." The comic strip was about the adventures of a young single woman living in the big city. Caroline lived in the Tribeca neighborhood of Manhattan, where she also worked, and eventually expanded her business to include greeting cards, books, and calendars. When she hired a rather stuffy artist/colorist named Richard Karinsky, played by Malcolm Gets, Caroline, much to her surprise, fell in love with him, although she had become engaged to Del Cassidy, played by Eric Lutes, who published Caroline's greeting cards. Richard, much to Caroline's chagrin, married an attractive, full-figured bartender named Julia, played by Sofia Milos. Listening to Caroline's various problems was her best friend, Annie, played by Amy Pietz. Tom La Grua ran the Italian restaurant Caroline and her friends frequented.

CARROLL, DIAHANN (CAROL DIAHANN JOHNSON 1935–)

Bronx-born New Yorker Diahann Carroll was the first African-American actress to have a leading role on a series of her own. Before she appeared on this show, *JULIA*, Carroll had won the *Chance of a Lifetime* talent show contest and played supporting roles in such important films as *Carmen Jones* (1954), *Porgy and Bess* (1959), *Paris Blues* (1961), and *Hurry Sundown* (1967). She also won a Tony Award for her starring role in Richard Rodgers's Broadway musical *No Strings* in the 1960s. In 1968, when *Julia* made its debut, Diahann Carroll suddenly became a major star. In 1974, Carroll played the leading role in the feature-length film *Claudine*. The less than successful *Diahann Carroll Show*, which was first seen in 1976, followed, and a more favorably received performance on the TV series *DYNASTY*, playing the pretentious Dominique Devereaux Lloyd (whose real name was Millie Cox) from 1984 to 1987, gave her career renewed vigor. A busy cabaret and nightclub singer, Carroll has been kept busy in recent years acting in TV miniseries, such as *Lonesome Dove* (1992), in the film *Eve's Bayou* (1997), and making guest appearances on *TOUCHED BY AN ANGEL* and *ELLEN*. Diahann Carroll's most recent major TV role was as Betty Hemings in the made-for-TV film *Sally Hemings: An American Scandal* (2000).

CARSON, JOHNNY (1925–)

For 30 years, comedian/TV host Johnny Carson was the popular star of the late night *TONIGHT SHOW* with Johnny Carson. Born in Corning, Iowa, but raised in Nebraska, Johnny began his performing career as a child, billing himself as "The Great Carson," and doing magic tricks at parties. He worked on radio after finishing his schooling, and then appeared on TV on WOW in Omaha, Nebraska, leaving for Hollywood in the early 1950s. In 1953, Carson got a job as a gag writer for *The RED SKELTON SHOW*, but in 1954, his wholesome look and good-natured quick wit soon led to TV-game-show hosting on such programs as *Who Do You Trust?* and *Earn Your Vacation.* Carson was

Johnny Carson (Author's collection)

chosen by NBC as the host of the *Tonight Show,* and on October 2, 1962, with Groucho Marx as his first guest, Carson made his debut and was an immediate success. He continued to entertain people as the star of the *Tonight Show* for the next 30 years. Johnny's last guest was Bette Midler on May 21, 1992. Over the years, Carson made many guest appearances on such popular TV series as *The* JACK BENNY PROGRAM, *The* UNITED STATES STEEL HOUR, GET SMART, *The* MARY TYLER MOORE SHOW, HERE'S LUCY, NIGHT COURT, NEWHART, CHEERS, *and The* SIMPSONS, among others. Since he left the *Tonight Show,* Carson has made only rare guest-starring appearances on television. Carson also played a former talk show host in the film *The Murdering Mom* (1993) and had a small, uncredited role in the film *The Newton Boys* (1998), but quadruple bypass heart surgery in 1999 forced Carson to curtail his performing activities.

CARTER, NELL (NELL RUTH HARDY 1948–)
African-American singer and actress Nell Carter took show business by storm as one of the stars of the Broadway musical sensation *Ain't Misbehavin'* in the 1970s, for which she won a Tony Award for her performance. Prior to that, Carter, who was born in Birmingham, Alabama, had sung in her church choir and appeared in music videos before going to New York and finding regular work as a

singer and actress. Roles in several off-Broadway shows and in the hit Broadway show *Hair,* and in the subsequent film version of that show followed. Carter became a regular on *The Misadventures of Sheriff Lobo* series in 1980, and then starred on her own series, GIMME A BREAK!, in 1981, playing a character named Nell Harper. *Gimme a Break!* was a success and had a large audience. Her next several series, *You Take the Kids* (1990), *Hangin' with Mr. Cooper* (1993–1995), and *Happily Ever After: Fairy Tales for Every Child* (1995), did not prove to be as popular as *Gimme a Break!.* Carter has continued to perform in nightclubs and cabarets, made occasional guest-starring appearances on TV series, was a semiregular panelist on the MATCH GAME series (1998), and played roles in such films as *The Crazysitter* (1995), *The Grass Harp* (1995), *Special Delivery* (1999), and *Sealed with a Kiss* (1999).

CASSIDY, DAVID (DAVID BRUCE CASSIDY 1950–)
The son of Broadway and television star Jack Cassidy, David Cassidy became an overnight sensation and a teenage heartthrob when he appeared in *The* PARTRIDGE FAMILY TV series with his stepmother, Shirley Jones, in 1979. Born in New York City while his father was starring on Broadway, David studied music and made his acting debut playing supporting roles on such TV series as ADAM-12, *The F.B.I.,* and *The* MOD SQUAD in 1970. That same year he was cast as Keith Partridge on the surprise hit of the 1970 television season, *The Partridge Family.* After the show was canceled, David starred on the ill-fated *David Cassidy—Man Undercover* series in 1978. Thereafter, Cassidy's acting career went into a decline, except for occasional roles in such made-for-TV films as *The Night the City Screamed* (1980) and in the feature film *Instant Karma* (1990). In recent years, Cassidy has concentrated on live concert stage appearances and has only occasionally guest-starred on TV series such as *The Ben Stiller Show* in 1992 and *The* JOHN LARROQUETTE SHOW in 1995.

CHAMBERLAIN, RICHARD (GEORGE RICHARD CHAMBERLAIN 1935–)
Few television actors were more popular than Richard Chamberlain in the 1960s. Chamberlain played the handsome young doctor, James Kildare, on one of several series with hospital settings seen during that decade, DR. KILDARE. The young actor, who was born in Beverly Hills, California, had just graduated from Pomona College in California when he was cast in the *Dr. Kildare* series and became an immediate TV star. Chamberlain subsequently appeared in a several films, such as *A Thunder of Drums* (1961), *Twilight of Honor* (1963), and *The Madwoman of Chaillot* (1969), but it was after a performance in a stage production of *Hamlet* in England, that Chamberlain's career took an unexpected change of direction. Drama critics were amazed by his remarkable portrayal of Shakespeare's tragic prince, as was the public when Cham-

berlain repeated his Hamlet role on a TV special. More important film and TV roles followed. He starred in the big-budgeted, if less than well-received, films *The Music Lovers* (1970), *The Three Musketeers* (1973), *The Towering Inferno* (1974), *The Man in the Iron Mask* (1976), and the very successful TV miniseries *Centennial* (1978), *Shogun* (1980), and *The Thorn Birds* (1983). In 1989, Chamberlain starred on the TV series *Island Son*, which was not successful. The actor has continued to appear in made-for-TV films, the most recent being *Too Rich: The Secret Life of Doris Duke* (1999) and *The Pavilion* (1999).

CHANCELLOR, JOHN (JOHN WILLIAM CHANCELLOR 1927–1996)

NBC television anchorman and news correspondent John Chancellor was born in Chicago, Illinois. Chancellor began his career in journalism as a copy boy at the *Chicago Sun Times*. He became a television reporter for NBC and hosted the local news at WMAQ in the 1950s. In 1958, Chancellor became NBC's Vienna bureau chief and covered the cold war. In 1961–1962, Chancellor was the host of *NBC News Today*. He continued working as an NBC correspondent, and then, from 1970 to 1982, was their chief news anchor on the *NBC Nightly News*. In 1982, Tom BROKAW took over the evening news assignment, but Chancellor continued to work on special assignments for NBC. Two years before illness and subsequent death from stomach cancer in 1996, Chancellor hosted the popular NBC documentary miniseries *Baseball*.

Charlie's Angels: Jaclyn Smith, Farrah Fawcett-Majors, and Kate Jackson (Author's collection)

CHARLES IN CHARGE

Oct. 1984–Apr. 1985	CBS	Wed. 8–8:30 P.M.
Apr. 1985	CBS	Sat. 8–8:30 P.M.
June 1985–July 1985	CBS	Wed. 8–8:30 P.M.
Jan. 1987–Dec. 1990	Syndicated Series	Various stations and times

Scott BAIO, because of his success as Chachi on the HAPPY DAYS series, was given his own TV series, *Charles in Charge*, in 1984. The show remained on the air for only a little over one season, but it did have an impressive number of fans during its brief run. Baio played a 19-year-old college student named Charles, who went to work as a "governess" for a busy working couple. Julie Cobb and James Widdoes played his employees, Jill and Stan Pembroke, and Jonathan Ward, April Lerman, and Michael Pearlman played their children, Douglas, Lila, and Jason. Willie Aames, who had been one of the stars of the EIGHT IS ENOUGH series, was seen as Charles's college friend, Buddy Lembeck. Occasionally, Ellen Travolta also appeared on the series as Charles's mother, Lillian.

CHARLIE'S ANGELS

Sept. 1976–Aug. 1977	ABC	Wed. 10–11 P.M.
Aug. 1977–Oct. 1980	ABC	Wed. 9–10 P.M.
Nov. 1980–Jan. 1981	ABC	Sun. 8–9 P.M.
Jan. 1981–Feb. 1981	ABC	Sat. 8–9 P.M.
June 1981–Aug. 1981	ABC	Wed. 8–9 P.M.

Three beautiful actresses, Kate JACKSON, Farrah FAWCETT-Majors, and Jaclyn SMITH, were the main reason for the success of the rather banal adventure series *Charlie's Angels*. For five years, they played three police-trained young women named Sabrina Duncan (Jackson), Jill Munroe (Fawcett-Majors), and Kelly Garrett (Smith), who worked for a wealthy, unseen boss who talked to them only on the telephone (the voice was that of actor John FORSYTHE). The girls helped Charlie resolve problems he was having at his various health spas, nightclubs, and other glamorous businesses he owned. Charlie's assistant, John Bosley, played by David Doyle, acted as an intermediary between the girls and their boss. In 1977, when Farrah Fawcett-Majors decided she had had enough of the series, she was replaced by Cheryl Ladd. In 1979, Kate Jackson left the series and was replaced by Shelley Hack. When Hack left the show, she was replaced by Tanya Roberts. *Charlie's Angels* was produced by Aaron Spelling, and 115 episodes of the series were filmed. In 2000, a *Charlie's Angels* motion picture, which starred an entirely different cast, revived interest in the series.

CHAYEFSKY, PADDY (SIDNEY AARON CHAYEFSKY 1923–1981)

One of television's most celebrated playwrights, Paddy Chayefsky was born in the Bronx, New York City. When he graduated from DeWitt Clinton High School, Chayefsky attended City College of New York. For a time, Chayefsky was a stand-up comic before he was drafted into the U.S. Army during World War II. While he was recovering from injuries received during the war, Chayefsky wrote his first play, and when discharged from the army, he found employment as a radio, and then television, writer. His realistic television dramas, which usually depicted the lives of ordinary people, became very popular on such early dramatic anthology shows as *The* PHILCO/GOODYEAR PLAYHOUSE and PLAYHOUSE 90 in the 1950s, and *Marty*, *The Bachelor Party*, and *The Catered Affair*, later became successful motion pictures. The three-time Academy Award–winning writer (for *Marty* in 1955, *The Hospital* in 1971, and *Network* in 1976) also provided the scripts for the successful films *The Americanization of Emily* (1964), *Paint Your Wagon* (1969), and *Altered States* (1980), which was adapted from his novel of the same name.

CHEERS

Sept. 1982–Dec. 1982	NBC	Thurs. 9–9:30 P.M.
Jan. 1983–Dec. 1983	NBC	Thurs. 9:30–10 P.M.
Dec. 1983–Aug. 1993	NBC	Thurs. 9–9:30 P.M.
Feb. 1993–May 1993	NBC	Thurs. 8–8:30 P.M.

The cast of *Cheers*. Sitting, Ted Danson and Kelsey Grammer; standing, Rhea Perlman, Woody Harrelson, John Ratzenberger, Kirstie Alley, George Wendt (Author's collection)

Few television situation comedies have won the affection and loyalty of TV critics and viewers that NBC's *Cheers* did. For 11 years, Thursday night became the night millions of devoted fans watched their beloved *Cheers*, and when the series finally departed the airwaves in 1993, the public outcry was unprecedented. The main setting of *Cheers* was a downtown bar in Boston, Massachusetts, called "Cheers." It was a place where good conversation, familiar faces, and some salty locker room jokes were common, and it was a place viewers, and the regular customers on the show, loved to be. The owner of the bar was a tall, lanky, former Boston Red Sox pitcher named Sam Malone, who was played by Ted Danson. Sam had an eye for the ladies. He was a recovering alcoholic who had sworn off liquor forever before he bought his bar. Helping behind the counter as a bartender was a former baseball manager and coach, Ernie Pantusso (called "Coach"), played by Nicholas Colasanto. Working at the bar as a waitress was a wisecracking, down-to-earth, tough little woman named Carla Tortelli LeBec, played by Rhea Perlman. Two of *Cheers*'s most loyal customers, who never seemed to spend time anywhere but at the bar, were a heavyset accountant who loved his beer, Norm Peterson, played by George Wendt, and a bragging but likable postman named Cliff Clavin, played by John Ratzenberger. When a young graduate student named Diane Chambers, played by Shelley Long, was jilted by her fiancée, she found herself in need of immediate employment and applied for the only job she felt she felt qualified for—a waitress at Cheers. Diane disliked Sam at first, in spite of his generous offer of a job, and the two often argued. Love eventually blossomed between them, and an off-again, on-again romance developed. When actor Nicholas Colasanto suddenly died, Sam, after a suitable period of mourning, hired a somewhat dim-but-lovable young bartender named Woody Boyd, played by Woody Harrelson. By this time, another regular customer at the bar, an obnoxious, insecure but highly amusing psychologist named Frasier Crane, played by Kelsey GRAMMER, appeared on the series. Frasier Crane had an overbearing, too-bright-for-her-own-good, pretentious wife named Dr. Lilith Sternin, played by Bebe Neuwirth, who also visited the bar on occasion. In 1987, after five years on the show, Shelley Long decided that she wanted to leave the series to pursue other career interests. She was replaced by Kirstie Alley, who played the bossy Rebecca Howe, who had been hired to manage Cheers when Sam sold the bar after Diane left him on the final episode of the 1985–1986 season. When *Cheers* returned for the 1986–1987 season, Sam, who had returned to Boston after taking an around-the-world trip, was broke and became a bartender at the establishment he had once owned. By the last episode of *Cheers*, Sam had regained ownership of the bar, but it soon closed forever. Sam finally did marry Diane when she returned to *Cheers* for a brief visit. The final, poignant shot on the series was of the remaining cast turning off the lights of the bar forever, and silently going home.

CHER

Feb. 1975–June 1975	CBS	Sun. 7:30–8:30 P.M.
Sept. 1975–Jan. 1976	CBS	Sun. 8–9 P.M.

After starring on a popular weekly variety show, *The SONNY AND CHER COMEDY HOUR*, for five years together, Sonny and Cher Bono were divorced, and both became the stars of separate TV variety shows. Sonny's solo show was called The *Sonny Comedy Revue* and was on the air for four months. Cher's show was simply called *Cher* and lasted for one full year. Cher's show presented her as a glamorous, appealing personality and solo performer, costumed in glamorous clothes that, more often than not, revealed her sleek, well-toned body. Even comedian Steve Martin and actress Teri Garr, who were frequent guest stars on the *Cher* show, as was the Bonos' daughter, Chastity, could not help to keep the show on the air. One month after the show was canceled, the *Sonny and Cher Show* resurfaced, reuniting the famous couple as a team, if not as husband and wife. This show remained on CBS for 2 years.

CHEVY SHOW WITH DINAH SHORE, THE

(see *Dinah Shore Show, The*)

CHEYENNE

Sept. 1955–Sept. 1959	ABC	Tues. 7:30–8:30 P.M.
Sept. 1959–Dec. 1962	ABC	Mon. 7:30–8:30 P.M.
Apr. 1963–Sept. 1963	ABC	Fri. 7:30–8:30 P.M.

In the mid-1950s to early 1960s, half-hour western adventure programs were among the most popular shows on television, and ABC offered a special, full-hour western, *Cheyenne*, as part of the *Warner Brothers Presents* series. The protagonist of *Cheyenne* was a character named Cheyenne Bodie, played by Clint WALKER, a muscular, tall, good-looking, adventure-seeker who roamed the Wild West in the days immediately following the Civil War. The public demanded to see more of *Cheyenne* and Walker, and during the 1956 season, *Cheyenne* became a series that alternated every other week with a show called *Conflict*. In 1957, *Cheyenne* alternated with the *SUGARFOOT* western series. Clint Walker quit the series in 1958 during a contract dispute with his bosses at Warner Brothers, and the show continued with Ty Hardin as Bronco Lane replacing the Cheyenne Bodie character. In 1959, Walker, his contract dispute with ABC resolved, returned as the star of *Cheyenne,* and *Bronco* became a separate series. As Cheyenne drifted from place to place, working as a ranch hand, a wagon train leader, and a lawman, to name just a few of the jobs he held, the series' popularity continued to grow. Warner Brothers spared no cost in making the weekly adventure series exciting and attractive. Because of the variety of *Cheyenne's* various settings, viewers saw something different each week, which surely helped keep the series on the air for eight seasons. *Cheyenne* was loosely based on the Warner Brothers' film *Cheyenne*, which had starred Dennis Morgan and was originally released in 1947.

CHICAGO HOPE

Sept. 1994	CBS	Sun. 8–9 P.M.
Sept. 1994	CBS	Thurs. 10–11 P.M.
Oct. 1994–Dec. 1994	CBS	Thurs. 9–10 P.M.
Dec. 1994–Sept. 1997	CBS	Mon. 10–11 P.M.
Oct. 1997–	CBS	Wed. 10–11 P.M.

In 1994, CBS, in an attempt to recapture some of the audience its rival, NBC, had won with their hospital series *ER*, launched a one-hour medical series of its own, *Chicago Hope*. Set in the fictitious Chicago Hope Hospital, the series was placed by CBS in the same time slot as NBC's *ER*. *Chicago Hope* was well received by critics, but failed to put a dent in the number of viewers watching *ER*. As a result, CBS moved *Chicago Hope* to another time slot. The original series, created by David E. Kelley, had an engaging cast that included Adam Arkin as surgeon Aaron Shutt; Roxanne Hart as his wife, nurse Camille Shutt; Mandy Patinkin as Dr. Jeffrey Geiger; E. G. Marshall as Dr. Arthur Thurmond; Hector Elizondo as chief surgeon Phillip Watters; Peter MacNicol as the hospital's lawyer, Alan Birch; Roma Maffia as Angela; Thomas Gibson as Dr. Daniel Nyland; Robyn Lively as nurse Maggie Atkinson; Diane Venora as Dr. Infante; Peter Berg as Dr. Billy Kronk; and Vondie Curtis-Hall as Dr. Dennis Hancock. The series was, at times, quirky, especially when Mandy Patinkin burst out in song as he operated on a patient, and when E. G. Marshall, as an aged doctor whose dementia has gotten the best of him, feebly fumbled about the hospital. Mandy Patinkin left the series after its first season, but returned several years later to appear as a semiregular. Over the years, other actors joined the cast and became popular characters with the show's ever-increasing number of viewers. They included Christine Lahti as Dr. Kathryn Austin, Jamey Sheridan as Dr. John Sutton, Vanessa L. Williams as Dr. Grace Carr, Ron Silver as Tommy Wilmette, and Eric Stolz as Dr. Robert Yates.

CHICO AND THE MAN

Sept. 1974–Jan. 1976	NBC	Fri. 8:30–9 P.M.
Jan. 1976–Mar. 1976	NBC	Wed. 9–9:30 P.M.
Apr. 1976–Aug. 1976	NBC	Wed. 9:30–10 P.M.
Aug. 1976–Feb. 1978	NBC	Fri. 8:30–9 P.M.
June 1978–July 1978	NBC	Fri. 8:30–9 P.M.

This ethnically oriented situation comedy series centered on two men from two very different backgrounds and generations who lived and worked in the barrio of East Los Angeles, California. Chico was an enterprising young Chicano automobile mechanic, played by Freddie Prinze, who was determined to prove himself worthy of becoming a partner in Ed Brown's ("the Man's") small, dilapidated auto garage/repair shop. The energetic, clever Chico Rodriguez and the cranky old Anglo–American owner of the shop, Ed Brown, played by veteran character actor Jack Albertson, had little in common, and their contrasting lifestyles was often the basis for the series' humor; but in spite of his apparent contempt for Chico, it became apparent that Ed, a rather lonely widower, was really flattered and touched by Chico's taking an interest in him and his business. When the series first went on the air, it was often criticized by Mexican-American groups that protested the fact that Freddie Prinze was not of Mexican descent, like his character Chico, but was of Puerto Rican and Hungarian extraction. When the series became a hit, increased understanding and appreciation for the Mexican-American community in Southern California developed, and when Mexican-American actors were added to the cast, the protests diminished. Appearing regularly on the series with Prinze and Albertson were Scatman Crothers as Louie, Bonnie Boland as Mabel, Isaac Ruiz as Mando, Ronny Graham as Rev. Bemis, Della Reese as Della Rogers, and the sexy Spanish performer Charo as Aunt Charo. In 1977, while the series was at the peak of its popularity, actor Freddie Prinze, who was 22 years old, committed suicide, and the show's producers considered canceling the series. The following season, however, actor Gabriel Melgar became Ed Brown's new young Mexican-American partner. The public could not accept anyone but Freddie Prinze as "the Man's" partner on *Chico and the Man,* and the series was canceled in 1978.

CHILD, JULIA (JULIA McWILLIAMS CHILD 1912–)

The grande dame of American cooking, Julia Child, whose fame came from her numerous cooking shows on

Julia Child (Author's collection)

television, as well as her expertise in the kitchen, was born in Pasadena, California, to wealthy parents. A pampered and curious child, Julia was encouraged to experiment with all sorts of activities while she was growing up and, in addition to interests in the arts and literature, she was also a fine athlete. During World War II, when she was in her early thirties, Julie held a job as a clerk with the Office of Strategic Services (OSS), which later became the CIA, and rose to the rank of a registrar with that organization, putting her in control of top-secret, sensitive wartime documents. In 1946, when she was in her mid-thirties, she married Paul Child. The couple remained happily married until Paul's death in 1996. When Julia Child was in her forties, she developed an interest in cooking and decided to study at the famed Cordon Bleu culinary school in Paris. The result of her training was a two-volume cookbook that she coauthored with French chefs Simone Beck and Louisette Bertholle called *Mastering the Art of French Cooking.* The book was an enormous success, and when Child returned to the United States, she was asked to star on a television cooking show on the Public Broadcasting System, *The* FRENCH CHEF, which made its debut in 1962. The show became popular and made Julia Child the most famous cook in the United States. Her forthright manner, casual reaction to on-camera mistakes (she often dropped food on the floor), and her devil-may-care attitude toward cooking, made her a well-loved television personality. *The French Chef* was on the air from 1962 until 1973, and those shows can still be seen regularly in reruns. In 1978, Julia hosted a new cooking series on PBS, *Julia Child & Company,* which featured celebrated guest chefs. Julia Child is still active on television, and her book *The Way To Cook,* published in 1989, has become one of the most successful cookbooks of all time.

CHINA BEACH

Apr. 1988	ABC	Tues. 9–11 P.M.
Apr. 1988–June 1988	ABC	Wed. 10–11 P.M.
Aug. 1988–Sept. 1988	ABC	Wed. 10–11 P.M.
Nov. 1988–Mar. 1990	ABC	Wed. 10–11 P.M.
Apr. 1990	ABC	Mon. 9–10 P.M.
July 1990–Aug. 1990	ABC	Wed. 10–11 P.M.
Aug. 1990–Dec. 1990	ABC	Sat. 9–10 P.M.
June 1991–July 1991	ABC	Tues. 10–11 P.M.
July 1991	ABC	Mon. 9–11 P.M.

In the 1980s, the American military involvement in Vietnam during the 1960s and 1970s, was not a particularly popular subject with many TV viewers; they wanted to forget that such an embarrassing war had ever happened. In spite of this, ABC's *China Beach,* which was set during those turbulent times, attracted a large audience by presenting soap opera–like stories that depicted the private lives of various women who were involved in the conflict. The series wisely took a popular, strongly antiwar stand. The "China Beach" of the series' title was a combination evacuation and U.S.O. entertainment center that was located near the large U.S. military base in Da Nang, Vietnam. Most of the show's episodes centered on Colleen McMurphy, a nurse played by Dana Delany, who had affairs with several men at the center, but who was in love with a married man, Dr. Dick Richard, played by Robert Picardo. Other regular characters featured on the series at various times were an ambitious U.S.O. singer, Laurette Barber, played by Chloe Webb; Red Cross worker Cherry White, played by Nan Woods, who was killed during the Tet offensive; officious Major Lila Garreau, played by Concetta Tomei, who married Sgt. Pepper of the motor pool, played by Tony Evans; K. C. Kolaski, played by Marg Helgenberger; Boone Lanier, played by Brian Wimmer; Wayloo Marie Holmes, played by Megan Gallagher; Pvt. Frankie Bunsen, played by Nancy Giles; Dodger, played by Jeff Kober; and Holly the Donut Dolly, played by Ricki Lake. Taking advantage of the U.S.O. aspect of the show, guest stars sometimes performed on the series. Nancy Sinatra made a cameo appearance on the series singing her hit song of the 1960s, "Those Boots Were Made for Walking." *China Beach's* theme song, "Reflections," sung by Diana Ross and the Supremes, was heard at the beginning of each episode. The show was created by Williams Broyles, Jr. and John Sacret Young.

CHiPS

Sept. 1977–Mar. 1978	NBC	Thurs. 8–9 P.M.
Apr. 1978	NBC	Sat. 8–9 P.M.
May 1978–Aug. 1978	NBC	Thurs. 8–9 P.M.
Sept. 1978–Mar. 1980	NBC	Sat. 8–9 P.M.
Mar. 1980–Mar. 1983	NBC	Sun. 8–9 P.M.
Apr. 1983–May 1983	NBC	Sun. 7–8 P.M.
May 1983–July. 1983	NBC	Sun. 8–9 P.M.

California Highway Patrol (CHiPs) officers Jon Baker and Frank "Ponch" Poncherello, played by Larry WILCOX and Erik ESTRADA, were motorcycle-riding partners whose police work and private lives were the main focus of this full-hour action-packed series, which was extremely popular with young viewers. Disagreements between Wilcox and Estrada led to Wilcox's leaving the series in 1982. Officer Poncherello had several other partners for the show's remaining one and a half years. Other regulars on the series included Robert Pine as Baker and Ponch's commanding officer, Sgt. Joe Getraer, Brodie Greer as Officer Barickza, Lou Wagner as police mechanic Harlan, Brianne Leary as Officer Sindy Cahill, Randi Oakes as Officer Bonnie Clark, Michael Dorn as Officer Turner, Tom Reilly as Officer Bobby "Hotdog" Nelson, Bruce Penhall as Nelson's half brother Officer Bruce Nelson, Tina Gayle as Officer Kathy Linahan, and former Olympic decathlon medalist Bruce Jenner as Officer Steve McLeish. The show became known for its many car crash scenes and highway chases. In all, 138 episodes of the series were filmed.

Erik Estrada (Ponch) and Larry Wilcox (Jon) of *ChiPs* (Author's collection)

CISCO KID, THE

1950–1956	Syndicated series	Various stations and times

One of television's earliest western series produced with younger viewers in mind, was *The Cisco Kid*, first seen in 1950. It was also the first filmed TV adventure series seen during those early years when shows were usually live. The hero of this very popular adventure program was a Mexican adventurer called the Cisco Kid, played by Duncan Renaldo. The Kid roamed the West on his horse, Diablo, with his trusted sidekick Pancho, played by actor Leo Carrillo, who rode a horse named Loco, at his side. Renaldo was in his fifties when *The Cisco Kid* was filmed and Carrillo was in his seventies, but this did not make them any less dashing or heroic, and Cisco and Pancho avenged the wronged and fought the bad guys wherever they found them, with amazing gusto. The Cisco Kid character was the creation of short story writer O. Henry, who had written stories about The Kid's adventures 50 years before he was seen on TV. In the O. Henry stories, Cisco was a bandito, but he became a hero when he was first seen in several silent films in the 1920s. *The Cisco Kid* was also a popular radio program before it became a TV series. In all, 156 episodes of *The Cisco Kid* were filmed for television, and they can still be seen in reruns.

CLARK, DICK (RICHARD WAGSTAFF CLARK 1929–)

The seemingly eternally young television host Dick Clark first came to the public's attention during the early days of rock and roll, when he hosted a popular TV teen dance show called AMERICAN BANDSTAND in 1957. Soon after he graduated from school, Clark, who was born in Mount Vernon, New York, became a radio disc jockey. While working at a radio station in Philadelphia, he was asked to replace *American Bandstand's* original host, Bob Horn. *Bandstand* was a successful local TV show that was seen on WFIL-TV in Philadelphia. The show's popularity and reputation grew, and by 1975 it had became a national network show. Dick Clark, who was in his mid-twenties, continued to host the show from 1957 until 1989. In 1960, the young TV personality's good looks led to an offer to appear in films. Clark's first film role was in *Because They're Young* (1960), and the following year he starred in *The Young Doctors* (1961). Clark subsequently hosted the *Missing Links* TV series in 1964 and the very successful *$10,000 PYRAMID* quiz show from 1973 to 1988. In 1984, Clark, with cohost Ed McMahon, emceed *TV's Bloopers and Practical Jokes* series, and in 1985 and 1986 he was the ringmaster of the *Circus of Stars* specials. In addition to his many TV hosting and acting appearances, Clark is also one of show business's most successful producers. He has produced numerous made-for-TV films and shows over the years, most notably *Murder in Texas* (1981), the *Donny and Marie Hour* (1998), WHO WANTS TO BE A MILLIONAIRE (1999), and *Greed* (1999). Dick Clark has also made numerous guest appearances on such popular TV series as PERRY MASON, The ODD COUPLE, FRIENDS, The DREW CAREY SHOW, and DHARMA & GREG, to name just a few.

COACH

Feb. 1989	ABC	Tues. 9:30–10 P.M.
Mar. 1989–June 1989	ABC	Wed. 9:30–10 P.M.
June 1989–Aug. 1989	ABC	Tues. 9:30–10 P.M.
Aug. 1989–Sept. 1989	ABC	Wed. 9:30–10 P.M.
Nov. 1989–Nov. 1992	ABC	Tues. 9:30–10 P.M.
Nov. 1992–Jul. 1993	ABC	Wed. 9:30–10 P.M.
July 1993–July 1994	ABC	Tues. 9:30–10 P.M.
Aug. 1994–Oct. 1994	ABC	Mon. 8–8:30 P.M.
Oct. 1994–Dec. 1994	ABC	Mon. 8–9 P.M.
Jan. 1995–Mar. 1995	ABC	Mon. 8:30–9 P.M.
Mar. 1995–May 1995	ABC	Wed. 9:30–10 P.M.
June 1995–Jan. 1996	ABC	Tues. 9:30–10 P.M.
Feb. 1996–May 1996	ABC	Tues. 8:30–9 P.M.
May 1996–Sept. 1996	ABC	Tues. 9:30–10 P.M.
Sept. 1996–Oct. 1996	ABC	Sat. 9–9:30 P.M.
Dec. 1996–Aug. 1997	ABC	Wed. 8:30–9 P.M.

For eight years, *Coach* was the America's favorite behind-the-scenes TV situation comedy with a sports setting as its background. Craig T. Nelson played Hayden Fox, a divorced football coach at Minnesota State University, whose team seemed to have a talent for losing games, until 1990, when they went on a winning streak. Jerry Van Dyke was Fox's "Screaming Eagles" assistant coach, Luther Van Dam; Clare Carey was Fox's daughter, Kelly (whom he hadn't seen for 16 years until she became a student at Minnesota State); Shelly Fabares played Fox's girlfriend, newscaster Christine Armstrong; Bill Fagerbakke played student Dauber Dybinski; and Kris Kamm played a young man who married and then divorced Kelly while both were still students. After years of having an on-again, off-again romance, Fox and Christine were finally married in 1993, much to the delight of the show's many fans. Also appearing on the series as regulars from time to time were Pam Stone as Judy Watkins, a women's basketball coach at MSU; Ken Kimmens and Georgia Engel as athletic director Howard Burleigh and his wife, Shirley; and Rita Taggart as Van Dams lady friend, Ruthanne.

COCA, IMOGENE (IMOGENE FERNANDEZ DE COCA 1908–2001)

As Sid CAESAR's costar on NBC's immensely popular YOUR SHOW OF SHOWS comedy/variety program from 1950 to 1954, comedienne Imogene Coca was one of television's earliest stars. Coca, who was born in Philadelphia, began her career as a child performer in vaudeville and on Broadway. She made her TV debut in 1949 on the *Admiral Broadway Revue*, and a year later was signed by NBC to star on *Your Show of Shows*. Hoping to become known as a solo performer on television, Coca left *Your Show of Shows* after four years to star on the ill-fated *Imogene Coca Show* in 1954. She reteamed with Sid Caesar on the *Sid Caesar Invites You* series in 1958, but the magic had gone out of their partnership, and the new show failed to attract an audience. In 1963, Coca starred on the situation comedy series *Grindl*, and then on the *It's About Time* series in 1966. Both of these series were failures. Over the years, Coca was featured in such films as *Under the Yum Yum Tree* (1963), *Rabbit Test* (1978), *Vacation* (1983), *Buy & Cell* (1989), the made-for-TV films *The Return of the Beverly Hillbillies* (1981) and *Alice in Wonderland* (1985), and the Broadway musical comedy *On the Twentieth Century*, before retiring in the early 1990s.

COLBYS, THE

Nov. 1985	ABC	Wed. 10–11 P.M.
Nov. 1985–Mar. 1987	ABC	Thurs. 9–10 P.M.

Despite its big-name Hollywood cast and the fact that it was a spin-off of the popular DYNASTY series, *The Colbys*, which was about life among the superrich of Los Angeles, failed to capture a sizable enough audience to keep it on the air for more than one and a half seasons. Even film stars Charlton Heston, Katherine Ross, Barbara STANWYCK, Ricardo MONTALBAN, and such well-known supporting players as Joe Campanella, Ken Howard, Kevin McCarthy, Michael Parks, and Gary Morris, who sometimes appeared on the series, could not make the show a hit. The series' major characters had originally been introduced to viewers on *Dynasty* at the beginning of the 1985 season. They included the very wealthy corporate executive Jason Colby, the father of *Dynasty's* Jeff Colby, played by Charlton Heston; Jason's wife, Sable Scott Colby, played by Stephanie Beacham; Sable's sister, Francesca, played by Katherine Ross; Jason's sister, Constance, played by Barbara Stanwyck; Jason and Sable's oldest daughter, Monica, played by Tracy Scoggins; and the Colby's son, Miles, played by Maxwell Caulfield. TV superstar Joan Collins, Alexis of *Dynasty*, was so disturbed by *The Colbys* debut on TV that she urged her fellow *Dynasty* cast members to have nothing to do with the series in an article published in *TV Guide* magazine.

COLGATE COMEDY HOUR, THE

Sept. 1950–Dec. 1955 NBC Sun. 8–9 P.M.

For five years, NBC's *Colgate Comedy Hour* was CBS's *The TOAST OF THE TOWN* (*The ED SULLIVAN SHOW*) only serious threat in the popular 8–9 P.M. Sunday night time slot. *The Colgate Comedy Hour* presented the first television appearances of some of show business's most celebrated stars, such as Eddie Cantor, Fred Allen, Spike Jones and his City Slickers, Jerry Lester, ABBOTT and COSTELLO, Tony Martin, and Phil SILVERS. *The Colgate Comedy Hour* was also the first major television variety series to originate from Hollywood. In addition to weekly variety shows that were hosted by big-name stars and that featured comedy sketches, songs, dances, and circus acts, the show occasionally presented full-length television adaptations of such well-known Broadway musicals as *Anything Goes*, which was seen on the show in 1954, starring Frank Sinatra and Ethel Merman. In 1954, *The Colgate Comedy Hour* began to present shows telecast from various locations such as the Jones Beach Amphitheater on Long Island, the S.S. *United States*, the Cocoanut Grove, the Hollywood Bowl in Los Angeles, and Pebble Beach, California. The cost of producing this spectacular and very expensive show was footed by the show's single sponsor, Colgate toothpaste. Having one company sponsor an entire show that bore its name was a holdover from the old radio days when a company's product became indelibly associated with a single program (e.g. *Oxydol's Own Ma Perkins*, the *Lux Radio Theater*, *The Ford Theater*, *The Jello Show with Jack Benny*, *Johnson's Wax's Fibber McGee and Molly*, etc.) Eventually, Colgate decided that the expense of producing the show was not cost-effective, and Colgate withdrew its sponsorship. NBC canceled the show in 1955, and all but but gave up its rights to compete with Ed SULLIVAN's *Toast of the Town* for the Sunday 8 P.M. time slot for the next 20 years.

COLLYER, BUD (CLAYTON JOHNSON HEERMANCE, JR. 1908–1969)

When television first began to replace radio as America's favorite home entertainment medium in the mid-to-late 1940s, as World War II ended, a handsome young radio actor and announcer, Bud Collyer, who was the voice of Superman/Clark Kent on radio, became one of the first performers to turn his attention to TV. Born in New York City, Collyer had entered radio as an announcer when he was barely out of school and was soon being featured on such popular radio programs as *The Cavalcade of America, Believe It or Not, Terry and the Pirates,* and such radio soap operas as *Just Plain Bill, Life Can Be Beautiful, The Road of Life, Kitty Kelly,* and *Joyce Jordan, Girl Intern.* Collyer's first major television assignment was as the the host of *Winner Take All* in 1948. He then hosted the BREAK THE BANK (1948), *Talent Jackpot* (1949), BEAT THE CLOCK (1950), MASQUERADE PARTY (1952), *Quick as a Flash* (1953), *Talent Patrol* (1953), *Feather Your Nest* (1954), TO TELL THE TRUTH (1956), and *Number Please* (1961) quiz and panel shows. In 1966, Collyer was also the voice of Superman/Clark Kent once again for *The New Adventures of Superman* TV cartoon series, as well as for *The Batman/Superman Hour* animated cartoon series. Bud Collyer died at the age of 61 of a circulatory ailment.

COLUMBO

Sept. 1971–Sept.1972	NBC	Wed. 8:30–10P.M.
Sept. 1972–July 1974	NBC	Sun. 8:30–10P.M.
Aug. 1974–Aug. 1975	NBC	Sun. 8:30–10:30P.M.
Sept. 1975–Sept. 1976	NBC	Sun. 9–11 P.M.
Oct. 1976–Sept. 1977	NBC	Sun. 8–9:30 P.M.
Feb. 1989–May 1989	ABC	Mon. 9–11 P.M.
Aug. 1989–July 1990	ABC	Sat. 9–11 P.M.
Aug. 1990	ABC	Sun. 9–11 P.M.
Jan. 1992–May 1992	ABC	Thurs. 8–10 P.M.
Nov. 1992–Feb. 1993	ABC	Sat. 8–10 P.M.

The one-and-a-half- and two-hour *Columbo* dramas that starred Peter FALK as the crafty Lt. Columbo, a somewhat seedy homicide detective with the Los Angeles police force, were among television's top-rated shows in the 1970s, and the Columbo character was brought back by popular demand twice in the 1980s and 1990s. At the beginning of each feature-length episode of *Columbo*, viewers witnessed murders committed by people who took ingenious means to avoid detection by the police. Although we knew who the murderers were, homicide detective Columbo had to use his talent for tricking criminals he suspected of wrongdoing into confessing their crimes. When it was originally aired in 1971, *Columbo* was one of three rotating shows seen on the NBC *Sunday Mystery Movie* series, along with McMILLAN AND WIFE and McCLOUD. NBC continued to present full-length made-for-TV *Columbo* films regularly, until Peter Falk, exhausted by the schedule of having to appear in so many feature-length films each year, decided to occasionally reprise his Columbo character. Interestingly, Peter Falk had not been the producers' first choice for the role of Lt. Columbo. In 1970, when the series was being developed by NBC, singer/actor Bing CROSBY had been offered the role. Crosby who, by that time was a millionaire many times over, thought that such an exhausting schedule would "interfere with [his] golf game," and turned the producers down. A spin-off series called *Mrs. Columbo*, aka *Kate Loves a Mystery,* which starred Kate Mulgrew, was produced in 1989. *Columbo's* wife had never been seen on the original series, and was just referred to in the original *Columbo* films.

COMBAT!

   Oct. 1962–Aug. 1967   ABC Tues. 7:30–8:30 P.M.

War dramas have not proved to be particularly popular with TV viewers over the years. One exception was *Combat!*, which was on ABC for five years and developed a large and loyal following. *Combat!*'s setting was Europe during World War II after the D-day invasion. The show was realistically gritty, and newsreel footage of actual World War II battles were often used on the series. The episodes ranged from bloody battle dramas to human interest stories, and even included a few humorous shows. Lt. Gil Hamley, played by Rick Jason, and Sgt. Chip Saunders, played by Vic Morrow, led a U.S. Army platoon with appropriate toughness and compassion. The platoon's comic hustler, Pvt. Braddock, was played by comedian Shecky Greene. Also featured on the series were Pierre Jal-

Morris the Cat (Author's collection)

bert as Pvt. Paul "Caj" (for Cajan) Lemay, Jack Hogan as Pvt. William G. Kirby, Dick Peabody as "Littlejohn," Steven Rogers as Doc Walton, and Tom Lowell as Pvt. Billy Nelson. *Combat!* was produced by Gene Levitt.

COMMERCIALS ON TELEVISION

When television was in its infancy in the late 1940s to early 1950s, programs were usually sponsored by a single company or product. Like radio, the sponsor's name and the name of the star of the program became synonymous. On radio, Jack Benny's program was called *The Jello (or Lucky Strike) Program Starring Jack Benny,* and other popular shows were *The Johnson's Wax Program with Fibber McGee and Molly, The Lux* (soap) *Radio Theater, Oxydol's* (detergent) *Own Ma Perkins, The United States Steel Hour,* and *The Voice of Firestone* (tires). Since early television shows were also usually sponsored by a single product or company, many shows also used the name of their sponsor's product in the title of the shows, e.g. *TEXACO* (oil) *STAR THEATER,* The *KRAFT* (cheese) *TELEVISION THEATER, GENERAL ELECTRIC* (appliances) *THEATER,* and *The COLGATE* (toothpaste) *COMEDY HOUR.* It was not at all unusual during TV's early years to see big-name stars acting as spokespersons for the sponsors of their shows. Bob Hope sold Pepsodent toothpaste, Bing Crosby sold Philco radios and phonographs, and Betty Furness actually became more famous as the spokeswoman for Westinghouse refrigerators on the *STUDIO ONE* dramatic anthology show than she was as a film actress. As the cost of single-show sponsorship became prohibitive, sponsors gave up taking on the entire cost of a program, and the networks began to sell 15-second, 30-second, and full-minute commercial spots on each show to individual advertisers that paid for the time. As a result, television commercials became as familiar to viewers as the shows on which they were seen, some of them running hundreds of times during a single season. Among the most memorable TV slogans and characters that became as familiar as the plots and characters of favorite TV shows over the last 50 years are:

> The White Knight: Ajax cleanser
> Speedy, an animated tablet (voiced by Richard Beals): Alka Seltzer
> "Look Mom, no cavities": Crest toothpaste
> "Hertz puts you in the driver's seat,": Hertz Rent a Car
> The Marlboro Man: Marlboro cigarettes
> "Does she or doesn't she?" Miss Clairol hair dye
> "Why don't you pick me up and smoke me sometime" (voiced by Edie Adams): Muriel cigars
> The dancing cigarette pack and matches: Old Gold cigarettes
> The Jolly Green Giant: frozen foods
> "You'll wonder where the yellow went.": Pepsodent toothpaste
> "Feel really clean.": Zest soap

"In New York, where there are more [Jews, Italians, Irish, Greeks, etc.] than in [Jerusalem, Venice, Dublin, Sparta, etc.], more people drink Rheingold than any other beer": Rheingold beer
Mr. Whipple's "Please don't squeeze the Charmin": Charmin toilet paper
"Ring around the collar": Wisk detergent
Talking Fruit of the Loom characters: Fruit of the Loom underwear
Miss Sweden, Gunilla Knutson's "Take it off . . . Take it all off.": Noxema shaving cream
"When you care enough to send the very best": Hallmark greeting cards
Dena Dietrich as Mother Nature saying, "It's not nice to fool Mother Nature": Chiffon margarine
"I can't believe I ate the whole thing": Alka Seltzer
Charlie Chan saying, "Get wise": Wise potato chips
Ronald McDonald and the McDonald characters: McDonald's fast food chain
Colonel Sanders: Kentucky Fried Chicken restaurants
"Mr. Perdue": Perdue chicken
O. J. Simpson running and jumping hurdles to catch an airplane: Hertz Rent a Car
Baseball player Joe DiMaggio: Mr. Coffee coffee-making machines
Clara Peller's "Where's the beef?": Wendy's fast food chain
Used car salesman Mad Man Muntz: Muntz used cars
Crazy Eddie: Crazy Eddie electronics stores
Mama Cass singing "Hurry on down to Hardee's": Hardee's restaurant chain
"Time to make the donuts": Dunkin donuts
The Pillsbury doughboy: Pillsbury flour
Morris the Cat: Nine Lives cat food
and many others

In the 1940s, the entire weekly production budget for a show like *The Texaco Star Theater*, including commercials, was $15,000, but by the mid-1970s, the price of putting one 30-second commercial on the air had risen to approximately $3,000 a second. During 1976, for example, the top 554 advertisers spent over $3 billion on television ads. In 1977, ads shown during the World Series cost $75,000 for 30 seconds, and those figures continued to rise throughout the 1980s and 1990s. At present, these figures have tripled, and commercial time on popular programs can currently cost advertisers whatever the traffic will allow.

COMMISH, THE

Sept. 1991–Jan. 1995	ABC	Sat. 10–11 P.M.
Feb. 1995–Apr. 1995	ABC	Thurs. 9–10 P.M.
May 1995	ABC	Sat. 10–11 P.M.
Aug. 1995–Sept. 1995	ABC	Thurs. 9–10 P.M.

This well-written police drama had an engaging cast and was popular with viewers for four years. The hero of the series was a police commissioner named Tony Scali of Eastbridge, a suburban town just north of New York City. The Brooklyn-born Scali, played by Michael Chiklis, was nicknamed "The Commish" by police officers under his jurisdiction. The Commish was tough on criminals, but he was a sweet, lovable man to his staff and family, and he would rather be having a meal with them than tracking down a crook. Tony's loving wife, Rachel, played by Theresa Saldana, was supportive and loyal, and his young adolescent son, David, played by Kaj-Erik Eriksen, was impressionable and naive, but was in total awe of his father. The series was based on the real-life experiences of Police Commissioner Tony Schembri of Rye, New York, and was created and written by Stephen J. Cannell. Schembri was an adviser for Cannell on several other police series he had written. Other regular characters on the series were the Scalis' baby daughter, Sarah Scali, played by Dayna Comborough and her twin sister Justine; Arnie Metzger, played by David Paymer; and Det. Irv Wallerstein, played by Alex Bruhanski. Also appearing on the series from time to time were Nicholas Lea, Gina Belafonte, Geoffrey Nauffts, Melinda McGraw, John Cygan, Kimberly Scott, Pat Bermel, Jason Scott Schombing, Michael Patten, David Ward, Ray Scivano, and Linda Durlow.

COMO, PERRY (PIERINO ROLAND COMO 1912–2001)

Singer Perry Como was a barber before he embarked on a career in show business in the 1930s. Como was born in Canonsburg, Pennsylvania, and his first major singing job was with the Ted Weems band in the late 1930s. In the six years he performed with the Weems band, Como made many hit recordings, including the best-selling "Temptation" and "Blue Moon." His success led to a radio show on which he costarred with singer Jo Stafford, *The Chesterfield Supper Club* in the 1940s, and then the *Perry Como Show*, which was on the air from 1953 until 1955. Perry's smooth and easygoing singing style and his dark good looks won him a contract to appear in films at MGM, and he was featured in *Something for the Boys* (1944), *Doll Face* (1945), *If I'm Lucky* (1946), and *Words and Music* (1948). Perry, or "Mr. C" as he was affectionately called, had his own television show on the air as early as 1948. For over 16 years, Perry's show was one of TV's most popular musical/variety programs on the air and made Como a major star. During that time, Como also made numerous recordings that became number one on the Hit Parade, including "Catch a Falling Star" and "It's Impossible." Into the late 1990s, Perry Como continued to make personal appearances in sold-out concerts throughout the United States.

CONNORS, CHUCK (KEVIN JOSEPH CONNORS 1921–1992)

Before becoming an actor, Chuck Connors, who was born in Los Angeles, California, was a professional baseball player. Connors played ball with the Montreal Royals of the International League and was scouted by the Major

Leagues. In 1951, the 6 foot, 5 inch Connors played baseball with the Chicago Cubs, but decided he wanted to play basketball and signed with the Boston Celtics. In 1958, Connors's good looks won him a featured role in the film *Pat and Mike*, starring Spencer Tracy and Katharine Hepburn, and he decided to make acting his career. Chuck became well known when he was cast as Lucas McCain on the western series *The RIFLEMAN* in 1958. The series became one of television's most popular programs and made Chuck Connors a TV star. Roles in such films as *Support Your Local Gunfighter* (1971) and *Airplane II* (1982) and popular made-for-TV miniseries and films such as *POLICE STORY* (1973) and *ROOTS* (1977) kept Connors in the spotlight. Connors remained busy as an actor until shortly before his death from lung cancer at the age of 71.

CONRAD, ROBERT (KONRAD ROBERT FALKOWSKI 1935–)

Before he became a television star playing Tom Lopaka on the *HAWAIIAN EYE* series in 1958, Robert Conrad had played supporting roles on *MAVERICK* and *Colt .45* (1959). Born in Chicago, Illinois, Conrad became interested in drama while he was attending Northwestern University in Evanston, Illinois. After appearing in various regional theater productions, Conrad went to Hollywood, where he soon found employment as an actor on television. After *Hawaiian Eye* left the air, Conrad starred in films such as *Palm Springs Weekend* (1963) and *Young Dillinger* (1965) before starring on his second TV series *The WILD, WILD WEST* in 1965. Many made-for-TV films and several less-than-successful TV series followed. He starred in the popular miniseries *Centennial* in 1978, as well as on several short-lived TV series, including *The D.A.* in 1970, *BAA BAA BLACK SHEEP* (1976), *The Duke* (1979), *A Man Called Sloane* (1979), *High Mountain Rangers* (1988), *Jesse Hawkes* (1989), and *High Sierra Search and Rescue* (1995), which featured his family in regular roles. In addition, he also starred in numerous TV films in the 1990s, including *Anything to Survive* (1990), *Mario and the Mob* (1992), *Sworn to Vengeance* (1993), and *New Jersey Turnpikes* (1999).

CONRAD, WILLIAM (WILLIAM CANN 1920–)

Actor, producer, director William Conrad, who was born in Louisville, Kentucky, was one of radio's busiest actors during the latter part of radio's Golden Age in the 1940s and 1950s. Before becoming an announcer at the age of 17 at radio station KMPC in Los Angeles, where he had moved with his parents, Conrad had worked as a newspaper reporter. Eventually, he became a radio actor and was radio's Marshall Matt Dillon on *Gunsmoke* from 1952 until 1961. He was also regularly heard on such popular radio shows as *Escape, Suspense, The Whistler,* and *The Screen Guild Players.* In addition to his work on radio, Conrad also appeared in many films as a supporting player, usually playing villains, throughout the 1940s and 1950s, including *The Killers* (1946), *Body and Soul* (1947), *Sorry, Wrong Number* (1948), *Arch of Triumph* (1948), *Any Number Can Play* (1949), *Johnny Concho* (1956), and many others. Conrad provided the voice-over narrative for several TV series, including *Escape* (1950), *The Bullwinkle Show* (1961–1973), *The Dudley Do-Right Show* (1969), *The Wild, Wild World of Animals* (1973), and *The Highwayman* (1988). But it was as the star of several TV series that William Conrad became best known. In 1971, Conrad was cast as the title character on the *CANNON* series, which was very well received and remained on the air for five years. He starred in another mystery/crime series, playing a sophisticated private detective, *NERO WOLFE,* in 1981, which lasted for only one season. His next starring role was as Jason Lochinvar (called "The Fat Man") on *JAKE AND THE FATMAN,* which was on the air for five seasons. William Conrad worked steadily on radio and television for over 50 years, and in addition to acting was also a successful producer and director of episodes of *GUNSMOKE, The RIFLEMAN,* and *NAKED CITY.* Conrad also produced the films *The Ride Back* (1957), *An American Dream* (1966), *The Cool Ones* 1967), and *Assignment to Kill* (1968), to mention just a few.

CONRIED, HANS (HANS GEORG CONRIED, JR. 1917–1982)

One of show business's most popular character actors, Hans Conried was born in Baltimore, Maryland, and grew up in New York City. Conried studied acting at Columbia University and appeared in several stage productions as a member of Orson Welles's Mercury Theatre Company before becoming a radio actor. Conried was one of the busiest performers on radio throughout the 1940s and 1950s and was heard regularly on such programs as *My Friend Irma, Suspense, Lights Out,* and many others. He also appeared as a supporting player in numerous films such as *Dramatic School* (1938), *Maisie Was a Lady* (1941), *Journey into Fear* (1942), and others. Conried was a regular on such TV series as *PANTOMIME QUIZ* in 1947, the TV version of *MY FRIEND IRMA,* playing his radio role of Professor Kropotkin, and *The Tony Randall Show* in 1976. But it was as Uncle Tonoose on the popular Danny *THOMAS MAKE ROOM FOR GrandDADDY* TV series that Conried is best remembered. In addition to his regular roles on TV series, Conried guest-starred on most of television's most successful shows, including *I LOVE LUCY, The BEVERLY HILLBILLIES, ALICE,* and *LAVERNE & SHIRLEY.* Hans Conried was also one of the busiest cartoon voice actors in Hollywood, and he provided voices for Disney's *Peter Pan* (1953) and the voice of Snidely Whiplash on the popular *Dudley Do-Right* cartoon series.

CONTINENTAL, THE

| Jan. 1952–Apr. 1952 | CBS | Tues./Thurs. 11:15–11:30 P.M. |
| Oct. 1952–Jan. 1953 | ABC | Tues./Fri. 11–11:15 P.M. |

When World War II ended in 1945, television had begun to establish itself as America's new home entertainment diversion for the few people who had TV receivers in those early days and who would watch almost anything that came on their home screens. One show, *The Continental*, which was seen late at night, after 11 P.M., was a particular early TV favorite with female viewers. "The Continental" was a sophisticated gentleman with a charming European accent named Renzo Cesana, who made the ladies' hearts flutter with his suave, continental, and very romantic monologues. Cesana was said to have been an Italian aristocrat and a member of one of Rome's most prominent families, but this speculation could never be substantiated. Before CBS gave Cesana a network show, which originated from New York City, he had been performing similar monologues on a local TV station in Los Angeles. For one year, The Continental was one of the most talked about performers on early television, but the novelty of his show soon wore thin, and when his first year on the air ended, Cesana almost immediately faded into obscurity.

CONVERSE, FRANK (1938–)

Frank Converse, who was born in St. Louis, Missouri, became a TV star overnight when he appeared in *N.Y.P.D.* in 1967, playing Det. Dr. Johnny Corso. Converse had previously been seen in the *Coronet Blue* series and in the films *Hour of the Gun* and *Hurry Sundown* in 1967. He became the star of the *Movin' On* TV series in 1974, which proved to be as successful as *N.Y.P.D.*, and he subsequently appeared in a series of made-for-TV films. In 1984, Converse became a regular on the ONE LIFE TO LIVE daytime serial drama and followed that with regular roles on the TV series *Dolphin Cove* in 1989 and the daytime dramas AS THE WORLD TURNS (1992) and ALL MY CHILDREN (1997). Frank Converse has, over the years, remained a busy guest star on such popular series as *The Young Lawyers*, STARSKY AND HUTCH, QUINCY, MAGNUM, P.I., LAW & ORDER, MURDER, SHE WROTE, and *The* PRACTICE.

CONWAY, TIM (THOMAS DANIEL CONWAY 1933–)

In order to avoid being confused with film actor Tom Conway, Tim Conway used the name "Tim" when he decided to become a performer after finishing his schooling in Willoughby, Ohio, where he was born. He was 23 years old and performing in a comedy club in 1956 when he was discovered by actress Rosemarie, who thought he was a very funny young man and who arranged for him to audition for *The* STEVE ALLEN SHOW. Allen hired Conway on the spot and made him a regular cast member on his TV show. In 1962, Conway joined the cast of the situation comedy series MCHALE'S NAVY, playing the role of Ens. Charles Parker. His hilarious characterization won him a TV series of his own, *The Tim Conway Show* in 1970. Unfortunately, the show was not a hit, but comedi-

enne Carol Burnett was sufficiently impressed with Conway's comic talents to offer him a regular spot on her popular CAROL BURNETT SHOW in 1975. Conway remained with Burnett's show until 1979, when Carol decided to end the series. In 1975, Tim Conway starred in the successful film *The Apple Dumpling Gang* and then appeared in *The Shaggy D.A.* (1976) and *Gus* (1976). When Carol Burnett decided to reunite her former *Burnett Show* cast for a new series, CAROL AND COMPANY in 1977, Conway was on hand for the reunion. In 1987, Conway made the first in a series of Dorf videos, *Dorf's Golf Bible*, which was followed by other Dorf comedy videos that, like the first video, became best-sellers. In 1990, Conway starred on the TV series *Tim Conway's Funny America* and followed up with his successful *Tim and Harvey in the Great Outdoors* (1998), with fellow Burnett show alumnus Harvey KORMAN. Conway was also the voice of Griff for the Disney film *Hercules* in 1998 and has guest-starred on the DIAGNOSIS MURDER, *The* DREW CAREY *Show*, *The* ROSEANNE *Show*, and MAD ABOUT YOU series.

COOPER, JACKIE (JOHN COOPERMAN, JR. 1922–)

A former child star born in Los Angeles, California, who appeared in the films *Sunny Side Up* (1929), *Skippy* (1931), *The Champ* (1931, with Charlie Chaplin), and *Treasure Island* (1934), Jackie Cooper's parents were in show business. Jackie literally grew up in movies. By the time he was an adolescent, Cooper was appearing in such films as *Ziegfeld Girl* (1941). Cooper joined the U.S. Navy at the onset of World War II. When the war ended, Cooper resumed his acting career and starred in the film *Kilroy Was Here* (1947). By the early 1950s, Cooper, although only in his thirties, was finding it increasingly difficult to get acting jobs, and so he began to work in television. In 1955, the actor starred in a television situation comedy series, THE PEOPLE'S CHOICE, playing Socrates "Sock" Miller. The show, Cooper, and a bassett hound named Cleo became favorites with TV viewers and the show had a healthy three-year run. *People's Choice* was canceled in 1958, but one year later Cooper starred on another TV series, *Hennessey*, playing Lt. Charles "Chick" Hennessey. This series was on the air for three years. Except for playing Clark Kent's editor, Perry White, in the *Superman* films in the 1970s, Jackie Cooper has mainly concentrated on directing TV shows such as MURDER, SHE WROTE, ST. ELSEWHERE, THE ROCKFORD FILES, and others. He had previously directed such classic TV series as *The* UNITED STATES STEEL HOUR, YOUR SHOW OF SHOWS, and *The* TWILIGHT ZONE when he was a young man.

COPS

Mar. 1989–June 1989	FOX	Sat. 9–9:30 P.M.
June 1989–July 1990	FOX	Sat. 8–8:30 P.M.
Aug. 1990–Dec. 1990	FOX	Sat. 9–9:30 P.M.

| Dec. 1990–July 1991 | FOX | Sat. 9–10 P.M. |
| July 1991–present | FOX | Sat. 8–9 P.M. |

This police documentary series, which was presented on the Fox network, began each episode with the theme song, "Bad Boys," performed by Inner Circle. As cameras followed real-life police officers around their headquarters, on street patrols and raids, at stakeouts, and even in their homes at times, viewers were treated to actual happenings in the private lives and careers of police officers. When the series made its debut, it was filmed in Broward County, Florida. Eventually, it was filmed at various actual locations throughout the United States, such as Los Angeles, Minneapolis, and even Anchorage, Alaska. One episode was filmed in Moscow and St. Petersburg in Russia, and other episodes were filmed in London, Hong Kong, and Central America. The success of *Cops* led to several imitations, such as *Detective*, *FBI—The Untold Story*, *Secret Service*, *True Detectives*, and *Real Stories of the Highway Patrol*, none of which enjoyed the success or longevity of *Cops*, one of the earliest contemporary REALITY TV shows.

COSBY, BILL (WILLIAM HENRY COSBY, JR. 1937–)

Actor/comedian Bill Cosby was born in the Mount Airy section of Germantown in Philadelphia. Cosby attended Germantown High School, but dropped out of school before he graduated to join the U.S. Navy. After being discharged from the navy, Cosby, who had earned a GED diploma, attended Temple University. While at Temple, Cosby became interested in becoming an entertainer and decided to pursue a career as a comedian. He developed a stand-up comedy act and began performing in various comedy clubs around the country. In 1964, Cosby was asked to join the cast of the TV series THAT WAS THE WEEK THAT WAS. This led to his first major acting assignment in 1965, when he became one of the stars of the I SPY series. The show was about two American undercover agents who worked in various locations around the world. Cosby played Alexander Scott, and Robert Culp played Kelly Robinson. The show was a success and remained on the air for three years, making Cosby a star. In 1969, Cosby starred on his first BILL COSBY SHOW, playing Chet Kincaid. The show ran for two years. In 1971, he appeared regularly on the PBS educational series *The* ELECTRIC COMPANY. In his stand-up act, Cosby often talked about kids he knew when he was growing up in Philadelphia. These kids became the characters on a successful TV cartoon series that made its debut in 1972, *Fat Albert and the Cosby Kids.* That same year, Cosby launched his *New Bill Cosby Show,* which was an hour-long variety show. This show was on the air for only one season, and was summarily canceled. After appearing in several films, including the box office success *Mother, Jugs & Speed* (1976), Cosby launched yet another variety show, *Cos,* which also failed to attract an audience.

Returning to films, Cosby appeared in *California Suite* (1978) and *The Devil and Max Devlin* (1981)

The Cosby Show: (standing in front, left to right) Lisa Bonet, Bill Cosby, Keshia Knight Pulliam, Phylicia Rashad; (back, left to right) Sabrina Le Beauf, Tempestt Bledsoe, and Malcolm Jamal-Warner (Author's collection)

before starring on the television series *The Cosby Show* (1984). The series was successful beyond Cosby's wildest dreams and made him a superstar and one of television's most highly paid performers. As Doctor Heathcliff (Cliff) Huxatble, Cosby played a well-educated African American whose professional and family life were beyond reproach. The series became an enormous hit and stayed on the air for eight years. When YOU BET YOUR LIFE, which had starred comedian Groucho Marx in the 1950s and 1960s, was revived in 1992, Cosby was the host. The series did not remain on the air long. In 1994, Cosby, in an attempt to try something totally different, starred on *The Cosby Mysteries* series, playing Guy Hanks, a former criminologist who comes out of retirement to solve crimes. It was on the air for just one year. In 1996, Cosby returned to TV with a new series, *Cosby,* on which he played Hilton Lucas, a character similar to the Heathcliff Huxtable role that had worked so well for him in the past. Several of the *Cosby Show's* original cast members joined him on the new show. The show was a success and continues to be one of television's most popular programs. Cosby's latest project is hosting *Kids Say the Darndest Things,* on which he interviews young children, employing the same good humor he used when talking to kids in his popular Jell-O commercials.

COSELL, HOWARD (HOWARD WILLIAM COHEN 1918–1995)

Before he became one of television's most famous sports commentators, Howard Cosell, who was born in Winston-Salem, North Carolina, was a lawyer. Cosell first gained the attention of sports fans as a sports announcer on the *N.F.L. Monday Night Football* specials. His staccato delivery, opinionated and occasionally humorous comments, and often outrageous questions when he was interviewing sports stars made him very popular with viewers. By 1971, Cosell had become recognizable enough to appear in Woody Allen's film *Bananas*, playing himself. Subsequent appearances on such TV shows as *The Connection* (1973), *The World's Greatest Athlete* (1973), SATURDAY NIGHT LIVE (1975), *Fighting Back* (1980), and acting roles in Woody Allen's film *Broadway Danny Rose* (1984) and *Shelly Duvall Presents: American Tall Tales and Adventures* followed. Cosell was seen posthumously in a clip of a World Series game in the film *Summer of Sam*, which was released in 1999.

COSTELLO, LOU (LOUIS FRANCIS CRISTILLO 1906–1959)

When he finished high school, Lou Costello, who was born in Paterson, New Jersey, went to Hollywood, hoping to break into show business, and he obtained work as a carpenter at Warner Brothers Studio. He eventually began to perform stunts in films that were made at Warner Brothers and, since people were always laughing at everything he did, he decided to become a comedian. In 1931, Costello was performing in a vaudeville comedy act when his partner at the time suddenly became ill. Bud ABBOTT, who had worked as a straight man with several other comedians, jumped in to help Costello out. The two men discovered that they worked extremely well together, and they decided to become a comedy team, with Costello playing the dim-witted clown and Abbott, the slick straight man. Before long, they began to get more important theatrical bookings, and when singer Kate Smith saw their act and asked them to appear on her popular radio show, the team performed their "Who's on First" baseball routine. Reaction to the routine was so positive that Abbott and Costello became regular performers on *The KATE SMITH EVENING HOUR*, and eventually the comedians were offered their own weekly radio show and signed a contract to appear in films. The team made their film debut at Paramount Pictures in the wartime comedy *Buck Privates* in 1941. The film also starred the Andrews Sisters. The comedy duo subsequently appeared in the hit Paramount film *Abbott and Costello in the Navy* in 1942, which also costarred the Andrews Sisters, and then appeared in several films at the Universal Studios, including *Abbott and Costello Meet Frankenstein* (1948); *Abbott and Costello Meet The Killer* (*Boris Karloff*–1949), *Meet Captain Kidd* (1952), etc. In 1951–1954, Abbott and Costello hosted *The* COLGATE COMEDY HOUR television variety show, and in 1952, they starred in a weekly syndicated series of filmed ABBOTT AND COSTELLO SHOW episodes that can still be seen on occasion. By 1957, Abbott and Costello decided that it was time to go their separate ways. Costello without Abbott, and Abbott without Costello, however, did not find themselves as much in demand as they had been as a team, and financial troubles soon ensued for both of them. Lou Costello appeared in several TV specials as a solo act, and in 1959, he had a role in the film *The 30 Foot Bride of Candy Rock*, which was released the year he died of a heart attack.

COURTSHIP OF EDDIE'S FATHER, THE

Sept. 1969–Sept. 1970	ABC	Wed. 8–8:30 P.M.
Sept. 1970–Sept. 1971	ABC	Wed. 7:30–8 P.M.
Sept. 1971–Jan. 1972	ABC	Wed. 8:30–9 P.M.
Jan. 1972–June 1972	ABC	Wed. 8–8:30 P.M.

This series, which was based on a novel by Mark Toby, was about a widower raising his young son alone. The father, Tom Corbett, played by Bill BIXBY, and his son, Eddie, played by Brandon Cruz, were seen in amusing episodes that sometimes revolved around Eddie's trying to match his father up with an attractive young woman. There was a simple charm to this series that viewers responded to favorably, and the show remained on the air for two and a half years, in spite of lukewarm reviews. Also appearing on the series were Mrs. Livingstone, Corbett's dependable, but often confused Oriental housekeeper, played by Academy Award–winning actress Miyoshi Umeki; Corbett's secretary, Tina, played by Kristina Holland; and his friend, photographer Norman Tinker, played by James Komack. Soon to be famous as a film star, Jodie Foster was also seen on the series playing Eddie's school friend, Joey Kelly, during the 1970–1971 and 1971–1972 seasons. *The Courtship of Eddie's Father's* theme music was "Best Friends" by Harry Nilsson.

COX, WALLY (WALLACE MAYNARD COX 1924–1973)

Mild-mannered Wally Cox, who was born in Detroit, Michigan, was a childhood friend and roommate of Marlon Brando when both were struggling young actors trying to find work in New York City. After appearing on the TV series *School House* in 1949, and acting in several television plays on GOODYEAR TELEVISION PLAYHOUSE dramatic anthology series in 1951, Cox was cast in the leading role of science teacher Robinson J. Peepers on the TV series MR. PEEPERS, a "live" television comedy, in 1952. Even though *Mr. Peepers* was aired for only three years, for the remainder of his career, Cox was always remembered for having played Mr. Peepers, and this apparently did not help the actor's career. After *Mr. Peepers* was canceled, Cox starred on *The Adventures of Hiram Holliday*, which was not a success. Thereafter, he played supporting roles in such films as *Something's Got to Give* (1962), *The Yellow Rolls-Royce* 1965), *The Night Strangler* (1973), and others, and appeared on the TV series *The HOLLYWOOD SQUARES* (1967–1973) as a regular panelist. He was also seen on *LOST IN SPACE*, *The MONKEES*, *HERE'S LUCY*, *IT TAKES A THIEF*, *The ODD COUPLE*, and *NIGHT GALLERY*. Wally Cox died at the age of 49 of tuberculosis.

CRANE, BOB (ROBERT EDWARD CRANE 1928–1978)

Before deciding to become an actor, Bob Crane, who was born in Waterbury, Connecticut, was a radio disc jockey. He was, in fact, the first disc jockey in the United States to earn a salary in excess of $100,000. When he was 33 years old, Crane quit radio to pursue an acting career. His first major acting assignments were playing Peter White on the *Return to Peyton Place* television series and a featured role in the film *Man-Trap* in 1961. From 1963 until 1965, Crane played Dr. Dave Kelsey on the popular *DONNA REED SHOW*. This led to his being cast as the leading character on the *HOGAN'S HEROES* situation comedy series in 1965. Loosely based on the hit play and film *Stalag 17*, *Hogan's Heroes* took place in a Nazi prisoner-of-war camp during World War II. Crane played Col. Robert Hogan, an American officer held prisoner by the Germans. The series proved to be very popular and remained on the air for six years, making Crane a TV star. After *Hogan's Heroes* was canceled in 1971, Crane found it increasingly difficult to find work as an actor. He had appeared in a well-received made-for-TV version of the popular play and film *Arsenic and Old Lace* in 1969, during *Hogan's Heroes'* run, but once the series was off the air, few major roles were offered to the actor. He did appear in the made-for-TV film *The Delphi Bureau* in 1972 and in the feature film *Superdad* in 1974, and occasionally guest-starred on such TV shows as *QUINCY*, *The LOVE BOAT*, and *The HARDY BOYS/NANCY DREW MYSTERIES*. Crane's series, *The Bob Crane Show*, made its television debut in 1975, but it failed to attract an audience and was canceled after only three months. Crane subsequently toured in dinner theater productions, until his untimely death in 1978, which was ruled a homicide. Crane's killer was never apprehended.

CRENNA, RICHARD (RICHARD ANTHONY CRENNA 1927–)

Few actors have worked as long or as steadily as Richard Crenna. Crenna was born in Los Angeles, where his mother managed a small hotel. When Richard finished high school, he enrolled at the University of Southern California, where he majored in theater arts. In 1946, when he was 19 years old, Crenna auditioned for and won the role of Oogie Pringle on *A Date With Judy* on radio. He next played the role of high school student Walter Denton on the *Our Miss Brooks* radio show in 1948. The series made a successful transition from radio to television in 1952, with Crenna re-creating his radio role of Walter Denton. *OUR MISS BROOKS* remained on TV until 1956. Soon after *Our Miss Brooks* ended its TV run, Crenna appeared as a country bumpkin named Luke McCoy on *The REAL McCOYS*. The series was also a success, and remained on the air from 1957 until

1963. His next TV series was *SLATTERY'S PEOPLE* in 1964, which did not prove to be as successful as either of his successes, and lasted for only one season. Crenna, however, continued to appear in numerous feature films, including *John Goldfarb, Please Come Home* (1965), *The Sand Pebbles* (1966), *Star!* (1968), *Marooned* (1969), *Jonathan Livingstone Seagull* (1973), *Body Heat* (1981), *First Blood* (1982), and *Rambo: First Blood Part II* (1985), as well as on the TV miniseries *Centennial* (1978) and the unsuccessful TV series *All's Fair* (1976) and *Look at Us* (1981). In the 1990s, Crenna continued to star in numerous TV and feature films, most notably as Det. Frank Janek in a series of made-for-TV mystery films, and *In The Name of Love: A Texas Tragedy* (1995), *20,000 Leagues Under the Sea* (1997), *To Serve and Protect* (1999), and others.

CRONKITE, WALTER (1916–)

For 19 years, from 1962 until 1981, Walter Cronkite was the anchorman of the *CBS Evening News*, and during that time he became one of the most respected and admired people in America. Born in St. Joseph, Missouri, but raised in Houston, Texas, Cronkite decided to become a journalist after reading about a foreign correspondent in a magazine. He attended the University of Texas, but left college to work at the *Houston Post* in 1935. He later went into broadcasting and worked at several midwestern

Walter Cronkite (Author's collection)

radio stations as an announcer and newscaster. During World War II, Cronkite worked as a correspondent for United Press, covering the European front. When World War II ended, Cronkite covered the Nuremberg war crime trials for United Press. In 1950, he joined the CBS radio and television network as a newscaster, and one of his major assignments was covering the national political conventions for CBS—a job he continued to perform for the next 29 years. From 1953 until 1957, Cronkite also hosted the popular CBS series YOU ARE THERE. This series, which had first been heard on radio, became a TV series. It used on-the-spot news coverage techniques, using newsmen, microphones, and then cameras to report such dramatized historical events as the signing of the Declaration of Independence, the landing of the Pilgrims on Plymouth Rock, Julius Caesar's assassination, and the eruption of Mt. Vesuvius at Pompeii in A.D. 79. Upon his retirement in 1981, Cronkite was awarded the Presidential Medal of Freedom, the highest honor a United States citizen can receive, for his work in television journalism. Some people believe that it was Cronkite's professional, level-headed compassion, and his totally human reporting of the assassination of President John F. Kennedy that helped the nation get through that terrible ordeal. Public opinion polls identified Cronkite as "the man Americans most trusted." During the United States's military involvement in the Vietnamese Civil War in the 1960s and 1970s, Cronkite said, when it became apparent that the United States was fighting a losing battle, "It is increasingly clear that the only rational way out will be to negotiate, not as victors, but as honorable people who lived up to the pledge to defend democracy." Cronkite made this statement after the Tet Offensive, and many people believed that his comments marked the turning point for United States's involvement in that unpopular military encounter and was one of the developments that apparently contributed to the United States's withdrawal from Vietnam in the early 1970s. Cronkite continued to appear on various news specials occasionally after his 1981 retirement, including such TV specials as *The Universe* in 1980, *Vietnam: A Television History,* in 1985, and, for PBS, *We're Back: A Dinosaur's Story* (1993), and *Fail Safe* (2000).

CROSBY, BING (HARRY LILLIS CROSBY 1904–1977)

Although he was one of the America's most successful and well-known pop singers, Bing Crosby seldom appeared on television. In the 1950s and 1960s, he made rare appearances on *The PHILCO TELEVISION PLAYHOUSE, The Ford Star Jubilee,* and *The HOLLYWOOD PALACE,* and it wasn't until 1964 that he tried a weekly series of his own, *The BING CROSBY SHOW.* Crosby admitted that he was "uncomfortable" appearing on television, and said that he felt "more at home" in the casual, less-pressured atmosphere of a recording, radio, or motion picture studio. He abandoned his regular TV series after just one year.

Bing Crosby was one of seven children born to Harry and Kate Crosby in Tacoma, Washington. Crosby studied law at Gonzaga University in Spokane, Washington, but was more interested in playing the banjo and the drums and singing with a college band. In 1925, Bing left Gonzaga and went to Hollywood, to pursue a career in show business. Before long, he was singing with the Paul Whiteman Orchestra and made his first hit record, "I Surrender, Dear." The record attracted the attention of CBS president Bill Paley, who signed Crosby to a contract to star on a regular program on CBS. In 1932, CBS broadcast his live performances in New York City for 20 consecutive weeks, and by the time the series of programs ended, Bing Crosby was a major star. His romantic "crooning" singing style caught the attention of listeners all across America. Crosby also appeared in several films in the early 1930s, including *Two Plus Fours* (1930), *The King of Jazz* (1930, performing with the Paul Whiteman Orchestra), *Check and Double Check* (1930, which starred radio's Amos and Andy), and *I Surrender, Dear* (1931), but when he became a popular radio personality, he starred in the major motion pictures *College Humor* (1933), *The Big Broadcast of 1936, Waikiki Wedding* (1937), *Sing You Sinners* (1938), and many other films. In 1940, Crosby teamed up with comedian Bob HOPE and actress Dorothy Lamour to star in *Road to Singapore* at Paramount Pictures, where all three were under contract. The film was so popular that Crosby, Hope, and Lamour appeared in many more "Road" films, including *Road to Zanzibar* (1941), *Road to Morocco* (1942), *Road to Victory* (1944), *Road to Hollywood* (1946), *Road to Utopia* (1946), *Road to Rio* (1947), *Road to Bali* (1952), and *Road to Hong Kong* (1962), which were all box office successes. In addition to his Road films, Crosby also appeared in such memorable films as *Holiday Inn* (1942, in which he introduced the classic Irving Berlin song "White Christmas"), *Going My Way* (1944, winning a Best Actor Academy Award), *White Christmas* (1954), *High Society* (1956), and countless others. Crosby was one of the on-screen narrators in *That's Entertainment!* (1974), which presented musical numbers from several MGM films of the past. Bing Crosby died while playing golf, his favorite pastime, after completing a tour of England that included a sold-out engagement at the London Palladium.

CULLEN, BILL (WILLIAM LAURENCE CULLEN 1920–1990)

Bill Cullen, who was born in Pittsburgh, Pennsylvania, was one of TV's most successful game show hosts. Throughout the 1950s, 1960s, 1970s, and into the 1980s, Cullen starred on an impressive number of TV game and panel shows. Even though he was frequently seen on television, few viewers were aware that Cullen had been crippled by polio when a child, and he walked with a pronounced limp. He usually hosted his shows sitting on a stool, or he sat behind a table during his panel show appearances. They did recognize him, however, for his trademarks: a close-cropped crewcut and his dark-framed eyeglasses. Before entering television, Cullen had worked as a radio announcer on such daytime serials as *This Is Nora Drake* and on the game shows *Winner Take All* and *Quick as a*

Flash. In 1952, Cullen was a panelist on the television game show *That Reminds Me*. He then hosted *Give and Take* (1952), *Who's There?* (1952), *Where Was I?* (1953), *Bank on the Stars* (1953), NAME THAT TUNE (1954–1955), *Place the Face* (1954–1955), *Down You Go* (1956), *The* PRICE IS RIGHT (1956–1965), TO TELL THE TRUTH (1969–1978), *Three on a Match* (1971), *The $10,000* PYRAMID (1974–1979), and many other quiz shows, and was a regular panelist on I'VE GOT A SECRET (1952–1967). The last game show Cullen hosted was called *Hot Potato*, which was seen in 1984. A heavy smoker most of his life, Cullen died of lung cancer at the age of 70.

CULP, ROBERT (1930–)

Robert Culp claims he wanted to be an actor from the time he was a little boy growing up in Oakland, California, where he was born. Culp became actively involved in drama department plays when he was in college, and after graduating he actively pursued a career as an actor. It wasn't until he was 35, however, that Culp became famous, when he played a starring role on the I SPY TV series. As a young actor, Culp had played major supporting roles on such television series as BONANZA, The RIFLEMAN, YOU ARE THERE, and The OUTER LIMITS. Once he appeared on *I Spy* as secret agent Kelly Robinson, he was kept constantly busy as a leading man in such subsequent series as The GREATEST AMERICAN HERO (1981), *I Spy Returns* (1994), and *Gargoyles* (1994), and in the feature films *Bob & Carol & Ted & Alice* (1969), *Big Bad Mama II* (1987), *The Pelican Brief* (1993), and many others. After *I Spy* ended its run, Culp continued to be a busy guest star on such TV movies and series as PERRY MASON, COLUMBO, The NAME OF THE GAME, The GOLDEN GIRLS, The NANNY, EVERYBODY LOVES RAYMOND, COSBY, and CHICAGO HOPE, and more recently has been featured in *Farewell My Love* (1999) and *Newsbreak, Hunger* and *Running Mates*, which were both released in 2000.

CUMMINGS, ROBERT (CHARLES CLARENCE ROBERT ORVILLE CUMMINGS 1908–1990)

One of the first well-known Hollywood film stars to appear on a television series, Robert Cummings made his initial appearance on the short-lived situation comedy series *My Hero* in 1952. His second TV series *Love That Bob* (also called *The* BOB CUMMINGS SHOW), however, was a success and remained on the air for four years, making him more famous than he had been as a movie star. Cummings, who was born in Joplin, Missouri, was educated at Carnegie Tech and the American Academy of Dramatic Arts and appeared on Broadway before acting in films. Believing stage producers would be more interested in hiring a sophisticated young actor from England than an American boy from Joplin, Missouri, Cummings passed himself off as an English actor named Blade Stanhope Conway. His ploy worked. When he was signed to a contract to appear in films, Cummings assumed that yet another fictional iden-

tity—that of a rich young actor from Texas named Bruce Hutchens—might help his career. In his early films Cummings was billed as Bruce Hutchens, but as his star began to rise, he began to use the name Robert Cummings. He eventually became one of Hollywood's most successful light comedians in the late 1930s and '40s. His film appearances included roles in *The Virginia Judge* (1935), *Hollywood Boulevard* (1936), *Wells Fargo* (1937), *One Night in the Tropics* (1940), *It Started with Eve* (1941), *Kings Row* (1942), *Princess O'Rourke* (1943), *Flesh and Fantasy* (1943), *You Came Along* (1943), *The Petty Girl* (1950), and *Dial M for Murder* (1954), to name just a few. By the early 1950s, Cummings's career hit a standstill, and good film roles became harder for him to get, even though he had retained his youthful appearance. His *Bob Cummings Show* made him a major star once again, and he continued to work on television, making only occasional film appearances, until the early 1970s, when he gradually began to fade from the spotlight. Cummings's last TV series was *My Living Doll*, which was seen in 1964. Cummings appeared in only 22 episodes of that series. His last television appearances were in two made-for-TV films, *The Great American Beauty Contest* and *Partners in Crime*, which were both released in 1973.

CYBILL

Jan. 1995–Sept. 1995	CBS	Mon. 9:30–10 P.M.
Sept. 1995–Apr. 1996	CBS	Sun. 8–8:30 P.M.
Apr. 1996–Feb. 1997	CBS	Mon. 9:30–10 P.M.
Mar. 1997–Dec. 1997	CBS	Mon. 9–9:30 P.M.
Mar. 1998–Apr. 1998	CBS	Wed. 8:30–9 P.M.
May 1998–June 1998	CBS	Mon. 9–9:30 P.M.
June 1998–July 1998	CBS	Mon. 9:30–10 P.M.

On the *Cybill* situation comedy series, actress Cybill SHEPHERD played Cybill Sheridan, a wisecracking, good-natured actress who lived in Los Angeles and whose personal and professional life was in a constant state of crisis. Since she was no longer young, the parts she was being offered were smaller and for much older women than she had been accustomed to. A soft touch, in spite of her flippant remarks, Cybill's first husband, Jeff Robbins, played by Tom Wopat, slept on the couch in her living room; her daughter Rachel, played by Dedee Pfeiffer, announced that Cybill was going to be a grandmother, which made her feel older, and her daughter Zoey, played by Alicia Witt, a moody 16-year-old, was also living with her. Cybill's best friend, Maryann Thorpe, played by Christine Baranski, was a divorced woman who had been to the Betty Ford Clinic to combat a drinking problem. Her husband, Dr. Richard Thorpe, played by Ray Baker, had left her well-off, and her major goal in life was to make her ex-husband's life as miserable as she could. Other characters who appeared regularly were Maryann's son, Jason, played by Danny Masterson; Ira Woodbine, played by Alan Rosenberg; Walter, played by Tim Macaulan; and Sean, played by Jay Paulson.

D

DAGMAR (VIRGINIA RUTH EGNOR AKA JENNY LEWIS C. 1921–2001)
When television was in its infancy in the early 1950s, a tall, buxom blonde named Dagmar (stage name of Jenny Lewis) became one of TV's most-talked-about performers. Dagmar was seen on the popular late evening program BROADWAY OPEN HOUSE, a show that starred comedian Jerry Lester. Playing the wide-eyed, sexy-looking, not-so-dumb blonde stooge to Lester's comic, Dagmar soon began to steal the show, and it was later rumored that Lester left the show when he learned that Dagmar was receiving more fan mail than he was. Born in Huntington, Virginia, Dagmar had gone to New York to become an actress, but had little luck and worked as a showgirl, until she became a member of the *Broadway Open House* cast. When the show left the air in 1951, Dagmar was, for a short time, a panelist on MASQUERADE PARTY and then suddenly disappeared from the show business spotlight. When Dagmar died in 2001, her death went unnoticed by the public who had adored her fifty years before.

DAKTARI

Jan. 1966–Sept. 1968	CBS	Tues. 7:30–8:30 P.M.
Sept. 1968–June 1969	CBS	Wed. 7:30–8:30 P.M.

Set in Africa, *Daktari* was actually filmed in "Africa, USA," which is a wild-animal refuge and park located near Los Angeles. The series centered on Dr. Marsh Tracy, played by Marshall Thompson, a veterinarian running an animal study center in Africa. Marsh was assisted by his daughter, Paula, played by Cheryl Miller; a young American game park assistant, Jack Dane, played by Yale Summers; and a native African, Mike, played by Hari Rhodes. Also seen regularly on the series were Hedley, an English game warden, played by Hedley Mattingly, Bart Johnson, a former ranger

and hunter who had become a guide for safaris, played by Ross Hagen; and a seven-year-old orphan named Jenny Jones, played by Erin Moran, who was later more prominently featured on HAPPY DAYS. Two nonhuman performers who appeared on the series that were popular with viewers were a lion named Clarence and a chimpanzee named Judy, who were the Tracy family's pets at the animal center.

DALLAS

Apr. 1978	CBS	Sat. 10–11 P.M.
Sept. 1978–Oct. 1978	CBS	Sun. 10–11 P.M.
Oct. 1978–Jan. 1979	CBS	Sun. 10–11 P.M.
Jan. 1979–Nov. 1981	CBS	Fri. 10–11 P.M.
Dec. 1981–May 1985	CBS	Fri. 9–10 P.M.
Sept. 1985–May 1986	CBS	Fri. 9–10 P.M.
Sept. 1986–May 1988	CBS	Fri. 9–10 P.M.
Oct. 1988–Mar. 1990	CBS	Fri. 9–10 P.M.
Mar. 1990–May 1990	CBS	Fri. 10–11 P.M.
Nov. 1990–Dec. 1990	CBS	Fri. 10–11 P.M.
Jan. 1991–May 1991	CBS	Fri. 9–10 P.M.

Dallas, produced by David Jacobs for Lorimar Productions, was a prime-time soap opera drama series. In the early 1960s, the evening series PEYTON PLACE had made its TV debut. It was the first evening serial drama presented on TV and became an enormously popular show and one of the longest-running programs on television at the time. *Dallas,* however, surpassed the popularity of *Peyton Place* and became one of the most successful and longest-running programs of any type on television. Thirteen years after the first episode of *Dallas* was aired, the program ended its run, much to the disappointment of millions of fans who would have kept watching the series for another 13 years. *Dallas* centered on two generations of the oil-rich Ewing family, who owned a sprawling ranch called South Fork, in Braddock County, Texas, near Dallas. Also seen on the series were two generations of the Barnes family, bitter rivals of the Ewings. The basic plot of the made-for-TV film that launched this series involved a Romeo and Juliet–like romance between the youngest Ewing son and one of the Barnes family's daughter. The original cast of *Dallas* included Jim Davis as Jock Ewing, the head of the Ewing family, a tough, self-made man; Barbara Bel Geddes as his wife, Eleanor or "Ellie," a practical, solid matriarch; Larry HAGMAN as their eldest son, John Ross, or "J. R.," an immoral, selfish man; Linda Gray as J. R.'s troubled wife, Sue Ellen; Patrick Duffy as the Ewings' youngest son, Bobby, certainly more decent than his brother, J. R.; Victoria Principal as Bobby's less troubled wife, Pamela (a member of the Barnes family); Ken Kercheval as Pamela's brother, lawyer Cliff Barnes; David Wayne as their father, William "Digger" Barnes; Charlene Tilton as Jock's granddaughter, Lucy; and Steve Kanaly as the Ewing ranch foreman, Ray Krebbs. As the years went on and *Dallas* remained one of America's favorite prime-time TV shows, the cast and story lines changed, but the series continued to remain popular until its very last episode. No one who followed the series would ever forget the "Who shot J. R.?" publicity campaign that followed the final episode of the

The Ewing family of *Dallas:* (clockwise from left) Patrick Duffy, Victoria Principal, Barbara Bel Geddes, Larry Hagman, Linda Gray, Jim Davis, and Charlene Tilton (Author's collection)

1983–84 season, when viewers had to wait for the series to return in the fall to find out if J. R. was alive or dead. Millions of viewers also tuned in to the first show of the 1984–85 season to find out who had fired the shot and discovered it was J. R.'s wife's half sister, Katherine Wentworth, played by Morgan Brittany, who was the culprit, and that J. R. was not killed in the incident but was very much alive. When Barbara Bel Geddes decided she was too ill to play Ellie in 1984, she was replaced by Donna Reed. Reed sued the producers of the series when Bel Geddes decided to return to the series and Reed's services were terminated. The success of the cliff-hanging shooting of J. R. started a series of cliff-hanging final-season episodes on the show, none of which equaled the impact, or the publicity, generated by the original J. R. shooting. The 1980–81 season ended with a body discovered floating in a swimming pool. Viewers once again had to wait for the next season's opening episode to find out the identity of the body in the pool. *Dallas* was the inspiration for a several similar evening serial drama series, including KNOTS LANDING, which was actually a spin-off of *Dallas*. When actor Patrick Duffy decided he wanted to leave the series, his character was apparently killed off at the end of the 1984–85 season.

DALY, JOHN (1914–1991)

Few people realize that the John Daly who wrote more than 60 books on such varied subjects as constitutional law and broadcasting techniques was the same John Daly who hosted the popular, long-running TV panel show WHAT'S MY LINE?. Daly was born in Johannesburg, South Africa, but immigrated to the United States with his parents when he was 10 years old. Entering broadcasting shortly after graduating from college, Daly was the original radio announcer for President Franklin D. Roosevelt's Fireside Charts radio broadcasts in the 1930s. He was also one of the announcers/reporters on CBS's YOU ARE THERE radio and TV programs. In 1948, Daly moderated the *America's Town Meeting* TV series, and in 1949, he appeared on the *Front Page* series. Daly was a regular panelist on *Celebrity Time* in 1950 and also became the host of the perennially popular *What's My Line?* that same year. *What's My Line?*, remained on the air for 17 years, its last telecast in 1967. For many people, the 10:30 Sunday evening time slot was when they watched *What's My Line?*, and the weekend just didn't seem over until the show ended. In addition to hosting *What's My Line?*, John Daly also hosted *We Take Your Word* (1950), moderated *It's News to Me* (1951), *Open Hearing* (1954), and narrated *The Voice of Firestone* music program (1958–59). Occasionally, Daly guest-starred on such TV series as *The Adventures of Superman*, FATHER KNOWS BEST, and GREEN ACRES. Daly virtually retired from television soon after *What's My Line?* left the air in 1967 and concentrated on being an author.

DANIEL BOONE

Sept. 1964–Aug. 1970   NBC   Thurs. 7:30–8:30 P.M.

Fess Parker as Daniel Boone (Author's collection)

Fess PARKER, who became famous playing Davy Crockett on TV in the 1950s, starred in the western/adventure series *Daniel Boone* 10 years after his immensely popular Crockett adventures were initially seen on the *Disneyland* anthology series. Loosely based on the life and times of early American frontiersman Daniel Boone, who settled in Kentucky in the 1770s, the series equaled the success of Parker's *Davy Crockett* adventures and enjoyed an impressive six-year run. In addition to Parker, also seen on the series were Ed Ames, who played Boone's friend, Mongo, a college-educated Cherokee; Pat Blair played Boone's wife, Rebecca; Albert Salmi played Boone's companion Yadkin; singer Jimmy Dean played Josh Clements, another companion; former football star Roosevelt Grier played Gabe Cooper, a runaway slave who became Boone's good fiend; Darby Hinton played Boone's son, Israel; Veronica Cartwright played Boone's daughter, Jemima; and Dallas McKennon played a character named Cincinnatus. In 1977, CBS made an attempt to revive the Boone character on *Young Daniel Boone*, but the series was canceled after only one month when it failed to attract an audience.

DANSON, TED (EDWARD BRIDGE DANSON III 1947–)

Born in San Diego, California, Ted Danson attended the Kent School for Boys in Connecticut and Stanford University before deciding he wanted to study drama at the celebrated Carnegie-Mellon University, and become an actor. After performing at the Beverly Hills Playhouse, where he studied acting with Milton Katselas, Danson's first major acting assignment was on the *Somerset* daytime drama series. Good supporting roles in such feature films as *The Onion Field* (1979) and *Body Heat* (1981) and TV appearances in B. J. AND THE BEAR, LAVERNE & SHIRLEY, MAGNUM P.I., TAXI, and other shows, led to his being cast in the leading role of Sam "Mayday" Malone on CHEERS. *Cheers* became one of television's most successful series, and was on the air for 11 years, making Danson a star. Danson's next TV series, *Ink* (1996), was less successful, but a second series, *Becker*, which made its TV debut in 1998, was more favorably received by critics and the public and, as of 2002, is still on the air. In addition to his work on TV, Danson also starred in such successful feature films as *Creepshow* (1982), *Three Men and a Baby* (1987), *Made in America* (1993), *Saving Private Ryan* (1998), and *Mumford* (1999), and he played Gulliver in the made-for-TV movie *Gulliver's Travels* (1996).

DANZA, TONY (ANTONIO IADANZA 1951–)

Like the character he played on TAXI, Tony Banta, Tony Danza was a boxer before he became an actor. Born in Brooklyn, New York, Danza attended the University of Dubuque, where he was active in sports. *Taxi* was Danza's first TV series, and his performance was so well received by the public that he became one of TV's most popular performers. After *Taxi's* run ended, Danza starred on another successful series, WHO'S THE BOSS?, playing a character named Tony Micelli. While he was on *Taxi* and *Who's the Boss?*, he also appeared in several films, including the made-for-TV film *Murder Can Hurt You* (1980) and the feature films *Going Ape!* (1981), *Cannonball Run II* (1984), *Freedom Fighter* (1988), *She's Out of Control* (1989), and *Mob Justice* (1992). While starring on *Who's the Boss?*, Danza also provided the voice of Mickey Campbell for the TV cartoon series *Baby Talk*. In 1994, Danza also provided the voice of Vinnie the alligator for the *The Mighty Jungle*. Two subsequent series, *Hudson Street* (1995) and *The Tony Danza Show* (1997), met with less success than his previous series, but he did appear in several well-received films, including *Dear God* (as himself, 1996), *The Girl Gets Moe* (1997), and the made-for-TV films *North Shore Fish* (1996), *12 Angry Men* (1997), *Noah* (1998), and others. In 2000, Danza joined the regular cast on the series *Family Law*.

DARK SHADOWS

June 1966– Apr. 1971	NBC	Mon.–Fri. 4–5 P.M.
Jan. 1991	NBC	Sun. & Mon. 9–11 P.M., Fri. 10–11 P.M.
Jan. 1991	NBC	Fri. 9–10 P.M.
Mar. 1991	NBC	Fri. 10–11 P.M.

Daytime TV's most unconventional serial, *Dark Shadows,* enjoyed a five-year run and attracted legions of loyal fans while it was on the air. The most popular character on this supernatural series was Barnabas Collins, a 200-year-old vampire played by Jonathan Frid. The show shifted back and forth between modern times (the 1960s–70s) and the past (the 1800s) and was set in the Collins's spooky family mansion, "Collins House," in Collinsport, Maine. All sorts of unusual characters such as ghouls, ghosts, and werewolves, and weird locales in haunted houses and graveyards, with violent thunderstorms and lots of fog for atmosphere, set the tone. Besides Barnabas Collins, other major characters included the governess of young David Collins, Victoria Winters, played by Alexandra Moltke; David, played by Joseph Gordon-Levitt at ege eight and David Hennessey as a young man; David's father, Roger Collins, played by Louis Edmonds; Elizabeth Collins, Roger's sister, played by veteran film star Joan Bennett; Dr. Julia Hoffman, a physician sent to cure Barnabas but who ended up falling in love with him, played by Grayson Hall; Quentin Collins, played by David Selby; Daphne Harridge, played by Kate JACKSON; Angelique, played by Lara Parker; and Reverend Task, played by Humphrey Bogart lookalike Jerry Lacy. The series was directed by Dan Curtis, who also produced the show with Robert Costello. In 1990, NBC announced plans to present an updated prime-time version of *Dark Shadows*. Ben Cross played the vampire Barnabas, and the prime-time cast included Joanna Going, film star Jean Simmons, Jim Fyfe, Roy Thinnes, Joseph Gordon-Levitt (who was in the original cast as a child actor), Barbara Steele, Ely Pouget, Barbara Blackburn, Lysette Anthony, and Michael Cavanaugh. The series lasted less than three months.

DATELINE NBC

Mar. 1992–present   NBC   Various days and times

After several attempts to produce a show that could compete with CBS's popular *60 MINUTES* news/magazine series, NBC finally came up with a show that attracted a respectable number of viewers with its *Dateline NBC*. Jane Pauley and Stone Phillips were the series coanchors. Over the years, Tom BROKAW, Katie Couric, Bryant Gumbel, and Maria Shriver have been contributing anchors on the show. The usual subjects of TV news magazine shows, such as government, business, show business, crime and other urban problems, sports, etc., are included at various times In November 1992, *Dateline NBC* generated quite a bit of controversy when it presented a feature that exposed the design faults of GM trucks, and it was revealed that *Dateline NBC* producers had placed explosives under the bodies of GM trucks that they used in a demonstration so that the trucks would explode on cue when they were crash-tested. GM executives exposed the fakery, and anchorman Stone Phillips presented an on-the-air apology to GM for the *Dateline NBC* report. In the wake of this incident, NBC News president Michael Gartner resigned.

In the early years of the 21st century, *Dateline NBC* has covered such contemporary news as the destruction of New York's World Trade Center by Islamic terrorists on September 11, 2001, as well as the impact this tragic event had on the economy and the personal lives of the survivors and victims' families; the ongoing Middle East crisis; the presidency of George W. Bush and his handling of the so-called war on terrorism; the activities of Islamic terrorist leader Osama Bin Laden; and other noteworthy items.

DAVE'S WORLD

Sept. 1993–Apr. 1994	CBS	Mon. 8:30–9 P.M.
Apr. 1994–June 1994	CBS	Mon. 8–8:30 P.M.
July 1994–Sept. 1995	CBS	Mon. 8:30–9 P.M.
Aug. 1995–Nov. 1995	CBS	Wed. 8:30–9 P.M.
Nov. 1995–Apr. 1996	CBS	Wed. 8–8:30 P.M.
Apr. 1996–June 1996	CBS	Mon. 8:30–9 P.M.
July 1996	CBS	Wed. 8–8:30 P.M.
Aug. 1996	CBS	Wed. 8:30–9 P.M.
Sept. 1996–Mar. 1997	CBS	Fri. 8–8:30 P.M.
Apr. 1997–May 1997	CBS	Wed. 8:30–9 P.M.
June 1997–July 1997	CBS	Fri. 8–8:30 P.M.
July 1997	CBS	Fri. 8–9 P.M.

Set in Miami, *Dave's World* situation comedy series was loosely based on the life and career of newspaper columnist Dave Barry, whose popular column "Barry's World," seen in syndication in hundreds of newspapers throughout the country, offered Barry's amusing comments about the ordinary events of everyday life. Harry ANDERSON, who had been one of the stars of the popular *NIGHT COURT* series, starred as Dave Barry; DeLane Matthews was his wife, Beth; Zane Carney was their eldest son, Tommy; Andrew Ducote was their youngest son, Willie; Shadoe Stevens was Dave's editor and friend, Kenny Beckett; Meshach Taylor was Dave's divorced pal, a plastic surgeon named Sheldon Baylor; J. C. Wendel was Dave's assistant, Mia; Tammy Lauren was Beth's sister, Julie; and Patrick Warburton was Mia's boyfriend, Eric. Dave was a grown-up Peter Pan–like man who never really grew up. He worked at home and took care of his house and kids while his wife was at work as a teacher; this provided much of the show's humor.

DAVID FROST SHOW, THE

July 1969–July 1972	Syndicated show	Various times and stations

Englishman David FROST, who had attracted the attention of American TV viewers on the popular *THIS WAS THE WEEK THAT WAS* series, was the host of this 90-minute talk show on which he interviewed some of the most celebrated people of the time. His interview with Elizabeth Taylor and Richard Burton, who were married at the time, was one of the most viewed shows of the 1960s. Frost used a probing, but good-natured style, asking questions other talk show hosts dared not ask. Frost's main appeal was that he always appeared to be genuinely interested in his guests and did not hesitate to use a bit of humor during his interviews. During the three years his American talk show was on the air, Frost commuted by air daily between London and New York in order to appear on his *London Weekly Television* program in England as well as on his New York–based *David Frost Show*. His hectic commuting schedule was much publicized. Music for Frost's show was provided by the Billy Taylor Orchestra. Syndicated by Westinghouse, all 750 shows were videotaped in New York. After his show ended its American run, Frost was seldom seen on TV in the United States, until he televised a much publicized, multipart interview with former President Richard M. Nixon in 1977.

DAVID LETTERMAN SHOW, THE

(see *Late Night with David Letterman*)

DAVID SUSSKIND SHOW, THE

1958–1987	Syndicated show	Various times and stations

Television's longest-running talk show both in length of time it was on the air and length of time each show was aired was *The David Susskind Show*. A syndicated show hosted by a former talent agent and Broadway and television producer, David SUSSKIND, the show was originally a New York City–based local program called *Open End*. It was seen in the 11 P.M. time slot. The show remained on the air until the subject or his fatigued guests were exhausted. Sometimes the show lasted well over two hours. Critics dubbed Susskind's program "Open Mouth," because it never seemed to come to an end. Susskind's guests were usually literate, well-spoken people and, more often than not, controversial. When Soviet leader Nikita Khrushchev visited the United States in 1960, Susskind managed to book him as a special guest. Khrushchev unashamedly used the opportunity to promote his nation's communistic ideals and governmental policies, and made Susskind visibly squirm with his relentless monologues. Race relations, the draft, the controversial war in Vietnam, sex change operations, I.Q. testing, organized crime, et al., were fair game on Susskind's show. In the early 1960s, the show was confined to a definite two hours, although the name remained *Open End*. When *The David Susskind Show* went into national syndication, it kept its basic format intact. During Susskind's last years on TV, his show was mainly seen on PBS stations, although many commercial stations continued to air it in selected cities.

DAVIS, ANN B. (ANN BRADFORD DAVIS 1926–   )

Ann B. Davis and her twin sister, Harriet, were born in Schenectady, New York. Although her twin sister pre-ferred anonymity, Ann B. Davis decided early in life that she wanted to be in show business. Her first important role was in the 1955 film *A Man Called Peter*. That same year, Ann was cast as Robert CUMMINGS's photography business assistant Charmaine "Schultzy" Schultz, on *Love That Bob* (later *The BOB CUMMINGS SHOW*). Davis played a not particularly attractive but very outspoken and funny woman who had a crush on her boss. The public loved the Schultzy character, and the actress who played her, and for the rest of her career, Davis was forever associated with the role of "Schultzy" and even billed herself as Ann "Schultzy" Davis at times. When *The Bob Cummings Show* left the air, Davis appeared in several films, such as *All Hands on Deck* (1961), and *Lover Come Back* (1961), and then became a regular on *The John Forsythe Show,* playing a receptionist, Miss Wilson. In 1969, Davis was signed to play housekeeper Alice Nelson on a situation comedy series, *The BRADY BUNCH*. The show became an even bigger hit than *The Bob Cummings Show,* and over the years, even after the original series was canceled, the Bradys and Alice kept resurfacing on TV. First, the Bradys and Alice reappeared on a weekly variety show, *The Brady Bunch Hour* (1977), and then on TV specials, *The Brady Girls Get Married* (1981) and *A Very Brady Christmas* (1988), and finally, in *The Bradys* TV series (1990), which was not a success. In 1995, *The Brady Bunch Movie,* a feature film, was released with a different cast from that seen on TV. Ann B. Davis did have a cameo role in the film as a trucker named Schultzy. When she retired from acting, Ann went to live with fellow parishioners of the Episcopalian religious community in San Antonio, Texas, where she is involved in prayer, Bible study, and charity work.

DAVIS, GAIL (BETTY JEANNE GRAYSON 1925–1997)

Television's sharp-shooting cowgirl, Annie Oakley, was played by a real-life cowgirl-turned-actress, Gail Davis. Davis, who was born in Little Rock, Arkansas, learned to ride a horse, shoot a gun, and rope steers at an early age, and toured the country in several rodeos before she was discovered by a movie scout and began to appear in films. In the late 1940s, Davis was seen in a succession of western TV shows and films, including *The LONE RANGER, The CISCO KID, Death Valley Days* (1952) on TV and the second-feature films *Sons of New Mexico* (1949), *The Far Frontier* (1948), *Law of the Golden West* (1949), *Indian Territory* (1950), *Yukon Manhunt* (1951), *Silver Canyon* (1951), *Winning of the West* (1953), and *Goldtown Ghost Riders* (1953), among others. In 1954, Davis was cast in the role of the legendary sharpshooter Annie Oakley on a television western adventure series that was produced with younger viewers in mind, *ANNIE OAKLEY*. Although only 81 episodes of the syndicated series were filmed, the show has been constantly seen in reruns over the past 40 years, and the names Gail Davis and Annie Oakley have became forever linked in the public's mind. After *Annie Oakley*'s initial run ended, Davis found it difficult to get work in films or on TV because she had become so closely associated with the Oakley role. She returned to performing in rodeos and Wild West shows and became one of the United States's most popular rodeo attractions. Davis made a rare appearance in the film *Coffy* in 1973 and was one of the voices for the *Race for Your Life, Charlie Brown* TV special in 1977.

DAVIS, JOAN (MADONNA JOSEPHINE DAVIS 1907–1961)

Joan Davis rivaled Lucille BALL as America's favorite television comedienne in the 1950s, and her situation comedy series, *I MARRIED JOAN,* was one of TV's earliest popular successes. Joan Davis was born in St. Paul, Minnesota, and entered show business when she was a young girl, performing in clubs and on the vaudeville circuit. Her comic, gangling appearance, mobile face, and squeaky voice made her an audience favorite, and in 1935, when she was 30 years old, she made her film debut playing a small but memorable part in *Way Up Thar.* More important comedy roles in such films as *Thin Ice* (1937), *Life Begins in College* (1937), *On the Avenue* (1937), *You Can't Have Everything* (1937), *My Lucky Star* (1938), *Sun Valley Serenade* (1941), *Show Business* (1944), *George White's Scandals* (1945), *If You Knew Susie* (1948), and *Harem Girl* (1952) made Davis one of Hollywood's most recognized funny ladies. In 1952, Davis took her very popular radio show, *I Married Joan,* to television. *I Married Joan* (also called *The Joan Davis Show*) was as successful on television as it had been on radio, and made Joan a TV, as well as a film, star. In 1955, Joan's health began to fail, and *I Married Joan,* in spite of its success, was taken off the air. Davis died of a heart attack at the age of 54 in 1961.

DAWBER, PAM (1951–)

Pam Dawber was a relatively inexperienced, unknown young actress when she was cast in a major role on a new TV situation comedy series called *MORK & MINDY* in 1978. Dawber, who was born in Detroit, Michigan, became an overnight star playing Mindy McConnell, a young lady who became involved with an eccentric alien from outer space named Mork, played by Robin WILLIAMS. The show was immensely popular and remained on the air for four years. When *Mork & Mindy* was canceled, Dawber starred in several made-for-TV films, including *Remembrance of Love* (1982), *The Little Mermaid* on *Faerie Tale Theatre* (1984), *Wild Horses* (1985), and *This Wife for Hire* (1985), and others, before starring in another TV situation comedy series called *My Sister Sam* in 1986. When *My Sister Sam* was canceled after two seasons, Dawber continued to appear in made-for-TV films such as *Your New Baby* (1989), *Face of Fear* (1990–1991), *Stay Tuned* (1992), *The Man With Three Wives* (1993), *A Child's Cry for Help* (1994), *A Stranger to Love* (1996), *I'll Remember April* (1999) and *Don't Look Behind You* (1999), among others.

DAWSON, RICHARD (COLIN EMM 1932–)

Richard Dawson, who was born in Great Britain and made his acting debut there, first came to the attention of the American public playing Cpl. Peter Newkirk on the hit situation comedy series *HOGAN'S HEROES* in 1965. The success of that show, which was set in a German prisoner of war camp during World War II, and his natural talent for telling jokes, led to appearances on *Can You Top This* as a joke teller in 1970. When *Can You Top This* was canceled, Dawson became a regular on *ROWAN AND MARTIN'S LAUGH-IN* from 1971 until 1973. While he was appearing on *Laugh-in,* Dawson also had a regular role on *The New Dick Van Dyke Show* (1973–74). But it was as television game show panelist and host that Richard Dawson gained his greatest success and finally became a TV star. He was a regular popular panelist on the *MATCH GAME '73* through '79 game/panel show series and became that program's favorite match guesser for most of the show's contestants, because he could usually match their answers and win them big money prizes. Dawson also hosted *MASQUERADE PARTY* in 1974 and followed that by hosting a revised *I'VE GOT A SECRET.* In 1976, Richard Dawson became the host of what would be his most celebrated game show, *FAMILY FEUD.* The show ran for a nine years on network, and then was seen for several years as a syndicated series. Among the series Dawson appeared on as an actor were *The DICK VAN DYKE SHOW, Love American Style* (1971, 1972), *The ODD COUPLE, MCMILLAN AND WIFE,* and *MAMA'S FAMILY.*

DAY, DORIS (DORIS KAPPELHOFF 1924–)

Actress/singer/film superstar Doris Day was born in Cincinnati, Ohio. Her parents were divorced when she was a child, and Doris was raised by her single mother. When she was a teenager, Doris was injured in an automobile accident and was hospitalized for a year, ending her dream of becoming a ballet dancer. In high school, Doris discovered that she had a talent for singing, and she auditioned for the Bob Crosby Band when it was playing an engagement in Cincinnati. Crosby signed her on the spot, and she sang with his band for a while before joining Les Brown and His Band of Renown in the early 1940s. Brown's hit recording of "Sentimental Journey," with Day singing the vocal, became a top-selling recording. Day's blond hair and fresh, freckle-faced, girl-next-door good looks brought her an offer to appear in films at Warner Brothers in 1947. Her first major role at Warners was in *Romance on the High Seas* (1948), and the film was so successful, Doris Day became a film star overnight. Day followed that success with well-received performances in such diverse films as *Calamity Jane* (1953), *Young at Heart* (1954), and Alfred Hitchcock's *The Man Who Knew Too Much* (1956), in which she sang another hit song, "Que Sera Sera." Starring roles in other romantic comedy films such as *Pillow Talk* (1959), *Lover Come Back* (1962), *That Touch of Mink* (1962), and *Please Don't Eat the Daisies* (1960) made her one of

Hollywood's top stars at the box office. In 1968, Day decided to appear in a TV series, which because of her celebrity status, was called *The DORIS DAY SHOW*. The series ran for five years and was consistently among the top shows in TV ratings. In 1973, Day decided to retire from films and network TV, and except for an easygoing talk show on cable TV called *Doris Day's Best Friends*, she remained relatively inactive as a performer. The show promoted her favorite cause, animal rights, and featured some of her famous show business friends as guests. Doris Day remains active in the animal rights movement and currently runs the Doris Day Animal Foundation in Carmel, California.

DAYS OF OUR LIVES
Nov. 1965–present NBC Mon.–Fri. Various times

"Like sands through the hourglass, so are the days of our lives..." For over 35 years, daytime serial fans have heard that familiar opening that heralds the beginning of another weekday episode of *Days of Our Lives*. Set in a town called Salem, the series originally centered on the Horton family, which consisted of Dr. Tom Reed and his wife, Alice, played by Macdonald Carey and Frances Reed; and their five children: a doctor, Tommy, played by John Lupton; Addie, played by Pat Huston and then Patricia Barry; Mickey, a lawyer, played by John Clarke; Marie, played by Maree Cheatham; and Bill, who was also a doctor, played by Paul Carr and then Ed Mallory and Christopher Stone. Other regular characters were psychiatrist Dr. Laura Spencer, who married Mickey Horton, played over the years by Floy Dean, Susan Flannery, Susan Oliver, Rosemary Forsythe, and Jamie Lyn Bauer; David Martin, played by Steven Mines and Clive Clerk; Susan Martin, played by Denise Alexander and Bennye Gatteys; Kitty Horton, who was married to Tommy, played by Regina Gleason; Tommy and Kitty's daughter, Sandy, played by Heather North, Martha Smith, and Pamela Roylance; Marie Horton's boyfriend, Tony Merritt, played by Dick Colla, Don Briscoe, and Ron Husmann; and many others. In 1970 Bill Hayes joined the cast as a former nightclub singer, Doug Williams, who fell in love with Addie Olsen's daughter, Julie, played by Susan Seaforth. One of the series most-viewed episodes was the wedding of Doug and Julie on October 1, 1976. The TV wedding was made even more exciting to viewers because they knew that Bill Hayes and Susan Seaforth had actually been married two years earlier in October 1974. Doug and Julie's on-again, off-again marriage, over the following several years, gained *Days of Our Lives* ever-increasing numbers of viewers. Over the years, there have been hundreds of additions to and changes in the cast, and only a very few of the original characters from the original show remain. *Days of Our Lives* was created by Ted Corday, Irna Phillips, and Allan Chase. In 1975, the show was the second daytime soap opera series to expand from a half-hour to a full hour each weekday, the first being CBS's *AS THE WORLD TURNS*.

In the 1990s and early 2000s, popular actors on the series included David Dowd (2002–) as the third "Austin Reed" seen on the show, Alison Sweeny (1992–) as Samantha "Sami" Brady, Lauren Koslow (1996–) as the second Kate Roberts, and Arianne Zuker (1998–) as Nicole Walker.

DEAN MARTIN SHOW, THE (DEAN MARTIN PRESENTS, THE DEAN MARTIN SUMMER SHOW, DEAN MARTIN'S COMEDY WORLD)
DEAN MARTIN PRESENTS (summer replacement show):

June 1968–Sept. 1968	NBC	Thurs. 10–11 P.M.
July 1969–Sept. 1969	NBC	Thurs. 10–11 P.M.
July 1970–Sept. 1970	NBC	Thurs. 10–11 P.M.
July 1972–Sept. 1972	NBC	Thurs. 10–11 P.M.
July 1973–Sept. 1973	NBC	Thurs. 10–11 P.M.

DEAN MARTIN COMEDY WORLD (summer replacement show):

June 1974–Aug. 1974	NBC	Thurs. 10–11 P.M.

DEAN MARTIN SUMMER SHOW (summer replacement show):

June 1966–Sept. 1966	NBC	Thurs. 10–11 P.M.
June 1967–Sept. 1967	NBC	Thurs. 10–11 P.M.
July 1971–Aug. 1971	NBC	Thurs. 10–11 P.M.

DEAN MARTIN SHOW, THE:

Sept. 1965–July 1973	NBC	Thurs. 10–11 P.M.
Sept. 1973–May 1974	NBC	Fri. 10–11 P.M.

Although singer Dean Martin had a weekly TV variety show that was on the air for over seven years and was seen during the regular season, he was also the star of several summer replacement series, using the same formula he had used on his regular TV show. The former partner of comedian Jerry Lewis, Martin became an even bigger star as a solo performer than he had been with Lewis, after he decided to leave the Martin and Lewis act. His weekly music/variety show became one of TV's most popular programs and was in the same time slot for many years. Viewers began to think of 10 o'clock on Thursday nights as Dean Martin time. Martin's casual, slow-and-easy, slightly inebriated manner of speaking and crooning a song, and his good-natured banter with celebrated guests, made *The Dean Martin Show* one of TV's highest-rated programs. Among the notable regulars and guests who appeared on Martin's shows over the years were Frank SINATRA (who was Martin's good friend and a frequent guest), Joey Heatherton, Nipsey Russell, Jackie COOPER, Paul Lynde, Lainie Kazan, Bobby Darin, Rip Taylor, Marion Mercer, Foster Brooks, Dom DeLuise, Marty Feldman, Rodney Dangerfield, Dan Rowan and Dick Martin, Vic Damone, Carol Lawrence, and the bands of Les Brown, Jack Parnell, and Eddie Kazam, to name just a few. A bevy of beautiful female dancers was always featured on the show, called the Goldiggers. Four of these women later became known as the Ding-a-Ling Sisters on the show. In 1973, Martin introduced his popular "roasts" of various celebrities on his show. On these roasts, a guest celebrity had a panel of fellow celebrities talk about his life and career using good-natured insults, put-downs and humorous remarks. This feature became so popular with viewers that when Martin's regular show left the air, he hosted occasional "Roast Specials," which could be seen periodically on NBC.

DEAR JOHN

Oct. 1988	NBC	Thurs. 9–9:30 P.M.
Oct. 1988–Jan. 1990	NBC	Thurs. 9:30–10 P.M.
Jan. 1990–Mar. 1990	NBC	Wed. 9:30–10 P.M.
May 1990–Oct. 1990	NBC	Wed. 9:30–10 P.M.
Oct. 1990–Dec. 1990	NBC	Wed. 9–9:30 P.M.
Dec. 1990–Mar. 1991	NBC	Sat. 10:30–11 P.M.
Mar. 1991–June 1991	NBC	Wed. 9:30–10 P.M.
July 1991	NBC	Sat. 10–10:30 P.M.
Aug. 1991–Sept. 1991	NBC	Sat. 9:30–10 P.M.
Sept. 1991–Oct. 1991	NBC	Fri. 9–9:30 P.M.
Oct. 1991–Jan. 1992	NBC	Fri. 9:30–10 P.M.
Apr. 1992	NBC	Wed. 9:30–10 P.M.
July 1992	NBC	Wed. 9:30–10 P.M.

Dear John: (sitting) Judd Hirsch; (standing, left to right) Jane Carr, Harry Groener, Jere Burns, and Isabella Hoffman (Author's collection)

Five years after his popular situation comedy series, *TAXI*, left the air, Judd HIRSCH returned to TV as the star of another series, *Dear John*. Hirsch played middle-aged John Lacey, whose wife had written him a "Dear John" letter telling him she no longer wished to be married to him. Devastated and confused by his newfound bachelor status, Lacey, a high school teacher in New Rochelle, New York, signed up for a weekly single people's support group called the "One-Two-One Club," which was held at the Rego Park Community Center. The group's leader was Louise Mercer, an English woman played by Jane Carr. Other members of the support group were Kirk Morris, a ladies' man who couldn't seem to get it into his head that he has been dumped by his partner, played by Jere Burns; the compassionate but out-of-touch Kate, played by Isabella Hoffman; Mrs. Margie Philbert, an elderly, somewhat dim, widow played by Billie Bird; Tom, an elderly man who never uttered a word, played by Tom Willett; Ralph, a shy toll collector, played by Harry Groener; and Mary Beth, a sexy, not-too-bright southern lady, played by Susan Walters. Occasional drop-ins at the One-Two-One group meetings were Ben, the community center maintenance man, played by William O'Leary, and Denise, who was the leader of the weight control group in the room next door at the Community Center. The series, based on an English series of the same name, stayed on the air for four years, but never reached the top-20 list of the Nielsen ratings. This was likely because NBC constantly shifted the show from one time slot to another, even though there were many viewers who found the series highly entertaining and were fiercely loyal to the program, following it to whatever time slot it was in.

DECEMBER BRIDE

Oct. 1954–June 1958	CBS	Mon. 9:30–10 P.M.
Oct. 1958–Sept. 1959	CBS	Thurs. 8–8:30 P.M.
July 1960–Sept. 1960	CBS	Fri. 9:30–10 P.M.
Apr. 1961	CBS	Thurs. 7:30–8 P.M.

An early television situation comedy series success that enjoyed a six-and-a-half-year run, with a few months off in between, *December Bride*, made its TV debut in 1954. The series was about an ideal mother and mother-in-law who could actually live with, and be loved by, her son-in-law. Veteran film character actress Spring BYINGTON played the dearly loved Lily Ruskin, and Frances Rafferty and Dean Miller played her daughter and son-in-law, Ruth and Matt Henshaw. Verna Felton, whose voice was certainly familiar to people who listened to the radio in the 1930s, '40s and '50s, played Lily's friend, Hilda Crocker. Hilda became the show's most popular comic character. Lily was an attractive widow, and her popularity with the older set made her a likely candidate for a second marriage; her first husband had died, leaving her a widow. Ruth and Matt were always looking for a suitable husband for Lily, but Hilda, who was less attractive than Lily, was always trying to trap a man. Harry Morgan, who later became famous as Col.

Sherman Potter on *M*A*S*H*, played Pete Potter, the Henshaw's amusing next-door neighbor who was always complaining about his bossy wife, Gladys, who never actually appeared on the show. Pete and Gladys became the central characters on one of television's first spin-off series, appropriately called *PETE AND GLADYS*. On this series, Gladys was indeed seen, and was played by Cara Williams.

DEFENDERS, THE

Sept. 1961–Sept. 1963	CBS	Sat. 8:30–9:30 P.M.
Sept. 1963–Nov. 1963	CBS	Sat. 9–10 P.M.
Nov. 1963–Sept. 1964	CBS	Sat. 8:30–9:30 P.M.
Sept. 1964–Sept. 1965	CBS	Thurs. 10–11 P.M.

The first of the realistic, law-oriented television series, *The Defenders* attracted a great deal of attention from viewers and critics when it made its debut in 1961. The series centered on the professional and private lives of two lawyers, a father and son, whose law firm, Preston and Preston, was a beehive of legal activity. The father, Lawrence Preston, played by E. G. Marshall, was a seasoned and sober attorney with 20 years experience. His son, Kenneth Preston, played by Robert Reed, was a recent law school graduate who was more inclined to take a humanistic, rather than a legalistic, approach to the law. The firm's secretary, Helen Donaldson, played by Polly Rowles, and Kenneth's girlfriend, Joan Miller, represented women's points of view. In the early 1960s, most television drama series avoided any hint of controversy, but *The Defenders* took on such unconventional topics as mercy killing, abortion, United States travel restrictions, and the blacklisting of people suspected of having Communist affiliations. The series was based on an original story by Reginald ROSE and was first seen as a two-part telecast on the popular *STUDIO ONE* dramatic anthology series. Ralph Bellamy and William SHATNER played the father and son lawyers on that TV drama, and Steve MCQUEEN, who later went on to TV and film stardom, played a young defendant accused of murder on one memorable episode of the series.

DeGENERES, ELLEN (1958–)

In 1994, when her situation comedy series *Ellen* made its debut, comedienne Ellen DeGeneres had already been hailed as "one of the funniest people in America," in 1982, and "the Best Female Club Standup" at the Comedy Awards in 1991. Her series was well received by viewers and critics alike, and it looked as if Ellen DeGeneres was on her way to becoming a superstar. *Ellen* was not DeGeneres's first appearance on a TV series. She had previously been seen on the *Open House* series, playing Margo Van Meter, from 1989 until 1990 and on *Laurie Hill,* as Nancy MacIntire, in 1992. She made her big-screen debut in *Coneheads* in 1993. DeGeneres, who was born and raised in New Orleans, Louisiana, had been a paralegal before deciding to become a comedienne. She performed her stand-up act in various comedy clubs before appearing on television and in films, but became nationally known only when *Ellen* made its debut. The show was a big success, but during its run, DeGeneres decided it was time to tell the world that she was a lesbian. "I'm a lesbian, an Aquarian, and a vegetarian," she reportedly said in April 1997. The reaction to her announcement ranged from her being named "Entertainer of the Year" by *Entertainment Weekly* in 1997, to having an ABC affiliate in Birmingham, Alabama, refuse to air the landmark episode on which she announced that the character she was playing on the series was also a lesbian. That episode earned ABC one of the largest audience ratings of the TV season. The controversy proved to be too much for ABC to handle, however, since *Ellen's* number of viewers began to diminish after the initial lesbian announcement was aired, and the show was canceled at the end of the 1997–98 season. After *Ellen,* the number of roles DeGeneres was offered were few, but she was seen in the previously filmed *Mr. Wrong,* and she played a small role in the film *Reaching Normal* (1999). She had larger roles in *Goodbye Lover* (1999) and *The Love Letter* (1999). She also appeared on TV in *If These Walls Could Talk 2* (2000), which she also produced with her partner at that time, Anne Heche. She also starred on several Home Box Office specials. Over the years, Ellen DeGeneres has also made guest starring appearances on *ROSEANNE, The LARRY SANDERS SHOW,* and *MAD ABOUT YOU.*

DeLUISE, DOM (1933–)

Even though comedian/actor Dom DeLuise is considered one of the funniest men in America by the public and by his fellow performers, he has never been a major success as the star of a TV series. Dom headlined two less-than-successful TV series, *LOTSA LUCK* (1973) and *The Dom DeLuise Show* (1987), and was the host of the *CANDID CAMERA* series for a short time in 1991. He was also a regular on the series *Roman Holidays* in 1972 and on a revival of *BURKE'S LAW* in 1994. The Brooklyn-born funny man did, however, make well-received regular appearances on such TV shows as *The Entertainers* (1964), *The Glen Campbell Goodtime Hour* (1969), and *The DEAN MARTIN SHOW* (1972–73). DeLuise enjoyed greater success as a supporting player in such memorable films as *The Glass Bottom Boat* (1966), *Norwood* (1970), *Blazing Saddles* (1974), *The Adventures of Sherlock Holmes' Smarter Brother* (1975), *Silent Movie* (1976), *The End* (1978), *The Cheap Detective* (1978), *Smokey and the Bandit II* (1980), *The Cannonball Run* (1981), *The Best Little Whorehouse in Texas* (1982), and *Robin Hood: Men in Tights* (1993), and starred in the film *Fatso* in 1980. In 1999, DeLuise was a regular on the *Walking after Midnight* series. The many other TV series Dom DeLuise has made guest-starring appearances on include *The MUNSTERS, The MUPPET SHOW, DIAGNOSIS MURDER, MARRIED . . . WITH CHILDREN, MURPHY BROWN,* and with his three sons, Peter, Michael, and David, *3RD ROCK FROM THE SUN.*

DENNIS THE MENACE

Oct. 1959–Sept. 1963   CBS   Sun. 7:30–8 P.M.

A popular cartoon character, Dennis the Menace, created and drawn by artist Hank Ketcham, became the hero of a television situation comedy series in 1959. Dennis was an impish little boy with blond hair and a cowlick, who always wore oversized overalls. He wasn't deliberately bad; he just seemed to make things worse when he was trying to be helpful. The role of Dennis on the *Dennis the Menace* series was played by Jay North, who, in the four years the show was on the air, grew from a child to a preadolescent. Dennis's long-suffering but loving parents, Henry and Alice Mitchell, were played by Herbert Anderson and Gloria Henry. The Mitchells' next-door neighbor, whom Dennis usually managed to upset, was the ever-exasperated Mr. George Wilson, played by Joseph Kearns. Wilson's more child-tolerant wife, Martha, was played by Sylvia Field. In 1962, a year before *Dennis the Menace* ended its TV run, Joe Kearns died and was succeeded by veteran radio and TV character actor Gale Gordon as John Wilson, George Wilson's brother. Sara Seeger played John Wilson's wife, Eloise. Much of the show's comedy revolved around the encounters between Dennis and Mr. Wilson. Usually adding to both of their problems was the Wilson's dog, Fremont. Also seen regularly on the show were Gil Smith as Dennis's pal, Joey MacDonald; Irene Tedrow as Mrs. Lucy Elkins; Billy Booth as Tommy Anderson; Jeannie Russell as Margaret Wade; Willard Waterman as Mr. Quigley; Mary Wickes as Mrs. Esther Cathcart; Kathleen Mulqueen as Grandma Mitchell; George Cisar as Sgt. Theodore Mooney; and Robert John Pittman as Seymour. Reruns of *Dennis the Menace* were immediately aired when the show ended its network run and were seen on Saturday mornings on NBC, even though the show was originally seen on the CBS network from October 1963 until September 1965. This was most unusual for a newly departed series. In all, 145 episodes of *Dennis the Menace* had been filmed during its four-year run. The series was produced by Harry Ackerman.

DENVER, BOB (ROBERT DENVER 1935–   )

Bob Denver, who is well known for playing two memorable roles on two different television situation comedy series, Maynard G. Krebs on The MANY LOVES OF DOBIE GILLIS and Willy Gilligan on GILLIGAN'S ISLAND, wasn't sure he wanted to be an actor when he finished his schooling, and for a time worked as a mailman and a teacher. Born in New Rochelle, New York, Denver attended college at Loyola-Marymount University in Los Angeles, where he appeared in plays with Dwayne HICKMAN. It was, in fact, Hickman, who had been signed to play the title role of Dobie Gillis on the new TV series, who arranged for his college friend Denver to take a screen test for the role of Maynard G. Krebs. The show was a hit and remained on the air for four years. After *Dobie Gillis* was canceled, Denver appeared in the films *Take Her, She's*

Mine (1963) and *For Those Who Think Young* (1964), and then won the title role on a new television series, *Gilligan's Island*, which no one believed was going to be a success. Everyone was surprised when the series became one of TV's most popular situation comedies and enjoyed a healthy three-year run. After *Gilligan's Island's* departure from TV, Denver appeared on three less-than-successful series, *The Good Guys* (1968), *Dusty's Trail* (1973), and *Far Out Space Nuts* (1975), before providing the voice for the Gilligan character on the cartoon series *The New Adventures of Gilligan* (1974–77). He followed this by playing Gilligan again on the TV specials *Rescue from Gilligan's Island* (1978), *Castaways on Gilligan's Island* (1979), and *The Harlem Globetrotters on Gilligan's Island* (1981), and once again provided Gilligan's voice for another cartoon series, *Gilligan's Planet* (1982). In 1988, Denver revived the role of his first TV character, Maynard G. Krebs in a TV special, *Bring Me the Head of Dobie Gillis*, which starred his old college pal, Dwayne Hickman. Over the years, Bob Denver has made guest-starring appearances on such series as *The FARMER'S DAUGHTER*, *The ANDY GRIFFITH SHOW*, *Love, American Style* (1969–74), *The LOVE BOAT*, *FANTASY ISLAND*, *ROSEANNE*, and *The SIMPSONS*, among others.

DEPUTY DAWG

1959–1971	Syndicated show	Various times and stations
Sept. 1971–Sept. 1972	NBC	Various times

The misadventures of an inept but lovable dog who enforced the law in the swampland of the Deep South became one of television's most endurable and favorite animated cartoon series, *Deputy Dawg*. Deputy Dawg's biggest problem as a law enforcer was keeping his friends Musky Muskrat, Vincent Van Gofer, and Ali Gator away from the hen house. Dayton Allen provided the voice for Deputy Dawg. The series was produced by affiliates of animator Paul Terry and his associates, who had been producing film cartoons since 1915 and who was a pioneer of filmed animation techniques. The *Deputy Dawg* cartoons were usually seen late Saturday afternoons, but between 1971 and 1972 it was a Saturday morning show on NBC.

DESIGNING WOMEN

Sept. 1986–Nov. 1986	CBS	Mon. 9:30–10 P.M.
Dec. 1986–Jan. 1987	CBS	Tues. 9:30–10 P.M.
Feb. 1987	CBS	Sun. 9–9:30 P.M.
Mar. 1987–Feb. 1988	CBS	Mon. 9:30–10 P.M.
Feb. 1988–June 1988	CBS	Mon. 8:30–9 P.M.
June 1988–Sept. 1989	CBS	Mon. 9:30–10 P.M.
Sept. 1989–Oct. 1989	CBS	Mon. 10–10:30 P.M.
Nov. 1989–June 1992	CBS	Mon. 9:30–10 P.M.
Aug. 1992–Sept. 1992	CBS	Mon. 9:30–10 P.M.
Sept. 1992–May 1993	CBS	Fri. 9–9:30 P.M.
May 1993	CBS	Mon. 9–10 P.M.

A favorite program of both television critics and the public, *Designing Women* was an engaging situation comedy series about four outspoken women who ran an interior design company. The women's company, Sugarbakers, operated out of a large suburban house in Atlanta, Georgia, that served as a combination office and showroom for their interior designs. The house was the residence of the formerly wealthy Sugarbaker family. Starring was Dixie Carter as the widowed Julia Sugarbaker, a literate and practical woman; Delta Burke as Julia's younger sister, Suzanne Sugarbaker, a self-centered, thrice-divorced, former beauty queen; Annie Potts as a divorced mother of two, Mary Jo Shively; and Jean Smart as the unmarried (when the series began), somewhat naive and down-to-earth Charlene Frazier. Also starring was Meshach Taylor as the women's African-American man Friday, ex-convict Anthony Bouvier. Occasionally seen on the series were Hal Holbrook (Dixie Carter's real-life husband) as Julia's suitor, Reese Watson; Richard Gilliland as Mary Jo's boyfriend, J. D. Shakelford; Alice Ghostley as Bernice Clifton; Olivia Brown as Vanessa, Anthony's girlfriend; and Priscilla Weems and Brian Lando as Mary Jo's kids, Claudia and Clinton. Gerald McRaney, who later married Delta Burke, played Suzanne Sugarbaker's former husband, Dash Goff, and Doug Barr played Bill Stillfield, whom Charlene met and married during the series' run. In 1992, when it ended its network run, the series, whose executive producers were the husband and wife team of Harry Thomason and Linda Bloodworth, was sold as a syndicated show to a record-breaking (for the time) 200 different television stations. *Designing Women's* theme song, heard at the beginning, and sometimes the end, of each show, was "Georgia on My Mind," performed by Doc Severinsen's orchestra, and during the 1991–92 season, by Ray Charles, who sang the vocal.

DeVITO, DANNY (DANNY MICHAEL DeVITO 1944–)

Multitalented actor, director, producer Danny DeVito, who was born in Neptune, New Jersey, studied acting at the American Academy of Dramatic Arts in New York City in the mid-1960s. Before he decided he wanted to be an actor, DeVito had worked as a hairdresser for his sister, who owned a beauty salon. While he was attending the American Academy, Danny's roommate was Michael Douglas. Danny's first role was a small one in the film *Dreams of Glass* in 1969. However, it was a role in the off-Broadway play *One Flew over the Cuckoo's Nest,* which he repeated in an Academy Award–winning film version of the play, that attracted the attention of Hollywood casting directors. Eventually, DeVito landed the role of Louie DePalma on the hit series TAXI in 1978. The series ran from 1978 until 1983. The diminutive DeVito's portrayal of the despotic taxi cab dispatcher DePalma made the actor a TV star, and soon DeVito was playing important roles in such major feature films as *Romancing the Stone* (1984) and *The Jewel of the Nile* (1985), both starring his American Academy of Dramatic Arts pal

Michael Douglas, and *Ruthless People* (1986), which costarred Bette Midler. He subsequently played major roles in *Tin Men* (1987), *Twins* (1988), *Other People's Money* (1991), *Batman Returns* (1992), *The Rainmaker* (1997), and *L. A. Confidential* (1997). In 1987, DeVito directed his first feature film, *Throw Momma From the Train,* and subsequently he directed *The War of the Roses* (1989), *Hoffa* (1992), and with his wife, Rhea Perlman, one of the stars of CHEERS, *Matilda* (1996). In 1994, DeVito produced the successful film *Pulp Fiction,* and then produced two other hit films, *Get Shorty* (1995) and *Out of Sight* (1998). DeVito also produced and costarred in the film *Man on the Moon,* which was about the short and unconventional life of one of his *Taxi* costars, Andy KAUFMAN. Among the numerous TV series Danny DeVito has made guest appearances on are STARSKY AND HUTCH, *Amazing Stories,* The SIMPSONS (as the voice of Herbert Powell), and *The* LARRY SANDERS SHOW.

DeWITT, JOYCE (1949–)

Best known for playing Janet Wood Dawson on the popular THREE'S COMPANY situation comedy series, actress Joyce DeWitt attended Bell State University in Muncie, Indiana, where she first became interested in acting. Born in Wheeling, West Virginia, DeWitt had appeared on the TV series *The Manhunter* (1974), BARETTA (1975), and *The Tony Randall Show* (1976) before she became one of the costars of THREE'S COMPANY in 1977. Disillusioned with show business by the time *Three's Company* left the air in 1984, due to numerous unpleasant encounters with fellow cast members and the show's producers, Joyce decided to travel around the world to study various religions. After many years out of the spotlight, DeWitt slowly began to return to acting, and in 1995, she appeared in the made-for-TV film *Spring Fling!,* and made guest-starring appearances on such TV series as CYBILL and *Living Single* (1998). In 2000, she played the hero's mom in the film *18.*

DHARMA & GREG

Sept. 1997–July 1998	ABC	Wed. 8:30–9 P.M.
July 1998–July 1999	ABC	Wed. 8–8:30 P.M.
July 1999–present	ABC	Tues. 9–9:30 P.M.

This situation comedy about a young married couple who came from two entirely different backgrounds certainly proved the adage "opposites attract." The "Dharma" of the series' title is a free-spirited young woman who is a yoga instructor and dog trainer. Dharma, like her unconventional former hippie parents, believes in the idea that people should live their lives on impulse. The "Greg" of the show's title, on the other hand, comes from a conservative background, and is a somewhat stiff, but lovable lawyer. The couple met on a subway platform, and for *Dharma & Greg* it was love at first sight. They were married the night they had their first date, much to the delight of Dharma's bohemian mom (who likes to paint in the nude) and dad, who was an antiwar radical in the 1960s. Greg's wealthy, country club parents, who are considerably less liberal than Dharma's parents, were less than pleased with Greg's choice of wife. Engaging actors Jenna Elfman and Thomas Gibson play Dharma Finkelstein and Greg Montgomery on the series. The couple's parents, Abby O'Neill Finkelstein and Larry Finkelstein, and Edward and Kitty Montgomery, are played by Mimi Kennedy and Alan Rachins, and Mitchell Ryan and Susan Sullivan respectively. Also seen on the series as regulars are Joel Murray as Greg's pal Pete, and Shae D'lyn as Dharma's oddball girlfriend, Jane.

DIAGNOSIS MURDER

Oct. 1993–Sept. 1995	CBS	Fri. 8–9 P.M.
Dec. 1995–Aug. 1996	CBS	Fri. 9–10 P.M.
Sept. 1996–July 1997	CBS	Thurs. 8–9 P.M.
July 1997–Jan. 1999	CBS	Thurs. 9–10 P.M.
Jan. 1999–Mar. 1999	CBS	Thurs. 8–9 P.M.
Apr. 1999	CBS	Thurs. 9–10 P.M.
July 1999–present	CBS	Thurs. 8–9 P.M.

Twenty-seven years after his popular situation comedy series The DICK VAN DYKE SHOW ended its run, Dick VAN DYKE returned to television as the star of an entirely different type of show—a murder/adventure program, *Diagnosis Murder*. On his new hit series, Van Dyke plays Dr. Mark Sloan, the chief of internal medicine at the fictional Community General Hospital in Los Angeles. Sloan had a talent for stumbling upon murders, and with the help of his assistants Dr. Jack Stewart, played by Scott BAIO, and when Baio left the series, Dr. Jesse Travis, played by Charles Schlatter, and Dr. Amanda Bentley Livingstone, played by Victoria Rowell, Sloan managed to solve weekly mysteries. That Sloan's son, Steve, played by Barry Van Dyke, was a police detective certainly came in handy when the hospital sleuths were solving cases. Also seen on the series are Michael Tucci as Norman Briggs and Delores Hall as Nurse Delores Mitchell. Dr. Mark Sloan was originally introduced to viewers on JAKE AND THE FATMAN. He was also the central character on three made-for-TV films before *Diagnosis Murder* became a TV series.

DICK CAVETT SHOW, THE

May 1969–Sept. 1969	ABC	Mon., Tues., Fri. 10–11 P.M.
Dec. 1969–Dec. 1972	ABC	Mon.–Fri. 11:30 P.M.–1 A.M.

In the late 1960s to early 1970s, talk show host Dick Cavett had one of the most popular late night TV shows on the air with his DICK CAVETT SHOW. Although Cavett conducted intelligent, lively interviews with guest celebrities from the worlds of show business, sports, and politics, and was the first TV star to have shows on daytime,

prime-time, and late evening hours, his show failed to attract the number of viewers it needed to keep it on the air, and to the disappointment of serious-minded viewers who wanted more in-depth interviews on their late night talk shows, *The Dick Cavett Show* was canceled after two and a half years. Appearing regularly on Cavett's show were musician Bobby Rosengarten and announcer Fred Foy. A daytime version of Cavett's talk show was presented in a 90-minute five-days-a-week version and also featured interviews and occasional musical numbers. Cavett was also the star of the *Dick Cavett Variety Show*, a one-hour show on CBS from August 1975 until September 1975. Even though such a celebrated star as Groucho Marx appeared on the series, it also failed to attract a sizable enough audience to keep it on the air.

DICK CLARK'S AMERICAN BANDSTAND

(see *American Bandstand*)

DICK VAN DYKE SHOW, THE

Oct. 1961–Dec. 1961	CBS	Tues. 8–8:30 P.M.
Jan. 1962–Sept. 1964	CBS	Wed. 9:30–10 P.M.
Sept. 1964–Sept. 1965	CBS	Wed. 9–9:30 P.M.
Sept. 1965–Sept. 1966	CBS	Wed. 9:30–10 P.M.

For five years, *The Dick Van Dyke Show* was one of America's favorite situation comedy series. The show,

The cast of the *Dick Van Dyke Show:* (left to right) Dick Van Dyke, Mary Tyler Moore, Morey Amsterdam, Rose Marie, Richard Deacon (Author's collection)

which starred Dick VAN DYKE as Rob Petrie, a TV comedy writer, was set behind the scenes of the fictional "Alan Brady Show." Also starring on the series were Mary Tyler MOORE as Rob's spirited wife, Laura Petrie, and Rose Marie and Morey Amsterdam as Rob's cowriters of "The Alan Brady Show," Sally Rogers and Maurice "Buddy" Sorrell. Also featured on the show were Larry Matthews as Rob and Laura's young son, Ritchie; Richard Deacon as the Brady show's pompous producer, Melvin Cooley; Carl Reiner as Alan Brady; and Jerry Paris and Ann Morgan Guilbert as Jerry and Millie Helper, the Petries' friends. Other less regular performers who made appearances on the show were Joan Shawlee as Buddy's wife, Viona; Tom Tulley and then J. Pat O'Malley as Rob's father, Sam; and Isabel Randolph and then Mabel Albertson as Rob's mother, Clara. Excellent writing and wonderful casting made this show one of TV's most successful and best-remembered sitcoms, although it took several seasons for the series to become a hit. *The Dick Van Dyke Show* was created by Carl Reiner, who played Alan Brady on the series. Sheldon Leonard was the show's producer. In all, 158 episodes of *The Dick Van Dyke Show* were filmed, many of them written by Bill Persky and Sam Denoff. In 1995, Reiner reprised his Alan Brady role on a nostalgic episode of *MAD ABOUT YOU*.

DICKINSON, ANGIE (ANGELINE BROWN 1931–)

Although she had previously appeared as a regular on the less-than-successful TV series *Men into Space* in 1959, film actress Angie Dickinson scored a major success playing Sgt. Suzanne "Pepper" Anderson on the action/adventure series *POLICE WOMAN* in 1974. The series enjoyed a healthy four-year run and made Dickinson ever more famous. Dickinson, who was born in Kulm, North Dakota, attended Immaculate Heart College and Glendale College before deciding to embark upon an acting career. The actress's first major assignment was in the film *Return of Jack Slade* in 1955, and she followed that with increasingly more important roles in such films as *Tension at Table Rock* (1956), *Rio Bravo* (1959), *The Sins of Rachel Cade* (1961), *The Killers* (1964), and *Big Bad Mama* (1974), before starring on the *Police Woman* series. After *Police Woman* left the air, Dickinson continued to play featured roles in such films as *Dressed to Kill* (1980), *Even Cowgirls Get the Blues* (1993), *Sabrina* (1995), and *Play It Forward* (2000), as well as several less successful films and TV series such as *The Orson Welles Show* (1979), *Cassie & Company* (1982), and the TV miniseries *Wild Palms* (1993).

DIFF'RENT STROKES

Nov. 1978–Oct. 1979	NBC	Fri. 8–8:30 P.M.
Oct. 1979–Oct. 1981	NBC	Wed. 9–9:30 P.M.
Oct. 1981–Aug. 1982	NBC	Thurs. 9–9:30 P.M.
Aug. 1982–Aug. 1985	NBC	Sat. 8–8:30 P.M.
Sept. 1985–Mar. 1986	NBC	Fri. 9–9:30 P.M.
June 1986–Aug. 1986	NBC	Sat. 8–8:30 P.M.

What happens when a wealthy white widower, who lives with his daughter in a luxury penthouse in New York City, adopts two underprivileged African-American orphan boys from Harlem? NBC's answer was, a great deal of fun is enjoyed by all. In this situation comedy, Conrad Bain played Philip Drummond, the wealthy gentleman, Dana Plato his biological daughter, Kimberly, and pint-sized, chubby-cheeked Gary Coleman and preadolescent Todd Bridges the black siblings, Arnold and Willis Jackson. Drummond's various white friends did countless double takes during the series' eight-year run whenever Drummond introduced Arnold and Willis as his "sons." Over the years, many characters came and went on the series. The Drummonds' housekeeper, Mrs. Edna Garrett, played by Charlotte Rae, left the series after one season to become a housemother at the Eastland School for Girls in a spin-off series, *The FACTS OF LIFE*, in 1979. She was replaced on *Diff'rent Strokes* by a housekeeper named Adelaide Brubaker, played by Nedra Volz. Other characters who appeared on the series were Pearl Gallagher, played by Mary Jo Catlett; Aunt Sophia, played by Dody Goodman; Dudley Ramsey, played by Shavar Ross; Mr. Ted Ramsey, played by Le Tari; Miss Chung, played by Rosalind Chao; Charlene DuPrey, played by Janet Jackson; Lisa Hayes, played by Nikki Swasey; Sam McKinney, played by Danny Cooksey; Robbie Jason, played by Steven Mond; and Charley, played by Jason Hervey. However, Gary Coleman became the show's major attraction, and his "Whatchoo you talkin' bout, Willis?" became a catchphrase that was often repeated by millions of devoted fans. Drummond's three children finally got a mother in 1984, when Philip married Maggie McKinney, played by Dixie Carter and then Mary Ann Mobley. Maggie was a feisty TV exercise show hostess. *Diff'rent Strokes* was created by Jeff Harris and Bernie Kukoff and developed by Norman LEAR's Tandem Productions.

DINAH SHORE SHOW, THE & DINAH SHORE CHEVY SHOW, THE

DINAH SHORE SHOW, THE:

Nov. 1951–July 1957	NBC	Tues. & Thurs. 7:30–7:45 P.M.

DINAH SHORE CHEVY SHOW, THE:

Oct. 1956–June 1957	NBC	Fri. 10–11 P.M.
Oct. 1957–June 1961	NBC	Sun. 9–10 P.M.
Oct. 1961–June 1962	NBC	Fri. 9:30–10:30 P.M.
Dec. 1962–May 1963	NBC	Sun. 10–11 P.M.

For six years, singer Dinah SHORE had a 15-minute, two-times-a-week musical/variety, early evening series on the air. Dinah sang hit songs of the day, as well as some standards. Her accompanyist, Ticker Freeman, occasionally performed piano solos. The Notables and then the Skylarks were Dinah's backup singers, and the orchestras of

Vic Shoen and then Harry Zimmerman provided musical accompaniments. On occasion, Dinah would chat with guest stars who visited the show. In 1956, Dinah was given a prime-time musical/variety, hour-long show, which was sponsored by Chevrolet. The show lasted for seven seasons and became one of television's most memorable and popular programs, and Dinah was America's favorite female singer in several fan magazine audience polls. In addition to Dinah's wonderful renditions of popular songs, elaborately staged musical numbers, complete with a singing chorus and dancers, big-name guest stars were featured on Dinah's show. Dinah always wore gorgeous gowns and beautifully designed costumes for her musical numbers, and the sets were more like those seen in expensively produced films, rather than the usual TV variety show. Dinah's warm and friendly style, her spirited singing of the sponsor's jingle, "See the U.S.A. in your Chevrolet," and the hearty kiss she blew to her audience at the end of each show became her trademarks and endeared her to millions of fans throughout the United States and Canada. One of her most memorable shows featured Dinah and Ella Fitzgerald singing a medley of their hits. Together, they were nothing short of sensational. In addition to Dinah, the show regularly featured the Harry Zimmerman, and then the Frank DeVol, Orchestras, the Skylarks, and the Even Dozen singers, and the Tony Charmoli and Nick Castle Dancers. When Dinah's regular weekly series left the air, she continued to star on occasional TV specials on NBC. Shore hosted a 90-minute daytime talk show called *Dinah* from 1974 until 1980. Henry Jaffee and Carolyn Raskin were the *Dinah* show's producers. In 1979, *Dinah* was retitled *Dinah and Friends,* and Shore shared the daily spotlight with a weekly cohost.

DING DONG SCHOOL

Dec. 1952–Dec. 1956	NBC	Mon.–Fri. 10–10:30 A.M.
1959	Syndicated show	Various times and stations

Designed for preschoolers, *Ding Dong School* was one of television's first educational programs for young children. The show was hosted by Dr. Frances Horwich, a plump, grandmotherly-looking woman, who was head of the Education Department at Roosevelt College in Chicago, and who was affectionately known as "Miss Frances" to her young fans. The title was given to the show by the three-year-old daughter of the programs producer, Reginald Werrenrath, after she watched the pilot of the show and noticed that Miss Frances rang a handheld school bell at the beginning of the show. NBC canceled the show in 1956, and a syndicated *Ding Dong School* series resurfaced in 1959. Unfortunately, the syndicated show failed to attract the attention of young viewers, and *Ding Dong School* and the popular and well-loved Miss Frances, who never talked down to her young viewers and always spoke with a gentle, calm voice, retired from television.

DISNEY, WALT (WALTER ELIAS DISNEY 1901–1966)

Walt Disney, whose name became forever linked with animated film cartoons, and later with several memorable children's television shows and theme parks, was born in Chicago. During World War I, when he was 16 years old, Disney lied about his age and joined the U.S. Army. Disney was stationed in Paris, France, but the war ended before he ever fought in a battle. Always a talented artist, Disney won a scholarship to the Kansas City Art Institute when he returned to the United States from overseas. At the institute, Walt met a fellow artist, Ub Iwerks. The two young men became friends and formed their own company, which produced a series of animated short-subject films called "Newman's Laugh-O-Grams." The company went bankrupt, but Disney and Iwerks went to Hollywood in 1923, formed a new company, and produced a series of new animated film shorts called "Alice Comedies." These short-subject films became very popular, and between 1923 and 1927, hundreds of "Alice Comedies" were produced.

In the late 1920s, Disney came up with a cartoon character he called Mickey Mouse and used the character as the star of three animated cartoons, the first being *Steamboat Willie* (1928). Mickey Mouse became popular with moviegoers, and Disney began to produce a series of film cartoons called "Silly Symphonies" that established him as one of Hollywood's most successful animators. In 1937, Disney had formed his Disney Studios production company and produced his first feature-length animated film, *Snow White and the Seven Dwarfs.* Most people believed a feature-length cartoon film was destined for failure, but *Snow White and the Seven Dwarfs* was an enormous hit, and Disney followed this with a series of successful feature-length animated films that have become classics, including *Pinocchio* (1940), *Fantasia* (1940), *Dumbo* (1941), and *Bambi* (1942). Disney was the first animator to combine live action and cartoon characters in a feature-length film in *Song of the South* (1946). He also produced his first feature-length nonanimated action film, *Treasure Island,* in 1950. The number of successful Disney films over the next several years was impressive and included such classics as *Cinderella* (1950), *Alice in Wonderland* (1951), *Peter Pan* (1953), *Lady and the Tramp* (1955), *Sleeping Beauty* (1959), and, released the year he died, *One Hundred and One Dalmatians* (1961). By 1954, Disney had recognized the growing popularity of television and produced a series called *Disneyland,* which he initially used to promote his new Disneyland theme park in California. He also produced the very popular children's program *The MICKEY MOUSE CLUB,* the Davy Crockett serial, which was seen on his *Disneyland* show, and the action/adventure *ZORRO* series. The Walt Disney Productions organization currently holds the record for receiving the most Academy Awards, 32.

Walt Disney (Author's collection)

DR. KILDARE

Sept. 1961–	NBC	Thurs. 8:30–9:30 P.M.
Sept. 1965		
Sept. 1965–	NBC	Mon./Tues. 8:30–9 P.M.
Aug. 1966		

Television series set in hospitals were all the rage in the 1960s, and NBC's *Dr. Kildare* was one of the most popular "hospital shows." Originally, Dr. Kildare, who was a young resident physician at the fictional metropolitan Blair General Hospital, was introduced to moviegoers in a series of popular films produced at MGM in the 1930s and 1940s, which starred Lew Ayres and Lionel Barrymoore. The television version of *Dr. Kildare* starred Richard CHAMBERLAIN as the young hospital intern, Dr. James Kildare, and Raymond Massey as his cantankerous but concerned mentor and senior staff physician, Dr. Leonard Gillespie. Each week, the various life-and-death situations encountered in all metropolitan hospitals were dramatic, and viewers made *Dr. Kildare* one of the top-rated shows for five years. Also appearing on the series regularly were

Eddie Ryder and Jud Taylor as Dr. Simon Agurski and Thomas Gersom, who were fellow interns of Dr. Kildare (and were seen during the 1961–62 season); Joan Patrick as hospital receptionist Susan Deigh (also seen during the 1961–62 season); Jean Inness as Nurse Fain; Steven Bell as Dr. Lowry; and Lee Kurty as Nurse Zoe Lawton. *Dr. Kildare* was produced by Norman Felton at the MGM Studios. Before it was a film, a radio show, and finally a TV program, *Dr. Kildare* was a series of short stories serialized in magazines that were written by Max Brand. Brand's inspiration for the Kildare character was a prominent urologist, Dr. George Winthrop Fish (1895–77).

DR. QUINN, MEDICINE WOMAN

Jan. 1993	CBS	Fri. 8–10 P.M.
Jan. 1993–Dec. 1997	CBS	Sat. 8–9 P.M.
Feb. 1998–June 1998	CBS	Sat. 8–9 P.M.

When *Dr. Quinn, Medicine Woman* made its TV debut as a made-for-TV film in 1993, no one thought it would become a popular series. Set in the Wild West of the 1860s, *Dr. Quinn, Medicine Woman* centered on a single female physician who, because opportunities for female doctors in the East were limited, migrated west from Boston to Colorado Springs in order to open her medical practice in a western frontier town. At first, Dr. Quinn is greeted with hostility by the townspeople who resent she is a woman. Viewers loved the TV film and the subsequent series, and they also responded favorably to the show's star, Jane Seymour, who played the physician, Dr. Michaela "Mike" Quinn. The response to the series was even more favorable when, after one of her patients died, Dr. Quinn adopted the woman's three orphaned children. The children, Matthew, Coleen, and Brian Cooper, were played by Chad Allen, Erika Flores and then Jessica Bowman, and Shawn Toovey. A handsome, rugged young widower, Byron Sully, played by Joe Lando, came into the family's life when he rented his homestead to Dr. Quinn and her children and subsequently became a love interest for Dr. Quinn. Other performers who appeared on the series when it was first aired were Diane Ladd as Charlotte Cooper, the mother of the three children Dr. Quinn later adopts; Orson Bean as storekeeper Loren Bray; Jim Knobeloch as barber Jake Slicker; Geoffrey Lower as Reverend Johnson; William Shockley as Hank, the bartender; and Helene Udy as Myra, a saloon girl. At the end of the 1994–95 season, to the delight of the show's loyal viewers, Dr. Quinn and Sully were married. They were even more delighted when the good doctor became pregnant in the series' following season. When CBS announced that it was going to cancel *Dr. Quinn, Medicine Woman* in 1998, thousands of protest letters were sent to the network. Jane Seymour, disappointed with the series' cancellation, appeared on several TV talk shows to generate popular support for her show. CBS, however, disappointed with the series' ratings, held firm, and *Dr. Quinn, Medicine Woman* became part of TV history in June 1998.

DONAHUE, PHIL (1935–)

One of television's most successful talk show hosts, Phil Donahue was born in Cleveland, Ohio. Donahue's father, Joseph, was a furniture salesman, and his mother, Catherine, sold shoes. After graduating from St. Edward's High School in Lakewood, Ohio, in 1955, Donahue, whose sister Elinor Donahue was an actress and one of the stars of the popular FATHER KNOWS BEST series, attended the University of Notre Dame in South Bend, Indiana. When he graduated from college, Donahue got a job as an announcer at KYW radio in Cleveland and then became a newscaster at WHIO in Dayton, Ohio, where he also hosted his first talk show on radio, *Conversation Piece*. In 1967, Donahue was hired by WLWD-TV in Dayton, where he became the host of a talk show that was produced for "women who think." His show involved a studio audience in the interviews, and the topics he employed were usually timely, informative, and often controversial. Donahue became the host of the nationally syndicated PHIL DONAHUE SHOW in 1970, and for the next 21 years

he remained one of television's most popular talk show hosts. By 1996, competition from countless other talk shows, most notably *The OPRAH WINFREY SHOW*, which shared the same time slot as Donahue's program, led to Donahue's show being dropped by many TV stations. Oprah generously acknowledged Donahue's contributions to talk show television by stating, "If there hadn't been a Phil, there wouldn't have been a me," when she heard about *The Phil Donahue Show's* cancellation. During his tenure on TV, Donahue won an impressive nine daytime Emmys as Outstanding Talk Show Host and a Lifetime Achievement Emmy in 1996. In 1992, Donahue, in addition to his regular, syndicated talk show, cohosted *This Week With Donahue and Pozner*, which also starred Vladimir Pozner, the former information chief of the Soviet Union. Except for occasional guest-starring cameo appearances on such series as ELLEN and FRASIER, Donahue retired from the television spotlight, except to promote various worthwhile causes with his wife, actress Marlo Thomas.

DONALD, PETER (1918–1979)

Peter Donald was born in Bristol, England, but spent most of his life in the United States. Donald was one of radio's most successful actors before he became a TV game show host during television's earliest years. A regular performer on such radio programs as *The Fred Allen Show* (playing Ajax Cassidy), *The Peter Donald Show*, and *Can You Top This?* (as the joke teller who told jokes sent in by listeners that comedians tried to "top" with jokes of their own on the same subject), Donald was the popular star/host of the *Prize Performance* (1950), and the MASQUERADE PARTY (1954–56) game show, on which he was also a panelist (1952–53).

DONNA REED SHOW, THE

Sept. 1958–Sept. 1959	ABC	Wed. 9–9:30 P.M.
Oct. 1959–Jan. 1966	ABC	Thurs. 8–8:30 P.M.
Jan. 1966–Sept. 1966	ABC	Sat. 8–8:30 P.M.

Academy Award–winning actress (*From Here to Eternity*, 1955) Donna REED became the star of a television situation comedy series appropriately titled *The Donna Reed Show* in 1958. The series was one of television's most popular domestic comedies, and the beautiful Ms. Reed became one of America's favorite TV personalities. On this series, Reed played Donna Stone, a "typical," All-American, stay-at-home wife and mother, whose husband, Alex, played by Carl Betz, was a pediatrician. The Stones had three children, Mary, Jeff, and Trisha, played by Shelley Fabares, Paul Petersen, and Patty Petersen. The family suffered through all the usual domestic trials and tribulations such as measles, problems with boyfriends and girlfriends, academics, fibs, et al., that are common in most TV family-oriented situation comedies of the late 1950s to early 1960s. The series, mainly because of the charm and beauty of its star, remained high in audience polls for an impressive eight years, making it one of television's longest-running sitcoms. The show's theme music, "Happy Days," introduced viewers to a half-hour of delightful, wholesome TV entertainment, and even TV critics agreed that *The Donna Reed Show* was well worth tuning in to see. Also appearing on the series as regulars were Kathleen Freeman as the Stones' nosy neighbor, Mrs. Wilgus; Harvey Grant and Darryl Richard as Jeff's friends, Philip and Smitty; Candy Moore as Bebe Barnes; and Bob Crane and Ann McCrea as the Stones' friends and neighbors, Dr. Dave and Madge Kelsey. At the height of the show's popularity, both Shelley Fabares and Paul Petersen launched singing careers and recorded several teenybopper hit songs, including Fabares's "Johnny Angel" and Petersen's "My Dad" and "She Can't Find Her Keys." Appearances by such recognizable performers as character actress Margaret DuMont of Marx Brothers films, singer James Darren, George Hamilton, and silent screen legend Buster Keaton, delighted viewers and kept them watching the show. Because of the popularity of series and its star, reruns of *The Donna Reed Show* began to appear on home screens as early as 1964 and ran concurrently with the first-run shows of the series until 1968. This was a first for a TV situation comedy.

DONNY AND MARIE (AKA *THE OSMOND FAMILY SHOW*)

Jan. 1976–May 1977	ABC	Fri. 8–9 P.M.
June 1977–Aug. 1977	ABC	Wed. 8–9 P.M.
Aug. 1977–Jan. 1978	ABC	Fri. 8–9 P.M.
Jan. 1979–May 1979	ABC	Sun. 7–8 P.M.

For three years, brother and sister Donny and Marie Osmond had a popular musical variety show on the air, which featured their singing and various guest stars from the entertainment world. When the series first went on the air, Donny was 18 years old and Marie was 16, and the show was directed mainly toward young viewers. Appearing on the show regularly with Donny and Marie were their brothers, Jimmy, Merrill, and Alan, who with Donny had previously scored a big success as the Osmond Brothers on *The ANDY WILLIAMS SHOW* and subsequently appeared on their own show, *The Osmonds*, in 1972–74. *The Osmond Family Show* made its debut in 1979, but was not successful. Donny and Marie's many hit recordings were highlighted on the show, and regular appearances by talented comic Paul Lynde, the Mormon Tabernacle Choir, and many guest stars, were often featured. In 1977, *Donny and Marie*, which had been taping its shows in a Hollywood studio, decided to tape the program in Donny and Marie's home state, Utah. The designer Bob Mackie (Cher's chief costume designer) was hired to "dress up" the show and make it a bit more trendy. These changes were only moderately successful, and two years later, the *Donny and Marie* show was canceled. In the late 1990s, after they had embarked on separate careers, Donny and Marie Osmond were reunited as the hosts of a syndicated television talk show, which was

canceled in 2000. The executive producer of the original *Donny and Marie* show was Raymond Katz, and the show's producers were Sid and Marty Krofft.

DOOGIE HOWSER, M.D.

Sept. 1989	ABC	Tues. 8:30–9 P.M.
Sept. 1989	ABC	Wed. 9:30–10 P.M.
Oct. 1989–Feb. 1992	ABC	Wed. 9–9:30 P.M.
Feb. 1992–May 1992	ABC	Wed. 8:30–9 P.M.
May 1992–Aug. 1992	ABC	Wed. 9–9:30 P.M.
Aug. 1992–Mar. 1993	ABC	Wed. 8:30–9 P.M.
June 1993–July 1993	ABC	Wed 8:30–9 P.M.

As if life isn't complicated enough for a 16-year-old boy, Douglas "Doogie" Howser, the hero of the *Doogie Howser, M.D.* situation comedy series, was a boy genius who finished high school in a record nine weeks, attended Princeton University when he was 10 years old, graduated from medical school when he was 14 years old, and became a resident physician at the Eastman Medical Center in Los Angeles when he was 16. As silly as all this seems, *Doogie Howser, M.D.* was a surprisingly good series, mainly due to the talent of the young actor who played Doogie, Neil Patrick HARRIS. In spite of his highly demanding job as a doctor, Doogie was every bit a typical 16-year-old boy as far as his private life was concerned. The usual awkwardness that goes along with being a teen becoming aware of sex and the larger world around him, as contrasted with his very grown-up professional responsibilities, accounted for much of the show's comedy. Doogie's father, David, also a doctor, was played by James B. Sikking, and his mother, Katherine, was played by Brenda Montgomery. They did what they could to keep Doogie on an even keel. Doogie's colleagues at the medical center were chief of services, Dr. Caulfield, played by Lawrence Pressman, and fellow resident physician, Dr. Jack McGuire, played by Mitchell Anderson. His not very smart buddy, Vinnie, was played by Max Casella. Also appearing on the series were Nurse Carly Springfield, played by Kathryn Layng, and Vinnie's girlfriend, Wanda, played by Lisa Dean Ryan. Another object of Doogie's affection was Janine, played by Lucy Boryer. As the series unfolded, Doogie eventually moved out of his parents' home and shared an apartment with his friend Vinnie. During the show's final season, Doogie had a new girlfriend, Michele, a nurse played by Robyn Lively. Prolific television show producer Steven Bochco created the *Doogie Howser, M.D.* series with David Kelly.

DORIS DAY SHOW, THE

Sept. 1968–Sept. 1969	CBS	Tues. 9:30–10 P.M.
Sept. 1969–Sept. 1973	CBS	Mon. 9:30–10 P.M.

In 1968, one of Hollywood's biggest and brightest performers, Doris DAY, became the star of a half-hour television situation comedy series, *The Doris Day Show.* On this series, which was an instant audience favorite from the first time it aired, Day played Doris Martin, a young widow with two sons to raise. When the series first went on the air, Doris had left her home in the big city and moved back to her family's ranch, owned by her father, Buck, played by veteran character actor Denver Pyle. Assisting Buck on the ranch was his hired hand, Leroy, played by James Hampton. Also living at the ranch was a housekeeper named Aggie, played by Fran Ryan. Aggie was replaced by Juanita, played by Naomi Stevens. Doris's sons, Billy and Tony, were played by Philip Brown and Todd Stark. Doris had a difficult time adjusting to the rural life on the ranch after so many years of living in the city. In the second season, Doris became a commuter when she took a job as a secretary at *New World* magazine in nearby San Francisco. Her boss at the magazine was Michael Nicholson, played by McLean Stevenson. One of the most popular characters on the show was Doris's prissy neighbor, Willard Jarvis, played by the very funny Billy DeWolfe, who had appeared with Day in several of her feature films and had become one of her closest friends. Also appearing on the series as regulars over the years were comedienne Kaye Ballard as Angie Palucci, and Bernie Kopell as Louie Palucci, who were the proprietors of an eatery that Doris frequented. For a short time, Peter Lawford appeared on the series, playing Doris's boyfriend, Dr. Peter Lawrence. *The Doris Day Show* was produced by Day's son, Terry Melcher.

DOUGLAS, MIKE (MICHAEL DOWD 1925–)

Mike Douglas, who is not to be confused with film actor Michael Douglas, was the host of a popular TV talk show, *The MIKE DOUGLAS SHOW*, which was one of the most popular daytime programs for over 20 years. Douglas, the singing voice of Prince Charming in the animated feature film *Cinderella* in 1950, and for many years a featured vocalist with several big-name bands, was born and raised in Chicago. In 1953, Douglas became a regular on *The Music Show*, before hosting his nationally syndicated talk show. When his long-running syndicated show ended in 1982, Douglas retired from television, except for rare appearances in such films as *The Incredible Shrinking Woman* (1981, playing himself), and *Birds of Prey* (1985). When he was hosting *The Mike Douglas Show*, Douglas guest-starred on such popular programs as *The JACKIE GLEASON SHOW*, *The ANDY WILLIAMS SHOW*, *The GREATEST AMERICAN HERO*, and *KNOTS LANDING*.

DOW, TONY (1945–)

Well known for playing Wally Cleaver in the situation comedy *LEAVE IT TO BEAVER*, Tony Dow, who was born in Hollywood to show business parents, was a child actor before winning the Wally role in 1957. The series made Dow one of the most famous TV personalities of the late 1950s. Two years after *Leave It to Beaver* left the air in 1963, Dow became a regular on the less suc-cessful *Never Too Young* series. He later played Ross Jeanelle on *GENERAL HOSPITAL* and had roles in such films as *Kentucky Fried Movie* (1977), the made-for-TV films *The Ordeal of Bill Carney* (1981), *Still the Beaver* (1983), and *High School U.S.A.* (1983). Dow also guest-starred on numerous TV series, such as *MY THREE SONS, EMERGENCY!, SIMON AND SIMON, KNIGHT RIDER, MURDER, SHE WROTE, CHARLES IN CHARGE*, and *DIAGNOSIS MURDER*. By 1994, Dow had become a successful producer and director. He produced the TV series *The HIGH LIFE* and *AIN'T MISBEHAVIN*, the made-for-TV film *The Adventures of Captain Zoom in Outer Space* (1995), and the feature film *It Came from Outer Space II* (1996). He directed episodes of *COACH*, as well as episodes of the TV series *Swamp Thing, Harry and the Hendersons, Murder Most Horrid, Star Trek—Deep Space Nine, Blue Heaven, Honey, I Shrunk the Kids: The TV Show, Crusade*, and *Cover Me: Based on the True Life of an FBI Family*.

DOWNS, HUGH (HUGH MALCOLM DOWNS 1921–)

Born in Akron, Ohio, Hugh Downs's first major television assignment was as the off-camera announcer on the popular TV children's show, *KUKLA, FRAN AND OLLIE*. Downs, a descendent of the legendary 19th-century frontiersman Davy Crockett, had his big on-camera break as the host of the *Home* TV series in 1954. Downs was the announcer on *Caesar's Hour*, which starred comedian Sid Caesar, from 1956 until 1957, and from 1958 until 1969, he was the host of the popular *Concentration* game show. He became well known to late-night TV viewers, however, as the sidekick/announcer on comedian Jack Paar's popular *TONIGHT SHOW* from 1957 until 1962. In 1962, Downs became the host of NBC's *TODAY* show, an early morning program, and in 1978, he coanchored the *20/20* series. Barbara Walters joined him as cohost in 1984. Hugh Downs remained one of TV's most familiar faces and occasionally hosted TV specials such as *Live from Lincoln Center, Danny Kaye: A Legacy of Laughter*, and *Tales from the Tomb: The Lost Sons of the Pharaoh* until his retirement in 1999.

DRAGNET

Jan. 1952–Dec. 1955	NBC	Thurs. 9–9:30 P.M.
Jan. 1956–Sept. 1958	NBC	Thurs. 8:30–9 P.M.
Sept. 1958–June 1959	NBC	Tues. 7:30–8 P.M.
July 1959–Sept. 1959	NBC	Sun. 8:30–9 P.M.
Jan. 1967–Sept. 1970	NBC	Thurs. 9:30–10 P.M.

Before it was one of television's most successful police/crime drama series, *Dragnet* was a popular radio program. First heard in 1949, radio's *Dragnet* was on the air for seven years, and from 1952 until 1956, it was simultaneously on radio and television. The television series ran for an additional three years after the radio show ended, before it, too, was canceled. Eight years later,

Dragnet returned to television for an additional two-year run. The star, director, and series' major force was Jack WEBB, who played the laid-back Los Angeles Police Department detective Joe Friday. Friday's flat, almost emotionless delivery, and his short, terse expressions such as, "Only the facts, ma'am," when he was questioning someone, and "It's my job, I'm a cop," when someone either praised or berated him, became familiar catchphrases for millions of viewers. The clipped, sparse dialogue used by the actors on this series became material for many parodies. In addition to Joe Friday, Barton Yarborough was heard on radio and briefly seen on the television series as Friday's partner, Sgt. Ben Romero. When Yarborough suddenly died after filming only three episodes of the television show, Friday's partner became Sgt. Ed Jacobs, played by Barney Phillips. Phillips remained on the series for the remainder of its first season. For the next season, Ben Alexander joined the cast as Friday's new partner, Sgt. Frank Smith, and remained with the series until it eventually left the air. Also appearing on the series was Herb Ellis as Officer Frank Smith. Few actresses were featured as regulars on *Dragnet*, but Dorothy Abbot did appear regularly as Ann Baker during the 1954 season, and Marjie Miller appeared as Sharon Maxwell, who worked in the Records Bureau of the L. A. Police Department, during the 1956 season and became a rare and short-lived romantic interest for Friday. The various episodes seen on *Dragnet* were reportedly based on actual police cases, and announcers Hal Gibney and then George Fenneman stated, "The story you have just seen is true . . . the names have been changed to protect the innocent," at the end of each show. In 1967, it reappeared on television with Jack Webb playing Sgt. Joe Friday and and Harry Morgan as his new partner, Officer Bill Gannon. The new

Dragnet series remained on the air for three seasons. A syndicated *Dragnet* series resurfaced in 1989 and featured Jeff Osterhage, Bernard White, Thalmus Rasulala, and Don Stroud in the cast, but without Jack Webb's unique presence, the series was doomed for failure and remained on the air for just one year.

DREW CAREY SHOW, THE

Sept. 1995–Feb. 1996	ABC	Wed. 8:30–9 P.M.
Apr. 1996–May 1996	ABC	Wed 8:30–9 P.M.
May 1996–Aug. 1996	ABC	Tues. 8:30–9 P.M.
Sept. 1996–Nov. 1996	ABC	Wed. 9:30–10 P.M.
Dec. 1996	ABC	Wed. 9–9:30 P.M.
Aug. 1997–Sept. 1997	ABC	Wed. 8–8:30 P.M.
Jan. 1998–Feb. 1998	ABC	Tues. 8–8:30 P.M.
Mar. 1999–Present	ABC	Thurs. 9–9:30 P.M.

Four single, working-class friends are the central characters on this half-hour situation comedy series that stars stocky, crew-cutted comedian Drew CAREY. Set in Cleveland, Ohio, Carey's actual hometown, Drew plays an underpaid assistant personnel director at the Winfred–Louder Department Store, who prefers to spend time in the kitchen of his home or at the Warsaw Tavern with his buddies, Oswald, a package deliverer and would-be disc jockey, Lewis, a janitor at the somewhat questionable Drugco Pharmaceutical Company, and Kate, a tomboy looking for love in all the wrong places. Oswald, Lewis, and Kate are played by Diedrich Bader, Ryan Stiles, and Christa Miller. Drew's major nemesis on the series is Mimi Bobek, a fat woman from hell at the department store, an oversized blonde who wears too much makeup and has a nasty attitude and mouth. The role is played by comedienne Kathy Kinney. When the series made its debut, Carey's boss at the department store was a loud-but-unseen Mr. Bell, whose voice was provided by Kevin Pollak. In 1997, Bell was replaced by the highly visible Nigel Wick, played by Craig Ferguson. Carey had several different girlfriends on the show over the years, but none of his romantic relationships ever seemed to work out for him. The highlights of several *Drew Carey Show* episodes were elaborately staged musical comedy fantasy numbers, in which everyone in the cast performed. One of these numbers parodied the hit film *The Full Monty*, which was about unemployed working-class men who decide to make extra money by performing a striptease act, à la the Chippendales. Drew's nightmare became a reality when his brother Steve married his archenemy Mimi Bobek.

DUCHOVNY, DAVID (DAVID WILLIAM DUCOVNY 1960–)

Born to comfortably well-off parents in New York City, David Duchovny, famous as Special Agent Fox William Mulder on the successful science fiction series *The X-FILES*, attended Princeton University as an undergraduate. After earning his B.A. degree, Duchovny attended graduate school at Yale University, where he studied

Dragnet featuring Jack Webb (Sgt. Joe Friday) and Ben Alexander (Off. Frank Smith) (Author's collection)

David Duchovny (Author's collection)

English literature. While at Yale, Duchovny became interested in acting and commuted to New York City regularly to attend acting classes. In 1987, Duchovny abandoned his graduate studies to pursue acting full time and won small roles in such films as *Working Girl* (1988, his film debut), and *Bad Influence* (1990), before landing a regular role on the TV series TWIN PEAKS in 1990, playing transsexual DEA Agent Dennis/Denise Bryson. Roles in such films such as *Chaplin* (1992), *Beethoven* (1992), and the *Red Shoe Diaries* made-for-TV films, led to his being cast in a starring role on *The X-Files* in 1993. After scoring a major success playing Agent Mulder, Duchovny starred in *The X-Files* (1998), for which he was paid a reported $6 million, and was then seen in *Return to Me* (2000). In 1996, David Duchovny was named one of the 50 most beautiful people in the world by *People* magazine. Choosing to focus on his film career, Duchovny left *The X-Files* in 2000.

DUKE, PATTY (ANNA MARIE DUKE 1946–)

Born in New York City, Patty Duke was a child actress who appeared on such early TV dramatic anthology series as *The Armstrong Circle Theatre* and *The UNITED STATES STEEL HOUR* in the 1950s. She was also a regular on the daytime drama series *The Brighter Day* (1958–59) and had an important role on the *Kitty Foyle* TV series (1958).

In the early 1960s, the young actress scored major stage and film successes as the deaf and blind, preadolescent Helen Keller, who became a renowned spokeswoman for the handicapped, in *The Miracle Worker*. By 1963, Patty was the star of a weekly situation series *The PATTY DUKE SHOW*, playing cousins Patty and Cathy Lane. The show became popular with young viewers and remained on the air for three successful seasons. By the time *The Patty Duke Show* ended its run, Duke was a young woman, and she soon became one of the busiest actresses in Hollywood, appearing in such films as *Valley of the Dolls* (1967), *Me, Natalie* (1969), and *Two on a Bench* (1971), and on many TV series and countless made-for-TV films, such as the miniseries *George Washington* (1984), *Fight for Life* (1987), *Fatal Judgement* (1988), *Everybody's Baby: The Rescue of Jessica McClure* (1989), *A Killer Among Friends* (1992), *Cries of the Heart* (1994), *Harvest of Fire* (1996), *Love Lessons* (2000), and many others, as well as the series *Amazing Grace* (1995). Because of the large number of made-for-TV films Patty Duke has appeared in, she has been given the unofficial title "Queen of TV Movies" by the entertainment industry.

DUKES OF HAZZARD, THE

Jan. 1979–Nov. 1981	CBS	Fri. 9–10 P.M.
Dec. 1981–Feb. 1985	CBS	Fri. 8–9 P.M.
June 1985–Aug. 1985	CBS	Fri. 8–9 P.M.

Good ol' country boys, souped-up cars and car crashes and chases, moonshine, and scantily clad young women were the major reasons this one-hour comedy/adventure series was a success. The two handsome young country bumpkins and the pretty girl who were the main characters on this rural comedy series were cousins Luke, Bo, and Daisy Duke, played by Tom WOPAT, John SCHNEIDER, and Catherine Bach. The Dukes lived in Hazzard County in the Deep South, and they had a penchant for getting into trouble. The series was very popular, especially with younger viewers who loved all the fast-paced action and slapstick comedy. The Dukes' Uncle Jesse, played by Denver Pyle, was constantly bailing the Duke boys out of the troubles they were always getting into with their chief nemeses in Hazzard County, the chubby, totally corrupt county commissioner, Jefferson Davis "Boss" Hogg, played by Sorrel Brooke, and Sheriff Roscoe Coltrane, Hogg's dumb stooge, played by James Best. Working for Hogg and Coltrane was Deputy Enos Strate, played by Sonny Shroyer, and then Deputy Cletus, played by Rick Hurst. The show's narration was provided by balladeer Waylon Jennings, who wrote and sang the series' theme song, "Good Ol' Boys," and provided an off-camera commentary about the action. In spite of the popularity of the Duke boys and Daisy, the real attraction for younger viewers was the car, a superduper 1969 souped-up Dodge Charger that the boys called "General Lee." The automotive acrobatics the General Lee performed staggered the imagination and certainly kept youngsters, and indeed many adults, glued to their

The Dukes of Hazzard: John Schneider (Bo Duke), Catherine Bach (Daisy Duke), and Tom Wopat (Luke Duke) (Author's collection)

television sets when the General Lee was in action. *The Dukes of Hazzard,* which was a lead-in show for the popular *DALLAS* series, was among the top 10 shows for three seasons from 1979 through 1982. Before the 1982–83 season began, actors John Schneider and Tom Wopat decided to boycott the program due to financial squabbles with the show's producers. Two new male Duke cousins were seen on the show for one year, Coy and Vance Duke, played by Byron Cherry and Christopher Mayer. The show's ratings fell drastically without Wopat and Schneider, and the following year, the two financially satisfied actors resumed their Luke and Bo Duke roles. By the time the series was canceled in 1985, 143 episodes of *The Dukes Of Hazzard* had been filmed. In 1983, an animated cartoon series, *The Dukes,* was seen on CBS's Saturday morning lineup of children's programs. The actors who were seen on the live-action show provided the cartoon voices for the same characters they played on the original series.

DuPONT SHOW OF THE WEEK, THE (AKA DuPONT SHOW OF THE MONTH, THE)

Sept. 1957–Mar. 1961	CBS	Sun. 10–11 P.M.
Sept. 1961–Sept. 1964	NBC	Sun. 10–11 P.M.

The E. I. DuPont company sponsored this one-hour television program that offered viewers a wide variety of enter-

tainment, from dramatic plays and documentaries, to light comedies and musical comedies and revues. One of the purposes of this series was to demonstrate the wide range of programs television could provide, and while it was on the air, *The DuPont Show of the Week* was one of TV's most popular programs. Three years before *The DuPont Show of the Week* was aired, DuPont sponsored *The DuPont Show of the Month,* which was seen on CBS and presented TV adaptations of such classic works of literature and the theater as *Hamlet, A Tale of Two Cities,* and *The Browning Version.* The first show presented on *The DuPont Show of the Week* series was a documentary about the novelist Ernest Hemingway. Later shows featured the famous clown Emmett Kelly, who narrated an informative documentary about life in the circus. Peter Lind Hayes narrated a program about the celebrated Broadway showman George M. Cohan. In addition, adaptations of such classic plays and novels as *A Tale of Two Cities* (with with Denholm Elliott, Gracie Fields, and George C. Scott), *The Red Mill* (an operetta with Harpo Marx, Mike Nichols, Elaine May, and Donald O'Connor), *Wuthering Heights* (with Richard Burton), *I, Don Quixote* (with Lee J. Cobb), and *Ethan Frome* (with Sterling Hayden), to name just a few, were presented on *The DuPont Show of the Month* series. Among other well-known actors who also appeared in the television plays were Eddie ALBERT, Martha Scott, Claude Rains, Zachary Scott, Walter Matthau, and Peter FALK. One of *The DuPont Show of the Week*'s most controversial programs was a no-holds-barred documentary about the backstage goings-on in the career of comedian Shelly Berman. Berman forcefully shoved a backstage worker during his show, an action caught by the cameras. Viewers were not amused by Berman's display of ego, and the comedian's career suffered considerably.

DURANTE, JIMMY (JAMES FRANCIS DURANTE 1893–1980)

Few entertainers have had the longevity and the adulation comedian Jimmy Durante enjoyed. For over 65 years, with his lovable, unpretentious stage presence, his gruff, New York–accented speech and mispronunciations of words, and his vaudeville-style singing and comic delivery, Durante was one of the most popular performers of the stage, films, radio, and finally, TV. Born in New York City, Jimmy, who taught himself to play the piano when he was a child, quit grade school in his early teens to play the piano in a Coney Island saloon. In the early 1920s, Durante formed a partnership with two vaudeville entertainers, Lou Clayton and Eddie Jackson, and the three men developed a successful act that toured the vaudeville circuit. Jimmy, the team's most popular asset, was soon appearing in such shows as *The Ziegfeld Follies of 1929* with his partners. In 1930, Durante, who by this time had been nicknamed "The Snozzola" and "The Schnoz," because of his large nose, made his film debut in an early "talking" picture, *Roadhouse Nights,* and soon become one of Hollywood's most sought-after comedians. Among the hundreds of films Durante appeared in over the years were *Blondie of the Follies* (1932), *Palooka* (1934), *George White's Scandals* (1934), *The Man Who Came to Dinner* (1942), *Jumbo* (1962) and *It's a Mad, Mad, Mad, Mad World* (1963). From 1943 until 1950, Jimmy was the star of *The Jimmy Durante Show* on radio, and in 1950, he became a television star, appearing as an alternate host on the FOUR STAR REVUE music/variety show. The other stars on this program were Danny THOMAS, Jack Carson, and Ed WYNN. Durante was also a frequent guest host on The COLGATE COMEDY HOUR (1950–55) and starred on his own JIMMY DURANTE SHOW from 1954 through 1956. A popular guest on such TV programs as *The MILTON BERLE SHOW*, *The Mothers-in-Law*, *The ANDY WILLIAMS SHOW*, and *The SONNY AND CHER COMEDY HOUR*, among others, Durante remained constantly in demand until shortly before his death in 1980.

DYNASTY

Jan. 1981–Apr. 1981	ABC	Mon. 9–10 P.M.
July 1981–Sept. 1983	ABC	Wed. 10–11 P.M.
Sept. 1983–May 1984	ABC	Wed. 9–10 P.M.
Aug. 1984–May 1986	ABC	Wed. 9–10 P.M.
Sept. 1986–May 1987	ABC	Wed. 9–10 P.M.
Sept. 1987–Mar. 1988	ABC	Wed. 10–11 P.M.
Nov. 1988–May 1989	ABC	Wed. 10–11 P.M.

Following CBS's lead, ABC offered a full-hour, prime-time soap opera of its own, *Dynasty,* created by Richard and Esther Shapiro, three years after CBS's successful DALLAS made its TV Debut. Like *Dallas, Dynasty* centered on a rich family, the Carringtons. The Carringtons lived in Denver, Colorado, and had made their money in the oil business. The series featured beautiful sets and costumes and some very glamorous people. Actor John FORSYTHE played Blake Carrington, the patriarch of the Carringtons and the head of the family's oil empire. Linda Evans played Krystle Jennings, a beautiful, divorced woman who married Blake on the first episode of the show. Pamela Sue Martin and then Emma Samms played Blake's untrustworthy and selfish daughter from his first marriage, Fallon Carrington. Al Corley and then Jack Coleman played Blake's bisexual son, Steven, who was idealistic and somewhat naive. Steven was killed off when an oil rig exploded (actor Corley had complained about his role on the show), but the part was recast and the character revived, and the audience was told Steven hadn't been killed at all, but had been badly burned and had undergone plastic surgery, explaining why a new actor was playing the role. Other actors originally seen on the series were John James as Fallon's young attorney/husband, Jeff Colby; Lloyd Bochner as Jeff's Uncle Cecil; Bo Hopkins as geologist Matthew Blaisdel, a former boyfriend of Krystle; Pamela Bellwood as Matthew's off-center wife, Claudia; Katy Kurtzman as the Blaisdels' daughter, Lindsay; Dale Robertson as Wildcatter Walter Lankersham; and Lee Bergere, Peter Mark Richman, and Andy Laird. During *Dynasty's* second season, English actress Joan Collins joined the cast as Blake's former wife, Alexis Carrington, who constantly plotted to make Blake's new wife, Krystle, miserable. Also added to the cast were James Farentino as Dr. Nick Toscanni and Heather Locklear as Krystle's niece, Sammy Jo Dean, who married Steven Carrington, but was paid by Alexis to leave him. At the end of the 1983–84 season, Diahann CARROLL joined the cast as Blake Carrington's African-American illegitimate sister, Dominique Deveraux. In the fall of 1985, *a Dynasty* spin-off, *The COLBYS,* made its debut and was on the air for two years. For the remaining four years that *Dynasty* was aired, there were numerous cast additions, and the show's various plots became increasingly bizarre. The show was canceled in 1989 after eight seasons of misery, mayhem, and a great deal of over-the-top "campy" action.

EARLY EDITION

Sept. 1996–Jan. 1998	CBS	Sat. 9–10 P.M.
Apr. 1998–June 1998	CBS	Sat. 9–10 P.M.
July 1998–2000	CBS	Sat. 8–9 P.M.

When *Early Edition* made its TV debut, few people projected success for a series about a young man who gets the next day's newspaper and knows what is going to happen a day before events occur. They were wrong. Viewers immediately took to the new series and its engaging young star, Kyle Chandler, who played Gary Hobson, the young man charged with trying to prevent disasters from happening. The next day's early edition newspaper was delivered each day at his apartment front door by a mysterious ginger-colored cat. Gary spent the rest of the day preventing bad things from happening that had appeared in the *Chicago Sun-Times*. Gary, the owner of a Chicago pub called McGinty's, apparently had plenty of free time during the day to accomplish his missions of mercy. The only people who were aware of the early editions that Gary received were his African-American employee, Marissa Clark, a blind girl played by Shanesia Davis-Wiliams, and his friend and partner, Chuck Fishman, played by Fisher Stevens. At the end of the 1998 season, Chuck moved to Hollywood to become a film producer, and Gary made Marissa his partner at McGintys'.

EAST SIDE/WEST SIDE

| Sept. 1963–Sept. 1964 | CBS | Mon. 10–11 P.M. |

Although it was on the air for only one year, the hour-long *East Side/West Side* drama series became the prototype for many similar low-keyed urban shows that followed. The excellent cast was headed by George C. Scott as Neil Brock, a social worker whose clients lived in the slums of New York City. Elizabeth Wilson played Frieda Hechlinger, Brock's boss at the welfare agency, and Cecily Tyson played Brock's coworker, Jane Foster. In an attempt to revise the show and make it more palatable to viewers, who seemed to shy away from the depressing subjects it dealt with, the show was altered when Brock went to work for a congressman in the series' midseason. The show's gritty portrayal of life among the underprivileged won praise from TV critics for its realism, but the show was years ahead of its time, and viewers found it difficult to accept the show's seedy atmosphere and characters, and it was canceled after completing little more than one season. *East Side/West Side* was one of the first TV series filmed on actual locations in New York City. It was produced by David SUSSKIND.

EASTWOOD, CLINT (CLINTON EASTWOOD, JR. 1930–)

Before he attracted the attention of television viewers as the laid-back cowboy Rowdy Yates on CBS's popular western series RAWHIDE in 1959, Clint Eastwood appeared in supporting roles in such second-rate films as *Francis in the Navy* (1955) and *Tarantula* (1955). Eastwood, born in San Francisco during the Great Depression, was the son of Clinton, Sr., and Ruth Eastwood. His father moved his family around California, looking for work, when Clint, Jr., was a boy, but the family finally settled in Oakland, California, where the younger Eastwood graduated from Oakland Technical High School in 1948. After finishing school, Clint went to work as a logger, a truck driver, and a steel-furnace stoker, before he was drafted into the U.S. Army. Stationed at Fort Ord in Monterey, California, Eastwood met actors David Janssen and Martin Milner, who had also been drafted. When

Eastwood was discharged, Jansseen and Milner, who were impressed with Clint's rugged good looks, convinced him to go to Hollywood to try to break into films. After a screen test, Eastwood was signed to a contract, earning $75 a week and was seen in several low-budget productions before winning the Rowdy Yates role on *Rawhide* in 1959. After *Rawhide*, Eastwood's acting career came to a standstill for a time, and upon the advice of his agent, the actor went to Italy, where American western films were all the rage, to star in a series of low-budget "spaghetti westerns." The films, to Eastwood's surprise, became immensely popular in the United States, as well as in Europe, and included such box office favorites as *A Fistful of Dollars* (1964), *For a Few Dollars More* (1965), and *The Good, the Bad and the Ugly* (1966). These films made Eastwood internationally known, and when he returned to Hollywood, he appeared in several big-budget films such as the musical *Paint Your Wagon* (1969), and then directed and starred in the film *Play Misty for Me* (1971), which earned him the respect of the film industry and led to superstardom in such action films as *Dirty Harry* (1971, as Harry Callahan), *Magnum Force* (1973), *Sudden Impact* (1983), *The Dead Pool* (1988), and the films *Bridges of Madison County* (1995), *Absolute Power* (1997), and *Space Cowboys* (2000). Eastwood continues to be one of Hollywood's most important actors, directors, and producers. In 1993 he won the Best Director Oscar for his film *Unforgiven*.

EBSEN, BUDDY (CHRISTIAN RUDOLPH EBSEN 1908–)

A performer who played two entirely different roles on television in two successful series—Jed Clampett on the situation comedy The BEVERLY HILLBILLIES, and the title role on the crime drama BARNABY JONES—Buddy Ebsen began his career as a dancer. Born in Belleville, Illinois, Ebsen took tap-dancing lessons with his sister, Vilma, when he was a boy, and when he finished school, Buddy and Vilma went to New York City to break into show business. Ebsen appeared in the dancing chorus of several Broadway shows in the late 1920s and early 1930s, and formed a vaudeville act with his sister. In 1935, Buddy and Vilma went to Hollywood, hoping to appear in films. Before long, Buddy's eccentric dancing style—he was extremely tall and gangling for a dancer—attracted attention, and he was cast in such films as *Hollywood Hobbies* (1939), *Captain January* (1936), *Broadway Melody of 1938*, and *Sing Your Troubles Away* (1942), dancing with such famous costars as Eleanor Powell and Shirley Temple. Ebsen was originally cast as the Tin Man in *The Wizard of Oz* in 1939, but when he developed an allergic reaction to the silver makeup his character had to wear, he was replaced by Jack Haley. In the 1940s, Ebsen returned to the stage and made only occasional appearances in films until the mid-1950s, when he was seen on the *Davy Crockett* (1954) and the *Northwest Passage* (1958) series and in *Breakfast at Tiffany's* (1961), playing straight non-dancing roles. In 1962, Ebsen became one of television's

most famous faces when he played Jed Clampett on *The Beverly Hillbillies*. Soon after that show was canceled, Ebsen appeared on the one-hour crime series *Barnaby Jones*, playing a private detective who comes out of retirement to run his old detective agency, after his son, who was also a P.I., is killed. When *Barnaby Jones* was canceled, Ebsen semiretired from show business and has only rarely guest-starred on various TV shows in recent years.

ED SULLIVAN SHOW, THE　(AKA THE TOAST OF THE TOWN)

June 1948	CBS	Sun. 9–10 P.M.
July 1948–Aug. 1948	CBS	Sun. 9:30–10:30 P.M.
Aug. 1948–Mar. 1949	CBS	Sun. 9–10 P.M.
May 1949–June 1971	CBS	Sun. 8–9 P.M.

Every Sunday for over 20 years, *The Ed Sullivan Show* was a showcase for some of the world's most celebrated performers. A wide variety of singers, comedians, actors, dancers, and various circus performers displayed their talents on *The Ed Sullivan Show* each week, and made it America's favorite television variety program for 23 years. Ed SULLIVAN was one of the first people in show business to acknowledge the potential of television for displaying the United States's and the world's finest artist's talents. He was a well-known New York–based entertainment columnist who had begun his broadcasting career on

Ed Sullivan

The historic appearance of the Beatles on *The Ed Sullivan Show:* (left to right) Ed Sullivan, Paul McCartney, George Harrison, Ringo Starr (above), John Lennon (Author's collection)

radio in 1931 hosting a talk/variety program. A somewhat stiff-looking man, who only rarely smiled, Sullivan readily admitted that he was not a performer. Sullivan never interfered with the work of artists who appeared on his show. He simply introduced them, and when they had finished their act, occasionally chatted with them and urged the audience to applaud them once again. Originally titled *The TOAST OF THE TOWN*, Sullivan's show began with a line of pretty girls (the June Taylor Dancers) dancing, as a chorus sung the program's theme song. Sullivan was then introduced by an off-camera announcer. The variety of entertainers that appeared on the first *Toast of the Town* telecast in 1948 gave an indication of the variety that viewers could expect on future shows. The first show included the comedy team of Dean MARTIN and Jerry Lewis, concert pianist Eugene List, and the Broadway songwriting team of Richard Rodgers and Oscar Hammerstein II. The show was an immediate success, and before long, it was America's foremost showcase for prac-

tically every entertainer in the United States, and even the world. Among the celebrities who made their TV debuts on *The Ed Sullivan Show* over the years were Bob HOPE, Lena Horne, Dinah SHORE, Eddie Fisher, and cartoonist/filmmaker Walt DISNEY. Two performances were among the most watched and publicized events in television history. Millions of curious viewers and devoted fans tuned in to watch singer Elvis Presley perform in 1956. Elvis was instructed by Sullivan to tone down his swiveling pelvic motions, which TV censors of that time considered too obscene to be seen on television. Cameras showed the singer only from the waist up, much to the disappointment of his adoring female fans. Another eagerly awaited TV performance occurred when the popular English rock and roll group the Beatles made their American TV debut on the *Ed Sullivan Show* on February 9, 1964. In addition, several performers such as comedians Alan King, Myron Cohen, and ventriloquist Señor Wences and his little hand puppet mouse, Topo Gigio, were on the show so many times, they practically became "regulars." Old-time vaudeville performers like Gallagher and Sheen and Sophie Tucker as well as popular stage and film stars such as Ethel Merman, Fred ASTAIRE, Hedy Lamarr, and Jane Powell, and rock and roll and soul performers such as the Supremes, the Rolling Stones, and James Brown appeared on the show. Everyone who was anybody in show business, either for a brief, bright moment or for half a century, made appearances on *The Ed Sullivan Show* between 1948 and 1971, keeping the show high in the TV ratings. By the 1970s, top performers had begun to demand large sums for a single appearance on the show, and Sullivan could not afford to book several major performers on any one show any longer. *The Ed Sullivan Show's* final telecast was seen in June 1971, when the series was retired from the air and became part of never-to-be-forgotten TV history. Ed Sullivan died three years after *The Ed Sullivan Show's* last telecast.

ED WYNN SHOW, THE

THE ED WYNN variety SHOW:

Oct. 1949–Dec. 1949	CBS	Tues. 9–9:30 P.M.
Jan. 1950–Mar. 1950	CBS	Sat. 9–9:30 P.M.
Apr. 1950–July 1950	CBS	Tues. 9–9:30 P.M.

THE ED WYNN situation comedy SHOW:

Sep. 1958–Jan. 1959	NBC	Thurs. 8–8:30 P.M.

Comedian Ed (the Perfect Fool) Wynn had been one of the United States's major stars on the vaudeville and Broadway stage, as well as on radio, when he made his TV debut in 1949 as one of the earliest pioneer performers to appear on the medium after World War II. Many people thought Wynn's half-hour television variety show would be a perfect vehicle for displaying Wynn's broad comic style. The show failed to attract a sizable enough audience, however, to keep it on the air more than one season, even though it featured some of the biggest names in show business, including Lucille BALL, Desi ARNAZ, Ben Blue, Buster Keaton, the Three Stooges, Leon Errol, Marie Wilson, and Joe E. Brown. *The Ed Wynn Show* was the first TV variety show to originate from Hollywood, and it was seen live on the West Coast, kinescoped, and then repeated for East Coast viewers later the same evening. At that time, most shows originated in New York and were kinescoped there and then seen on the West Coast. In 1958, Wynn came out of semiretirement to star in a second *Ed Wynn Show,* a situation comedy series. On this series, Wynn played an elderly widower named John Beamer whose son and daughter-in-law had died and left him to raise his two granddaughters. This show also failed to catch viewers' attention and was canceled after less than one full season.

EDEN, BARBARA (BARBARA JEAN MOORHEAD 1934–)

Although Barbara Eden made her film debut in *Back from Eternity* in 1956, and was subsequently featured in such

Barbara Eden on *I Dream of Jeannie* (Author's collection)

films as *Will Success Spoil Rock Hunter?,* (1957), *Twelve Hours to Kill* (1960), *Flaming Star* (1960), *The Wonderful World of the Brothers Grimm* (1962), *Seven Faces of Dr. Lao* (1964) and had starred on a TV situation comedy series, HOW TO MARRY A MILLIONAIRE (1957), it wasn't until she played Jeannie on the hit TV series I DREAM OF JEANNIE that she became a star. Eden was born in Tucson, Arizona, and attended Abraham Lincoln High School in San Francisco before embarking upon a career in show business. After her hit TV series *I Dream of Jeannie* left the air in 1970, Eden starred in a series of not very memorable made-for-TV films, before she became the star of another situation comedy, HARPER VALLEY P.T.A., which was based on a hit song, in 1981. Other made-for-TV films followed, and then Barbara appeared on the long-running DALLAS series as LeeAnn De La Vega, a role she played from 1990 to 1991. In 1991, Eden reprised her Jeannie role in a made-for-TV film *I Still Dream of Jeannie.* The actress has guest-starred on such TV series as BACHELOR FATHER, HIGHWAY PATROL, The MILLIONAIRE, PERRY MASON, GUNSMOKE, ROUTE 66, ADVENTURES IN PARADISE, The ANDY GRIFFITH SHOW, RAWHIDE, BURKE'S LAW, The ANDY WILLIAMS SHOW, and DONNY AND MARIE.

EDGE OF NIGHT, THE

Apr. 1956–Nov. 1975	CBS	Various daytime hours

Dec. 1975–Dec. 1984	ABC	Various daytime hours

For 19 years on CBS, and then for an additional nine years on ABC, *The Edge of Night* was one of television's most popular daytime serial dramas. The show was so popular with viewers, that thousands of letters protesting ABC's decision to cancel the program were received when it was announced that the show was to be terminated in 1984. When it was first seen on TV, *The Edge of Night* was a half-hour, five-days-a-week series and was scheduled during the late afternoon (therefore its title). Created by Irving Vendig, this soap opera was unlike any other daytime serial, since most of its story lines during the early years involved various crimes and court trials. The main character was an assistant district attorney, Mike Carr. As the series progressed, it became increasingly more romance-oriented.

The Edge of Night was produced by Procter and Gamble, and for the entire time it was on the air Henry Slesar was the show's head writer. From its debut in 1956 until 1962, Mike Carr was played by John Larkin, who had been lawyer Perry Mason on radio, before assuming the lead role on *The Edge of Night.* Larkin was replaced by Laurence Hugo, who played the role from 1962 until 1971, and then by Forrest Compton, who played Carr from 1971 until the series left the air in 1984. Carr's wife, Sarah Lane Carr, played by Teal Ames, was killed trying to save her daughter's life. This was one of the first deaths of a major character on a daytime TV series, and because Sarah was an extremely popular character, the number of letters protesting her demise was unprecedented. Both Larkin and Teal Ames appeared in front of the camera at the end of one of the shows to assure viewers that only the character, Sarah, and not the actress, Teal Ames, was dead.

Set in the town of Monticello, other characters seen on the show's early episodes were Sarah's brother, Jack Lane, played by Don Hastings (who later became a long-running character on AS THE WORLD TURNS); Betty Jane Lane, Jack's wife, played by Mary Alice Moore; Mattie Lane, Jack and Sarah's mother, originally played by Betty Garde and then by Peggy Allenby and Katherine Meskill; Winston Grimsley, a wealthy businessman who married Mattie, played by Walter Greaza; Bill Marceau, Monticello's chief of police, played by Carl Frank and then for many years by Mandel Kramer; Judy Marceau, his daughter, played by Joan Harvey; Martha, Bill Marceau's secretary and later wife, played by Teri Keane. Many of these actors remained on the series until shortly before it left the air. By the time *The Edge of Night* ended its run, an impressive 7,420 episodes of the series had been televised.

EDWARDS, DOUGLAS (1917–1990)

One of television's first network news anchormen, Douglas Edwards began his broadcasting career as a newscaster on CBS radio in 1942, switching to television in 1947. Edwards, born in Ada, Oklahoma, attended the University of Alabama, Emory University, and the University of Georgia. During World War II, CBS radio assigned Edwards to cover the war in London, where he worked with the legendary newsman Edward R. Murrow. Edwards anchored *Douglas Edwards and the News,* an evening news program, from 1948 until 1962. In 1962, Edwards was replaced by Walter CRONKITE on *The CBS Evening News,* but he continued to work at CBS until his retirement in 1988, hosting such programs as *Newsbreak, For Our Time,* and the *Mid-Day News.* In addition to his newsman chores, Edwards also hosted the MASQUERADE PARTY panel/quiz TV show and *The Armstrong Circle Theatre* dramatic anthology series from 1957 until 1961.

EDWARDS, RALPH (RALPH LIVINGSTONE EDWARDS 1913–)

Radio and TV announcer, actor, host, and producer, Ralph Edwards was born in Marino, Colorado, and attended UCLA before entering broadcasting as an announcer in 1936. Edward's conversational, casual style was unique at the time, and he attracted a great deal of attention from network officials and the public. During his radio days, Edwards was heard on such popular programs as *The Gumps, Against the Storm, Life Can Be Beautiful, The Original Amateur Hour,* and *Vic and Sade.* In 1940, Edwards created an audience-participation game show called TRUTH OR CONSEQUENCES, which he also hosted. The show, which had contestants performing outrageous, amusing acts such as swimming in a tank of Jell-O, blowing up as many balloons as possible, and trying to throw as large a number of rings around a spouse's head, which were described in detail to the radio-listening audience, became one of the most popular radio programs. In 1950, Edwards introduced *Truth or Consequences* to the TV audience. A natural for television, *Truth or Consequences* became an instant success and ran for an impressive 17 years. Edwards, who became busy with other projects, turned over his hosting chores to Jack Bailey in 1954, who was replaced by Bob Barker in 1956, when it became a syndicated show. For a few years in the 1940s, Edwards, because of his radio popularity, became a film actor and appeared in such films as *Radio Stars on Parade* (1945), *The Bamboo Blonde* (1946), and *Beat the Band* (1947). In 1952, Edwards introduced a series on television that became one of that medium's most successful shows, THIS IS YOUR LIFE. The show surprised a celebrity each week by announcing that his or her life was about to be featured on the show, and that people who had been a part of the celebrity's life (relatives, teachers, costars, etc.) would be appearing on the show as well. In 1954, Edwards hosted the series *Place the Face* (1953), *Funny Boners* (1954), and produced *It Could Be You* (1956), which did not prove as popular as either *Truth or Consequences* or *This Is Your Life,* and in 1982, Edwards gradually faded from the TV spotlight, although he continued to produce television programs.

EDWARDS, VINCE (VINCENT EDWARD ZOINO 1928–1996)

For five years in the early 1960s, Vince Edwards, who played the title role on the BEN CASEY hospital drama series, was one of the most popular actors on television. Edwards, born in Brooklyn, New York, was the son of Italian immigrant parents. In high school, Edwards was a state swimming champion, and he won a scholarship to Ohio State University. He made the Olympic swim team while in college, but an appendectomy put an end to his dream of Olympic glory. When Edwards appeared in a college play, he decided that he wanted to become an actor, and he enrolled at the American Academy of Dramatic Arts. Small roles on the stage followed, and in the 1940s, Edwards began an acting career, playing featured roles in such films as *Sailor Beware* (1951), *Mr. Universe* (1951), *Hiawatha* (1952), *I Am a Camera* (1955), *The Killing* (1956), *Murder by Contract* (1958), and *City of Fear* (1959). In 1961, Edwards was cast as Dr. Ben Casey on a new television series, *Ben Casey*. The show was an instant success and made Edwards a star. When *Ben Casey* left the air, Edwards appeared on the TV series *Matt Lincoln* (1970) and numerous made-for-TV films and several feature films, but his career never reached the heights he had enjoyed on *Ben Casey*. Edwards continues to appear in feature and made-for-TV films and was seen in *Dillinger* (1991), *Motorama* (1991), and *The Fear* (1995), and also guest-starred on such series as KNIGHT RIDER and MURDER, SHE WROTE.

EERIE, INDIANA

Sept. 1991–Nov. 1991	NBC	Sun. 7:30–8 P.M.
Dec. 1991–Feb. 1992	NBC	Sun. 7–7:30 P.M.
Mar. 1992	NBC	Sun. 7:30–8 P.M.
Mar. 1992–Apr. 1992	NBC	Sun. 7–7:30 P.M.

Although it was on the air for only one and a half years, this unusual series was very popular with youngsters, and attracted considerable attention among adult viewers as well. Produced by the same team that offered the UNSOLVED MYSTERIES series, to the *Eerie, Indiana* was about an imaginative 13-year-old boy who believed his new hometown was a strange place where supernatural things occurred. The boy, Marshall Teller, played by Omri Katz, and his friend, Simon Holmes, played by Justin Shenkarow, saw such weird things as a mocking raven who carried a glass eye in its beak, a mailman who carried a gun, and the supposedly dead Elvis Presley coming out of Marshall's suburban home. All these things could have logical explanations, but to Marshall and Simon they were cause for alarm. Marshall and Simon tagged and labeled all the evidence they found to prove that their hometown was indeed a hotbed of weird activities. Marshall's rather conventional family—his father, Edgar, an inventor for Things, Inc., played by Francis Guinan; his mother, Marilyn, played by Mary-Margaret Humes; and his sister, Syndi, played by Julie Condra—remained totally unaffected by Marshall's strange sightings and usually ignored Marshall and Simon's attempts to expose the supernatural things that were supposedly taking place in Eerie, Indiana. The series was created by Karl Schneider and Jose Rivera. In 1997, *Eerie, Indiana* was revived on the FOX network with a new cast and a new title, *Eerie, Indiana: The New Dimension*. Bill Switzer and Daniel Clark played Mitchell and Stanley, two new adolescents who also found their hometown somewhat odd.

EIGHT IS ENOUGH

Mar. 1977–May 1977	ABC	Tues. 9–10 P.M.
Aug. 1977–Mar. 1981	ABC	Wed. 8–9 P.M.
Mar. 1981–Aug. 1981	ABC	Sat. 8–9 P.M.

The "eight" in this series' title referred to the eight very different offspring of Tom Bradford, played by Dick VAN PATTEN, and his wife, Joan, played by Diana Hyland, on *Eight Is Enough*. The show was based on a novel of the same name by Thomas Braden, about what it is like to grow up in a large family. When Hyland died unexpectedly shortly after the show made its TV debut, Bradford became a widower on the series, and for a time, he struggled on alone supervising the upbringing of his eight children, ages eight to 23, until Sandra Sue Abbott ("Abby"), played by Betty Buckley, came into his life and took over the role of surrogate mother and confidante of the children. None of the Bradford children were anything alike, which allowed for many different story lines to develop on the show and kept viewers watching for four years. The Bradford children consisted of Nicholas (age eight), played by Adam Rich; Tommy (age 14), played by Willie Aames; Elizabeth (age 15), played by Connie Needham (Newton); Nancy (age 18), played by Dianne Kay; Susan (age 19), played by Susan Richardson; Joannie (age 20), played by Laurie Walters; Mary (age 21), played by Lani O'Grady; and David (age 23), originally played by Mark Hamill on the show's pilot and then, for most of the series' run, by Grant Goodeve. Over the four years the series was aired, the Bradford children grew up, fell in love, had boyfriend/girlfriend troubles, were married, had marital troubles, career troubles, fights with one another, and suffered through all the usual problems encountered by TV family members. In all, 112 episodes of *Eight Is Enough* were produced. Most of the cast was reunited for a made-for-TV film, *Eight Is Enough: A Family Reunion*, in 1987. Actress Mary Frann played the role of Abby in this production. They were reunited again in 1989 in another made-for-TV film, *An Eight Is Enough Wedding*, this time with actress Sandy Faison playing Abby. *Eight Is Enough* was created by Lee Rich and and Philip Caprice for Lorimar Productions.

ELLEN (AKA THESE FRIENDS OF MINE)

Mar. 1994–May 1994	ABC	Wed. 9:30–10 P.M.

Aug. 1994–Sept. 1994	ABC	Tues. 9:30–10 P.M.
Sept. 1994–Mar. 1995	ABC	Wed. 9:30–10 P.M.
Mar. 1995–Sep. 1995	ABC	Wed. 8:30–9 P.M.
Apr. 1995–May 1995	ABC	Tues. 9:30–10 P.M.
Sept. 1995–Nov. 1996	ABC	Wed. 8–8:30 P.M.
Dec. 1996–Feb. 1997	ABC	Wed. 9:30–10 P.M.
Mar. 1997–Apr. 1997	ABC	Tues. 8:30–9 P.M.
Apr. 1997–Mar. 1998	ABC	Wed. 9:30–10 P.M.
May 1998–July 1998	ABC	Wed. 9:30–10 P.M.

Similar in many ways to the successful *SEINFELD* situation comedy series, *Ellen* was about a group of friends who talked about the trivial, everyday events in their lives and shared confidences about one another's dates, sexual problems, and often, how to rid themselves of people they didn't like. Ellen Morgan, the heroine of the series, played by Ellen DEGENERES, was a bookstore/coffee shop manager. She was an insecure, but good-hearted, 30-year-old woman. Her inner circle of friends, when the series first went on the air, included her roommate, a slob, Adam Greene, played by Arye Gross; Ellen's longtime friend, Holly, played by Holly Fulger; and her wisecracking friend, Anita, played by Maggie Wheeler. In the *Ellen* show's second season, Holly and Anita departed and were replaced by a former childhood friend, a pushy woman named Paige, played by Joely Fisher, and Joe, played by David Anthony Higgins, who worked as a coffee server in the bookstore/coffee shop that Ellen now owned. Ellen's parents, Lois and Harold Morgan, who occasionally appeared on the series, were played by Alice Hirson and Steven Gilborn. Adam moved to London and left the series in 1995 and was replaced by Spence Kovack, played by Jeremy Piven, who became Ellen's new roommate. In 1997, Ellen decided to give up looking for the "perfect man" and announced to the world that it didn't matter anyway because she was, in fact, a lesbian. Her "coming out" episode, seen on April 30, 1997, attracted one of the largest audiences in television history, mainly due to the advance publicity and the fact that Degeneres had already previously admitted to the press that she was, and always had been, a lesbian. After the success of the "announcement" episode, *Ellen* began to lose viewers, and the final episode of the show was a spoof of Degeneres's show business career; she played a vaudeville performer in the 1920s, an early television star, and finally, as she is at present.

Eight Is Enough: (front row, left to right) Laurie Walters, Dick Van Patten, Adam Rich, Betty Buckley, Dianne Kay; (back) Susan Richardson, Connie Needham, Grant Goodeve, Willie Aames, and Lani O'Grady (Author's collection)

The cast of *Ellen*: (left to right) Joely Fisher, Jeremy Piven, Ellen DeGeneres, David Anthony Higgins, and Clea Lewis (Author's collection)

ELLERY QUEEN (THE ADVENTURES OF ELLERY QUEEN)

Oct. 1950–Dec. 1951	DUMONT	Thurs. 9–9:30 P.M.
Dec. 1951–Mar. 1952	ABC	Sun. 7:30–8 P.M.
Apr. 1952–Dec. 1952	ABC	Wed. 9–9:30 P.M.
Sept. 1958–Aug. 1959	NBC	Fri. 8–9 P.M.
Sept. 1975–Dec. 1975	NBC	Thurs. 9–10 P.M.
Jan. 1976–Sept. 1976	NBC	Sun. 8–9 P.M.

The Adventures of Ellery Queen had three incarnations on television, two in the 1950s and one in the 1970s. Ellery Queen, the master mystery writer sleuth whose father, Inspector Richard Queen, was a policeman, was created by mystery novelists Frederick Dannay and Manfred Bennington Lee. The books had originally been dramatized on a popular CBS radio series in 1939. A little more than a decade later, Ellery made his first television appearance. Richard Hart and then Lee Bowman played Ellery, and Florenze Ames played Inspector Richard Queen on the first *Ellery Queen* TV series, which ran for two years. The second series made its debut in 1958 and starred George Nader and then Lee Philips as Ellery, and Les Tremayne as Inspector Queen. It remained on the air for one season.

The third and final series, to date, starred Jim Hutton as Ellery and David Wayne as Inspector Queen and made its TV debut in 1975, remaining on the air for just one year. This series is fondly remembered, and viewers were disappointed when it was canceled. The format of the show was basically the same for all three TV versions, and the shows always ended with Ellery speaking to viewers, "Have you figured it out? Do you know who the murderer is?" before revealing the solution to the case.

EMERGENCY!

Jan. 1972–July 1972	NBC	Sat. 8–9 P.M.
Sept. 1972–Sept. 1977	NBC	Sat. 8–9 P.M.

Using a semidocumentary style that Jack WEBB had previously introduced in DRAGNET, *Emergency!* presented the life-and-death activities of the Los Angeles County Fire Department's Paramedical Rescue Service's Squad 51. The series centered on paramedics Roy DeSoto, played by Kevin Tighe, and John Gage, played by Randolph Mantooth, and followed the team's rescue victims into Rampart General Hospital, where the injured were treated by

Dr. Kelly Brackett, played by Robert Fuller; Nurse Dixie McCall, played by singer Julie London (Jack Webb's former wife); Dr. Joe Early, played by former bandleader Bobby Troup (London's current husband); and Dr. Mike Morton, played by Ron Pinkhard. Investigating many of the injured parties' misfortunes were Capt. Hammer, played by Dick Hammer, and Capt. Hank Stanley, played by Michael Norrell. Firemen Chet Kelly, Marco Lopez, and Mike Stoker, played by Tim Donnelly, Marco Lopez, and Mike Stoker respectively, were often involved in weekly rescues. The series remained popular for five years. In 1978, a two-hour *Emergency!* series was aired, which showed scenes from previous episodes of the series, and in 1973–76, *Emergency!* was seen as a Saturday morning cartoon series. *Emergency!* was produced by Robert A. Cinader for Jack Webb's Mark VII Productions.

EMERSON, FAYE (1917–1983)

Numerous sources claim that it was pioneer television performer Faye Emerson's name that was the inspiration for the "Emmy" Awards nickname. Emerson, born in Elizabeth, Louisiana, was a film actress in the 1940s and appeared in such films as *The Nurse's Secret* (1941), *Affectionately Yours* (1941), *Lady Gangster* (1942), *Destination Tokyo* (1943), *The Desert Song* (1943), *Hollywood Canteen* 1944), and many others, before becoming one of television's busiest actresses in 1948. Emerson appeared on such TV dramatic anthology programs as *The PHILCO TELEVISION PLAYHOUSE*, *The UNITED STATES STEEL HOUR*, *The GOODYEAR TELEVISION PLAYHOUSE* and on the *YOUR SHOW OF SHOWS* variety show, and as the star of her own series, *Paris Cavalcade of Fashions* in 1948, *The Faye Emerson Show* in 1950, and *Wonderful Town, U.S.A.* in 1951. In addition, Emerson became one of television's most popular game show hostesses and panelists, appearing on such programs as *Author Meets the Critic* (1952, as the show's moderator), *I'VE GOT A SECRET* (1952–58, as a panelist), and *Main Street to Broadway* (1953). In 1953, Faye, who had been previously married to President Franklin D. Roosevelt's son Elliott, also cohosted a series called *Faye and Skitch* with her then husband, Skitch Henderson. She was also the hostess of *Of All Things* in 1956 and a panelist on *What's In a Word* (1954) and *MASQUERADE PARTY* (1958–60). In the 1960s, Faye Emerson retired and settled into a life of relative obscurity, until her death from stomach cancer in 1983.

EMPTY NEST

Oct. 1988–June 1991	NBC	Sat. 9:30–10 P.M.
Aug. 1991–July 1994	NBC	Sat. 9–9:30 P.M.
Aug. 1994–Oct. 1994	NBC	Sat. 8:30–9 P.M.
Oct. 1994–Mar. 1995	NBC	Sat. 8–8:30 P.M.
June 1995–July 1995	NBC	Sat. 8–9 P.M.

Set in the same Miami neighborhood as NBC's hit series *GOLDEN GIRLS*, Empty Nest starred Richard MULLIGAN as Dr. Harry Weston, a pediatrician, whose wife, Libby, had died the year before. Although their three daughters were grown up, Dr. Weston's empty nest did not remain empty long, since two of his daughters, Barbara, a single undercover cop, and Carol, a neurotic divorcee, played by Kristy McNichol and Dinah Manoff respectively, moved back home to take care of their widowed father. Weston's youngest daughter, Emily, was away at college, and although she called home frequently, she never appeared on the series. As one of Miami's most eligible bachelors, Dr. Weston was constantly being pursued by elderly single women, including the Golden Girls themselves, played by Bea ARTHUR, Betty WHITE, and Rue MCCLANAHAN. As if having two daughters trying to run his life at home were not enough, Dr. Weston was also constantly being managed by his office receptionist, La Verne Todd a sharp-tongued woman with a thick Arkansas drawl, played by Park Overall. Weston's neighbor, Charley Dietz, played by David Leisure, was an offensive, skirt-chasing cruise ship employee who kept dropping in on Dr. Weston's home, trying to mooch a free meal and trade insults with Weston's daughter Carol. Harry Weston worried about his two at-home adult daughters, but he confided in his huge, hairy dog, Dreyfuss, who gave him his undivided attention. Other good friends were Weston's pediatric patients, including a little boy named Jeffrey Millstein, played by Edan Gross. In 1993, Estelle GETTY, as Sophia Petrillo of *Golden Girls*, which had departed the airwaves by that time, made frequent visits to Harry's home, searching for her former home. Sophia had returned to Shady Pines Retirement Home, located near Dr. Weston's house, as she constantly tried to run away from that dreaded institution.

EQUALIZER, THE

Sept. 1985–Mar. 1986	CBS	Wed. 10–11 P.M.
Mar. 1986–Aug. 1986	CBS	Tues. 10–11 P.M.
Sept. 1986–Feb. 1987	CBS	Wed. 10–11 P.M.
May 1987–June 1988	CBS	Wed. 10–11 P.M.
June 1988–Mar. 1989	CBS	Wed. 9–10 P.M.
Mar. 1989–May 1989	CBS	Thurs. 9–10 P.M.
June 1989–July 1989	CBS	Thurs. 10–11 P.M.
Aug. 1989–Sept. 1989	CBS	Thurs. 9–10 P.M.

When Robert McCall, a retired secret agent who had become disillusioned with the deceitful practices he had experienced during his years as a clandestine government operative, found himself idle, he decided to single-handedly champion the causes of people who found themselves victimized by forces beyond their control. Calling himself "The Equalizer" when he was a secret agent, McCall advertised in newspaper classified ads that his services were available, and it didn't take long for unfortunate victims to avail themselves of his services. With his young friend and confidante, the unconventional Mickey, doing most of his leg work for him, and his son, Scott, and various friendly members of the NYPD, assisting him from time to time,

McCall helped many unfortunates during the series' run. Even his former boss at the Agency, "Control," did what he could to help McCall. Robert McCall was played by British actor Edward Woodward. Mickey was played by Keith Szarabajka; Scott was played by William Zabka; Control was played by Robert Lansing; and Ron O'Neil, Chad Redding, and Eddie Jones were McCall's police department contacts. In 1987, Maureen Anderman joined *The Equalizer* as Pete O'Phelan, another former secret agent, who owned a small bistro that McCall often frequented.

ER

Sept. 1994	NBC	Mon. 9–11 P.M.
Sept. 1994–Feb. 1997	NBC	Thurs. 10–11 P.M.
Aug. 1997–present	NBC	Thurs. 10–11 P.M.

Set in the emergency room of Chicago's Cook County General Hospital, this one-hour dramatic series was the hit show of the 1994–95 season. Created by best-selling author Michael Crichton, who has a medical school degree, ER was similar to several series that had gone before it. ER was different, however, in that the fast-paced action, which was often filmed by cameras following the various doctors, nurses, and orderlies around the emergency room, gave the show a "breathless," realistic quality that was new to television. Sandwiched in between the dramatic hospital rescue scenes were personal stories about the loves and private lives of the people who worked in the hospital. At the center of ER's action were a womanizing, handsome pediatrician, Dr. Douglas Ross, played by George Clooney; Dr. Mark Greene, played by Anthony Edwards, a chief resident in the emergency room who had serious personal problems at home with a demanding lawyer wife; Jennifer, played by Christine Harnos, who was constantly on his back; Dr. Susan Lewis, played by Sherry Stringfield, a proper young woman always seeking "Mr. Right"; Dr. Peter Benton, played by Eriq LaSalle, a demanding African-American physician with a serious identity problem; Dr. John Carter, played by Noah Wyle, a sometimes inept last-year young resident; head nurse Carol Hathaway, played by Julianna Margulies, a troubled woman with a serious drug problem; and Dr. David Morgenstern, played by William H. Macy, the cranky head of the ER unit. Scurrying around the ER were various doctors, nurses, attendants, and orderlies played by Rick Rossovich, John Terry, Ellen Crawford, Abraham Benrubi, Conni Marie Brazleton, Yvette Freeman, Vanessa Marquez, and many others. In 1998, Kellie Martin joined the cast as the wide-eyed Lucy Knight, who worked for Nurse Hathaway when she opened a clinic. Recent changes included the return of cast member Sherry Stringfield and the departure of the highly popular Anthony Edwards.

ERNIE KOVACS SHOW, THE (AKA KOVACS UNLIMITED)

| Dec. 1952–Apr. 1953 | CBS | Tues. 8–9 P.M. |
| July 1956–Sept. 1956 | NBC | Mon. 8–9 P.M. |

Few comedians used television more effectively than Ernie KOVACS, often called a "comic genius." Kovacs' shows, which were not on the air as long as many people think, presented television comedy in a way no one before or after him has ever attempted. Just a few of the innovations Kovacs featured were blackouts; spoofs of TV commercials and TV programs; a group of musicians dressed in ape suits, the Nairobi Trio, which played classical music on various instruments; trick camera effects such as showing a fully dressed woman and several animals step out of a bathtub in which Kovacs was sitting and taking a bath; and an effeminate poet named Percy Dovetonsils, played by Kovacs with his hair plastered to his head and wearing thick, round glasses, who read his own poems from a large book. Other popular characters Kovacs played were Wolfgang Sauerbraten, a German disc jockey; Irving Wong, a Chinese songwriter; J. Walter Puppybreath; and Uncle Gruesome. Among Kovacs' regular cast were his wife, Edie Adams, who later became well known as the singer/spokeswoman for Muriel cigars who asked viewers "why don't you pick (me) up and smoke (me) sometime," and who did a perfect imitation of actress Marilyn Monroe; pianist Ernie Hartak and straight men Trigger Lund and Andy McKay. Regularly seen on the Kovacs shows were the features *You Asked to See It, Mr. Question Man,* and Clowdy Faire, Your Weather Girl. In the late 1950s to early 1960s, Kovacs was seen on several TV specials, but he did not have another regular on-the-air show after 1956. Kovacs' brilliant career was cut short in 1962, when he was killed in an automobile accident. In 1977, excerpts from several of his shows were aired in a special, *The Best of Ernie Kovacs.*

ERWIN, STUART (1903–1967)

After a long career as a film actor who appeared in hundreds of second-feature motion pictures beginning in 1929, Stu Edwin became one of television's first situation comedy stars when *The STU ERWIN SHOW* made its debut in 1950. Erwin, born in Squaw Valley, California, made his film debut at the age of 25 in *Mother Knows Best.* Before he entered films, Erwin had been a vaudeville performer. In 1929 alone, Erwin appeared in no less than 11 forgettable films, and was then appeared in the more successful films *The Playboy of Paris* (1930), *Working Girls* (1931), *The Big Broadcast* (1932), *The Crime of the Century* (1933), *Going Hollywood* (1933), *Palooka* (1934), *Pigskin Parade* (1936), *It Could Happen to You* (1939), *The Bride Came C.O.D.* (1941), and *Father Is a Bachelor* (1950), to name just a few. *The Stu Erwin Show* was a domestic comedy series in which Erwin played a bumbling husband and father of two daughters; he was the only male in a house full of women. The show remained popular for four years. After show left the air, Erwin was featured on several TV specials such as *Moochie of the Little League* (1959), in the films *For the Love of Mike* (1960) and *Son of Flubber* (1963), and was also a regular on the *Greatest Show on Earth* TV series in 1963. He also made guest-starring appearances on such series as *The ANDY GRIFFITH SHOW*, *PERRY MASON*, *The UNTOUCHABLES*, *WAGON TRAIN*, *GUNSMOKE*, *BONANZA*, *GREEN ACRES*, and *The BIG VALLEY*. Erwin's last appearance on TV came in the made-for-TV film *Shadow over Elveron* in 1968.

ESTRADA, ERIK (1949–   )

Before being cast as Officer Francis "Ponch" Poncherello on the TV police/adventure series *CHiPs*, which made him a star, Erik Estrada was featured in such films as *Parades* (1972), *The Cross and the Switchblade* (1972), *Airport 1975* (1974). *Midway* (1976), and *Trackdown* (1976), and was also seen on the *KOJAK, EMERGENCY!*, and *HAWAII FIVE-O* series, to name just a few. Estrada, born in New York City, was usually cast as a thug during his early career, but that changed once he played the heroic, handsome Officer Poncherello on *CHiPs*. The series was not on the air long before he began to receive thousands of letters from adoring female fans who were attracted to his dark, Latino looks. When *CHiPs* was canceled after six years on the air, Estrada starred in several feature films, none of which were very memorable, and he made guest-starring appearances on such series as *HUNTER*, *The Cosby Mysteries*, *CYBILL*, *L.A. LAW*, *The NANNY*, *SABRINA, THE TEENAGE WITCH*, and *WALKER, TEXAS RANGER*, among others. In the early 1990s, Estrada had a regular role on a popular Mexican *telenovela* (soap opera). Since Estrada did not speak Spanish, the actor had his lines fed to him through an earphone during the taping of the show.

ETHEL AND ALBERT

Apr. 1953–Dec. 1954	NBC	Sat. 7:30–8 P.M.
June 1955–Sept. 1955	NBC	Mon. 9:30–10 P.M.
Oct. 1955–July 1956	NBC	Fri. 10–10:30 P.M.

Few series captured the everyday, ordinary conversations of a married couple as accurately as *Ethel and Albert*. The carefully executed scripts of this domestic comedy were so realistic, many viewers thought that the dialogue was improvised by an actual husband and wife. For six years, *Ethel and Albert* was a popular radio program on ABC, and in 1951, it made a successful transition to television when it became a segment on *The KATE SMITH EVENING HOUR*. Peg LYNCH, who both wrote the scripts and played Ethel, and Alan Bunce, who played Albert, reprised their radio roles for television. The down-to-earth, familiar squabbles and exchanges that occurred between the happily married, but very human, Ethel and Albert Arbuckle, who lived in Sandy Harbor, were masterpieces of observation, and Lynch's scripts are still being performed in little theaters and at nostalgia conventions all around the country, giving testimony to their timelessness. In 1953, NBC made *Ethel and Albert* a weekly series, which remained on the air for three years. Trivial, but highly amusing subjects such as blown fuses, forgotten anniversaries, business trips, shopping, dinners

Ethel and Albert starring Peg Lynch and Alan Bunce (Author's collection)

that go bad, nosey neighbors, etc., were some of the commonplace incidents depicted in Lynch's scripts. What was familiar to any married couple was the way Ethel and Albert talked to each other, and that was what made *Ethel and Albert* so endearing.

EVENING SHADE

Sept. 1990–Nov. 1990	CBS	Fri. 8–8:30 P.M.
Nov. 1990–June 1991	CBS	Mon. 8–8:30 P.M.
June 1991	CBS	Mon. 9:30–10 P.M.
July 1991–May 1994	CBS	Mon. 8–8:30 P.M.

In spite of its impressive cast of well-known actors, its amiable and comfortably familiar small-town setting, and its well-written scripts, *Evening Shade* failed to attract the attention of viewers, and the show was canceled after just one year. Burt REYNOLDS played the show's central character, Wood Newton. Newton had been a star athlete in Evening Shade High School in Arkansas, went to college on an athletic scholarship, became a professional football player, retired, and then returned to Evening Shade to coach the Evening Shade Mules football team at the same high school he had attended as a boy. In spite of Wood's background, however, the Mules had failed to win a game in two years. Other cast members on *Evening Shade* included Marilu HENNER as Wood's wife, Ada, to whom he had been married for 16 years, and their four children, Taylor, a quarterback on the high school team, Molly, Will, and the baby, Emily, who was born shortly after the series first went on the air; they were played by Jay R. Ferguson, Melissa Martin (and then Candace Hutson), Jacob Parker, and Alexa Vega respectively. Other regular characters on the series were Wood's friends Dr. Harlan Eldridge, played by veteran character actor Charles Durning; Ponder Blue, the philosophical owner of Ponder Blue's Barbecue Villa, played by Ossie Davis; Evan Evans, Ada's father, played by Hal Holbrook; Frieda Evans, Ada's pushy aunt, played by Elizabeth Ashley; Merleen Eldridge, Dr. Eldridge's young wife, a former stripper, played by Ann Wedgeworth; and Herman Stiles, a wimpy-looking math teacher, whom Wood took under his wing, amusingly played by Michael Jeter, who became the series' most popular character. *Evening Shade* was created by Linda Bloodworth-Thomason, who had previously been responsible for the successful DESIGNING WOMEN series.

EVERETT, CHAD (RAYMOND LEE CRAMTON 1936–)

Before becoming a television star playing Dr. Joe Gannon on the popular MEDICAL CENTER series, Chad Everett was a regular on The DAKOTAS western series in 1963, and appeared in such films as *The Chapman Report* (1962), *The Singing Nun* (1965), and *The Impossible Years* (1968), among others. Everett was born in South Bend, Indiana, and after attending college, he embarked upon an acting career. Small roles on the stage and on such TV series as *Bronco, 77* SUNSET STRIP, HAWAIIAN EYE, CHEYENNE, ROUTE 66, and The MAN FROM U.N.C.L.E., in the late 1950s to early 1960s, eventually led to *Medical Center*. After *Medical Center* left the air, the handsome actor failed to land another starring role that capitalized on his popularity, but he kept busy appearing in supporting roles in such films as *The Firechasers* (1970), and the TV miniseries *Centennial* (1978) and *The French Atlantic Affair* (1979). Eventually, he did play a leading role on the less than successful

Hagen TV series (1980). In 1981, Everett starred on another ill-fated series, *The Rousters,* and in 1994, starred on the more slightly more successful *McKenna* series. Supporting roles in such films as *Airplane II: The Sequel* (1982), *Fever Pitch* (1985), *Official Denial* (1994), *Psycho* (1998), and in the made-for-TV films *Freefall* (1999) and *Mulholland Dr.* (2001) followed. Everett was also a frequent guest star and semiregular on such series as MURDER, SHE WROTE, CYBILL, TOUCHED BY AN ANGEL, CAROLINE IN THE CITY, JUST SHOOT ME, and *Melrose Place.*

EVERYBODY LOVES RAYMOND

Sept. 1996–Feb. 1997	CBS	Fri. 8:30–9 P.M.
Mar. 1997–June 1998	CBS	Mon. 8:30–9 P.M.
June 1998–Aug. 1998	CBS	Mon. 8:30–9:30 P.M.
Aug. 1998–Sept. 1998	CBS	Mon. 9–10 P.M.
Sept. 1998	CBS	Mon. 9–9:30 P.M.
Apr. 1999–present	CBS	Wed. 8–8:30 P.M.

Comedian Ray Romano plays Raymond Barone, the married father of three children who is a successful sportswriter for *New York Newsday*. Raymond loves his wife, Debra, played by Patricia Heaton, and his children, daughter Ally and twin sons Michael and Geoffrey, played by Madylin Sweeten and Sawyer and Sullivan Sweeten. Raymond's life would be perfect, except that his house is across the street from his parents, Marie and Frank Barone, played by Doris Roberts and Peter Boyle, who are always dropping in on Ray and his family. Marie and Frank constantly try to impose their way of doing things on him. Raymond's older brother, Robert, a hulking, divorced policeman, played by Brad Garrett, lives with his parents, and Raymond is constantly asked to reassure his somewhat insecure brother that he is not the loser his parents seem to think he is. *Everybody Loves Raymond* is loosely based upon Ray Romano's real-life experiences, which were the basis for his stand-up comedy act. The popular series has been consistently nominated for Emmy Awards since it made its TV debut in 1996.

F TROOP

| Sept. 1965–Aug. 1966 | ABC | Tues. 9–9:30 P.M. |
| Sept. 1966–Aug. 1967 | ABC | Thurs. 8–8:30 P.M. |

An incompetent troop of post–Civil War soldiers stationed in the fictional Fort Courage, located somewhere out in Missouri, were the main characters in this western spoof. Leading the bungling F Troop was Capt. William Parmenter, played by Ken Berry. Under his command were Sgt. Morgan O'Rourke, played by Forrest Tucker; Cpl. Randolph Agarn, played by Larry Storch; the troop's bugler, Hannibal Dobbs, played by James Hampton; and Troopers Duffy and Vanderbilt, played by Bob Steele and Joe Brooks. Frequent visitors to the fort were Wrangler Jane (Jane Angelica Thrift), a pretty-but-rough Calamity Jane–like character, played by Melody Patterson; and the Indians, Chief Wild Eagle, played by Frank deKova, and Crazy Cat, played by Don Diamond. Most of the humor on this situation comedy came from the troop's total ineptitude and constant bungling. A hilarious assortment of Native American characters, played by well-known performers, included Roaring Chicken, played by the ancient (by that time) character actor Edward Everett Horton, and his aging Indian princess daughter, played by Cathy Lewis; the 147-year-old Flaming Arrow, played by Phil Harris; Bald Eagle, played by Don Rickles; and Wise Owl, an Indian detective, played by Milton Berle. Also appearing in some very funny episodes of *F Troop* were comedian Paul Lynde as Sgt. Ramsden, a singing Mountie, and Henry Gibson, as Wrongo Starr, a jinxed cavalry trooper. *F Troop* was produced by Hy Averback, who also produced *At Ease, The Don Rickles Show, Mrs. G. Goes to College,* and *Needles and Pins.*

F-Troop: (sitting) Ken Berry (Capt. William Parmenter), Melody Patterson (Jane); (standing) Forrest Tucker (Sgt. O'Rourke) and Larry Storch (Cpl. Agarn) (Author's collection)

FACTS OF LIFE, THE

| Aug. 1979–Sept. 1979 | NBC | Fri. 8:30–9 P.M. |
| Mar. 1980–May 1980 | NBC | Fri. 8:30–9 P.M. |

June 1980–July 1980	NBC	Wed. 9:30–10 P.M.
Aug. 1980–Oct. 1980	NBC	Fri. 8:30–9 P.M.
Nov. 1980–Oct. 1981	NBC	Wed. 9:30–10 P.M.
Oct. 1981–Aug. 1985	NBC	Wed. 9–9:30 P.M.
Sept. 1985–June 1986	NBC	Sat. 8:30–9 P.M.
June 1986–May 1987	NBC	Sat. 8–8:30 P.M.
June 1987–July 1987	NBC	Wed. 9–9:30 P.M.
July 1987–Sept. 1988	NBC	Sat. 8–8:30 P.M.

The Facts of Life was a spin-off of the popular DIFF'RENT STROKES series, and the star of this new show, Charlotte Rae, who played Mrs. Edna Garrett on *Diff'rent Strokes*, repeated her role. Mrs. Garrett, the Drummond's housekeeper on *Diff'rent Strokes*, became a housemother at a prestigious private girls' school called Eastland. Mrs. Garrett, a kindhearted, understanding woman, was in charge of the wealthy, attractive 15-year-old Blair Warner, played by Lisa Whelchel; Nancy Olson, a well-adjusted and confident 14-year old, played by Felice Schachter; Sue Ann Weaver, also 14, cute and boy-crazy, played by Julie Piekarski; Dorothy "Tootie" Ramsey, 11, the resident gossip, played by Kim Fields; and Natalie Green, a plump, lovable, and trusting girl played by Mindy Cohn. By the second season, two of the girls at the Eastland school, Nancy and Sue Ann, had departed, leaving Blair, Tootie, and Natalie as occupants in Mrs. Garrett's house. A 16-year-old tomboy named Jo Polniaczek, played by Nancy McKeon, then

The Facts of Life: (sitting, left to right) Mindy Cohn (Natalie), Nancy McKeon (Jo), and Kim Fields (Tootie); (standing, left to right) Lisa Whelchel (Blair) and Charlotte Rae (Mrs. Garrett) (Author's collection)

joined the girls at Eastland. As the series continued, many new developments took place. In addition to her housemother duties Mrs. Garrett became Eastland's dietitian, and another new character, Howard the cook, played by Hugh Gillan, joined the cast. The headmaster at Eastland, Mr. Bradley, played by John Lawlor, was succeeded by Mr. Harris, played by Kenneth Mars, and then by Mr. Parker, played by Roger Perry, whose daughter, Molly, was played by Molly Ringwald. Blair eventually graduated from Eastland, and attended nearby Langley College; Mrs. Garrett opened a gourmet food shop, "Edna's Edibles"; Jo joined Blair at Langley College; Mrs. Garrett eventually left Eastland altogether in 1986, her housemother role taken over by Cloris LEACHMAN playing Beverly Ann Stickle in 1986. Two years after Leachman joined the cast, *The Facts of Life* was canceled.

FALCON CREST

Dec. 1981–May 1985	CBS	Fri. 10–11 P.M.
Sept. 1985–Mar. 1990	CBS	Fri. 10–11 P.M.
Apr. 1990–May 1990	CBS	Thurs. 9–10 P.M.

Another prime-time soap opera that capitalized on the success of DALLAS was *Falcon Crest*. Like *Dallas*, *Falcon Crest* centered on wealthy ruthless people, but this time they were wine-rich and not oil-rich. Academy Award–winning actress Jane Wyman played Angela Channing, an autocratic, power-hungry woman who owned a winery, Falcon Crest, and ran her business with ruthless authority. The winery was located in the fictitious Tuscany Valley, located in the Napa Valley near San Francisco. In addition to Wyman, the original cast featured Robert Foxworth as Angela's nephew, Chase Gioberti, who came into his share of the Falcon Crest winery when his father mysteriously died; Abby Dalton as Angela's divorced daughter, Julia Cumson; Lorenzo Lamas as Julia's son, Lance Cumson, who frequently conspired with Angela; Margaret Ladd as Angela's unstable daughter, Emma Channing; Susan Sullivan as Chase's wife, Maggie; Jamie Ross as Chase and Maggie's daughter, Victoria; William R. Moses as their son, Cole; Chau-Li Chi as the Channings' butler; and Nick Ramos, Mario Marcelino, Stephen Elliott, Douglas Channing, Ana Alicia, Carlos Romero, David Selby, Shannon Tweed, Sarah Douglas, Mel Ferrer, Roy Thinnes, Cliff Robertson, Mary Kate McGreehan, Laura Johnson, and former film star Lana Turner as Chase's mother, Jacqueline Perrault, who was eventually killed wrestling for a gun with Julia Cumson at the end of the 1982–83 season. *Falcon Crest* enjoyed its most popular year during the 1983–84 season. Remaining on the air for an impressive nine years, the series added many new names to its roster of famous performers over the next several years, including Italian film star Gina Lollobrigida, Parker Stevenson, J. Paul Freeman, English film star Simon MacCorkindale, former pop star Apollonia Kotero, Cesar Romero, Morgan Fairchild, Kim Novak, DAYS OF OUR LIVES star Kristian Alfonzo, and many other actors who had less recognizable names. By the

1989–90 season, *Falcon Crest* had dropped to number 63 of TV's most popular 100 shows, and the producer decided it was time to cancel the series. Interestingly the show was popular enough for Spring Mountain Vineyards, where exteriors for the series were filmed, to market two wines using "Falcon Crest" as a label.

FALK, PETER (1927–   )

Although Peter Falk's list of acting credits is formidable, he is best known for playing the somewhat scruffy police detective. Columbo on the popular COLUMBO made-for-TV films. Originally one of three alternating detective movies seen on NBC's *Sunday Mystery Movie* series, *Columbo* has been on television from 1971 until (as of this writing) 2000, when the TV film *Columbo: Murder With Too Many Notes* was aired. Peter Falk was born in New York City, but moved to Ossining, New York, with his parents, where he attended Ossining High School. He first became interested in acting when he substituted for a boy who was playing a detective in a school play but who became ill. Falk's parents were not too keen on his becoming an actor, so he attended college and became a certified public accountant, working for the Budget Bureau of the state of Connecticut. Not able to forget his dream of becoming an actor, Falk studied with celebrated acting coaches Eva Le Gallienne and Sanford Meisner in New York, and eventually began to get work in off-Broadway plays in New York City. An operation for cancer that removed one of his eyes when he was three years old put a damper on his becoming a leading man, so Falk became a character actor, appearing on such television series as NAKED CITY, The UNTOUCHABLES, HAVE GUN WILL TRAVEL, ALFRED HITCHCOCK PRESENTS, The TWILIGHT ZONE, and WAGON TRAIN in the late 1950s and early 1960s, and in such feature films as *Pretty Boy Floyd* (1960), *Murder, Inc.* (1960), *Pocketful of Miracles* (1961), *It's a Mad, Mad, Mad, Mad, Mad World* (1963), *Robin and the 7 Hoods* (1964), and *Brigadoon* (1966). In 1968, Falk played Lt. Columbo for the first time in a made-for-TV film *Prescription: Murder*. He subsequently played Columbo in over 60 TV films in the years that followed. In addition to playing Columbo, Falk also appeared in such successful feature films as *Murder by Death* (1976), *The Great Muppet Caper* (1981), *The Princess Bride* (1987), and more recently, *Lakeboat, Enemies of Laughter, 3 Days of Rain, Made,* and *Corky Bonono,* all released in 2000 and 2001.

FAME

| Jan. 1982–Aug. 1983 | NBC | Thurs. 8–9 P.M. |

Although it was on TV only briefly, the drama series *Fame,* based on a popular film of the same name, is fondly remembered by many viewers. The series took place at New York City's famed High School for the Performing Arts and was about inner city youths who wanted to become actors, dancers, and singers. The young people exhibited enthusiasm, energy, and raw talent. Featured on the show were Bruno Martelli, played by Lee Curreri, a talented, if arrogant, keyboard musician; Coco Hernandez, played by Erica Gimpel, a career-driven singer and dancer; Danny Amatullo, played by Carlo Imperato, a would-be comedian; Doris Schwartz, played by Valerie Landsburg, an actress-writer-comedienne who had a big ego in spite of her pleasant demeanor; Leroy Johnson, played by Gene Anthony Ray, a gifted dancer from the black ghetto; Montgomery MacNeil, played by P. R. Paul, whose mother was a well-known actress; and Julie Miller, played by Lori Singer, a cellist who was an outsider from Grand Rapids, Michigan. Also appearing as regulars were Debbie Allen as the hard-driving dance teacher Lydia Grant; Albert Hague as music teacher Benjamin Shorofsky; Michael Thoma as drama teacher Mr. Crandall; and Carol Mayo Jenkins as an English teacher Elizabeth Sherwood. Debbie Allen, Albert Hague, Gene Anthony Ray, and Lee Curreri repeated their roles in the popular film.

FAMILY

Mar. 1976–Feb. 1978	ABC	Tues. 10–11 P.M.
May 1978	ABC	Tues. 10–11 P.M.
Sept. 1978–Mar. 1979	ABC	Thurs. 10–11 P.M.
Mar. 1979–Apr. 1979	ABC	Fri. 8–9 P.M.
May 1979	ABC	Thurs. 10–11 P.M.
Dec. 1979–Feb. 1980	ABC	Mon. 10–11 P.M.
Mar. 1980	ABC	Mon. 9–10 P.M.
June 1980	ABC	Wed. 8–9 P.M.

An evening soap opera that was first seen as a miniseries and then became a weekly program, *Family* centered on the problems of the middle-class Lawrence family of Pasadena, California. A low-keyed, gentle, family-oriented series, ABC did everything in its power to keep *Family* on the air, mainly in order to silence critics who were saying that television programs were becoming much too violent. The patriarch of the family, Doug Lawrence, played by James Broderick, was an independent, kindly lawyer. His wife, Kate, played by Sada Thompson, was even-tempered and sensible. The Lawrence's three children were Nancy, Willie, and Letitia (aka Buddy). Nancy was played by Elayne Heilveil and then for most of the series by Meredith Baxter Birney. Gary Frank and Kristy McNichol played Willie and Buddy. On the series' first episode, Nancy discovered that her husband, Jeff, played by John Rubinstein, was having an affair. Willie, young, vulnerable, and idealistic, then became interested in an unwed mother, but eventually fell in love with a girl who had a terminal illness. With her parents involved in trying to solve the problems of their two oldest children, Buddy, feeling unwanted, ran away from home. While Kate was trying to deal with all her children's problems, she discovered that she had breast cancer, and then Doug was temporarily blinded in an automobile accident. The family dealt with dying grandparents, Doug's alcoholic sister's misadventures, and numerous other domestic problems during the series' four turbulent, but audience-pleasing, years on the air. *Family* was created by Jay Presson Allen and was produced by Mike Nichols, Aaron SPELLING, and Leonard Goldberg.

FAMILY FEUD

July 1976–June 1985	ABC	Mon.–Fri. Various times
1977–1983	Syndicated series	Various times and stations
1988–1995	Syndicated series	Various times and stations
July 1988–May 1991	CBS	Mon.–Fri. Daytime
June 1992–Sept. 1993	CBS	Mon.–Fri. Daytime

One of the many game/panel shows produced by Mark GOODSON and Bill TODMAN, *Family Feud* was a popular program that pitted two families against each other as they tried to match responses to questions previously given to 100 people. Five family members played on each of the two teams. Richard DAWSON hosted both the network and the syndicated daytime shows, and he is the host most closely identified with the series. Dawson's affectionate treatment of contestants on the show and his gentle chiding made him extremely popular with both the families who were competing and with the studio and viewing audiences. In 1988, when *Family Feud* returned to the air after a five-year absence on both CBS and as a syndicated show, Ray Combs was its host. The series was revived again in 1992–93, after one year off the air, as an hour-long network show called *The New Family Feud*. Another syndicated *Family Feud* series surfaced in 1994 with Richard Dawson returning as host, much to the delight of viewers. This show was also one hour long. Special *Family Feud* shows featured teams of famous sports stars, show business celebrities, and the casts of TV series competing against each other.

FAMILY MATTERS

Sept. 1989–Apr. 1991	ABC	Fri. 8:30–9 P.M.
Apr. 1991–May 1991	ABC	Fri. 9–9:30 P.M.
May 1991–Aug. 1991	ABC	Fri. 8:30–9 P.M.
Aug. 1991–May 1997	ABC	Fri. 8–8:30 P.M.
June 1997–Aug. 1997	ABC	Sat. 8–8:30 P.M.
Sept. 1997–Oct. 1997	CBS	Fri. 8–8:30 P.M.
Nov. 1997–Jan. 1998	CBS	Fri. 9–9:30 P.M.
June 1998–July 1998	CBS	Fri. 9–9:30 P.M.

The amusing problems of a middle-class African-American family were the focus of this half-hour situation comedy that was very popular for seven years. *Family Matters* was a spin-off of *Perfect Strangers,* on which Jo Marie Payton, who played a leading role on *Family Matters,* had attracted attention as a sarcastic elevator operator. *Family Matters* centered on the Winslow family, who lived in a suburb of Chicago. Carl, a heavyset policeman always blustering about one thing or another, was played by Reginald VelJohnson; his sharp-tongued wife, Harriette, was played by Jo Marie Payton; their children, Eddie (age 15), Laura (age 13), and Judy (age nine), were played by Darius McCrary, Kellie Shanygne Williams, and Jaimee Foxworth; Grandma Winslow was played by Rosetta LeNoire; Harriette's recently widowed sister, Rachel, was played by Thelma Hopkins; and Rachel's infant son, Richie, was played by Joseph and Julius Wright, and as he grew older by Bryton McClure. The real star of the show, however, was a teenaged nerd, a neighbor of the Winslow family named Steve Urkel, who was played by Jaleel White. Steve had a mad crush on Laura, and was constantly dropping in on the Winslow home. Steve Urkel's oversized glasses, his too-short trousers, which he wore up by his chest, his high-pitched nasal voice, and his awkward, grasshopperlike walk, had viewers doubled over with laughter the entire seven years the series was on the air. In 1995, Urkel moved in with the Winslows when his parents left the country without him. When *Family Matters* came to the end of its run in 1998, Urkel and Laura, who were 20 years old by that time, had miraculously become engaged. Urkel had helped Carl get a promotion to captain on the police force, and he had become the first student astronaut after he won a contest. When he blasted off on a shuttle to outer space, the mission went wrong, but Steve performed a space walk, removed a satellite that had crashed into the shuttle, and saved the day. *Family Matters* was created by William Bickley and Michael Warren. The theme song was "What a Wonderful World," sung by Louis Armstrong, when the series first went on the air, but in 1989, it became "As Days Go By."

FAMILY TIES

Sept. 1982–Mar. 1983	NBC	Wed. 9:30–10 P.M.
Mar. 1983–Aug. 1983	NBC	Mon. 8:30–9 P.M.
Aug. 1983–Dec. 1983	NBC	Wed. 9:30–10 P.M.
Jan. 1984–Aug. 1987	NBC	Thurs. 8:30–9 P.M.
Aug. 1987–Sept. 1987	NBC	Sun. 8–9 P.M.
Sept. 1987–Sept. 1989	NBC	Sun. 8–8:30 P.M.

Family Ties was the situation comedy that made Michael J. FOX a star. Alex P. Keaton, a conservative 1980s young man was the son of former hippie parents who themselves were young in the 1960s, Elyse and Steve Keaton, played by Meredith Baxter Birney and Michael Gross. The show reflected the changes that the United States was going through politically at the time when Ronald Reagan was elected president. The series was set in Columbus, Ohio. The patriarch of the Keaton family, Steven, still embraced the liberal ideals of his youth, even though he was, by that time, the manager of public TV station WKS-TV, and his wife, Elyse, was an architect. Seventeen-year-old son Alex, was a totally materialistic reactionary who even had a picture of ultraconservative William F. Buckley, Jr., on the wall over his bed. The Keatons' two other children, Mallory and Jennifer, played by Justine Bateman and Tina

The Keatons of *Family Ties:* (front) Michael J. Fox, Meredith Baxter Birney, Tina Yothers; (back) Michael Gross, Justine Bateman (Author's collection)

FANTASY ISLAND

Jan. 1978–Aug. 1979	ABC	Sat. 10–11 P.M.
Aug. 1979–Oct. 1979	ABC	Fri. 8–9 P.M.
Oct. 1979–Aug. 1984	ABC	Sat. 10–11 P.M.
Sept. 1998–Dec. 1998	ABC	Sat. 9–10 P.M.
Jan. 1999–present	ABC	Sat. 10–11 P.M.

Because of the success of THE LOVE BOAT and its idealized cruises, ABC decided to launch similar series. *Fantasy Island* was an hour-long series about people who are guests on an exotic tropical island somewhere in the South Pacific, where their wildest dreams come true. The proprietor of the Fantasy Island resort was Mr. Roarke, played by Ricardo Montalban, who made sure his guests received the most fulfilling vacation possible. His diminutive assistant on the island was Tattoo, played by Herve Villechaize. At the beginning of each week's drama, Roarke and Tattoo were seen waiting to greet their guests who were arriving by airplane. Viewers looked forward to hearing Tattoo exclaim "Da plane . . . da plane," as the airplane bearing the weekly guests approached the airfield. During the series' 1981–82 season, Wendy Schaal joined Montalban and Villechaize as a regular on the show, playing Roarke's goddaughter, Julie, and in 1983, Christopher Hewett became Roarke's new assistant, Lawrence. Usually there were two major stories each week, and the show's action shifted back and forth between them, as the characters' fantasies were fulfilled. Guests on *Fantasy Island* consisted of a

Yothers, were also children of the 1980s. Mallory would wear only designer jeans and thought that most things, especially politics, were boring. Jennifer, on the other hand, was only nine years old when the series first went on the air, and she just wanted to be a kid. A new baby of the family, Andrew, played by Brian Bonsall, was born during the series' run. Other regular characters featured Ellen Reed, Alex's first girlfriend, played by Tracy Pollan (who became Fox's real-life wife); Laureen Miller, Alex's next girlfriend, played by Courteney Cox; Nick Moore, Mallory's sculptor boyfriend, played by Scott Valentine; and Alex's somewhat dim friend, Irwin "Skippy" Handelman, played by Marc Price. The often contrasting attitudes of the loving and devoted parents and their bewildering offspring led to much of the show's comedy. As *Family Ties* progressed, the show continued to parody Reagan-era values, but it also tackled more serious themes, such as teenage drunk driving accidents, racial prejudice, and Steven's sudden heart attack. By the time the series left the air, after seven successful seasons, Alex had graduated from college and accepted a good job at a large Wall Street firm. *Family Ties* was created by Gary David Goldberg. The show's theme song was "Without Us" by Jeff Barry and Tom Scott, which was sung by Johnny Mathis and Deniece Williams.

Ricardo Montalban (Mr. Rourke) and Herve Villechaize (Tattoo) of *Fantasy Island* (Author's collection)

wide variety of people played by well-known actors from other TV series, and occasionally from films, and included such familiar faces as Henry Gibson, Georgia Engel, Marcia Strassman, Christopher George and Dennis James. Roddy McDowell was a semiregular on the show and played Mr. Mephistopheles. *Fantasy Island's* exterior scenes were filmed at the Arboretum, a real tropical paradise located 23 miles from Los Angeles. In 1999, *Fantasy Island* was revived with English actor Malcolm McDowell playing Mr. Rourke. That series was not a success and remained on the air for less than a full season. The original series was produced by Aaron SPELLING and Leonard Goldberg.

FARMER'S DAUGHTER, THE

Sept. 1963–Nov. 1963	ABC	Fri. 9:30–10 P.M.
Dec. 1963–Sept. 1964	ABC	Wed. 8:30–9 P.M.
Sept. 1964–June 1965	ABC	Fri. 8–8:30 P.M.
June 1965–Oct. 1965	ABC	Mon. 9:30–10 P.M.
Nov. 1965–Sept. 1966	ABC	Fri. 9:30–10 P.M.

Based on a popular 1947 film that won Loretta YOUNG an Academy Award as Best Actress of the Year, *The Farmer's Daughter* was a half-hour situation comedy about a Swedish–American farm girl named Katrin "Katy" Holstrum, who goes to Washington to seek the help of her congressman, Glen Morley, to keep her family's farm, and she remains in Washington as the governess of Morley's two motherless sons. Katy was played by Inger Stevens, Morley by William Windom, and Morley's young sons, Steve (age four) and Danny (age eight) by Mickey Sholdar and Rory O'Brien. Also seen regularly was Morley's mother, played by Cathleen Nesbitt, and the Morley's butler, Cooper, played by Philip Coolidge. Appearing occasionally were Alice Frost and Walter Sande as Katy's parents, Mama and Pappa Holstrom, and Nancy DeCarl as Katy's girlfriend, Pam. Predictably, Katy and Morley fell in love, and in one of the most viewed telecasts of the time, they were married on November 5, 1965. The event was heavily publicized, and the famous Washington hostess and former ambassador to Luxembourg, Pearl Mesta, even threw a party to commemorate the event. It was attended by members of the cast and over 300 Washington, D.C., notables. In spite of the popularity of this episode, *The Farmer's Daughter* failed to retain the audience it needed to keep it on the air, and in 1966, after three seasons, the show was canceled.

FATHER DOWLING MYSTERIES, THE

Jan. 1989–Mar. 1989	NBC	Fri. 8–9 P.M.
Jan. 1990–July 1991	ABC	Thurs. 8–9 P.M.
Aug. 1991	ABC	Thurs. 9–10 P.M.
Aug. 1991–Sept. 1991	ABC	Thurs. 8–9 P.M.

Even though it was canceled by NBC after only three months, *Father Dowling Mysteries* was picked up by ABC the following year and ran for two years. When the series left the air in 1992, many viewers expressed their disappointment at the cancellation and wrote letters of protest to ABC.

Catholic priest Father Frank Dowling, played by Tom BOSLEY, seemed to have a talent for stumbling upon murders, in addition to performing his sacred duties. Dowling was assisted in his crime-solving activities by young Sister Stephanie (aka Sister Steve), played by Tracy Nelson, who had a rather worldly background and could pick locks, cut a deck of cards like a professional dealer, and was totally streetwise. Father Dowling and Sister Steve managed to gain entry to places ordinary people might not so easily infiltrate, which made their mystery-solving that much more successful. Working at St. Michael's rectory, where Father Dowling lived, was Marie, a busybody housekeeper, played by veteran character actress Mary Wickes. Marie often became involved in Father Dowling and Sister Stephanie's various capers. Also living at the rectory was a young priest, Father Prestwick, played by James Stephens, who was in a world of his own and never understood what was going on around him. *The Father Dowling Mysteries* series was based on the mystery novels of Ralph McInerny.

FATHER KNOWS BEST

Oct. 1954–Mar. 1955	CBS	Sun. 10–10:30 P.M.
Aug. 1955–Sept. 1958	NBC	Wed. 8:30–9 P.M.
Sept. 1958–Sept. 1960	CBS	Mon. 8:30–9 P.M.
Oct. 1960–Sept. 1961	CBS	Tues. 8–8:30 P.M.
Oct. 1961–Feb. 1962	CBS	Wed. 8–8:30 P.M.
Feb. 1962–Sept. 1962	CBS	Mon. 8:30–9 P.M.
Sept. 1962–Dec. 1962	ABC	Sun. 7–7:30 P.M.
Dec. 1962–Apr. 1963	ABC	Fri. 8–8:30 P.M.

The legendary *Father Knows Best* situation comedy was one of television's earliest and most fondly remembered family series. The show was purportedly about the typical American family of the 1950s, and became the inspiration for similar family-oriented TV situations comedies. The star of *Father Knows Best*, Robert YOUNG, was already a familiar face to millions of moviegoers throughout the 1930s and 1940s. Young played Jim Anderson, the wise, loving, sensible, reliable husband of Margaret Anderson, a patient, understanding, loyal wife and mother who was totally devoted to her family. Margaret was played by Jane WYATT. Jim and Margaret Anderson's three children were Betty, a girl of 17 when the series first went on the air, played by Elinor Donahue; James, Jr., aka Bud, a rambunctious adolescent boy of 14, played by Billy Gray; and the "baby" of the family and father's pet, nine-year-old daughter Kathy, aka Kitten, played by Lauren Chapin. The Andersons lived in a comfortable, large, and beautiful home in Springfield, located somewhere in the Midwest. Jim Anderson made a good living working for the General Insurance Company, Betty was a stay-at-home wife and mother, and their three children were swell youngsters. Originally a popular radio program that made its debut in 1949, *Father Knows Best* moved to television when the radio show left the air in 1955. Other regular characters on the series were Miss Thomas, played by Sarah Selby; Ed and Myrtle Davis, played by Robert Foulk and Vivi Jannis; Dotty Snow, played by Yvonne Lime; Kippy Watkins, played by Paul Wallace; Claude Messner, played by Jimmy Bates; Doyle Hobbs, played by Roger Smith; Ralph Little, played by Robert Chapman; April Adams, played by Sue George; and Joyce Kendall, played by Jymme (Roberta) Shore. Natividad Vacio played the Andersons' gardener, Frank "Fronk" Smith, a newly naturalized American citizen. In all, 208 episodes of *Father Knows Best* were filmed between 1955 and 1960. This was the only time in television history that a show had left the air at the peak of its popularity. The series remained on the air for two more years of reruns.

Interestingly, in spite of critical praise for the show when it first appeared, the series was not particularly popular with the public, and it was canceled by CBS after 26 weeks. The following season, the series resurfaced with a new sponsor, a new time slot, and a new network, NBC. Two years later, CBS obtained the series once again. By that time, it was an unqualified success. *Father Knows Best* was produced by Eugene B. Rodney, who owned the rights to the series with Robert Young.

FAWCETT, FARRAH (MARY FARRAH LENI FAWCETT 1947–)

Before Farrah Fawcett was an actress, she was a successful model. Born in Corpus Christi, Texas, Fawcett had become a model shortly after graduating from school. In the mid-1960s, Farrah decided to become an actress, and after making an appearances on *The Dating Game* in 1965, her good looks soon landed her roles on such series as *The FLYING NUN, I DREAM OF JEANNIE, DAYS OF OUR LIVES, The PARTRIDGE FAMILY,* and *The SIX MILLION DOLLAR MAN,* which starred the man who became her

Father Knows Best: (clockwise from bottom left) Billy Gray, Elinor Donahue, Robert Young, Jane Wyatt, and Lauren Chapin (Author's collection)

husband, Lee Majors. Fawcett made her film debut in the French-language film *Un homme qui me plaît* in 1969, and she won a role in the much anticipated film version of the novel *Myra Breckinridge* in 1970. The film proved to be a disappointment to critics and filmgoers alike, and it became box office poison. Other roles in films, and as a regular on the *Harry O* series, led to her being cast as one of the three beauteous Angels on a show that became one of 1976's biggest hits, CHARLIE'S ANGELS. Fawcett played Jill Monroe on *Charlie's Angels*, and in less than a year she was one of the most photographed and famous women in Hollywood. In 1976, Farrah was named one of the 12 "Most Promising Faces" of the year in John Willis's *Screen World* annual. Fawcett broke her contract with the producers of *Charlie's Angels* in 1987, which resulted in a lawsuit. After several less than memorable appearances in a few feature films, Farrah appeared in a made-for-TV film in 1986, *The Burning Bed,* and appeared in a film adaptation of the off-Broadway play *Extremities*. Fawcett's acting won critical praise and established her as a serious actress, revitalizing her career. Important roles in many made-for-TV and feature films, as well as guest-starring appearances on *The LARRY SANDERS SHOW, Johnny Bravo* (1997), and ALLY MCBEAL, followed. In 1999, Fawcett was paid an impressive $750,000 for starring in the TV film *Silk Hope*.

FELDON, BARBARA (BARBARA HALL 1932–   )

Even though Barbara Feldon played only one major role on television, Agent 99 on the amusingly inventive comedy series GET SMART, the show and the role became so popular that Feldon is one of TV's most memorable stars. Born in Pittsburgh, Pennsylvania, Barbara graduated from the Carnegie Institute of Technology in 1955 with a B.A. degree in fine arts. A very intelligent woman, Feldon appeared on the popular TV quiz show *The $64,000 QUESTION,* answering questions about Shakespeare, and she won an impressive $64,000 on the show. After appearing in several stage plays in summer stock and in touring companies, Barbara began to appear on television shows. A role on the popular MAN FROM U.N.C.L.E series led to Feldon's being cast on *Get Smart,* which made her a star. Guest-starring appearances on such shows as ROWAN AND MARTIN'S LAUGH-IN, CHEERS, MAD ABOUT YOU, and *Something So Right* (1997), as well being a regular on *The Marty Feldman Comedy Machine* in 1972, *The Dean Martin Comedy World* in 1974, and starring roles in several made-for-TV films, kept her busy throughout the 1970s and 1980s. In recent years, Feldon narrated *The Dinosaurs!* animated film series, and in 1995 once again played Agent 99 on a revised, but unsuccessful, new version of *Get Smart*.

FIELD, SALLY (SALLY MARGARET FIELD 1946–   )

Two-time Academy Award–winning actress Sally Field, the daughter of actress Margaret Field, began her acting career as the star of two successive popular TV series, GIDGET in 1965 and *The FLYING NUN* in 1967. Her only TV appearance prior to winning the role of Gidget, which attracted a considerable following among younger viewers, was as a contestant on *The DATING GAME* in 1965. Field, who was born in Pasadena, California, claims she always knew she was going to be an actress. After one year on the *Gidget* series playing Frances "Gidget" Lawrence, an idealized California teenage girl, and a more impressive three years as Sister Bertrille (Elsie Ethrington) on *The Flying Nun,* Field appeared in several less than memorable TV films and in *The Girl with Something Extra* (1973–74) series. The starring role in the TV film *Sybil* in 1976, in which she played a woman with 16 personalities, won praise from the TV critics and changed the direction of her career. Starring roles in the feature films *Smokey and the Bandit* (1977), *Hooper* (1978), and *The End* (1978), all of which costarred Burt Reynolds, led to her Academy Award–winning roles in *Norma Rae* (1979) and *Places in the Heart* (1984). It was after winning her award for *Places in the Heart* that Field delivered her oft-quoted, tearful "You like me . . . You really like me," acceptance speech. Field has remained constantly in demand ever since, and has appeared in such successful films as *Punchline* (1988), *Steel Magnolias* (1989), *Soapdish* (1991), *Mrs. Doubtfire* (1993), *Forrest Gump* (1994), and *Where the Heart Is* (2000). Field has also made guest-starring appearances on such popular TV series as MARCUS WELBY, M.D., NIGHT GALLERY, *The LARRY SANDERS SHOW, MURPHY BROWN* and ER.

FIRST HUNDRED YEARS, THE

Dec. 1950–June 1952	CBS	Mon–Fri. Various daytime hours

The First Hundred Years was CBS's first television soap opera series. This daytime soap opera dealt with the lighter side of being married and starred Jimmy Lydon and Olive Stacey and then Anne Sergent as Chris and Connie Thayer, who were newlyweds. Also appearing regularly on the series were Robert Armstrong and Nana Bryant as Connie's parents, Mr. and Mrs. Martin; Don Tobin and Valerie Cossart as Chris's parents, Mr. and Mrs. Thayer, and Nancy Malone as Connie's kid sister, Margie. In 1952, CBS canceled *The First Hundred Years* and replaced it with the daytime serial *The GUIDING LIGHT,* which is still on the air.

FISH

Feb. 1977–May 1977	ABC	Sat. 8:30–9 P.M.
June 1977–Aug. 1977	ABC	Thurs 9:30–10 P.M.
Aug. 1977–Nov. 1977	ABC	Sat. 8–8:30 P.M.
Jan. 1978–Apr. 1978	ABC	Thurs. 8:30–9 P.M.
May 1978–June 1978	ABC	Thurs. 9:30–10 P.M.

On this spin-off of the popular BARNEY MILLER situation comedy, Abe Vigoda and Florence Stanley recreated their

Barney Miller roles of police detective Phil Fish and his wife, Bernice. When the series began, Fish and Bernice had moved out of their New York City apartment and into a rundown house to become the foster parents of five racially diverse juvenile delinquents for the "Persons in Need of Supervision" (P.I.N.S) city agency. The kids included Loomis, played by Todd Bridges, Victor, played by John Cassisi, Mike, played by Lenny Bari; Jilly, played by Denise Miller, and Diane, played by Sarah Natoli. Fish and Bernice's attempts to keep the young people in their charge on a straight and narrow path was the basis for much of the show's comedy. Also appearing on the series was Barry Gordon as a not very helpful psychologist, Charlie Harrison. When *Fish* first went on the air, Abe Vigoda appeared on this series as well as on *Barney Miller* for several months. *Fish* was produced by Norman Barasch and Roy Kammerman.

FLEMING, ART (1924–1995)

The original host of *JEOPARDY!*; Art Fleming was also the host of such popular game shows as *PANTOMIME QUIZ* (1947), one of television's earliest panel shows, and *Doctor I.Q.* (1953), in addition to hosting *Jeopardy!* (1964) and *The All New Jeopardy!* (1978). An actor as well as a TV host, Fleming appeared in such films as *A Hatful of Rain* (1957), *MacArthur* (1977), and *Airplane II: The Sequel* (1982, playing himself), and he was a regular on the *International Detective* TV series. Upon leaving network television in 1982, Fleming moved to St. Louis and worked at the CBS-owned radio station KMOX as the host of *Games People Play*. Fleming also hosted a nationally syndicated radio show about the golden days of radio, *When Radio Was*, before retiring from broadcasting in 1993.

FLINTSTONES, THE

Sept. 1960–Sept. 1963	ABC	Fri. 8:30–9 P.M.
Sept. 1963–Dec. 1964	ABC	Thurs. 7:30–8 P.M.
Dec. 1964–Sept. 1966	ABC	Fri. 7:30–8 P.M.

The Flintstones, which was produced by William Hanna and Joseph Barbera, was a prime-time cartoon series loosely based on Jackie GLEASON's popular *HONEYMOON-ERS* series. Set during the prehistoric Stone Age, the series revolved around a caveman named Fred Flintstone and his wife, Wilma, Stone Age versions of Gleason's Ralph and Alice Kramden of *The Honeymooners,* and even sounded a bit like them. Fred and Wilma's friends, who lived in a neighboring cave, were Barney and Betty Rubble. Baby Pebbles was Fred and Wilma's daughter, and Bam Bam was Barney and Betty's son. The voices for these characters were provided by Alan Reed (Fred), Jean Vander Pyl (Wilma), Mel Blanc (Barney), Bea BENADERET and then Gerry Johnson (Betty), Jean Vander Pyl (Pebbles), and Don Messick (Bamm Bamm). Mel Blanc also provided the voice for the Flintstones' pet dinosaur, Dino. *The Flint-*

stones was produced with adults, as well as children, in mind, and many of the amusing incidents were directed toward more mature audiences. In 1962, *The Flintstones* and *Beany and Cecil* became the first cartoon series to be telecast in color. Many *Flintstones* specials followed. In 1972–73, *The Flintstones Comedy Hour* aired on CBS, followed by *The Flintstones Show* (CBS 1973–74), *The New Fred and Barney Show* (NBC 1979), *Fred and Barney Meet the Thing* (NBC 1979), *Fred and Barney Meet the Schmoo* (NBC 1979–80), *The Flintstones Comedy Show* (NBC 1980–82), *Flintstones Funnies* (NBC 1982–84), and *The Flintstones Kids* (ABC 1986–88). Henry Corden provided the voice of Fred, and Gay Autterson the voice of Betty for the later shows.

FLIP WILSON SHOW, THE

Sept. 1970–June 1971	NBC	Thurs. 7:30–8:30 P.M.
Sept. 1971–June 1974	NBC	Thurs. 8–9 P.M.

African-American comedian Flip WILSON had an hour-long weekly variety show on TV for three years that was very popular. Wilson was the first black man to star on a TV series of his own. Wilson often appeared as several characters who became enormously popular, including the sassy, swinging Geraldine Jones, a liberated black woman with a very jealous boyfriend named "Killer"; Reverend Leroy of the Church of What's Happening Now, a dishonest preacher who liked the ladies; private detective Danny Danger; and Herbie, the Good Time ice cream wagon man. An oft-repeated catchphrase, "The Devil made me do it," became familiar to fans of the show. Also appearing regularly on *The Flip Wilson Show* were the Jack Regas Dancers and the George Wyle Orchestra. Many notable show business stars made guest appearances on the show. In its first two seasons on the air, *The Flip Wilson Show* was number two in the list of top shows according to the Nielsen ratings.

FLIPPER

Sept. 1964–Sept. 1967	NBC	Sat. 7:30–8 P.M.
Jan. 1968–June 1968	NBC	Sun. 6:30–7 P.M.
June 1968–Sept. 1968	NBC	Sun. 7–7:30 P.M.

A dolphin named Suzy starred as Flipper on this half-hour children's adventure series, which is well remembered by anyone who grew up in the late 1960s and watched television. Flipper resided at chief ranger Porter Ricks's Coral Key Park, Florida, shore-side home. Ricks, played by Brian Kelly, was a widower with two children, Sandy, his 15-year-old daughter, played by Luke Halpin, and Bud, his 10-year-old son, played by Tommy Norden. Flipper was Bud's pet dolphin, and he was both a friend and a helper to all the members of the Ricks family. Each week, Flipper rescued people in trouble, helped Porter, Bud, and Sandy take down evildoers, and generally made himself useful. Also appearing on the series when it first went on

Luke Halpin (center) and Suzy (Flipper) (Author's collection)

the air was Andy Devine as Hap Gorman, an old marine carpenter who told a lot of stories about the old days, and, during the series' last year, Ulla Stromstedt as Ulla Norstrand, an oceanographer.

FLYING NUN, THE

Sept. 1967–Jan. 1969	ABC	Thurs. 8–8:30 P.M.
Feb. 1969–Sept. 1969	ABC	Thurs. 7:30–8 P.M.
Sept. 1969–Jan. 1970	ABC	Wed. 7:30–8 P.M.
Jan. 1970–Sept. 1970	ABC	Fri. 7:30–8 P.M.

Sister Bertrille, whose name was Elsie Ethington, was a novice nun played by Sally FIELD who lived at the ancient Convent San Tanco on a hilltop near San Juan, Puerto Rico. Sister Bertrille, a delight to all who knew her, had one talent no other nun had—she could fly. A stiff wind would catch the starched cornette she wore and lift her slight 90 pounds from the ground, and off she flew. Need-less to say, Sister Bertrille's aerodynamics led to many unusual adventures. Not amused by her unusual abilities was the mother superior at her convent, played by Madeleine Sherwood, who would have preferred that Sister Bertrille were less conspicuous. Also appearing on the series were Marge Redmond as Sister Jacqueline, Alejandro Rey as Carlos Ramirez, Shelly Morrison as Sister Sixto, Linda Dangcil as Sister Ana, Vito Scotti as Police Captain Gaspar Formento, and Manuel Padilla, Jr., as Marcello, an orphan boy Sister Bertrille befriended. Surprisingly, *The Flying Nun* was praised for "humanizing nuns," by several religious orders. *The Flying Nun* was based on the novel *The Fifteenth Pelican* by Tere Rios.

FORD, TENNESSEE ERNIE (ERNEST JENNINGS FORD 1919–1991)

Country/western singer Tennessee Ernie Ford had three successful and successive prime-time variety shows on the air from 1955 to 1957, 1957 to 1961, and 1962 to 1965. Ford, who was born in Bristol, Tennessee, was a top recording artist before becoming a television star, and in 1990, he was inducted into the Country Music Hall of Fame. Ford's first television appearance was on *Old American Barn Dance* show in 1953. He subsequently appeared on *I LOVE LUCY* in 1954 and 1955, playing "Cousin Ernie" in the episodes "Tennessee Ernie Hangs On," and "Tennessee Bound." His easygoing, deep-voiced singing, and his pleasant personality and sense of humor made him a natural to star on a TV series of his own. In 1954, Ford hosted the *Kollege of Musical Knowledge,* which had been a successful radio program hosted by bandleader Kay Kyser. When his TV variety show made its debut in 1956, Tennessee Ernie soon became one of America's favorite performers. After his weekly variety shows left the air, Ernie frequently appeared as a semiregular guest star on *The ANDY WILLIAMS SHOW*, and then all but disappeared from TV, except for rare appearances as a guest star on TV variety shows, and mainly concentrated on his recording career and personal concert appearances.

FOREVER KNIGHT

May 1992–Aug. 1993	CBS	Tues. 11:30 P.M.–12.30 A.M.
Aug. 1993	CBS	Fri. 12:35–1:35 A.M.
Nov. 1993–Aug. 1994	CBS	Tues. 12:35–1:35 A.M.
Sept. 1994–Sept. 1996	Syndicated series	Various times and networks

Originally seen as a late-late-night offering on CBS *Forever Knight* later became more widely known as one of the most-watched syndicated TV programs. The hero was Nick Knight, a 700-year-old vampire who wanted to be a mortal being and who went to work (during the after-dark-to-dawn hours, of course) as a detective on a big city police force. Knight, played by Geraint Wyn Davies, went to war against criminals and other vampires who resented his heroic new lifestyle. Also appearing on the series were Catherine Disher as Dr. Natalie Lambert, the only nonvampire who knew the truth about Knight's background; John Kapelos as Knight's sarcastic partner, Don Schanke; vampires Lacroix and Janette, who was Knight's former girlfriend, played by Nigel Bennett and Deborah Duchene; Gary Farmer as Knight's boss, Capt. Stonetree, and then Natsuko Ohama, as his new boss, Capt. Amanda Cohen. The show, filmed on location in Toronto, can still be seen on the USA cable network, as well as on other independent TV stations.

FORSYTHE, JOHN (JOHN LINCOLN FREUND 1918–)

One of television's most familiar faces and voices for over 40 years, John Forsythe is best remembered for playing the leading roles on *BACHELOR FATHER* and *DYNASTY*, and as the voice of Charlie on *CHARLIE'S ANGELS*. Forsythe, who was born in Penn's Grove, New Jersey, was the son of a Wall Street businessman. Much to the disappointment of his father, young Forsythe decided to become an actor while he was still in school. After graduating from college, Forsythe was heard on several radio soap operas and secured roles in regional theater productions, before signing a contract with Warner Brothers to appear in films. In 1943, he appeared in *Destination Tokyo* before he joined the army during World War II. Forsythe appeared in the Army Air Corps show *Winged Victory,* which toured the nation in order to generate the sale of war bonds and to encourage people to support the war effort. When the war ended, Forsythe returned to New York and resumed his acting career, and was one of the cofounders of the Actor's Studio. In 1957, Forsythe starred on his first TV series, *Bachelor Father,* which was on the air for five years. His next series, *The John Forsythe Show,* which made its debut in 1965, proved less successful than *Bachelor Father*. In the 1970s, Forsythe had important roles in the feature films *In Cold Blood* (1967) and *Topaz* (1969) and the TV films *Terror on the 40th Floor* (1974) and *The Deadly Tower* (1975). In 1976, Forsythe, who in his younger days had been the public address announcer for the Brooklyn Dodgers, became the unseen voice of Charlie Townsend on *Charlie's Angels,* which was an enormous success. The actor continued to appear in TV and feature films throughout the 1970s. In 1981, Forsythe appeared as Blake Carrington, the patriarch on the popular *Dynasty* evening soap opera. Numerous starring roles on TV series and in such feature films as *Sizzle* (1981), *On Fire* (1987), *Opposites Attract* (1990), and regular roles on *The Powers That Be* (1992) and the *I Witness Video* (1992) TV series, and the TV film *Journey to the Center of the Earth* (1999) followed.

FOUR STAR REVUE

Sept. 1952–Sept. 1954	CBS	Thurs. 8:30–9 P.M.
Oct. 1954–Sept. 1956	CBS	Thurs. 9:30–10 P.M.

This early dramatic anthology series presented different half-hour TV plays, and originally starred four of Hollywood's most prominent performers: Charles Boyer, Dick Powell, Rosalind Russell, and Joel McCrea. When Russell and McCrea decided to bow out of the project, they were replaced by David Niven and Ida Lupino. The four stars alternated as the major performers on the semiweekly dramas. Although the stars played varied roles in different plays, one character who appeared often was a nightclub owner named Willie Dante, played by Dick Powell. Over the four years this series was on the air, Ronald Colman, Merle Oberon, Joan Fontaine, Teresa Wright, and Frank Lovejoy were also featured on the show. Originally an alternating series, *Four Star Revue* expanded to a weekly offering in September 1953.

FOX, MICHAEL J. (MICHAEL ANDREW FOX 1961–)

Canadian-born Michael J. Fox decided he wanted to be an actor when he was still attending school in Edmonton,

Alberta. Before he graduated, Fox went to Hollywood and soon won a role on the *Leo and Me* series in 1976. Appearances on such TV shows as *Letters from Frank,* TRAPPER JOHN, M.D., and in the feature film *Midnight Madness* (1980), the TV series *Palmerstown, U.S.A.,* and the film *Class of 1984,* led to his being cast as the conservative teenage son of former hippies, Alex P. Keaton, on FAMILY TIES. The show made him a star. Roles in such feature films as *Teen Wolf* (1985), *Poison Ivy* (1985), the phenomenally successful *Back to the Future* films (1985, 1989, 1990), *The Secret of My Succe$s* (1987), *Doc Hollywood* (1991), *The American President* (1995), and others, made Fox a superstar. In 1996, Fox returned to television on SPIN CITY, which became very popular. He subsequently appeared in the films *Mars Attacks!* (1996), and *Stuart Little* and *Stuart Little 2* (1999, 2001, as the voice of Stuart). In January 2000, Fox announced that he was leaving his successful *Spin City* series because he had Parkinson's disease, which had begun affect his ability to perform. In addition to acting, Fox was the executive producer of *Spin City* and *Anna Says* series, and of the feature film *Coldblooded* (1995). He also directed episodes of the TV series *Tales from the Crypt* (1989) and the TV film *The Trap* (1991).

FOXX, REDD (JOHN ELROY SANFORD 1922–1991)

African-American comedian Redd Foxx's stand-up comedy act was considered too vulgar for television, so he rarely appeared on TV programs that usually featured popular comedians. Foxx, who born in St. Louis, Missouri, and was one-quarter Seminole Indian, struggled for many years as a performer in various comedy clubs throughout the United States, but in 1972, at the age of 50, he became a star overnight when he appeared on the TV series SANFORD AND SON. Although he had previously been a guest star on the TV series *The Name of the Game* in 1968, and appeared in the feature film *Cotton Comes to Harlem* (1970), his memorable portrayal of Fred Sanford, the junkyard owner on *Sanford and Son,* catapulted him into superstardom. Appearances in the feature film *Norman . . . Is That You?* (1976), and on the less than successful TV series *The Redd Foxx Comedy Hour* in 1977, *Sanford* in 1980, and *The Redd Foxx Show* in 1986 followed. Foxx played two important roles in the films *Ghost of a Chance* (1987) and *Harlem Nights* (1989) before returning to television as Alfonso Royal on the *The Royal Family* in 1991. A heart attack while *The Royal Family* was in production suddenly ended Foxx's life at the age of 68.

FRANCIS, ARLENE (ARLINE FRANCIS KAZANJIAN 1907–2001)

For over 17 continuous years on network television, and then for an additional seven years in syndication, Arlene Francis became a well-known TV personality to millions of television viewers as a panelist on the long-running WHAT'S MY LINE series. An pioneer performer on TV, Francis, who was born in Boston, Massachusetts, was a successful radio personality and actress who was heard on such popular radio programs as the *Hour of Charm* musical show and the *Betty and Bob* soap opera before entering TV. Francis was featured on YOUR SHOW OF SHOWS in 1950, and acted on *The* UNITED STATES STEEL HOUR dramatic anthology program in 1953. Arlene made her TV debut as the hostess of *Blind Date* in 1949, and as a young actress previously been featured in the films *Murders in the Rue Morgue* (1932), *Too Much Johnson* (1938), *Stage Door Canteen* (1943), and *All My Sons* (1948), and was frequently seen on the Broadway stage in such plays as *Once More With Feeling.* While she was appearing on *What's My Line?,* Francis also hosted *Answer Yes or No* (1950), *By Popular Demand* (1950), *Prize Performance* (1950), *That Reminds Me* (1952), *Who's There?* (1952), *Talent Patrol* (1954), and *Home,* and she had a major role in the film *One, Two, Three* (1961), which costarred James Cagney. Before Francis died from Alzheimer's disease, she was last seen on television in 1983 as a guest star on SCARECROW AND MRS. KING.

FRANCISCUS, JAMES (JAMES GROVER FRANCISCUS 1934–1991)

James Franciscus, one of television's most famous fictional teachers, Mr. Novak, on the hit TV series MR. NOVAK, was born in Clayton, Missouri. Franciscus's father was a pilot who was killed in action during World War II, and the Franciscus family had a difficult time financially when the war ended. Hard work won him a scholarship to Yale University, from which he graduated with a B.A. degree in English and theater. Roles on such early television dramatic anthology series as STUDIO ONE and *The* WESTINGHOUSE DESILU PLAYHOUSE in the 1940s and 1950s, and as a supporting player on a HAVE GUN WILL TRAVEL episode, led to his being cast on NAKED CITY as Det. James "Jimmy" Halloran, a role that finally put him in the spotlight. In 1961, Franciscus starred on a second TV series *The Investigators,* which proved to be less successful than *Naked City,* but in 1963, he became John Novak, the handsome high school teacher on the well-received *Mr. Novak* series. Roles in such feature films as *The Outsider* (1961), *Youngblood Hawke* (1964), *Beneath the Planet of the Apes* (1970), *Jonathan Livingston Seagull* (1973, as the voice of Jonathan), *The Greek Tycoon* (1978), and leading roles on the TV series *Longstreet* (1971–72), *Doc Elliott* (1974), and HUNTER, and many others, kept Franciscus steadily employed. As one of the cofounders of Omnibus Productions, Franciscus produced many film adaptations of classic books such as *Heidi, Kidnapped, Jane Eyre, David Copperfield,* and *The Red Pony.* Over the years Franciscus was a frequent guest star on several series such as *The* TWILIGHT ZONE, *The* MILLIONAIRE, RAWHIDE, *The* GENERAL ELECTRIC THEATER, DR. KILDARE, and *The F.B.I.,* to name just a few. Franciscus, a heavy smoker, remained active until shortly before his death in 1991 from complications brought on by chronic emphysema.

FRANK SINATRA SHOW, THE

Oct. 1950–June 1951	CBS	Sat. 9–10 P.M.
Oct. 1951–Apr. 1952	CBS	Tues. 8–9 P.M.
Oct. 1957–June 1958	ABC	Fri. 9–9:30 P.M.

Even though he had had a very successful career as a singer/entertainer, Frank Sinatra was in one of his several career declines when he first agreed to appear on television. One of the earliest performers to venture into television after World War II when TV was in its infancy, Sinatra's first weekly musical/variety show was a one-hour program scheduled opposite Milton BERLE's very successful *TEXACO STAR THEATER*. In addition to Sinatra, this early TV show also featured comedians Ben Blue and Sid Fields, and Erin O'Brien, singer Roberta Lee, and Axel Stordahl and His Orchestra as regulars. When the show was canceled, after struggling along for one and a half seasons, Sinatra avoided appearing on a regular television show for five years, and mainly concentrated on guest appearances on other performers' TV shows. In 1957, Sinatra was convinced to try another weekly show of his own. By this time, however, Sinatra's career had taken a turn for the better. He had won an Academy Award as Best Supporting Actor for his work in *From Here to Eternity*, and the singer/actor was paid a reported $3 million by ABC to appear on their network. The shows, with Sinatra in complete control, were one-third dramas starring Sinatra, one-third variety shows, and one-third dramas starring other performers. Nelson Riddle, the arranger for many of Sinatra's hit recordings, was the show's musical director, and guests included such big-name entertainers as Bob HOPE and Peggy Lee, and Sinatra's daughter, Nancy, who made her TV debut on the show. Sinatra was said to have had little time to rehearse his weekly half-hour show, and the result was a disaster. It was canceled after less than a full season. Thereafter, Sinatra confined his television appearances to guest-starring on other performers' shows and, much later, on occasional TV specials of his own.

FRANKLIN, BONNIE (1944–)

Bonnie Franklin, who was born in Santa Monica, California, began her career playing small parts in such Hollywood films as *The Kettles in the Ozarks* (1956), *The Wrong Man* (1956), and *A Summer Place* (1959). As a featured performer on Broadway Franklin attracted the attention of theater critics for her performance in the musical comedy *Applause* in 1970. She then went back to Hollywood, where she made numerous guest-starring appearances on such TV series as *The MAN FROM U.N.C.L.E*, *Please Don't Eat the Daisies* (1965–67), and *The MUNSTERS*. In 1975, Franklin was cast as Ann Romano Royer, a divorced woman who had two young daughters to raise, on *ONE DAY AT A TIME*. The series was an enormous hit and enjoyed an impressive nine-year run, making it one of television's most successful situation comedies. While she was appearing on *One Day at a Time*, Franklin also starred in several TV films, including *A Guide for the Married Woman* (1978), *Breaking Up Is Hard to Do* (1979), *Portrait of a Rebel: The Remarkable Mrs. Sanger* (1980, as Margaret Sanger), and *Your Place . . . or Mine* (1983). In the 1990s, Franklin appeared as a guest star on *Hearts Are Wild* (1992), *BURKE'S LAW*, and *Almost Perfect* (1996).

FRASIER

Sept. 1993–Sept. 1994	NBC	9:30–10 P.M.
Sept. 1994–Sept. 1996	NBC	9–9:30 P.M.
June 1998–July 1998	NBC	9–9:30 P.M.
Sept. 1998–present	NBC	9–9:30 P.M.

In 1993, Kelsey GRAMMER repeated the Dr. Frasier Crane role he had made famous on the enormously popular *CHEERS* series on his own show, *Frasier*. On this series, psychiatrist Dr. Frasier Crane had divorced his overbearing wife, Lilith, left Boston (where *Cheers* had taken place), and moved to Seattle to become a radio talk show host who gave advice to callers at station KACL. Frasier's Seattle apartment was a strikingly modern place with wonderful views of the city. His ex-Marine, retired cop father, Martin, played by John Mahoney, a somewhat grumpy man, moved in with Frasier, bringing along his favorite well-worn, ratty-looking lounge chair and his beloved dog,

Frank Sinatra (left) and the rest of the Rat Pack: (left to right) Dean Martin, Peter Lawford, Joey Bishop, and Sammy Davis, Jr. (sitting) (Author's collection)

The cast of *Frasier*: (clockwise from left) Peri Gilpin (Roz), David Hyde Pierce (Niles), Kelsey Grammer (Frasier), John Mahoney (Martin), Jane Leeves (Daphne), Dan Butler (Bulldog), and Eddie (Author's collection)

Eddie, played by Moose. Because his father was disabled, Frasier hired an English at-home care worker, Daphne Moon, played by Jane Leeves, to look after him. Frasier's younger look-alike (albeit more frail) brother, Dr. Niles Crane, played by David Hyde PIERCE, also a psychiatrist, often dropped by to complain about his overbearing wife, Maris, who was never seen. Before long, the very funny Niles became one of the series' most popular characters. At KACL, Frasier's call-scanner and producer, Roz Doyle, played by Peri Gilpin, and fellow broadcaster Bob "Bulldog" Briscoe, played by Dan Butler, who was a macho sportscaster, are constant thorns in Frasier's side, although later Roz became more of a friend than a nemesis to Frasier. Gil Chesterton, the restaurant critic at the station, played by Edward Hibbert, KACL station manager Kate Costos, played by Mercedes Ruehl, and Sherry Demsey, who was Martin Crane's girlfriend, played by Marsha Mason, made occasional appearances on the show. Several of Kelsey Grammer's fellow *Cheers* cast members, including Shelley Long, Ted Danson, Woody Harrelson, and his former wife on *Cheers*, Lilith, played by Bebe Neuwirth, have made appearances on *Frasier*.

As *Frasier* progressed, characters changed and new story lines were developed. Niles became romantically involved with his father's caretaker, Daphne, and Frasier fell in love with his former nemesis, Roz Doyle, who worked with him at KACL.

FRAWLEY, WILLIAM (WILLIAM CLEMENT FRAWLEY 1887–1966)

Well known to viewers as the incomparable Fred Mertz on *I LOVE LUCY*, character actor William Frawley was born in Burlington, Iowa. As a boy, Frawley sang solos at St. Paul's Catholic Church and performed at the Burlington Opera House, and he decided that he would pursue a career as an actor as soon as he got older. After a short stint as a stenographer for the Union Pacific Railroad, Frawley went into vaudeville with his brother, Paul, singing duets. He then became part of an act that starred pianist Franz Rath. Teaming with Edna Louise Broedt, who became his wife, Frawley toured the Orpheum and Keith vaudeville circuits and then went on to Broadway, where he appeared in numerous musicals and revues. Although he made his first film appearance in 1916 in *Lord Loveland Discovers America,* it wasn't until 1929 that Frawley began his career as one of Hollywood's most visible character actors. His hundreds of motion picture appearances included roles in such memorable films as *Fancy That* (1929), *Roberta* (1935), *Roxie Hart* (1942), *Going My Way* (1944), *Miracle on 34th Street* (1947), *The Babe Ruth Story* (1948), many *Blondie* films, and *Abbott and Costello Meet the Invisible Man* (1951). But it wasn't until he played Fred Mertz on *I Love Lucy* in 1951, and on the subsequent *Lucy–Desi Comedy Hour* in 1957, that William Frawley became a recognized show business name. In 1960, Frawley had a featured role on another hit series, *MY THREE SONS,* playing Bud O'Casey. Poor health, however, forced him to leave this series, and in 1966, Frawley, who was 79 years old, died after suffering a heart attack while walking along Hollywood Boulevard after seeing a film.

FREEBIE AND THE BEAN

| Dec. 1980–Jan. 1981 | CBS | 9–10 P.M. |

Although it was on the air for only one season, many viewers fondly remember *Freebie and the Bean,* which was based on a 1974 movie of the same name that starred James Caan and Alan Arkin. Freebie and Bean were two plainclothes policemen who worked on special assignments for the San Francisco District Attorney's office. Det. Sgt. Tim Walker, aka "Freebie," played by Tom Mason, and Det. Sgt. Dan Delgado, aka "Bean," played by Hector Elizondo, were, although apparently totally mismatched, an effective crime-fighting team. Swinging single Freebie and serious-minded family man Bean, who had a wife and two children, often found themselves in conflict about how certain cases should be handled, but they always got the results they wanted. Their boss, D.A. Walter W. Cruikshank, played by William Daniels, overlooked many of their more obvious faults, because of their effective detective work. Assisting the team on occasion was Rodney Blake, aka "Axie," played by Mel Stewart, a mechanic at the police garage. The show might have been a longer running success, had it not been scheduled opposite the very popular *LOVE BOAT,* which completely overshadowed *Freebie and the Bean* in viewer polls.

FRENCH CHEF, THE (JULIA CHILD & COMPANY, BAKING WITH JULIA, JULIA & JACQUES COOKING AT HOME, JULIA CHILD: LESSONS WITH MASTER CHEFS)

1962–1973 (*The French Chef*)	PBS	Various days and times
1978–1979 (*Julia Child & Company*)	PBS	Various days and times
1996–1997 (*Baking with Julia*)	PBS	Various days and times
2000 (*Julia & Jacques Cooking at Home*)	PBS	Various days and times
2001–2002 (*Julia Child: Lessons with Master Chefs*)	PBS	Various days and times

The indomitable chef Julia CHILD took television by storm when she first appeared on a cooking show on the Public Broadcasting System. Her hearty humor and unconventional kitchen behavior as she prepared wonderful food from her best-selling cookbook, *Mastering the Art of French Cooking,* included such outrageous actions as dropping a chicken on the floor, brushing it off, and saying, "You're alone in the kitchen," as well as suffering from an occasional failed soufflé, provided many laughs for her viewers, but always gave useful instructions about how to cook incredibly good meals. Julia's later series, *Julia Child & Company* (1978–79), which featured master chefs from around the world who prepared food from their most prized recipes, and the 1990s series *Baking with Julia,* which was taped when Julia was well into her eighties, had Julia mainly watch and assist great bakers as they prepared pies, cookies, and other mouthwatering baked goods, also proved very popular, and the shows are still being televised as of this writing.

FRESH PRINCE OF BEL AIR, THE

Sept. 1990–June 1995	NBC	Mon. 8–8:30 P.M.
June 1995–July 1995	NBC	Mon. 8–9 P.M.
July 1995–May 1996	NBC	Mon. 8–8:30 P.M.
May 1996–Sept. 1996	NBC	Mon. 8–9 P.M.

Engaging African-American actor, comedian, and rapper Will Smith starred as a youth from the ghetto of West Philadelphia who is sent to Bel Air, in Los Angeles, to live with wealthy relatives when things got too hot for him back East. Will's rich and conservative Uncle Philip Banks, played by James Avery, his wife, Vivian, played by Janet Hubert-Whitten and then Daphne Maxwell Reid, and their spoiled children, preppy son Carlton and snobby daughter Hilary, played by Alfonso Ribeiro and Karyn Parsons, did little to hide their disdain for Will's behavior. Their youngest daughter, Ashley, played by Tatyana M. Ali, was the only member of the Banks family who saw eye-to-eye with Smith. The proper family butler, Geoffrey, played by Joseph Marcell, in spite of his imperious demeanor, was surprisingly sympathetic to Will. During the 1993–94 season, Carlton and Will graduated from prep school, enrolled at the University of Los

Angeles, and shared the Banks's pool house as a bachelor pad. Subsequently, Aunt Vivian gave birth to the Banks's fourth child, Nicky, who the next season suddenly appeared on the show as a five-year-old, played by Ross Bagley. Then Will's ex-girlfriend from Philadelphia, Jackie, played by Tyra Banks, showed up to make things uncomfortable for Will. On the series' final episode, the Banks had put their Bel Air mansion up for sale. The potential buyers, Mr. Drummond and Arnold (Conrad Bain and Gary Coleman) from *DIFF'RENT STROKES,* considered buying the house, but it was bought by George and Louise Jefferson (Sherman Hemsley and Isabel Sanford), who had formerly been seen on *The JEFFERSONS.* The Jeffersons' former maid, Florence (Marla Gibbs) also made an appearance on *The Fresh Prince of Bel Air's* final show.

FRIENDS

Sept. 1994–Feb. 1995	NBC	Thurs. 8:30–9 P.M.
Feb. 1995–Aug. 1995	NBC	Thurs. 9:30–10 P.M.
Aug. 1995–present	NBC	Thurs. 8–8:30 P.M.

Like *SEINFELD,* a situation comedy about a group of friends, this show centered on six bright young people who lived in

The cast of *Friends:* (bottom) Courtney Cox, Matt LeBlanc; (middle) Jennifer Aniston, Lisa Kudrow; (top) Matthew Perry and David Schwimmer (Author's collection)

the same apartment building in New York City's Greenwich Village and enjoyed hanging out together and having fun. The six friends included Monica Geller, played by Courteney Cox, a young woman trying to find "Mr. Right," and a sort of a den mother to the crowds, which included her brother, Ross, whose wife had left him, played by David Schwimmer; her other roommates, Rachel Green, played by Jennifer Aniston, and flakey Phoebe Buffay, played by Lisa Kudrow; and Chandler Bing, played by Matthew Perry, and Joey Tribbiani, played by Matt LeBlanc, who shared another apartment in the same building. When they weren't hanging out in their apartments, the friends usually congregated at the Greenwich Village Central Perk coffeehouse, where they discussed dates and dating, work and working, and one another. Also appearing on occasion were Christina Pickles and Elliott Gould as Monica and Ross's parents; Tom Selleck as Monica's much-older boyfriend, Richard; Jane Sibbett as Carol, Ross's lesbian ex-wife; and Jessica Hecht as Susan, Carol's rather grim companion.

Friends was created by David Crane and Marta Kaufman. The first year on the air, *Friends* placed eighth in the Nielsen ratings of television's most popular shows. Several of the show's major cast members, including Lisa Kudrow, David Schwimmer, and Matthew Perry, subsequently became film stars, in addition to appearing on this hit TV series.

FROM THESE ROOTS

June 1958–Dec. 1961　NBC　Mon.–Fri. Various times

Although it has not been on the air for 40 years, the daytime serial *From These Roots*, created by Frank Provo, is still fondly remembered by older viewers as one of their favorite soap operas. Fiercely loyal fans never got over that it was canceled at the height of its popularity, and nostalgically recall incidents from the show; in various fan magazine polls, they claim it was one of television's top-quality serial dramas.

Produced by Paul Lammers and directed by Don Wallace, *From These Roots* centered on Ben Fraser, the elderly editor of the Stratfield *Record*, played by Rod Henrickson and then Jack Macauley; his fiction-writing daughter Liz, played by Ann Flood; his daughter Emily Fraser Benson, played by Helen Shields; and his son Frank, Jr., played by Frank Marth. Also featured prominently in the cast were Julie Bovasso and then Tresa Hughes as Rose Corelli Fraser, Ben, Jr.'s, wife; Len Wayland and then Tom Shirley as Dr. Buck Weaver; Billie Lou Watt as Buck's wife, Maggie Barker Weaver; Robert Mandan, as playwright David Allen (who eventually married Liz Fraser); Audra Lindley as Laura Tompkins; Millette Alexander as Gloria Sexton; Henderson Forsythe as Jim Benson (Emily Fraser's husband); Craig Huebing as Tom Jennings; David Sanders as Bruce Crawford; and Vera Allen as Ben, Sr.'s, maid, Kass. Over the three years the show was aired, 915 episodes were televised.

FROST, DAVID (DAVID PARADINE FROST 1939–)

David Frost, who was born in Tenterden, Kent, England, is remembered as one of television's most successful interviewers. Originally seen in the United States on *This Was the Week That Was* in 1962, Frost later appeared as a reporter on *The V.I.P.s* series in 1963, a reprised version of *That Was the Week That Was* in 1964, and *The Frost Report* in 1966, *Frost on Sunday* in 1968, *Frost on Saturday* in 1968, *The David Frost Show* in 1969, *Frost Over America* in 1971, and *Headliners With David Frost* in 1978. Frost, knighted by Queen Elizabeth II in 1993, is perhaps best remembered, however, for his probing, in-depth television interview of former president Richard M. Nixon, who had resigned in disgrace after the Watergate scandal.

FUGITIVE, THE

Sept. 1963–Aug. 1967　ABC　Tues. 10–11 P.M.

For four years, millions of viewers tuned in faithfully to watch Dr. Richard Kimble, who had been falsely accused of killing his wife, run away from the law as he searched for the one-armed man he knew was responsible for his wife's death. Dr. Kimble, played by David JANSSEN, was relentlessly pursued by Lt. Philip Gerard, played by Barry Morse, who was convinced Kimble was guilty of his wife's murder. Each episode was filled with suspense and breathless escapes, as Kimble traveled around the country, avoiding capture, and following leads concerning the whereabouts of the one-armed man. The final episode of *The Fugitive*, on which the one-armed man (played by Bill Raish) finally plunged to his death and Lt. Gerard realized that he had been wrong about Dr. Kimble's being guilty of murder, was viewed by more people than had ever watched a single episode of a television show: 72 percent of the viewing public, which was not topped until the opening episode of *DALLAS* revealed who shot J. R., aired 13 years later. A successful film version of *The Fugitive* starring Harrison Ford and Tommy Lee Jones was released in 1993, and an all-new *Fugitive* series emerged in 2000.

Quinn Martin was the executive producer of *The Fugitive*, which was narrated by William Conrad, whose deep, resonant voice heralded each program's opening and repeated the show's premise for viewers.

FULL HOUSE

Sept. 1987	ABC	Tues. 8:30–9 P.M.
Sept. 1987–Feb. 1988	ABC	Fri. 8–8:30 P.M.
Mar. 1988–July 1989	ABC	Fri. 8:30–9 P.M.
Aug. 1989–Aug. 1991	ABC	Fri. 8–8:30 P.M.
Aug. 1991–Aug. 1995	ABC	Tues. 8–8:30 P.M.

Set in San Francisco, this lighthearted situation comedy posed a rather serious question: How does a young, single father cope when his wife suddenly dies and leaves him with three young children to raise? The young father, a sportscaster named Danny Tanner, played by comedian Bob Saget, enlisted the aid of two other young men, his brother-in-law Jesse Cochran/Katsopolis, a rock and roll performer who wanted only to party, played by John Stamos, and his friend, Joey Gladstone, an aspiring comic, played by David Coulier, to help him take care of his three children: 10-year-old Donna Jo, aka D.J., played by Candace Cameron; five-year-old Stephanie, played by Jodie Sweetin; and six-month-old Michele, alternately played by the identical twins Mary Kate and Ashley Fuller Olsen. Over the eight years the series was on the air, viewers literally watched the Tanner children grow up, and by the time the series ended its run in 1995, baby Michele, who was still being played at different times by one or the other Olsen twin, was eight years old. Other characters on the series were Lori Loughlin as Rebecca, John Aprea as Nick Coughlan/Katsopolis, Yvonne Wilder as Irene Coughlan/Katsopolis, Gail Edwards as Vicki Larson, and Blake Tuomy-Wilhoit, Dylan Tuomy-Wilhoit, Tahj Mowry, Jurnee Smollett, Sara Moonves, Blake McIver Ewing, and Marla Sokoloff. *Full House* was created by Jeff Franklin.

FUNICELLO, ANNETTE (ANNETTE JOANNE FUNICELLO 1942–)

The MICKEY MOUSE CLUB's most famous Mouseketeer, Annette Funicello, was born in Utica, New York. When she was a child, her parents, convinced that their pretty and talented daughter could be a star, moved to Hollywood. Annette auditioned for various television and film roles. Catching the eye of Walt Disney, who was casting a new daytime TV series for children that was to be called *The Mickey Mouse Club,* Annette was immediately hired upon finishing her audition. Both her parents and Walt Disney's faith in the young performer proved justified when she became one of the most popular members of *The Mickey Mouse Club* cast the moment she stepped in front of the TV cameras in 1955. Placed under exclusive contract to Walt Disney Productions, Annette was seen on the *Disneyland: The Fourth Anniversary Show* in 1957,

the short-lived *Annette* TV series in 1958, and as a regular on *The New Adventures of Spin and Marty* series, all produced by Disney. In 1959, Annette became a regular on the popular show MAKE ROOM FOR DADDY, starring Danny THOMAS. As she grew up, Annette starred in a series of extremely popular feature-length teen-oriented films, including *The Shaggy Dog* (1959), *Babes in Toyland* (1961), *Beach Party* (1963), *Muscle Beach Party* (1964), *Bikini Beach* (1964), *Pajama Party* (1964), *How to Stuff a Wild Bikini* (1965), *Beach Blanket Bingo* (1965), and the 1979 TV series *Easy Does It,* which also starred her *Beach Party* costar Frankie Avalon. Over the years, Annette also made guest-starring appearances on such TV series as ZORRO, LOVE AMERICAN STYLE (1969–74), *The* LOVE BOAT, FANTASY ISLAND, GROWING PAINS, and FULL HOUSE. In 1987, while she was making the film *Back to the Beach* with Avalon, Annette discovered that she had multiple sclerosis, and she underwent brain surgery. Although her performing activities have been greatly reduced, Annette still makes occasional public appearances, usually on behalf of the Annette Funicello Fund for Neurological Disorders, a charitable organization that she founded.

FUNT, ALLEN (1914–1999)

In 1948, during television's earliest years, Allen Funt, who was born in New York City, introduced his popular CANDID CAMERA show, which had originally been heard on radio as *Candid Microphone* in 1947, to TV viewers. The show, which can still be seen regularly, became an American, and indeed a worldwide, institution, and Funt's name has become indelibly etched in viewers' minds together with his creation. A talented man who also wrote and directed the films *What Do You Say to a Naked Lady?* (1970) and *Money Talks* (1972), Funt kept busy producing various editions of *Candid Camera* until 1992, when a stroke, from which he never fully recovered, forced him into retirement. Funt's son, Peter, continues his father's lifework as the producer of *Candid Camera* productions.

GABOR, EVA (1919–1995)

One of three beautiful daughters born to Jolie Gabor, Eva Gabor, like her mother and sisters, was born in Budapest, Hungary. In the 1930s, before World War II broke out in Europe, Jolie immigrated to the United States with her teenage daughters, and before long Eva had embarked upon a career as a film actress. Her first important featured role as an actress was in *Pacific Blackout* (1941). She followed that with appearances in *The Forced Landing* (1941), *Star Spangled Rhythm* (1942), *A Royal Scandal* (1945), *The Wife of Monte Cristo* (1946), *Captain Kidd and the Slave Girl* (1954), *The Last Time I Saw Paris* (1954), *Gigi* (1958), *Youngblood Hawke* (1964), and other films, before being cast in the recurring role of Lisa Douglas, a wealthy socialite who finds herself living in a less than luxurious rural area on several episodes of the hit TV series PETTICOAT JUNCTION. With Eddie ALBERT as her husband, Oliver, Gabor became the costar of a spin-off series called GREEN ACRES, which became as big a hit as *Petticoat Junction*. *Green Acres* remained on the air for six years and was one of the most popular situation comedy series on the air during its time. When *Green Acres* ended its run, Eva became a regular panelist on the MATCH GAME '74, '75, '76, '77, '78, and '79 series, and had important roles in such films as *Nutcracker Fantasy* (1979), *The Princess Academy* (1987), *Rescuers Down Under* (1990, as the voice of Miss Bianca), and appeared on the less successful TV series *Bridges to Cross* in 1986. Eva was also a popular guest star on such TV shows as *Your Show Time*, The COLGATE COMEDY HOUR, The PHILCO TELEVISION PLAYHOUSE, ADVENTURES IN PARADISE, The UNITED STATES STEEL HOUR, HERE'S LUCY, The ADVENTURES OF ELLERY QUEEN, BURKE'S LAW, and other programs throughout the 1950s, '60s, '70s, and '80s.

GALE STORM SHOW, THE (AKA OH, SUSANNA)

Sept. 1956–Apr. 1959	CBS	Sat. 9–9:30 P.M.
Oct. 1959–Mar. 1960	ABC	Thurs. 7:30–8 P.M.

One year after her popular TV situation comedy series MY LITTLE MARGIE left the air, Gale STORM returned to TV with another series, OH, SUSANNA, which, shortly after its premiere, changed its name to *The Gale Storm Show*. On this series, Gale played Susanna Pomeroy, a social director on a luxury ocean liner named the S.S. *Ocean Queen*. Her best friend was the ship's beauty parlor operator, Esmerelda Nugent, played by comedienne ZaSu Pitts. The two spent a great deal of time getting under the skin of Capt. Huxley, played by Roy Roberts. Also adding to the captain's frustrations was Cedric, an impish little fellow played by Jimmy Fairfax, who had a talent for getting into trouble. Three years after *The Gale Storm Show* made its debut on CBS, it went into syndication and was seen on ABC for the remainder of time it was aired.

GALLOPING GOURMET, THE

1968–1971	Syndicated series	Various times and stations

Chef Graham Kerr, with a wineglass usually clutched in his hand, and a humorous approach to preparing food, became one of television's most popular cooking instructors of the late 1960s. Kerr's syndicated series, on which he prepared gourmet dishes, was noted for his somewhat unconventional way of cooking; sometimes the dishes came out perfect, and sometimes not so perfect. Originally called *The Galloping Gourmet* because of Kerr's somewhat erratic physical movements, the show was produced by Kerr's wife, Treena, at CJOH in Ottowa, Canada. In the mid-1970s after a few years' hiatus, Kerr returned to television with another syndicated cooking show simply called *Graham Kerr*. Because Kerr and his producer/wife had apparently found religion and sworn off alcoholic beverages and rich food, the wineglass was no longer featured on the show, and he prepared on his new series mainly low-fat and low-cholesterol dishes. Although the new show attracted a loyal following, it certainly had fewer viewers than his more outrageous and original previous series.

GARLAND, BEVERLY (BEVERLY LUCY FESSENDEN 1929–)

Beverly Garland, who was born in Santa Cruz, California, says she knew she was going to be an actress from the time she was a little girl. In her teens, Beverly studied acting under Anita Arliss, the sister of the renowned stage and screen actor George Arliss, and she acted in little theater productions in Glendale, California, and then in Phoenix, Arizona, when her parents moved there. In Phoenix, Garland worked on radio before making her screen debut in *D.O.A.* in 1950. That same year, she made her TV debut on the series *Mama Rosa*, and thereafter had important roles in such films as *Fearless Fagan* (1952), *Problem Girls* (1953), *Two Guns and a Badge* (1954), *The Desperado* (1954), *Swamp Women* (1955), *The Desperate Hours* (1955), *The Steel Jungle* (1956), and *The Joker Is Wild* (1957). In 1957, Garland was cast as Casey Jones on the TV series *Decoy*, which enjoyed only a brief run but led to other roles in films and eventually won Garland the leading role opposite Bing CROSBY on his TV show. In 1969, Garland played Fred MACMURRAY's girlfriend, and then wife, Barbara Harper Douglas, on MY THREE SONS. More screen roles and the regular running role of Dottie West on SCARECROW AND MRS. KING followed. Garland continued to be one of Hollywood's busiest performers throughout the 1970s, '80s, and '90s, and had another regular role on the LOIS AND CLARK: *The New Adventures of Superman* series. In 1997, Garland joined the cast of the daytime soap opera PORT CHARLES, playing Estelle. Among Garland's formidable list of guest-starring appearances on various TV series are *The* LONE RANGER, ZANE GREY THEATER, RAWHIDE, *The* TWILIGHT ZONE, LARAMIE, WANTED: DEAD OR ALIVE, GUNSMOKE, *The* FUGITIVE, *The* WILD, WILD WEST, *The Mothers-in-Law* (1968), HERE'S LUCY, and many others.

GARNER, JAMES (JAMES SCOTT BUMGARNER 1928–)

Popular television and motion picture actor James Garner, who starred on TV's MAVERICK and ROCKFORD FILES, was born in Norman, Oklahoma. Garner, part Cherokee Indian, grew up in Oklahoma, where his father was a carpet-layer. Dropping out of school when he was 16 years old, Garner worked at various low-paying jobs before joining the U.S. Army in the early 1950s. Wounded in action during the Korean conflict, Garner was awarded a Purple Heart. In 1954, after his discharge from the army,

a friend got him a nonspeaking role in the Broadway play *The Caine Mutiny Court-Martial,* and from then on Garner actively pursued a career as an actor. Small roles on several TV programs led to a Warner Brothers' contract to appear in films. At Warners, Garner was cast in *The Girl He Left Behind* (1956), which led to his being cast as Brett Maverick on TV's *Maverick,* which was also produced by Warner Brothers. The series, and Garner, were enormous successes, and *Maverick* made him a star. After his success in *Maverick,* Garner was given roles in such popular feature films as *The Thrill of It All* (1963), *Move Over, Darling* (1963), *The Great Escape* (1963), and *The Americanization of Emily* (1964), establishing him as one of Hollywood's major leading men. He enjoyed less success, however, in the films that followed and on the TV series *Nichols,* which made its debut in 1971. In 1974, Garner starred on another TV series, *The Rockford Files,* another major success for him, and once again the actor established himself as one of TV's most popular stars. After *The Rockford Files* left the air, Garner appeared in such important films as *The Glitter Dome* (1984), *Murphy's Romance* (1985), *Barbarians at the Gate* (1993), and *Maverick* (1994, a remake of his TV series with Mel Gibson playing his son). Garner also continued to make *Rockford Files* TV films throughout the 1980s and 1990s.

GARROWAY AT LARGE

Apr. 1949–July 1949	NBC	Sat. 10–10:30 P.M.
July 1949–June 1951	NBC	Sun. 10–10:30 P.M.
Oct. 1953–June 1954	NBC	Fri. 8–8:30 P.M.

Former radio disc jockey Dave GARROWAY introduced his low-keyed humor and casual, relaxed manner to television audiences during television's earliest years in the late 1940s, and his style proved perfect for the small home screens. Garroway's show, *Garroway At Large,* was a musical revue and chat show that originated from Chicago and featured a cast of regulars, singers Connie Russell, Jack Haskell, Jill Corey, the Songsmiths Quartet, the Daydreamers, and the Cheerleaders, comedian Cliff Norton, dancers Russell and Aura, and Ken Spaulding and Diane Sinclair, and the orchestras of Joseph Gallichio and Skitch Henderson. After his theme music, "Sentimental Journey," was played, Garroway strolled around the studio, interviewing performers and guests, and chatting with technicians, and he let viewers get a firsthand look at a TV studio behind the scenes. There were no elaborate sets or fancy costumes, just simple, unadulterated television, and viewers loved Garroway and his show. The original *Garroway at Large* was canceled in 1951. It resurfaced in 1973, but remained on the air for only one season, before Garroway left to become the anchor of NBC's original TODAY show.

GARROWAY, DAVE (DAVID CUNNINGHAM GARROWAY 1913–1982)

With his familiar sign-off "Peace," his casual, low-keyed and relaxed style, and his occasional impatience with

Dave Garroway (Author's collection)

June 1950–July 1950	CBS	Mon.–Fri. 7–7:30 P.M.
July 1950–Sept. 1950	CBS	Mon., Tues., Thurs., Fri. 7–7:30 P.M.
Aug. 1950–Sept. 1950	CBS	Wed. 8–9 P.M.
Oct. 1951–Dec. 1951	CBS	Thurs. 8–8:30 P.M.
Sept. 1958–June 1964	CBS	Tues. 10–11 P.M.
Sept. 1966–Jan. 1967	CBS	Sun. 9–10 P.M.

Garry Moore, whose short-cropped crew haircut became his trademark, arrived on television in the early 1950s, after starring on a popular radio program with comedian Jimmy DURANTE. Moore's first TV series was a five-day-a-week summer replacement variety show that featured singers Denise Lor and Ken Carson, and announcer Durwood Kirby. Many comedians who appeared on Moore's show regularly made their television debuts on his program, including Don ADAMS, Wally COX, Kaye Ballard, George GOBEL, Milt Kamen, Don KNOTTS, and Jonathan WINTERS. *The Garry Moore Show,* which was produced by Herb Sanford and directed by Clarence Schimmel, was heard on radio as well as seen on TV. It featured comedy sketches, musical numbers, and chatter, and had a relaxed, familiar quality that made it popular with viewers. After the show's initially successful telecasts, it was expanded to a full hour, but in that format, it remained on the air for less than a year. In 1958, Moore returned to television with a new series that became one of TV's most successful variety shows. Moore's new hour-long show had a big budget and featured lavishly staged musical numbers, numerous guest stars, a popular weekly feature called "That Wonderful Year," which each week highlighted events and entertainments from past years, and a fine cast of talented regulars that included his previous announcer, Durwood Kirby, as well as Marion Lorne, a dithery, stammering character actress who had scored a major success on the MR. PEEPERS show in the early 1950s, comedienne/singer Carol BURNETT (from 1959 to 1962) and then Dorothy Loudon (from 1962 to 1964), Alan FUNT and his CANDID CAMERA films, and, over the years, Chuck MCCANN, John Byner, Jackie Vernon, Paul Barbutti, the Buster Davis Singers, the George Becker Singers, the Paul Godkin Dancers, the Ernest Flatt Dancers, the Bob Hamilton Dancers, and the Howard Smith, Irwin Kostal, and Bernie Green Orchestras. Moore's evening show was produced by Joe Hamilton and Bob Banner. This popular series could have continued for many, many years, but in 1964, Moore decided he had to get a rest from the tiring weekly grind of putting on a fast-paced, elaborate variety show, and he announced his decision to end his weekly show. After a well-earned rest, Moore returned to television in 1966 with a new, less elaborate variety and comedy show that featured his old sidekick Durward Kirby. The new show was short-lived and was canceled after only a few months. Moore gradually faded from the spotlight, and only occasionally performed on television thereafter. Moore's 1966 series was produced by Sylvester "Pat" Weaver.

incompetence, Dave Garroway became one of television's earliest star/personalities. Garroway, who made full use of the medium's unique properties, was a radio disc jockey before entering TV in the late 1940s, and he even played the role of a disc jockey in the 1948 film *I Surrender Dear.* Born in Schenectady, New York, Garroway entered radio shortly after graduating from college, and made his TV debut as the host of one of television's earliest successes, *GARROWAY AT LARGE,* in 1949. Appearances on NBC's enormously popular *YOUR SHOW OF SHOWS* variety series in 1950 further established him as one of TV's major stars. In 1952, Garroway became the first host of NBC's early morning *TODAY* show and set the format that was followed by all the program's subsequent hosts. Garroway then hosted the *Wide Wide World* series in 1955, and began to exhibit fits of temperament and bad temper on the show. As if overnight, Garroway suddenly disappeared from TV screens in the early 1960s, and except for a rare guest-starring stint on the *Alias Smith and Jones* series in 1971, and as a voice-only performer on the *Jack Frost* TV film, Garroway disappeared from public view. In 1982, the public and members of the television community were shocked to learn that Dave Garroway had committed suicide at his home, apparently depressed at having been passed over and forgotten by the industry he loved.

GENE AUTRY SHOW, THE

July 1950–July 1953	CBS	Sun. 7–7:30 P.M.
July 1953–Sept. 1954	CBS	Tues. 8–8:30 P.M.
Sept. 1954–Aug. 1956	CBS	Sat. 7–7:30 P.M.

In 1950, singing cowboy film and radio performer Gene AUTRY brought his formidable talents to television as the star of a weekly, prime-time, half-hour series. With his sidekick, comedian Pat Buttram, and his horse, Champion, Autry, who was not a lawman, helped others maintain law and order in the Wild West, singing an occasional cowboy ballad, on what became one of the most popular children's western series on TV. Autry's shows, which were produced by his own production company, made the cowboy star millions of dollars, especially when the shows went into continuous reruns in the years that followed, and made Autry one of the wealthiest men in Hollywood. *The Gene Autry Show* spawned two successful spin-off series, ANNIE OAKLEY and *The Adventures of Champion* (1955–1956).

GENERAL ELECTRIC THEATER

| Feb. 1953–Sept. 1962 | CBS | Sun. 9–9:30 P.M. |

When this long-running dramatic anthology series first went on the air in 1953, *General Electric Theater* was an alternating series with *The Fred Waring Show*. Half-hour television plays were presented on alternating weeks that had a wide variety of themes and featured everything from westerns to biblical dramas to contemporary comedies. Many notable stars movies and the theater guest-starred on the show over the eight years the series was aired, and included such well-known names as Tony Curtis, Broderick Crawford, James Stewart, Michael LANDON, Robert CUMMINGS, Phyllis Thaxter, Burgess Meredith, Sir Cedric Hardwicke, Ward BOND, June Havoc, Alan Ladd, Jane Wyman, Barry Fitzgerald, Cornel Wilde, Myrna Loy, Jack BENNY, Bette Davis, Anne Baxter, Joseph Cotten, Fred MACMURRAY, Gene Tierney, Joan Crawford, Harry Belafonte, Rosalind Russell, Harpo, Groucho, and Chico MARX, Ernie KOVACS, Peggy Lee, Fred ASTAIRE, Sammy Davis, Jr., Nancy Davis Reagan (who appeared with her husband, Ronald Reagan), and Barbara STANWYCK, to name just some. During the series' 1954–1962 seasons, Ronald Reagan was the show's host, and he occasionally appeared in one of the plays. In 1962, another series called *General Electric True* surfaced and ran for one season. This series was a weekly dramatic anthology that presented dramatizations of true stories that had appeared in *True* magazine. Some performers on this series were Jerry Van Dyke, Arte Johnson, Robert Vaughn, and Victor Buono.

GENERAL HOSPITAL

| Apr. 1963–present | ABC | Mon.–Fri. Various times |

One of television's most popular daytime dramas, *General Hospital,* created by Doris and Frank Hursley, was a half-

hour program when it was first aired in 1963, and was not particularly well received by the public or critics when it made its debut. Under the supervision of Gloria Monty, who took over the producing chores in the late 1970s, the show's popularity steadily grew, until in 1980, it was the top-rated daytime drama. In 1976, the show was expanded to 45 minutes and was seen five day a week, and then expanded to a full hour, five times a week in 1978. In November 1981, an episode that featured the on-screen wedding of the popular *General Hospital* characters Luke Spencer and Laura Vining, played by Anthony Geary and Genie Francis, with the wicked Helena Cassadine in the background, played by Elizabeth Taylor (a fan of the show, who appeared on a few episodes just for the fun of it), attracted more viewers than any other single soap opera in TV history. Set at the fictional General Hospital, the show's original cast included former major-league baseball player John Beradino (who died in 1996 and was the last original cast member still on the show) as Dr. Steve Hardy; Emily McLaughlin (who died in 1991) as nurse Jessie Brewer; Lucille Wall as head nurse Lucille March; Rachel Ames as Lucille's sister, nurse Audrey March, who married Dr. Steve but then divorced him; Ross Elliott, and then Peter Hansen, as lawyer Lee Baldwin; as well as Roy Thinnes, Rick Falk, Robert Hogan, Craig Huebing, Martin West, Carolyn Craig, K. T. Stevens, Allison Hayes, Indus Arthur, Dean Harens, Paul Savior, Don Chastain, Barry Atwater, Catherine Farrar,

Emily McLaughlan (Jessie) and John Beradino (Dr. Steve Hardy) celebrate at *General Hospital's* seventh anniversary party (Author's collection)

Jennifer Billingsley, Ed Platt, Peggy McCay, Shelby Hiatt, Ray Girardin, Julie Adams, Denise Alexander, Denise Wilson, Kim Hamilton, Robin Blake, Adolph Caesar, Richard Dean Anderson, Susan Brown, Joan Tompkins, Stuart Damon, Lesley Woods, John Stamos, and many others. In 1987, executive producer Gloria Monty, who had guided *General Hospital* to success, left the show and was succeeded by H. Wesley Kenney. He in turn was succeeded by Joseph Hardy in 1989. Gloria Monty returned as the show's executive producer in 1990, but was succeeded by Wendy Riche in 1992.

By the 2000s, Sally Struthers, one of the stars of ALL IN THE FAMILY, the 1970s situation comedy series, had joined the cast as the third actress to play the role of Jennifer Smith on *General Hospital*; Lilly Melgar rejoined the cast as Lily Rivera Corinthos; Robin Christopher appeared as Skye Chandler-Quartermaine; Stephanie Allen was seen as the fourth Leslie Lu Spencer; Tamara Brawn was the second Carly Benson; Marc Brett was seen as Zander Smith; Jensen Buchanan played Melissa Bedford; Steve Burton reappeared as Jason Morgan; Tiernan Cunningham was seen as Michael Quartermaine; and Linda Dano was seen as Rae Cummings.

GEORGE BURNS AND GRACIE ALLEN SHOW, THE

Oct. 1950–Mar. 1953	CBS	Thurs. 8–8:30 P.M.
Mar. 1953–Sept. 1958	CBS	Mon. 8–8:30 P.M.

The husband and wife comedy team of George BURNS and Gracie ALLEN, who had begun their partnership in vaudeville in the late 1920s, appeared in many films and had a hit radio show from 1935 until 1950. They arrived on television in 1950. The team had one of the most popular situation comedy series on the air for eight years, until ill health forced Gracie Allen to retire from show business in 1958. *The George Burns and Gracie Allen Show* followed the same successful pattern their stage and radio act had enjoyed for over 30 years. George was the cigar-smoking straight man, who loved to sing but had an awful singing voice, and he patiently endured the scatterbrained comments and actions of his lovable wife, Gracie. On their TV series, George and Gracie lived in a comfortable, middle-class home. Their next door neighbors and friends were Blanche and Harry Morton, played by Bea BENADERET and Hal March and then John Brown, Fred Clark, and Larry Keating. Regular visitors to George and Gracie's home were announcers Bill Goodwin and Harry Von Zell, who delivered commercials and often participated in the show's story line. Later, George and Gracie's real-life adopted son, Ronnie Burns, joined the cast, playing himself. Originally telecast live from New York City every other Thursday night, the show became a once-a-week, filmed TV series that originated from the West Coast in 1952. By the time *The George Burns and Gracie Allen Show* left the air in 1958, the team's familiar closing—George saying, "Say good night, Gracie," and Gracie responding, "Good night, Gracie"—had become part of American TV history.

GEORGE GOBEL SHOW, THE

Oct. 1954–June 1957	NBC	Sat. 10–10:30 P.M.
Sept. 1957–Mar. 1959	NBC	Tues. 8–9 P.M.
Oct. 1959–June 1960	CBS	Sun. 10–10:30 P.M.

Soft-spoken, low-keyed, and mild-mannered comedian George GOBEL, who became familiarly known as "Lonesome George" to his many fans, starred on a popular weekly variety/situation comedy series for six years, and then all but disappeared from the public spotlight, except for occasional guest-starring appearances on panel shows. Each week, George opened his show with a monologue and then was seen in sketches that were usually about the problems the mild-mannered George was having with his wife, Alice. Alice was played by Jeff Donnell and then by Phyllis Avery. When the series moved from NBC to CBS in 1959, the Alice character was dropped. George Gobel was one of television's most successful comedians, and his familiar expressions, "Well, I'll be a dirty bird," and "We don't hardly get those no more," became oft-quoted catchphrases for millions of viewer-fans. When his show was on CBS, it alternated with *The JACK BENNY SHOW*, and was aired for only one season.

GERALD McBOING BOING SHOW, THE

May 1956	CBS	Sunday afternoons
May 1958–Oct. 1958	CBS	Fri. 7:30–9 P.M.

The popular TV cartoon series *The Boing Boing Show*, was first seen as a Sunday afternoon children's program, and for a short time in 1958, it was an early evening offering on the CBS network. The series featured a character named Gerald McBoing-Boing, who could not speak, but communicated by using gestures and various noises. Announcer/moderator Bill Goodwin was always available to translate what Gerald was trying to say when it became difficult to understand him. The show was very successful with young, and even many adult, viewers, for the entire time it was aired.

GERTRUDE BERG SHOW, THE

Oct. 1961–Jan. 1962	CBS	Wed. 9:30–10 P.M.
Jan. 1962–Apr. 1962	CBS	Thurs. 9:30–10 P.M.

Gertrude BERG, who became well known to viewers as Molly Goldberg on *The GOLDBERGS* in the late 1940s–early 1950s, returned to television in 1961 as the star of a new show called *The Gertrude Berg Show*. Similar to *The Goldbergs*, which Berg wrote as well as starred in, on this new show Berg played a Jewish woman named Sarah Green, an older and more worldly version of Molly Goldberg. Sarah was a widow who decided in her declining years that she wanted to be better educated, and enrolled in college. Her English teacher, Professor Grayson, played by Sir Cedric Hardwicke, was an exchange teacher from Cambridge, England. Sarah lived in a boardinghouse managed by a crusty woman named Maxfield, played by Mary Wickes. Joe Caldwell, played by Skip Ward, was an 18-year-old who also lived at Maxfield's boardinghouse and became Sarah's friend and confidante. Also appearing on the series in regular roles were Marion ROSS, Leo Penn, Paul Smith, Aneta Corsaut, and Karyn Kupcinet. Originally titled *Mrs. G. Goes to College*, the show's name was changed after a few months to capitalize on Gertrude Berg's well-known name.

GET SMART

Sept. 1965–Sept. 1968	NBC	Sat. 8:30–9 P.M.
Sept. 1968–Sept. 1969	NBC	Sat. 8–8:30 P.M.
Sept. 1969–Feb. 1970	CBS	Fri. 7:30–8 P.M.
Apr. 1970–Sept. 1970	CBS	Fri 7:30–8 P.M.
Jan. 1995–Feb. 1995	FOX	Sun. 7:30–8 P.M.

In the 1960s, films and TV series featuring secret agents such as James Bond, John Steed of *The AVENGERS*, and John Drake of *SECRET AGENT* were very popular. With this in mind, Mel Brooks and Buck Henry developed a spoof of these shows with their TV series called *Get Smart*. The hero of Brooks and Henry's hilarious, if sophomoric, situation comedy series was an agent named Maxwell Smart, played by comedian Don ADAMS. Smart was an enthusiastic, but totally inept, often confused bumbler, who battled the evil Professor Siegfried, played by Stacy Keach, Sr., and his assistant, Starker, played by King Moody, who worked for the mysterious K.A.O.S. organization. Maxwell Smart worked for "The Chief," Thaddeus, played by Edward Platt, who was the head of the U.S. Intelligence Agency C.O.N.T.R.O.L. that was located in Washington, D.C. Working with Smart was a beautiful and intelligent young woman agent simply known as Agent 99, played by Barbara FELDON. *Get Smart* was an extremely funny series and proved popular with both young and adult viewers. Max's favorite expression, "Would you believe . . . " followed by an improbable explanation of something he wished not to reveal, became a popular catchphrase. Twenty-five years after the original series left the air, it was revived in a new series seen on the FOX network. Don Adams, who reprised his role of Maxwell Smart on the new series, was now the "Chief" of C.O.N.T.R.O.L., and Barbara Feldon, once again playing Agent 99, was a congresswoman. Smart and Agent 99 had been married and had a son, Zach, played by Andy Dick, who was a nerd and who also worked for C.O.N.T.R.O.L., as a researcher. Another new character was Max's flighty secretary, Trudy, played by Heather Morgan. The show, which was only a pale imitation of the original series, was canceled after only seven episodes.

GETTY, ESTELLE (ESTELLE SCHER GETTLEMAN 1924–)

Estelle Getty, who was born in New York City, did not begin her professional acting career until she was 54 years old. A former housewife and mother, Getty was first seen playing a teacher in the film *Team-Mates* (1978). Small roles in *Tootsie* (1982), *Deadly Force* (1983), and *Mask* (1985), and in the TV films *Victims for Victims: The Theresa Saldana Story* (1984) and *No Man's Land* (1984), led to her being cast as Sophia Petrillo, Bea ARTHUR's 80-year-old Italian mother on *GOLDEN GIRLS*. The show and Getty were an enormous hit, and the actress won an Emmy in 1988 for her performance as Sophia on the series. While *Golden Girls* was still on the air. Getty appeared in the TV film *Copacabana* (1985), and in the feature films *Mannequin* (1987), *Stop! or My Mom Will Shoot* (1992). In 1992, Bea Arthur had had enough of *Golden Girls* and departed the series, but Estelle and the two other stars, Betty WHITE and Rue MCCLANAHAN, decided to keep the characters on the air without Arthur, and the three appeared in a new series called *The GOLDEN PALACE*. Unfortunately, the series was not a success and was canceled after one season. Getty had previously repeated her Sophia Petrillo role on *EMPTY NEST* in 1988. After *The Golden Palace* left the air, Getty guest-starred on *HOLLYWOOD SQUARES*, *The JOHN LARROQUETTE SHOW*, *TOUCHED BY AN ANGEL*, *MAD ABOUT YOU*, and *Duckman*, and appeared in the films *A Match Made in Heaven* (1997), *The Million Dollar Kid* (1999), and *Stuart Little* (1999).

GIFFORD, KATHIE LEE (KATHRYN LEE EPSTEIN 1953–)

Born in Paris, France, where her father was stationed as a member of the armed forces, Kathie Lee Gifford moved about quite a bit as a child, but graduated from high school in Bowie, Maryland. After winning the Maryland Junior Miss contest when she was 17 years old, Kathie Lee, who had been a cheerleader in high school, attended Oral Roberts University, where she majored in drama and music. In 1977, Kathie Lee appeared on the *NAME THAT TUNE* TV quiz show as a regular singer, and then in 1978, appeared as Kathie Lee Johnson, one of the "Honeys," on the syndicated TV series *Hee Haw Honeys*. Kathie Lee was a frequent substitute host on *GOOD MORNING AMERICA* from 1982 until 1987. Kathie Lee Gifford finally became a major TV personality when she was hired to be Regis Philbin's costar on the *LIVE WITH REGIS AND KATHIE LEE* morning talk show in 1989. In addition to that show, Kathie Lee also made guest-starring appearances on *SEINFELD*, *TOUCHED BY AN ANGEL*, *SPIN CITY*, *DIAGNOSIS MURDER*, *CAROLINE IN THE CITY*, and *The SIMPSONS*, and had featured roles in such films as *The First Wives Club* (1996) and *Dudley Do-Right* (1999), and was the voice of Echidna in the film *Hercules* in 1998. In July 2000, Kathie Lee left *Live with Regis and Kathie Lee* to pursue other career interests.

GILBERT, MELISSA (MELISSA ELLEN GILBERT 1964–)

Born into a show business family in Los Angeles, Melissa Gilbert began her professional acting career when she was nine years old and appeared on an episode of *GUNSMOKE*.

Roles on such TV shows as EMERGENCY! led to her being cast as Laura Ingalls on the TV series LITTLE HOUSE ON THE PRAIRIE, which became extremely popular with viewers and remained on the air for nine years. While appearing on *Little House on the Prairie*, Melissa also made guest-starring appearances on such shows as *The LOVE BOAT* and *Faerie Tale Theatre*, and also starred in the TV films *The Miracle Worker* (1979, as Helen Keller), *The Diary of Anne Frank* (1980, as Anne Frank), and *Splendor in the Grass* (1981), among others. By the time *Little House on the Prairie* ended its TV run in 1983, Gilbert went on to star in countless other TV films such as *Family Secrets* (1984), *Blood Vows: The Story of a Mafia Wife* (1987), *Without Her Consent* (1990), *With Hostile Intent* (1993), *House of Secrets* (1993), *Cries from the Heart* (1994), *Seduction in a Small Town* (1997), *Switched at Birth* (1999), *From Dusk Till Dawn 3: The Hangman's Daughter* (2000), and others. She also starred on the less successful TV series *Stand by Your Man* (1992), *Batman: The Animated Series* (1992–93, voice), and *Sweet Justice* (1994–95), and guest-starred on such series as BABYLON 5, *The OUTER LIMITS*, and TOUCHED BY AN ANGEL. Gilbert is the youngest person ever to receive a star on the Hollywood Walk of Fame.

GILLIGAN'S ISLAND

Sept. 1964–Sept. 1965	CBS	Sat. 8:30–9 P.M.
Sept. 1965–Sept. 1966	CBS	Thurs. 8–8:30 P.M.
Sept. 1966–Sept. 1967	CBS	Mon. 7:30–8 P.M.

Gilligan (Bob Denver) and the Skipper (Alan Hale, Jr.) of *Gilligan's Island* (Author's collection)

Although it is one of television's most fondly remembered situation comedy series, *Gilligan's Island* was on the air for only three years, and was disliked by critics when it made its debut in 1964. The series involved a group of sightseers who, while out on a boat called *The Minnow*, become marooned on a remote island somewhere in the South Pacific after they are thrown off course during a violent storm and their boat is destroyed. The castaways, an unlikely group of travelers, included the jolly captain of *The Minnow*, Jonas Grumby (the Skipper), played by Alan Hale, Jr.; Gilligan, his flaky, young, one-and-only crew member, played by Bob DENVER; Thurston Howell III, a pompous-but-good-natured millionaire, and his dithery wife, Lovey, played by Jim BACKUS and Natalie Shafer respectively; Ginger Grant, a gorgeous redheaded movie star, played by Tina Louise; Roy Hinkley, a stuffy young high school science teacher called "the Professor," played by Russell Johnson; and Mary Ann Summers, a country girl who was visiting California when she decided on impulse to go out on the boat to sightsee, played by Dawn Wells. One of the questions viewers kept asking during the show's run was, if, as the series' opening theme song stated, *The Minnow* was supposed to be going on a three-hour sightseeing tour, how did the castaways manage to have so many clothes with them? The castaways were, after all, marooned on the desert island for years, and the Howells and Ginger seemed to wear a new outfit on each week's episode. Even though *Gilligan's Island's* fans were mainly preadolescents, the show also became popular with many adults, and after it was canceled, the show became the most successful rerun in the 1960s and 1970s. In 1974, an animated cartoon version of the show called *The New Adventures of Gilligan's Island* made its debut on ABC and remained on the air for three years. A second *Gilligan's Island* cartoon series, *Gilligan's Planet*, emerged in 1982, and ran for two years. In 1978, NBC decided to reunite the original cast of the show in a special TV film in which the castaways were finally rescued. The original series had ended rather abruptly, leaving the castaways stranded on the island. The entire original cast agreed to appear on the show, with the exception of Tina Louise, who had demanded more money to reprise her role than NBC was willing to pay. Judith Baldwin played the part. The reunion show, *Rescue from Gilligan's Island*, was aired as a two-part special, and was a big success, attracting millions of viewers who wanted to know what had happened to the castaways. *Gilligan's Island* was created and produced by Sherwood Schwartz.

GIMME A BREAK!

Oct. 1981–Aug. 1982	NBC	Thurs. 9:30–10 P.M.
Sept. 1982	NBC	Thurs. 9–9:30 P.M.
Oct. 1982–Dec. 1982	NBC	Sat. 9–9:30 P.M.
Jan. 1983–Aug. 1983	NBC	Thurs. 9–9:30 P.M.
Aug. 1983–Sept. 1984	NBC	Thurs. 8–8:30 P.M.
Sept. 1984–Nov. 1984	NBC	Sat. 8:30–9 P.M.
Dec. 1984–Aug. 1985	NBC	Sat. 9–9:30 P.M.

Sept. 1985–June 1986	NBC	Sat. 8–8:30 P.M.
July 1986–Mar. 1987	NBC	Wed. 9:30–10 P.M.
Mar. 1987–May 1987	NBC	Tues. 9–9:30 P.M.

Fresh from Broadway and her Tony Award–winning performance in the musical *Ain't Misbehavin'*, the rotund African-American singer/actress Nell CARTER made her TV debut as the star of an old-fashioned situation comedy series called *Gimme a Break!*, which was about a fun-loving woman named Nellie Ruth "Nell" Harper, who takes charge of the family of white police chief Carl Kanisky, played by character actor Dolph Sweet, when Kanisky's beloved wife dies, leaving him with three young daughters to raise. The daughters, Katie, Julie, and Samantha (aka Sam), were played by Kari Michaelson, Lauri Hendler, and Lara Jill Miller. Also featured on the series were Howard Morton as an odd police officer named Ralph Simpson; John Hoyt and Jane Dulo as Grandpa and Grandma Kanisky; Pete Schrum as Uncle Ed Kanisky; and Joey Lawrence, Thelma Hopkins, Matthew Lawrence, Paul Sand, Rosetta LeNoir, and Rosie O'Donnell, who played Maggie O'Brien. Because Nell Carter was a rather heavyset woman, lots of good-natured fat jokes prevailed. The 1985–86 season began on a sad note when it was announced that Police Chief Kanisky had died, leaving Nell to raise the three Kanisky girls by herself (at the time, it was rumored that actor Dolph Sweet had had enough of Carter's outbreaks of temper and wanted off the series). The man of the house then became Jonathan Maxwell, played by Jonathan Silverman, who had married Julie at the end of the previous season. The series managed to remain on the air for an impressive six years, despite NBC's many changes in the show's time slot, making it difficult for viewers to keep track of the series. The February 23, 1985, episode was presented "live," a rare event for TV, in order to generate new interest in the series, whose popularity had begun to fade. *Gimme a Break!* was created by Mort Lachman and Sy Rosen.

GLEASON, JACKIE (HERBERT JOHN GLEASON 1916–1987)

One of television's, and indeed show business's, most beloved performers, Jackie Gleason was born in Brooklyn, New York. Leaving high school before he graduated, Gleason went to work at various odd jobs to help support his family. While in his late teens, Gleason grew interested in performing and began to sing and tell jokes at local saloons. Eventually, Gleason became a comic in burlesque and in vaudeville and went to Hollywood, where the heavyset comedian began to get small supporting roles in such films as *Steel Against the Sky* (1941), *Navy Blues* (1941), *Springtime in the Rockies* (1942), *Orchestra Wives* (1942), *All Through the Night* (1942), and *Escape from Crime* (1942). Discouraged with the way his film career was going, Gleason returned to performing in nightclubs, but in 1949, he was cast as Chester A. Riley on the TV situation comedy series *The LIFE OF RILEY*. When actor William Bendix, who had created the role of Riley on radio, decided he wanted to play the part on television, Gleason was replaced. That same year, however, Gleason became one of the hosts of the popular *Cavalcade of Stars* (1949–52) TV variety series, on which he introduced his later-to-be-famous Ralph Kramden character in several *Honeymooners* sketches. The character, and Gleason, were major successes, and in 1952, Gleason became the star of his own *JACKIE GLEASON SHOW*, on which *The Honeymooners* once again was frequently featured. In 1955, due to popular demand, Gleason starred in a regular *HONEYMOONERS* series, which, by that time, was already a TV classic. Trying to break away from his Ralph Kramden image, Gleason appeared in the TV series *You're in the Picture* in 1961, and made his debut that same year as a serious actor in *The Hustler*. Film critics and the public were amazed at Gleason's serious acting talents, and the rotund performer, in addition to hosting *The Jackie Gleason Show: The American Scene Magazine* TV series, was soon in demand as a film actor. He appeared in such successful films as *Gigot* (1962), *Requiem for a Heavyweight* (1962), *Soldiers in the Rain* (1963), and *Papa's Delicate Condition* (1963). In 1966, Gleason returned to television as the star of a new *Jackie Gleason Show*, and subsequently appeared in such hit films as *Don't Drink the Water* (1969), *Smokey and the Bandit* and *Smokey and the Bandit II* and *III* (1977, 1980, 1983), *The Sting II* (1983), and *Nothing in Common* (1986), his last film, among others. In 1987, Gleason, known for his heavy drinking and other excesses, died of liver and colon cancer in Fort Lauderdale, Florida.

GOBEL, GEORGE (1919–1991)

Comedian George Gobel, known to his fans as "Lonesome George," was born in Chicago, Illinois. The low-keyed, meek Gobel made his debut as a stand-up comedian, and in 1954, he attracted the attention of the public as a guest on *The Spike Jones Show*. That same year, Gobel was given a weekly variety/situation comedy series of his own, *The GEORGE GOBEL SHOW*, and the comedian soon became one of the most popular entertainers on television. By 1959, the public had become tired of Gobel and his show. Guest-starring appearances on such TV series as MY THREE SONS, DEATH VALLEY DAYS, F TROOP, *Love American Style* (1969–74), and *The Fall Guy* (1981–86), and regular appearances on *The HOLLYWOOD SQUARES*, *The Eddie Fisher Show* (1957–59), and in such films as *Rabbit Test* (1978), *A Guide for the Married Woman* (1978), and *Better Late Than Never* (1979), followed. Gobel is, however, perhaps best known for playing Mayor Otis Harper on the TV series HARPER VALLEY P.T.A. Gobel's last major TV appearance was in the TV film *Alice in Wonderland* in 1985, in which he played "The Gnat."

GODFREY, ARTHUR (ARTHUR MORTON GODFREY 1903–1983)

The legendary TV personality Arthur Godfrey, who throughout the 1950s was one of the most influential

Arthur Godfrey (Author's collection)

men on television, was born in New York City. As a young man, Godfrey joined the navy, and upon being discharged, entered radio as an announcer at WFBP in Baltimore, Maryland, where he also sang and played his ukulele on a local show. Godfrey then became a staff announcer for NBC, but it was an early morning Washington D.C.–based radio show for CBS that catapulted him into national prominence. His gentle hawking of various sponsors' products and his comforting, sensitive coverage of President Franklin D. Roosevelt's funeral in 1945 made him a household name. In 1948, Godfrey took his formidable talents to television as the star of ARTHUR GODFREY'S TALENT SCOUTS, which was heard and seen on both radio and television. The show was an immediate hit, and the following year, Godfrey became the host of a TV variety series, ARTHUR GODFREY AND HIS FRIENDS, which became one of the most popular shows on television. He subsequently hosted *Arthur Godfrey and His Ukulele, Arthur Godfrey Time,* and *The Arthur Godfrey Show.* By the late 1950s, Godfrey's on-air firing of regular cast member Julius LaRosa, and his growing arrogance in general, had begun to annoy viewers, and they began to turn off his shows. In 1960, Godfrey resurfaced cohosting CANDID CAMERA with Alan FUNT. In 1966, Godfrey was seen as Doris DAY's father in the film *The Glass Bottom Boat,* but he was by that time less in demand. Except for occasional appearances in

such TV and feature films as *Handle with Care* (1977), *The Great Bank Hoax* (1977), *Flatbed Annie & Sweetie-pie: Lady Truckers* (1977), and *Angel's Brigade* (1979), Godfrey all but disappeared from the public spotlight. He died, relatively unknown to younger generations of television viewers, in 1983 at the age of 80.

GOLDBERGS, THE

Jan. 1949–Feb. 1949	CBS	Mon. 8–8:30 P.M.
Mar. 1949–Apr. 1949	CBS	Mon. 9–9:30 P.M.
Apr. 1949–June 1951	CBS	Mon. 9:30–10 P.M.
Feb. 1952–July 1952	CBS	Mon./Wed./Fri. 7:15–7:30 P.M.
July 1953–Sept. 1953	CBS	Fri. 8–8:30 P.M.
Apr. 1954–Oct. 1954	DUMONT	Tues. 8–8:30 P.M.

Gertrude BERG's popular program, *The Goldbergs,* on radio from 1929 until 1950, in 1949 was one of the first domestic comedy series to make a successful transition from radio to television. *The Goldbergs,* was written by and starring Gertrude Berg as Molly Goldberg, a lovable, nurturing, and forever-wise Jewish mother, who lived in apartment 3B at 1030 East Tremont Avenue in the Bronx, New York. Molly's family, her husband, Jake, played by Philip Loeb and then by Harold J. Stone and Robert H. Harris; her teenage son, Sammy, played by Larry Robinson and then Tom Taylor; her daughter, Rosalie, played by Arlene McQuade; and her Uncle David, played by Eli Mintz, were a close-knit, working-class family who encountered all the usual problems most TV families have to deal with in their everyday lives. Since Molly, Jake, and Uncle David were first-generation Americans and spoke with heavy eastern European accents, their mispronunciations and malapropisms were the source of much of the show's humor. A recurrent scene on each week's show had Molly leaning out of her apartment window, calling, "Yoo hoo, Mrs. Bloom," whenever she had something good to gossip about with her neighbor, who lived in the apartment next door. Mrs. Bloom was played by Olga Fabian. Other characters who appeared on the show regularly were Dora Barnett, Sammy's fiancée, and her mother, Carrie, played by Betty Bendyke and then Ruth Yorke, and neighbors Daisy and Henry Carey, played by Susan Steel and Jon Lormer. During its earliest years, *The Goldbergs,* like most TV shows of the time, was telecast live, which often made for amusing on-camera mistakes, such as windows that wouldn't open, lines forgotten, and characters who were late for a scene. The show was canceled after five seasons, but could have remained on the air for many more years, except that in 1951, Philip Loeb was blacklisted when he was accused of having left-wing sympathies. In the anticommunist 1950s, this sort of accusation was sure death to an actor's career. In 1955, Loeb, who was never able to reclaim his acting career, committed suicide. *The Goldbergs* never recaptured the popularity it had enjoyed before Loeb's tragic death.

GOLDEN GIRLS, THE

Sept. 1985–July 1991	NBC	Sat. 9–9:30 P.M.
Aug. 1991–Sept. 1991	NBC	Sat. 8–8:30 P.M.
Sept. 1991–Sept. 1992	NBC	Sat. 8:30–9 P.M.

The unlikely heroines of this very popular, highly amusing situation comedy series were three over-50 widows who lived together in Miami. Dorothy Zbornak, an outspoken, divorced substitute teacher, was played by Bea ARTHUR; Rose Nylund, an unsophisticated, scatterbrained woman from the Minnesota farm country, was played by Betty WHITE; and their Miami home's owner, Blanche Devereaux, an attractive, sex-obsessed southern belle, was played by Rue McCLANAHAN. Also living with the three women was Dorothy's 80-year-old mother, Sophia Petrillo, played by Estelle Getty, who, before she went to live with Dorothy, Rose, and Blanche, had resided at the dreaded Shady Pines retirement home before it burned to the ground. Sicilian-born Sophia was a firecracker of a woman who, in spite of her advanced age, could always be depended upon to put her three housemates in their place when the situation called for it. Appearing on the series regularly was Stanley Zbornak, Dorothy's no-good ex-husband, who had left her for a younger woman and then been dumped himself, played by Herb Edelman. Harold Gould was also featured on the series for several

The Golden Girls: (clockwise from left) Estelle Getty (Sophia), Rue McClanahan (Blanche), Betty White (Rose), and Bea Arthur (Dorothy) (Author's collection)

seasons as Rose's boyfriend, Miles Webber. Rose later discovered that Miles was a former mob accountant who had turned state's evidence and was in the Witness Protection Program and had to leave town when his true identity was discovered. *The Golden Girls,* which won 10 Emmy Awards, was a Nielsen top-10 show for the first five years it was on the air. On the show's final episode, wedding bells rang for Dorothy and Blanche's visiting uncle Lucas, played by Leslie Nielson. *The Golden Girls,* whose memorable theme song was "Thank You for Being a Friend," was created by Susan Harris. The series' executive producer was Gail Parent.

GOLDEN PALACE, THE

| Sept. 1992–Aug. 1993 | CBS | Fri. 8–8:30 P.M. |

A sequel to the popular GOLDEN GIRLS series, *The Golden Palace* featured three of the stars of *Golden Girls,* Rue McCLANAHAN, Betty WHITE, and Estelle GETTY, playing the roles they had played on the former series: Blanche Devereaux, Rose Nylund, and Sophia Petrillo. On this series, Blanche had sold her Miami home after Dorothy Zbornak, played by Bea ARTHUR, left to get married, and the remaining three housemates bought a small Art Deco hotel in the South Bay section of Miami Beach. Also appearing on the series were Cheech Marin as Chuy Castillos, their Mexican-born chef, Don Cheadle as Roland Wilson, the women's Black manager/desk clerk, and Billy L. Sullivan as Oliver Webb, a young boy who does odd jobs at the hotel. The series, without Bea Arthur's caustic wit, failed to attract an audience, and the show was canceled after only one year on the air.

GOMER PYLE, U.S.M.C.

Sept. 1964–June 1965	CBS	Fri. 9:30–10 P.M.
Sept. 1965–Sept. 1966	CBS	Fri. 9–9:30 P.M.
Sept. 1966–Aug. 1967	CBS	Wed. 9:30–10 P.M.
Sept. 1967–Sept. 1969	CBS	Fri. 8:30–9 P.M.
July 1970–Sept. 1970	CBS	Wed. 8–8:30 P.M.

After playing the lovable, naive gas station attendant Gomer Pyle on *The* ANDY GRIFFITH SHOW, Jim NABORS was offered a situation comedy series of his own. Nabors played the same country bumpkin with the high-pitched voice and pronounced southern drawl, who kept saying, "Golllllie!" whenever confronted with an unusual situation, that he had played on *The Andy Griffith Show.* Gomer, however, had left Mayberry, North Carolina, and joined the U.S. Marine Corps. Stationed at Camp Henderson, Gomer's nemesis was a tough Marine sergeant, Vince Carter, played by Frank Sutton, who was constantly dumbfounded by Gomer's naiveté. Other regular characters seen on the series were Pvt. Gilbert "Duke" Slater, played by Ronnie Schell; Cpl. Chuck Boyle, played by Roy Stuart; Frankie Lombardi, played by Ted Bessell; Bunny, played by Barbara Stuart; Pvt. Lester Hummel, played by William Christopher; and Col. Edward Gray, played by Forrest Compton. Also featured on the series were Tommy Leonetti as Sgt. Hacker, Larry Hovis as Larry, and Elizabeth MacRae as Lou Anne Poovie. Over the six years the series was aired, Sgt. Carter eventually became Gomer's protector and friend in spite of his never-ending exasperation with Gomer's naive, often silly, behavior. *Gomer Pyle* was produced by the same men who had produced *The Andy Griffith Show,* Sheldon Leonard and Aaron Ruben, and by the time it left the air, 150 episodes had been completed.

GONG SHOW, THE

June 1976–July 1978	NBC	Various daytime hours
1976–1980	Syndicated show	Various times and stations
1988	Syndicated	Various times and stations

Chuck BARRIS, a diminutive, perennially stoned-looking man, created and coproduced *The Gong Show* and was also its host. The premise was simple. Unusual variety acts were performed before a panel of three celebrity judges who rated them on a scale of one to 10, or hit a large gong, putting them off the show before they finished their performances. The acts usually ranged from bad to downright silly, and more often than not they were gonged. People whistled through their noses, fat ballerinas danced in tutus, dogs sang, sopranos wailed, elderly people danced, and inept magicians bungled. All were given a chance to compete with one another for the show's prize money, $516.32 on the weekday show and $712.05 on the evening show. When the show was on NBC, contestants could win as much as $1,000. Two out of 10 people who appeared on the show had talent and they usually won the prizes. Some contestants were so popular with the studio audience that they returned as regulars on the show. One such contestant was Gene-Gene, the Dancing Machine, a middle-aged black man who tap-danced softly in place, but barely moved. The show's staff, the celebrity/panelists, and even the studio audience, would throw all sorts of objects at him as he danced, but he remained oblivious. Another contestant-turned-regular was the Unknown Comic, who after his appearance on the show often appeared as a panelist. The Unknown Comic, who wore a paper bag over his head, told jokes and never revealed his real identity on the show. Sometime later he was revealed to be one Murray Langston. Regular panelists included Jaye P. Morgan, whose sexy comments made her an audience favorite, film critic Rex Reed, Arte Johnson, Michele Lee, Jamie Farr, Rip Taylor, Phyllis Diller, and Steve Garvey. Announcer/host Gary Owens hosted *The Gong Show* during its first year as a syndicated show, before Barris took over the hosting chores. In 1988, *The Gong Show*

was revived with Don Bleu hosting, but without Barris, the show proved only mildly amusing.

GOODMAN, JOHN (1952–)

Before John Goodman became well known as Roseanne Barr's husband, Dan Conner, on the popular ROSEANNE sitcom series, he had appeared in major supporting roles on *The* EQUALIZER and MOONLIGHTING and in the feature films *Jailbait Babysitter* (1978), *The Survivors* (1983), *Revenge of the Nerds* (1984), *Raising Arizona* (1987), *The Big Easy* (1987), and *Punchline* (1988), among others. Goodman, who was born in St. Louis, Missouri, was a graduate of Southwest Missouri State, where he majored in drama. Before finding work as an actor, Goodman, a burly, heavyset man, was a bouncer in a nightclub. After his success on *Roseanne,* Goodman became one of the most sought-after character actors in Hollywood, and he played major roles in such feature films as *Stella* (with Bette Midler, 1990), *Arachnophobia* (1990), *The Babe* (1992), *Kingfish: A Story of Huey P. Long* (1995), *Blues Brothers 2000* (1998), *Bringing Out the Dead* (1999), and *O Brother, Where Art Thou?* (2000), as well as a TV version of Tennessee Williams's *A Streetcar Named Desire* (1995). In addition, Goodman is one of SATURDAY NIGHT LIVE's most popular guest hosts. Equally at home playing serious or comic roles, Goodman has been featured on GRACE UNDER FIRE, *Soul Man* (1997–98), *The* SIMPSONS (1998) (as the voice of Meathook), and *Futurama* (1999).

GOOD MORNING AMERICA

Nov. 1975–present	ABC	Mon.–Fri. 7–9 A.M.

Good Morning America was the first network show to give NBC's popular early morning program TODAY serious competition. The ABC show, like *Today,* is a combination news, interview, special features program, and was originally hosted by David Hartman, who remained with the program until 1987. Nancy Dussault was Hartman's first cohost. When Dussault departed the show in 1977, she was replaced by Sandy Hill, who left the program in 1980. Joan Lunden then took over the job of cohost with Hartman. Regularly featured were columnist Jack Anderson, humorist/author Erma Bombeck, celebrity gossip columnist Rona Barrett, newsman Geraldo Rivera, magazine editor Helen Gurley Brown, former Olympian Bruce Jenner and his wife, Chrystie, and physicians Dr. Timothy Johnson and then Dr. Lendon Smith. In 1987, David Hartman left the show and was replaced by Charles Gibson. By 1982, *Good Morning America* had replaced NBC's *Today* show as America's favorite early morning program.

GOOD TIMES

Feb. 1974–Sept. 1974	CBS	Fri. 8:30–9 P.M.
Sept. 1974–Mar. 1976	CBS	Tues. 8–8:30 P.M.
Mar. 1976–Aug. 1976	CBS	Tues. 8:30–9 P.M.

Sept. 1976–Jan. 1978	CBS	Wed. 8–8:30 P.M.
Jan. 1978–May 1978	CBS	Mon. 8–8:30 P.M.
June 1978–Sept. 1978	CBS	Mon. 8:30–9 P.M.
Sept. 1978–Dec. 1978	CBS	Sat. 8:30–9 P.M.
May 1979–Aug. 1979	CBS	Wed. 8:30–9 P.M.

A spin-off of the popular situation comedy series MAUDE, which had been a spin-off of ALL IN THE FAMILY, *Good Times* starred Esther ROLLE as Florida Evans, who had been Maude's maid. Florida and her husband, James, played by John Amos, were a working-class black couple who had three children: James, Jr. (called "J.J."), played by Jimmie WALKER, Thelma, played by BernNadette Stanis, and Michael, played by Ralph Carter. The Evans family lived in a high-rise ghetto apartment on the South Side of Chicago. Florida and James Evans were a hard-working couple, even though James was often out of work, who tried to guide their children toward better lives. J. J., who was 17 when the series first went on the air, was always looking for a get-rich-quick scheme that would get him out of the ghetto. His catchphrase, "Dy-no-mite," whenever things were looking good, became familiar to millions of viewers who became fans of the show, and even appeared on T-shirts at the height of the show's popularity. Thelma was 16 when the show began, and Michael was 10. Other regular characters on the series were Willona Woods, Florida's pretty next-door apartment neighbor and best friend, played by Ja'net DuBois; Carl Dixon, played by Moses Gunn; Nathan Bookman, played by Johnny Brown; Penny Gordon Woods, played by future pop-star Janet Jackson (sister of Michael Jackson); Keith Anderson, played by Ben Powers; and Sweet Daddy, played by Theodore Wilson. At the beginning of the 1976–77 season, John Amos decided that he wanted to leave the series, and his character went to Mississippi to work. During the season, it was learned that James had been killed in an accident, leaving Florida a widow. The following year, Esther Rolle decided that she, too, had had enough of the series after three years and what she felt were less than satisfying scripts for her character. The show, with Jimmie Walker as its star, continued without Florida and James, and limped along for an additional year. The die, however, had been cast, and *Good Times* was canceled when the 1978–79 season ended. Norman LEAR, who had produced both *All in the Family* and *Maude*, Allan Manings, Austin and Irma Kalish, and Norman Paul were the series' executive producers. By the time *Good Times* left the air, 133 episodes had been filmed.

GOODSON-TODMAN (MARK GOODSON 1915–1992; BILL TODMAN 1916–1979)

Radio and television producers Mark Goodson and Bill Todman's names became synonymous with game shows and panel shows. The production partners' first TV game show was on the Mutual Broadcasting System and was called *Pop the Question*. Contestants threw darts at balloons to determine the value of their prizes. The team's most successful collaborations were the long-running TV panel shows WHAT'S MY LINE? TO TELL THE TRUTH, and I'VE GOT A SECRET, and the game show BEAT THE CLOCK. Goodson and Todman also produced the series *The Web* in 1950, and *The Richard Boone Show* (1963–64). After Bill Todman's death in 1979, Mark Goodson continued to be active as a television and film producer, until his death from cancer in 1992.

GOODYEAR TV PLAYHOUSE

| Oct. 1951–Sept. 1957 | NBC | 9–10 P.M. |
| Sept. 1957–Sept. 1960 | NBC | 9:30–10 P.M. |

Goodyear Tires sponsored this hour-long, early TV dramatic anthology program that remained on the air longer than any other series of its kind. Every other week for six years, a live, hour-long original TV drama, alternating with the PHILCO TELEVISION PLAYHOUSE and later with *The Alcoa Hour*, was presented. Fred Coe was the talented producer who guided the series to success. Original television plays that became classics and which were later adapted into successful feature films had their beginnings on *Goodyear TV Playhouse*. Paddy CHAYEFSKY wrote his critically acclaimed dramas *The Catered Affair* and *Marty* for *Goodyear TV Playhouse*, and other writers whose works were presented on this series included Tad Mosel, Robert Alan Auther, Horton Foote, N. Richard Nash, J. P. Miller, Reginald ROSE, Sumner Locke Elliot, David Shaw, Gore Vidal, and Calder Willingham. Many celebrated performers appeared on the series, including Rod Steiger (who originated the role of Marty), Roddy McDowall, Eli Wallach, Walter Matthau, Kim Stanley, Gene Kelly, Eva Marie Saint, Cyril Ritchard, Martin Balsam, Tony RANDALL, Julie Harris, Paul Newman, Grace Kelly, Veronica Lake, and Lillian and Dorothy Gish, to name just a few. A partial list of players and plays seen on *Goodyear TV Playhouse* in the mid-to-late 1950s included Julie Harris and Leslie Nielsen in *October Story*, Jose Ferrer in an adaptation of Rostand's *Cyrano de Bergerac* (Ferrer repeated this role in a film and won an Academy Award), Eva Marie Saint and Phyllis Kirk in *Wish on the Moon*, Lili Darvis and Eileen Heckart in *My Lost Saints*, E. G. Marshall in *Old Tasselfoot*, John Cassavetes and Glenda Farrell in Reginald Rose's *The Expendable House*, Martin Balsam, Sydney Poitier, and *Don Murray* in Robert Alan Aurthur's *A Man Is Ten Feet Tall*, Thelma Ritter in Paddy Chayefsky's *The Catered Affair*, Jack Warden and Lee Grant in Aurthur's *Shadow of the Champ*, and many others. In September 1957, the series temporarily became known as *Goodyear Theater*, and featured a rotating roster of stars, including Robert Ryan, David Niven, Jane Powell, Jack Lemmon, and Charles Boyer, but by February, 1958, the show's title once again became *Goodyear TV Playhouse*. During its last two years, performers on the show included Peter Lawford, Paul Douglas, Edward G. Robinson, Ray Milland, Jackie COOPER, Gig Young, Erroll Flynn, Thomas Mitchell, and Eddie ALBERT.

GRACE UNDER FIRE

Sept. 1993–Mar. 1994	ABC	Wed. 9:30–10 P.M.
May 1994–Sept. 1994	ABC	Wed. 9:30–10 P.M.
Sept. 1994–Mar. 1995	ABC	Tues. 9:30–10 P.M.
Mar. 1995–Nov. 1996	ABC	Wed. 9–9:30 P.M.
Dec. 1996–July 1997	ABC	Wed. 8–8:30 P.M.
Aug. 1997–Sept. 1997	ABC	Tues. 8:30–9 P.M.
Nov. 1997–Dec. 1997	ABC	Tues. 8–8:30 P.M.
Jan. 1998–Feb. 1998	ABC	Tues. 9:30–10 P.M.

Comedienne Brett Butler played Grace Kelly, a working-class woman who had just broken up with her physically abusive husband after eight years of marriage, on the *Grace Under Fire* situation comedy series. Grace, who referred to her ex-husband as a "knuckle-dragging, cousin-loving, beer-sucking redneck," had decided it would be better to raise her three children by herself than to continue to be abused by her no-good husband, Jim, who only periodically showed up on the series, and was played by Geoff Pierson. The couple's three children, Quentin, Elizabeth, and Patrick, were played by Jon Paul Steuer and then Sam Horrigan, Kaitlin Cullum, and twins Dylan and Cole Sprouse. Grace found a job working at an oil refinery and often traded insults with her apelike coworkers, but had lots of support from her friends Nadine and Wade Swoboda, played by Julie White and Casey Sander. During the 1995–96 season, Grace was promoted at the oil refinery and had a boyfriend, Rick Brawshaw, an oil refinery executive, played by Alan Autry. When Grace and Rick eventually broke up, Grace began to date other men, and entered night school to better herself. Also appearing on the series as regulars at different times were Julia Duffy, Lauren Tom, Tom Poston, Paul Dooley, William Fichtner, Louis Mandylor, Walter Olkewicz, Valri Bromfield, and Dave Florek. The series, which was very popular, was suddenly canceled in the middle of the 1997–98 season. It was rumored that Brett Butler, because of excessive drinking and overwork, was losing control of herself on the set, and finding it increasingly difficult to make rational decisions.

Grace Under Fire was created by Chuck Lorre, who was also creative director of the series when it first went on the air. Lorre resigned in the middle of the show's first season because of "creative differences" with the show's star. *Grace Under Fire* was the first American TV series to be telecast regularly in Russia, and for the first several seasons, it placed among the top 10 shows in the Nielsen ratings.

GRAHAM, BILLY (WILLIAM FRANKLIN GRAHAM, JR., 1918–)

Evangelist Billy Graham was one of the first preachers to recognize the potential of television to reach a large audience for teaching the gospel. His television specials, which made him one of the most recognized people in the United States, attracted millions of viewers. Graham, who was born in Charlotte, North Carolina, attended Wheaton College and upon graduation entered the ministry as the pastor of the First Baptist Church of Western Springs, Illinois. In 1947, Graham organized a revival team that toured the nation. While leading a revival meeting in Los Angeles in 1949, Graham attracted the attention of many Hollywood personalities, and his charismatic preaching and handsome, youthful looks led to his being asked to preach on television. In 1950, his *Hour of Decision* series became one of the country's most watched religious programs, and he went on to make several religion-oriented films, including *Souls in Conflict* (1955), *Wiretapper* (1956), *The Restless Ones* (1965), *For Pete's Sake* (1966), *Time to Run* (1973), *The Prodigal* (1983), *Caught* (1987), and *Come the Morning* (1993). In 1980, Graham, who had said a prayer at President Richard Nixon's inauguration and became one of Nixon's closest advisers, appeared on a new television series simply called *Billy Graham*. A TV special, *Crusade: The Life of Billy Graham*, attracted a formidable audience in 1993.

GRAMMER, KELSEY (ALLEN KELSEY GRAMMER 1955–)

Kelsey Grammer is the only television actor to have been nominated for Emmy Awards for playing the same character, Frasier Crane, on three different TV shows: CHEERS, WINGS (for a guest appearance), and FRASIER. Before Grammer, who was born on St. Thomas in the Virgin Islands, became Frasier Crane, a role for which he will always be remembered, he was a relatively unsuccessful actor who had played only a small role in a TV film version of Shakespeare's *Macbeth* (1982) and appeared in a supporting role in the miniseries *Kennedy* (1983). In 1984, a role on the daytime serial drama ANOTHER WORLD and a semiregular role, Frasier Crane, on the popular *Cheers* situation comedy, suddenly made viewers sit up and take notice. As Crane, a depressed psychiatrist who frequented the Cheers pub in Boston in order to get away from his domineering wife, Lilith, Kelsey Grammer suddenly became one of *Cheers'* most popular characters and an instant TV star. In 1993, after appearing in several feature and TV films such as *George Washington* (1984), and *Dance 'Til Dawn* (1988), Grammer reprised his popular Frasier Crane role on a series of his own, *Frasier*. Like *Cheers*, *Frasier* was an enormous success, and, as of this writing, after seven years on the air, it is still one of the most popular shows on television. Over the years, in addition to playing Frasier Crane, Grammer also appeared in such films as *Down Periscope* (1996), *The Real Howard Spitz* (1998), has been one of the voices of characters in the hit films *Anastasia* (1997), *Animal Farm* (1999), and *Toy Story 2* (1999), and guest-starred on such TV series as *Star Trek: The Next Generation* (1992), *The JOHN LARROQUETTE SHOW, JUST SHOOT ME*, and provided the voice of Robert "Sideshow Bob" Underdunk Terwilliger on *The SIMPSONS* cartoon series.

GRAVES, PETER (PETER AURNESS 1926–)

Peter Graves, whose brother James Aurness played Matt Dillon on the popular GUNSMOKE series for many years, was born in Minneapolis, Minnesota. Following in his big brother's footsteps, Peter went to Hollywood after finishing his schooling to pursue a career as an actor in the late 1940s. After appearing in such feature films as *Mrs. Fitzherbert* (1947), *Red Planet Mars* (1952), and *Beneath the 12-Mile Reef* (1953), Graves appeared on his first TV series *Where's Raymond?* in 1953. An important role as a Nazi spy in *Stalag 17* (1953) led to more important film roles in *East of Sumatra* (1953), *Killers from Space* (1954), *Robber's Roost* (1955), *The Court-Martial of Billy Mitchell* (1955), *Night of the Hunter* (1955), *Canyon River* (1956), and regular roles on the TV series *Whiplash* and *Court Martial*. Graves was kept busy as a supporting player until he was cast in the role that finally made him a star, Jim Phelps on MISSION IMPOSSIBLE. Roles in the box office favorites *Airplane!* and *Airplane II* (1980 and 1982) and countless other films followed. In 1987, Graves became one of the hosts of the popular A&E show BIOGRAPHY, a program he still hosts as of this writing. In 1988, Graves revived his role of Jim Phelps on a new, not very successful *Mission Impossible* series, and was also seen in the *7th Heaven* (1997-2000) series, which also proved to be short-lived. Over the years, in addition to appearing on regular TV series and in films, Peter Graves has guest-starred on numerous TV series, including *Cimarron City*, *The* KRAFT SUSPENSE THEATRE, *The* VIRGINIAN, *Laredo*, *Branded*, *The F.B.I.*, FANTASY ISLAND, BUCK ROGERS IN THE 25TH CENTURY, SIMON AND SIMON, MURDER, SHE WROTE, GOLDEN GIRLS, BURKE'S LAW, and DIAGNOSIS MURDER.

GREAT GILDERSLEEVE, THE

1955	Syndicated series	Various stations and times

Water Commissioner Throckmorton P. Gildersleeve of Summerfield, a character originally heard on the *Fibber McGee and Molly* radio show in the early 1940s, became the central character of a radio program and then a syndicated television situation comedy series called *The Great Gildersleeve* in 1955. Actor Willard Waterman, who took over the role of Gildersleeve when Harold Peary, who had created the role but quit during the series' original radio run, also starred on TV in the title role of Gildersleeve, and Lillian Randolph, who had also been heard on the radio series, re-created her role of Birdie, Gildersleeve's African-American housekeeper on the TV program. The parts of Gildersleeve's niece and nephew, Marjorie and Leroy Forrester, who became their bachelor/uncle Gildersleeve's wards when their parents died, were played by Stephanie Griffin and Ronald Keith. Willis Bouchey played Mayor Terwilliger, Forrest Lewis re-created his radio role of Peavey the druggist, Shirley Mitchell played Gildersleeve's southern belle girlfriend, Leila Ransom, a role she had also played on radio, and Barbara Stuart played Gildy's secretary, Bessie, on the TV series.

GREAT PERFORMANCES

1974–present	PBS	Various times

Classical music concerts, operas productions, dance programs, and occasional Broadway play and musical comedy presentations were well represented on the Public Broadcasting System's *Great Performances* series. Among the memorable dramatic miniseries seen on this series was the popular and critically acclaimed adaptation of Evelyn Waugh's *Brideshead Revisited*, which was broadcast in 1982 and featured Anthony Andrews, Jeremy Irons, Laurence Olivier, Claire Bloom, Diana Quick, John Gielgud, and Nikholas Grace. Other popular productions seen on *Great Performances* were *Jennie: Lady Randolph Churchill*, which starred Lee Remick, a dramatization of Dorothy Parker's *Big Blonde* with Sally Kellerman, *Judy Garland: The Concert Years*, *Irving Berlin's America*, *The Ebony Tower* with Laurence Olivier, Gilbert and Sullivan's *The Mikado*, *Baryshnikov Dances Ballanchine*, *Hamlet* with Kevin Kline, Peter Sellars's production of *The Marriage of Figaro*, Maggie Smith and Natasha Richardson in Tennessee Williams's *Suddenly Last Summer*, Paddy CHAYEFSKY's *The Mother*, with Anne Bancroft, Anne Meara, and John Cusack, and *The Music of Kurt Weill*, among others.

GREATEST AMERICAN HERO, THE

Mar. 1981–May 1981	ABC	Wed. 8–9 P.M.
Aug. 1981–Aug. 1982	ABC	Wed. 8–9 P.M.
Sept. 1982–Nov. 1982	ABC	Fri. 9–10 P.M.
Jan. 1983–Feb. 1983	ABC	Thurs. 8–9 P.M.

A parody of all the many superhero TV series, films, and comic books, *The Greatest American Hero* starred William Katt as Ralph Hanley (originally named "Hinkley" until a man named John Hinckley attempted to assassinate President Ronald Reagan), a curly-headed high school teacher in Los Angeles, who came upon extraterrestrial beings while on a field trip in the desert and received from them an incredible red suit that enabled him to fly. FBI agent Maxwell, played by Robert CULP, convinced Ralph to use the suit to fight crime. In addition to Maxwell, only Ralph's girlfriend, Pam Davidson, played by Connie Sellecca, knew the truth about the power of Ralph's suit. In spite of problems with the character's name, Hinkley, and several other production setbacks, the series managed to remain on the air for two years before it was canceled.

GREEN ACRES

Sept. 1965–Sept. 1968	CBS	Wed. 9–9:30 P.M.
Sept. 1968–Sept. 1969	CBS	Wed. 9:30–10 P.M.
Sept. 1969–Sept. 1970	CBS	Sat. 9–9:30 P.M.
Sept. 1970–Sept. 1971	CBS	Tues. 8–8:30 P.M.

Green Acres, a spin-off of the popular rural situation comedy series PETTICOAT JUNCTION, was an equally popular series that placed in the top 20 on the Nielsen ratings for the first four years it was aired. The leading characters were Oliver Wendall Douglas, a wealthy Manhattan lawyer who decided he had had enough of big-city life in

Green Acres: Eva Gabor (Lisa) and Eddie Albert (Oliver) (Author's collection)

New York and bought a run-down place in the country so that he could be closer to nature, and his wife, Lisa, who wanted to go back to the couple's penthouse apartment the moment she set foot on country soil. Oliver and Lisa, played by Eddie ALBERT and Eva GABOR, of the famous Hungarian-born Gabors (mother Jolie and sisters Zsa Zsa and Magda), lived on a farm located on the outskirts of Hooterville, which was also the setting of *Petticoat Junction.* The farm, which the Douglases named Green Acres, had not been lived on for years and was a run-down mess. Much of the show's humor was based upon the fact that the Douglases were totally unprepared to live under such primitive conditions. Lisa's gorgeous gowns, jewelry, and negligees were amusingly out of place in the dump the Douglases lived in. Among the funny characters who appeared regularly were Mr. Haney, a shrewd country man who knew a couple of city rubes when he saw them, and had sold Lisa and Oliver the farm, sight unseen; Fred and Doris Ziffel, Lisa and Oliver's neighbors, who owned a pig farm, played by Hank Patterson and Barbara Pepper and then Fran Ryan; Ed Dawson, the Douglases' inept handyman, played by Tom Lester; storekeeper Sam Drucker, played by Frank Cady; and Hank Kimball, the local agricultural agent, played by Alvy Moore. One of the show's most popular performers, however, was a pig named Arnold, Fred Zeffel's pet. Arnold became one of the show's major attractions during the last few years

Green Acres was on the air. Since both *Green Acres* and *Petticoat Junction* were set in Hooterville, characters from both series appeared on each other's shows. *Green Acres* was produced by Jay Sommers. In 1990, most of the cast was reunited in a TV movie, *Return to Green Acres.*

GREENE, LORNE (1915–1987)

Lorne Greene, who was born in Ottawa, Ontario, had a long and distinguished career in films and on TV. Perhaps best known for playing the patriarch of the Cartwright family, Ben Cartwright, on the extremely successful TV western series BONANZA, Greene first started acting in school plays while he was attending Canada's Queen's University. After he graduated from Queen's University, Greene's deep, resonant voice got him a job as a radio announcer, and within a few years, he was one of Canada's top newscasters. During World War II, while he was working for the Canadian Broadcasting Company, Greene was dubbed "The Voice of Doom," because of his gloomy news reports about the war. In the early 1950s, Greene left Canada and went to Hollywood, determined to break into films. He was soon appearing on such popular television programs as YOU ARE THERE, *Star Stage* (1955–56), ALFRED HITCHCOCK PRESENTS, *The* ALCOA HOUR, *The* UNITED STATES STEEL HOUR, WAGON TRAIN, and CHEYENNE, and had supporting roles in such films as *The Silver Chalice* (1954), *Peyton Place* (1957), and *The Buccaneer* (1958). In 1959, Greene was cast as Ben Cartwright on *Bonanza,* and the role made him a major TV star. After *Bonanza* left the air in 1973, Greene continued to appear in major films such as *Earthquake* (1974), and on TV in the miniseries ROOTS (1977), the TV film *The Trial of Lee Harvey Oswald* (1977), and the TV series BATTLESTAR GALACTICA in 1978, and *Code Red* in 1981. Greene's last major appearance, before he died of pneumonia at the age of 72 in 1987, was in the film *The Alamo: Thirteen Days to Glory,* playing General Sam Houston.

GREENE, RICHARD (1918–1985)

England's legendary medieval bandit, Robin Hood, became the hero of a weekly television adventure series, *The* ADVENTURES OF ROBIN HOOD, in 1955, and English actor Richard Greene played Robin. Greene, who was born in Plymouth, in Devon, had been one of Hollywood's handsomest leading men before he played Robin Hood for five years on television. Greene made his film debut in 1938 in *Submarine Patrol,* and his good looks made him an immediate favorite with filmgoers. Roles in such films as *Kentucky* (1938), *My Lucky Star* (1938), *Stanley and Livingstone* (1939), *The Hound of the Baskervilles* (1939), *Little Old New York* (1940), *Forever Amber* (1947), *Lorna Doone* (1951), *Captain Scarlett* (1953), and many others, followed. In 1960, when *The Adventures of Robin Hood* suspended production, Greene played Robin once more in the feature film *Sword of Sherwood Forest.* Greene later appeared in films such as

Island of the Lost (1967) and *The Blood of Fu Manchu* film serial (1968), and on the unsuccessful TV series *Scarf Jack* (1980). Greene and his movie star wife, Patricia Medina, at the height of his popularity, were named "Hollywood's most attractive couple." The actor died in relative obscurity at the age of 67, after suffering cardiac arrest following a fall in his home.

GRIFFIN, MERV (1925–)

Before he became one of Hollywood's most successful businessmen, Merv Griffin was a popular TV talk show host who pioneered the type of interview show that is so common on television today. Born in San Mateo, California, Griffin became a band singer shortly after graduating from school, and his recording of "I've Got A Lovely Bunch of Coconuts" sold millions of copies. In 1951, Griffin made his film debut in the western *Cattle Town,* and followed that with supporting roles in *So This Is Love* (1953), *By the Light of the Silvery Moon* (1953), *The Charge at Feather River* (1953), *Phantom of the Rue*

Morgue (1954), and *The Boy from Oklahoma* (1954). In 1954, Griffin also appeared on his first TV series, *Summer Holiday,* a musical/variety show, and then he became a regular vocalist on *The Robert Q. Lewis Show* in 1955. In the late 1950s, Griffin hosted the game shows *Play Your Hunch* (1958–62) and *Keep Talking* (1959–60). *The MERV GRIFFIN SHOW* made its debut in 1962, and soon became America's favorite TV chat program. Wise real estate investments and a good business sense led to Griffin's producing a series of shows that became long-running, financially successful enterprises: *JEOPARDY!* in 1964, *WHEEL OF FORTUNE* in 1975, *Dance Fever* in 1979, a series that capitalized on the disco dance craze, as well as the TV series *Ruckus* in 1991.

GRIFFITH, ANDY (ANDREW SAMUEL GRIFFITH 1926–)

When he was a young boy growing up in Mount Airy, North Carolina, during the height of the Great Depression, Andy Griffith, who loved to sing, dreamed of becoming an opera singer. When he grew older, Griffith

Merv Griffin (Author's collection)

decided he wanted to be a Moravian preacher, and in 1944, he enrolled as a pre-divinity student at the University of North Carolina. In college, Griffith became involved with drama department plays, and by the time he graduated with a degree in music in 1949, he knew that he wanted to be a singer/actor. For three years after he graduated, Griffith taught high school music. While he was teaching, Griffith and his wife, Barbara, developed a monologue for him called "What It Was Was Football," which capitalized on his story-telling skills, and he soon found employment performing his monologue in various clubs around the South. A record featuring Griffith's monologue became one of the most popular comic spoken-word records of all time. Traveling to New York City, Griffith performed his monologue on *The ED SULLIVAN SHOW*, which led to his being cast as Will Stockdale in the TV version of Ira Levin's play *No Time for Sergeants* in 1954. In 1955, when *No Time for Sergeants* was produced on Broadway, Griffith repeated his role of Stockdale and won critical acclaim. After appearing in the Broadway musical *Destry Rides Again* in the 1960s, and winning a Tony nomination, Griffith went to Hollywood to appear in films. His film debut in *A Face in the Crowd,* directed by Elia Kazan, in 1957, won the actor rave reviews. In 1960, after appearing as a guest on *MAKE ROOM FOR DADDY*, Griffith was given a series of his own, *The ANDY GRIFFITH SHOW*, playing the lovable, widower/father Sheriff Andy Taylor, who had a small son. The series became a long-running hit, remaining on the air for eight seasons. *The Andy Griffith Show* is among the most fondly remembered programs and best-loved series ever aired. After starring in several films and attempting to duplicate his *Andy Griffith Show* success on such less admired TV series as *The Headmaster* (1970–71), *The New Andy Griffith Show* (1971), *Salvage 1* (1979), and *Best of the West* (1981–82), Griffith finally found a character and a TV show that was almost as successful as his *Andy Griffith Show*. *MATLOCK* made its debut in 1986. It was about a lawyer in Atlanta, Georgia, who has talent for defending innocent people who had seemingly impossible cases. *Matlock* remained on the air for six seasons. Griffith continues to be active in films and on TV.

GRIZZLY ADAMS

(see *Life And Times of Grizzly Adams, The*)

GROWING PAINS

Sept. 1985–Mar. 1986	ABC	Tues. 8:30–9 P.M.
May 1986–Mar. 1988	ABC	Tues. 8:30–9 P.M.
Mar. 1988–Aug. 1990	ABC	Wed. 8–8:30 P.M.
Aug. 1990–Aug. 1991	ABC	Wed. 8:30–9 P.M.
Aug. 1991–Sept. 1991	ABC	Fri. 9:30–10 P.M.
Sept. 1991–Jan. 1992	ABC	Sat. 8:30–9 P.M.
Feb. 1992–Apr. 1992	ABC	Sat. 9:30–10 P.M.
May 1992–July 1992	ABC	Wed. 8:30–9 P.M.
July 1992–Aug. 1992	ABC	Thurs. 8:30–9 P.M.

For seven years, America watched a young man named Mike Seaver, who was 15 years old when *Growing Pains* first went on the air, and his sister and brother, Carol and Ben, 14 and nine years old, grow up before their very eyes. Mike, who was engagingly played by Kirk CAMERON, and Carol and Ben, played by Tracey Gold and Jeremy Miller, were typical young TV characters, and their parents, Dr. Jason Seaver and his wife, Maggie, played by Alan Thicke and Joanna Kerns, went through the usual parental concerns as their offspring grew from children to young adults. Since the senior Seaver, Jason, was a psychiatrist, he was far wiser than most parents when it came to understanding his children's "growing pains," but that did not make those problems any the less troublesome. Mike was a bit lazy as far as schoolwork was concerned, and he loved to hang out and have a good time. His mother called him "a hormone with feet," because of his adolescent preoccupation with the opposite sex. Carol was brainy, and Ben wanted to be just like his older brother. The Seavers lived in a comfortable house in a New York City suburb on Long Island. James had his office at home, Maggie worked as a reporter for the *Long Island Herald*, and Mike and Carol attended Thomas E. Dewey High School. In 1988, the Seavers had a fourth child, Chrissy, alternately played by twins Kristen and Kelsey Dohring and then as an older child by Ashley Johnson. As the hit series continued, Mike, who became the show's major attraction and a teenage heartthrob, graduated from high school, went to college, decided to become an actor, and fell in love many times. By the time *Growing Pains* left the air in 1992, Carol had graduated from college and Ben was attending college. Other characters who appeared regularly on the series were Richard Stabone, nicknamed "Boner," Mike's friend, played by John Andrew Koening; Maggie's parents Ed and Kate Malone, played by Gordon Jump and Betty McGuire; Mike's buddy, Eddie, played by K. C. Martel; and Coach Lubbock, played by Bill Kirchenbauer. Chelsea Noble and Julie McCullough played two of Mike's more serious love interests. During the series' final season, Mike moved back home and lived in an apartment that had formerly been the Seavers' garage. His roommate was a tough, streetwise young man named Luke Brower, played by Leonardo DiCaprio, a homeless 15-year-old Mike had befriended. When *Growing Pains* made its debut, many viewers thought it was a revised version of the *Growing Paynes* TV series that had been a far less successful TV show of the late 1940s.

GUIDING LIGHT

June 1952–present   CBS   Mon.–Fri. Various times

Although the daytime drama *Guiding Light* made its TV debut in 1952, the program had first been heard as a five-day-a-week radio show in 1937. Created by Irna Phillips when it was on radio, *The Guiding Light,* as it was then called, centered on a minister and his daughter, Rev. Rutledge and Mary, who lived in the town of Springfield. During the *Guiding Light*'s radio run, the German–American Bauer family eventually replaced Dr. Rutledge and Mary, who disappeared from the series in the early 1940s. By the time the series made its television debut, the Bauers were firmly established as the series' main characters. When head writer Irna Phillips left the show to write other soap operas, AS THE WORLD TURNS and ALL MY CHILDREN, she was succeeded by Agnes Nixon, who remained in charge until the mid-1970s. Originally a 15-minutes-a-day TV program, *Guiding Light* was expanded to a half-hour, five-days-a-week series in 1969, and then to a full hour, Monday through Friday series in 1977. The original TV cast of *Guiding Light* included Theo Goetz as Papa Bauer; Lyle Sudrow and then Ed Bryce as his son, Bill; Charita Bauer as Bill's wife, Bertha, or "Bert"; Jone Allison and then Ellen Demming as Meta Bauer; Helen Wagner and then Lisa Howard as Trudy Bauer; Christopher Walken (then known as Ron Walken) and then Michael Allen, Paul Prokop, Gary Pillar, Bob Pickering, and Don Stewart as lawyer Michael Bauer, Bill and Bert's son; Pat Collins, Bon Gentry, Matt Hulswit, Richard van Vleet and then Peter Simon as Dr. Ed Bauer, also Bill and Bert's son; Les Damon, Bernard Hughes, Sydney Walker and then William Roerick as Dr. Bruce Banning, Meta's husband; Herb Nelson as Joe Roberts, Bert's second husband when Bill Bauer died; and Susan Douglas, James Lipton, Whit Conner, Zina Bethune, Nancy Malone, Ellen Weston, Sandy Dennis, John Gibson, and many others in major roles. Among the popular principal players who were introduced to viewers in the 1960s and into the 1970s were Kathryn Hays, Stefan Schnabel, Milette Alexander, Jan Sterling, Augusta Dabney, Barbara Berjer, James Earl Jones, Billy Dee Williams, William Beaudine, Chris Sarandon, Christina Pickles, Tudi Wiggins, and Rosetta LeNoire, to name just a few. One of the most popular villains on *Guiding Light* was a character who remained on the series until well into the 1990s, Roger Thorpe, played by Michael Zaslow, who married Holly Norris, played by Maureen Garrett. Garrett also remained on the series and can still be seen playing the role.

Also in the 1970s, the working-class Reardon family began to dominate *Guiding Light*'s story lines. Gregory Beecroft played Tony Reardon; Lisa Brown played his troublesome sister, Nola Readon; and Ellen Parker played their older sister, Maureen Readon. Michael Tylo played the mysterious Quint McCord, later known as Quentin Chamberlaine, who married Nola. Lee Lawson played their mother, Bea. Also prominent in the late 1970s to 1980s were the wealthy Chamberlaine and Lewis families. Anna Stuart, and then for many years Maeve Kinkead, played the rich and spoiled, but later redeemed, Vanessa Chamberlaine; and William Roerick, who had previously been seen as another character on the series, played Vanessa's wealthy father, Henry Chamberlaine. Rebecca Hollen played Trish Lewis, Robert Newman played her brother Josh Lewis, Jordan Clarke and then for a short while Geoffrey Scott played Billy Lewis, and Larry Gates played their oil-rich father H. B. Lewis.

The superrich Spaulding family and the less privileged Shayne family dominated the series in the 1980s and 1990s, although the Bauers and Chamberlaines were still very much in evidence. The temptress Reva Shayne, played by Kim Zimmer, who won several daytime Emmy Awards for playing Reva, married all three Lewis men, Josh, Billy, and their father, H. B. The wealthy Spauldings included the opportunistic Alan Spaulding, played for many years by Chris Bernau and then Daniel Pilon and then for many years, Ron Raines; Alan's sister Alexandra, played by Beverlee McKinsey and then Marj Dusay; and Alan's son, Philip, played by Jarrod Ross, John Bolger, and for many years, Grant Aleksander. Other popular characters on the series during the 1980s and 1990s were lawyer Ross Marler, played for many years by Jerry Ver Dorn; Krista Tesreau; Kimberly Simms; Ann Hamilton; and Barbara Crampton as Mindy Lewis, Billy's daughter; Judi Evans and Beth Chamberlin as Beth Raines; Tina Sloan as Beth's mother, Lillian; Carl Tye Evans and Rick Hearst as Alan Michael Spaulding; Frank Dicopoulos as Frank Cooper; Beth Ehlers as Harley Davidson Cooper; Jason Deas as their father, Buzz Cooper; Jean Carol as Nadine Cooper; Melissa Hayden as Bridget Reardon; Mark Derwin as A. C. Mallet; and Jeff Phillips, Leonard Stabb, and Sean McDermott as Hart Jessup Thorpe.

GUILLAUME, ROBERT (ROBERT WILLIAMS 1927–)

Robert Guillaume, who became well known for playing Benson, first on the SOAP situation comedy series and then on his own BENSON series, was born in St. Louis, Missouri, and began his performing career as a singer. After a few minor appearances on several TV shows such as MARCUS WELBY, M.D., Guillaume appeared on Broadway in the musical comedy *Purlie* in the early 1970s, and won a Tony Award as Best Supporting Actor in a Musical. Returning to TV, Guillaume appeared on the GOOD TIMES series. In 1977, Guillaume was cast as the wiser-than-his-employer butler Benson on *Soap*, and then played Benson again on the spin-off series *Benson*. Roles in such feature films as *Seems Like Old Times* (1980), *Prince Jack* (1984), and on the successful TV miniseries *North and South* (1985), and other TV and feature films, as well as guest-starring appearances on such TV series as The JEFFERSONS, ALL IN THE FAMILY, and L.A. LAW, in addition to his regular TV series, kept Guillaume busy throughout the 1970s and 1980s. In the 1980s, Guillaume returned to the stage and appeared in the musical *Phantom of the Opera*, playing the leading role and surprising everyone with his wonderful singing voice. In the 1990s Guillaume continued to appear on TV series such as DIAGNOSIS MURDER, SAVED BY THE BELL, BURKE'S LAW, The FRESH PRINCE OF BEL AIR, and TOUCHED BY AN ANGEL, and also appeared in many TV films. In 1998, Guillaume played the running role of Isaac Jaffe on *Sports Night*. When he suffered a minor stroke in 1999, while on the set of *Sports Night*, Guillaume and the show's producers decided to have the character have a stroke as well. Guillaume went back to work, and in 2000, he provided one of the voices for the animated film *The Adventures of Tom Thumb and Thumbelina*.

GUMBY SHOW, THE

Mar. 1957–Nov. 1957	NBC	Sat. 10:30–11 A.M.
1966	Syndicated	Various times and stations
1988	Syndicated	Various times and stations

Although not a success when it was originally aired in 1957, 30 years later a syndicated version of the *Gumby* children's show was very well received and can still be seen in syndication in various parts of the country. First seen on *HOWDY DOODY* in the early 1950s, Gumby was not a puppet or a live character, but was a combination of live animation and stop-motion photography. A large eraserlike character, Gumby and his "claymates" and his pet horse Pokey were involved in numerous misadventures on the program. Bobby Nicholson was the original host of the *Gumby* series, and Nicholson was replaced by Pinky Lee. The revival of *The Gumby Show* in 1985 introduced several new children's show hosts to viewers, including Shari Lewis and her puppet Lambchop, and the remarkable Mr. Wizard, who was in reality Don Herbert.

GUNSMOKE

Sept. 1955–Sept. 1961	CBS	Sat. 10–10:30 P.M.
Sept. 1961–Sept. 1967	CBS	Sat. 10–11 P.M.
Sept. 1967–Sept. 1971	CBS	Mon. 7:30–8:30 P.M.
Sept. 1971–Sept. 1975	CBS	Mon. 8–9 P.M.

The popular western series *Gunsmoke,* which was continuously on the air for 18 years (20 years with immediate prime-time reruns), was, when it departed the airwaves in 1975, the longest-running and most popular program ever presented on television. Before *Gunsmoke* was on television, it was a radio series first heard in 1952 and starred William CONRAD as U.S. Marshal Matt Dillon and Parley Baer as Dillon's deputy, Chester. When the program became a TV series in 1955, an entirely different cast played the roles on TV, although the radio show continued for another six years, finally ending its run in 1961. The television cast of *Gunsmoke* consisted of James ARNESS as Marshall Dillon, a lawman in Dodge City, Kansas (John Wayne had originally been offered the TV role, but turned it down); Milburn Stone as Dr. ("Doc") Galen Adams; Amanda Blake as Kitty, the owner of Dodge City's Long Branch

Gunsmoke: (left to right) Milburn Stone (Doc), Dennis Weaver (Chester), Amanda Blake (Kitty), and James Arness (Matt) (Author's collection)

Saloon, who was Dillon's close friend (and some thought lover); and Dennis Weaver as Deputy Chester Goode. During the many years the show was aired, other regular characters included Festus Hagen, played by Ken Curtis, who replaced Chester when Dennis Weaver went on to other projects; Quint Asper, played by Burt REYNOLDS; Sam, the bartender, played by Glenn Strange; and Clayton Thaddeus Greenwood, played by Roger Ewing. Other performers who played regular roles on *Gunsmoke* included Buck Taylor, Fran Ryan, Ted Jordan, Woody Chambliss, George Selk, Dabbs Greer, James Nusser, Howard Culver, Tom Brown, John Harper, Sarah Selby, Roy Roberts, Charles Wagenheim, Pat Hingle, and Hank Patterson.

For nine years, *Gunsmoke* was produced by Norman Macdonnell, who had also produced the radio show. In 1964, after a falling out with the show's star, James Arness, Macdonnell left the series as producer and was succeeded by Phillip Leacock. John Mantley replaced Leacock as *Gunsmoke*'s producer in 1967. Several feature-length, TV *Gunsmoke* films were produced between 1987 and 1994, all starring James Arness as Dillon.

HADLEY, REED (REED HERRING 1911–1974)

During his long and prosperous film career, tall, dark, and slender Reed Hadley usually played either villains or officers of the law, and his deep, resonant voice made him one of Hollywood's most successful off-screen narrators. It wasn't until he appeared on the television series RACKET SQUAD and *The Public Defender* (1954–55) that Hadley became a "name" performer. A popular radio actor who played western hero Red Ryder and many other roles, Hadley was born in Petrolia, Texas. He made his screen debut in 1937 in *Hollywood Stadium Mystery*. Hundreds of supporting roles in such films as *Orphan of the Street* (1938), *The Great Adventures of Wild Bill Hickok* (1938), *Diamond Horseshoe* (1945), *A Bell for Adano* (1945), *Leave Her to Heaven* (1945), *13 Rue Madeleine* (1946), *The Iron Curtain* (1948), and *I Shot Jesse James* (1949) led to his being cast as Capt. John Braddock on *Racket Squad*. In 1954, Hadley had his second major TV role, playing Det. Lt. Joe White on the *Public Defender* series. Hadley continued to appear in films and to guest-star on such TV series as *The Restless Gun*, WAGON TRAIN, BAT MASTERSON, RAWHIDE, PERRY MASON, and GREEN ACRES until shortly before his death in 1974. His last major film appearance was in *Brain of Blood* in 1972, two years before the actor died of a heart attack.

HALE, BARBARA (1921–)

Before Barbara Hale played the role that made her famous, Della Street on the long-running PERRY MASON TV series, she was a successful film actress. Born in DeKalb, Illinois, Barbara wanted to be an artist and attended the Chicago Academy of Fine Arts after graduating from high school. In order to pay her expenses at the academy, Barbara worked as a model for the artist who drew the "Ramblin' Bill" comic strip. When she posed for magazine layouts, her good looks attracted the attention of a Hollywood talent scout who signed her to a contract. As a studio contract player, Barbara played many small roles in such films as *Mexican Spitfire's Elephant* (1942, her film debut), *The Seventh Victim* (1943), *Higher and Higher* (1944), *Heavenly Days* (1944), several *Falcon* films (1944), and *West of the Pecos* (1945). The roles Hale played grew increasingly larger, and soon she was playing leading ladies in such popular films as *Jolson Sings Again* (1949) and *Lorna Doone* (1951). In 1957, Hale was cast as Della Street, lawyer Perry Mason's loyal secretary, a role she played for the next 38 years, from 1957 until 1995. After the original *Perry Mason* series left the air, Hale appeared on numerous TV *Perry Mason* films.

HALL, MONTY (MAURICE HALPRIN 1923–)

Popular TV game show host Monty Hall, who is best known as the emcee of the popular and long-running LET'S MAKE A DEAL, was born in Winnipeg, Canada. Before entering TV, Hall worked on radio. He made his first major TV appearance as the host of the *Keep Talking* game show in 1958. After hosting the *Video Village* series, Hall became the host of the show that made him a household name, *Let's Make a Deal*, in 1963. The show was one of the most popular daytime game series on television for the following 28 years. During this time, Hall also hosted the game shows *It's Anybody's Guess* (1977), BEAT THE CLOCK, and *Split Second* (1986). He also played himself on such TV series as *The FLIP WILSON SHOW*, *The ODD COUPLE*, and *Wait Till Your Father Gets Home* (1972–74). Hall was also the producer of *It's Anybody's Guess*.

HALLMARK HALL OF FAME, THE

Jan. 1952–present   Various networks and times

A television staple for over 45 years, the *Hallmark Hall of Fame* drama series has been seen on all three major networks. Originally a once-a-week, half-hour show called *The Hallmark Playhouse*, it first aired in 1952. From 1955 until the present, *The Hallmark Hall of Fame* has been seen as a series of specials. The series, which has been sponsored by the Hallmark Greeting Card company for the many years it has been on the air, originally featured Sarah Churchill (British Prime Minister Winston Churchill's actress daughter) as its host and occasional star. Mildred Freed Alberg produced the series for several seasons. She was succeeded by George Schaefer. During its first three years, live adaptations of such celebrated plays as *Hamlet* with Maurice Evans, *Moby Dick* with Victor Jory, *Alice in Wonderland* with Eva Le Gallienne, and *Macbeth* with Maurice Evans and Judith Anderson were featured. When *The Hallmark Hall of Fame* became a series of occasional specials after 1955, outstanding productions of such classics *The Taming of the Shrew* with Maurice Evans and Diane Cilento, *The Green Pastures* with Frederick O'Neill and Eddie "Rochester" Anderson, *Hans Brinker* with Tab Hunter, *A Doll's House* with Julie Harris, and *The Tempest* with Maurice Evans, Roddy McDowell, and Richard Burton were presented. In the 1960s and 1970s, the show presented *Victoria Regina* with Julie Harris, *Little Moon of Alban* with Julie Harris and Dirk Bogarde, *The Fantasticks* with John Davidson and Bert Lahr, *The Man Who Came to Dinner* with Orson Welles, *Brief Encounter* with Richard Burton and Sophia Loren, and *Return Engagement* with Elizabeth Taylor, to name just a few. In the 1980s and 1990s, the series presented productions of *Casey Stengel* with Charles Durning, *Promise* with James GARNER and James Woods, *Foxfire* with Jessica Tandy and Hume Cronyn, *O, Pioneers!* with Jessica Lange, *Sarah, Plain and Tall* with Glenn Close and Christopher Walken, *The Piano Lesson* with Charles S. Dutton, Carl Gordon, and Alfre Woodard, and many other outstanding productions.

HAPPY DAYS

Jan. 1974–Sept. 1983	ABC	Tues. 8–8:30 P.M.
Sept. 1983–Jan. 1984	ABC	Tues. 8:30–9 P.M.
Apr. 1984–May 1984	ABC	Tues. 8:30–9 P.M.
June 1984–July 1984	ABC	Thurs. 8–8:30 P.M.

When *Happy Days* made its TV debut on January 15th, 1974, critics didn't think that a situation comedy about a conventional family living in the suburbs of Milwaukee, Wisconsin, in the 1950s, would be a success. The country had, after all, just come through the Vietnam War, and was undergoing radical social changes. The critics were wrong. Nostalgia for the more predictable times of the past was apparently just what the public wanted. The show surprised everyone by becoming one of television's most popular and long-running shows, placing in the top 20 in the Nielsen ratings, and remaining on the air for an impressive 10 seasons. Ron HOWARD, who was already well known to viewers who had watched him grow up as Opie, Sheriff Taylor's little boy on *The ANDY GRIFFITH SHOW*, played a typical teen, Richard "Richie" Cunningham. With his friends Warren "Potsie" Weber and Ralph Malph, played by Anson Williams and Donny Most, he suffered through most of the problems and frustrations encountered by teenage boys, such as trouble in school, trouble with parents, troubles with girls, troubles that ensued because of rash behavior, troubles due to a lack of money, etc. Richie's parents, Howard and Marion Cunningham, played by Tom BOSLEY and Marion ROSS, were loving and, especially Marion, understanding. Mr. Cunningham was sometimes confused by his son's behavior, but he was always supportive when he had to be. Richie's college-bound older brother, Chuck, played by Gavan O'Herlihy and then Randolph Roberts, was usually too busy to know what his younger brother was doing, and Richie's sister, Joannie, played by Erin Moran, was usually dazzled by her brother's behavior. An unlikely friend of Richie's was a leather-jacketed tough guy from Brooklyn, Arthur Fonzarelli, nicknamed "the Fonz," or "Fonzie," played by Henry WINKLER, Fonzie was a slick, fast-talking, cool womanizer who always had sound

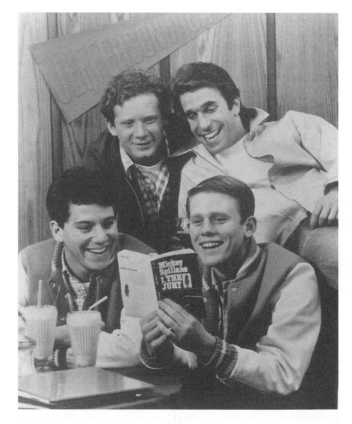

The *Happy Days* gang: (front) Anson Williams, Ron Howard; (rear) Donny Most and Henry Winkler (Author's collection)

advice to offer his somewhat square friends. After only a short time on the air, Fonzie became the show's major attraction, and playing the character made Henry Winkler a TV superstar. Other characters who also became popular were Alfred Delvecchio, played by Al Molinaro, who owned the local teen hangout; Pinky Tuscadero, played by Roz Kelly, the Fonz's female counterpart; and Charles "Chachi" Arcola, played by Scott BAIO, Fonzie's younger cousin from New York. *Happy Days* was created by Garry MARSHALL, who had previously written *The DICK VAN DYKE SHOW* and *The LUCY SHOW*. Happy Days had two successful spin-off series, *LAVERNE & SHIRLEY*, which starred Penny MARSHALL and Cindy WILLIAMS, who had made appearances on *Happy Days*, and *MORK & MINDY*, which came about after a popular story on *Happy Days* in which Mork, an alien played by Robin WILLIAMS, appeared. The less successful *JOANIE LOVES CHACHI*, which starred Erin Moran and Scott Baio, was also a spin-off of *Happy Days*, but it did not remain on the air long. (In 1970, a variety show with the title *Happy Days* featured such performers as Louis Nye,

Chuck MCCANN, Bob and Ray [Bob Elliott and Ray Goulding], and others, but it remained on the air for only seven months before it was canceled.)

HARDY BOYS/NANCY DREW MYSTERIES, THE

Jan. 1977–Jan. 1979	ABC	Sun. 7–8 P.M.
June 1979–Aug. 1979	ABC	Sun. 7–8 P.M.

Prolific young people's adventure and mystery novel writer Edward Stratemeyer, who wrote under the name Franklin W. Dixon, among others, created the popular Tom Swift, Rover Boys, and Hardy Boys series. The Hardy Boys books were turned into a television show that alternated weekly with a series about "girl sleuth" Nancy Drew, a character created by Carolyn Keene, whose book series was later absorbed by the Stratemeyer publishing syndicate. The TV series was called *The Hardy Boys/Nancy Drew Mysteries*. The two teenage sons of world-famous investigator Fenton Hardy, 16- and 18-year-old Joe and Frank Hardy, were the major characters

The Hardy Boys: Shaun Cassidy (left) and Parker Stevenson (Author's collection)

on *The Hardy Boys* series. The boys had inherited their father's sleuthing talents and became involved in ghost-chasing, missing-people cases, exposing smugglers, and solving various other mysteries. Shaun Cassidy and Parker Stevenson played Joe and Frank Hardy, and Edmund Gilbert played their father, Fenton, on this series. Also appearing on the series regularly were Lisa Eilbacher as Callie Shaw and Edith Atwater as Aunt Gertrude. *Nancy Drew Mysteries* starred Pamela Sue Martin as Nancy, a young girl who had a talent for stumbling upon and solving mysteries. In 1978, the Hardy Boys and Nancy Drew joined forces on one weekly show. Pamela Sue Martin left the show at that time and was replaced by Janet Louise Johnson. Also appearing on the *Nancy Drew* segments was William Schallert as Nancy's father, Carson Drew, a criminal lawyer. Glen A. Larsen was the show's executive producer; he produced the series in association with Universal Television.

HARPER VALLEY P.T.A.

Jan. 1981–Aug. 1981	NBC	Fri. 8–8:30 P.M.
Oct. 1981–Nov. 1981	NBC	Thurs. 8–8:30 P.M.
Dec. 1981–Jan. 1982	NBC	Sat. 8–8:30 P.M.
Jan. 1982–Feb. 1982	NBC	Sat. 8:30–9 P.M.
Apr. 1982–June 1982	NBC	Sat. 8–8:30 P.M.
July 1982–Aug. 1982	NBC	Sat. 8:30–9 P.M.

Barbara EDEN, who for many years played Jeannie on the popular *I DREAM OF JEANNIE* situation comedy series, played Stella Johnson, a liberated woman fighting hypocrisy in a small southern town called Harper Valley. The series was based upon Jeannie C. Riley's hit song of 1968, "Harper Valley P. T. A.," and a subsequent film that also starred Barbara Eden. On the series, Stella, a single mother, wore short skirts, flirted with men, said what she thought, and generally upset many pompous, self-righteous citizens in the town of Harper Valley. When Stella joined the P.T.A. at the school her daughter, Dee, played by Jenn Thompson, attended, much to the horror of other board members, she is elected to the P.T.A.'s board of directors. The snobbish members of the P.T.A. board try to eject her, so Stella decides to expose the hypocrisy of the stuffy matrons. The various adulterous, alcoholic, underhanded actions of Harper Valley's less liberal citizens become fair game for Stella. Stella's principal adversary in Harper Valley is wealthy Flora Simpson Reilly, played by Anne Francine; Reilly is the major force behind ejecting Stella from the board. Also appearing on the series were George GOBEL as Mayor Otis Harper, Jr., Fannie Flagg as Cassie Bowman, Bridget Hanley as Wanda Reilly Taylor, Suzi Dean as Scarlett Taylor, Rod McCary as Bobby Taylor, Christopher Stone as Tom Meachum, Gary Allen as Norman Clayton, Edie McClurg as Willamae Jones, Mari Gorman as Vivian Washburn, Robert Gray as Cliff Willoughby, Vic Dunlop as George Kelly, Kevin Scannell as Coach Burt Powell, and Mills Watson as Winslow Homer.

HARPER, VALERIE (1940–)

Before becoming famous as Rhoda Morgenstern on *The MARY TYLER MOORE SHOW*, Valerie Harper, who was born in Suffern, New York, was a dancer who appeared in the musicals *Rock, Rock, Rock* and *L'il Abner* in the late 1950s. After scoring a major success as Mary Richards's best friend, Rhoda, a role she played for four years, Harper appeared on her own series, *RHODA*, a spin-off of *The Mary Tyler Moore Show*, in 1974. Roles in such films as *Freebie and the Bean* (1974), *Chapter Two* (1979), *The Last Married Couple in America* (1980), and *Blame It on Rio* (1984), and TV films such as *Night Terror* (1977), *The Shadow Box* (1980), *The Day the Loving Stopped* (1981), *Don't Go to Sleep* (1982), and *An Invasion of Privacy* (1983) led to a second starring role on the TV series *Valerie* in 1986. When Jason Bateman, playing Valerie's son, became a teenage heartthrob and virtually became the star of Harper's show, the series name was changed to *The Hogan Family* and Harper was all but written off her own show. When Harper protested, the producers fired her. She successfully sued them for "wrongful firing" and was awarded $1.4 million. After this incident, Harper for a time found it difficult to find work on TV, since she had gone against the establishment. Eventually, she began to appear on such successful TV films as *Strange Voices* (1987) and *The People Across the Lake* (1988). In 1990, Harper starred on another series, *City*, but the show was not a success. She continued to guest-star on such series as *Missing Persons* (1993), *TOUCHED BY AN ANGEL*, *Promised Land* (1996–), and *SEX AND THE CITY*, and in 2000, she reprised her role of Rhoda Morgenstern in a TV film, *Mary and Rhoda*, which costarred Mary Tyler Moore.

HARRIS, NEIL PATRICK (1973–)

After attending high school with Freddie Prinze, Jr., Neil Patrick Harris, who was born in Albuquerque, New Mexico, where his parents were lawyers, became a star overnight when he was cast as Doogie Howser on a series that became a big success, *DOOGIE HOWSER, M.D.* Before playing Doogie, Harris, an accomplished magician, as well as a juvenile actor, appeared on such series as *B. L. Stryker* (1989–90), and in the films *Purple People Eater* (1988), *Clara's Heart* (1988), and the TV films *Too Good to Be True* (1988) and *Home Fires Burning* (1989). After four successful seasons on *Doogie Howser, M.D.*, Harris was kept busy appearing in such TV films as *For Our Children* (1993), *A Family Torn Apart* (1993), *Snowbound: The Jim and Jennifer Stolpa Story* (1994), *My Antonia* (1995), and *The Man in the Attic* (1995), and in the feature films *Animal Room* (1995), *Starship Troopers* (1997), and *The Proposition* (1998). In 1999, Harris played Henry McNeeley on the TV series *Stark Raving Mad*.

HART TO HART

Aug. 1979–Oct. 1979	ABC	Sat. 10–11 P.M.
Oct. 1979–July 1984	ABC	Tues. 10–11 P.M.

This popular mystery/adventure series starred Robert WAGNER and Stephanie POWERS as Jonathan and Jennifer Hart, a wealthy married couple who kept stumbling upon crimes. Jonathan Hart was a self-made millionaire who headed the Hart Industries conglomerate, and his wife, Jennifer, was a former freelance journalist. The Harts were international jet-setters, stylish, sophisticated, and urbane. Their gravel-voiced chauffeur and butler, Max, played by veteran character actor Lionel Stander, looked after the couple like a doting parent, and often assisted when they were trying to solve a crime. *Hart to Hart* was the brainchild of the prolific, best-selling author Sidney Sheldon. Aaron SPELLING and Leonard Goldberg were the show's executive producers. By the time *Hart to Hart* left the air, 112 episodes had been filmed.

HASSELHOFF, DAVID (1952–)

When he was seven years old, David Hasselhoff, who was born and raised in Baltimore, Maryland, decided that he wanted to be an actor, and so his parents enrolled him in dancing, singing, and acting lessons. Because of his father's job, the Hasselhoff family moved from place to place frequently. Eventually, they settled in the Los Angeles area. After acting in various amateur and semiprofessional stock companies, Hasselhoff was cast on the daytime serial drama *The YOUNG AND THE REST-LESS*, playing a handsome young physician named Dr. "Snapper" Foster. The character in the person of the attractive young actor became enormously popular, and in less than a year, he was offered a starring role on an evening series, *KNIGHT RIDER*, by NBC's Brandon Tartikoff. *Knight Rider* was a success, and Hasselhoff won a People's Choice "Most Popular Actor on TV" Award. At this time, Hasselhoff also launched his singing career and recorded a hit song, "Looking for Freedom." In 1989, Hasselhoff returned to television as the star of a new series, *BAYWATCH*, playing a head lifeguard, Mitch Buchannan, who was the single father of a young son. The series was panned by TV critics, but the public loved watching all the half-clothed young men and young women running around on the beach, saving people from drowning, and falling in love with one another. NBC bowed to the critics and canceled the show after just one season. Hasselhoff, however, was convinced that there was an audience for *Baywatch*. With several partners, Hasselhoff bought the rights to the show and began to produce new episodes of *Baywatch* and placed the series in syndication. Eventually, Hasselhoff's faith in the show paid off, and *Baywatch* was soon being seen in 140 countries throughout the world, including the United States, and was watched by over 1 billion viewers. The revenues from *Baywatch* made Hasselhoff, who continued to appear on and produce the show, a very rich man. In addition to *Baywatch,* Hasselhoff also appeared in and produced the TV film *Nick Fury: Agent of S.H.I.E.L.D.* in 1998. He also produced and starred in the miniseries *Shaka Zulu: The Citadel* in 2000.

HAVE GUN WILL TRAVEL

Sept. 1957–Sept. 1963   CBS   Sat. 9:30–10 P.M.

One of several TV western series that were popular in the late 1950s, *Have Gun Will Travel* starred Richard BOONE as Paladin, a West Point–educated, literate, and sophisticated man, who, after fighting in the Civil War, headed west, where he became a high-priced, trouble-shooting gun-for-hire. His home base was the fancy Hotel Carlton in San Francisco. Paladin always gave out a calling card that read, "Have gun will travel. Wire Paladin, San Francisco." Something of a dandy, Paladin wore fine clothes, which were always black, and enjoyed good food, the arts, and intelligent conversation. Occasionally, when he felt the situation warranted it, Paladin even brought to justice the very people who hired him. When *Have Gun Will Travel* first went on the air, Paladin always had his messages delivered to him at the Hotel Carlton. They were always handed to him by "Hey Boy," an Asian man working at the hotel, played by Kam Tong, After a few seasons, the messages were delivered by a young Asian girl, "Hey Girl," played by Lisa Lu. *Have Gun Will Travel* was an enormous hit and ranked among the top five shows on television the first season it was aired. The show's theme song, "The Ballad of Paladin," became a top-selling recording in the early 1960s.

HAWAII FIVE-O

Sept. 1968–Dec. 1968	CBS	Thurs. 8–9 P.M.
Dec. 1968–Sept. 1971	CBS	Wed. 10–11 P.M.
Sept. 1971–Sept. 1974	CBS	Tues. 8:30–9:30 P.M.
Sept. 1974–Sept. 1975	CBS	Tues. 9–10 P.M.
Sept. 1975–Nov. 1975	CBS	Fri. 9–10 P.M.
Dec. 1975–Nov. 1979	CBS	Thurs. 9–10 P.M.
Dec. 1979–Jan. 1980	CBS	Tues. 9–10 P.M.
Mar. 1980–Apr. 1980	CBS	Sat. 9–10 P.M.

During the 12½ years it was on prime-time television, the police drama *Hawaii Five-O* had one of TV's most loyal audiences, and the show was among the most viewed shows on television. Set in Honolulu, Hawaii, the law enforcers depicted on *Hawaii Five-O* were not members of the Honolulu Police Department, as most people thought. The Hawaii Five-O unit was part of the Hawaiian State Police force and was accountable directly to the governor of the state of Hawaii. Jack LORD played the show's central character, Det. Steve McGarrett, a tough, no-nonsense policeman who headed the Five-O team that fought the Hawaiian underworld and solved various other statewide crimes. One of McGarrett's main adversaries was the evil Wo Fat, played by Khigh Dhiegh, a criminal genius who periodically turned up to make McGarrett and his men's job more difficult. Assisting McGarrett were Det. Danny "Danno" Williams, played by James MacArthur, an idealistic young police officer, and the older-and-wiser officer of the law, Det. Chin Ho Kelly, played by Kam Fong. Assisting them was a heavyset Native Hawaiian, Det. Kono Kalakaua, played by an actor named Zulu. Their boss,

Governor Philip Grey, was played by Richard Denning. Also appearing regularly on the series were Al Harrington as Det. Ben Kakua, Harry Endo as Che Fong, Al Eben as Doc Bergman, Maggi Parker as May, Peggy Ryan as Jenny Sherman, Laura Sode as Luana, Herman Wedermeyer as Duke Lukela, Morgan White and then Glenn Cannon as the state's attorney general, William Smith as James "Kimo" Carew, Moe Keale as Truck Kealoha, and Sharon Farrell as Lois Wilson. The Iolani Palace, where Hawaii Five-O's offices were located, had, at one time, housed the Hawaiian State Legislature. The series was created by Leonard Freeman, who was *Hawaii Five-O*'s executive producer, until his death in 1973.

HAWAIIAN EYE

Oct. 1959–Sept. 1962	ABC	Wed. 9–10 P.M.
Oct. 1962–Sept. 1963	ABC	Tues. 8:30–9:30 P.M.

This detective series introduced such later-to-be-famous performers as Robert CONRAD, Connie STEVENS, and Troy Donahue to the American public and was very popular during the four years it was aired, although it was often confused with another series called *77 SUNSET STRIP*. Both series centered on several attractive young people who worked in a private detective agency and conducted investigations for an odd assortment of clients. Robert "Bob" Conrad played Tom Lopaka, a detective at the P. I. agency whose offices were located in the Hawaiian Village Hotel in Honolulu. Lopaka's partner, Tracy Stele, was played by Anthony Eisley. Often assisting the two young detectives was addlepated singer/photographer Cricket Blake, who worked at the hotel, played by Connie Stevens. Also offering the detectives assistance was cab driver Kazuo Kim, nicknamed Kim Kim, played by Poncie Ponce, and, later during the series' run, detective Greg MacKenzie, played by Grant Williams. Added to the show later was Philip Barton, the hotel's social director, played by Troy Donahue, who joined the others in their crime-solving activities. Because of his blond, boy-next-door good looks, Donahue became one of the show's major attractions. Other performers who made appearances on the show were Chad EVERETT and Jack Nicholson. William T. Orr produced the series for the Warner Brothers Studios.

HAZEL

Sept. 1961–July 1964	NBC	Thurs. 9:30–10 P.M.
Sept. 1964–Sept. 1965	NBC	Thurs. 9:30–10 P.M.
Sept. 1965–Sept. 1966	CBS	Mon. 9:30–10 P.M.

America's favorite domestic, Hazel, who had been a popular *Saturday Evening Post* magazine cartoon character created by Ted Key, arrived on television in 1961 with Academy Award– and Tony-winning actress Shirley BOOTH playing the role of Hazel. Hazel Burke was a down-to-earth, plain-talking, loving housekeeper who worked as a combination maid/nanny/cook and main adviser to the Baxters, George and Dorothy, played by Don DeFore and Whitney Blake. Hazel could always be depended upon to know exactly what needed to be done during emergencies, and she always offered sound advice when it was called for. She was also a patient, supportive, and loving nanny to the Baxters' young son, Harold, played by Bobby Buntrock. The Baxters' zany next-door neighbors were Harriet and Herbert Johnson, played by Norma Varden and Donald Foster. Other characters who appeared regularly were Rosie, played by Maudie Prickett, and the Baxters' friends, Deidre and Henry Thompson, played by Cathy Lewis and Robert P. Lieb. When *Hazel* moved from NBC to CBS in 1965, Hazel went to work for George Baxter's brother, Steve, and his wife, Barbara, played by Ray Fulmer and Lynn Borden. Viewers were told George and Dorothy Baxter and their son, Harold, had moved to the Middle East, where George's company had transferred him. In its first season, *Hazel* was among the top-10 shows on television, according to the Nielsen ratings. The series was produced by James Fonda for Screen Gems.

HEAD OF THE CLASS

Sept. 1986–Feb. 1987	ABC	Wed. 8:30–9 P.M.
Apr. 1987–June 1989	ABC	Wed. 8:30–9 P.M.
Aug. 1989–Aug. 1990	ABC	Wed. 8:30–9 P.M.
Sept. 1990–Jan. 1991	ABC	Tues. 8:30–9 P.M.
May 1991–June 1991	ABC	Tues. 8:30–9 P.M.

Created by Michael Elias and Rich Eustis, and based upon Eustis's personal experiences as a substitute teacher in New York City, *Head of the Class* starred Howard Hesseman as Charles Moore, a substitute teacher at Fillmore High School who was hired to take over the Individual Honors Program (IHP) class. Although Moore's students were book-smart enough, he soon realized that they had a lot to learn about life, and he made it his mission to expose them to certain of life's realities. Fillmore's principal, Dr. Harold Samuels, played by William G. Schilling, did not appreciate Moore's nonacademic approach and often became a stumbling block that the teacher and his students had to circumvent. All Dr. Samuels cared about was that Moore's students win the city's Academic Olympics contests. The school's assistant principal, Bernadette Meara, played by Jeannetta Arnette, did what she could to support Moore. Moore's class members consisted of the grade-obsessed Maria Borges, played by Leslie Bega; the nerd Arvod Engen, played by Dan Frischman; preppy and pretty Darlene Merriman, played by Robin Givens; book-loving Simone Foster, played by Khrystyne Haje; exchange student Jawaharlal Choudhury, played by Jory Husain; heartthrob Alan Pinkard, played by Tony O'Dell; brainy tough guy Eric Mardian, played by Brian Robbins; art-loving Sarah Nivens, played by Kimberly Russell; heavyset science fiend Dennis Blunden, played by Dan Schneider; 12-year-old prodigy Janice Lazorrotto, played by Tannis Vallely; fast-talking T. J., played by Rain Pryor; horny Alex Torres, played by Michael DeLorenzo; normal Viki Amory, played by Lara

Piper; artistic Aristotle McKenzie, played by DeVoreaux White; and Jasper Kwong, played by Jonathan Ke Quan. After four seasons, Howard Hesseman decided he wanted to quit the series. He was replaced by Scottish comedian Billy Connolly, who played substitute teacher Billy MacGregor. In 1988, *Head of the Class* became the first American television series to film an episode in the Soviet Union.

HEE HAW

June 1969–Sept. 1969	CBS	Sun. 9–10 P.M.
Dec. 1969–June 1970	CBS	Wed. 7:30–8:30 P.M.
Sept. 1970–July 1971	CBS	Tues. 8:30–9:30 P.M.
1971–1993	Syndicated series	Various times and stations

Using a format similar to the successful *LAUGH-IN* variety show of the 1960s, *Hee Haw* was a country music and comedy–oriented variety show that featured blackout sketches, musical numbers, and guest-starring appearances by some of the most famous names in country music. County singers Roy Clark and Buck Owens hosted the show, performed many of their hit songs, and often appeared in skits. Corny one-liners, silly running gags, an abundance of full-figured pretty girls, and typical country

Hee Haw: Marianne Gordon, Roy Clark, and Buck Owens (Author's collection)

humor kept the show at the top of the ratings throughout the United States for two years. In 1971, while *Hee Haw* was on the top-20 Nielsen list of popular shows, CBS decided to cancel the program in order to "deruralize" its programming, since most advertisers wanted to concentrate on selling their products to the larger urban audiences. The show promptly went into syndication and managed to remain on the air for 22 additional years. Among *Hee Haw*'s original cast members were the Hager twins (Jim and Jon), Louis M. "Grandpa" Jones, Lulu Roman, Cathy Baker, Jennifer Bishop, Archie Campbell, Don Harron, Gunilla Hutton, Claude "Jackie" Phelps, Don Rich, Jimmy Riddle, Jeannine Riley, Alvin "Junior" Samples, Diana Scott, David "Stringbean" Akeman, Gordie Tapp, Mary Taylor, Sheb Wooley, the Buckaroos, the Hee Haw Band, and the Nashville Edition. Additional semiregulars included "Cousin Minnie" Pearl, George Lindsay, Barbi Benton, Misty Rowe, Roy Acuff, Slim Pickens, Jonathan WINTERS, Dub Taylor, Rev. Grady Nutt, and Kathie Lee Johnson (Kathie Lee GIFFORD).

HEMSLEY, SHERMAN (SHERMAN ALEXANDER HEMSLEY 1938–)

Although he appeared in the successful Broadway musical comedy *Purlie* (1970) and had regular roles on such TV series as *AMEN* (1986–90), *Dinosaurs* (1992), *Townsend Television* (1993), and *Goode Behavior* (1996), African-American actor Sherman Hemsley will always be remembered as George Jefferson, the crusty dry cleaning store owner who moved "on up to a deluxe apartment in the sky." Before he became an actor, Hemsley, who was born in Philadelphia, worked at various jobs, but even though he was a frequent performer on the stage, it wasn't until he played George Jefferson, Archie Bunker's next-door neighbor on the enormously successful *ALL IN THE FAMILY*, that he became a star. In 1975, *The JEFFERSONS*, which starred Hemsley and Isabel Sanford, who had originated the roles of George and Louise Jefferson on *All in the Family*, became one of the most successful television spin-off series of all time. In addition to his starring roles on TV series, Hemsley has also appeared in many feature films, including *Stewardess School* (1987), *Ghost Fever* (1987), *Club Fed* (1990), *Mr. Nanny* (1993), *The Misery Brothers* (1995), *Senseless* (1998), *Screwed* (2000), and others, and made guest appearances on such popular TV series as *The LOVE BOAT, FANTASY ISLAND, ER, The FRESH PRINCE OF BEL AIR, DESIGNING WOMEN, BURKE'S LAW, FAMILY MATTERS*, and *The HUGHLEYS*.

HENDERSON, FLORENCE (FLORENCE AGNES HENDERSON 1934–)

The youngest of 10 children born to a sharecropper and his homemaker wife, Florence Henderson was born in Dale, Indiana. After finishing high school, Florence went to New York City, determined to break into show business. Before long, she was appearing in the chorus of several Broadway shows. Eventually, Henderson was selected by composer Richard Rodgers and lyricist Oscar Hammerstein II to play the leading role of Laurie in the touring company of their musical comedy success *Oklahoma!* During the late 1950s to early 1960s, Henderson was one of the busiest actresses in New York and was regularly seen on such television programs as *The TONIGHT SHOW*, from 1958 to 1962, *The Jack Paar Show, Sing Along* (1958), *TODAY*, and *The Oldsmobile Music Theatre* (1959). She also frequently guest-starred on such shows as *The UNITED STATES STEEL HOUR*. Returning to Broadway, Henderson starred in the musical comedy *The Girl Who Came to Supper*. In 1969, she was cast as Carol Ann Brady, the mother of three daughters who married a widower with three sons on *The BRADY BUNCH*. Although she continued to appear in occasional *Brady Bunch* specials and TV films after the regular series was canceled in 1974, Henderson also appeared as a guest star on many TV series such as *HART TO HART, ALICE, MURDER, SHE WROTE, ROSEANNE, CAROLINE IN THE CITY, ELLEN,* and others, and had featured roles in the films *Naked Gun 33 1/3* (1994), *The Brady Bunch Movie* (1995, playing Grandma). In 1999, Henderson became one of the cohosts on the *Later Today* magazine show.

HENNER, MARILU (MARY LUCY DENISE PUDLOWSKI 1952–)

A talented singer and dancer who appeared in the chorus of such Broadway shows as *Over Here*, a musical comedy that starred the Andrews Sisters in the 1970s, Marilu Henner, was born in Chicago to hard-working parents. After finishing high school, Marilu went to New York City to break into show business and eventually, after numerous auditions, found work in the chorus of several Broadway shows. During her run in *Over Here*, Marilu dated actor John TRAVOLTA, who had a featured role in the show, and they remained close friends after the show ended. Henner's big break didn't occur on the stage, but on TV, when she was cast as Elaine Nardo on *TAXI*. The situation comedy series became one of television's most successful programs. When *Taxi* left the air in 1983, Henner appeared in feature films such as *The Man Who Loved Women* (1983), *Cannonball Run II* (1984), *Perfect* (1985), *Grand Larceny* (1987), and several TV films. In 1990, Henner played Burt Reynolds's wife, Ava Evans Newton, on the TV series *EVENING SHADE*, and subsequently hosted an unsuccessful talk show, *Marilu*, in 1994. Roles in such highly rated TV films as *My Son Is Innocent* (1996), *Titanic* (1996, as Molly Brown), and a cameo appearance as herself in the Andy Kaufman film biography, *Man on the Moon* (1999) followed. In the late 1990s, Henner returned to Broadway, replacing one of the stars of the musical comedy *Chicago*.

HENSON, JIM (JAMES MAURY HENSON 1936–1990)

One of the greatest puppeteers of all time, Jim Henson originally began puppeteering as a means of getting into television and had never seriously considered a career in puppetry. After graduating from Northwestern High School in Hyattsville, Maryland, and then attending the University of Maryland, Henson, who was born in Greenville, Mississippi, worked at various jobs and eventually settled in Washington, D.C. After hounding the programming director at a Washington, D.C., TV station, Henson was finally given the opportunity to work on an after-the-eleven o'clock news puppet show called *Sam and Friends*. The show became very popular, and before long, Henson and his puppets were seen in numerous commercials in the Washington area, and then around the country. Henson and his puppets made guest appearances on *The Jimmy Dean Show* and introduced Rowlf the Dog, a character that became very popular. Appearances on several TV shows and in-person performances around the country followed.

In 1965, Henson produced a short film that featured his puppets, *Time Piece*. This led to his being asked to participate in a project produced by the Children's Television Workshop for the Public Broadcasting System called *SESAME STREET*. Henson, with his partner, Frank Oz, created characters for the show, which was directed toward preschool youngsters and was designed to teach them the alphabet and counting, as well as how to get along with one other. The puppet characters Henson created for the show became extremely popular with young viewers and, interestingly enough, their parents. They included Kermit the Frog, Miss Piggy, the Cookie Monster, Bert and Ernie, Big Bird, Oscar the Grouch, and many others. Bert and Ernie even became popular commercial spokesmen. *Sesame Street* was an enormous hit, and within a year, Henson had become the most famous puppeteer in the world.

In 1976, in addition to continuing to supervise the puppets on *Sesame Street* and providing the voices for many of the characters on the show, Henson and Frank Oz developed *The MUPPET SHOW* for commercial television, which became a successful network program and featured celebrated guest stars who vied to be booked on the show. Many films followed, such as *The Muppet Movie* (1979), *The Great Muppet Caper* (1981), *The Dark Crystal* (1982, which did not feature Henson and Oz's usual puppets), and *The Muppets Take Manhattan* (1984), produced and directed by Henson and featuring his puppet creations, as well as his voice. Henson's untimely death in 1990 occurred on the weekend before he was to sell his company to the Disney organization, which currently owns all rights to Henson's former properties.

HERB SHRINER SHOW, THE/HERB SHRINER TIME

Nov. 1949–Feb. 1950	CBS	Mon./Tues./Thurs.–Sat. 7:55–8 P.M.
Oct. 1951–Apr. 1952	ABC	Thurs. 9–9:30 P.M.
Oct. 1956–Dec. 1956	CBS	Tues. 9–9:30 P.M.

Hailed as the successor to the legendary Indiana-born humorist and homespun philosopher of the 1920s and 1930s, Will Rogers, Herb Shriner was one of early television's first major stars. Shriner, who had first come to the public's attention as the star of his own radio show in the 1940s, arrived on television in 1949, with a five-day-a-week show that featured comedy chatter, musical selections, and occasional guests. His show became a five-times-a-week evening attraction in 1949. On this show, Shriner performed well-received short monologues. In 1951, Shriner moved to prime-time TV with a program called *Herb Shriner Time*, which not only presented his tall tales, but also featured comedy skits and many famous guest stars. The show was canceled after only one season, but Shriner returned to prime-time with another series, *The Herb Shriner Show*, a variety show that featured a format similar to his previous program, in 1956. It was not successful and was canceled after only two and a half months on the air. After this, Shriner appeared as a guest star on several comedy/variety programs and occasionally was featured on *The ED SULLIVAN SHOW*, but for all intents and purposes his star had set, and he gradually faded from public view.

HERMAN, PEE-WEE
(see Reubens, Paul)

HICKMAN, DWAYNE (1934–)
Born in Los Angeles to show business parents, Dwayne Hickman, who is best known for playing Dobie Gillis in *The MANY LOVES OF DOBIE GILLIS* TV series of the late 1950s–early 1960s, was, like his brother, Darrel Hickman, a successful child actor before he became a TV star. Dwayne was featured in such films as *Melodies Old and New* (1942, his film debut), *The Secret Heart* (1946), *Her Husband's Affairs* (1947), *My Dog Rusty* (1948), *Rally 'Round the Flag, Boys!* (1958), and appeared on episodes of *The LONE RANGER* and *WAGON TRAIN* He was also a regular on *Love That Bob* (aka *The BOB CUMMINGS SHOW*) in 1995. After *Dobie Gillis* left the air, Hickman had featured roles in the films *Cat Ballou* (1965) and *How to Stuff a Wild Bikini* (1965), and guest-starred on such series as *Kolchak: The Night Stalker* (1974–75), *ELLERY QUEEN*, *MURDER, SHE WROTE*, *Clueless* (1998–99), and others. He has also directed episodes of *DESIGNING WOMEN* and *Harry and the Hendersons,* and appeared in several TV films. Hickman's last major film appearance to date was in the 1998 film *A Night at the Roxbury.*

HIGHLANDER: THE SERIES

1992–1999 (with reruns)	Syndicated series	Various times and stations

The success of the syndicated fantasy/action series *Highlander* was in large part due to its handsome, athletic star Adrian Paul. The series, which was based on the 1986 feature film *Highlander,* was about 400-year-old Scotsman Duncan McCloud, who was one of a small number of immortals inhabiting Earth. Not all the immortals who were seen on this show were as good or moral as Duncan McCloud. The immortals fought one another with swords, and their duels always ended with a ritualistic beheading. The survivor of the duel then took over the powers of the immortal who had been killed. Ultimately, only one immortal was to be left on Earth, and hopefully, it would be the virtuous Duncan McCloud. If the final survivor was one of the evil immortals who roamed the planet, Earth would be condemned to "an eternity of darkness." Also appearing on the series was Alexandra Vandernoot as McCloud's mortal girlfriend, Tessa Noel. Tessa, one of a few people who knew the truth about McCloud's immortality, ran an antique shop. Shocked viewers registered their complaints when Tessa was killed off after the series' second season. Also aware of McCloud's immortality was a young man named Richie Ryan, played by Stan Kirsch, who later discovered that he, too, was an immortal. One of a group of mortals known as the Watchers, because they observed but did not interfere with the immortals, was Joe Dawson, played by Jim Byrnes, who became a friend and supporter of McCloud. After Tessa's death, McCloud, following a considerable period of grief, eventually found a new girlfriend, a surgeon named Anne Lindsey, played by Lisa Howard. Randi McFarland, a reporter at KCLA played by Amanda Wyss, TV, was always trying to find out what she could about the strange beheadings that were taking place. She and McCloud's fellow immortal, and former lover, Amanda Darieux, played by Elizabeth Gracen were, for a time, featured regularly on the series. In all, 119 episodes of *Highlander* were filmed between 1992 and 1998, and the series can still be seen on various cable stations and as a late-night network offering.

HIGHWAY PATROL

1955–1959	Syndicated series	Various times and stations

Academy Award–winning actor Broderick Crawford starred on this action/adventure series that was one of television's most viewed syndicated shows. Crawford played Chief Detective Dan Matthews, the head of the state police's highway patrol in an unnamed western state. The patrol cars tracked down hijackers, smugglers, and robbers on the state's highways. Most of the show's action took place out of doors. Announcer Art Gilmore was the series' unseen narrator. In all, 156 episodes of the show were filmed.

HILL STREET BLUES

Jan. 1981	NBC	Thurs./Sat. 10–11 P.M.
Jan. 1981–Apr. 1981	NBC	Sat. 10–11 P.M.
Apr. 1981–Aug. 1981	NBC	Tues. 9–10 P.M.
Oct. 1981–Nov. 1986	NBC	Thurs. 10–11 P.M.
Dec. 1986–Feb. 1987	NBC	Tues. 9–10 P.M.
Mar. 1987–May 1987	NBC	Tues. 10–11 P.M.

For six years, the police drama series *Hill Street Blues* was one of the most popular shows on television. The series was about police officers assigned to the Hill Street Station, located in a depressed urban ghetto in a large eastern American city. The show was noted for its original, gritty, and realistic depictions of big city police officers' professional and personal lives. In command of the officers at the Hill Street Station was Capt. Frank Furillo, played by Daniel J. Travanti, a quiet, strong leader who had to cope with the usual bureaucracy that exists in big city service departments, as well as handle the everyday problems that occurred on the streets and in the lives of his staff. The police officers under Furillo's command were Sgt. Phil Esterhaus, played by Michael Conrad; Officer Bobby Hill, played by Michael Warren; Officer Andy Renko, played by Charles Haid; Det. Mike Belker, played by Bruce Weitz; Lt. Ray Calletano, played by Rene Enriquez; and Det. Neal Washington, played by Taurean Blacque. Also appearing on the series as police officers at the Hill Street Station were James Sikking, Joe Spano, Gerry Black, Richard Hirschfield, Ed Mariano, Jon Cypher, Ken Olin, Robert Clohessy, David Selburg, and, as Lt. Norman Buntz, Dennis Franz. Playing major female roles were Veronica Hamel as Joyce Davenport, a public defender who dated and eventually married Furillo; Barbara Bosson as Fay Furillo, Capt. Furillo's ex-wife; and several female officers under Furillo's command, played by Betty Thomas, as Officer/Sgt. Lucille Bates; and Lisa Sutton, Mimi Kuzyk, and Megan Gallagher. Also appearing in the series on a semiregular basis were George Wyner as Asst. District Attorney Irwin Bernstein, J. A. Preston as Mayor Ozzie Cleveland, and Trinidad Silva, Jeffrey Tambor, Judith Hansen, and Robert Prosky. *Hill Street Blues,* which was developed by NBC's president Fred Silverman, was produced by MTM productions' Michael Kozoll and Stephen Bochco. Even though the series received rave reviews from TV critics when it was first aired, viewers were slow to discover the show. After several adjustments were made concerning the best time to air the show, it gradually began to attract an audience and eventually became one of the most popular shows on television, winning numerous Emmy and viewer poll awards.

HILLIARD, HARRIET (AKA HARRIET NELSON NÉE PEGGY LOU SYNDER 1909–1994)

Before she became known as America's favorite wife and mother on *The ADVENTURES OF OZZIE AND HARRIET,* Harriet Hilliard was a successful band singer and film actress. Born in Des Moines, Iowa, Hilliard began her career as a teenage singer in local talent contests. A Hollywood talent scout discovered Hilliard during a singing engagement and signed her to a contract. Her first film role was in 1932 in *The Campus Mystery,* playing a coed. Increasingly larger roles followed in such films as *Follow the Fleet* (1936), in which her singing attracted considerable attention and led to many radio show appearances, and larger roles in the films *New Faces of 1937, The Life of the Party* (1937),

Cocoanut Grove (1938), *Confessions of Boston Blackie* (1941), *Jukebox Jenny* (1942), *Swingtime Johnny* (1943), *Hi, Good Lookin'* (1943), and others. In 1944, Harriet, who had been a regular on the *Red Skelton Show* radio programs, joined her husband, bandleader Ozzie Nelson, at the microphone as the star of a situation comedy called *The Adventures of Ozzie and Harriet,* which became one of radio's most popular programs, remaining on the air for nine years. In 1952, Harriet and Ozzie appeared in a feature film, *Here Come the Nelsons,* which led to their entry into television with their situation comedy series. The show, which later also featured the Nelson's real-life sons, David and Ricky, became one of TV's highest-rated shows and remained on the air for an impressive 14 continuous years. In 1973, Harriet once again teamed up with her husband, Ozzie, in the TV series *Ozzie's Girls,* which did not prove to be as successful as their *Ozzie and Harriet Show.* Hilliard was subsequently seen only occasionally on television in such projects as the miniseries *Once an Eagle,* and in such TV films as *Death Car on the Freeway* (1979), *The First Time* (1982), and *The Kid with the 200 I.Q.* (1983). In 1989, Hilliard made her last television appearance, as a nun named Sister Agnes, on her granddaughter Traci Nelson's series, *The FATHER DOWLING MYSTERIES.*

HIRSCH, JUDD (1935–)

An Emmy Award–winning actor for his performance on *TAXI,* Judd Hirsch had no idea that he was going to be an actor when he was majoring in physics in college. Born in the Bronx, New York, Hirsch, who had attended De Witt Clinton High School before entering college, made his film debut in 1973 playing an uncredited role in *Serpico.* Regular roles on such TV series as *The Law* (as Murray Stone) and *Delvecchio* (1976), as Sergeant Dominick Delvecchio), in TV films *Fear on Trial* (1975), *The Legend of Valentino* (1975), and in the feature film *King of the Gypsies* (1978), led to his being cast as Alex Rieger, the role that made him famous, on *Taxi.* The show became one of television's most successful series and made Hirsch a star. The series remained on the air for five years and won practically every major award. While he was appearing on *Taxi,* Hirsch was also seen in such feature films as *Ordinary People* (1980), *Without a Trace* (1983), and *Teachers* (1984), and in several TV films. In 1985, Hirsch appeared on the less successful TV series *Detective in the House,* and in 1988, he starred on the more popular *DEAR JOHN* series. Roles in many TV films, and a cameo appearance playing himself in the film *Man on the Moon* in 1999, a film biography of his *Taxi* costar Andy Kaufman, followed.

HITCHCOCK, ALFRED (ALFRED JOSEPH HITCHCOCK 1899–1980)

Even though Alfred Hitchcock was one of England's and Hollywood's most celebrated film directors and producers, he is also fondly remembered as the producer, sometimes director, and regular host of two very successful television series, *ALFRED HITCHCOCK PRESENTS,* which ran from 1955–1965, and *The Alfred Hitchcock Hour,* which was on television from 1961–1965. Hitchcock's corpulent frame, his slow, mannered speech, and his imposing countenance were already familiar to audiences thanks to his habit of making cameo appearances in his many films. Born in London, England, where his father was a grocer, Hitchcock studied engineering at St. Ignatius College, a Jesuit school, before deciding to study art at the University of London. In 1920, after working as a technician at a cable company and in the advertising department of a large London department store, Hitchcock was hired as a draftsman by a London film studio. Hitchcock worked his way up to scriptwriting, then to assistant directing, and finally to directing. His first directing assignment was a low-budget melodrama called *The Pleasure Garden* in 1925. His first important film was *The Lodger,* which he directed in 1926. He followed that up with the even more successful *The Man Who Knew Too Much* (1934), *The 39 Steps* (1935), and *The Lady Vanishes* (1938), which established him as one of England's best film directors. In 1940, Hitchcock went to Hollywood, where he directed *Rebecca* (1940), which was an enormous artistic and financial success. Successful Hollywood films such as *Foreign Correspondent* (1940), *Suspicion* (1941), *Shadow of a Doubt* (1943), *Lifeboat* (1944), *Spellbound* (1945), *Rope* (1948) *Notorious* (1946), *Strangers on a Train* (1951), *Rear Window* (1954), *Vertigo* (1958), *North by Northwest* (1959), and *Psycho* (1960) followed. Although he never received an Academy Award for his work in films, Hitchcock was knighted by Queen Elizabeth II for his achievements in cinema. Hitchcock's last film, *Family Plot,* was released in 1976, five years before his death at the age of 80.

HODGE, AL (ALBERT HODGE 1912–1979)

Al Hodge, who was the voice of the Green Hornet and many other characters on radio in the 1930s and 1940s, earned a place for himself in television's Hall of Fame by playing Captain Video on the fondly remembered early series CAPTAIN VIDEO, a popular children's adventure show in the early 1950s. Born in Ravenna, Ohio, where his parents owned a dry-cleaning business, Hodge majored in drama at the University of Miami in Oxford, Ohio, and worked as an actor in summer stock before entering radio as a staff member at WXYZ in Detroit, Michigan. There Hodge directed and acted on such memorable radio programs as *Challenge of the Yukon, The Lone Ranger, Ned Jordan, Secret Agent,* and *The Green Hornet.* Hodge also played the part of Tex Mason on radio's *Bobby Benson* adventures. Moving to New York City in the 1940s, Hodge was soon heard on such popular daytime radio soap operas as *The Romance of Helen Trent* and *Ma Perkins.* After serving in the U.S. Navy during World War II, Hodge returned to radio and was heard on such programs as *Gangbusters, Mr. District Attorney, Mr. Keen, Tracer of Lost Persons,* and many others. In 1951, Hodge was cast as Captain Video. After *Captain Video* left the air in 1955, Hodge continued to work as a voice-over performer for film documentaries, foreign film dubbing, and cartoon characters, and made guest appearances on such TV series as NAKED CITY, The UNITED STATES STEEL HOUR, *Michael Shayne* (1960–61), HAWAIIAN EYE, and *Angel* (1960–61), but he never again achieved the success or attention he had enjoyed as Captain Video. Hodge died an alcoholic, alone and forgotten, in 1979. At the time of his death, Hodge was living on his $63-a-week Social Security check.

Alfred Hitchcock (Author's collection)

HOGAN'S HEROES

Sept. 1965–Sept. 1967	CBS	Fri. 8:30–9 P.M.
Sept. 1967–Sept. 1969	CBS	Sat. 9–9:30 P.M.
Sept. 1969–Sept. 1970	CBS	Fri. 8:30–9 P.M.
Sept. 1970–July 1971	CBS	Sun. 7–8 P.M.

By 1967, CBS believed that enough years had gone by to diminish the memory of many of the horrors of World War II, which had ended 22 years earlier. The network felt that a situation comedy set in a prisoner of war (POW) camp during the war would, by that time, be acceptable to the public. They were right, and *Hogan's Heroes,* set in a POW camp during World War II, became a hit and was on the air for six seasons. The leader of a group of Allied prisoners of war at Stalag 13 was Col. Robert Hogan, played by Bob CRANE. His nemesis at the camp was the bumbling, status-conscious Nazi commandant Col. Wilhelm Klink, played by Werner Klemperer. As Col. Hogan and his men plotted escapes, tricked Klink and his guards into giving them various privileges, and made the most of bad situations, they always made fools of their Nazi captors. Among the POWs under Hogan's command were French Cpl. Louis LeBeau, played by Robert Clary; British Cpl. Peter Newkirk, played by Richard DAWSON; Sgt. James Kinchloe, played by Ivan Dixon; Sgt. Richard Baker, played by Kenneth Washington; and Sgt. Andrew Carter, played by Larry Hovis. One of the show's most amusing and popular characters was a fat, inept prison guard named Sgt. Hans Schultz, played by John Banner, who inadvertently always seemed to play right into Col. Hogan and his men's hands. A catchphrase often quoted by fans was Schultz's "I know nothing," when his ineptitude was about to be exposed. Also appearing on the series was a pretty German girl named Helga, played by Cynthia Lynn, who lived in a town close to the prison compound. Lynn was replaced by Sigrid Valdis, who played the part of Hilda in later episodes of the show. *Hogan's Heroes* was created by Bernard Fein and Albert S. Ruddy and produced by Ed Feldman for Bing Crosby Productions. In all, 168 episodes of the series were filmed.

HOLLIDAY, POLLY (1937–)

Polly Holliday became well known for playing the gum-chewing, somewhat bossy waitress with a heavy Southern drawl and upswept blond hair, Florence Jean Castleberry or "Flo," as she was called, on the *ALICE* and the *Flo* situation comedies. She began her career as a stage actress in regional and off-Broadway plays. Holliday, who majored in drama in college, was indeed, like Flo Castleberry, a daughter of the Deep South, born in Jasper, Alabama. Her first major television appearance was on the daytime drama SEARCH FOR TOMORROW in 1974, playing a menacing prison inmate and was seen in such other films as *Pittsville* (1974), *W. W. and the Dixie Dancekings* (1975), *Distance* (1975), and in the TV films *The Silence* (1975) and *Luke Was There* (1976), which led to her being cast as Flo on *Alice* in 1976. In 1980, Holliday was given a spin-off series of her own, *Flo*, playing the same character she had played on *Alice*, when her character became one of the major reasons for *Alice's* success. While she was on *Alice* and on *Flo*, Holliday continued to perform in other projects and had featured roles in the films *All the President's Men* (1976), *The One and Only* (1978), and starred in the TV version of the popular stage play *You Can't Take It With You* (1979). After *Flo* was canceled when it did not prove to be as successful as *Alice*, Holliday continued to appear in films such as *Gremlins* (1984) and *Mrs. Doubtfire* (1993), and was a regular on the *Stir Crazy* (1985–86) and John Grisham's *The Client* (1996) TV series, as well as starring in many TV films. The actress also made many guest-starring appearances on such series as GOLDEN GIRLS, Amazing Stories, and *The EQUALIZER*, and was a semiregular on

HOME IMPROVEMENT. Holliday's last major film appearance of the 1990s was in *The Parent Trap* in 1998.

HOLLYWOOD PALACE, THE

Jan. 1964–May 1967	ABC	Sat. 9:30–10.30 P.M.
Sept. 1967–Jan. 1968	ABC	Mon. 10–11 P.M.
Jan. 1968–Feb. 1970	ABC	Sat. 9:30–10:30 P.M.

When The Hollywood Palace, a big-budget, lavish, weekly variety show, made its debut in 1967, it was ABC's Saturday night answer to CBS's popular Sunday night variety program *The ED SULLIVAN SHOW*. Hollywood Palace, telecast live from ABC's newly refurbished El Capitan Theater in Hollywood, which had been renamed The Palace, featured Bing CROSBY as its host on the premiere show. Film star Mickey Rooney, dancer Bobby Van, singer Nancy Wilson, comedian Bob NEWHART, Bing's son Gary, and various magicians, singers, dancers, and circus acts made guest appearances on the first telecast. Other hosts, (Bing Crosby subsequently hosted over 30 shows) were Fred ASTAIRE, Jimmy DURANTE, Sid CAESAR, Imogene COCA, Don ADAMS, and Milton BERLE, to name just a few. Among the many celebrated entertainers who performed on the show over the six years it was aired were Ed Wynn, Frank Sinatra, Judy Garland, the Rolling Stones, and many other top-name acts. When it first went on the air, *The Hollywood Palace* was called *The Saturday Night Hollywood Palace*. In 1973 and 1977, two attempts were made to revive the series, but both attempts ended in cancellation after less than a season. During the show's first few months Raquel Welch, not yet famous, held up cards announcing the various acts. Mitchell Ayres and his orchestra provided music for the show. *The Hollywood Palace's* executive producer was Nick Vanoff. The series was produced by Bill Harbach, and was directed by Grey Lockwood.

HOLLYWOOD SQUARES

Oct. 1966–June 1980	NBC	Mon.–Fri. Various daytime hours
Jan. 1968–Sept. 1968	NBC	Fri. 9:30–10 P.M.
1972–1980	Syndicated show	Various times and stations
1986–1989	Syndicated show	Various times and stations
1998–present	Syndicated show	Various times and stations

This durable game show features nine celebrities who sit in nine squares in large tic-tac-toe boxes. As in tic-tac-toe, one of two players earns either an X or an O by agreeing with, or turning down, an answer given by one of the celebrities in one of the nine boxes. The celebrities either answer the question correctly or bluff their way into making the contestant believe that they know the right answer. Two players, seated on either side of the show's host, compete with each other, and the first contestant to match three squares, up and down, side to side, or diagonally, completing a tic-tac-toe, win the round. At the end of the game, the contestant with the highest number of points wins the match and is given the chance to match one celebrity for a grand prize.

Peter Marshall was the show's original host/moderator from 1966 until 1983. Celebrities who regularly sat in squares on the show during those years were Paul Lynde, who always sat in the center square, George GOBEL, Rose Marie, Cliff Arquette (as Charley Weaver), Wally COX, John Davidson, and many others. In 1986, when a new daytime syndicated version of *Hollywood Squares* surfaced, John Davidson was the program's host. Shadoe Stevens took over the center spot in 1998. In the late 1990s comedienne/actress Whoopi Goldberg acquired the rights to the series and became the regular center square on the show, which was then hosted by Tom Bergeron. Guest celebrities who regularly sit in the squares on this latest syndicated version of the show, which, as of this writing, is still on the air, include the comedians Bruce Vilanche, Caroline Rhea, and Gilbert Gottfried.

In 2001, Henry Winkler (Fonzie of HAPPY DAYS), replaced Whoopi Goldberg on occasion as the center square on the show. Among the many guest stars who currently appear on *Hollywood Squares* regularly are: Jason Alexander, Michael Badalucco, Antonio Banderas, Garth Brooks, Carol Burnett, Dyan Cannon, Carol Channing, Carmen Electra, Kathie Lee Gifford, Danny Glover, Melanie Griffith, Richard Hatch (the first SURVIVOR winner), Star Jones, Little Richard, Camryn Manheim, Rosie O'Donnell, Donny Osmond, Paula Poundstone, Debbie Reynolds, Doris Roberts, Al Roker, Rita Rudner, Martin Short, the Smothers Brothers, Robert Wagner, and Raquel Welch, among others.

HOME IMPROVEMENT

Sept. 1991–Aug. 1992	ABC	Tues. 8:30–9 P.M.
Aug. 1992–Sept. 1994	ABC	Wed. 9–9:30 P.M.
Mar. 1994–May 1994	ABC	Wed. 8–8:30 P.M.
Sept. 1994–July 1996	ABC	Tues. 9–9:30 P.M.
Apr. 1997–May 1997	ABC	Tues. 8–8:30 P.M.
Sept. 1997–Oct. 1997	ABC	Tues. 8–8:30 P.M.
Feb. 1998–May 1998	ABC	Tues. 8–8:30 P.M.
July 1998–May 1999	ABC	Tues. 8–8:30 P.M.
Apr. 1999–May 1999	ABC	Fri. 8–8:30 P.M.

Comedian Tim ALLEN starred on this situation comedy series that was based on material he used in his stand-up comedy act. Allen played Tim Taylor, the host of a handyman TV cable show sponsored by Binford Tools. The show was called *The Tool Man,* and took place in Detroit, Michigan. Tim Taylor offered his viewers advice as to how to fix various things that were broken around the house, and he peppered his advice with a lot of gentle humor. He usually ended up telling his viewers that what they really needed was "more power." At home, Tim Taylor was less than an expert at repairing things, which made him the butt of many

jokes. Tim's wife, Jill Taylor, played by Patricia Richardson, and his two young sons, Brad and Randy, played by Zachery Ty Bryan and Jonathan Taylor Thomas, lovingly and patiently endured Tim's klutzy behavior at home. Tim often confided in his next-door neighbor, Wilson Wilson, played by Earl Hindman, who was never clearly seen and always talked to Tim from behind a fence that divided their backyards. At the TV studio where *The Tool Man* was produced, Tim was assisted by Al Borland, played by Richard Karn, who usually knew much more about how to repair things than Tim did. A buxom blonde named Lisa, who was called "the tool girl," played by Pamela Anderson, offered visual incentive to Tim's mainly male viewers to watch the show. Lisa handed Tim tools when he needed them and generally just looked attractive. When Pamela Anderson left the series in 1993, she was replaced by Debbie Dunning, who played another pretty "tool girl" assistant named Heidi.

HOMETIME

1987–present	PBS	Various times

This half-hour home-building and repair show, which is seen on various Public Broadcasting System stations, has been popular with home improvement and building advocates, as well as with would-be do-it-yourself builders and decorators, for more than 13 years. Dean Johnson has been the chief builder/repairer for all 13 seasons the show has been aired. JoAnne Liebeler was his female counterpart for four years, and was replaced by Susanne Egli in 1991. Egli remained with the show for two seasons and was replaced by Robin Hartl, who is still working with Johnson, as of this writing. *Hometime* is one of PBS's most popular home shows, and only THIS OLD HOUSE attracts more viewers.

HOMICIDE: LIFE ON THE STREET

Jan. 1993	NBC	Sun. 10:25–11:25 P.M.
Feb. 1993–Mar. 1993	NBC	Wed. 9–10 P.M.
Jan. 1994	NBC	Thurs. 10–11 P.M.
Oct. 1994–May 1998	NBC	Fri. 10–11 P.M.
Sept. 1998–Aug. 1999	NBC	Fri. 10–11 P.M.

This police show was noted for its gritty depiction of life in the densely populated, less privileged streets of a large American city, in this case, Baltimore, Maryland. Based on David Simon's book *Homicide: A Year on the Killing Streets,* the television series was produced by Barry Levinson and Tom Fontana. Mostly filmed at actual locations in Baltimore, the show had the look of a documentary that was reporting events as they happened. This was mainly due to the handheld cameras that were used to follow the actors around, as is the case in some TV-news crime coverage. When the show first went on the air, Ned Beatty played Det. Stanley Bolander; Richard Belzer played Det. John Munch; Yaphet Kotto played Lt. Al Giardello; Melissa Lee played

Det. Kay Howard; Daniel Baldwin played Det. Beau Felton; Andre Braugher played Det. Frank Pembleton; Clark Johnson played Det. Meldrick Lewis; and John Polito played Det. Steve Crosetti. Joining the cast for the 1994 season were Kyle Secor as Det. Tim Bayliss and Isabella Hoffman as Lt. Megan Russert. In 1995, Reed Diamond and Harlee McBride joined the cast as Det. Mike Kellerman and Medical Examiner Dr. Alyssa Dyer.

HONEY WEST

Sept. 1965–Sept. 1966 ABC Fri. 9–9:30 P.M.

Although the *Honey West* detective/drama series was on the air for only one year, it is fondly remembered by many TV viewers. *Honey West* was one of very few mystery/crime shows that featured a female in the major role. Honey West, played by veteran film and TV actress Anne Francis, was a private detective who had inherited her P. I. business from her late father. Her father's partner, Sam Bolt, played by John Ericson, reluctantly agreed to continue working with Honey, who to him seemed much too pretty and feminine to be a very effective detective. He soon discovered that Honey, who had a pet ocelot named Bruce that she adored, was an expert at judo and karate, and owned an impressive arsenal of unusual weapons. She often did her private detecting work out of a traveling office/spying van that was disguised as a delivery truck and had the name "H. W. Bolt & Co., TV Service" on its side. The show occasionally featured Irene Hervey as Honey's Aunt Meg. *Honey West* originally appeared as a character on *BURKE'S LAW*. Honey West was produced by Four Star Films.

HONEYMOONERS, THE

Oct. 1955–Feb. 1956 CBS Sat. 8:30–9 P.M.
Feb. 1956–Sept. 1956 CBS Sat. 8–8:30 P.M.
Jan. 1971–May 1971 CBS Sun. 10–11 P.M.

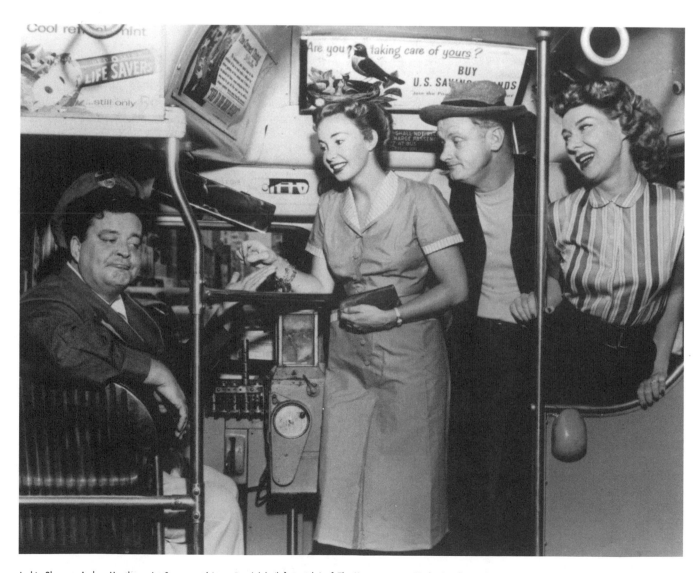

Jackie Gleason, Audrey Meadows, Art Carney, and Joyce Randolph (left to right) of *The Honeymooners* (Author's collection)

Although *The Honeymooners* was seen on television for only less than one and a half years as a regular TV series, Honeymooners sketches were often featured on other shows, such as *Cavalcade of Stars,* from 1951 until the mid-1970s. After the prime-time, weekly *Honeymooners* series was aired, it continued to be seen as occasional sketches on *The JACKIE GLEASON SHOW* in 1961. *The Honeymooners'* major characters were bombastic bus driver Ralph Kramden; his long-suffering, but sharp-tongued wife, Alice; a sewer worker/friend of Ralph's, Ed Norton; and Ed's supportive wife, Trixie. Ralph and Alice, the honeymooners of the show's title, were not newlyweds, but were a couple approaching middle age. The show's title, therefore, was tongue-in-cheek. The Kramdens lived in a cold-water flat in Brooklyn, and most of the Honeymooners' actions took place in the Kramden's sparsely furnished, dreary kitchen. Ralph, played by Jackie GLEASON, was a portly loudmouth who drove a bus for the city. A colorful loser, Ralph was always looking for a quick way to get rich, and was constantly being brought back to reality by his loving, practical wife, Alice, originally played by Pert Kelton on the *Cavalcade of Stars* for many years, by Audrey Meadows, and finally by Shelia MacRae. Ed Norton, played by Art CARNEY, and his wife Trixie, originally played by Joyce Randolph and then by Jane Kean, lived in the same apartment building as the Kramdens. Ed, who was not very bright, was always getting caught up in one of Ralph's get-rich-quick schemes. In 1985, fans of *The Honeymooners* were delighted to learn that kinescopes of several old *Honeymooners* sketches, not seen since they were originally aired between 1952 and 1957, had been uncovered. When they were shown as *The Honeymooners Lost Episodes* on the Showtime network, millions of viewers tuned in to see the long-forgotten episodes, which were offered with other more familiar episodes of the series.

HOOTENANY

Apr. 1963–Sept. 1963	ABC	Sat. 8:30–9 P.M.
Sept. 1963–Sept. 1964	ABC	Sat. 7:30–8:30 P.M.

This folk and country-music jamboree was taped before different live audiences at various college campuses around the country every week for one and a half years. Capitalizing on the popularity of the country and folk-music craze among young people in the United States during the early 1960s, *Hootenanny* featured some of the top folk performers, such as the Smothers Brothers, the Limelighters, and the Chad Mitchell Trio, and popular country music artists such as the Carter Family and Josh White. The show might have been a longer-running hit than it was, had it not refused to book folk acts that had been branded as having left-wing sympathies in those Communist witch-hunting years. Such popular performers as the Weavers and singer Pete Seeger were barred from the show. Big-name folk and country acts such as the Kingston Trio, Joan Baez, and Peter, Paul, and Mary refused to appear because of these unjust actions.

William "Bill" Boyd as Hopalong Cassidy (Author's collection)

HOPALONG CASSIDY

June 1949–Oct. 1949	NBC	Fri. 8–9 P.M.
Apr. 1950–Dec. 1951	NBC	Sun. 6–7 P.M.
1952–1953	Syndicated	Various times and stations
1953–present	Syndicated	Various times and stations

Western star William BOYD first starred as the western hero Hopalong Cassidy in a series of 66 films that were made between 1935 and 1948. Realizing the potential market for the *Hopalong Cassidy* films as television properties series when TV was in its infancy and looking for new shows, Boyd bought the rights to his old films. Editing the films into 30- and 60-minute segments, *Hopalong Cassidy* made its debut on TV in 1949. The series was an immediate success, and Boyd produced 52 new episodes of *Hopalong Cassidy* adventures especially for TV. Hopalong Cassidy was a true "Knight of the Old West," who could always be depended upon to be moral and upstanding and to apprehend the bad guys and bring them to justice. Always dressed conservatively in black, Cassidy rode a white horse named Topper, who became almost as famous as Hopalong himself. His sidekicks in the original films were played by Gabby Hayes and Andy Clyde. For the newly produced TV episodes, Hopalong, or "Hoppy" as he was familiarly called, had actor Edgar Buchanan as his crusty old sidekick. When William Boyd died in 1972, at the age of 74, he was one of the richest men in Hollywood.

HOPE, BOB (LESLIE TOWNES HOPE 1903–   )

Although he never had a regular television series, perennially popular comedian Bob Hope starred on numerous *Bob Hope Show* TV specials from the early 1950s until well into the 1980s, and infrequently after that. Born in London, England, but raised in Cleveland, Ohio, after his parents immigrated to the United States at the turn of the century, Hope began performing when he was four years old. By 1920, Hope was a vaudeville headliner and performed, "songs, patter and eccentric dancing" throughout the United States. In 1933, Hope made his Broadway debut in the musical comedy *Roberta*, and won both critical and public acclaim. Broadway appearances in *The Ziegfeld Follies of 1935* and the musical *Red, Hot and Blue*, which costarred Ethel Merman, led to a weekly NBC radio show, *The Pepsodent Show*, which became very popular and made Bob Hope a household name. In 1938, Hollywood beckoned, and soon Hope was appearing in a string of successful films such as *The Big Broadcast of 1938* (his film debut) and many other box office hits. In 1940, Hope costarred with singer Bing CROSBY in the film *Road to Singapore*, which led to a series of financially successful and popular "Road" pictures with Crosby. Major films such as *The Ghost Breakers* (1940), *My Favorite Brunette* (1947), *The Paleface* (1948), *Sorrowful Jones* (1949), and *The Lemon Drop Kid* (1951) established Hope as one of Hollywood's favorite film comedians. Hope made his first foray into television in 1947, when he appeared on a telecast by KTLA, the West Coast's first television station. In the early 1950s, Hope appeared on such TV shows as *The TONIGHT SHOW* and *I LOVE LUCY*, and telecasts of his annual Christmas show, which was shown internationally to United States troops stationed all around the world, were seen. During World War II, and the Korean War, Hope became famous for his front-line visits to entertain members of military serving abroad, and he continued to perform for the troops even during peacetime. Hope earned the title "U.S.O.'s Ambassador of Good Will" for his efforts on behalf of the U.S. military. From 1963 until 1967, Hope hosted, and sometimes performed on, *Bob Hope Presents the Chrysler Theatre* series. Over the years, Hope also frequently hosted the annual Academy Award ceremonies, beginning in 1939 and continuing until well after the Academy Awards were first seen on television. Among the awards Hope has been given during his long and celebrated career were the Jean Hersholt Humanitarian Award, the People's Choice Award from 1975 to 1979 as "Favorite All-Around Male Entertainer," and, in 1985, the prestigious Kennedy Center Honors for lifetime achievement. Hope, who continued to perform regularly well into the 1990s, was knighted by Queen Elizabeth II in 1998.

HORTON, ROBERT (MEADE HOWARD HORTON 1924–   )

Before he became well known to television viewers as Flint McCullough, and then Shenandoah on *WAGON TRAIN* and *A Man Called Shenandoah* in the late 1950s to early 1960s, Robert Horton, who was born in Los Angeles, in the shadow of the big television and film studios, appeared as a featured player on such TV series as *ALFRED HITCHCOCK PRESENTS*, *The Barbara Stanwyck Show* (1960–61), and *The UNITED STATES STEEL HOUR*, in such feature films as *The Tanks Are Coming* (1951), *Apache War Smoke* (1952), *Bright Road* (1953), *Prisoner of War* (1954), *Men of the Fighting Lady* (1954), and was a regular on the short-lived TV series *King's Row* in 1955. When *A Man Called Shenandoah* was canceled in 1966, Horton continued to appear in featured roles in such TV films as *The Dangerous Days of Kiowa Jones* (1966), *The Spy Killer* (1969), and *Foreign Exchange* (1970), and played Whit McColl on the long-running daytime drama *AS THE WORLD TURNS* in 1983–84.

HOT L BALTIMORE

Jan. 1975–June 1975   ABC   Fri. 9–9:30 P.M.

Even though it was on the air for less than six months, the *Hot L Baltimore* situation comedy series had a large and loyal following that was more than just slightly upset

Bob Hope (Author's collection)

when ABC decided to cancel the program. One of the most controversial series produced in the 1970s, *Hot L Baltimore* was the first show on TV to bring sexual innuendos and racy dialogue into American homes, which were the major reasons ABC decided to drop the series in spite of its considerable audience. Produced by Norman LEAR, who had already broken new ground with his *ALL IN THE FAMILY* series, *Hot L Baltimore* was set in the sleazy and seedy Hotel Baltimore, whose letter "e" was missing from the neon sign in front of the hotel. The odd assortment of characters regularly seen on the show were Bill Lewis, the hotel's clerk, played by James Cromwell; April, Lewis's robust and rotund girlfriend, played by Conchata Ferrell; Clifford, the harried manager, played by Richard Masur; Suzy Marta Rocket, a Colombian prostitute, played by Jeannie Linero; Millie, an unemployed waitress, played by Gloria LeRoy; Jackie, a lesbian, played by Robin Wilson; the ancient Mr. Morse, played by Stan Gottlieb; George and Gordon, a homosexual couple, played by Lee Bergere and Henry Calvert; Charles, the philosopher, played by Al Freeman, Jr.; and the eccentric Mrs. Belloti, played by Charlotte Rae. The series, based on a successful off-Broadway play by Lanford Wilson, had as its executive producer Rod Parker and was produced by Ron Clark and Gene Marcione for the Lear organization.

HOTEL

Sept. 1983–May 1984	ABC	Wed. 10–11 P.M.
June 1984–July 1984	ABC	Tues. 9–10 P.M.
Aug. 1984–Mar. 1987	ABC	Wed. 10–11 P.M.
May 1987–Sept. 1987	ABC	Wed. 10–11 P.M.
Sept. 1987–Jan. 1988	ABC	Sat. 10–11 P.M.
Mar. 1988–May 1988	ABC	Thurs. 9–10 P.M.
June 1988–Aug. 1988	ABC	Sat. 10–11 P.M.

The weekly, hour-long series *Hotel*, which followed the lead of such popular evening serials as *DALLAS* and *FALCON CREST*, was based on Arthur Hailey's steamy, bestselling novel *Hotel*. A large, elegant hotel called St. Gregory's, located in the posh Nob Hill section of San Francisco, was the show's setting. The series was produced by Aaron SPELLING and Douglas S. Cramer, who also produced the popular *The LOVE BOAT* series. *Love Boat* and *Hotel* had a lot of things in common. Both series had a cast of regulars, and both featured weekly guest stars who were the center of different stories that took place on the cruise ship and at the hotel each week. Originally, legendary film actress Bette Davis was signed to play the owner of the hotel, Laura Trent, but illness forced her to leave the series, and she was replaced by Anne Baxter, who played the part of Laura's sister-in-law, Victoria Cabot. James Brolin played Peter McDermott, the manager of the hotel, and Connie Sellecca played Christine Francis, the assistant manager. Other regular characters included Mark Denning, the director of guest relations, played by Shea Farrell; Billy Griffin, the hotel's chief of security, played by Nathan Cook; desk clerk Megan Kendall, played by Heidi Bohay; bellhop Dave Kendall, who was Heidi's husband, played by Michael Spound; and Julie Gillette, the hotel's manager of information, played by Shari Belafonte-Harper. When Anne Baxter died prematurely and unexpectedly in 1985, a power struggle for control of the hotel between Charles Cabot, played by Efrem ZIMBALIST, Jr., and Elizabeth Bradshaw Cabot, the new owner, Jessica Cabot, played by Dina Merrill, and Jake Cabot, played by Ralph Bellamy, ensued. Among the many performers who guest-starred on various episodes of the show were Shirley JONES, Morgan Fairchild, Stewart Granger, Pernell Roberts, Arte Johnson, LIBERACE, Donald O'Connor, Connie STEVENS, McLean Stevenson, Lynn Redgrave, and Peter Marshall. The exteriors for *Hotel* were filmed at the famed Fairmont Hotel in San Francisco.

HOUSE CALLS

Dec. 1979–Mar. 1980	CBS	Mon. 9:30–10 P.M.
May 1980–Sept. 1982	CBS	Mon. 9:30–10 P.M.

House Calls was based upon a motion picture that starred Walter Matthau and Glenda Jackson. The premise of the show was simple. When surgeon Charley Michaels, played by Wayne ROGERS, dates a hospital administrator, Ann Anderson, played by Lynn Redgrave, when both work at Kensington General Hospital in San Francisco, numerous problems ensue. Dr. Michaels is a free spirit who does not particularly care about following rules and regulations, and Ann is a stickler for following correct procedures, leading to much of the series' comedy. In addition to Michaels and Anderson, other amusing characters who worked at the hospital included the somewhat senile chief of surgery, Dr. Amos Wetherby, played by David Wayne; the neurotic Dr. Norman Solomon, played by Ray Buktenica; head nurse Bradley, played by Aneta Corsaut; a peculiar gray lady, Mrs. Phipps, played by Deedy Peters; and the humorless hospital administrator, Conrad Peckler, played by Mark L. Taylor. When Redgrave left the show after a dispute with the producers about breast-feeding her newborn baby on the set, she was replaced by Sharon Gless, who played hospital administrator Jane Jeffreys.

HOWARD, RON (RONALD WILLIAM HOWARD 1954–)

Few performers are lucky or talented enough to have regular roles on two popular television shows and then go on to become one of Hollywood's most successful film directors, but that is exactly what happened to Ron Howard. Born in Duncan, Oklahoma, Ron began acting at the tender age of two. His parents, Rance and Jean Howard, were both actors, and Rance was also a director and a writer, so show business was in Ron Howard's blood. His earliest performances came on such shows as *The KRAFT SUSPENSE THEATRE* and *The RED SKELTON SHOW*, and he

Ron Howard, with Howdy Doody (background) and Buffalo Bob Smith (Photofest)

was seen on DENNIS THE MENACE, *The* FUGITIVE, and *The* BIG VALLEY before he was six years old. When he was five years old, he appeared in the film *The Journey* with Yul Brynner and Deborah Kerr. In 1960, Ron was cast as Opie Taylor, the young son of Sheriff Andy Taylor on *The* ANDY GRIFFITH SHOW, which became one of television's most durable and popular series, running for an impressive eight years. He also appeared in such feature films as *Door-to-Door Maniac* and *The Music Man,* as well as on the TV series *The Land of the Giants* and *Daniel Boone,* TV film *Smoke,* and with his brother Clint, also an actor, *The Wild Country* (1971). In 1973, Howard, who by that time was in his teens, was cast in the George Lucas film *American Graffiti,* playing a small-town teenager of the 1950s. The film was an enormous success and led to Howard's being cast as Richie Cunningham on a new situation comedy series, HAPPY DAYS, in 1973. *Happy Days* became a very successful show, and Howard remained with the show for seven years. In 1977, Howard directed his first feature film, *Grand Theft Auto,* and subsequently directed the extremely popular *Splash,* with Tom Hanks and Daryl Hannah (1984), *Cocoon* (1985), and the less successful *Willow* (1988), *Backdraft* (1991), and *Far and Away* (1992). Howard's next directing efforts included the critically acclaimed *Apollo 13* (1995), *Ransom,* with Mel Gibson (1996) and *EdTV* (1999). In addition to acting and directing, Ron Howard also produced the successful TV series SPORTS NIGHT.

HOWARD STERN SHOW, THE (ALSO *THE HOWARD STERN RADIO SHOW*)

| 1990–1992 | Syndicated show | Various times and stations |
| 1998–2001 | CBS | Sat. 11:30 P.M.–12:30 A.M. |

Howard Stern is a radio talk show "shock jock," the self-proclaimed "King of All Media," whose outrageous, profane, and sexually explicit early morning radio talk/music show made him one of broadcasting's most talked-about hosts. He also became the target of numerous Federal Communications Commission (FCC) investigations and fines. In 1990, Stern became the host of a syndicated TV talk show, which featured guest stars from the world of show business and other lesser known personalities from the more seamy side of life. It also featured Stern's cast of radio show regulars that included Robin Quivers, a newswoman who was coaxed into remaining on mike after she had delivered the morning news early in Stern's radio career and who eventually became Stern's on-the-air voice of reason, giving him a degree of credibility; comedy writer and stand-up comic Jackie "the Jokeman" Martling; Fred "Frightening Fred" Norris, who provided sound effects for the show and acted in skits with other cast regulars and guests; Gary "Babbabooey" Dell'Abate, the much maligned Adelphi University graduate who was Stern's producer; and "Stuttering John" Melendez, who asked rude questions of celebrities at various premieres, award-show ceremonies, and other "on the scene" events.

In the mid-1990s, the Entertainment Cable Network (E!), began to videotape Stern's early morning radio show, which originated from the radio studios of WXRK in New York City, and show the programs on its network. The show was a success and was watched by millions of Stern's loyal fans six nights a week from 11 to 12 P.M. In 1998, CBS began to produce carefully edited excerpts from Stern's E! shows, and telecast these shows once a week on the 11:30 P.M. Saturday spot opposite NBC's popular SATURDAY NIGHT LIVE. Stern's show, which featured famous celebrity guests, as well as a menagerie of Stern's "Wack Pack" favorites such as K. C. Armstrong, a muscular, good-looking assistant producer on the show; Ralph Cirella, Stern's judgmental hair stylist, who feels that he is an expert evaluator of feminine perfection; Scott the engineer, who worked on Stern's radio show and was always being accused of messing things up; Benjy Bronk, an overweight intern-turned-segment producer, who will do anything, including making an ass of himself, to get air time; Ronnie, Howard's highly critical limousine driver, Beetlejuice, an undersized black man with a tiny head and a large sexual appetite; Hank, the Angry Dwarf; Nichole Bass, a female bodybuilder whom Howard insisted was really a man (a test proved him wrong); Croix, a spacey, elderly exotic dancer who insisted she is an "architect," and Crackhead Bob, Elephant Boy, Big Foot (a giant of a man), the King of All Backs; Shelly, the Angry Black; OJ Mask, High Pitched Eric; Vin the Retard; Wood Yi (a "dirty old man" who reads one-line comments); Joe Can-

acters Smith introduced on that show was a marionette named Elmer, who always greeted his audience by saying "Howdy doody." The character became very popular with Smith's young viewers, and when NBC asked Smith to star on an early morning children's show in 1947, Smith decided to center the show on the Elmer character, whom he named Howdy Doody. First called *Puppet Playhouse,* the new NBC show, after one year on the air, changed its name to *The Howdy Doody Show.* The show was set in Doodyville, a circus town populated by puppets and people. An audience of children attended the telecasts each morning, and they were eventually dubbed "The Peanut Gallery." In addition to live sketches, child chat, and songs, the program featured short films and a running story involving the citizens of Doodyville. Smith's assistant on the show was Clarabell, a clown originally played by Bob KEESHAN, who later became known as Captain Kangaroo, and then played by Bobby Nicholson. Nicholson later played Doodyville storekeeper Cornelius Cobb, and Lew Anderson took over the Clarabell role. Other popular regular characters included Chief Thundercloud, played by Bill LeCornec, Princess Summerfall Winterspring, played by Judy Tyler (who was killed in an automobile accident in 1957) and then by Linda Marsh, who took over the role before becoming a puppet character on the show; Bison Bill, played by Ted Brown, who took over for Smith when he was on vacation; and Ugly Sam the wrestler, played by Dayton Allen. Popular puppet characters included Phineas T. Bluster, Dilly Dally, Flub-a-dub (a pet with body parts from eight different animals), Captain Scuttlebutt, private eye John J. Fadoozle, Don Jose Bluster, Hector Hambock, and Howdy's sister, Heide Doody. Most of the puppet's voices were provided by Smith. Ruyfus Rose was the show's chief puppeteer, and he was assisted by Rhoda Mann and Dayton Allen. The show's popular theme song was "It's Howdy Doody Time," sung to the tune of "Ta-Ra-Ra Boom-de-ay." On the show's last telecast, after 2,343 performances, Clarabell the Clown, who only honked a horn and never spoke, sadly said, "Goodbye, kids," as the last show ended.

Howard Stern (Author's collection)

cer; Captain Janks; Slow Adam; Daniel Carver, the Ku Klux Klan advocate; Gary the Retard; Crazy Alice; and porn stars Kendra Jade, Amy Lynn, Brandy Rodrick, Houston, Janine Lindenmueller, and Janet Jameson, among many others, who only too willingly removed their tops to reveal their breasts, as well as any other part of their anatomy Howard wished to see.

Some of the Stern show's most popular sketches are "Homeless Jeopardy," "Who Wants to be a Turkish Millionaire," and "Wack Pack Squares." Stern's Saturday night show on CBS steadily outrated NBC's popular *Saturday Night Live,* and is especially popular with males between the ages of 18 and 49.

HOWDY DOODY SHOW, THE

Dec. 1947–Aug. 1948	NBC	Fri. 5:30–6:30 P.M.
Aug. 1948–June 1956	NBC	Mon.–Fri. 5:30–6:30 P.M.
June 1956–Sept. 1960	NBC	Sat. 10–10:30 A.M.
1976	Syndicated	Mornings, Mon.–Fri.

One of television's most beloved and well-remembered early morning children's shows, the *Howdy Doody Show,* which was on the air continuously for over 18 years, starred Bob "Buffalo Bob" SMITH, a former singer who had previously hosted the *Triple B Ranch* show on radio. One of the char-

H.R. PUFNSTUF

Sept. 1969–Sept. 1971	NBC	Sat. 10–10:30 A.M.
Sept. 1972–Sept. 1973	ABC	Sat. 11:30 A.M–12 P.M.

Produced by Sid and Marty Krofft, the *H. R. Pufnstuf* puppet show was the first of many Saturday morning programs produced by the Krofft brothers. The half-hour show centered on the adventures of Jimmy, a boy who had a magic flute he named Freddie, and who was stranded on an enchanted island. The mayor of the island was a gentle dragon named H. R. Pufnstuf, a strange-looking beast who presided over an equally strange-looking bunch of island inhabitants. An evil witch named Miss Witchiepoo menaced Jimmy and tried to steal his magic flute. Jimmy was played by Jack Wild, and Billie Hayes played the wicked Miss Witchiepoo, who were the only nonpuppet characters on the show.

HUCKLEBERRY HOUND (AKA THE HUCKLEBERRY HOUND SHOW)

1958–1962	Syndicated	Various times and stations

The first of several successful animated cartoon series produced expressly for television by William Hanna and Joseph Barbera for their Hanna-Barbera Productions, *Huckleberry Hound* was an Emmy Award–winning series that featured a lovable dog who would try anything once. Huckleberry Hound had many occupations over the years, but he began his career as a police officer who sniffed out a gorilla that was missing from a zoo. He was also a mail carrier, a truant officer, an explorer, a mounted police officer, a firefighter, and even a dogcatcher at different times. The series also introduced characters named Yogi Bear, the intelligent Ursine–American who lived in Jellystone Park; Park and Pixie Dixie, a pair of mice who were always being chased by a cat named Mr. Jinx; and Hokey Wolf, a scheming wolf who was always being duped. The series was immensely popular with young viewers and spurred several successful animated cartoon spin-off series including *Yogi Bear, Quick Draw McGraw,* and *The FLINTSTONES.* Huckleberry Hound's southern voice was provided by Daws Butler. Each episode of the show cost a meager $2,800, which was extremely reasonable for the time. Hanna and Barbera called the technique they used to film their series "limited animation," since it greatly reduced the number of drawings needed to complete a full cartoon.

HUDSON, ROCK (ROY HAROLD SCHERER, JR. 1925–1985)

One of Hollywood's most successful leading men, Rock Hudson became the star of a popular TV series, MCMIL-LAN AND WIFE, in 1971, after a long and distinguished career as a film star. Hudson, who was born in Winnetka, Illinois, was the son of an auto mechanic and a telephone operator, who were divorced when Hudson was eight years old. Although he was always interested in acting, Hudson was never given a part in a school play because he had trouble remembering lines. When he graduated from high school, Hudson went to work for the postal department, and during World War II served as a Navy airplane mechanic. When the war ended, Hudson went to work as a truck driver in Los Angeles, where he hoped to break into films. Eventually, his handsome looks and muscular body did get him a screen test when he was discovered by a talent scout. Hudson's first film role was in *Fighter Squadron* in 1948, in which he had one line. His good looks attracted filmgoers' attention, and he began getting increasingly larger roles in such films as *Undertow* (1949), *Winchester '73* (1950), *Tomahawk* (1951), *Iron Man* (1951), *Has Anybody Seen My Gal?* (1952), *The Lawless Breed* (1952), *Bengal Brigade* (1954), *Magnificent Obsession* (1954), and *Never Say Goodbye* (1956), among others. In 1956, Hudson was cast in a leading role in his first really important motion picture, *Giant,* and won an Academy Award nomination as Best Actor. This led to a starring role *A Farewell to Arms* (1957). Hudson then costarred in a series of extremely popular romantic comedies with Doris DAY, which began with *Pillow Talk* in 1959, that established him as Hollywood's most popular leading man. Roles in numerous films followed. In 1971, Hudson starred on the *McMillan and Wife* TV series, playing Police Commissioner Stewart "Mac" McMillan. Hudson also had roles in the miniseries *Wheels* in 1978, *The Martian Chronicles* in 1980, and on the unsuccessful TV series *The Devlin Connection* in 1982, and in a more successful appearance on *DYNASTY,* playing Daniel Reece from 1984 to 1985. Hudson's last major appearance was in the film *The Ambassador* in 1984. He died from complications due to AIDS in 1985.

HULLABALOO

Jan. 1965–May 1965	NBC	Tues. 8:30–9:30 P.M.
June 1965–Aug. 1965	NBC	Tues. 10–11 P.M.
Sept. 1965–Aug. 1966	NBC	Mon. 7:30–8 P.M.

One of television's attempts to capitalize on the popularity of the rock and roll music craze of the 1960s was NBC's *Hullabaloo,* a big budget variety show that featured top rock and roll recording artists. The show, produced by Gary Smith for NBC, featured 10 good-looking R&R dancer regulars, six girls and four boys, who, as the Hullabaloo Dancers, became very popular, dancing to music provided by Peter Matz. Different hosts, including Paul Anka, Jack Jones, Frankie Avalon, Annette FUNICELLO, Jerry LEWIS (who hosted when his rock-star son, Gary Lewis, performed on the show), and others, presided over the weekly proceedings. Among the name performers who guest-starred on the program were the Supremes, the Ronettes, Sonny and CHER, and, in a weekly segment hosted by rock impresario Brian Epstein that originated from London during the first three months the show was aired, Gerry and the Pacemakers, Marianne Faithful, Herman's Hermits, and the Moody Blues. After Brian Epstein left the show, his most celebrated clients, the Beatles, made an appearance on *Hullabaloo* in January 1966.

HUNT, HELEN (HELEN ELIZABETH HUNT 1963–   )

Academy Award–winning actress Helen Hunt, who is perhaps best known on television for playing Jamie Buchman on MAD ABOUT YOU, is the daughter of TV director Gordon Hunt, who directed episodes of COACH, FRASIER, CAROLINE IN THE CITY, and MAD ABOUT YOU, to name just a few. Helen, who was born in Los Angeles, began acting when she was a child and was seen in many TV commercials before she was 10 years old. She then appeared on the *Amy Prentiss* TV series in 1974. Regular roles on such series as *Swiss Family Robinson* (1975–76), *The Fitzpatricks* (1977–78), ST. ELSEWHERE, *It Takes Two* (1982–83), *My Life and Times* (1991), and appearances in numerous TV films, as well as guest appearances on such shows as *The MARY TYLER MOORE SHOW, KNOTS LAND-*

ING, FAMILY, *The* FACTS OF LIFE, GIMME A BREAK!, *Highway to Heaven*, and CHINA BEACH, followed. Hunt was also seen in such films as *Waiting to Act* (1985), *Trancers* (1985), *Peggy Sue Got Married* (1986), *The Frog Prince* (1988), *Into the Badlands* (1991), and *Mr. Saturday Night* (1992), before being cast as Paul Reiser's wife, Jamie, on *Mad About You*. In spite of her busy work schedule as a young actress, Helen managed to attend Providence High School in Burbank, California, and even went to U.C.L.A. for one month, before acting assignments forced her to leave college. In 1997, Hunt received an Academy Award for her performance as Carol Connelly in the film *As Good as It Gets,* which costarred Jack Nicholson, and subsequently appeared in the film *Twister* (1996), the Lincoln Center production of Shakespeare's *Twelfth Night* (aired on TV, 1998), and the films *From Alice to Ocean* (2000), *Pay It Forward* (2000), and *Cast Away* (2000), among others. In 1998, Hunt was named one of *People* magazine's "50 Most Beautiful People." For the final season of *Mad About You*, Helen Hunt and her costar, Paul Reiser, each received $1 million per episode for their work on the series, which made her one of television's highest-paid stars.

HUNTER

Sept. 1984	NBC	Tues. 9–10 P.M.
Sept. 1984–Jan. 1985	NBC	Fri. 9–10 P.M.
Mar. 1985–Feb. 1986	NBC	Sat. 10–11 P.M.
Mar. 1986–Aug. 1986	NBC	Tues. 9–10 P.M.
Aug. 1986–Dec. 1987	NBC	Sat. 10–11 P.M.
Dec. 1987–Mar. 1988	NBC	Tues. 9–10 P.M.
Mar. 1988–Apr. 1990	NBC	Sat. 10–11 P.M.
Apr. 1990–May. 1990	NBC	Mon. 9–10 P.M.
June 1990–Aug. 1990	NBC	Sat. 10–11 P.M.
Aug. 1990–Feb. 1991	NBC	Wed. 10–11 P.M.
Mar. 1991–Apr. 1991	NBC	Fri. 9–10 P.M.
May 1991–June 1991	NBC	Fri. 8–9 P.M.
Aug. 1991	NBC	Fri. 10–11 P.M.

During the seven years the *Hunter* police drama was aired, NBC changed the day and time the series was aired so many times, viewers found it difficult to remember when to watch the show. The main character was Det. Sgt. Rick Hunter of the Los Angeles Police Department, who was played by Fred Dryer, a former professional football player turned actor. Hunter's successive police department partners were all attractive young women: Det. Sgt. Dee Dee McCall, played by Stepfanie Kramer for six years, then Det. Sgt. Joanne Malenski, played by Darlanne Fluegel for one year, and finally Sgt. Chris Novak, played by Lauren Lane. Also appearing regularly on the series were James Whitmore, Jr., as Sgt. Bernie Terwilliger;

Arthur Rosenberg as Capt. Lester Cain; John Amos as Capt. Dolan; Bruce Davison as Capt. Wyler; Charles Hallahan as Capt. Charlie Devane; John Shearin as Lt. Ambrose Finn; Richard Beauchamp as Carlos; Garrett Morris as Arnold "Sporty" James; Perry Cook as Barney; and Rudy Ramos as Reuben Garcia. After six years in the homicide division of the L.A.P.D., Hunter was transferred to the city's elite Metro Division, where he took on a wider variety of high-profile cases. *Hunter* was produced by Stephen J. Cannell Productions.

HUNTLEY, CHET (CHESTER ROBERT HUNTLEY 1911–1974)

Television news anchorman Chet Huntley, who became well known on the *Huntley-Brinkley Report* news program on NBC, was born in Cardwell, Montana. Huntley began his broadcasting career as a radio announcer, and was heard on such radio programs as *The Big Street* and *The Next Voice You Hear* early in his career. He also narrated the films *Gung Ho!, I Cheated the Law, Arctic Manhunt,* and *Mau-Mau* in the 1940s and early 1950s. In 1957, Huntley became a familiar face and voice to millions of TV viewers when he coanchored the *Huntley-Brinkley Report* news program with David BRINKLEY on NBC. He also hosted the *Chet Huntley Reporting* news program. Huntley's cool, deliberate style, coupled with Brinkley's urbane wit, made *The Huntley-Brinkley Report* America's favorite evening news program. The team especially excelled at covering the national political conventions. Both The *Huntley-Brinkley Report* and Chet Huntley won many Emmy and Peabody Awards for excellence in TV journalism, before Huntley retired due to illness.

HUTCHINS, WILL (MARSHALL LOWELL HUTCHASON 1932–)

Even though many people believed the slow-talking, easygoing Will Hutchins, who made his TV debut as Tom "Sugarfoot" Brewster on the TV western series SUGARFOOT, was a real cowboy, he was actually born in Los Angeles. In addition to his starring role on *Sugarfoot*, Hutchins also made guest appearances on such popular western series as MAVERICK, CHEYENNE, Bronco (1961), and GUNSMOKE in the late 1950s and early 1960s, and also appeared on the PERRY MASON and EMERGENCY! programs. Hutchins also starred on the TV series *Hey, Landlord* in 1966 and BLONDIE (as Dagwood Bumstead) in 1968. He played featured roles in several films, including *Lafayette Escadrille* (1958), *No Time for Sergeants* (1958), *Claudelle Inglish* (1961), *Merrill's Marauders* (1962), *Spinout* (1966), *The Shooting* (1967), *Clambake* (1967), *Slumber Party '57* (1977), and after a brief period in retirement, *Maverick* (1994), and *Gunfighter* (1998).

I

I DREAM OF JEANNIE

Sept. 1965–Sept. 1966	NBC	Sat. 8–8:30 P.M.
Sept. 1966–Aug. 1967	NBC	Mon. 8–8:30 P.M.
Sept. 1967–Aug. 1968	NBC	Tues. 7:30–8 P.M.
Sept. 1968–Aug. 1969	NBC	Mon. 7:30–8 P.M.
Sept. 1969–Sept. 1970	NBC	Tues. 7:30–8 P.M.

Barbara EDEN starred as Jeannie, a skimpily clad, 2,000-year-old, beautiful, and still youthful genie, who was trapped in a lamp for centuries, waiting to be summoned by a mortal being who would free her and allow her to do her new owner's bidding. The lamp was found by astronaut Capt. Tony Nelson, played by Larry Hagman, when his spaceship landed somewhere in the desert, and he released Jeannie and her magical powers. Nelson took the lamp back to Corona Beach, Florida, where his base was located. The base psychiatrist, Dr. Alfred Bellows, played by Hayden Rorke, became convinced that Nelson was suffering from delusions caused by exposure to the sun while he was in the desert, when Jeannie the genie refused to perform any of her magic for anyone but Nelson. Jeannie's unfamiliarity with life in the 20th century, and the fact that she had fallen in love with Nelson, confused Jeannie and led to much of the show's comedy. She became especially agitated when Nelson's former girlfriend, Melissa, the general's daughter, played by Karen Sharpe, appeared on the scene. Melissa's father, Gen. Martin Peterson, was played by veteran character actor Barton MacLane. Capt. Roger Henley, Nelson's fellow astronaut and buddy, was the only other person besides Nelson who knew about Jeannie's magical powers. Also appearing on the series during the show's last season on the air was Roger's old girlfriend, Lisa, played by Farrah FAWCETT. Eventually, Jeannie and Tony Nelson found love, and on the last six months the series was on the air, they were a somewhat unconven-

tional married couple. *I Dream of Jeannie* was created by Sidney Sheldon, who was also the executive producer of the series for Screen Gems. In 1987, a TV film *I Dream of Jeannie: Fifteen Years Later,* resurfaced, with Barbara Eden looking remarkably well-preserved, re-creating her role of Jeannie. Wayne Rogers played Nelson in the TV film. Since censors were extremely prudish when the original *I Dream of Jeannie* was filmed, the 1987 TV film was the first time viewers glimpsed Barbara Eden's navel.

I'LL FLY AWAY

Oct. 1991	NBC	Mon. 8–10 P.M.
Oct. 1991–Jan. 1992	NBC	Tues. 8–9 P.M.
Feb. 1992–May 1992	NBC	Fri. 9–10 P.M.
Aug. 1992–Feb. 1993	NBC	Fri. 10–11 P.M.

In spite of television critics' and loyal fans' attempts to keep this award-winning TV series on the air, *I'll Fly Away* never attracted a sizable enough audience to warrant its continuance for longer than two years. The series, created by Joshua Brand and John Falsey, was concerned with race relations in the South during the late 1950s. It starred Sam Waterston as Forrest Bedford, an idealistic, liberal-minded prosecutor in Bryland County, who later became a United States attorney. Other characters regularly seen in major story lines on the series were Bedford's black housekeeper, Lily Harper, played by Regina Taylor; Bedford's older son, Nathan, played by Jeremy London; his daughter, Francie, played by Ashlee Levitch; his younger son, John Morgan, played by John Aaron Bennett; Bedford's love interest, lawyer Christina Le Katzis, played by Kathryn Harrold (Bedford's wife had been institutionalized after suffering a nervous breakdown); Lily's father, Lewis, played by Bill Cobbs; Lily's daughter, Adelaide, played by Zelda Harris; and wrestling coach Zolli-cofer Weed, played by Brad Sullivan. Following its cancel-lation by NBC in 1993, the 38 episodes of the series, which had been filmed for the program's original run, were purchased by the Public Broadcasting System and were shown as reruns during their 1993–94 season.

I LOVE LUCY

Oct. 1951–June 1957	CBS	Mon. 9–9:30 P.M.
Apr. 1955–Oct. 1955	CBS	Sun. 6–6:30 P.M.
Oct. 1955–Apr. 1956	CBS	Sat. 6:30–7 P.M.
Sept. 1957–May 1958	CBS	Wed. 7:30–8 P.M.
July 1958–Sept. 1958	CBS	Mon. 9–9:30 P.M.
Oct. 1958–May 1959	CBS	Thurs. 7:30–8 P.M.
July 1959–Sept. 1959	CBS	Fri. 8:30–9 P.M.
Sept. 1961	CBS	Sun. 6:30–7 P.M.

Most TV fans—if not all—have heard of *I Love Lucy*. Even though the series ended its original run in the late 1950s, there has never been a time when *I Love Lucy* has not been on TV, because it has been in constant reruns ever since ending production in 1957. When CBS originally asked Lucille BALL to star on a television version of her hit radio program, *My Favorite Husband,* which had been on the air for three years, Ball decided that she would agree to appear on a TV series only if her husband, Cuban-born singer and bandleader Desi ARNAZ could be her costar. CBS agreed, and Ball and her *My Favorite Husband*'s head writer and producer, Jess Openheimer, and writers Bob Carroll, Jr., and Madelyn Pugh, with Arnaz, developed *I Love Lucy* for television. The show featured Arnaz and Ball as Ricky a heavily accented Cuban bandleader, and Lucy Ricardo, his zany, scatterbrained wife who was always getting into trouble. Also featured were William FRAWLEY and Vivian VANCE, as Ricky and Lucy's neighbors and good friends, Fred and Ethel Mertz. Ethel was always involved in Lucy's scatterbrained schemes, which usually exasperated Desi and left Fred either bemused or confused. Lucy Ricardo, whose maiden name was MacGillicuddy, was a frustrated performer who wanted more than any-thing to be successful at something. Desi performed in, and later owned, the Tropicana Club in Manhattan, where the Ricardos and the Mertzes lived. The show, soon after it made its debut in 1951, became the most popular show on television. One of the most anticipated TV events of the 1950s was the birth of Lucy and Ricky's son, Little Ricky, played by Richard Keith. Since Lucille Ball was actually pregnant when episodes dealing with her character's preg-nancy were shown, viewers were delighted when the birth of a son, Desiderio Alberto Arnaz IV, took place on the same night the Ricardos' son, Ricky, Jr., was introduced to TV viewers. Also appearing on occasion were Jerry Haus-ner as Jerry the agent, Elizabeth Patterson as Mathilda Trumbull, Doris Singleton as Caroline Appleby, Kathryn Card as Mrs. MacGillicuddy, and Mary Jane Croft and Frank Nelson as Betty and Ralph Ramsey. Among viewers' favorite *I Love Lucy* shows, which they watched over and

The cast of *I Love Lucy:* (left to right) Desi Arnaz, Lucille Ball, Richard Keith, Vivian Vance, and William Frawley (Author's collection)

over again, were when Lucy tried to get a job on Ricky's new TV variety show doing a health tonic commercial; when Lucy and Ethel get a job in a chocolate factory and are overwhelmed as chocolates keep coming at them on a conveyor belt; the time Lucy presses grapes with her feet in a barrel with an Italian peasant woman during a visit to Italy; and when Lucy gets pinned to the wall of her apart-ment when she puts too much yeast in the homemade bread she is trying to bake.

One of the wisest things Lucy and Desi decided to do was to film, rather than kinescope, their show. This meant that their shows could be seen with the same clarity as the original telecasts, which made them more marketable as reruns. Because of the unprecedented success of *I Love Lucy* Lucille and Desi were eventually able to form their own production company, Desilu, which produced many hit TV shows. When they sold the rights to their proper-ties several years later, they became among the richest people in Hollywood.

I MARRIED JOAN

Oct. 1952–Apr. 1955	NBC	Wed. 8–8:30 P.M.

Popular Hollywood screen and radio comedienne Joan DAVIS was one of the earliest major stars to commit to a regular situation comedy series on television. Davis's origi-nal show, *Leave It to Joan,* which had been one of radio's most popular comedy programs from 1943 until 1950, was given a new title, *I Married Joan,* when it moved to

TV in 1952. The series costarred Joan's radio husband, Jim BACKUS. Joan played Joan Stevens, the trouble-prone wife of a domestic court judge, Bradley Stevens, played by Backus. Each week, Judge Stevens told the couple before him in court that he had had similar domestic problems to theirs, at home. The scene then shifted to the Stevens's home as the judge and his zany wife, Joan, worked through their domestic problems. During the series' first season the Stevens's next-door neighbor and Joan's frequent cohort was a large woman named Minerva Parker, played by Hope Emerson. The following two seasons, Davis's real-life daughter, Beverly Wills, appeared as Joan's college-age sister, Beverly. Also appearing regularly were Dan Tobin as the Stevens's prissy friend, Kerwin, Geraldine Carr and Shelia Bromley as Mabel and Janet, Sandra Gould as Mildred Webster, and Hal Smith as Charlie. The series was produced by Dick Mack. In all, 98 episodes of *I Married Joan* were completed.

I SPY

Sept. 1965–Sept. 1967	NBC	Wed. 10–11 P.M.
Sept. 1967–Sept. 1968	NBC	Mon. 10–11 P.M.

The *I Spy* adventure series was different from most espionage series in that the two leading characters on the show, Kelly Robinson and Alexander Scott, approached their missions with considerable good humor in addition to action-packed cloak-and-dagger activities. Robinson and Scott, played by Robert CULP and Bill COSBY, were two American undercover agents who, while pretending to be a top-seeded tennis player and his trainer, were in reality dedicated to serving their government as international spies. Both men were well educated and sophisticated. Kelly had indeed played on two Davis Cup tennis teams before becoming a government agent, and he was a former law student at Princeton University. Scott was a multilingual graduate of Temple University and a former Rhodes scholar. Cosby, who was a stand-up comedian before starring on *I Spy,* had the distinction of being the first African-American performer to play a major role on a dramatic series on American television.

    I Spy was produced by Sheldon Leonard, Mort Fine, and David Friedkin. Robert Culp and Bill Cosby were reunited as Robinson and Scott in a TV film *I Spy Returns* in 1994. A series with the same title, an anthology of spy stories of the present and past and hosted by film actor Raymond Massey playing Anton the spy master, had originally been aired in 1956. The series was not successful and was canceled after only a few episodes.

I'M DICKENS—HE'S FENSTER

Sept. 1962–Sept. 1963	ABC	Fri. 9–9:30 P.M.

This slapstick comedy about two construction workers named Harry Dickens and Arch Fenster starred John Astin and Marty Ingels in the title roles. The two men were always getting themselves into hazardous situations, both at work and at home. Arch Fenster was a single man who was very irresponsible, and Harry Dickens, who was married and definitely more sober than Fenster, was always having to get the two of them out of trouble. Dave Ketchum and Henry Beckman played Mel Warshaw and Mulligan, two friends and fellow workers of Dickens and Fenster. Emmaline Henry played Arch's wife, Katie, and former bandleader Frank DeVol played Myron Bannister, the boys' balding boss. The series was produced by Leonard Stern.

IN LIVING COLOR

Apr. 1990	FOX	Sun. 9:30–10 P.M.
Apr. 1990–May 1990	FOX	Sat. 9–9:30 P.M.
May 1990–Aug. 1990	FOX	Sun. 9:30–10 P.M.
Sept. 1990–Mar. 1992	FOX	Sun. 8–8:30 P.M.
Mar. 1992–Apr. 1992	FOX	Sun. 8:30–9 P.M.
Apr. 1992–Aug. 1993	FOX	Sun. 8–8:30 P.M.
Dec. 1992–Aug. 1994	FOX	Thurs. 9–9:30 P.M.
Oct. 1993	FOX	Fri. 11 P.M.–12 A.M.
Nov. 1993–Jan. 1994	FOX	Fri. 11:30 P.M.–12 A.M.

One of the Fox network's longest-running and most popular shows, *In Living Color,* was created by, written and produced by, and starred the talented black comedian/actor Keenen Ivory Wayans. A variety/comedy show similar to NBC's popular SATURDAY NIGHT LIVE, *In Living Color* featured mainly African-American performers. The show spoofed films, TV series, celebrities, commercials, political figures, and black stereotypes in hilarious satirical sketches enacted by a talented group of performers. Among some of the more memorable recurring skits were "Men in Films," which featured two gay critics, Blaine Edwards and Antoine Mayweather, who commented on current movies; "Hey, Mom," which centered on the everyday problems of the Hedley family, who were hardworking blacks from the West Indies; "The Buttmans," a family who had buttocks where their foreheads should be; and "The Home Boys," Wiz and Ice, two young black con artists. Appearing on the show as regulars were James (Jim) Carrey (one of the few white performers on the show), Kelly Coffield, Kim Coles, Tommy Davidson, David Alan Grier, T'Keyah "Crystal" Keymah, Damon Wayans, Kim Wayans, Shawn Wayans, Steve Park, Jamie Foxx, Marlon Wayans, Alexandra Wentworth, Twist (Leroy Casey), Anne-Marie Johnson, Jay Leggett, Chris Rock, Carol Rosenthal, Marc Wilmore, Reggie McFadden, and the very popular Fly Girls, an energetic group of dancers who at one time included Jennifer Lopez.

IN THE HEAT OF THE NIGHT

Mar. 1988	NBC	Sun. 9–11 P.M.
Mar. 1988–May 1988	NBC	Tues. 9–10 P.M.
July 1988–Sept. 1988	NBC	Tues. 9–10 P.M.
Dec. 1988–Jan. 1992	NBC	Tues. 9–10 P.M.
Jan. 1992–June 1992	NBC	Tues. 8–9 P.M.
June 1992–July 1992	NBC	Sun. 8–9 P.M.

Oct. 1992–Aug. 1993	CBS	Wed. 9–10 P.M.
Jan. 1994–May 1994	CBS	Wed. 9–10 P.M.
July 1994	CBS	Thurs. 8–9 P.M.

Dubbed "the show with nine lives" by people in the television industry, *In the Heat of the Night* was a series that came and went from home screens for six years. When it made its debut in 1988, the police/drama series starred Carroll O'CONNOR as Chief Sheriff Bill Gillespie of Sparta, Mississippi. The series also starred Howard Rollins as Chief of Detectives Virgil Tibbs, a black man, who was forced on Chief Gillespie by the mayor of his town, who was hoping to attract more black voters in a coming election. Anne-Marie Johnson played Tibbs's wife, Althea, who was less than pleased with her husband's relocation to a white-dominated southern town. Tibbs eventually earns the respect and friendship of Gillespie, because of his upright, fair-minded, and competent police work. Also appearing on the series regularly were Alan Autry as Sgt./Capt. Bubba Skinner; David Hart as Det./Sgt. Parker Williams; Christian LeBlanc as Dep. Junior Abernathy; Peter Gabb as Dep. Horace Goode; Hugh O'Connor (Carroll O'Connor's son) as Dep./Lt. Lonnie Jamison; Dennis Lipscomb as Mayor Findley; and, as the years went on, Randall Franks, Geoffrey Thorne, Lois Nettleton, Crystal Fox, Denise Nicholas (as Gillespie's black girlfriend, a city counselor), Dan Biggers, Wilbur Fitzgerald, Dee Shaw, Tonea Stewart, Harvey E. Lee, Jr., Mark Johnson, C. C. Taylor, Thom Gossom, Jr., Jen Harper, Carl Weathers, and Barbara Lee-Belmonte. When Carroll O'Connor was forced to leave the series temporarily during the 1988–89 season to undergo heart surgery, Joe Don Baker filled in for him as Chief of Police Tom Dugan. The TV series was based on the 1967 Academy Award–winning film *In the Heat of the Night,* which starred Rod Steiger and Sidney Poitier.

INCREDIBLE HULK, THE

May 1978–Jan. 1979	CBS	Fri. 9–10 P.M.
Jan. 1979	CBS	Wed. 8–9 P.M.
Feb. 1979–Nov. 1981	CBS	Fri. 8–9 P.M.
May 1982–June 1982	CBS	Wed. 8–9 P.M.

This action/adventure series, which was directed toward younger viewers, was about a research scientist named David Banner, played by Bill BIXBY, who, while experimenting with various ways of determining the effect of stress on physical strength, is accidentally exposed to a massive dose of radiation that gives him supernatural strength whenever he becomes emotionally upset. David, who was normally a quiet, reserved man, became a huge, green, brutish hulk when he was upset. When Banner's change took place, strongman Lou Ferrigno took over the role. Also appearing on the series, which was based on a Marvel Comics character, was Jack Colvin as Jack McGee, a reporter for the *National Register,* who was constantly trying to expose the truth about the Hulk's identity. Kenneth Johnson was *The Incredible Hulk*'s executive pro-

ducer, and James D. Parriott and Chuck Bowman produced the series for Universal Television. Several *Incredible Hulk* TV films surfaced after the series left the air, with Bixby and Ferrigno re-creating their original roles.

INSPECTOR GADGET

1983–1985   Syndicated   Various times and stations

The half-hour *Inspector Gadget* cartoon series, a Japanese-made production, featured "the world's most clever detective." The inspector was a master of gadgets and carried such objects as a jet-propelled copter hat that flew him from place to place, mechanical arms that could be expanded to unlimited lengths by pushing a button, and instant radar. Inspector Gadget used these devices to fight the evil MAD organization, which was headed by the villainous Dr. Claw. Assisting the inspector were his niece, Penny, and her dog, Brain, who certainly had the better brain of the two. Inspector Gadget's voice was provided by Don ADAMS, who had played Maxwell Smart on GET SMART.

IRONSIDE

Sept. 1967–Sept. 1971	NBC	Thurs. 8:30–9:30 P.M.
Sept. 1971–Nov. 1971	NBC	Tues. 7:30–8:30 P.M.
Nov. 1971–Jan. 1975	NBC	Thurs. 9–10 P.M.

After his long-running series PERRY MASON left the air, Raymond BURR made a triumphant return to television in a new series, *Ironside,* which enjoyed a healthy eight-year run. On this series, Burr played Robert Ironside, who had been chief of detectives for the San Francisco Police Department for many years, before he was shot by an assassin and left crippled from the waist down. Confined to a wheelchair and retired from the police force, Ironside eventually convinced his old friend Police Commissioner Randall, played by Gene Lyons, to allow him to remain on the force as a special consultant. Assisting Ironside were two former cops, Det. Sgt. Ed Brown, played by Don Galloway, and Policewoman Eve Whitefield, played by Barbara Anderson. An ex-juvenile delinquent, Mark Sanger, played by Don Mitchell, became Ironside's bodyguard. At the end of the 1970–71 season, Barbara Anderson left the series and was replaced by Elizabeth Baur as Policewoman Fran Belding. The executive producer of *Ironside* was Joel Rogosin.

IT TAKES A THIEF

Jan. 1968–Aug. 1969	ABC	Tues. 8:30–9:30 P.M.
Aug. 1969–Jan. 1970	ABC	Thurs. 10–11 P.M.
Jan. 1970–Sept. 1970	ABC	Mon. 7:30–8:30 P.M.

It Takes a Thief was one of those TV series on which the name of the major character became as well known as the show's title (as was the case with Archie Bunker of ALL IN THE FAMILY). The character in this case was Alexander Mundy, a professional thief and sophisticated and cultured gentleman who was a very successful crook, until he was caught by the police. Mundy was played by Robert WAGNER. While serving time in the San Jobel Prison, Mundy was recruited by a representative of the U.S. government spy agency, the SIA, to work for them on various assignments stealing important secrets from various European cold war enemies. Mundy, who was somewhat of a ladies' man, was always getting involved with one pretty woman after another, but this never made him fail in his missions. Also appearing on the series in regular roles were Malachi Throne as Mundy's boss, Noah Bain, Edward Binns as Wallie Powers, Mundy's SIA contact, and his father, Alister Mundy, who had taught Alexander everything he knew about being a thief. The role was played by veteran film star Fred ASTAIRE. The series was produced by Universal TV.

IT'S GARRY SHANDLING'S SHOW

Mar. 1988–July. 1989	FOX	Sun. 9–9:30 P.M.
July 1989	FOX	Sun. 9:30–10 P.M.
July 1989–Aug. 1989	FOX	Sun. 10–10:30 P.M.
Aug. 1989–Mar. 1990	FOX	Sun. 10:30–11 P.M.

The imaginative situation comedy series *It's Garry Shandling's Show* was rejected by all three major networks before it was finally bought by the innovative FOX network. The series, which starred low-keyed comedian Garry Shandling, was a clever parody of such TV shows as *SATURDAY NIGHT LIVE, LATE NIGHT WITH DAVID LETTERMAN, MOONLIGHTING*, and others, with Shandling basically playing himself—an offbeat comic who found it somewhat difficult to deal with the world outside. On the series, Shandling talked to viewers, made observations as the various scenes on the show were being seen, allowed his studio audience to roam about the set, and took phone calls from viewers, while playing a character who was himself the star of a TV show. *It's Garry Shandling's Show* was given rave reviews by critics, who were delighted with its new approach to TV situation comedy. Among Shandling's regular cast members, who were also given license to comment on the proceedings, were Barbara Cason as Shandling's mother; his friend, Pete Schumaker, played by Michael Tucci; Pete's bright young son, Grant, played by Scott Nemes; Jackie Schumaker, played by Bernadette Birkett; Shandling's friend, Nancy Bancroft, played by Molly Cheek; and his nosy next-door neighbor, Leonard Smith, played by Paul Willson. Also appearing on the series were Ian Buchanan as Ian and Jessica Harper as Phoebe Bass, who became Shandling's girlfriend and eventually married him on the show. The series was created by Shandling and former *Saturday Night Live* writer Alan Zweibel.

I'VE GOT A SECRET

June 1952–June 1953	CBS	Thurs. 10:30–11 P.M.
July 1953–Sept. 1961	CBS	Wed. 9:30–10 P.M.
Sept. 1961–Sept. 1962	CBS	Mon. 10:30–11 P.M.
Sept. 1962–Sept. 1966	CBS	Mon. 8–8:30 P.M.
Sept. 1966–Apr. 1967	CBS	Mon. 10:30–11 P.M.
June 1976–July 1976	CBS	Tues. 8–8:30 P.M.

One of television's most enduring game/panel shows, *I've Got a Secret* made its debut in 1951 and finally left the air in 1976, after 15-year run. Four panelists questioned people who had secrets and tried to determine what the secret was. If the panel failed to guess the guest's secret, the contestant was given a financial reward. On the original show, the setting of *I've Got a Secret* was a courtroom. On each show, a guest celebrity also appeared and had the panel guess what his or her secret might be. Garry MOORE moderated the proceedings from its debut in 1952 until 1964. He was succeeded by Steve ALLEN, who hosted the show from 1964 until 1967, and then by Bill CULLEN when the series was revived in 1976. The panelists who were on the show longest were Bill Cullen (1952–67), Henry Morgan (1952–67 and 1976), Faye EMERSON (1952–58), Jayne Meadows (1952–59), Betsy Palmer (1957–67), and Bess Myerson (1958–67). Also serving on the panel for shorter periods of time were Louise Allbritton (1952), Laura Hobson (1952), Walter Kiernan (1952), Orson Bean (1952), Melville Cooper (1952), Kitty Carlisle (1951–53), Laraine Day (1952), Eddie Bracken (1952), Pat Collins (1976), Richard DAWSON (1976), and Elaine Joyce (1976). The show was created and produced by GOODSON–TODMAN Productions, and its executive producer was Gil Cates.

I've Got a Secret: Bess Myerson, Henry Morgan, Garry Moore, Bill Cullen, and Betsy Palmer (Photofest)

JACK BENNY PROGRAM, THE

Oct. 1950–June 1959	CBS	Sun. 7:30–8 P.M.
Oct. 1959–June 1960	CBS	Sun. 10–10:30 P.M.
Oct. 1960–June 1962	CBS	Sun. 9:30–10 P.M.
Sept. 1962–June 1963	CBS	Tues. 9:30–10 P.M.
Sept. 1963–Sept. 1964	CBS	Tues. 9:30–10 P.M.
Sept. 1964–Sept. 1965	CBS	Fri. 9:30–10 P.M.
Aug. 1977	CBS	Tues. 8–8:30 P.M.

For 26 years, from 1932 until 1958, *The Jack Benny Program* was one of the most popular programs on radio. One of the first prominent comedians to realize that television was the wave of the future, Jack BENNY transferred his radio show intact to television in 1950, and for eight years his show was seen, as well as heard, on both radio and television. Benny's regular television show continued for seven more years after his radio show was canceled. The cast of Jack Benny's TV shows remained basically the same, since his entire cast had all become almost as famous as Benny himself. His wife, Mary Livingston, was a favorite on Jack's radio and TV shows, although Mary was never really comfortable appearing on television and gradually all but disappeared from the TV show. Other regulars included Benny's corpulent announcer, Don Wilson, who was with Jack throughout his radio and TV careers; the gravel-voiced Eddie "Rochester" Anderson, who played Jack's black valet on the show; and Irish tenor Dennis Day, who was with Benny for many years on both radio and television. Performers who had been supporting players on Benny's radio show and who were also seen on television included the unctious "Floorwalker," played by Frank Nelson, who always greeted Jack with a long, drawn-out "Yeeeeeees?"; the versatile Mel Blanc, who played Jack's violin teacher, Monsieur LeBlanc, the familiar train announcer who always stated that the train was heading for "Anaheim, Azusa and Cucamonga," and also played many other characters on Jack's shows; the hard-boiled, blond bombshell Iris Adrian, whose loud voice burst many an eardrum on the show; Bea BENADERET and Sandra Gould, two Brooklyn-accented telephone operators who occasionally dated Jack and commented on his cheapness; and the Yiddish-accented Mr. Kitzel, played by Artie Auerbach, who always sang "Pickle in the middle with the mustard on top," as he sold his frankfurters. All provided Jack's audiences with plenty of laughs. Many of Benny's radio show routines were transferred intact to television and included Jack's never admitting to be any older than 39; Jack's reputation for being a miser who kept his money locked in a vault in the basement of his Beverly Hills home (the vault was guarded by a man who had not seen the light of day for years); and Jack's pet polar bear, Carmichael, who also guarded his vault and once ate the gas man. Jack's movie career was always being spoofed on the show, and the cast and guests appeared in many take-offs of Benny's, as well as other popular movies: Jack's famous pause when he was thinking over something he did not particularly wish to answer, and then when pushed, always said, "I'm thinking . . . I'm thinking," became as familiar to TV viewers as they had been to radio listeners. Among the famous performers who made their TV debuts on Benny's show were Humphrey Bogart, Marilyn Monroe, Claudette Colbert and Basil Rathbone, and a young comedian named Johnny Carson, who made one of his first important appearances on TV on Jack's show in 1952. After about 15 years as a regular performer on television, Benny decided to end his regular show and confine his TV appearances to occasional guest-starring stints on various situation comedies and variety shows. Benny, however, never lost the popularity he had enjoyed on radio and TV. The legendary comedian died in August 1977.

The executive producer of Benny's TV show was Ralph Levy and his producer was Hildy Marks, who was his brother-in-law. Benny's brilliant writers for both his radio and TV shows included Sam Perrin, George Balzer, Hal Goodman, and Al Gordon.

JACKIE GLEASON SHOW, THE

Sept. 1952–June 1955	CBS	Sat. 8–9 P.M.
Sept. 1956–June 1957	CBS	Sat. 8–9 P.M.
Oct. 1958–Jan. 1959	CBS	Fri. 8:30–9 P.M.
Sept. 1962–May 1968	CBS	Sat. 7:30–8:30 P.M.
Sept. 1968–Sept. 1970	CBS	Sat. 7:30–8:30 P.M.

Comedian Jackie GLEASON had several *Jackie Gleason Shows* on the air from 1952 until 1970. Before having a show that featured his name, Gleason had starred on the *Cavalcade of Stars,* which was seen on the DuMont network from the summer of 1950 until CBS offered the rotund comedian a staggering (for the time) $8,000 a week (he was being paid $1,000 a week by DuMont) to appear on their network in a regular weekly series in 1952. It was on this show that Gleason introduced his celebrated Ralph Kramden character on "The Honeymooners" sketches. The sketches featured Art CARNEY as Kramden's friend and next-door neighbor, Ed Norton, and Pert Kelton as his wife, Alice. Jackie's first *Jackie Gleason Show* for CBS was telecast live from New York City, and many of his DuMont show cast members were also seen on the CBS show, including Art Carney, the June Taylor Dancers, and the Ray Bloch Orchestra. Audrey Meadows and Joyce Randolph joined the Gleason show as Alice Kramden and Trixie Norton when the comedian began to once again feature his celebrated Honeymooners sketches on his show.

Among the many characters Gleason played on his variety series, several of which had first been introduced on his DuMont show, were the Poor Soul, Joe the Bartender, the Loudmouth, Reggie Van Gleason III, Rudy the Repairman, and Fenwick Babitt. Jackie's expressions "Awaaaaay we go," and "A little traveling music, please," before he went into another sketch, his title of "The Great One," and his catchphrase, "How sweet it is," became as familiar to viewers as the comedian himself. The original CBS *Jackie Gleason Show* ran for three years, but the popularity of "The Honeymooners" sketches led to his dropping the variety show format and appearing in a weekly situation comedy series, *The HONEYMOONERS,* which replaced his variety show for the 1955–56 season.

In fall 1958, Gleason returned with another variety show format. Most of his former regular cast members had left the show by this time. Jackie's frequent second banana on this series was comedian Buddy Hackett. In 1962, after hosting the less than successful quiz show, *You're in the Picture,* and an even less successful Jackie Gleason talk show, Jackie returned to his variety show format and starred in a new series, *The Jackie Gleason Show: The American Scene Magazine.* Featured on this new show were comedienne/actress Alice Ghostley, who played a lovelorn tenement dweller, Barbara Heller as Christine Clam, Frankie Fontaine as the drunkard Crazy Guggenheim, and Sue Ann Landon. Wayne Newton became a protégé of Gleason's and made frequent guest-starring appearances on the show. In 1966, Art Carney joined Gleason once again on another Jackie Gleason variety show that originated from Miami, and "The Honeymooners" sketches were revised, this time featuring Gleason and Carney as Ralph Kramden and Ed Norton and Shelia MacRae and Jane Kean, as their wives, Alice and Trixie. Jack Philbin was the executive producer of Gleason's final regular weekly TV variety show, and the program was produced by Ronald Wayne and directed by Frank Bunetta.

JACKSON, KATE (1949–)

Before Kate Jackson attracted the attention of TV viewers by playing Daphne Harridge in the offbeat gothic vampire/horror daytime series DARK SHADOWS in 1971, she had played only minor roles on such series as BONANZA. After appearing on *Dark Shadows,* the Birmingham, Alabama–born Jackson became a regular on the prime-time adventure series The ROOKIES, which became one of the 1970s' most popular shows. Leading roles in such scream-fest films as *Limbo* (1972), *Killer Bees* (1974), *Death Cruise* (1974), and *Death Scream* (1975) followed. In 1976, Jackson was cast as Sabrina Duncan, one of three lovely detectives on the CHARLIE'S ANGELS adventure series. The series and the three "angels," Kate Jackson, Jaclyn SMITH, and Farrah FAWCETT, were huge hits, and Jackson, Smith, and Fawcett became enormous TV stars. In addition to appearing on *Charlie's Angels,* Jackson was featured in such films as *Thunder and Lightning* (1977), *Dirty Tricks* (1981), and *Making Love* (1982), and in many other roles in TV films, which eventually led to another hit TV series, SCARECROW AND MRS. KING, on which she played Amanda King, opposite Bruce BOXLEITNER. Jackson continued to star in numerous TV films, and was recently seen in *Satan's School for Girls* (2000), another of her long string of horror film appearances.

JAFFE, SAM (SHALOM JAFFE 1891–1984)

New York City–born Sam Jaffee was a celebrated character actor in films and on television before he played the role that made him most famous, Dr. David Zorba on the BEN CASEY television series. Before he became known as Dr. Zorba, Jaffee played major roles in such film classics as *The Scarlet Empress* (1934), *Lost Horizon* (1937), *Gunga Din* (1939, playing Gunga Din), *13 Rue Madeleine* (1946), *Gentlemen's Agreement* (1947), *The Asphalt Jungle* (1950), *The Day the Earth Stood Still* (1951), and *Ben-Hur* (1959), and was a frequent guest star on such TV series as *Westinghouse Desilu Playhouse* (1958–1960), ALFRED HITCHCOCK PRESENTS, *The Westerner* (1960), *The UNTOUCHABLES, NAKED CITY,* and BONANZA. After *Ben*

Casey left the air, Jaffee continued to appear in numerous films and TV series until his death in 1984 at the age of 90. One of his last appearances was as Father Knickerbocker in the film *Nothing Lasts Forever* (1984), which was released the same year that he died.

JAG

Sept. 1995–Feb. 1996	NBC	Sat. 8–9 P.M.
Mar. 1996–July 1996	NBC	Wed. 8–9 P.M.
July 1996	NBC	Sat. 8–9 P.M.
Jan. 1997–Mar. 1997	CBS	Fri. 9–10 P.M.
Mar. 1997–Apr. 1997	CBS	Fri. 8–9 P.M.
May 1997–Aug. 1997	CBS	Fri. 9–10 P.M.
Sept. 1997–present	CBS	Tues. 8–9 P.M.

This legal/adventure series starred David James Elliott as Lt. Harmon "Harm" Rabb, Jr. and Tracey Needham as Lt. (jg) Meg. Austin, two lawyers assigned to the Judge Advocate General's Office of the U.S. Navy, or JAG as it is commonly called, when it made its debut in 1995. Although most of their assignments dealt with members of the military, Lt. Rabb and Lt. (jg) Austin were sometimes asked to defend civilians as well, and their job took them all over the world. Rabb, who was the son of a navy pilot who went missing in action during the Vietnam War, was haunted by his father's disappearance and never gave up hope that one day he would be found. When the series moved from NBC to CBS in 1997, after two years on the air, Lt. (jg) Austin was replaced by marine Maj. Sarah "Mac" MacKenzie, played by Catherine Bell, who became Rabb's new partner. Also appearing on the series were W. K. Stratton as Cmdr. Teddy Lindsey, Andrea Thompson as Cmdr. Allison Krennick, Patrick Labyorteaux as Lt. (jg) Bud Roberts, John M. Jackson as Adm. A. J. Chegwidden, Steven Culp as Agent Clayton Webb, Karri Turner as Ens. Harriet Sims, and Chuck Carrington as Petty Officer Tiner.

JAKE AND THE FATMAN

Sept. 1987	CBS	Sat. 10–11 P.M.
Sept. 1987–Feb. 1988	CBS	Tues. 9–10 P.M.
Mar. 1988–May 1988	CBS	Wed. 9–10 P.M.
June 1988–Sept. 1988	CBS	Wed. 8–9 P.M.
Mar. 1989–June 1992	CBS	Wed. 9–10 P.M.
June 1992–Sept. 1992	CBS	Sat. 10–11 P.M.

Jason Lochinvar McCabe, nicknamed the "Fatman" because of his large size, was a hard-boiled district attorney in a large, unidentified southern California city. McCabe, played by William CONRAD, was a former policeman who had a reputation for being tactless and persistent and using unconventional methods when investigating a case. Assisting McCabe was Jake Styles, played by Joe Penny, a hip young stud, who often went undercover when he was conducting an investigation for McCabe. Also on McCabe's staff at the district attorney's office were Derek Mitchell, an enthusiastic, if somewhat rash, young man,

played by Alan Campbell, and McCabe's outspoken secretary, Gertrude, played by Lu Leonard. One of the most popular characters on the show was McCabe's pet bulldog, an ancient canine named Max, who oddly resembled McCabe and was constantly at his side. In *Jake and the Fatman's* second season, McCabe retired from politics and moved to Hawaii, where he opened a private detective agency. Jake and Derek joined McCabe in Hawaii, doing most of the leg work for the fat McCabe, who usually remained in his office. One year later, McCabe, along with Jake, Derek, and of course Max, moved back to the mainland, taking his Hawaiian secretary, Lisbeth Berkeley-Smythe, played by Olga Russell, with him. The mayor of the large southern California city, where he had formerly been the district attorney, asked McCabe to investigate corruption in the D. A.'s office.

JAMES AT 15

Oct. 1977–Mar. 1978	NBC	Thurs. 9–10 P.M.
June 1978–July 1978	NBC	Thurs. 9–10 P.M.

One of television's more serious attempts to explore the problems of adolescents was *James at 15*. The series starred Lance Kerwin as James Hunter, an intelligent, sensitive boy growing up in the 1970s. When James's college professor father, Paul Hunter, played by Linden Chiles, moved from Oregon to Boston, after accepting another teaching job, James's life was thrown into turmoil, as he was forced to accept new friends and a new environment. James's sympathetic mother, Joan Hunter, played by Lynn Carlin, did what she could to make the move less problematic for James, but in spite of his family's support, James runs away from home. After he returns home, he slowly begins to adjust to life in his new home. Other characters regularly seen on the series were James's sisters, Sandy and Kathy, played by Kim Richards and Deidre Berthrong; Sly Hazeltine, James's new African-American friend, played by David Hubbard; his female friend, Marlene Mahoney, played by Susan Myers; and his teacher, Mr. Shamley, played by Jack Knight. The show's title changed from *James at 15* to *James at 16* when one of the show's most controversial episodes was aired. The episode involved James's loss of virginity after he met an attractive Swedish exchange student named Christina Killberg, played by Kirsten Baker. Many viewers were outraged that premarital sex by teens was portrayed as something acceptable, and thousands of letters of protest were sent to NBC by disgruntled viewers. The publicity this episode generated did not stop NBC from canceling the series at the end of its first and only season. The show's original executive producers were Martin Manulis and Joe Hardy, who were replaced by Ron Rubin.

JANSSEN, DAVID (DAVID HAROLD MEYER 1931–1980)

Although David Janssen began his career as a child actor and was featured in such films as *Swamp Fire* (1946) when he was 15 years old, he is best remembered for starring roles on two very successful television shows, RICHARD DIAMOND, PRIVATE DETECTIVE and The FUGITIVE. As a young actor, Janssen, who was born in Naponee, Nebraska, but moved to Southern California with his family when he was a small child, appeared on such TV series as ZANE GREY THEATER and YOU ARE THERE, and had roles in many films, including *Yankee Buccaneer* (1952), *Francis Goes to West Point* (1952), *Bonzo Goes to College* (1952), *All That Heaven Allows* (1955), *To Hell and Back* (1955), *Francis in the Navy* (1955), *Showdown at Abilene* (1956), and *Never Say Goodbye* (1956), among others. All this led to his being cast as Richard Diamond on the television series. Important roles in numerous films and on TV shows, such as *Lafayette Escadrille* (1958), *Darby's Rangers* (1958), *Dondi* (1961), ROUTE 66, and NAKED CITY followed. In 1961, Janssen was cast as Dr. Richard Kimble on *The Fugitive* inspired by the actual case of Dr. Sam Shepherd, which had made headlines in the late 1950s. The show was about a doctor falsely accused of murdering his wife, who escapes the law and spends countless hours running away and hiding as he tries to find the one-armed man whom he knows is his wife's actual killer. The series became one of television's most popular programs and made Janssen a star. Important roles in such films as *The Shoes of the Fisherman* (1968) and *The Green Berets* (1968), and subsequent leading roles on the TV series *O'Hara, U.S. Treasury,* which was not very successful, and the more successful *Harry-O* series, as well as many appearances in feature films and in the popular TV miniseries *Centennial* and *The Word,* kept Janssen busy until the late 1970s, when he was diagnosed with heart trouble. Janssen died at the age of 49 of a massive heart attack in 1980.

JEFF FOXWORTHY SHOW, THE

Sept. 1995	ABC	Tues. 8:30–9 P.M.
Sept. 1995–Jan. 1996	ABC	Sat. 8–8:30 P.M.
Feb. 1996	ABC	Sat. 8:30–9 P.M.
Sept. 1996–May 1997	NBC	Mon. 8–8:30 P.M.

Comedian Jeff Foxworthy, a "good ole boy" whose humorous observations about rural white male behavior made him a popular comedian, starred on a weekly TV situation comedy that was on the air for one and a half years. Originally, Foxworthy owned a small heating and air-conditioning company in Indiana on the series. His wife, Karen, a nurse, was played by Anita Barone, and his bright son, Matt, was played by Haley Joel Osment, and they often criticized their less sophisticated husband and father. Walt Bacon and Russ Francis, played by Matt Clark and Matt Borlenghi, were Jeff's two rather dim employees, and the sarcastic Sandi, Karen's friend and fellow nurse, was played by Sue Murphy. Craig Lesko, the Foxworthy's condescending neighbor at The Hunt Club at Avon housing development where they lived, was played by Steve Hytner, and Karen's parents, Elliott and Lois, who were less than pleased with their

daughter's choice of husband, were played by Dakin Matthews and Bibi Besch. When *The Jeff Foxworthy Show* moved to NBC from ABC for the 1996–97 season, Jeff and Karen had somehow found a second son, Justin, who was played by Jonathan Lipnicki. The Foxworthys had moved to Atlanta, where Jeff's southern brand of humor seemed much more at home. Jeff's overpowering father, Big Jim Foxworthy, played by G. W. Bailey, also joined the cast when the family moved to Atlanta.

JEFFERSONS, THE

Jan. 1975–Aug. 1975	CBS	Sat. 8:30–9 P.M.
Sept. 1975–Oct. 1976	CBS	Sat. 8–8:30 P.M.
Nov. 1976–Jan. 1977	CBS	Wed. 8–8:30 P.M.
Jan. 1977–Aug. 1977	CBS	Mon. 8–8:30 P.M.
Sept. 1977–Mar. 1978	CBS	Sat. 9–9:30 P.M.
Apr. 1978–May 1978	CBS	Sat. 8–8:30 P.M.
June 1978–Sept. 1978	CBS	Mon. 8–8:30 P.M.
Sept. 1978–Jan. 1979	CBS	Wed. 8–8:30 P.M.
Jan. 1979–Mar. 1979	CBS	Wed. 9:30–10 P.M.
Mar. 1979–June 1979	CBS	Wed. 8–8:30 P.M.
June 1979–Sept. 1982	CBS	Sun. 9:30–10 P.M.
Sept. 1982–Dec. 1984	CBS	Sun. 9–9:30 P.M.
Jan. 1985–Mar. 1985	CBS	Tues. 8–8:30 P.M.
Apr. 1985	CBS	Tues. 8:30–9 P.M.
June 1985	CBS	Tues. 8:30–9 P.M.
June 1985–July 1985	CBS	Tues. 8–8:30 P.M.

The Jeffersons' familiar theme song began:

Movin' on up to the East Side
To a deluxe apartment in the sky
Movin' on up to the East Side
We finally got a piece of the pie . . .

The Jeffersons, George and Louise (whom George affectionately called Weezie), were played by Sherman HEMSLEY and Isabel SANFORD. Before they got a series of their own, the Jeffersons had been characters on the very successful ALL IN THE FAMILY series, playing the bigot Archie Bunker's next-door neighbors, who owned a dry-cleaning business. George Jefferson was as bigoted against white people as Archie Bunker was against blacks, and Archie and George's ridiculously hostile exchanges and insults resulted in many laughs on the show. The spin-off series, *The Jeffersons,* became almost as popular with viewers as *All in the Family,* and remained on the air for an impressive 10 years. Also appearing on *The Jeffersons* was their son, Lionel, originally played by Mike Evans then by Damon Evans, and finally by Mike Evans once again. When the Jeffersons expanded their business and bought a chain of dry-cleaning establishments, their fortune changed for the better, and the family left the Bunkers and their Queens, New York, neighborhood and settled in a luxurious penthouse apartment on the prestigious Upper East Side of Manhattan in New York City. Their neighbors in their new high-rise apartment building included a towering, gawky Englishman named Harry Bentley, played by Paul Benedict, and a wealthy white man named Tom Willis and his black wife, Helen, played by Franklin Cover and Roxie Roker. Belinda Tolbert played Lionel's girlfriend, and later wife, Jenny Willis (Tom and Helen's daughter). Among the show's most amusing characters were the opinionated Olivia Jefferson, George's overbearing mother, played by Zara Cully, and Florence Johnson, the Jeffersons' independent, bossy African-American maid, played by Marla Gibbs. Ned Wertimer played Ralph, the Jeffersons' apartment house doorman; Ernest Harden, Jr., played Marcus Garvey; Jay Hammer played Allan Willis (Jenny's white half brother); Danny Wells played Charlie, the owner of a tavern that George and Tom Willis bought; and Ebonie Smith was Lionel and Jenny's baby daughter, Jessica. *The Jeffersons* was created by Don Nicholl, Michael Ross, and Bernie West and developed by Norman LEAR.

JENNINGS, PETER (PETER CHARLES JENNINGS 1938–)

ABC's major anchorman, Peter Jennings, was born in Toronto, Ontario, dropped out of high school, and later attended Carleton University and Rider College, before embarking upon a career in broadcasting. Jennings's father, Charles Jennings, was a pioneer radio newsman in Canada and was active in developing early television news programming in that country, so young Peter practically grew up in the broadcasting industry. After years of delivering local news first in Canada and then in the United States, Jennings went to work for the American Broadcasting Company. In 1965, Jennings became ABC's *Evening News* anchorman. After a brief hiatus, he returned to the anchorman's chair at ABC in 1978, and has remained in that seat ever since. In addition to his ABC *Evening News* assignment, Jennings has also hosted various specials for ABC, including *Hiroshima: Why the Bomb Was Dropped* and *The Century*, which was seen in conjunction with the publication of the best-selling book of the same name, which Jennings coauthored with Todd Brewster.

JEOPARDY!

Mar. 1964–Jan. 1975	NBC	Various times
1974	Syndicated	Various times and stations
Oct. 1978–Mar. 1979	NBC	Various times
1984–present	Syndicated	Various times and stations
June 1990–Sep. 1990	ABC	Sat. 8–8:30 P.M.
1998–present	Syndicated	Various times and stations

Jeopardy! is America's only game show in which contestants are provided with answers and must supply the right questions. On the show, three contestants win cash by providing the correct questions to answers supplied by the show's host. The answers are seen on a board with 30 squares, five squares in each of six categories. Contestants attempt to be the first to click in and provide the question to the information given by the show's host to win the total amount for that answer. The contestant with the most cash at the end of the show is the only one of the three contestants to receive any money. The other two contestants win consolation prizes. The series was the brainchild of performer/producer Merv GRIFFIN. Originally, the show was hosted by Art Fleming. In 1984, after a hiatus, *Jeopardy!* returned to home screens with Alex TREBEK as its host. At present, *Jeopardy!* is one of the most popular first-run syndicated series on the air. In 1990, a once-a-week, prime-time version of the show was presented on ABC and was called *Super Jeopardy!* It did not prove to be as successful as the five-day-a-week early evening version of the show, and the series was canceled after less than a full season on the air. In 1998, a daytime version of the show called *Rock 'n' Roll Jeopardy!*, with Jeff Probst hosting, was aired on cable TV; all the categories were rock and roll oriented. Music videos and audio clips were frequently used as the answers provided on this series.

JERRY SPRINGER SHOW, THE

1992–present	Syndicated	Mon.–Fri. Various stations

A former mayor of Cincinnati, Jerry SPRINGER became the host of one of television's most controversial daytime talk shows in the early 1990s. The program became well known for its often violent physical confrontations and outbursts of emotion that occurred among guests on the show. Springer himself once described his show as "silly." Many critics and viewers found the show upsetting because of the "low-life" problems on which it focused. Some of the seamier subjects featured on the show in just two months in 1995 were "Mate Swapping," "Strip Club Denizens," and "Pinups and Prostitutes."

JETSONS, THE

Sept. 1962–Sept. 1963	ABC	Sun. 7:30–8 P.M.
Sept. 1963–Apr. 1964	ABC	Sat. 10–10:30 A.M.
Sept. 1964–Sept. 1965	CBS	Sat. 9–9:30 A.M.
Oct. 1965–Sept. 1967	NBC	Sat. 10–10:30 A.M.
Sept. 1969–Sept. 1971	CBS	Sat. 10:30–11 A.M.
Sept. 1971–Sept. 1976	NBC	Sat. 9–9:30 A.M.
Feb. 1979–Sept. 1981	NBC	Sat. 10:30–11 A.M.
Sept. 1982–Apr. 1983	NBC	Sat. 11–11:30 A.M.
1985, 1987	Syndicated	Various times and stations

This animated cartoon series about a modern space-age family named the Jetsons was originally presented as an evening program, but never attracted an audience. When it became apparent to network officials at ABC that the series simply was not appealing to adults, the show was switched to daytime hours on Saturday and then Sunday, and almost immediately became one of the most viewed children's shows on the air. Produced by William Hanna and Joseph Barbera, who had also launched the popular *FLINTSTONES* cartoon series several years earlier, *The Jetsons* featured a family (obviously modeled after the Flintstones) who lived in a 1960s version of the future. The Jetsons lived at the Skypad Apartments and had a robot for a maid. The family dog was called Astro. The head of the family, George Jetson, was a likable bungler. His wife, Jane, was practical and sensible, and they had two children, Judy and Elroy. George worked at Spacely Sprockets, where he developed products that he hoped would impress his overbearing boss, and compete with his company's largest competitor, Coswell's Cogs. The actors who provided the voices for the characters were George O'Hanlon (George Jetson); Penny Singleton (who had played Blondie in films and on radio, was the voice of Jane Jetson); Mel Blanc (Mr. Spacely, George's boss); Janet Waldo (Judy Jetson); Daws Butler (Leroy); and Don Messick (Astro, the dog). *The Jetsons* is one of the most popular cartoon series ever to be aired on television.

JIMMY DURANTE SHOW, THE

Oct. 1954–June 1956	NBC	Sat. 9:30–10 P.M.
June 1957–Sept. 1957	CBS	Sat. 8–8:30 P.M.
Sept. 1957	CBS	Sat. 8:30–9 P.M.

JIMMY DURANTE PRESENTS THE LENNON SISTERS:

Sept. 1969–Jan. 1970	ABC	Fri. 10–11 P.M.
Feb. 1970–July 1970	ABC	Sat. 9:30–10:30 P.M.

Jimmy DURANTE enjoyed a long and prosperous career on the stage, in films, and on radio and became the star of the first weekly variety show to use the star's name, *The Jimmy Durante Show*, in 1954. Appearing as regulars were Eddie Jackson (Durante's old vaudeville partner), pianist Jules Buffano, drummer Jack Roth, the Durante Girls, and the Ray Bargy Orchestra. Durante made good use of all the old vaudeville routines that had made him a star, including frequent references to his large nose (his familiar nickname was "the Schnozzola), his signature song, "Ink-a-Dink-a-Doo," and his famous closing line, "Goodnight, Mrs. Calabash, wherever you are," which he always said prior to walking offstage as a single spotlight followed him. Jimmy's first television show was *The TEXACO STAR THEATER*, and Durante alternated as the show's star every other week with dancer Donald O'Connor. Jimmy's shows on this series were all presented live, whereas O'Connor's shows were filmed. In 1969, one year after they ended their long relationship with bandleader Lawrence Welk, the singing Lennon Sisters, costarred with Durante on a weekly, hour-long variety show called *Jimmy Durante Presents the Lennon Sisters* (1969–70). Appearing as guests on the show were such popular performers as Jack BENNY, Phyllis Diller, Bob HOPE, and singer Glen Campbell. In spite of the show's talented cast and big-name guest stars, it failed to attract an

audience and was canceled after one season. After 1970, Durante continued to appear on television regularly as the star of numerous TV specials, and he remained active on TV until shortly before his death in 1980.

JOANIE LOVES CHACHI

Mar. 1982–Apr. 1982	ABC	Tues. 8:30–9 P.M.
Sept. 1982–Dec. 1982	ABC	Thurs. 8–8:30 P.M.
May 1983–Sept. 1983	ABC	Tues. 8:30–9 P.M.

Because the characters they played on *HAPPY DAYS* situation comedy were so popular, Erin Moran and Scott BAIO, who played Joanie Cunningham and Chachi Arcola on that show, were given a series of their own, *Joanie Loves Chachi*, in 1982. Baio had become a teenage heartthrob playing Arthur Fonzarelli, or "The Fonz's," cousin "Chachi" Arcola on *Happy Days*. On this spin-off series, Chachi had moved to Chicago, to pursue a career as a singer. Joining him was a major character on *Happy Days*, Richie Cunningham's sister, Joanie. Joanie and Chachi had developed a relationship while on *Happy Days*, and Joanie shared Chachi's dream of being a singer. Also appearing on series were Chachi's mother, Louise Delvecchio, played by Ellen Travolta, and Chachi's stepfather, Al Delvecchio, played by Al Molinaro. Even though such amusing characters as Bingo, a spaced-out drummer, played by Robert Peirce; Annette, Chachi's chubby cousin, played by Winifred Freedman; her brother, Mario, played by Derrel Maury; and Annette and Mario's father, Uncle Rico, played by Art Metrano, who became Joanie and Chachi's agent when they embarked upon a singing career, *Joanie Loves Chachi* never became the hit show its producers had hoped it would be, and the series was canceled when it ranked number 68 in the Nielsen ratings during the 1982–83 season.

JOHN LARROQUETTE SHOW, THE

Sept. 1993	NBC	Thurs. 9:30–10 P.M.
Sept. 1993–Mar. 1994	NBC	Tues. 9:30–10 P.M.
Mar. 1994–Apr. 1994	NBC	Tues. 9–10 P.M.
June 1994	NBC	Tues. 9–10 P.M.
July 1994–Aug. 1994	NBC	Tues. 9–9:30 P.M.
Sept. 1994–Mar. 1995	NBC	Tues. 9:30–10 P.M.
May 1995–Sept. 1995	NBC	Tues. 9:30–10 P.M.
June 1995	NBC	Sat. 9–9:30 P.M.
July 1995	NBC	Sat. 9–10 P.M.
July 1995–Aug. 1995	NBC	Tues. 8:30–9 P.M.
Sept. 1995–Nov. 1995	NBC	Sat. 9–9:30 P.M.
Dec. 1995–June 1996	NBC	Tues. 9:30–10 P.M.
Aug. 1996–Oct. 1996	NBC	Wed. 8:30–9 P.M.

Television situation comedy series are usually light and cheerful affairs, but *The John Larroquette Show* was quite the opposite. It was a somewhat dark, although often very funny, rather somber show. *TV Guide* magazine actually dubbed *The John Larroquette Show* "sitcom noir." Set in a seedy bus terminal called "The Crossroads," located in the seamier part of town in St. Louis, Missouri, the series starred John LARROQUETTE, who one year before, was on the hit sitcom NIGHT COURT. On *The John Larroquette Show,* Larroquette played John Hemingway, a well-educated, often married and divorced man, who had lost his family and his job because of his alcoholism and who accepted a job as all-night manager at the bus terminal. Hemingway's loud, sarcastic, wise, and very funny Latina assistant. Mahalia Sanchez, played by Liz Torres, knew more about running the terminal than he did. Also working at the terminal were Dexter Wilson, played by Daryl "Chill" Mitchell, a young black man with a chip on his shoulder who ran the terminal's snack bar, and Gene, played by Chi McBride, a large, angry man who was the janitor at the terminal but hated having to clean it. Frequent visitors at the terminal were Carly Watkins, a hooker with a heart of gold who used the bus station as her headquarters, played by Gigi Rice; Oscar, the homeless bum who used the terminal as his bedroom; Catherine Merrick, played by Alison LaPlaca, who bought the bar located in the terminal and used it as a place to launch and showcase her torch-singing career and who became a love interest for Hemingway; Max Dumas, played by John F. O'Donohue; and Police Officers Hampton and Eggers, played by the tall and lumbering Lenny Clarke and the small and feisty Elizabeth Berridge. The third season the show was on the air, major changes took place. In an attempt to lighten the show up a bit for the 1995 season, although loyal fans liked the series just as it was, NBC decided that Hemingway would be the daytime manager at the terminal. They believed that this would give the show a brighter look and feeling. Oscar the bum took a job running the newsstand, Carly met a millionaire and quit being a prostitute, and Hemingway was reunited with his two kids, Rachel and Tony, played by Mayim Bialik and Omri Katz, neither of whom knew of each other's existence. Donna Mills also turned up as one of Hemingway's ex-wives, Carol. The show was canceled a few weeks into the 1996–97 season. That it had been scheduled opposite the popular ROSEANNE show when it made its debut, and then opposite the successful HOME IMPROVEMENT show, did not help *The John Larroquette Show,* in spite of its clever scripts and talented cast of actors, to gain a large enough audience to keep it on the air.

JOHNSON, DON (DONNIE WAYNE JOHNSON 1949–   )

Don Johnson, who first attracted the attention of TV viewers as one of the stars of the innovative and successful crime drama series MIAMI VICE, began his performing career not as an actor, but as a rock singer. Johnson, who was born in Flat Creek, Missouri, began singing and playing the guitar while attending Wichita South High School in Wichita, Kansas. Johnson's first professional acting job was in the San Francisco–based American Conservatory Theatre production of the rock musical *Your Own Thing,* which led to his being offered a full drama scholarship to the University of Kansas. When he graduated from college,

Johnson went to Hollywood and made five pilots for TV shows at NBC. Unfortunately, none came to fruition. In 1965, Johnson appeared on *The Dating Game* as a contestant, and his good looks attracted the attention of casting directors, who soon found him work as an actor in such series as *The Rookies* (1972–76), KUNG FU, *The STREETS OF SAN FRANCISCO,* and *Big Hawaii* (1977), and in such films as *The Magic Garden of Stanley Sweetheart* (his film debut in 1970), *Zachariah* (1971), *The Harrad Experiment* (1973), and *A Boy and His Dog* (1975). Johnson also appeared in numerous TV films, including *Cover Girls* (1977), *Pressure Point* (1978), *Ski Lift to Death* (1978), *First, You Cry* (1978), *The Rebels* (1979), and *Amateur Night at the Dixie Bar and Grill* (1979). In 1980, Johnson appeared in his first starring role on a TV series, *From Here to Eternity,* playing Jefferson "Jeff" Davis Prewitt. The show was not a success, but after roles in several additional TV films, Johnson starred on a second TV series, *Miami Vice,* playing Police Detective James "Sonny" Crockett. The show and Johnson were enormous successes. Johnson continued to star in feature films such as *Cease Fire* (1985), *Dead Bang* (1989), *Paradise* (1991), and *Born Yesterday* (1993), and others, while appearing on *Miami Vice* and then after the series left the air. In 1996, Johnson appeared on another action/crime drama series that became as successful as *Miami Vice,* NASH BRIDGES. Johnson continues to be active in films, as well as on television.

JONATHAN WINTERS SHOW, THE

Dec. 1967–Dec. 1968	CBS	Wed. 10–11 P.M.
Dec. 1968–May 1969	CBS	Thurs. 8–9 P.M.

Although the immensely talented and unique comedian/actor Jonathan WINTERS frequently guest-starred on many popular TV variety and talk shows, including *The GARRY MOORE SHOW* and *The TONIGHT SHOW,* as well as on several TV specials, he starred on only one, relatively short-lived *Jonathan Winters Show* on television. All of Winters's familiar characters such as Maud Frickert, Willard (in the "Couple Up The Street" sketches), and Jack Armstrong—the All-American Boy, in a take-off of the popular children's adventure series, were seen on the show. Appearing with Winters were Abby Dalton and Dick Curtis, and at various times, Alice Ghostley, Pamela Rodgers, Paul Lynde, Georgene Barnes, Jerry Rannow, Cliff Arquette as "Charlie Weaver," and The Establishment, the Bob Banas Dancers, the Tony Charmoli Dancers, the Wisa D'Orso Dancers, and the Paul Weston and Earl Brown Orchestras. In 1972, Winters appeared in a syndicated series called *The Wacky World of Jonathan Winters,* which did not remain on the air long. This series also featured Marion Mercer and the Soul Sisters. In 1980, Winters became a semiregular on the popular MORK & MINDY series playing the alien Mork's full-grown son, Mearth, who had been born when an egg popped out of Mork's navel. The chemistry between Winters and Robin WILLIAMS, who had similar approaches to comedy, was magic, but it failed to keep *Mork & Mindy* on the air longer than one additional season.

JONES, SHIRLEY (SHIRLEY MAE JONES 1934–)

When Shirley Jones was born in Smithton, Pennsylvania, her parents had a premonition that their lovely baby girl was destined to be a famous entertainer and named her after the movies' most popular performer of that time, child star Shirley Temple. Jones began her formal training as a singer when she was 12 years old, and after she graduated from high school, she went to New York City to audition for Rodgers and Hammerstein's casting director. Impressed with Shirley's beauty and lovely, trained singing voice, Rodgers and Hammerstein immediately signed her to play a nurse in their new musical comedy *South Pacific*. One year later, she was cast in the leading role of Laurie in Rodgers and Hammerstein's long-awaited film version of their hit musical *Oklahoma!* (1955). The film made Jones a star overnight, and the leading role of Julie in Rodgers and Hammerstein's film version of their stage success *Carousel* (1956) followed. In the late 1950s, musicals had begun to lose favor with filmgoers, and Shirley decided to pursue a nonmusical acting career. She appeared in such films as *Never Steal Anything Small* (1959) and *Pepe* (1960) and completely took Hollywood by surprise when she won an Academy Award as Best Supporting Actress in the film *Elmer Gantry* (1960). In 1962, she returned to musicals and starred in the film version of the hit musical comedy *The Music Man*. Even though Shirley was mainly playing dramatic roles in films during the 1960s and 1970s, she continued her active singing career by frequently guest-starring on such TV shows as *The ANDY WILLIAMS SHOW*. In 1970, Jones was cast as Shirley Partridge, playing the singing matriarch of a talented musical family on the TV series *The PARTRIDGE FAMILY*. To everyone's surprise, the series was a huge hit and actually became the role for which Shirley is perhaps best remembered. Roles in several feature and TV films, and guest appearances on such TV shows as *McMILLAN AND WIFE*, *MURDER, SHE WROTE*, *EMPTY NEST*, *BURKE'S LAW*, *Something So Right* (1996–98), *The DREW CAREY SHOW*, and *SABRINA, THE TEENAGE WITCH* kept Jones busy throughout the 1980s and 1990s. Jones had regular roles on the TV series *Shirley* in 1979, which was not a success, in the revival of the *Burke's Law* series in 1994, and on *Melrose Place* in 1998, as well. Jones's last film role, to date, was in *Shriek If You Know What I Did Last Friday the 13th* (2000).

JUDY GARLAND SHOW, THE

Sept. 1963–Mar. 1964	CBS	Sun. 9–10 P.M.

Although her weekly variety show was on the air for less than one full season, the legendary film star Judy Garland's TV series is fondly remembered by anyone who saw it. Guided by young George Schlatter, who later steered *ROWAN AND MARTIN'S LAUGH-IN* to success, Judy's show was modeled after a very popular special in which she appeared in the spring of 1962. Schlatter was fired from the series after producing five shows when the program failed to make a dent in the audience that was watching the very popular *BONANZA* series opposite Garland's show. By the time it left the air four months later, *The Judy Garland Show* had gone through two more producers as it attempted to find a format and an audience. Among the many guests who appeared with Judy were her daughter, Liza Minnelli, Mickey Rooney, Ray Bolger (who had played the Scarecrow in the film hit *The Wizard of Oz* in 1939), and special guest appearances by Frank Sinatra, Dean MARTIN, and others. By the time Garland's series left the air, Garland had finally found a format that worked for her, but it was too late. Perhaps if she had simply stood in front of the cameras and sang her heart out, without comedy sketches and big production numbers and famous guest stars, as she did on the last few shows, *The Judy Garland Show* might have been a bigger hit than it was.

JULIA

Sept. 1968–Jan. 1971	NBC	Tues. 8:30–9 P.M.
Jan. 1971–May 1971	NBC	Tues. 7:30–8 P.M.

Actress/singer Diahann CARROLL was the first African-American performer to star on a weekly situation comedy, Julia, playing a black woman who was not a domestic, but rather a well-educated, intelligent, professional woman. Carroll played Julia Baker, an independent young nurse whose husband had been killed in Vietnam and who was raising her young son alone. Julia's son, Corey, played by Marc Copage, was an engaging boy who was curious and loving. Julia's fellow nurse at the hospital where she worked was Hannah Yarby, played by Lurene Tuttle, and her mentor at the hospital was Dr. Martin Chegley, played by veteran film actor Lloyd Nolan. When the series first went on the air, network executives were afraid that the public would not accept a series that had a totally integrated cast and that treated the characters as equals and not adversaries. Their fears were unfounded and the show soon became one of America's favorite series. Also appearing on the program were Betty Beaird as Marie Waggedorn, Michael Link as Earl J. Waggedorn, Mary Wickes as Dr. Chegley's wife, Melba, Ned Glass as Sol Cooper, and Eddie Quillan, Paul Winfield (as Julia's love interest, Paul Cameron), Hank Brandt, Fred Williamson (as Julia's second love interest, Steve Bruce), Janear Hines, Richard Steele, and Stephanie James. *Julia* was produced by Hal Kanter for 20th Century Fox.

JUNGLE JIM

1955	Syndicated	Various times and stations

Former film Tarzan Johnny Weissmuller played James Bradley, a guide and adventurer in Africa whom the natives called "Jungle Jim," on this half-hour weekly syndicated series. The series costarred Martin Huston as Bradley's young son, Skipper, and featured Norman Frederic as his East Indian aide, Kassim, and Tamba, the chimpanzee, who bore a remarkable resemblance to Tarzan's pet chimp Cheetah. *Jungle Jim* was an action-packed series, and in the first episode alone, Jungle Jim fought natives, lions, and crocodiles and battled a raging jungle fire. Even though Weissmuller was no longer the athlete he had once been as an Olympic swimming champion, and was obviously older and overweight, he insisted on performing all his own stunts on the show. After *Jungle Jim* ended production in 1957, Weissmuller rarely appeared on television thereafter and concentrated on his swimming pool construction business.

JUST SHOOT ME

Mar. 1997	NBC	Tues. 9:30–10 P.M.
Mar. 1997	NBC	Wed. 9:30–10 P.M.
July 1997–Mar. 1998	NBC	Tues. 9:30–10 P.M.
Feb. 1998–May 1998	NBC	Thurs. 8:30–9 P.M.
May 1998–June 1998	NBC	Tues. 9:30–10 P.M.
June 1998–Aug. 1998	NBC	Thurs. 9:30–10 P.M.
Aug. 1998–Sept. 1998	NBC	Tues. 9:30–10 P.M.
Sept. 1998	NBC	Tues. 9–10 P.M.
July 1999–	NBC	Tues. 8–8:30 P.M.

This situation comedy series that takes place in the offices of a sleazy women's fashion magazine, *Blush,* stars Laura San Giacomo as Maya Gallo, a journalist with high ideals, who was fired from her job as a TV news writer for standing up for her beliefs and ended up working for her father, Jack Gallo, played by George Segal, who owns the magazine. Other characters who work at the magazine are Nina, a bossy and scheming former model who serves as *Blush's* editor, played by Wendie Malick; Elliott, a somewhat hysterical, balding photographer at the magazine, played by Enrico Colantoni; and Dennis Finch, a sneaky, back-stabbing young executive assistant, played by former *SATURDAY NIGHT LIVE* performer David Spade. Not long after the series made its debut, Dennis, a character whose two-faced, self-serving actions kept people laughing, became the most popular character on the show. Never seen, but often talked about, was Ally, the womanizing Jack's fourth wife, a former classmate of Maya's.

K

KAPLAN, GABE (1945–)

Former stand-up comedian Gabe Kaplan, who was born in Brooklyn, New York, was first seen on television on the *POLICE STORY* series in 1973. In 1975, he created and starred on a series called *WELCOME BACK, KOTTER*, which was about a special-education high school teacher, Gabe Kotter, who teaches a group of tough Brooklyn boys at James Buchanan High School, which was Kaplan's actual alma mater. The series was a huge success, remained on the air for four years, and was one of the top-30 shows during the 1975–76, 1976–77, and 1977–78 seasons. When *Welcome Back, Kotter* ended its run in 1979, Kaplan made only occasional guest appearances in such films as *Fast Break* (1979), *Nobody's Perfekt* (1981), the TV miniseries *Lewis & Clark* (1981), *Groucho* (1982, as Groucho Marx), and *The Hoboken Chicken Emergency* (1984). Kaplan also made guest appearances on *Police Story* and *MURDER, SHE WROTE*. In 1996, Kaplan came out of semiretirement, after mostly concentrating on his financial investments, to appear in the series *Mr. Rhodes*, on which he re-created his role of teacher Gabe Kotter.

KATE AND ALLIE

Mar. 1984–May 1984	CBS	Mon. 9:30–10 P.M.
Aug. 1984–Sept. 1986	CBS	Mon. 9:30–10 P.M.
Sept. 1986–Sept. 1987	CBS	Mon. 8–8:30 P.M.
Sept. 1987–Nov. 1987	CBS	Mon. 8:30–9 P.M.
Dec. 1987–June 1988	CBS	Mon. 8–8:30 P.M.
July 1988–Aug. 1988	CBS	Sat. 8–8:30 P.M.
Aug. 1988–Sept. 1988	CBS	Mon. 9–9:30 P.M.
Dec. 1988–Mar. 1989	CBS	Mon. 8:30–9 P.M.
Mar. 1989–June 1989	CBS	Mon. 10:30–11 P.M.
June 1989–Sept. 1989	CBS	Mon. 8–8:30 P.M.

Two divorced women, Kate McArdle and Allie Lowell, who had three children between them, joined forces and shared a large Greenwich Village apartment in New York City on the lighthearted situation comedy *Kate and Allie*. The women, who had been friends in high school, soon found that they had very different lifestyles. Kate, played by Susan Saint James, was a contemporary, career-oriented woman, if sometimes a bit flighty. Allie, played by Jane Curtin, was a conservative homebody who preferred making pies to going out to work. Kate had one child, Emma, played by Ari Meyers, a teenager who had inherited her mother's casual attitude about life, and Allie's children, Chip and Jennie, played by Frederick Koehler and Allison Smith. By the time the series left the air, all three children were college age. Charles Lowell, Allie's ex-husband, played by Paul Hecht, often picked his kids up to take them on outings, and later in the series remarried. Kate and Allie dated several men during the series run, including Ted Bartelo, played by George Salata, and Bob Barsky, played by Sam Freed, whom Allie eventually married. Lou Carello, the super at their apartment building, played by Peter Onorati, was always trying to make time with a totally turned-off Kate. *Kate and Allie* was created by Sherry Koben, who got the idea for the show when she attended her high school graduation class's tenth anniversary reunion and discovered how many of her fellow female classmates were divorced.

KATE SMITH EVENING HOUR, THE (ALSO *THE KATE SMITH HOUR* & *THE KATE SMITH EVENING HOUR*)

THE KATE SMITH HOUR:

Sept. 1950–June 1954	NBC	Daytime

THE KATE SMITH EVENING HOUR:
Sept. 1951–June 1952   NBC   Wed. 8–9 P.M.

THE KATE SMITH EVENING HOUR:
Jan. 1960–July 1960   CBS   Mon. 7:30–8 P.M.

One of radio's most successful performers, singer Kate Smith was first seen on television in a daytime talk show, *The Kate Smith Hour,* which followed the same format as her popular daytime radio show on which she interviewed celebrities, chatted with her manager and partner Ted Collins, and sang contemporary and standard songs. Smith's first evening show, *The Kate Smith Evening Hour,* featured guest stars from Hollywood and Broadway who performed excerpts from their films and plays, and various dancers, singers, magicians, and occasional acrobats. Ted Collins was also on hand to host the TV show. Regularly featured on the program was a domestic comedy skit, *Ethel and Albert,* that had been a popular radio show written by and starring Peg LYNCH as Ethel, and featuring Alan Bunce as Albert, a couple with the same problems most couples encounter during the course of their marriage. Two performers who were rarely seen on television made their debuts on Kate's show. One was the controversial African-American entertainer Josephine Baker, and the other was bandleader Tommy Dorsey, who performed with his orchestra. On Smith's daytime show her familiar theme song was "When the Moon Comes Over the Mountain," but on her evening variety show, Kate performed "God Bless America" as her theme. In 1960, Kate Smith returned to prime-time television with a brand new half-hour variety program that featured singing and dancing, celebrity guests, and occasional production numbers.

KAUFMAN, ANDY (ANDREW GEOFFREY KAUFMAN 1949–1984)

Comedian Andy Kaufman, who became famous playing the foreign-born Latka Gravas on the successful *TAXI* situation comedy series, was born in New York City to an affluent family and grew up in Great Neck, New York. An unusual child, Kaufman spent hours in his bedroom working on various comedy routines that he later used as part of his stand-up comedy nightclub act. In 1967, Kaufman graduated from high school and received a notice that he was to be drafted into the U.S. Army. He received a 4-F classification from the army when army doctors determined that he was psychologically unfit, which was perhaps a portent of things to come in Andy's life. At Boston's Graham Junior College, Kaufman studied radio and television production and produced, directed, and starred in his own show, *Uncle Andy's Playhouse,* at the college TV station. After finishing his schooling, Kaufman began to perform his comedy routines in various comedy clubs in New York City and was discovered by Improvisation Comedy Club owner, Budd Friedman, who arranged for him to perform in various comedy clubs around the country. His strange act either delighted or repelled his audiences, but it led to a debut on

national TV on the *Dean Martin Comedy Hour* in 1974. This led to appearances as a regular guest on the popular SATURDAY NIGHT LIVE, and as a guest star on such shows as *Van Dyke and Company, The TONIGHT SHOW* starring Johnny Carson, *The MIKE DOUGLAS SHOW, The Dating Game,* and the *Fridays* comedy show. In 1979, Kaufman booked Carnegie Hall for a concert that featured his comedy routines. After the show, all 2,800 members of the audience were treated to milk and cookies at a Manhattan cafe. The featured role on *Taxi,* and appearances in two less than successful films, *In God We Tru$t* (1980) and *Heartbeeps* (1981) followed. Unhappy with appearing on a scripted TV sitcom, Kaufman began to misbehave on the *Taxi* set, but remained with the show until it ended its run in 1983. Stints as a professional wrestler, which many suspected was a setup, and occasional appearances on TV followed, but one year after *Taxi's* demise, Kaufman was diagnosed with lung cancer, and the comedian died at the age of 35.

KEESHAN, BOB (ROBERT KEESHAN 1927–)

TV's beloved Captain Kangaroo, Bob Keeshan, was born in Lynbrook on Long Island in New York, and made his television debut as Clarabell the Clown on the *Puppet Playhouse,* which became best known as *The HOWDY DOODY SHOW,* in 1947. Keeshan became an entertainer after serving in the U.S. Marine Corps and was one of TV's pioneer performers. In 1955, Keeshan became the star of a morning children's program on CBS, CAPTAIN KANGAROO. The show, which became one of TV's most popular shows for children, was on the air for a continuous 29 years, with Keeshan remaining at its helm for the entire run. Keeshan, who was elected to the Clown Hall of Fame, made guest-starring appearances on several shows, including *The ANDY WILLIAMS SHOW* and *MURPHY BROWN* in the 1960s though the 1980s, and even though he had retired, he was seen playing himself on *The Stupids* in 1996.

KEN MURRAY SHOW, THE (AKA *TIME TO SMILE*)

Jan. 1950–June 1952   CBS   Sat. 8–9 P.M.
Feb. 1953–June 1953   CBS   Sun. 9:30–10 P.M.

Ken MURRAY, a comedian who began his career as a teenager in the 1920s and had the first commercial program on television in 1930, became the host of a weekly musical/variety show on CBS in 1950. *The Ken Murray Show* was one of early television's most successful programs and starred Murray, who also produced the show, as host. The show featured top celebrity guests and a large cast of regulars that at different times included former *Our Gang* film comedy's child star Darla Hood, Joe Wong, Tony Labriola, Jack Mulhall, Betty Lou Walters, The Enchanters singing group, comedian Joe Besser, singer Art Lund, Pat Conway, Jane Bergmeier, Lillian Farmer, singer Anita Gordon, singer Johnny Johnston, and a pretty, wide-eyed cowgirl with a deadpan expression who stole the show each week, Laurie Anders. Anders's catch-phrase, "Ah love the wide open spaces," was quoted by everyone who had a television set at the time and was familiar with the show. In between the musical acts and comedy sketches, Murray informally chatted with guests and talked directly to viewers at home. The program, which began as an alternating show, became a weekly show a few months after it went on the air, and then in 1953, returned to being an alternating show with *The ALAN YOUNG SHOW*, using the title *Time to Smile*.

KING FAMILY SHOW, THE

Jan. 1965–Sept. 1965	ABC	Sat. 7:30–8:30 P.M.
Sept. 1965–June 1966	ABC	Sat. 8–8:30 P.M.
Mar. 1969–Sept. 1969	ABC	Wed. 8:30–9 P.M.

The King Sisters (Yvonne, Luise, Marilyn, Alyce, Maxine, and Donna), who were a popular singing group during the big-band era of the 1940s, returned to show business with a weekly TV musical variety show in the mid-1960s. For a time, the show was very popular with viewers. In addition to the sisters, the show also featured Luise's husband, Alvino Rey, and his orchestra, and over 35 other members of the King family (including the girls' father, who was 79 years old), who sang, danced, and certainly were living proof that a family that played together, stayed together. The original King Sisters' brothers, husbands, cousins, nephews and nieces, and their children, even infants and pretoddlers, made appearances on the show. The show was a spin-off of a King Sisters' successful appearance on *The HOLLYWOOD PALACE*. In spite of the program's original impact, *The King Family Show's* novelty soon wore off, and after a brief hiatus from 1966 until 1969, and then a short revival in 1969, the show faded from the spotlight and became part of television's history.

KING OF QUEENS, THE

Sept. 1988–July 1999	CBS	Mon. 8:30–9 P.M.
July 1999–present	CBS	Mon. 8–8:30 P.M.

Kevin James plays the hard-working IPS delivery driver Doug Heffernan, who lives in the borough of Queens in New York City, on this half-hour situation comedy series. Doug's wife, Carrie, played by Leah Remini, is as attractive woman who works in an upscale law firm in Manhattan. Doug's favorite pastime is hanging out with his buddies Deacon, Spence, and Richie, played by Victor Williams, Patton Oswalt, and Larry Romano, in the basement of his house. When his hangout is taken over by Carrie's widowed father, Arthur Spooner, a sarcastic, difficult-to-get-along-with man, played by Jerry Stiller, who refuses to move to a retirement home, Doug's leisure time is interrupted, until Doug and his friends decide to hang out in the Hefferman garage. His life is further complicated when Carrie's younger sister, Sara, an aspiring actress, moves in with then to save money.

KING, LARRY (LAWRENCE HARVEY ZEIGER 1933–   )

One of television's favorite talk show hosts, Larry King, who was born in Brooklyn, began his broadcasting career in 1957. Before becoming the host of his popular *LARRY KING LIVE* show on CNN in 1987, King was the host of a popular Washington-based radio call-in show. In addition to his talk show appearances, King has also been featured in such motion pictures as *Ghostbusters* (1984), *Eddie and the Crusaders II: Eddie Lives!* (1989), *Crazy People* (1990), *Dave* (1993), *Courage Under Fire* (1996), *Primary Colors,* (1998), *Enemy of the State* (1998), and on the TV series *MURPHY BROWN*, *The SIMPSONS*, *The MUPPETS*, *SPIN CITY*, and *FRASIER*, always playing himself. King is noted for having been married seven times and for saying, "Before they made you they broke the mold," on his show, which he considers a put-down.

KLUGMAN, JACK (1922–   )

Jack Klugman, who was born in Philadelphia, became a familiar face to TV viewers in the 1950s when he was seen in hundreds of dramatic anthology shows, such as *Hollywood Screen Test* (1948–53), *The UNITED STATES STEEL HOUR*, *GOODYEAR TELEVISION PLAYHOUSE*, *The PHILCO TELEVISION PLAYHOUSE*, *The Alcoa Hour* (1955–57), and on such classic series as *ALFRED HITCHCOCK PRESENTS*, *GUNSMOKE*, *NAKED CITY*, *The TWILIGHT ZONE*, *The DEFENDERS*, and *The UNTOUCHABLES*. Klugman was also featured in such films as *Apache Gold* (1952), *12 Angry Men* (1957), *I Could Go on Singing* (1963), *The Detective* (1968), and others. He also costarred with Ethel Merman on Broadway in the musical comedy *Gypsy* in the late 1950s, and was a regular on the *The Greatest Gift* and *Harris Against the World* TV series in 1954 and 1964. In 1970, Klugman was cast as Oscar Madison on the TV version of Neil Simon's hit play *The Odd Couple*. The series became one of television's all-time favorite shows and made Klugman a TV superstar. Not one to rest on his laurels, after *The ODD COUPLE* left the air, Klugman continued to appear as a guest star on television shows and in films, and eventually landed another starring role on a TV series that became a hit, *QUINCY*, in 1976. Early in the 1990s, Klugman developed throat cancer and had part of his larynx removed, leaving his voice extremely gruff. Nonetheless, Klugman continued to appear in such TV and feature films as *The Odd Couple: Together Again* (1993), *Dear God* (1996), and *The Twilight of the Golds* (1997), and guest-starred on the TV series *DIAGNOSIS MURDER* and *Brother's Keeper*.

KNIGHT RIDER

Sept. 1982	NBC	Sun. 8–10 P.M.
Oct. 1982–Aug. 1983	NBC	Fri. 9–10 P.M.
Aug. 1983–Mar. 1985	NBC	Sun. 8–9 P.M.
Mar. 1985–Apr. 1985	NBC	Fri. 8–9 P.M.
Apr. 1985–Aug. 1985	NBC	Sun. 8–9 P.M.
Aug. 1985–Dec. 1985	NBC	Fri. 8–9 P.M.

| Jan. 1986–Apr. 1986 | NBC | Fri. 9–10 P.M. |
| May 1986–Aug. 1986 | NBC | Fri. 8–9 P.M. |

Among the most successful TV shows of the 1982–83 season was NBC's *Knight Rider,* an adventure program that featured David HASSELHOFF as Michael Knight, a young ex-cop who was shot in the face and given a new face and identity by a dying millionaire who charged him to fight for law and justice using the supercar KITT (Knight Industries Two Thousand) which he had developed. The car, a customized Pontiac Trans-Am that could cruise at 300 miles per hour, leap up to 50 feet in the air, and was loaded with flame throwers, smoke bombs, and infrared devices, became the real star of the show. The debonair and sophisticated Englishman Devon Miles, played by Edward Mulhare, coordinated the crime-fighting activities for Knight Industries and assisted Knight in his pursuits of law and justice. Bonnie Barstow, played by Patricia McPherson, and then April Curtis, played by Rebecca Holden, were KITT's master mechanics and sometimes accompanied Knight on his missions. KITT's voice was supplied by actor William Daniels. Peter Parros joined the cast for the 1985–86 season, playing Reginald Cornelius III ("RC3"), who drove a specially equipped truck that hauled KITT from place to place. *Knight Rider* was developed by Brandon Tartikoff, who was the head of programming at NBC in 1982. Ninety episodes of *Knight Rider* were produced during the five years the series was in production. In 1991, Hasselhoff re-created his Michael Knight role in a TV movie, *Knight Rider 2000.*

KNOTS LANDING

Dec. 1979–Mar. 1980	CBS	Thurs. 10–11 P.M.
June 1980–Mar. 1981	CBS	Thurs. 10–11 P.M.
June 1981–Oct. 1981	CBS	Thurs. 10–11 P.M.
Nov. 1981–Mar. 1982	CBS	Thurs. 9–10 P.M.
Mar. 1982–Mar. 1983	CBS	Thurs. 10–11 P.M.
June 1983–June 1986	CBS	Thurs. 10–11 P.M.
Sept. 1986–Nov. 1986	CBS	Thurs. 9–10 P.M.
Nov. 1986–Mar. 1993	CBS	Thurs. 10–11 P.M.
May 1993	CBS	Thurs. 9–11 P.M.

For 21 years, from December 1979 through May 1993, Thursday night television belonged to *Knots Landing,* the evening soap opera series. Following the lead of the popular DALLAS evening serial drama, from which it was a spin-off, *Knots Landing* concentrated on the comings and goings of two of *Dallas's* Ewing family members—the weak-willed Gary Ewing, played by Ted Shackelford, and his wife, Valene Ewing Gibson Waleska, played by Joan Van Ark, who lived on a quiet cul-de-sac in the Southern California community of Knots Landing, where Gary, the former alcoholic, black sheep of the Ewing family and Val had moved after he divorced and then remarried her. Also prominently featured in the original *Knots Landing* episodes were Gary and Val's neighbors and friends who also lived in the cul-de-sac: Sid and Karen Fairgate, played

by Don Murray and Michelle Lee, who were Gary's boss at Knots Landing Motors, and his wife; Kenny and Ginger Ward, played by James Houghton and Kim Lankford, a recording executive and his wife; and Richard and Laura Avery, played by John Pleshette and Constance McCashin, an obnoxious, aggressive womanizing lawyer and his wife. As the series went into its second, third, and beyond seasons, these characters separated, were divorced, died, and changed in other ways. Added to the cast over the years were Donna Mills, who played Abby Cunningham, who then became Abby Ewing, and then Abby Sumner, a mother of two, looking for love in all the wrong places; Earl Trent, played by Paul Rudd, a member of Alcoholics Anonymous, whom Gary introduced to his friends. Subsequently, the cast changed regularly and included such prominent players as stage and screen actress Julie Harris, singer Jon Cypher, film actors Millie Perkins, Lisa Hartman, Alec Baldwin, Howard Duff, Ava Gardner, Ruth Roman, Red BUTTONS, Michael York, Michelle Phillips (formerly of the Mamas and the Papas singing group), France Nuyen, TV star Betsy Palmer, and many others who played major roles on the series at various times. Over the years there was occasional interplay between characters on *Knots Landing* and *Dallas.* Gary's brothers often turned up at Knots Landing, and Gary and Val periodically visited the Ewing ranch on the outskirts of Dallas. *Knots Landing,* which was created by David Jacobs, had its last hurrah as a two-hour special on which most of the loose ends that had developed during the series run were finally tied up. It was preceded by a one-hour special called "Knots Landing Block Party," on which members of the cast, past and present, reminisced about their experiences on the show.

KNOTTS, DON (JESSE DONALD KNOTTS 1924–)

Don Knotts, who achieved fame playing Barney Fife, a popular character on *The* ANDY GRIFFITH SHOW, was born in Morgantown, West Virginia. Before attending high school in Morgantown, he performed as a ventriloquist and comedian at church and school functions, and after finishing high school, he headed for New York, determined to break into show business. When he failed to find employment as a performer, Knotts returned home and enrolled at the University of West Virginia. Dissatisfied with life as a student and since it was in the middle of World War II, Knotts joined the army and toured the South Pacific as a comedian in a G.I. variety show called *Stars and Gripes.* When the war ended, Knotts returned to college, and upon graduation, he once again went to New York to pursue his dream of becoming an entertainer. This time, he easily found work on television as a regular on the SEARCH FOR TOMORROW daytime serial in 1951, and on Broadway in 1958 in a stage comedy, *No Time for Sergeants,* which starred Andy GRIFFITH, who became Knott's lifelong friend, and later costar on *The Andy Griffith Show.* Knotts first became well known to TV viewers, however, as a regular on *The STEVE ALLEN SHOW* from

1956 until 1960. He then appeared in the film version of *No Time for Sergeants* in 1958. From the moment he appeared on *The Andy Griffith Show* playing Deputy Barney Fife, Don Knotts secured a place for himself as one of America's favorite performers, and he won three Emmy Awards as Outstanding Supporting Actor for his work on that show. In 1964, Knotts appeared in his first starring role in a film in *The Incredible Mr. Limpet,* and he followed that up with leading roles in such film comedies as *The Ghost and Mr. Chicken* (1966), *The Reluctant Astronaut* (1967), *The Shakiest Gun in the West* (1968), and Disney's *The Apple Dumpling Gang* (1975), which were all hits at the box office. In 1979, Knotts became a regular on the popular THREE'S COMPANY series, playing eccentric landlord Mr. Furley, and from 1988 until 1992, he occasionally appeared on his friend Andy Griffith's show MAT-LOCK. In the late 1990s, Knotts was seen in such films as *Big Bully* (1996), *Cats Don't Dance* (1997, as the voice of T. W. Turtle), *Pleasantville* (1998, as the TV repairman), and in 2000, *Lady and the Tramp II: Scamp's Adventure* (as the voice of the dogcatcher).

KOJAK

Oct. 1973–Sept. 1974	CBS	Wed. 10–11 P.M.
Sept. 1974–Sept. 1975	CBS	Sun. 8:30–9:30 P.M.
Sept. 1975–Jan. 1977	CBS	Sun. 9–10 P.M.
Jan. 1977–Sept. 1977	CBS	Mon. 10–11 P.M.
Sept. 1977–Dec. 1977	CBS	Sun. 10–11 P.M.
Dec. 1977–Apr. 1978	CBS	Sat. 10–11 P.M.
Nov. 1989–June 1990	CBS	Sat. 9–11 P.M.

Kojak was originally a character on a 1973 TV film *The Marcus-Nelson Murders,* written by Abby Mann. On the subsequent TV series, New York City police detectives Theo Kojak and Frank McNeil, played by Telly SAVALAS and Dan Frazer, had been partners early in their careers, but McNeil worked his way up to chief of detectives at the 13th Precinct in Manhattan South. The independent Lt. Kojak, was something of a rebel in the police department, who insisted on doing things his way, no matter who was in charge, even if it was his good friend and former partner, McNeil. Working with Kojak was plainclothesman Lt. Bobby Crocke, played by Kevin Dobson, who was as close to being a partner of Kojak as anyone on the force could be. Also working with Kojak were Det. Stavros, played by Savalas's brother, George Savalas, Dr. Rizzo, played by Vince Conti, and Det. Saperstein, played by Mark Russell. With his trademark lollipop, his outspoken, streetwise ways, and his bald pate, Kojak, as played by Telly Savalas, became one of television's most unforgettable characters. For the five years it was on the air, *Kojak* was also one of TV's most popular programs.

In all, 118 episodes of *Kojak* were filmed between 1973 and 1978. The series was produced by Jack Laird for Universal Television. In 1989, 11 years after the original *Kojak* series was canceled, Telly Savalas returned to television in the role he had made famous, and several

Telly Savalas as Kojak (Author's collection)

new *Kojak* TV films were produced as part of the ABC *Mystery Movie* series. In the cast with Savalas in these films were Andre Braugher, Kario Salem, Candace Savalas, and Charles Cioffi.

KORMAN, HARVEY (HARVEY HERSCHEL KORMAN 1927–)

Before he became familiar to millions of fans on *The* CAROL BURNETT SHOW, actor/comedian Harvey Korman, who was born in Chicago, was a successful character actor seen on such popular TV shows as *The* UNTOUCH-ABLES, PERRY MASON, EMPIRE, *The* MUNSTERS, F TROOP, and *The* WILD, WILD WEST, and appeared in the films *Living Venus* (1960), *Gypsy* (1962), and *Lord Love a Duck* (1966). Korman was also a regular on *The Danny Kaye Show* from 1964 to 1967. It wasn't until he joined the cast of the *Carol Burnett* variety show in 1967, however, that Korman's name became familiar to the public. While appearing on the BURNETT show, Korman also appeared in such popular films as *Huckleberry Finn* (1974) and *Blazing Saddles* (1974), as well as on such TV shows as *The* LOVE BOAT. In 1977, Korman rejoined Carol Burnett on the *Carol Burnett and Friends* series, and was subsequently seen on *The Tim Conway Show* and MAMA'S FAM-ILY with fellow Burnett show alumni Tim CONWAY and Vicki LAWRENCE. Constantly busy as a much sought-after character actor throughout the 1980s and '90s, Korman appeared in the films *History of the World: Part 1* (1981),

Curse of the Pink Panther (1983), *The Munchies* (1987), *Radioland Murders* (1994), *The Flintstones in Viva Rock Vegas* (2000), on the TV series *Leo & Liz in Beverly Hills* (1986), *The Nutt House* (1989), and HOLLYWOOD SQUARES, and as a guest star on such series as ROSEANNE, ELLEN, DIAGNOSIS MURDER, and ER.

KOVACS, ERNIE (ERNEST KOVACS 1919–1962)

One of television's most creative and innovative performers, Ernie Kovacs was born in Trenton, New Jersey. After completing high school, Kovacs studied acting, determined to became a famous performer. Early acting jobs with several stock companies on Long Island and a column he wrote for the *New Jersey Trentonian* kept him busy until he finally sold an idea for a TV show to NBC in 1951. NBC liked the show, which was called *Time for Ernie,* and on the show Kovacs introduced many entirely TV-oriented, zany, imaginative characters and routines that could be successful only on television. He followed this show with *Ernie in Kovacsland,* also in 1951, and then *The* ERNIE KOVACS SHOW in 1952–54 (originally titled *Kovacs Unlimited*), and the *Take a Guess, Gamble on Love, One Minute Please, Time Will Tell,* and *The Tonight Show* TV series in 1953 and 1954. In 1956, Kovacs made his film debut in *Showdown at Ulcer Gulch* and followed that up with appearances in a series of successful films that included *Operation Mad Ball* (1957), *Bell, Book and Candle* (1958), *It Happened to Jane* (1959), *Our Man in Havana* (1959), *North to Alaska* (1960), *Strangers When We Meet* (1960), and *Five Golden Hours* (1961), which was his last film appearance. In 1962, Kovacs's career was cut tragically short when he was killed in an automobile accident.

KRAFT TELEVISION THEATRE

May 1947–Dec. 1947	NBC	Wed. 7:30–8:30 P.M.
Jan. 1948–Oct. 1958	NBC	Wed. 9–10 P.M.
Oct. 1953–Jan. 1955	ABC	Thurs. 9:30–10:30 P.M.

The Kraft Foods Co. was the sole sponsor of this dramatic anthology series that was the first hour-long series of this kind on television. During the 11 years it was on the air, *Kraft Television Theatre* presented 650 plays, which were, for the most part, presented live, and employed 3,955 actors in over 6,750 roles. The series first production was "Double Door," which starred John BARAGREY. It originated from a small converted radio studio at NBC. For many years, announcer Ed Herlihy, the Kraft Company's longtime spokesman, introduced the various dramas seen on the series. During the show's early years, each hour-long play cost $3,000 to produce, but by 1958, when the series departed the airwaves, each show cost $165,000. Scripts produced on the show ranged from plays written by Shakespeare to those by contemporary playwrights, and practically every major dramatist was represented on the

series at one time or another. Over the years, among the outstanding performers and plays that were seen on *The Kraft Television Theater* were James Dean in "A Long Time Till Dawn" (1953); Rod SERLING's "Patterns" starring Ed Begley, Richard Kiley, and Everett Sloane (1955); Eugene O'Neill's "The Emperor Jones," with Ossie Davis and Everett Sloane (1955); Rod Serling's "The Blues of Joey Minotti," with Constance Ford and Dan Morgan (1953); F. Scott Fitzgerald's "The Diamond as Big as the Ritz," with Signe Hasso, Robert Montgomery, and Lee Remick (1955); John F. Kennedy's (a U.S. senator at the time) "A Profile In Courage" (1956), with James Whitmore; "A Night To Remember" (1956), an adaptation of the book about the final hours of the *Titanic,* which employed over 107 actors and was directed by George Roy Hill; Simon Winchelberg's "The Sea Is Boiling Hot" (1958), with Earl Holliman and Sessue Hayakawa; "The Singing Idol" (1957) with Tommy Sands and Fred Clark; and "Drummer Man" (1957) with Sal Mineo. Other prominent actors seen during the 11 years the show was aired were Art CARNEY, E. G. Marshall, Jack Lemmon, Anthony Perkins, Joanne Woodward, Giselle MacKenzie, Julius LaRosa, Cyril Ritchard, Rod Steiger, Grace Kelly, Cloris LEACHMAN, and Paul Newman, to name just a few. Many producers and directors worked on *Kraft Television Theatre,* including Stanley Quinn, Maury Holland, Henry Hermann, Richard Dunlap, Fielder Cook, William Graham, Norman Morgan, David SUSSKIND, Robert Herridge, Alex March, George Roy Hill, and Buzz Kulik. *Kraft Television Theatre* was one of the finest programs produced during television's "Golden Years" in the 1950s.

KUKLA, FRAN AND OLLIE

Nov. 1948–June 1954	NBC	Various times
Sept. 1954–Aug. 1957	ABC	Various times
Sept. 1961–June 1962	NBC	Various times
1969–1971	PBS	Various times

Puppet master Burr TILLSTROM's first TV show was on a local NBC station in Chicago in 1947 and was called *Junior Jamboree.* NBC officials were so impressed with the show, and with Tillstrom's ability to handle all the puppets by himself as well as provide voices for the puppet characters, that they decided to give him a network series of his own the following year. With singer and actress Fran ALLISON interacting with the puppets, Tillstrom's puppets became very real characters to viewers, and interestingly, to adults as well as to children who were soon watching the show on a regular basis. The entire action of the show took place in front of the proscenium arch of the Kuklapolitan Puppet Theater with Fran standing next to the stage and talking to the puppets who appeared within the arch. The likable, patient Fran, the only live character who appeared on the show, and her fellow "Kuklapolitan Players," which included the hand puppets (who continued to be handled and voiced by Burr Tillstrom): Kukla (Russian for "doll"), a serious, bulbous-

Kukla, Burr Tillstrom, Ollie, and Fran Allison (left to right) (Photofest)

nosed, bald little fellow; Ollie (Oliver J. Dragon), a lovable, gentle, and somewhat goofy dragon; the wiry and clever Fletcher Rabbit; the crackle-voiced, gullible, and totally likable Beulah (Beauh) the Witch; the funny, sometimes overbearing, but kind-hearted diva Madame Ophelia Oglepuss; her boyfriend, the long-winded southerner Colonel Crackie; Dolores Dragon, Ollie's young niece; the fidgety Mercedes Olivia Dragon, Ollie's mother; and Cecil Bill, who used only the sounds "doi-de-doi-doi" when he communicated with Fran and his fellow puppets, delighted viewers with their musical revues, backstage activities, holiday celebrations and parties, and everyday problems at their Kuklapolitan Playhouse. Their Thanksgiving pageants, Christmas musicales, operetta spoofs of such shows as Gilbert and Sullivan's *The Mikado,* and various other exchanges among the characters on the show, became classics and are as fondly remembered today as when they were originally aired over 50 years ago. In addition to their regular five-day-a-week, two-day-a-week, and one day-a-week shows, Tillstrom, Fran, and

the puppets also appeared as guest stars on many popular TV variety programs, and from 1969, to 1971, they had a regular program on the PBS network. *Kukla, Fran and Ollie* was produced for many years by Beulah Zachary, for whom the Beulah the Witch was named. *Kukla, Fran and Ollie* remains, in many people's minds, one of television's most beloved and popular shows of all time.

KUNG FU

Oct. 1972–Nov. 1972	ABC	Sat. 8–9 P.M.
Jan. 1973–Aug. 1974	ABC	Thurs. 9–10 P.M.
Sept. 1974–Oct. 1974	ABC	Sat. 9–10 P.M.
Nov. 1974–Jan. 1975	ABC	Fri. 8–9 P.M.
Jan. 1975–June 1975	ABC	Sat. 8–9 P.M.

Although few people think of it as such because of its decidedly Oriental flavor, the *Kung Fu* TV series was a western, which was set in the American West of the late 1800s. The hero of the series, Kwai Chang Caine, played by David Carradine, had been born in China of American and Chinese parents and, when orphaned as a child, had been raised by the monks of the Shaolin Temple. Tutored in "the mystic philosophy of internal harmony" and "the oneness of all things," Caine had a firm belief in nonviolence. He had also been trained in the ancient art of kung fu, however, in order to defend himself when necessary. Forced to leave China when he accidentally killed a member of the Chinese royal family, Caine relocated to the western United States to search for his long-lost half brother, as he avoided capture by Chinese imperial agents and American bounty hunters who were constantly tracking him down. Also appearing on the series regularly were Chinese-American actors Keye Luke, as Master Po, and Philip Ahn, as Master Kan, his teachers in China (who were often seen in flashbacks); Radames Pera, who played Caine as a boy (also seen in flashbacks); and Season Hubley, who played Margit McLean, Caine's American cousin. The series was created by Ed Spielman and developed by Herman Miller, who produced it with Alex Beaton. Jerry Thorpe was the show's executive producer. In 1993, a sequel called *Kung Fu: The Legend Continues,* a syndicated show, surfaced with David Carradine repeating his original role.

L

L.A. LAW

Oct. 1986–Nov. 1986	NBC	Fri. 10–11 P.M.
Dec. 1986–Aug. 1990	NBC	Thurs. 10–11 P.M.
Oct. 1990–Feb. 1993	NBC	Thurs. 10–11 P.M.
Apr. 1993–Dec. 1993	NBC	Thurs. 10–11 P.M.
Feb. 1994–May 1994	NBC	Thurs. 10–11 P.M.

One of the most successful programs that made its debut during the 1986–87 season was *L.A. Law*, which was created by Steven Bochco, who was responsible for the popular HILL STREET BLUES series, and Terry Louise Fisher, a former deputy district attorney in Los Angeles and the creator of CAGNEY AND LACEY. *L.A. Law's* action centered on the high-powered L.A. law firm of McKenzie, Brackman, Chaney and Kuzak, which handled both criminal and civil cases. The central characters included Leland McKenzie, the fatherly senior partner, played by Richard Dysart; Douglas Brackman, Jr., an egocentric, balding lawyer who was always trying to emulate his successful father, who was also a lawyer, played by Alan Rachins; Michael Kuzak, a softhearted, intelligent younger partner, played by Harry Hamlin; Grace Van Owen, the idealistic deputy D.A. (obviously patterned after T. L. Fisher), who was also Kuzak's lover, played by Susan Dey; Ann Kelsey, one of the law firm's female partners, played by Jill Eikenberry; Stuart Markowitz, the firm's tax attorney, played by Michael Tucker; Arnie Becker, the firm's womanizing divorce lawyer, played by Corbin Bernsen; Victor Sifuentes, a young Hispanic lawyer brought into the firm in order to satisfy racial quotas, played by Jimmy Smits; Abby Perkins, a young intern at the firm, played by Michele Greene; Roxanne Melman, the firm's receptionist, played by Susan Ruttan; Jonathan Rollins, a young black lawyer at the firm, played by Blair Underwood; and Benny, a mentally handicapped office worker at the firm, played by Larry Drake. Other actors who appeared as regulars were Diana Muldaur (as lawyer Rosalind Shays), Ellen Drake (as Elizabeth Brand), Joanna Frank (as Shelia Brackman), Patricia Huston (as Hilda Brunschweiger), Cynthia Harris (as Iris Hubbard), Joyce Hyser (as Alison Gottlieb), Dann Florek (as David Myer), Nancy Vawter (as Dorothy Wyler), Jennifer Hetrick (as Corrine Hammond), Renee Jones (as Diane Moses), Vincent Gardenia (as Murray Melman), Sheila Kelley (as Gwen Taylor), John Spencer (as Tommy Mullaney), Amanda Donohoe (as Cara Jean Lamb), Cecil Hoffman (as Zoey Clemmons), Tom Verica (as Billy Castroverti), Conchata Ferrell (as Susan Bloom), Michael Cumpsy (as Frank Kittridge), A. Martinez (as Daniel Morales), Alan Rosenburg (as Eli Levinson), Debi Mazar (as Denise Ianello), Alexandra Powers (as Jane Halliday), Liza Jane (as Melinda Paros), and Kathleen Wilhoite (as Rosalie).

LAND OF THE GIANTS

Sept. 1968–Sept. 1970	ABC	Sun. 7–8 P.M.

Taking its lead from the popular science fiction adventure series LOST IN SPACE, which had made its debut two years earlier, *Land of the Giants* was directed toward younger viewers and was about seven space travelers who became stranded on an Earthlike planet where the human inhabitants were 12 times their size. Giant children, huge pets, and immense insects continuously menaced the seven as they attempted to repair their spacecraft so that they could return to Earth. Featured on the series were Gary Conway as Capt. Steve Burton, the spacecraft's pilot; Don Matheson as Mark Wilson, the ship's engineer-tycoon; Stefan Arngrim, as a 12-year-old passenger on the spacecraft; Barry Lockridge, who had a dog named Chipper;

Don Marshall as the ship's copilot, Dan Erikson; Deanna Lund as passenger Valerie Scott, a rich heiress; Heather Young as stewardess Betty Hamilton; Kurt Kasznar as the troublesome and mysterious Cmdr. Alexander Fitzhugh; and Kevin Hagen as the Giant Inspector Kobrick, who kept track of what the Earth people were doing. The executive producer of this series was Irwin Allen, who budgeted each episode at the unheard of, for the time, $250,000 for each weekly show.

LAND OF THE LOST

Sept. 1974–Nov. 1976	NBC
Feb. 1978–Sept. 1978	NBC
June 1985–Dec. 1985	CBS
June 1987–Sept. 1987	CBS
Sept. 1991–Sept. 1994	ABC

This live-action Saturday morning children's adventure series was produced by Sid and Marty Krofft. The series centered on the Marshall family: Ranger Rich Marshall, played by Spencer Milligan, and Will and Holly Marshall, his son and daughter, played by Wesley Eure and Kathy Coleman, who are trapped behind a one-way time barrier after surviving a plunge over a waterfall that could have been fatal. The Marshalls battled giant prehistoric monsters, befriended a group of apelike people called the Pakunis, and avoided their reptilian enemies, the Sleestacks, who were determined to destroy them. After two seasons, Ranger Rich disappeared during an earthquake (actor Spencer Milligan left the series, hoping to find more challenging acting jobs), and his place was taken by his brother, Jack Marshall, played by Ron Harper, who had been searching for his relatives and who also became trapped in the same time barrier that his relatives had been lost in.

LANDON, MICHAEL (EUGENE MAURICE OROWITZ 1936–1991)

The star of three popular shows, BONANZA, LITTLE HOUSE ON THE PRAIRIE, and Highway to Heaven, Michael Landon was a talented javelin thrower in high school who had no idea he would one day became an actor. The son of a New York City publicist and his actress/wife, Eli and Peggy (O'Neill) Orowitz, Landon was born in Forest Hills, Queens, New York, but grew up in Collingswood, New Jersey. Because his father was Jewish and his mother Irish Catholic, Landon often felt out of place in school and was a poor student, barely graduating from high school. His athletic abilities, however, won him a scholarship to the University of Southern California. Devastated when a torn arm ligament ended his dream of becoming a sports star, Landon left college and, for a time, supported himself as a gas station attendant, a blanket salesman, and a stock boy. While he was working in a North Hollywood warehouse, Landon was discovered by a Warner Brothers executive who thought Landon's good looks might get him work as an actor. After taking acting classes, Landon changed his

name from Eugene Orowitz to Michael Landon, a name he picked out of the phone book, and began to audition for roles in films and TV shows. A natural actor, Landon soon found work on TV in such series as The Cavalcade of America (1952–57), and in 1956, he was cast in his first feature film, These Wilder Years. One year later, Landon won the leading role in the film I Was a Teenage Werewolf, which led to his being cast in one of the leading roles on Bonanza, "Little Joe" Cartwright. The series was a tremendous success. While Landon was appearing in Bonanza, he became interested in television production, and when the series ended after 14 years on the air, Landon decided to use his behind-the-scenes knowledge to produce, and star in, a series of his own, Little House on the Prairie. The show became a huge hit and ran for an impressive eight years from 1974 to 1982. Landon then produced two less than successful spin-off series, Little House: A New Beginning and Father Murphy (1981–84). In 1984, Landon produced and starred in the series Highway to Heaven, which was also a success, but in 1991, it was discovered than Landon, only 55 years old, had pancreatic cancer. The actor died that same year, at the height of his career.

LANSBURY, ANGELA (ANGELA BRIGIT MACGILL LANSBURY 1925–   )

The multitalented star of films, the stage, and television, Angela Lansbury was born in London, England. Her mother, a music hall entertainer and actress named Moyna MacGill, left England to escape the blitz bombing of London during World War II and went to New York City, where she tried to find work on Broadway. Not meeting with much success, MacGill went to Hollywood, where she did find work as a character actress in films. It was her daughter, the pretty teenager Angela Lansbury, however, who landed a contract at the MGM Studios and won an Academy Award as Best Supporting Actress for her first film, Gaslight (1944). At MGM, Angela appeared in such films as The Picture of Dorian Gray (1945), The Harvey Girls (1946), and The Three Musketeers (1948), and in Cecil B. DeMille's Samson and Delilah (1949). In the 1950s, Lansbury frequently guest-starred on such TV series as ROBERT MONTGOMERY PRESENTS, The Lux Video Theatre (1950–57), Schlitz Playhouse of Stars (1951–59), FOUR STAR REVUE, YOUR SHOW OF SHOWS, GENERAL ELECTRIC THEATER, The Fireside Theatre (1949–63), Stage 7 (1954–55), Front Row Center (1949–50), Screen Directors Playhouse (1955–56), and PLAYHOUSE 90. Because she looked older than her actual years, even though she was still in her twenties, Lansbury began to play important character roles in such critically acclaimed films as The Long, Hot Summer (1958), The Dark at the Top of the Stairs (1960), and The Manchurian Candidate (1962), and appeared on Broadway in Hotel Paradiso (1957) and the musicals Mame and Sweeney Todd in the 1960s and 1970s. In 1984, Lansbury became the star of the one-hour mystery series MURDER, SHE WROTE, playing a mystery novelist named Jessica Beatrice (J. B.) Fletcher. The show and Lansbury became well known and loved by millions of viewers

Angela Lansbury (Author's collection)

and remained on the air for 12 seasons. Constantly busy as an actress in films and on television, Lansbury was also heard as the singing voice of Mrs. Potts in the Disney animated cartoon *Beauty and the Beast* (1991) and as the voice of the Dowager Empress Marie in Disney's *Anastasia* (1997). Lansbury can still be seen playing Jessica Fletcher in occasional *Murder, She Wrote* TV films.

LARROQUETTE, JOHN (JOHN BERNARD LARROQUETTE 1947–   )

A two-time Emmy Award–winning actor for his work on the NIGHT COURT TV series, John Larroquette was born in New Orleans, Louisiana. As a young man, Larroquette diligently worked to lose his Louisiana drawl in order to work on radio when he finished school. He succeeded, and he was employed for several years as a radio disc jockey. In the late 1960s, Larroquette went to Hollywood, determined to become a TV and film actor. By the early 1970s, he was appearing on such TV series as SANFORD AND SON, ELLERY QUEEN, KOJAK, The SONNY AND CHER COMEDY HOUR, DALLAS, THREE'S COMPANY, MORK & MINDY, and REMINGTON STEELE, and in such feature films as *The Texas Chain Saw Massacre* (1974), *Heart Beat* (1980), *Cat People* (1982), *Meatballs Part II* (1984), and others, and as a regular on such TV series as *Doctors' Hospital* (1975–76) and BAA BAA BLACK SHEEP. In 1984, Larroquette was cast as the flip Assistant D.A. Daniel

"Dan" Fielding on the TV series *Night Court.* The series made Larroquette a star, and he continued to appear in such films as *Star Trek III: The Search for Spock* (1984), *Blind Date* 1987), *Tune in Tomorrow* (1990), and *Madhouse* (1990). In 1992, Larroquette starred on *The JOHN LARROQUETTE SHOW,* which, although it remained on the air for three years, was not the success he had hoped it would be. In 1999, Larroquette appeared in a second less than successful series, *Payne,* but he also had roles in the film *Isn't She Great* (2000), and the TV miniseries *The 10th Kingdom* (2000).

LARRY KING LIVE (AKA *THE LARRY KING SHOW*)

Mar 1983–July 1983	Syndicated	Various times and stations
1985–1993	CNN	Mon.–Fri. Various times
1993–present	CNN	Mon.–Sat. Various times

The popular star of a Washington D.C.–based radio show, Larry King took his successful interview/call-in show to television in 1985. One of cable TV's best-known programs, *Larry King Live* attracted a large audience as King interviewed some of the most successful and controversial people in the United States and the world. During national elections, many Democratic and Republican party candidates, as well as several third-party candidates, appeared on King's show. Millionaire Ross Perot, who ran for the presidency as a third-party candidate, announced on King's show that he was going to run for the nation's highest office. Such celebrities as President Bill Clinton, singer/actress Barbra Streisand, mogul Ted Turner, PLO leader Yasir Arafat, and late-night talk show host David Letterman are among the many who have appeared on King's show.

LARRY SANDERS SHOW, THE

Aug. 1992–present	Syndicated	Various times and stations

Garry Shandling's second parody of late-night talk shows was a spoof called *The Larry Sanders Show,* on which Shandling played a fictitious TV host named Larry Sanders. Created by Garry Shandling and Dennis Klein, the show featured Jeffrey Tambor as Hank Kingsley, Sanders's sidekick; Rip Torn as Artie, the show's pompous producer; Megan Gallagher as Sanders's wife, Jeannie; Janeane Garofalo as Paula, the show's talent booker; Linda Doucett as Beverly, Larry's assistant; Jeremy Piven and Wallace Langham as writers for the show; Kathryn Harrold as Shandling's ex-wife, Francine; and Scott Thompson as Brian, Hank's gay assistant. *The Larry Sanders Show* featured such celebrated guest stars as Roseanne, Sharon Stone, and Peter Falk. The behind-the-scenes segments of the show became well known for the use of salty language.

LASSIE

Sept. 1954–June 1955	CBS	Sun. 7–7:30 P.M.
Sept. 1955–Sept. 1971	CBS	Sun. 7–7:30 P.M.

This long-running children's adventure series, which was on the air for a continuous 17 years, was based on the popular book and film *Lassie Come Home* by Eric Knight, about a boy and his loyal, courageous collie dog, Lassie. When the series first went on the air, Lassie's owner was a young boy named Jeff Miller, played by Tommy Rettig. Jeff lived on a farm outside a town called Calverton with his widowed mother, Ellen, played by Jan Clayton, and his grandfather, played by George Cleveland. After many adventures with Jeff, a runaway orphan boy named Timmy, played by Jon Provost, was taken in by the Miller family and became Lassie's new friend. In fall 1957, Grandpa Miller died (actor George Cleveland had also died), so Ellen and Jeff sold the farm to the Martin family, Ruth and Paul, played by Cloris LEACHMAN and then by June Lockhart, and Hugh Reilley, who adopted Timmy, since they were childless. In 1964, the Martins sold the farm, and Lassie was left in the care of Cully Wilson, played by Andy Clyde, an elderly man with a good heart. Lassie soon found herself with a new master, a ranger named Corey Stuart, played by Robert Bray. As the years went on, Lassie remained but cast members changed, and her costars for the next several years included Jed Allen, Jack De Mave, Ron Hayes, Skip Burton, Joshua Albee, Larry WILCOX, Larry Pennell, Pamelyn Ferdin, and Sherry Boucher. By September 1971, Lassie had swum her final lap, chased her last villain, saved her final master, and overcome her last hardship, and the dog many viewers wished they owned retired from first-run television, to be seen on reruns for the next 30 years and beyond.

LATE NIGHT WITH DAVID LETTERMAN

Feb. 1982–May 1987 12:30–1:30 A.M.	NBC	Mon.–Thurs.
June 1987–Aug. 1991 12:30–1:30 A.M.	NBC	Mon.–Fri.
Sept. 1991–Sept. 1993 12:35–1:35 A.M.	NBC	Mon.–Fri.

In the time slot following NBC's popular *TONIGHT SHOW*, which starred Johnny CARSON, there was another talk show, *Late Night with David Letterman*, which featured a format similar to *The Tonight Show*, but had a host who was nothing like Carson, David LETTERMAN. With his orchestra leader, Paul Shaffer, as his foil, Letterman's casual and somewhat smug approach to talk show hosting, his midwestern sense of humor, his seemingly meaningless banter with Shaffer and his guests, Letterman offered a new look for late night talk shows. Letterman's "Stupid Pet Tricks," "Small Town News" (reports he read aloud that had appeared in small-town newspapers around the country), "Brush with Greatness," and "Nightcap Theater" segments on the show became much-anticipated nightly events

to loyal fans of the show. Letterman was especially adept at poking fun at show business happenings and celebrities, and he didn't spare famous guests from good-natured ribbing. Larry "Bud" Melman, a short fat man who wore thick glasses, was a regular on the show and performed various chores for Letterman, such as handing out hot towels to passengers at the Port Authority Bus Terminal as their buses arrived and passing out fliers in front of the Soviet Embassy, urging people entering and leaving the embassy to defect. Frequent guest stars were Pee Wee HERMAN, Sandra Bernhard, Jay LENO, Richard Lewis, Rita Rudner, Elayne Boosler, Brother Theodore, Carol Leifer, George Muller, the show's writers Chris Eliot, whom Letterman called "the guy under the seats," and "the fugitive," and Gerard Mulligan, Larry Jacobson, and Steve O'Donnell. In 1992, Letterman was passed over to host *The Tonight Show*, when Johnny Carson decided to retire. Jay Leno took over as Carson's replacement. One year later, Letterman left NBC to host *The LATE SHOW WITH DAVID LETTERMAN* at CBS, in a time slot opposite Leno's *Tonight Show*.

LATE SHOW WITH DAVID LETTERMAN, THE

Aug. 1993–present	CBS	Mon.–Fri. 11:35 P.M.–12:35 A.M.

When David LETTERMAN became the host of *LATE NIGHT WITH DAVID LETTERMAN*, opposite NBC's *TONIGHT SHOW*, hosted by Jay LENO, he became the first real threat to the popularity of that show. Letterman's laid-back approach to talk show hosting attracted increasingly large audiences, and the highest ratings in that time period has seesawed back and forth between the two shows ever since Letterman's show made its debut in 1993. Paul Shaffer, the orchestra leader from *Late Night with David Letterman* on NBC, was also featured on Letterman's new show. Also seen regularly were Calvert DeForrest and, from 1994 until 1996, Leonard Tepper. Telecast from the famous CBS Ed Sullivan Theater in midtown Manhattan, *The Late Show with David Letterman* became known for frequent forays onto the streets of New York, where David, who usually remained in the studio, chatted with customers at cafes and delicatessens on a "Meet Our Neighbors" segment, which made celebrities of such unlikely people as store clerks Sirajul and Mujibar Rahman, and deli owner Rupert Lee, as well as Letterman's mother, Dorothy, who covered the Winter Olympics in Lillehammer, Norway, for the show. When the show premiered, only one station failed to carry it. That was in Sioux City, Iowa, which became known as the "home office" of the show's popular "Late Show Top Ten List." Other segments on the show, in addition to the numerous celebrity guest stars and people in the news, included "David Talks to Kids," "Stupid Human Tricks," and "The CBS Mail Bag."

LAUGH-IN

(see *Rowan and Martin's Laugh-In*)

LAVERNE & SHIRLEY

Jan. 1976–July 1979	ABC	Tues. 8:30–9 P.M.
Aug. 1979–Dec. 1979	ABC	Thurs. 8–8:30 P.M.
Dec. 1979–Feb. 1980	ABC	Mon. 8–8:30 P.M.
Feb. 1980–May 1983	ABC	Tues. 8:30–9 P.M.

Laverne De Fazio and Shirley Feeney, played by Penny MARSHALL and Cindy WILLIAMS, were two young women living in Milwaukee, Wisconsin, who were life-long friends working on an assembly line in the Shotz Brewery in the *Laverne & Shirley* situation comedy. Laverne was rash and defensive, and Shirley was naive and trusting. Before they became the major attractions on the show, the girls had been introduced to TV viewers on the popular HAPPY DAYS series, which like *Laverne & Shirley,* was set in the 1950s. For the 1978–79 season, the girls and the show moved into the 1960s. Also seen as regulars on the show were Lenny Kosnowski and Andrew "Squiggy" Squiggman, two oddball truck driver/neighbors of Laverne & Shirley, played by Michael McKean and David L. Lander. Other characters featured on the series were the amorous Carmine Raguzo, called "the big Ragu," played by Eddie Mekka; Laverne's father, Frank, who owned "The Pizza Bowl" restaurant, played by Phil Foster; Laverne & Shirley's landlady and later, Laverne's stepmother, Mrs. Edna Babish De Fazio, played by Betty Garrett; Rosie Greenbaum, played by Carole Ita White; Sonny St. Jacques, played by Ed Marinaro; and Rhonda Lee, played by Leslie Easterbrook. During the series' seven and a half years on the air, 178 episodes were filmed.

LAVIN, LINDA (1937–)

Linda Lavin, who is perhaps best known for playing Alice on television, first became interested in acting when she was in school in Portland, Maine, where she was born. Lavin first worked on the stage, appearing in regional theater productions and in off-Broadway and Broadway plays before becoming a semiregular on the popular BARNEY MILLER TV show, playing Detective Janice Wentworth in 1975. The following year she was given her own series, ALICE, which was based on the hit movie *Alice Doesn't Live Here Anymore.* The series was a success, and Linda remained on the show for the next six years. Roles in such TV films as *Another Woman's Child* (1983), *Lena: My 100 Children* (1987), *I Want to Go Home* 1989), *Stolen Memories: Secrets from the Rose Garden* (1995), and *For the Children: The Irvine Fertility Scandal* (1996), among others, followed. Lavin also appeared as a regular on the TV series *Room for Two* (1992) and *Conrad Bloom* (1998), which were less than successful. Lavin has made guest appearances on such TV series as The MUPPET SHOW, The MARY TYLER MOORE SHOW, and TOUCHED BY AN ANGEL. In addition to her acting assignments, Lavin has also been a successful producer, with the TV films *Another Woman's Child* (1983), *A Place to Call Home* (1987), *The Sunset Gang* (1991), and *Stolen Memories: Secrets from the Rose* Garden (1995).

LAW & ORDER

Sept. 1990–Oct. 1990	NBC	Thurs. 10–11 P.M.
Oct. 1990–Apr. 1991	NBC	Tues. 10–11 P.M.
June 1991–Jan. 1992	NBC	Tues. 10–11 P.M.
Jan. 1992–June 1992	NBC	Tues. 9–10 P.M.
June 1992–July 1992	NBC	Fri. 10–11 P.M.
Aug. 1992–Feb. 1997	NBC	Wed. 10–11 P.M.
Mar. 1997	NBC	Thurs. 10–11 P.M.
Apr. 1997–June 1998	NBC	Wed. 10–11 P.M.
June 1998–July 1998	NBC	Sun. 10–11 P.M.
Mar. 1999–Apr. 1999	NBC	Mon. 9–10 P.M.
July 1999–	NBC	Mon. 9–10 P.M.

Set in New York City, this popular police/legal drama series features two different segments. The first half of the show features the police investigation of a crime, and the second half concentrates on the court battle that ensues after the criminals are arrested. Actual high-profile cases, taken directly from the news, are used as the basis for the stories on this series, although they are fictionalized and never use the names of real people. The first part of the program often employs handheld cameras, giving the show an immediate, news-reporting appearance, which was supported by the location shooting on the streets of New York City. When the series made its debut, New York City Police Det. Mike Logan and Det. Sergeant Max Greevey, played by Christopher Noth and George Dzundza, were in charge of the police investigations. They reported to Capt. Donald Cragen, played by Dann Florek. In 1991, Greevey was replaced by Det. Phil Carreta, played by Paul Sorvino, and in 1992, Carreta was replaced by Det. Lennie Briscoe, played by Jerry Orbach. Logan disappeared from the series in 1995 and was replaced by Det. Reynaldo "Rey" Curtis, played by Benjamin Bratt. In 1993, Capt. Greegan's replacement was Lt. Anita Van Buren, played by S. Epatha Merkerson. On the legal half of the series, Assistant District Attorney Ben Stone, played by Michael Moriarty, was in charge of the cases that resulted from an arrest. Stone was assisted by Asst. D.A. Paul Robinette, played by Richard Brooks, from 1990 until 1993. From 1991 until 1994, Carolyn McCormick appeared as Dr. Elizabeth Olivet, who gave medical advice to the lawyers. In 1994, Sam Waterston, as Asst. D.A. Jack McCoy, replaced Stone. He was assisted by Asst. D.A. Claire Kincaid, played by Jill Hennessy until 1996, and Asst. D.A. Jamie Ross, played by Carey Lowell, and then by Asst. D.A. Abbie Carmichael, played by Angie Harmon. The district attorney, Adam Schiff, was always played by Steven Hill. Controversy ensued when Michael Moriarty left the series. The show's producer, Dick Wolf, had locked horns with Moriarty when the actor complained about what he felt was "government's interference with free speech," when politicians became critical of the violence seen on TV, and on *Law & Order* in particular. Dick Wolf had bowed to government pressure and softened the show's scripts somewhat, and Moriarty quit the series in protest, which led to hundreds of letters of complaint.

As of 2002, actors Jerry Orbach, Jesse L. Martin, and S. Epatha Merkerson were still representing the New York City Police Department on the series, and Sam Waterston, Elizabeth Rohm, and Dianne Weist, the city's legal department. In 1999, a spinoff series called *Law & Order: Special Victims Unit* aired to an enthusiastic audience. The new series, which runs concurrently with *Law & Order*, delves into the darker side of the criminal world in New York City and centers around detectives in a new elite force, the Special Victims Unit. The detectives investigate and prosecute various sex crimes while trying to balance their work and private lives. Featured on *Law & Order: Special Victims Unit* are Christopher Meloni as Det. Elliot Stabler, Mariska Hargitay as Det. Olivia Benson, Richard Belzer as Det. John Munch, Dann Florek as Capt. Donald Cragen, Stephanie March as Assistant District Attorney Alexandra Cabot, Ice-T as Det. Odafin "Fin" Tutuola, and B. D. Wong as police psychiatrist George Huang. A second *Law & Order* spinoff, called *Law & Order: Criminal Intent*, appeared in 2001. This series, which ran concurrently with *Law & Order* and *Law & Order: Special Victims Unit* at different prime-time hours, depicts the criminal justice system from the criminal's point of view. The show stars Vincent D'Onofrio as Det. Robert Goren, Kathryn Erbe as Det. Alexandra Eames, Jamey Sheridan as Capt. James Deakins, and Courtney B. Vance as Assistant District Attorney Ronald Carver.

LAWMAN, THE

| Oct. 1958–Apr. 1962 | ABC | Sun. 8:30–9 P.M. |
| Apr. 1962–Oct. 1962 | ABC | Sun. 10:30–11 P.M. |

Film actor John RUSSELL played Marshal Dan Troop on this western adventure series set in the late 1800s. The series was very popular with viewers in the late 1950s and early 1960s. Troop was the chief lawman, firm but fair, in the wild western town of Laramie. The lawman had a fatherly relationship with his young deputy, Johnny McKay, played by Peter Brown. Also appearing as regulars were Bek Nelson as Dru Lemp and Dan Sheridan as Jake, who provided some of the lighter moments. For the show's second season, Peggy Castle joined the cast as Lily Merrill. Lily was the owner of the Birdcage Saloon, and the role was more than slightly reminiscent of popular saloon owner Miss Kitty, a major character on the hit series *GUNSMOKE*.

LAWRENCE, VICKI (1949–)

Vicki Lawrence, who was born in Inglewood, California, was a member of The Young Americans choral group when a journalist reviewing one of the group's concerts mentioned her strong resemblance to TV comedienne Carol BURNETT in his review. Lawrence sent the review to Burnett, who arranged for her to audition for her popular TV show. Impressed with Lawrence's singing and acting talents, Burnett hired her as a regular member of her cast in 1967. In 1972, Lawrence had a number one record on the Billboard Hot 100 pop charts, "The Night the Lights Went Out in Georgia." When *The CAROL BURNETT SHOW* left the air in 1979, Lawrence appeared on the TV series *Supertrain,* which was not a success, but in 1983, she reprised a role she had played on *The Carol Burnett Show,* and starred in a situation comedy called *MAMA'S FAMILY,* playing Thelma "Mama" Harper. The show was a network series on NBC for two years, and then it was even more successful when it became a syndicated program. In 1987, Lawrence became one of TV's few game show hostesses when she appeared on the *Win, Lose or Draw* show. Lawrence and Carol Burnett were reunited in 1991 for the short-lived second *Carol Burnett Show,* and in 1992, Lawrence starred on a TV series of her own, *Vicki,* which proved to be short-lived. Regular roles on the TV series *Fox After Breakfast* (1996), and as a regular panelist on the revived *MATCH GAME* (1998), as well as guest-starring on such TV series as *LAVERNE & SHIRLEY, ROSEANNE, All-American Girl* (1995), *BURKE'S LAW,* and *ALLY MCBEAL,* has kept Lawrence busy over the years.

LAWRENCE WELK SHOW, THE

July 1955–Sept. 1963	ABC	Sat. 9–10 P.M.
Sept. 1963–Jan. 1971	ABC	Sat. 8:30–9:30 P.M.
Jan. 1971–Sept. 1971	ABC	Sat. 7:30–8:30 P.M.
1971–1982	Syndicated	Various times and stations

Bandleader Lawrence WELK and his Champagne Music Makers, a popular dance band in the 1930s and 1940s, were first seen on television as a summer replacement in 1955. In spite of poor reviews from TV critics, the show went on to become one of TV's longest-running and most popular programs, remaining on the air for a continuous 27 years. Welk's theme music "Bubbles in the Wine," which was played as soap bubbles swirled behind the band; his polka-dancing with whomever his current "Champagne Lady" was at the time; his large cast of regular singers and dancers; and Welk himself, with his slight German accent (even though he was born in the United States) and his "a-one and a-two" down beat before each number began and "Wunnerful . . . wunnerful" when each song ended, became familiar to millions of loyal viewers over the years. The show proved to be especially popular with senior citizens, who longed to hear the popular music of their past, without having to listen to the all-too-common rock and roll beat that had begun to dominate pop music.

Cast members of the Welk show became familiar "friends" to dedicated viewers, who knew everything about their favorites, including when they were married, had children, appeared on other shows, etc. Among Welk's original cast members were his first "Champagne Lady," singer Alice Lon (who left the show in 1959); his second "Champagne Lady," Norma Zimmer (who remained with the show until it left the air in 1982); tenor Jim Roberts; accordionist Myron Floren; pianist and organist Jerry Burke; baritone and saxophone player Dick Dale; pianist and bass singer Larry Hooper; violinist Dick Kesner; singer violinist Bob Lido; pianist Tiny Little, Jr.; guitarist Buddy Merrill; gravel-voiced trumpeter Rocky Rockwell; and The Sparklers Quartet.

Other favorite regulars added to the cast as the show endured were the very popular Lennon Sisters (Dianne, Peggy, Kathy, and Janet); vocalist Larry Dean; pianist Frank Scott; vocalist Maurice Pearson; Irish tenor Joe Feeney; tap dancer Jack Immel; hymn singer Alvan Ashby; Dixieland clarinetist Pete Fountain; ragtime pianist Jo Ann Castle; violinist Jimmy Getzoff; dance team Bobby Burgess and Barbara Boylan, who was replaced by Cissy King, and then by Elaine Niverson; violinist Joe Livoti; pianist organist Bob Ralston; dancer Art Duncan; vocalist Steve Smith; vocalist Natalie Nevins; The Blenders vocal quartet; vocalist Lynn Anderson; vocalist Andra Willis; vocalist Tanya Falan Welk; vocalist Sandi Jensen; vocalist Salli Flynn; The Hotsy Totsy Boys; vocalist Clay Hart; and Ralna English Hovis, Mary Lou Metzger, Guy Hovis, Peanuts Hucko, Anacani, Tom Netherton, Ava Barber, Kathy Sullivan, Shelia and Sherry Aldridge, David and Roger Otwell, and Jim Turner. The Welk show's musical numbers became increasingly more elaborate over the years, and the program featured various "theme" shows, such as special Thanksgiving, Halloween, Christmas, and Easter programs, and shows that had barn dance, ice-skating, film, dance party, social get-together, birthday party, etc., settings. In 1971, *The Lawrence Welk Show* left network television and became a syndicated show. New shows continued to be produced for the next 11 years and attracted a sizable number of new viewers as well as keeping fans who remained faithful to the program. In later years, early shows were rereleased under the title *Memories with Lawrence Welk*, which, in addition to the previously seen staged production numbers, also featured interviews and comments by former Welk show regulars. For a time, the Public Broadcasting System also telecast old Lawrence Welk programs.

LEACHMAN, CLORIS (1926–)

Before she became known as Phyllis Lindstrom on *The MARY TYLER MOORE SHOW*, and then in the *PHYLLIS* series, Cloris Leachman had regular roles on the TV series *Bob and Ray* (1951) and *LASSIE* (1957–8), and appeared as a guest star on such TV series as *Actor's Studio* (1949), *Danger* (1952), *The PHILCO TELEVISION PLAYHOUSE* (1950, 1954), *ALFRED HITCHCOCK PRESENTS* (1955), *The ZANE GREY THEATER* (1956), *GUNSMOKE* (1956, 1961),

Alcoa Presents (1959), *Westinghouse Desilu Playhouse* (1960), *THRILLER* (1960), *The TWILIGHT ZONE* (1961), *The UNTOUCHABLES* (1962), *ROUTE 66* (1962), *WAGON TRAIN* (1962), *PERRY MASON* (1966), *BIG VALLEY* (1967), *MARCUS WELBY, M.D.* (1970), and many other shows. Before Leachman played Phyllis, she appeared in such films as *Kiss Me Deadly* (1955), *The Chapman Report* (1962), *Lovers and Other Strangers* (1970), and *The Last Picture Show* (1971), for which she won a Best Supporting Actress Academy Award.

Leachman, who was born in Des Moines, Iowa, attended Northwestern University, where she became interested in acting. In 1946, Cloris won the Miss Chicago beauty contest, and was encouraged to go to New York to try to break into show business. After appearing on the stage in New York and in plays at various regional theaters throughout the United States, Leachman went to Hollywood, where she soon became a busy supporting actress in films and on TV. After her success as Phyllis Lindstrom on *The Mary Tyler Moore Show*, Leachman was kept constantly busy, appearing in films such as *Dillinger* (1973), *Young Frankenstein* (1974), *Daisy Miller* (1974), *Crazy Mama* (1973), *High Anxiety* (1977), *The Muppet Movie* (1979), *The Beverly Hillbillies* (1993), *Never Too Late* (1997), and *Hanging Up* (2000), among others, and was a regular on such TV series as *FACTS OF LIFE* (1986–88), *The Nutt House* (1989), and *Thanks* (1999). Leachman has also made guest appearances on such shows as *The NANNY*, *TOUCHED BY AN ANGEL*, and *Norm* in recent years.

LEAR, NORMAN (MILTON LEAR 1922–)

TV producer Norman Lear was born in New Haven, Connecticut. After attending Emerson College in Boston for one year, Lear got a job as a writer for the *The Ford Star Revue* in 1950. In 1959, Lear formed Tandem Productions with Bud Yorkin and produced a number of films and TV shows. His impressive list of television shows included *The ANDY WILLIAMS SHOW*, *ALL IN THE FAMILY*, *SANFORD AND SON*, *MAUDE*, *GOOD TIMES*, *ONE DAY AT A TIME*, and *The JEFFERSONS*, and a few less than successful series such as *HOT L BALTIMORE*, *The Nancy Walker Show* (1976), *Forever Fernwood* (1977), *All That Glitters* (1977), *A Year at the Top* (1977), *The Baxters* (1979–1981), *Hanging In* (1979), a.k.a. *Pablo* (1984), *Sunday Dinner* (1991), *The Powers That Be* (1992), *704 Hauser* (1994) and *Channel Umptee-3* (1997). Lear also produced several successful major motion pictures, including *Come Blow Your Horn* (1963), *Never Too Late* (1965), *Divorce American Style* (1967), *The Night They Raided Minsky's* (1968), *Start the Revolution Without Me* (1970), *Cold Turkey* (1971), *Fried Green Tomatoes* (1991), and *Way Past Cool* (2000). One of Lear's most controversial and innovative TV projects was a quirky evening soap opera series called *MARY HARTMAN, MARY HARTMAN*. A dedicated political liberal, Lear founded People for the American Way in 1981.

LEAVE IT TO BEAVER

Oct. 1957–Mar. 1958	CBS	Fri. 7:30–8 P.M.
Mar. 1958–Sept. 1958	CBS	Wed. 8–8:30 P.M.
Oct. 1958–June 1959	ABC	Thurs. 7:30–8 P.M.
July 1959–Sept. 1959	ABC	Thurs. 9–9:30 P.M.
Oct. 1959–Sept. 1962	ABC	Sat. 8:30–9 P.M.
Sept. 1962–Sept. 1963	ABC	Thurs. 8:30–9 P.M.

A true classic among early television situation comedies, *Leave it to Beaver* was a family-oriented program that focused on the life of a boy named Theodore "Beaver" Cleaver, played by Jerry MATHERS, and was told through his eyes. When the series began, Beaver was seven years old, and by the time the last episode of the series was seen, he was 13. His older brother, Wally, played by Tony DOW, was 12 when the series began and 18 when it ended its run. The Beaver and Wally's parents, June and Ward Cleaver, were played by Barbara Billingsley and Hugh Beaumont. The Cleavers lived in Mayfield in a typically middle-class suburban home. Ward Cleaver was an accountant and an understanding, patient father. June Cleaver was a stay-at-home mom, also understanding and patient. Wally was an athletic, all-American boy, and the Beaver was a boy who always seemed to get into trouble even though he was usually trying to do the right thing. Other regular characters on the show were Wally's shifty friend, Eddie Haskell, played by Ken Osmond, whose overly charming and friendly demeanor when he was in the company of Mr. and Mrs. Cleaver, and especially the Beaver, belied his contempt for them. Frank Bank played Wally's chubby friend, Clarence "Lumpy" Rutherford; Richard Deacon played Lumpy's father, Fred Rutherford, who was also Ward Cleaver's boss; Diane Brewster was the Beaver's second grade teacher at the Grant Avenue Elementary School, Miss Canfield; Sue Randall was the Beaver's third grade teacher, Miss Landers; Doris Packer was the Grant Avenue School's principal, Mrs. Cornelia Rayburn; Rusty Stevens was the Beaver's friend, Larry Mondello; Madge Blake was Mrs. Mondello; and Burt Mustin was Gus, the old man at the fire station. Over the years, other characters appeared on the series, including Beaver's friends: Whitey Whitney, played by Stanley Fafara; Gilbert Bates, played by Stephen Talbot; Richard Rickover, played by Richard Correll; Tooey, played by Tiger Fafara; Chester, played by Buddy Hart; and the Beaver's enemy at school, Judi Hensler, played by Jeri Weil. Wally's high school sweetheart, Mary Ellen Rogers, was played by Pamela Beaird.

Leave It to Beaver was created by, written by, and produced by Joe Connelly and Bob Mosher. In 1983, the cast (except for Hugh Beaumont who had died a year earlier) were reunited in a TV movie, *Still the Beaver*, which proved very popular.

The cast of *Leave it to Beaver:* (clockwise from top) Tony Dow (Wally Cleaver), Hugh Beaumont (Ward Cleaver), Jerry Mathers (Theodore "The Beaver" Cleaver), and Barbara Billingsley (June Cleaver) (Author's collection)

LEE, PINKY (PINCUS LEFF 1907–1993)

A comedian and TV child show host, Pinky Lee was born in St. Paul, Minnesota, and went on the stage when he was a very young boy. Considering that his earliest years as a performer were spent in vaudeville and burlesque, it is surprising that Pinky's greatest fame came from hosting a popular children's TV series, *The PINKY LEE SHOW*, first in 1950, again in 1954, and then as the emcee of the popular *GUMBY* show in 1957. In 1943, Lee made his film debut in *Lady of Burlesque*, a mystery that starred Barbara STANWYCK, and was based on Gypsy Rose Lee's bestselling book *The G String Murders*. He subsequently appeared in the films *Earl Carroll Vanities* (1945), *Blonde Ransom* (1945), *One Exciting Week* (1946), and *That's My Gal* (1947), before becoming one of the first entertainers to make a foray into television, which had just begun to capture the public's attention in 1950. In addition to his two *Pinky Lee* shows and *Gumby*, Lee also appeared on the situation comedy series *Those Two* in 1951 as well as in the films *South of Caliente* (1951), *Pals of the Golden West* (1951), and *Hawaiian Nights* (1953). Except for rare appearances as a guest on TV talk and panel shows, Lee all but disappeared from the spotlight in the late 1950s, but he did resurface in an uncredited appearance in the film *Ocean's Eleven*, in 1960. For the next 33 years, Pinky Lee was not seen on TV, films, or on the stage. The comedian died in 1993 at the age of 86, remembered only by the many now-grown children he had entertained on television.

LENO, JAY (JAMES DOUGLAS MUIR LENO 1950–)

Before he took over Johnny CARSON's hosting chores on NBC's *TONIGHT SHOW* in 1992, comedian Jay Leno was one of the busiest stand-up comics in the United States and usually made more than 300 appearances at comedy clubs and on TV in a single year. Leno had also been a regular on television as early as 1977, when he appeared on *The Marilyn McCoo and Billy Davis, Jr. Show.* He played supporting roles on such TV series as *GOOD TIMES* in 1976, *ALICE*, in 1981, and *LAVERNE & SHIRLEY* in 1979 and 1983. Jay Leno, whose father was an insurance salesman and his mother a housewife, was born in New Rochelle, New York, but was raised in Andover, Massachusetts. When Leno was in the fifth grade, his teacher wrote on his report card, "If Jay spent as much time studying as he does trying to be a comedian, he'd be a big star," which turned out to be prophetic. After attending Emerson College in Boston, where he majored in speech therapy, Leno began to perform stand-up comedy in local nightclubs and eventually became a warm-up act for the Johnny Mathis and Tom Jones concert tours. In 1996, Leno won an Emmy Award for his hosting of the *Tonight Show.* Since becoming the permanent *Tonight Show* host, Leno has made guest-starring appearances on such TV series as *FRASIER, The FRESH PRINCE OF BEL AIR, HOME IMPROVEMENT, MAD ABOUT YOU, JAG, HOMICIDE: Life on the Streets, WINGS, SEINFELD, The NANNY, ELLEN, 3RD ROCK FROM THE SUN, BAYWATCH, CAROLINE IN THE CITY, The Muppets Tonight,* and *The West Wing.* He has also used his voice in the cartoon series *SOUTH PARK* and *The SIMPSONS,* and played himself in such films as *Wayne's World 2* (1993), *Major League II* (1994), *The Flintstones* (1994), *The Birdcage* (1996), *Contact* (1997), *Wag the Dog* (1997), *EdTV* (1999), and *The House of COC* (1999). In 1993, Leno's contract with *The Tonight Show* was extended for five years at $440 million dollars. In 1998, he signed a contract to continue to appear on *The Tonight Show* for $100 million for five additional years.

LESTER, JERRY (1910–1995)

One of television's earliest stars, Jerry Lester had a show on the air in 1951 that was the forerunner of all the late-night talk/variety shows that followed, *BROADWAY OPEN HOUSE.* The show, which featured Lester's stand-up comedy routines, as well as skits, variety acts, and a little bit of chatter, became extremely popular with late-night viewers for the short time it was on the air. Lester, who was born in Chicago, began his career in vaudeville, but until he entered television, he met with only moderate success as a performer. In 1933, Lester had appeared in the film *Arizona to Broadway,* but his film career failed to take off, and except for an appearance in the film *Sleepytime Gal* in 1942, he mainly performed his stand-up comedy act in nightclubs. In spite of his success on *Broadway Open House,* Lester, who had a dispute with the show's producers, left the series. He subsequently appeared as a panelist on *The NAME'S THE SAME* in 1951, but after that, was rarely seen on television, except for an appearance on *The MONKEES* TV series in 1967. He did, however, appear in the films *The Rookie* (1959), *The Godmothers* (1973), and *Smokey and the Bandit II* (1980). His last major film appearance was in *Hardly Working* in 1980.

LET'S MAKE A DEAL

Prime time:

May 1967–Sept. 1967	NBC	Sun. 8:30–9 P.M.
Feb. 1969–May 1969	ABC	Fri. 9–9:30 P.M.
May 1969–Jan. 1970	ABC	Fri. 7:30–8 P.M.
Jan. 1970–Jan. 1971	ABC	Sat. 7:30–8 P.M.
Jan. 1971–Aug. 1971	ABC	Mon. 7:30–8 P.M.

Daytime:

Dec. 1963–Dec. 1968	NBC	Various daytime hours
Dec. 1968–July 1976	ABC	Various daytime hours
1971–1976	Syndicated	Various daytime hours
1980	Syndicated	Various daytime hours
1984–1985	Syndicated	Various daytime hours

The long-running, popular game show *Let's Make a Deal* required no skill, knowledge, or special abilities for contestants to win wonderful prizes that included automobiles, major household appliances, vacations, and cash, or occasionally such unwelcome gifts as a pig in a pen, or a wheelbarrow full of fertilizer, if they were unlucky. Before each show, 39 members of the studio audience, who usually wore attention-getting costumes and outfits in order to get noticed by the show's host, Monty Hall, were chosen and asked if they had something to trade for a prize or cash. At the end of each show, contestants who had won the greatest amount of money (prize values were totaled) were asked to pick one of three doors and trade whatever they had already won for a "Big Deal" of the day, which was worth at least $10,000.

Host Monty Hall developed and produced the show with his partner, Stefan Hatos. Courteous and pleasant, even to aggressive contestants who were sometimes positively obnoxious, Hall was always a perfect host and gentleman. Assisting Hall was announcer Jay Stewart and model Carol Merrill. Almost 4,000 *Let's Make a Deal* shows were produced during the series' network years alone. In 1990, *Let's Make a Deal* resurfaced as a daytime show produced by the Disney/MGM Studios with Bob Hilton acting as host.

LETTERMAN, DAVID (DAVID MICHAEL LETTERMAN 1947–)

Late-night TV talk show host David Letterman was born in Indianapolis, Indiana, and attended Broad Ripple High

David Letterman (Author's collection)

School, where he was voted "Class Smart Alec," which certainly defined his later-to-be-famous TV personality. Known for his gap-toothed, mischievous grin, his offbeat humor, and satiric edge and smugness, Letterman majored in broadcasting at Ball State University, from which he graduated with a B.A. degree in broadcasting in the 1960s. After working as a radio announcer, a TV weatherman, and a local talk show host, Letterman became a TV game show panelist on *The GONG SHOW* in 1976. He subsequently appeared on the TV series *The Starland Vocal Band Show* in 1977, *Mary* in 1978, and *Fast Friends* in 1979, before becoming the host of a daytime talk show mainly directed toward women, *The DAVID LETTERMAN SHOW* in 1980. This led to his late, late-night talk show, *LATE NIGHT WITH DAVID LETTERMAN*, in 1982. When Johnny CARSON retired from *The TONIGHT SHOW* in 1993, everyone assumed that Letterman would be his replacement. When NBC announced that Jay LENO was to be Carson's replacement, Letterman left NBC and became the host of *The LATE SHOW WITH DAVID LETTERMAN*, opposite *The Tonight Show*. In addition to his talk show hosting, Letterman has also produced such TV shows as *The Building* (1993), *The Bonnie Hunt Show* (1995), *The High Life* (1996), and the very popular *EVERYBODY LOVES RAYMOND* (1996), in addition to producing his own shows.

LEVENSON, SAM (1911–1980)

Humorist Sam Levenson, who was born in New York City, was a schoolteacher before he became a popular TV game show panelist. One of TV's earliest familiar faces, Levenson was first seen on a show called *This Is Show Business,* which was on the air from 1949 until 1956. Moderated by Clifton Fadiman, *This Is Show Business* featured guest performers who displayed their talent and talked about problems they were having in show business. In addition to panelist Levenson and host Fadiman, the show also featured playwright and wit George S. Kaufman as a regular panelist. On December 21, 1952, Levenson became involved in a controversial program on which the always acerbic Kaufman, who was talking about the overcommercialization of Christmas, remarked, "Let's make this one program on which no one sings 'Silent Night.'" In spite of Levenson's attempts to excuse Kaufman's remarks, hundreds of letters were sent to CBS complaining about the playwright's anti-Christmas comments and demanding that he be fired from the program. Levenson continued to appear on the program, but Kaufman was indeed temporarily removed from the show. In addition to *This Is Show Business,* Levenson had a show of his own, *The Sam Levenson Show,* during the 1950–51 television season. In addition, he was also a frequent guest panelist on the popular *WHAT'S MY LINE* program, and was a regular panelist on *MASQUERADE PARTY* show from 1958 to 1960. By the 1970s, Levenson had, for all intent and purposes, abandoned TV as a performer, but he continued to remain active as a writer and TV columnist, making infrequent guest appearances on game and panel shows until shortly before his death in 1980.

LEWIS, JERRY (JOSEPH LEVITCH 1926–)

Zany comedian Jerry Lewis, who was born and raised in Newark, New Jersey, claims that he was thrown out of school for punching the principal of his high school when he heard him make anti-Semitic comments. Not a very good student, Lewis who had been dubbed "the class comic" by fellow students, left school and, although still in his teens, he began to pursue a career as a comedian in vaudeville, performing a stand-up comedy act, and in the "Borscht Belt" hotels of New York's Catskill Mountains, where he became a particular favorite of patrons at Brown's Hotel. His career did not go very far, however, until he teamed up with an Italian-American singer named Dean MARTIN, who performed on a bill with Lewis. The two worked so well together, combining Martin's laid-back, handsome good looks and Lewis's hyperactive, almost frantic simpleton characterizations. They were soon booked into some of the more celebrated hotels and nightclubs in New York City, and eventually attracted the attention of Hollywood talent scouts, who thought they would be perfect in films. In 1949, Martin and Lewis made their screen debuts in the film *My Friend Irma,* which was a hit. They followed that with appearances in the films *My Friend Irma Goes West* (1950) and *At War with the Army* (1950). Martin and Lewis became the stars of the television comedy/variety show *The COLGATE COMEDY HOUR* in 1950, rotating with Fred Allen and Eddie Cantor as the show's stars. They remained with the series until 1955. While appearing on *The Colgate Comedy Hour,* the team also starred in such films as *Sailor Beware* (1951), *That's My Boy* (1951), *Jumping Jacks* (1951), *The Stooge* (1953), *Scared Stiff* (1953), *The Caddy* (1953), and *Artists and Models* (1955), to name just a few, and their popularity continued to increase.

In 1956, Martin and Lewis, who were by then the world's most successful comedy team, decided to end their partnership and go their separate ways. On his own, Lewis became the number one comedian in films in 1957, 1959, and from 1961 through 1967. He starred in such films as *The Sad Sack* (1957), *Cinderfella* (1960), *The Errand Boy* (1961), and *The Nutty Professor* (1963). In 1963, Lewis became the star of the weekly television series *The Jerry Lewis Show,* which proved to be less successful than his films. He continued to star in films and became extremely popular with French moviegoers, earning the nickname "Le Roi du Crazy" (the King of Crazy) in France and eventually earning the French Legion of Honor in 1984 for his work in films. Success on television once again evaded him in 1967, when he starred on a second *Jerry Lewis Show,* which also failed to attract an audience. Lewis was, however, by that time a successful film director, as well as a film star. His film comedies include *The Bellboy* (1960), *The Nutty Professor* (1963), and many others.

Lewis's annual telecasts on which he solicited pledges of money to fight muscular dystrophy made him one of the best-known fundraisers in the world, and he was nominated for a Nobel Prize for his work on behalf of MDA. In addition to roles in such films as *The King of Comedy* in 1983, Lewis continued to guest-star on such TV series as *BATMAN, The SONNY AND CHER COMEDY HOUR, MAD ABOUT YOU, The Martin Short Show,* and many other shows. He also had a regular role on the *WISEGUY* series in 1988–89. Lewis continues to remain active as a film actor, director, and producer, and in 1995, he became the highest-paid performer on Broadway when he played the Devil in a revival of the musical comedy *Damn Yankees.*

LEWIS, ROBERT Q. (ROBERT GOLDBERG 1920–1991)
In the 1950s and early 1960s, television personality Robert Q. Lewis was one of America's most familiar faces, and many people believed that he would become a star to rival such successful TV personalities as Arthur GODFREY, Ed SULLIVAN, and Steve ALLEN. Robert Q. Lewis, who was born in New York City, was, before he became a TV celebrity, a radio announcer and show host. In 1950, Lewis appeared on TV shows of his own, *The ROBERT Q. LEWIS SHOW* (1950–51 and 1954–56), and subsequently became the host of such popular early TV game shows as *The NAME'S THE SAME, MASQUERADE PARTY, Play Your Hunch* (1962–63), *Make Me Laugh*

(1958), and *Got the Message* (1964). By the 1960s, Lewis's popularity had begun to diminish, but he did appear as a supporting player in such films as *Good Neighbor Sam* (1964), *Ski Party* (1965), *How to Succeed in Business Without Really Trying* (1967), and in 1986, *Mr. Chauffeur,* playing the role of an unnamed businessman. In the 1960s, at the peak of his popularity, Lewis had guest-starred on such series as *BEWITCHED* and *Branded* (1965). Known to be a heavy smoker, Lewis died of emphysema in 1991, forgotten by the industry he had pioneered.

LEWIS, SHARI (SHARI HURWITZ 1933–1998)
Puppeteer/ventriloquist Shari Lewis, whose best-known hand puppets were Lamb Chop, Charley Horse, and Hush Puppy, was born in New York City. Shari, who wanted to be a performer from the time she was a small child, began her career as an actress in 1953, and appeared on *The UNITED STATES STEEL HOUR.* After developing Lamb Chop and perfecting her skills as ventriloquist, Shari was soon booked on such talent/variety shows as *The ED SULLIVAN SHOW* and *SHOWER OF STARS,* and in 1960, she became the star of a children's TV series of her own called *The Shari Lewis Show.* After guest-starring on such TV series as *Car 54, Where Are You?* and in 1968 appearing on *The Banana Splits Adventure Hour,* providing the voice for the Princess Nidor character, Shari once again had another regular TV series called *The Shari Show* in 1975. Shari continued to appear on numerous shows throughout the 1980s, and returned to TV as the star of *Lamb Chop's Play-Along* (1992) and *The Charley Horse Music Pizza* 1998), and became a familiar face on the PBS network, before dying of cancer at the age of 65.

LIBERACE (WLADZIU VALENTINO LIBERANCE 1919–1987)
Legendary entertainer/pianist Liberace was born into a musically talented family in West Allis, Wisconsin. Liberace's father was a French horn player for the Milwaukee Symphony for many years, and he encouraged his son's musical talents on the piano, an instrument his mother and sister also played. When he was four years old, Liberace could play any tune he heard, by ear, and he made his debut as a professional pianist when he was 14 years old. In high school, "Lee," as he was nicknamed, played piano in a musical combo group called The Mixers. As a teenager, Liberace began playing piano in the nightclub circuit, using the name Walter Busterkeys, but it was on television in the early 1950s that Liberace first attracted the attention of the general public. In 1950, he was featured on a late-night, and then an early evening program. His tuxedo, ever-present candelabra on his piano, and his romantic, almost simpering manner of speaking, became familiar to early television viewers, and he soon became one of the most talked-about and publicized entertainers on early TV. In 1955, Liberace made his first appearance as a film star in *Sincerely Yours,* which was not particu-

Liberace (Author's collection)

Nakuma, played by Don Shanks, Grizzly Adams built a log cabin and lived in perfect harmony with nature. A bear cub Adams had found abandoned and named "Ben" grew up to become his closest companion and even shared the cabin with Adams.

Grizzly Adams had numerous adventures battling nature and various intruding strangers who passed through the wilderness where Adams lived. A frequent visitor to Adams's cabin was the young son of a neighboring farmer, Robbie Cartman, played by John Bishop. Robbie enjoyed listening to Grizzly Adams's tales about life in the wilderness. Based on a film that also starred Dan Haggerty, *The Life and Times of Grizzly Adams* took full advantage of the fact that Haggerty had been an animal trainer before he became an actor, and his scenes with his costar, Ben the Bear, reflected the unusual rapport that can exist between a human and an animal of the wilderness.

There actually was a mountain man named Grizzly Adams, who although born in Massachusetts, spent most of his life in the undeveloped Sierra Nevada Mountains. The real Grizzly Adams had toured with P. T. Barnum's traveling side show. Charles E. Sellier, Jr., was the executive producer of the TV series.

LIFE GOES ON

Sept. 1989	ABC	Tues. 10–11 P.M.
Sept. 1989	ABC	Fri. 9–10 P.M.
Sept. 1989–Mar. 1992	ABC	Sun. 7–8 P.M.
May 1993–Aug. 1993	ABC	Sun. 7–8 P.M.

This family-oriented, weekly dramatic series was a groundbreaking TV program that was the first series centered on a character with Down syndrome. Young teenager Charles "Corky" Thatcher, was played by Christopher Burke, who was fortunate in that he had a loving and supportive family that consisted of his mother and father, Drew and Libby Thatcher, played by Bill Smitrovich and Patti Lupone (a musical comedy actress who was the star of *Evita* on Broadway before becoming one of the stars of *Life Goes On*), and two sisters, Rebecca "Becca" Thatcher, played by Kellie Martin, and Paige Thatcher, played by Monique Lanier, and then by Tracey Needham. Corky had all of the same problems so-called normal male adolescents experienced, such as problems in school, with girls, and with self-esteem. Corky's father was a former construction worker who had opened a restaurant, and his mother was a former advertising executive who at the age of 40 had given birth to her son, Corky. Corky was born with Down syndrome, and Libby always felt guilty about having a child at such an advanced age. Corky's sister was Drew's daughter from his first marriage, and Becca was torn between her sense of responsibility for her younger brother and her desire to fit in with other students in her school. In 1992, Corky fell in love with a girl named Amanda, played by Andrea Friedman, who also had Down syndrome, and the couple eloped. Becca fell in love with several less than desirable young men, and Paige, after

larly popular with filmgoers. Successful appearances as a guest star on such shows as *The ANDY WILLIAMS SHOW, BATMAN, The MONKEES, HERE'S LUCY,* and *The MUPPET SHOW,* however, added to his popularity, and by the late 1960s, Liberace, who by that time was performing mainly in live concerts and in Las Vegas, was one of the five highest-paid entertainers in show business. Liberace's elaborately produced nightclub and theater shows made him a superstar, and his beaded, brocaded, diamond- and jewel-encrusted costumes and spectacular stage effects became legendary. During his career, Liberace, who was given the title "Mr. Showmanship" by TV columnists, earned two Emmy Awards for TV specials and had five million-selling record albums.

THE LIFE AND TIMES OF GRIZZLY ADAMS, THE
Feb. 1977–July 1978   NBC   Wed. 8–9 P.M.

Although Dan Haggerty played the title character on this western adventure series set in the 19th century, *The Life and Times of Grizzly Adams,* the real star of the show was a lovable pet grizzly bear named Ben. Grizzly Adams was a man who had been accused of a crime he did not commit, and who retreated to the mountains to live in relative obscurity. With the help of his friend, Mad Jack, played by Denver Pyle, and his Native American "blood brother," many troublesome years, finally married, and eventually divorced, a young man named Michael Romanov, played by Lance Guest. The show's theme music, already familiar to many viewers, was "Ob-La-Di, Ob-La-Da," by the Beatles, which was sung by Patti Lupone and the cast as the opening credits of the show rolled. (The song's chorus includes the phrase "life goes on.")

LIFE IS WORTH LIVING

Feb. 1952–Apr. 1955	DuMont	Tues.	8–8:30 P.M.
Oct. 1955–Apr. 1956	ABC	Thurs.	8–8:30 P.M.
Oct. 1956–Apr. 1957	ABC	Mon.	9–9:30 P.M.

The star of this early prime-time television show was a bishop of the Catholic Church, Fulton J. SHEEN, who, speaking directly into the cameras, delivered weekly lessons in morality, which although like sermons, were certainly less formal. Bishop Sheen delivered his talks in a charming and well-spoken manner. The series, *Life is Worth Living*, became one of television's most popular programs in the early 1950s, and had a large audience that made it the most successful religious program in TV history. Before he became a TV celebrity, Bishop Sheen of New York had a regular show on the radio. As Bishop Sheen spoke, he often punctuated his remarks by scrawling on a blackboard to emphasize a point, and as he spoke, one of his stagehands, whom he called "angels," would wipe the blackboard clean. In the cold war days of the 1950s, many of Sheen's programs were concerned with "the evils of communism." On one of his most publicized programs in 1953, Bishop Sheen read the burial scene from Shakespeare's *Julius Caesar*, and substituted the names of Caesar, Cassius, Marc Antony, and Brutus (ancient Roman leaders) with the names Stalin, Beria, Malenkov, and Vishinsky (Soviet Union leaders), saying Stalin was like Caesar (who had been murdered by his underlings). Sheen ended the reading with Shakespeare's phrase, "must one day meet his judgment." Quite by coincidence, the next day, Stalin, the Russian dictator, suffered a stroke and a week later, he was dead, which made Sheen's telecast seem almost prophetic. Four years after his ABC series ended, Sheen returned to television with a syndicated show called *The Bishop Sheen Program*, which ran from 1963 until 1968. Bishop Sheen always ended his telecasts by saying, "God love you."

LIFE OF RILEY, THE

Oct. 1949–Mar. 1950	NBC	Tues.	9:30–10 P.M.
Jan. 1953–Sept. 1956	NBC	Fri.	8:30–9 P.M.
Oct. 1956–Dec. 1956	NBC	Fri.	8–9:30 P.M.
Jan. 1957–Aug. 1958	NBC	Fri.	8:30–9 P.M.

The Life of Riley was first heard as a radio program in 1943 and starred film character actor William BENDIX in the title role of Chester A. Riley, a blue-collar worker who worked in an aircraft plant and lived with his wife and two children in a typical working-class neighborhood in Cali-

fornia. In 1949, the popular radio program became a half-hour weekly television series that starred comedian Jackie GLEASON in the Chester A. Riley role. Rosemary DeCamp played Riley's wife, Peg, Lanny Rees played his teenage son, Junior, and Gloria Winters played his daughter, Babs. Also seen on this series were Sid Tomack as Riley's friend and neighbor, Jim Gillis, and John Brown, as Riley's friendly undertaker/friend, Digby "Digger" O'Dell. The series was canceled after one season, but in 1953, *The Life of Riley* returned to television with the actor who had played the role on the successful radio series, William Bendix. Film actress Marjorie Reynolds played the role of his wife, Peg, Wesley Morgan played his son, Junior, and Lugene Sanders played his daughter, Babs. Also featured on this version of the show were Tom D'Andrea as Jim Gillis, Gloria Blondell as his wife, Honeybee Gillis, and Gregory Marshall as their son, Egbert Gillis. Much of the show's comedy revolved around Riley's mispronunciation of words and his ill-advised interventions in minor problems. One of Riley's catchphrases that became known to millions of fans was, "What a revoltin' development this is," uttered when his misinterpretations of events led to confusion. Peg Riley, a long-suffering wife and mother, was the real anchor of the family, and could always be depended upon to give sound and loving advice to her children and her husband. Junior and Babs were teenagers who encountered the usual problems of TV young people. Tom McKnight was the producer of the second version of the series.

LIFE WITH FATHER

Nov. 1953–May 1954	CBS	Sun.	7–7:30 P.M.
Aug. 1954–Dec. 1954	CBS	Tues.	10–10:30 P.M.
Jan. 1953–July 1955	CBS	Tues.	8–8:30 P.M.

The lives of an upper middle-class American family who lived in New York City at the turn of the 20th century (1900) was the focus of this half-hour weekly situation comedy series that was produced by Ezra Stone (radio's Henry Aldrich). Based on a series of essays by Clarence Day, Jr., that had appeared in *Harper's* magazine and a subsequent long-running Broadway play of the same name, the *Life with Father* TV series starred Leon Ames as Clarence Day, Sr., a prosperous banker and autocratic father of four sons. Day's softhearted and loving wife, Vinnie, was played by Lurene Tuttle. The couple's four sons were Clarence, Jr., originally played by Ralph Reed, and then by Steven Terrell; Whitney, played by Richard Keith, and then by B. G. Norman and Freddy Ridgeway; Harlan, played by Harvey Grant; and John, played by Freddie Leiston, and then Malcolm Cassell. Mrs. Clarence Day, Jr., the wife of the show's author, who was a special consultant for the series, insisted that all the actors who played the Days' sons actually had red hair, as her real-life husband and his brothers did, even though the series was broadcast in black and white, and no one would have known what the actors' hair color was. The show's producers honored Mrs. Day's demand.

LIFESTYLES OF THE RICH AND FAMOUS

July 1986–	ABC	Mon.–Fri. 12–12.30
Aug. 1986		P.M. & 12–12:30 A.M.
Sept. 1986	ABC	Fri. 12–12.30 P.M.
		& 12–12:30 A.M.
Jan. 1984–	Syndicated	Various times
Sept. 1996		and stations

Celebrity reporter Robin Leach was the host of this series that took Leach and his viewers into the glamorous homes of world-famous people. Leach's guided tours, with the famous owners usually in attendance, became popular with viewers who wanted to see how "the other half" lived. The words "elegant," "glamorous," "luxurious," "exclusive," and "fantastic" were often used by Leach to describe the celebrities' homes. The series proved so successful that two spin-off series, also hosted by Leach, *Fame, Fortune and Romance* and *Runaway with the Rich and Famous,* followed. In 1994, Leach and his costar, Shari Belafonte, hosted the syndicated version of the original show, which had changed its title to *Lifestyles with Robin Leach and Shari Belafonte.*

LIGHTS OUT

| July 1949–Aug. 1949 | NBC | Tues. 9–9:30 P.M. |
| Nov. 1949–Sept. 1952 | NBC | Mon. 9–9:30 P.M. |

One of radio's most successful mystery/suspense programs, Arch Oboler's *Lights Out,* which had been on and off the air from 1935 until 1947, found its way to television as a weekly half-hour series. Originally hosted by Jack LaRue (1949–50), and then by Frank Gallop (1950–52), the *Lights Out* television series, like the radio program, presented chilling tales that usually sent shivers down viewers' spines. During the program's opening, viewers saw a pair of evil-looking eyes, a bloody hand reaching to turn out the lights, and then heard a sinister laugh and the words, "Lights out, everybody . . . " This set the stage for the half-hour frightening story that followed. When *Lights Out* was first telecast, relatively unknown actors were featured, but by 1950, well-known stars such as Boris Karloff, Billie Burke, Burgess Meredith, Leslie Neilsen, Basil Rathbone, Eddie ALBERT, Raymond Massey, and Yvonne De Carlo were featured in major roles on the show. *Lights Out* was first seen on TV as early as 1946, as part of a series of four specials produced by Fred Coe.

LINDEN, HAL (HAROLD LIPSHITZ 1931–)

Best known for playing the title character on the *BARNEY MILLER* situation comedy, Hal Linden was born in New York City. After graduating from college, Linden embarked upon a career as an actor. Unhappy with his surname, Hal decided to change it to Linden after seeing a sign at the Linden, New Jersey, train station while traveling from Philadelphia, where he was living at the time, to an acting job in New York City. Linden's fine singing voice won him roles in several musicals, and in 1960 he appeared in the film musical *Bells Are Ringing* and in the 1960s he was a regular on the SEARCH FOR TOMORROW TV soap opera series. In 1970, Linden returned to Broadway and starred in the musical comedy *The Rothschilds,* winning a Tony Award as Best Actor in a Musical. It wasn't until he was cast as police captain Barney Miller on the *Barney Miller* situation comedy series, however, that Linden became a familiar face to prime-time television viewers. Barney Miller was one of the hit shows of the 1975–76 season and made Linden a TV star. Roles in such TV films as *How to Break Up a Happy Divorce* (1976), *When You Comin' Back, Red Ryder?* (1979), *Father Figure* (1980), *The Other Woman* (1983), *Blacke's Magic* (1986), *Dream Breakers* (1989), *The Colony* (1995), and *Jump* (1999), and as a regular in the series *Jack's Place* (1992) and *The Boys Are Back* (1994), which failed to attract audiences, followed.

LINKLETTER, ART (ARTHUR GORDON KELLY 1912–)

Born in Moose Jaw, Saskatchewan, Canada, Art Linkletter began his career in American broadcasting at radio station KGB in San Diego in 1933. It wasn't until 1942, however, that Linkletter, who had worked as radio announcer, became the host of the radio show *People Are Funny* in 1942 that he became well known. *People Are Funny* was seen on television as early as 1946, but became a regular TV offering in 1954. As on the successful radio show, Linkletter interviewed ordinary people chosen from the studio audience, and then asked them to perform a stunt that would indeed prove that "people [were] funny." Linkletter had previously hosted other TV interview shows, including *Life with Linkletter* (1950), and *House Party* (1952) and was also seen in the feature film *Champagne for Caesar* (1950). In 1952 and 1954, Linkletter hosted two shows for the Disney Company, *Dateline: Disney* and *Dateline: Disneyland,* and in the 1950s, Linkletter also made guest-starring appearances on such TV shows as The ZANE GREY THEATER, WAGON TRAIN, BATMAN, HERE'S LUCY, and *Kids Say the Darndest Things.* After hosting the TV series *The Art Linkletter Show* in 1963 and *Hollywood Talent Scouts* in 1965, Linkletter retired from the spotlight, but remained active as a TV producer. In 1999, Linkletter resurfaced briefly to play himself in the film *Let Me In, I Hear Laughter.*

LITTLE HOUSE ON THE PRAIRIE

| Sept. 1974–Sept. 1976 | NBC | Wed. 8–9 P.M. |
| Sept. 1976–Mar. 1983 | NBC | Mon. 8–9 P.M. |

Based on the best-selling books by Laura Ingalls Wilder about a family that lived in the developing American West of the 1870s, this popular television series starred Michael LANDON as homesteader Charles Ingalls; Karen Grassle as his wife, Caroline Ingalls; and Melissa Sue

Cast members of *Little House on the Prairie*.

Shannen Doherty; and schoolteacher Etta Plum, played by Leslie Landon (Michael Landon's daughter). Although he continued to produce the series, Michael Landon was rarely seen on the series during its final season, 1981–82. As *Little House on the Prairie: A New Beginning,* one more season was squeezed out of the series, but the series finally ended its run in 1983.

LIVE WITH REGIS AND KATHIE LEE (LIVE WITH REGIS AND KELLY AFTER AUGUST 2000)

Sept. 1989–Present Syndicated Mon–Fri. 9–10 A.M.

The TV talk/magazine show, *Live with Regis and Kathie Lee,* which airs live five days a week, follows a format that first became popular on radio in the 1940s on such early morning "breakfast" shows as *Dorothy and Dick, Tex and Jinx,* the *Fitzgeralds,* and *The Breakfast Club.* During their morning chats at the beginning of each show, the show's hosts, the often cantankerous but always lovable Regis PHILBIN and from 1989 until 2000, Kathie Lee GIFFORD (who departed the show in the summer of 2000 to pursue other career interests) talked about events they had attended in New York City, where the show originated, current happenings in the news and in the world of show business, and their families. Philbin's wife, Joy, was a frequent cohost on the show. Kathie Lee gave birth to both of her children, Cody and Cassidy, during the time

Anderson, and Melissa GILBERT, the twins Lindsay and Sidney Greenbush (who alternated in a role), and the twins Wendi and Brenda Turnbeaugh (who also alternated in a role), as the Ingalls' four daughters Mary (the eldest daughter), Laura (the second eldest daughter, from whose point of view the story unfolded), Carrie, and Grace (who was born during the 1977–78 season). Also regularly seen on the series playing neighbors of the Ingalls family in the small town of Walnut Grove were Victor French and Bonnie Bartlett as Isaiah and Grace Edwards; Richard Bull and Katherine MacGregor as storekeeper Nels Oleson and his overbearing wife, Harriet; Jonathan Gilbert as the Olesons' son, Willie; Alison Arngrim as the Olesons' nasty daughter, Nellie; Charlotte Stewart as schoolteacher Miss Beadle; Dabbs Greer as Reverend Robert Alden; Ted Gehring as banker Ebenezer Sprague; Kevin Hagen as Doctor Baker; Tracie Savage as Laura Ingalls's friend, Christy; Merlin Olsen and Hersha Parady as Jonathan Garvey and his wife, Alice; and Patrick Laborteaux as the Garveys' son, Andy. As the series continued, other characters were added, including Almanzo Wilder, played by Dean Butler, who married Laura during the 1980–81 season; Cassandra and James, played by Missy Francis and Jason Bateman, two orphans the Ingalls family adopted; blacksmith John Carter and his wife, Sarah, played by Stan Ivar and Pamela Roylance; the Carters' son, Jason, played by David Friedman; Almanzo's niece, Jenny, played by

Kathie Lee Gifford and Regis Philbin (Author's collection)

she was appearing on the show, and audiences followed both of her pregnancies as if awaiting the birth of a dear friend's child. Kathie Lee often mentioned her husband, sportscaster Frank Gifford, and her children. The show's producer, Michael Gelman, was often brought on camera when either Regis or Kathie Lee referred to him. Kathie Lee often complained about some slight she felt she had suffered because of him. The second half of the show featured well-known celebrities from the world of TV, films, and the Broadway stage, and occasionally politics, who were usually promoting a current project. Regular appearances were made by such experts as The Love Chef, celebrity correspondent Claudia Cohen, and, by far the most popular regular guest on the show, the zany garden expert Mrs Greenthumbs (comedienne/writer Cassandra Danz). The hilarious Mrs. Greenthumbs gave amusing and informative gardening advice and usually traveled with Regis and his cohost whenever the show went to such places as Hawaii, Canada, or New Orleans. She also occasionally filled in as an out-of-studio, on-location interviewer as needed. In spite of network attempts to attract audiences in the time slot opposite *Live,* the program remains extremely popular. Kelly Rippa replaced Gifford in 2000.

LLOYD, CHRISTOPHER (1938–)

Before playing "Reverend Jim" Ignatowski, the shell-shocked-from-drugs cab driver on the popular series *TAXI,* Christopher Lloyd made a memorable film debut as a mental patient named Taber in the Academy Award–winning film *One Flew Over the Cuckoo's Nest* in 1975. Born in Stamford, Connecticut, Lloyd spent years trying to establish himself as an actor before landing the attention-getting role of Taber on the Broadway stage, which he re-created for the film version of the play. It was *Taxi,* however, that won Lloyd two Emmy Awards and made him a familiar name and face to millions of viewers. After his debut on *Taxi,* Lloyd went on to become one of Hollywood's most successful character actors, and he appeared in numerous films and television series playing a wide variety of roles. Lloyd's notable film appearances include *The Lady in Red* (1979), *Butch and Sundance: The Early Days* (1979), *The Onion Field* (1979), *National Lampoon Goes to the Movies* (1981), *The Legend of the Lone Ranger* (1981), *To Be or Not to Be* (1983), *Star Trek III: The Search for Spock* (1984), *Back to the Future* (1985), *Who Framed Roger Rabbit* (1988), *Back to the Future II* (1989), *Back to the Future III* (1990), *The Addams Family* (1991), *Addams Family Values* (1993), *Angels in the Outfield* (1994), *Changing Habits* (1997), *Anastasia* (1997) as the voice of Rasputin), *Man on the Moon* (1999), and *Chasing Destiny* (2000), to name just a few. Lloyd also appeared as a guest star on such TV series as *BARNEY MILLER, CHEERS,* and *SPIN CITY,* and was, in addition to *Taxi,* a regular on the TV series *Street Hawk* (1985), *Back to the Future* (1991–93), and *Deadly Games* (1995).

LOIS & CLARK: THE NEW ADVENTURES OF SUPERMAN

Sept. 1993–Dec. 1996	ABC	Sun. 8–9 P.M.
Jan. 1997	ABC	Sun. 7–8 P.M.
Mar. 1997	ABC	Sun. 7–8 P.M.
Apr. 1997–June 1997	ABC	Sat. 8–9 P.M.

This quirky science fiction/adventure series was about the youthful Clark Kent and Lois Lane characters of Superman fame. The emphasis on this series, which was tailor made for the 1990s, was not on action and adventure, although the series did contain the usual Superman bad guys and fights and flights, but on the romantic tensions that existed between Clark and his fellow reporter on the Metropolis *Daily Planet* newspaper, Lois Lane. Clark Kent/Superman was engagingly played by Dean Cain, and Lois Lane was played by Teri Hatcher. Other familiar Superman characters who appeared on this updated version of the familiar story were *The Daily Planet's* managing editor, Perry White, played by Lane Smith; the newspaper copyboy, Jimmy Olsen, played by Michael Landes, and then by Justin Whelan; the villainous Lex Luthor, played by John Shea; and Clark/Superman's adoptive parents, Jonathan and Martha Kent, played by Eddie Jones and K Callan. Also appearing on the series was a character named Catherine "Cat" Grant, who was played by Tracy Scoggins. In the series' final episodes, Lois finally figured out that Clark and Superman were one and the same person, and when Clark proposed marriage to her

Dean Cain and Teri Hatcher of *Lois and Clark* (Author's collection)

during the 1995–96 season, Lois accepted. On a trip back to Superman's home planet, Krypton, during the 1996–97 season, Superman and Lois discovered that the "man of steel" had previously become betrothed to a woman named Zara, played by Justine Bateman, which gave the newlyweds trouble for a while. On the last episode, Lois and Clark had resolved any problems they had with Zara, and had decided to parent a superbaby.

LONE RANGER, THE

Sept. 1949–Sept. 1957	ABC	Thurs. 7:30–8 P.M.
June 1950–Sept. 1950	ABC	Fri. 10–10:30 P.M.

Originally one of radio's most successful western adventure programs, which was on the air from 1933 until 1955, *The Long Ranger* made its debut as a television series in 1949 with Clayton MOORE playing the Lone Ranger and Native American Jay SILVERHEELS playing his "faithful Indian companion Tonto." Moore played the Ranger role for 221 of the episodes that were filmed between 1949 and 1957; actor John Hart played the role on 26 episodes between 1951 and 1953. At least once a year, the series repeated the story of how the Lone Ranger originated. He was a Texas Ranger named John Reid, who was the only survivor when a group of his fellow Rangers was ambushed and killed by the evil Butch Cavindish and his Hole-in-the-Wall gang. Seriously wounded in the attack, Reid was found dying by an Indian named Tonto, who nursed him back to health and became his devoted friend and outlaw-fighting companion. Deciding not to reveal his true identity, but to retain an air of mystery, Reid donned a black mask, and sometimes disguised himself as a cowboy or a miner in order to remain anonymous. Riding his "great white horse, Silver," the Lone Ranger, with Tonto riding his horse, Scout, at his side, patrolled the plains, seeking out bad guys and acting as a champion for law and order throughout the western United States. The original radio program was the brainchild of George W. Trendle and Fran Striker, and the TV series followed the lead of its radio predecessor. The Lone Ranger on both his radio and TV adventures used only silver bullets in his two six-shooters, but shot only to wound, and not kill, his adversaries; never used profane language or was, in any way, rough; never consorted with loose women, or any women for that matter; and was always a heroic role model for the younger generation. During the course of the series, the Lone Ranger's nephew, Dan Reid, whose father had been killed in the same ambush that had wounded the Lone Ranger, became the Ranger's/John Reid's ward when his mother died.

Few people who ever heard it could forget *The Lone Ranger's* spirited opening, which was read on both radio and TV by announcer Fred Foy, that stated, "A fiery horse with the speed of light and a hearty Hi-Yo Silver. The Lone Ranger rides again," as the strains of the show's theme music, Rossini's *William Tell* Overture, swelled. An animated version of *The Lone Ranger* surfaced in Septem-

The Lone Ranger (Clayton Moore) and Tonto (John Silverheel) (Author's collection)

ber 1969, and remained a Saturday morning favorite with young viewers for three years as part of the *Tarzan/Lone Ranger Hour*.

LORD, JACK (JOHN JOSEPH PATRICK RYAN 1920–1998)

Perhaps best known for playing police detective Steve McGarrett on the *HAWAII FIVE-O* television series, Jack Lord, who was born in New York City, was, in addition to being an actor and director, a talented artist who had two of his oil paintings purchased by the Metropolitan Museum of Art in New York City and the British Museum of Modern Art in England. Before becoming world famous as McGarret on *Hawaii Five-O*, Jack Lord was active on the stage in New York City and was frequently featured on such TV series as *SUSPENSE*, *The PHILCO TELEVISION PLAYHOUSE*, *STUDIO ONE*, *HAVE GUN WILL TRAVEL*, *GUNSMOKE*, *BONANZA*, *The UNTOUCHABLES*, *RAWHIDE*, *NAKED CITY*, *WAGON TRAIN*, *The F.B.I*, *The VIRGINIAN*, *The FUGITIVE*, and *The MAN FROM U.N.C.L.E*. Lord also had major roles in such feature films as *The Court Martial of Billy Mitchell (1955)*, *The Vagabond King (1956)*, *God's Little Acre (1958)*, *Dr. No (1962)*, and *Ride to Hangman's Tree (1967)*. In addition to appearing in the leading role on Hawaii Five-O, Lord directed many episodes of the series. After *Hawaii Five-O* ended its successful TV run in 1980, Lord virtually retired from show business. A cultured man who loved reading poetry aloud on the set of his TV show, and painting in the study of his Hawaiian home, Lord lived a reclusive life until he died of congestive heart failure at the age of 77 in 1998.

LORETTA YOUNG SHOW, THE (AKA A LETTER TO LORETTA)

| Sept. 1953–June 1958 | NBC | Sun. 10–10:30 P.M. |
| Oct. 1958–Sept. 1961 | NBC | Sun. 10–10:30 P.M. |

Academy Award–winning actress Loretta YOUNG arrived on TV in 1953, generating a great deal of publicity. At that time, few major Hollywood stars would venture into the new medium, believing their film careers would be over if they condescended to go to work for "the enemy" of films, television. Young's TV show, which was mainly directed toward women, was a half-hour dramatic anthology program that featured her in different roles each week that were written to showcase her versatility as an actress. One of Young's television trademarks was the dramatic way she appeared on camera each week. Bursting through a door, Young, wearing a strikingly different and glamorous gown or dress each week, would sweep onstage, walk up to the camera, greet her viewers, and introduce whatever play she was going to enact on that week's show. At the end of each telecast, Loretta once again addressed her viewers and read a bit of poetry or a passage from the Bible that emphasized the point or the message of the play in which she had just appeared.

When it first went on the air, Young's show was called Letter To Loretta, since Loretta read a letter, reportedly written by a viewer asking for advice from the star. She then proceeded to answer the letter in the form of the weekly drama. In 1954, the "letter" idea was abandoned, and the series changed its name to The Loretta Young Show. The wide variety of roles Loretta played on this series certainly proved her versatility as an actress. Over the years, Loretta was seen as diverse characters of all ages, such as a Japanese war bride, an actress, housewife, a reporter, an empress, a farmer's wife, a businesswoman, etc. Among the leading men who appeared with Young on the series were Ricardo MONTALBAN (who appeared on the show nine times), John Newland (who costarred with Loretta 13 times), and Everett Sloane, Eddie ALBERT, George Nader, Hugh O'BRIEN, Craig STEVENS, Claude Atkins, Ralph Meeker, James Daly, Stephen McNally, and Regis Toomey. From 1960 until 1964, NBC ran reruns of The Loretta Young Show on weekday afternoons, calling the show The Loretta Young Theater. In 1972, Young sued NBC, saying that her contract had been violated when the syndicated series the company released, contrary to her contract, showed the star with outdated hair styles and fashions. The star was awarded a reported $599,000 to settle the case.

LOST IN SPACE

Sept. 1965–Sept. 1968 CBS Wed. 7:30–8:30 P.M.

For three years, the science fiction series Lost in Space, which was seen in the early evening hours and produced with younger viewers in mind, was one of the most popular children's shows on television. The plot of the show was simple: A family of space travelers named the Robinsons, who lived in the distant future, became lost in space as their craft is traveling from Earth on a five-year voyage to a distant planet in the Alpha Centauri star system. The ambitions and wicked Dr. Zachary Smith, who was traveling with the Robinsons, inadvertently sabotaged the spaceship's control system as he attempted to manipulate the program of a robot whose writing was tied into the spaceship's control system. This diverted the spaceship's course and left the occupants hopelessly lost in space. The Robinson family consisted of Professor John Robinson, played by Guy WILLIAMS; his wife Maureen, played by June Lockhart; and their children Judy, Will, and Penny, played by Marta Kristen, Billy Mumy, and Angela Cartwright. Dr. Smith was played by Jonathan Harris, the spaceship's copilot, Don West, was played by Mark Goddard, and the Robot was played by Bob May, with Duck Tufeld doing his voice. As the series unfolded, Dr Smith constantly tried to make deals with various aliens on the planets they visited, enlisting their aid in helping him to get back to Earth, leaving the Robinsons to fend for themselves as they wandered around the the universe, landing on strange and often hostile planets, encountering aliens, and dealing with malfunctioning equipment. Each episode usually ended with a cliff-hanging event, which made viewers want to tune in again to find out how the situation had been resolved. In all, 83 hour-long episodes of Lost in Space were filmed. Irwin Allen created the series and was the show's executive producer.

LOTSA LUCK

| Sept. 1973–Jan. 1974 | NBC | Mon. 8–8:30 P.M. |
| Jan. 1974–May 1974 | NBC | Fri. 8:30–9 P.M. |

In spite of the formidable comic talents of Dom DeLuise playing Stanley Belmont, the clerk in a New York City bus company's lost and found department, Lotsa Luck failed to attract an audience and was canceled when one full season ended. Most of the show's action took place, not at the bus station's lost and found department, but in Stanley's home, where he lived with his bossy mother, played by Kathleen Freeman, his sister, Olive, played by Beverly Sanders, and Olive's unemployed, lazy husband, Arthur, played by Wynn Irwin. Jack Knight played Stanley's uncomplicated friend Bummy. The series was based on the hit British TV series On the Busses.

LOU GRANT

| Sept. 1977–Jan. 1978 | CBS | Tues. 10–11 P.M. |
| Jan. 1978–Sept. 1982 | CBS | Mon. 10–11. P.M. |

On the final episode of the popular MARY TYLER MOORE situation comedy series, which was seen in September

Lost in Space (Left to right.) Angela Cartwright, Mark Goddard, Marta Kristen, Jonathan Harris, June Lockhart, Billy Mumy and (standing above him), Guy Williams (Author's collection)

1977, the entire news staff at WJM-TV, Minneapolis, Minnesota, where Mary Richards and her boss, Lou Grant, worked, were fired. Lou Grant, who was 50 years old at the time, moved to Los Angeles, where he got a job as the city editor on the *Los Angeles Tribune*. This was the basis of the Lou Grant spin-off series that starred actor Ed ASNER, who had become extremely popular with viewers as a cast member on The *Mary Tyler Moore Show*. Unlike that series, *Lou Grant* was not a situation comedy. It was newspaper drama series that featured mystery, crime, and action-filled stories. In addition to the Lou Grant character, also appearing on the series were the autocratic owner of the newspaper, Margaret Pynchon, played by Nancy Marchand (who later became better known for playing Livia Soprano on the popular *Sopranos* series); Lou's boss, the managing editor of the newspaper, Charlie Hume, played by Mason Adams; the hotshot investigative reporter for *The Tribune*, Joe Rossi, played by Robert Walden; an ambitious young newspaper reporter, Carla Mardigan, played by Rebecca Balding, who was replaced by reporter Billie Newman McCovey, played by Linda Kelsey; Art Donovan, Lou Grant's assistant city editor, played by Jack Benson; and Dennis "Animal" Price, an unconventional newspaper photographer, played by Daryl Anderson. Even though the series was highly rated and very popular with viewers, it was canceled by CBS after its fifth season. CBS claimed the *Lou Grant* series was losing viewers, but most observers felt that the real reason the show was canceled was because the show's star, Ed Asner, was publicly critical of American involvement in Central American political affairs at the time, and CBS allegedly decided to make Asner less visible to the public by canceling his series.

LOVE, AMERICAN STYLE

Sept. 1969–Jan. 1970	ABC	Mon. 10–11 P.M.
Jan. 1970–Sept. 1970	ABC	Fri. 10–11 P.M.

| Sept. 1970–Jan. 1971 | ABC | Fri. 9:30–10 P.M. |
| Jan. 1971–Jan. 1974 | ABC | Fri. 10–11 P.M. |

Love, American Style was unusual in that it was a comedy anthology series that presented two or three different comedy/romance stories of various lengths on a single episode, each separated by brief blackouts. The cast that played the various roles in the different stories included Bill Callaway, Phyllis Elizabeth Davis, Buzz Cooper, Jaki De Mar, Mary Grover, James Hampton, Stuart Margolin, Lynne Marta, Barbara Minkus, Bernie Kopell, Tracy Reed, and Richard Williams. The series was produced by Arnold Margolin and Jim Parker. Writers for the show included Frank Buxton, Jerry Rannow, George Strangis, Ed Scharlach, and Doug Tibbles.

LOVE BOAT, THE

Sept. 1977–Jan. 1978	ABC	Sat. 10–11 P.M.
Jan. 1978–Sept. 1985	ABC	Sat. 9–10 P.M.
Sept. 1985–May 1986	ABC	Sat. 10–11 P.M.
June 1986–Sept. 1986	ABC	Fri. 10–11 P.M.

When Jack Jones's voice was heard singing the theme song at the beginning of each episode of the popular *Love Boat,* viewers knew they were in for one full hour of romance and comedy on this series, which was set on a luxury cruise ship called the *Pacific Princess.* Patterned after ABC's successful LOVE, AMERICAN STYLE series, *The Love Boat* featured different stories, all set on the cruise ship and its ports of call, and these stories usually centered on the diverse passengers on each week's cruise. The crew of the *Pacific Princess* were the only regular characters on the show and sometimes they became the focus of one of the stories. Gavin MacLeod played the ship's skipper, Captain Merrill Stubing; Bernie Kopell played the ship's physician, Dr. Adam Bricker; Fred Grandy played the ship's assistant purser, Burl "Gopher" Smith; Ted Lange played the ship's bartender, Isaac Washington; and Lauren Tewes played the ship's social director, Julie McCoy In 1979, Jill Whelan, who played Stubing's illegitimate daughter, Vicki, joined the cast. Lauren Tewes was replaced during the 1984–85 season by Pat Klous, who played the ship's new social director, Judy McCoy. Ted McGinley also joined the cast of regulars as ship's photographer, Ashley "Ace" Covington, during the 1984–85 season. In 1985, the *Pacific Princess*'s name was changed to the *Royal Princess* and eight beautiful singer/dancers were added to the regular cast. Many well-known show business personalities of the past and present showed up as passengers on the cruises, and viewers were always delighted to see one of their film or TV favorites. One particularly nostalgic *Love Boat* cruise featured Broadway stars Ethel Merman and Carol Channing and film stars Van Johnson and Ann Miller, as well as singer Della Reese, playing passengers on the ship who became entangled in various romantic escapades. The executive producers of *The Love Boat* were Aaron SPELLING and Douglas

S. Cramer. One of the series' directors rather accurately described *The Love Boat* as "love and pap."

LOVE OF LIFE

| Sept. 1951–Feb. 1980 | CBS | Mon.–Fri. various daytime hours |

One of television's earliest daytime serial successes, *Love of Life* made its debut in 1951 and remained on TV for 28 years. Created by John Hess, the series executive producer for many, many years was daytime TV's legendary Roy Winsor. During the series' last few years on television, former child actor Darrel Hickman was the show's executive producer. For most of the series' run, the plots centered on two very different sisters—the noble, long-suffering Vanessa Dale and her selfish opportunistic sister, Margaret "Meg" Dale. In the late 1950s, Meg was written off the show, but returned in 1973, and she became one of the show's most popular characters. The role of Vanessa was played over the years by Peggy McKay (1951–55), Bonnie Bartlett (1955–59), and for most of the series' run, Audrey Peters (1959–80). Meg was originally played by Jean McBride (1951–56) and then, after a 17-year absence, by Tudi Wiggins (1973–80). When the series was first aired, the program was set in a town called Barrowsville, but the show's location eventually changed to Rosehill, where the series remained until it was canceled in 1980. Other popular characters who appeared on the show over the years were Van and Meg's mother, Sarah, who was played by Jane Rose, and then by Joanna Roos; Van and Meg's father, Will Dale, played by Ed Jerome; Meg's first husband, Charles Harper, played by Paul Potter; Meg and Charles's, son, Benno, played by Dennis Parnell, Tommy White, Christopher Reeve, and Chandler Hill Harbin over the years; and Van's husband, lawyer Paul Raven, played by Richard Coogan. As the series continued, various younger characters were featured in various story lines, with Vanessa and then Meg remaining pivotal throughout the series' run. Among the many actors who were featured on the series playing both short- and long-term roles, at one time or another, were Martin Balsam, Warren Beatty, Peter FALK, Annie Jackson, Donald Symington, Lauren Gilbert, Ann Loring, Ron Tomme, Lee Lawson, Jerry Lacy, Frances Sternhagen, Paul Michael Glaser, Tony Lo Bianco, Roy Scheider, Nancy Marchand, Deborah Courtney, Bigitta Tolksdorf, Natalie Schafer, and Geraldine Brooks.

LUCILLE BALL SHOW, THE
(see *Lucy Show, The*)

LUCKY PUP

| Aug. 1948–Sept. 1948 | CBS | Mon./Wed./Fri. Various times |
| Sept. 1948–Sept. 1950 | CBS | Mon.–Fri. 6:30–6:45 P.M. |

Jan. 1949–June 1951 CBS   Sat. Various half hours
between 6:00 and
7:15 P.M.

The husband-and-wife team of Hope and Morey Bunin
were the producers and chief puppeteers of this popular
15-minute, five-day-a-week serialized puppet show with a
circus setting. The show, which was sponsored by Good
and Plenty candy, featured a cute little hand puppet dog
named Lucky Pup, who had been "lucky" enough to
inherit 5 million. Lucky was the star attraction in the
"Bunin Circus," which in addition to the pup, featured
the hand puppets Jolo the Clown, who was Lucky's friend
and protector, and the villainous puppet Foodini the
Great, a magician who kept plotting to get Lucky's fortune away from him. Aiding Foodini was the puppet Pin-
head, Foodini's faithful but inept accomplice. In time,
Foodini became so popular with young viewers that he
became the major character on one of television's first
spin-off series, *Foodini the Great,* on the ABC network.

LUCY SHOW, THE (AKA THE LUCILLE BALL SHOW)

Oct. 1962–June 1964	CBS	Mon. 8:30–9 P.M.
Sept. 1964–July 1965	CBS	Mon. 9–9:30 P.M.
Sept. 1965–June 1967	CBS	Mon. 8:30–9 P.M.
Sept. 1967–Sept. 1971	CBS	Mon. 8:30–9 P.M.
Sept. 1971–Sept. 1974	CBS	Mon. 9–9:30 P.M.

After Lucille BALL and her husband, Desi ARNAZ, decided
to end their popular *I LOVE LUCY* series, Ball became the
star of her own weekly situation comedy series, *The Lucy
Show.* Appearing with Ball on her new series was her *I
Love Lucy* costar Vivian VANCE, who continued to play
straight woman to Lucy's comic character. When this
series first went on the air, Ball played Lucy Carmichael, a
widow with two children named Chris and Jerry, played
by Candy Moore and Jimmy Garrett. Lucy had moved
from the city to suburban Danfield, Connecticut, with her
divorced friend, Vivian Bagley, played by Vivian Vance.
The two women, who were desperately hoping to find
new husbands, had numerous misadventures, and both
eventually took part-time jobs at the Danfield First
National Bank, where their boss was the short-tempered,
ever-exasperated Theodore J. Mooney, played by Gale
Gordon. In 1965, Vance left the series as a regular performer, and Lucy Carmichael moved to San Francisco,
where she got a job at the Westland Bank. Quite by coincidence, Mr. Moody had also moved to San Francisco and
had become the vice president at the Westland Bank,
where Lucy continued to make his life difficult. The president at the Westland Bank was Harrison Cheever, played
by Roy Roberts. Lucy's daughter, Chris, did not move to
San Francisco with Lucy, and her friend Vivian only occasionally visited Lucy in her new home. Her new regular
friend and constant companion was a character named
Mary Jane Lewis, played by Mary Jane Croft. In 1968,
Lucy moved once again, this time to Los Angeles, and her

name was changed to Lucy Carter. In L.A., Lucy got a job
at the Unique Employment Agency. Lucy was still a
mother of two children, but the characters were then
being played by Lucy's real-life children, Lucie and Desi,
Jr. Gale Gordon, who had also moved to Los Angeles,
continued to be Lucy's ever-blustering adversary, playing a
character named "Uncle Harry" Carter, who was her
brother-in-law.

LUDDEN, ALLEN (ALLEN ELLSWORTH 1917–1981)

One of television's most respected game show hosts, Allen
Ludden, who was born in Mineral Point, Wisconsin, was a
teacher before he became a broadcaster and the moderator
of the *G.E. College Bowl* television game show in 1959.
The *G.E. College Bowl* pitted teams from two different colleges against each other. The teams tried to be the first to
ring a buzzer and answer questions about various academic
subjects such as literature, mathematics, and science. In
1961, Ludden became the host of the *PASSWORD* series,
which became one of the most popular game shows on television. The series remained on the air until 1975. Ludden
also hosted *The Joker's Wild* (1972), *Stumpers!* (1976), and
Liar's Club (1977), and was a panelist on the *MATCH GAME
P.M.* series (1975). In 1966, Ludden appeared on the *BAT-
MAN* series, playing a character named David Dooley. He
also played himself in a 1972 episode of the series *The ODD
COUPLE.* Shortly before his untimely death from cancer in
1981, Ludden hosted the *Password Plus* series, which was
a revival of his successful *Password* game show.

LUPTON, JOHN (1928–1993)

Best known for playing Tom Jeffords on the popular TV
western series *BROKEN ARROW* from 1956 until 1960,
John Lupton was born in Highland Park, Illinois. When he
was 23 years old, Lupton got his first big break as an actor
on the *WANTED: DEAD OR ALIVE* TV series. He subsequently appeared on such TV series as *Yancy Derringer*
(1959), *Black Saddle* (1959), *PERRY MASON, RICHARD DIA-
MOND, GUNSMOKE, LARAMIE, WAGON TRAIN, ALFRED
HITCHCOCK PRESENTS, RAWHIDE, The VIRGINIAN, I SPY,
CANNON, The ROCKFORD FILES, CHARLIE'S ANGELS,* and
many others. From 1967 until 1972, and then from 1975
until 1979, Lupton played Dr. Tommy Horton, Jr., on the
DAYS OF OUR LIVES daytime series. Among the memorable
feature films Lupton appeared in were *The Band Wagon*
(1953), *Julius Caesar* (1953), *Seven Angry Men* (1955),
Battle Cry (1955), *The Greatest Story Ever Told* (1965),
The World's Greatest Athlete (1973), *Airport 1975* (1974),
The Young Runaways (1978), and *Body Shot* (1993).

LYNCH, PEG (MARGARET FRANCES LYNCH 1916–)

The creator, writer, and star of the *ETHEL AND ALBERT*
radio and television programs, Peg Lynch was born in
Lincoln, Nebraska. Lynch began her broadcasting career
in 1938, working as a jack-of-all trades at a small radio

station in Minnesota. Moving to Chicago, Lynch began to write a series of sketches about a young married couple and the little problems they had to deal with in their everyday lives, which became very popular with listeners. In 1944, Lynch moved to New York, and officials at the Blue Network, which had formerly been owned by NBC network, asked to her to develop a program for their new network. *Ethel and Albert* was the result. Although Lynch was the program's writer, because no one else could read the female character she had developed to the producer's satisfaction, she also became the show's leading actress. Lynch's formidable talents as writer and actress were the primary reasons for the show's subsequent success. In 1951, while her radio show was still on the air, Lynch performed her *Ethel and Albert* sketches on TV on *The KATE SMITH EVENING HOUR* as a semiregular attraction. From 1953 through 1956, *Ethel and Albert* then became a half-hour weekly situation comedy series and was seen in subsequent years on all three major networks, ABC, CBS, and NBC. Lynch's domestic comedy skits continued to delight radio listeners on *The Couple Next Door* in the mid-1950s, and were revived on a series called *The Little Things in Life,* which was one of four programs on the *Radio Playhouse* program, which tried to bring back radio drama to the airwaves in the mid-1970s. Lynch still performs her timeless comedy sketches at colleges and universities around the country, and her one-act plays, which have been published by the Samuel French Company, are as relevant today as they were when she first wrote them for radio and TV in the 1940s–1950s.

MacGYVER

Sept. 1985–Jan. 1986	ABC	Sun. 8–9 P.M.
Jan. 1986–July 1986	ABC	Wed. 8–9 P.M.
Aug. 1986	ABC	Wed. 9–10 P.M.
Sept. 1986–May 1987	ABC	Mon. 8–9 P.M.
June 1987–Sept. 1987	ABC	Wed. 9–10 P.M.
Sept. 1987–May 1988	ABC	Mon. 8–9 P.M.
June 1988–Sept. 1988	ABC	Sun. 8–9 P.M.
Oct. 1988–Aug. 1989	ABC	Mon. 8–9 P.M.
Aug. 1989–Sept. 1989	ABC	Sun. 8–9 P.M.
Sept. 1989–Dec. 1991	ABC	Mon. 8–9 P.M.
May 1992–June 1992	ABC	Thurs. 9–10 P.M.
July 1992–Aug. 1992	ABC	Sat. 8–9 P.M.

The success of the action/adventure series *MacGyver*, which was on the air for seven years, was largely due to the charm of the actor who played the title role, Richard Dean Anderson, and the show's appeal to young people. MacGyver was a former Special Services agent who worked for the Phoenix Foundation, a think tank dedicated to exposing and eliminating evil forces around the world. MacGyver was an expert at managing to infiltrate the bad guys' domains, and because of his expertise at using ordinary objects to get out of any problem, he was able to extricate himself from danger. MacGyver's boss was Peter Thornton, played by Dana Elcar, the Director of Field Operations for the Phoenix Foundation. As the series progressed, it became increasingly more concerned with such social issues as teenage runaways, the environment, and politics. Mayim Bialik was, for a time, a regular on the series playing MacGyver's teenage friend, Lisa. Michael Des Barres was also seen regularly as MacGyver's major nemesis, the evil Murdoc. On the last episode of the show, MacGyver discovered that he fathered a son, who was by then a teen, named Sean "Sam" Malloy, played by

Dalton James. At the end of the last show, MacGyver and Sam set off on their motorcycles together to look for new adventures.

MacMURRAY, FRED (FREDRICK MARTIN MacMURRAY 1908–1991)

For over 30 years, before he became one of America's favorite television fathers on the popular situation comedy series *MY THREE SONS*, Fred MacMurray was one of Hollywood's most successful film actors. Born in Kankakee, Illinois, to Maleta and Frederick MacMurray, Fred, whose father was a successful concert violinist, sang and played in an orchestra as a young man in order to pay his tuition at Carroll College in Wisconsin. After playing with another orchestra in Chicago for a year after he graduated, he joined the orchestra when it went to Hollywood and made several recordings with them and also appeared as an extra in films. MacMurray then joined yet another band, the California Collegians, and when the band went to New York City, MacMurray went with them and was asked to appear in a Broadway revue called *Three's a Crowd*. His collegiate good looks won him a role in the musical *Roberta* in 1935, as well as a contract to appear in films at Paramount Pictures. Over the next 30 years, Fred appeared in such popular motion pictures as *Alice Adams* (1935), *The Trail of the Lonesome Pine* (1936), *Sing You Sinners* (1938), *Too Many Husbands* (1940), *Take a Letter, Darling* (1942), *Double Indemnity* (1944), *Murder, He Says* (1945), *The Egg and I* (1947), *The Miracle of the Bells* (1948), *The Caine Mutiny* (1954), *The Shaggy Dog* (1959), *The Apartment* (1960), *The Absent-Minded Professor* (1961), *Son of Flubber* (1963), and *The Happiest Millionaire* (1967), establishing himself as one of Hollywood's most successful leading men, as well as starring on his own TV series *My Three Sons* from 1960 until 1972. After the show left the air, MacMurray continued to appear in films, and infrequently on TV, and was seen in *The Chadwick Family* (1974), *Herbie Day at Disneyland* (1974), and *The Walt Disney Comedy and Magic Revue* (1985) on TV, and in the films *Charley and the Angel* (1973), and *The Swarm* (1978), before retiring in the late 1980s.

MAD ABOUT YOU

Sept. 1992–Jan. 1993	NBC	Wed. 9:30–10 P.M.
Feb. 1993–July 1993	NBC	Sat. 9:30–10 P.M.
July 1993–Aug. 1995	NBC	Thurs. 8–8:30 P.M.
Aug. 1995	NBC	Thurs. 8:30–9 P.M.
Sept. 1995–Jul. 1996	NBC	Sun. 8–8:30 P.M.
Aug. 1996–Dec. 1998	NBC	Tues. 8–8:30 P.M.
Dec. 1998–Jan. 1999	NBC	Mon. 9–9:30 P.M.
Feb. 1999–May 1999	NBC	Mon. 8:30–9 P.M.
May 1999–July 1999	NBC	Mon. 9–9:30 P.M.
Aug. 1999	NBC	Thurs. 10:30–11 P.M.

Created by Paul REISER and Danny Jacobson, the situation comedy series *Mad About You* centered on a newly married young couple, Paul and Jamie Buchman, who were played by Paul Reiser and Helen HUNT. The Buchmans lived in New York City and came from two very different backgrounds. Paul was an excitable, somewhat neurotic freelance documentary filmmaker, and Jamie worked as an executive for a large public relations firm.

Mad About You: Paul Reiser and Helen Hunt with Murray the dog (Author's collection)

The newlyweds lived in a high-rise apartment building, and the comedy on the series usually revolved around the little things in life that most couples face when they set up housekeeping and lovingly try to adjust to each other's idiosyncrasies. When asked what his series was about, Paul Reiser once stated, "The feeling of this show should be like a couple's car ride home after a party, when you can finally say what you've been thinking all night. It's what the world is like behind closed doors." Other regular characters on the series during its early years were Jamie's innocently insensitive single sister, Lisa Stemple, played by Anne Elizabeth Ramsay; Paul's sloppy bachelor friend, Jay Selby, played by Tommy Hinkley; Fran and Dr. Mark David Devanow, Paul and Jamie's friends, played by Leila Kenzle and Richard Kind; Paul's cousin, Ira Buchman, played by John Pankow; and Jamie and Paul's well-loved dog, Murray. Making occasional appearances over the years were Judy Geeson as Maggie; Paxton Whitehead as Hal; Jeff Garlin as Marvin; Cynthia Harris and Louis Zorich as Paul's parents, Sylvia and Burt Buchman; Robin Bartlett as Paul's sister, Debbie Buchman; and, on a few later episodes of the series, Carol BURNETT and Carroll O'CONNOR as Jamie's parents, Theresa and Gus Stemple. As the series continued, Paul and Jamie worked their way through various problems and adjustments, such as a near breakup of their marriage and the birth of their child, Mabel, but the loving couple's relationship managed to endure.

MAGIC CLOWN, THE

Sept. 1949–June 1954   NBC   Sun. 8:30–8:45 A.M.

This Sunday morning children's show was produced in front of a live audience of kids who participated in a wide variety of magic tricks and games. The program was hosted by Zovella, the Magic Clown, who was an illusionist and prestidigitator. He delighted children with his magic, and the show was a weekly "must-see" program with young viewers. *The Magic Clown*, which was written and directed by Al Garry, was sponsored by the Bonomo Candy Company (Turkish Taffy).

MAGIC COTTAGE, THE

July 1949– Feb. 1951	DuMont	Mon.–Fri. 6:30–7 P.M.

Pat Meikle was the fairy princess/hostess of the popular early television children's program *The Magic Cottage*. The show, which was seen five days a week on the DuMont network, was telecast live from New York City's Wanamaker's department store, and children could watch the live show from outside the display window of the store. Meikle was a teacher and an artist who sketched animated characters and told nap-time stories in daily serialized episodes, assisted by an animated English-speaking pigeon named Wilmer. She also offered a wide variety of games and contests that children could play. The show, which was preceded by Meikle's earlier daytime program *The T.V. Babysitter,* was produced by Pat Meikle's husband, Hal Cooper. At the beginning of each show, young viewers were told the Magic Cottage was a place where "everything and anything can happen and does happen," and as far as they were concerned, it certainly was.

MAGILLA GORILLA SHOW, THE

Jan. 1964–	Syndicated	Various times
Jan. 1965		and stations
Jan. 1966–	ABC	Sat. 11:30–12 A.M.
Sept. 1967		

The Magilla Gorilla Show was a children's program produced by the Hanna and Barbera Studios and featured a gorilla named Magilla, who lived in a pet store window. The owner of the pet store, Mr. Peebles, was constantly trying to sell Magilla to anyone who came into his store, but the ape was always returned to the store by whomever bought him. Among the customers who bought Magilla were an odd hunter who was in the "monkey business," a football coach, and a wealthy socialite. Also seen on this show on other segments were such things as "Mush Mouse and Punkin' Puss," which was about a mouse and a cat who always quarreled, and Sheriff Ricochet Rabbit ("Bing-bing-bing!") of the Wild West. The voices of the characters on the show were provided by Allan Melvin (as Magilla and Punkin' Puss), Howard Morris (as Mr. Peebles and Mush Mouse), Dan Messick (as Ricochet), Daws Butler (as Breezly), and Mel Blanc (as Droop-a-Long Deputy and Sneezely Seal). When *The Magilla Gorilla Show* was first on the air, it was sponsored by the Ideal Toy Company. Like many of the Hanna-Barbera productions, *The Magilla Gorilla Show* was revived in the 1970s and as part of a new program called *Yogi's Gang.*

MAGNUM, P.I.

Dec. 1980–Aug. 1981	CBS	Thurs. 9–10 P.M.
Sept. 1981–Apr. 1986	CBS	Thurs. 8–9 P.M.
Apr. 1986–June 1986	CBS	Sat. 10–11 P.M.
June 1986–Aug. 1986	CBS	Tues. 9–10 P.M.
Sept. 1986–May 1987	CBS	Wed. 9–10 P.M.
July 1987–Feb. 1988	CBS	Wed. 9–10 P.M.
June 1988–Sept. 1988	CBS	Mon. 10–11 P.M.

The beautiful Hawaiian landscape was the setting for the detective/adventure series *Magnum, P.I.* which starred actor Tom SELLECK as a Vietnam War veteran turned private detective, Thomas Sullivan Magnum. *Magnum, P.I.* replaced the popular HAWAII FIVE-O series on CBS when that show departed the airwaves, and the characters on *Magnum, P.I.* frequently referred to Steve McGarrett and his *Hawaii Five-O* policemen on the new show. Thomas Magnum was a private investigator who lived in the

guest house on the fabulous Hawaiian estate of the wealthy writer Robin Masters (whose voice was only heard and was provided by no less a celebrated name than Orson Welles). Magnum obtained his enviable living arrangement in exchange for providing the security of guarding the Masters estate. Also living at the estate, which Masters rarely visited, was an Englishman named Jonathan Quayle Higgins III, played by John Hillerman, who ran the estate for its absent owner, and who had two large Doberman pinschers named Zeus and Apollo that guarded the estate with Magnum but frequently were at odds with him. Higgins was fastidious, disciplined, and somewhat prissy, the exact opposite of Magnum, who was laid-back and casual, and the two occupants of the estate often clashed. Assisting Magnum with his private detective assignments were Magnum's African-American service buddy, T. C. (Theodore Calvin), played by Roger E. Mosley, and his other service buddy, Rick Wright (who hated his real name, Orville), played by Larry Manetti, who, when the series first went on the air, managed a nightclub that resembled Rick's Place in the film *Casablanca.* Later in the series Rick became the managing partner with Robin Masters of the exclusive King Kamehameha Beach Club. Occasionally, Magnum and his two friends were assisted in their private detective activities by a shady character named Ice Pick, played by Elisha Cook, Jr., and Assistant D.A. Carol Baldwin, played by Kathleen Lloyd, who was a friend of Magnum's. Also appearing on the series as semiregulars were Kwan Hi Lim as police detective Lt. Tanaka, Jeff MacKay as Magnum's navy buddy, Mac Reynolds, who provided Magnum with useful information as needed, and Gillian Dobb as Agatha Chumley.

MAHONEY, JOCK (JACQUES O'MAHONEY 1919–1989)

Before Jock Mahoney, who is perhaps best known for playing Yancy Derringer on television, became an actor, he was an outstanding athlete at the University of Iowa, where he excelled at swimming, basketball, and football. Mahoney, who was born in Chicago, enlisted in the U.S. Marine Corps during World War II and was a fighter pilot and an instructor during the war. After his discharge from the Marines, Mahoney went to Hollywood, where he became a stunt man in films, doubling for famous actors such as Erroll Flynn, John Wayne, and Gregory Peck. Mahoney's big break as an actor came when Gene AUTRY signed him to star on a TV series called *The Range Rider* in 1951. In 1958, Mahoney won the role of Yancy on *Yancy Derringer* and followed that up by playing Tarzan in two feature films, *Tarzan Goes to India* (1962) *and Tarzan's Three Challenges* (1963). Mahoney also appeared in such films as *Once Before I Die* (1965), *The Love Bug* (1968), *The Bad Bunch* (1973), and *The End* (1978) and guest-starred on such TV series as BATMAN, EMERGENCY!, BANACEK, KUNG FU, *The STREETS OF SAN FRANCISCO, B. J. AND THE BEAR,* and *The Fall Guy.*

MAJOR DAD

Sept. 1989	CBS	Mon. 8–8:30 P.M.
Sept. 1989–Sept. 1990	CBS	Mon. 8:30–9 P.M.
Sept. 1990–June 1991	CBS	Mon. 8:30–9 P.M.
June 1991–July 1991	CBS	Mon 8–8:30 P.M.
July 1991–Sept. 1992	CBS	Mon. 8:30–9 P.M.
Sept. 1992–Apr. 1993	CBS	Fri. 8:30–9 P.M.
May 1993–Sept. 1993	CBS	Mon. 8:30–9 P.M.

Major John D. "Mac" MacGillis, played by Gerald McRaney, was the main character on this situation comedy series. MacGillis was a conservative, spit-and-polish Marine officer who was stationed at Camp Singleton in San Diego, California, where he lived a well-ordered life until he fell in love with Polly Cooper, played by Shanna Reed, a liberal, unconventional reporter who had met MacGillis when she interviewed him for a local newspaper. Polly, a widow with three children, and Mac were married after a whirlwind three-week courtship, and Mac suddenly found his ordered life turned upside down when he became surrounded by females. Polly's three daughters were Elizabeth Cooper (age 15), played by Marisa Ryan; Robin Cooper (age 11), played by Nichole Dubuc; and Casey Cooper (age six), played by Chelsea Hertford. Other regular characters on the series were Mac's staff members: the easy-to-please 2nd Lt. Gene Holowachuk, played by Matt Mulhern; the quick-tongued Sgt. Byron James, played by Marlon Archey; and the perky secretary, Merilee Gunderson, played by Whitney Kershaw. Major MacGillis and his new family relocated to Camp Holister, near Washington, D.C., for the show's second season. Added to the cast were Beverly Archer as Gunnery Sgt. Alva "Gunny" Bricker, who soon became one of the most popular characters on the show, and Chance Michael Corbitt as the commanding officer's grandson, Jeffrey. During the series' final season, Camp Hollister was threatened with possible closure, reflecting what was actually happening to military bases throughout the United States at that time. On a November 1990 episode that commemorated the 215th anniversary of the Marine Corps, Dan Quayle, then the vice president of the United States, made an appearance.

MAJORS, LEE (HARVEY LEE YEARY 1941–   )

Best known as television's SIX MILLION DOLLAR MAN, Lee Majors, who was born in Wyandotte, Michigan, starred in no less than six other TV series during his long and successful career: The VIRGINIAN from 1970 until 1971, Owen Marshall: Counselor at Law in 1971, The BIONIC WOMAN in 1976, The Fall Guy in 1981, Tour of Duty in 1990, and Raven in 1991–1993. Majors, who made his first principal acting appearance in the film Straight-Jacket in 1964, subsequently appeared on The BIG VALLEY series and in the film Will Penny (1968), before getting his first major role on The Virginian. When he was married to FARRAH FAWCETT, Lee and Farrah were among Hollywood's most photographed couples. In recent years, Majors has been seen in featured roles in such films as Trojan War (1997), Chapter Zero (1999), and Primary Suspect (2000).

MAKE ROOM FOR DADDY (THE DANNY THOMAS SHOW/MAKE ROOM FOR GRANDDADDY)

Sept. 1953–June 1956	ABC	Tues. 9–9:30 P.M.
Oct. 1956–Feb. 1957	ABC	Mon. 8–8:30 P.M.
Feb. 1957–July 1957	ABC	Thurs. 9–9:30 P.M.
Oct. 1957–Sept. 1964	CBS	Mon. 9–9:30 P.M.
Apr. 1965–Sept. 1965	CBS	Mon. 9:30–10 P.M.
Sept. 1970–Jan. 1971	ABC	Wed. 8–8:30 P.M.
Jan. 1971–Sept. 1971	ABC	Thurs. 9–9:30 P.M.

Comedian Danny THOMAS was the star of one of television's longest-running family comedies of the 1950s and 1960s, Make Room for Daddy. After three seasons on the air, the show changed its name to The DANNY THOMAS SHOW. The show ended its run in 1965, but in 1970, after a six-year absence, Thomas returned to TV as the star of a new situation comedy series, playing the same character he had played on Make Room for Daddy; however, in his new series, Make Room for Granddaddy, Danny was a grandfather. On the original show, Thomas was a nightclub singer and comedian named Danny Williams, whose domestic problems stemmed from his frequent absences from home and the adjustments he had to make as a husband and father when he returned home. When the series first went on the air, the show's title stemmed from the fact that whenever Williams returned home after an

Make Room For Daddy: Rusty Hamer, Penny Parker, and Danny Thomas. (Author's collection)

engagement, his wife and kids always stated that they had better "make room for Daddy." When the series was originally aired in 1953, Jean Hagen played Danny's wife, Margaret, but when Hagen decided to leave the show in 1956 (her character died), she was replaced by Marjorie Lord as Danny's new wife, Kathy (nicknamed "Clancy"), a widow he had met and married after his first wife's death. Rusty Hamer played Danny and Margaret's son, Rusty, and Sherry Jackson, and then Penny Parker, played their daughter, Terry. Kathy's daughter from her first marriage, Linda, played by Angela Cartwright, joined the cast of *Make Room for Daddy* in 1957 and became Danny's adopted daughter. Among the show's most popular characters on the original series were the family's African-American maid, Louise, played by Louise Beavers, and then by Amanda Randolph, and Danny's foreign-born eccentric uncle, Tonoose, played by Hans Conried. Also seen on the original and revised programs were Horace McMahon as Horace, Ben Lessy as Benny, Mary Wickes as Liz, Sheldon Leonard as Danny's agent, Phil Brokaw, Pat Harrington, Jr., as Part Hannigan, Annette FUNICELLO as Gina, Sid Melton as Uncle Charley Halper (who owned the Copa Club, where Danny frequently performed), and Pat Carroll as his wife, Bunny Halper, Roosevelt Grier as Rosey Robbins, Michael Hughes as Michael, and Stanley Myron Handelman as Henry. Many well-known show business celebrities made guest appearances on Thomas's 1970 series, *Make Room for Granddaddy,* including Lucille BALL, Milton BERLE, Bob HOPE, and Frank Sinatra. Unfortunately, these stars did not help to keep the new series on the air, and *Make Room for Granddaddy* was canceled after one year. *The Danny Thomas Show's* familiar theme music was "Londonderry Air" ("Danny Boy").

MAMA

July 1949–July 1956	CBS	Fri. 8–8:30 P.M.

The family-oriented television series *Mama* was one of the most popular early programs on the air for seven years and was the prototype for the many "growing family" series that followed. A lighthearted account of family life in San Francisco at the turn of the century (1900), *Mama* was based on a novella, *Mama's Bank Account,* by Kathryn Forbes, and a subsequent Broadway play, *I Remember Mama,* by John Van Druten. The major characters on this warm and loving series were a Norwegian immigrant woman, Marta "Mama" Hansen, played by Peggy WOOD; her husband, Lars "Papa" Hansen, played by Judson Laire; and their children, adolescents Nels, played by Dick VAN PATTEN, and Katrin (who narrated each week's episode), played by Rosemary Rice, and the baby of the family, Dagmar, originally played by Iris Mann (in 1949), and then by Robin Morgan for most of the show's run. Each week's episode began with a grown-up Katrin sitting at a desk, writing her remembrances of her childhood in San Francisco, and then the story unfolded. Mama Hansen was the practical, loving matriarch and

"rock" of the family, who could always be depended upon for a solution to whatever problem her family might be having. Other characters regularly seen on the series were Mama's sister, Aunt Jenny, played by Ruth Gates; Mama's gruff and often overbearing Uncle Chris, played by Malcom Keen, and then by Roland Winters; Mama's younger sister, Aunt Trina, and her husband, Gunnar Gunnerson, played by Alice Frost and Carl Frank; and cousin Ingeborg, played by Patty McCormack. *Mama* was telecast live, rather than filmed, each week, and therefore reruns of this very popular series, except for a very few kinescoped episodes, do not exist. *Mama* was produced and directed by Ralph Nelson, was later produced by Carol Irwin.

MAMA'S FAMILY

Jan. 1983–June 1983	NBC	Sat. 9–9:30 P.M.
Aug. 1983–Dec. 1983	NBC	Thurs. 8:30–9 P.M.
Jan. 1984–May 1984	NBC	Sat. 9:30–10 P.M.
June 1984–July 1984	NBC	Sat. 9–9:30 P.M.
July 1984–Sept. 1984	NBC	Sat. 9:30–10 P.M.
June 1985–Aug. 1985	NBC	Sat. 9:30–10 P.M.
Sept. 1986–Sept. 1990	Syndication	Various times and stations

Mama Thelma Harper of *Mama's Family* was first introduced to the public as a character in a sketch on *The CAROL BURNETT SHOW*. The character, played by Vicki LAWRENCE, a regular cast member on the Burnett show, a became very popular with viewers, and four years after *The Carol Burnett Show* departed the airwaves, a regular weekly spin-off series, *Mama's Family,* starring Lawrence as Mama Harper, surfaced. *Mama's Family* was set in the fictional southern town of Raytown. In addition to Lawrence as the cantankerous, mean-spirited old matriarch of a dysfunctional family, the series also starred Ken Berry as her somewhat dim recently divorced son, Vint, who had moved back to Mama's house; Eric Brown as Vint's teenage son, Buzz; Karen Argoud as Vint's teenage daughter, Sonia; Dorothy Lyman as the Harpers' next-door neighbor, Naomi Oates, who later married Vint; Rue McCLANAHAN as Mama's sister, Fran, who was a writer for the Raytown newspaper; Betty WHITE as Mama's daughter, Ellen; and Harvey KORMAN as the sophisticated and urbane Alistaire Quince. Korman, as Quince, introduced each episode of the show. Carol BURNETT appeared on occasion as Mama's demeaned but indomitable daughter, Eunice. Burnett had played the same character on the original sketches that had introduced the Harper family to viewers. Harvey Korman originally played Eunice's long-suffering husband, Ed, on the *Burnett Show* sketches. When *Mama's Family* went into syndication, new characters on the series were Bubba Higgins, Eunice's and

Ed's son, played by Alan Kayser, and Iola Boylan, Mama's next-door neighbor, who had a crush on Vint, played by Beverly Archer.

MAN AGAINST CRIME

Oct. 1949–Mar. 1952	CBS	Fri. 8:30–9 P.M.
Apr. 1952–June 1952	CBS	Thurs. 9–9:30 P.M.
Oct. 1952–June 1953	CBS	Wed. 9:30–10 P.M.
July 1953–Oct. 1953	CBS	Fri. 8:30–9 P.M.
Oct. 1953–Apr. 1954	DuMont	Sun. 10:30–11 P.M.
Oct. 1953–July 1954	NBC	Sun. 10:30–11 P.M.
July 1956–Aug. 1956	NBC	Sun. 10–10:30 P.M.

A tough private detective named Mike Barnett was the "man against crime" on this television detective/drama series set in New York City that was very popular with viewers in the late 1940s to mid-1950s. Barnett, who fought crime with his brain and not his brawn, was played by film actor Ralph Bellamy from 1949 through 1954, and then by Frank Lovejoy in a revived version of the show in 1956. In summer 1951, when Bellamy went on vacation, Robert Preston appeared as Mike Barnett's brother, Pat Barnett. From 1949 until fall 1952, the series was telecast live from Thomas A. Edison Studios in the Bronx, New York. In 1952, the series was filmed, and it was one of the first TV shows to use various locations in and around the city as backgrounds. When CBS dropped the show in 1953, it was picked up by the DuMont and NBC networks, and for a short while it was seen on both networks. After a two-year hiatus, *Man Against Crime* was revived on NBC with Frank Lovejoy playing the Barnett role, but it was on the air only as a summer replacement, and then disappeared.

MAN FROM ATLANTIS, THE

Sept. 1977	NBC	Thurs. 9–10 P.M.
Oct. 1977–Jan. 1978	NBC	Tues. 8–9 P.M.
Apr. 1978–July 1978	NBC	Tues. 8–9 P.M.

The Man from Atlantis was a science fiction/adventure series that starred Patrick Duffy as Mark Harris, who, though he appeared human, had been born in the ocean and had gill tissues rather than lungs. Harris was able to breathe air and walk around just like any other human for no longer than 12 hours before he had to return to the sea. Harris could swim like a dolphin and had superhuman strength and endurance. He had been found by Dr. Elizabeth Merrill when he washed ashore, unconscious. Dr. Merrill nursed Harris back to health, and when he had recovered, he agreed to join the doctor and her fellow scientists from the Foundation of Oceanic Research in a project to learn more about life undersea. As the scientists and Harris traveled around in a craft called Cetacean, they encountered evil scientists such as Dr. Schubert, played by Victor Buono, and his assistant, Brent, played by Robert Lussier, who tried to steal their information for financial

gain. Also appearing regularly was Alan Fudge as the foundation's director, C. W. Crawford; Richard Williams as Jomo; J. Victor Lopez as Chuey; Jean Marie Hon as Jane; and Anson Downes as Allen. The executive producer was Herbert F. Solow. *The Man from Atlantis* was the first American series to be purchased by the People's Republic of China for distribution in that country.

MAN FROM U.N.C.L.E., THE

Sept. 1964–Dec. 1964	NBC	Tues. 8:30–9:30 P.M.
Jan. 1965–Sept. 1965	NBC	Mon. 8–9 P.M.
Sept. 1965–Sept. 1966	NBC	Fri. 10–11 P.M.
Sept. 1966–Sept. 1967	NBC	Fri. 8:30–9:30 P.M.
Sept. 1967–Jan. 1968	NBC	Mon. 8–9 P.M.

The "U.N.C.L.E." in the title of this television series was the United Network Command for Law and Enforcement, an organization that fought the international crime syndicate THRUSH. U.N.C.L.E. was headquartered in New York, and two of its agents, American Napoleon Solo, played by Robert VAUGHN, and Russian Illya Kuryakin, played by David MCCALLUM, were teamed to do battle with THRUSH. The director of the U.N.C.L.E. organization was Mr. Waverly, played by Leo G. Carroll, who coordinated the agents' efforts. Solo was a sophisticated man of the world, and Kuryakin was introverted and shy, but the two worked well together as they traveled around the world fighting THRUSH's evil activities. As the series progressed, the plots of each episode became more and more far-fetched, and in 1966 a spin-off series, *The Girl from U.N.C.L.E.*, surfaced, expanding *The Man from U.N.C.L.E.* from one to two hours a week. *The Girl from*

Man from U.N.C.L.E: (left to right) Leo G. Carroll, Robert Vaughn, David McCallum (Author's collection)

U.N.C.L.E. was canceled after one season, and *The Man from U.N.C.L.E.* reverted to its one-hour-a-week format, remaining on the air for one more year. In all, 132 episodes were filmed. In 1983, Vaughn and McCallum, as Solo and Kuryakin, were reunited in a TV film *The Return of the Man from U.N.C.L.E.*, which attracted a large audience who fondly remembered the original series, which during its second season was on the Nielsen list of top 20 shows on television.

MANNIX

Sept. 1967–Sept. 1971	CBS	Sat. 10–11 P.M.
Sept. 1971–Sept. 1972	CBS	Wed. 10–11 P.M.
Sept. 1972–Dec. 1972	CBS	Sun. 9:30–10:30 P.M.
Jan. 1973–Sept. 1974	CBS	Sun. 8:30–9:30 P.M.
Sept. 1974–June 1975	CBS	Sun. 9:30–10:30 P.M.
July 1975–Aug. 1975	CBS	Wed. 10–11 P.M.

For eight years, *Mannix* was one of television's most popular detective/adventure series. The series starred Mike Connors as Joe Mannix, a Los Angeles private eye who worked for a sophisticated detective agency called Intertect. The company used computers and other electronic devices in its detective work, but Mannix seemed happiest when he was employing his own intuition and his fists when working on a case. At the beginning of the series' second season, Mannix had left Intertect and opened an agency of his own in a small office on the ground floor of the building in which he lived. His girl Friday and good friend, Peggy Fair, played by African-American actress Gail Fisher, assisted Mannix in the office, as did his friend, Lou Wickham, played by Joe Campanella, who had been Mannix's boss when he worked at Intertect. Known as one of television's most violent series, the highlight of each program was usually a brawl that resulted in bodies strewn all over the place. Also featured on the series were Robert Reed as Lt. Adam Tobias and Ward Wood as Lt. Art Malcolm of the L.A. Police Department. *Mannix* was produced by Bruce Geller for Paramount TV.

MAN WITH A CAMERA

Oct. 1958–Mar. 1959	ABC	Fri. 9–9:30 P.M.
Oct. 1959–Feb. 1960	ABC	Mon. 10:30–11 P.M.

Film star Charles BRONSON's first major exposure as an actor was on the *Man with a Camera* television series. Bronson played a former combat photographer during World War II, Mike Kovac, who became a freelance photographer who sold his photos to newspapers, police departments, insurance companies, and private individuals. The type of assignments Mike usually had made him more of a private detective than a photographer. Appearing regularly on the series with Bronson were Ludwig Stossel as his father, Anton Kovac, who, on occasion, assisted his son, and James Flavin as New York City police detective Lt. Donovan.

MANY LOVES OF DOBIE GILLIS, THE

Sept. 1959–Sept. 1962	CBS	Tues. 8:30–9 P.M.
Sept. 1962–Sept. 1963	CBS	Wed. 8:30–9 P.M.

In the late 1950s to early 1960s, one of the most popular series on TV was *The Many Loves of Dobie Gillis*. Dobie Gillis was a typical American teenage boy who was interested in fast cars, pretty girls, and money. Dobie's father was a grocer and not very rich, so the fast cars and money eluded the teen, but Dobie still had his interest in pretty girls to keep him occupied. Dobie, played by Dwayne HICKMAN, had a best friend who was an unconventional fellow named Maynard G. Krebs, played by Bob DENVER. Maynard was a "beatnik" and not in the least bit interested in work and therefore was not a particularly good influence on Dobie. Dobie's parents, Herbert T. and Winifred (Winnie) Gillis, played by Frank Faylen and Florida Friebus, tried to understand their bewildering offspring, but were usually confused by his adolescent behavior. One girl who had a crush on Dobie was Zelda Grey, played by Sheila James. Zelda was a bookworm and not particularly attractive, but she pursued Dobie with relentless vigor. Dobie's major nemesis during the series' early years was the handsome and popular Milton Armitage, played by Warren Beatty. Milton made Dobie feel less than adequate in the girl department. In 1960, Milton was replaced by a character named Chatsworth Armitage, Jr., a rich fellow classmate of Dobie's who, like Milton, always tried to better Dobie. In 1961, Dobie and Maynard enlisted in the army, but their army experience lasted only into the next season, and at the beginning of the 1961–62 season, the boys had enrolled at St. Peter Prior Junior College. In 1977, 15 years after the original *Dobie Gillis* series was on TV, CBS launched a pilot for a revised series, but the show was abandoned before it found a new audience. Dobie had married Zelda, and had settled down to working in his father's grocery store. The idea did not appeal to viewers who remembered Dobie's youthful exuberance. Dobie Gillis and his friends were based on characters created by author Max Shulman.

MARCH, HAL (1920–1970)

The host of one of television's most successful game shows, *The $64,000 QUESTION*, Hal March was born in San Francisco. March began his show business career as a comedian, partnering with comic Bob Sweeney. As "Sweeney & March," the comedy team enjoyed considerable success performing in nightclubs and on television in the late 1940s to early 1950s, until they decided to go their separate ways. Before becoming a television game show host, March was an actor and had featured roles in such films as *Ma and Pa Kettle Go to Town* (1950), *The Eddie Cantor Story* (1953), *Yankee Pasha* (1954), and *The Atomic Kid* (1954), and was a regular on such TV series as *The GEORGE BURNS AND GRACIE ALLEN SHOW*, *The RCA Victor Show* (1951–53), *MY FRIEND IRMA*, and *The Imogene Coca Show* (1954–55). March also appeared on such TV shows as *I LOVE LUCY* and *Life with Elizabeth* (1953). In 1955, March became the host of what became one of television's most successful game shows, *The $64,000 Question*. In the late 1950s, however, many TV game shows became embroiled in a scandal of rigging answers so that contestants could win big prize money and keep the public interested in their shows. Although *The $64,000 Question* was not specifically accused of wrongdoing, all the TV game shows of the time suddenly disappeared from the home screens. March subsequently appeared in such films as *Send Me No Flowers* (1964) and *A Guide for the Married Man* (1967), but his career never reached the heights it had while he was hosting *The $64,000 Question*. In 1970, while March was cohosting the *It's Your Bet* TV game show, he suffered a heart attack and died.

MARCUS WELBY, M.D.

Sept. 1969–May 1976	ABC	Tues. 10–11 P.M.

When *Marcus Welby, M.D.* made its television debut in 1969, the series almost instantly became one of the biggest hit shows on the ABC lineup, and subsequently, it became one of the most successful shows in the history of the ABC network. The longtime star of the very popular FATHER KNOWS BEST series, Robert YOUNG, played the title role on the *Marcus Welby, M.D.* series, and it was mainly his comforting and familiar presence that first drew viewers to the show. Welby was a kindly, 60-something physician who practiced general medicine in Santa Monica, California. Welby was dedicated to his patients, whose various illnesses became the basis for each week's episode. Assisting Dr. Welby was a young physician named Dr. Steven Kiley, played by James Brolin, who contracted to work with Welby for one year before resuming his training as a neurologist. Although there was tension between the older and younger doctors, since Kiley treated the psychological nature of the patient and Welby favored treating the "whole patient," the two doctors become fond of each other, and Kiley decided to remain with Welby after the year ended. Other regulars on the series included Elena VERDUGO as the doctor's lovable and able, well-meaning, but sometimes opinionated office nurse, Consuelo Lopez; Sharon Gless as Nurse Kathleen Faverty; Anne Schedeen as Welby's daughter, Sandy, who came to live with the good doctor in the show's last season; and Sandy's son, six-year-old Phil, played by Gavin Brendan. During the show's first season, Welby had a girlfriend named Myra Sherwood, played by veteran actress Anne Baxter, but Myra departed for places unknown before the show's second season began.

Over the years, Welby and his staff dealt with a wide variety of medical problems, such as tumors, diabetes, drug addiction, amnesia, blindness, and strokes, which kept viewers tuning in to see what new illness Welby and his crew encountered and treated. In 1975, love found Dr. Kiley in the person of Janet Blake, played by Pamela Hensley, who was a public relations director at the Hope Memorial Hospital. The show's ratings soared when Kiley and Blake were married on the October 21, 1975, episode.

Marcus Welby, M.D. was created by David Victor, who also produced the show.

MARRIED . . . WITH CHILDREN

Apr. 1987–Oct. 1987	FOX	Sun. 8–8:30 P.M.
Oct. 1987–July 1989	FOX	Sun. 8:30–9 P.M.
July 1989–Nov. 1993	FOX	Sun. 9–9:30 P.M.
Nov. 1993–Jan. 1994	FOX	Sun. 9–10 P.M.
Jan. 1994–Apr. 1995	FOX	Sun. 9–9:30 P.M.
Apr. 1995–May 1995	FOX	Sun. 9–10 P.M.
May 1995–Jan 1996	FOX	Sun. 9–9:30 P.M.
Jan. 1996–Feb. 1996	FOX	Sun. 9–10 P.M.
Mar. 1996–Apr. 1996	FOX	Sun. 9–9:30 P.M.
Apr. 1996–May 1996	FOX	Sun. 9–10 P.M.
May 1996–July 1996	FOX	Sun. 9–9:30 P.M.
July 1996–Aug. 1996	FOX	Sun. 8:30–9 P.M.
Sept. 1996–Oct. 1996	FOX	Sat. 9–9:30 P.M.
Nov. 1996–Dec. 1996	FOX	Sun. 7–8 P.M.
Jan. 1997	FOX	Mon. 9:30–10 P.M.
Feb. 1997–May 1997	FOX	Mon. 9–9:30 P.M.
Jan. 1997–July 1997	FOX	Mon. 9–10 P.M.

"Love and Marriage," as sung by Frank Sinatra, introduced each episode of the FOX situation comedy series *Married . . . with Children*, which was certainly not the typical television family-oriented series. The Bundys, the

Married with Children: (clockwise from left) Christine Applegate (Kelly Bundy), Amanda Bearse (Marcy Rhoades), David Garrison (Steve Rhoades), Katey Segal (Peggy Bundy), Ed O'Neill (Al Bundy), and David Faustino (Bud Bundy) (Author's collection)

family featured on this unconventional series, were not lovable, and their dysfunctional behavior made even the most hardened viewer wince with alarm as they reacted to one another and to various domestic situations with insensitive and unabashed selfishness. The Bundys lived in suburban Chicago. The patriarch was Al Bundy, played by Ed O'Neill. Al was a shoe salesman whose chauvinistic attitudes and coarse behavior could easily have earned him the title of "Swine of the Millennium." Al's wife, Peggy, played by Katey Segal, was not much better than Al. Peggy, Al's wife of 15 years, was a lazy slattern who never cooked or cleaned their house and certainly could have given Al a run for his money for the "Swine" title. The Bundys' semidelinquent teenage children, Kelly, played by Christina Applegate, a terrible teen who was self-centered and mean-spirited, and Bud, played by David Faustino, who was as rotten as his sister, were usually at each other's throats when not showing contempt for their parents. Even though *Married . . . with Children* was the most successful series on the new FOX network, which had just surfaced when the series was first seen, it drew the wrath of many critics and viewers because of its outspoken, often raunchy, approach to TV comedy. Sex was frequently discussed, and one of the program's running jokes involved Al's bedroom prowess, or lack of it, according to the forever frustrated Peggy, who could never seem to get Al to respond to her. The Bundys' dog, Buck, also occasionally figured into the plots. Also appearing regularly were the Bundys' newlywed neighbors, Steve and Marcy Rhoades, played by David Garrison and Amanda Bearse, who were madly in love, until Al and Peggy started to tell them all about marriage, as they saw it. The series' popularity continued to grow, the more heinous the situations the family found itself engaged in.

In 1991, due to Segal's actual pregnancy, the producers decided to have both Peggy and Marcy become pregnant. When Segal lost her baby during pregnancy, the plot of *Married . . . with Children* changed, and Peggy's pregnancy was revealed to have been one of Al's nightmares. In 1992, the six-year-old son of one of Peggy's cousins moved in with the Bundys, but the character disappeared after a few months with no explanation. Kelly got a job as a waitress in a diner during the 1992 season, and Bud had begun to attend college and got a part-time job as a driving tester for the Bureau of Motor Vehicles.

Also appearing on the series during its long run were Ted McGinley as Jefferson D'Arcy, Shane Sweet as Seven Wanker, Dan Tullus, Jr., as Officer Don, Harold Sylvster as Al's fellow shoe salesman at Gary's Shoe Emporium, Tom McCleister as Ike, Pat Millicano as Sticky, E. E. Bell as Bob Rooney, Tim Conway as Efram Wanker, Peg's mother's (who was never seen) husband, and Janet Carroll as Gary, Al's verbally abusive boss and the owner of the shoe store where he worked.

By 1994, *Married . . . with Children* had become the longest-running situation comedy series on network television, with 200 episodes. The series continued for another three years, and eventually went into reruns, becoming one of television's perennial favorites on cable.

Married . . . with Children was developed for television by Ron Leavitt and Michael Moye, who had been writers for *The JEFFERSONS* for many years. Concerning *Married . . . with Children's* origins, Moye once said, "We'd always hated the typical family on television. It just makes us sick, basically." The Bundys on his show were certainly anything but a "typical" TV family.

MARSHALL, GARRY (GARRY KENT MARSHALL 1934–)

The creator, producer, and frequent director of such successful television series as *HAPPY DAYS*, *LAVERNE & SHIRLEY*, *The ODD COUPLE*, *MORK & MINDY* and *Who's Watching the Kids*, to name just a few, Garry Marshall was born in New York City. After graduating from DeWitt Clinton High School in New York, Garry attended Northwestern University in Evanston, Illinois, where he majored in television and film production. Garry's first job after graduating from college was as a comedy writer, and in 1961 he became a script supervisor for the television series *The Joey Bishop Show*. Among Marshall's TV producing credits, in addition to the shows cited above, are *Me and the Chimp* (1972), *Blansky's Beauties* (1977), and *Herndon* (1983).

Garry Marshall (Author's collection)

Marshall also produced the films *How Sweet It Is!* (1968), *Evil Roy Slade* (1971), *Young Doctors in Love* (1982), and *The Twilight of the Golds* (1997). His credits as a director, in addition to his TV hits, include films *The Flamingo Kid* (1984), *Pretty Woman* (1990), and *Runaway Bride* (1999). A talented actor as well as an accomplished producer and director, Marshall has been featured in such films as *Lost in America* (1985), *A League of Their Own* (1992), and *Hocus Pocus* (1993), and on the TV series *The Ugliest Girl in Town* (1968), and MURPHY BROWN, among others.

MARSHALL, PENNY (CAROLE PENNY MARSHALL 1942–)

Best known for her performances on television as Myrna Turner on *The* ODD COUPLE, Miss Larson on *The* BOB NEWHART SHOW, and Laverne De Fazio on LAVERNE & SHIRLEY, Penny Marshall, the sister of producer/director Garry MARSHALL, was born in the Bronx in New York City. Like her brother, in addition to acting, Penny also became a successful producer and director and was largely responsible for the success of such celebrated films as *Big* (1988), *A League of Their Own* (1992), *Renaissance Man* (1994), and *The Preacher's Wife* (1996). Few people know that Marshall was one of the four finalists for the role of Gloria on ALL IN THE FAMILY, but the role was given to Sally Struthers. Marshall, however, went on to become one of TV's most familiar faces and, in addition to appearing on *The Odd Couple, Bob Newhart,* and *Laverne & Shirley* shows, she was also featured on such TV series as *Banacek, The* MARY TYLER MOORE SHOW, HAPPY DAYS, MORK & MINDY, BOSOM BUDDIES, and TAXI, and was heard as the voice of Lucille Botzcowski (aka Ms. Botz) on a popular episode of *The* SIMPSONS.

MARTHA RAYE SHOW, THE

| Sept. 1955–May 1956 | NBC | Tues. 8–9 P.M. |

Although she was one of four stars who alternated every four weeks on NBC's FOUR STAR REVUE from 1951 through 1953, and appeared in many specials from 1953 until 1955, comedienne Martha RAYE had her own weekly show on NBC, *The Martha Raye Show,* during the 1955–56 season. Raye's broad, slapstick style, her mugging and her loud, comic song renditions made her one of television's most popular comediennes. Boxing champion Rocky Marciano was a regular on her weekly series, which told a different story each week with Marciano usually playing Martha's boyfriend. The show was set in a nightclub, which was the perfect setting for the numerous comic sketches, singing, and musical production numbers featured on each week's show.

MARTHA STEWART LIVING

| 1993–present | Syndicated series | Various times and stations |

Martha Stewart, the undisputed diva of all things in the home including cooking, decorating, gardening, housekeeping, and home repairs, and who was a frequent guest on numerous TV shows through the 1980s and early 1990s, brought her formidable talents to television on a half-hour weekly internationally distributed show of her own in 1993. Stewart's very successful book *Entertaining* (1983) led to a veritable cottage industry for Ms. Stewart. Currently, her tips can be seen on the CBS network as well as on reruns of her previous shows on various cable outlets.

MARTIN

Aug. 1992–Aug. 1993	FOX	Thurs. 8:30–9 P.M.
Aug. 1993–July 1994	FOX	Sun. 8–8:30 P.M.
Aug. 1994–July 1995	FOX	Thurs. 8–8:30 P.M.
Aug. 1995	FOX	Thurs. 8:30–9 P.M.
Sept. 1995–Oct. 1995	FOX	Sat. 8–8:30 P.M.
Nov. 1995–Feb. 1996	FOX	Sun. 8:30–9 P.M.
Feb. 1996–May 1996	FOX	Thurs. 8:30–9 P.M.
May 1996–Aug. 1997	FOX	Thurs. 8–8:30 P.M.

Before he became one of Hollywood's most popular film comedians, Martin Lawrence starred on a very successful weekly comedy show on FOX, *Martin,* a situation comedy based on a character Martin introduced in his stand-up comedy act, Martin Payne. Payne was a sexist, wisecracking talk show host on a Detroit radio station, WZUP. Also appearing on the series with Lawrence were Tisha Campbell as Payne's girlfriend, Gina Waters, who was a marketing executive at WZUP and put up with Payne because she loved him, Tichina Arnold as Pam James, Gina's sarcastic secretary who disliked Payne; Carl Anthony Payne II and Thomas Mikal Ford, who played Payne's friends, Cole Brown and Tommy Strong, who seemed to have nothing better to do but hang out at Payne's apartment; Garrett Morris as the radio station's arrogant owner; Jonathan Gries, the show's only white character, as Shawn the station handyman; and Martin Lawrence, playing a second role on the show, Sheneneh Jenkins, a flashy bimbo who lived in the apartment across the hall from Payne. Lawrence also appeared as several other characters on the show. *Martin* was one of the FOX network's most popular shows for the entire five years it was aired.

MARTIN, DEAN (DINO PAUL CROCETTI 1917–1995)

Before Dean Martin, who was born in Steubenville, Ohio, decided to become a professional singer, he was a prizefighter, a steel mill worker, a gas station attendant, and a gambler. In 1946, while he was singing in an upstate New York resort hotel, Martin met a comedian named Jerry LEWIS. The two performers decided to form a comedy team, with Martin singing and acting as the straight man, and Lewis acting as the clown. The team worked well together, and they were soon performing in some of the biggest nightclubs in the country, as well as appearing on various popular radio programs. Hollywood beckoned, and soon Martin and Lewis were appearing in one successful film comedy after another, including *My Friend Irma*

(1950, their film debut), *At War with the Army* (1950), *Sailor Beware* (1951), *That's My Boy* (1951), *Scared Stiff* (1953), *The Caddy* (1953), and *Artists and Models* (1955), among numerous others. In 1950, the team of Martin and Lewis also starred on a television variety show program, *The COLGATE COMEDY HOUR*. By 1957, personality differences led to the team's splitting up, and the two entertainers went their separate ways.

Martin went on to appear in 51 films as both a comic and a serious actor. Among the box office successes Martin starred in were *The Young Lions* (1958), *Some Came Running* (1958), *Rio Bravo* (1959), *Ocean's Eleven* (1960), *Bells Are Ringing* (1960), *Come Blow Your Horn* (1963), *Toys in the Attic* (1963), and *Robin and the 7 Hoods* (1964, one of several films Martin appeared in with his "Rat Pack" buddies, Frank Sinatra, Sammy Davis Jr., and Peter Lawford). In 1965, Martin starred on his own TV series, *The DEAN MARTIN SHOW*, which became one of TV's top-rated shows and remained on the air for nine years. Martin continued to star in such films as *Airport* (1970), *The Cannonball Run* (1981) and *Cannonball Run II* (1984), and hosted a series of popular Celebrity Roast specials on television (he had originally introduced Celebrity Roasts on his popular weekly TV series).

In 1985, Martin came out of semiretirement to star in an ill-fated TV series called *Half Nelson*, which was based on his 1985 film of the same name. A heavy cigarette smoker all his life, Dean Martin died of respiratory failure at the age of 78.

MARTIN KANE, PRIVATE EYE

Sept. 1949–June 1954   NBC   Thurs. 10–10:30 P.M.

One of television's earliest detective/drama series, NBC's *Martin Kane, Private Eye* starred four Hollywood leading men during the five years it was on the air. The series, which was telecast live, originally featured William Gargan, who had played the role on radio, as Martin Kane. In 1951, Gargan was replaced by Lloyd Nolan, who played the role for one year, and then by Lee Tracy, for one year, and Mark Stevens, also for one year. Originally, Kane was a smooth-talking private detective who worked closely with the police department in New York City. As the series progressed, Kane became more tough and less smooth, and his liaison with the police diminished. Most of the crimes Kane worked on were murders.

In 1953, the series name was shortened to *Martin Kane*, and the program became more mystery- and suspense-oriented. Also appearing on the series were Walter Kinsella as Kane's assistant, Happy McMann, and Fred Hillebrand as Lt. Bender, Horace McMahon as Capt. Willis, Nicholas Saunders as Sgt. Ross, Walter Greaza as Capt. Leonard, Frank Thomas as Capt. Burke, and King Calder as Lt. Grey, all of the New York City Police Department.

In 1957, three years after it departed network television, the series resurfaced as a syndicated show called *The New Adventures of Martin Kane*. On this series, Kane had moved to London, and the role was played by TV's original Martin Kane, William Gargan.

MARTINDALE, WINK (WINSTON CONRAD MARTINDALE 1934–   )

Wink Martindale, the host of several popular television game shows, was born in Jackson, Tennessee, and began his career on radio. In 1958, Martindale appeared as himself in the film *Let's Rock*, and he subsequently hosted *What's This Song* (1965), *Dream Girl of '67* (1966), *How's Your Mother-in-Law?* (1967), *Everybody's Talking* (1967), *Can You Top This?* (1970), *Words and Music* (1970), and *Gambit* (1972). When he hosted *The New Tic Tac Dough* (1978–85) and *High Rollers* (1987–88) game shows, however, Wink Martindale's name became well known to television viewers. Martindale also hosted the *Trivial Pursuit* (1993) and *Debt* (1996) game shows.

MARX, GROUCHO (JULIUS HENRY MARX 1890–1977)

Long before he was the host of the very successful *YOU BET YOUR LIFE* TV game show in 1950, comedian Groucho Marx was, with his brothers Harpo, Chico, and Zeppo, one of show business's most successful entertainers. Born in New York City, the bushy-browed, cigar-smoking wise-cracker, who sported a painted-on mustache, was a headliner in vaudeville and appeared in many Broadway revues before he and his brothers went to Hollywood and became popular film stars. After a sensational success in their first film, *The Cocoanuts,* in 1929, the Marx Brothers went on to star in such later-to-be-classic films as *Animal Crackers* (1930), *Monkey Business* (1931), *Horse Feathers* (1932), *Duck Soup* (1933), *A Night at the Opera* (1935), *A Day at the Races* (1937), and *Room Service* (1938), and the less memorable *Go West* (1940), *Copacabana* (1947), and other films, before hosting *You Bet Your Life*, first on radio in 1948, and then on television in 1950. *You Bet Your Life* remained one of television's most popular game shows until it left the air in 1961.

Over the years, Groucho guest-starred on such notable TV shows as *The JACK BENNY PROGRAM*, *The MILTON BERLE SHOW*, *The GENERAL ELECTRIC THEATER*, *I DREAM OF JEANNIE*, *The JACKIE GLEASON SHOW*, *The DICK CAVETT SHOW*, and *The New Bill Cosby Show*. With such memorable lines as, "I resign. I wouldn't want to belong to any club that would have me as a member," "Marriage is a wonderful institution, but who wants to live in an institution," and "Either he's dead or my watch has stopped," Groucho established himself as one of show business's most original wits.

MARY HARTMAN, MARY HARTMAN

1976–1977   Syndicated series   Various times and stations

A quirky but funny spoof of television daytime serials, *Mary Hartman, Mary Hartman,* created by Gail Parent,

Ann Marcus, Jerry Adelman, and Daniel Gregory Browne and developed by Norman LEAR, was a late-night soap opera that took TV by storm when it made its debut in 1976. The heroine of this hilarious, unconventional series was a pigtailed Ohio housewife who wore gingham dresses and lived in a world where TV commercials were as important as real-life problems. The housewife was Mary Hartman, and she was brilliantly played by Louise Lasser. Set in the fictional town of Fernwood, the plots of the series were totally unsuitable for daytime TV but perfect for late-night adult viewers, since they usually revolved around sexual situations and various unpleasant happenings. On the first episode, a mass murder took place, and the show ended with the heroine having a mental breakdown in front of millions of people as she was appearing as a guest on a TV talk show.

In addition to Mary Hartman, other unusual, but oddly familiar, characters seen on the series included Mary's impotent husband, Tom, played by Greg Mullavey; her daughter, Heather, played by Claudia Lamb, who was held hostage by a mass murderer; her grandfather, Raymond Larkin, played by Victor Killan, who was well known by everyone in Fernwood as a "flasher," who repeatedly exposed himself; her addle-brained mother, Martha Shumway, played by Dodie Goodman; her father, George Shumway, played by Philip Bruns, who strangely disappeared one night; her best friend, Loretta Haggers, played by Mary Kay Place, who was a country-western singer who became paralyzed; and Loretta's husband, Charley Haggers, played by Graham Jarvis. Other performers who played a wide assortment of disturbed and/or unusual characters on the series were Sparky Marcus as Jimmy Joe Jeeter, Dabney Coleman as Merle Jeeter, Marian Mercer as Wanda Jeeter, Martin Mull as Garth Gimble, Susan Browning as Pat Gimble, Shelly Fabares as Eleanor Major, Dennis Burkley as Mac Slattery, Judy Kahan as Penny Major, Richard Hatch as Harmon Farinella, Severn Darden as Popesco, Randall Carver as Jeffrey deVito, Shelley Berman as Mel Beach, Renee Taylor as Anabelle, Orson Bean as Reverend Brim, and James Staley as Dr. Szymon.

When Lasser decided to leave the series in 1977, after 325 episodes had been seen, the producers attempted to keep the show alive with a new title, *Forever Fernwood*. Without Lasser as Mary Hartman, however, the show was not a success and was canceled after one season.

MARY TYLER MOORE SHOW, THE

Sept. 1970–Dec. 1971	CBS	Sat. 9:30–10 P.M.
Dec. 1971–Sept. 1972	CBS	Sat. 8:30–9 P.M.
Sept. 1972–Oct. 1976	CBS	Sat. 9–9:30 P.M.
Nov. 1976–Sept. 1977	CBS	Sat. 8–8:30 P.M.

Although it eventually became one of television's best-loved situation comedy series, when *The Mary Tyler Moore Show* made its debut in 1971, few people thought it would be a success. The heroine of this series, Mary Richards, played by Mary Tyler MOORE, was, after all, a

The cast of the *Mary Tyler Moore Show:* (top) Valerie Harper (Rhoda Morgenstern), Ed Asner (Lou Grant), Cloris Leachman (Phyllis Lindstrom), (bottom) Gavin MacLeod (Murray Slaughter), Mary Tyler Moore (Mary Richards), and Ted Knight (Ted Baxter) (Author's Collection)

career-oriented woman in her thirties who was sensitive, compassionate, and highly moral. Compared to top popular series of the time, such as ALL IN THE FAMILY and MAUDE, whose comedy depended mainly upon satire, *The Mary Tyler Moore Show* was sincere and sweetly funny.

When the series made its debut, Mary Richards had recently moved to Minneapolis to find new friends and a new job after a disappointing breakup with a boyfriend. Although she would have preferred to get married and have children, Mary was a responsible young woman and ambitious to make a go of it on her own. Hired as an assistant producer in the news department of the WJM-TV television station, Mary moved into an apartment in a rambling old Victorian home in Minneapolis, determined to get on with her life. At WJM, Mary's coworkers in the news department consisted of her cantankerous, unsentimental but somehow lovable boss, Lou Grant, played by Ed ASNER; the sharp but downtrodden head news writer at the station, Murray Slaughter, played by Gavin MacLeod; the pompous, not particularly bright news anchorman at the station, Ted Baxter, played by Ted Knight; and Gordon "Gordy" Howard, the news department's weatherman, played by John Amos. At home, Mary soon found a close friend, Rhoda Morgenstern, played by Valerie HARPER, a 30-something young Jewish woman from New York City who lived in a tiny attic apartment in the same building as Mary and worked as a window dresser at a Minneapolis department store. Mary's well-meaning but self-centered landlady was Phyllis Lindstrom, played by Cloris LEACHMAN, whose husband, Lars, was talked about but never seen, with an adolescent daughter named Bess, played by Lisa Garritsen. Appearing semiregularly on the series was Joyce Bulifant as Murray Slaughter's wife, Marie.

As the series progressed and gained steadily in popularity, Georgia Engel as Georgette Franklin Baxter, Ted's sweet-but-dim girlfriend, who later became Ted's wife, and Betty WHITE as WJM's hostess of the "Happy Homemaker Show," Sue Ann Nivens, a woman in her forties who desperately tried to attract any man she could, joined the cast. The Gordy character departed the series in 1973, Rhoda tearfully left the show in 1974, supposedly to go back to New York (in reality Valerie Harper had been given a spin-off series of her own, *RHODA*), and Phyllis and Bess Lindstrom left the show for a spin-off series of their own, *PHYLLIS*, in 1975. By the time *The Mary Tyler Moore Show* ended its seven-year run, it was one of the most popular and successful shows on television, and millions of loyal fans shed a tear as the staff at WJM-TV gave each other a group hug as they said good-by for the last time and went their separate ways.

M*A*S*H

Sept. 1972–Sept. 1973	CBS	Sun. 8–8:30 P.M.
Sept. 1973–Sept. 1974	CBS	Sat. 8:30–9 P.M.
Sept. 1974–Sept. 1975	CBS	Tues. 8:30–9 P.M.
Sept. 1975–Nov. 1975	CBS	Fri. 8:30–9 P.M.
Dec. 1975–Jan. 1978	CBS	Tues. 9–9:30 P.M.
Jan. 1978–Sept. 1983	CBS	Mon. 9–9:30 P.M.

When the last original episode of *M*A*S*H* was aired on February 28, 1983, the curtain came down on one of television's most successful programs. The special two-and-a-half-hour final episode, which was titled "Good-by, Farewell and Amen," was one of the most widely viewed television shows of all time, and 77 percent of all people watching television that evening were said to have been watching *M*A*S*H*. Over the 11 years *M*A*S*H* was on prime-time TV, millions of people had grown to love the characters and felt as if they knew them personally. Based on a 1970 Robert Altman film about a Mobile Army Surgical Hospital unit stationed in Korea during the 1950s conflict in that country, the mobile hospital unit moved their tents from one site to another in order to be as close to the fighting lines as possible. The United States was part of the the United Nations force that had been assigned to defend noncommunist South Korea from an invasion by the commumnist North Korean government. The actual Korean conflict lasted only three years, but *M*A*S*H* was on the air for 11 years.

Alan ALDA played Capt. Benjamin Franklin Pierce, nicknamed "Hawkeye," a surgeon in the 4077th M*A*S*H unit, who had been drafted back into military service when his reserve unit in Crabapple, Maine, was recalled into active duty at the beginning of the Korean conflict. Hawkeye's refusal to conform to army rules and regulations did not affect his skill as a surgeon, or his trying to keep things on as light a note as possible considering the horrors of war all around him. Hawkeye's roommate and fellow surgeon, Capt. John "Trapper John" McIntyre, who had also been recalled into active service, played by Wayne ROGERS, became Hawkeye's closest friend and joined him in various off-hours escapades. Unlike Hawkeye, Trapper John was married and longed to return to his wife and family in the United States. Also appearing as major characters on the original series were McLean Stevenson as chief surgeon Lt. Col. Henry Blake, Hawkeye's and Trapper John's commanding officer, who was easy-going and usually avoided executing his authority as commanding officer; Loretta SWIT as Major Margaret "Hot Lips" Houlihan, the misunderstood head nurse of the mobile hospital unit; Larry Linville as Major Frank Burns, a conservative, by-the-book surgeon who objected to Hawkeye's and Trapper John's liberal views, but, although married, was having an affair with "Hot Lips" Houlihan; Gary Burghoff as Cpl. Walter "Radar" O'Reilly,

The cast of *M*A*S*H*: (top) William Christopher (Father Francis Mulcahy), Jamie Farr (Cpl. Max Klinger), David Ogden Stiers (Maj. Charles Emerson Winchester), (middle) Mike Farrell (Capt. B.J. Hunnicut), Alan Alda (Capt. Benjamin Franklin "Hawkeye" Pierce), Henry Morgan (Col. Sherman Potter), and (bottom) Loretta Swit (Maj. Margaret "Hot Lips" Houlihan) (Author's collection)

an unsophisticated, boyish, and strangely clairvoyant company clerk, who, although young, practically single-handedly ran the entire hospital unit; William Christopher as the unit's kindly and understanding chaplain, Father Francis Mulcahy; and Jamie Farr as an orderly, Cpl. Max Klinger, who usually dressed in women's clothes in a desperate attempt to get a discharge from military service, but could always be depended upon to help out during a crisis. In 1975, Wayne Rogers and McLean Stevenson decided that they wanted to leave the series to pursue other career interests. Rogers was replaced by actor Mike Farrell, who played a character named Capt. B. J. Hunnicut. Hunnicut became Hawkeye's new roommate, fellow surgeon, friend, and partner in various hospital shenanigans. Like Trapper John, Hunnicutt was a married man who looked forward to being reunited with his wife and family back in the United States. McLean Stevenson was replaced by veteran character actor Henry Morgan, who became the military unit's new commanding officer, a crusty but lovable old man named Col. Sherman Potter. In 1977, Larry Linville also left the series and was replaced by David Ogden Stiers, who played a stuffy Boston-bred surgeon, Maj. Charles Emerson Winchester. Other semiregular characters who appeared during the 11 years the show was on the air were Dr. Sidney Freedman, an army psychiatrist played by Allan Arbus; Capt. Calvin Spaulding, played by Loudon Wainwright III; Lt. Kellye Nakahara, a nurse, played by Kellye Nakahara, who had originally been a nonspeaking extra, but over the years had become a supporting character on the series; Igor Straminsky, the company cook, played by Jeff Maxwell; Sgt. Zale, played by Johnny Haymer, and Sgt. Luther Rizzo, played by G. W. Bailey.

By the time *M*A*S*H* finally ended its long TV run in 1983, it was the third highest-rated program in the country according to the A. C. Nielsen Company poll of viewers. It had been among the top 10 shows on television for eight years and was a top-20-rated show for 10 years. The series' memorable theme music was "Suicide Is Painless" by Johnny Mandel, originally written for the movie.

MASQUERADE PARTY

July 1952–Aug. 1952	NBC	Mon. 8–8:30 P.M.
June 1953–Sept. 1953	CBS	Mon. 9:30–10 P.M.
June 1954–Sept. 1954	CBS	Mon. 9:30–10 P.M.
Sept. 1954–June 1956	ABC	Wed. 9–9:30 P.M.
June 1956–Dec. 1956	ABC	Sat. 10–10:30 P.M.
Mar. 1957–Sept. 1957	NBC	Wed. 8–9:30 P.M.
Aug. 1958–Sept. 1958	CBS	Mon. 8:30–9 P.M.
Oct. 1958–Sept. 1959	NBC	Thurs. 10:30–11 P.M.
Oct. 1959–Jan. 1960	CBS	Mon. 7:30–8 P.M.
Jan. 1960–Sept. 1960	NBC	Fri. 9:30–10 P.M.

Over the eight years the *Masquerade Party* game/panel show was on television, it was hosted by six well-known TV personalities, including (in the order they hosted the show) Bud COLLYER (1952), Douglas EDWARDS (1953), Peter DONALD (1954–6), Eddie Bracken (1957), Robert Q. LEWIS (1958), and Bert PARKS (1959–60). The premise of this show was simple: a guest celebrity who was heavily costumed and disguised with elaborate makeup appeared before three or four panelists who tried to guess who he or she was by asking questions about the person and his or her disguise. The costume and makeup the guest wore usually was a clue to his or her identity. During the time *Masquerade Party* was aired, no less than 19 stars appeared on the show, including Peter Donald (who later served as moderator), Ilka Chase, John S. Young, Madge Evans, Buff Cobb, Ogden Nash, Bobby Sherwood, DAGMAR, Mary Healy, Betsy Palmer, Frank Parker, Johnny Johnston, Jonathan WINTERS, Jinx Falkenburg, Pat Carroll, Audrey Meadows, Lee Bowman, Faye EMERSON, and Sam LEVINSON. Richard Dawson hosted a revived edition of *Masquerade Party* after a 14-year absence from home screens during the 1974–75 season. The series, which was syndicated, was produced by Stefan Hatos and Monty Hall. Bill Bixby, Lee Meriwether, and Nipsey Russell were panelists on the syndicated show.

MASTERPIECE THEATRE

Jan. 1971–present	PBS	Various times

For over 30 years, *Masterpiece Theatre* has been presenting multipart adaptations of famous works of literature, which have been produced mainly by the British Broadcasting Company (BBC) in England. The series is seen in the United States on Public Broadcasting System stations and is funded by the Mobil Oil Company. Originally, the series was hosted by Alistair Cooke (1971–93), and Russell Baker took over the hosting chores in October 1993.

Presented on this program during the first season were (1971–72) *The First Churchills,* Henry James's *The Spoils of Poynton,* Dostoevsky's *The Possessed,* and Balzac's *Pere Goriot,* among others: Thomas Hardy's *Jude the Obscure,* Dostoevsky's *The Gambler,* Tolstoy's *Resurrection,* Stella Gibbons's *Cold Comfort Farm, The Six Wives of Henry VIII* (in six segments), *Elizabeth R* (in six segments with Glenda Jackson as Elizabeth I), and James Fenimore Cooper's *The Last of the Mohicans.*

The second season (1972–73) included Thackeray's *Vanity Fair,* Balzac's *Cousin Bette, The Moonstone, Tom Brown's Schooldays,* Aldous Huxley's *Point Counter Point,* and Henry James's *The Golden Bowl.*

The third season's (1973–74) offerings were *Clouds of Witness, The Man Who Was Hunting Himself, The Unpleasantness at the Bellona Club, The Little Farm,* and 13 episodes of *Upstairs Downstairs,* which was the story of a wealthy family that lived in London (upstairs) and their servants (downstairs). Created by Jean Marsh, who appeared as one of the servants, and Eileen Atkins, the series was so popular with viewers that over the next several years (1974–77), 55 episodes in all of *Upstairs Downstairs* were presented on *Masterpiece Theatre.*

Fourth season (1974–75) presentations included *Murder Must Advertise, Upstairs Downstairs* (13 additional episodes), *Country Matters, Vienna 1900: Games with Love and Death,* and *The Nine Tailors.*

Included during the fifth season (1975–76) were *Shoulder to Shoulder, Notorious Woman* (about author George Sand), *Upstairs Downstairs* (13 additional episodes), Somerset Maugham's *Cakes and Ale* and *Sunset Song.*

The sixth season (1976–77) featured Gustave Flaubert's *Madame Bovary,* and *How Green Was My Valley, Five Red Herrings, Upstairs Downstairs* (the final 16 episodes), and *Poldark.*

The seventh season included (1977–78) *Dickens of London* (in 10 parts), Robert Graves's *I, Claudius* (in 13 segments, with Derek Jacoby as Claudius), Tolstoy's *Anna Karenina,* and *Our Mutual Friend.*

The eighth season (1978–79) presented *The Mayor of Casterbridge* (seven parts, with Alan Bates), *The Duchess of Duke Street* (15 segments), *Country Matters,* and *Lillie* (13 episodes about Lillie Langtry).

The ninth season (1979–80): *Kean, Love for Lydia, Prince Regent, The Duchess of Duke Street* (15 more further episodes), and *Disraeli: Portrait of a Romantic.*

The tenth season (1980–81): Jane Austen's *Pride and Prejudice, Testament of Youth, Danger UXB,* and *Therese Raquin.*

The eleventh season (1981–82): *A Town Like Alice, Edward and Mrs. Simpson, The Flame Trees of Thika, I Remember Nelson, Love in a Cold Climate,* and *Flickers.*

The twelfth season (1982–83): *To Serve Them All My Days, The Good Soldier, Winston Churchill: The Wilderness Years, On Approval, Drake's Venture, Private Schultz,* and D. H. Lawrence's *Sons and Lovers* (in seven segments).

The thirteenth season (1983–84): *Pictures, The Citadel, The Irish R. M., The Tale of Beatrix Potter,* and *Nancy Astor.*

The fourteenth season (1984–85): Anthony Trollope's *Barchester Chronicles, The Jewel in the Crown* (the highly acclaimed 14-segment series about life in colonial India), *All for Love* (five single plays presented under one title), and *Strangers and Brothers.*

The fifteenth season (1985–86): *The Last Place on Earth,* Dickens's *Bleak House* (in eight segments), *Lord Mountbatten: The Last Viceroy* in six parts), *By the Sword Divided* (in nine segments), and *The Irish R. M.*

The sixteenth season (1986–87): John Mortimer's *Paradise Postponed* (in 11 episodes), *Goodbye Mr. Chips, Lost Empires, Silas Marner, Star Quality, The Death of the Heart,* and *Love Song.*

The seventeenth season (1987–88): *The Bretts* (an eight-part production with the theater as its background), Jane Austen's *Northanger Abbey, Sorrell and Son, Fortunes of War* (seven segments with Kenneth Branagh and Emma Thompson), Thomas Hardy's *Day at the Fair,* and Dickens's *David Copperfield* (in five segments).

The eighteenth season (1988–89): John le Carre's *A Perfect Spy* (in seven parts), *Heaven on Earth* (a CBC/BBC coproduction), *A Wreath of Roses, A Very British Coup, All Passion Spent, Talking Heads* (with Maggie Smith), *Christabel, The Charmer,* and six new episodes of *The Bretts.*

The nineteenth season (1989–90): *And a Nightingale Sang, Precious Bane, Glory Enough for All, A Tale of Two Cities* (in four segments), *The Yellow Wallpaper, After the War* (in 10 parts), *The Real Charlotte, The Dressmaker* (a two-hour play with Joan Plowright), *Traffik,* and *Piece of Cake.*

The twentieth season (1990–91): Harold Pinter's *The Heat of the Day, The Ginger Tree,* P. G. Wodehouse's *Jeeves and Wooster* (in five segments), *House of Cards,* and *Summer's Lease.*

The twenty-first season (1991–92): *A Matter of Quality* (with Denholm Elliott and Glenda Jackson), *Sleepers, She's Been Away, Parnell and the Englishwoman, Titmuss Regained, Paradise Postponed* (a three-part sequel to the original production), Eliot's *Adam Bede,* Ibsen's *A Doll's House, Clarissa* (in three parts), *A Perfect Hero* (in four parts), and *Portrait of a Marriage.*

The twenty-second season (1992–93): *A Question of Attribution, The Best of Friends, Momento Mori* (with Maggie Smith), *The Secret Agent* (with David Suchet)—at the end of this presentation, Alistair Cooke bade viewers farewell as *Masterpiece Theatre's* host—*Jeeves and Wooster* (additional new episodes), *The Countess Alice, The Blackheath Poisonings, Hedda Gabler, The Black Velvet Gown, Calling the Shots* (with Lynn Redgrave), and *Dr. Finlay.*

The twenty-third season (1993–94; Russell Baker was introduced as the series's new host): *Selected Exits* (with Anthony Hopkins), *Jeeves and Wooster* (several new episodes), the 1991 film *Where Angels Fear to Tread, Sharpe's Rifles, Sharpe's Eagle, To Play the King, House of Cards* (a sequel to the original production), *Body and Soul* (in four parts), *Middlemarch* (in six segments), the 1993 film *A Foreign Field* (with Alec Guinness and Lauren Bacall), and Ingmar Bergman's *The Best Intentions.*

The twenty-fourth season (1994–95): *The Blue Boy* (with Emma Thompson), *The Rector's Wife, Dandelion Dead, Doctor Finlay II* (in six parts), the 1991 film *Impromptu, Jeeves and Wooster* (several new episodes), *The Cinder Path,* Dickens's *Martin Chuzzlewit* (in five segments), Dickens's *Hard Times,* the 1993 film *Much Ado About Nothing* (with Kenneth Branagh and Emma Thompson). and three more *Sharpe* episodes.

The twenty-fifth season (1995–96): Edith Wharton's *The Buccaneers* (three segments), *The Great Kandinsky, Prime Suspect: The Lost Child* (with Helen Mirren), *The Choir* (four episodes), *The Politician's Wife, The Final Cut, Prime Suspect: Inner Circles, Heavy Weather, The Peacock Spring* (three segments), *Bramwell* (four segments), *Prime Suspect: Scent of Darkness, Signs and Wonders, Interview Day.*

The twenty-sixth season (1996–97): Daniel Defoe's *Moll Flanders,* Arthur Miller's *Broken Glass, Bramwell: Series 2,* Joseph Conrad's *Nostromo, A Royal Scandal, Breaking the Code, Prime Suspect,* Jane Austen's *Persuasion,* DuMaurier's *Rebecca.*

The twenty-seventh season (1997–98): *The Mill on the Floss, The Tenant, The Moonstone, Bramwell: Series 3* (four segments), *Rhodes* (three segments), *Reckless* (three segments), *Wingless Bird,* Wilkie Collins's *The Woman in White, Painted Lady,* Thomas Hardy's *Far from the Madding Crowd.*

The twenty-eighth season (1998–99): *King Lear* (with Ian Holm), Emily Bronte's *Wuthering Heights, A Respectable Trade, Unknown Soldier, The Prince of Hearts,* Dickens's *Our Mutual Friend* (three episodes), *Bramwell: Series 4* (six segments), *Cider with Rosie, Reckless: The Sequel,* DuMaurier's *Frenchman's Creek,* Dickens's *Great Expectations, Goodnight, Mr. Tom.*

Over the years, *Masterpiece Theatre* has received numerous awards, including over 30 Emmys for outstanding drama and outstanding performances, six International Emmys, 10 Peabody Awards, and many others.

MATCH GAME (AKA MATCH GAME P.M.)

Dec. 1962–Sept. 1969	NBC	Various times
July 1973–Apr. 1979	CBS	Various times
1975–1981	Syndicated	Various times and stations
July 1990–Mar. 1992	ABC	Various times
1985	Syndicated	Various times and stations

The prolific TV game show producers GOODSON-TODMAN produced this popular program that was seen in both daytime and prime-time hours. The series was hosted by Gene RAYBURN and, over the years, featured Richard DAWSON, Brett Somers, and Charles Nelson Reilly (regular panelists for most of the series' run), and Fannie Flagg and Betty WHITE (longtime regulars), and Dick Martin, Richard Paul, Nipsey Russell, Patti Deutsch, Mary Wickes, Marcia Wallace, Lee Meriwether, Debralee Scott, Jack KLUGMAN, Elayne Joyce, and many others as members of a six-panel group that attempted to match the endings of sentences that were given by two competing contestants on the program. The sentence endings usually had double-entendre or sexual connotations. The contestant who matched the most celebrities went on to try to win more money by matching one or more of the panel members by finishing a sentence with the same word(s). After its original runs ended, the series was resurrected in 1990, and again in 1998, also as a syndicated show with Ross Shafer, and then Michael Berger, acting as hosts. *Match Game* is one of the most popular rerun shows seen on the Game Show Network.

MATHERS, JERRY (1948–   )

Before playing Theodore "Beaver" Cleaver on the late 1950s–early 1960s family-oriented situation comedy LEAVE IT TO BEAVER, Jerry Mathers was a child actor in such films as The *Trouble with Harry* (1955), *The Seven Little Foys* (1955), *That Certain Feeling* (1956), and *The Deep Six* (1957), and on the TV series LASSIE. Born in Sioux City, Iowa, Mathers began work as an actor almost immediately after arriving in Hollywood with his parents in the early 1950s. His brother, Jimmy, was also a successful child actor. *Leave It to Beaver* made Jerry one of the country's most recognized faces and the series one of America's most beloved programs. After six years on the series, Mathers virtually retired from show business, finding it difficult to land roles since he had become so identified with the Beaver part in viewers' minds. In 1983, Mathers resurfaced in a TV film *Still the Beaver,* playing the role he had made famous, as a grown-up Theodore Cleaver. An attempt to revive *Leave It to Beaver* in 1985 in a series called *Still the Beaver* was unsuccessful. Recently, Mathers has been seen in supporting roles in such films as *Back to the Beach* (1987) and *Sexual Malice* (1994) and has made guest-starring appearances on such series as MARRIED . . . WITH CHILDREN and DIAGNOSIS MURDER.

MATLOCK

Sept. 1986	NBC	Sat. 10–11 P.M.
Sept. 1986–Sept. 1991	NBC	Tues. 8–9 P.M.
Oct. 1991–Aug. 1992	NBC	Fri. 8–9 P.M.
Jan. 1993–Feb. 1993	ABC	Thurs. 8–9 P.M.
Feb. 1993–May 1993	ABC	Thurs. 8–10 P.M.
May 1993–July 1993	ABC	Thurs. 8–9 P.M.
July 1993–June 1994	ABC	Thurs. 9–10 P.M.
July 1994	ABC	Thurs. 8–10 P.M.
Aug. 1994	ABC	Thurs. 8–9 P.M.
Oct. 1994–Jan. 1995	ABC	Thurs. 9–10 P.M.
Feb. 1995	ABC	Thurs. 8–9 P.M.
Apr. 1995	ABC	Thurs. 8–9 P.M.
July 1995–Sept. 1995	ABC	Thurs. 8–9 P.M.

The star of the popular and long-running ANDY GRIFFITH SHOW, Andy GRIFFITH, returned to regular TV after an 18-year absence as the star of a new series, *Matlock,* in 1986. As the hero of this legal drama/mystery series, Benjamin L. Matlock, Griffith played a lawyer in Atlanta, Georgia, who, although unassuming, was a clever and canny southerner. Matlock was Harvard-educated and one of the top defense lawyers in Atlanta, similar to Perry Mason in that he always managed to establish his client's innocence in a last-minute courtroom revelation. Assisting Matlock was his daughter, Charlene, also a lawyer, played by Linda Purl, and Tyler Hudson, played by Kene Holliday, an African-American stock market expert, whom Matlock kept convincing to do the legwork for his cases. Matlock lived in a large, 100-year-old house in Willow Springs, Georgia, where he often spent time contemplating his next move in a court case by strumming on his banjo. In 1986, Matlock's daughter, Charlene, departed the series, and was replaced by another daughter, Leanne McIntyre, played by Brynn Thayer. Conrad McMaster, played by Clarence Gilyard, Jr., replaced Tyler as Ben's legman, and he was replaced by lawyer Cliff Lewis, played by Daniel Roebuck. Other characters who became regulars and semiregulars on the series included Michelle Thomas, who became Ben's junior partner, played by Nancy Stafford; Cliff's eccentric father, Billy Lewis, played by Warren Frost; Cassie Phillips, an eager law clerk, played by Kari Lizer; Les Calhoun, Ben's old army buddy and neighbor, played by Don KNOTTS, Assistant D.A. Julie March, played by Julie Sommars; D.A. Lloyd Burgess, played by Michael Durrell; Police Lt. Bob Brooks, played by David Froman; Matlock's final investigator, Jerri Stone, played by Carol Huston; and Judges Irene Sawyer and Richard Cooksey, played by Lucille Meredith and Richard Newton. *Matlock* was produced by Fred Silverman.

MAUDE

Sept. 1972–Sept. 1974	CBS	Tues. 8–8:30 P.M.
Sept. 1974–Sept. 1975	CBS	Mon. 9–9:30 P.M.
Sept. 1975–Sept. 1976	CBS	Mon. 9:30–10 P.M.
Sept. 1976–Sept. 1977	CBS	Mon. 9–9:30 P.M.
Sept. 1977–Nov. 1977	CBS	Mon. 9:30–10 P.M.
Dec. 1977–Jan. 1978	CBS	Mon. 9–9:30 P.M.
Jan. 1978–Apr. 1978	CBS	Sat. 9:30–10 P.M.

Maude was a spin-off of the popular ALL IN THE FAMILY series. The bigot Archie Bunker was first confronted by his wife, Edith's, liberal, outspoken cousin, Maude, on an episode of *All in the Family,* and the public's reaction to the character was positive enough to have the show's producer, Norman LEAR, decide to make Maude the leading character in a series of her own. The character's popularity was, in large part, due to the comedic talents of Bea ARTHUR. Maude Findley lived in the suburban town of Tuckahoe, New York, with her fourth husband, Walter Findley, played by Bill Macy, and her divorced daughter, Carol, played by Adrienne Barbeau, and Carol's young son, Phillip, played by Brian Morrison, and then by Kraig Metzinger. Walter Findley owned Findley's Friendly Appliances, and was a good provider who patiently endured his brutally frank, liberated wife's unconventional views. When the series made its debut, the Findleys had a cleaning lady named Florida Evans, played by African-American actress Esther ROLLE. When Florida left *Maude* for a spin-off series of her own, GOOD TIMES, in 1974, a blowsy Englishwoman named Mrs. Naugatuck and played by Hermione Baddeley became the new housekeeper. Also appearing regularly on the series were Conrad Bain and Rue McCLANAHAN as Maude's friends and neighbors, Dr. Arthur and Vivian Harmon. John Amos, who joined Esther Rolle on *Good Times,* played Florida's husband, Henry Evans, who appeared on the series on occasion. Even though *Maude* was a situation comedy, the plots of the weekly episodes often centered on such serious subjects as politics, abortion, and menopause, which often shocked viewers and led to a great deal of viewer mail, but kept people watching the series for six seasons.

MAVERICK

Sept. 1957–Sept. 1961	ABC	Sun. 7:30–8:30 P.M.
Sept. 1961–July 1962	ABC	Sun. 6:30–7:30 P.M.

In the late 1950s to early 1960s, the heroes of most of the many western series on television were fairly familiar characters. They were usually serious, staunch defenders of the downtrodden who chased and fought lawbreakers and defended the weak. Bret Maverick was an exception. A true maverick in every sense of the word, Bret Maverick, as played by James GARNER, was a dapper gambler who was something of a coward, but who had a distinctive sense of humor. The series, and its star, Garner, became enormously popular with viewers soon after *Maverick* made its TV debut. The wisecracking, quick-witted Bret was joined by his serious brother, Bart Maverick, played by Jack Kelly, after the show was on the air for two months. Neither brother was a typical western hero. They were just as happy to sneak out of town than face an angry desperado, thought nothing of cheating at cards, and neither was particularly adept with a gun.

Appearing on occasion with the Maverick brothers were Efrem ZIMBALIST, Jr., as Dandy Jim Buckley, and Richard Long as Gentleman Jim Darby, who were the brothers' friends, fellow gamblers, and competitors. Bret had a major nemesis in the person of Samantha Crawford, played by Diane Brewster, who always seemed to out-con the usually clever con-man/gambler. In 1960, James Garner left the series and the Warner Brothers Studios, where the program was produced, after demanding and being refused a better contract and a higher salary. Roger MOORE, playing a character named Cousin Beauregarde Maverick, who had fought in the Civil War with distinction and moved to England (where he picked up his English accent), was brought in to replace Garner. Beauregarde and Bart, however, could not draw audiences as James Garner did, and although the series limped along for an additional two years, it was finally canceled in July 1962.

MAX HEADROOM

Mar. 1987–May 1987	ABC	Tues. 10–11 P.M.
Aug. 1987–Oct. 1987	ABC	Fri. 9–10 P.M.

Although the *Max Headroom* series was on the air for only a year and a half, it was an innovative program that attracted a great deal of attention. The setting of this unconventional series was the rather dim and grim future, when television ruled and could be seen not only in homes, but even embedded into trash cans in the city's slums. Thousands of TV stations competed for audiences in a totally materialistic society where commercials were taken as gospel and the inventive Japanese were the winners in the ratings wars. Max Headroom, whose voice was provided by Matt Frewer, was a computer-generated television "star" who appeared on TV screens at odd times, making sarcastic comments about his human creators. Max was seen on the highly rated Channel 23, and had been created by a young boy named Bryce Lynch, played by Chris Young, who had used an ace TV reporter named Edison Carter, also played by Matt Frewer, as a model for the Max Headroom character. Like Edison, Max had a mind of his own, even though unlike Edison, the computer-generated Max looked rather mechanical, spoke with a lisp, and moved oddly. Other characters who appeared on the series were Theora Jones, played by Amanda Pays, who monitored Max's movements in a control room; Max's chief rivals and sometimes allies, Blank Reg and his partner Dominique, played by William Morgan Sheppard and Concetta Tomei; and Murray, played by Jeffrey Tambor, the newsroom director. The Max Headroom character was originally conceived by Peter Wagg, the producer of a 1984 British television movie. Max became so popular with viewers that he was eventually seen on the Cinemax network conducting interviews and in Coca-Cola commercials.

McCALLUM, DAVID (DAVID KEITH McCALLUM 1933–)

Before television viewers came to know David McCallum as Illya Kuryakin on The MAN FROM U.N.C.L.E., he was a popular actor in England who made a dozen films, including an award-winning performance in Billy Budd (1962). Born in Glasgow, Scotland, McCallum, whose parents were both professional musicians, was slated for a career as an oboist. After studying music at the Royal Academy of Music in London, he became interested in acting and enrolled at the Royal Academy of Dramatic Art.

While enjoying his success on The Man From U.N.C.L.E., McCallum appeared in such films as The Greatest Story Ever Told (1965), One of Our Spies is Missing (1966), and The Karate Killers (1967, as Illya Kuryakin). After The Man From U.N.C.L.E left the air in 1968, McCallum continued to be seen in hundreds of films and TV shows, including How to Steal the World (1968), Teacher, Teacher (1969), Frankenstein: The True Story (1972), The Invisible Man film and TV series (1975), King Solomon's Treasure (1977), The Return of the Man from U.N.C.L.E. TV film (1983), The Man Who Lived at the Ritz TV miniseries (1988), Titanic: The Legend Lives On (Narrator, 1994), as well as playing regular roles on such TV series as Sapphire and Steel (1979), As the World Turns (1983), Cluedo (1991), Trainer (1991), and VR.5 (1995). Among the well-known television series McCallum has made guest appearances on are The OUTER LIMITS, PERRY MASON, NIGHT GALLERY, MARCUS WELBY, M.D., The SIX MILLION DOLLAR MAN, HART TO HART, MATLOCK, ALFRED HITCHCOCK PRESENTS, MURDER, SHE WROTE, and LAW AND ORDER.

McCAMBRIDGE, MERCEDES (CARLOTTA MERCEDES AGNES MCCAMBRIDGE 1918–)

Mercedes McCambridge, who won an Academy Award as Best Supporting Actress for her performance in All the King's Men (1949), was one of radio's most successful actresses before appearing in films and on television. Orson Welles once called McCambridge "the world's greatest radio actress," and she was regularly heard on such classic radio programs as The Inner Sanctum, Gangbusters, Big Sister, Studio One, The Ford Theater, One Man's Family, I Love a Mystery, and hundreds of others. Born in Joliet, Illi-

nois, McCambridge joined the acting staff at NBC when an executive at that station saw her perform while she was still in school, and signed her to a contract. After McCambridge won the Academy Award in 1949, she continued to appear in such films as The Scarf (1951), Johnny Guitar (1954), Giant (1956, for which she received another Academy Award nomination), Suddenly Last Summer (1959), and, as the voice of the Devil, in The Exorcist (1973). She also appeared on numerous television programs from 1949 on, including her own TV series, Wire Service (1956), and WAGON TRAIN, RAWHIDE, BONANZA, LOST IN SPACE, BEWITCHED, and CHARLIE'S ANGELS. In addition to her work on radio, in films, and on television, McCambridge has also been active on the stage, and appeared on Broadway and in touring company productions of such plays as Who's Afraid of Virginia Woolf, Agnes of God, 'Night, Mother, and Lost in Yonkers.

McCANN, CHUCK (CHARLES McCANN 1934–)

One of television's busiest character actors, Chuck McCann, was born in Brooklyn, New York, but raised in Queens. He began his career on TV as the host of a popular children's program when he was scarcely out of high school. Chuck's appearances as Little Orphan Annie and other hilarious characters on this show, which was seen on the DuMont TV station in New York, are still fondly remembered by older viewers. McCann has had regular roles and/or provided the voices for various characters on such TV series as Cool McCool (1966), Turn-On (1969), HAPPY DAYS, Far Out Space Nuts (1975), Van Dyke and Company (1976), All That Glitters (1977), A New Kind of Family (1979–1980), Scooby and Scrappy-Doo (1979–1983), The Drak Pack (1980), Pac-Man (1982–1984), Santa Barbara (1984), G.I. Joe (1983–1986), DuckTales (1987–1990), Ring Raiders (1989), Tale Spin (1990–1994), Where's Waldo? (1991), The Toxic Crusaders (1991), On the Air (1992), The Fantastic Four (1994), Iron Man (1994), Invasion (1997), and The Powerpuff Girls (1998). The actor has also had featured roles in numerous feature films, including The Heart Is a Lonely Hunter (1968), The Projectionist (1971), The Girl Most Likely To . . . (1973), Herbie Rides Again (1974), the TV film Mae West (1982, as W. C. Fields), Robin Hood: Men in Tights (1993), and Dracula: Dead and Loving It (1995). McCann has also made guest appearances on such popular TV series as The JETSONS, KOJAK, COLUMBO, STARSKY AND HUTCH, CHiPs, The GREATEST AMERICAN HERO, ST. ELSEWHERE, DIFF'RENT STROKES, Sliders, SABRINA, THE TEENAGE WITCH, and MAD ABOUT YOU.

McCLANAHAN, RUE (EDDI RUE McCLANAHAN 1934–)

Born in Healdton, Oklahoma, Rue McClanahan made her debut in New York City in the 1960s, appearing in such off-Broadway plays as a revival of Dark of the Moon and also had featured roles in such films as The Grass Eater (1961), Five Minutes to Love (1963), and The People Next

Door (1970). Discovered by TV producer Norman LEAR, McClanahan made her first major television appearance on Lear's popular ALL IN THE FAMILY series and subsequently appeared on Lear's series MAUDE, playing Maude's next-door neighbor, Vivian Harmon. In 1978, McClanahan had a regular role on the unsuccessful series *Apple Pie*, and then appeared as Aunt Fran on MAMA'S FAMILY from 1983 until 1985. It was, however, as Blanche Marie Hollingsworth Devereaux on the hit TV series THE GOLDEN GIRLS, which made its debut in 1985, that McClanahan had her biggest success and became one of America's major performers. *The Golden Girls* remained one of TV's highest-rated shows until 1992, when it left the air. McClanahan continued to play Blanche Devereaux on the less successful *Golden Palace* series, which was on the air for just one season. McClanahan has continued to appear regularly in numerous TV films such as *Nunsense* and *Nunsense 2: The Sequel* (1993, 1994), *Innocent Victims* (1996), *Safe Harbor* (1999), and The *Moving of Sophia Myles* (2001), to name just a few. Over the years, the actress has also made guest appearances on such popular TV series as *The LOVE BOAT, GIMME A BREAK, NEWHART, ALICE, MURDER SHE WROTE, MURPHY BROWN, EMPTY NEST, BOY MEETS WORLD, BURKE'S LAW, TOUCHED BY AN ANGEL, The JOHN LARROQUETTE SHOW, Remember WENN*, and *Promised Land*, among others.

McCLOUD

Sept. 1970–Oct. 1970	NBC	Wed. 9–10 P.M.
Mar. 1971–Aug. 1971	NBC	Wed. 9–10 P.M.
Sept. 1971–Aug. 1972	NBC	Wed. 8:30–10 P.M.
Sept. 1972–Aug. 1975	NBC	Sun. 8:30–10 P.M.
Sept. 1975–Aug. 1976	NBC	Sun. 9–11 P.M.
Oct. 1976–Aug. 1977	NBC	Sun. Various times

Arriving in New York City from Taos, New Mexico, chasing escaped prisoners, Deputy Marshal Sam McCloud, played by Dennis WEAVER, found his strong-arm methods out of place. Remaining in New York on temporary assignment after the escaped prisoners were apprehended, McCloud tried to learn and adapt to the methods used by the city police, but often found it difficult. Assigned to Manhattan's 27th Precinct, McCloud often locked horns with his boss, Chief Peter B. Clifford, played by J. D. Cannon, but his unusual and peculiarly western police methods often brought about justice when the city's more sophisticated methods failed to do so. Working with McCloud was Police Sgt. Joe Broadhurst, played by Terry Carter. Also seen regularly on the series were Diana Muldaur as Chris Coughlin, who was a writer and a love interest of McCloud's, and Ken Lynch as Sgt. Grover. When *McCloud* first premiered in 1970, it was the first of four miniseries aired under the title of *Four-in-One*; the other programs in this series were *San Francisco International Airport*, NIGHT GALLERY, and *The Psychiatrist*. It then became part of NBC's Mystery Movie series. *McCloud* was, by far, one of the most successful pro-

grams seen in this series and remained on the air in various formats for the next seven years. Glen A. Larson was the executive producer of *McCloud*. In 1989, Dennis Weaver revived his McCloud role in a TV movie, *The Return of Sam McCloud*, on the CBS. McCloud had become a U.S. senator.

McGAVIN, DARREN (1922–)

Darren McGavin, who was born in San Joaquin, California, began his acting career soon after graduating from high school. When he was 23, McGavin appeared in his first film, *She Wouldn't Say Yes* (1945), playing the small role of The Kid. He subsequently played a tech sergeant in the film *Kiss and Tell* (1945), and played a larger role in *Queen for a Day* (1951), before landing the title role in the television version of the popular *Casey Crime Photographer* radio program. Steadily employed thereafter, McGavin was seen in the films *The Man with the Golden Arm* (1955), *The Court-Martial of Billy Mitchell* (1955), *Summertime* (1955), and *Beau James* (1957), before starring in his second TV series, MIKE HAMMER, in 1958–59. Regular roles on such TV series as *Riverboat* (1959–61), *The Outsider* (1968–69), *Kolchak: The Night Stalker* (1974–75, which he also produced), and *Small & Frye* (1983), and in such films as *Anatomy of a Crime* (1969), *Mrs. Polifax—Spy* (1971), *Brinks: The Great Robbery* (1976), *Waikiki* (1980), *Captain America* (1992), and *Small Time* (1998), as well as guest-starring appearances on such TV films and miniseries as *The Outsider* (1967), *Something Evil* (1972), *Ike: The War Years* (1978), *My Wicked, Wicked Ways* (1985), *Inherit the Wind* (1988), *Around the World in Eighty Days* (1989), *The American Clock* (1993), and *A Perfect Stranger* (1994), and appearances on *The GOODYEAR TELEVISION PLAYHOUSE, The PHILCO TELEVISION PLAYHOUSE, ALFRED HITCHCOCK PRESENTS, The Alcoa Hour, RAWHIDE, The VIRGINIAN, GUNSMOKE, The MAN FROM U.N.C.L.E, MISSION: IMPOSSIBLE, MAGNUM, P.I., MURPHY BROWN, MURDER, SHE WROTE, BURKE'S LAW, The COMMISH, TOUCHED BY AN ANGEL*, and THE X-FILES, among others, have made Darren McGavin well known and successful.

McHALE'S NAVY

| Oct. 1962–Sept. 1963 | ABC | Thurs. 9:30–10 P.M. |
| Sept. 1963–Aug. 1966 | ABC | Tues. 8:30–9 P.M. |

Academy Award–winning actor Ernest BORGNINE starred on this situation comedy series that was about one of the most oddball crews in the U.S. Navy. Lt. Cdr. Quinton McHale, played by Borgnine, was a con man and a devout gambler and found himself involved in misadventures similar to those Phil SILVERS had encountered in his hit series about life in the U.S. Army, YOU'LL NEVER GET RICH. The men under McHale's command loved their leader, even though he was often involved in schemes that usually got him in trouble with his long-suffering boss, Capt. Wallace B. Binghamton, played by Joe Flynn. Also appearing in the series with Borgnine and Flynn were Tim CONWAY as the trouble-prone Ens. Charles Parker, Carl Ballantine as Lester Gruber, Gary Vinson as George "Christy" Christopher, Billy Sands as Harrison "Tinker" Bell, Edson Stroll as Vigil Edwards, Jane Dulo as Nurse Molly Turner, Gavin MacLeod as Joseph "Happy" Haines, John Wright as Willy Moss, Yoshio Yoda as Fuji Kobiaji, Bob Hastings as Lt. Elroy Carpenter, Henry Beckman as Gen. Douglas Harrigan, Simon Scott as Gen. Bronson, Dick Wilson as Dino Baroni, Jay Novello as Mayor Mario Lugatto, and Peggy Mondo as Rosa Giovanni.

When the series first went on the air, McHale and his crew were stationed on the island of Taratupa in the South Seas, but at the beginning of the series' last season, the entire crew was assigned to duty in Italy. By the time *McHale's Navy* left the air in 1966, it had completed 130 episodes and had become one of the longest-running TV shows that had a military setting.

McKAY, GARDNER (1932–2001)

Even though he appeared on a television network series for only three years, Gardner McKay was, between 1959 and 1968, one of show business's most publicized, if not particularly active, young actors. An exceptionally handsome man whose looks, more than anything else, accounted for his show business celebrity, McKay was discovered in 1959 when a TV producer saw him and decided to ask the attractive 20-year-old young man to star on a new television series called *ADVENTURES IN PARADISE*. The series and Gardner McKay became instant successes.

McKay, who was born in New York City, was the son of an advertising executive and his wife, Deane and Catherine McKay. While he was attending Cornell University, his father died and McKay left college and went to work at his father's advertising agency. He left the agency after six months. A talented sculptor, McKay had one of his works displayed at the Metropolitan Museum of Art when he was 20 years old, and he also appeared in an uncredited role in the film *Raintree County* (1957). He was also seen on the TV series *Boots and Saddles* (1957), before he became the star of *Adventures in Paradise* series.

Unhappy with his life as an actor, McKay decided to quit show business to see the world. He hiked along the Amazon River in Brazil, rode camels in Egypt, and worked as a crewman on yachts in the Caribbean. McKay briefly returned to acting in 1964 and in 1968, appearing in the film *The Pleasure Seekers* and playing himself in a documentary called *I Sailed to Tahiti with an All Girl Crew*. In 1968, McKay quit show business once and for all. He married Madeleine Madigan in 1980 and concentrated on becoming a writer, working as a drama critic for the L. A. *Herald Examiner* from 1979 until 1981. His first novel, *Toyer,* was published in 1999.

McQUEEN, STEVE (TERENCE STEVEN McQUEEN 1930–1980)

Before he became a successful film actor, Steve McQueen first came to the attention of the public on television, appearing on such dramatic anthology shows as *The GOODYEAR TELEVISION PLAYHOUSE*, The *UNITED STATES STEEL HOUR*, and *STUDIO ONE*, and as the star of the western adventure series *WANTED: DEAD OR ALIVE*. Born in Beech Grove, Indiana, McQueen served in the U.S. Marine Corps after graduating from high school. After completing his stint in the Marines, Steve, who was always a bit of a rebel, was expelled from the Carnegie Institute of Technology (now Carnegie-Mellon University), where he was majoring in drama, for riding a motorcycle through the college's fine arts building. One of two actors who was accepted for admission to the Actor's Studio (the other was Martin Landau), McQueen impressed everyone with his acting prowess, and before long, in the late 1950s, the talented McQueen had become active as an actor on the developing new medium, television. His performance on *Wanted: Dead or Alive* led to a contract, and by the 1960s, McQueen was the highest-paid star in films. His impressive list of film credits included starring roles in *The Great St. Louis Bank Robbery* (1959), *The Magnificent Seven* (1960), *Love with the Proper Stranger* (1963), *The Great Escape* (1963), *Bullitt* (1968), *The Thomas Crown Affair* (1968), *The Reivers* (1969), *Papillon* (1973), *The Towering Inferno* (1974), *An Enemy of the People* (1977), and *The Hunter* (1980), which was his final film. Steve McQueen died of cancer when he was only 50 years old, in 1980.

McMILLAN AND WIFE

Sept. 1971–Aug. 1972	NBC	Wed. 8:30–10 P.M.
Sept. 1972–July 1974	NBC	Sun. 8:30–10 P.M.
Sept. 1974–July 1975	NBC	Sun. 8:30–10:30 P.M.
Sept. 1975–Aug. 1976	NBC	Sun. 9–11 P.M.
Dec. 1976–Aug. 1977	NBC	Sun. 8–9:30 P.M.

Rock HUDSON was the star of *Mcmillan and Wife*, which was a series of one-and-a-half-hour TV films, as well as a two-hour series. Hudson played San Francisco Police Commissioner Stewart McMillan, and his energetic wife, Sally, was played by Susan ST. JAMES. Sally had a talent for stumbling upon crimes that she always got her husband to investigate. This police drama/comedy was in the spirit of the Thin Man films and radio and TV programs, always with a good deal of humor involved in their exploits, as well as danger. Providing many of the show's laughs was comedienne Nancy Walker as the McMillans' housekeeper, the sarcastic, sharp-tongued Mildred. John Schuck played McMillan's earnest assistant, Sgt. Charles Enright, on the series. At the end of the 1975–76 season, both Susan Saint James and Nancy Walker left the series. Mildred was replaced by another housekeeper, Agatha, who was Mildred's sister, played by Martha RAYE. McMillan, or "Mac," as he was called, also acquired a new assistant, Sgt. Maggio, played by Richard Gilliland. Leonard B. Stern was the executive producer of *McMillan and Wife* for Universal Television.

MEDIC

Sept. 1954–Nov. 1956   NBC   Mon. 9–9:30 P.M.

This mid-1950s television series was a medical drama that featured stories taken from the files of the Los Angeles County Medical Association and starred Richard BOONE as Dr. Konrad Styner. The series was one of the first of television's "realistic" programs, and episodes of *Medic* were filmed at actual hospitals and clinics and used real doctors and nurses. Boone, as Dr. Styner, was the host of the series, and he introduced each episode by describing the doctor being featured and saying, "guardian of birth, healer of the sick, and comforter of the aged," since the weekly dramas usually revolved around the struggle to preserve life, and the bad, as well as the good, that came out of those struggles.

MEDICAL CENTER

Sept. 1969–May 1973   CBS   Wed. 9–10 P.M.
May 1973–Sept. 1976   CBS   Mon. 10–11 P.M.

The Medical Center of this series was located in Los Angeles and was part of a large university. Dr. Paul Lochner, played by James Daly, was the medical center's chief of staff. He was a kind and compassionate physician who guided his staff with wisdom and intelligence. Dr. Lochner's young assistant at the center was Dr. Joe Gannon, played by Chad EVERETT, who was an associate professor in charge of surgery, and later the director of student health services. Also appearing on the series in regular roles were Audrey Totter as Nurse Wilcox, the center's efficient head nurse; Jayne Meadows as Nurse Chambers; Corinne Camacho as Dr. Jeanne Bartlett; Chris Hutson as Nurse Courtland; Fred Holliday as Dr. Barnes; Jane Dulo as Nurse Murphy; Barbara Baldavin as Nurse Holmby; Virginia Hawkins as Nurse Canford; Daniel Silver as the center's anesthesiologist; Eugene Peterson as Dr. Weller; Ed Hall as Dr. Bricker; Louise Fitch as Nurse Bascomb; and Martin E. Brooks as Lt. Samuels.

The program was the first TV drama to successfully present the personal as well as the professional lives of medical personnel and became the prototype for the numerous hospital-background series that followed. O. J. Simpson and Cicely Tyson guest-starred on the series's premiere episode, "The Last Ten Yards." Frank Glicksman and Al C. Ward were the series's executive producers.

MEET MILLIE

Oct. 1952–June 1953   CBS   Sat. 9:30–10 P.M.
June 1953–Aug. 1953   CBS   Sat. 9–9:30 P.M.
Aug. 1953–Sept. 1953   CBS   Sat. 9:30–10 P.M.
Oct. 1953–Feb. 1954   CBS   Sat. 7–7:30 P.M.
Mar. 1954–Mar. 1956   CBS   Tues. 9–9:30 P.M.

For four years, *Meet Millie*, which had originally been a radio series and for a time was both heard on radio and seen on television, was one of TV's most popular programs. The heroine, Millie Bronson, played by Elena VERDUGO, was a young, middle-class secretary who lived with her mother, Mama Bronson, played by Florence Halop, in a New York apartment. It was Mama Bronson's aim to marry Millie off to an eligible bachelor, and she kept introducing her independent daughter to one young man after another. Millie, however, was intent on marrying her boyfriend, Johnny Boone, Jr., played by Ross Ford, the son of her boss, played by Earl Ross, and then by Roland Winters. Johnny's snobbish mother was played by Isabel Randolph. Also featured on the series was Virginia Vincent as Millie's best friend, Gladys. One of the series' most popular characters, however, was the Bronsons' neighbor, the mild-mannered Alfred Prinzmetal, played by Marvin Kaplan, who had a mad crush on Millie. *Meet Millie* was one of the first series telecast from CBS's Television City facility in Hollywood.

MEET THE PRESS

Nov. 1947–present   NBC   Weekly

Created by Martha Rountree, *Meet the Press* was originally heard on radio as early as 1945 and became a television series usually seen on Sunday mornings since 1947. The series usually features as guests political figures who are grilled by four journalists. The format has not changed in the 55 years plus it has been on both radio and television. For many years Lawrence E. Spivak, the editor of *American Mercury* magazine, was a regular panelist, and Rountree, during the show's earliest years, acted as the program's moderator. In 1953, Spivak bought Rountree's interest in the program, and for the next 22 years, until 1975, he was the series' moderator. NBC newsman Bill Monroe became the program's moderator when Spivak retired. In 1984, Marvin Kolb became *Meet the Press's* moderator, and in 1987, Chris Wallace took over, followed by Garrick Utley in 1988, who remained on the show until 1991 when Tim Russert took over as moderator. One of the series' most frequent guests has been former U.S. senator Robert Dole of Kansas.

MERV GRIFFIN SHOW, THE

Oct. 1962–Mar. 1963	NBC	Mon.–Fri. 4–4:45 P.M.
1965–1969	Syndicated	Various times and stations
Aug. 1969–Feb. 1972	CBS	Mon.–Fri. 11:30 P.M.–1 A.M.
1972–1986	Syndicated	Various times and stations

One of the pioneers of the TV talk show, Merv GRIFFIN had a popular program on the air for 24 years. Griffin's easy-going, show business savvy, good-natured interviews with various guests from the entertainment world, and occasionally the political arena, made his program one of TV's most-watched talk shows. Griffin's announcer/cohost on the series was the English actor who was known for playing butlers in hundreds of films, Arthur Treacher. Griffin, who had been a singer/actor before turning to the TV talk format, often sang on his program. Mort Lindsey and his orchestra provided the music for the show. Griffin was known for attracting some of the biggest names in show business as guests, mainly due to the deferential manner in which he conducted his interviews. On the first show of his series on CBS, Griffin's impressive list of guests included Woody Allen, film star Hedy Lamarr, Moms Mabley, Ted Sorenson, and Leslie Uggams. For several years, Griffin was the only serious competition to Johnny CARSON. After he ended his talk show, Merv Griffin went on to become one of Hollywood's most successful entrepreneurs and became the producer of several important game shows and the owner of several hotels and restaurants.

Don Johnson and Philip Michael Thomas of *Miami Vice* (Author's collection)

MIAMI VICE

Sept. 1984	NBC	Sun. 10–11 P.M.
Sept. 1984–May 1986	NBC	Fri. 10–11 P.M.
June 1986–Mar. 1988	NBC	Fri. 9–10 P.M.
Apr. 1988–Jan. 1989	NBC	Fri. 10–11 P.M.
Feb. 1989–May 1989	NBC	Fri. 9–10 P.M.
June 1989–July 1989	NBC	Wed. 10–11 P.M.

Using the glamor and excitement of Miami Beach as its background, the *Miami Vice* police/adventure series attracted a good deal of attention and became noted for its exciting, throbbing music, its distinctive look (the plainclothes detectives wore pastel sports jackets over T-shirts and exterior scenes were shot against the Art Deco backgrounds of Miami Beach), and its two good-looking major characters, police detectives Det. James "Sonny" Crockett and Det. Ricardo Tubbs, played by Don JOHNSON and Phillip Michael Thomas. Crockett was a tough guy Miami vice squad detective who lived on a sailboat called *St. Vitus Dance,* and had a pet alligator named Elvis. Tubbs was an African-American, ex–New York City cop who had originally gone to Miami to track down a drug dealer who had murdered his brother. As different as they were, the two men worked well together as they sped around in Sonny's flashy black Ferrari Spider sports car. The team was supported by their moody superior, Lt. Martin Costillo, played by Edward James Olmos, and two female undercover cops, Det. Gina Novaro Calabrese and Det. Judy Joplin, played by Saundra Santiago and Olivia Brown. Also appearing on the series regularly were Michael Talbot as Det. Sam Switek, John Diehl as Det. Larry Zito, Martin Ferrero as Izzy Moreno, and singer Sheena Easton as Caitlin Davies. *Miami Vice* was one of the most "hip" series of the 1980s, and was especially popular with younger viewers. The show often featured well-known celebrities in cameo roles, including singers Phil Collins, Ted Nugent, James Brown, and the Fat Boys, Watergate felon G. Gordon Liddy, boxing promoter Don King, comic Tommy Chong, and Chrysler's former chairman of the board, Lee Iacocca. The series was the brainchild of NBC president Brandon Tartikoff. Writer/producer Anthony Yerkovich, who had mainly been responsible for the successful *HILL STREET BLUES,* wrote the pilot of *Miami Vice,* and Michael Mann became the series' executive producer.

MICKEY MOUSE CLUB, THE (ALSO *THE NEW MICKEY MOUSE CLUB*)

As THE MICKEY MOUSE CLUB:

Oct. 1955–Sept. 1957	ABC	Mon.–Fri. 5–6 P.M.
Oct. 1957–Sept. 1959	ABC	Mon.–Fri. 5–5:30 P.M.
1962–1965 (reruns)	Syndication	Various times and stations
1975 (reruns)	Syndication	Various times and stations

As THE NEW MICKEY MOUSE CLUB:

1976–1979 (reruns)	Syndication	Various times and stations

As THE MICKEY MOUSE CLUB:

1989–1994	Disney Channel	Various times

By the time film animator Walt DISNEY brought his *Mickey Mouse Club* series to television, his animated characters Mickey Mouse, Donald Duck, Goofy, et al., were already famous, and Walt Disney's name was well known to millions of people throughout the world. In 1955, television executives were looking for new programming for children, and Walt Disney's five-days-a-week show was tailor-made to appeal to younger viewers. The series, which was hosted by Jimmy Dodd, featured a group of talented young people and their adult leaders, and presented musical numbers performed by the club members, occasional films such as Disney's *Spin and Marty, The Hardy Boys, Annette, Clint and Mac,* and *Corky and the White Shadow,* and various cartoons, sketches, newsreels, etc. Dodd and the young club members, who were called "Mouseketeers," wore hats with mouse ears and T-shirts with their names printed on them. Assisting Dodd was another adult, Disney animator Roy Williams, who because of his size was called a "Mooseketeer."

Each day, an animated Mickey Mouse opened the show by telling the audience what the format of the show would be that day. Monday was "Fun With Music" day, which featured the Mouseketeers in a wide variety of songs, dances, and sketches. Tuesday was "Guest Star" day, and celebrated guests would appear on the show with the Mouseketeers. Wednesday was "Anything Can Happen Day," and everything from art lessons, travel films, and news reports were seen. Thursday was "Circus Day," and the Mouseketeers, dressed as circus performers, introduced various circus acts that performed for the viewers at home. Friday was "Talent Roundup Day," and the Mouseketeers, dressed in western costumes, introduced children who were performing on TV for the first time.

Among the original show's talented Mouseketeer club members were Nancy Abbate, Billie Jean Beanblossom, Dennis Day, Dickie Dodd, Mary Espinosa, Judy Harriet, John Lee Joann, Bonni Lou Kern, Bobby Burgess, Carl "Cubby" O'Brien, Karen Pendleton, Darleen Gillespie, Sharon Baird, Tommy Cole, Lonnie Burr, Doreen Tracey, Johnny Crawford, Don Grady, Mary Sartori, Bronson Scott, Michael Smith, Ronnie Steiner, Mark Sutherland, Don Underhill, and the most popular Mouseketeer of all, Annette FUNICELLO. On the first few shows of the series the Mouseketeers also included Paul Peterson and Tim and Mickey Rooney, Jr., the sons of the well-known film actor. Annette became so popular with viewers that she was eventually given a film serial of her own that was shown on the series. Annette went on to star in many Disney feature films as she grew into young adulthood.

By the end of its first year on television, *The Mickey Mouse Club* had attracted over 10 million viewers and was the most popular late afternoon children's show on the air. Only 10 members of the original Mouseketeer cast remained: Burgess, O'Brien, Pendleton, Gillespie, Baird, Cole, Burr, Tracey, Crawford, Grady, and Funicello. Numerous Mickey Mouse products such as mouse-ear hats, T-shirts, Mickey jack-in-the-boxes, Mickey Mouse Club books, and records became best-selling items all around the world.

Produced for the ABC network by Bill Walsh, *The Mickey Mouse Club* remained popular with viewers until Disney decided the series had run its course and suspended production in 1959. The original series was subsequently released as a syndicated show and is seen at various times and on many different stations around the country. The show continued to attract sizable audiences. In 1976, the Disney organization produced *The New Mickey Mouse Club,* which was also seen in syndication. The new group of Mouseketeers, unlike the original series, was multiracial and included Pop Attmore as host, and Scott Craig, Nita DeGiampaolo, Mindy Feldman, Angelo Florez, Allison Fonte, Shawnte Northcutte, Kelly Parsons, Julie Piekanski, Todd Turquand, Lisa Whelchel, and Carrie Wong. Ron Miller was the executive producer. In 1989, a new *Mickey Mouse Club* series surfaced that was decidedly updated and, like *The New Mickey Mouse Club,* featured multiethnic Mouseketeers, as well as rap music, computer graphics, music videos, etc. Fred Newman and Mowava Pryor were the adult hosts of the show.

MIKE DOUGLAS SHOW, THE (AKA *THE MIKE DOUGLAS ENTERTAINMENT HOUR*)

1963–1982	Syndicated	Various times and stations

For 19 years, talk show host Mike DOUGLAS, who had begun his career as a big band vocalist, was the amiable host of one of television's most successful talk programs, *The Mike Douglas Show.* Douglas began his TV career as the host of a daytime variety show that originated in Chicago. The show was on the air from 1953 until 1955. In 1961, he hosted a daily, 90-minute talk show from Cleveland. The show was nationally syndicated in 1963, and in 1965, Douglas moved his program to Philadelphia, where it remained for the next 13 years. Each week, Douglas shared the hosting chores with a guest celebrity, the first being singer Carmel Quinn, formerly of *The ARTHUR GODFREY SHOW.* In 1978, Douglas moved the show to Los Angeles, where it was easier to book big-name guests as cohosts. The show's first producer was Woody Frasier, and subsequent producers included Jack Reilly, Brad Lachman, Vince Calandra, and E. V. DiMassa. In 1967, *The Mike Douglas Show* was the first syndicated TV series to win an Emmy Award. During its last few months on TV, the show was known as *The Mike Douglas Entertainment Hour* and concentrated mainly on variety show attractions.

MIKE HAMMER: PRIVATE EYE (AKA *MICKEY SPILLANE'S MIKE HAMMER*)

As MIKE HAMMER:

1957–1958	Syndicated	Various times and stations

As MICKEY SPILLANE'S MIKE HAMMER:

Jan. 1984	CBS	Thurs. 9–10 P.M.
Jan. 1984–Apr. 1984	CBS	Sat. 10–11 P.M.

Apr. 1984–Sept. 1984	CBS	Thurs. 10–11 P.M.
Sept. 1984–Jan. 1985	CBS	Sat. 9–10 P.M.
May 1985–July 1985	CBS	Sat. 10–11 P.M.
Apr. 1986–May 1986	CBS	Tues. 9–10 P.M.
Sept. 1986–Oct. 1986	CBS	Sat. 9–10 P.M.
Nov. 1986–Sept. 1987	CBS	Wed. 8–9 P.M.

As MIKE HAMMER, PRIVATE EYE:

| 1997–1998 | Syndication | Various times and stations |

Author Mickey Spillane's hard-boiled private detective, Mike Hammer, was first seen on TV in 1955, with Darren MCGAVIN in the title role. The half-hour, weekly series, which was syndicated, filmed 78 episodes. McGavin played Hammer with a touch of humor, which was not exactly what Spillane had in mind when he wrote his detective novels. In 1984, Stacy Keach played the title role of Mike Hammer on a CBS network program that remained on and off the air for three years. *Mickey Spillane's Mike Hammer: Murder Me, Murder You*, was seen in 1983 on the CBS network, and the well-received film, which had two subsequent TV films released in 1983–84, became a TV series in 1984. The series, like TV films, were excessively violent, generating negative criticism from the press and a certain segment of the public. It also led to an increased numbers of curious viewers. Hammer was a not particularly likeable character as played by Keach. He was a womanizer, often resorted to brawling, and chain-smoked and drank heavily. Also featured on the series was Don Stroud as Hammer's friend, Capt. Pat Chambers of the New York City Police Department, who often gave Hammer assistance when he was working on a case. Hammer's nemesis on the series was District Attorney Barrington, played by Kent Williams, who was humorless and abhorred Hammer's reckless demeanor. Also appearing on the series were Lindsay Bloom as Hammer's pretty secretary, Velda, Danny Goldman as Hammer's street source, Ozzie the Answer, and Donna Denton as a mysterious woman known only as "The Face," who made brief appearances on each episode. Lee Benton played Jenny, the bartender at Hammer's favorite saloon hangout. At Keach's insistence, all of the filming for the *Mike Hammer* series was done in New York. The series was interrupted in 1984, when Keach was arrested in England for the possession of cocaine and served time in jail in that country. When he returned to the United States, Keach appeared in a TV film, *The Return of Mickey Spillane's Mike Hammer*. The final episode of the CBS series was seen in September 1987. After a 10-year hiatus, in 1997, Stacy Keach returned as Mike Hammer in a new syndicated series, *Mike Hammer: Private Eye*, but the syndicated series suspended production after one year on the air.

MILLER, MARVIN (MARVIN MUELLER 1913–1985)

Before Marvin Miller became famous as Michael Anthony, the man who handed out a million dollars to lucky people who had been chosen by his wealthy boss, John Beresford

Tipton, to be benefactors of his generosity, he was one of radio's most successful performers. Born in St. Louis, Missouri, Marvin Miller used his rich baritone voice to find employment as a radio announcer in the 1930s, after graduating from Washington University. On radio, Miller was heard on such celebrated programs as *The Andrews Sisters Show, Mary Noble, Backstage Wife, The Billie Burke Show, Captain Midnight, A Date with Judy, Father Knows Best, The Guiding Light, Jack Armstrong, the All-American Boy, One Man's Family, The Red Skelton Show, The Road of Life, The Romance of Helen Trent, The Whistler,* and *Songs by Sinatra.* In addition to his radio work, Miller was also a successful film actor and had roles in hundreds of films from the 1940s through the early 1980s, including *Johnny Angel* (1945), *Dead Reckoning* (1947), *Smuggler's Island* (1951), *Hong Kong* (1951), *Off Limits* (1953), *When the Girls Take Over* (1962), *Hell on Wheels* (1967), *Where Does It Hurt?* (1972), *The Naked Ape* (1973), *Kiss Daddy Goodbye* (1981), and his last film, *Hell Squad* (1985). On television, in addition to appearing on the popular THE MILLIONAIRE series from 1955 until 1960, Miller was featured on the TV series *Mysteries of Chinatown* (1949) and *Space Patrol* (1951), and his voice was regularly heard on such programs as *The Gerald McBoing-Boing Show, The Famous Adventures of Mr. Magoo,* and *The Pink Panther Show.* Miller also guest-starred on such TV series as MAKE ROOM FOR DADDY, *The* JACK BENNY PROGRAM, BAT MASTERSON, PERRY MASON, BATMAN, MISSION: IMPOSSIBLE, KOJHAK: NIGHT STALKER, and WONDER WOMAN.

MILLER, MITCH (MITCHELL WILLIAM MILLER 1911–)

Orchestra conductor/choral director/record producer Mitch Miller became an unlikely TV star when his popular SING ALONG WITH MITCH show became one of the most watched programs on television in 1961. Miller, who was born in Rochester, New York, began his career in music as an oboist and played with several classical music orchestras throughout the 1930s and 1940s. In 1950, Miller joined the staff at Columbia Records as a scout and producer of such popular performers as Doris DAY and Johnny Mathis. Virtually unknown to the public until he began hosting his *Sing Along with Mitch* program on NBC, Miller's spirited conducting and good-natured hosting, with the help of his regular cast of choristers and soloists, revived the singalong fad of earlier days and, for a time, had everyone in America singing along with the Mitch Miller company of performers each week. After *Sing Along with Mitch* left the air, Miller has been a guest conductor with several symphony orchestras around the country.

MILLIONAIRE, THE

| Jan. 1955–Sept. 1960 | CBS | Wed. 9–9:30 P.M. |

For a half hour each week, millions of viewers tuned into *The* MILLIONAIRE. They were drawn to the series as they daydreamed that one day they might become the beneficiary of the million-dollar check that was being given away tax-free by an enormously wealthy old gentleman named John Beresford Tipton. Tipton had decided that he might be able to do some good by giving away his fortune to various unsuspecting strangers. Only Tipton's hand was seen handing his secretary, Michael Anthony, played by Marvin MILLER, the weekly check for $1 million he wanted him to give to a specified recipient whom Tipton had read or heard about and decided to reward with his money. The way the weekly recipients of the million dollars responded to the news that they were sudden millionaires, and the way they handled their new found fortune, was the basis of each week's drama. Tipton made only one request of the new millionaires: that they never reveal who their mysterious benefactor was, or they would have to forfeit the money. The mellifluous, deep voice of John Beresford Tipton belonged to longtime Hollywood radio and film character actor and announcer Paul Frees. Even though the series was canceled in 1959, it was seen in reruns from 1959 until 1963, and remained a favorite show of viewers until it left the air. The executive producer of *The Millionaire* was Don Fedderson, who made sure that his wife, Tido Fedderson, appeared as an extra in every episode of the series.

MILTON BERLE SHOW, THE (AKA *THE TEXACO STAR THEATER*)

June 1948–June 1956	NBC	Tues. 8–9 P.M.
Oct. 1958–May 1959	NBC	Wed. 9–9:30 P.M.
Sept. 1966–Jan. 1967	NBC	Fri. 9–10 P.M.

Milton Berle was the comedian who became known as "Uncle Miltie" and "Mr. Television" to millions of early TV viewers. His weekly variety show, originally called *The TEXACO STAR THEATER*, was the most popular program on the air in the late 1940s to early 1950s, and Tuesday night became the night to stay home to watch *The Milton Berle Show*. Berle first appeared on *Texaco Star Theater* on June 8, 1948, but when the show made its debut, he was not its only star. During the summer of 1948, in addition to Berle, comedians Harry Richman, George Price, Henny Youngman, Morey Amsterdam, Jack Carter, and Peter DONALD alternated as the show's weekly star, but Berle, who was by far the most popular, became the show's permanent host and star in September 1948. Berle had been a successful comedian and had appeared in films, on the nightclub circuit and vaudeville stage, and on his own radio show. On television, however, Berle enjoyed his greatest success and popularity and was said to be responsible for more television sets being sold than any other post–World War II performer. Millions of people who were waiting to see if TV was "just a fad" bought TV receivers to see for themselves what all the fuss was about.

Berle's comedy was outrageous and very visual, which was one of the major reasons he became such a success on TV. Each show opened with four men dressed as Texaco servicemen singing "Oh, we're the men of Texaco . . . we work from Maine to Mexico, . . . " They then introduced the star of the show: "And now," they would say, "the man with jokes from the Stone Age . . . Milton Berle!" Milton would then make his entrance, dressed as a caveman. Each week, Berle appeared in a different outlandish costume. One week he was dressed as Brazilian bombshell Carmen Miranda (Berle often appeared in drag on his shows); another time he appeared as a tramp, then as a clown, and then as Gorgeous George, the popular wrestling star, etc. The format of the show remained the same the entire eight years the original show was on the air. There were always numerous sight gags. Berle told many one-line jokes that he openly admitted he had "borrowed" from every other comedian in America, appeared in sketches wearing wild-looking costumes, and used numerous props.

Berle also introduced many guest stars who appeared on his show over the years. Regulars who appeared on *The Milton Berle Show* included pitchman Sid Stone, who talked fast and gave the commercials for the show, always saying, "A wright, I'll tell ya what I'm gonna do!"; Stone was replaced by Danny O'Day, and O'Day was subsequently replaced by Jack Lescoulie; Ruth Gilbert as Berle's secretary, Max; Arnold Stang as Francis, an NBC stagehand whom Max had a crush on; Fatso Marco as Marko Marcelle; Irving Benson as Sidney Sphritzer; and Bobby Sherwood, Jack Collins, and Milton Frome. Berle's orchestra leaders included Alan Roth (1948–55) and Victor Young (1955–56). Each program ended with Berle singing his theme song, "Near You."

In 1953, Texaco dropped out as the sponsor of *The Texaco Star Theater, Starring Milton Berle*, but the show continued as *The Buick-Berle Show*. The show ended its run in 1956, when the public lost interest in Berle's brand of comedy.

Two years later, Berle resurfaced as the star of *Milton Berle Starring in the Kraft Music Hall*, which was, like his original program, a variety show. Each show began with Berle giving a comedy monologue and then appearing in a series of sketches with guest stars. Berle was far less outlandish in this series than he had been in his first TV show. Billy May led the orchestra on this series. Berle's new, more restrained image did not prove to be very popular with viewers, and the show was canceled after one season.

In 1966, after a seven-year absence from regular TV, Milton Berle once again starred in another *Milton Berle Show*. This time, Berle's variety show featured two young singers, Bobby Rydell and Donna Loren, as regulars, in order to appeal to younger TV audiences. When viewers failed to respond to the new show, Rydell and Loren disappeared after a few months. Also seen on this show was Irving Benson, who played a heckler in the audience. Bill Dana was the show's producer, and he also appeared on the show as a comic character named Jose Jimenez. Numerous guest stars such as Bob HOPE and Lucille BALL were recruited to help bolster the show, but nothing could help and it was canceled after one year on the air, devastated in the ratings by its competition, the popular *MAN FROM U.N.C.L.E.* series.

MINER, WORTHINGTON (WORTHINGTON C. MINER 1900–1982)

One of television's most influential and innovative producer/directors, Worthington Miner was born in New York City. Miner was the man mainly responsible for the success of the dramatic anthology program *STUDIO ONE*, which was a series that presented live, hour-long dramas during television's early years. Miner's bold and imaginative camera techniques and dramatic innovations set the stage for many similar TV drama shows that followed. In addition to *Studio One*, Miner also produced such popular series as *The Kaiser Aluminum Hour*, MEDIC, *The Play of the Week*, and *Frontier*. In addition to his work on television, Miner also produced the films *Coriolanus* (1951) and *The Pawnbroker* (1964).

MISSION: IMPOSSIBLE

Sept. 1966–Jan. 1967	CBS	Sat. 9–10 P.M.
Jan. 1967–Sept. 1967	CBS	Sat. 8:30–9:30 P.M.
Sept. 1967–Sept. 1970	CBS	Sun. 10–11 P.M.
Sept. 1970–Sept. 1971	CBS	Sat. 7:30–8:30 P.M.
Sept. 1971–Dec. 1972	CBS	Sat. 10–11 P.M.
Dec. 1972–May 1973	CBS	Fri. 8–9 P.M.
May 1973–Sept. 1973	CBS	Sat. 10–11 P.M.
Oct. 1988–Jan. 1989	ABC	Sun. 8–9 P.M.
Jan. 1989–July 1989	ABC	Sat. 8–9 P.M.
Aug. 1989	ABC	Thurs. 9–10 P.M.
Sept. 1989–Dec. 1989	ABC	Thurs. 8–9 P.M.
Jan. 1990–Feb. 1990	ABC	Sat. 8–9 P.M.
May 1990–June 1990	ABC	Sat. 8–9 P.M.

The opening of each episode of the *Mission: Impossible* adventure series, which dealt with international intrigue, was one of the most memorable lead-ins in television history. The leader of the Impossible Mission Force (IMF), who were highly trained government agents specializing in secret, undercover government operations, received secret instructions on a miniature tape recorder hidden in unlikely places such as back alleys, on a seaside cliff, in the backseat of an abandoned automobile in a junk yard, etc. "Your mission," the voice on the tape would say, "should you decide to accept it, is . . . ," and then the voice would give a description of the problem. After the IMF leader had heard the instructions, the tape immediately self-destructed, and the throbbing *Mission: Impossible* theme music, written by Lalo Schifrin, would be heard as the show's credits rolled.

During the first year the series was telecast, 1966, Stephen Hill was seen as the IMF's leader, Daniel Briggs, but it is Peter GRAVES, who played James Phelps for the rest of the series' six-year run, and then when the program was revived in 1988 for another two years, who is best remembered as the team's leader. Other members of the team, who were all expert actors who could pretend to be anyone they had to be to accomplish their missions, were the beauteous Cinnamon Carter, played by Barbara Bain, the master of disguises Robin Hand, played by Martin Landau, the clever African-American engineer agent of the team, Barney Collier, played by Greg Morris, and strongman Willie Armitage, played by Peter Lupus. When Barbara Bain and Martin Landau left the cast in 1969, they were replaced by Lesley Ann Warren and Leonard NIMOY as Dana Lambert and Paris. Sam Elliot joined the cast as Doug in 1970, and in 1971 Lynda Day George replaced Lesley Ann Warren as Lisa Casey. Barbara Anderson joined the cast in 1972.

Each episode of the show ended with the thwarted villains left to deal with the consequences of their evil actions that had been exposed by the clever IMF team, and the show's theme music once again swelled as the team safely departed the scene where their successful ruse had just taken place.

After a 15-year absence, *Mission: Impossible* returned to the airwaves, with Peter Graves once again playing Jim Phelps and a new cast that included Thaao Penghis as Nicholas Black, Antony Hamilton as Max Harte, Phil Morris (Greg Morris's son) as Grant Collier, Terry Markwell as Casey Randall (who was replaced by Jane Badler as Shannon Reed), and Bob Johnson, who had the same role on the original series, as the voice that gave the team their instructions at the beginning each show. The series was canceled after less than two years on the air. Bruce Geller was the executive producer of this long-running and popular series.

MR. ADAMS AND EVE

Jan. 1957–Feb. 1958	CBS	Fri. 9–9:30 P.M.
Feb. 1958–Sept. 1958	CBS	Tues. 8–8:30 P.M.

Film star Ida Lupino and her husband, radio and film actor Howard Duff, starred in this half-hour situation comedy series playing husband and wife film stars, Eve Drake and Howard Adams. Each week Eve and Howard battled studio bosses, dealt with difficult agents, competed with each other for attention, and encountered various problems at the studio in this comedy series that was in the tradition of the Preston Sturges screwball comedies. Alan Reed played the couple's crafty studio boss, J. B. Hafter, and also featured on the series were Hayden Rorke and Olive Carey as their friends Steve and Elsie.

MR. AND MRS. NORTH

Oct. 1952–Sept. 1953	CBS	Fri. 10–10:30 P.M.
Jan. 1954–July 1954	NBC	Tues. 10:30–11 P.M.

Writers Frances and Richard Lockridge's husband-and-wife team of detectives Pam and Jerry North, who had been heard on a successful radio series since 1942, arrived on television in 1952 with Barbara Britton and Richard Denning playing the amateur detectives who always seemed to be stumbling upon various crimes that they inevitably solved. The Norths lived in New York City's Greenwich Village, and were lucky enough to have the occasional assistance of their friend Det Lt. Bill Weigand of the New

York City Police, played by Francis De Sales, in their crime-solving activities. Pam was eager, pretty, and clever, and Jerry was patient, loving, and supportive. *Mr. and Mrs. North,* which had first been introduced to the public in a series of stories in *The New Yorker* magazine, had, before it was heard on radio and seen on television, been a successful play on Broadway, as well as a popular film.

MR. BELVEDERE

Mar. 1985–Apr. 1985	ABC	Fri. 8:30–9 P.M.
Aug. 1985–Mar. 1987	ABC	Fri. 8:30–9 P.M.
May 1987–Sept. 1987	ABC	Fri. 8:30–9 P.M.
Oct. 1987–Jan. 1988	ABC	Fri. 9–9:30 P.M.
Jan. 1988–Feb. 1988	ABC	Fri. 8:30–9 P.M.
Mar. 1988–July 1989	ABC	Fri. 9–9:30 P.M.
Aug. 1989–Sept. 1989	ABC	Fri. 8:30–9 P.M.
Sept. 1989–Dec. 1989	ABC	Sat. 8–8:30 P.M.
July 1990	ABC	Sun. 8:30–9 P.M.

Based on a series of popular films of the 1940s that starred Clifton Webb in the title role, *Mr. Belvedere* arrived on television in 1985 with Christopher Hewett playing Belvedere. Mr. Lynn Belvedere was an unlikely housekeeper who ran the household and took care of the children of a widower, sportswriter George Owens, played by Bob Uecker, and his wife, Marsha, who had gone back to college, played by Ilene Graff. The children included Kevin (age 16), Heather (age 14), and Wesley (age eight), played by Rob Stone, Tracy Wells, and Brice Beckham, who were precocious and sometimes difficult, but were easily handled by the very proper, eccentric Englishman, Mr. Belvedere, who had formerly worked for no less a member of the British gentry than Winston Churchill, and who always seemed to know just what to do with the Owens's kids and keep them, as well as the family dog, Spot, under control. Each weekly episode ended with Belvedere writing about the events of his day in a diary. This situation comedy series remained on the air at various times over a period of five years. By the time it left the airwaves, Marsha had graduated from college and was working at her first job, and Kevin had become a college student. Over the years, singer Robert Goulet made occasional appearances on the show and even sang at Mr. Belvedere's wedding on the last episode of the series. Before he appeared in films and on this television series, the Mr. Belvedere character, which was created by Gwen Davenport, was the hero of a popular novel. Christopher Hewitt was cast in the role of Belvedere after three other well-known actors had filmed earlier pilots that failed to materialize as a regular series, Reginald Gardner, Hans Conried, and Victor Buono.

MISTER ED

Oct. 1961–Sept. 1962	CBS	Sun. 6:30–7 P.M.
Sept. 1962–Mar. 1963	CBS	Thurs. 7:30–8 P.M.
Mar. 1963–Oct. 1964	CBS	Sun. 6:30–7 P.M.
Dec. 1964–Sept. 1965	CBS	Wed. 7:30–8 P.M.

Following the example of the highly successful *Francis, the Talking Mule* film series of the 1940s and 1950s, CBS launched a situation comedy about a talking horse named Mister Ed. The series, which starred Alan YOUNG as the mild-mannered Wilbur Post, a young architect who, when he became tired of city life, decided to move to the country. Wilbur and his wife, Carol, played by Connie Hines, bought a big country house that had all of the country attractions they had hoped to find, and one thing they had not counted on. The former owners had left a palomino horse in the barn, named Mister Ed, whom Wilbur discovered talked (the voice of Mister Ed was supplied by the veteran western character actor Allan "Rocky" Lane). From 1961 until 1964, Larry Keating and Edna Skinner played Wilbur and Carol's next-door neighbors, Roger and Kay Addison. From 1964, until the series left the air two years later, Leon Ames and Florence MacMichael played the Posts, new neighbors, Gordon and Winnie Kirkwood. Although many celebrated guest stars made brief appearances on the show, one of the most memorable visits to Mister Ed's stable was made by the film world's queen of the double entendre, Mae West. Her sexy exchanges with Wilbur's horse had people talking about the episode she appeared on for years and almost caused the show to be canceled by outraged critics, who felt that West's presence on a show that was seen during the early evening hours when children were watching TV was unpardonable. The episode was, to most people, extremely funny. *Mister Ed's* executive producer was Al Simon, and Arthur Lubic was the series' producer director.

MR. I MAGINATION

May 1949–July 1949	CBS	Sun. 7–7:30 P.M.
July 1949	CBS	Sun. 7:30–8 P.M.
Aug. 1949–Sept. 1949	CBS	Sun. 7:30–7:55 P.M.
Oct. 1949–June 1951	CBS	Sun. 6:30–7 P.M.
Jan 1952–Feb. 1952	CBS	Sun. 6:30–7 P.M.
Feb. 1952–Apr. 1952	CBS	Sun. 6–6:30 P.M.

Several years before *CAPTAIN KANGAROO* and *MR. ROGER'S NEIGHBORHOOD* graced the airwaves, the *Mr. I Magination* series, which used the same format as these shows, was a very popular children's program that was originally seen once a week during the early evening hours on Sundays. Each week the show's host, Paul Tripp, who was called Mr. I Magination, dressed in train engineer coveralls and cap, encouraged children to use their imaginations and act our their fantasies as he spun his homey philosophy, and created a wonderful imaginary environment for them to enjoy. The series presented sketches that used music and puppets, as well as "live" characters, and was directed toward the preschoolers in the television audience. Appearing with Tripp were his wife, Ruth Enders, and Ted Tiller, Joe Silver, and Richard BOONE. Paul Tripp, who was only 23 years old when the series first aired in 1949, not only played the show's title character, but was also the series' creator, producer, and chief writer.

Tripp also wrote several children's books, most notably *Tubby the Tuba,* and after *Mr. I Magination* left the air, he hosted two popular local TV shows for children and had featured roles in several films and Broadway plays.

MR. NOVAK

Sept. 1963–Aug. 1965   NBC   Tues. 7:30–8:30 P.M.

For two seasons, *Mr. Novak* was popular with viewers, although it was never one of the top-20-rated shows according to the Nielsen television ratings. Mr. Novak was a good-looking young high school English teacher, played by James FRANCISCUS. The frustrations, rewards, and challenges that the inexperienced new teacher encounters when dealing with rebellious adolescents were the basis of most of the episodes of this dramatic series. Set in the fictional Jefferson High School in Los Angeles, the series also featured Dean Jagger as Jefferson's principal, Albert Vane, and Burgess Meredith as his replacement, Martin Woodridge; Jeanne Bal as Novak's fellow teacher and friend, Jean Pagano; Jim Hendriks as Larry Thor; Marion Ross as school nurse Miss Bromfield; and Steve Franken, Donald Barry, Marian Collier, Vince Howard, André Phillippe, Stephen Roberts, Kathaleen Ellis, Marjorie Corley, Phyllis Avery, William Zuckert, David Sheiner, Peter Hansen, and Irene Tedrow as Novak's fellow teachers. The series was produced by MGM, and E. Jack Neuman was the series' executive producer.

MR. PEEPERS

July 1952–Sept. 1952	NBC	Thurs. 9:30–10 P.M.
Oct. 1952–July 1953	NBC	Sun. 7:30–8 P.M.
Sept. 1953–June 1955	NBC	Sun. 7:30–8 P.M.

Mr. Peepers is a TV series that is fondly remembered from the years immediately following World War II. This gentle, good-natured series, which was telecast live from New York, starred Wally COX as Robinson Peepers, a shy, quiet teacher who was always trying to do the right thing, but who usually had his good deeds backfire on him. Mr. Peepers taught science at Jefferson High School. His best friend was a fellow teacher, Harvey Weskitt, played by Tony RANDALL, who taught history. Weskitt's confidence and straightforwardness contrasted sharply with his friend, Mr. Peepers. Other major characters on the series were Nancy Remington, the school nurse, played by Patricia Benoit, whom Peepers had a crush on, and the dithery English teacher Mrs. Gurney, played by Marion Lorne, whose husband, Gabriel, played by Joseph Foley, was Jefferson's principal the first season the show was aired. Other characters who appeared regularly were music appreciation teacher Rayola Dean, who was Mr. Peepers's girlfriend when the series was first aired, played by Norma Crane; Charlie Burr, played by David Tyrell; Superintendent Bascom, played by Gage Clark; Nancy Remington's father and mother, played by Ernest Treux and Sylvia Field; Harvey Weskitt's wife, Marge, played by Georgann Johnson; Mr. Hansen, played by Arthur O'Connell; Frank Whip, played by Jack Warden; Mr. Peeper's mother, played by Ruth McDevitt; his sister, Agnes, played by Jenny Egan; and his Aunt Lil, played by Reta Shaw. The fine ensemble acting and its amusing but real story lines made the show truly memorable. The show's popularity really soared when a romance developed between the mild-mannered science teacher, Peepers, and school nurse, Nancy Remington. When they were finally married during the 1953–54 season, millions of viewers tuned in to witness the proceedings. In their initial review of the *Mr. Peepers* show, *TV Guide* magazine said that the series "[came] close to being the perfect TV show," and loyal fans of the series certainly agreed.

MISTER ROGERS' NEIGHBORHOOD

1968–present   PBS   Mon.–Fri. Various times

The creator/host of a long-running children's program, Fred ROGERS was first seen by his preschool TV audience on a local, 15-minute, five-days-a-week show that was seen in Toronto, Ontario, as early as 1963. Mr. Rogers's warm, friendly chats with his preschooler friends, his fun activities, songs, and stories, and his easy-to-understand explanations of things that to adults might seem obvious, as well as his daily visits by toy train to the world of make-believe, where his many puppet and live action "friends" reside, and his songs and stories, made *Mister Rogers' Neighborhood* a most successful, award-winning children's program. Mr. Rogers's credo, which he repeated many times over the years, was, "I want every child to know that he or she has something lovable and worth expressing." Also appearing on the series, in addition to Rogers, who also produced the program and provided the voices for many of the puppet characters, were Betty Aberlin as Lady Aberlin, Joe Negri as the town handyman, Don Brocket as Fire Chief Brocket, David Newell (who was also the show's associate producer) as Mr. McFeeley of the Speedy Delivery service, Frances Clemons as Officer Clemons, and Bob "Bob Dog" Trow, who also provided puppet character voices for the show. The inhabitants of Rogers' Land of Make Believe included such favorites as the "live" Lady Elaine (Fairchild), and puppets King Friday XIII, the shy Daniel, the Striped Tiger, and Henrietta Pussycat. For most of the series' run, it originated from Philadelphia. In 2000, Rogers announced that no new episodes of *Mister Rogers' Neighborhood* would be taped.

MOD SQUAD, THE

| Sept. 1968–Aug. 1972 | ABC | Tues. 7:30–8:30 P.M. |
| Sept. 1972–Aug. 1973 | ABC | Thurs. 8–9 P.M. |

The United States of the 1960s was a country in which many social changes were taking place, and many of the conventions of the past were being discarded by much of the youth of the country. Some young people were called "hippies," and they advocated an antiwar, prolove, unisexual, free-spirited way of life. The TV series *The Mod Squad,* which featured a trio of youthful "hippie cops," attracted a considerable following during the six years it was on the air. The three major characters were young people who were on probation after being convicted of committing various infractions of the law. They had been recruited into a special undercover youth squad whose purpose was to uncover adult criminals who preyed on young people in Southern California. The three young hippie-cops included Pete Cochran, played by Michael Cole, a boy from a wealthy family, who had stolen a car and who was told to leave home by his parents; Linc Hayes, played by Clarence Williams III, an African-American young man from the Los Angeles ghetto of Watts who had been arrested for rioting and looting; and Julie Barnes, played by Peggy Lipton, the daughter of a San Francisco prostitute, who had run away from home and been arrested for vagrancy. They had been recruited by Capt. Adam Greer, played by Tige Andrews, to work for the L.A. Police Department as undercover agents. During the series' first season, the three young cops rode around in a battered old station wagon they called "Woody," but Woody was disposed of at the beginning of the show's second season, being driven off a cliff.

Clarence Williams III (Linc Hayes), Peggy Lipton (Julie Barnes), and Michael Cole (Pete Cochran) of *The Mod Squad* (Author's collection)

The Mod Squad was the brainchild of Bud Ruskin, a former cop and P.I., who was a member of an undercover squad while he was working for the Los Angeles Sheriff's Department. By the time *The Mod Squad* left the air in 1973, the youth movement had begun to mellow, mainly due to the fact that the Vietnam War, which was one of their major targets for change, had begun to wind down and rebellion had begun to ebb.

MONKEES, THE

Sept. 1966–Aug. 1968   NBC   Mon. 7:30–8 P.M.

Considering that it was on the air for only two seasons, *The Monkees* television series is still fondly remembered by viewers who were in their teens when it was first aired. Using the successful format of a hit film that starred the Beatles, *A Hard Day's Night,* which had a slight plot that strung together songs, visual effects, and slapstick comedy routines, TV producers Bert Schneider and Robert Rafelson formed a group of young men to appear in a series about a rock and roll group similar to the Beatles. From the over 400 performers who auditioned for the show, four entirely different, previously unknown to each other, young men were hired to play a rock and roll group called the Monkees on the new TV series. The four consisted of Micky Dolenz, an actor and singer who had previously appeared on TV in the series *Circus Boy;* Davy Jones, a British singer who had appeared in such stage productions as *Oliver!* on London's West End and Broadway; and Peter Tork and Mike Nesmith, who had musical backgrounds and had worked in rock and roll bands. As part of their contracts, the group, in addition to appearing on the TV series, also made records together as "The Monkees." The series, as well as the group's recordings, proved to be very popular with younger members of the TV audience. During the first year the series was aired, albums recorded under "The Monkees" name sold more than 8 million copies. In the 1980s, three of the group's original members, Jones, Dolenz, and Tork, appearing as The Monkees, were reunited for a successful concert tour. Toward the end of the tour, Nesmith joined the group for a few concerts. An unsuccessful attempt to revive the series in 1987, *The New Monkees,* failed to attract an audience, and only a few episodes of the show were aired before the program was canceled.

MONTALBAN, RICARDO (1920–)

The debonair, handsome Latin American actor Ricardo Montalban, who is perhaps best known to TV viewers as Mr. Roarke on the FANTASY ISLAND series, was born in Mexico City, to comfortably well-off parents. Montalban decided that he wanted to be an actor while he was in his teens, and by the time he was in his early twenties, he was one of Mexico's most popular film actors. In 1947, Montalban signed a contract with MGM Studios to appear in films in the United States, and made his debut as the leading man in *Fiesta*, opposite the popular actress/swimming star Esther Williams. He became instantly popular with the filmgoing audiences and was subsequently seen in such successful films at MGM as *Neptune's Daughter* (1949, also with Esther Williams), *Battleground* (1949), and *Two Weeks with Love* (1950). Over the next 25 years, Montalban continued to appear in numerous films and as a guest star on such television series as WAGON TRAIN, ADVENTURES IN PARADISE, ALFRED HITCHCOCK PRESENTS, *The* UNTOUCHABLES, BEN CASEY, *The* MAN FROM U.N.C.L.E, *The* WILD, WILD WEST, STAR TREK, MISSION: IMPOSSIBLE, IT TAKES A THIEF, GUNSMOKE, and HERE'S LUCY. After his success as the star of the *Fantasy Island* series, Montalban appeared as a regular on such series as *How the West Was Won*, *The* COLBYS, *Heaven Help Us* (1994), and provided his voice for the series *Freakazoid!* (1994). He also played prominent roles in the films *Star Trek II: The Wrath of Khan* (1982, as Khan), *Cannonball Run II* (1984), and *The Naked Gun: From the Files of Police Squad!* (1988).

MONTGOMERY, ELIZABETH (1933–1995)

The daughter of Elizabeth Allen and Robert MONTGOMERY, who were both successful actors, Elizabeth Montgomery, who was born in Hollywood, attended the Spence School in New York City and then the American Academy of Dramatic Arts, determined to follow in her parents' footsteps and become an actress. Elizabeth made her acting debut on a series that was produced by her father, ROBERT MONTGOMERY PRESENTS, in 1950, and was then seen in over 200 live television shows over the next several years. In addition, Montgomery also appeared in such successful films as *The Court-Martial of Billy Mitchell* (1955) and *Johnny Cool* (1963) and guest-starred on such TV series as ALFRED HITCHCOCK PRESENTS, *The* UNTOUCHABLES, *The* TWILIGHT ZONE, THRILLER, BURKE'S LAW, RAWHIDE, *and* 77 SUNSET STRIP. The role that made her famous, however, was Samantha the witch on the highly successful TV situation comedy BEWITCHED, which she starred in from 1964 until 1972. After *Bewitched* left the air, Montgomery appeared in what became an impressive list of memorable TV films, including the critically acclaimed *A Case of Rape* (1974), *The Legend of Lizzie Borden* (1975), and *Black Widow Murders* (1993). Elizabeth Montgomery died of cancer at the age of 62.

MONTGOMERY, ROBERT (HENRY MONTGOMERY, JR. 1904–1981)

Before he was the producer, director, and occasional star of one of television's most successful dramatic anthology shows, ROBERT MONTGOMERY PRESENTS, which was on the air from 1950 until 1957, Robert Montgomery was a popular film star. Montgomery, who was the son of the president of the New York Rubber Company, lived a privileged life as a youth. When his father died while Robert was still in school, the family's fortune suddenly disappeared, and Montgomery went to work at various jobs before leaving his home in Beacon, New York, and went to New York

City to become a writer. On the advice of a friend, Montgomery decided to become an actor and worked on the stage for a time before entering films. His first film role was in *So This Is College* in 1929, and he subsequently appeared in such important films as *Private Lives* (1931, with Norma Shearer), *The Last Mrs. Cheyney* (1937), *Night Must Fall* (1937, playing a role that won him a nomination for a Best Actor Academy Award), *Here Comes Mr. Jordan* (1941), and hundreds of other popular films.

In 1941, Montgomery became a member of the Naval Reserve and when the United States entered World War II in December of that year, Montgomery became a PT boat commander in the Pacific. He later participated in the D-day invasion of Europe as an officer on a U.S. destroyer. In 1945, when the war ended, Montgomery returned to the screen and starred in *They Were Expendable*, which was about PT-boat operations during the war.

Montgomery's first directorial assignment was an innovative film in which he also played the role of Private Detective Philip Marlowe. The film, *Lady in the Lake* (1946), was filmed from Marlowe's point of view, and Marlowe was seen only when his image appeared in a mirror. All the actors in the film talked directly to the camera, as if they were addressing Marlowe. In 1955, Montgomery directed the hit Broadway play *The Desperate Hours*, and then hosted, directed, produced, and appeared on his own TV series *Robert Montgomery Presents*.

Montgomery turned to politics after his TV series left the air, and in addition to being the four-term president of the Screen Actors Guild, he organized the Hollywood Republican Committee, which helped elect Dwight D. Eisenhower to the presidency of the United States. In his declining years, Montgomery, bitter about his inability to launch another hit TV series, wrote a book about the "mediocrity of television programming."

MOONLIGHTING

Mar. 1985	ABC	Sun. 9–11 P.M.
Mar. 1985–Apr. 1985	ABC	Tues. 10–11 P.M.
Aug. 1985–Sept. 1988	ABC	Tues. 9–10 P.M.
Dec. 1988–Feb. 1989	ABC	Tues. 9–10 P.M.
Apr. 1989–May 1989	ABC	Sun. 8–9 P.M.

Moonlighting, a detective comedy/drama series, was a fast-paced, witty program that did not take itself too seriously and was called "the show that knows it's on television," by its creator Glenn Gordon Caron. The major characters were Maddie Hayes, played by Cybill SHEPHERD, a former high-fashion model who discovered that her business manager had embezzled most of her earnings, and David Addison, played by Bruce WILLIS, a brash private detective who worked at the Blue Moon Detective Agency, which was one of the only assets left from Maddie's lost funds. Addison convinced a reluctant Maddie to keep her interest in the P.I. agency and go to work at the agency herself, keeping him on the staff. The chemistry between the two stars proved to be just right, and the 1940s-like witty, overlap-

Cybill Shepherd and Bruce Willis of *Moonlighting* (Author's collection)

ping dialogue, as well as the puns, rhymes, in-jokes, and double entendres, were slick, funny, and sophisticated. The series found favor with a large number of viewers who especially enjoyed Maddie's weekly icy rejection of Addison's amorous advances. Also appearing regularly on the series was Allyce Beasley as the detective agency's lisping, wide-eyed secretary, Agnes Dipesto. In spite of persistent production problems, *Moonlighting* enjoyed high ratings and was in the top-20 list of TV series during the 1985–86 season, its first year on the air. Scheduling problems because of Willis's budding film career and Shepherd's pregnancy caused delays in taping new episodes of the series during its second year, but the public kept demanding to see more, and *Moonlighting* limped along for two more fun-filled, if interrupted, years, finally ending production at the end of the 1988–89 season. Also appearing as regulars on the series were Curtis Armstrong as Herbert Viola, the agency's accountant; Eva Marie Saint and Robert Webber as Maddie's parents (seen during the 1987–88 season); and Jack Blessing as MacGillicuddy. Before the show's final season began, a power struggle between Cybill Shepherd and the series' creator/producer, Caron, forced Caron to resign, and Jay Daniels became *Moonlighting*'s executive producer. The various delays, conflicts, and controversies took their toll on the series, and *Moonlighting* finished a disappointing 41st in the Nielsen ratings during its final season on the air.

MOORE, CLAYTON (JACK CARLTON MOORE 1914 OR 1908–1999)

Forever identified with the role of the Lone Ranger, which he played on TV, in films, and in commercials for over three decades, Clayton Moore was born in Chicago. He began his career in show business when he was eight years old and worked as a circus acrobat. By 1934, Moore was an aerialist with the circus and appeared at the World's Fair. A handsome young man, Clayton, or Jack as he was then called, went to New York, where he soon found work as a male model. This led to appearances as a bit player in films and, because of his circus background, stunt work in Hollywood. Before long, Moore was cast in major roles in such second-feature films as *The Son of Monte Cristo* (1940), *Kit Carson* (1940), *Outlaws of Pine Ridge* (1942), *The Crimson Ghost* (1946), *Jesse James Rides Again* (1947), *Ghost of Zorro* (1949), and many others, eventually earning the unofficial title of "King of the B (second-feature) Films," among Hollywood insiders. In 1949, Moore was cast in the role that would, for the rest of his career, be permanently identified with him, the Lone Ranger, in a successful TV series that ran from 1949 until 1951, and then after a brief hiatus, from 1954 to 1957. Moore also played the Lone Ranger in two very successful films, *The Lone Ranger* (1956) and *The Lone Ranger and the Lost City of Gold* (1958), while continuing to play roles in numerous other films, because the Lone Ranger wore a mask and was not easily identifiable. Moore was making appearances as the Lone Ranger until the year he died, 1999, at the reported age of 85.

MOORE, GARRY (THOMAS GARRISON MORFIT 1915–1993)

In 1935, when Garry Moore made his radio debut on *The Ransom Sherman Show,* his name was Tom Morfit. The producers of the show were not pleased with his real name and conducted a contest to find him a new one. A woman from Pittsburgh proposed the name Garry Moore, won the contest, and Tom Morfit was known forever after as Garry Moore. He was born in Baltimore, Maryland, and his big break came, however, when he became popular comedian Jimmy DURANTE's partner and straightman on radio's *The Jimmy Durante–Garry Moore Show* in the 1940s. This led to *The Garry Moore Show* (also for radio) in 1949, and subsequent hosting assignments on such successful radio game shows as *Beat the Band* and *Take It or Leave It.* Moore also hosted the *Camel Caravan* and *Breakfast in Hollywood* shows on radio. In 1950, Garry Moore made his TV debut on a daytime variety show called *The Garry Moore Show,* which remained on the air until 1958. He also hosted the very popular I'VE GOT A SECRET game/panel show from 1952 until 1964, and a successful evening version of *The Garry Moore Show* from 1958 until 1967. From 1969 through 1977, Moore hosted the TO TELL THE TRUTH game/panel show and then quietly retired from the spotlight.

MOORE, MARY TYLER (1936–)

One of television's most beloved stars, Mary Tyler Moore, who was born in Brooklyn, New York, began her show business career as a dancer soon after she graduated from high school. When she was 19 years old, Mary was appearing on television as "Happy Hotpoint," the Hotpoint Appliance TV elf, in commercials that were seen during THE ADVENTURES OF OZZIE AND HARRIET in 1955. In 1959, Moore was cast as a character named Sam, who was seen only from the waist down, on the

RICHARD DIAMOND, PRIVATE DETECTIVE series, which was on the air from 1957 until 1960. In 1961, Mary Tyler Moore won the role of Laura Petrie opposite Dick VAN DYKE on The DICK VAN DYKE SHOW, which became one of TV's most successful situation comedy series and made Mary a TV star. After several less than successful attempts to become a film star in such movies as Thoroughly Modern Millie (1967), What's So Bad About Feeling Good? (1968) and Run a Crooked Mile (1969), Mary returned to television as the star of her own show, The MARY TYLER MOORE SHOW, which proved to be one of television's most successful programs and made her a TV legend. The show left the air in 1977, while it was still very popular. In 1978 and 1979, Moore starred in two other TV shows, Mary and The Mary Tyler Moore Hour, but in 1980, she tried film work once again and this time received critical acclaim for her performances in Ordinary People (1980) and Six Weeks (1982).

In addition to appearing in two new TV series, Mary in 1985 and Annie McGuire in 1988, she continued to appear in films. In 1995, Moore became a cast member of the TV series New York News, which was not a success, and in 2000 she reprised her role of Mary Richards in a TV film that costarred her Mary Tyler Moore Show costar, Valerie HARPER, which was titled Mary and Rhoda. Over the years, in addition to her starring roles in films and on television, Mary Tyler Moore has also made memorable guest appearances on such TV shows as 77 SUNSET STRIP, HAWAIIAN EYE, The MILLIONAIRE, WANTED: DEAD OR ALIVE, FRASIER, and ELLEN.

MOORE, ROGER (ROGER GEORGE MOORE 1927–)

Roger Moore was one of the actors who played James Bond after Sean Connery abandoned the role. The six Bond films Roger Moore appeared in were all box office hits and included Live and Let Die (1973), The Man with the Golden Gun (1974), The Spy Who Loved Me (1977), Moonraker (1979), For Your Eyes Only (1981), and A View to a Kill (1985). Roger Moore, who was born in London, was a successful film actor in Great Britain and the United States before assuming the Bond role and was well known to television viewers in both countries as Simon Templar on the mystery/adventure series The SAINT, which was on the air from 1962 until 1969. Before starring on The Saint, Moore was a regular in the TV series Ivanhoe (1958, as Ivanhoe), The Alaskans (1959), and MAVERICK (1960–61, as Beau Maverick). After The Saint was canceled, he was seen on The Persuaders (1971) series.

Among the memorable films Moore appeared in are The Last Time I Saw Paris (1954), The Sins of Rachel Cade (1961), and The Cannonball Run (1981), among others. Moore appeared on the stage in the musical comedy Aspects of Love in 1990, which was his debut as a singer, but he left the show days before it opened because he felt his singing voice was inadequate. In 1999, Moore was a regular on The Dream Team TV series and also narrated and hosted The James Bond Story.

MORAN, ERIN (1961–)

Born in Burbank, California, where many of Hollywood's film and television studios are located, Erin Moran began appearing in such films as How Sweet It Is! (1968) and Watermelon Man (1970) while she was still a child. In 1972, Moran became a regular cast member on The Don Rickles Show, playing Janie Robinson. But it was as Joanie Cunningham on the popular TV series HAPPY DAYS, that Erin enjoyed her greatest success as an actress and became a well-known face to millions of television viewers. In 1982, Moran starred with Scott Baio on the JOANIE LOVES CHACHI TV series, which was a spin-off of Happy Days, playing the same character she played on that show. Moran had a major role in the film Galaxy of Terror (1981) and played herself in the film Dear God (1996). Among the numerous TV shows Erin Moran has guest-starred on are MY THREE SONS, Family Affair, GUN-SMOKE, The WALTONS, The LOVE BOAT, MURDER, SHE WROTE, and DIAGNOSIS MURDER.

MORK & MINDY

Sept. 1978–Aug. 1979	ABC	Thurs. 8–8:30 P.M.
Aug. 1979–Dec. 1979	ABC	Sun. 8–8:30 P.M.
Jan. 1980–Feb. 1982	ABC	Thurs. 8–8:30 P.M.
Apr. 1982–May 1982	ABC	Thurs. 8:30–9 P.M.
May 1982–June 1982	ABC	Thurs. 8–8:30 P.M.

A spin-off of a February 1978 episode seen on the popular HAPPY DAYS series, Mork & Mindy featured comedian Robin WILLIAMS as an alien named Mork from the planet Ork. On the original Happy Days episode, Mork had landed on Earth and decided to kidnap Richie Cunningham of Happy Days to take him back to his home planet as a pet. The Mork character was so well received by viewers, that Williams was given a series of his own in fall 1978. In addition to Williams, Mork & Mindy also starred Pam DAWBER as Mindy Beth McConnell, a human who had befriended the human-looking, but decidedly strange-acting alien Mork and let him stay in the attic of her apartment house in Boulder, Colorado. Mindy worked in a music store owned by her father, Frederick McConnell, played by Conrad Janis, a conservative man who was scandalized that his daughter had arranged for a strange man to live in her building. Her grandmother, Cora, played by Elizabeth Kerr, however, was delighted with the arrangement. As he attempted to adjust to Earth's odd way of doing things, Mork made many un-Earthly blunders, which resulted in most of the comic situations that occurred on the show. The Mork character was particularly suited to the unusual comedic talents of Robin Williams, whose improvisational acting on the series seemed natural, considering he was playing an alien from another world, and hilarious. Also appearing on the series regularly were Jeffrey Jacquet as Eugene, Tom POSTON as Franklin Delano Bickley, Jay Thomas and Gina Hecht as Remo and Jean DeVinci, Jim Staahl as Nelson Flavor, Crissy Wilzak as Glenda Faye "Crissy" Comstock, Robert

Donner as the alien Exidor, and Foster Brooks as Mr. Miles Sternhagen. The voice of Mork's Orkan leader was provided by Ralph James.

By 1981, Mork & Mindy, in spite of their differences, had fallen in love and were married, and the couple honeymooned on Mork's home planet, Ork. Shortly after their marriage, it was Mork who gave birth to a baby when an egg simply popped out of his navel. The half alien–half human baby, named Mearth, played by comedian Jonathan WINTERS, was a full-grown man who was 225 pounds and looked middle-aged but babbled like a baby. Mearth called Mork "Mommy," and Mindy, "Shoe." The improvisational exchanges between Robin Williams and Jonathan WINTERS, both masters of improvisational acting, kept the producers of the show in a constant state of anxiety, but delighted viewers. At the end of each episode, Mork always reported back to his leader on Ork, speaking in a strange language, and signed off by twisting his ears and muttering, "Na nu, na nu," which was Orkan for "goodbye."

In June 1982, Mork said his last "na nu," and the series became part of television history. Mork & Mindy was created and produced by Garry Marshall, who was also responsible for Happy Days, and Joe Glausberg and Dale McRaven.

MOTHERS-IN-LAW, THE

Sept. 1967–Sept. 1969   NBC   Sun. 8:30–9 P.M.

Although they had been TV neighbors in suburban Los Angeles for 15 years, the Hubbards and the Buells were very different people on The Mothers-in-Law situation comedy series. When their children married each other, the two couples became in-laws. Eve Hubbard, played by Eve ARDEN, was the matriarch of the conservative Hubbard family and Kay Buell, played by Kaye Ballard, was the extremely unconventional matriarch of the Buells. Eve's husband, Herb, played by Herbert Rudley, was a politically conservative golfer, while Kay's husband, Roger, played by Roger Carmel, and then by Richard Deacon, was a liberal television writer who was always reading his scripts to anyone he came in contact with. The two couples' children, Jerry and Susie Buell, played by Jerry Fogel and Deborah Walley, were always running interference between their parents. The series' executive producer was Desi ARNAZ, who also appeared on the show on occasion as a bullfighter named Raphael del Gado.

MOVIES ON TELEVISION

Although the major Hollywood film studios were extremely worried when commercial television surfaced in the late 1940s, fearing that the new medium might steal paying customers away from movie theaters, they were sure TV was just a passing fad. By the 1950s, TV had become the filmmakers' major competitor, and movie companies, in an attempt to curb TV's popularity, refused to allow any recently released films to be shown on television. The films that were sold to television, therefore, were old films like King Kong (1933), silent films from the 1920s, old westerns like the Hopalong Cassidy films, and mystery film potboilers such as the Charlie Chan and Philo Vance series as well as many other second-feature films and serials from the 1930s and 1940s. The first attempt to get high-quality feature films on television was made by the DuMont TV station in New York, not by one of the three major networks, ABC, NBC, or CBS. In 1948, the local New York station WPIX signed an agreement with English producer Alexander Korda to broadcast 24 major British films with such English stars as Laurence Olivier, Vivien Leigh, and Charles Laughton, and their popularity with viewers signaled what the future held for the Hollywood film studios.

It wasn't until 1961, however, that a relatively recent motion picture was aired on TV. NBC bought the rights to show the popular 20th Century Fox film How to Marry a Millionaire, which starred Marilyn Monroe, Lauren Bacall, and Betty Grable, on their new series Saturday Night at the Movies, which premiered on September 23, 1961. The response to the new series was so overwhelmingly positive that the film industry decided it couldn't ignore the financial rewards of showing some films on television, and it began to release recent films to the television networks. The highest single-showing feature films seen on television since Saturday Night at the Movies made its debut are (in the order of their ratings by number of viewers) Gone With the Wind, The Day After, Airport, Love Story, Jaws, The Poseidon Adventure, True Grit, The Birds, Patton, The Bridge on the River Kwai, The Godfather, Jeremiah Johnson, Ben-Hur, Rocky, Little Ladies of the Night, Helter Skelter, The Burning Bed, The Wizard of Oz, Born Free, The Sound of Music, Bonnie and Clyde, The Ten Commandments, and The Night Stalker.

Unquestionably, the three most popular films that have been seen on television, which have been seen by more people than any other films (taking individual local station, network presentations, and cable station showings into account) are Gone With the Wind, Casablanca, and The Wizard of Oz. Realizing that there was a demand for original feature-length films to be shown on television, producers began to offer made-for-TV films in 1964, when Universal Pictures produced See How They Run especially for television. Shortly thereafter producers began to make TV films as pilots for new series. By the 1986–87 season, filmmakers were producing fewer than 100 films for theatrical release, but made over 300 feature-length TV films.

As first-run movies were usually available on DVDs and videocassettes within a year after their release on pay-for-view satellite and cable stations in the 1990s, the networks had to wait longer periods of time to present current feature films on their stations. Some popular films were not broadcast by national networks until several years after theatrical release, and even films that were as old as 10 years turned up as movies of the week on the networks.

MULLIGAN, RICHARD (1932–2000)

Before making his film debut in *Love with the Proper Stranger* in 1963, Richard Mulligan appeared in many stage plays in New York and on tour. Born in New York City, Richard's brother was film director Robert Mulligan, who helped him find work in films when he first arrived in Hollywood. His talent, however, landed him roles in such films as *The Group* (1966), *Little Big Man* (1970, as General George Custer), *From the Mixed-Up Files of Mrs. Basil E. Frankweiler* (1973), and *Meatballs Part II* (1984), and as a regular on the TV series *The Hero* (1966), *Diana* (1973), SOAP (as Burt Campbell), and EMPTY NEST, playing Dr. Harry Weston, the role he is perhaps best remembered for. In addition, Mulligan also guest-starred on such popular series as *I DREAM OF JEANNIE, BONANZA*, The PARTRIDGE FAMILY, CHARLIE'S ANGELS, The LOVE BOAT, The TWILIGHT ZONE, GUNSMOKE, The GOLDEN GIRLS, and The JOHN LARROQUETTE SHOW.

MUNSTERS, THE

(also The Munsters Today)

Sept. 1964–Sept. 1966   CBS   Thurs. 7:30–8 P.M.

As The Munsters Today:
Oct. 1988–Sept. 1991   Syndication   Various times and stations

In 1964, two television situation comedy series that featured bizarre, ghoulish families who lived in spooky mansions made their TV debuts, and both became favorites with viewers and enjoyed two-year runs that ended in September 1966. One of the series was called *The ADDAMS FAMILY* and the other *The Munsters*. *The Munsters* starred Fred Gwynne and Yvonne DeCarlo as Herman and Lily Munster, a couple who strongly resembled the Frankenstein monster and the Bride of the Frankenstein monster. Far from being frightening, however, the Munsters, in spite of their strange monster looks, were a gentle, loving couple who just happened to have some unusual habits. Herman and Lily had two children: a son named Edward Wolfgang "Eddie" Munster, played by Butch Patrick, who looked like the Wolf Man in miniature, and a perfectly normal-looking, blonde daughter named Marilyn Munster, whom everyone in the family considered sadly abnormal, played by Beverly Owen, and then by Pat Priest, who resembled Marilyn Monroe. Living with the Munsters was Grandpa Munster, played by Al Lewis, who looked a good deal like Count Dracula of horror movie fame. The family pet was a dinosaur named Spot. The Munsters lived at 1313 Mockingbird Lane in a mansion that was cobweb-covered, furnished in heavy Victorian, and dismal. The Munsters were, in spite of their spooky looks, a "typical American family." Twenty years after the original series departed the airwaves, *The Munsters* was revived as a syndicated show that starred an entirely new cast that included John Schuck as Herman Munster, Lee Meriwether as Lily, Jason Marsden as

The Munsters: (clockwise from top) Fred Gwynne (Herman Munster), Beverly Owen (Marilyn Munster), Al Lewis (Grandpa Munster), Butch Patrick (Eddie Munster, and Yvonne DeCarlo (Lily Munster) (Author's collection)

Eddie Munster, Hilary VanDyke as Marilyn Munster, and Howard Morton as Grandpa Munster. Even though the series was on the air one year longer than the original program, it was never as popular as the first *Munsters* show. *The Munsters* was created by Joe Connelly and Bob Mosher, who had previously worked together on *LEAVE IT TO BEAVER*.

MUPPET SHOW, THE

1976–1981   Syndicated   Various times and stations

In the best tradition of the innovative *KUKLA, FRAN & OLLIE* TV series, which combined puppets and live performers, *The Muppet Show* offered TV viewers a half hour of charming, fun-filled entertainment. The Muppets, originally a group of puppet characters who had become well known on PBS's *SESAME STREET*, emerged as the major characters on this variety show, which featured a different big-name celebrity as a guest star and was hosted by Kermit the Frog, whose voice was supplied by and actions manipulated by Muppet creator Jim HENSON.

Among the popular Muppets who appeared regularly on the series were the overstuffed, vain Miss Piggy, who was determined to be a show business "star"; Rowlf, the

The Muppets with creator Jim Henson (Author's collection)

shaggy piano-playing dog; Fozzie Bear; Dr. Teeth and his Electric Mayhem band (which featured Floyd, the spaced-out guitarist and Animal, the drummer); Dr. Benson Honeydew; the maniacal Swedish Chef, Gonzo, who always tried to open the show with a failed trumpet fanfare; and two crusty, hard-of-hearing old men, Statler and Waldorf, who sat in the balcony of the Muppet Theater, yelling insults and criticizing the action; along with many other creative and amusing characters.

Guests on *The Muppet Show*, who usually vied to appear on the show, included such notable performers as George BURNS, Zero Mostel, Steve Martin, Rudolf Nureyev, Elton John, Beverly Sills, and Peter Sellers. The puppeteers who worked on *The Muppet Show* included Jim Henson, who handled Kermit, Swedish Chef, Capt. Link Heartthrob the Pig, hero of the Pigs in Space skits, and Rowlf; Frank OZ, who was responsible for Miss Piggy, Fozzie Bear, Animal, and many other puppets and later became a coproducer of the series and Muppet feature films that followed; and Richard Hunt, Dave Goelz, Jerry Nelson, Erin Ozker, Louise Gold, Kathryn Miller, and Steve Whitmire.

By the time *The Muppet Show* departed the airwaves in 1981, 400 Muppet characters had been introduced to an adoring public. In 1991, *The Muppets Tonight* series surfaced with Bill Baretta, Kevin Clash, Dave Goelz, Brian Henson, Jerry Nelson, Steve Whitmire, and Frank Oz handling the puppets and providing the voices for the characters. Jim Henson, who had died before this new series was aired, was sadly missing from the new series.

MURDER, SHE WROTE

Sept. 1984–May 1991	CBS	Sun. 8–9 P.M.
June 1991–July 1991	CBS	Sun. 9–10 P.M.
July 1991–Sept. 1995	CBS	Sun. 8–9 P.M.
Aug. 1995–June 1996	CBS	Thurs. 8–9 P.M.
Apr. 1996–Aug. 1996	CBS	Sun. 8–9 P.M.

Hollywood and Broadway star Angela LANSBURY played a middle-aged widow and mystery novelist named Jessica Fletcher, who wrote under the name J. B. Hetcher, on this cozy whodunit TV series that remained on the air for five years before settling into endless reruns. Jessica lived in the picturesque Maine coastal town of Cabot Cove, where everyone knew one another and where an alarming number of murders seemed to take place, which Jessica always managed to solve. A former substitute teacher and amateur detective, Jessica had become a celebrity late in life when her first mystery was published and became enormously successful. She took full advantage of her newfound money and celebrity to travel widely, especially when the number of crimes that could possibly have taken place in a small town in Maine became more and more improbable.

When the series was first aired, Tom BOSLEY played Sheriff Amos Tupper, whom Jessica assisted whenever a crime took place in Cabot Cove. When Bosley decided to leave the series in 1988, Ron Masak took over his job as Sheriff Mort Metzger. Often becoming involved in Jessica's crime-solving missions was Dr. Seth Hazlitt, played by William Windom, Cabot Cove's physician, who was one of Jessica's best friends. During its earliest years, *Murder, She Wrote* became known for featuring guest appearances by some of Hollywood's most famous former stars, many of whom had worked with Lansbury when she was under contract to MGM Studios in the 1940s and 1950s. Among the guests during these years were Kathryn Grayson, Ruth Roman, Margaret O'Brien, Gloria DeHaven, Van Johnson, Julie Adams, and Tom Drake. Appearing regularly on the series were Richard Paul as Cabot Cove's mayor, Sam Booth, Michael Horton as Grady Fletcher, Jessica's nephew, and Keith Michell as Jessica's British friend, Dennis Stanton, a former jewel thief who often helped her solve crimes when Jessica was visiting San Francisco. Lt. Perry Catalano, of the San Francisco Police Department, played by Ken Swoford, often became involved in Jessica and Stanton's crime-solving activities.

In 1991, although she maintained her home in Cabot Cove and returned there periodically to solve a mystery or two, Jessica lived in New York City five days a week, where she taught a class in criminology at Manhattan University. The number of crimes Jessica stumbled upon in New York City seemed much more probable, and the series continued along with Jessica uncovering murderer after murderer until 1996, when the series was abruptly canceled by CBS, much to Angela Lansbury's, and the viewers', surprise. Thousands of letters arrived at CBS protesting the show's demise, but it remained off the air.

The series was created especially for Angela Lansbury by Richard Levinson, William Link, and Peter S. Fisher when Lansbury failed to obtain the TV rights to play Agatha Christie's sleuth Miss Marple, a role she had played in a film, since the BBC in England had already contracted to film a series in that country. After *Murder, She Wrote* ended its initial run, Lansbury continued to make TV films, still playing Jessica Fletcher, and these films and the character continued to be popular with large numbers of viewers.

MURPHY BROWN

Nov. 1988–Feb. 1997	CBS	Mon. 9–9:30 P.M.
Apr. 1997–May 1997	CBS	Mon. 8:30–9 P.M.
June 1997–Sept. 1997	CBS	Mon. 9:30–10 P.M.
Oct. 1997–Jan. 1998	CBS	Wed. 8:30–9 P.M.
Apr. 1998–May 1998	CBS	Mon. 9:30–10 P.M.
July 1998–Aug. 1998	CBS	Mon. 9:30–10 P.M.

Set at a Washington, D.C., television studio, this situation comedy was about a fictional weekly news magazine show, *F.Y.I.,* that was seen on Wednesday nights and was in its twelfth successful year when the *Murphy Brown* series made its premiere. Murphy Brown, played by Candice BERGEN, was the veteran star reporter of the *F.Y.I.* series and was hardly the easiest person in the world to work with or live with. Opinionated, independent, sarcastic, and ambitious, Murphy was determined to retain her place of importance in the male-dominated news-reporting business. She lived life to the fullest, drinking and smoking in excess, which landed the character in the famous Betty Ford Clinic in California, where she underwent treatment for her addictions. She was, in spite of herself, a successful, competent TV reporter and an impressive on-camera presence. Appearing as regular characters with Murphy were the show's stuffy, 25-year veteran anchorman, Jim Dial, played by Charles Kimbrough; *F.Y.I.*'s investigative reporter, Frank Fontana, Murphy's longtime friend, played by Joe Regalbuto; the pretty, young, new kid on the show, Corky Sherwood, a former Miss America who became a featured reporter on the *F.Y.I.* show mainly because of her perky personality and good looks, played by Faith Ford; and the show's executive producer, who was extremely young, naive, nervous, and somewhat neurotic, whom Murphy was always able to better, played by Grant Shaud. Also appearing on the series during its first several years, were Robert Pastorelli as Edwin Bernecky, a handyman who was endlessly working on Murphy's house who became one of her best friends; and Pat Corley as Phil; Ritch Brinkley as Carl Wishinsky; John Hostetter as John, the stage manager; Scott Bakula as Peter Hunt, a globe-trotting reporter who became involved in a torrid affair with Murphy; veteran stage and film actress Colleen Dewhurst, who played Murphy's mother on several episodes of the series; and Dyllan Christopher and then Haley Joel Osment as Avery Brown, Murphy's son, whose birth, since Murphy was not married, caused considerable controversy in the press and criticism from several conservative camps.

When Murphy's baby, who was fathered by Murphy's ex-husband, Jake, played by Jay Thomas, after a brief encounter between the former couple, was born in May 1992, it became the center of a controversy that is perhaps unique in television history. The then vice president of the United States, Dan Quayle, delivered a speech in San Francisco that centered on the "deterioration of family life in America," mentioning the *Murphy Brown* show in particular, saying it "doesn't help matters when primetime TV has Murphy Brown, a character who supposedly epitomizes today's intelligent, highly paid professional woman [mocks] the importance of fathers by bearing a child alone and calling it just another lifestyle choice." *Murphy Brown*'s producer, Diane English, was quick to respond to the vice president's criticism and replied, "If he believes that a woman cannot adequately raise a child without a father, then he'd better make sure abortion remains safe and legal." The publicity generated by this controversy certainly did not detract from the show's popularity: ratings increased, and the series remained on the air for an additional five years.

During the years *Murphy Brown* was aired, it became known for Murphy's having a different secretary every week

Murphy Brown: (left to right) Charles Kimbrough (Jim), Candice Bergen (Murphy), Joe Regalbuto (Frank), Faith Ford (Corky), and Grant Shaud (Miles) (Author's collection)

because of Murphy's "difficult" personality and impossible demands on them. By the time *Murphy Brown* departed the airwaves in 1998, Murphy had had 93 secretaries.

MURRAY, ARTHUR & KATHRYN (MOSES TEICHMAN 1895–1991 & KATHRYN KOHNFELDER 1906–1999)

For 10 years from 1950 until 1960, Arthur Murray and his wife, Kathryn, had one of the most popular shows on television. The show was called *The ARTHUR MURRAY PARTY* and the Murrays hosted each week's program. Arthur Murray was born in New York City, and after a brief stint as a dancer on the vaudeville stage and on Broadway, he opened a school to teach ballroom dancing to novices in New York City. The school was a big success, and soon there were Arthur Murray Dance Schools opening all across the country. Murray, who was himself an expert dancer, made guest appearances in films such as *Cuban Rhythm* (1941) and *Jiggs and Maggie in Society* (1947). It was Murray's wife, Kathryn, who was born in Jersey City, New Jersey, and had been a dance instructor in one of Arthur's studios before she married him, who had the bright idea to bring Murray's dance school techniques to television, and in 1950 the *Arthur Murray Party Time* program made its premiere. The idea proved a good one, and soon people all across the country were tuning in to see the Murrays' weekly dance parties. After their TV series was canceled, the Murrays continued to operate their dance schools for a time, but eventually retired from the spotlight, except for occasional guest appearances on various TV talk shows.

MURRAY, KEN (1903–1988)

Brash comedian Ken Murray, who was known for his *Ken Murray Blackout* stage shows in the 1930s and 1940s, was the star of one of television's first successful variety shows, *The KEN MURRAY SHOW*, which premiered in 1950. Murray, who was born in New York City, had been a performer on the vaudeville stage in the 1920s and made his film debut in 1929 in *Half Marriage*. Murray subsequently appeared in the long-running *Blackouts* stage show and in such films as *Ladies of the Jury* (1932), *Brother Could You Spare a Million?* (1933), *Swing, Sister, Swing* (1938), *Bill and Coo* (1947), *Red Light* (1949), and others, before entering television. After his TV series was canceled, Murray continued to appear in such films as *The Marshal's Daughter* (1953), *The Man Who Shot Liberty Valance* (1962), *Son of Flubber* (1963), *The Way West* (1967), and *Won Ton Ton, The Dog Who Saved Hollywood* (1976), before retiring in the early 1980s. Murray was also a successful producer and was in charge of the films *Bill and Coo* and *The Marshal's Daughter*, which he also appeared in.

MURROW, EDWARD R. (EGBERT ROSCOE MURROW 1908–1965)

Before he became one of television's most admired news personalities, Edward R. Murrow was a dominant figure on radio. During the early years of World War II, before the United States entered the war, Murrow's dramatic, on-the-scene broadcasts to America from Europe as he covered the German occupation of Austria in 1938, the Nazi blitzkrieg of Czechoslovakia, and the bombing of London in 1939, made him one of the most recognized voices in the United States. Born in Greensboro, North Carolina, Murrow had entered radio shortly after he graduated from Washington State College, where he majored in political science, speech, and international relations. After the war, Murrow continued to comment on the postwar news for CBS, and in 1951, he hosted one of television's most successful news magazine shows, SEE IT NOW. His series PERSON TO PERSON, on which he interviewed many political figures such as Jacqueline Kennedy, President Ben-Gurion of Israel, and the duke and duchess of Windsor, also became one of the most popular programs on television in the early 1950s. Murrow interviewed his guests from the CBS studio, and they answered him live from their homes, and the show became a weekly must for millions of viewers. Murrow was known for ending all of his programs with the expression, "Good night and good luck." A longtime heavy cigarette smoker, Murrow died of brain cancer at age 57 in 1965.

MY FAVORITE MARTIAN

Sept. 1963–Sept. 1966	CBS	Sun. 7:30–8 P.M.

The *My Favorite Martian* situation comedy series starred Ray Walston as a Martian whose spacecraft had crashed on Earth. The Martian was found by a reporter for *The Los Angeles Sun*, Tim O'Hara, played by Bill BIXBY, and taken back to his rooming house to recuperate. To avoid alarm, Tim told people the Martian was his "Uncle Martin," and since the Martian looked human and spoke English, people believed him. The Martian, however, had amazing inhuman supernatural abilities. He could make himself invisible, move things by just looking at them, and had an advanced knowledge of technology. Tim lived in a rooming house owned by Mrs. Lorelei Brown, played by Pamela Britton. During the show's first season, Mrs. Brown had a daughter named Angela, played by Ann Marshall, who departed the series after one year. Mrs. Brown, Tim's boss, Mr. Harry Burns, played by J. Pat O'Malley, and Mrs. Brown's boyfriend, police detective Bill Brennan, played by Alan Hewitt, did not know the truth about "Uncle Martin's" real identity, but they were always suspicious and thought that something was peculiar about him. *My Favorite Martian*'s 107 filmed episodes were produced by Jack Chertok.

MY FRIEND IRMA

Jan. 1952–Mar. 1952	CBS	Tues. 10:30–11 P.M.
Apr. 1952–June 1953	CBS	Fri. 8:30–9 P.M.
Oct. 1953–June 1954	CBS	Fri. 10–10:30 P.M.

When the *My Friend Irma* show made its television debut in 1952, it was already one of America's most popular radio shows, and had been on the air since 1947. When CBS decided to present its successful comedy on television as well as on radio, the voices of the *My Friend Irma*'s major characters were already well known, and so the same performers were cast on the television series. On both the radio and TV series, Marie WILSON played Irma Peterson, a somewhat dim-witted blonde whose wacky illogical remarks kept people laughing for years, and Cathy Lewis played her intelligent, levelheaded roommate, Jane Stacy. The girls both worked as secretaries in New York. Gloria Gordon, who was also heard on the radio series, played the girl's landlady, Mrs. O'Reilly, on the TV series. Irma's fast-taking, con-man boyfriend, Al, was played by Sig Tomack. Jane's boyfriend, who was also her boss, was Richard Rhinelander III, played by Brooks West. Irma's long-suffering, always exasperated boss, Mr. Clyde, was played by Don McBride. One of the most popular characters on the series was one of the boarders at Mrs. O'Reilly's boardinghouse, Professor Kropotkin, played by Sid Arno on the TV series (Hans CONRIED, who had originated the role on radio, did not make the transition from radio to TV). One of Hollywood's most recognizable character actresses, Margaret Dumont, played the snooty Mrs. Rhinelander, Richard's mother. Also appearing on the series were Hal MARCH as Joe Vance, Richard Eyer as Bobby Peterson, Mary Shipp as Kay Foster, and John Carradine as Mr. Corday. *My Friend Irma* was created by Cy Howard. The TV series was produced by Nat Perrin and directed by former film actor Richard Whorf.

MY LITTLE MARGIE

June 1952–Sept. 1952	CBS	Mon. 9–9:30 P.M.
Oct. 1952–Nov. 1952	NBC	Sat. 7:30–8 P.M.
Jan. 1953–July 1953	CBS	Thurs. 10–10:30 P.M.
Sept. 1953–Aug. 1955	NBC	Wed. 8:30–9 P.M.

Gale STORM starred as Margie Albright, a 20-year-old woman determined to save her handsome, 50-year-old widowed father, Verne Albright, played by Charles Farrell, from the wiles of various women who were out to trap him into marriage. Margie did, however, approve of her father's friend Roberta Townsend, played by Hillary Brooke, and did what she could to encourage their relationship. Verne worked as an executive with the investment-counseling firm of Honeywell and Todd, and the Albrights lived in a Fifth Avenue apartment in New York City. Verne's cantankerous boss, Mr. Honeywell (Mr. Todd was never seen) was played by veteran character actor Clarence Kolb. Their neighbor in the next-door apartment was an amusing woman named Mrs. Odets, played by Gertrude W. Hoffman, who became one of the series' most popular characters. Also appearing on the series were African-American comedian Willie Best, who played a stereotypical handyman named Charlie. *My Little Margie* was also heard on radio from 1952 until 1955, the same years it was seen as a TV series. Both the radio and TV series were produced by Hal Roach, Jr. and

My Little Margie starred Charles Farrell and Gale Storm (Author's collection)

Roland Reed and was originally aired on television as a summer replacement. In all, 126 episodes of *My Little Margie* were filmed and were widely syndicated after its original run ended, throughout the 1950s and 1960s.

MY MOTHER THE CAR

Sept. 1965–Sept. 1966   NBC   Tues. 7:30–8 P.M.

Although it was on the air for only one year, *My Mother the Car* was one of the most talked-about television situation comedy programs of the 1965–66 season. This imaginative series centered on a talking car, whose voice was supplied by Ann SOTHERN. The hero of the series was a small-town lawyer named Dave Crabtree, played by Jerry Van Dyke, who discovered the talking car while he was visiting a used-car lot searching for an inexpensive luxury car but became strangely attracted to a 1928 Porter automobile. When Crabtree got behind the wheel of the car, it talked to him and told him that it was the reincarnation of his deceased mother. Against the advice of his wife, Barbara, played by Maggie Pierce, and to the delight of his children, Cindy and Randy, played by Cindy Eilbacher and Randy Whipple, Crabtee bought the car, and the funny episodes that followed involved his adventures with the car. The villain of the series was a character named Capt. Manzini, an antique car collector who was always trying to get the car away from Crabtree. The series was created by Allan Burns and Chris Hayward and produced by Rod Amateau.

MY THREE SONS

Sept. 1960–Sept. 1963	ABC	Thurs.	9–9:30 P.M.
Sept. 1963–Sept. 1965	ABC	Thurs.	8:30–9 P.M.
Sept. 1965–Aug. 1967	CBS	Thurs.	8:30–9 P.M.
Sept. 1967–Sept. 1971	CBS	Sat.	8:30–9 P.M.
Sept. 1971–Dec. 1971	CBS	Mon.	10–10:30 P.M.
Jan. 1972–Aug. 1972	CBS	Thurs.	8:30–9 P.M.

For 12 years the *My Three Sons* situation comedy was one of the most popular programs on television. The series starred film actor Fred MacMURRAY as Steve Douglas, a widowed father with three sons to raise, first with the help of his father-in-law, Michael Francis "Bub" O'Casey, played by William FRAWLEY, and when Frawley departed the series in 1965 because of failing health, Bub's brother, Uncle Charlie O'Casey, played by William Demarest. Douglas's sons, Mike (18 when the series first aired), Robbie (14), and Chip (seven) were played by Tim Considine, Don Grady, and Stanley Livingston. The family lived at 837 Mill Street in a small midwestern town where Steve was a consulting aviation engineer. The problems that resulted from living in a totally male-inhabited home was the basis for much of the show's comedy during its early years.

As the show continued, many other characters were introduced to viewers. After two years on the air, Tim Considine decided that he no longer wanted to be on the series, and so his character, Mike, married his girlfriend, Sally, played by Meredith MacRae, and the newlyweds moved to a different city. In order to justify the show's title, Steve adopted a new son, an orphan named Ernie, played by Barry Livingstone. The family moved from the Midwest to Los Angeles during the 1967–68 season. Robbie fell in love with a girl named Katie, played by Tina Cole, the two were married, and eventually Katie gave birth to triplet boys in 1968, which enabled the series to maintain its "three sons" theme. In 1969, love found Steve Douglas in the person of Ernie's teacher, Barbara Harper, played by Beverly Garland, and Steve and Barbara were married on a much viewed episode of the series. During the 1970–71 season, Chip, who was 17 years old, eloped with his sweetheart, Polly Williams, played by Ronne Troupe. Other characters who appeared on the series during its long and successful run were Jean Pearson and her parents, played by Cynthia Pepper, Robert P. Lieb, and Florence MacMichael, the Pfeiffers, Sudsy and his parents, played by Ricky Allen, Olan Soule, and Olive Dunbar, and many others. The executive producer of *My Three Sons* was Don Fedderson.

MYSTERY!

Feb. 1980–present	PBS	Various times

This popular Public Broadcasting System series was originally hosted by Gene Shalit when it was first aired in 1980, and has subsequently been hosted by film actor Vincent Price, and then by British actress Diana Rigg, who is the show's current hostess. The series, which presents mystery programs that, for the most part, were produced in England, has over the years included such British series as Leo McKern as barrister Horace Rumpole in John Mortimer's *Rumpole of the Bailey* programs, Hywel Bennett and Judy Parfit in four *Malice Aforethought* programs, the *Sergeant Cribb* series, and other popular British-produced series that featured Jeremy Brett and David Burke as Sherlock Holmes and Dr. Watson in numerous *Sherlock Holmes* dramas, David Suchet as Agatha Christie's Belgian detective Hercule Poirot in a series of mystery dramas, Michael Gambon as Chief Inspector Maigret, Patrick Malahide as Inspector Alleyn, Derek Jacobi as Brother Cadfael, and Helen Mirren as Deputy Chief Inspector Jane Tennison in a series of mystery dramas called *Prime Suspect,* to name just a few.

N

NABORS, JIM (1930–)

From the moment he made his TV debut as a country bumpkin named Gomer Pyle on *The ANDY GRIFFITH SHOW* in 1963, Jim Nabors has been one of television's favorite performers. Nabors, who was born in Sylacauga, Alabama, and who played the simple, kindhearted, naive mechanic Gomer, became so popular after one season on that show he was given a spin-off series of his own, *GOMER PYLE, U.S.M.C.*, which was a big success and ran for six years. Since Nabors played a nasal-voiced southern country boy as Gomer, viewers were amazed when the actor appeared on *The Danny Kaye Show* in 1963 and sang in a perfectly normal, deep baritone voice. Subsequently, his vocal renditions were heard on such programs as *The LUCILLE BALL SHOW*, *The CAROL BURNETT SHOW*, *The SMOTHERS BROTHERS COMEDY HOUR*, and *The MUPPET SHOW*, and on a music/variety series of his own *The Jim Nabors Hour* in 1969. Other less successful TV appearances included regular roles on *The Lost Saucer* (1975), *The Krofft Supershow* (1976), and *Buford and the Galloping Ghost* (1979). In addition, Nabors was also featured in such films as *A Different Approach* (1978), *The Best Little Whorehouse in Texas* (1982), *Cannonball Run II* (1984), and the TV film, *Return to Mayberry* (1986). Nabors still appears as a singing guest star on TV on occasion. "When He Spoke" is a collection of religious songs.

NAKED CITY

Sept. 1958–Sept. 1959	ABC	Tues. 9:30–10 P.M.
Oct. 1960–Sept. 1963	ABC	Wed. 10–11 P.M.

One of the first TV series to film at actual locations in New York City, *Naked City* was a gritty, realistic police drama series that became the prototype for many series that fol-lowed. The series centered on a seasoned police officer, Det. Dan Muldoon, played by John McIntire, and his young sidekick, Det. Jim Halloran, played by James FRANCISCUS. The team ran down various muggers, thieves, smugglers, and sundry other urban criminals who inhabited the city's seamier areas. After its first successful season on the air, *Naked City* underwent a major cast change when Det. Muldoon was killed in the crash of his police car while chasing a criminal. Lt. Mike Parker, another seasoned police veteran, played by Horace McMahon, became Det. Halloran's new partner. During the 1960–61 season, Det. Halloran departed, and he was replaced by Det. Adam Flint, played by Paul Burke. Also making her debut during this season was Flint's girlfriend, Libby, played by Nancy Malone, who became one of the show's most popular characters. Patrolman Frank Acaro, played by Harry Bellaver, who had been seen on previous episodes in a supporting capacity, became a major character during the 1960–61 season. The series' theme music, "Somewhere in the Night," aka "The Naked City Theme," by Billy May and Milton Raskin, became one of television's first theme songs to make the hit parade. The show's opening narrative, which began, "There are eight million stories in the Naked City," became familiar to many more millions throughout the United States. Many later-to-be-famous performers made appearances on *Naked City*, including Robert Redford, Sandy Dennis, Jon Voight, Peter Fonda, and Dustin Hoffman. *Naked City's* executive producer was Herbert B. Leonard.

NAME OF THE GAME, THE

Sept. 1968–Sept. 1971	NBC	Fri. 8:30–10 P.M.

Three performers, Robert STACK, Tony Franciosa, and Gene BARRY, appeared in three different stories under the title *The Name of the Game* on this one-and-a-half-hour adventure series. Although all three actors played characters who were connected with a publishing firm named Howard Publications located in Los Angeles, the three were featured in different episodes. Gene Barry played Howard Publications' dynamic owner, Glenn Howard, who confronted business and political enemies and lived a uniquely flamboyant life in his segments of *The Name of the Game*. Tony Franciosa played Jeff Dillon, an aggressive former newsboy who had worked his way up to being an investigative correspondent for Howard Publications. Robert Stack played Dan Farrell, a former FBI agent who had gone into publishing because he felt he would able to make the public more aware of the dangers of organized crime in America as the editor of Howard Publishing's *Crime* magazine. A major character who appeared on all three segments of the series was an ambitious, intelligent-if-somewhat eccentric editorial assistant named Peggy Maxwell, played by Susan ST. JAMES, who came in contact with all of the three men. Also appearing on occasion were reporters Joe Sample, Andy Hill, and Ross Craig, who were played by Ben Murphy, Cliff Potter, and Mark Miller. Each of the three segments were produced by different men. Richard Irving produced Gene Barry's segments, E. Jack Neuman, and then Leslie Stevens, produced Tony Franciosa's segments, and David Victor produced the Robert Stack episodes. *The Name of the Game* was based on a TV film, *Fame Is the Name of the Game,* which was originally aired in November 1966. The series, which was budgeted at $400,000 per episode, was said to be the most expensive TV series produced up until that time.

NAME THAT TUNE

June 1953–June 1954	NBC	Mon. 8–8:30 P.M.
Sept. 1954–Mar. 1955	CBS	Thurs. 10:30–11 P.M.
Sept. 1955–Sept. 1958	CBS	Tues. 7:30–8 P.M.
Sept. 1958–Oct. 1959	CBS	Mon. 7:30–8 P.M.

Even though the premise of this music quiz show was rather simple, *Name that Tune* managed to keep viewers tuning in for six years. Contestants on *Name That Tune* vied with each other to be the first to identify a tune played by the orchestra or sung by one of the program's regular vocalists. When a contestant thought he or she knew the name of the song, he or she raced to ring a bell located 25 feet away. The contestant who named the most tunes was given the chance to win a $1,600 jackpot by identifying seven songs in 30 seconds.

Over the years, Red Benson (1953), Bill CULLEN (1954–55), and George De Witt (1955–59) were the show's hosts. Later, the producers introduced the big-money "Golden Medley Marathon" segment, during which competing teams could win as much as $5,000 a week for a maximum of five weeks. In 1970, a syndicated series version of *Name That Tune* surfaced with Richard Hayes as host. It was also revived in 1974 by NBC as a

daytime quiz show with Dennis James as the program's host. Tom Kennedy hosted another syndicated version of *Name That Tune* in 1977, which was called *The $100,000 Name That Tune* that featured Kathie Lee Johnson (later GIFFORD) as one of its vocalists. In 1984, Jim Lange hosted yet another syndicated version of *The $100,000 Name That Tune,* which lasted for one year. *Name That Tune* was created by Harry Salter, and the producers of this series over the years included Ralph EDWARDS, who was responsible for the 1970s versions of the show.

NAME'S THE SAME, THE

Dec. 1951–Nov. 1952	ABC	Wed. 7:30–8 P.M.
Dec. 1952–Aug. 1954	ABC	Tues. 10:30–11 P.M.
Oct. 1954–June 1955	ABC	Mon. 7:30–8 P.M.
June 1955–Sept. 1955	ABC	Tues. 10–10:30 P.M.
Sept. 1955–Oct. 1955	ABC	Fri. 10–10:30 P.M.

For five years in the early 1950s, *The Name's the Same* was one of television's most popular game/panel shows. Contestants on the show had names that were the same as famous people or familiar objects, and it was the panelist's job to guess what their name was by asking them a series of questions. Jane Alexander was on the panel for the show's entire run, and other celebrities on the panel over the years included Abe Burrows (1951–52), Meredith Willson (1951–53), Bill Stern (1953–54), Gene RAYBURN (1953–55), Roger Price (1954–55), and Audrey Meadows (1955). Mike WALLACE, Basil Rathbone, Carl Reiner, and Jerry LESTER were also panelists for shorter periods of time. *The Name's the Same* was produced by Mark GOODSON and Bill TODMAN.

NANCY DREW/HARDY BOYS MYSTERIES, THE

(see *Hardy Boys/Nancy Drew Mysteries, The*)

NANNY, THE

Nov. 1993–Dec. 1993	CBS	Wed. 8:30–9 P.M.
Dec. 1993–Sept. 1994	CBS	Wed. 8–8:30 P.M.
June 1994	CBS	Mon. 8:30–9 P.M.
July 1994–Sept. 1996	CBS	Mon. 8–8:30 P.M.
Aug. 1995–Sept. 1995	CBS	Wed. 8–9 P.M.
Sept. 1996–Feb. 1999	CBS	Wed. 8–8:30 P.M.
May 1999–June 1999	CBS	Wed. 8–9 P.M.

The improbable idea of a pretty, flashy, heavily New York–accented Jewish girl from middle-class Queens, New York, becoming the nanny for the three children of a successful British-born theatrical producer who lived in a town house on Manhattan's posh East Side was the premise of this popular situation comedy series that enjoyed a six-year TV run. The nanny, Fran Fine, played by Fran Drescher, had talked her way into getting the job, even though she had no previous experience as a nanny and had worked as a cosmetics saleslady in a New York

Charles Shaughnessy (Maxwell Sheffield) and Fran Drescher (Fran Fine) of *The Nanny* (Author's collection)

department store. Her boss, a good-looking Englishman named Maxwell Sheffield, played by Charles Shaughnessy, soon became Fran's object of affection, and for most of the series she used every means at her disposal to attract Mr. Sheffield. The Sheffield children, Maggie, who was 14 when the series was first aired, played by Nicholle Tom, Brighton, age 10, played by Benjamin Salisbury, and Grace, age six, played by Madeline Zima, loved Nanny Fine's unconventional behavior and liberal attitudes about child-rearing. The Sheffields' butler, Niles, played by Daniel Davis, was also amused by and quite fond of Fran, but Mr. Sheffield's assistant, Chastity Clare "C. C." Babcock, played by Lauren Lane, who had designs of her own on her boss, despised the nanny and did everything in her power to make the free-spirited nanny look bad. Fran's best friend, Val Toriello, played by Rachel Chagall, Fran's blowsy mother, Sylvia Fine, played by Renee Taylor, and her grandmother, Yetta, played by Ann Morgan Guilbert, paid frequent visits to the Sheffield home to offer Fran support and their own brand of advice, which was often not exactly what was needed. In time, Fran and Maxwell Sheffield did become romantically involved, much to the delight of everybody but C. C. Babcock, and were married during the last season the series was aired. The series was created by Fran Drescher and her husband, Peter Marc Jacobson, who was also the program's executive producer.

NANNY AND THE PROFESSOR

Jan. 1970–Aug. 1970	ABC	Wed. 7:30–8 P.M.
Sept. 1970–Sept. 1971	ABC	Fri. 8–8:30 P.M.
Sept. 1971–Dec. 1971	ABC	Mon. 8–8:30 P.M.

British actress Juliet Mills and American actor Richard Long starred as the title characters in this half-hour situation comedy series whose title, *Nanny and the Professor,* revealed the show's basic premise. Mills played a young nanny named Phoebe Figalilly, who took care of the three children of the widowed Professor Howard Everett, played by Long. The children, 12-year-old Hal Everett, played by David Doremus, eight-year-old Butch, played by Trent Lehman, and five-year-old Prudence, played by Kim Richards, were a handful for the young woman, but she proved to be the best role model for the children after four previous housekeeper/nannies had failed to control the precocious Everett trio. In addition to the professor and the children, the household also consisted of the huge family sheep dog, Waldo, a guinea pig named Myrtle, and numerous other pets. Phoebe, who had unusual psychic abilities, eventually won the hearts of everyone in the Everett home. In fall 1971, character actress Elsa Lanchester joined the cast as Phoebe's aunt, Aunt Henrietta. *Nanny and the Professor* was produced by Charles B. Fitzsimmons.

NASH BRIDGES

| Mar. 1996–May 1996 | CBS | Fri. 10–11 P.M. |
| July 1996–present | CBS | Fri. 10–11 P.M. |

Don JOHNSON, who had previously starred on the successful *MIAMI VICE,* is the title character on the action/police drama program *Nash Bridges,* which also features Cheech Marin as his amusing former police partner and friend, a private detective named Joe Dominguez, who often becomes involved in Bridges' cop capers. Nash Bridges, who is the head of a special investigations unit for the San Francisco Police Department, is a laid-back and friendly fellow who calls everyone "Bubba." Although successful in his professional life, he has an unusual amount of trouble in his private life.

Nash's team of fellow police officers includes Evan Cortez, played by Jaime P. Gomez, a womanizing young man who idolized Nash; Rick Betinna, played by Daniel Roebuck, who is Nash's chief rival in the department; and Bryn Carson, played by Mary Mara, a sexy, tough cop who is definitely her own woman.

At home, Nash tried to balance his police work with raising his teenage daughter, Cassidy, played by Jodi Lyn O'Keefe, and also take care of his retired father, a former longshoreman, played by James Gammon. In addition to his action-packed cases, Nash also had to deal with several women who always complicate his life. Married and divorced twice, Nash and his first wife, Lisa, played by Annette O'Toole, who gave Nash custody of Cassidy, were always trying to get back together. His second wife,

Kelly, played by Serena Scott Thomas, who came from a socially prominent family, had divorced Nash because he would not quit the police force. In addition to his daughter and father, Nash's sister, Assistant D.A. Stacy Bridges, played by Angela Dohrmann, who was a lesbian, also lived with Nash for a time, further complicating his life.

The success of *Nash Bridges* is certainly due to its unusual balance of fast action-packed situations and quirky domestic complications.

NAT "KING" COLE SHOW, THE

Nov. 1956–June 1957	NBC	Mon. 7:30–7:45 P.M.
July 1957–Sept. 1957	NBC	Tues. 10–10:30 P.M.
Sept. 1957–Dec. 1957	NBC	Tues. 7:30–8 P.M.

At a time when African-American performers did not have network variety shows of their own, singer Nat "King" Cole starred on the first TV series to feature a black performer, *The Nat King Cole Show*. Initially a 15-minute program, it featured Cole singing his hit recordings and other popular songs of the past and present in the casual, husky-voiced style that made him famous. The show was expanded to a half-hour format for its second, and final, year on the air but it failed to attract much of an audience. Every major black entertainer made guest appearances on Cole's program (at minimum salary because of trouble obtaining sponsors), and the list of formidable performers included gospel singer Mahalia Jackson, bandleader Count Basie, singers Ella Fitzgerald, Pearl Bailey, Harry Belafonte, Billy Eckstine, Sammy Davis, Jr., the Mills Brothers, and Cab Calloway. Other well-known performers such as Frankie Laine, Peggy Lee, Gogi Grant, Tony Martin, Mel Tormé, Tony Bennett, and Stan Kenton also made appearances on Nat's show. Among the regulars who performed were the Bouteneers, the Herman McCoy Singers, the Randy Van Horne Singers, the Jerry Graff Singers, the Cheerleaders, and Nelson Riddle and His Orchestra.

NELSON, DAVID (1936–)

The elder son of show business legends Ozzie and Harriet NELSON, David Nelson was born in New York City while his bandleader father and vocalist mother were performing in that city. David made his debut as an actor playing himself on The ADVENTURES OF OZZIE AND HARRIET radio show in the late 1940s, and when that show went to television in 1952, David re-created his role. That same year *The Adventures of Ozzie and Harriet* TV series made its debut, David had appeared in the film *Here Come the Nelsons* with his mother and father and younger brother, Ricky. While he was appearing on the TV series, David also had major roles in the films *Peyton Place* (1957), *The Big Circus* (1959), *The Remarkable Mr. Pennypacker* (1959), *Day of the Outlaw* (1959), and *The Big Show* (1961), but when the TV series ended, David left the spotlight to pursue his interest in producing and directing.

NELSON, HARRIET

(see Hilliard, Harriet)

NELSON, OZZIE (OSWALD GEORGE NELSON 1906–1975)

Ozzie Nelson, who was born in Jersey City, New Jersey, attended Rutgers University, where he studied law before he decided to embark upon a career in show business. Always interested in music, Ozzie formed a band, and while playing in a supper club attracted the attention of radio network officials. Ozzie and his band were soon heard on such radio programs as *The Joe Penner Show, The Red Skelton Show,* and *Ripley's Believe It or Not,* and featured in films like *Sweetheart of the Campus* (1939), *Strictly in the Groove* (1942), *Honeymoon Lodge* (1943), *Hi, Good Lookin'* (1944), and *People Are Funny* (1946). In 1944, Ozzie and his wife, vocalist Harriet HILLIARD, whom he had met while both were appearing on *The Red Skelton Show,* starred on a half-hour situation comedy series on radio playing a husband and wife who, like themselves, had two young sons. The radio show, *The Adventures of Ozzie and Harriet,* made a successful transition from radio to television in 1952 and became one of TV's most successful, long-running family-oriented series. A producer and director, as well as performer, Nelson was mainly responsible for his son Ricky NELSON's, rise as one of rock and roll's most popular stars.

NELSON, RICKY (ERIC HILLIARD NELSON 1940–1985)

Popular rock and roll performer Ricky Nelson, the son of Ozzie and Harriet (HILLIARD) NELSON, made his acting debut on his parents' radio show, *The Adventures of Ozzie and Harriet,* in the late 1940s playing himself. Ricky, who was born in Teaneck, New Jersey, made a successful transition from radio to television with his parents when *The ADVENTURES OF OZZIE AND HARRIET* made its debut as a TV series in 1952. Ricky grew up to be a handsome young man and began singing rock and roll songs on the program that became best-selling recordings and made him a teenager's heartthrob. Guest-starring appearances on such programs as *The ANDY WILLIAMS SHOW,* major roles in such films as *Rio Bravo* (1959), *The Wackiest Ship in the Army* (1960), and *Love and Kisses* (1965), and the *Malibu U* TV series (1967), as well his continuing singing career, established Ricky Nelson as one of America's most popular performers. Nelson's life was cut tragically short when he was killed in an airplane accident at the age of 45 in 1985.

NERO WOLFE

Jan. 1981–Apr. 1981	NBC	Fri. 9–10 P.M.
Apr. 1981–Aug. 1981	NBC	Tues. 10–11 P.M.

Although it was seen for less than one full TV season, the *Nero Wolfe* detective/crime drama series is fondly remembered by many viewers, who were very upset when NBC decided to cancel the show after only eight months on the air. Mystery writer Rex Stout's heavyset, orchid-loving, reclusive private detective, Nero Wolfe, played by veteran character actor William CONRAD, was a well-known character to mystery lovers as the hero of several novels, as well as of a radio series and many films. Wolfe lived in a Manhattan town house where he tended his beloved orchids in a specially built greenhouse, and he seldom ventured out of doors. He left all the footwork to his assistant, Archie Goodwin, played by Lee Horsley, but he was always able to solve any mystery by using his well-developed powers of analytical deduction. Other members of Nero's staff included Saul Panzer, played by George Wyner, who assisted Archie in his investigations; Fritz Brenner, Wolfe's gourmet cook, played by George Voskovec; and Theodore Horstman, Wolfe's much-valued horticulturist, played by Robert Coote. Appearing on the series regularly was Allan Muller, who played Police Inspector Crumer, who often sought Nero Wolfe's advice when working on a case. *Nero Wolfe* was produced by Ivan Goff and Ben Roberts for Paramount Television.

NEWHART

Oct. 1982–Feb. 1983	CBS	Mon. 9:30–10 P.M.
Mar. 1983–Apr. 1983	CBS	Sun. 9:30–10 P.M.
Apr. 1983–May 1983	CBS	Sun. 8:30–9 P.M.
June 1983–Aug. 1983	CBS	Sun. 9:30–10 P.M.
Aug. 1983–Sept. 1986	CBS	Mon. 9:30–10 P.M.
Sept. 1986–Aug. 1988	CBS	Mon. 9–9:30 P.M.
Aug. 1988–Mar. 1989	CBS	Mon. 8–8:30 P.M.
Mar. 1989–Aug. 1989	CBS	Mon. 10–10:30 P.M.
Aug. 1989–Oct. 1989	CBS	Mon. 10:30–11 P.M.
Nov. 1989–Apr. 1990	CBS	Mon. 10–10:30 P.M.
Apr. 1990–May 1990	CBS	Mon. 8:30–9 P.M.
May 1990–July 1990	CBS	Mon. 10–10:30 P.M.
July 1990–Aug. 1990	CBS	Fri. 9–9:30 P.M.
Sept. 1990–	CBS	Sat. 9–9:30 P.M.

Bob Newhart's most successful television situation comedy series, *Newhart,* which made its debut four years after his previous popular series, The BOB NEWHART SHOW, left the air, proved an even bigger success than that long-running show. On *Newhart,* Bob played Dick Loudan, a New York writer of "How To" books, who decided to buy and renovate an old inn that was originally built in 1774 in Norwich, Vermont, putting his "how-to" knowledge to practical use. Dick and his less-than-enthusiastic wife, Joanna, played by Mary Frann, called their New England hotel the Stratford Inn. It didn't take long for Dick to realize that running an inn was more complicated than he had expected. Helping him run the inn was a colorful local character named George Utley, played by Tom Poston, whose family had been caretakers at the inn for more than 100 years. Kirk Devane, played by Steven Kampmann, owned the Minuteman Cafe and Gift shop, which was next to the Stratford Inn and became one of Dick and Joanna's best friends. Kirk was engaged to a professional clown named Jennifer, played by Jennifer Holmes.

In 1984, a pretentious and wealthy young student from nearby Dartmouth College, Cindy, played by Rebecca York, decided to take a job at the Stratford Inn as a maid to find out what being "average" was like. When Cindy departed the series in 1984, reportedly to continue her studies in England, her cousin, an equally pretentious and inept young woman named Stephanie, played by Julia Duffy, took her place, and soon became one of the series' most popular comic characters. In addition to running his inn, Dick became the host of a local talk show called "Vermont Today," and his young producer, Michael Harris, played by Peter Scolari, a fast-talking, nervous young man, soon began dating Stephanie. The two were the perfect prototypes for a yuppie couple of the 1980s, and soon both were the show's most popular supporting characters. Three amusing local bumpkins, brothers named Larry, Darryl, and Darryl, played by William Sanderson, Tony Papenfuss, and John Voldstad, who were totally inept, worked as handymen at Dick's Stratford Inn. Larry did all of the talking for the trio and the two Darryls never uttered a word.

During the 1988–89 season, Michael lost his job at the TV station and became a shoe salesman, which caused the status-conscious Stephanie to have a nervous breakdown and break up their relationship. The couple eventually made up, were married, and the following fall, Stephanie became pregnant and once again took up residence at the Stratford Inn.

On the final episode of *Newhart,* a Japanese businessman had bought the entire town of Norwich, including the Stratford Inn, because he wanted to turn the area into a golf course. Everything that had happened on the *Newhart* series, however, turned out to be a bad dream that Bob Hartley, the character Newhart played on *The Bob Newhart Show* was having. Suzanne PLESHETTE, who played Bob Hartley's wife, Emily, on the original series, was at his side when he awakened, and she brought him back to reality.

NEWHART, BOB (GEORGE ROBERT NEWHART 1929–)

Before Bob Newhart became a professional comedian, he was an accountant who created monologues as a diversion. Newhart, who was born and lived in Chicago, amused his friends with these monologues, and they encouraged him to perform them in comedy clubs around the city. Newhart was a satirist whose monologues usually centered on the amusing things that happen to white-collar workers at home and in the office. In 1960, his act attracted the attention of a recording executive who signed him to a contract. The album, *The Button Down Mind of Bob Newhart,* became a best-seller and went to number one on the charts, surpassing best-selling Elvis Presley albums and *The Sound of Music.* The success of Newhart's album led to regular appearances on The ANDY WILLIAMS SHOW and The TONIGHT SHOW.

In 1961, Newhart starred on his first television series, *The BOB NEWHART SHOW,* which was only moderately successful. This was followed by a regular role on *The Entertainers* series in 1964. In 1972, Newhart's second *Bob Newhart Show,* a situation comedy, became popular and was on the air for six successful seasons. Newhart appeared in several films, including *Thursday's Game* (1974), *First Family* (1980), *Little Miss Marker* (1980), and then returned TV in 1982 as the star of a new situation comedy series called *NEWHART,* which also became a hit and remained on the air for eight seasons. A third series, *Bob,* which made its debut in 1992, proved less successful, as did a series called *George & Leo* (1997), which were both on the air for just one season. In 1998, Newhart provided the voice of Leonard the Polar Bear for the TV animated film, *Rudolph the Red-Nosed Reindeer.*

NEWLYWED GAME, THE

(also The New Newlywed Game)

| July 1966–Dec. 1974 | ABC | Sat. & Mon. 8–8:30 P.M. |
| 1977–1980 | Syndicated | Various times and stations |

As THE NEW NEWLYWED GAME:

| 1985–1990 | Syndicated | Various times and stations |

The Newlywed Game made its TV debut as an early evening attraction on ABC in 1966 and remained on that network until 1974. The series returned as a syndicated daytime program in 1970 and ran for three years. It resurfaced once again as a syndicated show in 1985 when *TV Guide* magazine called it "the worst piece of sleaze on television today." Hosted by Bob Eubanks for most of its incarnations, Paul Rodriguez took over the hosting chores in 1989 for the show's final season. The premise of the show was simple. Four newly married couples competed against one another as they attempted to match answers to questions asked by the show's host. As the husband, or wife, was offstage, the host solicited answers to silly, often very suggestive, questions, and when the partners returned, they attempted to match the answers their spouses had given and win points. The couple that matched each other's answers most often was judged the winner. The series was the brainchild of Chuck BARRIS, who was also responsible for *The GONG SHOW* and *The DATING GAME.*

NEWS ON TELEVISION (NATIONAL NETWORK NEWS)

During television's early days, news programs followed the same format that had been used by the national radio networks. News was usually presented in five- and 15-minute segments in the morning, at noon, in the early evening, and at 11 o'clock. As television replaced radio as America's most popular home entertainment and information medium, news gradually increased to half-hour broadcasts, and full-hour news magazine programs.

The major network news histories were as follows:

American Broadcasting Company

Aug. 1948–Oct. 1952	Mon.–Sat. 7–7:15 P.M.
Oct. 1952–Dec. 1952	Mon. 9–10 P.M. Wed. 8–9 P.M. Thurs. 8–8:30 P.M.
Oct. 1952–Jan. 1953	Fri. 8:30–9:30 P.M.
Oct. 1952–Aug. 1953	Sun. 8–9 P.M.
Aug. 1998–Sept. 1998	Thurs. 10–11 P.M.

MON.–FRI. EARLY EVENING:

Oct. 1953–May 1959	Mon.–Fri. 10:30–10:45 P.M.
May 1959–Jan. 1967	Mon.–Fri. Various early evening hours (15 min.)
Jan. 1967	Mon.–Fri. Various early evening hours (30 min.)

MON.–FRI LATE NIGHT:

Sept. 1958–May 1959	Mon.–Fri. 10:30–10:45 P.M.
Oct. 1961–Jan. 1965	Mon.–Fri. 11–11:30 P.M.
Mar. 1980–Jan. 1981	Mon.–Thurs. 11:30 P.M.–12 A.M.
Jan. 1981–Mar. 1981	Mon.–Thurs. 11:30 P.M.–12 A.M.
Mar. 1981–Apr. 1983	Mon.–Fri. 11:30 P.M.–12 A.M.
Apr. 1983–Feb. 1984	Mon.–Fri. 11:30 P.M.–12 A.M.
Feb. 1984–Apr. 1993	Mon.–Fri. 11:30 P.M.–12 A.M.
Jan. 1992–	Mon.–Thurs. 2–6 A.M.
Apr. 1993–	Mon.–Fri. 11:35–12:05 A.M.

The first regularly scheduled TV news program on ABC was *News and Views,* which premiered in August 1948 and featured H. R. Baukhage and Jim Gibbons. In 1951, it was replaced by *After the Deadlines.* Offering news as an alternative to prime-time entertainment, ABC presented their *All Star News* program in 1952, which was seen for a half hour in the middle of the evening. The program featured Pauline Frederick, Bryson Rash, Gordon Fisher, and Leo Cherne, but it was not successful. ABC returned to the 15-minute news format in 1953 with veteran newsman John DALY acting as the anchorman. In 1960, when Daly left ABC, he was followed by Bill Lawrence, Al Mann, and John Cameron Swayze, who took over the early evening newscasts. In fall 1961, ABC introduced its first five-days-a-week, 11 o'clock newscast, which was anchored by Ron Cochran, and then by Murphy Martin and Bob Young. In 1963, ABC abandoned this weekday format in favor of a Saturday/Sunday news program that was called *ABC Weekend News* and featured, at different times, Bob Young, Tom Jarriel, Max Robinson, Britt Hume, Bill Beutel, and Sylvia Chase. The regular ABC early evening national news program has been hosted over the years by Ron Cochran (1963–65), and then by Peter JENNINGS (1965–68), Frank Reynolds (1968–83), Howard K. Smith (1970–75), Harry Reasoner (1971–83), and Barbara WALTERS (1976–83). In 1983, Peter Jennings, who, for a time, had been ABC's London correspondent, became the sole ABC evening news anchorman, a job he continues to hold as of this writing.

Columbia Broadcasting System

May 1948–Sept. 1953	Mon.–Fri. 7:30–7:45 P.M.
Sept. 1955–Aug. 1963	Mon.–Fri. 7:15–7:30 P.M.
Sept. 1963–	Mon.–Fri. Various times (30 minutes) in the early evening
WEEKENDS:	
Aug. 1948–present	Early evening: Various times (usually 6:30 & 7 P.M.) Late evening Various times (usually 11 P.M.)

Douglas EDWARDS, who had been reading the news at CBS radio for many years, became that network's first major television news anchorman from 1948 until 1962, when Walter CRONKITE became CBS Evening News major news anchorman. Cronkite remained in the network's national news anchor chair even longer than Edwards, retiring in 1981, when Dan RATHER replaced him. In 1983, Connie Chung joined Rather as coanchor in an attempt to boost CBS's news show ratings. Cronkite initially anchored the Sunday evening CBS news program as well, with other well-known CBS commentators and correspondents such as Eric Sevareid, Harry Reasoner, Dan Rather, Bon Shieffer, Morton Dean, Ed Bradley, Charles Osgood, Susan Spencer, Bill Plante, and Russ Mitchell as regular anchormen from 1963 until 1997 when the regular Sunday national news programs were canceled.

National Broadcasting Company

Apr. 1944–July 1944	Various times between 8 & 9 P.M. (10–15 min)
Aug. 1944–July 1945	Mon. 8–8:10 P.M.
July 1945–June 1946	Sun. 8–8:15 P.M.
June 1946–Dec. 1946	Mon./Thurs. 7:50–8 P.M.
Dec. 1946–Oct. 1947	Mon. 9–9:10 P.M.
Dec. 1946–Oct. 1947	Thurs. 7:50–8 P.M.
Nov. 1947–Dec. 1947	Wed. 8:45–9 P.M.
Feb. 1948–Feb. 1949	Mon.–Fri. 8:45–9 P.M.
June 1948–Sept. 1948	Sun. 7:50–8 P.M.
Sept. 1948–Feb. 1949	Sun. 7:20–7:30 P.M.
Feb. 1949–Sept. 1957	Mon.–Fri. 7:45–8 P.M.
Apr. 1949–Feb. 1950	Sat. 7:45–8 P.M.
July 1949–Oct. 1949	Sun. 7–7:30 P.M.
Sept. 1957–Sept. 1963	Mon.–Fri. 6:45–7 P.M.
Oct. 1961–Oct. 1965	Sat. 6–6:15 P.M.
Sept. 1963–present	Mon.–Fri. Various 30 minutes
Sept. 1965–Aug. 1967	Sun. 6–6:30 P.M.
Oct. 1965–present	Sat. 6:30–7 P.M.
Sept. 1957	Sun. 6:30–7 P.M.
July 1982–Dec. 1983	Mon.–Thurs. 1:30–2:30 A.M.
July 1982–Dec. 1983	Fri. 2–3 A.M.
Nov. 1991–Sept. 1998	Mon.–Sun. 3–4:30 A.M.

The National Broadcasting Company was the industry's pioneer network. David Sarnoff, who had been the president and major force behind the National Broadcasting Company from 1926 until 1949, from the time it was part of the RCA Corporation, began experimenting with television in the 1920s and exhibited a television receiver at the RCA pavilion at the New York World's Fair in 1939. NBC was the first network to telecast news programs as early as 1939, and was the first major network to originate regular news telecasts. The well-known radio commentator Lowell Thomas simulcasted his popular Sunoco News show on both radio and on television to local TV viewers in the New York City area lucky enough to have a television receiver in their homes. During the World War II years 1941–45, NBC continued to telecast news of war events. When the war ended, NBC telecast its regular news program, the *NBC Television Newsreel*, which gained a sponsor, the Esso Oil company, that was seen two nights a week. In 1948, NBC offered the first Monday through Friday news show, *The Camel News Caravan*, sponsored by Camel cigarettes, which featured John Cameron Swayze as its anchorman. In October 1956, Swayze was replaced by Chet HUNTLEY and David BRINKLEY, whose weekly nighttime news show, *The Huntley-Brinkley Report*, became one of television's most popular news programs. Huntley and Brinkley's nightly closing, "Good Night, Chet," "Good night, David," replaced John Cameron Swayze's closing, "Glad we could get together," as television's most familiar news show closings. After 14 years on the air, Huntley and Brinkley left the air as regular anchormen and John CHANCELLOR and Frank McGee alternated as anchors seven nights a week on *The NBC Nightly News*. In 1971, Chancellor became the sole anchor of the NBC news show, a position he held for the next 11 years. For three of these years, Chancellor shared the anchorman spot with David Brinkley, who returned to the nightly NBC news from 1976 until 1979. Tom BROKAW and Roger Mudd replaced Chancellor in 1982, but after one year Mudd departed the show and Brokaw became NBC's major and only nightly news anchorman. Among the weekend news anchors at NBC were Sander Vanocur, Ray Sherer, Robert MacNeil, Frank McGee, Garrick Utley, Floyd Kalber, Tom Snyder, Chris Wallace, John Palmer, and John Hart. Beginning in 1977, female anchors Catherine Mackin, Jessica Savitch, Jane Pauley, Connie Chung, Giselle Fernandez, and Maria Shriver became permanent fixtures on NBC's weekend and weekday news programs.

Fox Network

In 1987 Rupert Murdoch's Fox network began to telecast evening national news programs from various cities in the United States using different local news teams.

NEWSRADIO

Mar. 1995–May 1995	NBC	Tues. 8:30–9 P.M.
Aug. 1995–Jan. 1996	NBC	Tues. 8:30–9 P.M.
Jan. 1996–July 1996	NBC	Sun. 8:30–9 P.M.
June 1996–Aug. 1996	NBC	Tues. 8:30–9 P.M.
Sept. 1996–Feb. 1997	NBC	Wed. 9–9:30 P.M.
Mar. 1997–June 1997	NBC	Wed. 8–8:30 P.M.
June 1997–Aug. 1997	NBC	Sun. 8:30–9 P.M.
June 1997–July 1997	NBC	Wed. 8–9 P.M.
July 1997–Mar. 1998	NBC	Tues. 8:30–9 P.M.
Mar. 1998–May 1998	NBC	Wed. 8–8:30 P.M.
May 1998–Aug. 1998	NBC	Tues. 8:30–9 P.M.
Sept. 1998–Dec. 1998	NBC	Wed. 9:30–10 P.M.
Nov. 1998–July 1999	NBC	Tues. 8:30–9 P.M.

The fictional WNYX was the setting for the situation comedy series *Newsradio* which centered on the premise that working at a radio station that produced a news show could be loads of fun. The major character on this series was Dave Nelson, played by Dave Foley, an enthusiastic, naive young man who had just arrived in New York from Wisconsin to work as the news director at the all-news radio station. Nelson was the latest of several previous station directors who had been hired and then fired by the station's overbearing, unpredictable owner, Jimmy James, played by Stephen Root. Working at the station were the major anchors, Bill McNeal, played by Phil Hartman, and Catherine Duke, played by Khandi Alexander, who were egocentric and often difficult, but were mostly supportive to Dave; the inept, always nervous station reporter, Matthew Brock, played by Andy Dick; the slick, manipulative maintenance man, Joe Garelli, played by Joe Rogan; and the gum-chewing, wisecracking, knowing secretary, Beth, played by Vicki Lewis. Also working at the station was Lisa Miller, played by Maura Tieney, a smart, pretty producer who thought that she was going to get the station director's job before Dave appeared on the scene. Even though there was friction between Dave and Lisa, they found themselves attracted to each other and became involved in an on-again, off-again romance. The tragic murder of one of the show's stars, Phil Hartman, in 1998

affected the comedic impact of the show, and the series began to drop in the TV ratings. The audience was told Bill McNeal, the character Hartman played on the show, had died of a heart attack. He was replaced by an insecure anchorman named Max Lewis, played by Jon Lovitz, but in spite of Lovitz's hilarious addition to the show, it was canceled before the 1999–2000 season commenced.

NIELSEN, LESLIE (LESLIE WILLIAM NIELSEN 1926–)

Before Leslie Nielsen became the star of numerous film comedies that satirized the many disaster and adventure movies that were prevalent in the 1970s and 1980s, he was a well-respected serious actor who began his career during television's early live years in the late 1940s to early 1950s. Nielsen, who was born in Regina, Saskatchewan, was the son of a Canadian mountie who was a strict disciplinarian, and a mother who was born in Wales but immigrated to Canada in the mid-1920s. Against his father's wishes, Nielsen studied at the Academy of Radio Arts in Toronto before he moved to New York City, where he studied acting at the Neighborhood Playhouse. A talented and good-looking young man, Leslie soon found acting jobs on such early television shows as SUSPENSE, STUDIO ONE, The PHILCO TELEVISION PLAYHOUSE, The GOODYEAR TELEVISION PLAYHOUSE, Tales of Tomorrow, and ALFRED HITCHCOCK PRESENTS and became one of television's busiest performers. Regular roles on such TV series as *Swamp Fox* (1959), *The New Breed* (1961), PEYTON PLACE (1965), *The Bold Ones: The Protectors* (1969), *Bracken's World* (1970), *The Explorers* (host, 1973–76), KUNG FU, and guest-starring appearances on such series as *The* FUGITIVE, *The* MAN FROM U.N.C.L.E., WAGON TRAIN, The WILD, WILD WEST, GUNSMOKE, *The* BIG VALLEY, *Night Gallery*, M*A*S*H*, HAWAII FIVE-O, KOJAK, CANNON, *The* LOVE BOAT, VEGA$, MURDER, SHE WROTE, WHO'S THE BOSS, and GOLDEN GIRLS followed. In addition to his work on TV, Nielsen also appeared in such feature films as *Forbidden Planet* (1956), *Tammy and the Bachelor* (1957), *Night Train to Paris* (1964), and many others, before starring in *The Naked Gun: From the Files of Police Squad!* in 1988, a hilarious spoof of police procedure films. The success of this film led to starring roles in a series of very funny film parodies that included *Naked Gun 2¹/₂: The Smell of Fear* (1991), *Naked Gun 33¹/₃: The Final Insult* (1994), *Dracula: Dead and Loving It* (1995), *Mr. Magoo* (1997), and *Family Plan* (1997), to name just a few. During his long and illustrious career, Leslie Nielsen has appeared in over 1,500 TV shows and over 50 feature films.

NIGHT COURT

Jan. 1984–Mar. 1984	NBC	Wed. 9:30–10 P.M.
May 1984–Mar. 1987	NBC	Thurs. 9:30–10 P.M.
Mar. 1987–June 1987	NBC	Wed. 9–9:30 P.M.
June 1987–July 1987	NBC	Wed. 9:30–10 P.M.
July 1987–Aug. 1987	NBC	Wed. 9–9:30 P.M.
Aug. 1987–Mar. 1988	NBC	Thurs. 9:30–10 P.M.

Mar. 1988–Apr. 1988	NBC	Fri. 9–9:30 P.M.
May 1988–Sept. 1988	NBC	Thurs. 9:30–10 P.M.
Oct. 1988–Aug. 1990	NBC	Wed. 9–9:30 P.M.
Sept. 1990–Jan. 1991	NBC	Fri. 9–9:30 P.M.
Jan. 1991–Nov. 1991	NBC	Wed. 9–9:30 P.M.
Dec. 1991–May 1992	NBC	Wed. 9:30–10 P.M.
May 1992–June 1992	NBC	Sun. 9:30–10 P.M.
June 1992–July 1992	NBC	Wed. 9:30–10 P.M.

Night Court was a situation comedy set in a New York City courthouse where people arrested for a wide variety of crimes during overnight hours were brought for sentencing. The judge at the court was a boyish judiciary who wore blue jeans under his judge's robe, had a flip manner that often bothered his staff, and seemed unlikely to succeed at his job. The judge, Harry T. Stone, played by Harry Anderson, had, to everyone at the courthouse's surprise, positive results when it came to dealing with the odd assortment of characters who appeared before him. Working with Stone were Laura Wagner, played by Karen Austin, the court clerk who had a crush on Stone; Selma Hacker, played by Selma Diamond, a tough court matron who chain-smoked and had a caustic sense of humor; bald-headed Bull, played by Richard Moll, a very tall, somewhat dim bailiff at the courthouse; District Attorney Dan Fielding, played by John LARROQUETTE, a well-dressed, sex-starved, and sarcastic man who represented the state; and an African-American legal aid lawyer, Liz Williams, played by Paula Kelly. At the end of the first season, court clerk Lana was replaced by Mac Robinson, played by Charlie Robinson. Selma Dia-

Night Court: (left to right) Selma Diamond, Charlie Robinson, Richard Moll, Ellen Foley, John Larroquette, and (seated) Harry Anderson (Author's collection)

mond departed the series after the 1984–85 season, and her character was replaced by a matron named Florence Kleiner, played by Florence Halop. Halop was replaced after the 1985–86 season by yet another matron named Roz Russell, played by Marsha Warfield. Billie Young, played by Ellen Foley, and then Christine Sullivan, played by Markie Post, replaced the Liz Williams character after the first season. Other recurring characters who made frequent appearances on *Night Court* were the unpleasant street reporter Al Craven, played by Terry Kiser, a runaway orphan named Leon, played by Bumper Robinson; Art Fensterman, the maintenance man at the courthouse, played by Mike Finneran; Mac's Asian wife, Quan Lee, played by Denise Kumagi; an ex–mental patient named Buddy Ryan, played by John Astin, who turned out to be Judge Harry Stone's father; an attractive newspaper reporter named Margaret Turner, played by Mary Cordette, whom Judge Stone dated; and a blind newsstand owner named Jack Griffin, played by S. Marc Jordan. Singer Mel Tormé, who was Judge Stone's idol, was a frequent guest star on the series. After eight years of courtroom nonsense and many laughs, *Night Court* left the air, much to the disappointment of its legions of fans.

NIGHT STALKER, THE (AKA KOLCHAK: THE NIGHT STALKER)

Sept. 1974–Dec. 1974	ABC	Fri. 10–11 P.M.
Jan. 1975–July 1975	ABC	Fri. 8–9 P.M.
Aug. 1975	ABC	Sat. 8–9 P.M.

Actor Darren MCGAVIN starred in this tongue-in-cheek hour-long series about a seedy crime reporter for the Independent News Service. Carl Kolchak specialized in stories about occult happenings. On this series, a strange mixture of reality and fantasy, McGavin brought a good deal of charm to his Kolchak characterization. The series' stories, although often scary, were always laced with wisecracks and considerable humor, as the intrepid reporter ran into an odd assortment of vampires, werewolves, zombies, Jack the Ripper–like murderers, swamp monsters, and other more supernatural oddities. Kolchak's boss at the News Service, Tony Vincenzo, played by Simon Oakland, was usually skeptical about Kolchak's reports of strange happening around the city. His fellow reporter at INS was Ron Updyke, played by Jack Grinnage, and the ancient advice to the lovelorn columnist for the News Service, Emily Cowles, played by Ruth McDevitt, were tolerant of Kolchak's odd behavior and reports. Also appearing on the series regularly were John Fielder as Gordy Spangler and Carol Ann Susi as Monique Marmelstein. *Night Stalker* filmed 21 episodes after it made its initial debut as two successful TV films in 1972 and 1973. Paul Playden and Cy Chermak produced the series for McGavin, who was its executive producer.

NIMOY, LEONARD (1931–)

Before he became forever identified with the role of Spock, the half-Vulcan science officer on the *STAR TREK* series,

Leonard Nimoy was a versatile and successful actor who appeared in numerous films and TV shows playing more normal characters. Nimoy, who was born in a poor neighborhood in Boston, began acting in community theaters at the tender age of eight. He made his film debut in 1951, and played small roles in the films *Queen for a Day* and *Rhubarb*. Larger roles in such films as *Zombies of the Stratosphere* (1952), *Francis Goes to West Point* (1952), and *Them!* (1954), and regular roles on such television series as GENERAL HOSPITAL followed. In 1966, Nimoy was cast in the role of Spock on the *Star Trek* series. When that show was canceled, Nimoy became a member of the cast of the MISSION: IMPOSSIBLE series, which he was on from 1969 until 1971. Starring roles as Spock in several successful *Star Trek* feature films followed. In addition to writing several volumes of poetry, hosting the popular *In Search of . . .* and *Ancient Mysteries* series, Nimoy has also made appearances on the stage in touring productions of *Fiddler on the Roof, Oliver!, Camelot,* and *Equus.* Over the years, Nimoy has also made guest appearances on such TV series as PERRY MASON, *The* VIRGINIAN, GUNSMOKE, *The* MUPPET SHOW, and *The* SIMPSONS. He also directed episodes of *Mission: Impossible, Star Trek,* and *Night Gallery,* among others. In 1998, Nimoy appeared in NBC's TV version of *Brave New World.*

NO TIME FOR SERGEANTS

Sept. 1964–Sept. 1965   ABC   Mon. 8:30–9 P.M.

Based on a popular novel by Mac Hyman that became a successful Broadway play and film that starred Andy GRIFFITH, *No Time for Sergeants,* which was produced by Warner Brothers Studio, was about a country bumpkin who was in the U.S. Air Force, Airman Will Stockdale, played by Sammy Jackson. Stockdale, a country boy, was constantly amazed by the world he discovered when he joined the Air Force, but he was enthusiastic and resourceful and was always eager to improve things at Oliver Air Force Base, where he was stationed. Sgt. King, Stockdale's always exasperated NCO, played by Harry Hickox, and the base's commanding officer, Col. Farnsworth, played by Hayden Rorke, were usually dumbfounded by Will's behavior and country logic. Airman Ben Whitledge, played by Kevin O'Neal, was Stockdale's buddy on the base, and Millie Anderson, played by Laurie Sibbald, was his girlfriend. Also appearing on the series on occasion were Andy Clyde as Millie's grandpa, Jim Anderson, Paul Smith as Captain Martin, Michael McDonald as Pvt. Jack Langdon, George Murdock as Capt. Krupnick, Greg Benedict as Pvt. Benedict, and Joey Tata as Pvt. Mike Neddick.

NORTH, JAY (1951–)

Born in Hollywood, child actor Jay North is best remembered for playing Dennis Mitchell on the popular TV situation comedy DENNIS THE MENACE from 1959 until 1963. Previously in the 1950s, North was seen on such popular TV series as WANTED: DEAD OR ALIVE and *The* DONNA REED SHOW. After *Dennis the Menace* left the air, North appeared as a guest on such TV series as WAGON TRAIN, *The* MAN FROM U.N.C.L.E., and MY THREE SONS, and played featured roles in the films *Zebra in the Kitchen* (1965) and *Maya* (1966). In 1967, he had a regular role on the TV series *Maya,* but his on-camera appearances subsequently diminished as North began to grow into young adulthood. He provided his voice for characters in such animated cartoon series as *The Banana Splits Adventure Hour* (1968), *Here Comes the Grump* (1969), *The Pebbles and Bamm-Bamm Show* (1971), *The Flintstones Comedy Hour* (1972), and *Fred Flintstone and Friends* (1977), before deciding to return to private life. In the 1980s, North made a brief comeback and was seen in the film *Scout's Honor,* playing the father of the film's juvenile character.

NORTHERN EXPOSURE

July 1990–Aug. 1990	CBS	Thurs. 10–11 P.M.
Apr. 1991–Dec. 1994	CBS	Mon. 10–11 P.M.
Jan. 1995–Mar. 1995	CBS	Wed. 10–11 P.M.
July 1995–Aug. 1995	CBS	Wed. 9–10 P.M.

The one-hour drama/comedy series *Northern Exposure* made its debut on television as a summer replacement. The public's reaction to the series was so favorable, the following spring it became a regularly scheduled program on CBS and remained on the air for five seasons. The charm of this engaging series was in large part due to its picturesque Alaskan setting, with its beautiful scenery and unique lifestyle, and a wonderful set of eccentric characters who inhabited the fictional town of Cecily. When Dr. Joel Fleischman, played by Rob Morrow, graduated from Columbia University Medical School at the age of 27, he expected to spend four years in the Alaskan city of Anchorage to repay the state of Alaska for financing his medical education. To his dismay, he was assigned to be the only doctor in the small town of Cecily (population 813) when the town's only doctor suddenly died. Adjusting to life in Cecily, which was in the middle of nowhere, with its primitive conditions and quaint customs, was not easy for Fleischman who wanted only to get home to New York City and his fiancée.

Among the many regulars whom Fleischman encountered in Cecily were a pretty, feisty, independent air-taxi pilot named Maggie O'Connell, who owned the cabin Fleischman lived in and thought that he was a pretty wimpy character, played by Janine Turner; a former astronaut and the president of the Cecily Chamber of Commerce, Maurice Minnfield, played by Barry Corbin, who was the most enterprising citizen in Cecily; Holling Vincoeur, the retired adventurer and owner of the town's saloon, played by John Cullum; Holling's 18-year-old girlfriend, Shelly Tambo, played by Cynthia Geary, who eventually married the much older Holling; the offbeat disc jockey at the town's only radio station, Chris Stevens, played by John Corbett; a young half–Native American assistant to Minnfield, Ed Chigliak, played by Darren E.

Burrows, who was determined to eventually become a filmmaker; Fleischman's always levelheaded Eskimo assistant, Marilyn, played by Elaine Miles; and the ancient but sturdy Ruth Anne Miller, played by Peg Phillips, who owned Cecily's general store. Other characters also seen on the series were Rick Pederson, played by Grant Goodeve, who was Maggie's boyfriend and was killed by a falling satellite at the end of the first season; Mike Monroe, played by Anthony Edwards, a lawyer who was allergic to toxics in the environment and lived in a huge plastic bubble on the outskirts of Cecily and for a while had a romance with Maggie; Dave the cook at Holling's saloon, played by William J. White; and a mountain man named Adam, played by Adam Arkin.

When *Northern Exposure* ended its run, Dr. Fleischman returned to New York even though he had finally begun to have a much-anticipated relationship with Maggie O'Connell, who decided to remain in Cecily. *Northern Exposure* was created by Joshua Brand and John Falsey, who were also responsible for the ST. ELSEWHERE series. The exteriors of *Northern Exposure* were not filmed in Alaska, but in the small town of Roslyn, Washington, which, because of the series success, became a popular tourist attraction.

NOVA

| Mar. 1974–present | PBS | Various times |

These documentaries about various scientific subjects are some of the Public Broadcasting System's most popular offerings. Produced by WGBH-TV in Boston, with the American Association for the Advancement of Science, the episodes are usually one hour in length and deal with such subjects as, "Can We Make a Better Doctor?," "Can You Believe TV Ratings?," "How To Create a Junk Food," "The Secrets of the Psychics," "Little Creatures Who Run the World," and "Mystery of the Senses," to mention just a few of the many subjects featured on the series during its first 26 years.

NURSES, THE

Sept. 1962–Dec. 1962	CBS	Thurs. 9–10 P.M.
Jan. 1963–Sept. 1964	CBS	Thurs. 10–11 P.M.
Sept. 1964–Sept. 1965	CBS	Tues. 10–11 P.M.

For three years, the professional and personal lives of nurses were the focus of a one-hour dramatic series called *The Nurses*, which featured Shirl Conway as Liz Thorpe, the head nurse at a New York City hospital, and Zina Bethune as a naive 17-year-old student nurse, Gail Lucas. Two doctors, the older and more experienced Dr. Ted Steffin, played by Joe Campanella, and the younger intern, Dr. Alex Tazinski, played by Michael Tolan, were also prominent on the series. Appearing in regular major roles were Edward Binns as Dr. Anson Kiley and Stephen Brooks as Dr. Ned Lowry. The series, which was filmed on location in New York City, became a daytime serial when it ended its prime-time run. The cast changed, but *The Nurses* retained its New York hospital setting. The daytime version of the program was on the air until 1967. In 1991, a series called simply *Nurses* made its TV debut. It was a half-hour situation comedy and starred Stephanie Hodge, Arnetia Walker, Mary Jo Keenan, Jeff Altman, Ada Maris, Kip Gilman, Carlos LaCamara, Florence Stanley, Markus Flanagan, David Rasche, and Loni Anderson. The series was on the air for three seasons, ending its run in June 1994.

NYPD BLUE

| Sept. 1993–July 1998 | ABC | Tues. 10–11 P.M. |
| Oct. 1998–present | ABC | Tues. 10–11 P.M. |

The creation of Stephen Bochco, *NYPD Blue* is a police-procedural series that, when it was first premiered, was controversial because of its nudity and salty language, not usually seen or heard on prime-time TV. The gritty, realistic series was, however, well written and acted, and absorbingly depicted the professional and personal lives of members of the New York City Police Department.

When it was first aired, the principal characters were Det. John Kelly, played by David Caruso, and Det. Andy Sipowicz, played by Dennis Franz. Major regular supporting characters were Lt. Arthur Fancy, played by James McDaniel, Laura Hughes Kelly, played by Sherry Stringfield; Officer Janice Licalsi, played by Amy Brenneman; Officer/Det. James Martinez, played by Nicholas Turturro; and Asst. D.A. Sylvia Costas, played by Sharon Lawrence. The two main characters, Kelly and Sipowicz, were as different as two sides of a coin. Kelly, a 15-year police department veteran, was compassionate and subdued, even in the face of terrible events. His partner, Sipowicz, was intolerant of the low-life characters he often encountered in his job. Kelly's ex-wife, Laura, a lawyer, loved him but couldn't deal with the unpredictability his job caused, and his new girlfriend, Officer Janice Licalsi, also had trouble balancing her private and professional lives. During the second season, Sipowicz became involved romantically with Asst. D. A. Sylvia Costas, and his private and professional life were often in juxtaposition.

In 1994, David Caruso left the series, hoping to capitalize on his *NYPD* popularity by becoming a star in films. Sherry Stringfield also departed the series in 1994. Other characters regularly seen on the show were Det. Greg Medavoy, played by Gordon Clapp; Donna Abandando, played by Gail O'Grady; Det. Bobby Simone, played by Jimmy Smits, who dominated many of the episodes; Det. Adrienne Lesnick, played by Justine Miceli; Det. Diane Russell, played by Kim Delaney; Gina Colon, played by Lourdes Benedicto; Officer Abby Sullivan, played by Paige Turco; and Det. Jill Kirkendall, played by Andrea Thompson. In 1998, Rick Schroder joined the cast as Sipowicz's new young partner, Det. Danny Sorenson. Mark-Paul Gosselaar and Charlotte Ross joined the regular cast of *NYPD Blue* in 2001.

O

O'BRIAN, HUGH (HUGH CHARLES KRAMPE 1925–)

In the 1950s, westerns were among television's most successful shows, and WYATT EARP, which starred Hugh O'Brian in the title role, was one of the most popular shows on the air. Hugh O'Brian was born in Rochester, New York, and embarked upon a career as an actor shortly after finishing his schooling. By the time O'Brian was 25 years old, he was appearing in such films as *Rocketship X-M* (1950), *The Return of Jesse James* (1950), *Never Fear* (1950), *Little Big Horn* (1951), *Son of Ali Baba* (1952), *The Battle at Apache Pass* (1952), *The Man from the Alamo* (1953), *The Lawless Breed* (1953), *There's No Business Like Show Business* (1954), *Saskatchewan* (1954), and *White Feather* (1955). It was not until he played the role of Wyatt Earp on the television series THE LIFE AND LEGEND OF WYATT EARP that O'Brian became a familiar name and face to millions of TV viewers. He had previously made guest-starring appearances on such TV series as PLAYHOUSE 90 and *The Westinghouse Desilu Playhouse* in the early 1950s. After *Wyatt Earp* left the air in 1961, after six successful seasons, O'Brian continued to appear in such films as *Feathertop* (1961), *Come Fly With Me* (1963), *Ten Little Indians* (1966), *Wild Women* (1970), *Killer Force* (1975), *The Shootist* (1976), *Game of Death* (1978), and the TV film *The Seekers* (1979), playing regular roles on the TV series *Search* (1972), and the miniseries *Greatest Heroes of the Bible* (1978), and guest-starring on such TV shows as *The* VIRGINIAN, PERRY MASON, *The Alfred Hitchcock Hour*, POLICE STORY, CHARLIE'S ANGELS, and *The* LOVE BOAT. For the next 10 years O'Brian appeared only rarely on television and in films; however, he was featured in a 1984 episode of the popular series MURDER, SHE WROTE. In 1988, O'Brian, who had been working in dinner and regional theaters throughout the country, appeared in the film *Twins*, and subsequently was seen in *Doin' Time on Planet Earth* (1988) and *Gunsmoke: The Last Apache* (1990). O'Brian reprised his role of Wyatt Earp on television in the TV film *The Gambler Returns: The Luck of the Draw*, and

Hugh O'Brian (Author's collection)

262

once again played Earp in the 1994 film, *Wyatt Earp: Return to Tombstone.*

O'CONNOR, CARROLL (1924–2001)

Carroll O'Connor became world famous playing Archie Bunker, the bigot everyone loved to hate on ALL IN THE FAMILY. But before that he had a successful acting career on the stage and in films. Like Archie Bunker, O'Connor was a native New Yorker; unlike Archie, he was a college graduate. He earned an undergraduate degree and a master's degree, in speech, from the University of Montana, and later attended college in Ireland. O'Connor first appeared on the stage while a student in Ireland, and he made his Broadway debut in 1958. Soon he logged numerous guest appearances on such TV series as ADVENTURES IN PARADISE, The UNITED STATES STEEL HOUR, The UNTOUCHABLES, NAKED CITY, The OUTER LIMITS, The FUGITIVE, The MAN FROM U.N.C.L.E., I SPY, GUNSMOKE, and The WILD WILD WEST, and appeared in such films as *By Love Possessed* (1961), *Cleopatra* (1963), *Hawaii* (1966), *The Devil's Brigade* (1968), *Fear No Evil* (1969), and *Kelly's Heroes* (1970), among many others. In the late 1960s TV producer Norman LEAR cast O'Connor as Archie Bunker in the series that would air in 1971 as *All in the Family.* The success of that program made O'Connor a star. Barely a decade later, he was earning an unprecedented $250,000 a week, making him one of the highest-paid actors in the world. In 1988, O'Connor starred on his second hit TV series, IN THE HEAT OF THE NIGHT, which was also a long-running hit and remained on the air for six seasons. During the 1990s, O'Connor continued to appear in *In the Heat of the Night* TV films, as well as appearing as Gus Stemple on the popular MAD ABOUT YOU series, and as Jacob Gordon on the PARTY OF FIVE series. O'Connor was last seen on film in *Return to Me* in 2000. He died the following year.

ODD COUPLE, THE

Sept. 1970–Jan. 1971	ABC	Thurs. 9:30–10 P.M.
Jan. 1971–June 1973	ABC	Fri. 9:30–10 P.M.
June 1973–Jan. 1974	ABC	Fri. 8:30–9 P.M.
Jan. 1974–Sept. 1974	ABC	Fri. 9:30–10 P.M.
Sept. 1974–Jan. 1975	ABC	Thurs. 8–8:30 P.M.
Jan. 1975–July 1975	ABC	Fri. 9:30–10 P.M.
Oct. 1982–Feb. 1983	ABC	Fri. 8:30–9 P.M.
May 1983	ABC	Fri. 8–8:30 P.M.
May 1983–June 1983	ABC	Thurs. 8:30–9 P.M.

Neil Simon's hit Broadway play *The Odd Couple,* which also became a successful film, arrived on television as a situation comedy series in 1970. The leading characters were Felix Unger and Oscar Madison, played by Jack KLUGMAN and Tony RANDALL. Felix and Oscar were two entirely different, middle-aged, divorced single men who decided to split their expenses by sharing an apartment. The two men were indeed an odd couple. Felix, a photographer, was a prim and proper conservative who liked everything done "by the book," as well as a fastidious housekeeper and a gourmet cook. Oscar, a sportswriter, was sloppy, casual, and gruff, couldn't care less about living in a tidy apartment, and preferred junk food to gourmet feasts. Also appearing was Al Molinaro, Oscar's poker-playing pal Murray Greshler, who was a New York City cop. Making periodic guest appearances were Garry Walberg, Ryan MacDonald, and Larry Gelman, as three of Oscar's other poker-playing friends, Speed, Roy, and Vinnie; Monica Evans and Carol Shelly as the Pidgeon sisters, Cecily and Gwen, two talkative English girls who were neighbors of Felix and Oscar; Joan Hotchkis as Dr. Nancy Cunningham, who dated Oscar during the series first several seasons; Elinor Donahue as Miriam Welby, who was Felix's female friend; Penny MARSHALL as Myrna Turner, Oscar's kooky secretary; Brett Somers (who was actually Jack Klugman's wife) as Oscar's ex-wife, Blanche; and Janis Hansen as Felix's ex-wife, Gloria.

The Odd Couple was produced by Garry Marshall and Sheldon Keller. Seven years after the original *Odd Couple* series departed the airwaves, it resurfaced in 1982 as a series called *The New Odd Couple,* which starred two African-American actors, Ron Glass and Demond Wilson, as Felix Unger and Oscar Madison. The series, which remained on the air for less than one full season,

Tony Randall and Jack Klugman of *The Odd Couple* (Author's collection)

also featured John Schuck, Christopher Joy, Bart Braverman, Sheila Anderson, Ronalda Douglas, Liz Torres, and Jo Marie Payton-France. An animated version of *The Odd Couple,* which was called *The Oddball Couple,* had been previously aired from 1975 until 1977.

O'DONNELL, ROSIE (ROSEANNE TERESA O'DONNELL 1962–)

The popular TV talk show host Rosie O'Donnell was born in Commack, Long Island, New York, to Irish-American parents, the middle child of five in the family. Rosie, whose mother died when she was 10 years old, claims that she spent many hours every day watching television, and developed a lifelong interest in everything connected with show business. Voted the most popular girl in her high school class, Rosie attended Boston University for one year, but dropped out to pursue a career in show business. In the early 1980s, O'Donnell began performing a stand-up comedy act at clubs around the country, and won the $20,000 prize on STAR SEARCH as a contestant on that series. This led to her being cast as a regular on GIMME A BREAK (1986–87) and *Stand By Your Man* (1992), as well as major supporting roles in such films as *A League of Their Own* (1992), *Another Stakeout* (1993), *Sleepless in Seattle* (1993), *The Flintstones* (1994), *I'll Do Anything* (1994), *Now and Then* (1995), and *Harriet the Spy* (1996). O'Donnell also has made numerous guest appearances on such TV series as BEVERLY HILLS 90210, *The* LARRY SANDERS SHOW, *The* NANNY, SPIN CITY, SUDDENLY SUSAN, MURPHY BROWN, and ALLY MCBEAL. In 1996, O'Donnell became the star of her own show, *The* ROSIE O'DONNELL SHOW, which became one of the most popular daytime syndicated TV talk shows on the air. In addition to her five-days-a-week talk show, O'Donnell continued to appear in such films as *The Twilight of the Golds* (1997), *Wide Awake* (1998), and provided the voices for the character of Terk in the animated feature film *Tarzan* (1999). O'Donnell's talk show went off the air in 2001.

OH SUSANNA

(see *Gale Storm Show, The*)

OLYMPIC GAMES ON TELEVISION

It was not until the 1960s that the Olympics were telecast almost in their entirety as special events. By the late 1990s, the summer and winter Olympics every four years had become one of the popular events in television and were being watched by millions of people throughout the world.

The preparations for televising the Olympics begin months before the actual games are televised. Countless miles of trenches are dug to hide the TV and power cables needed to televise the games. Huge platforms to support the hundreds of cameras needed to cover all the events are placed at strategic locations everywhere the events are taking place. In order to assure the uninterrupted power needed to televise the games, independent power supplies and backup supplies are built. Complicated telephone and intercom systems are constructed so that the many reports for the various contests can be coordinated properly.

In addition to the sporting events shown on the Olympic telecasts, viewers have also witnessed various political situations that have taken place during the modern Olympic games. In 1956, the world watched TV reports, from Melbourne, Australia, of protest by Egypt, Iraq, and Lebanon of the seizure of the Suez Canal, and the Netherlands, Spain, and Switzerland protested the U.S.S.R.'s invasion of Hungary. During the 1968 Olympics, in Mexico City, two black American athletes used the victory podium to protest the United States's race policies. In 1972, the world was shocked when it witnessed the massacre of 11 Israeli athletes participating in the Olympic games being held in Munich, Germany, by Palestinian terrorists. In 1976, 26 nations made the news by refusing to attend the Montreal, Canada, Olympics, in a protest relating to South Africa's apartheid policies. When the U.S.S.R invaded its neighbor Afghanistan, the United States and 40 other nations boycotted the 1980 Olympics. Four years later, during the 1984 summer games held in Los Angeles, the U.S.S.R. and several of its Eastern Bloc allies stole the spotlight by boycotting the games to demonstrate that they, like the Western nations, had the power to disrupt the Olympic games. Again, during the summer games in 1988, six nations boycotted the games, but the television reports of the games once again concentrated on the athletes and their sporting events, and the boycotts apparently ceased to be an effective means of politicizing the Olympics.

Although the modern Olympics made world-famous superstars of such sports figures as track and field's Jesse Owens, figure skater Sonja Henie, and swimmer Johnny Weissmuller in the 1920s and 1930s, television made well-known celebrities of many more sports people, whose feats millions of viewers witnessed as they watched the Olympics on TV. A partial list of some of the most publicized and popular gold medalists of recent TV times should surely include American track and field star Carl Lewis, who won four gold medals at the 1984 Olympics in Los Angeles, and subsequently won gold medals at the 1988, 1992, and 1996 Olympics; speed skater Bonnie Blair, who captured the hearts of people all over the world when she became the only woman to win five gold medals in Olympic competitions in the winter games at Calgary in 1988, and won several more gold medals at the 1992 and 1994 winter Olympics in Albertville, France, and Lillehammer, Norway; field and track stars, the Joyner family, Jacqueline Joyner-Kersee, Alfrederick Alphonzo Joyner, and Delores Florence Griffith Joyner (best known by her nickname "Flo-Jo"), who who won gold medals at the 1984, 1966, and 1992 games; swimmer Mark Spitz, who became a TV superstar when he won a record seven gold medals at the 1972 Olympic games; figure skaters Peggy Fleming, who captured the gold medal at the 1968 winter Olympics in Grenoble, France, and Dorothy Hamill, who captured the gold medal at the 1976 winter games; American track and field star

Bruce Jenner, who stunned the world with his Olympic victory in the decathlon at the 1976 games in Montreal; diver Greg Louganis, who won a silver medal when he was 16 years old at the 1976 Olympics, and then won four gold medals at the 1984 and 1988 Olympic games; figure skater Katarina Witt, an East German skater who won two Olympic gold medals at the 1984 and 1988 winter games.

The 1992 Summer Olympics took place in Barcelona and marked the entry of professional athletes into competition when the U.S. basketball team took the court, featuring several professional players. In 1996, a bombing in Centennial Park, which had been constructed for the Olympics, marred the games in Atlanta. After the 1996 games the Olympics then moved to a split schedule, alternating winter and summer games every two years. The 1998 winter games took place in Nagano, where Tara Lipinski upset favorite Michelle Kwan in the figure skating competition. Summer games were held in Sydney in 2000 with the following winter games in Salt Lake City in 2002.

OMNIBUS

Nov. 1952–Oct. 1953	CBS	Sun. 4:30–6 P.M.
Oct. 1953–Apr. 1956	CBS	Sun. 5–6:30 P.M.
Oct. 1956–Mar. 1957	ABC	Sun. 9–10:30 P.M.
Oct. 1957–May 1959	NBC	Sun. 9–10:30 P.M.

For seven years, *Omnibus* was one of the most critically acclaimed programs on television. Underwritten by the Ford Foundation, *Omnibus,* which was hosted by Alistair Cooke, who later hosted PBS's popular MASTERPIECE THEATRE series, was first seen on late Sunday afternoons. The series presented everything from documentaries, to musicals and well-known and written-for-TV plays. During the series' first season, such diverse offerings as James Agee's continuing story *Mr. Lincoln,* three Maxwell Anderson plays, Russian playwright Anton Chekhov's play *The Bear,* the Metropolitan Opera production of *Die Fledermaus,* the Agnes DeMille ballet *Three Maidens and the Devil,* G. B. Shaw's play *Arms and the Man,* among others, were presented. Over the years, such widely diverse programs as highlights from the successful musical comedy *Oklahoma!,* Shakespeare's *King Lear,* which starred Orson Welles in his TV debut, concerts conducted by Leonard Bernstein, documentary films about undersea explorer Jacques Cousteau, Christopher Plummer in the ancient Greek *Oedipus Rex, The Empty Chair,* with George C. Scott and Peter Ustinov, and Gilbert and Sullivan's operetta *H.M.S. Pinafore,* were featured. *Omnibus* was originally produced by Robert Saudek and then by Fred Rickey. In 1980, *Omnibus* resurfaced as a series of irregularly scheduled specials with Hal Holbrook as its regular host.

ON THE ROAD WITH CHARLES KURALT

As an evening program:

June 1983	CBS	Sun. 8–8:30 P.M.
June 1983–Aug. 1983	CBS	Sun. 8–8:30 P.M.

CBS News commentator Charles Kuralt first offered his *On the Road* essays about life in America as segments that were seen for many years on the *CBS Evening News* as early as 1967. The show became a regular morning attraction on Sundays, where it remained for over 15 years, and for a time was seen as an evening attraction on CBS in 1983. The series presented weekly features about people, places, and historical events that defined what life in the United States was all about. Each week, Kuralt went to a different location in the United States and chatted with ordinary citizens. Among the people and events Kuralt covered were shoe salesman at work, the annual whistler's convention, a small bottling plant in South Carolina, a man who made everything from a Ferris wheel to a clock out of toothpicks, life among real cowboys, and a junk mail collector who used his collection for heating his house.

ONE DAY AT A TIME

Dec. 1975–July 1976	CBS	Tues. 9:30–10 P.M.
Sept. 1976–Jan. 1978	CBS	Tues. 9:30–10 P.M.
Jan. 1978–Jan. 1979	CBS	Mon. 9:30–10 P.M.
Jan. 1979–Mar. 1979	CBS	Wed. 9–9:30 P.M.
Mar. 1979–Sept. 1982	CBS	Sun. 8:30–9 P.M.
Sept. 1982–Mar. 1983	CBS	Sun. 9:30–10 P.M.
Mar. 1983–May 1983	CBS	Mon. 9:30–10 P.M.
June 1983–Feb. 1984	CBS	Sun. 8:30–9 P.M.
Mar. 1984–May 1984	CBS	Wed. 8–8:30 P.M.
May 1984–Aug. 1984	CBS	Mon. 9–9:30 P.M.
Aug. 1984–Sept. 1984	CBS	Sun. 8–8:30 P.M.

The situation comedy series *One Day at a Time,* which was about a divorced woman who has two teenage daughters to raise, starred Bonnie FRANKLIN as the mother, Ann Romano, and Mackenzie PHILLIPS and Valerie BERTINELLI as her daughters, Julie and Barbara. The three lived in an apartment in Indianapolis, Indiana, Ann's hometown. The superintendent at the apartment building, Dwayne Schneider, played by Pat Harrington, Jr., was a tattooed dope who thought of himself as a great lover and who provided many of the series' laughs. Other characters on the series were Ann's romantic interest, David Kane, played by Richard Masur, who left the series in 1976; Ann's neighbor, the outspoken, brassy Ginny Wroblicki, played by Mary Louise Wilson; and Ann's ex-husband, Ed Cooper, played by Joe Campanella, who made occasional appearances on the show.

In time, Ann finally managed to get a good job as an account executive for the Connors and Davenport Advertising Agency, Julie married an airline flight steward named Max Horvath, played by Michael Lembeck, and Ann became involved with a man named Nick Handris, played by Ron Rifkin, who was divorced and had a young son, Alex, played by Glenn Scarpelli. Barbara married her boyfriend, dental student Mark Royer, played by Boyd Gaines, during the 1982–83 season. When Mackenzie Phillips, who had left the series to treat a serious drug addiction, returned temporarily, but left the series once again, Bonnie Franklin and Valerie Bertinelli decided that they wanted to leave the series after the 1983–84 season ended. *One Day at a Time,* which was created by Whitney Blake and Allan Manings, was developed for television by Norman LEAR.

ONE LIFE TO LIVE

July 1968–present   ABC   Various daytime

Agnes Nixon, who also created the popular daytime serial drama series ALL MY CHILDREN, apprenticed under the prolific radio and TV soap opera writer Irna Phillips. *One Life to Live* made its daytime TV debut in 1968. Set in a typical American suburban town called Lanview, *One Life to Live,* from its earliest days stressed various ethnic situations and such diverse ethnic groups as Jews, WASPs, Poles, and African Americans that figured prominently on the series. Over the years the series has been produced at different times by Doris Quinlin, Joseph Stuart, Jean Arley, Paul Rauch, Linda Gottlieb, and Susan Bedsow Morgan. When the program was first aired, it was a half-hour Monday through Friday program, but it expanded to a 45-minute, five-days-a-week format in July 1976, and then to one hour, five days a week in January 1978. The original cast of *One Life to Live* included Ernest Graves, and then Shepperd Strudwick, and finally Tom O'Rourke as a newspaper publisher named Victor Lord; Gillian Spencer, and then Christine Jones, and finally Erika Slezak, who still plays the role, as Lord's daughter Victoria, aka Vicki; Trish Van Devere, and then Lynn Benisch as Lord's daughter Meredith, who died early in the series' run; Lee Patterson as reporter Joe Riley, who married and later divorced, Vicki; Patricia Roe, and then Alice Hirson as Joe's sister, Eileen Riley Siegel; Allan Miller as Eileen's husband, Dave Siegel, who died of a heart attack; Lee Warrick, and then Leonie Norton, as the Siegels' daughter, Julie; and Bill Fowler, and then William Cox, and finally Tom Berenger as the Siegels' son, Timmy, who died in a fall. Among the actors who appeared on the series over the next 20 years and played characters who were very popular were Doris Belack (Anna Woleck), Ellen Holly (Carla Gray), Lillian Hayman (Sadie Gray), John Cullum (Artie Duncan), Tommy Lee Jones (Dr. Mark Toland), Millee Taggart (Millie Parks), Francesca James (Marcy Wade), Marilyn Chris (Wanda Webb), Robin Strasser (Dr. Dorian Cramer), Donald Madden (John Douglas), Farley Granger (Dr. Will Vernon), Teri Keane (Naomi Vernon), Krista Tesreau (Tina Clayton), Joan Copeland (Gwendolyn Abbott), Frank Converse (Harry O'Neill), Brian Davies (Scott Edgar), Christine Jones (Pamela Buchanan), and Joe Lando (Jake Harrison), among many others.

During the 1980s, *One Life to Live* often used fantasy story lines, which was unusual for the time. Vicki had an out-of-body experience while she was on an operating table, Clint Buchanan time-traveled to the Wild West of the 1880s, and the "lost city" of Eterna, which was located near Lanview, was discovered. The story lines often met with unfavorable comments by TV critics who preferred their soap operas to be more domestic and less fantastic.

In the 1990s, several well-known actors played regular roles on *One Life to Live,* including Yasmine Bleeth (Lee Ann Demarest), Ann Flood (Mrs. Guthrie), Carole Shelley (Babs Bartlett), Roy Thinnes (Sloan Carpenter), Eileen Heckart (Wilma Burr), Shirley Stoler (Gert Mulligan), and Bethel Leslie (Ethel Crawford). Several guest stars have made special appearances on *One Life to Live* over the years, including Dr. Joyce Brothers, Erika Slezak's father, popular character actor Walter Slezak, John Beradino, Sammy Davis, Jr., and Mary Stuart, who for many years was the major character on the SEARCH FOR TOMORROW daytime series.

ONE MAN'S FAMILY

Nov. 1949–Jan. 1950	NBC	Fri. 8–8:30 P.M.
Jan. 1950–May 1950	NBC	Thurs. 8:30–9 P.M.
July 1950–June 1952	NBC	Sat. 7:30–8 P.M.

One of radio's most successful and long-running series, *One Man's Family,* which was on the air continuously for 26 years, from 1933 until 1959, arrived on television in 1949, but remained on TV for only three years. Most Americans were thoroughly familiar with the Barbour family, who lived in the Seacliff area of San Francisco in a house that overlooked the Golden Gate Bridge. Henry Barbour, the elderly patriarch of the family who was a semiretired stock broker, played on radio for many years by J. Anthony Smythe, was played by Bert Lytell, and Fanny Barbour, his wife, played on radio by Minetta Ellen, and then Mary Adams, was played on TV by Marjorie Gateson. The Barbour children included their eldest son, Paul, who had been a pilot during World War II, played on TV by Russell Thorson; their daughter, Hazel, played on TV by Lillian Schaaf; their twins the free-spirited Claudia, who was played on TV by Nancy Franklin, and then by Eva Marie Saint, and Clifford, played by Frank Thomas, Jr., and then by Billy Idelson and James Lee; and their youngest son, Jack, played by Arthur Cassell, and then by Richard Wigginton. Paul's love interest, Beth Holly, was played by Mercedes MCCAMBRIDGE, and then by Susan Shaw. Hazel's husband, Bill Herbert, was played by Les Tremayne, and then by Walter Brooke. Paul's ward, Teddy Lawton, was played by Madeline Belgard, and Claudia's husband, Captain Nicholas Lacey, was played by Lloyd Bochner. Unlike the radio series, which over the 26 years it was on the air developed a large and loyal following, many of whom spent their holidays listening to the Barbours enjoy their family gatherings, wrote to the members of the family regularly and sent them birthday, get-well, and anniversary cards, and became entirely involved with no less than four generations of the Barbour clan, the TV series was not on the air long enough to attract as loyal a following. Both the radio and TV versions of *One Man's Family* were written by Carlton E. Morse. In 1954, a daytime version of *One Man's Family* surfaced, but it was can-

The cast of *One Man's Family:* Marjorie Gateson and Bert Lytell (Mother and Father Barbour) surrounded by their TV children and grandchildren (Author's collection)

celed after less than one full season. The program continued on radio, however, with many of the original cast playing the roles they had originated in the early 1930s, and it remained popular with listeners until the program finally departed the airwaves in 1959.

ONE STEP BEYOND (AKA *ALCOA PRESENTS*)
Jan. 1959–Oct. 1961   ABC   Tues. 10–10:30 P.M.

This series, a half-hour anthology program about the occult, was directed and hosted by John Newland. The series reportedly presented actual case histories of various supernatural events that had been dramatized for the program. Ghosts and extrasensory perception were frequent themes on the show. Twenty years later, in 1978, Newland returned to host a second series about the occult called

The Next Step Beyond, which, in spite of the fact that it was in color and not black and white like its predecessor, failed to attract an audience and was canceled before one season had been completed.

OPERATION PETTICOAT

Sept. 1977–May 1978	ABC	Sat. 8:30–9 P.M.
May 1978–June 1978	ABC	Thurs. 8:30–9 P.M.
June 1978–Aug. 1978	ABC	Fri. 8:30–9 P.M.
Sept. 1978–Oct. 1978	ABC	Mon. 8:30–9 P.M.
June 1978–Aug. 1979	ABC	Fri. 8–8:30 P.M.

Operation Petticoat was a half-hour situation comedy series set during World War II, that starred John Astin as Lt. Cdr. Matthew Sherman, a navy career officer who is anxious to see action before the war ends. When he finally gains command of a submarine named *Sea Tiger,* he is disappointed to learn that the submarine has sunk dockside. Numerous problems ensue for Sherman as he attempts to patch up his submarine. His problems are compounded when he rescues five army nurses at sea, played by Yvonne Wilder, Melinda Naud, Jamie Lee Curtis, Dorrie Thompson, and Bond Gideon, and by a self-serving supply officer, Lt. Nick Holden, played by Richard Gilliland, who wants to avoid combat as much as Sherman wants to join the fight.

During *Operation Petticoat's* first season, it failed to attract a very large audience, and when it returned for a second season, it featured an entirely new cast. The submarine's new skipper was Lt. Cdr. Haller, played by Robert Hogan, and there were new nurses, led by Jo Ann Pflug, as Lt. Katherine O'Hara, but the new cast also failed to attract an audience, and the show was canceled after only four episodes. The series was based on a successful 1959 film with the same title that starred Cary Grant and Tony Curtis, whose daughter, Jamie Lee Curtis, was featured in the original TV series. Leonard B. Stern was the series' executive producer, and David J. O'Connell and Si Rose produced the series for Universal.

OPRAH WINFREY SHOW, THE

Sept. 1986–present	Syndicated	Mon.–Fri., Various times and networks

Oprah WINFREY was the first African-American woman to host a successful daytime talk show on television, and she became one of the wealthiest performers of the last two decades of the 20th century. Oprah, who began her career on television as a news anchorwoman in Nashville, Tennessee, later cohosted a local talk show in Baltimore, and then moved to Chicago, where, in 1984, she became the hostess of another local talk show called *A.M. Chicago.* In 1986, her show, *The Oprah Winfrey Show,* was syndicated nationally, and in 1988, Oprah acquired the ownership of her series, purchased a production studio in Chicago. In one year her program became so popular that she had become the richest woman in television. Seen for one hour, five days a week, each *Oprah Winfrey Show* usually features a single topic or guest, and is taped before a live audience that is always encouraged to ask questions of Oprah and her guests. According to the show's former producer, Debra DiMaio, who departed the show in 1994, *The Oprah Winfrey Show* is "emotionally oriented," and Oprah often reacts to her guests, as well as the topics, with tears of sympathy, outrage, and compassion, and occasionally hugs guests and audience members.

Among the topics on the program are child abuse, racial prejudices, and self-improvement. Oprah, who is constantly fighting a battle of weight gain and loss, often talks about her weight on her show and gives her audience, which is primarily female, various plans and theories about losing weight and proper diets. In 1996,

Oprah, who is an avid reader, began to feature various authors and book selections that she felt her audience might enjoy, or should read for one reason or another. She discontinued this as a monthly feature in 2002. *The Oprah Winfrey Show* remained at the top of the daytime ratings throughout the 1990s and continues to be one of television's most popular daytime talk shows.

ORIGINAL AMATEUR HOUR, THE

Jan. 1948–Sept. 1949	DUMONT	Sun. 7–8 P.M.
Oct. 1949–Jan. 1952	NBC	Tues. 10–11 P.M.
Jan. 1952–Sept. 1952	NBC	Tues. 10–10:45 P.M.
Apr. 1953–Sept. 1954	NBC	Sat. 8:30–9 P.M.
Oct. 1955–Dec. 1955	ABC	Sun. 9:30–10 P.M.
Jan. 1956–Feb. 1956	ABC	Sun. 9:30–10:30 P.M.
Mar. 1956–Sept. 1956	ABC	Sun. 9–10 P.M.
Oct. 1956–Mar. 1957	ABC	Sun. 7:30–8:30 P.M.
Apr. 1957–June 1957	ABC	Sun. 9–10 P.M.
July 1957–Sept. 1957	NBC	Mon. 10–10:30 P.M.
Sept. 1957–Dec. 1957	NBC	Sun. 7–7:30 P.M.
Feb. 1958–Oct. 1958	NBC	Sat. 10–10:30 P.M.
May 1959–June 1959	CBS	Fri. 8:30–9 P.M.
July 1959–Oct. 1959	CBS	Fri. 10:30–11 P.M.
Mar. 1960–Sept. 1960	ABC	Mon. 10:30–11 P.M.

One of the first popular radio shows of the 1930s and 1940s to make a successful transition to television was *The Original Amateur Hour* talent contest program. Hosted by Ted Mack, the television version featured the same variety of performers such as singers, spoon players, and comedians that had been heard on the popular radio show, which was originally hosted by "Major" Edward Bowes, who died shortly before the show arrived on television. Although thousands of performers got their start on *The Original Amateur Hour,* only a few went on to become well known to the public. Frank Sinatra was one of the radio version's most celebrated contestants. The TV version marked the first major appearances of singers Gladys Knight and Pat Boone. On August 10, 1954, the show celebrated its 1,001st broadcast with a show that featured some of the most memorable winners who had been heard and seen over the years. The show was also famous for the dancing pack of Old Gold cigarettes and the smaller matchbox that tap danced as part of the Old Gold commercials. Dennis James was the show's announcer. In 1992, a revised version surfaced on cable's Family Channel as *The New Original Amateur Hour,* hosted by Willard Scott, but the show failed to attract an audience and was canceled after 13 programs.

OUR MISS BROOKS

Oct. 1952–June 1955	CBS	Fri. 9:30–10 P.M.
Oct. 1955–Sept. 1956	CBS	Fri. 8:30–9 P.M.

The popular *Our Miss Brooks,* which made its debut on radio in 1948, became an equally popular situation comedy series on television in 1952. The show starred Eve ARDEN as Connie Brooks, a love-starved single high school English teacher and a thorn in the side of Madison High's blustery, pompous school principal, Osgood Conklin, played by Gale Gordon. The object of Connie's unflattering affection was handsome high school science teacher Philip Boynton, played by Robert Rockwell. Other regulars on the series, who, like Eve Arden and Gale Gordon, had originated their roles on radio, were Richard CRENNA, who played Walter Denton, Connie's adolescent student, who drove her to school each day; Jane Morgan, who played Connie's landlady, Mrs. Margaret Davis; and Gloria McMillan, who played Mr. Conklin's teenage daughter, Harriet. Also regularly featured were Leonard Smith as the dim high school athlete, Stretch Snodgrass; Mary Jane Croft as Connie's rival, Miss Daisy Enright; Virginia Gordon, and then Paula Winslowe, as Osgood Conklin's wife, Martha; Joseph Kearns as school superintendent Mr. Stone; and Jesslyn Fox, Ricky Vera, Bob Sweeney, Nana Bryant, Isabel Randolph, Gene BARRY, William Ching, and Hy Averback. In 1955, when the series began to fall in the ratings, the setting of the show was changed to Mrs. Nestor's Private Elementary School, where Connie Brooks got a new job. The new locale did not help the show's ratings, and the series was canceled in 1956 after four years on the air. *Our Miss Brooks* was produced by Larry Berns and directed by Al Lewis.

OUTER LIMITS, THE

Sept. 1963– Sept. 1964	ABC	Mon. 7:30–8:30 P.M.
Sept. 1964– Jan. 1965	ABC	Sat. 7:30–8:30 P.M.
1995–present	SHOWTIME	Various times

The *Outer Limits* science fiction anthology series, which was created and produced by Leslie Stevens, had one of the most unforgettable openings on television. The voice of Control (Vic Perrin from 1963 until 1965, and Kevin Conway in 1965) said, "There is nothing wrong with your television set. Do not attempt to adjust the picture. We are controlling transmission. We will control the horizontal. We will control the vertical. We can change the focus to a soft blur—or sharpen it to crystal clarity. For the next hour sit quietly and we will control all that you see and hear. You are about to participate in a great adventure. You are about to experience the awe and mystery which reaches from the inner mind to . . . *The Outer Limits!*" The weekly sci-fi tales that followed were interesting and well produced, and the casts, which included such well-known performers as Robert CULP, Martin Sheen, Bruce Dern, William SHATNER, Sally Kellerman, Martin Landau, Cliff Robertson, and others, was always first rate. The series was revived in 1992 on the Showtime Cable Network, 30 years after the original series was aired. *Outer Limits* has recently been seen on the Sci-Fi Channel and late night on CBS.

OZ, FRANK (RICHARD FRANK OZNOWICZ 1944–)

Puppeteer/producer/director Frank Oz, who, with Jim HENSON, was responsible for the success of The Muppets, was born in Hereford, England, but immigrated to the United States, where he developed his interest in puppetry. In 1969, Oz, as one of the puppeteers on the new, innovative Public Broadcasting System's children's series SESAME STREET, embarked upon a project that would make him one of the most successful and highly regarded men in television and films. As the voice and manipulator of such characters as Bert, Grover, Cookie Monster, Prince Charming, Harvey Kneeslapper, and Professor Hastings, Oz contributed to the success of *Sesame Street*. In 1976, Oz and fellow puppeteer Jim Henson, introduced their *MUPPET SHOW* to prime-time viewers. The show was a great success, and the characters Oz created for the show, which included Miss Piggy, Fozzie Bear, Sam the Eagle, and The Swedish Chef, became major attractions and were subsequently seen in the feature films *The Muppet Movie* (1979), *The Great Muppet Caper* (1981), *The Muppets Take Manhattan* (1984), *The Muppet Christmas Carol* (1992), and others. In addition to his Muppet shows and movies, Oz was the voice of Yoda for the *Star Wars* films, and is the voice of Yoda in Episodes I, II, and III (scheduled for 2005). He directed *The Dark Crystal* (1982), *The Muppets Take Manhattan* (1984), *Little Shop of Horrors* (1986), *Dirty Rotten Scoundrels* (1988), *The Indian in the Cupboard* (1995), and many other successful films. In 1996, Oz revived his Muppet characters for a new *Muppets Tonight* TV series, and in 1990 he was, once again, the voice of Miss Piggy, Fozzie the Bear, Animal, and Sam the Eagle in the film *Muppets From Space*.

OZZIE AND HARRIET

(see *Adventures of Ozzie and Harriet, The*)

P

PAAR, JACK (HAROLD PAAR 1918–)

In addition to Steve ALLEN, most observers credit Jack Paar with being the originator of the talk show format that became the prototype for such successful subsequent show hosts as Johnny CARSON, David LETTERMAN, and Jay LENO. Jack Paar, who was born in Canton, Ohio, quit school when he was 16 years old and went to work as a radio announcer. While serving in the U.S. Army during World War II, Paar entertained troops as a comedian in the South Pacific. When the war ended, Paar went to Hollywood, where he had minor roles in such films as *Variety Time* (1948), *Easy Living* (1949), *Walk Softly, Stranger* (1950), *Love Nest* (1951), and *Footlight Varieties* (1951), before becoming the host of his first TV series, *Up to Paar*, in 1952. Paar subsequently hosted the *Bank on the Stars* TV game show in 1953 and was seen in the film *Down Among the Sheltering Palms* (1953), before joining the staff at NBC-TV. In 1957, Paar replaced Steve Allen as the host of the late-night *TONIGHT* show. A natural conversationalist and interviewer, Paar became so popular that the show was renamed *The Jack Paar Show* in 1958. Paar became known for his on-and off-the-air feuds with various celebrities and politicians, and in the mid-1960s, he decided that he had had enough of television performing, retired from the spotlight, and bought a local television station in Poland, Maine, appearing on television only on rare occasions thereafter.

PANTOMIME QUIZ (AKA STUMP THE STARS)

July 1950	CBS	Mon. 9:30–10 P.M.
July 1950–Sept. 1950	CBS	Mon. 8–8:30 P.M.
July 1951–Aug. 1951	CBS	Mon. 8–8:30 P.M.
Jan. 1952	NBC	Wed. 10:30–11 P.M.
Jan. 1952–Mar. 1952	NBC	Wed. 10–10:30 P.M.
July 1952–Sept. 1952	CBS	Fri. 8:30–9 P.M.
July 1953–Aug. 1953	CBS	Fri. 8–8:30 P.M.
Oct. 1953–Apr. 1954	DUMONT	Tues. 8:30–9 P.M.
July 1954–Aug. 1954	CBS	Fri. 8–8:30 P.M.
Jan. 1955–Mar. 1955	ABC	Sun. 9:30–10 P.M.
July 1955–Sept. 1955	CBS	Fri. 8–8:30 P.M.
July 1956–Sept. 1956	CBS	Fri. 10:30–11 P.M.
July 1957–Sept. 1957	CBS	Fri. 10:30–11 P.M.
Apr. 1958–Sept. 1958	ABC	Tues. 9:30–10 P.M.
June 1959–Sept. 1959	ABC	Mon. 9–9:30 P.M.
Sept. 1962–Sept. 1963	CBS	Mon. 10:30–11 P.M.

For over 13 years, the popular *Pantomime Quiz* TV game show was seen at various times, mainly as a summer replacement. The show, which began as a local series in the Los Angeles area, was based on the popular parlor game charades. Two teams of four members each competed as the team members attempted to have their team guess a famous phrase, a literary work, a motto, etc., as they acted out each word in the puzzle in the shortest amount of time. Home viewers were asked to send in suggestions for puzzles. Over the years, Mike Stokey and Pat Harrington, Jr., were the show's hosts. The long list of regular team members included Hans CONRIED, Vincent Price, Adele Jergens, Jackie Coogan, John Barrymore, Jr., Dave Willock, Rocky Graziano, Dorothy Hart, Robert Clary, Peter DONALD, Carol Haney, Milt Kamen, Jan Clayton, Elaine Stritch, Jerry LESTER, Carol BURNETT, Stubby Kaye, Dick VAN DYKE, Fred Clark, Robert STACK, Angela LANSBURY, Orson Bean, Rose Marie, John Carradine, Howard Morris, Tom Poston, Beverly GARLAND, Sebastian Cabot, Ross Martin, Diana Dors, Mickey Manners, and Ruta Lee. *Pantomime Quiz* was also seen as a daytime show in 1959 with Mike Stockey, who was also the program's producer, acting as host.

PAPER CHASE, THE

Sept. 1978	CBS	Sat. 8–9 P.M.
Sept. 1978–	CBS	Tues. 8–9 P.M.
Jan. 1979		
Feb. 1979	CBS	Tues. 10–11 P.M.
Mar. 1979–	CBS	Tues. 8–9 P.M.
July 1979		
1983–1986	SHOWTIME	Various times

The hero of this weekly series was a law student, John T. Hart, whose rural upbringing in Iowa did not prepare him for the realities of the very competitive and ruthless atmosphere that existed in law school. Hart, played by James Stephens, often had difficulty dealing with his imperious professor at the law school, Charles W. Kingsfield, Jr., played by John Houseman, who was the world's leading authority on contract law and was both admired and hated by his students because of his overbearing manner. Hart was a member of a study group of young law students who worked together sharing notes and assignments. Members of the group, whose private lives were, like Hart's, often the focus of weekly episodes of the show, included Franklin Ford III, played by Tom Fitzsimmons, who had organized the study group; Thomas Craig Anderson, played by Robert Ginty; Willis Bell, played by James Keane; Elizabeth Logan, played by Francie Tacker; and Jonathan Brooks, played by Jonathan Segal, who was the only married member of the group. Brooks's wife, Ashley, was played by Deka Beaudine.

At Ernie's pizza joint, where Hart worked part time to support himself in school, he met Carol, played by Carole Goldman, a waitress who admired Hart's intelligence but couldn't understand his dedication to his studies. The pizza parlor's owner, Ernie, was played by Charles Hallahan. Also seen regularly was Mrs. Nottingham as Professor Kingsfield's loyal secretary, played by Betty Harford. Appearing on later episodes of the series were Jack Manning as Dean Rutherford, Jessica Salem as Mallison, Stanley De Santis as Gogorian, Jane Kaczmarek as Connie Lehman, Michael Tucci as Gerald Golden, Clare Kirkconnell as Rita Harriman, Andrea Millan as Laura, Penny Johnson as Vivian, Lainie Kazan as Rose Samuels, Peter Nelson as Tom Ford, and Diana Douglas as Professor Tyler. *The Paper Chase* was based on a novel by John Jay Osborne, Jr., which had been made into a film in 1973. The final show of the last 36 episodes that were produced by the Showtime network in the 1980s was titled "The Graduation."

PARKER, FESS (FESS ELISHA PARKER JR. 1925–)

Before he became famous as Davy Crockett on the Walt Disney Studio's television adventures, Fess Parker, who was born in Fort Worth, Texas, played small roles in such films as *Untamed Frontier* (1952), *Springfield Rifle* (1952), *Them!* (1954), and was a regular on the ANNIE OAKLEY TV series (1954). Parker was a college athlete and studied drama before embarking upon a career in show business when he graduated. The popularity of the *Davy Crockett* TV series led to a starring role as Crockett in the Disney feature film *Davy Crockett and the River Pirates* (1956). In addition to playing Crockett, Parker was also seen in the films *The Great Locomotive Chase* (1956), *Westward Ho the Wagons!* (1956), *Old Yeller* (1957), *The Light in the Forest* (1958), *Alias Jesse James* (1959), *The Hangman* (1959), *The Jayhawkers!* (1959), and *Hell Is for Heroes* (1962). In 1962, Parker was featured in the TV film version of *Mr. Smith Goes to Washington,* and in 1964, he starred on the TV series DANIEL BOONE and became as identified with that character as he had been with Davy Crockett. Parker also guest-starred on such TV series as DRAGNET, DEATH VALLEY DAYS, and *The* ANDY WILLIAMS SHOW. After *Daniel Boone* left the air, Parker retired from acting and went into real estate.

PARKS, BERT (BERT JACOBSON 1914–1992)

Born in Atlanta, Georgia, Bert Parks, who is perhaps best known for hosting the annual Miss America contest, was a radio announcer before he entered television as the host of the game show *Party Line* in 1947. Parks subsequently hosted an impressive number of television game shows, including BREAK THE BANK, *The Big Payoff, Double or Nothing, Balance Your Budget* (1952–53), *Two in Love* (1954), *Giant Step* (1956–57), *Hold That Note* (1957), MASQUERADE PARTY, *County Fair* (1958–59), *Bid 'n Buy* (1958), and *Yours for a Song* (1961–62). Parks also hosted the *Circus* (1971) TV series and appeared in the film *Shining Star* (1975) and played himself in the film *The Freshman* (1990). Over the years, Parks made guest-starring appearances on such series as HONEY WEST, *The* JACKIE GLEASON SHOW, ELLERY QUEEN, *The* BIONIC WOMAN, W.K.R.P. IN CINCINNATI, ROSEANNE, and NIGHT COURT.

PARTRIDGE FAMILY, THE

Sept. 1970–June 1973	ABC	Fri. 8:30–9 P.M.
June 1973–Aug. 1974	ABC	Sat. 8–8:30 P.M.

Even though it was on the air for just four years, *The Partridge Family* situation comedy series is among television's best-remembered programs. The series, which was loosely based on the real-life experiences of a popular singing family called the Cowsills, was about a widowed suburban mother of six who, at her children's urging, records a song with them in their garage. The song, titled "I Think I Love You" (which actually became a real-life hit) is sold to a record company and is a surprise hit. The Partridge family then sets off in a wildly painted old school bus to perform all across the country.

The weekly episodes of the series depicted the family's adventures on the road as rock and roll performers, as well as in their California home. The widow, Shirley Partridge, was played by Academy Award–winning actress, Shirley JONES, and her talented children: Keith, played by

The Partridge Family: (top) Susan Dey (Laurie), David Cassidy (Keith), Shirley Jones (Shirley), (middle) Susan Crough (Tracy), James Gelbwaks (Christopher), Danny Bonaduce (Danny), and (bottom) David Madden (Reuben Kinkaid) (Author's collection)

David Cassidy, who became a teenage heartthrob because of the series' success; Laurie, played by Susan Dey; Danny, played by Danny Bonaduce; Christopher, played by James Gelbwaks, and then by Brian Forster, and Tracy, played by Susan Crough. The family's child-hating agent, Reuben Kinkaid, was played by David Madden. During the 1973–74 season, a neighbor of the Partridge family, Ricky Stevens, joined the family at the microphone. The 96 episodes were produced by Bob Claver. In 1974, the same year the original series was canceled, an animated cartoon version of *The Partridge Family* surfaced and remained on the air for one year.

PARTY OF FIVE

Sept. 1994–Dec. 1994	FOX	Mon. 9–10 P.M.
Dec. 1994–Mar. 1995	FOX	Wed. 9–10 P.M.
June 1995–Apr. 1997	FOX	Wed. 9–10 P.M.
Aug. 1997–May 1999	FOX	Wed. 9–10 P.M.

When their parents were killed in an accident, the five Salinger children, who live in San Francisco, do everything they can to keep their family together. The eldest son, Charlie, played by Matthew Fox, was appointed legal guardian of the younger children, and he works as a bartender at Salinger's restaurant, which had been owned by his father, to support his siblings. Bailey was played by Scott Wolf, Julia was played by Neve Campbell, Claudia, was played by Lacey Chabert, and Owen, originally was played by Brandon and Taylor Porter, and then by Jacob Smith. Charlie eventually hired Kirsten Bennett, who was a graduate student in child psychology, to be the younger children's nanny. Kate, Bailey's girlfriend, was played by Jennifer Blanc, Claudia's violin teacher, Ross, was played by Mitchell Anderson, Jill was played by Megan Ward, Artie was played by Michael Shulman, Julia's boyfriend, Justin, was played by Michael Goorjian, Sarah was played by Jennifer Love Hewitt, and the Salinger restaurant's manager, Joe, was played by Tom Mason. *Party of Five* was created by Christopher Keyser and Amy Lippman.

PASSWORD (AKA *PASSWORD PLUS* & *SUPER PASSWORD*)

Jan. 1962–Sept. 1962	CBS	Tues. 8–8:30 P.M.
Sept. 1962–Mar. 1963	CBS	Sun. 6:30–7 P.M.
Mar. 1963–Sept. 1963	CBS	Mon. 10–10:30 P.M.
Sept. 1963–Sept. 1964	CBS	Thurs. 7:30–8 P.M.
Sept. 1964–Sept. 1965	CBS	Thurs. 9–9:30 P.M.
Apr. 1967–May 1967	CBS	Mon. 10–10:30 P.M.
1967–1969	Syndicated	Various times
Apr. 1971–Jun. 1975	ABC	Various times
Jan. 1979–Mar. 1982	NBC	Various times
Sept. 1984–Mar. 1989	NBC	Various times

Over a period of 28 years, *Password* was one of television's most popular quiz shows. Hosted for most of its years by Allen LUDDEN, *Password* pitted two teams against each other. One of the two-member team players was a guest celebrity, and the other a viewer producers had selected. One of the team was shown a "password," and he or she had to use one-word clues to have the team member guess the password. If the password was guessed with just one clue, they won the most points for their team, and less as more than one clue was given. The first team to score 25 points won the game and proceeded to the "lightning round," where a player won $50 for each word he or she could identify in 60 seconds.

Mark GOODSON and Bill TODMAN were the producers of the series, which was seen on both prime-time and daytime hours at different times. In 1979, when the series was seen on NBC's daytime schedule, it was titled *Password Plus.* The two teams no longer played for points, but for money that they won not by guessing the passwords, but by guessing a second word or phrase suggested by each of the passwords.

Allen LUDDEN remained as the host of series until he suffered a heart attack in 1980. He was replaced by Tom Kennedy. In 1984, the series returned to NBC, hosted by Bert Convy, as *Super Password,* and remained on the air until 1989. One well-publicized side note concerning this series involved one contestant who was arrested after winning $58,600 when he was identified by a viewer who recognized him as a fugitive from an insurance fraud case.

PATTY DUKE SHOW, THE

Sept. 1963–Aug. 1966   ABC   Wed. 8–8:30 P.M.

Teenage actress Patty DUKE, who had won an Academy Award for her performance in *The Miracle Worker* in 1962, had the dual role of cousins, Patty and Cathy Lane, on a half-hour weekly situation comedy series *The Patty Duke Show*, which made its TV debut in 1963. The series also starred William Schallert as Patty's ever-patient, magazine editor father, Martin Lane. The cousins couldn't have been more different. Patty was a gum-chewing teenager who loved to listen to Paul Anka records and have slumber parties with her girlfriends. Patty's cousin, Cathy, was a Scottish girl who had arrived in the United States to live with her Uncle Martin, and spoke with a Scottish burr and played the bagpipes. Because they looked so much alike, the cousins enjoyed confusing everyone in their Brooklyn Heights neighborhood by switching identities every now and then. Even Patty's father and mother, Natalie, played by Jean Byron, and her younger brother, Ross, played by Paul O'Keefe, were fooled by the girls' exchange of identities. The girls especially enjoyed teasing Patty's boyfriend, Richard Harrison, played by Eddie Applegate, about who was who. Also seen on the series on occasion were John McGiver as Martin Lane's boss, J. R. Castle; Kitty Sullivan, as Patty's enemy, Sue Ellen Turner; Skip Hinnant as Cathy's occasional boyfriend,

The Patty Duke Show: (from left) Jean Byron (Natalie Lane), Patty Duke (Patty and Cathy Lane), William Schallert (Martin Lane), and Paul O'Keefe (Ross Lane) (Author's collection)

Ted; Alberta Grant as the girls' friend, Maggie; Robyn Miller as Roz; and Kelly Wood as Gloria.

PAUL WINCHELL-JERRY MAHONEY SHOW, THE (AKA *THE BIGELOW SHOW, THE SPEIDEL SHOW, THE PAUL WINCHELL SHOW, WINCHELL AND MAHONEY, CARTOONIES, WINCHELL AND MAHONEY TIME*)

Sept. 1950– June 1953	NBC	Mon. 8–8:30 P.M.
Aug. 1953– May 1954	NBC	Sun. 7–7:30 P.M.
Nov. 1954– Feb. 1956	NBC	Sat. 10:30–11 A.M.
Sept. 1957– Apr. 1961	ABC	Sun. 5–5:30 P.M.
Apr. 1963– Sept. 1963	ABC	Sat. 12–12:30 P.M.
1965	Syndicated	Mon.–Fri. Mornings, various times

Ventriloquist Paul Winchell and his dummy, Jerry Mahoney, were featured on several shows that were produced with younger viewers in mind from television's earliest days in the 1950s until well into the 1960s. Winchell's first TV show presented a variety of songs and comedy and featured Dorothy Claire, announcer Jimmy Blaine, and a very young comedienne named Carol BURNETT in the regular cast. The main feature of the show was the conversations Winchell had with his wisecracking dummy, Jerry Mahoney. Winchell also introduced a second dummy, a thick-headed bumpkin named Knucklehead Smiff, on this show. Winchell's second regular TV series featured films, games, contests, and direct conversations with young viewers at home. Winchell's third regular series featured all the ingredients of his former programs, and introduced a comedian named Frank Fontaine. The show's opening and closing theme songs, "Scottie-wattie-doo-doo" and "Friends We'll Always Be," became well known to Winchell's many fans. Paul Winchell's subsequent syndicated programs followed the same format as his previously successful shows. Other performers who appeared in various Winchell/Mahoney shows were Diane Sinclair, Ken Spaulding, Mary Ellen Terry, Margaret Hamilton, and the John Gart Orchestra.

PEE-WEE'S PLAYHOUSE

Sept. 1986–Sept. 1988 CBS   Sat. 10–10:30 A.M.
Sept. 1988–July 1991   CBS   Sat. 11:30 A.M.–12 P.M.

Paul REUBENS, who became known as the comic character with a high-pitched, nasal voice and a bow tie, Pee-wee HERMAN, was the host of a children's series called *Pee-wee's Playhouse*, which was an odd, almost surreal, live-action show that featured talking furniture, puppets, and robots as well as live action, special effects, visits by celebrities, and vintage cartoons. Appearing with Pee-wee on the show were Lynne Stewart as Miss Yvonne, Johann

Carlo as Dixie, Gilbert Lewis and William Marshall as King Cartoon, Gregory Harrison as Conky the Robot, S. Epatha Merkerson as Reba, John Paragon as the disembodied genie head, Jambi, Shawn Weiss as Elvis, Diane Yang as Cher, Natasha Lyonne as Opal, and Wayne White, George Michael McGrath, Larry Fishburne, Suzanne Kent, Alison Mork, and Ric Heitzman as various other characters. The show remained popular with viewers the entire time it was on the air, but it was abruptly canceled by CBS when Reubens was arrested for indecent exposure at a Florida adult cinema in 1991.

PEOPLE'S CHOICE, THE

> Oct. 1955–Dec. 1955   NBC   Thurs. 8:30–9:30 P.M.
> Jan. 1956–Sept. 1958   NBC   Thurs. 9:00–9:30 P.M.

Former child film actor Jackie COOPER became one of television's earliest stars in 1955, when he appeared in the situation comedy series *The People's Choice*. Cooper played Socrates (Sock) Miller, a government naturalist who became a councilman in the town of New City, Oklahoma. Socrates was dedicated to doing the "right thing" in his community, which often got him in trouble with the town's corpulent and pompous mayor, John Peoples, played by Paul Maxey. It didn't help matters that Socrates's girlfriend was Mayor Peoples's daughter, Amanda (Mandy), played by Pat Breslin. In spite of the fact that Socrates was the focus of most episodes, the real attraction on the show was a lovable basset hound named Cleo, who was Socrates's pet. Although no one in the cast could hear her, Cleo made many comments to the TV audience about what was happening on the show, as voiced by actress Mary Jane Croft. At the end of the show's second season, Sock and Mandy were married, and Sock got a job selling homes in the town of Barkerville. Sock and Mandy were given one of the homes in Barkerville to live in, and Sock's friend, the freeloading Rollo, played by Dick Wesson, had a room in their home. Also featured on the series were Margaret Irving as Socrates's Aunt Gus, Leonid Kinskey as Pierre, and John Stephenson as Roger Cratcher.

PEOPLE'S COURT, THE

> 1981–1993   Syndicated   Various times and stations
> 1997–present   Syndicated   Various times and stations

This half-hour, syndicated series, which was usually seen during the daytime hours, featured Judge Joseph A. Wapner, a retired judge of the California Superior Court. Judge Wapner sat in judgment on cases that involved domestic and small claims matters. The parties who appeared on the program agreed to be bound by Judge Wapner's rulings and could recover up to $1,500, with the defender receiving $25, and a successful defendant would split $500 with the plaintiff. The producers of the show were diligent in bringing real cases before Judge Wapner. Doug Llewelyn hosted the show and interviewed the liti-

gants at the end of their case. Rusty Burrell was Judge Wapner's longtime bailiff. In 1997, former New York City mayor Ed Koch became the show's judge, and Carol Martin became the show's host. Harvey Levin, who was also the show's coexecutive producer, interviewed litigants after their cases had been heard, and Josephine Ann Longobordi was the bailiff. When Ed Koch left the show, the series subsequently featured Judge Jerry Sheindlin, the husband of Judge Judy (Judith Sheindlin), who had a similar courtroom show on the air.

PERKINS, MARLIN (ROBERT MARLIN PERKINS 1900–1986)

Zoologist Marlin Perkins, who had two successful television shows about animals, began his zoology studies in 1921. While he was working as the curator for Chicago's Lincoln Park and the St. Louis Forest Park zoos, Perkins began broadcasting his observations about animals over local Chicago radio station WBKB. In 1950, television executives at NBC decided that a show about animals and zoos might prove popular with young people and hired Perkins to host a series called ZOO PARADE. The show, cohosted by Jim Hurlbut, became a Sunday afternoon hit, and remained on the air for seven seasons. A second successful series, *Mutual of Omaha's Wild Kingdom*, also hosted by Perkins, focused on the animals of Africa and India and was filmed on location. Reruns of *Wild Kingdom* can still be seen in syndication and on PBS stations. Perkins remained active in television until shortly before his death at the age of 86.

PERRY COMO SHOW, THE (AKA *THE CHESTERFIELD SUPPER CLUB* & *THE KRAFT MUSIC HALL*)

> | Dec. 1948–Jan. 1949 | NBC | Fri. 7–7:15 P.M. |
> |---|---|---|
> | Jan. 1949–June 1949 | NBC | Fri. 11–11:15 P.M. |
> | Oct. 1949–June 1950 | NBC | Sun. 8–8:30 P.M. |
> | Oct. 1950–June 1955 | CBS | Mon./Wed./Fri. 7:45–8 P.M. |
> | Sept. 1955–June 1959 | NBC | Sat. 8–9 P.M. |
> | Sept. 1959–June 1963 | NBC | Wed. 9–10 P.M. |

Singer Perry COMO was one of the first major performers to venture into television in the late 1940s. Como, who was one of show business's most successful entertainers in the late 1940s, appeared on a TV version of his hit radio show, *The Chesterfield Supper Club*, which was heard for 15 minutes every Friday evening at 7 P.M. The show was expanded to three nights a week in 1949 and was heard in the early evening hours and then at 11 P.M. The show featured Como singing his hit recordings as well as standard tunes, and featured the Fontane Sisters (Marge, Bea, and Geri), the Ray Charles Singers, the Louis Da Pron Dancers, the Peter Gennaro Dancers, and the Mitchell Ayres Orchestra. Guests included Nat "King" Cole, Burl Ives, and Patti Page. In 1950, Como left NBC and went to CBS, where he starred on a 15-minute, three-times-a-week show and then in 1955, he was seen on a prime-time show, *The Perry*

Como Show, on Saturday nights, once again on NBC. Perry's theme song, "Dream Along with Me," became well known to millions of viewers. During the series' run, Kraft took over its sponsorship and announcer Frank Gallop assumed a regular role on the show. In addition to songs and staged musical numbers, Como's *Kraft Music Hall* also featured comedy skits with "The Kraft Music Hall Players," Kaye Ballad, Don ADAMS, Sandy Stewart, Jack Duffy, Paul Lynde, and Pierre Olaf. Among the many announcers, other than Frank Gallop, featured on Como's shows were Martin Block, Durward Kirby, Dick Stark, and, during its Kraft years, Ed Herlihy. Como's regular weekly shows ended in 1963, but the singer, remained popular with viewers, was seen on television every five or six weeks on various Kraft Music Hall specials from 1963 until 1967, and less frequently on specials after 1967. He died in 2001.

PERRY MASON

Sept. 1957–Sept. 1962	CBS	Sat. 7:30–8:30 P.M.
Sept. 1962–Sept. 1963	CBS	Thurs. 8–9 P.M.
Sept. 1963–Sept. 1964	CBS	Thurs. 9–10 P.M.
Sept. 1964–Sept. 1965	CBS	Thurs. 8–9 P.M.
Sept. 1965–Sept. 1966	CBS	Sun. 9–10 P.M.
Sept. 1973–Jan. 1974	CBS	Sun. 7:30–8:30 P.M.

Mystery writer Erle Stanley Gardner's famous defense attorney, Perry Mason, who had been heard on a popular radio program from 1943 through 1955, arrived on television in 1957 and became one of that medium's most popular programs. For nine years, from 1957 until 1966, for a brief time in 1973, and then as numerous feature-length TV films, *Perry Mason* had a loyal following. A good deal of the show's success was due to the commanding presence of the actor who played Perry Mason, Raymond BURR. A large, burly man, Burr had a sturdy appearance and a confident, calm manner that made people believe he could win every case he argued in court, as indeed he did on this series. Mainly a courtroom drama, Mason, with his colleagues, secretary Della Street, played by Barbara Hale, and private investigator Paul Drake, played by William Hopper, were thorns in the side of D. A. Hamilton Burger, played by William Talman, who was usually thwarted by the team who invariably came up with an irrefutable defense for their client just as the trial was ending. At the end of every *Perry Mason* episode, Perry, Della, and Paul always recapped just how they had managed to solve the case and clear their client. Other regular characters on the series were Police Lt. Arthur Tragg, played by Ray Collins; David Gideon, played by Karl Held; Lt. Anderson, played by Wesley Lau; Lt. Steve Drumm, played by Richard Anderson; Sgt. Brice, played by Lee Miller; and Terrance Clay, played by Dan Tobin.

Over the nine-year period the series was aired, Mason lost only one case, in 1963, when his client did not reveal information that would have exonerated her. By that time, Raymond Burr had had enough of playing Mason and went on to star in another successful series, *IRONSIDE*. In 1973, *Perry Mason* was revived with an entirely new cast that included Monte Markham as Mason, Sharon Acker as Della Street, Albert Stratton as Paul Drake, Dane Clark as Lt. Tragg, and Harry Guardino as Hamilton Burger. The revival was not successful and was canceled before it had completed one full season. In 1985, 12 years after Raymond Burr had quit the series, he returned as Perry Mason in a reunion TV film, *Perry Mason Returns,* which also starred Barbara Hale re-creating her role of Della Street. This led to two or three TV *Perry Mason* films a year, that starred Burr and Hale, which continued to be made until 1993, and ended shortly before Burr passed away of kidney failure. These TV films included *Perry Mason Returns* (1985), *The Case of the Shooting Star* (1986), *The Case of the Notorious Nun* (1986), *The Case of the Lost Love* (1987), *The Case of the Sinister Spirit* (1987), *The Case of the Murdered Madam* (1987), *The Case of the Scandalous Scoundrel* (1987), *The Case of the Avenging Ace* (1988), *The Case of the Lady in the Lake* (1988), *The Case of the Lethal Lesson* (1989), *The Case of the Musical Murder* (1989), *The Case of the All-Star Assassin* (1989), *The Case of the Poisoned Pen* (1990), *The Case of the Desperate Deception* (1990), *The Case of the Silenced Singer* (1990), *The Case of the Defiant Daughter* (1990), *The Case of the Ruthless Reporter* (1991), *The Case of the Maligned Mobster* (1991), *The Case of the Glass Coffin* (1991), *The Case of the Fatal Fashion* (1991), *The Case of the Posthumous Painter* (1992), *The Case of the Reckless Romeo* (1992), *The Case of the Heartbroken Bride* (1992), *The Case of the Skin-Deep Scandal* (1993), *The Case of the Telltale Talk Show Host* (1993), and *The Case of the Killer Kiss* (1993).

PERSON TO PERSON

Oct. 1953–June 1959	CBS	Fri. 10:30–11 P.M.
Oct. 1959–Sept. 1960	CBS	Fri. 10:30–11 P.M.
Sept. 1960–Dec. 1960	CBS	Thurs. 10–10:30 P.M.
June 1961–Sept. 1961	CBS	Fri. 10:30–11 P.M.

The celebrated newscaster Edward R. MURROW had a very popular interview show on the air in the mid-to-late 1950s called *Person to Person.* Murrow conducted his interviews live as he sat in a comfortable easy chair in the CBS studios, whereas the famous people he interviewed were televised from their homes. The celebrities came from the worlds of show business, politics, literature, and science and included such well-known people as Marilyn Monroe and Zsa Zsa Gabor; politicians Sam Rayburn, Fidel Castro, Senator John F. Kennedy, and Tom Dewey; author John Steinbeck; A. C. Nielsen of the TV Nielsen Ratings company; conductor Leopold Stokowski and his heiress wife, Gloria Vanderbilt; baseball player Roy Campanella; and many others. In 1959, Murrow began to curb his television activities and Charles Collingswood became the show's new host. Collingswood decided to venture out of the studio, and many of the interviews he conducted were filmed on location all over the world. *Person to Person* was produced by Murrow, with Jesse Zousmer and John Aaron.

PETE AND GLADYS

Sept. 1960–Sept. 1962   CBS   Mon. 8–8:30 P.M.

On one of TV's first spin-off series, Pete and Gladys were characters who had originally been introduced on the popular *DECEMBER BRIDE* situation comedy series. Although the sardonic Pete was seen on that series, his wife, Gladys, remained anonymous until she emerged as an on-camera character on the *Pete and Gladys* program. Pete and Gladys Porter were played by Henry (Harry) Morgan and Cara Williams. Also featured on the series was veteran character actress Verna Felton, who played the same character she had played on *December Bride,* Hilda Crocker. The way Cranky Pete often made sarcastic remarks made about his sincere and ingenuous, if scatterbrained, wife, Gladys, was often the basis of the show's comedy. Also seen on the series were Gale Gordon as Gladys's Uncle Paul; Peter Leeds and Shirley Mitchell as Pete and Gladys's next-door neighbors, George and Janet Colton; Frances Rafferty, who had been one of the stars of *December Bride,* as an entirely different character named Nancy, who was a friend of Gladys; and Bill Hinnant as Gladys's nephew, Bruce, who lived with the Porters and attended a nearby college. Also seen on the series at various times were Barbara Stuart as Alice; Ernest Truex as Pop; Alvy Moore as Howie; Barry Kelley as Pete's boss, Mr. Slocum; Helen Kleeb, and then Lurene Tuttle as his wife; and Mina Kolb and Joe Mantell as Peggy and Ernie Briggs. Park Levy was the series' executive producer.

PETER GUNN

Sept. 1958–Sept. 1960   NBC   Mon. 9–9:30 P.M.
Oct. 1960–Sept. 1961   ABC   Mon. 10:30–11 P.M.

Detective/adventure series were very popular on television in the late 1950s to early 1960s, and *Peter Gunn,* produced by Blake Edwards, was one of the viewers' favorite shows during those years. The title character of the *Peter Gunn* series was a handsome, debonair private detective, played by film star Craig STEVENS, who was very popular with the ladies. When he wasn't trying to solve a case for a client, Gunn spent a lot of time at a nightclub called Mother's, where his girlfriend, Edie Hart, played by Lola Albright, was a featured singer. Also seen regularly on the series were Herschel Bernardi as police Lt. Jacoby, and Hope Emerson, and then Minerva Urecal, as the owner of Mother's. Original jazz music, written especially for the show by Henry Mancini, spawned two successful, best-selling record albums, "The Music From Peter Gunn," and "More Music From Peter Gunn."

PETTICOAT JUNCTION

Sept. 1963–Sept. 1964   CBS   Tues. 9–9:30 P.M.
Sept. 1964–Aug. 1967   CBS   Tues. 9:30–10 P.M.
Sept. 1967–Sept. 1970   CBS   Sat. 9:30–10 P.M.

The rural community of Hooterville was the setting for the situation comedy series *Petticoat Junction,* which

Peter Gunn: Craig Stevens and Lola Albright (Author's collection)

starred Bea BENADERET as Kate Bradley, who owned the Shady Rest Hotel and who had three beautiful and buxom daughters: Billie Jo Bradley, played by Jeannine Riley (1963–65), Gunilla Hutton (1965–66), and then Meredith MacRae (1966–70); Bobby Jo Bradley, played by Pat Woodell (1963–65), and then Lori Saunders (1965–70); and Betty Jo Bradley, played by Linda Kaye (née Henning). Helping Kate and her daughters run their small country hotel was Kate's Uncle Joe Carson, played by veteran film character actor Edgar Buchanan. The Bradleys' nemesis, Homer Bedloe, played by Charles Lane, was the vice president of the C. F. & W. Railroad, who was determined to put Kate out of business by closing down the steam-driven train that ran through Hooterville and scrap its only engine, the Cannonball, putting its two engineers, Charlie Pratt and Floyd Smoot, played by Smiley Burnette and Rufe Davis, out of jobs. In 1965, a spin-off of *Petticoat Junction,* a series called GREEN ACRES, surfaced, and two characters from that series frequently turned up on *Petticoat Junction*—farmer Newt Kelly, played by Kay E. Kuter, and Eb Dawson, played by Tom Lester. During the 1966–67 season, a pilot named Steve Elliott, played by Mike Minor, crashed his airplane outside Hooterville, was nursed back to health by the Bradleys, and eventually married Betty Jo Bradley.

Other characters regularly seen over the years were Homer Bedloe, played by Charles Lane; Sam Drucker,

Petticoat Junction (Author's collection)

played by Frank Cady; Norman Curtis, played by Roy Roberts; Selma Plout, played by Virginia Sale; and then by Elvia Allman; Henrietta Plout, played by Susan Walther, and then by Lynette Winter; Dr. Barton Stuart, played by Regis Toomey; Wendell Gibbs, played by Byron Foulger; Bert Smedley, played by Paul Hartman; Kathy Jo Elliott, played by Elna Hubbell; Jeff Powers, played by Geoff Edwards; and Orrin Pike, played by Jonathan Daly.

Petticoat Junction suffered a severe blow when the series' star, Bea Benaderet, died suddenly during the 1968–69 season. To fill the void created by the loss of this character, June Lockhart joined the cast as Dr. Janet Craig, who became Hooterville's physician when the town's previous doctor, Dr. Stuart, retired. The absence of Bea Benaderet proved to be fatal to the series, and *Petticoat Junction* was canceled one year later. Paul Henning, who had previously been responsible for creating the successful BEVERLY HILL-BILLIES series, created and was the executive producer of *Petticoat Junction*, which was produced by Dick Wesson.

PEYTON PLACE

Sept. 1964–June 1965	ABC	Tues./Thurs. 9:30–10 P.M.
June 1965–Oct. 1965	ABC	Tues./Fri. 9:30–10 P.M.
Nov. 1965–Aug. 1966	ABC	Mon./Tues./Thurs. 9:30–10 P.M.
Sept. 1966–Jan. 1967	ABC	Mon./Wed. 9:30–10 P.M.
June 1967–Aug. 1967	ABC	Mon./Tues. 9:30–10 P.M.
Sept. 1967–Sept. 1968	ABC	Mon./Thurs. 9:30–10 P.M.
Sept. 1968–Jan. 1969	ABC	Mon. 9–9:30 P.M. Wed. 8:30–9 P.M.
Feb. 1969–June 1969	ABC	Mon. 9–9:30 P.M.

For five years, millions of Americans did not miss a single episode of TV's first successful evening soap opera, *Peyton Place*. Like Grace Metalious's best-selling book and the subsequent hit feature film, the TV version of *Peyton Place* depicted the "hidden" life of a supposedly typical, respectable-looking, small New England town. The TV series made its debut in 1964 and soon became one of the country's most talked-about new programs.

On the surface, everything in Peyton Place seemed dull and ordinary, but what was going on behind closed doors would shock even the most open-minded viewer.

Illegitimate births, incest, teenage sex, and the like were common occurrences in the town, and viewers couldn't get enough of the series.

When the program began, the central characters included Constance Mackenzie/Carson, played by Dorothy Malone, who owned the town's bookstore. Constance had given birth to a girl out of wedlock, and the girl, Allison, played by Mia Farrow, was 18 years old when the series began. In 1965, Constance finally married Allison's father, Elliott Carson, played by Tim O'Connor. Other major characters on the series were Dr. Michael Rossi, played by Ed Nelson, whom viewers always hoped Constance would marry; the town's aging patriarch, Martin Peyton, played by George Macready, and for a while Wilfred Hyde-White during Macready's illness, a character that was not seen when the series first went on the air, but was often talked about and who became an important character as the series progressed; Peyton's grandson, Rodney Harrington, played by Ryan O'Neal, with whom Allison was in love; Steven Cord, played by James Douglas, a young man with a questionable past; Betty Anderson, played by Barbara Parkins, who tricked Rodney into marriage and then later married Steven Cord; Rita Jacks, played by Patricia Morrow, from the "other side of the tracks" who, much to the distress of the Peyton/Harrington clan, married Norman Harrington, played by Christopher Connelly, Rodney's younger brother; Rita's mother, long-suffering Ada Jacks, played by Evelyn Scott, who owned the town saloon; Matthew Swain, played by Warner Anderson, who was the editor of the town's newspaper, *The Clarion;* Betty Anderson's mother, Julie, played by Kasey Rogers; and Steven Cord's mother, Hannah Cord, played by Ruth Warrick.

Also appearing on the series in important roles during the five-year period the series was on the air were Henry Beckman as Betty's father, George; Paul Langton as Rodney and Norman's father, Leslie Harrington; Kent Smith as Dr. Robert Morton; Richard Evans as Paul Hanley, Frank Ferguson as Eli Carson; Erin O'Brien-Moore as Nurse Choate; Mariette Hartley as Dr. Claire Morton; Leslie Nielsen as Dr. Vincent Markham; William Smithers as David Shuster; Gail Kobe as Doris Schuster; Kimberly Beck as Kim Schuster; Patrick Whyte as lawyer Theodore Dowell; Lee Grant as Stella Chernak; Don Quine as Joe Chernak; Bruce Gordon as Gus Chernak; David Canary as Dr. Russ Gehring; John Kerr as D.A. John Fowler; Joan Blackman as his wife, Marion; Lana Wood as Sandy Webber; Gary Haynes as Chris Webber; Stephen Oliver as Lee Webber; Susan Oliver as Ann Howard; Leigh Taylor-Young as Rachel Welles; John Kellogg as Jack Chandler; Gena Rowlands as Adrienne Van Leyden; Dan Duryea as Rita Jack's father, Eddie; Elizabeth "Tippy" Walker as Carolyn Russell; Joe Maross as Fred Russell; Barbara Rush as Marsha Russell; Bob Hogan as the randy Rev. Tom Winter; Diana Hyland as Susan Winter; Percy Rodriguez as Dr. Harry Miles; Glynn Turman as Lew Miles; Joyce Jillson as Jill Smith; and Michael Christian as Dr. Rossi's brother, Joe.

Even though *Peyton Place* made Mia Farrow a star, she decided to leave the series early in its run after two seasons had been completed. Thousands of letters of protest regarding her departure were written to the series' producers demanding to know what had happened to her. In 1965, Dorothy Malone became ill, and she was replaced, temporarily, by Lola Albright.

In all, 514 episodes of *Peyton Place* were filmed. It was produced for 20th Century Fox Television by Paul Monash. In 1972, a daytime serial version of *Peyton Place* called *The Return to Peyton Place* surfaced. This series, which ran from April 1972 until January 1974, featured Kathy Glass, Bettye Ackerman, Susan Brown, Warren Stevens, Guy Stockwell, Joe Gallison, Mary K. Wells, Lawrence Casey, Yale Summers, Ron Russell, Patricia Morrow, Julie Parish, Lynn Loring, Evelyn Scott (re-creating her role as Ada Jacks), John Levin, John Hoyt, Frank Ferguson (from the original cast), Dina Fantini, and Ben Andrews, among others, in the cast.

PHIL DONAHUE SHOW, THE
1970–1996   Syndicated   Various times and stations

Talk show host Phil DONAHUE's first chat program was a local show that originated in Dayton, Ohio, in 1967. By 1970, Donahue had a nationally syndicated series and his TV audience grew steadily larger. In 1977, Donahue moved his show from Dayton to Chicago, and the program became known simply as *Donahue.* Donahue's hour-long show usually centered on a single topic, and he skillfully involved his studio audience in the program, which made his show different from the other talk shows at the time. Later, talk show hostess Oprah WINFREY credited Donahue with giving her the format of audience involvement that certainly contributed to her success. In 1985, Donahue moved his show from Chicago to New York City, where he felt he would get a wider variety of guests. One of the most memorable programs of his first year in New York was a show in which he conducted a "citizens' summit," with hookups between the United States and the U.S.S.R., during which citizens of both countries could ask one another questions. In 1987, Donahue gained a great deal of publicity when he donned women's clothing on a show that was concerned with men who enjoyed dressing in ladies' clothes. By 1990, other talk shows began to attract larger audiences than Donahue, and the subjects covered became increasingly more sensational in an attempt to lure viewers back to his show. During this time such topics as "Husbands Learn How to Become Exotic Dancers," "Multiple Personalities," "Country Music Female Impersonators," "Penthouse Pets," and "Teenage Prostitutes" were presented, but the writing was already on the wall, and by 1996, Donahue's ratings had declined sufficiently to warrant the show's cancellation.

PHIL SILVERS SHOW, THE (AKA *YOU'LL NEVER GET RICH & SERGEANT BILKO*)
Sept. 1955–Oct. 1955   CBS   Tues. 8:30–9 P.M.

| Nov. 1955–Feb. 1958 | CBS | Tues. 8–8:30 P.M. |
| Feb. 1958–Sept. 1959 | CBS | Fri. 9–9:30 P.M. |

Fast-talking comedian Phil SILVERS displayed his comedic talents as the star of a TV situation comedy series originally called *You'll Never Get Rich,* and later, *The Phil Silvers Show,* in 1955. The series, was about a slick, fast-talking, and opportunistic army master sergeant named Ernie Bilko stationed in a fictional army post in Kansas named Fort Baxter. With little to do at the peacetime army post, Bilko spent most of his time gambling, thinking up various money-making schemes, and wiggling out of the trouble that he got into with his superior at the base, Col. John Hall, played by Paul Ford. Bilko's schemes rubbed off on his men, who, like Bilko, were usually pulling the wool over the eyes of the other soldiers at Fort Baxter. Bilko's object of affection during the series' early years was WAC Sgt. Joan Hogan, played by Elisabeth Fraser, who worked at the base's headquarters. Among the regulars on the series were Harvey Lembeck as Cpl. Rocco Barbella; Herbie Faye as Pvt. Sam Fender; Maurice Gosfield as Pvt. Dwayne Doberman; Joe E. Ross as Sgt. Rupert Ritzik; Allan Melvin as Cpl. Henshaw; Billy Sands as Pvt. Dino Parelli, Mickey Freeman as Pvt. Zimmerman; and Jimmy Little as Sgt. Grover. Other regular characters included Beatrice Pons as Sgt. Ritzik's nagging wife, Emma; Nicholas Saunders as Col. Hall's adjutant, Capt. Barker; and Hope Sansberry as Col, Hall's wife, Nell. As the series continued, Sgt. Bilko's platoon included Tige Andrews as Pvt. Gander; P. Jay Sidney as Pvt. Palmer, Walter Cartier as Pvt. Dillingham, Jack Healy as Pvt. Mullen, Bernie Fein as Pvt. Gomez; Maurice Brenner as Pvt. Fleishman, Terry Carter as Pvt. Sugarman, Ned Glass as Sgt. Andy Pendleton; and Gary Clarke as Sgt. Zewicki. Among the guest stars who made appearances on *The Phil Silvers Show* were Margaret Hamilton, who had played the Wicked Witch in *The Wizard of Oz;* Fred Gwynne, who later played Herman Munster on *The* MUNSTERS; Dick VAN DYKE; Alan ALDA (in his first major TV appearance); Dody Goodman, and Dick Cavett, among others. *You'll Never Get Rich/The Phil Silvers Show* was created by Nat Hiken.

PHILBIN, REGIS (REGIS FRANCIS XAVIER PHILBIN 1931–)

Regis Philbin, one of America's favorite talk and game show hosts, was born in New York City and attended Cardinal Hayes High School in the Bronx. The son of Italian- and Irish-American parents, Regis graduated from Notre Dame University and then began his career in show business as a stagehand at KCOP-TV in Los Angeles and eventually became a stand-up comic. In the 1960s, Philbin made appearances on such TV series as GET SMART, *The Joey Bishop Show,* and *The* BIG VALLEY. He then hosted local talk shows such as *Regis Philbin's Saturday Night in St. Louis* and *A.M. Los Angeles* in the mid-1970s, and was a regular on the TV series *The Neighbors* (1975) and *Almost Anything Goes* (1975).

In 1989, Philbin became the star of LIVE WITH REGIS AND KATHIE LEE (now *Live with Regis and Kelly*), which also starred Kathie Lee GIFFORD. The show became one of daytime TV's most successful early morning talk programs. In summer 2000, when Kathie Lee decided to leave the show, Regis carried on alone. The new *Live with Regis* enjoyed even greater success with him as sole host, with various guest-star cohosts that frequently included his wife, Joy Senese. In addition to his five-day-a-week talk show, Philbin has also been active as a guest star on such TV series as MAD ABOUT YOU, *The* FRESH PRINCE OF BEL-AIR, SPIN CITY, DIAGNOSIS MURDER, CAROLINE IN THE CITY, and *The* SIMPSONS, and in such films as *Funny About Love* (1990), *Night and the City* (1992), *The Emperor's New Clothes* (1993, as the Emperor), *Perry Mason: The Case of the Telltale Talk Show Host* (1993), and others, usually playing himself. In 1999, at age 65, Philbin became the host of one of the most successful quiz programs in television's history, WHO WANTS TO BE A MILLIONAIRE.

PHILCO TELEVISION PLAYHOUSE, THE (AKA THE PHILCO/GOODYEAR TELEVISION PLAYHOUSE)

| Oct. 1948–Oct. 1955 | NBC | Sun. 9–10 P.M. |

The Philco Television Playhouse, which featured prominent actors in live, weekly, hour-long dramas, was one of television's most popular early programs. In the late 1940s to early 1950s, live drama programs such as STUDIO ONE, GOODYEAR TV PLAYHOUSE and PLAYHOUSE 90 had large audiences, and *The Philco Television Playhouse,* sponsored by the Philco Electronics Company, was considered one of the best shows of its type on the air. Hosted by Bert Lytel during its first year, the show presented TV adaptations of famous novels, short stories, and plays, such as Rostand's *Cyrano de Bergerac* with José Ferrer (later made into a feature-length film), *Dinner at Eight* with Peggy Wood and Dennis King, and *Counselor at Law* with Paul Muni. Over the next six years, the series continued to present outstanding live television dramas that included *October Story* with Julie Harris and Leslie Nielsen, *Marty* with Rod Steiger and Nancy Marchand, *Wish on the Moon* with Eva Marie Saint, *The Catered Affair* with Thelma Ritter, *A Man Is Ten Feet Tall* with Sidney Poitier, Don Murray, and Martin Balsam, and many other plays. Featured on the series at various times were such popular performers as Anthony Quinn, Paul Newman, Grace Kelly, Lillian Gish, Walter Matthau, and Charlton Heston. Among the celebrated writers who wrote original plays for the series were Paddy Chayefsky, Tad Mosel, Robert Alan Arthur, Horton Foote, N. Richard Nash, J.P. Miller, Sumner Locke Elliot, David Saw, Gore Vidal, and Calder Willingham. The man behind the success of the series was a young producer named Fred Coe, who was determined to introduce new and previously untried writers and performers to his viewers, as well as showcase the work of established writers and performers.

PHILLIPS, MACKENZIE (LAURA MACKENZIE PHILLIPS 1959–)

Mackenzie Phillips, the daughter of John Phillips of the famous Mamas and the Papas singing group, was born in Alexandria, Virginia. Mackenzie made her first important appearance as an actress on the popular MARY TYLER MOORE SHOW in 1970. She subsequently was one of the many soon-to-be-famous actors that included Harrison Ford, Richard Dreyfuss, Suzanne SOMERS, Ron HOWARD, and Cindy WILLIAMS who were featured in the 1973 hit film *American Graffiti*. In 1975, Phillips became one of the stars of the situation comedy ONE DAY AT A TIME, which became one of television's most popular programs. In addition, Phillips also appeared in such films as *Rafferty and the Gold Dust Twins* (1975), as a young Eleanor Roosevelt in the TV film *Eleanor and Franklin* (1976), *More American Graffiti* (1979), and others. When *One Day at a Time* was in its third season, Phillips was arrested for cocaine possession, and her career went into a decline. In 1980, Mackenzie was fired from the series because of her unpredictable behavior, but after she went into drug rehab, she returned to the hit show in 1981. Unfortunately, her good behavior did not last, and once again she was fired from the series in 1983. After several difficult years fighting her various addictions, Mackenzie finally shook her drug habit and resumed her career, appearing on such TV series as BEVERLY HILLS, 90210, MELROSE PLACE, NYPD BLUE, CAROLINE IN THE CITY, WALKER, TEXAS RANGER, CHICAGO HOPE, and The OUTER LIMITS. For a time, Mackenzie toured with her father's group as a featured singer. In 1996, Phillips was a regular cast member on the GUIDING LIGHT daytime drama series, and she had a featured role in the film *When* in 1999.

PHYLLIS

Sept. 1975–Jan. 1977	CBS	Mon. 8:30–9 P.M.
Jan. 1977–July 1977	CBS	Sun. 8:30–9 P.M.
Aug. 1977	CBS	Tues. 8:30–9 P.M.

One of three series that were spin-offs of the popular MARY TYLER MOORE SHOW, Phyllis (the others were RHODA and LOU GRANT) starred Cloris LEACHMAN as Phyllis Lindstrom, Mary Richards's 40-something, ego-involved landlady in Minneapolis. Phyllis's husband, Lars, who had never actually been seen on the *Mary Tyler Moore Show*, but was often talked about, had died, and Phyllis and her teenage daughter, Bess, played on both series by Lisa Gerritsen, had moved to San Francisco to live with Lars's scatterbrained mother, Audrey, played by Jane Rose, and Audrey's second husband, Judge Jonathan Dexter, played by Henry Jones. Joining the cast shortly after *Phyllis* made its debut was Judge Dexter's ancient mother, Sally "Mother" Dexter, played by Judith Lowry, who soon became one of the show's most popular characters.

In San Francisco, Phyllis went to work as the inept assistant to Julie Erskine, played by Liz Torres, a commercial photographer. During the series' second season, Phyllis went to work as an administrative assistant to a member of the San Francisco Board of Supervisors, Dan Valenti, played by Carmine Caridi. One of the show's most hilarious sequences, however, involved Bess's engagement to a young man named Mark, played by Craig Wasson, who although of normal height, had parents who were midgets. Phyllis's shocked, speechless, and dazed response when she meets Mark's parents for the first time, and Mother Dexter's insistence on calling them "cute," is remembered as a classic television moment.

During a break in the production, Judith Lowry died unexpectedly, and shortly after, the series was canceled. Ed Weinstein and Stan Daniels were the show's executive producers. It was produced by MTM Enterprises, which also produced *The Mary Tyler Moore Show*.

PICKET FENCES

Sept. 1992–Mar. 1993	CBS	Fri. 10–11 P.M.
Apr. 1993–Aug. 1993	CBS	Thurs. 10–11 P.M.
Aug. 1993–July 1995	CBS	Fri. 10–11 P.M.
Dec. 1993–Mar. 1994	CBS	Fri. 12:35–1:45 A.M.
June 1994–July 1994	CBS	Thurs. 10–11 P.M.
Aug. 1995–Sept. 1995	CBS	Fri. 9–11 P.M.
Sept. 1995–Nov. 1995	CBS	Fri. 9–10 P.M.
Dec. 1995–Feb. 1996	CBS	Fri. 10–11 P.M.
June 1996	CBS	Wed. 9–10 P.M.

One of the more unusual series to arrive on television, *Picket Fences* was a quirky, hour-long serialized drama that took place in a town called Rome in Wisconsin. Although the town appeared perfectly normal, odd things happened that made it anything but typical. The main characters on the series were the Brock family, which consisted of Sheriff Jimmy Brock, played by Tom Skerritt; his wife, Dr. Jill Brock, who was the town's physician, played by Kathy Baker; and their three children, 16-year-old Kimberly, played by Holly Marie Combs, 11-year-old Matthew, played by Justin Shenkarow, and eight-year-old Zach, played by Adam Wylie. Other regular characters included Sheriff Brock's two overly enthusiastic deputies, Officers Kenny Locas and Maxine Stewart, played by Costas Mandylor and Lauren Holly; his nosey, diminutive, middle-aged receptionist, Ginny, played by Zelda Rubinstein, who, when she retired, was found frozen in her refrigerator in a later episode of the show; an eccentric medical examiner, Carter Pike, played by Kelly Connell; a pushy defense attorney named Douglas Wambaugh, played by Fyvush Finkel; the town's cantankerous old judge, Henry Bone, played by Ray Walston, in whose courtroom a great deal of the show's action took place; and the series' final mayor, Laurie Bey, played by the Academy Award–winning deaf actress Marlee Matlin.

Out-of-the-ordinary things kept occurring in the town of Rome, such as the murder of an actor who was playing the Tin Man in a community theater stage production of *The Wizard of Oz*, by an overdose of nicotine, a student bringing a severed head to class for show-and-tell; a midget riding an elephant he had brought to town to save it from its abusive handlers; a male victim of date rape; a serial bather who broke into various homes in the town, took a bath, and left rings of dirt in the tubs; a woman who killed her husband with a steamroller and blamed the killing on menopause; parents who were refused permission to freeze their son shortly before he died of leukemia; the death of a man whose fat wife rolled over him while they were in bed sleeping; and a series of murders with the bodies found in freezers, which became known as the "freezer murders," and included the murder of the town's mayor, Ed Lawson, played by Richard Masur. (It was finally discovered that the mayor's wife had done the killings.)

Although critics loved the series for its complex stories and unexpected events, and even though the series had developed a cult following, *Picket Fences* was canceled when it failed to attract a sizable enough audience to warrant its continuance after four years. One of the series' chief writers and major influences was David E. Kelley, who was also the show's executive producer.

PIERCE, DAVID HYDE (1959–)

Before playing Dr. Niles Crane on the successful television situation comedy series FRASIER, David Hyde Pierce starred in a series of less than memorable films such as *Rocket Gibraltar* (1988), *Vampire's Kiss* (1989), and *Little Man Tate* (1991), and had a regular role on the ill-fated TV series *The Powers That Be* (1992). Pierce, who has won several Emmy Awards for his portrayal of the intelligent, if out of touch, Dr. Niles Crane on *Frasier,* graduated from Yale University before he embarked upon a career as an actor. Born and raised in Saratoga Springs, New York, Pierce claims that he always wanted to be an actor, and when he graduated from Saratoga Springs High School in 1977, he was named Best Dramatic Arts Student. After a brief time working as a security guard, Pierce began getting roles in regional theater productions and in films. Hired because he looked like he could be the brother of *Frasier's* star, Kelsey GRAMMER, Pierce soon became one of the show's most popular characters. After his debut on *Frasier,* Pierce has been featured in such films as *Nixon* (1995), *A Bug's Life* (1998, as the voice of Slim), *Hercules* (1998, as the voice of Daedalus), *Wet Hot American Summer* (2000), and *Osmosis Jones* (2000), and has guest-starred on such series as CAROLINE IN THE CITY and The SIMPSONS (as the voice of Cecil Terwilliger).

PINKY LEE SHOW, THE

Jan. 1954–Aug. 1955	NBC	Mon.–Fri. 5–5:30 P.M.	
Sept. 1955–May 1956	NBC	Mon.–Fri. 5–5:30 P.M.;	
		Sat. A.M.	

Although Pinky LEE, who had been a stage and film comedian, first appeared on television in *Those Two* in 1951, a weekly musical variety series that costarred actress/singer Vivian Blaine, he become one of television's most memorable children's show hosts in 1954 in a five-days-a-week series called *The Pinky Lee Show.* Pinky spoke to children on their level, and with his funny hat and checkered costume, his lisp, and his flair for being silly and even somewhat mischievous, he was childlike himself, which endeared him to his young viewers. Each show opened with a funny song and dance that began, "Yo ho, it's me, my name is Pinky Lee," and then he told stories, played games, talked to puppets and children, and generally wildly frolicked around the studio, usually catching his staff off guard with his delightful improvising, as his studio and viewing audience of youngsters squealed with laughter. During a regular segment of the show called "Mr. and Mrs. Grumpy," Pinky, as a character named Pinky the Clown, displayed a more serious side of himself, playing a sometimes sad clown. Also appearing on the show with Pinky were Roberta Shore, Mel Konetz, Barbara Lake, Jane Howard, and Jimmy Brown.

PLAYHOUSE 90

Oct. 1956–Jan. 1960	CBS	Thurs. 9:30–11 P.M.
July 1961–Sept. 1961	CBS	Tues. 9:30–11 P.M.

Considered one of the finest programs ever presented on television, *Playhouse 90* was a drama anthology series that offered 90 minutes of outstanding drama each week, and during the 1959–60 season, a series of specials. The series had a large budget that allowed it to employ the very best writers, actors, and technology available. Over 100 mostly live plays were produced, including many of the best-remembered and critically acclaimed TV plays of the past century. Among the most notable plays presented on *Playhouse 90* were *Requiem for a Heavyweight* and *The Miracle Worker,* both of which became award-winning feature films.

Martin Manulis was the series producer, and the first play presented on the series was Rod Serling's *Forbidden Area* with a cast that included Charlton Heston, Tab Hunter, Diana Lynn, Vincent Price, and Jackie Coogan. Serling's chilling drama about a down-and-out boxer, *Requiem for a Heavyweight* with Jack Palance, Keenan Wynn, Kim Hunter, and Ed WYNN, followed. It won an Emmy Award as Best Single Program of the Season, and *Playhouse 90* won an Emmy for being Best New Series. Also seen during the series' first season were such diverse offerings as Kay Thompson's *Eloise,* with Evelyn Rudie, Ethel Barrymore, Louis Jourdan, and Miss Thompson; *So Soon to Die,* with Richard Basehart; William Gibson's award-winning *The Miracle Worker,* which was about the intellectual awakening of the deaf and mute Helen Keller, with Patty McCormack, Teresa Wright, and Burl Ives; the classic comedy *Charley's Aunt,* with Jeanette MacDonald and Art Carney; *Three Men on a Horse,* with Carol Channing and Johnny CARSON; *Child of Trouble,* with Lillian Roth; and *Without Incident* with Errol Flynn, to mention just a few.

Over the next five years, *Playhouse 90* continued to offer an impressive number of quality productions that included *The Dark Side of the Earth* with Earl Holliman and Kim Hunter; *The 80 Yard Run* with Paul Newman; *The Male Animal* with Andy GRIFFITH; *The Days of Wine and Roses* (which became a hit film), with Charles Bickford, Piper Laurie, and Cliff Robertson; Joseph Conrad's *Heart of Darkness* with Oscar Homolka and Eartha Kitt, *Face of a Hero* with Jack Lemmon; *Child of Our Time* with Maximilian Schell; Ernest Hemingway's *For Whom the Bell Tolls*, with Jason Robards, Jr., Maria Schell, Maureen Stapleton, Eli Wallach, and Broderick Crawford; Abby Mann's *Judgment at Nuremburg* with Claude Rains, Melvyn Douglas, and Maximilian Schell; *Misalliance* with Claire Bloom; *Alas, Babylon* with Dana Andrews, Don Murray, Kim Hunter, Barbara Rush, and Burt Reynolds; *Journey to the Day* with Mike Nichols; *In the Presence of Mine Enemies* with Charles Laughton, Arthur Kennedy, and Robert Redford; *Last Clear Chance* with Paul Muni; *The Helen Morgan Story* with Polly Bergen; *The Plot to Kill Stalin* with Melvyn Douglas, Oscar Homolka, Eli Wallach, E. G. Marshall, Luther Adler, and Thomas Gomez, *The Time of Your Life* with Jackie GLEASON, Betsy Palmer, and Jack KLUGMAN; and *Old Man* with Sterling Hayden, among many others. One of the series' most frequent directors was John Frankenheimer, who later became a successful film director. Other *Playhouse 90* directors included Fred Coe, Franklin Schaffner, George Roy Hill, Alex Segal, and Robert Stevens.

PLESHETTE, SUZANNE (1937–)

For six years, from September 1972 until August 1978, Suzanne Pleshette, was Bob NEWHART's wife, Emily Hartley, on the very popular *BOB NEWHART SHOW*. Pleshette, who was born in New York City, was the daughter of Eugene Pleshette, who managed the Paramount and Brooklyn Paramount theaters in New York during the big-band era. Suzanne attended New York's High School of Performing Arts and then majored in theater arts at Syracuse University and Finch College, before studying at the famed Neighborhood Playhouse and at Sanford Meisner's acting school. In the late 1950s and throughout the 1960s, Pleshette began getting increasingly larger roles on such television shows as *Alcoa Presents*, *ADVENTURES IN PARADISE*, *ALFRED HITCHCOCK PRESENTS*, *NAKED CITY*, *ROUTE 66*, *The Dick Powell Show*, *WAGON TRAIN*, *The WILD, WILD WEST*, *The FUGITIVE*, *The F.B.I.*, *IT TAKES A THIEF*, *DR. KILDARE*, *MARCUS WELBY, M.D.*, *IRONSIDE*, and *BONANZA*, and in the feature films *The Geisha Boy* (1958), *Rome Adventure* (1962), *The Birds* (1963), *Youngblood Hawke* (1964), *The Ugly Dachshund* (1966), *If It's Tuesday, This Must Be Belgium* (1969), and *Support Your Local Gunfighter* (1971). In 1972, Pleshette was on *The Bob Newhart Show*, and she subsequently appeared in the films *Oh, God! Book 2* (1980), *The Star Maker* (1981), and others, on her own TV series, *Suzanne Pleshette Is Maggie Briggs* (1984), as well as the series

Bridges to Cross (1986), *Nightingales* (1989), *The Boys Are Back* (1994), and in the title role in the TV film *Leona Helmsley: The Queen of Mean* (1990). In 1998, Pleshette provided the voice of Zira for the film *The Lion King II: Simba's Pride* (1998).

POLICE STORY

Sept. 1973–Sept. 1975	NBC	Tues. 10–11 P.M.
Sept. 1975–Oct. 1975	NBC	Tues. 9–10 P.M.
Nov. 1975–Aug. 1976	NBC	Fri. 10–11 P.M.
Aug. 1976–Aug. 1977	NBC	Tues. 10–11 P.M.
Oct. 1988–Dec. 1988	ABC	Sat. 9–11 P.M.

Police Story, which was created by former Los Angeles police officer Joseph Wambaugh, was a realistic, documentary-style series whose weekly episodes centered on the ordinary details of police work and the lives of police officers. The episodes, however, also contained the more dramatic aspects of police work such as drug busts, drunk drivers, as well as forced retirement and work-related stress, often dealing with the psychological effects of police work.

Two of *Police Story*'s episodes were spun off into other series: "The Gamble" (1974), which became *POLICE WOMAN*, with Angie DICKINSON playing the role of Sgt. Pepper Anderson, and "The Return of Joe Forrester," (1975), which became *Joe Forrester*, with Lloyd Bridges. More than 10 years after the original *Police Story* series left the air, four new TV films were produced during the 1988–89 TV season. Actors who played police officers in these films included Ken Olin, Robert CONRAD, and Jack Warden.

POLICE WOMAN

Sept. 1974–Oct. 1975	NBC	Fri. 10–11 P.M.
Nov. 1975–Aug. 1977	NBC	Tues. 9–10 P.M.
Oct. 1977–Dec. 1977	NBC	Tues. 10–11 P.M.
Dec. 1977–Mar. 1978	NBC	Wed. 10–11 P.M.
Mar. 1978–May 1978	NBC	Thurs. 10–11 P.M.
June 1978–Aug. 1978	NBC	Wed. 10–11 P.M.

Angie DICKINSON starred as policewoman Sgt. Suzanne "Pepper" Anderson on this police drama series that was popular for four years. Pepper was a Los Angeles Police Department undercover agent who worked on a vice squad with two other undercover policemen, Det. Joe Styles, played by Ed Bernard, and Det. Pete Royster, played by Charles Dierkop. The team reported to Lt. Bill Crowley, played by Earl Holliman. In her police work Pepper had to pretend to be everything from a prostitute to a criminal's girlfriend, and her assignments were usually very dangerous. Also seen on a semiregular basis during the series' first season was Pepper's handicapped sister, Cheryl, played by Nichole Kallis. The executive producer of *Police Woman* was David Gerber, and the series was produced by Douglas Benton.

POLITICALLY INCORRECT

July 1993–Dec. 1996	Syndicated	Prime time and
		late night
Jan. 1997–present	ABC	12:05–12.35 A.M.

The half-hour chat show *Politically Incorrect*, hosted by comedian Bill Maher, features discussions by a panel of celebrities and semicelebrities who discuss the current political and social scene in a humorous manner. Usually, four panelists from the world of show business, and sometimes politics, give their not always informed views on such subjects as Bill Clinton's personal life, abortion rights, gun control, animal rights, and other current events, as Maher asks questions and moderates the discussion. The series originally made its debut as a weekly program, but moved to late weeknights in January 1994, and for a time could be seen on prime time in October 1994.

POVICH, MAURY (1939–)

The son of well-known *Washington Post* columnist Shirley Povich, talk show host Maury Povich was born in Washington, D.C. After finishing school, Maury followed in his father's footsteps and, for a time, worked as a journalist before entering television. In 1991, Povich became the host of *The Maury Povich Show*, which he also produced. This syndicated series became one of TV's most popular talk shows. Povich, who married TV news anchorwoman Connie Chung in 1984. also hosted the *Imagemaker* (1986), *A Current Affair* (1986–95), and *Twenty One* (2000–01) TV series. and guest-starred on such TV series as WINGS and *Dream On.*

POWERS OF MATTHEW STAR, THE

| Sept. 1982–Aug. 1983 | NBC | Fri. 8–9 P.M. |
| Aug. 1983–Sept. 1983 | NBC | Sun. 7–8 P.M. |

Although it lasted only one year, *The Powers of Matthew Star* was an interesting TV science fiction series that was popular with the younger TV audience. Originally scheduled to make its debut in 1981, production of the series was delayed for one year when Peter Barton, who played the show's major character, Matthew Star, was injured while filming an early episode when he fell on a magnesium flare during filming. Matthew was a young man who, although he looked like any other student at Crestridge High School, was actually a crown prince from a planet named Quadris. Matthew had been sent to Earth by his father when he was overthrown by evil usurpers. Matthew's father wanted his son to develop the powers of telepathy and telekinesis on Earth so that he could return to Quadris and fight the evil beings who had taken over his planet. Matthew had a Quadrian guardian to look after him on Earth, whose name was Walt Shepherd. Walt kept the prince hidden from their enemies, who kept appearing on Earth disguised as humans or as robots, and who tried to destroy Matthew. Even though he was certainly different from the other kids at Crestridge High, he tried to have as normal a life on Earth as possible. He excelled at sports, had a human girlfriend named Pam Elliott, played by Amy Steel, and a cute human buddy named Bob Alexander, played by Chip Frye. Midway through the series' first year, the show's producers decided that in order to make the show more exciting, Matthew and Walter should go to work for the federal government as agents. James Karen joined the cast as Matthew's and Walter's government liaison, Major Wymore.

POWERS, STEFANIE (STEFANIA ZOFIA FEDERKIEWICZ 1942–)

Before Stefanie Powers became the star of the HART TO HART TV series, she appeared as a regular on such less-than-successful series as *The Girl From U.N.C.L.E.* and *The Feather and Father Gang*, and was a featured player in over 200 TV episodes. Born in Hollywood, Powers attended Hollywood High School with Linda Evans and took ballet lessons with Natalie Wood and Jill St. John. When she was 15 years old, Powers signed a contract with Columbia Pictures. Powers left Columbia, where she was supposed to play Maria in the film version of *West Side Story*, when she was replaced by Natalie Wood. The studio thought Stefanie was too young to play the part and wanted to capitalize on Natalie Wood's increasing popularity. After concentrating on her education for about five years, Powers returned to acting and was seen on such television series as BONANZA, ROUTE 66, IT TAKES A THIEF, KUNG FU, The STREETS OF SAN FRANCISCO, BANACEK, CANNON, MCMILLAN AND WIFE, The ROOKIES, The ROCKFORD FILES, and The BIONIC WOMAN, and was featured in such films as *McLintock* (1963), and *The Magnificent Seven Ride!* (1972), before becoming the star of the successful *Hart to Hart* series.

Powers continued to remain active on TV in films after *Hart to Hart* left the air, and she also starred in several stage plays such as the musical comedy *Applause* in an off-Broadway production. She also became the hostess on the newly formed Romance Network on cable TV in the late 1990s.

In the early 1990s, Powers, with her *Hart to Hart* costar, Robert WAGNER, began to make a series of feature-length *Hart to Hart* TV films that introduced the character she played on the series, Jennifer Hart, to a whole new audience of viewers. Powers is also well known for her active involvement in philanthropic causes such as the William Holden Wildlife Foundation. The actress most recently starred in the TV film *Someone Is Watching* (2000).

PRACTICE, THE

Mar. 1997–Apr. 1997	ABC	Tues. 10–11 P.M.
July 1997–Jan. 1998	ABC	Sat. 10–11 P.M.
Jan. 1998–Aug. 1998	ABC	Mon. 10–11 P.M.
Aug. 1998–present	ABC	Sun. 10–11 P.M.

The Emmy Award–winning legal drama *The Practice* is about a small law firm, Donnell and Associates, that specializes in criminal cases. The firm, located in a low-rent district in Boston, generally handles clients who are from the dregs of society and are quite often guilty of the crimes they have been charged with. The various episodes of *The Practice* center on the pretrial actions of members of the firm, the subsequent trials, and the personal lives of the lawyers at Donnell and Associates. Bobby Donnell, played by Dylan McDermott, is the young head of the law firm who does what he has to in order to win a case, even if this means turning a deaf ear on truth. Donnell's fellow lawyers are Eugene Young, played by Steve Harris, who is a confident and competent, if a bit too serious, African-American attorney; Eleanor, played by Camryn Manheim, who is a somewhat pushy, idealistic young woman; Lindsay Dole, played by Kelli Williams, is an ambitious young graduate of Harvard Law School and who, during the show's early episodes, formed a romantic relationship with her boss, Bobby Donnell; Rebecca Washington, played by Lisa Gay Hamilton, an African-American paralegal when the series began and then an attorney at the firm, who struggles with trying to balance what is right with what is legally possible; and Jimmy Berluti, played by Michael Badalucco, a kindhearted, idealistic young lawyer who, before he joined Donnell and Associates, had run TV ads to attract clients to his private practice. Also working at the firm is Lucy Hatcher, played by Marla Sokoloff, the company's very young receptionist/secretary. Constantly trying cases against Donnell and Associates, and yet a close friend of the attorneys at the firm, is Asst. D. A. Helen Gamble, played by Lara Flynn Boyle, who for a time had an affair with Bobby Donnell. Holland Taylor and Linda Hunt are also regularly seen playing judges on the series, and the judge Taylor played had a torrid affair with Jimmy Berluti.

PRETENDER, THE

Sept. 1996	NBC	Thurs. 10–11 P.M.
Sept. 1996–May 1997	NBC	Sat. 9–10 P.M.
June 1997–Sept. 1997	NBC	Sat. 8–9 P.M.
Nov. 1997–Jan. 1998	NBC	Sat. 8–9 P.M.
Jan. 1998–Apr. 1998	NBC	Sat. 9–10 P.M.
May 1998	NBC	Sat. 8–9 P.M.
July 1998–Aug. 1998	NBC	Wed. 8–9 P.M.
Aug. 1998–Sept. 1998	NBC	Sat. 8–9 P.M.
Oct. 1998–Dec. 1998	NBC	Sat. 9–10 P.M.
Jan. 1999–Feb. 1999	NBC	Sat. 8–9 P.M.
Feb. 1999–May 1999	NBC	Sat. 9–10 P.M.
June 1999–2000	NBC	Sat. 8–9 P.M.

The science fiction series *The Pretender* began with the statement "There are extraordinary individuals among us known as pretenders . . . geniuses with the ability to insinuate themselves into any walk of life, to literally become anyone." The hero of this series, Jarod Russell, played by Michael T. Weiss, was a child prodigy who had been taken away from his parents as an infant and raised to be a "pretender" in a facility known as "the Centre." The man in charge of the Centre was a psychiatrist named Dr. Sidney Greene, played by Patrick Bauchau, who sold his extraordinary mental ability to develop pretenders to the highest bidder. When he was grown, Jarod managed to escape from the Centre's heavily guarded facilities, where he was being held captive. While he was on the run from the Centre's agents, he attempted to expose the Centre's activities and find out who he really was. Using his highly developed abilities to become anyone he wanted, Jarod worked as a doctor, a pilot, a sea captain, or whatever else, in order to accomplish his mission, helping the many people he came in contact with along the way. One of the Centre's agents, who was constantly trying to track down Jarod and kill him before he exposed their questionable activities, was the alluring Miss Parker, played by Andrea Parker. Also trying to track down Jarod before he closed down their illegal activities was the Centre's Brigitte and Mr. Lyle, played by Pamela Gidley and Jamie Denton. As the series continued, Miss Parker gradually discovered the truth about her own abduction by the Centre, and joined Jarod in his mission to expose the Centre. Other characters who appeared regularly on the series were Angel, played by Paul Dillon, who had been driven mad as the Centre attempted to turn him into a pretender, and Boots, played by Jon Gries, who was the Centre's computer nerd. Canceled in 2000, *The Pretender* resurfaced on cable.

PRICE IS RIGHT, THE

Nov. 1956–Sept. 1963	NBC	Various times
Sept. 1963–Sept. 1965	ABC	Various times
1972–present	CBS	Various times
1984	Syndicated	Various times and stations
1994	Syndicated	Various times and stations

The perennial game show favorite *The Price Is Right*, which as of this writing has been on the air continuously for 30 years, was produced by Mark GOODSON and Bill TODMAN. The show has been seen in both daytime and prime-time slots. For the initial nine years the show was on the air, Bill CULLEN was the show's host. On the original version of the series, which was a half-hour program, four contestants were seated behind "tote" machines. After being shown various items of merchandise, each of the four contestants in turn would place a bid on the item(s), and the contestant whose bid was highest, without going over the amount of the suggested list price of the item(s) won the merchandise. Certain items called for "one bid only."

After seven years on NBC, the program moved to ABC in 1963, where it ran for two more years in both daytime and prime-time hours. Announcer Don Pardo introduced the host and described the items that were to be bid on. *The Price Is Right* left the air in 1965, but after a seven-year break, two versions of the program resurfaced as both a syndicated and a CBS network show in 1972. Called *The New Price Is Right,* the syndicated show was hosted by Dennis James and the network show by Bob BARKER, who at present still hosts the series. In 1975, with Barker solely at the helm, *The Price Is Right* became the first regularly scheduled game show to be expanded to one full hour. By the 1980s *The Price Is Right* had become television's longest-running daily game show.

Johnny Olson was the series original announcer, and the show's format had changed considerably from when it had made its debut in the mid-1950s. When Olson died in 1985, he was replaced by announcer Rod Roddy, who took over calling out "Come on down" and then announcing the name of the contestant selected from the studio audience who would, when four contestants had been brought forward, bid on an item displayed by Barker. Again, the contestant who came closest to the bid without going over the suggested retail price was brought onstage and could play a game that could win another, more impressive, prize. At the end of each half of the one-hour show, three of the contestants who had been called onstage spun a wheel with various dollar amounts on it, and the one of the three who, after a total of two possible spins, came up with the highest total sum without going over one dollar, was selected to be one of the final two contestants to make bids on two showcases that contained thousands of dollars worth of prizes that could include, appliances, furniture, trips, and cars. Assisting Barker onstage were models called "Barker's Beauties," who demonstrated the products being given away, set up games that the contestants played, and added a bit of glamour to the proceedings. The three Barker's Beauties who were on the show for the longest period were Holly Hollstrom, Dian Parkinson, and Janice Pennington. For one month in 1985, Barker also hosted a prime-time version of the show; and the daytime version of the show was hosted by Tom Kennedy. Barker returned to host the popular daytime show, and to this day is the program's host.

PRINZE, FREDDIE (FREDERICK KARL FRUETZEL 1954–1977)

Born in New York City of Hungarian–Jewish and Puerto Rican parents, Freddie Prinze attended Fiorello La Guardia High School of the Performing Arts in that city before embarking upon a career in show business that proved to be tragically short. Prinze's big break came in 1974 when he was cast as Chico Rodriguez in the television situation comedy series CHICO AND THE MAN. The show's popularity catapulted Prinze into national prominence, and he was soon named "the most promising new face in show business." He subsequently appeared in the TV films *Joys* (1976) and *The Million Dollar Rip-Off* (1976). Unable to deal with his sudden success, Prinze became addicted to drugs and was arrested for driving a car while under the influence of methaqualone. At the height of his popularity, Prinze committed suicide while under the influence of drugs. He was 23 years old at the time. Freddie Prinze, Jr., who, as of this writing has a successful acting career of his own, is Freddie's son, and was an infant when his father died.

PRISONER, THE

June 1968–Sept. 1968	CBS	Sat. 7:30–8:30 P.M.
May 1969–Sept. 1969	CBS	Thurs. 8–9 P.M.

Even though only 17 episodes of *The Prisoner* were aired, it was one of the most original series ever seen on American television and had a devoted, if limited, number of loyal viewers during its tenure. Filmed in England, the series starred Patrick McGoohan as the Prisoner Number 6. Prisoner Number 6 was a government agent who had resigned from his position and been summarily abducted and imprisoned by the government and placed in a strange, surreal community. Prisoner Number 6 retained the secret information he had been exposed to, and it was apparent that someone wanted to make sure he never revealed what he knew. At times, it seemed as if his captors were trying only to test his loyalty, but his captors were seldom seen, and they always had different faces when they did appear. Even though the community in which Prisoner Number 6 was imprisoned was an attractive little town surrounded by a forest, mountains, and the sea, it became apparent to Number 6 that there was no escaping from the place, no matter how "ideal" it appeared. On the final episode of the series, Prisoner Number 6, who had consistently outwitted his captors, was given an astonishing offer. He was asked to be the community's leader. In the end, Prisoner 6 did escape and the community was destroyed. *The Prisoner* was created, produced, and occasionally written by its star, Patrick McGoohan. Also appearing on the series as a regular was Angelo Muscat as "The Butler."

PRIVATE BENJAMIN

Apr. 1981	CBS	Mon. 8–8:30 P.M.
Oct. 1981–Jan. 1982	CBS	Mon. 8–8:30 P.M.
Jan. 1982–Mar. 1982	CBS	Mon. 8:30–9 P.M.
Apr. 1982–Sept. 1982	CBS	Mon. 8–8:30 P.M.
Sept. 1982–Jan. 1983	CBS	Mon. 8:30–9 P.M.
May 1983–Sept. 1983	CBS	Mon. 8:30–9 P.M.

The hit film *Private Benjamin*, which starred Goldie Hawn, became a television situation comedy series in 1981 and starred Lorna Patterson in the title role. Private Judy Benjamin was a spoiled New York socialite who decided to enlist in the U.S. Army in order to expand her horizons. Since she was accustomed to the finer things in life, such as designer clothes and gourmet food, Judy found it hard to adjust to the life of an army private. Stationed at the fictional Fort Bradley, Private Benjamin was a thorn in the side of her commanding officer, Capt. Doreen Lewis, played by Eileen Brennan, who had the difficult job of trying to turn the rich girl into a soldier. Judy's fellow recruits included Private Maria Gianelli, a tough, streetwise girl who had chosen the army as an alternative to jail, played by Lisa Raggio; Private Rayleen White, from the ghetto in Detroit, played by Joyce Little; Private Barbara Ann Glass, a naive country girl who loved country music and often burst into song, played by Joan Roberts; Private Carol Winter, the company's resident obnoxious snitch, played by Ann Ryerson; Private Luanne Hubble, played by Lucy Webb; Private Harriet Dorsey, played by Francesca Roberts; Private Jackie Sims, played by Damita Jo Freeman; and Private Stacey Kouchalakus, played by Wendie Jo Sperber. The girls' drill sergeant was Sgt. Ted Ross, played by Hal Williams. The base's publicity-seeking, pompous commanding officer was Col. Lawrence Fielding, played by Robert Mandan. Eileen Brennan and Hal Williams re-created the roles they had played in the original film, but in 1982, Brennan was injured in an automobile accident and Polly HOLLIDAY replaced her for one episode before the show was canceled. During the show's 1980–81 season, it was number five in the Nielsen ratings, but the show's popularity soon after began to diminish.

PRIVATE SECRETARY

Feb. 1953–June 1953	CBS	Sun. 7:30–8 P.M.
June 1953–Sept. 1953	NBC	Sat. 10:30–11 P.M.
Sept. 1953–June 1954	CBS	Sun. 7:30–8 P.M.
June 1954–Sept. 1954	NBC	Sat. 10:30–11 P.M.
Sept. 1954–Mar. 1957	CBS	Sun. 7:30–8 P.M.
Apr. 1957–Sept. 1957	CBS	Tues. 8:30– P.M.

For four years, the popular situation comedy series *Private Secretary,* which starred Ann SOTHERN as Susie McNamara, the private secretary, seesawed back and forth between CBS and NBC. The series, which was Sothern's first foray into television, centered on a secretary who was attractive and competent, but kept getting mixed up in the personal life of her boss, a theatrical agent named Peter Sands, played by Don Porter. Receptionist Vi Praskins, played by Ann Tyrrell, was Susie's friend at the office. Susie's friend Sylvia, played by Joan Banks, was often competing with Susie for the attention of their handsome boss. Also appearing on the series was Jesse White as Peter's cigar-smoking competitor in the talent business, Cagey Calhoun. During the show's last season Louis Nye and Ken Berry appeared as characters named Delbert and Woody. *Private Secretary* was produced by Jack Chertok, and the series was directed by Christian Nyby. During its first season, *Private Secretary* alternated every other week with *The JACK BENNY PROGRAM.* (See also ANN SOTHERN SHOW, The).

PRODUCERS' SHOWCASE

Oct. 1954–May 1957	NBC	Mon. 8–9:30 P.M.

Producers' Showcase, supervised by Fred Coe, was a one-and-a-half-hour live drama anthology series of specials that was seen on NBC in the mid-to-late 1950s. Many memorable television performances were seen on this series during the three years it was aired. Stage star Mary Martin was featured in a musical comedy adaptation of Barrie's *Peter Pan,* which was so well received it was repeated the following year, and several times thereafter, with Martin as Peter and Cyril Ritchard as Captain Hook repeating their original roles. Other memorable performers and productions that were featured on this lavishly produced series included Humphrey Bogart, Henry Fonda, and Lauren Bacall in *The Petrified Forest;* Frank Sinatra, Paul Newman, and Eva Marie Saint in a musical adaptation of Thornton Wilder's *Our Town;* dancers Margot Fonteyn and Michael Soames in two ballets, *Sleeping Beauty* and *Cinderella;* Lee J. Cobb, Ruth Roman, Joseph Wiseman, and Nehemiah Persoff in Delbert Mann's production of *Darkness at Noon;* Trevor Howard and Ginger Rogers in *Tonight at 8:30;* Nina Foch, Joseph Cotten, and Margaret Sullavan in Arthur Penn's production of *State of the Union;* legendary stage actress Katherine Cornell making her TV debut in *The Barretts of Wimpole Street,* with Anthony Quayle and Nancy Coleman; Louis Armstrong, Kay Starr, Buster Keaton, and Dick Haymes in the musical *The Lord Don't Play Favorites;* Audrey Hepburn, Mel Ferrer, Judith Evelyn, and Raymond Massey in *Mayerling;* stage legends Alfred Lunt and Lynn Fontanne in *The Great Sebastians;* Broadway musical comedy star Barbara Cook in *Bloomer Girl;* Joel Grey, Celeste Holm, Billy Gilbert, Cyril Ritchard, Arnold Stang, and Peggy King in a musical adaptation of *Jack and the Beanstalk;* Claire Bloom and John Neville in Shakespeare's *Romeo and Juliet;* and Fredric March, Claire Trevor, and Geraldine Fitzgerald in *Dodsworth.*

PROFILER

Sept. 1996–May 1997	NBC	Sat. 10–11 P.M.
May 1997–July 1997	NBC	Fri. 10–11 P.M.
Nov. 1997–July 1998	NBC	Sat. 10–11 P.M.
Oct. 1998–2000	NBC	Sat. 10–11 P.M.

The action/adventure series *Profiler* centers on a forensic psychologist named Dr. Samantha "Sam" Waters, played by Ally Walker, who has the skill to visualize what had happened at various crime scenes, and can mentally envision both the victim and the criminal at those scenes. Dr. Waters's abilities were especially useful to the F.B.I., until she became involved with an unseen serial killer known as Jack of All Trades, played by Dennis Christopher, who became obsessed with Dr. Sam and killed her husband. Dr. Sam retired to the country with her young daughter Cloe, played by Caitlin Wachs (age seven), and from 1996 by Evan Rachel Wood, and her best friend, Angel Brown, played by Erica Gimpel. Before long, her mentor, F.B.I. Agent Bailey Malone, played by Robert Davi, convinced her to return to work at the Violent Crimes Task Force in Atlanta, Georgia. Dr. Sam was sent to the scenes of violent crimes to "profile" the scene of the crime at various localities around the country. On the same investigative team as Dr. Sam is Det. John Grant, played by Julian McMahon; Dr. Nathan Brubaker, a idealistic former attorney, played by Michael Whaley; Grace Alvarez, a forensic pathologist, played by Roma Maffia; Det. Marcus Payton, who was skeptical of Dr. Sam's abilities, played by Shiek Mahmoud-Bey; and George Friley, the team's computer hacker, played by Peter Frechette.

PROVIDENCE

Jan. 1999–present	NBC	Fri. 8–9 P.M.

When her mother suddenly died, Dr. Sydney Hansen, played by Melina Kanakaredes, a successful plastic surgeon who reconstructed the faces of celebrities in Hollywood, decided to return home to Providence, Rhode Island, to take care of her dysfunctional family. The family included her veterinarian father, Dr. Jim Hansen, who had an easier time relating to animals than he did to people, played by Mike Farrell; her sister Lynda, played by Concetta Tomei; her troubled sister, Joanie, who had an illegitimate child, played by Paula Cale; and her younger brother, Robbie, played by Seth Peterson. Sydney was determined to take charge of the family to help them cope with their unhappy lives, and in spite of the constant meddlesome advice given to her by the ghost of her dead mother (which was actually Sydney's way of making decisions), she moved home and became the family's anchor and counselor. In order to support herself, Sydney took a job helping the poor at a downtown clinic run by Helen Reynolds, played by Leslie Silva, who became her best friend. In spite of its soap-opera-like premise, *Providence*, mainly due to its excellent acting and well-written scripts, was one of the surprise hits of the 1999–2000 television season.

P.T.L. CLUB, THE

1976–1987 Syndicated Various times and stations

At its height, *The P.T.L. Club* televangelism program reached 13 million viewers. ("P.T.L." stood for "praise the lord" or "people that love.") The show was hosted by Pentecostal Assemblies of God minister Jim Bakker and his wife, Tammy Faye, who had begun their TV careers as hosts of a children's religious show in 1964 in Portsmouth, Virginia. When evangelist/broadcasting executive Pat Robertson saw the show, he signed up the Bakkers to host *The 700 Club*, a religious talk show on Robertson's Virginia Beach–based Christian Broadcasting Network. In 1972, the Bakkers left Robertson's network and relocated to Charlotte, North Carolina, where they set up their P.T.L. Club and began their popular TV series, which remained on the air until 1987, when a scandal involving Jim Bakker's finances forced the series to be canceled and Bakker retired from his ministry.

PUNKY BREWSTER

Sept. 1984–May 1985	NBC	Sun. 7:30–8 P.M.
June 1985–Apr. 1986	NBC	Sun. 7–7:30 P.M.
May 1986–Sept. 1986	NBC	Sun. 7:30–8 P.M.

"Punky" Brewster, whose real first name was Penelope, was a spirited seven-year-old girl who lived in Chicago and had a lot of problems, but was always optimistic. Abandoned by her parents, Punky, played by Soleil Moon Frye, moved into an empty apartment where she lived until being discovered by the building's cantankerous manager and sometime photographer, a confirmed bachelor named Henry Warnimont, played by George Gaynes. Won over by Punky's charm, Warnimont convinced authorities to allow Punky and her adorable puppy to live with him. Before long, Punky was making the cranky old man's life brighter, and each week's episode usually revolved around how Punky and Henry adjusted to living with each other. Also seen on the series were the building's odd maintenance man, Eddie Malvin, played by Eddie Deezen; Cherie Johnson, Punky's friend and playmate, played by Cherie Johnson; Margaux Kramer, Punky's conceited classmate, played by Susie Garrett; Margaux's mother, Mrs. Kramer, played by Loyita Chapel; Punky's friend, Allen Anderson, played by Casey Ellison; and Punky's teachers, Mrs. Morton, played by Dody Goodman, and Mike Fulton, played by T. K. Carter. *Punky Brewster* was developed for television by Brandon Tartikoff, who was NBC's head of programming. An animated version of *Punky Brewster* called *It's Punky Brewster* was aired on Saturday mornings from 1985 through 1987 and then from 1988 through 1989.

QUANTUM LEAP

Mar. 1989	NBC	Sun. 9–11 P.M.
Mar. 1989–Apr. 1989	NBC	Fri. 9–10 P.M.
May 1989	NBC	Wed. 10–11 P.M.
Sept. 1989–Aug. 1990	NBC	Wed. 10–11 P.M.
Aug. 1990–Jan. 1991	NBC	Fri. 8–9 P.M.
Mar. 1991–July 1992	NBC	Wed. 10–11 P.M.
June 1992–July 1992	NBC	Tues. 9–10 P.M.
Aug. 1992–Apr. 1993	NBC	Tues. 8–9 P.M.
Aug. 1993	NBC	Sun. 7–8 P.M.

On this imaginative science fiction series, Dr. Sam Beckett, played by Scott Bakula, was a physicist who bounced around in time assuming the identity of various people in the past, after an experiment he was involved in went wrong. He could time travel only within his own life span (the mid-1950s through the 1980s), and he could change events only if the change was for the better in the lives of the people whose bodies he was inhabiting. Historical events, such as assassinations, wars, etc., could not be altered in any way. Dr. Beckett appeared as himself to TV viewers, but to those around him, he was the person whose body he had assumed. The only person from his own time that Dr. Beckett could communicate with was Al Calavicci, played by Dean Stockwell, who was known as "The Observer." Al, who was a former U.S. Navy admiral, could be seen only by Dr. Beckett as a hologram. He told Dr. Sam what was going to happen to the person whose body he was trapped in by consulting a handheld computer he called "Ziggy" that contained information about future events. Only small children and animals could also see Al. Over the years the series was aired, Dr. Beckett, who desperately longed to return to his own time, assumed the identities of a wide variety of individuals, including an elderly black man in the Deep South before the civil rights movement, an attractive, sexually harassed secretary, a trapeze artist, a blind concert pianist, a teenage hot rodder, and a pregnant girl who was about to give birth. Such controversial social subjects as racism, the war in Vietnam, prejudices against the mentally retarded, the problem of being a single parent, and others were addressed. When the series came to end in 1993, after three and a half years on the air, viewers were told that Dr. Beckett never returned home.

QUEEN FOR A DAY

Jan. 1956–Sept. 1960	NBC	Various daytime hours
Sept. 1960–Oct. 1964	ABC	Various daytime hours
1970	Syndicated	Various daytime hours

The female contestant who could evoke the greatest amount of sympathy from the studio audience with her tale of personal hardship and/or domestic turmoil was judged "Queen for a Day" on this series that was popular with daytime viewers in the mid-to-late 1950s and into the mid-1960s. The woman chosen as Queen was rewarded with various prizes and crowned by the show's host. A popular radio show in the 1940s, *Queen for a Day* arrived on television in 1956 with Jack Bailey, who hosted the radio show, also in charge of the proceedings on TV. Originating from Hollywood, the series was the most popular daytime series on television the first year it was aired, and during its second season, it was expanded from one half-hour a day to 45 minutes. Jeannie Cagney was featured as the show's fashion commentator. In 1970, the series was revived as syndicated show with Dick Curtis acting as host, but it remained on the air for less than one full season.

QUINCY, M.E.

Oct. 1976–Nov. 1976	NBC	Sun. 9:30–11 P.M.
Feb. 1977–May 1977	NBC	Fri. 10–11 P.M.
June 1977–July 1977	NBC	Fri. 9:30–11 P.M.
July 1977–Aug. 1978	NBC	Fri. 10–11 P.M.
Sept. 1978–Apr. 1980	NBC	Thurs. 9–10 P.M.
Apr. 1980–June 1983	NBC	Wed. 10–11 P.M.
June 1983–Sept. 1983	NBC	Sat. 9–10 P.M.
Sept. 1983	NBC	Mon. 10–11 P.M.

Jack KLUGMAN starred as a medical examiner for the Los Angeles County Coroner's Office, known simply as Quincy, on this police drama series that was one of the most popular series on the air from the mid-1970s into the early 1980s. Quincy had given up a lucrative medical practice to go to work for the coroner's office, and he often became involved in the investigations of the bodies that arrived in his laboratory for autopsy, much to the chagrin of his immediate supervisor, Dr. Robert Astin, played by John S. Ragin. Assisting Quincy at the lab was Sam Fukiyama, a Japanese-American lab technician, played by Robert Ito. Police department detectives with whom Quincy often became involved as both friends and fellow investigators included Lt. Frank Monohan, played by Garry Walberg, and Sergeant Brill, played by Joseph Roman. Much of Quincy's off-duty hours were spent dining at Danny's Place, where Quincy and his pals would discuss cases and their solutions. The restaurant's proprietor, Danny Tovo, was played by Val Bisoglio. Lynette Mettey played Quincy's girlfriend, Lee Potter, on the series' early episodes, and Anita Gillette (who had played Quincy's deceased wife in an early episode) as Dr. Emily Hanover became his female interest on the show's later episodes. Quincy and Emily were eventually married on a spring 1983 episode. Although viewers never knew Quincy's first name, his business card, seen on one show, read, "Dr. R. Quincy." The series, which began as one of the four rotating TV films on the NBC *Sunday Mystery Movie* series (COLUMBO, MCCLOUD, and MCMILLAN AND WIFE were the other three), became an hour-long series in 1977. Glenn Larson, who created the series, was the show's executive producer, and Robert F. O'Neill was the series' supervising producer.

QUIVERS, ROBIN (ROBIN OPHELIA QUIVERS 1952–)

Controversial radio and TV talk and music show host Howard STERN's sidekick, Robin Quivers first joined Stern at the radio microphones at DC 101 in Washington, D.C. Quivers soon became an important asset to Stern's radio, and later television, shows. Born in Baltimore, Maryland, Quivers graduated from the University of Maryland with a degree in nursing and was a second lieutenant in the U.S. Air Force Reserve before beginning her career as a news reporter at WIOO-AM in Carlisle, Pennsylvania. Once she joined the regular cast of *The Howard Stern Show,* Robin became invaluable to Stern as someone who kept his wild antics and shockingly frank comments in their proper place. Quivers was featured in *Howard Stern's Butt Bongo Fiesta* special (1992), on the *Howard Stern TV Series* (1994), and in the film *Private Parts* (1997), which was about Howard Stern's private life and career, and *The HOWARD STERN RADIO SHOW,* a popular late-night TV series that is seen on the CBS network. In addition, Quivers has made notable guest-starring appearances on such TV series as *The FRESH PRINCE OF BEL AIR, The LARRY SANDERS SHOW,* and *The Magic Hour* (1998). Quivers is the author of a best-selling autobiography, *Quivers,* published in 1995.

RACKET SQUAD

June 1951–Dec. 1952	CBS	Thurs. 10–10:30 P.M.
Jan. 1953–July 1953	CBS	Thurs. 10:30–11 P.M.
July 1953–Sept. 1953	CBS	Mon. 9–9:30 P.M.

One of television's earliest post–World War II police procedure series, *Racket Squad* starred Reed Hadley as Capt. John Braddock of the San Francisco Police Department's Racket Squad. Braddock did not deal with violent crimes, but reported on and investigated various confidence games. Based on actual cases from the files of police departments throughout the United States, *Racket Squad* described in detail how con men cheated unsuspecting citizens into giving them their money. One year before *Racket Squad* became a national program, it was seen as a syndicated show, with Reed Hadley, who was on both the syndicated and CBS series, the show's only regular character. The half-hour series was produced by Hal Roach, Jr., and Carroll Case and directed by Jim Timling.

RAMAR OF THE JUNGLE

1952–1954 Syndicated Various times and stations

Film star Jon Hall played Dr. Tom Reynolds, a physician and researcher who worked in the "jungles" of Kenya, where he was called "Ramar" (which meant "great white doctor") by the natives, on this early, syndicated TV series. On the adventure-filled episodes, which were filmed with younger viewers in mind, Ramar, who had been raised in the jungle by missionary parents, searched for cures for exotic ailments while he battled restless natives, killer cannibal tribes, bungling assistants, and the wild animals of the jungle. Also appearing regularly on the 52 episodes of *Ramar of the Jungle* was Ray Montgomery as Ramar's colleague, Dr. Howard Ogden, and M'liss McClure as his female friend. Ramar visited India on occasion, and when he was in that country, Victor Millan was seen as his Indian guide, Zahir. *Ramar of the Jungle* was produced by Harry S. Rothschild and Leon Fromkess for their Eagle-Lion's Productions.

RANDALL, TONY (LEONARD ROSENBERG 1920–)

After attending Northwestern University in Evanston, Illinois, Tony Randall, who was born in Tulsa, Oklahoma, entered radio and television as an actor and was on such popular radio programs as *I Love a Mystery* and on such early TV shows as ONE MAN'S FAMILY, The PHILCO TELEVISION PLAYHOUSE, *The Alcoa Hour, The Westinghouse Desilu Playhouse, The Alfred Hitchcock Hour,* and *Here's Lucy.* He was best known, however, for playing Harvey Weskitt, the best friend and fellow teacher of Wally COX on MR. PEEPERS. After his success on that show, Randall appeared in a series of popular feature films, including *How to Be Very, Very Popular* (1955), *Will Success Spoil Rock Hunter?* (1957), *Pillow Talk* (1959), *The Mating Game* (1959), and *Send Me No Flowers* (1964), before becoming one of the stars of *The ODD COUPLE* in 1970. *The Odd Couple* enjoyed a profitable 12-year run and made Randall one of America's most recognized and successful actors. After his success on that show, Randall starred on the *The Tony Randall Show* and *Love, Sydney,* and was featured in such films as *The King of Comedy* (1983, playing himself), and several popular TV films. Randall, who has stated that "the theater is [his] first love," founded and is one of the directors of the National Actors Theatre in New York City, which produces stage plays.

RAT PATROL, THE

Sept. 1966–Sept. 1968   ABC   Mon. 8:30–9 P.M.

The half-hour war drama/adventure series *Rat Patrol* was, for the two years it remained on the air, a favorite program of many viewers. The series, which often featured humorous scenes, as well as exciting battle sequences, starred Chris George as Sgt. Sam Troy, Gary Raymond as Sgt. Jack Moffitt, Lawrence Casey as Pvt. Mark Hitchcock, Justin Tarr as Pvt. Tully Pettigrew, and Hans Gudegast (later known as Eric Braeden) as Hauptman (Capt.) Hans Dietrich of the Rat Patrol. Troy, Moffitt, Casey, and Pettigrew were four young commandos, three Americans and one Englishman, called the Rat Patrollers, who were fighting General Rommel's Afrika Korps in North Africa during World War II. General Dietrich, of the German army, was their usual enemy. The show, whose exterior scenes were filmed in Spain, was produced by Stanley Sheptner, and then by Lee Rich.

RATHER, DAN (DAN IRVIN RATHER. JR. 1931–   )

CBS Evening News anchorman Dan Rather was born in Wharton, Texas. After graduating from college, Rather joined the staff at a local Houston television station as a news reporter. He joined the CBS Dallas News Bureau in 1962 and then served as White House correspondent from 1964 through 1974, where he filed special reports like *The White House Tapes: The President's Decision,* during President Richard M. Nixon's tenure. From 1975 until 1981, Rather was one of the interviewers on the popular CBS program *60 MINUTES.* In 1981, he became the anchorman of the *CBS Evening News,* and in 1988, he became one of the featured interviewers on CBS's popular *48 Hours.* He continues to serve as anchor and managing editor of *CBS Evening News.*

RAWHIDE

Jan. 1959–Apr. 1959	CBS	Fri. 8–9 P.M.
May 1959–Sept. 1963	CBS	Fri. 7:30–8:30 P.M.
Sept. 1963–Sept. 1964	CBS	Thurs. 8–9 P.M.
Sept. 1964–Sept. 1965	CBS	Fri. 7:30–8:30 P.M.
Sept. 1965–Jan. 1966	CBS	Tues. 7:30–8:30 P.M.

When viewers heard the theme song "Rawhide," sung by Frankie Laine, they knew that they were in for a full hour of adventure on CBS's popular western series *Rawhide.* It was the story of the adventures of the cattle drives that were regularly made from North Texas to Sedalia, Kansas, during the latter part of the 19th century. The series featured Eric Fleming as Gil Favor, the trail boss, and Clint EASTWOOD as Rowdy Yates, a young, ramrod cattle rustler who became trail boss when Fleming left the series in 1965 and remained with the series the entire time it was on the air. Also appearing were Jim Murdock as Harkness "Mushy" Mushgrove, Paul Brinegar as the cattle drivers' cook, Wishbone; Sheb Wooley as Pete Nolan (1959–65);

Rocky Shahan as Joe Scarlett (1959–64); Robert Cabal as Hey Soos Patines (1961–64); Steve Raines as Jim Quince; Charles Gray as Clay Forrester (1962–63); John Ireland as Jed Colby (1965–66); and Raymond St. Jacques as Solomon King (1965–66). Over the seven years the series was on the air, it was produced by Charles Marquis Warren, the creator of the series, and then Endre Bohem, Vincent Fennelly, Bernard Kowalski, Bruce Geller, Endre Bohem once again, and finally Ben Brady.

RAYBURN, GENE (EUGENE RUBESSA 1917–1999)

Before he became one of television's best-known personalities, Gene Rayburn, the host of the popular game show *MATCH GAME,* was a successful performer on radio, the announcer on the popular *TONIGHT* show on NBC, and the host of many other panel and game programs. Born in Christopher, Illinois, Rayburn entered radio shortly after finishing his schooling, and in the early 1950s had a successful morning talk show, *Rayburn and Finch,* on the air in the late 1940s. Rayburn appeared as a panelist on *THE NAME'S THE SAME* (1951–55) and subsequently hosted *The Sky's the Limit* (1954–56), *Make the Connection* (1955), *Musical Chairs* (1955), *Choose Up Sides* (1956), *Play Your Hunch* (1958), and *Dough Re Mi* (1958–60). It was, however, as the host of the popular *Match Game* that Rayburn enjoyed his greatest success. *Match Game* made its debut on television in 1962, but it was not a success at first. In 1975, the series was revived and became one of the most popular game shows on television, remaining on network TV and in syndication for the next five years. Except for rare guest-starring appearances, Rayburn disappeared from the spotlight after *Match Game* left the air, but resurfaced briefly to host the *BREAK THE BANK* game show in 1985. During the height of his success as the host of *Match Game,* Rayburn made several guest-starring appearances on *The LOVE BOAT* and was seen as "The Quiz Master" on an episode of *FANTASY ISLAND* in 1982.

RAYE, MARTHA (MARGARET TERESA YVONNE REED AKA O'REED 1916–1994)

The daughter of vaudeville performers, comedienne Martha Raye made her stage debut when she was a small child, and went on to become one of America's most successful singer/comediennes, as a major performer on the stage, in films, and on radio and television. Born in Butte, Montana, where her parents were appearing in a vaudeville show, Martha first became well known to the general public when Paramount Pictures signed her to appear in the film *Rhythm on the Range* with Bing CROSBY in 1936. Her boisterous, big-mouthed comic style and her energetic singing of novelty musical numbers made her an instant favorite with the movie going public, and she soon appeared in a series of popular films, usually playing the man-hungry second female lead, including *The Big Broadcast of 1938, College Holiday* (1936), *Waikiki Wedding, Artists & Models,* and *Double or Nothing* (all in 1937),

The Big Broadcast of 1938, The Boys From Syracuse (1940), *Hellzapoppin* (1941), and *Pin-Up Girl* (1944).

During World War II, Martha was a tireless performer who entertained millions of GIs, both on the home front and on the front lines overseas, and her wartime adventures were chronicled in the film *Four Jills in a Jeep* in 1944. In 1947, Martha costarred with Charlie Chaplin in the critically acclaimed film *Monsieur Verdoux.*

After the war, Martha became one of Hollywood's first major stars to appear on television. She was one of the four alternating stars of the *Four Star Play House* TV variety show from 1951 to 1953, and starred on a popular variety show of her own, *The MARTHA RAYE SHOW,* from 1955 until 1956. The comedienne continued to keep busy throughout the 1950s as a frequent guest star on such TV shows as *The ANDY WILLIAMS SHOW* and *LOVE, AMERICAN STYLE.* In 1976, Martha joined the cast as a regular on the *McMILLAN AND WIFE* TV series, and subsequently was a regular on the *ALICE* series from 1982 to 1984. In 1981, Raye appeared as Berthe in a TV adaptation of the successful stage musical *Pippin.* Increasing bad health curtailed Raye's performing activities in the late 1980s to early 1990s, and she died in 1994 after a long illness.

READING RAINBOW

1983–present	PBS	Mon–Fri. Various times

The half-hour, five-days-a-week series *Reading Rainbow* is hosted by LeVar Burton, who made his television debut playing the young African abducted into slavery, Kunta Kinte, in the acclaimed TV miniseries *ROOTS* in 1977. The reading series was developed by the Public Broadcasting System especially to encourage children to become better readers. The programs consist of stories, films, and discussions about books and any reading problems children might be having, and attempts to help youngsters overcome any fears that interfere with their ability to read. *Reading Rainbow* is considered by most television critics and educators to be one of the best educational programs on the air, and is watched by millions of young viewers daily.

REALITY TV

The first important TV "reality program" (consisting of nonfiction, unscripted but artificially contrived situations featuring nonactors), was *CANDID CAMERA,* which was first telecast in 1948. Other popular early "reality" shows on TV were *THE PEOPLE'S COURT,* which for many years featured real life judge Joseph A. Wapner, a syndicated show that made its debut in 1981; *Cops* (1989), in which a camera crew follows police officers on a typical workday; *AMERICA'S MOST WANTED* (1986), which reenacted unsolved crimes in an ostensible bid to publicize and therefore solve them; and *AMERICA'S FUNNIEST HOME VIDEOS* (1990). It wasn't until 2000, however, encouraged by the success of *SURVIVOR,* that reality shows began to saturate primetime TV. Among the more popular network reality shows are: *The Amazing Race* (CBS) on which a group of contestants in teams of two races to various exotic locales all over the world in an attempt to win a million-dollar prize; *The Bachelor* (ABC), in which a group of young women vie for the affections of, and possible marriage to, a good-looking, prosperous young man; *Big Brother* (CBS), which places a group of young people in a shared house and has the roommates periodically vote one of the group out of the house in an attempt to be the last person living in the house; *Boot Camp* (Fox), which depicts life in a military-style training camp; *Crime and Punishment,* which is basically a "real" version of the popular *LAW & ORDER* program; *Fear Factor* (NBC), in which contestants attempt to face their worst fears, such as getting into a tank with hundreds of snakes or jumping off a high cliff into a body of water; *The Mole* (ABC), which plants a spy or "mole" amidst of group of people who attempt to discover who "the mole" is, as well as try to avoid being ratted on by other members of the group, which would lead to being voted off the show; and *Temptation Island* (Fox), which records events at a resort community designed to tempt players to leave their girlfriends or boyfriends.

REAL McCOYS, THE

Oct. 1957–Sept. 1962	ABC	Thurs. 8:30–9 P.M.
Sept. 1962–Sept. 1963	CBS	Sun. 9–9:30 P.M.

When writers Irving and Norman Pincus first proposed the idea of a situation comedy set in rural America and about a family of hillbillies, most network officials thought the series was doomed for failure, but ABC decided to take a chance. To everyone's surprise the show, called *The Real McCoys,* became a hit and remained on the air for an impressive six years. The series, produced by Danny Thomas Productions, starred veteran film character actor Walter BRENNAN as Grandpa Amos McCoy, a crusty old codger who liked to meddle in other people's business. Grandpa's family consisted of his grandson, Luke McCoy, played by Richard CRENNA, and Luke's new wife, Kate McCoy, played by Kathy Nolan; Luke's teenage sister, "Aunt" Hassie, played by Lydia Reed; and Luke's younger brother, Little Luke, played by Michael Winkelman. Also appearing regularly on the series were the McCoys' musical farmhand, Pepino Garcia, played by Tony Martinez; their argumentative neighbor, George MacMichael, played by Andy Clyde; and George's sister, Flora, played by Madge Blake, who had her heart set on marrying a reluctant Grandpa McCoy. In 1962, when the series moved to the CBS network, Luke was a widower (Kathy Nolan had decided to leave the series), and many of the show's new stories involved Grandpa's attempt to match up his grandson with a new wife. Janet DeGore joined the cast in 1963 as the McCoys' neighbor, a young widow named Louise Howard, who had a son, Greg, played by Butch Patrick. Joan Blondell also joined the cast as Louise's aunt, Winifred. The executive producer of *The Real McCoys* was Irving Pincus, who had created the series, and Danny Arnold was the show's producer.

REASONABLE DOUBTS

Sept. 1991	NBC	Thurs. 10–11 P.M.
Sept. 1991–Jan. 1992	NBC	Fri. 10–11 P.M.
Feb. 1992–Mar. 1992	NBC	Tues. 10–11 P.M.
June 1992–July 1992	NBC	Fri. 9–10 P.M.
Aug. 1992–Jan. 1993	NBC	Tues. 9–10 P.M.
Mar. 1993–Apr. 1993	NBC	Sat. 10–11 P.M.
Apr. 1993	NBC	Tues. 8–9 P.M.
June 1993–July 1993	NBC	Sat. 10–11 P.M.

Academy Award–winning actress Marlee Matlin, who is hearing impaired, played a hearing-impaired assistant D.A. named Tess Kaufman on the police drama series *Reasonable Doubts,* which was created by Robert Singer. Assigned to the felony division of the Chicago District Attorney's office, Tess was a first-rate, sensitive lawyer who was teamed up with a hard-boiled policeman who believed in being unusually tough on criminals. The policeman, Dicky Cobb, played by Mark Harmon, had been assigned to work with Tess, in spite of their differences, because he understood sign language and could communicate easily with the deaf Assistant D. A. William Converse-Roberts played the team's boss, Chief Arthur Gold; Tess's estranged husband, a philanderer who was also an attorney, Bruce Kaufman, was played by Tim Grimm; and Dicky's manipulative and jealous girlfriend, Kay Lockman, played by Nancy Everhard, caused Tess and Dicky trouble in their private lives. Maggie Zombro, a combative attorney often pitted against Tess, was played by Kay Lenz. Also appearing on the series were Vanessa Angel as police officer Peggy Eliot, and Jim Pirri on occasion as Tess's sometimes boyfriend, Asher. Much of the show's dialogue was in sign language, which Dicky often translated aloud so that viewers would understand what was being said. Matlin, as Tess Kaufman, could speak, but with difficulty.

REBEL, THE

Oct. 1959–Sept. 1961	ABC	Sun. 9–9:30 P.M.
June 1962–Sept. 1962	NBC	Wed. 8:30–9 P.M.

Nick Adams, playing an ex-Confederate soldier named Johnny Yuma, was the only regular character on the western adventure series *The Rebel.* At the end of the Civil War in the late 1800s, Yuma traveled from town to town in the Wild West, defending the innocent against the various criminal elements, as well as helping them solve certain moral issues, as he searched for inner peace. The show's theme song, "The Ballad of Johnny Yuma," sung by Johnny Cash, became familiar to millions of viewers who watched the series each week for three seasons. Goodson-Todman Productions, which usually produced game and panel shows for television, produced *The Rebel* in association with Celestial Productions and Fen-Ker-Ada Productions.

RED BUTTONS SHOW, THE

Oct. 1952–Dec. 1952	CBS	Tues. 8:30–9 P.M.
Dec. 1952–Jan. 1953	CBS	Sat. 9–9:30 P.M.
Jan. 1953–June 1954	CBS	Mon. 9:30–10 P.M.
Oct. 1954–May 1955	NBC	Fri. 8–8:30 P.M.

One of the first performers to become a major star via television in the early 1950s was comedian Red BUTTONS. Buttons, who later in his career won a Best Supporting Actor Oscar for a dramatic performance in the film *Sayonara,* starred in a weekly variety series that featured monologues, dance numbers, and a much-publicized song he called the "Ho-Ho" song, during which he placed his hands together, leaned his head against them at an amusing angle, and hopped around the stage, singing "Ho-Ho, He-He, Ha-Ha." For some reason, the song became a national craze, and it is cited by many as the most memorable thing about Buttons's show. Also featured were a company of regulars who sang, danced, and performed in sketches with Red that included at different times during the show's three-year run, Dorothy Jolliffe, Pat Carroll, Beverly Dennis, Jeanne Carson, Sara Seeger, Jimmy Little, Ralph Stanley, Sammy Birch, Allan Walker, Joe Silver, Betty Ann Grove, Phyllis Kirk, Paul Lynde, Bobby Sherwood, and the Elliot Lawrence Orchestra. Among the funny recurring characters Buttons played on the show were a punchy boxer named Rocky Buttons; a little boy named Kupie Kid; Sad Sack; and the dim-minded German, Keegelfaven. *The Red Buttons Show* was produced by Jess Kimmell and directed by Peter Kass.

RED SKELTON SHOW, THE

Sept. 1951–June 1952	NBC	Sun. 10–10:30 P.M.
Sept. 1952–June 1953	NBC	Sun. 7–7:30 P.M.
Sept. 1953–June 1954	CBS	Tues. 8:30–9 P.M.
July 1954–Sept. 1954	CBS	Wed. 8–9 P.M.
Sept. 1954–Dec. 1954	CBS	Tues. 8–8:30 P.M.
June 1955–June 1961	CBS	Tues. 9:30–10 P.M.
Sept. 1961–June 1962	CBS	Tues. 9–9:30 P.M.
Sept. 1962–June 1963	CBS	Tues. 8:30–9:30 P.M.
Sept. 1963–June 1964	CBS	Tues. 8–9 P.M.
Sept. 1964–June 1970	CBS	Tues. 8:30–9:30 P.M.
Sept. 1970–Mar. 1971	NBC	Mon. 7:30–8 P.M.
June 1971–Aug. 1971	NBC	Sun. 8:30–9 P.M.

Comedian Red SKELTON, who enjoyed success on the stage, in films, and on radio, also had one of the longest-running, most successful comedy variety shows on television. Skelton's comedic talents were especially well suited to television because he was essentially a visual comic. One of the first entertainment-world superstars to have a weekly show on television, Skelton's show remained popular with viewers for over 20 years, and when his weekly show ended its run, SKELTON continued to star on periodic specials for the next 20 years.

Many of the wonderfully funny characters Red introduced on his television show had previously been heard, but not seen, on his successful radio show, which was on the air from 1939 until 1953. These characters included his "Mean Widdle Kid," who always said "I dood it," in the wake of the chaos he usually caused; the country bumpkin, Clem Kadiddlehopper; the inept Sheriff Dead-eye of the Wild West; the punch-drunk boxer, Cauliflower McPugg; the always drunk Willie Lump-Lump; the con artist, San Fernando Red; Bolivar Shagnasty; and Freddie the Freeloader, a character who performed in pantomime and was created especially for television.

Red's show always opened with a monologue, which was followed by various sketches and performances by well-known guest stars, that in 1964 included the celebrated rock and roll group, the Rolling Stones, in a rare television appearance. Orchestra leader David Rose provided the music for Red's shows on both radio and television. Other regulars who appeared with Skelton over the years were Carol Worthington, Chanin Hale, Jan Arvan, Bob Duggan, Peggy Rea, Brad Logan, Elsie Baker, Jackson Bostwick, Yvonne Ewald, Dorothy Love, John Magruder, Ida Mae McKenzie, Janos Prohaska, Mike Wagner and the Burgundy Street Singers. Skelton always ended his shows by saying, "God Bless."

REED, DONNA (DONNA BELLE MULLENGER 1921–1986)

For eight years, from 1958 through 1966, Academy Award–winning actress Donna Reed had one of the most popular situation comedy series on television. Reed, who was born in the small town of Denison, Iowa, grew up on a farm. A beautiful child and then a beautiful young woman, Donna won a beauty contest in Denison when she was in high school, and upon graduation, she attended Los Angeles City College in Hollywood where she studied drama and appeared in several college plays, planning to pursue her dream of becoming an actress. In college she won the title "Campus Queen," which helped attract the attention of a Hollywood talent scout at MGM Studios, who was so impressed with her beauty that he encouraged his superiors to sign her to a contract. Donna had a small role in the film *The Get-Away* (1941), and subsequently had small roles in MGM's *Babes on Broadway* (1941), *The Bugle Sounds* (1941), *The Courtship of Andy Hardy* (1942), and *The Man From Down Under* (1943). In 1944, Donna won the leading female role in the film *See Here, Private Hargrove,* which impressed film critics and established her as one of Hollywood's most promising new stars. In 1945, Reed had the leading ingenue role in the film *The Picture of Dorian Gray,* which was her most important film role up until that time. It was, however, in 1946, that Donna Reed played her most memorable film role—Mary Hatch in the Christmas classic *It's a Wonderful Life*. In 1953, Reed won an Academy Award for her portrayal of a prostitute in the film *From Here to Eternity*. After starring in the films *The Caddy* (1953, opposite comedian Jerry Lewis), *The Far Horizons* (1955), and *The Whole Truth* (1958), Reed decided to try television and accepted the leading role on *The DONNA REED SHOW*. The show was a success, and before long, Donna Reed had become America's favorite television wife and mother, and over the years she was nominated for the "Best Actress in a Television Series Award" every year from 1959 through 1962. When the show ended its run, Donna retired from show business, but came out of retirement in 1974 to appear in the film *The Yellow-Headed Summer*. During the 1984–85 TV season, Reed accepted the role of Ellie Ewing Farlow on the hit TV series *DALLAS*, replacing Barbara Bel Geddes in the role for one season. Two weeks before her 65th birthday, Donna Reed died unexpectedly of pancreatic cancer.

REEVES, GEORGE (GEORGE KEEFER BREWER 1914–1959)

To millions of TV viewers, George Reeves *was* Superman, a role he played in hundreds of TV shows and films. Few people realize, however, that Reeves was a competent actor who played many other roles during his long performing career. Born in Woolstock, Iowa, but raised in Pasadena, California, Reeves received an B.A. degree from Pasadena Junior College before embarking upon a career as an actor. One of Reeves's first acting jobs was as one of the Tarlton Twins in the classic film *Gone With the Wind* in 1939. He subsequently appeared in such films as *Four Wives* (1939), *The Monroe Doctrine* (1939), *Virginia City* (1940), *Knute Rockne: All American* (1940), *'Til We Meet Again* (1940), *The Strawberry Blonde* (1941), *Blood and Sand* (1941), *So Proudly We Hail!* (1943), *Winged Vic-*

George Reeves as Superman (Author's collection)

tory (1944), *Jungle Jim* (1948), *Special Agent* (1949), and *Superman and the Mole Men* (1951), which led to his playing the Superman/Clark Kent role on the subsequent very successful TV series *The Adventures of Superman,* which began filming in 1951. Reeves became so identified with the part that he found it increasingly difficult to get any other roles in films or on TV. His last film appearance was in *Westward Ho the Wagons!* (1956). Reeves committed suicide in 1959 at the age of 45.

REGIS AND KATHIE LEE SHOW, THE
(see *Live With Regis And Kathie Lee*)

REISER, PAUL (1957–)
Before he became the producer and star of the popular television situation comedy series *MAD ABOUT YOU,* Paul Reiser was a successful stand-up comedian and actor. Reiser was born in New York City and attended Stuyvesant High School and the State University of New York at Binghamton, where he majored in music. After completing his education, Reiser embarked upon a career in comedy, and in addition to appearing in numerous comedy clubs, he also worked as an actor in such films as *Diner* (1982), *Odd Jobs* (1984), *Beverly Hills Cop* (1984), *Aliens* (1986), *Cross My Heart* (1987), *Beverly Hills Cop II* (1987), *Crazy People* (1990), and *The Marrying Man* (1991), in the TV film *You Ruined My Life* (1987), on the TV special *Paul Reiser Out on a Whim* (1988), and as a regular on the TV series *My Two Dads* (1987). Reiser formed his own production company, which he called "Nuance," after a speech the character he played in *Diner* delivered, and in 1992 produced his own TV series, *Mad About You,* which became one of TV's top-rated programs. While *Mad About You* was being aired, Reiser continued to star in such films as *Family Prayers* (1993), *The Tower* (1993), *Mr. Write* (1994), *Bye Bye, Love* (1995), and *The Story of Us* (1999). In 1999, Reiser and his *Mad About You* costar, Academy Award–winning actress Helen Hunt, were paid an astounding $1 million per episode for their final season on that series.

REMINGTON STEELE
Oct. 1982–Mar. 1983	NBC	Fri. 10–11 P.M.
Mar. 1983–Dec. 1983	NBC	Tues. 9–10 P.M.
Jan. 1984–Feb. 1986	NBC	Tues. 10–11 P.M.
Feb. 1986–Aug. 1986	NBC	Sat. 10–11 P.M.
Feb. 1987	NBC	Tues. 10–11 P.M.
Mar. 1987	NBC	Mon. 10–11 P.M.

When an intelligent young society woman named Laura Holt, played by Stephanie Zimbalist, decided to open her own private detective agency that would cater to the needs of wealthy society clients on the detective drama series *Remington Steele,* she found that people were reluctant to use her services because she was a woman. Her solution was to invent an imaginary male boss for her company whom she called "Remington Steele." When her clients demanded to meet the nonexistent Mr. Steele, Laura hired a debonair, attractive man whose real name and identity remained a mystery, but who filled the bill, played by Irish actor Pierce BROSNAN. Holt's company flourished, and the mysterious Mr. Steele became the company's major asset. A fan of old-time Hollywood movies, Steele often enacted scenes from classic films when working on a case, and before long, the attractive pair became romantically, as well as professionally, involved. Appearing as regulars on the series were James Read as Murphy Michaels, who was Laura's original partner but left the series after the 1983 season, reportedly to form his own agency; Janet DeMay as Bernice Foxe, the agency's secretary who ran off after the 1982–83 season to marry a saxophone player; and Doris Roberts, who played Mildred and joined the cast in 1983 and remained with the series until it departed the airwaves in 1987.

REUBENS, PAUL (PAUL RUBENFELD AKA PEE-WEE HERMAN AND PAUL MALL 1952–)
Paul Reubens, who became well known as TV's Pee-wee Herman on the popular children's show *PEE-WEE'S PLAYHOUSE,* was born in Peekskill, New York. After finishing his schooling, Reubens served in the U.S. Marine Corps, and when his service ended he was given an honorable discharge. Reubens decided that he wanted to be a comedian and began to perform in various comedy clubs and was a contestant on the popular *GONG SHOW* in the 1970s. In the 1980s, Reubens appeared on *Pray TV,* and had small roles in the films *Midnight Madness* (1980), *The Blues Brothers* (1980), *Cheech & Chong's Next Movie* (1980), and *Dream On* (1981), before starring on his own TV series, *The Pee-wee Herman Show* in 1981, introducing his Pee-wee character. He subsequently appeared in several additional films, including *Pandemonium* (1982), *Meatballs: Part II* (1984), and as Pinocchio in a *Faerie Tale Theatre* production in 1983. In 1985, Reubens starred as Pee-wee Herman in the film *Pee-wee's Big Adventure* and also appeared on a new TV series, *Pee-wee's Playhouse,* a show that he produced, directed, and starred in that became very successful with young viewers and made Pee-wee Herman, if not Paul Reubens, a household name. In 1991, Reubens was arrested for indecent actions performed in a movie theater in Florida, and his career was temporarily curtailed. He subsequently appeared in the film *Buffy the Vampire Slayer* (1992), *The Nightmare Before Christmas* (1993), as the voice of Lock), on the TV series *MURPHY BROWN* (as Andrew J. Lansing III), *Matilda* (1996), *Dr. Doolittle* (1998, as the voice of the Raccoon), *Blow* (2001), and others, and hosted the TV game show *You Don't Know Jack* (2001), which was based on the CD-ROM game of the same name. Over the years, Reubens made memorable guest-starring appearances on such shows as *MORK & MINDY* and *EVERYBODY LOVES RAYMOND,* among others.

REYNOLDS, BURT (BURTON LEON REYNOLDS JR. 1936–)

Before he became an actor, Burt Reynolds, who was born in Waycross, Georgia, was an aspiring football player whose athletic career was cut short when he was involved in a serious automobile accident that damaged his knee. In college, Reynolds became interested in acting and began appearing in school plays, and when he left school he went to Hollywood determined to break into films. Before long he was seen playing small roles on such TV series as ZANE GREY THEATER, M Squad, ROUTE 66, PERRY MASON, and FLIPPER, but Reynolds's big break occurred when he won the role of Ben Frazer on the TV series RIVERBOAT in 1959. In 1962, he joined the regular cast of GUNSMOKE, playing Quint Asper, a role he played until 1965. In 1966, and 1970, Reynolds starred on two TV series of his own, Hawk, which had a brief run, and Dan August. In 1972, Reynolds was cast in his first major feature film, Deliverance, and his performance was so impressive that he became an instant film star. Major roles followed in such box-office favorites as Smokey and the Bandit (1977), Cannonball Run (1981), and The Best Little Whorehouse in Texas (1982). Reynolds also became a film director during this time, and he directed the successful film Sharkey's Machine in 1981. In 1989, Burt Reynolds returned to television as the star of the B. L. Stryker, and the following year he directed and starred on the situation comedy EVENING SHADE, which proved only moderately successful and remained on the air for only one season. Reynolds enjoyed a film comeback in Boogie Nights in 1997, playing a role that won him an Academy Award nomination as Best Supporting Actor.

REYNOLDS, MARJORIE (MARJORIE GOODSPEED 1916–1997)

When Marjorie Reynolds, who is perhaps best known for playing Peg Riley on The LIFE OF RILEY, was a child, she appeared in silent films such as Scaramouche (1923). By the early 1930s, Reynolds, who was born in Bhul, Idaho, but moved to Hollywood with her parents when she was an infant, was a promising young starlet who appeared in such movies as Wine, Women and Song (1933), Collegiate (1936), Murder in Greenwich Village (1937), Streets of New York (1939), Tillie the Toiler (1941), and numerous other second-feature films. In 1942, Reynolds won the leading female role opposite Bing CROSBY in the immensely popular film Holiday Inn, which led to other important roles in such films as Dixie (1943), Duffy's Tavern (1945), and Heaven Only Knows (1947). Reynolds entered television in 1953 when she played the long-suffering, but loving wife of Chester A. Riley. Reynolds played Peg Riley until the show left the air in 1958, and subsequently appeared in the films Juke Box Rhythm (1959), The Silent Witness (1962), and on the TV miniseries Pearl (1978) before retiring from show business in the early 1980s.

RHODA

Sept. 1974–Sept. 1975	CBS	Mon. 9:30–10 P.M.
Sept. 1975–Jan. 1977	CBS	Mon. 8–8:30 P.M.
Jan. 1977–Sept. 1978	CBS	Sun. 8–8:30 P.M.
Sept. 1978–Dec. 1978	CBS	Sat. 8–8:30 P.M.

When Rhoda made its debut as a weekly half-hour situation comedy series in 1974, viewers were already familiar with the show's title character, Rhoda Morgenstern. Rhoda had been a regular character on the popular MARY TYLER MOORE SHOW, and Rhoda was that show's first successful spin-off series. When she first appeared, Rhoda, who was played by Valerie HARPER, was a young woman from New York City who had low self-esteem. Rhoda worked as a window dresser in a Minneapolis department store and had a tiny attic apartment in the same building as Mary Richards, who eventually became her best friend. When Rhoda left Minneapolis to return home to New York, she got a job and a new boyfriend, Joe Gerard, played by David Groh, who owned the New York Wrecking Company. Living in the same building as Rhoda was her younger sister, Brenda, played by Julie Kavner, who was a bank teller also with low self-esteem. A frequent visitor to the girls' apartments was their mother, Ida Morgenstern, played by Nancy Walker, and on occasion, their father, Martin, played by Harold Gould. Other characters who were seen on the show regularly included Carlton, the unseen doorman at Rhoda's apartment building whose voice was supplied by Lorenzo Music (one of Rhoda's coproducers); Nick Lobo, Brenda's boyfriend, who was an accordionist, played by Richard Masur; Myrna Morgenstein, played by Barbara Sharma, a former classmate of Rhoda's who went to work for Rhoda when she formed her own freelance window-dressing company; Joe's employee at the Wrecking Company, Justin Culp, played by Scoey Mitchell; Gary Levy, an aggressive boutique owner, played by Ron Silver; and Rhoda's stewardess friend, Sally Gallagher, played by Anne Meara. Also appearing on the series over the years were Kenneth McMillan as Rhoda's boss, Jack Doyle, and Nancy Lane as Tina Molinari. Early in the series, Rhoda and Joe were married, and as time went on were eventually divorced. Ida Morgenstern's husband left her toward the end of the series, and she became a single woman like both of her daughters.

The executive producers of Rhoda were James L. Brooks and Allan Burns for MTM (Mary Tyler Moore) Productions from 1974 until 1978, and Charles Brown was executive producer for the series' final season.

RICH MAN, POOR MAN (BOOKS I AND II)

Feb. 1976–Mar. 1976	ABC	Mon. 10–11 P.M. (Orig. mini-series)
Sept. 1976–Mar. 1977	ABC	Tues. 9–10 P.M. (Book II)
May 1977–June 1977	ABC	Tues. 9–11 P.M. (Rerun of Book I)

Irwin Shaw's epic best-selling book Rich Man, Poor Man was the basis of one of television's landmark miniseries, which chronicled the lives of the Jordache family, and was primarily concerned with the very different lives of two brothers, Rudy and Tom Jordache, played by Peter Strauss and Nick Nolte. *Rich Man, Poor Man* was an enormously successful series, and it became the inspiration for the numerous serialized versions of novels and stories that followed, including the phenomenally successful miniseries *ROOTS*. First seen as a 12-part series, *Rich Man, Poor Man* rated third in the Nielsen top shows in 1976, and won an impressive 23 Emmy nominations. In fall 1976, a 21-part continuation of the original miniseries was released, but failed to capture the ratings or the awards received by the original production. The series revolved around Axel and Mary Jordache, played by Edward ASNER and Dorothy McGuire and their two sons, the good son, Rudy, and the troubled son, Tom. Also seen on the original series were Susan Blakely as Julie Prescott, the object of both the boys' affection; Bill Bixby as Willie Abbott; Robert Reed as Teddy Boylan; Ray Milland as Duncan Calderwood; Kim Darby as Virginia Calderwood; Talia Shire as Teresa Santoro; Lawrence Pressman as Bill Benton; and Kay Lenz as Kate. The second book of *Rich Man, Poor Man* featured several additional performers, including Gregg Henry as Tom's son, Wesley Jordache; James Carroll Jordan as Julie's son, Billy Abbott; Susan Sullivan as Maggie Porter; William Smith as Anthony Falconetti; Dimitra Arliss as Marie Falconetti; Sorrell Booke as Phil Greenberg; Peter Haskell as Charles Estep; Laraine Stephens as Claire Estep; Penny Peyser as Romana Scott; John Anderson as Scotty; Peter Donat as Arthur Raymond; Cassie Yates as Annie Adams; Barry Sullivan as Senator Paxton; G. D. Spradlin as Senator Dillon; and Philip Abbott as John Franklin. Universal Television produced both miniseries. Harve Bennett was the original series executive producer, and Jon Epstein was the show's producer. Book II of *Rich Man, Poor Man* had Michael Gleason as its executive producer, and Epstein also produced this series.

RICHARD DIAMOND, PRIVATE DETECTIVE

July. 1957–Sept. 1957	CBS	Mon. 9:30–10 P.M.
Jan. 1958–Sept. 1958	CBS	Thurs. 8–8:30 P.M.
Feb. 1959–Sept. 1959	CBS	Sun. 10–10:30 P.M.
Oct. 1959–Jan. 1960	NBC	Mon. 7:30–8 P.M.
June 1960–Sept. 1960	NBC	Tues. 9–9:30 P.M.

Before he played Richard Kimball on the successful TV series *The FUGITIVE* in 1963, David JANSSEN played a private eye named Richard Diamond on the half-hour *Richard Diamond, Private Detective* series. The soft-spoken, serious Diamond, an ex–New York City policeman, often solicited the help of NYPD friends such as Lt.Dennis "Mac" McGough, played by Regis Toomey, to help him with his cases. After a year and a half on the air, Diamond relocated to Los Angeles, where he acquired a regular girlfriend, Karen Wells, played by Barbara Bain. In Los Angeles, Diamond used an answering service to get his phone messages. The voice of the receptionist who took his calls belonged to a girl named Sam, whose face was never seen, but whose sultry voice and lovely legs became popular attractions on the show. The voice and legs belonged to Mary Tyler MOORE, and then to Roxanne Brooks. In Los Angeles, Diamond once again had a friend in the Police Department, Lt. Pete Kile, played by Russ Conway, but he also had an enemy named Sgt. Alden, played by Richard Devon, who was always out to get him. The series was produced by Dick Powell's Four Star Productions. Powell had played the Richard Diamond character on the radio version of the show from 1949 through 1952.

RICKI LAKE

1993–present Syndicated Mon.–Fri. Various times

A former teen actress named Ricki Lake, who had been discovered by filmmaker John Waters and was one of the stars of his film *Hairspray*, and who had also been a regular on the *CHINA BEACH* TV series, suddenly emerged as a talk show hostess on a five-days-a-week series that bore her name, *The Ricki Lake Show*, in 1993. The one-hour show usually featured such topics as "Jilted Lovers," "Promiscuous Teenagers," "Who Was My Father," "My Best Friend Stole My Boyfriend," "Mothers and Daughters Who Don't Get Along," "Problems with Mother's Boyfriends," and other subjects that especially appealed to young female viewers and made it one of the more popular daytime talk shows on the air.

RIFLEMAN, THE

Sept. 1958–Sept. 1960	ABC	Tues. 9–9:30 P.M.
Sept. 1960–Sept. 1961	ABC	Tues. 8–8:30 P.M.
Oct. 1961–July. 1963	ABC	Mon. 8:30–9 P.M.

Chuck CONNORS starred as Lucas McCain, a homesteader in the Old West whose wife died and left him with a young son, Mark McCain, played by Johnny Crawford, to raise by himself on this weekly western adventure series. Connors, who had been a professional baseball player before becoming an actor, began his acting career on this critically acclaimed series, set in the fictional western town of North Fork, New Mexico, which had a law-enforcing marshal named Micah Torrence, played by Paul Fix, who frequently called upon Lucas to help him deal with various outlaws in the town. Lucas was an expert marksman who never went anywhere without his Winchester lever-action rifle that had a large ring that cocked the rifle when Lucas had to draw on someone. Appearing as a romantic interest for Lucas from 1960 through 1962 was Joan Taylor as Miss Milly Scott, who owned the town's general store. During the 1962 season, a woman who was a goodhearted con artist, Lou Mallory, played by Patricia Blair, joined the series. Also appearing regularly on the series were Bill Quinn as Sweeney, the bartender, and Hope Summers as Hattie Denton. By the time the series left the air, after four seasons, Mark McCain, who was 12 when the series began, had grown into adolescence and was beginning to show the usual signs of teenage rebelliousness associated with 16-year-old boys. Over the years Arthur Gardner, Arnold Laven, and Jules Levy produced the series for Dick Powell's Four Star Films. In 1990, Chuck Connors and Johnny Crawford were reunited on an episode of the western series *Paradise*.

RIN TIN TIN

(see *Adventures of Rin Tin Tin, The*)

RIPTIDE

Jan. 1984–Feb. 1986	NBC	Tues. 9–10 P.M.
Mar. 1986–Apr. 1986	NBC	Fri. 8–9 P.M.

Riptide, about two beach bums who decide to become private detectives, starred Perry King and Joe Penny as Cody Allen and Nick Ryder. The men's office was located in Cody's cabin cruiser, *The Riptide,* which was docked at Pier 56 in King's Harbor, and also from their favorite hangout, the Straightaway Restaurant, which was owned by a character named Straightaway, played by Gianni Russo. Cody and Nick occasionally used Nick's old but serviceable helicopter, *The Screaming Mimi,* Cody's speedboat, and, during the 1984 season the services of a character named Mama Jo, played by Anne Francis, and the all-girl crew of her charter boat, *The Barefoot Contessa,* as well as those of the awkward computer hacker, Murray "Boz" Bozinsky, played by Thom Bray. Kirk "The Drool" Dooley, a dock boy, played by Ken Olandt, often did legwork for Cody and Nick. Also appearing on the series at different times were Jack Ging and June Chadwick, as police lieutenants Ted Quinlan and Joanna Parisi. Stephen J. Cannell created and produced the series for his Stephen J. Cannell Productions.

RITTER, JOHN (JONATHAN SOUTHWORTH RITTER 1948–)

The son of famous cowboy star Tex Ritter, John Ritter was born in Burbank, California. After graduating from the University of Southern California, where he majored in drama, Ritter, who had decided to follow in his father's footsteps and become an actor, began to appear on such TV series as *Dan August* and HAWAII FIVE-0, before being cast in the regular role of Reverend Matthew Fordwick on the successful WALTONS TV series. Supporting roles in the films *The Other* (1972), *The Stone Killer* (1973), and *Nickelodeon* (1976), led to his being cast as Jack Tripper on the THREE'S COMPANY situation comedy. The series was a tremendous hit and made Ritter a TV superstar. While appearing on *Three's Company,* Ritter continued to appear in such feature and TV films as *Ringo* (1978), *The Comeback Kid* (1980), *They All Laughed* (1981), *The Flight of Dragons* (1982), *Love Thy Neighbor* (1984), and others. In 1984, Ritter revived his *Three's Company* role on a new TV series, *Three's a Crowd,* which was not successful. He continued to appear in films and in 1987 starred on another TV series, *Hooperman,* which also

proved to be less than successful and was canceled after a short time on the air. Roles on numerous TV series, such as *Anything But Love,* The ROPERS, DAVE'S WORLD, NEWSRADIO, TOUCHED BY AN ANGEL, *King of the Hill,* BUFFY THE VAMPIRE SLAYER, ALLY MCBEAL, VERONICA'S CLOSET, CHICAGO HOPE, and many others, the TV films *The Dreamer of Oz* (1990, playing *Wizard of Oz* author L. Frank Baum), *Hearts Afire* (1992), *Heartbeat* (1993), *Unforgivable* (1996), a critically acclaimed performance in the feature film *Sling Blade* (1996), and numerous other projects, have made Ritter one of the busiest character actors in show business. As of this writing, Ritter's most recent appearance was in the film *Panic* (2000).

RIVA, MARIA (MARIA SIEBER AKA MARIA MANTON C. 1924–)

The daughter of a legendary film star of the 1930s and 1940s, Marlene Dietrich, Maria Riva was born in Germany and became one of early television's most active and successful actresses. When she was a child, Maria appeared in several of her mother's films, including *The Scarlet Empress* (1934, playing her mother as a child), and *The Garden of Allah* (1936, playing a schoolgirl). When World War II ended in 1945, Maria, who was classically trained as an actress, began to appear in a wide variety of roles on such live dramatic anthology programs as STUDIO ONE, The PHILCO TELEVISION PLAYHOUSE, *The Motorola TV Hour,* and as Queen Catherine the Great, a role her mother had played in the 1930s, on the CBS TV series YOU ARE THERE. Throughout the 1950s, Maria continued to appear on hundreds of dramatic anthology programs and became one of TV's most recognized faces. Suddenly, when the 1950s ended, Maria retired from the spotlight to raise her children, but in 1988, the actress resurfaced briefly to appear in the film *Scrooged* with Bill Murray, playing a character named Mrs. Rhinelander. Her comeback was short-lived, and once again, when good acting jobs failed to materialize, she retired. In 1997, Maria once again came out of retirement to appear in the TV miniseries *Murder One: Diary of a Serial Killer.*

RIVERBOAT

Sept. 1959–Jan. 1960	NBC	Sun. 7–8 P.M.
Feb. 1960–Jan. 1961	NBC	Sun. 7:30–8:30 P.M.

Seven years before the space ship *Enterprise* became familiar to millions of viewers on the STAR TREK TV series, another ship called *The Enterprise* was transporting people up and down the Mississippi, Missouri, and Ohio Rivers in the 1840s. *Riverboat* was an hour-long adventure series that was set on a 100-foot boat owned by Gary Holden, a former rumrunner, soldier, swordsman, and dockworker, played by Darren MCGAVIN. Holden was a good-natured, fun-loving romantic who had won the boat in a game of chance and was determined to turn his winning into a profitable business. Working with Holden was Ben Fraser, a boat pilot who was written off the series during its first season, played by Burt REYNOLDS. Also appearing on the series as regular characters were crew members Travis, played by William D. Gordon, who also left the series during its first season; Carney, played by Richard Wessell; Joshua, played by Jack Lambert; Chip, played by Mike McGreevey; Pickalong, played by Jack Mitchum; Terry Blake, played by Bart Patten; and Bill Blake, played by Noah Beery, Jr. Forty-four episodes of *Riverboat* were filmed before the series was canceled in 1961.

RIVERS, JOAN (JOAN ALEXANDRA MOLINSKY 1933–)

Versatile comedienne Joan Rivers was born in Brooklyn, New York, and attended Barnard College, where she majored in English and anthropology, before embarking upon a career as a stand-up comic shortly after she graduated from college. After years of appearing in comedy clubs around the country, Joan made her acting debut in the film *The Swimmer* in 1968, and that same year was seen on television in an episode of *Here's Lucy*. In 1969, Rivers starred on a TV series of her own, *The Joan Rivers Show*, which was not successful, and in 1971, she narrated "The Adventures of Letterman," for PBS's *The Electric Company* series. As a semiregular panelist on the HOLLYWOOD SQUARES game show during the 1975–76 season, a regular substitute guest host on NBC's TONIGHT SHOW from 1983 to 1986, and an actress in such films as *The Muppets Take Manhattan* in 1984, Joan kept busy on television and in films. Rivers became the regular host of CBS's *Late Show* during the 1986–87 season, and returned to *Hollywood Squares* as the "Center Square" panelist from 1987 through 1989. In the 1990s, Rivers appeared in such films as *Serial Mom* (1994), and played Meredith Dunston on the ANOTHER WORLD daytime soap opera in 1997, and herself on ALL MY CHILDREN in 1997. Currently, Rivers appears regularly with her daughter, Melissa, as a hostess on E! (Entertainment) Channel specials and sells her own line of jewelry on the QVC shopping network, as well as appearing regularly as a guest on such TV shows as *Live with Regis and Kelly* and SUDDENLY SUSAN, playing a character named Edie.

ROBERT MONTGOMERY PRESENTS (AKA LUCKY STRIKE THEATER, THE JOHNSON'S WAX PROGRAM, THE RICHARD HUDNUT SUMMER THEATER, ETC.)

Jan. 1950–June 1957 NBC Mon. 9:30–10:30 P.M.

Film star Robert MONTGOMERY produced the big-budget dramatic anthology series *Robert Montgomery Presents*, which presented live adaptations of novels and stage plays, as well as original TV dramas, during television's early years. When the series first aired in 1950, TV adaptations of such successful films as *Rebecca* and *Dark Victory* were seen, but after a few months adaptations of works other than films became more prominent. The first production presented on *Robert Montgomery Presents* was an adaptation of W. Somerset Maugham's *The Letter*, which had been a best-selling novel, as well as a successful stage play and film. Other critically acclaimed productions included Helen Hayes in *Victoria Regina*, Van Heflin in *Arrowsmith*, Barbara Bel Geddes in *The Philadelphia Story*, Kim Hunter in *Rise Up and Walk*, Joanne Woodward, making her first important TV appearance, in *Penny*, Jack Lemmon in *Dinah, Kip and Mr. Bigelow*, Ed Begley, Dorothy Gish, Vaughn Taylor, and James Dean in *Harvest*, Louis Jourdan in *Wages of Fear*, Phyllis Kirk, John Newland, and Gena Rowlands in *The Great Gatsby*, Elizabeth Montgomery (Robert Montgomery's daughter, who made many appearances on the program) in *Top Secret*, James Cagney, in his first major TV appearance, in *Soldiers from the Wars Returning*, Claudette Colbert in *After All These Years*, and Peter Falk in *Return Visit*, to name just a few. One of the more spectacular productions was a drama about the explosion of the dirigible *Hindenburg*, which at the end of the drama presented interviews with real-life survivors of the tragedy.

During the summer months from 1952 through 1956, *Robert Montgomery Presents* offered the public a repertory company of actors that included Jan Miner, John Newland, Anne Seymour, Cliff Robertson, Vaughn Taylor, Elizabeth Montgomery, Charles Drake, Margaret Hayes, Augusta Dabney, House Jameson, Dorothy Blackburn, Eric Sinclair, Mary K. Wells, John Gibson, Tom Middleton, and others, playing a wide variety of roles in many different TV plays.

ROBERT Q. LEWIS SHOW, THE (AKA ROBERT Q'S MATINEE)

July 1950–Sept. 1950	CBS	Sun. 9–9:15 P.M.
Sept. 1950–Jan. 1951	CBS	Sun. 11–11:15 P.M.
Jan. 1954–May 1956	CBS	Daytime

Genial game and talk show host, panelist Robert Q. LEWIS, who sometimes substituted for CBS's popular host Arthur GODFREY, hosted a prime-time series of his own, *The Robert Q. Lewis Show*, as well as two daytime variety programs. On his prime-time series, which was seen for 15 minutes once a week, Lewis, whose dark-rimmed spectacles became his trademark, interviewed various celebrity guests. Lewis's first daytime series, *Robert Q.'s Matinee*, was a 45-minutes show that remained on the air for 14 weeks. A popular feature on this show was Lewis's weekly "Breadwinner of the Week," during which Lewis interviewed someone with an unusual job who worked in the New York City area. His second daytime series, also called *The Robert Q. Lewis Show*, remained on the air for two years and featured such regulars as Jaye P. Morgan, Jan Arden, Betty Clooney, Jane Wilson, Lois Hunt and Earl Wrightson, Merv Griffin, Julann Wright, the Chordettes, dancer choreographer Don Liberto, and announcer Lee Vines.

ROBERTA QUINLAN SHOW, THE (AKA THE MOHAWK SHOWROOM)

May 1949–Nov. 1951	NBC	Tues. & Thurs.
		Mon., Wed., &
		Fri. evenings

As a tom-tom beat out an accompaniment to the sponsor's theme, "Car-pets-from-the-looms-of-Mohawk," Morton Downey, who originally hosted this 15-minutes, two and three times a week show, announced that it was time to hear singer/pianist Roberta Quinlan perform standard and hit songs of the day on this early television program. Quinlan, dressed in an evening gown and sitting at a piano, and sang her way into becoming one of television's first performers who became known primarily as a television personality.

ROBERTS, PERNELL (PERNELL ELVIN ROBERTS 1928–)

Pernell Roberts became best known as Ben Cartwright's eldest son, Adam, on the BONANZA western series. Before he became a member of the the cast in 1959, Roberts, who was born in Waycross, Georgia, appeared on such TV series as *Bronco* and *Cimarron City* and had small roles in the films *The Sheepman* (1958) and *Desire Under the Elms* (1958). The success of *Bonanza* made Roberts an instant TV star, but he left the series in the middle of its run in a salary dispute with the producers, and his career came to a sudden halt. He continued to appear on hundreds of TV shows such as *The VIRGINIAN*, *The BIG VALLEY*, *The WILD WILD WEST*, *MISSION: IMPOSSIBLE*, *GUNSMOKE*, *The NAME OF THE GAME*, *HAWAII FIVE-O*, *BANACEK*, *ELLERY QUEEN*, *The ROCKFORD FILES*, *The MAN FROM ATLANTIS*, *QUINCY*, and *DIAGNOSIS MURDER*, among others, and had featured roles in such films as *The Errand Boy* (1961), *Four Rode Out* (1969), and *Tibetana* (1970), and had regular roles on the TV series *Alien Lover* (1975), *Centennial* (1978), *TRAPPER JOHN, M.D.* (1979), as well as hosting the TV series *FBI: The Untold Stories* (1991). Roberts nevertheless failed to become the "star" his promising debut on *Bonanza* and the popularity he enjoyed because of the show had indicated he would be.

ROBERTSON, DALE (DAYLE LYMOINE ROBERTSON 1923–)

A true son of the West, Dale Robertson, who was born in Harrah, Oklahoma, first became well known to TV viewers as Jim Hardie on the *Tales of Wells Fargo* western series. Robertson was a popular film star before he entered television. A handsome, dark-haired young man with an appealing smile, Robertson got his first big acting break in films because an agent thought he looked and sounded like a young Clark Gable, which indeed he did. Robertson's first film role was in *The Boy with Green Hair* in 1948, and, because he "clicked" with filmgoers, he subsequently played increasingly larger roles in such films as *Flamingo Road* (1949), *The Girl from Jones Beach* (1949), *Two Flags West* (1950), *Call Me Mister* (1951), *Take Care of My Little Girl* (1951, which really established him as a film star), *The Outcasts of Poker Flats* (1952), *O'Henry's Full House* (1952), *The Farmer Takes a Wife* (1953), *Sitting Bull* (1954), and *Hell Canyon Outlaws* (1957), before appearing on the TV series *Tales of Wells Fargo*. Although he did appear in several feature films after *Wells Fargo* left the air, Robertson concentrated on his television appearances and guest-starred on such series as *FANTASY ISLAND* and *MURDER, SHE WROTE*, and was a regular on *The Iron Horse* (1966), *DEATH VALLEY DAYS* (1968–72), *American Horse and Horseman* (1973), *DYNASTY* (1981), and *J. J. Starbuck* (1987).

ROBIN HOOD

(see *Adventures of Robin Hood, The*)

ROBOCOP

1994–1995	Syndicated	Various days and times

The science fiction series *Robocop* was a live-action, cartoonlike show based on the violent 1987 hit film of the same name. It was set in the 21st century in Delta City, a controlled environment run by a company called Omni Consumer Products (OCP). OCP had a hand in just about everything that happened in Delta City and controlled everything in the community including the local government and the products citizens of the city bought, and had even taken over the highly technological RoboCop Police Department. Former cop Alex Murphy (aka RoboCop), played by Richard Eden, who had been killed in a shootout had his human remains implanted in a high-tech cyborg body. Murphy, who had a lot of his own personality remaining, patrolled Delta City, a dangerous place that was adjacent to the "Old" city of Detroit. Also appearing on the series was Yvette Niper as Murphy's human partner in the police department, Lisa Madigan. Blu Mankuma played RoboCop's boss, Sgt. Stan Parks; Andrea Roth played a secretary named Diana Powers, whose brain had been stolen by a mad scientist and who existed inside a computer; David Gardner played the head of the evil OCP empire, who was called "The Chairman"; Sarah Campbell played a young orphan named Gadget; Dan Duran and Erica Ehm played Bo Harlan and Rocky Crenshaw, the coanchors of a three-minute TV news program called "Media Bank"; Jennifer Griffin played Murphy's wife, Nancy; and Peter Costigan played Murphy's son, 13-year-old Jimmy. The show's main antagonists were a mad scientist named Dr. Cray Z. Mallardo; John Rubenstein, who played a slippery character named Chip Chaykin; and James Kidnie, who played the villainous Pudface Morgan, who had been disfigured by toxic waste.

ROCKFORD FILES, THE

Sept. 1974–May 1977	NBC	Fri. 9–10 P.M.
June 1977	NBC	Fri. 8:30–9:30 P.M.
July 1977–June 1979	NBC	Fri. 9–10 P.M.
Feb. 1979–Mar. 1979	NBC	Sat. 10–11 P.M.
Apr. 1979–Dec. 1979	NBC	Fri. 9–10 P.M.
Mar. 1980–Apr. 1980	NBC	Thurs. 10–11 P.M.
June 1980–July 1980	NBC	Fri. 9–10 P.M.

James GARNER, who had first come to the attention of the public as the star of the TV western adventure series *MAVERICK*, returned to television after starring in several feature films in 1974. Garner's new series, *The Rockford Files,* was a detective drama series. Garner played Jim Rockford, a private detective and former convict who had been imprisoned for a crime he did not commit but was exonerated when new evidence surfaced. Because of his own experience with the law, Rockford specialized in cases that seemed hopeless, and his talent for uncovering evidence that had been overlooked by the police did not endear him to law-enforcement officials, especially Police Det. Dennis Becker, played by Joe Santos, with whom Rockford had a love/hate relationship. Rockford worked out of his house trailer, which was at the beach near Los Angeles. He charged $200 a day plus expenses, which made him a rather expensive P.I. Assisting Rockford, with his investigations were his father, a retired trucker named Joseph "Rocky" Rockford, played on the pilot by Robert Donley, and in the series by Noah Beery, Jr., and his girlfriend/attorney Beth Davenport, played by Gretchen Corbett from 1974 until 1976. Also appearing on the series regularly were Stuart Margolin as Evelyn "Angel" Martin, a former cellmate of Rockford's when he was in prison, Bo Hopkins as John Cooper (1978–79), Tom Atkins as Lt. Alex Diehl (1974–76), James Luisi as Lt. Doug Chapman (1976–80), and, during the last season, Tom SELLECK as Lance White, a fellow private eye who always seemed to get things to work out for him without much effort. Stephen J. Cannell and Roy Huggins created the series, and The executive producer was Meta Rosenberg. In 1994, Garner, Margolin, and Santos were reunited for a two-hour TV film, *The Rockford Files: I Still Love L.A.*

ROCKY JONES, SPACE RANGER

Jan. 1952–1954	Syndicated	Various times and stations

Among television's most successful science fiction shows produced for younger viewers during the early 1950s was *Rocky Jones, Space Ranger,* which starred Richard Crane as the commander of the spaceship The Orbit Jet, Rocky Jones, who worked for the United Worlds; Sally Mansfield as his navigator; Vena Ray; Scotty Becket as Rocky's copilot, Winky; Maurice Cass as Professor Newton; and Robert Lyden as Bobby, a space ranger.

As the crew of The Orbit Jet cruised space defending democracy wherever it was in danger from hostile aliens from planets other than Earth, they had many adventures over the three years the show was aired. Unlike similar shows of the time such as *TOM CORBETT, SPACE CADET,* and *CAPTAIN VIDEO,* which had relatively small budgets, *Rocky Jones* had a large budget for the time and had realistic settings, well-done special effects, and sophisticated story lines. Unlike other science fiction shows for children in the late 1940s to early 1950s, *Rocky Jones* was filmed and not produced live. Produced by Roland

Reed Productions, the series was filmed at the Hal Roach Studios in Hollywood.

ROGERS, FRED (FRED MCFEELY ROGERS 1928–)

One of television's most celebrated children's show hosts, Fred Rogers hosted and produced the *MR. ROGERS' NEIGHBORHOOD* program. Born and raised in Latrobe, Pennsylvania, Rogers, who became an ordained Presbyterian minister, was attending college in the late 1940s when, while watching a local children's program, he first realized the potential of the new medium for teaching children. Soon after graduating from college, Rogers decided to try to find work on television in order to be a minister to young children. In order to learn what TV was all about, he got a job working backstage for western character actor George "Gabby" Hayes on his TV show for children. Hayes gave Rogers a bit of advice he never forgot: "When I'm looking at the camera," Hayes said, "I think of that one little buckaroo out there. That's who I talk to." Soon after, Rogers got a camera job working on an early morning kid's show that starred starred a lady known simply as "Josie." It was on this show that Rogers, working as a puppeteer, first introduced several characters he later used on his own TV show—Daniel the Striped Tiger and King Friday the 13th. Like Fran ALLISON of the *KUKLA, FRAN & OLLIE* series, Josie would stand in front of a backdrop and talk to Fred's puppet characters. Since he often had to run around behind the backdrop and did not want to be heard, he began his later-to-be-famous practice of wearing sneakers. On his own show, *Mr. Rogers' Neighborhood,* Fred

Mister Rogers (Author's collection)

changed his shoes for sneakers at the beginning of each show. The sweaters that the soft-spoken, gentle Rogers always wore on his shows were all handmade by his mother, and like his sneakers, became one of his trademarks. The show and Rogers, who had a wonderful way of talking to youngsters on their own level, became one of PBS's most successful children's offerings and remained on the air continuously for over 30 years, earning Fred Rogers numerous awards. Occasionally, Rogers makes guest-starring appearances in films and on TV shows and has been featured as himself in the film *Casper* (1995), and *Arthur* (voice, 1996), and as Mr. James in DR. QUINN, MEDICINE WOMAN (1993).

ROGERS, ROY (LEONARD FRANKLIN SLYE 1911–1998)

Roy Rogers, perhaps the most famous radio, film, and television cowboy of all time, was born in Cincinnati, Ohio, but moved to Hollywood when he was 18 years old. A talented country-western singer and guitar player, Rogers got jobs with such groups as the Hollywood Hillbillies, the Rocky Mountaineers, the Texas Outlaws, and his own group, the International Cowboys. In 1934, Rogers, who was at that time known as Leonard Slye (his real name) and then Dick Weston, and finally Roy Rogers, formed a new group with Bon Nolan and Tim Spencer that was called the Sons of the Pioneers, which became enormously popular. Their songs "Cool Water" and "Tumbling Tumbleweeds" became best-selling recordings. In time, Rogers' handsome, wholesome good looks attracted the attention of Hollywood talent scouts, and in 1935 he made his film debut as Dick Weston in *Way Up Thar*. As Leonard Slye, he appeared in *The Old Homestead* (1935) and several other second-feature films, usually playing a cowboy. In 1936, he appeared with the Sons of the Pioneers in the film *Rhythm on the Range*, which

Roy Rogers and Dale Evans (Author's collection)

starred Bing CROSBY and Martha RAYE. The following year, *Under Western Stars* (1938) made him an instant cowboy star. Over the next 30 years, Rogers, who became known as the "King of the Cowboys," starred in over 100 second-feature films, as well as the very successful *Son of Paleface* (1952) with Bob HOPE. Rogers also had his own radio show from 1944 until 1955, and with his wife and film costar Dale Evans, he had one of the most successful cowboy series on television, The ROY ROGERS SHOW, from 1951 through 1957. He was elected to the Country Music Hall of Fame in 1980 as a member of the Sons of the Pioneers and also in 1988 as a solo singer. Few entertainers enjoyed the public acclaim and success Roy Rogers did, and the singer/actor became a legend in his own time.

ROGERS, WAYNE (1933–)

Before he became famous for playing Capt. "Trapper John" McIntyre on the hit television series M*A*S*H in 1972, Wayne Rogers played Luke Perry on the TV series *Stagecoach West* (1960), had small roles in the films *Odds Against Tomorrow* (1959), *The Glory Guys* (1965), *Chamber of Horrors* (1966), *Cool Hand Luke* (1967), and *WUSA* (1970), and was featured on such TV series as The ZANE GREY THEATER, WANTED: DEAD OR ALIVE, GUNSMOKE, ALFRED HITCHCOCK PRESENTS, GOMER PYLE, USMC, HONEY WEST, The FUGITIVE, COMBAT, The F.B.I., and The BIG VALLEY. The success of M*A*S*H made Rogers one of TV's most sought-after actors in Hollywood, but early in its run, Rogers decided to leave the series when the producers asked him to sign a morality clause, but refused his demand that they sign one as well. The producers of M*A*S*H sued Rogers for breach of contract, but they lost the suit because Rogers had not signed a formal contract at the time. The following year, Rogers starred on the less-than-successful TV series *City of Angels*, and in 1979, he appeared with Lynn Redgrave on the series HOUSE CALLS. He subsequently appeared in such films as *Having Babies II* (1977), *The Top of the Hill* (1980), *The Hot Touch* (1981), *The Gig* (1985), *The Killing Time* (1987), *Passion and Paradise* (1989), *Ghosts of Mississippi* (1996), and *Frozen with Fear* (2000), and starred on the TV series *High Risk* (1988). In addition to his acting career, Rogers is also a successful producer of such TV films as *The Perfect Witness* (1989), *Money Plays* (1997), and *Nobody Knows Anything* (1998), and in the 1980s, guest-starred frequently on the series MURDER, SHE WROTE.

ROLLE, ESTHER (1920–1998)

Television viewers best remember African-American actress Esther Rolle as Florida Evans, a role she played on the highly successful TV series MAUDE and GOOD TIMES. Esther, who was born in Pompano Beach, Florida, made her acting debut on the stage, but in 1971, she first became familiar to viewers as Sadie Gray on the popular daytime serial drama series ONE LIFE TO LIVE. This led to her being cast as Beatrice Arthur's housekeeper, Florida, on *Maude*.

The outspoken Florida became an audience favorite, and in 1974, Rolle repeated her Florida role on a spin-off series, *Good Times,* which became even more popular than *Maude.* Unhappy with the quality of scripts she was given, Rolle left *Good Times* in 1979, and appeared in such films as *I Know Why the Caged Bird Sings* (1979), *Driving Miss Daisy* (1989), *How to Make an American Quilt* (1995), and in such TV films as *See China and Die* (1980), *The Mighty Quinn* (1989), *A Raisin in the Sun* (1989), *Message from Nam* (1993), *Scarlett* (1994, as Mammy in the *Gone With the Wind* sequel), as well as being a regular on the *Singer & Sons* (1990) TV series.

ROLLER DERBY ON TELEVISION

From 1949 through 1951, ABC's Roller Derby telecasts were among the most popular programs on the air. Before television emerged as America's favorite entertainment medium, few people had heard of the roller derby, but its fast-paced team races had everyone who owned a TV receiver in those years tuning in regularly to watch all of the exciting action as skaters raced one another around the rink. Roller derby was actually more like a violent free-for-all than a sporting event, as team members tried to knock one another off their feet or out of the rink as they whirled around. The sport, which included elements of skating, rugby, wrestling, and football, remained somewhat vague as far as actual rules and regulations were concerned, but no one seemed to mind. Two teams competed against each other, the men of one team against the men in the other team, the women against the women. ABC's show was usually seen three times a week and originated from various locations around New York City, including the 14th Regiment Armory in Brooklyn, as well as arenas on Long Island and in New Jersey. Ken Nydell was the Roller Derby's official announcer for ABC, and he gave a play-by-play of the skating competitions as the two teams skated around an oval track. The New York Chiefs were the home team, and they skated against such teams as the San Francisco Bay Bombers, and the Midwest Pioneers, among others. Also featured on the Roller Derby broadcasts were Joe Hasel (1949–50), Howard Myles (1950–51), and Ed Begley (1951). Fans of the sport made folk heroes of the various team members, and few people who ever watched roller derby on TV could forget a fearless, tough young woman skater named Tuffy Brasuhn, or an attractive blonde named Pat Gardner.

ROOKIES, THE

Sept. 1972–Sept. 1975	ABC	Mon. 8–9 P.M.
Sept. 1975–Apr. 1976	ABC	Tues. 9–10 P.M.
May 1976–June 1976	ABC	Tues. 10–11 P.M.

Three young rookie police officers, Terry Webster, Willie Gillis, and Mike Danko, played by Georg Stanford Brown, Michael Ontkean, and Sam Melville, were the major characters on the police/adventure series *The Rookies.* The three young cops, who worked for the Los Angeles Police Department, were a new college graduate, a former government social worker, and a soldier who had been recently discharged from the army. The trio was dedicated to using new, more humane methods of conducting police business, which often pitted them against their boss, Lt. Eddie Ryker, played by Gerald S. O'Laughlin, who had a more traditional approach to police work. Also appearing as regulars on the series were Kate JACKSON as Officer Danko's wife, Jill, who was a registered nurse, and Bruce Fairbairn, during the 1974–76 season, as Officer Chris Owens, who replaced Officer Gillis. The series was produced by Aaron SPELLING and Leonard Goldberg, who had previously been responsible for the successful series MOD SQUAD, and later produced the popular CHARLIE'S ANGELS series.

ROOM 222

Sept. 1969–Jan. 1971	ABC	Wed. 8:30–9 P.M.
Jan. 1971–Sept. 1972	ABC	Wed. 8–8:30 P.M.
Sept. 1971–Jan. 1974	ABC	Fri. 9–9:30 P.M.

Like the popular English film *To Sir, with Love,* which starred Sidney Poitier as a black secondary school teacher who teaches his underprivileged students some important lessons about life, *Room 222* was a schoolroom situation comedy series that starred Lloyd Haynes as Pete Dixon, an African-American teacher with a similar mission. At different times, his students at Walt Whitman High School in Los Angeles, who eventually grew to appreciate Dixon's concern and ability to communicate with them, included Alice Johnson, played by Karen Valentine; Richie Lane, played by Howard Rice; Helen Loomis, played by Judy Strangis; Jason Allen, played by Heshimu; Al Crowley, played by Pendrant Netherly; Bernie, played by David Jolliffe; Kim, played by Carol Green; Cleon, played by Ty Henderson; Pam, played by Ta-Tanisha; and Larry, played by Eric Laneuville. Dixon's fellow educator and girlfriend was a guidance counselor named Liz McIntyre, played by Denise Nicholas, and his superior at Walt Whitman was the school's sarcastic principal, Seymour Kaufman, played by Michael Constantine. *Room 222* was developed for ABC by James L. Brooks, and the series was produced and directed by Gene Reynolds.

ROOTIE KAZOOTIE

Dec. 1952–May 1954	ABC	Sat. 11–11:30 A.M.
Dec. 1950–Sept. 1952	NBC	Mon.–Fri. 6–6:15 P.M.

For four years, *Rootie Kazootie* was one of children's favorite TV programs. The star of the program was a hand puppet named Rootie Kazootie, a Little Leaguer who wore a baseball cap jauntily tilted on his head and who talked to the human regulars on the show, Tod Russell and John Vee. Rootie Kazootie's name came from the fact that he was always rooting and tooting on his kazoo. Other puppets on the show included Rootie's puppet girlfriend, Polka

Dottie; El Squeako Mouse; Rootie's arch enemy, Poison Zoomack; and Rootie's ever faithful, lovable dog, Gala Poochie, who were manipulated and voiced by puppeteers Paul Ashley and Frank Milano. The show took place in the Rootie Kazootie Club House, and the various episodes of the program usually involved Rootie and his friends in amusing escapades that were eventually resolved on the Friday show of the five-days-a-week program. When the show moved from NBC to ABC in 1952, it was expanded to a full 30 minutes and was seen one day a week with a live audience of youngsters who answered questions about science, American history, geography, etc. Also seen on the Saturday early evening show were vintage short films from silent movie days that starred the Keystone Cops, Charlie Chase, and Edgar Kennedy.

ROOTS AND ROOTS: THE NEXT GENERATIONS

Jan. 1977	ABC	9–11 P.M. or 10–11 P.M. for 8 days (rerun)
Feb. 1978	ABC	8–11 P.M. or 9–11 P.M. for 5 days (Roots)
Feb. 1979	ABC	8–10 P.M. or 9–10 P.M. for 7 days (Roots: TNG)
May 1981–July 1981	ABC	Sun. 7–9 (rerun)

Alex Haley's epic saga of an African man named Kunta Kinte, who was captured, shipped to America, and sold into slavery, and subsequent generations of his ancestors, was adapted for television by William Blinn and became one of TV's most talked-about, award-winning, and watched miniseries. Approximately 100 million people faithfully viewed every episode of the miniseries. Kunta Kinte, Haley's ancestor, was born in 1750 in Gambia, Africa, to a couple named Binta and Omoro, played by Cicely Tyson and Thalmus Rasulala. After a happy childhood, when Kunta Kinte, played by LeVar Burton, grew into young manhood, his life drastically changed when slave traders trapped him and sold him into slavery. Shipped to America on a boat commanded by a conscience-ridden seaman named Capt. Davies, played by Edward ASNER, and his mean-spirited third mate, Slater, played by Ralph Waite, Kunta Kinte never lost his desire to escape from captivity, and in America, endured many hardships. As an older adult, Kunta Kinte, who was then played by John Amos, married and had a daughter named Kizzy, played by Leslie Uggams. As time went on, Kunta Kinte died, Kizzy had a son who became known as Chicken George, later played as an adult by Ben Vereen, the Civil War came and went, and the slaves became free men and women. As the series ended, Kunta Kinte's great-great-grandson, Tom, played by George Stanford Brown, who was by this time a free man, struck out to start a new life in Tennessee.

Among the numerous celebrities who appeared on the series were Maya Angelou, O. J. Simpson, Moses Gunn, Louis Gossett, Jr., Lorne Greene, Lynda Day George, Vic Morrow, Robert Reed, Gary Collins, Raymond St. Jacques, Sandy Duncan, Chuck CONNORS, Lawrence Hilton-Jacobs, John Schuck, Macdonald Carey, Olivia Cole, Scatman Crothers, George Hamilton, Carolyn Jones, Ian McShane, Lillian Randolph, Richard Roundtree, Lloyd BRIDGES, and Burl Ives.

Because of its unprecedented popularity, *Roots* returned in February 1979 as a five-part miniseries called *Roots: The Next Generation,* which picked up the story of Alex Haley's family where the original series left off. This series began in 1882, and Kunta Kinte's great-great-grandson, Tom, had established himself as a blacksmith in Tennessee. Through the turn of the century, post–World War I years, and finally into the World War II years, the family saga continued as Haley's ancestors came and went, enduring continuing racial prejudice. Haley was a character on the series, played by Damon Evans as a young man, and then by James Earl Jones. *As Roots: The Next Generations* came to an end, Haley went back to Africa, determined to trace his family roots, and he first became aware of Kunta Kinte, whose memory had been kept alive by African tribesmen, and the story verbally related to Haley reinforced the account of Kunta Kinte's life his family had also passed down to him. Among the notable actors who appeared on *Roots: The Next Generations* were Beah Richards, Olivia De Havilland, Richard THOMAS, Irene Cara, Harry Morgan, Henry Fonda, Ruby Dee, Rosey Grier, Paul Winfield, Christoff St. John, Damon Evans, Debbie Allen, and Marlon Brando, as the white supremacist leader George Lincoln Rockwell. David L. Wolper was the executive producer of both *Roots* and *Roots: The Next Generations.*

ROPERS, THE

Mar. 1979–Apr. 1979	ABC	Tues. 10–10:30 P.M.
Aug. 1979–Sept. 1979	ABC	Sun. 8:30–9 P.M.
Sept. 1979–Jan. 1980	ABC	Sat. 8–8:30 P.M.
Jan. 1980–Mar. 1980	ABC	Sat. 8:30–9 P.M.
May 1980	ABC	Thurs. 9:30–10 P.M.

The Ropers were characters originally seen on the popular *THREE'S COMPANY* situation comedy. Norman Fell and Audra Lindley, who played the bickering Ropers, who were neighbors of *Three's Company's* Jack Tripper, Janet Ward, and Chrissy Snow, were given a half-hour spin-off series of their own due to the popularity of the characters they played. The Ropers had moved from the apartment building he owned in Santa Monica to a condominium in posh Cheviot Hills, California. Appearing on the series with the Ropers were their snobbish neighbor, a balding realtor named Jeffrey P. Brooks III, played by Jeffrey Tambor, who felt that the Ropers were bringing down the neighborhood because of their trashy behavior. Helen Roper, however, found a friend in Brooks's wife, Anne, played by Patricia McCormack. Also appearing on the series were Evan Cohen as Anne and Jeffrey's son, David; Dena Dietrich as Helen's snobbish sister, Ethel; Rod Colbin as Hubert; and Louise Vallance as a Jenny Ballinger, an art student who rented a

Roseanne and John Goodman (Author's collection)

room at the Ropers' apartment. One of the most popular performers on the show was Helen's little dog, Muffin. The executive producers of *The Ropers* were Don Nicholl, Michael Ross, and Bernie West.

ROSE, REGINALD (1921–2002)

In the years following World War II, when television first began to emerge as America's major source of home entertainment, live TV dramas such as KRAFT TELEVISION SUSPENSE THEATRE, STUDIO ONE, and PLAYHOUSE 90 were very popular. Among the earliest successful playwrights who provided original dramas for these TV programs was New York City–born Reginald Rose. Rose provided scripts for GOODYEAR TELEVISION PLAYHOUSE, *Studio One*, *Playhouse 90*, and *The DU PONT SHOW OF THE MONTH*. Rose's courtroom drama *12 Angry Men*, which he had originally written for CBS's *Studio One*, subsequently became a successful film, has been adapted for the stage, and is currently studied by American high school and college students as part of the English curriculum. Other successful projects Rose worked on were the TV series *Crime in the Streets* (1956), *Dino* (1957), *Man of the West* (1958), *The Man in the Net* (1959), the miniseries *The Sacco-Vanzetti Story* (1960), and *Studs Lonigan* (1979). In 1961, Rose created the very successful TV courtroom drama *The DEFENDERS*, which was the first TV series to deal with the

ethical questions raised by criminal behavior such as capital punishment, abortion, criminal insanity, and even cannibalism. In 1987, Rose wrote the screenplay for the successful TV film *Escape from Sobibor*, which was about a group of Jewish concentration camp prisoners who, during World War II, revolted against their captors and escaped from their imprisonment. In 1997, Rose's celebrated play *12 Angry Men* was given a new production as a TV special.

ROSEANNE

Oct. 1988–Feb. 1989	ABC	Tues. 8:30–9 P.M.
Feb. 1989–Sept. 1994	ABC	Tues. 9–9:30 P.M.
Sept. 1994–Mar. 1995	ABC	Wed. 9–9:30 P.M.
Mar. 1995–May 1995	ABC	Wed. 8–8:30 P.M.
May 1995–July 1995	ABC	Wed. 9:30–10 P.M.
Aug. 1995–Sept. 1995	ABC	Tues. 8:30–9 P.M.
Sept. 1995–Aug. 1997	ABC	Tues. 8–8:30 P.M.

The comedienne ROSEANNE Barr, later known as Roseanne Arnold and simply as Roseanne, took her stand-up act to television as the star of a half-hour situation comedy playing the same character she had developed for her comedy club appearances. On the series, Roseanne played Roseanne Conner, the down-to-earth, sarcastic wife of beefy building contractor Dan Conner, played by John GOODMAN. The couple lived in a small home in Lanford, Illinois, with their three children: eldest daughter, 13-year-old Becky, played by Lecy Goranson until 1993, and then by Sarah Chalke until the series left the air in 1997; their 11-year-old daughter, Darlene, played by Sara Gilbert; and their six-year-old son, D. J., played by Michael Fishman. Also appearing as regular characters were Roseanne's police officer sister, Jackie Harris, played by Laurie Metcalf; Roseanne's thrice-married friend, Chrystal Anderson, who worked with Roseanne at a plastics factory, played by Natalie West; and, during the show's first season, the supervisor at the factory, Booker Brooks, played by George Clooney. The show was an immediate success and became second-highest rated on the Nielsen ratings for the 1988–89 season.

From the outset, the show was plagued with problems as Roseanne constantly fought with the series' creator, Matt Williams, as well as the program's producers, writers, and director, Ellen Falcon, for control of the show. During the 1990–91 season of *Roseanne,* the comedienne's husband at that time, Tom Arnold, became an occasional cast member of the show, playing Dan's pal, Arnie Merchant/Thomas, and Roseanne Barr used his name and became Roseanne Arnold. Over the years the show was on the air, her character changed jobs several times, working in a beauty salon and then as a waitress at Rodbell's Coffee Shop, and various characters came and went as regulars, including Martin Mull as her gay boss at the coffee shop, Leon Carp; Michael Des Barres as Leon's companion, Jerry; and Bonnie Sheridan as the waitress Bonnie. During the 1991–92 season, Dan opened his own motorcycle business which failed, and then went to work in a municipal job. Jackie and Roseanne opened up their own lunch room called Lanford Lunch Box. Jackie quit the police department and became a long-distance truck driver, and Academy Award–winning actress Estelle Parsons joined the cast as Roseanne's and Jackie's troublesome mother, Bev.

By the time *Roseanne* reached its seventh season, Roseanne had divorced Tom Arnold and became known simply as Roseanne, and as the series wound down, the character Roseanne became pregnant with a baby boy who was "born" on the Halloween 1995 episode of the show and named Jerry Garcia Conner. In 1993, *Roseanne* won the prestigious Peabody Award, and in spite of the program's enormous popularity, it never won an Emmy until the show was in its fourth season. By the time *Roseanne* left the airwaves in 1997, Roseanne was one of the most successful women on television and was earning an estimated $1 million an episode for her work on the show.

ROSEANNE (NÉE ROSEANNE CHERRIE BARR, AKA ROSEANNE ARNOLD 1952–   )

Actress/comedienne Roseanne was born in Salt Lake City, Utah, to blanket salesman Jerry Barr and his wife, Helen. One of four children, Roseanne claims her "whole life was a dichotomy." Her parents were Jewish, but when Roseanne was three years old, she hit her head on a kitchen table and was paralyzed for a while, and her mother called local Mormon ministers to pray over her. When she recovered, Roseanne attended Jewish schools, but her mother also sent her to the Mormon church on Sundays, which led to early childhood confusion about her identity. Roseanne's father was a devotee of comedians, and every Sunday he would sit his whole family down to watch the popular comedians of the day perform on *The ED SULLIVAN SHOW.* Roseanne's favorite comedians were Jack BENNY, Lenny Bruce, and Mort Sahl, whom she imitated whenever a group of friends and family were gathered. When she was 15 years old, Roseanne suffered from a case of Bell's palsy, which paralyzed her face. Disgusted with her appearance, Roseanne began to escape from reality by drinking and smoking marijuana. Her parents committed her to the Utah State Hospital when her behavior became too erratic, and it turned out to be one of the most important experiences of her life. At 17, Roseanne left Salt Lake City and her parents' home and settled in Georgetown, Colorado, where she met a man named Bill Pentland, fell in love with him, and was married in 1974. She settled down as a wife and mother for several years, and the couple had three children. Soon Roseanne became restless with her domesticity, and after attending a local comedy club, decided she wanted to pursue a career as a comedienne. Performing at comedy clubs around the western United States, Roseanne developed an act, and after an appearance at the Comedy Store in Los Angeles, she was asked by the club's owner, Mitzi Shore, to move to Los Angeles to become a regular performer at the club. Before long, Roseanne was appearing on such TV shows as *The TONIGHT SHOW,* and her act, which was mainly about her own domestic frustrations and sexual disillusionment, became the basis for the situation comedy series *ROSEANNE,* which became one of the most popular shows on TV and remained on the air from October 1988 until August 1997. In 1998, Roseanne became the host of a daytime syndicated talk show, *The Roseanne Show,* which failed to attract an audience and was canceled during its second season. Currently, Roseanne heads her own production company called Full Moon and High Tide, and she continues to make guest appearances on various TV shows and to search for suitable properties for herself.

ROSIE O'DONNELL SHOW, THE

1996– 2002   Syndicated   Mon.–Fri. Various
daytime hours

In 1996, stand-up comedienne/actress Rosie O'DONNELL became the host of a five-days-a-week daytime talk show that, unlike many of the more sensational talk shows on the air, concentrates on the more positive aspects of daily living. The show has a decidedly child-oriented approach, and Rosie and her guests demonstrate various crafts, cooking, and gardening techniques. Rosie conducts interviews with many celebrated performers, novelists, and political figures. A dedicated TV viewer, Rosie often chats about such popular shows as WHO WANTS TO BE A MILLIONAIRE, on which she appeared as a celebrity contestant and won $500,000 for her favorite charity, and the much-ballyhooed *Survivor* series. A single mother of two adopted children, Rosie often focuses on such subjects as child abuse and child rearing, and frequently talks about her favorite actor, Tom Cruise, and her good friend, pop singer Madonna. O'Donnell decided to leave the program in 2002 when it was announced that comedienne Caroline Ray of SABRINA THE TEENAGE WITCH would host a new show in the time slot.

ROSS, MARION (1928–)

Perhaps best known for playing Marion Cunningham, Richie's mother on the successful HAPPY DAYS situation comedy series, Marion Ross, who was born in Albert Lea, Minnesota, began her acting career in the early 1950s shortly after she graduated from college. Ross had small roles in such films as *Forever Female* (1953), *Sabrina* (1954), *The Glenn Miller Story* (1954), *Lust for Life* (1956), *Some Came Running* (1958), *Teacher's Pet* (1958), and *Operation Petticoat* (1959). In 1961, Ross became a regular cast member on the *Gertrude Berg* show, and subsequently appeared as a regular on such TV shows as MR. NOVAK, *Paradise Bay* (1965), and *Any Second Now* (1969), before becoming one of the stars of *Happy Days* in 1974. The series remained on the air for 10 years and made Ross a familiar face to millions of viewers. In 1991, Ross starred on the critically acclaimed series BROOKLYN BRIDGE, playing Grandmother Sophie Berger, and although the series attracted considerable praise from the critics, it failed to attract a sizable enough audience to keep it on the on the air longer than two seasons. Over the years, Ross was one of television's busiest actresses and made guest appearances on such shows as ROUTE 66, HAWAII FIVE-O, The BRADY BUNCH, MISSION: IMPOSSIBLE, LOVE, AMERICAN STYLE, EMERGENCY!, The LOVE BOAT (on which she was also a regular during the 1985–86 season), MacGYVER, NIGHT COURT, TOUCHED BY AN ANGEL, BURKE'S LAW, The DREW CAREY SHOW, and That 70s Show. Ross has also been frequently seen on the stage, and in 1987, she starred on Broadway in a revival of the popular comedy *Arsenic and Old Lace* with Jean STAPLETON.

ROUTE 66

Oct. 1960–Sept. 1964   CBS   Fri. 8:30–9:30 P.M.

In the early 1960s, many young Americans had wanderlust and traveled across the country trying to find a place for themselves in a changing, evolving society. The TV series *Route 66* capitalized on this craze. The heroes of the series were two young men, Tod Stiles and Buz Murdock, played by Martin Milner and George Maharis, who traveled around in Buz's Corvette in search of adventure. They came

from two very different backgrounds. Tod was the son of wealthy parents, who discovered upon his father's death, that most of the family's fortune was gone. Buz was the son of poor parents who had grown up in the slums of the Hell's Kitchen section in New York City. The series was filmed on location in various places in the United States as the boys traveled around the country. In 1962, George Marharis decided to leave the series, even though it was very popular with viewers, and he was replaced by Glenn Corbett, who played a Vietnam War veteran named Linc Case, who joined Tod in his travels. Among the celebrated performers who made guest appearances on the series were Alan ALDA, Joey Heatherton, Robert Redford, Rod Steiger, and Ethel Waters, the noted black singer/actress whose performance on the series won her an Emmy Award nomination. The theme music from *Route 66,* written by Nelson Riddle, became a top-selling recording in 1962. Herbert B. Leonard was the executive producer of the series for Screen Gems. In 1993, a less successful revived version of the series that starred James Wilder and Dan Cortese surfaced. Wilder played Buz Murdock's son, who had inherited the old Corvette and decided to relive his father's adventures. The series remained on the air for one season.

ROWAN AND MARTIN'S LAUGH-IN

Jan. 1968–May 1973   NBC   Mon. 8–9 P.M.

One of television's most innovative programs in the late 1960s, *Laugh-in* starred the comedy team of Dan Rowan and Dick Martin, and was a fast-moving, brassy combination of short skits, sight gags, one-line jokes, and songs that usually concluded with a blackout. The show was an immediate sensation, and well-known figures from the worlds of show business and politics vied to make a guest appearance on the show. The regular, in addition to Rowan and Martin who acted as hosts and also appeared in skits, included an impressive array of talented comedians. Over the five years the series was aired, the cast included comedienne Ruth Buzzi and announcer Gary Owens (both of whom remained with the series the entire time it was on the air), Judy Carne (1968–70), Eileen Brennan (1968), Goldie Hawn (1968–70), Arte Johnson (1968–71), Henry Gibson (1968–71), Roddy-Maude Roxby (1968), Jo Anne Worley (1968–70), Larry Hovis (1968, 1971–72), Pigmeat Markham (1968–69), Charlie Brill (1968–69), Dick Whittington (1968–69), Mitzi McCall (1968–69), Chelsea Brown (1968–69), Alan Sues (1968–72), Dave Madden (1968–69), Teresa Graves (1969–70), Jeremy Lloyd (1969–70), Pamela Rodgers (1969–70), Byron Gilliam (1969–70), Ann Elder (1970–72), Lily Tomlin (1970–73), Johnny Brown (1970–72), Dennis Allen (1970–73), Nancy Phillips (1970–71), Barbara Sharma (1970–72), Harvey Jason (1970–71), Richard DAWSON (1971–73), Patti Deutsch (1972–73), Jud Strunk (1972–73), Brian Bressler (1972–73), Sarah Kennedy (1972–73), Donna Jean Young (1972–73), Tod Bass (1972–73), Lisa Farringer (1972–73), and Willie Tyler and Lester (1972–73).

Some of the regular features of the show were the "Cocktail Party," "Letters to Laugh-In," "the Flying Fickle Finger of Fate Award," "Laugh-In Looks at the News" (of the past, present, and future), "Hollywood News" with Ruth Buzzi, the torso of a well-shaped, heavily tattooed woman in a bikini undulating to dance music, and, at the end of each show, small windows that cast members kept popping open and delivering one-line jokes or having a bucket of water thrown at them. Catchphrases such as "Is that a chicken joke?" (delivered by Jo Anne Worley), "You bet your bippy" (Dick Martin's familiar response), "Sock it to me" (which ended up with a splash of water thrown at Judy Carne's face), "Very in-ter-essting!" (said by Arte Johnson as a German army officer), "Look that up in your Funk and Wagnall's," "Beautiful Downtown Burbank" (which described the location of the studio where the series was filmed), and "Here come de judge," became American catchphrases because of their frequent use on the series. George Schlatter and Ed Friendly, and then Paul Keyes, were the executive producers of the series.

ROXANNE (ROXANNE ARLEN 1931–1989)

One of the first models to become well known to the public solely because of her appearance on a television show was a beautiful young blond woman known simply as Roxanne. Roxanne was the Vanna WHITE of the early 1950s, although her reign did not last as long as White's. Roxanne was an assistant and product demonstrator on the popular BEAT THE CLOCK quiz show from 1950 until 1955. Her stunning good looks impressed producers, and after *Beat the Clock* left the air, Roxanne was given featured roles in such films as *Illegal* (1955), *Battle Cry* (1955), *Hot Rod Girl* (1956), *The Best Things in Life Are Free* (1956), *Slim Carter* (1957), *Gypsy* (1962, as the stripper Miss Electra), *A House Is Not a Home* (1964), and *The Loved One* (1965). Among the TV series Roxanne made guest appearances on were ALFRED HITCHCOCK PRESENTS, PERRY MASON, CHEYENNE, NAKED CITY, and BEWITCHED. By the mid-1960s, Roxanne's career was going nowhere, and she decided to retire from show business. The actress lived in relative obscurity until her death at the age of 58 in 1989.

ROY ROGERS SHOW, THE

(also THE ROY ROGERS & DALE EVANS SHOW)

Dec. 1951–Jan. 1952	NBC	Sun. 6–6:30 P.M.
Aug. 1952–June 1957	NBC	Sun. 6:30–7 P.M.
Sept. 1963–Dec. 1962	ABC	Sat. 7:30–8:30 P.M.

Hollywood's singing King of the Cowboys Roy ROGERS, who starred in hundreds of second-feature western films in the 1930s and 1940s, arrived on television in the early 1950s with a half-hour western adventure series that was directed mainly toward younger viewers. The series featured Roy as a cowboy at the Double R Bar Ranch, who fought for law and order in the West and occasionally burst out into song. Also seen on the show were Roy's real-life wife, cowgirl Dale Evans, and his bumbling sidekick, Pat Brady, who brought some comic relief to the show. Among the most popular performers on the series was Roy's horse, Trigger, Dale's horse, Buttermilk, and Pat's horse, Nellybelle. Even though the series ceased production in 1957, reruns of the show were seen on the CBS network on Saturday mornings from January 1961 until September 1964. From September 1962 through December 1962, Roy and Dale were featured in a full-hour musical/variety program called *The Roy Rogers & Dale Evans Show*. Roy's old sidekick Pat Brady was also seen on the program, as were former rodeo-performer/singer Kirby Buchanon, Kathy Taylor, Cliff Arquette, Roy's former singing group the Sons of the Pioneers, and Ralph Carmichael and his Orchestra. The show often featured circus and rodeo acts as well as numerous musical numbers and comedy skits.

RUN FOR YOUR LIFE

Sept. 1965–Sept. 1967	NBC	Mon. 10–11 P.M.
Sept. 1967–Sept. 1968	NBC	Wed. 10–11 P.M.

Ben Gazzara starred as a 35-year-old lawyer named Paul Bryan, who was intelligent, handsome, successful, and rich, but who had an incurable disease, chronic myelocytic leukemia. Even though he knew he had only a few years to live, Bryan, instead of waiting to die, quit his job and sought adventure wherever he could find it, constantly living on the edge with, obviously, nothing to lose. *Run for Your Life* was the brainchild of Roy Huggins, who had been responsible for the successful series The FUGITIVE.

RUSSELL, JOHN (WILLIAM LAWRENCE RUSSELL 1921–1991)

The former star of numerous Hollywood second-feature films, the tall, dark, and handsome John Russell, who perhaps became best known for playing Marshal Dan Troop on the popular LAWMAN western television series in the late 1950s, was born in Los Angeles. After attending the University of Southern California, where he was a student athlete, Russell served in the U.S. Marine Corps during World War II, and won a battlefield commission after being decorated for valor at the battle of Guadalcanal. After the war and his much-publicized heroism, that Hollywood talent scouts decided the handsome young man might be a success in films. Appearances in such films as *Within These Walls* (1945), *A Bell for Adano* (1945), *Forever Amber* (1947), *Sitting Pretty* (1948), *Slattery's Hurricane* (1949), *The Fat Man* (1951), *Fair Wind to Java* (1953), *Jubilee Trail* (1954), and *The Last Command* (1955), among many others, established Russell as one of Hollywood's busiest actors. In 1955, Russell starred on his first TV series, *Soldiers of Fortune*, and then in 1958, he starred on *The Lawman* series. Russell continued to be active in films such as *Rio Bravo* (1959), *Apache Uprising*

(1966), *Alias Smith and Jones* (1970), *Fugitive Lovers* (1975), *The Outlaw Josey Wales* (1976), and *Pale Rider* (1985, as Clint EASTWOOD's nemesis, Bloody Bill Anderson). In 1979, the actor starred on the short-lived TV series *Jason of the Star Command*. Over the years, the actor was also a frequent guest star on such TV series as MAVERICK, CHEYENNE, DANIEL BOONE, IT TAKES A THIEF, and GUNSMOKE. John Russell's last appearance was in the film *Under the Gun* in 1989.

RYAN'S HOPE

July 1975–Jan. 1989   ABC   Various daytime hours

Even though by TV soap opera standards it had a relatively short, 11-year run, the daytime serial drama *Ryan's Hope* had fiercely loyal fans and is fondly remembered by both television critics and viewers. Created by Claire Labine and Paul Avila Mayer, who also served as the show's executive producers during its earliest years, *Ryan's Hope* was named for a fictional tavern on Manhattan's West Side. Most of the action took place either at the tavern or at Riverside Hospital. Featured in the series original cast were Faith Catlin as Dr. Faith Coleridge; Justin Deas as Dr. Bucky Carter; Bernard Barrow as the proprietor of the Ryan's Hope Tavern, Johnny Ryan; Helen Gallagher as Johnny's wife, Maeve; Michael Hawkins as their son, Frank; Ilene Kristen as Frank's wife, Delia; Malcolm Groome as Dr. Pat Ryan, who was Johnny and Maeve's youngest son; Kate Mulgrew as Mary Ryan, Johnny and Maeve's daughter; Diana Van Der Vlis as Dr. Nell Beaulac; John Gabriel as Nell's husband, Seneca; Frank Latimore as Dr. Ed Coleridge; Nancy Addison (later Altman) as Jillian Coleridge; Ronald Hale as Dr. Roger Coleridge; Michael Levin as Jack Fenelli; Michael Fairman as Nick Szabo; Earl Hindman as Bob Reid; Hannibal Penney, Jr., as Clem Moultrie; and Rosalinda Guerra as Romona Gonzalez.

Over the next 11 years numerous characters were added to and dropped from the series. Among the actors who appeared on the program were Catherine Hicks, Andrew Robinson, Kathleen Tolan, Nicolette Goulet, Tom MacGreevey, Dennis Jay Higgins, Julia Barr, Rosetta LeNoir, Jose Aleman, Ana Alicia Ortiz, Louise Shaffer, Jadrien Steele, Jason Adams, Fat Thomas, Lisa Sutton, Megan McGracken, Nana Tucker, John Blazo, Robert Finoccoli, Patrick James Clarke, Sarah Felder, Ann Gillespie, Marg Helgenberger, Carrell Myers, Barbara Blackburn, Pauline Flanagan, and Patrick Hogan. Other well-known actors who had regular roles on *Ryan's Hope* over the years were Maureen Garrett, Peter Haskell, Nell CARTER, Yasmine Bleeth, Kathleen Widdoes, Gloria DeHaven, Harve Presnell, Christian Slater, Sylvia Sidney, Nancy Coleman, Jacqueline Brookes, and Rosemary Prinz.

True to its New York City West Side Irish background, *Ryan's Hope* ended with longtime cast member Helen Gallager, who had been a Broadway musical comedy star, singing "Danny Boy" on the show's final episode.

SABRINA THE TEENAGE WITCH

Sept. 1996–Oct. 1996	ABC	Fri. 8:30–9 P.M.
Oct. 1996–Sept. 1997	ABC	Fri. 9–9:30 P.M.
Sept. 1997–Sept. 1998	ABC	Fri. 8–8:30 P.M.
Dec. 1998–May 1998	ABC	Fri. 9–9:30 P.M.
Sept. 1998–present	ABC	Fri. 9–9:30 P.M.

A surprise hit of the 1996–97 season, the situation comedy series *Sabrina the Teenage Witch* centered on the life of a teenage girl who was to all appearances as normal as every other girl at Westbridge High School, but who was really a witch. When she turned 16, however, strange things began to happen to her, such as being able to bring dead frogs back to life in her biology class and levitate in her sleep. Sabrina, played by Melissa Joan Hart, lived with her two eccentric aunts, who, like Sabrina, just happened to be witches. The aunts, sweet and lovable Aunt Hilda Spellman, played by Caroline Rhea, and acerbic Aunt Zelda Spellman, played by Beth Broderick, and her dead father, Sam, who talked to her through a picture of himself, began to tutor Sabrina in the fine art of witchcraft. A mischievous warlock named Salem, who had been turned into a sarcastic-talking black cat (voiced by Nick Bakay) and made to do penance for past misdoings, often commented on what was going on in Sabrina's house. Other characters who regularly appeared on the series were Sabrina's biology teacher, Mr. Pool, played by Paul Feig; her best friend, Jenny, played by Michelle Beaudoin; her male friend, Harvey, who had a crush on her, played by Nate Richert; and the stuck-up cheerleader, Libby, played by Jenna Leigh Green. During the series' second season, several new characters appeared such as Westbridge High School's vice principal, Willard Kraft, played by Martin Mull; the Quizmaster, who gave Sabrina a series of tests in order for her to receive her witch's license, played by Alimi Ballard; and Sabrina's new best friend, Valerie, played by Lindsay Sloane. Before it became a successful TV series, Sabrina had been a character in the *Archie Show* in 1970, and then, in 1971, was the main character on the *Sabrina the Teenage Witch* cartoon series. In 1977, the character was seen on a cartoon series called *Superwitch,* and subsequently appeared in a popular live-action feature film that was also called *Sabrina, the Teenage Witch.*

SAINT, THE

May 1967–Sept. 1967	NBC	Sun. 10–11 P.M.
Feb. 1968–Sept. 1968	NBC	Sat. 7:30–8:30 P.M.
Apr. 1969–Sept. 1969	NBC	Fri. 10–11 P.M.

The first airing of *The Saint* mystery/adventure series on television was a syndicated program produced in Great Britain by ITC and starred Roger Moore as Simon Templar, who was better known as "The Saint." Templar traveled around the world solving crimes, and was as well known to members of society as he was to police departments on five continents. His calling card was a picture of a stick figure with a halo over its head. In the United States, the series was originally seen on NBC on Sundays at 10 P.M., then on Saturdays at 7:30 P.M. and finally on Fridays, once again at 10 P.M. The series also featured British actors Winsley Pithey, Norman Pitt, and Ivor Dean as Inspector Claude Teal of Scotland Yard. In 1979, a new version of *The Saint, The Return of the Saint,* emerged on CBS with Ian Ogilvy playing Simon "The Saint" Templar. Both series were based upon the character created by Leslie Charteris for a series of novels in the 1930s and 1940s. *The Saint* had previously been aired as a radio show starring Vincent Price as Simon Templar from 1945 until 1951.

ST. ELSEWHERE

Oct. 1982–Aug. 1983	NBC	Tues. 10–11 P.M.
Aug. 1983–May 1988	NBC	Wed. 10–11 P.M.
July 1988–Aug. 1988	NBC	Wed. 10–11 P.M.

Unlike most popular television hospital drama series, *St. Elsewhere* was a realistic depiction of what happens in an actual hospital. There were no miracle cures, only occasional happy endings, and the physicians and nurses were seen as both good and bad with their fair share of human frailties. The show's title was a nickname for a hospital called St. Eligius, which was located in a seamier part of town in Boston. The personal and professional experiences of the staff at St. Elsewhere were the major focus of each week's episode, but the stories of various patients were also featured each week. Dr. Donald Westphall, played by Ed Flanders, was St. Eligius's chief of staff, and other regular characters on the series included Dr. Mark Craig, an egotistical heart surgeon, played by William Daniels; Dr. Auschlander, a veteran doctor who was fighting cancer, played by Norman Lloyd; Dr. Ben Samuels, played by David Birney, who was a free-spirited young man who had slept with just about every female at St. Elsewhere; Dr. Wayne Fiscus, played by Howie Mandell, who was having an affair with a pathologist at the hospital, Dr. Cathy Martin, played by Barbara Whinnery; the dedicated physician Dr. Jack Morrison, played by David Morse, who often neglected his young wife who then died, leaving him feeling guilty about his neglect; Dr. Annie Cavanero, played by Cynthia Sikes, who often became too emotionally involved with her patients' problems; Dr. Elliot Axelrod, played by Stephen Furst, as an overweight physician who was constantly battling his obesity; and African-American physician Dr. Phillip Chandler, played by Denzel Washington, who was always trying to prove his worth. Other popular regular characters were Dr. Victor Ehrich, played by Ed Begley, Jr.; Dr. Peter White, played by Terence Knox; Dr. Hugh Beale, played by G. W. Bailey; Nurse Helen Rosenthal, played by Christina Pickles; Dr. V. J. Kochar, played by Kavi Raz; Dr. Wendy Armstrong, played by Kim Miyori; Nurse Shirley Daniels, played by Ellen Bry; Orderly Luther Hawkins, played by Eric Laneuville; Joan Holloran, played by Nancy Stafford; Dr. Robert Caldwell, played by Mark Harmon; Dr. Michael Ridley, played by Paul Sand; Mrs. Ellen Craig, played by Bonnie Bartlett; Nurse Lucy Papandrao, played by Jennifer Savidge; Dr. Jacqueline Wade, played by Sagan Lewis; Orderly Warren Coolidge, played by Byron Stewart; Dr. Emily Humes, played by Judith Hansen; Dr. Alan Poe, played by Brian Tochi; Nurse Peggy Shotwell, played by Saundra Sharp; Mrs. Hufnagle, played by Florence Halop; Dr. Roxanne Turner, played by Alfre Woodard; Ken Valere, played by George Deloy; Terry Valere, played by Deborah May; Dr. Seth Griffin, played by Bruce Greenwood; Dr. Pauline Kiem, played by France Nuyen; Dr. Carol Novino, played by Cindy Pickett; and Dr. John Dideon, played by Ronny Cox. The series was created by Joshua Brand and John Falsey, and was produced by MTM Enterprises, which had previously produced the popular *HILL STREET BLUES* police drama series that used basically the same episodic format as *St. Elsewhere*.

SAINT JAMES, SUSAN (SUSAN JANE MILLER 1946–)

The star of such successful television series as *The NAME OF THE GAME, MCMILLAN AND WIFE*, and *KATE AND ALLIE*, Susan St. James, was born in Los Angeles, and began her acting career shortly after finishing her schooling. St. James's first major TV appearance was on an episode of *IRONSIDE* in 1967. After several regular appearances playing various roles on the *IT TAKES A THIEF* series, St. James starred on *The Name of the Game* from 1968 until 1971, when she starred with Rock Hudson on the *McMillan and Wife* series. Appearances in such TV films as *Scott Free* (1976), *Desperate Women* (1978), *Sex and the Single Parent* (1979), *The Girls in the Office* (1979), *S.O.S. Titanic* (1979), and in the films *Love at First Bite* (1979), *How to Beat the High Co$t of Living* (1980), and *Don't Cry, It's Only Thunder* (1982), followed. After starring on the popular *Kate and Allie* situation comedy series from 1984 to 1989, St. James decided to retire from show business to concentrate on her personal life. In 1995, St. James made a guest-starring appearance on an episode of *The DREW CAREY SHOW*, playing the mother of a regular character on the show, Kate.

SAJAK, PAT (1946–)

Best known as the host of the long-running, successful game show series *WHEEL OF FORTUNE*, Pat Sajak, who was born in Chicago, began his career in show business as a disc jockey while serving in U.S. Army in Vietnam. After he was discharged from the army, Sajak got a job as a weatherman at WSM-TV in Nashville, Tennessee, before moving to KNBC in Los Angeles. His popularity as a weathercaster won him the hosting job on *Wheel of Fortune* in 1981. Sajak has made several guest appearances, usually playing himself on such TV series as *GIMME A BREAK!, SANTA BARBARA, RUGRATS, The LARRY SANDERS SHOW*, and playing Dr. Brian Brandon on *The COMMISH*. In 1989, Sajak was given a chance to host his own late-night talk show opposite NBC's *TONIGHT SHOW* on CBS. The show was not a success and was canceled after one season.

SALES, SOUPY (MILTON SUPMAN 1926–)

Soupy Sales, the host of numerous children's TV shows and a frequent panelist on game shows throughout the 1960s and 1970s, was born in Franklinton, North Carolina. Soupy first came to the attention of the general public in 1959, when, after several years of performing stand-up comedy and hosting several local children's television shows, he appeared on an ABC national show for children. Soupy's local TV show, *Soupy's On*, had caught the attention of ABC network officials, who offered

Soupy a weekday evening network show that originated from Detroit. The show featured jokes, slapstick comedy (including numerous pies in Soupy's face), songs, puns, silent film classics, and sketches with an assortment of puppets. Soupy became enormously popular with adult, as well as child, viewers, and he subsequently appeared in the films *Critic's Choice* (1963) and *Birds Do It* (1966). In 1968, Soupy became a regular panelist on the popular WHAT'S MY LINE panel show, and he made guest appearances on such series as ROUTE 66 and The BEVERLY HILL-BILLIES. In 1979, Soupy hosted the *Junior Almost Anything Goes* TV series and was also seen and heard as a regular on the *Sha Na Na* and *Donkey Kong* (1983) series. Soupy has kept busy acting in films and appearing on television shows as a guest star and recently has had featured roles in such films as *The Making of . . . And God Spoke* (1993), *Conundrum* (1998), *Holy Man* (1998), *Everything's George* (2000), and *Palmer's Pick Up* (1999), and guest-starred on such TV series as WINGS and BOY MEETS WORLD.

SALLY JESSY RAPHAEL SHOW, THE

    1985–present   Syndicated   Mon.–Fri. Various
                                     daytime hours

A former radio talk show host who wore glasses and seemed like she could be anyone's next-door neighbor, Sally Jessy Raphael brought her talent to make people open up and talk to television in the mid 1980s. Sally's show encouraged studio audience participation and dealt with a wide variety of subjects. The format became standard fare for other talk shows. In the early 1990s, Raphael's show fell victim to various hoaxes. A man claimed that he was impotent, but it was later revealed that the same man had previously been seen on *Geraldo* and claimed that he was an unmarried virgin. On another of Sally's shows, a woman claiming she was a superior sex partner turned out to have appeared on another TV show claiming she was a woman who "hated sex." In spite of these blunders *The Sally Jessy Raphael Show* prospered, and over the years Sally has delved into such interesting subjects as "School Bullies," "Girls with Embarrassingly Sexual Mothers," "Videotaped Indiscretions," "Women with Low Self-Esteem," "Female Criminals," and "Sexual Teens."

SANFORD, ISABEL (1917–)

Before she became a well-known TV personality, African-American actress Isabel Sanford was a Broadway performer who had appeared in hundreds of plays for over 30 years before moving to Hollywood in the early 1960s. Sanford, who was born in New York City, is perhaps best known for playing Louise "Weezie" Jefferson on ALL IN THE FAMILY and its successful spin-off series, The JEFFER-SONS. The actress's first major TV appearance was on the BEWITCHED series, playing Aunt Jenny. She was subsequently featured in such films as *Guess Who's Coming to Dinner* (1967), *Pendulum* (1968), *The Red, White and Black* (1971), and *The Great Man's Whiskers* (1971), and on such TV series as LOVE, AMERICAN STYLE, The MARY TYLER MOORE SHOW, KOJAK, and VEGA$, before landing the role of Archie and Edith Bunker's next-door neighbor. Sanford continued appearing in feature films such as *Lady Sings the Blues* (1972) and *The New Centurions* (1972). In 1975, Sanford, with Sherman HEMSLEY, became the major players on the successful spin-off series *The Jeffersons*. After the show left the air, Sanford continued to remain active as a guest star on such TV series as LOIS AND CLARK, ROSEANNE, CYBILL, and *The* FRESH PRINCE OF BEL AIR, and in the films *Pucker Up and Bark Like a Dog* (1990), *South Beach* (1992), *Sprung* (1997), and in the TV film *Jackie's Back!* (1999).

SANFORD AND SON

    Jan. 1972–Sept. 1977   NBC   Fri. 8–8:30 P.M.

Risqué nightclub comic Redd FOXX played a junkyard owner, Fred Sanford, and Demond Wilson played his son and reluctant partner, Lamont, on this situation comedy series that enjoyed a successful five-year run on NBC. Foxx was perfectly contented with being his own boss even though the junkyard never yielded very much income, but Lamont had better ideas of how he would like to spend his working hours. Fred's wife, Elizabeth, who had died many years earlier, was constantly being referred to, and Fred, when he was confronted with a situation he found objectionable, especially Lamont's threat to quit the family business, would often feign a heart attack, saying, "I'm coming, Elizabeth, I'm coming," which never really fooled anyone, especially not Lamont, who loved his father but was never really fooled by his manipulative shenanigans. The series, rated among the top 10 shows according to the Nielsen ratings, was developed for television by Norman LEAR and Bud Yorkin and was Lear's second hit show following his successful ALL IN THE FAMILY series. Other recurring characters included Fred's girlfriend, Nurse Donna Harris, whom he was always promising to marry, played by Lynn Hamilton; Aunt Esther Anderson, Fred's sister-in-law, who owned the run-down Sanford Arms rooming house and was always at odds with Fred, played by LaWanda Page; and Lamont's girlfriend, Janet Lawson, a divorcée with a young son, played by Marlene Clark. Other popular characters on the series during its five-year tenure were Melvin, played by Slappy White; Bubba Hoover, played by Don Bexley; Police Officers Swanhauser and Smith ("Smitty"), played by Noam Pitlik and Hal Williams; Aunt Ethel, played by Beah Richards; Julio Fuentes, played by Greg Sierra; Rollo Larson, played by Nathaniel Taylor; Grady Wilson, played by Whitman Mayo; Officer Hopkins, played by Howard Platt; Ah Chew, played by Pat Morita; Woody Anderson, played by Raymond Allen; and Roger Lawson, played by Edward Crawford. In 1977, both Redd Foxx and Demond Wilson decided to leave the series to pursue other career

Redd Foxx (left) and Richard Pryor of *Sanford and Son* (Author's collection)

interests. The series' producer, Norman Lear, valiantly tried to keep the series on the air as *The Sanford Arms*, but viewers were not interested in the Sanfords without Fred and Lamont, and *Sanford Arms* was canceled after one month. Bud Yorkin was *Sanford and Sons* executive producer. Aaron Rubin, and then Saul Turtletaub and Bernie Orenstein produced the show for Lear and Yorkin.

SANTA BARBARA

July 1984–Jan. 1993   NBC   Mon.–Fri. Various
                                 daytime hours

Santa Barbara was a daytime drama series that did not take itself very seriously, and even though it was on the air for just nine years (a relatively short run as soap operas go), and never attracted legions of viewers, it won two daytime Emmy Awards as Best Daytime Drama in 1988 and 1989. Originally produced by Bridget and Jerome Dobson, who were the head writers for the daytime

drama series GENERAL HOSPITAL, AS THE WORLD TURNS, and GUIDING LIGHT, the Dobsons sold their right to the show in 1985 to World Television. In 1991, the Dobsons regained control of *Santa Barbara*. When the series premiered, stage and film star Dame Judith Anderson, and then shortly after the show surfaced, Janis Paige as Minx Lockridge, was the matriarch of the show's major family. Nicolas Coster played Minx's son, Lionel; Louise Sorel played Lionel's wife, Augusta; Julie Ronnie, followed by Susan Marie Snyder and Shell Danielson, played Lionel and Augusta's daughter, Laken Lockridge; and John Allen Nelson, and then Scott Jenkins and finally Jack Wagner, played their son, Warren. The head of the rival Capwell clan, Channing Creighton (C. C.) Capwell, was played in turn by Peter Mark Richman, Paul Burke, Charles Bateman, and Jed Allen; Shirley Field, and then Marj Dusay was C. C.'s first wife, Pamela; Judith McConnell played C. C.'s second wife, an actress named Sophia Wayne; Lane Davies, Terry Lester, and Gordon Thomson played C. C.'s son, Mason; Robin Wright, and then Kimberly McArthur,

Carrington Garland, and Eileen Davidson, played C. C. and Sophia's daughter, Kelly Capwell; Marcy Walker played Eden Capwell (who became one of television's longest-suffering daytime drama characters); Todd McKee and Michael Brainard played C. C. and Sophia's son, Ted; Robert Wilson played Channing Capweel, Jr., who was actually the son of Lionel Lockridge and Sophia; and A. Martinez played Cruz Castillo, who married Eden and became one of *Santa Barbara's* most popular characters. Over the years, an impressive number of characters came and went, and among the popular actors and actresses who frequented the series were Linda Gobboney, Robin Mattson, Carmen Zapata, Justin Deas, David Haskell, Jon Cypher, and former Olympic champion runner Florence Griffith Joyner.

SATURDAY NIGHT LIVE

   Oct. 1975–Present   NBC Sat. 11:30 P.M.–1 A.M.
   (also)
   Oct. 1979–Mar. 1980 NBC   Wed. 10–11 P.M.
   Mar. 1980–Apr. 1980 NBC   Fri. 10–11 P.M.

When NBC launched its late Saturday night, one and a half hour, live variety/comedy show, which was directed mainly toward young adult viewers, no one thought the series would be a success. To everyone's surprise, this series developed for NBC by Dick Ebersol and produced by Lorne Michaels became one of the 1975–76 season's most popular shows. In less than a year, many young people in America were talking about, and tuning in to see, the show. Each week featured a guest celebrity emcee and a group of regulars called "The Not Ready For Prime Time Players." Many of the cast members were drafted from the popular *Second City*, a Chicago-based improvisational theater club, and the original cast included Chevy Chase, Dan Aykroyd, John Belushi, Jane Curtin, Garrett Morris, Laraine Newman, and Gilda Radner. Comedian George Carlin was the show's first guest host, and a wide variety of guest emcees over the years included such diverse personalities as presidential press secretary Ron Nessen, consumer advocate Ralph Nader, state legislator Julian Bond, and many rock and motion picture stars. Popular regular weekly segments on the show included "Weekend Update," a satire of news programs that originally featured Chevy Chase, and then Jane Curtin and Dan Aykroyd as anchor people, and, most notably, Gilda Radner as a news correspondent named Roseann Roseannadanna; the Coneheads, a family of aliens, played by Jane Curtin, Dan Aykroyd, and Laraine Newman, who had pointed heads but attempted to blend into American society and hoped not to be noticed; and "Samurai Warrior," about the adventures of an Oriental swordsman, played by John Belushi. When Chevy Chase departed the series at the beginning of the 1976–77 season, he was replaced by comedian Bill Murray. In 1979, Belushi and Aykroyd decided to leave the series to pursue other interests, and in 1980, producer Lorne Michaels and Curtin,

Morris, Radner, Newman, Murray, and Don Novello, who joined the cast and had appeared as a cleric named Father Guido Sarducci, also left the series.

When the show returned for a new season, Jean Doumanian was the series' producer and the new "Not Quite Ready for Prime Time Players" included Gilbert Gottfried, Charles Rocket, Joe Piscopo, Denny Dillon, Ann Risley, and Gail Mathias and a young black comedian named Eddie Murphy, who appeared on show irregularly. The public was not happy about the cast changes, and the show's ratings during the 1980–81 season fell drastically. Doumanian was dismissed, and Dick Ebersol, who had developed the series for NBC, took over as the show's producer. For the 1981–82 season, everyone in the cast but Joe Piscopo and Eddie Murphy were replaced, and the new cast included Robin Duke (1981–84), Christine Ebersole (1981–82), Mary Gross (1981–85), Tim Kuzurinsky (1981–84), Tony Rosato (1981–82), Brian Doyle-Murray (1981–82). In 1982, Julia Louis-Dreyfus, Brad Hall, and Gary Kroeger joined the cast, and in 1983, John Belushi's brother, Jim, became a cast member. Billy Crystal, Martin Short, Rich Hall, Christopher Guest, Harry Shearer, and Pamela Stephenson joined Dreyfus, Kroger, and Belushi. Lorne Michaels returned as *Saturday Night Live's* producer in the spring of 1985, and the following fall a new cast of players was introduced. It included Joan Cusack, Robert Downey, Jr., Nora Dunn, Anthony Michael Hall, Jon Lovitz, Randy Quaid, Terry Sweeney, Danitra Vance, and, on occasion, A. Whitney Brown, Don Novello, and Damon Wayans. Michaels's cast failed to please the audience, and the next season a new cast of regulars appeared. With only Lovitz and Dunn remaining from the previous season, this cast included Dana Carvey, Phil Hartman, Jan Hooks, Victoria Jackson, Dennis Miller, and Kevin Nealon. Finally, the new group of performers seemed to please the show's fans as much as the show's original cast, and such regular segments as Dana Carvey's "Church Lady," and his impersonations of President George Bush, as well as Dunn's outrageous talk show hostess "Pat Stevens," Lovitz's "Master Thespian," and Miller's new "Weekend Update" segment became viewer favorites.

One of the show's writers, Al Franken, also became a frequent performer, and in 1988, Mike Myers and Ben Stiller joined the the series as regular cast members. The cast of the 1991–92 season included Carver, Myers, Jackson, Hartman, Nealon, and newcomers Chris Rock, Chris Farley, Rob Schneider, David Spade, Julia Sweeney, Ellen Cleghorne, Tim Meadows, Adam Sandler, and Siobhan Fallon. The cast, except for Jackson and Fallon, returned for the 1992–93 season, and newcomer Melanie Hutsell joined the group. Michael McKean joined the cast in 1994. Hartman, Hutsell, Schneider, and Sweeney left the cast before the 1994–95 season began, and they were replaced by Chris Elliott and Janeane Garofalo. Garofalo left midseason and two new performers, Morwenna Banks and Molly Shannon, took her place. McDonnell, Mark McKinney, Meadows, Shannon, and Spade returned for the next season and were joined by Jim Brewer, Will

Ferrell, Darrell Hammond, David Koechner, Cheri Oteri, and Nancy Walls.

Several of *Saturday Night Live's* sketches became successful in feature films, including Carvey and Myers "Wayne's World," and "The Coneheads," as well as Julia Sweeney's hilarious character "Pat," a person whose gender was impossible to determine by mere appearance.

Over the years, rock and roll music has been an important feature on the weekly shows, and such celebrated rock performers as the Rolling Stones, Tracy Chapman, Sting, Paul McCartney, and Bonnie Raitt have made guest-starring appearances. The show's regular band was originally led by Howard Shore, and then by Paul Shaffer and G. E. Smith. In September 1989, *Saturday Night Live* celebrated its fifteenth year on the air with a retrospective show that featured performers and taped sketches from previous shows.

SAVAGE, FRED (FREDRICK AARON SAVAGE 1976–)

Fred Savage, who became well known as Kevin Arnold on the successful situation comedy series *The WONDER YEARS*, was the youngest person ever to be nominated for an Emmy Award as Best Leading Performer. Savage, whose brother, Ben, is also an actor, was born in Chicago, and was first seen on TV on the revived *TWILIGHT ZONE* series in 1985. He subsequently appeared on the TV series *Morningstar/Eveningstar* (1986), played the grandson in the film *The Princess Bride* (1987), and was featured on the series *Runaway Ralph* (1988), before becoming a star on *The Wonder Years*. After that show left the air, Savage appeared in the TV film *No One Would Tell* (1996) and in the film *A Guy Walks Into a Bar* (1997), and then decided to complete his schooling at Stanford University. In 1997, Savage decided to take a year off from his studies at Stanford to star in a new situation comedy series called *Working*. In 1998, Savage was the narrator of the animated feature film *The Jungle Book: Mowgli's Story*.

SAVALAS, TELLY (ARISTOTLE SAVALAS 1924–1994)

Telly Savalas, who was known for his gruff manner and his bald pate, was one of TV's most successful characters, the Greek–American police detective Theo Kojak on the *KOJAK* police drama series. The son of Greek immigrants, Savalas was born in Garden City, Long Island, New York, and shortly after graduating from high school served in World War II. When the war ended, Savalas studied psychology and then worked as a journalist for ABC News. In the 1950s, Savalas decided to become an actor, and by the late 1960s to early 1970s, he was one of Hollywood's busiest character actors, appearing in such films as *The Young Savages* (1961), *The Interns* (1962), *Birdman of Alcatraz* (1962), *The Greatest Story Ever Told* (1965, as Pontius Pilate), *Ghengis Khan* (1965), *The Dirty Dozen* (1967), *Mackenna's Gold* (1969), *Kelly's Heroes* (1970), and *Pancho Villa* (1972, as Pancho Villa), and on such TV

series as *The FUGITIVE, BONANZA,* and *The VIRGINIAN.* Savalas also had a regular role on the TV series *Acapulco* (1961). In 1973, Savalas first played the role that eventually made him one of the best-known personalities on television, Lt. Theo Kojak, in the TV film *The Marcus-Nelson Murders.* The film was one of the top-rated shows of the TV season, and that same year, Savalas played the Kojak role on a one-hour-a-week series, *Kojak,* which remained on the air as a weekly series until 1978. After *Kojak* was canceled, Savalas kept busy appearing in such films as *Beyond the Poseidon Adventure* (1979), *Fake-Out* (1982), *Alice in Wonderland* (1985, as the Cheshire Cat), and in a series of TV feature-length *Kojak* films. Savalas also made guest appearances on such shows as *The EQUALIZER* and *The COMMISH.* The actor's final film, *Backfire!,* was released in 1995, one year after he died from prostate cancer.

SAVED BY THE BELL (ALSO *SAVED BY THE BELL: THE COLLEGE YEARS* AND *SAVED BY THE BELL: THE NEW CLASS*)

Aug. 1989–Sept. 1993	NBC	Sat. mornings
Sept. 1993–Feb. 1994	NBC	Tues. 8–8:30 P.M. (TCY)
Sept. 1993–2000	NBC	Sat. mornings (TNC)

Although many Saturday morning TV shows were animated cartoons, NBC launched a live-action situation comedy series with younger viewers in mind called *Saved by the Bell* in 1989, and the series became one of the most popular shows among teenagers in the early 1990s. Young actor Mark-Paul Gosselaar played the girl-crazy teenager Zack Morris, a student at Bayside High School in Palisades, California. Zack talked directly to his viewers as he narrated each week's episode. His schoolmates were played by Mario Lopez as pal A. C. Slater; Tiffani-Amber Thiessen as Kelly Kapowski; Elizabeth Berkley as Jessie Spano; Lark Voorhies as Lisa Turtle; Dustin Diamond as the nerdy Screech Powers; Ed Alonzo as Max; and Leanna Creel as Tory. Bayside High School's principal, Richard Belding, was played by Dennis Haskins. When the series first went on the air, it was given two prime-time airings before settling into its Saturday morning time slot. In an attempt to turn the series into a permanent prime-time show, NBC presented two specials, "Saved by the Bell—Hawaiian Style," and "Saved by the Bell Goes to College" during the 1992–93 season. In 1993, most of the Saturday morning cast moved to prime time with a series called *Saved by the Bell: The College Years,* and an entirely new cast was assembled to appear on the Saturday morning show, which was called *Saved By the Bell: The New Class.* Dennis Haskins continued to be seen as Principal Richard Belding of Bayside High School, but new students on the Saturday morning show included Hammersmith, played by David Byrd; Tommy Dee Deluca, played by Jonathan Angel; Weasel the nerd, played by Isaac Lidsky; Lindsay Warner, played by Natalie Cigliuti; Meghan, played by Bianca Lawson; Vicki, played by Bonnie Russavage; and football captain Crunch Grabowski, played by Ryan

Hurst. In fall 1994, original cast member Dustin Diamond returned to the Saturday morning show as Principal Belding's administrative assistant, Samuel "Screetch" Powers. Also seen on the series were Christian Oliver as Brian Keller, Sarah Lancaster as Rachel Myers, Spankee Rogers as Bobby Wilson, Richard Lee Jackson as Ryan Parker, Salim Grant as R. J. "Hollywood" Collins, and Samantha Becker as Maria Lopez.

SCARECROW AND MRS. KING

Oct. 1983–Sept. 1986	CBS	Mon. 8–9 P.M.
Sept. 1986–Feb. 1987	CBS	Fri. 8–9 P.M.
May 1987–Sept. 1987	CBS	Thurs. 8–9 P.M.

The "Scarecrow" in the title of the *Scarecrow and Mrs. King* adventure/espionage series referred to an agent for a secret government organization, Lee Stanton, played by Bruce BOXLEITNER. "Mrs. King" was a bored, suburban divorcee and mother, Amanda King, played by Kate JACKSON, who helped "Scarecrow" as he dodged various Russian spies. Amanda proved to be so good at assisting "Scarecrow" that she was recruited by his boss, Billy Melrose, played by Mel Stewart, to be Stanton's partner. Amanda's family, which included her mother, Dotty West, played by Beverly GARLAND, and her children, Philip and Jamie, played by Paul Stout and Greg Morton, were never quite sure what Amanda was up to, or what her relationship with Stanton was about. In order to keep her agent work a secret, Amanda took a part-time job with the International Federal Film Company, which was a cover firm for the government agency she was actually working for. Other regular characters on the series were Francine Desmond, played by Martha Smith, a sharp-tongued operative for the agency; Stanton's favorite source of information was T. P. Aquinos, played by Raleigh Bond; Amanda's ex-husband, Mr. King, who was played by Sam Melville, finally appeared on the series on a 1985 episode. The Scarecrow and Mrs. King, whose personal relationship had been developing with their professional one, were married in February 1987, seven months before the last episode of the series was aired. The series was filmed in Washington, D.C., which gave the show an aura of authenticity.

SCHNEIDER, JOHN (JOHN RICHARD SCHNEIDER 1960–)

John Schneider's big break came when he was cast as a country bumpkin named Bo Duke on the adventure/situation comedy series, *The DUKES OF HAZZARD*. The series became one of the the late 1970s' to early 1980s' most popular shows. Schneider, who was 19 years old at the time, had already been acting for 12 years. He was born in Mt. Kisco, New York, and his mother and father were divorced when he was two years old. His mother, who was interested in show business, began to take her son to TV and theatrical auditions. Before long, his good looks brought him work in TV commercials and in several plays. When he was 14, John and his mother moved to

Atlanta, Georgia, where the boy continued to perform in local theatrical productions. In 1977, he won a small role in *Smokey and the Bandit*, which was filming in the Atlanta area, and when the film was completed, John and his mother moved to Hollywood to advance his career. At his audition for *The Dukes of Hazzard*, John pretended to be a country boy, like the character Bo Duke, saying that he was from a place named Snellville in Georgia. He got the part, and after several successful seasons, John launched a career as a country singer, and had several hit recordings including "I've Been Around Enough to Know" and "Country Girls." After *The Dukes of Hazzard* left the air, Schneider continued to appear in such films as *The Cocaine Wars* (1986) and *Ministry of Vengeance* (1989), and in the TV films *Gus Brown and Midnight Brewster* (1985) and *Christmas Comes to Willow Creek* (1987). He also had regular roles on the less-than-memorable TV series *Wild Jack* (1989), *Grand Slam* 1990), *Second Chances* (1993), and *Heaven Help Us* (1994), and the more successful VERONICA'S CLOSET and DR. QUINN, MEDICINE WOMAN. In 1997, Schneider hosted the TV series *Ordinary/Extraordinary*, and in 2000, he appeared in the film *Snow Day*.

SCOOBY-DOO

Sept. 1969–Aug. 1976	CBS	Sat. mornings
Sept. 1976–Sept. 1986	ABC	Sat. mornings

The highly successful Saturday morning cartoon show *Scooby-Doo* was produced by Hanna-Barbera Productions and featured a cowardly Great Dane named Scooby-Doo and four teenage detectives named Daphne, Freddy, Shaggy, and Velma. Over the years, several different formats of *Scooby-Doo* have been aired. The first half-hour series made its initial appearance on CBS-TV as *Scooby-Doo: Where Are You?* in 1969, which ran for three years. It then became known as *The New Scooby-Doo Movies* in 1972. In 1976, *Scooby-Doo* moved to ABC and became known as *The Scooby-Doo/Dynomutt Hour*, which, in addition to Scooby-Doo, also featured a segment with a bionic dog named Dynomutt, who, with the Blue Falcon, battled crime. In 1977, the hour-long show was expanded to two hours, and several new cartoon segments were shown under the title *Scooby's All-Star Laff-a-Lympics*. In 1978, Scooby was featured in two Saturday morning cartoon shows, the half-hour *Scooby-Doo: Where Are You?* and the 90-minute *Scooby's All Stars*. In 1979, Scooby and his nephew, Scrappy, were seen in *Scrappy and Scooby-Doo*, and in 1980 reruns were shown as *Scooby's Laff-a-Lympics*. Also in 1980, Scooby received second billing in a new cartoon series, *The Richie Rich/Scooby-Doo Show*. Over the next six years, new adventures titled *Scooby & Scrappy-Doo/The Puppy's New Adventures*, which was aired in 1982, *The Puppy's Further Adventures*, *The Best of Scooby-Doo*, and *The New Scooby and Scrappy-Doo* seen in 1983, *The New Scooby-Doo Mysteries* and *Scary Scooby Funnies* aired during the 1984–85 season, and during the 1985–86 season, *The 13 Ghosts of Scooby-Doo* and *Scooby's Mystery Funhouse* were aired. Although Scooby-Doo retired in 1986, another incarnation of the fabulous Great Dane reappeared on a cartoon series called *A Pup Named Scooby-Doo* in 1988.

CBS programming chief Fred Silverman had originally come up with the name "Scooby-Doo" for the Hanna-Barbera Productions cartoon character in 1969. Silverman heard Frank Sinatra use the words "scooby-doo" in his hit recording of "Strangers in the Night," and thought it was different enough to become a memorable name for the new Great Dane cartoon sleuth being developed for his network, which indeed it was.

SEA HUNT

Feb. 1958–1961   Syndicated   Various times and stations

Lloyd BRIDGES was the sole regular on the half-hour TV adventure series *Sea Hunt*. One of the few early syndicated television series to attract a sizable audience, *Sea Hunt* was a series that the major networks had all turned down, believing the underwater setting was limited. They were proved wrong, and *Sea Hunt* enjoyed a healthy four-year run with 156 episodes. Bridges played Mike Nelson, a former U.S. Navy frogman who became a freelance underwater investigator at the end of World War II. Nelson worked for various insurance companies and used his underwater skills to locate and recover stolen goods from sunken ships, as well as find and identify airplanes downed during the war, and generally battle countless criminals who roamed the seven seas. As the series unfolded, Nelson became increasingly more involved in dangerous assignments that involved national security matters. Producer Ivan Tors said of *Sea Hunt*, "We weren't sure at first how much underwater stuff we could get by with . . . We soon found out that was what the audience wanted . . . water, water, and more water." Approximately 50 per cent of the series action took place underwater as the show entered its second season, and the remainder of the action mostly took place aboard Nelson's boat, the *Argonaut*. In order to make sure the show was authentic in its depiction of deep-sea activities, Tors hired frogman Jon Lindbergh, the son of world famous flyer Charles Lindbergh, the first man to fly solo across the Atlantic Ocean in the 1920s, to act as the series' underwater sequence adviser. The effective photography for the series was executed by world-famous underwater photographer Lamar Boren.

SEARCH FOR TOMORROW

Sept. 1951–Mar. 1982 CBS   Various daytime hours
Mar. 1982–Dec. 1986 NBC   Various daytime hours

When the long-running daytime drama series *Search for Tomorrow* left the air after 35 years of continuous tears and turmoil, scores of viewers wrote letters protesting the decision to terminate the show. Over the years, *Search for Tomorrow* had become one of the viewers' favorite daytime drama series, and it had been on the air for as long as most of its fans had been alive. Over 9,000 episodes had been telecast during the show's 35-year tenure, and the central character, the four-times married, three-times widowed Joanne Gardner Barron Tate Vincente Tourneur, played by Mary Stuart for the entire 35-years, had became as familiar to viewers as members of their own families. Joanne was a woman who overcame many difficulties in life but always managed to maintain her dignity.

Search for Tomorrow was created by Roy Winsor for CBS in 1951. Winsor served as the show's executive producer when the series first aired, and Charles Irving was the series' first producer and director. Subsequent producers were Frank Dodge, Bernie Sofronski, Mary-Ellis Bunim, Joanna Lee, Ellen Barrett, and John Whitesell. The show's first head writer was the prolific Agnes Nixon, who was succeeded by Irving Vendig shortly after the series made its debut. When first aired, it was, like most daytime serials of the time, a 15-minute, 5-days-a-week show. In September 1968, it was one of the first TV "soap operas" to expand to 30 minutes, Monday through Friday.

Search for Tomorrow, which was set in a fictional town called Henderson, in addition to Mary Stuart, had a large company of regular players over the years. Among them were Johnny Sylvester as Joanne's first husband, Keith Barron; and Lynn Loring, Nancy Pinkerton, Abigail Kellogg, Patricia Harty, Trish Van Devere, Gretchen Walther, Melissa Murphy, Melinda Plank, Leigh Lassen, Tina Sloan, Jacqueline Schultz (as Joanne's daughter, Patty Barron), Cliff Hall and Bess Johnson (as Joanne's in-laws), Harry Holcombe, and then Eric Dressler (as Joanne's father), Melba Rae (as Joanne's best friend, Marge Bergman), Larry Haines (who played Stu Bergman for most of the years the program was aired); Ellen Spencer, Sandy Robinson, Fran Sharon, Nancy Franklin, Marion Hailey, Millee Taggart (who all played Marge and Stu's daughter, Janet, at one time or another); Peter Broderick, Ray Bellaran, John James, Mitch Litrofsky and Robert LuPone (as Marge and Stu's son, Tommy Bergman); Joanna Roos, Nydia Westman, Peter Lazar (as Jimmy Bergman), Coe Norton (as Dr. Ned Hilton); Terry O'Sullivan, and then Karl Weber (as Joanne's second husband, Arthur Tate); and Jeffrey Krolik (Mary Stuart's real-life son, as Joanne and Arthur's son, Duncan Eric Tate).

Other well-known or later-to-be-well-known performers who appeared on *Search for Tomorrow* as regulars during the 35 years the show was aired were Lee Grant, Nita Talbot, Constance Ford, Don Knotts, Donald Madden, David O'Brian, George Maharis, Robert Mandan, George Gaynes, Virginia Gilmore, Lesley Woods, Joan Copeland, Lenka Peterson, Jill Clayburgh, Lilia Skala, Natalie Schafer, Val Dufour, Anthony George (as Joanne's third husband, Dr. Tony Vincente), Hal Linden, Billie Lou Watt, Anne Revere, Wayne Rogers, Robby Benson, Kevin Kline, and John Aniston (as Joanne's fourth husband, Martin Tourneur).

During *Search for Tomorrow's* final years, the show had begun to deemphasize Mary Stuart's character, Joanne, and many critics felt that it was what caused viewers to finally lose interest in the series. Even the formidable talents of the show's final producer, John Whitesell, failed to save the program. On the show's final episode, Joanne Tourneur turned to loyal friend Stu Bergman, and uttered the show's last line, "Tomorrow . . . I can't wait."

SECRET AGENT

Apr. 1965–Sept. 1965	CBS	Sat. 9–10 P.M.
Dec. 1965–Sept. 1966	CBS	Sat. 8:30–9:30 P.M.

Even though *Secret Agent,* a series that originated in Great Britain as *Danger Man,* was on American prime-time television for just one and a half years, it had a large and loyal audience. The series, which was about a special security agent/spy named John Drake, who worked for NATO, was set in various locations throughout Europe. Drake was a smooth operator who had numerous encounters with enemy spies from Eastern bloc nations and was often seen in the company of beautiful women. Patrick McGoohan starred as Drake and was the only regular on the series. Even though Drake's mission was to "preserve world peace and promote brotherhood between people and nations," he was one of television's most violent heroes and often had violent encounters with his adversaries. *Secret Agent* was one of the few series on American television in the 1960s that was produced in Great Britain, and before it was seen on TV in the United States it had been a successful series throughout Europe. The show's theme song, "Secret Agent Man," which was sung by Johnny Rivers as the series' opening titles rolled, became familiar to millions of viewers on both sides of the Atlantic, and is fondly remembered by fans of the show. In all, only 35 episodes of the series were filmed by the British producers, ATV.

SECRET STORM, THE

Feb. 1954–Feb. 1974   CBS   Various daytime hours

For 20 years, CBS's daytime drama *The Secret Storm* was one of television's most popular soap operas, and when the series was suddenly canceled by CBS, due to declining audiences, millions of fans registered their disappointment. For many years, the series was produced by Gloria Monty, and Joe Manetta was the series' producer during the programs later seasons. Throughout the 1950s, and well into the 1960s, the show usually centered on the Ames family of Woodbridge. When the series was sold by its sponsor, American Home Products, to CBS in the late 1960s, the Ames family gradually all but disappeared from the show.

When *The Secret Storm* made its debut in 1954, it was a 15-minute, five-days-a-week, Monday-through-Friday offering, but it was expanded to 30 minutes, on Monday to Friday in June 1960. Featured as the show's patriarch, Peter Ames, were Peter Hobbs from 1954 until 1960, Cec Linder from 1960 until 1964, Ward Costello from 1964 until 1966, and Lawrence Weber from 1966 until 1968. Peter was the father of three, who had become a widower the first week the series was on the air when his wife was killed in an automobile accident. Peter's children, who were all young adults, were Susan Ames, his eldest daughter, played by Jean Mowry, and then by Rachel Taylor, Mary Foskett, and Judy Lewis (film star Loretta Young's daughter). His son, Jerry Ames, was originally played by Robert Morse, and then by Warren Berlinger, Wayne Tippit, Peter White, and Stephen Bolster. Peter's youngest daughter, Amy Ames, was played by Jada Rowlands, Beverly Lunsford, and Lynne Adams. Peter's father-in-law, Judge J. T. Tyrell, was played by Russell Hicks, and other regular cast members in the earliest years included Marjorie Gateson as Peter's mother-in-law, Grace Tyrell; Haila Stoddard as Peter's sister-in-law, Pauline, Virginia Dwyer as the Ames's housekeeper, Jane Edwards; and Ed Bryce, James Vickery, Donny Melvin, Joan Hotchkis, June Graham, Carl King, Frank Sutton, Jane McArthur, Jim Pritchett, Don Galloway, David O'Brien, Ed Griffith, John BARAGREY, Polly Childs, Pamela Raymond, Lori March, Bibi Besch, Roy Scheider, Diana Muldaur, Nick Coster, Jed Allen, Ryan MacDonald, Conrad Fowkes, Linden Chiles, Julie Wilson, Jane Rose, Jacqueline Brooks, Robert Sherwood, Jack Ryland, Robert Loggia, Laurence Luckinbill, Christina Crawford (film star Joan Crawford's daughter), Jeffrey Lynn, Marla Adams, Diane Dell, Terry Falis, Judy Safran, Bernie Barrow, David Ackroyd, Dennis Cooney, Barbara Rodell, Peter MacLean, Joel Crothers, James Grover, Stephanie Braxton, David Gale, Frances Sternhagen, Troy Donahue, Jennifer Darling, Gordon Rigsby, Alexander Scourby, Terry Kiser, James Storm, Jeff Pomerantz, Audre Johnson, Dan Hamilton, Ellen Barber, Sidney Walker, Joe Ponazecki, Patrick Fox, Madeline Sherwood, Richard Venture, Roberta Royce, Susan Sudert, Philip Bruns, Mary K. Wells, Diane Ladd, Scott Medford, and Nicholas Lewis. *The Secret Storm* was created by veteran daytime writer Roy Winsor, who was also responsible for SEARCH FOR TOMORROW.

SEE IT NOW

Nov. 1951–Apr. 1952	CBS	Sunday afternoon
Apr. 1952–June 1953	CBS	Sun. 6:30–7 P.M.
Sept. 1953–July 1955	CBS	Tues. 10:30–11 P.M.
Sept. 1955–July 1958	CBS	Various times

The dean of television news programs, CBS's Edward R. MURROW, hosted this quality news program that became the prototype for the many in-depth TV documentary/news shows that followed. On the very first *See It Now* telecast, Murrow showed a live shot of the Atlantic Ocean on one side of the TV screen and the Pacific Ocean on the other side of the screen to demonstrate the scope of TV saying, "We are impressed by a medium through which a man sitting in his living room has been able for the first time to look at two oceans at once."

Subjects ranged from serious probes of contemporary political figures, as when he criticized U. S. Senator Joseph McCarthy for his obsessive attacks of Americans whom McCarthy viciously accused of being communists or communist sympathizers during the cold war, to the lighthearted, as in his folksy interview with American primitive artist Grandma Moses, a woman who had gained fame when she was well into her eighties. Although Murrow also interviewed celebrities on his prime-time PERSON TO PERSON program, his interviews on *See It Now* were generally more serious, and Murrow often covered controversial subjects such as the recriminations of atomic scientists, and smoking and cancer. Ironically, Murrow was himself a heavy smoker and often puffed away on cigarettes while on camera on both *See It Now* and *Person to Person*. On occasion, Murrow took his show on the road, as when he visited soldiers at the front during the Korean War. Murrow always ended his telecasts by saying, "Good night . . . and good luck." Unfortunately, his luck did not hold out, and this most respected man in the news business died of lung cancer in 1965, at the age of 57.

SEINFELD

May 1990–July 1990	NBC	Thurs. 9:30–10 P.M.
Jan. 1991–Feb. 1991	NBC	Wed. 9:30–10 P.M.
Apr. 1991–June 1991	NBC	Thurs. 9:30–10 P.M.
June 1991–Dec. 1991	NBC	Wed. 9:30–10 P.M.
Dec. 1991–Jan. 1993	NBC	Wed. 9–9:30 P.M.
Feb. 1993–Aug. 1993	NBC	Thurs. 9:30–10 P.M.
Aug. 1993–Sept. 1998	NBC	Thurs. 9–9:30 P.M.
Jan. 1998–Sept. 1998	NBC	Wed. 8:30–9 P.M.

During the earliest episodes of this half-hour situation comedy, stand-up comedian Jerry SEINFELD performed parts of his real-life comedy routine as part of the show, which was about a young stand-up (named Jerry Seinfeld) and his friends who lived in New York City. Most of the action took place in Jerry's apartment, and the stories centered on the innocent misadventures Jerry and his self-absorbed young friends dealt with on a day-to-day basis, such as where they should eat, whom they should date and why they were dating who they were, why they weren't getting what they wanted out of life, how to deal with parents, where they had parked their car in the parking garage, etc. The series, according to Seinfeld, was "a show about nothing." His three costars included Julia Louis-Dreyfus, who played Jerry's girlfriend and then friend, Elaine Benes; Jason Alexander, who played George Costanza, Jerry's best friend, a worrywart who was a real estate agent when the series was first aired; and Michael Richards, who played Cosmo Kramer, Jerry's eccentric neighbor who was always trying to come up with a way to make a fast buck and constantly wandered in and out of Jerry's Upper West Side apartment. Other regular characters included George's ever-shouting parents, Estelle and Frank Costanza, played by Estelle Harris and Jerry Stiller, who were as neurotic as George; Jerry's out-of-touch parents, who lived in Florida, Helen and Morty Seinfeld, played by Liz Sheridan and Barney Martin; Jerry's archenemy, the postal worker, Newman, who lived in Jerry's apartment building, played by Wayne Knight; Jerry's Uncle Leo, played by Len Lesser; and Elaine's sometime boyfriend, the compliant David Puddy, played by Patrick Warburton. Also appearing as regulars on occasion were Sandy Baron as Jack Klompus, Richard Fancy as Mr. Lippman (Elaine's boss), Bob Balaban as Russell Dalrimple, Heidi Swedberg as Susan Biddle Ross (George's ill-fated girlfriend), Peter Crumbie as "Crazy Joe" Davola (Elaine's comical stalker), Danny Woodburn as Mickey Abbott (Kramer's undersized friend), Ian Abercrombie as Justin Pitt (Elaine's hapless boss), Steve Hytner as Kenny Bania (Jerry's rival comedian), Bryon Cranston as Dr. Tim Whatley (Jerry's pragmatic dentist), Richard Herd as Wilhelm (George's boss when he went to work for the Yankees), John O'Hurley as J. Peterman, and Phil Morris as Jackie Chiles (Kramer's pompous attorney).

Jerry, George, Elaine, and Kramer frequently hung out at Monk's diner, as well as in Jerry's small apartment. Memorable episodes included "The Pez Dispenser"; the episode on which Elaine showed a bit more skin on her Christmas card photo than she had intended; the episode on which Jerry and his gang take on the tyrannical owner

The cast of *Seinfeld:* Michael Richards as Cosmo Kramer, Julia Louis-Dreyfus as Elaine Benes, Jerry Seinfeld as himself, and Jason Alexander as George Costanza (Author's collection)

of a take-out restaurant, "the Soup Nazi"; the show on which Jerry wears a silly pirate shirt for an appearance on *The Tonight Show;* the "backwards episode" on which the scenes were shown in reverse order (the final scene, a wedding in India first, and the scenes concerning how they got to the wedding leading up to the ceremony, beginning 13 years earlier; the gang's encounter with the "Bubble Boy," a child forced to live in a plastic tent because of a malady; and the infamous Puerto Rican Day Parade episode, which, because of the chaotic way the parade was depicted, met with criticism from New York's Puerto Rican community.

In December 1997, when the show was at the height of its popularity, Jerry Seinfeld announced that it was the last season *Seinfeld* would be on the air. On the last episode of the show, Jerry and his pals, Elaine, George, and Kramer, were put on trial and convicted of crimes against common decency, and were sentenced to spend one year in jail. Many of the people seen on previous episodes made guest appearances, giving testimony concerning the self-centered way Jerry, Elaine, George, and Kramer had been behaving over the past eight years. Jerry decided to make the best of the situation and immediately began to perform his stand-up act for uninterested inmates.

SEINFELD, JERRY (JEROME SEINFELD 1954–)

Jerry Seinfeld, who was born in Brooklyn, New York, but spent most of his childhood in Massapequa, Long Island, claims that he knew he was going to be a comedian when he was eight years old. After attending Oswego and Queens Colleges, Jerry developed a comedy act that he first performed in the New York City comedy club Catch a Rising Star, and then in comedy clubs throughout the United States. During the 1970s, Seinfeld had as many as 300 club dates a year, and in 1976, he was featured on a Rodney Dangerfield TV special. In 1980, Seinfeld was a semiregular on the BENSON TV series, playing the role of Richie, but it was in 1981 that his big break came when he performed a five-minute comedy guest spot on NBC's popular late night TONIGHT SHOW with Johnny CARSON. He subsequently was seen on *The Tommy Chong Roast* TV special and on his own TV special, *The Seinfeld Chronicles,* in 1989. Jerry's act centered on his frank observations about the absurdities of everyday life. In the late 1980s, NBC approached Seinfeld about developing and starring in a pilot for a situation comedy series. After visiting a grocery store and making jokes about the store's produce, Jerry and his friend Larry David came up with the idea to center his new TV sitcom on wry observations about everyday life. The show made its debut in 1990, but it was not an immediate success. Its popularity increased, however, when its time slot was changed to the half hour that followed the successful NBC show CHEERS. The SEINFELD show's popularity steadily increased, and before long, everyone in America seemed to be talking about the new show that was supposed to be "about nothing," but somehow managed to deal with such previously taboo-for-TV

subjects as masturbation, breast implants, oral sex, body odor, nose picking, etc. In 1998, Jerry Seinfeld decided to return to his first love, performing his comedy routines in clubs around the country, and announced that his weekly show would be terminated after eight successful years. By the time Seinfeld retired from television, he was one of the wealthiest performers in the United States, but he did indeed return to performing stand-up comedy on TV and in nightclubs around the country and has been seen on the TV special *Jerry Seinfeld Live on Broadway: I'm Telling You for the Last Time* (1998), *Saturday Night Live: 25th Anniversary* (1999), and *Pros and Cons* (1999).

SELLECK, TOM (1945–)

Tom Selleck, the star of the successful TV series MAGNUM, P.I., and numerous feature films, was born in Detroit, Michigan. Selleck attended the University of Southern California on a basketball scholarship, where he claims he majored in acting, after being unable to sign up for architecture courses that were all filled up when he went to register. In the early 1970s, after seriously studying acting with Milton Katselas at the Beverly Hills Playhouse, Selleck embarked upon his acting career and landed roles on the TV series *Lancer* (1969), *The F.B.I.,* and MARCUS WELBY, M.D., and in the films *Myra Breckinridge* (1970) and *The Movie Murderer* (1970). In the 1990s, Selleck was seen on

Tom Selleck (Author's collection)

such series as *The STREETS OF SAN FRANCISCO* and *CHARLIE'S ANGELS*, but it was a regular role on the daytime serial drama series *The YOUNG AND THE RESTLESS* in 1973 that first attracted the attention of the public. Selleck continued to appear in ever larger roles on TV and in such films as *Midway* (1976), *Bunco* (1977), and *Coma* (1978). In 1979, Selleck became a regular on *The ROCKFORD FILES*, playing a character named Lance White, and in 1980, he was seen on his own TV series, *Magnum, P.I.,* playing Thomas Sullivan Magnum, the role that made him a star. The series remained on the air for eight seasons. During and after his appearances on *Magnum, P.I.,* Selleck was seen in such films as *High Road to China* (1983), *Runaway* (1984), *Lassiter* (1984), *Three Men and a Baby* (1987) *An Innocent Man* (1989), *Quigley Down Under* (1990), *3 Men and a Little Lady* (1990), *Mr. Baseball* (1992), *Christopher Columbus: The Discovery* (1992), and *Folks* (1992). In 1994, after guest-starring on several episodes of the show, Selleck became a semiregular on the popular television sitcom *FRIENDS*. In the late 1990s to early 2000s, Selleck continued to remain active and was seen in the films *Ruby Jean and Joe* (1996), *Open Season* (1996), *In & Out* (1997), *The Love Letter* (1999), *Running Mates* (2000), and was a regular on the TV series *The Closer* (1998). Selleck was chosen by *People* magazine as one of the "50 most beautiful people in the world" in 1998.

SENATE CRIME HEARINGS

In 1951, it seemed as though everyone in America who owned a television set was watching the live televised Senate hearings on organized crime activities in the United States. The televised hearings, which were chaired by Senator Estes Kefauver of Tennessee, made nationally recognized celebrities of such unlikely people as Senator Kefauver himself, Senator Charles Tobey, attorney Rudolph Halley, gang moll Virginia Hill, and mobster Frank Costello (whose face was never seen, but whose hands betrayed his discomfort at being called to task for his past criminal activities). The hearings were a revelation to millions of Americans who had never seen the Senate at work before, and many people became aware, for the first time, of the power of the Fifth Amendment, which grants citizens the right to refuse to answer questions on the grounds that it might tend to incriminate them, a right many crime figures called before the committee used in an attempt to avoid possible prosecution.

SERGEANT BILKO/YOU'LL NEVER GET RICH

(see *Phil Silvers Show, The*)

SERGEANT PRESTON OF THE YUKON

Sept. 1955–Sept. 1958   CBS   Thurs. 7:30–8 P.M.

First heard as a radio series in 1947, *Sergeant Preston of the Yukon* was created by the man who first introduced *The Lone Ranger* and *The Green Hornet* to radio listeners, George W. Trendle. The television series, which was set in the wilds of the Klondike, starred Richard Simmons, a former World War II pilot who had little previous acting experience, in the title role as the Royal Canadian Mounted policeman who, with his trusted canine companion, Yukon King, always managed to apprehend the bad guys and secure the safety of the Northwest. The series was set in 19th-century Canada, where criminals sought to take advantage of the Gold Rush that was taking place in western North America. Preston's father, a former Mountie himself, had been killed while tracking down a criminal at large, and Preston, a graduate law student when his father died, swore to avenge his father's death and enlisted in the Royal Canadian Mounted Police. Preston did indeed capture his father's killer and remained in the Mounted Police to track down many other criminals. In 1958, George Trendle Enterprises sold its interest in the series to the Wrather Corporation, who revived the 104 episodes that had been filmed and reran them on the NBC network from October 1963 through April 1964. During the series' original run, *Sergeant Preston of the Yukon* was sponsored by the Quaker Oats Company. In the 1970s, it resurfaced as a syndicated series that reran original episodes of the show.

SERLING, ROD (EDWIN RODMAN SERLING 1924–1975)

Television writer, producer, and personality Rod Serling, whose series *The TWILIGHT ZONE* became a TV classic, was born in Syracuse, New York, but moved to Binghamton, New York, as a child and completed his schooling in that city. Serling, a boxer and paratrooper before he began writing for television, was one of the original "angry young men" of post–World War II America. In the 1950s, Serling became one of several writers who wrote quality scripts for such popular early dramatic anthology series as *The KRAFT TELEVISION PLAYHOUSE*, the *UNITED STATES STEEL HOUR*, and *PLAYHOUSE 90*. Serling's television plays *Patterns* and *Requiem for a Heavyweight* also became successful motion pictures and are considered television classics. In 1959, Serling produced and was the host of *The Twilight Zone,* a science fiction/suspense series that was one of TV's most popular programs throughout the 1960s. He also wrote the original script for the film *Planet of the Apes* (1968). Always something of a maverick, Serling, who was an outspoken critic of such things as the United States's military involvement in Vietnam and racism in the United States in the 1960s, was eventually ignored by the major television networks, who found his stands on political issues too controversial. Serling's last major TV series was *NIGHT GALLERY*, which was produced in 1970. In 1983, Serling's play "It's A Good Life" was used as the third segment in the feature film *Twilight Zone: The Movie*. Unfortunately, Serling had died in 1975, and was not alive to appreciate the renewed interest in his work.

SERPICO

Sept. 1976–Jan. 1977   NBC   Fri. 10–11 P.M.

David BIRNEY played Frank Serpico, an idealistic New York City undercover policeman who bucked heads with his fellow officers on this hour-long police drama series that was based on a hit film of the same name, which starred Al Pacino. As an undercover police officer, Serpico often had to deal with drug dealers, racketeers, and corrupt politicians, which made his work extremely dangerous. Also regularly appearing on the series was full-time undercover cop Tom Sullivan, played by Tom Atkins, who worked with Serpico and was his "contact" with the police department when Serpico was working under cover. Frank Serpico was an actual person, and the original book upon which the film and TV show were based had been a best-seller in the 1960s. The executive producer of *Serpico* was Emmet G. Lavery. The series was produced in association with Paramount Television and NBC-TV.

SESAME STREET

Nov. 1969–present   NET (later PBS)   Afternoons

Unquestionably, *Sesame Street* is one of the most important shows for children ever produced for television. It was developed by Joan Ganz Cooney, the executive direc-

Bob McGrath, Roscoe Orman, and Loretta Long (foreground) of *Sesame Street* (Photofest)

tor of the Children's Television Workshop, a company formed in 1967 especially to produce *Sesame Street* that is presently simply called Sesame Workshop, with support from the United States Office of Education, the Ford Foundation, and the Carnegie Corporation. The series was designed especially to teach the alphabet, numbers, and correct English usage to preschool youngsters in an entertaining manner through song, skits, puppetry, and animation. The five-days-a-week, Monday-through-Friday series is set on a city street, because it is primarily directed toward inner-city preschoolers, but the show has proved popular with children from all backgrounds. Each show is "sponsored" by a letter in the alphabet or by a number, which are featured in commercial-like spots on the show. Story lines often include such topics as friendship, empathy for others, how to resolve conflicts, etc.

The cast of *Sesame Street* includes live actors and puppets. Members of the show's original cast of live performers included Loretta Long as Susan; Matt Robinson and Roscoe Orman as Gordon; Bob McGrath as Bob; Will Lee as storekeeper, Mr. Hooper; Northern J. Calloway as David; Emilio Delgado as Luis; and Sonia Manzano as Maria. The popular puppets, who were called "Muppets," that appeared on the series were created by master puppeteer Jim HENSON, and included such unforgettable characters as Bert and Ernie, Grover, Oscar the Grouch, the Cookie Monster, and Big Bird (a person, first puppeteer Frank OZ, and then Carroll Spinney, dressed in a bright yellow bird costume). Over the years the original music for the series was composed by Jeff Moss and Joe Raposo.

During its long and successful run, *Sesame Street* has dealt with a wide variety of life-and-death situations, in addition to its overtly instructional content. When elderly character actor Will Lee, who played Mr. Hooper, died, the series dealt with death as one of the things people encounter in life and talked openly about Mr. Hooper's death. The series also celebrated the TV wedding of *Sesame Street* characters Maria and Luis in 1988. In 1992, when Jim Henson, one of the major forces behind the success of *Sesame Street,* died unexpectedly, the producers of the series chose not to drop the characters whose voices he provided on the show, but to retain the characters and in a sense honor him, by having actor Steve Whitmire, who sounded exactly like Henson, continue to provide the voices of the characters Henson had played.

In 1993, the set of *Sesame Street* was enlarged for the 25th anniversary of the show. In addition to the row of tenement buildings and stores usually seen on the series, the Furry Arms Hotel and the Finders Keepers thrift shop, which was operated by comedienne Ruth Buzzi, who played a character named Ruthie, were also seen. Nine-year-old Tarah Lynne Shaeffer joined the cast that same year as Tarah, a young girl with a disability. Other children who became permanent members of the cast included Desiree Casado as Gabriella and Imani Patterson as Miles. Also added to the cast over the years were Alison Batlett O'Reilly as Gina, Linda Bove as Linda, and Alan Muroaka as Alan. Among the talented puppeteers who currently contribute their talents to *Sesame Street,* in addition to the gifted Jim Henson and Frank Oz, are Pam Arciero (Grundgetta Grouch), Fran Brill (Zoe, Roxy Marie, Prairie Dawn), Kevin Cash (Elmo, Hoots, Baby Natasha), Bruce Connelly (Barkley), Stephanie D'Abruzzo (Elizabeth), John E. Kennedy (various Honkers and Dingers), David Rudman (Baby Bear, Two-Headed Monster, Davey Monkey, Humphrey, Sonny Friendly, Norm), Judy Sladky (Alice Snuffleupagus), Carroll Spinney (Big Bird, Oscar the Grouch), Alice Dinnean Vernon (Mama Bear, Goldilocks), Matt Vogel (various characters), and Steve Whitmore (Kermit the Frog, Rizzo the Rat).

Certainly one of the most honored series ever seen on television, *Sesame Street* has won well over 75 Emmy Awards, more than any other show, and has also won two George Foster Peabody Awards, four Parents' Choice Awards, an Action for Children's Television Special Achievement Award, and the Prix Jeunesse International. Lou Berger is the head writer of *Sesame Street* and Michael Loman is the show's executive producer (Arlene Sherman is co–executive producer), and Michael Reazi is the show's musical director. The original goal of the people who created *Sesame Street* over 30 years ago was "to deliver academic and social education that will prepare children for grade school."

77 SUNSET STRIP

Oct. 1958–Oct. 1959	ABC	Fri. 9:30–10 P.M.
Oct. 1959–Sept. 1962	ABC	Fri. 9–10 P.M.
Sept. 1962–Sept. 1963	ABC	Fri. 9:30–10:30 P.M.
Sept. 1963–Feb. 1964	ABC	Fri. 7:30–8:30 P.M.
Apr. 1964–Sept. 1964	ABC	Wed. 10–11 P.M.

77 Sunset Strip was one of the first of several private detective shows in the late 1950s–early 1960s that gave P.I.'s a more glamorous look. Set in Hollywood, the private detectives Stuart Bailey, played by Efrem ZIMBALIST, Jr., and Jeff Spencer, played by Roger SMITH, were, unlike most of the Hollywood based P.I.'s who were seen before them, well-educated and sophisticated men. Bailey had been an officer in the OSS, spoke many languages and was suave and cultured; Spencer was a former government undercover agent who had a law degree. The office was located at 77 Sunset Strip in Hollywood. Dino's Restaurant was located next door to the office, and the restaurant's good-looking young parking lot attendant, Gerald Lloyd Kookson III, nicknamed "Kookie," played by Edd BYRNES, often became involved in Bailey's and Spencer's cases. Kookie, who was constantly combing his hair (a hit song of the day was "Kookie, Kookie, Lend Me Your Comb") used jive talk and generally provided comic relief. Numerous "jive" expressions Kookie used on the series became catchphrases for young people all across America. Kookie, for example, called things he liked "the ginchiest," described sleep as "piling up the z's," and, when he was delivering a message for the agency said that he "was playing pigeon." Byrnes temporarily left the series after the second season after

demanding a more important role because of his character's popularity. He was replaced by soon-to-be movie star Troy Donahue. When Byrnes returned to the series, it was as a partner at the Bailey/Spencer Detective Agency. Other regular characters on the series were Roscoe, a racetrack tout who often provided information to the P.I.'s, who was played by Louis Quinn; switchboard operator Suzanne Fabray, who was played by Jacqueline Beer; Police Lt. Gilmore, played by Byron Keith; Rex Randolph, played by Richard Long, who was a partner at the agency during the series' 1960–61 season; Kookie's parking lot replacement, J. R. Hale, played by Robert Logan; and, during the show's final years, the agency secretary, Hannah, played by Joan Staley. In 1963, Warner Brothers, who produced the series, dropped everyone but Efrem Zimbalist, Jr., from the cast in an attempt to revive the show's waning popularity. The series' original producer, Roy Huggins, had previously been replaced by Howie Horowitz, and then by William CONRAD, an actor/producer who later became known as TVs Cannon and Jake on *JAKE AND THE FAT MAN.*

SHATNER, WILLIAM (1931–)

Before William Shatner played Captain James Tiberius Kirk on the celebrated TV science fiction series STAR TREK in 1966, he was the star of such plays as *The World of Susie Wong* on Broadway, and made numerous guest-starring appearances on such television programs as *GOODYEAR TELEVISION PLAYHOUSE, STUDIO ONE, The UNITED STATES STEEL HOUR, The TWILIGHT ZONE, ROUTE 66, The OUTER LIMITS, The MAN FROM U.N.C.L.E., ALFRED HITCHCOCK PRESENTS, DR. KILDARE, NAKED CITY, The NURSES, The FUGITIVE, The BIG VALLEY,* and *GUNSMOKE* in the 1950s and 1960s. He also appeared in such films as *Oedipus Rex* (1957), *The Brothers Karamazov* (1958), *The Intruder* (1961), *Judgment at Nuremberg* (1961), and was a regular on the TV series *For the People* (1965). Shatner was born in Montreal, Quebec, where he attended McGill University and became interested in theater arts. After finishing his schooling, he headed for New York City, determined to break into show business. It wasn't long before he was appearing in stage productions and making appearances on TV. It was his role on *Star Trek,* however, that made him a star. Even though *Star Trek* was on the air for just three years, it attracted legions of loyal viewers and made Shatner one of the most recognized actors in the world. After *Star Trek* was canceled, Shatner continued to appear in such films as *The Andersonville Trial* (1970), and in a series of very profitable *Star Trek* feature films, including *Star Trek: The Motion Picture* (1979), *Star Trek II: The Wrath of Khan* (1982), *Star Trek III: The Search for Spock* (1984), *Star Trek IV: The Voyage Home* (1986), *Star Trek V: The Final Frontier* (1989), and *Star Trek VI: The Undiscovered Country* (1991), as well as starring on the *T. J. Hooker* series, appearing as a regular on such TV series as *Rescue 911* (1989), *3rd Rock From the Sun* (1996, as The Big Giant Head/Stone Phillips), as well as in numerous TV films. Among the TV series Shatner has guest-starred on since his regular appearance on the *Star Trek* series are BARNABY JONES, *The* SIX MILLION DOLLAR MAN, KUNG FU, COLUMBO, *The* ROOKIES, HOW THE WEST WAS WON, MORK & MINDY, *The* FRESH PRINCE OF BEL AIR, and *The Muppets Tonight.* Shatner continues to be an active performer in films and on television and has recently been seen in *First Men on the Moon* (1999), *Falcon Down* (2000), and *Miss Congeniality* (2000).

SHEEN, BISHOP FULTON J. (1895–1979)

One of television's earliest major personalities was a Roman Catholic priest, Fulton J. Sheen, who popularized religion through his mesmerizing talks. Bishop Sheen, who was Msgr. Fulton J. Sheen when he entered television, was born in El Paso, Illinois, and even before he was seen on television, he was considered one of the most brilliant and persuasive members of the Catholic clergy. Ordained in 1919, Sheen did graduate work in Rome and Louvain, Belgium, and in 1925, he became a member of the faculty of St. Edmund's College in Great Britain. From 1927 to 1950, he was a philosophy professor at the Catholic University of America in Washington, D.C. Over the years, Sheen wrote many books, including the best-selling *Walk with God* (1965) and *The Moral Universe* (1967), but it was his television series *Life Is Worth Living*, which became a top-rated program in the 1950s, for which he is best remembered. Sheen, who had been consecrated auxiliary bishop in 1951, resigned his position as head of the Rochester, New York, diocese in 1966, in order to devote his final years to writing and making public appearances mainly throughout the United States and Canada.

SHEENA, QUEEN OF THE JUNGLE

1955–1956   Syndicated   Various Times and stations

The popular heroine who appeared in *Jumbo* comic books, drawn and written by S. M. Iger and Will Eisner in the 1930s and 1940s, Sheena, Queen of the Jungle, became the major character on a 30-minute, syndicated TV adventure series in 1955. The series, which was mainly directed toward young viewers, starred Irish McCalla in the title role. The series featured lots of jungle action for young viewers to enjoy and often had Sheena battling and befriending wild animals and hostile natives. The series was set in Kenya, Africa, but was actually filmed in Mexico, and featured Sheena's pet chimpanzee, Chim (played by Neal the Chimp), and Sheena's handsome trader friend, Bob, who was played by Christian Drake. In all, only 26 episodes were ever produced, but lots of people, especially males, fondly remember the voluptuous Sheena and her skimpy leopard-skin costume. People often ask whatever happened to McCalla after *Sheena* left the air, since she appeared in only a few B films after the show departed the airwaves. Her fans will be happy to know Irish McCalla became a successful painter after leaving show business in the early 1960s.

Irish McCalla as Sheena, Queen of the Jungle (Author's collection)

SHEPHERD, CYBILL (1950–   )

The star of two successful TV series, MOONLIGHTING and CYBILL, Cybill Shepherd was born in Memphis, Tennessee, and began her career as an actress when she was still in her teens and was discovered by film director Peter Bogdanovich, who gave her the leading ingenue role in his film *The Last Picture Show* in 1971. Shepherd, who had a longtime relationship with Bogdanovich and also dated Elvis Presley when she first went to Hollywood, continued to appear in such films as *The Heartbreak Kid* (1972), *Daisy Miller* (1974), *At Long Last Love* (1975), *Taxi Driver* (1976), *Silver Bears* (1977), *The Lady Vanishes* (1979), and *The Return* (1980), but her film career gradually faded as her relationship with Bogdanovich wound down. In 1983, Shepherd starred on the unsuccessful TV series *The Yellow Rose*, but in 1985, she starred on *Moonlighting* with Bruce Willis, which became the hit series that finally brought Shepherd the stardom that had eluded her. After *Moonlighting* left the air, Shepherd appeared in such films as *Chances Are* (1989), *Texasville* (1990), *Once Upon a Crime* (1992), and *The Last Word* (1994), and in 1995, she once again became the star of a hit TV show, a situation comedy called *Cybill*. In the late 1990s to early 2000's, Shepherd continued to appear in such TV films as *Journey of the Heart* (1997), and in the feature films *The Muse* (1999, playing herself), and *Marine Life* (2000).

SHIELDS AND YARNELL

| June 1977–July 1977 | CBS | Mon. 8:30–9 P.M. |
| Jan. 1978–Mar. 1978 | CBS | Tues. 8:30–9 P.M. |

In the late 1970s, the talented mime team of Robert Shields and Lorene Yarnell, who made their TV debuts on a summer replacement show, became the stars of a weekly half-hour TV variety show that in addition to their mime routines also featured songs, dancing, and comedy sketches. *Shields and Yarnell* was briefly popular with the public. In addition to Shields and Yarnell, who were married, and had begun their careers as mimes on the streets of San Francisco during the 1960s, also seen on the series were Ted Ziegler (1977), Joanna Cassidy (1977), Gailard Sartain (1978), John Bloom (1978), Flip Reade (1978), and the Norman Maney Orchestra. One of the series' most popular recurring skits involved the adventures of a couple named the Clinkers, a pair of awkward robots who were trying to adjust to life in the suburbs. In spite of its early success, the popularity and novelty of the show soon began to wear thin, and when the series was placed opposite ABC's very successful *LAVERNE & SHIRLEY*, it failed to attract a sizable enough audience for CBS to keep it on the air, and the show was unceremoniously canceled midseason in 1978. The executive producer and director of the *Shields and Yarnell* show was Steve Bender, and the series was produced by Frank Peppiatt and John Aylesworth.

SHINDIG

Sept. 1964–Jan. 1965	ABC	Wed. 8:30–9 P.M.
Jan. 1965–Sept. 1965	ABC	Wed. 8:30–9:30 P.M.
Sept. 1965–Jan. 1966	ABC	Thurs./Sat. 7:30–8 P.M.

In the mid 1960s, two rock and roll music/dance shows, *HULLABALOO* and *Shindig*, were popular with young people for a brief period. *Shindig* was a fast-moving, music-filled half-hour show that was seen on ABC, and like NBC's *Hullabaloo* it featured top recording artists of the day who performed their latest hit tunes. The show was hosted by West Coast disc jockey Jimmy O'Neill, and featured were a company of regular dancers in elaborate production numbers. Each week a "disc pick of the week" was chosen. The first telecast of *Shindig* starred singer Sam Cooke. Featured on the show were the Everly Brothers, the Righteous Brothers, the Wellingtons, the Blossoms (featuring Darlene Love), teen heartthrob Bobby Sherman and comedian Alan Sues, who later became a regular on *ROWAN AND MARTIN'S LAUGH-IN*. Musical accompaniments were provided by a group called the Shindogs and included, at different times, James Burton, Delaney Bramlett, Chuck Blackwell, Joey Cooper, Glen Hardin, Don Preston, and Leon Russell. During its second season on the air, also seen on the show were such celebrated rock and pop performers as the Rolling Stones, the Beatles, Sonny (BONO) and CHER, Donna Loren, Glen Campbell, the Beach Boys, Chuck Berry, and Neil Sedaka. Although Elvis Presley never performed on *Shindig,* an entire half-hour program centered on his hit songs. As the series continued, non–rock and roll performers like musical legend Louis Armstrong and film star Mickey Rooney, vaudeville comic Ed Wynn, actress Zsa Zsa Gabor, and on a special Halloween show, horror film star Boris Karloff, made guest appearances on the show. *Shindig* was developed for television by Jack Good, a British producer who had produced similar shows in England. The series' executive producer was Leon I. Mirell, and the program was produced by Dean Whitmore.

SHINING TIME STATION

| 1990–1993 | PBS | Mon–Fri. |
| | | Various daytime hours |

Set in a magical train station, *Shining Time Station* was a PBS half-hour children's series that encouraged youngsters to use their imaginations. The series had originally been produced in Great Britain in 1982 as *Thomas the Tank Engine and Friends*. Featured on the American version were Didi Conn as Stacy Jones, the female station manager; Brian O'Connor as Schemer; Leonard Jackson as Harry, the engineer; Nicole Leach as Tanya; Jason Wiliner as Matt; and former Beatle Ringo Starr, who had narrated the original British series, as (through trick photography) an 18-inch-tall character who could appear or disappear in a cloud of smoke at will as Mr. Conductor. In 1992, when Ringo Starr decided to leave the series, comedian George Carlin replaced him as Mr. Conductor.

SHIRLEY TEMPLE'S STORYBOOK/THE SHIRLEY TEMPLE SHOW (AKA *SHIRLEY TEMPLE THEATER*)

| Jan. 1959–Dec. 1959 | ABC | Mon. 7:30–8:30 P.M. |

As SHIRLEY TEMPLE THEATER:

| Sept. 1960–Sept. 1961 | NBC | Sun. 7–8 P.M. |

The most famous child film star of the 1930s, Shirley Temple became the hostess of a weekly fairy tale television anthology series as a young adult in the late 1950s. Shirley acted as the show's hostess, narrator, and sometimes star on this series of famous stories for children that often included musical numbers. Among the stories adapted for TV on this series were such time-proven classics as *Winnie the Pooh, Babes in Toyland, The Prince and the Pauper, Beauty and the Beast, Rumplestilskin, Rapunzel, Mother Goose, The Land of Oz,* and many others. Among the well-known performers who starred on the hour-long dramas were Charlton Heston, Agnes Moorehead, Carol Lynley, Elsa Lanchester, Jonathan WINTERS, Kurt Kasznar, Lorne GREENE, and Rex Thompson. After one year on ABC, *Shirley Temple's Storybook* was canceled, but resurfaced six months later as a series of specials on NBC called the *Shirley Temple Theater* and remained on the air for another full year. The executive producer of this series was William H. Brown, Jr., and the show was produced by William Asher.

SHOGUN

| Sept. 15, 1980– | NBC | Mon–Fri. 8 P.M. |
| Sept. 19, 1980 | | |

The 12-hour, five-part miniseries *Shōgun* was one of the most viewed specials ever presented on television. Adapted from James Clavell's epic novel about a European who is one of the first non-Asians to set foot in feudal Japan in the early 1600s, the series starred Richard CHAMBERLAIN as the European, John Blackthorne, who was the English pilot of a Dutch ship that was wrecked off the Japanese coast. Japanese actor Toshiro Mifune costarred as Toranga, a Japanese warlord who takes Blackthorne under his wing. Also appearing on the series were Yoko Shimada as Lady Mariko, with whom Blackthorne falls in love, John Rhys-Davies as a Portuguese emissary named Rodrigues; Damien Thomas as the missionary Father Alvito; Frankie Sabai as Yabu; Nobuo Kaneko as Toranga's archenemy, Ishido; and Alan Badel as Dell' Auqa. The series was adapted for television by Eric Bercovici. Filmed on location in Japan, the series was one of the first programs on American TV to use the actual language people in the film were speaking (in this case Japanese) with subtitles underneath. English was used only when the characters were speaking English. When the series was rerun in 1983, it had added narration by Orson Welles to further explain what was being said by the foreign actors.

SHORE, DINAH (FRANCES ROSE SHORE 1916–1994)

Dinah Shore was the first female star to have her own prime-time TV variety show on the air, and was one of the first female performers to host a regular talk show on TV. Born in Winchester, Tennessee, she was stricken with polio when she was a child, but recovered after receiving treatment by the famous Sister Kenny. A popular student in high school, Frances was a cheerleader at Hume-Fogg High in Nashville, Tennessee, where her parents had moved when she was a toddler. After high school, Shore attended and graduated from Vanderbilt University in 1938, where she had majored in sociology. Always interested in singing, she took voice and acting lessons while she was in college, and after she graduated, she auditioned for and won an assignment to sing on radio station WSM in Nashville. Shore left Nashville in late 1938 and went to New York City, where her smooth singing style won her a job as a vocalist at local radio station at. She made her first record with bandleader Xavier Cugat and his orchestra. When she scored a major success with a recording of the song "Dinah," Shore decided to change her name from Frances Shore to Dinah Shore, which she thought sounded more theatrical. Before long, she became a regular on the popular *Eddie Cantor Show* on radio, and her renditions of such songs as "Blues in the Night," and later "Buttons and Bows," made her one of America's favorite songstresses. In addition to her work on radio, at the height her popularity she also appeared in such films as *Thank Your Lucky Stars* (1943), *Up in Arms* (1944), *Belle of the Yukon* (1944), *Till the Clouds Roll By* (1946), and *Aaron Slick From Punkin Crick* (1952). In addition to her work in films and on the radio during World War II Shore also made numerous appearances performing for U.S. soldiers in U.S.O. (United Service Organization) shows at military installations throughout the world.

Shore, who also had a radio program of her own in the 1940s, performed on television when that medium was in its infancy in 1951. Her 15 minute, twice-a-week TV show featured various guest stars in a mostly musical format. In 1956, Shore launched an evening musical variety show sponsored by Chevrolet that was one of television's most popular programs until 1962. Soon after, she became the hostess of a regular daytime daily talk show called *Dinah's Place,* which became the standard for talk shows that followed it like OPRAH, *The SALLY JESSY RAPHAEL SHOW,* and ROSIE. In 1970, Shore hosted a second talk show that was called *Dinah and Her New Best Friends,* and then in 1974, a show that was simply called *Dinah!.* Over the years, Shore guest-starred on such TV series as *The COLGATE COMEDY HOUR,* CIMARRON CITY, *Here's Lucy,* ALICE, and MURDER, SHE WROTE.

SHOWER OF STARS

| Sept. 1954–Apr. 1958 | CBS | Thurs. 8:30–9:30 P.M. |

The hour-long, early television series *Shower of Stars* was seen once a month in the time slot usually occupied by the series *Climax.* Both series were sponsored by the Chrysler Corporation, and both were hosted by film actor William Lundigan. Later, the series was hosted for a time by film and radio comedian Jack BENNY. *Climax* was a dramatic series that usually featured suspenseful stories, whereas *Shower of Stars* was a lighthearted musical comedy program that featured hour-long adaptations of familiar works such as Charles Dickens's *A Christmas Carol,* which starred Fredric March as Scrooge, and a shortened version of the Broadway musical *Lend an Ear* with Edgar Bergen (without his dummy, Charlie McCarthy), Sheree North, and Mario Lanza. Among the luminaries who made several appearances on *Shower of Stars* were film star Betty Grable and her bandleader husband, Harry James, comedian Ed WYNN, Broadway's Ethel Merman, film and TV comic Red SKELTON, singer Frankie Laine, Shirley MacLaine, Van Johnson, and orchestra leader/singer Bob Crosby. Jack Benny, who hosted the series for a while and was the program's most familiar face, starred in many of the *Shower of Stars* telecasts until the series left the air in 1958.

SHRINER, HERB (HERBERT ARTHUR SCHINER 1918–1970)

Hoosier comedian/raconteur Herb Shriner, who was compared to Will Rogers, popular stage, film, and radio star of the 1930s, was seen on television as early as 1949 on a show of his own called *The Herb Shriner Show.* The

Indiana-born, homespun yarn spinner first came into prominence on radio when he was featured on such programs as NBC's *Big Show, The Camel Caravan,* and on his own *Herb Shriner Time* in 1948. Shriner also hosted the TV game show *Two For the Money* from 1952 until 1956. Shriner was a frequent guest star on such shows as YOUR SHOW OF SHOWS in 1951 and *The ANDY WILLIAMS SHOW* in 1962. In 1970, Shriner was killed in an automobile accident.

SILVERHEELS, JAY (HAROLD J. SMITH 1912–1980)

Native American actor Jay Silverheels, who became famous as Tonto on *The LONE RANGER* TV series and feature films, was born on the Six Nations Reserve in Brantford, Ontario, Canada. A star lacrosse player and a professional boxer before he decided to become an actor, Silverheels worked as a stuntman in films as early as 1938, and then played supporting roles in such films as *The Sea Hawk, Too Many Girls, Valley of the Sun, Good Morning, Judge, Song of the Sarong, Canyon Passage, Northwest Outpost, Unconquered, Fury at Furnace Creek,* and *Laramie,* and many others in the 1940s. In the 1950s, Silverheels was one of the most prominent Native American actors in the world and was seen in such films as *Broken Arrow, Red Mountain, Last of the Comanches, The Battle at Apache Pass, Drums Across the River, The Vanishing American, Return to Warbow,* as well as his most famous role, Tonto on *The Lone Ranger* television series, first seen in 1949 and in production until 1957, and in several *Lone Ranger* feature films, including *The Lone Ranger* (1956) and the *The Lone Ranger and the Lost City of Gold* (1958), with Clayton Moore playing The Lone Ranger. Although he was forever after identified with the Tonto role, Silverheels did appear as other characters in such films as *True Grit* (1969), *Santee* (1973), *The Man Who Loved Cat Dancing* (1973), *Cat Ballou* (1971), and as a guest star on such TV series as RAWHIDE, *Branded, The* VIRGINIAN, DANIEL BOONE, *The* BRADY BUNCH, and CANNON. During his later years, Silverheels was an active spokesman for the improvement of the way Native Americans were portrayed on television and in films.

SILVER SPOONS

Sept. 1982–Sept. 1984	NBC	Sat. 8:30–9 P.M.
Sept. 1984–May 1985	NBC	Sun. 7–7:30 P.M.
June 1985–Mar. 1986	NBC	Sun. 7:30–8 P.M.
May 1986–Sept. 1986	NBC	Sun. 7–7:30 P.M.

Ricky Stratton, played by Ricky Schroeder, was a mature-for-his-age 12-year-old who taught his childlike father, Edward Stratton III, played by Joel Higgins, a thing or two about being an adult. A very intelligent, good-looking boy, Ricky Stratton had been brought up by his divorced mother and then sent to a military school. Ricky convinced his wealthy father to let him live with him. The elder Stratton had never really grown up and his mansion was filled with video games, stuffed animals, and a child's railroad that he rode through the rooms of his home. During the course of the series, Ricky taught his dad what it was to be a father, and the two developed a close, loving relationship. Also appearing on the series was Edward's secretary, Kate Summers, played by Erin Gray, who was in love with Edward and eventually married him during the 1984–85 season. Leonard Lightfoot played Edward's lawyer, Leonard Rollins; Franklyn Seales played his stuffy business manager and friend, Dexter Stuffins. Occasionally appearing on the series were John Houseman as grandfather Edward Stratton II, Corky Pigeon as Ricky's nerdy friend Freddy Lippencottleman, Alfonso Ribeiro as Alfonso Spears, Bobby Fite as I.T. Martin, Ray Walston as Uncle Harry, Jason Bateman as Ricky's sly friend, Derek Taylor, and Billy Jacoby as Brad. When the original series ended its original TV run, 22 additional episodes were filmed and were shown in first-run syndication.

SILVERS, PHIL (PHILIP SILVERSMITH 1911–1985)

Fast-talking, forever-smiling comedian Phil Silvers, who was born in New York City, was a star on the stage, in films, and on television, but became most familiar as the lovable con-man, Master Sergeant Ernest T. Bilko on the very successful *The PHIL SILVERS SHOW,* called *You'll Never Get Rich* when it was first aired. After becoming a headliner in vaudeville and burlesque in the 1930s, Silvers made his film debut in *Hit Parade of 1941* and soon became one of Hollywood's favorite funny men, usually appearing as the second lead in such films as *Lady Be Good* (1941), *Ice-Capades* (1941), *The Wild Man of Borneo* (1941), *Tom, Dick and Harry* (1941), *My Gal Sal* (1942), *Coney Island* (1943), *Four Jills in a Jeep* (1944), *Cover Girl* (1944), and *Diamond Horseshoe* (1945). Silvers also starred on Broadway in *Do Re Mi* in 1960. Silvers made his TV debut in 1948 as the host of *The Arrow Show* variety series, but continued to appear in such films as *Summer Stock* (1950), *Top Banana* (1953), and *Lucky Me* (1954). In 1955, Silvers played Sgt. Bilko on his own TV series *The Phil Silvers Show,* which became one of America's favorite programs and remained on the air for four years. Silvers was seen on *The New Phil Silvers Show* in 1963, which was not as successful as his first TV series, and that same year he was one of a stellar list of comedian/actors who starred in the popular film *It's a Mad, Mad, Mad, Mad World.* Throughout the 1960s and 1970s, Silvers continued to appear in such popular films as *A Funny Thing Happened on the Way to the Forum* (1966), *A Guide for the Married Man* (1967), *Hollywood Blue* (1970), *Won Ton Ton, the Dog Who Saved Hollywood* (1976), *The Cheap Detective* (1978), *Goldie and the Boxer* (1979), and *The Happy Hooker Goes Hollywood* (1980). Over the years, Silvers also made frequent guest-starring appearances on such TV series as GILLIGAN'S ISLAND, *The* BEVERLY HILLBILLIES (on which he played a recurring character, Shifty Shafer), *Kolchak: The Night Stalker, S.W.A.T., The* LOVE BOAT, CHARLIE'S ANGELS, FANTASY ISLAND, and CHIPS, among others.

SIMON & SIMON

Nov. 1981–Mar. 1982	CBS	Tues. 8–9 P.M.
Apr. 1982	CBS	Thurs. 9–10 P.M.
July 1982–Apr. 1986	CBS	Thurs. 9–10 P.M.
Apr. 1986–June 1986	CBS	Thurs. 8–9 P.M.
June 1986–Sept. 1986	CBS	Tues. 8–9 P.M.
Sept. 1986–Nov. 1986	CBS	Thurs. 8–9 P.M.
Dec. 1986–Jan. 1987	CBS	Thurs. 8:30–9:30 P.M.
Jan. 1987–May 1987	CBS	Thurs. 9–10 P.M.
July 1987–May 1987	CBS	Tues. 8–9 P.M.
Dec. 1987–Aug. 1988	CBS	Thurs. 9–10 P.M.
Oct. 1988–Dec. 1988	CBS	Sat. 9–10 P.M.

Andrew Jackson (A. J.) and Rick Simon, played by Jameson Parker and Gerald McRaney, were two brothers who were partners in a small private detective agency called Simon and Simon. A. J. was a blond, conservative, and clean-cut young man who lived in a spotless apartment located behind their office, in San Diego, California, whereas Rick was a dark-haired liberal who always wore blue jeans and rode around in a beat-up old truck. There was much sibling rivalry between the two men, and their mother, Gloria Simon, played by Mary Carver, often had to ride interference between the two. Across the street from the Simon brothers' office was the office of their chief rival in the P.I. business, Myron Fowler, played by Eddie Barth. Myron's daughter, Janet, played by Jeannie Wilson, worked as a secretary for her father, but sometimes got the chance

Simon and Simon: (left) Gerald McRaney (Rick Simon), and Jameson Parker (A.J. Simon) (Author's collection)

to be a detective herself working for the Simon brothers, which distressed her father. When Janet graduated from law school, she became an assistant district attorney, which often strained her relationship with the Simon brothers. Also appearing as regular characters on the series were police officers Det. Marcel "Downtown" Brown, played by Tim Reid; Officer Nixon, played by Scott Murphy; Lt. Abigail Marsh, played by Joan McMurtey; and Officer Susie, played by Donna Jepson.

SIMPSONS, THE

Dec. 1989–Aug. 1990	FOX	Sun. 8:30–9 P.M.
Aug. 1990–Apr. 1994	FOX	Thurs. 8–8:30 P.M.
Apr. 1994–May 1994	FOX	Thurs. 8–9 P.M.
May 1994–July 1994	FOX	Thurs. 8–8:30 P.M.
Aug. 1994	FOX	Sun. 8–9 P.M.
Sept. 1994–Oct. 1994	FOX	Sun. 8–8:30 P.M.
Oct. 1994–Dec. 1994	FOX	Sun. 8–9 P.M.
Dec. 1994–Apr. 1996	FOX	Sun. 8–8:30 P.M.
Jan. 1995–Feb. 1995	FOX	Sun. 7–7:30 P.M.
Apr. 1996–May 1996	FOX	Sun. 8–9 P.M.
May 1996–Aug. 1996	FOX	Sun. 8–8:30 P.M.
Oct. 1996–July 1998	FOX	Sun. 8–8:30 P.M.
Aug. 1998–Present	FOX	Sun. 8–8:30 P.M.

The FOX network's outrageous prime-time cartoon series *The Simpsons,* which was directed at adult audiences, became one of the most popular programs on the air in the late 1980s and throughout the 1990s. Created by Matt Groening, the series, which centered on the dysfunctional Simpson family who lived in the "typical American town" of Springfield, which has most of the things contemporary American towns have (and hardly make for an idyllic place to live): a mall, a prison, a dump site, a mountain of burning trees, toxic waste, and a nuclear power plant. The head of the Simpson family, Homer Simpson (whose voice was supplied by Dan Castellaneta), was, when the series began, a lazy, incredibly stupid building inspector at a plant whose boss referred to him as "bonehead." When he wasn't trying to avoid work, Homer spent most of his time guzzling beer at Moe's Tavern and bowling at Barney's New Bowlerama. Homer's loving wife and mother of his two children was Marjorie Bouvier Simpson, called Marge (her voice supplied by Julie Kavner), who was the family peacemaker. Marge had an enormous blue beehive hairdo that was held together by a single bobby pin. Marge and Homer's youngest child was Maggie, an infant who had just started walking when the series first went on the air and always had a pacifier in her mouth. Maggie watched everything that was going on around her and often communicated by sign language. Lisa Marie Simpson (voiced by Yeardley Smith), who was Maggie's older sister, was an eternally optimistic second-grade student when the series began, who played the saxophone and was, by far, the smartest person in her family. Although she was an A student in school, other members of the Simpson family never seemed to notice or care. Bartholomew Jo-Jo Simpson, called Bart (voiced by Nancy Cartwright), the Simpson son, was an obnoxious, sarcastic, fourth-grade boy who had spiked hair, and rode around town on a skateboard. Other recurring characters were Barney, Grandpa Simpson, Mayor Joe Quimby, and Krusty the Klown (all voiced by Dan Castellaneta), Patty Bouvier, Selma Bouvier, Grandma Jackie Bouvier (all voiced by Julie Kavner), Bart's teacher Mrs. Edna Krabapple (voiced by Marcia Wallace), Charles Montgomery Burns, Waylon Smithers, Principal Seymour Skinner, Ned Flanders, Itchy, Scratchy, and Otto Mann (all voiced by Harry Shearer), Moe Szyslak, Apu Nahasapeemapetilon, Chief Clancy Wiggum, and Dr. Nick Riviera (voiced by Hank Azaria), Millhouse van Houten, Janey Hagstrom, Jimbo Jones, and Dolph (voiced by Pamela Hayden), Agnes Skinner, Ms. Albright, Mrs. Glick (voiced by Tress MacNeillie), Maude Flanders, Luanne van Houten, Helen Lovejoy, Elizabeth Hoover (voiced by Maggie Roswell), and Lionel Hutz and Troy McClure (voiced by Phil Hartman).

Among the numerous guest stars who have supplied voices or music to *The Simpsons* over the years are: Albert Brooks, Penny Marshall, Harvey Fierstein, James Earl Jones, Tony Bennett, Larry King, Jon Lovitz, Danny DeVito, Tracey Ullman, Ringo Starr, Jackie Mason, Steve Allen, Spinal Tap, Joe Frazier, Bob Hope, Dr. Joyce Brothers, Barry White, Bette Midler, Elizabeth Taylor, George Harrison, the Ramones, James Brown, Ernest Borgnine, James Woods, Kathleen Turner, James Taylor, Winona Ryder, Michelle Pfeiffer, Meryl Streep, Anne Bancroft, Mel Brooks, Mandy Patinkin, Mickey Rooney, Glenn Close, Bob Newhart, Smashing Pumpkins, Stephen Jay Gould, John Waters, David Hyde Pierce, David Duchovny, Jay Leno, Bob Denver, Steve Martin, Lisa Kudrow, Ron Howard Alec Baldwin, Moody Blues, Cyndi Lauper, Dolly Parton, Elton John, Mel Gibson, Garry Marshall, John Goodman, the Who, Aerosmith, and Britney Spears, among others.

The popularity of *The Simpsons* continues into the 2000s. DVDs of the series were released in 2002, as was a new set of *Simpsons* trading cards. That same year, an episode of *The Simpsons* was in the news when the Rio de Janeiro tourism office threatened to sue the producers of the show, believing that the episode portrayed Rio in an unflattering light. Apparently, the threat was never carried out.

SINCLAIR, MARY (1922–2000)

Few actresses who appeared on television in the late 1940s, when television was in its infancy, were busier than Mary Sinclair. Born in San Diego, California, Sinclair was a "dark haired, hazel-eyed beauty," according to *Life* magazine, and had been a fashion model in Hollywood before deciding that she wanted to be an actress and setting off for New York City to conquer Broadway. After a few minor roles in several stage plays, Sinclair met and eventually married the legendary Broadway director George Abbott, and with his influence, she managed to obtain a

contract with CBS television and began to play regular major roles on such popular live television anthology series as STUDIO ONE, *Starlight Theatre, Fireside Theater, Alcoa Presents,* PLAYHOUSE 90, and on such series as *Climax!, Tales of Tomorrow, Suspense, Danger, The Web, Sherlock Holmes,* PETER GUNN, and *The* UNTOUCHABLES. In two years in the early 1950s, Sinclair appeared on 36 live television dramas and played such classic heroines as Hester Prynne in *The Scarlet Letter,* Jane in *Jane Eyre,* Catherine in *Wuthering Heights,* Jo in *Little Women,* Bernice in "Bernice Bobs Her Hair," and Esmerelda in *The Hunchback of Notre Dame.* That Sinclair was a "quick study" and could remember lines from scripts after seeing them just a few times made her a natural for early TV, when many of the shows were presented live. In 1954, Sinclair starred on a series of her own that proved to be less than successful, *Woman with a Past,* and then in 1959, the actress suddenly disappeared from the TV spotlight at the height of her career. In 1975, Sinclair temporarily came out of retirement to play a supporting role in the film *Alice Goodbody.* She resurfaced in the mid-1980s playing small roles in the films *Robbery* (1985) and *Room to Move* (1987), before once again retreating into retirement.

SING ALONG WITH MITCH

Jan. 1961–Apr. 1961	NBC	Fri. 9–10 P.M.
Sept. 1961–Sept. 1962	NBC	Thurs. 10–11 P.M.
Sept. 1962–Sept. 1963	NBC	Fri. 8:30–9:30 P.M.
Sept. 1963–Sept. 1964	NBC	Mon. 10–11 P.M.
Apr. 1966–Sept. 1966	NBC	Fri. 8:30–9:30 P.M.

Record producer Mitch MILLER, who was the head of Columbia Records, was one of the major forces behind many of the most popular shows that were recorded in America in the 1950s. Miller even had a major recording hit of his own when he conducted the chorus and orchestra for the record "The Yellow Rose of Texas," which became a best-seller. The energetic, bearded Miller became a TV personality when he conceived, and then hosted a series that featured popular vocal music in the early 1960s. *Sing Along with Mitch* featured a large male chorus called "The Sing Along Gang." Individual members of the chorus also sang solos on the show. Also featured were "The Sing Along Kids," and several female vocalists, including Leslie Uggams, Diana Trask, Carolyn Conway, Gloria Lambert, Louise O'Brien, and Sandy Stewart. Elaborate production numbers spotlighted "The James Starbuck Dancers." The show featured familiar popular songs of the past and encouraged viewers to sing along with the chorus and soloists, running the lyrics to the songs at the bottom of the screen. By 1964, the public began to grow tired of the show, and it was canceled by NBC. In spring 1966, *Sing Along with Mitch* briefly resurfaced as a summer replacement, but then faded into obscurity as fall arrived. At the peak of its popularity, the show was among the most viewed programs on television, and Miller recorded several "Sing Along" albums that all became best-sellers.

SISTERS

May 1991–June 1991	NBC	Sat. 10–11 P.M.
Aug. 1991–May 1993	NBC	Sat. 10–11 P.M.
June 1993–July 1993	NBC	Thurs. 10–11 P.M.
Aug. 1993–Apr. 1995	NBC	Sat. 10–11 P.M.
Sept. 1995–May 1996	NBC	Sat. 10–11 P.M.

The four Reed sisters, Alex, Teddy, Georgie, and Frankie, were the major characters on this domestic drama that depicted the various rivalries, turmoil, and emotional entanglements that occurred among siblings living in a typical small American city, Winnetka, Illinois. Alex Halsey Barker, the eldest sister, played by Swoozie Kurtz, the well-to-do wife of a plastic surgeon, had no idea her marriage was about to end. The youngest sister, Frankie, played by Julianne Phillips, was an ambitious marketing analyst who was madly in love with a man named Mitch Margolis, played by Ed Marinaro. Georgie Whitsig, a real estate agent who was married to an eccentric out-of-work fellow named John, was played by Garrett M. Brown. Teddy Reed, an unmarried, free-spirited artist who on and off was an alcoholic, was played by Sela Ward. When the Reed sisters went home to look after their mother, Beatrice, played by Elizabeth Hoffman, following their father's death, all the old problems they had faced as young women resurfaced, forcing them to deal with them once and for all. Other characters who were prominent on the series were Alex's daughter, Reed Halsey, played by Kathy Wagner, and then Ashley Judd; Teddy's daughter, Cat Margolis, played by Heather McAdam; and Georgie's sons, Evan and Trevor Whitsig, played by Dustin Berkovitz and Ryan Francis. Weekly episodes began with the sisters sitting in a steam room, chatting about their lives, and the stories unfolded in much the same way daytime soap operas develop and included such concerns as illicit affairs, medical problems such as cancer and anorexia, careers vs. domestic responsibilities, rape, plane crashes, and drugs. During the show's 1992–93, the sisters discovered they had another sibling, a half sister named Dr. Charlotte "Charley" Bennett, played by Jo Anderson, and then by Shelia Kelly, who was the illegitimate daughter of their father and who eventually was accepted into the Reed family. Other characters who figured into the various story lines included Dr. Wade Halsey, played by David Dukes; Victor Runkle, played by David Gianopoulos; Judge Truman Ventnor, played by Philip Sterling; Simon Bell, played by Mark Frankel; Kirby Philby, played by Paul S. Rudd; Big Al Barker, played by Robert Klein; Norma Lear, played by Nora Dunn; Det. James Falconer, played by George Clooney; Dr. David Caspian, played by Daniel Gerroll; Lucky, played by John Wesley Shipp; Roxie, played by Kathryn Zaremba; Daniel Albright, played by Gregory Harrison; Officer Billy Griffin, played by Eric Close; Brian Kohler-Voss, played by Joe Flanigan; and Dr. Gabriel Sorenson, played by Stephen Collins. As the series came to an end, Frankie left town to pursue a career in business, Georgie was divorced, Cat became a policewoman, Teddy was shot during a carjacking but survived and married the surgeon who saved her life, Georgie received her degree from college and wrote a thesis about her sisters, and Mother Beatrice had a stroke and died, leaving Alex as the family matriarch to scatter her ashes over her beloved rose garden. *Sisters* began as a seven-episode miniseries, but proved so popular with viewers that it was turned into a weekly series and remained on the air for five seasons.

SIX MILLION DOLLAR MAN, THE

Jan 1974–Oct. 1974	ABC	Fri. 8:30–9:30 P.M.
Nov. 1974–Jan. 1975	ABC	Fri. 9–10 P.M.
Jan. 1975–Aug. 1975	ABC	Sun. 7:30–8:30 P.M.
Sept. 1975–Jan. 1978	ABC	Sun. 8–9 P.M.
Jan. 1978–Mar. 1978	ABC	Mon. 8–9 P.M.

Colonel Steve Austin was the world's first bionic man. Austin, played by Lee MAJORS, was a handsome, athletic American astronaut who was badly injured in an accident while on a training mission. In order to save his life, the government decided to operate on Austin using a sophisticated procedure developed by Dr. Rudy Wells, first played by Alan Oppenheimer, and then by Martin E. Brooks, that replaced human parts with expensive (thus the show's title) atomic-powered electromechanical parts that gave Austin supernatural physical powers. Austin did indeed recover from his injuries, but he became part human–part cyborg. His legs enabled him to run at great speeds, and his left eye could see through anything and had a built-in grid screen and a telescopic capability. Because of his special abilities, Austin went to work performing dangerous missions for the Office of Scientific Information. Austin's boss was Oscar Goldman, played by Richard Anderson. Goldman's secretary, Peggy Callahan, played by Jennifer Darling (aka Sharon Farrell) was occasionally seen on the series as well. As the series unfolded, Austin discovered that he was not the only cyborg working for the government. A race car driver named Barney Miller, played by Monte Markham, had also been given the same operation as Austin, but had, unfortunately, turned into an evil force, and the two bionic men eventually fought to the death, with the good guy, Austin, emerging as the victor. Shortly later, a bionic woman named Jaime Sommers, played by Lindsay Wagner, emerged and became a love interest for Austin before departing for her own spin-off series, *The BIONIC WOMAN*. On *Six Million Dollar Man*, Jamie died when her bionic parts went wrong, but she was revived in time to appear on her own series the following season. During the 1976–77 season, yet another bionic being, this time a boy named Andy Sheffield, called the Bionic Boy, played by Vincent Van Patten, appeared to assist Austin with his dangerous assignments. Originally introduced as a monthly feature on ABC's *Suspense Movie* series in 1973, *The Six Million Dollar Man* was based on the book *Cyborg* by Martin Caidin. Harve Bennett Productions produced the series in association with Universal Television.

$64,000 QUESTION, THE
(also $64,000 Challenge)

THE $64,000 QUESTION:

June 1955–June 1958	CBS	Tues. 10–10:30 P.M.
Sept. 1958–Nov. 1958	CBS	Sun. 10–10:30 P.M.

THE $64,000 CHALLENGE:

Apr. 1956–Sept. 1958	CBS	Sun. 10–10:30 P.M.

In the mid-1950s, quiz shows that gave away big money prizes were all the rage on television. One of the most popular of these shows was *The $64,000 Question,* hoisted by Hal MARCH. The TV series was an inflated version of a popular 1940's–1950s radio program called *The $64 Question.* On the TV show, contestants could win one of the largest amounts of money ($64,000) ever given away by a radio or TV program up until that time if they could answer an increasingly complex series of questions about a subject in which the contestant claimed to be an expert. If the contestant answered the first question correctly he or she was awarded $64, and the amount won doubled with each succeeding question up to the top prize of $64,000. If contestants reached the $8,000 level and then failed to answer the next question, they received a Cadillac automobile as a consolation prize. Contestants could quit at any point in the game and receive the money they had won up until that point. After the $8,000 question had been answered, contestants were required to answer any other question from a soundproof, glass isolation booth (called the Revlon isolation booth for the show's sponsor). Most of the contestants were chosen because they appeared to have an ability to generate empathy from the studio and viewing audience, because of their outgoing personality or because they had expertise on an unlikely subject. Among the most memorable contestants who appeared on the show were Redmond O'Hanlon, a New York City policeman who won $16,000 because he knew a great deal about William Shakespeare and his plays. A shoemaker from the Bronx, Gino Prato, took home $32,000 because he was an expert on opera; housekeeper Catherine Kreitze won $32,000 as a Bible expert; Bill Pearson, a jockey who was an art expert, won $64,000; Dr. Joyce Brothers, who later became a TV personality in her own right, won $64,000 because of her knowledge of boxing, and then later won $70,000 more on a spin-off series, *The $64,000 Challenge;* an 11-year-old genius named Robert Strom won an amazing $224,000 for appearing on both *The $64,000 Question* and *The $64,000 Challenge;* Teddy Nadler topped Strom's earnings by winning $252,000 after answering the top questions of both shows. In 1958, rumors had already begun to circulate that the big money quiz programs were "fixed" and that the producers of the shows were giving contestants the answers before they went on the air in order to make the show more exciting and to keep viewers tuning in to see the excitement each week. A disappointed loser on the big money quiz show *Dotto* told the press that the show he had appeared on was rigged. Because many people were becoming suspicious that so many people were winning so much money on these shows, the networks decided to drop their big money game shows rather than become involved in scandals that might occur. *The $64,000 Question* and *The $64,000 Challenge* both became victims of CBS's decision to check out of the business of telecasting big money shows.

60 MINUTES

Sept., 1968–Jan. 1972	CBS	Tues. 10–11 P.M.
Jan. 1972–June 1972	CBS	Sun. 6–7 P.M.
Jan. 1973–June 1973	CBS	Sun. 6–7 P.M.
June 1973–Sept. 1973	CBS	Fri. 8–9 P.M.
Jan. 1974–June 1974	CBS	Sun. 6–7 P.M.
July 1974–Sept. 1974	CBS	Sun. 9:30–10:30 P.M.
Sept. 1974–June 1975	CBS	Sun. 6–7 P.M.
July 1975–Sept. 1975	CBS	Sun. 9:30–10:30 P.M.
Dec. 1975–Present	CBS	Sun. 7–8 P.M.

CBS-TV's highly successful news magazine series *60 Minutes* opens, like a magazine, with a table of contents that tells viewers what stories (usually three major stories per show) are going to be covered on the show that evening. The credits for each story are superimposed over a stopwatch that indicates how much of the 60-minute time slot is left. The series specializes in investigating political and social events and newsworthy stories that are sometimes controversial, as well as spotlighting personalities currently in the news. People from the worlds of politics, business, athletics (professional and amateur), entertainment, art, music, and literature, and even ordinary citizens who have done something notable, are often highlighted. Over the years, the series, which became one of television's most successful top-rated programs, featured such stories as the American military involvement in Vietnam during the 1970s, "The Poppy Fields of Turkey—The Heroin Labs of Marseilles—The N.Y. Connection," "Local News Shows and the Ratings," the Watergate scandal, and other controversial subjects. Regular correspondents have been Mike WALLACE (1968–present), Harry Reasoner (1968–70, 1978–91), Morley Safer (1970–present) Dan RATHER (1975–81), Andy Rooney (1978–present), Ed Bradley (1981–present), Diane Sawyer (1984–89), Meredith Vieira (1989–91), Steve Kroft (1969–present), and Leslie Stahl (1991–present). During the 1970s, *60 Minutes* often featured debates on various subjects, and regular debaters included James J. Kilpatrick (1971–79), Nicholas Von Hoffman (1971–74), and Shana Alexander (1975–79). In 1996, the producers brought back the debate feature (after several years' absence) called "Point Counterpoint." The debaters on the new segment were outspoken newspaper columnists Molly Ivins and Stanley Crouch, and author P. J. O'Rourke. The debaters' unusually negative remarks were so poorly received that the segment was canceled after only two months. *60 Minutes* always ends with one of its correspondents reading letters sent to CBS by viewers, commenting on the various stories they had seen on the show. The executive producer of *60 Minutes* is Don Hewitt. It has been on the air continuously for almost 30 years and currently holds the record as the longest-running continuous prime-time series on television.

SKELTON, RED (RICHARD BERNARD SKELTON 1913–1997)

Popular comedian Red Skelton, a major star in all show business mediums, stage, radio, films, and television, was born in Vincennes, Indiana, the son of a former circus clown turned grocer and a cleaning woman. Red made his performing debut at the age of seven, when he was introduced at a vaudeville show by the well-known comic Ed Wynn. When he was 10 years old, Red left home and joined a traveling medicine show as an assistant. The show toured the Midwest, and when he was 15 years old, Red, who had pursued his father's former career and become a professional clown, toured the vaudeville stage circuit as a comedian who specialized in pantomime. When he was 17, Red met and fell in love with Edna Marie Stilwell, who was an usher at one of the vaudeville theaters Red was appearing in. The couple married, and Edna became Red's chief writer and manager. Soon after Edna took charge of his career, Red was appearing on Broadway and had his own weekly radio show as early as 1937. In 1938, Red appeared in the film *Having Wonderful Time,* and attracted the attention of studio officials at MGM Studios who signed him to a seven-year contract. Red soon became one of filmgoers' favorite comedians and played major roles in such popular films as *Lady Be Good* (1941), *Panama Hattie* (1942), *I Dood It* (1943, whose title was taken from one of Red's stock gag lines and was the film that made him a star), *Du Barry Was a Lady* (1943), *Bathing Beauty* (1944), *The Show-Off* (1946), *Merton of the Movies* (1947), *The Fuller Brush Man* (1948), *Neptune's Daughter* (1949), and *Three Little Words* (1950), to name just a few. In 1951, Skelton starred on his first TV series, *The RED SKELTON SHOW,* which remained on the air for the following 20 years. The numerous funny characters Red introduced on his show included Clem Kaddiddlehopper, George Appleby, and the seagulls Gertrude and Heathcliff, who continued to delight viewers for decades. Although he concentrated on his television show, Red occasionally appeared in films such as *The Clown* (1952), *Around The World in Eighty Days* (1956, in a cameo role), *Those Magnificent Men in Their Flying Machines* (1965), and, after his regular TV show was canceled, on television specials such as *Freddy the Freeloader's Christmas Dinner* (1981). He also guest-starred on the *The Lucy-Desi Comedy Hour* (1959, playing himself) and *The Westinghouse Desilu Playhouse* (1960, in "The Man in the Funny Suit"), for his former frequent costar at MGM, Lucille BALL. Skelton continued to make public appearances until shortly before his death at the age of 84 in 1997.

SLATTERY'S PEOPLE

Sept. 1964–Dec. 1964	CBS	Mon. 10–11 P.M.
Dec. 1964–Nov. 1965	CBS	Fri. 10–11 P.M.

Veteran radio and television actor Richard CRENNA starred as James Slattery, the minority leader in a fictional state legislature, on this political drama series. Both Slattery's political and personal life were the focus of the series. The idealistic Slattery was a state representative who was deeply interested in reform and was always deeply involved in various social causes. Also appearing on the series was Paul Geary as Slattery's energetic young aide, Johnny Ramos; Maxine Stuart as Slattery's secretary, B. J. Clawson; Ed ASNER as Frank Radcliff, and Tol Avery as Slattery's adversary, House Speaker Bert Mertcalf. When *Slattery's People* returned for a brief second season, Alejandro Rey, as Mike Valera, and Francine York, as Wendy Wendkowski, had replaced Geary and Stuart as Slattery's aide and secretary. James Moser was the series creator, and the program was produced by Michael Rapf for Bing Crosby Productions.

SMILIN' ED'S GANG (ALSO *THE BUSTER BROWN TV SHOW WITH SMILIN' ED MCCONNELL AND THE BUSTER BROWN GANG/ ANDY'S GANG*)

Aug. 1950– May 1951	NBC	Sat. 6:30–7 P.M.
Aug. 1951– Apr. 1953	CBS	Sat. 10:30–11 P.M.
Aug. 1953– Apr. 1955	ABC	Sat. 10:30–11 A.M.

As ANDY'S GANG:
Aug. 1955–Dec. 1960	NBC	Sat. 9:30–10 A.M.

Heavyset, lovable children's story-telling host, Ed McConnell, who, for many years had a popular children's show on radio throughout the 1930s, 1940s, and into the 1950s, was one of the first kid show hosts to make a successful transition from radio to television in the early 1950s. McConnell's 30-minute show used many of the same features that had made his radio show a long-running success. On each Saturday "club meeting," kids were treated to stories, memorable puppet characters such as Midnight the Cat, Squeaky the Mouse, Froggy, the mischievous Gremlin, as well as real-life characters such as the frustrated professor, played by Billy Gilbert, Shortfellow the Poet, played by Alan Reed, and on occasional filmed adventure stories, Gunga Ram, the Jungle Boy. For many years Smilin' Ed's show was sponsored by Buster Brown shoes. When host Ed McConnell died suddenly in the middle of the 1954–55 season, the network continued to play reruns of previous shows. For the 1955–56 season, actor/comedian Andy Devine became the new host of the series, which followed the same format as Smilin' Ed's program, but was called *Andy's Gang.* Devine, who was as well loved by children as Smilin' Ed, remained on the air until 1960.

SMITH, "BUFFALO BOB" (RICHARD SCHMIDT 1917–1998)

For 13 years, from 1947 until 1960, "Buffalo Bob" Smith hosted one of the most popular children's programs ever

Buffalo Bob Smith (Author's collection)

lerina when she was growing up in Houston, Texas. Always a beautiful child and then young woman, Jaclyn, who graduated from high school and then studied drama at Trinity University, played small roles in plays produced by various regional theaters after she graduated, and eventually she went to New York City, where she landed a small role in the Broadway productions of *West Side Story, Gentlemen Prefer Blondes* and *Bye, Bye Birdie*. A theatrical agent convinced Jaclyn that her looks made her perfect to appear in TV commercials, and in 1974, she became the spokeswoman/model for Breck shampoo. In 1975, Jaclyn moved to Hollywood, where she soon was seen as a guest star on such series as *The PARTRIDGE FAMILY, The ROOKIES, MCCLOUD* and *Switch* (1975), before landing the regular role of Kelly Garrett in 1976 on Aaron SPELLING's *Charlie's Angels* When the series left the air in 1981, Smith appeared in numerous TV films and miniseries such as *Jacqueline Bouvier Kennedy* (1981, as Jackie Kennedy), *Rage of Angels* (1983), *George Washington* (1984), *Sentimental Journey* (1984), *Windmills of the Gods* (1988), and *The Bourne Identity* (1988). In 1989, Smith starred on the short-lived TV series *Christine Cromwell*. When the series was unceremoniously canceled, Smith returned to making TV films such as *The Rape of Dr. Willis* (1991), *In the Arms of a Killer* (1992), *Family Album* (1994), *Married to a Stranger* (1997), *Freefall* (1999), and many others, earning her the unofficial title of "queen of the TV movies."

SMITH, ROGER (1932–)

In 1958, Roger Smith had a very good year as far as acting is concerned—he played Patrick Dennis, Auntie Mame's nephew in the hit film *Auntie Mame*, and he was cast in the major role of Jeff Spencer on the TV action series *77 SUNSET STRIP*. Prior to 1958, Smith had appeared on the *FATHER KNOWS BEST* series, playing the running character of Doyle Hobbs, had roles in the films *No Time to Be Young* (1957), *Operation Mad Ball* (1957), and *Man of a Thousand Faces* (1957), and had featured roles on the TV series *West Point* (1956) and *WAGON TRAIN*. After *77 Sunset Strip* ended in 1963, Smith appeared in the films *Never Steal Anything Small* (1959) and *For Those Who Think Young*, and starred on the series *Mr. Roberts* (1965), playing the title role. After appearances in the films *Criminal Affair* (1967) and *Rogues' Gallery* (1968), and guest appearances on such TV series as *HULLABALOO*, Smith virtually disappeared from the acting spotlight.

SMOTHERS BROTHERS HOUR, THE/THE SMOTHERS BROTHERS COMEDY SHOW

As THE SMOTHERS BROTHERS SHOW:
Sept. 1965–Sept. 1966   CBS   Fri. 9:30–10 P.M.

As THE SMOTHERS BROTHERS COMEDY HOUR:
Feb. 1967–June 1969   CBS   Sun. 9–10 P.M.

seen on television, *HOWDY DOODY* (also known as *The Puppet Playhouse, The Howdy Doody Show*, and *The Buffalo Bob Show*). Born in Henderson, North Carolina, Smith was one of the first performers to host a children's show on television in the years immediately following World War II. His show, a local TV program, attracted the attention of officials at NBC who were looking for shows to present on their fledgling TV network, and they signed Smith to a contract when they saw how popular his local children's show was. In 1948, Smith also hosted *The Gulf Road Show* for NBC-TV. *Puppet Playhouse/The Howdy Doody Show*, which featured Smith and a cowboy marionette (voiced by Smith), was an immediate and enormous success and became one of NBC's children's show staples. After *Howdy Doody* was canceled in 1960, Smith toured the country appearing in live shows for children at schools, civic auditoriums, and theaters. In 1974, Smith made a guest-starring appearance on *HAPPY DAYS* playing a character named Robert E. Smith (because of "rights" problems with NBC), with Ron Howard dressed and made up to look like Howdy Doody. Credited as Buffalo Bob Smith, he appeared in the film *Problem Child 2* in 1991, playing a character named Father Flanagan.

SMITH, JACLYN (ELLEN JACLYN SMITH 1947–)

One of the three actresses who starred on the popular *CHARLIE'S ANGELS* series, Jaclyn Smith aspired to be a bal-

July 1970–Sept. 1970	ABC	Wed. 10–11 P.M.
Jan. 1975–May 1975	ABC	Mon. 8–9 P.M.
Mar. 1988–May 1988	CBS	Wed. 8–9 P.M.
Jan. 1989–Feb. 1989	CBS	Sat. 9–10 P.M.
Aug. 1989	CBS	Wed. 8–9 P.M.

Tom and Dick Smothers, a duo of comedians/musicians who had appeared in various comedy clubs and became popular with young people in the early-to-mid-1960s, appeared on their first television series, a situation comedy called *The Smothers Brothers Show,* in 1965. On this series, Dick Smothers played a rising young executive at Pandora Publications. Instead of enjoying his life as a well-to-do bachelor, Dick was constantly being done in by his older brother, Tom Smothers, who had disappeared at sea, but two years later came back as an angel assigned to do good works on Earth. Not a very capable angel, Tom always had to seek the advice of his younger brother while on his missions. In spite of the fact that Tom played an angel on the series, the story lines basically duplicated material used by the Smothers Brothers in their popular comedy act and best-selling record albums. Also appearing on the series were Roland Winters as Leonard J. Costello, Dick's boss at Pandora Publications; Harriet MacGibbon as Leonard's wife; and Ann Elder as Dick's girlfriend, Janet. The series was not particularly successful, but one year later, in 1967, the Smothers Brothers appeared on a second TV series, a variety show called *The Smothers Brothers Comedy Hour,* which became one of the most popular programs on television. Tom, who played the guitar and was the less brilliant of the two brothers and who had a problem thinking logically and made all sorts of odd remarks, was the comic in the act. Dick, who played the bass fiddle, was the more intelligent straight man of the act. The show featured comedy and musical routines by the Smothers Brothers, who acted as the show's hosts, amusing editorials unusually critical of American military and social policies that were delivered by comedian Pat Paulsen, guest appearances by various big name performers, and regular appearances by Leigh French (1967–69, 1975), Bob Einstein (as Officer Judy, 1967–69, 1975), the Louis Da Pron Dancers (1967–68), the Ron Poindexter Dancers (1968–69), the Anita Kerr Singers (1967), the Jimmy Joyce Singers (1967–69), Nelson Riddle and His Orchestra (1967–69), the Denny Vaughn Orchestra (1970), Mason Williams (1967–69), Jennifer Warnes (aka Warren, 1967–69), John Hartford (1968–69), Sally Struthers (1970), Spencer Quinn (1970), Betty Aberlin (1975), Steve Martin (1975), Nino Senporty (1975), and the Marty Paich Orchestra (1975). Because of the show's anti-Vietnam War stance, and its advocacy of the free-living lifestyle of young people in the 1960s, *The Smothers Brothers Comedy Hour* became very controversial, and when CBS began to censor much of the show's material, the Smothers Brothers protested and publicly denounced the censorship, which did not endear them to network officials. The show was unceremoniously dropped at the height of its popularity in 1970, and except for a brief reappearance in 1975, the Smothers Brothers became personae non grata as TV stars. In 1988, Tom and Dick resurfaced in another *Smothers Brothers Comedy Hour* that once again featured Pat Paulsen, and also featured Jim Stafford, Geoffrey Lewis, and the Larry Cansler Orchestra, and then the Jack Elliott Orchestra. Unfortunately, time had taken its toll, and although the Smothers Brothers were still very amusing comedians, the public's interest in the show had waned. The revised show departed the airwaves one year after its first telecast.

SMURFS, THE

Sept. 1981– Sept. 1989	NBC	Sat. mornings
1989–1990	Syndicated	Mon.–Sun. Various times and stations

The animated cartoon series *Smurfs* became the most popular children's show on television shortly after it made its debut in 1981. Within a few months, it seemed as if everyone under 10 was talking about the adventures of a lovable group of small blue humanoids who lived peaceful lives in the forest, keeping out of the way of their archenemy, the evil Gargamel, who was always trying to capture one of them. Created by Belgian artist Peyo Culliford in 1957, the characters first became successful in Europe. In the 1970s, Smurf toys began to appear in America, and children became attracted to the Smurf characters and urged their parents to buy the toys. When the then-president of NBC, Fred Silverman, was asked by his daughter to buy Smurf toys for her, Silverman decided there was sufficient interest in the United States to warrant a cartoon series using the Smurfs. The show was an enormous hit among young TV viewers. Animated at the Hanna-Barbera Studios, the series featured such winning characters as Brainy, Greedy, Grouchy, et al., each representing certain emotions familiar to children. Talented voice-over actors Don Messick, Rene Auberjonois, and ventriloquist Paul Winchell (as the evil Gargamel), among others, provided the voices of characters on the series. In 1989, *Smurfs* left network television and its Saturday morning time slot, and for one year it was a syndicated daily series. *Smurfs* continues to be seen in reruns in more than 100 cities in the United States as well as in various places throughout the world.

SOAP

Sept. 1977–Mar. 1978	ABC	Tues. 9:30–10 P.M.
Sept. 1978–Mar. 1979	ABC	Thurs. 9:30–10 P.M.
Sept. 1979–Mar. 1980	ABC	Thurs. 9:30–10 P.M.
Oct. 1980–Jan. 1981	ABC	Wed. 9:30–10 P.M.
Mar. 1981–Apr. 1981	ABC	Mon. 10–11 P.M.

The most talked-about series of the 1977–78 season, a parody of daytime dramas, *Soap* was created and produced for television by Susan Harris. *Soap* was a half-hour, prime-time spoof of all the typical soap opera subjects such as infidelity, amnesia, sibling rivalries, etc., that fans had become accustomed to. From the day the show made its debut, protests from various religious and ethnic groups regarding the show's irreverent treatment of minorities, religious fanatics, etc., began to flood ABC offices. The resulting publicity made even more people want to tune in to see what all the fuss was about, and they weren't disappointed. The series featured such previously taboo-for-TV subjects as impotence, extramarital affairs, organized crime, and transexualism. Norman LEAR had previously introduced the public to the late-night TV soap opera/comedy *MARY HARTMAN, MARY HARTMAN,* and *Soap* was no more shocking than that series had been

Soap was set in the "typical" American upscale town of Dunn's River, Connecticut. Like so many daytime dramas, *Soap* had two families, one rich and one middle class, as its central characters. The patriarch of the show's wealthy family, Chester Tate, played by Robert Mandan, was a womanizing "dirty old man," and his wife, Jessica, played by Katherine Helmond, was a liberal socialite. During the show's first season, Jessica was convicted of murder, but the audience was later told "she didn't really do it," and during the second season, Jessica was freed from prison. The Tates' children, were Eunice, played by Jennifer Salt, Corinne, played by Diana Canova, and Billy, played by Jimmy Baio. Robert GUILLAUME played the Tates' sarcastic African-American cook/butler, Benson. Also living with the Tates was Jessica's father, called "the Major," played by Arthur Peterson. The middle-class family on the series, the Campbells, was headed by Jessica's sister, Mary Campbell, played by Cathryn Damon. Her second husband, Burt, was played by Richard MULLIGAN and her children from her first husband were the macho Danny Dallas, who became tied to "the mob," played by Ted Wass, and Jodie Dallas, a homosexual who wanted to undergo a sex-change operation, played by Billy Crystal. Other regular characters on the series included the crime boss head known simply as "the Godfather," played by Richard Libertini; Burt's handsome tennis-pro son, Peter Campbell, played by Robert Urich, who was murdered by one of the many young women he had slept with; and the convicted murderer, Dutch, played by Donnelly Rhodes. Also appearing at various times were Kathryn Reynolds as Claire, Jay Johnson as Chuck aka Bob Campbell, Bob Seagren as Dennis Phillips, Sal Viscuso as Father Timothy Flotsky, Rebecca Balding as Carol David, Dinah Manoff as Elaine Lefkowitz, Caroline McWilliams as Sally, John Byner as Police Det. Donahue, Randee Heller as Alice, Peggy Pope as Mrs. David, Candace Azzara as Millie, Marla Pennington as Leslie Walke, Lynne Moody as Polly, Roscoe Lee Browne as Saunders (who replaced Benson as the Tates' butler, when *BENSON* went on to become a spin-off series of *Soap*), Allan Miller as Dr. Posner, Eugene Roche as lawyer E. Ronald Malla, Gregory Sierra as Carlos, known as "el Puerco," Barbara Rhoades as Maggie, and Jesse Welles as Gwen.

The protests demanding that the show be taken off the air continued the entire time *Soap* was on, from 1977 until April 1981. One of the most determined critics of the series was the Rev. Everett Parker. Reverend Parker claimed that *Soap* was "a deliberate effort to break down any resistance to whatever the industry [television] wants to put into prime time. Who else but the churches," Rev. Parker continued, "is going to stand against the effort of television to tear down our moral values and make all of us into mere consumers?" In spite of Rev. Parker's attacks, *Soap* continued to be among America's top-rated programs, and it was among the top-20 programs, according to the Nielsen ratings, the first two years it was on the air. The series, following the lead of radio soap operas, had an unseen announcer, Rod Roddy, who reminded viewers of who and what the show's characters and plot were about.

SOMERS, SUZANNE (SUZANNE MARIE MAHONEY 1946–)

Suzanne Somers, who first attracted the attention of filmgoers by playing the small role of the blonde in the T-Bird in *American Graffiti* in 1973, and later went on to star on one of television's most popular situation comedies, *THREE'S COMPANY* in 1977, was born into a family of modest circumstances in San Bruno, California. Suzanne's father loaded beer onto boxcars and her mother was a homemaker. When they were growing up, Suzanne and her three siblings lived in constant fear of being killed by their abusive, alcoholic father. Suzanne was a talented youngster who, although she was a poor student, excelled in the arts and won a college music scholarship when she graduated from high school. Unfortunately, Suzanne was pregnant and was not able to attend college, but she married her child's father and gave birth to a boy, Bruce. Unhappy with her marriage, Suzanne left her husband and went to San Francisco where she found employment as a model. In 1974, Somers got a job on television as a model/assistant on the game show *High Rollers,* which was hosted by her soon-to-be husband, Alan Hamel. After she appeared in *American Graffiti,* Somers found that she was suddenly in demand as an actress and played increasingly larger roles in such films as *Magnum Force* (1973), and on the TV series *The ROCKFORD FILES* and *STARSKY AND HUTCH.* In 1977, she won the role of the sexy-but-dim blonde Chrissy Snow on the TV series *THREE'S COMPANY,* which became an enormous success and made Suzanne a star. At the beginning of the 1980–81 season of *Three's Company,* because of the success of the show, Somers asked for a raise from $30,000 an episode to $150,000 an episode and demanded an unprecedented 10 percent ownership of the show. The producers refused to give in to her requests, and Somers eventually left the show. Although she concentrated on performing in nightclubs after she left *Three's Company,* Somers also appeared on the less-than-top-rated TV series *She's the Sheriff* (1987), *Step by Step* (1991), *The Suzanne Somers Show* (1994), and, in recent years, as one of the hosts of the *CANDID CAMERA* series. She has also been featured in the TV miniseries *Hollywood Wives* (1985), and in TV films *Rich Men, Single Women* (1990), *Keeping Secrets*

(1991), *Seduced by Evil* (1994), *Serial Mom* (1994), *Love-Struck* (1997), *No Laughing Matter* (1998), *The Darklings* (1999), and as herself in *Say It Isn't So* (2000). Currently, Somers is frequently seen on the Home Shopping Network, where she promotes and sells her own line of clothes, jewelry, and exercise equipment.

SONNY AND CHER COMEDY HOUR, THE

(also The Sonny and Cher Show)

Aug. 1971–Sept. 1971	CBS	Sun. 8:30–9:30 P.M.	
Dec. 1971–June 1972	CBS	Mon. 10–11 P.M.	
Sept. 1972–Dec. 1972	CBS	Fri. 8–9 P.M.	
Dec. 1972–May 1974	CBS	Wed. 8–9 P.M.	

As THE SONNY AND CHER SHOW:

Feb. 1976–Jan. 1977	CBS	Sun. 8–9 P.M.	
Jan. 1977–Mar. 1977	CBS	Fri. 9–10 P.M.	
May 1977–Aug. 1977	CBS	Mon. 10–11 P.M.	

In the summer of 1971, Sonny Bono and his wife, CHER, who had several hit recordings in the 1960s, appeared on television as the stars and hosts of a summer replacement music/variety show called *The Sonny and Cher Comedy Hour*. To everyone's surprise the series became immediately popular with viewers, who had already begun to be nostalgic for the music and stars of the previous decade. Sonny and Cher were offered a regular show the following December. In addition to elaborate musical numbers that featured Sonny and Cher's previous hits, standard songs were also offered, as well as comedy sketches and appearances by various guest stars from the entertainment world. One of the biggest surprises, however, was the comedic chemistry that existed between Sonny and Cher and their husband and wife sketches, with Cher usually putting down her husband; delighted viewers kept asking for more. Comic segments on the show included "the Vamp," on which Cher appeared as some of the world's most notorious women; the "Sonny's Pizza" segment that featured Sonny as the dumb owner of a pizzeria and Cher as his beautiful, sexy waitress; "the Dirty Linen" segment, with Cher as a gum-chewing housewife named Laverne who was always giving her advice about men to her friend Olivia, played by Teri Garr; and a "headlines" section, during which items in the news, both past and present, and music and sketches from the period being shown, were featured. Often Sonny and Cher and their guests appeared in short operettas based on actual operas, TV commercials, TV programs. etc. Seen regularly on the series, in addition to Sonny and Cher and Teri Garr (1973–74) were their young daughter, Chastity (1973–77), Tom Solari (1971–72), Ted Ziegler, Clark Carr (1971–72), Freeman King (1971–74), Murray Langston (1971–74), Peter Cullen (1971–74), the Jimmy Dale Orchestra (1971–73), the Marty Paich Orchestra (1973–74), Steve Martin (1972–73), Billy Van (1973–76), Bob Einstein (1973–74), Gailard Sartain (1976), Jack Harrell (1976), mimes Shields and Yarnell (1976–77), the Tony Mordente Dancers (1973–74), the Earl Brown Singers (1971–74), and the Harold Battiste Orchestra (1976–77). Sonny and Cher's theme song was "The Beat Goes On," which had been a best-selling recording for the team in the 1960s. In 1974, the team decided to go their separate ways, and Sonny appeared on own show, *The Sonny Comedy Revue*, in 1974, which without Cher proved less than successful. The team, although maritally separated, reunited for the *Sonny and Cher Show* in 1976, and the new show, although it was not as popular as their original series, remained on the air for just one and a half years.

Sonny Bono and Cher of *The Sonny and Cher Comedy Hour* (Author's collection)

SOTHERN, ANN (HARRIETTE ARLENE LAKE 1901–2001)

A major film star in the 1930s and 1940s, Ann Sothern was one of Hollywood's first leading ladies to star on a television series in the 1950s. Sothern first starred as Susie McNamara on the very successful PRIVATE SECRETARY series in 1953, and then as Katy O'Connor on The ANN SOTHERN SHOW. In 1965, Ann supplied the voice of Gladys Crabtree on the quirky series MY MOTHER THE CAR. Born in Valley City, North Dakota, Ann Sothern began her film career as an extra in *Broadway Nights* in 1927. Eventually cast as a light comedienne, Ann bleached her red hair blond and began to get increasingly larger roles in such films as *Hearts in Exile* (1929), *Hold Everything* (1930), *Whoopee!* (1930), and *Kid Millions* (1934). After working at MGM Studios and on Broadway, Ann signed a contract to appear in films at Columbia Pictures in 1934. Dropped by

Columbia in 1936, Ann's contract was picked up by RKO Pictures, where she played leading roles in such less than memorable films as *Dangerous Number* (1937) and *She's Got Everything* (1938). After playing Jean Livingstone in the hit film *Trade Winds* in 1938, Sothern was signed to a contract at the prestigious MGM Studios. In 1939, Sothern played a tough, wisecracking showgirl named Maisie Ravier in the film *Maisie*, which proved to be very popular with filmgoers. Sothern made many more *Maisie* films at MGM and was also featured in such box office favorites as *Lady Be Good* (1941), *Cry 'Havoc'* (1943), *Thousands Cheer* (1943), *April Showers* (1948), *Words and Music* (1948), and *Nancy Goes to Rio* (1950). On loan to 20th Century Fox Studios, Sothern played one of the most memorable roles of her long career, Rita Phillips, in the award-winning film *A Letter to Three Wives* (1949). Her film career waning, Sothern decided to star on a television series in 1953, and became an even bigger star on television than she had been in films. After her TV series *My Mother the Car* was canceled, Sothern continued to appear on TV and in films on occasion. In 1985, she played a major comedy supporting role in a TV remake of *A Letter to Three Wives*, and in 1987 she was nominated for an Academy Award as Best Supporting Actress for playing Tisha Doughty in the film *The Whales of August*. Ann Sothern died at the age of 91, after having one of the longest and most successful careers in show business history.

SOUL TRAIN

1971–present Syndicated Various times and stations

Similar to Dick CLARK's *AMERICAN BANDSTAND*, the syndicated TV series *Soul Train* featured African-American music and a group of about 75 teenagers who danced to the music of hit recording artists who appeared as guests on the show and lip-synched as their records were played. Created by and starring Don Cornelius, the show was first seen as a local program in Chicago, but later moved to Hollywood, where it became a syndicated series. Cornelius quit hosting the series in 1993.

SOUPY SALES SHOW, THE (AKA SOUP'S ON, LUNCH WITH SOUPY SALES)

July 1955–Aug. 1955	ABC	Mon.–Fri. Early evening
Oct. 1959–June 1960	ABC	Sat. Mornings
Dec. 1960–Mar. 1961	ABC	Sat. Mornings
Jan. 1962–Apr. 1962	ABC	Fri. evenings
1965–1967	Syndicated	Various days and times
1979	Syndicated	Various days and times

Zany TV children's show host Soupy SALES was first seen on a local show in Detroit in 1953 that was called *Soup's On*. The show attracted the attention of officials at the ABC TV network who offered Sales a 15-minute, five-days-a-week national children's program that was first telecast in 1955. *The Soupy Sales Show* became very popular with viewers, young and old alike. Soupy then moved from Detroit to Los Angeles, where once again he hosted a local show for several years before returning to network television in fall 1959 with a five-days-a-week show that remained on the air until 1961. Early in 1962, Soupy appeared in a Friday evening show for ABC, and then, in 1964, he hosted a syndicated children's show that originated from New York City. In 1979, he hosted another syndicated show that lasted just one season. The format for Soupy's success as a children show host was simple. Sales was a naturally funny man who had a mobile face and was a good mime. His slapstick comedy made children as well as adults laugh, and his customary pie-in-the-face, which he received on all of his many TV shows, became one of his trademarks. Soupy had several regular characters that appeared on his shows, including two huge, bigger-than-life dogs, White Fang and Black Tooth, who showed only their immense paws; Herman the Flea; Marilyn Man Wolfe; and the popular Pookie the Lion, who appeared in various costumes with Soupy when he read stories. The show always contained silly puns, short silent films, skits, songs, and advice for children such as tips on good nutrition. Often, guest stars such as Frank Sinatra, Steve Lawrence, Sammy Davis, Jr., Dean MARTIN, Perry COMO, Jimmy DURANTE, Bob HOPE, and Tony Curtis made surprise visits to Soupy's show to have a custard pie thrown in their faces at the end of a telecast. The audience always had to guess just who was knocking on Soupy's door to receive the pie. Often the technicians behind the cameras could be heard laughing at the program's wild happenings, which added to the fun. One of Soupy's pranks cost him a one-week suspension from ABC. With time to fill at the end of a show, Soupy told his young viewers to send in "the little green pieces of paper" they found in their parents pocketbooks. Children took the joke seriously and sent Soupy over $20,000, mostly in play money. Soupy returned any money to children who took him seriously. Instead of upsetting the public, the prank actually endeared him to many older viewers who thought it was a funny joke and remember the incident to this day.

SPACE PATROL

Sept. 1950–Dec. 1950	ABC	Mon.–Fri. 5:45–6 P.M.
Jan. 1951–June 1951	ABC	Sun. 4:30–5 P.M.
June 1951–Sept. 1951	ABC	Sat. 6–6:30 P.M.
Sept. 1951–June 1952	ABC	Sun. 6–6:30 P.M.
June 1951–Mar. 1955	ABC	Sat. 11–11:30 A.M.

The best-remembered live science fiction shows of post–World War II television are *CAPTAIN VIDEO*, which originated from New York City, and *Space Patrol*, which was telecast from Hollywood. At its height in 1952, *Space Patrol* was the most popular action/adventure show on TV and was seen by more children and adults than any other similar show. Although it was an inexpensive show to produce, costing a mere $2,500 an episode, *Space Patrol* is said to have earned as much as $35 to $40 million in revenues for products such as space suits, ray guns, helmets, comic books, records, etc., that were sold in retail stores. The series starred Ed Kemmer, a former World War II pilot, as Commander Buzz Corey, the head of the Space Patrol, a 30th-century security force that policed space for the United Planets. Assisting Corey was his spaceship copilot on the *Terra*, Happy, played by Lyn Osborn. Also appearing on the series were Nina Bara as Tonga and Virginia Hewitt as Carol. Tonga, who was first seen as a villainess during the series' early years, eventually became a friend of the Space Patrol, and Carol was the daughter of Secretary-General Karlyle, played by Norman Jolley, and was as close as any other girl to being Buzz Corey's girlfriend. Also seen on the series was Ken Mayer as Major Bobby Robinson, the secretary chief of the universe. Some of Buzz and Happy's most memorable adversaries on the series were characters called "the Space Spider," the wild men of Prycyon, Captain Dagger, played by Glenn Strange, who piloted a spaceship called *The Jolly Roger*, and the evil "Black Falcon," played by Bela Kovacs, who was also called Prince Baccarratti, the man who ruled Planet X. Occasionally seen on the series was Marvin Miller as the villainous master of disguises, Mr. Proteus. The daily, and then weekly, episodes of the series were narrated off-camera by Jack Narz, who later became a TV game show host. *Space Patrol* garnered several awards from various parents' organizations for being one of TV's most "wholesome" programs, and was lauded for its scientific content, imagination, and humor. After the series left the air in 1955, kinescoped, individual episodes of *Space Patrol*, which had been a live program, surfaced on the USA cable network's *Night Flight* in recent years, much to surprise and delight of the show's many original fans.

SPECIALS ON TELEVISION

Although nonregularly scheduled "specials" appeared on television as early as 1939, they were infrequent, and often went virtually unnoticed until 1954, when NBC's president Sylvester "Pat" Weaver introduced "Spectaculars," which were expensively produced, early color special programs for the public's entertainment. CBS and ABC soon followed NBC's lead and began to offer "Special" programs as well. Over the years, many specials caught the attention of television viewers and are among TV's best-remembered offerings. To list all of the thousands of special programs that have been televised over the year would require a volume in itself, but below, in alphabetical order, is a list of some of the most successful, best-remembered specials that have appeared on TV between 1954 and 1990:

Ain't Misbehavin'

A two-hour adaptation of the award-winning 1978 Broadway musical that was first seen on June 21, 1982,

and starred members of the original Broadway cast, Nell CARTER, Andre De Shields, Ken Page, Armelia McQueen, and Charlaine Woodard.

Alan King Specials

Comedian Alan King starred on 12 hour-long specials that, like his act, poked fun at contemporary life. Guests on King's various shows included such popular entertainers as Shirley JONES, Liza Minnelli, Tony RANDALL, Buddy Hackett, Totie Fields, Phil Harris, James Coco, "Mama Cass" Elliot, Jack KLUGMAN, David Steinberg, Don KNOTTS, Angie DICKINSON, Elliott Reid, Hal LINDEN, and many others.

Amahl and the Night Visitors

Gian Carlo Menotti's Christmas opera about a poor crippled boy who joins the three Wise Men on their trip to Bethlehem to see the Christ child was written especially for television and was first presented on December 24, 1951, and was seen on many subsequent specials. Chet Allen played Amahl on the first telecast of the opera, which was presented on *The HALLMARK HALL OF FAME*.

Andy Williams Specials

Singer Andy WILLIAMS, who had a regularly scheduled show on TV for several years, starred on at least 19 specials from 1962 through 1987. Guests on Williams's specials included Ann-Margret, Dick VAN DYKE, Andy GRIFFITH, Joey Bishop, the Osmond Brothers, Lee Remick, Jane Wyman, Peggy Lee, Fred MACMURRAY, Maureen O'Hara, Claudine Longet, Ray Charles, Cass Elliot, Art Garfunkel, Aretha Franklin, Petula Clark, Flip WILSON, the Lennon Sisters, Topo Gigio, and Pope John Paul II, among others.

Annie Get Your Gun

Broadway star Mary Martin starred on this November 1957 two-hour television adaptation of the popular musical comedy. Also starring was John Raitt. On March 19, 1967, Ethel Merman appeared in a second adaptation of the musical she had starred in on Broadway. Bruce Yarnell and Jerry Orbach also appeared in the cast on this special.

Anything Goes

Cole Porter's Broadway show *Anything Goes* was a TV special on NBC in 1950 and 1954. The October 2, 1950, special starred Martha RAYE and the February 28, 1954, version starred the show's original Broadway star, Ethel Merman, and featured Frank Sinatra and Bert Lahr.

Applause

The Broadway musical adaptation of the film *All About Eve*, that starred Lauren Bacall, was seen as a TV special on March 15, 1973, with Bacall re-creating her award-winning role.

Arthur Godfrey Specials

CBS's popular star Arthur GODFREY had several specials on television from 1959 until 1979. The specials included *Arthur Godfrey in Hollywood*, *Arthur Godfrey and the*

Sounds of New York, Arthur Godfrey Loves Animals, and *Arthur Godfrey's Thanksgiving Special.* In addition to many of his ARTHUR GODFREY AND HIS FRIENDS regulars, guests also included Jackie GLEASON, Phil Foster, Mel Blanc, Shari LEWIS, Jack Cassidy, Steve ALLEN, and others.

Barbara Mandrell Specials

Country singer Barbara Mandrell starred on several TV specials in 1985 and 1986, including *Barbara Mandrell's Something Special, Barbara Mandrell: The Lady Is a Champ,* and *Barbara Mandrell's Christmas . . . A Family Reunion.*

Barbra Streisand Specials

Singer Barbra Streisand's TV specials include (but are not limited to) the memorable *My Name Is Barbra* (April 29, 1965), *Color Me Barbra* (March 20, 1966), *Barbra Streisand: A Happening in Central Park* (September 15, 1968), *Barbra Streisand and Other Musical Instruments* (November 2, 1973), *Barbra Streisand—Putting It Together: The Making of the Broadway Album* (January 11, 1986), and *Barbra Streisand: One Voice* (December 27, 1986).

Barry Manilow Specials

Pop singer Barry Manilow starred on three well-received TV specials, including *The Barry Manilow Special* (March 2, 1977), *Barry Manilow: One Voice* (April 5, 1979), and *Barry Manilow: Big Fun on Swing Street* (March 7, 1988).

Battle of the Network Stars

Each year, from 1976 until 1988, ABC-TV aired this series of specials that pitted stars from the ABC, CBS, and NBC network shows against one another in a series of athletic events. Produced over the years by Roone Arledge, Don Ohlmeyer, Barry Frank, and Bill Garnett, the series featured Howard Cosell and guests as hosts.

Beach Boys Specials

Rock and roll's Beach Boys starred on seven specials on TV from 1976 through 1989. Guests on the shows included Dan Aykroyd, John Belushi, Glenn Campbell, Julio Iglesias, and others.

Bette Midler Specials

Singer Bette Midler displayed her formidable talents on television in several 60-minute TV specials between 1976 and 1988. They included *The Bette Midler Show* (June 19, 1976), *Bette Midler—Ol' Red Hair Is Back* (December 7, 1977), *Bette Midler—Art or Bust* (August 19, 1984), and *Bette Midler's Mondo Beyondo* (March 19, 1988).

Bill Cosby Specials

Comedian Bill COSBY's 60-minute TV specials featured sketches and monologues and included *The Bill Cosby Special* (March 20, 1968), *Bill Cosby Does His Own Thing* (February 9, 1969), *The Second Bill Cosby Special* (March 11, 1969), *The Third Bill Cosby Special* (April 1, 1970), *The Bill Cosby Special, Or?* (March 2, 1971), *Cos: The Bill Cosby Comedy Special* (November 10, 1975).

Bing Crosby Specials

Crooner Bing CROSBY, who was a major star in films and on radio and had hundreds of top-selling recordings throughout the 1930s, 1940s, and 1950s, starred on a series of TV specials that included *The Bing Crosby Special* (January 3, 1954), *The Bing Crosby Special* (April 25, 1954), *Bing Crosby and His Friends* (January 12, 1958), *The Bing Crosby Special* (October 2, 1958), *The Bing Crosby Special* (March 2, 1959), *The Bing Crosby Special* (September 19, 1959), *The Bing Crosby Special* (February 29, 1960), *The Bing Crosby Special* (October 5, 1960), *The Bing Crosby Special* (March 22, 1961), *The Bing Crosby Springtime Special* (May 14, 1962), *The Bing Crosby Christmas Show* (December 14, 1962), *The Bing Crosby Special* (November 7, 1963), *The Bing Crosby Special* (February 15, 1964), *The Bing Crosby Special* (October 23, 1968), *Bing Crosby-Carol Burnett—Together Again for the First Time* (December 17, 1969), *Bing Crosby—Cooling It* (April 1, 1970), *Bing Crosby's Christmas Show* (December 16, 1970), *Bing Crosby and the Sounds of Christmas* (December 14, 1971), *Christmas with the Bing Crosbys* (December 10, 1972), *Bing Crosby's Sun Valley Christmas Show* (December 9, 1973), *Bing Crosby and Friends* (October 9, 1974), *Christmas with the Bing Crosbys* (December 15, 1974), *Merry Christmas, Fred, from the Crosbys* (December 2, 1975), *Bing Crosby's White Christmas (Dec. 1, 1976), Bing! . . . A 50th Anniversary Gala* (March 20, 1977), and *Bing Crosby's Merry Olde Christmas* (November 30, 1977). Among the many guests who appeared with Crosby on his specials over the years were his wife, Kathryn Grant, Jack BENNY, Howard Keel, Fred MacMURRAY, Dean MARTIN, Mahalia Jackson, Patti Page, Louis Armstrong, Peggy Lee, Rosemary Clooney, Johnny Mercer, Maurice Chevalier, Flip WILSON, Edie Adams, Bob HOPE, Mary Martin, Michael LANDON, Bernadette Peters, Pearl Bailey, Paul Anka, Sandy Duncan, Donald O'Connor, Debbie Reynolds, the Mills Brothers, Bette Midler, and Crosby's children Dennis, Philip, Lindsay, Mary, Harry, and Nathaniel.

Bob Hope Specials

Comedian Bob HOPE was one of the first major entertainers to be regularly seen on television during the years immediately following World War II, and he had first appeared on television on special telecasts in the 1930s. Hope starred on over 250 specials from the 1950s into the 1990s, and these appearances are too numerous to list on these pages. These shows featured monologues, sketches, song and dance numbers, and of course, always ended with his theme song, "Thanks for the Memory." Hope's specials included Christmas shows, USO shows before U.S. troops both in this country and abroad, and several specials that costarred his long-time radio and film pal Bing CROSBY. Among the hundreds of guest stars who appeared with Hope on his TV specials over the years were Beatrice Lillie, Dinah SHORE, Peggy Lee, Frank Sinatra, Lucille BALL, Bob Crosby, Marilyn Maxwell, Lily Pons, Bob CUMMINGS, former first lady Eleanor Roosevelt, Eddie Cantor, Sid CAESAR, Jimmy DURANTE, Rex Harrison, Jerry Colonna, Fred MacMurray, Rosemary Clooney, Frances Langford, Nelson Eddy, ABBOTT and COSTELLO, Dean MARTIN, Phil Harris, Dorothy Lamour, Cass Daley, Jack BENNY, Zsa Zsa Gabor, William Holden, Pearl Bailey, Kathryn Grayson, Vic Damone, Jane Russell, Steve ALLEN, Milton BERLE, Joan DAVIS, Perry COMO, Eddie Fisher, Lana Turner, Betty Grable, Harry James, Hedda Hopper, Patti Page, Ronald Reagan, James GARNER, Fabian, Frank Sinatra, Annette FUNICELLO, Anne Bancroft, George BURNS, Cyd Charisse, Ray Charles, Red BUTTONS, Ingrid Bergman, Glen Campbell, Shirley JONES, Johnny CARSON, Sammy Davis, Jr., Boy George, Kirk Cameron, Bea ARTHUR, Tony RANDALL, Burt REYNOLDS, Garth Brooks, Walter CRONKITE, and many, many others. Comedienne Phyllis Diller appeared on Hope's specials so many times, she could almost be called one of his regulars.

Charlie Brown Specials

Since the 1960s, one of America's most beloved comic strips, Charles Schultz's *Peanuts,* has regularly appeared on television in a series of popular specials. Charlie, the main character of the comic strip, a boy for whom things always seem to go wrong, and his pals Lucy, Linus (and his ever-present baby blanket), Sally, and everyone's favorite dog, Snoopy, have been delighting viewers, young and old alike, in such special features as *A Charlie Brown Celebration; A Charlie Brown Christmas; Happy Anniversary, Charlie Brown; Happy New Year, Charlie Brown; It's the Easter Beagle, Charlie Brown; Play It Again, Charlie Brown; It's Your First Kiss, Charlie Brown; Snoopy Comes Home; Snoopy—The Musical; This Is America, Charlie Brown; You Don't Look Forty, Charlie Brown;* and *You're the Greatest, Charlie Brown,* among many others. Over the 25-year-plus period the specials have been aired, the voice of Charlie Brown has been supplied by Casey Carlson, Peter Robbins, Todd Barber, Liam Martin, Kaleb Henley, Wendell Burton, Duncan Watson, and others.

A Christmas Carol

Charles Dickens's classic Christmas story, *A Christmas Carol,* has been seen on television as a Christmas special many times, and was first adapted for television in 1947, with character actor John Carradine enacting the miserly Ebenezer Scrooge character. Also starring as Scrooge over the years have been Dennis King (1948), puppeteer Rufus Rose in a Rufus Rose Marionette version of *A Christmas Carol* in 1948, Sir Ralph Richardson (1951), Fredric March (1954), and Richard Hilger (1982).

Cinderella

Three different television adaptations of the classic fairy tale *Cinderella* have attracted considerable attention among viewers and TV critics. In 1967, a much bally-hooed musical version of the story by Broadway's Richard

Rodgers and Oscar Hammerstein II starred Lesley Ann Warren as Cinderella and featured Ginger Rogers, Walter Pidgeon, Jo Van Fleet, Celeste Holm, Stuart Damon, Pat Carroll, and Barbara Ruick. Two ballet versions of the tale, were presented in 1957, and then again in 1981, videotaped in London and featured Margot Fonteyn (1957) and Leslie Collier (1981) as Cinderella.

Circus of the Stars

From 1977 through 1992, 17 *Circus of the Stars* specials have been aired on TV featuring well-known celebrities from the world of show business performing circus acts. Among the performers who have acted as ringmasters over the years have been John Forsythe, Lucille BALL, Bernadette Peters, Lauren Bacall, Sammy Davis, Jr., Lloyd BRIDGES, Rock HUDSON, Angela LANSBURY, Bob NEWHART, Scott BAIO, Vincent Price, Martha RAYE, Isabel SANFORD, Dick CLARK, Merv GRIFFIN, Bea ARTHUR, Richard CRENNA, Whoopi Goldberg, Mickey Rooney, Leslie Nielsen, and others. Entertainers who have appeared on the *Circus of the Stars* specials as circus acrobats, jugglers, aerialists, tightrope walkers, clowns, animal trainers, etc, have been Ed ASNER, Lynda Carter, Peter Fonda, Jack KLUGMAN, Jamie Lee Curtis, Tab Hunter, Roddy McDowell, Linda Blair, Tracy Nelson, Nell CARTER, Jane Powell, Lorenzo Lamas, Lynn Redgrave, William Katt, Sherman HEMSLEY, Harry Anderson, and many others.

Dean Martin Celebrity Roasts and Specials

Between 1974 and 1984, Dean MARTIN hosted a series of "roasts" on which a guest celebrity from the world of show business would be "honored" by his or her peers, by being good-naturedly chided. Over the years, stars who were honored on these special telecasts that were produced and directed by Greg Garrison were Bob HOPE (October 31, 1974), Telly SAVALAS (November 15, 1974), Jackie GLEASON (February 27, 1975), Joe Gariagola (May 25, 1976), Redd FOXX (November 26, 1976), Danny THOMAS (December 15, 1976), Angie DICKINSON (February 8, 1977), Gabe KAPLAN (February 21, 1977), Ed ASNER (March 2, 1977), Peter Marshall (May 2, 1977), Dean Haggerty (November 2, 1977), Frank Sinatra (February 7, 1978), Jack KLUGMAN (March 17, 1978), Jimmy Stewart (May 10, 1978), George BURNS (May 17, 1978), Betty WHITE (May 31, 1978), Joan Collins (February 23, 1984), Red BUTTONS (March 14, 1984), and Michael LANDON (December 7, 1984). Among the many "roasters" who appeared on the show were Jack BENNY, Milton BERLE, Howard Cosell, Phyllis Diller, Sid CAESAR, Art CARNEY, Steve ALLEN, Don Rickles, Nipsey Russell, Eve ARDEN, Joey Bishop, Ruth Buzzi, Foster Brooks, Rip Taylor, Dom DE LUISE, Gene Kelly, Allen LUDDEN, Nell CARTER, Rich Little, and many others.

In addition to his regularly scheduled TV shows, Martin also starred in occasional specials that were seen in the late 1950s to early 1960s. These 60-minute programs were produced by Hubbell Robinson and Jack Donohue. Among Dean's guests on these shows were

James Mason, Frank Sinatra, Bon HOPE, Donald O'Connor, Mae West, Don KNOTTS, and Andy GRIFFITH.

Dinah Shore Specials

Singer Dinah SHORE, who had several long-running regular series on the air, also starred in numerous TV specials over the years. From 1954 through 1957, Dinah appeared in at least ten 60-minute specials called either *The Dinah Shore Show* or *The Dinah Shore Special*. Again, from 1961 through 1963, Dinah appeared in a second series of 12 specials. The singer also appeared in a series of specials sponsored by Purex called *The Dinah Shore Purex Specials* in 1964 and 1965. Frank Sinatra was a frequent guest on these specials, and also making appearances were Betty Grable, Perry COMO, Art CARNEY, Shirley MacLaine, George Montgomery, James GARNER, Dean MARTIN, Jack Lemmon, Rose Marie, Polly Bergen, Harry Belafonte, Lucille BALL, Jack BENNY, Burt REYNOLDS, Ricardo MONTALBAN, and others.

Fred Astaire Specials

Hollywood dance star Fred ASTAIRE first appeared on television on May 5, 1960, in an hour-long program called *The Fred Astaire Special,* which featured Astaire's new TV dance partner, Barrie Chase. He appeared on a second *Fred Astaire Special,* again with Barrie Chase as his dance partner, on February 2, 1968. In 1980, Astaire was seen on two syndicated documentary specials, *Fred Astaire: Puttin' on the Top Hat* and *Fred Astaire: Change Partners and Dance.*

Garfield Cartoon Specials

Cartoonist Jim Davis's popular comic strip character Garfield, the lazy, self-serving, pasta-loving cat, was featured on a series of 30-minute specials seen on the CBS network between 1982 and 1991. The shows had such titles as *Here Comes Garfield, Garfield on the Town, Garfield In Paradise, Garfield Goes Hollywood, A Garfield Christmas, Garfield's Thanksgiving Special,* and *Garfield Gets a Life,* among others. Lorenzo Music provided the voice of Garfield for the specials.

George Burns Specials

Veteran show business comedian George BURNS, in addition to starring on his series with his wife, Gracie ALLEN, also starred on several TV specials from as early as 1959 until well into the 1990s. Burns's first special was called *George Burns in the Big Time* (November 17, 1959), and his last special was called *George Burns's 95th Birthday Party.* Among the numerous guest stars who appeared on George's specials over the years were Jack BENNY, Eddie Cantor, Bobby Darin, George Jessel, Madeline Kahn, Walter Matthau, Bob HOPE, Milton BERLE, Steve ALLEN, Carol Channing, Bill COSBY, and others.

Jack Benny Specials

Comedian Jack BENNY, in addition to his regular TV shows, hosted a series of 60-minute variety show specials that were seen two or three times a year from 1955 until 1958 (producer Irving Fein), from 1959 through 1963 (producers Bud Yorkin, and then Ralph Levy), and from 1965 through 1974. Benny also starred on the *Jack Benny Birthday Special* (February 17, 1969), *Jack Benny's New Look* (December 7, 1969), *Jack Benny's 20th Anniversary TV Special* (November 16, 1970), *Everything You Always Wanted to Know About Jack Benny and Were Afraid to Ask* (March 10, 1971), *Jack Benny's First Farewell Show* (January 18, 1973), and *Jack Benny's Second Farewell Show* (January 24, 1974). In addition to Benny's regular radio and TV show cast members Mary Livingstone (Benny's wife), Eddie "Rochester" Anderson, Dennis Day, Mel Blanc, Don Wilson, Joseph Kearns, Sheldon Leonard, Frank Nelson, and Phil Harris, specials guest stars over the years included George BURNS (on many shows), Gracie ALLEN, Peggy Lee, Shirley MacLaine, Johnny Ray, Carol Channing, Hermione Gingold, Betty Grable, Raymond BURR, Bob HOPE, Lucille BALL, Johnny CARSON, Dick CLARK, Phyllis Diller, Jack Lemmon, Walter Matthau, Gregory Peck, Frank Sinatra, Dean MARTIN, Redd FOXX, and many others.

Jack Paar Specials

The TONIGHT SHOW's host Jack PAAR hosted several TV specials, including *Jack Paar Presents* (April 26, 1960), with Cliff Arquette, Shelly Berman, Elaine May, and Mike Nichols as guests, *A Funny Thing Happened on the Way to Hollywood* (May 14, 1967), *Jack Paar and a Funny Thing Happened Everywhere* (December 6, 1967), *Jack Paar and His Lions* (September 8, 1969), *The Jack Paar Diary* (October 5, 1970), *Jack Paar Comes Home* (November 19, 1986), and *Jack Paar Is Alive and Well* (December 19, 1987).

Jerry Lewis Specials

In addition to his perennial telethons for the handicapped, comedian Jerry LEWIS hosted several special, hour-long, *Jerry Lewis Shows* in 1957, 1958, and 1960. Guests who appeared on Lewis's specials at different times included Ernie KOVACS, Eydie Gorme, Rowan and Martin, Sammy Davis, Jr., Betty Grable, Sophie Tucker, Everett Sloane, Louis Prima and Keely Smith, opera star Helen Traubel, Tony Bennett, and Eddie Fisher.

Johnny Cash Specials

Popular country singer Johnny Cash was the star of numerous specials between 1974 and 1985. Among the specials Cash hosted were *Johnny Cash Ridin' The Rails—The Great American Train Story* (November 22, 1974), *The Johnny Cash Christmas Special* (December 6, 1976 and November 30, 1977), *Johnny Cash Spring Fever* (May 7, 1978), *Johnny Cash: The First 25 Years* (May 8, 1980), *Johnny Cash and the Country Girls* (April 29, 1981, with his wife and frequent special costars, June Carter, Rosanne Cash, Wilma Lee Cooper, Emmylou Harris, and Minnie Pearl), *Johnny Cash: Cowboy Heroes* (May 6, 1982), and *The Johnny Cash 10th Anniversary*

Christmas Special (December 10, 1985), to name just a few. Over the years Cash's guests included Roy Clark, Ray Charles, Waylon Jennings, Anne Murray, Roy Acuff, Larry Gatlin, Glen Campbell, and on many occasions, the Carter family.

Julie and Carol at Carnegie Hall

Singer/actress Julie Andrews and comedienne Carol BUR-NETT starred on this critically acclaimed special on June 11, 1962. They followed up this hour-long variety show with similar hour-long TV specials, *Julie and Carol at Lincoln Center* (December 7, 1971) and *Julie and Carol: Together Again* (December 13, 1989). Andrews also appeared in several TV specials of her own, including *Julie and Dick in Covent Garden* (April 21, 1974) with Dick VAN DYKE, *Julie and Jackie: How Sweet It Is* (May 22, 1974), with Jackie GLEASON, *Julie Andrews: One Step into Spring* (March 9, 1978), *The Julie Andrews Show* (November 11, 1965), *The Julie Andrews Special* (November 9, 1969), *Julie Andrews: The Sounds of Christmas* (December 16, 1987), *The Julie Andrews Special* (syndicated show, February, 1968), *Julie— My Favorite Things* (April 18, 1975), and *Julie on Sesame Street* (November 23, 1973).

Kennedy Center Honors Specials

Each year a program is held that honors individuals who during their lifetimes have made significant contributions to American culture through the performing arts. The Kennedy Honors shows began in 1978 and have continued to this day. Among the notables who were honored on this annual special telecast between 1978 and 1992 were singer Marian Anderson, dancer Fred ASTAIRE, choreographer George Balanchine, composer Richard Rodgers, pianist Arthur Rubenstein, composer Aaron Copland, singer Ella Fitzgerald, actor Henry Fonda, choreographer Martha Graham, playwright Tennessee Williams, conductor Leonard Bernstein, actor James Cagney, choreographer Agnes de Mille, actress Lynn Fontanne, opera singer Leontyne Price, bandleader Count Basie, actor Cary Grant, actress Helen Hayes, choreographer Jerome Robbins, pianist Rudolph Serkin, stage director George Abbott, actress Lillian Gish, bandleader Benny Goodman, dancer Gene Kelly, conductor Eugene Ormandy, choreographer Katherine Dunham, director Elia Kazan, singer Frank Sinatra, actor James Stewart, composer Virgil Thompson, singer Lena Horne, comedian/actor Danny Kaye, composer Gian-Carlo Menotti, playwright Arthur Miller, violinist Isaac Stern, choreographer Merce Cunningham, actress Irene Dunne, comedian Bob HOPE, composer Alan Jay Lerner and lyricist Frederick Loewe, opera singer Beverly Sills, comedienne Lucille BALL, singer Ray Charles, actor Hume Cronyn, violinist Yehudi Menuhin, actress Jessica Tandy, choreographer Antony Tudor, singer Perry COMO, actress Bette Davis, singer Sammy Davis, Jr., violinist Nathan Milstein, choreographer Alwin Nikolas, choreographer Alvin Ailey, comedian George BURNS, actress Myrna Loy, violinist Alexander Schneider, producer Roger I. Stevens, singer

Harry Belafonte, actress Claudette Colbert, dancer Alexandra Danilova, singer/actress Mary Martin, composer William Schuman, actress Katharine Hepburn, opera singer Risé Stevens, composer Jule Styne, film director Billy Wilder, country singer Roy Acuff, writers/lyricists Betty Comden and Adolph Green, tap dancers the Nicholas Brothers, actor Gregory Peck, musician Lionel Hampton, actor Paul Newman, actress Ginger Rogers, conductor cellist Mstislav Rostropovich, and choreographer Paul Taylor.

King Family Specials

The King Sisters, Yvonne, Luise, Marilyn, Alyce, Maxine, and Donna, who were a popular singing team during the 1940s, starred on a series of 60-minute TV specials with their musical families, that included guitarist Alvino Rey, their parents, and countless brothers, cousins, in-laws, children, et al., between 1964 and 1974, in addition to appearing on their own regular show from 1965 through 1969. The first special, *The King Family,* was seen on August, 29, 1964, and led to their weekly regular series. The King's last special, a syndicated show called *Home for Christmas With the King Family* was seen in December 1974.

Life's Most Embarrassing Moments Specials

From April 27, 1983, until May 24, 1986, a series of nine specials that featured bloopers made by celebrities of the entertainment, political, athletic, and TV news world were seen on 60-minute specials aired on ABC. The guest stars who hosted these shows were John Ritter on the original show, and then for the remaining shows, Steve ALLEN.

Lily Tomlin Specials

Comedienne Lily Tomlin, who first came to the attention of TV viewers on the *ROWAN AND MARTIN LAUGH-IN* series, had a series of successful specials that began with *The Lily Tomlin Show* on March 16, 1973. She subsequently was featured on the specials *Lily* (November 2, 1973), *The Lily Tomlin Special* (July 25, 1975), *Lily— Sold Out* (February 3, 1981), and *Lily For President* (May 20, 1982).

Mac Davis Specials

Country and western singer Mac Davis starred on 13 TV specials between 1973 and 1983 that included *I Believe in Music* (November 24, 1973), *The Mac Davis Christmas Special* (December 14, 1975), *You Put the Music in My Life* (May 11, 1978), *The Mac Davis 10th Anniversary Special: I Still Believe in Music* (May 26, 1980), and others. Among Mac's guests on these popular shows were Rita Coolidge, Kris Kristofferson, Liza Minnelli, Neil Sedaka, Roy Clark, Richard THOMAS, Raquel Welch, Shields and Yarnell, Art CARNEY, Donna Summer, Bernadette Peters, Kenny Rogers, Robert URICH, Anne Murray, Dean MARTIN, Melissa Manchester, Gladys Knight and the Pips, Barbara Mandrell, and Ronnie Milsap, among others.

Magic of David Copperfield Specials

As early as 1978, magician David Copperfield starred on special TV shows that highlighted his amazing illusionary skills. These 60-minute specials were first telecast on October 27, 1978. In all, 15 *Magic of David Copperfield Specials* were produced between 1978 and 1993 alone. Guests of Copperfield's shows have included Valerie Bertinelli, Sherman HEMSLEY, Bill BIXBY, Susan Anton, Morgan Fairchild, Ricardo Montalban, Peggy Fleming, Jane Seymour, James Earl Jones, and Wayne Gretzky, among others.

Night of 100 Stars, The

On March 8, 1982, an elaborate special was seen that featured 100 of the world's most celebrated performers who donated their talents for the benefit of the Actor's Fund of America. Taped at New York City's famed Radio City Music Hall, among the big-name stars that appeared on the show were Jane Alexander, Steve ALLEN, June Allyson, Don Ameche, Bea ARTHUR, Pearl Bailey, Warren Beatty, Harry Belafonte, Tony Bennett, Milton BERLE, George BURNS, Ellen Burstyn, James Caan, James Cagney, Carol Channing, CHER, Arlene Dahl, Bette Davis, Robert De Niro, Danny DEVITO, Alfred Drake, Alice Faye, Jane Fonda, Ruth Gordon, Larry Hagman, Julie Harris, Helen Hayes, Lena Horne, Van Johnson, Diane Keaton, Howard Keel, Gene Kelly, Richard Kiley, Alan King, Janet Leigh, Myrna Loy, Mary Martin, Ethel Merman, Ann Miller, Liza Minnelli, Mary Tyler MOORE, Paul Newman, Jerry Orbach, Al Pacino, Gregory Peck, Anthony Quinn, Tony RANDALL, Christopher Reeve, Ginger Rogers, Mickey Rooney, Jane Russell, Alexis Smith, James Stewart, Elizabeth Taylor, Cecily Tyson, Liv Ullmann, Peter Ustinov, Orson Welles, Robin WILLIAMS, and many, many others. A second *Night of 100 Stars* surfaced on March 11, 1985, with many of the same stars who appeared on the first special making return appearances and many additional stars appearing for the first time, including Lucille BALL, Anne Baxter, Lloyd BRIDGES, Yul Brynner, Red BUTTONS, Michael Caine, Joan Collins, Olivia de Havilland, Angie DICKINSON, Michael J. FOX, Lillian Gish, Gene Hackman, Dustin Hoffman, Danny Kaye, Burgess Meredith, Jim NABORS, Bob NEWHART, Jack Palance, Sidney Poitier, Jane Powell, Vincent Price, William SHATNER, Dinah SHORE, Lana Turner, Dick VAN DYKE, Henny Youngman, and others.

Our Town

Thornton Wilder's classic play about two families who live in a small town in New England in the early 1900s, *Our Town*, in addition to being adapted for the regular TV series *ROBERT MONTGOMERY PRESENTS* (April 10, 1950), was on *The Pulitzer Prize Playhouse* (December 1, 1950) and was also seen as a 90-minute and as a two-hour special three different times on television. The best remembered of the three special TV productions of *Our Town* starred Frank Sinatra as the Narrator/Stage Manager, and Eva Marie Saint and Paul Newman as small-town next-door neighbors, and then lovers, Emily and George. This production, which aired on September 19, 1955, on NBC, and featured special musical numbers written especially for the play by Nelson Riddle, including the song "Love and Marriage," sung by Sinatra, which became a top-10 hit on the song charts. Four years later, on November 13, 1959, a second special production of *Our Town* was seen on NBC and featured Art CARNEY as the Stage Manager, and Kathleen Widdoes and Clint Kimbrough as Emily and George. On May 30, 1971, a third special production of *Our Town* was aired starring Hal Holbrook as the Stage Manager and Glynnis O'Connor and Robby Benson as Emily and George.

Paul Lynde Specials

Comic actor Paul Lynde, who was regularly seen as the center square on the popular HOLLYWOOD SQUARES game show series, starred on six 60-minute specials called *The Paul Lynde Comedy Hour* (November 6, 1975; April 23, 1977; May 20, 1978) and *The Paul Lynde Halloween Special* (October 29, 1976), *Paul Lynde at the Movies* (March 24, 1979), and *Paul Lynde Goes M-A-A-A-AD*. Lynde's guest stars included the Osmond Brothers, Margaret Hamilton (*The Wizard of Oz's* Wicked Witch of the West), Tony RANDALL, Gary Coleman, Vicki LAWRENCE, Betty WHITE, and others.

Perry Como Specials

Between 1963 and 1986, popular singer Perry COMO appeared in over 40 TV specials after his regularly scheduled show left the air. Como's specials were among the top-rated shows and included such titles, in addition to *The Perry Como Special*, as *Perry Como's Thanksgiving Show, The Perry Como Christmas Show, The Perry Como Springtime Special, Perry Como's Summer Show, The Perry Como Winter Show, The Perry Como Valentine Special, The Perry Como Sunshine Show, Perry Como's Lake Tahoe Holiday, Perry Como's Christmas in Mexico, Perry Como's Spring in New Orleans, Perry Como's Olde English Christmas, Perry Como's Bahama Holiday, Perry Como's Spring in San Francisco, Perry Como's Christmas in Paris, Perry Como's Christmas in New York, Perry Como: Las Vegas Style,* and others. Among the hundreds of guest stars who appeared on Como's various specials over the years were June Allyson, George BURNS, Anne Bancroft, the Lennon Sisters, Bobby Vinton, Liza Minnelli, Carol BURNETT, Don ADAMS, Art CARNEY, Flip WILSON, the Muppets, Debbie Reynolds, Paul Lynde, the Carpenters, Chet Atkins, Bob HOPE, Anne Murray, Dick VAN DYKE, Rich Little, Shirley JONES, Bernadette Peters, Debby Boone, Burt REYNOLDS, and Angie DICKINSON, to name just a few.

Peter Pan Specials

One of television's best-remembered 1950s specials was the musical version of James Barrie's classic children's story *Peter Pan*, with Broadway star Mary Martin as the boy who never grew up, Peter Pan, and featured music by Mark Charlip and Jule Styne. First seen on the NBC network on March 3, 1955, and subsequently aired on January 9,

1956, and seen again on December 8, 1960, in addition to Mary Martin as Peter, the casts included Cyril Ritchard as Captain Hook and Kathleen Nolan as Wendy, and Margalo Gilmore, Richard Harrington, Joseph Stafford, Joe E. Marks, Michael Allen, Tommy Halloran, Helen Halliday, Norman Shelly, and Sondra Lee in 1955 and 1956; and actress Lynn Fontanne as the Narrator on the 1960 telecast. On December 12, 1976, a fourth production of the musical fantasy *Peter Pan* was aired on a special *HALLMARK HALL OF FAME* telecast and starred Mia Farrow as Peter Pan, Danny Kaye as Captain Hook, Briony McRoberts as Wendy, and Virginia McKenna, Paula Kelly, Ian Sharrock, Adam Stafford, Peter O'Farrell, and others.

Red Skelton Specials

In 1954, 1959, 1960, 1982, 1983, and 1984, TV and film comedian Red SKELTON, in addition to his regularly scheduled shows, periodically starred on a series of television specials with titles that included *The Red Skelton Revue, The Red Skelton Chevy Special, The Red Skelton Times Special, Red Skelton's Christmas Dinner, Red Skelton's Funny Faces,* and *Red Skelton: A Royal Performance.* Skelton's special guests on these shows included the Ames Brothers, Tony Curtis, LIBERACE, James Arness, Rhonda Fleming, Lionel Hampton, Burl Ives, Tommy Sands, Frank Sinatra, George Raft, Bobby Rydell, Dinah SHORE, Vincent Price, and Tudi Wiggins, among others.

SPELLING, AARON (1923–)

One of television's most prolific producers, Aaron Spelling was born in Dallas, Texas, and attended Forest Avenue High School there before graduating from Southern Methodist University in Dallas with a bachelor of fine arts degree. Spelling began his TV career as a writer and sold his first script to *Jane Wyman Theater* and wrote several plays for such early TV shows as *PLAYHOUSE 90.* After writing the pilot show for Four Star Productions, Spelling was hired as a producer on the series and subsequently went to work for comedian Danny THOMAS, eventually forming Thomas-Spelling Productions. In 1972, Spelling went out on his own and formed Spelling Productions and also formed a partnership with Leonard Goldberg called Spelling-Goldberg Productions. In 1986, Spelling's company went public as Spelling Entertainment, Inc. Among the numerous memorable TV shows Aaron Spelling has either produced or been associated with are such classic series as *DANIEL BOONE, HONEY WEST, The MOD SQUAD, TWO FOR THE MONEY, The ROOKIES, S.W.A.T., STARSKY AND HUTCH, FAMILY, CHARLIE'S ANGELS, FANTASY ISLAND, The LOVE BOAT, VEGA$, HART TO HART, DYNASTY, BEVERLY HILLS, 90210, BURKE'S LAW, SUNSET BEACH,* and many others.

SPENSER: FOR HIRE

Sept. 1985–Oct. 1985	ABC	Fri. 10–11 P.M.
Oct. 1985–Sept. 1986	ABC	Tues. 10–11 P.M.
Sept. 1986–May 1987	ABC	Sat. 10–11 P.M.
June 1987–Sept. 1987	ABC	Tues. 10–11 P.M.
Sept. 1987–Jan. 1988	ABC	Sun. 8–9 P.M.
Jan. 1988–June 1988	ABC	Sat. 10–11 P.M.
June 1988–Aug. 1988	ABC	Wed. 10–11 P.M.
Aug. 1988–Sept. 1988	ABC	Sat. 10–11 P.M.

Robert URICH starred as Robert B. Parker's literate Boston detective Spenser on this hour-long series. The well-read Spenser, who was a former boxer, a gourmet cook, and had an office in a converted firehouse, drove around Boston in an old Mustang, but he was a first-rate private detective whose clients preferred a P.I. with a bit of class. Assisting Spenser was a tall, somewhat threatening-looking black man named Hawk, played by Avery Brooks. Hawk worked freelance, and his sinister appearance often belied his clear-headed, logical approach to tracking down criminals. Spenser's Boston police department buddy, Lt. Martin Quirk, played by Richard Jaeckel, and his sloppy, wisecracking assistant, Sgt. Frank Belson, played by Ron McLarty, often helped Spenser when the P.I. needed help while working on a case. Spenser's girlfriend, Susan Silverman (played by Barbara Stock) who was a school guidance counselor, departed the series after the show's first season, and Spenser's major female involvement became Asst. D.A. Rita Fiori, played by Carolyn McCormick during the series' 1986–87 season. The series, which was filmed on location in Boston, was closely supervised by *Spenser's* creator, novelist Robert B. Parker. After the regular series departed the airwaves, the character of Spenser returned as the main character in several TV films that also starred Robert Urich.

SPIN CITY

Sept. 1996–Sept. 1997	ABC	Tues. 9:30–10 P.M.
Aug. 1997–Sept. 1997	ABC	Wed. 8:30–9 P.M.
Sept. 1997–July 1998	ABC	Wed. 8–8:30 P.M.
July 1998–July 1999	ABC	Tues. 9–9:30 P.M.
Mar. 1999–Apr. 1999	ABC	Thurs. 9:30–10 P.M.
Jul. 1999–Apr. 2002	ABC	Thurs. 8–8:30 P.M.

The New York City political arena was the background for this topical situation comedy series that starred Michael J. FOX as a young deputy mayor, Michael Flaherty, who was a spokesman for the bumbling Mayor Randall Winston, played by Barry Bostwick. The series accurately depicted the materialistic nature of many young people in the 1980s and became one of the top-rated shows in the late 1990s. Mike Flaherty was a master at covering for his handsome but inept boss and explaining away the mayor's numerous blunders. Most of the show's action takes place in the mayor's office, and Mike's staff included the ambitious Stuart Bundek, played by Alan Ruck, who was always trying to earn points with Mayor Winston; the mayor's loud-mouthed press secretary, Paul Lassiter, played by Richard Kind; the naive young speech writer from the Midwest, James Hobert, played by Alexander Gaberman (later Chaplin); the office accountant, Nikki Faber, played by Connie Britton, who had a rather chaotic personal life; and the homosexual African-American activist/attorney Carter Heywood, played by Michael Boatman. Mike's girlfriend was an aggressive news reporter named Ashley Shaeffer, played by Carla Gugino. Mayor Winston's former wife, the bitchy Helen Winston, played by Deborah Rush, was seen during the 1996–97 season. Also featured regularly was Faith Prince as Claudia Sacks, Jennifer Esposito as Stacy Paterno, Victoria Dillard as Janelle, and Taylor Stanley as Karen. Michael J. Fox decided to leave the series at the end of the 1999–2000 season due to declining health caused by Parkinson's disease. During his last season on the air, Heather Locklear joined the cast, and when Fox left the series, his job in Mayor Winston's office was filled by actor Charlie Sheen.

SPORTS ON TELEVISION

The most popular sporting events currently seen on television are baseball, football, golf, basketball, hockey, auto racing, horse racing, boxing and soccer. The Olympics and various college sporting events are also periodic popular contemporary TV sports attractions.

The first sport to capture the attention of television viewers was wrestling (see WRESTLING ON TELEVISION). Wrestling proved a perfect sport for the technically primitive new medium because it took place indoors and was relatively cheap to produce. The roller derby (see ROLLER DERBY ON TELEVISION) was similarly suited. Both pro wrestling and roller derby had more entertainment than sports value, and were mainly staged for viewers' enjoyment. But the "real sports" of baseball, football, and basketball were a different story.

In 1947, the first World Series, between the New York Yankees and the Brooklyn Dodgers, was seen in New York City, Philadelphia, Washington, D.C., and Schenectady. Very few people owned television sets in 1947, so those lucky enough to see the games on TV were quick to mention highlights, such as when pinch hitter Cookie Lavagetto doubled off the Ebbets Field wall with two out in the ninth inning, to spoil Bill Bevens' no-hitter and win the game for the Dodgers, 3-2. Each year, as more people all across America began to acquire television receivers, the annual telecasts of World Series games (and to a lesser extent the All Star games) became eagerly anticipated events. Most baseball games, however, are seen not nationally, but as local or regional programs, at the discretion of individual teams, which may limit telecasts of games in order to induce fans to attend games in home ball parks. For several years in the 1950s and 1960s, the CBS television network telecasted its *Game of the Week* which featured Dizzy Dean and Buddy Blattner as commentators. Leo Durocher and Lindsey Nelson (who later became the TV voice of the New York Mets) were NBC's baseball commentators. Joe Garagiola was one of the first baseball commentators to interject a bit of humor and irreverence into his baseball commentary. Within the past several years, the Fox network has become the dominant baseball broadcasting network, but many baseball games can be seen on cable and satellite pay-for-view stations.

Autumn and winter are when many TV sports enthusiasts turn their attention to football. Early in the emergence of television as a major entertainment medium, professional football grew into TV's first and foremost sports attraction. Telecasts of Saturday and Sunday afternoon college football games, as well as the dozen or so College Bowl games which were invented expressly for television, have been popular TV attractions for more than 50 years, but professional football is the number-one draw of all of the sports events seen on television each year. The rights to televise the National Football League (NFL) games, as well as the less influential American League (AL) events, were the objects of bitter bidding wars between the networks, with amounts paid for the rights increasing each year. By the 1960s, the NFL began to profit not only from the lucrative television rights deals, but also from increased stadium ticket sales derived from the interest in football generated by its exposure on television. In 2001, the NFL, which had long been the leader in generating TV sports events revenue, added an Internet deal worth $300 million to its $17.6 billion television rights deal.

Among early sportscasters and commentators who enjoyed celebrity because of their football game coverage were Norman Sper, who in the 1950s had a popular show on TV called *Norman Sper and His Football Forecasts,* and Red Grange and Lindsey Nelson, who began telecasting *The Game of the Week* on the NBC network in 1955.

Unlike football, golf was not a particularly popular sport with viewers of early TV. Although golf was seen on occasional weekends in the 1950s and 1960s, it seldom attracted the sizeable audiences sponsors required to make it worthwhile to support. Various big-money tournaments and weekly filmed series were created expressly for television, augmenting the telecasts of such live events as the U.S. Open, the Masters, and the PGA Championship. Such golfing masters as Arnold Palmer, "Slammin'" Sam Snead, Jack Nicklaus and Gene Sarazen (who became a sportscaster for *Wonderful World of Golf*), became household names mainly because of the occasional coverage they received well into the 1970s and 1980s. Golf enjoyed an enormous surge of interest in the late 1990s with the arrival of a young man named Tiger Woods, who had grown from a child golfing prodigy to one of the greatest adult golfers in the world. By the beginning of the 21st century, Tiger Woods was, along with basketball great Michael Jordan, one of the most famous athletes in the world, and golfing became one of the most viewed sports on TV. By June 2002, Woods had won both the Masters and the U.S. Open, the first golfer to do so since Jack Nicklaus won both titles 30 years before, TV networks that currently benefit from the growth of golf as a nationally popular sport are ABC, CBS, NBC, ESPN, USA, and the Golf Channel, which are all part of the new PGA Tour TV deal signed in July 2001.

During television's early years, televised professional basketball games were few and far between. Coverage of college basketball games was more extensive, but in the late 1950s, the National Basketball Association (NBA) successfully convinced the TV networks that there was an audience for pro basketball games, and the sport became more visible on home screens all across the United States. By the 1970s and 1980s, talented basketball players such as Kareem Abdul-Jabbar, Earvin "Magic" Johnson and Larry Bird had become sports superstars thanks to their appearances on television. It was, however, a young player named Michael Jordan whose incredible talent was spotlighted on TV, who made basketball one of the most-watched sports on TV. When Jordan decided to retire from the game in 1999, NBA TV and ticket revenue sagged. Between 1999 and 2001, the basketball playoff ratings dropped 36 percent to 4.9. (While retired from the professional basketball scene, Jordan played professional baseball.) He soon decided to return to professional basketball and end his retirement in 2001, presumably helping to increase NBA revenue once again.

From the late 1950s through the 1990s, boxing, hockey, and horse racing, as well as the quadrennial Winter and Summer Olympics, were among television viewers' favorites. In the 1950s, boxing was shown twice a week on network television, on Wednesday and Friday evenings. Boxing fans were treated to bouts between such celebrated pugilists as Ray Robinson, Rocky Marciano, Willie Pep, Archie Moore, Cassius Clay (aka Muhammad Ali), and others. By the mid-1960s, boxing's popularity with TV viewers had waned, and it wasn't until the 1980s and 1990s that the sport once again began to gain popularity as championship fights were aired on cable television stations. Boxers such as George Foreman, Lennox Lewis, Evander Holyfield, and Mike Tyson (who also became known for his outrageous and sometimes criminal out-of-the-boxing-ring antics) came to the forefront and drew viewers who had cable or satellite receivers to their TVs again. Among the better-known boxing announcers from the late 1950s through the 1970s were Russ Hodges (who was the voice of the Wednesday night fights in the early years), Jimmy Powers (who announced the Friday night fights), Jack Drees (who took over the Wednesday night fight hosting chores in the late 1950s), and Don Dunphy, formerly a radio fight announcer, who became the sportscaster of *The Saturday Night Fights* in 1960. Dr. Joyce Brothers, a psychologist and TV personality, who once won the top money prize on THE $64,000 QUESTION, often appeared at the bouts to comment about the proceedings. By 2001, televised boxing's popularity had declined due to numerous postponements of major fights.

In spite of its continued popularity among sports enthusiasts, hockey has never had a large television audience. In recent years, the National Hockey League (NHL) has not been a ratings winner for the ABC network or ESPN cable network, which telecast its events. The NHL's five hockey matches telecast by ABC in 2001 averaged a 1.6 rating, up 14 percent over the five games aired in the spring of 2000, which indicated that the number of hockey fans tuning in was certainly growing.

Television's coverage of auto racing has changed dramatically in the first years of the 21st century, with a new NASCAR television contract in 2001, extension of the Indy Racing League contract with ABC and ESPN, and a new CART television agreement with CBS and Fox, which replaced an earlier contract with long-time TV partners ABC and ESPN, networks that on occasion covered auto races in the 20th century.

National TV coverage of horse racing has been largely confined to the Triple Crown events (the Kentucky Derby, Belmont Stakes, and the Preakness Stakes) and, infrequently, other races. The annual running of the Kentucky Derby at Churchill Downs is an eagerly awaited TV sporting event. Regional TV hookups bring Saturday horse-racing features from major tracks around the country to viewers in several sections of the United States. Among the most celebrated horse-racing announcers in TV history are Clem McCarthy and Fred Capossela, who covered numerous events in the 1950s and 1960s.

Without question, soccer, a sport that was all but ignored by U.S. broadcasts in the 20th century, began to attract a wide TV audience at the beginning of the 21st century. The emergence of the U.S. soccer team as a major international player in 2002 has resulted in increased TV viewer numbers. Like the NBA, Major League Soccer got a new rights deal after the 2001 season, when its initial contracts with ESPN and ABC expired. ESPN announced that it viewed Major League Soccer as "an integral part of its commitment to soccer" and promised increased soccer coverage on TV.

Among the sportscasters and sports commentators, in addition to those mentioned above, who became TV stars in their own right were: wrestling's Dennis James, Dumont network commentator; Ted Husing; Bill Stern; Red Barber; Harry Wismer; Marty Glickman; Mel Allen; Tommy Harmon; and Bud Palmer, who covered a wide variety of sporting events for various television networks. In recent years familiar sportscaster names who have covered national sporting events for various TV networks have included Frank Gifford, Marv Albert, and Bob Costas.

SPRINGER, JERRY (GERALD SPRINGER 1944–)

Few television personalities have made the successful transition from the world of politics to the world of show business as talk show host Jerry Springer has done. Springer, who was born in London, but moved to the United States with his parents when he was a boy, entered politics shortly after finishing his schooling, and as a young man was elected mayor of Cincinnati, Ohio. Capitalizing on his ability to entertain, the personable Mayor Springer guest-starred on the MARRIED . . . WITH CHILDREN TV series in 1987, and in 1991, he was given a national talk of his own, *The Jerry Springer Show*, which became famous for people fighting onstage and using foul language and obscene gestures, as well as for such controversial guests as strippers, prostitutes, criminals, and various other unusual characters. In 1999, the violence on his show had become so rampant that a strict nonviolence rule was enforced by Springer.

In addition to his popular weekday show appearances, Springer has also been featured on several TV specials and in films such as *The Best of Ed's Night Party* (1996), *Jerry Springer: Too Hot for TV!* (1997), *Meet Wally Sparks* (1997, as himself), *Killer Sex Queens from Cyberspace* (1998, as himself), *Kissing a Fool* (1998, as himself), *Austin Powers: The Spy Who Shagged Me* (1999, as himself), and *Jerry Springer on Sunday* (1999). Springer has also made guest-starring appearances on such TV series as *Night Stand*, ROSEANNE, *The X-FILES*, *The Wayans Brothers*, *The SIMPSONS*, SABRINA, THE TEENAGE WITCH, and *Mad TV*.

STACK, ROBERT (ROBERT LANGFORD MODINI 1919–)

Although Robert Stack is perhaps best known for playing G-Man Eliot Ness on *The UNTOUCHABLES* TV series, he was not the first choice for the role. Film stars Van Johnson and Van Heflin were both offered the role before Stack, and they decided against appearing on a regular TV series. Stack, who was born in Los Angeles, like Johnson and Heflin, had been a movie star in films as early as 1939, when his youthful good looks landed him a major role in *First Love* when he was just 20 years old. He subsequently appeared in such films as *A Little Bit of Heaven* (1940), *Badlands of Dakota* (1941), and *Men of Texas* (1942), before serving in the U.S. Navy during World War II. When the war ended, Stack resumed his film career and appeared in many films, including *Fighter Squadron* (1948), *A Date with Judy* (1948), *Miss Tatlock's Millions* (1948), *The Bullfighter and the Lady* (1951), *Bwana Devil* (1952), *Good Morning, Miss Dove* (1955), *The Tarnished Angel* (1957), and *John Paul Jones* (1959), before receiving the leading role of Eliot Ness on *The Untouchables*. After the show left the air, Stack continued to appear in such films as *The Caretakers* (1963) and *Is Paris Burning?* (1966), and had regular roles on the television series *The NAME OF THE GAME*, *Strike Force* (1981), *It's a Great Life* (1985), FALCON CREST, and, most notably, as the host of the TV documentary series *Most Wanted* from 1976 through 1977. In 1998, Stack was heard as Bob the Narrator on the *Hercules* TV series. Stack has also guest-starred on the series MURDER, SHE WROTE, SUDDENLY SUSAN, and DIAGNOSIS MURDER, among others.

STANWYCK, BARBARA (RUBY STEVENS 1907–1990)

One of Hollywood's most popular leading ladies, Barbara Stanwyck, who had been a major film star for over 30 years before she first appeared on television in 1960 on *The Barbara Stanwyck Show*, scored her greatest success on TV playing Victoria Barkley on the TV western series *The BIG VALLEY*. Born in Brooklyn, New York,

before she entered show business, Stanwyck worked as a telephone operator, and she took dance classes determined to become a chorus girl on Broadway. Her determination paid off, and when she was only 17 years old, Stanwyck got a job in the chorus of a Broadway musical. In 1928, after appearing in *Broadway Nights,* which was filmed in New York, Stanwyck moved to Hollywood and began what became one of the most successful acting careers in films. Increasingly larger roles in such films as *Ten Cents a Dance* (1931), *The Miracle Woman* (1931), *So Big!* (1932), *Baby Face* (1933), *Annie Oakley* (1935), *Stella Dallas* (1937, which made her a star), *Union Pacific* (1939), *Golden Boy* (1939), *The Lady Eve* (1941), *Ball of Fire* (1941), *Meet John Doe* (1941), *Lady of Burlesque* (1943), *Double Indemnity* (1944), *Christmas in Connecticut* (1945), *The Two Mrs. Carrolls* (1947), *B. F.'s Daughter* (1948), *The Furies* (1950), *Titanic* (1953), *Executive Suite* (1954), and *The Maverick Queen* (1956), and many, many others, followed. After starring on *The Big Valley* from 1966 through 1969, Stanwyck continued to appear in films, and in 1983, she was seen as Mary Carson in the successful TV miniseries *The Thorn Birds*. From 1985 through 1986, Stanwyck was a regular on the popular DYNASTY series. She also played Constance "Conny" Colby Patterson on *The Colbys* series in 1985, and made guest-starring appearances on such TV series as *The Ford Theater* (1952), *The ZANE GREY THEATER*, WAGON TRAIN, RAWHIDE, *The UNTOUCHABLES*, and CHARLIE'S ANGELS.

STAPLETON, JEAN (JEANNE MURRAY 1923–)

Loved by millions of TV viewers as Edith Bunker on ALL IN THE FAMILY, Jean Stapleton, who was born in New York City and who considers herself first and foremost a stage actress, made her first television appearance on *The PHILCO TELEVISION PLAYHOUSE* in 1948, and was subsequently seen on the *Woman with a Past* series in 1954. In 1960, Stapleton repeated the role she had first been seen in on Broadway in the film *Bells Are Ringing,* and throughout the 1960s she made guest appearances on such TV series as NAKED CITY and ROUTE 66, although she mostly concentrated on her stage career. Stapleton also had featured roles in the films *Up the Down Staircase* (1967), and *Cold Turkey* (1971), before being cast as Edith Bunker in *All in the Family* by producer Norman LEAR, who remembered her because of her memorable performance as a baseball player's wife in the film of *Damn Yankees*. Her role on *All in the Family,* which she played from 1971 until 1980, made her a major star and led to her being cast in a wide variety of roles on the stage, in such TV films as *You Can't Take It With You* (1979), *Aunt Mary* (1979), *Jack and the Beanstalk* (1982), *Eleanor, First Lady of the World* (1982, as Eleanor Roosevelt), *Cinderella* (1984), *A Matter of Sex* (1984), and *Dead Man's Folly* (1986), as well as in the film *The Buddy System* (1984) and on the TV series *Bagdad Cafe* (1991). In 1983, in order to return to the stage, Stapleton turned down the role of Jessica Fletcher on the TV series MURDER, SHE WROTE, which was eventually played by Angela LANSBURY. In more recent years, in addition to playing Mrs. Piggle-Wiggle on the 1994 TV series *Mrs. Piggle-Wiggle*, she has had major roles in the films *Michael* (1996) and *You've Got Mail* (1998), and was featured on the TV miniseries *The Great War* (1996), and the TV film *Chance of a Lifetime* (1998), and provided the voice of Mrs. Jenkins for the animated film *Pocahontas II: Journey to the New World* (1998). Stapleton has also made guest appearances on such TV series as SCARECROW AND MRS. KING, GRACE UNDER FIRE, CAROLINE IN THE CITY, MURPHY BROWN, and TOUCHED BY AN ANGEL.

STAR SEARCH/ED McMAHON'S STAR SEARCH

1983–1995 Syndicated Various times and stations

Star Search, which starred Ed McMahon as master of ceremonies, introduced a wide variety of talented singers, comedians, dancers, actors, and other entertainers and gave them their first national television exposure. *Star Search* was a weekly, hour-long talent show on which performers competed in eight categories, including vocal group, stand-up comedy, solo vocalist, dance, drama (with the aid of a well-known actor or actress such as Joan Collins or Anthony Geary of GENERAL HOSPITAL). The talent was rated by a panel of agents and producers, and the weekly winner returned on the next show to compete with new challengers, hoping to gain a long run. The longest-running acts returned each spring to compete against one another for the title of Best New Star. In 1992, a five-days-a-week version of the series surfaced, but it was canceled after only a few months. The show's title was changed in the mid-1990s to *Ed McMahon's Star Search.* The series was produced by Disney-MGM Studios and originated from Orlando, Florida. Former MTV veejay Martha Quinn announced the vocalist section of the show. One of *Star Search's* longest-reigning talents was a baby-faced singer named Sam Harris. Also introduced on the series were the country music group Sawyer Brown, singer Tiffany, actors Brian Bloom, later of AS THE WORLD TURNS, Amy Stock of DALLAS, Ami Dolenz of *General Hospital,* and comedians Sinbad, Rick Ducommun, Dennis Miller, and Kim Coles. The acting part of the competition was dropped during the 1991–92 season, and additional musical categories such as junior vocalist, teen vocalist, adult dance, junior dance, and teen dance were also featured.

STARSKY AND HUTCH

Sept. 1975–Sept. 1976	ABC	Wed. 10–11 P.M.
Sept. 1978–Jan. 1978	ABC	Sat. 9–10 P.M.
Jan. 1978–Aug. 1978	ABC	Wed. 10–11 P.M.
Sept. 1978–May 1979	ABC	Tues. 10–11 P.M.
Aug. 1979	ABC	Tues. 10–11 P.M.

In its first season on television, *Starsky and Hutch,* a police drama, was in the top 20 on the Nielsen chart of popular TV programs. The show's popularity, however, proved to be short-lived, and although it remained on the air for three more seasons, the series never again appeared on the top-20 list. The major characters on this fast-paced series, which was created by William Blinn, were two young undercover plainclothes officers who lived and worked in Los Angeles, Dave Starsky, played by Paul Michael Glaser, and Ken Hutchinson, played by David Soul. Starsky and Hutch were both fun-loving bachelors, but they came from two entirely different backgrounds. Starsky was a dark-haired, streetwise tough guy, and Hutch was a fair-haired, well-educated, soft-spoken fellow. The two men, however, were perfectly matched as a team, and their differences actually added to their effectiveness as policemen who tracked down a wide assortment of prostitutes, pimps, muggers, dope pushers, and organized crime hoodlums. The partners' commanding officer, Capt. Harold Dobey, played by Bernie Hamilton, and their frequent informant, nicknamed Huggy Bear, played by Antonio Fargas, were also seen regularly. Sequences that proved popular with younger viewers involved racing through the streets of the city in Starsky's bright red hot rod, a 1974 Ford Torino. *Starsky and Hutch's* executive producers were Aaron SPELLING and Leonard Goldberg.

STAR TREK

Sept. 1966–Aug. 1967	NBC	Thurs.	8:30–9:30 P.M.
Sept. 1967–Aug. 1968	NBC	Fri.	8:30–9:30 P.M.
Sept. 1968–Apr. 1969	NBC	Fri.	10–11 P.M.
June 1969–Sept. 1969	NBC	Tues.	7:30–8:30 P.M.

The original *Star Trek* science fiction series was on the air for only three seasons, but it earned a substantial and long-lasting cult following. Set in the 23rd century, *Star Trek* centered on the adventures of the crew of the starship *Enterprise* as they conducted their reconnaissance mission to explore previously unexplored worlds in the universe for the United Federation of Planets. As they traveled around space on a five-year mission "to seek out new life and new civilization," the crew of the *Enterprise* encountered two hostile alien races, the Klingons and the Romulans, with whom they often had to do battle. The 79 episodes of the original series were often concerned with the differences between the imperfect but essentially noble human Earthlings and other life forms that existed in outer space, from gaseous beings to almost humanlike species the crew of the *Enterprise* encountered. Captain James T. Kirk, who was the commander of the *Enterprise,* was played by William SHATNER. On the pilot for the series, the commander of the *Enterprise* was named Captain Pike, played by film actor Jeffery Hunter, who died before the series began its run. Footage from this pilot was used in the two-part "The Menagerie" episode. The first officer on the *Enterprise,* Mr. Spock, played by

Leonard NIMOY, was the half alien–half human son of the ambassador to Earth from the United Federation planet of Vulcan and his human wife. Spock had inherited the pointed ears and mind-reading intelligence of his alien father, but had little of his mother's human emotionality. Also serving as members of the crew on the *Enterprise* were the level-headed chief medical officer, Dr. Leonard McCoy (nicknamed "Bones"), played by DeForest Kelley; Yeoman Janice Rand (during the 1966–67 season), played by Grace Lee Whitney; the navigator, Sulu, played by George Takei; Communications Officer Lt. Uhura, played by Nichelle Nichols; Chief Engineer Montgomery Scott ("Scotty"), played by James Doohan; nurse Christine Chapel, played by Majel Barrett; and assistant navigator Ens. Pavel Chekhov (1967–69), played by Walter Koenig. Placing 52nd in the TV ratings, *Star Trek* was canceled in 1969, but gradually gained a loyal audience when it was shown in reruns. In 1973, *Star Trek* resurfaced as a Saturday morning animated cartoon series that featured the voices of original cast members. This half-hour show was produced by Norm Prescott and Lou Scheimer and featured many episodes that were based on original *Star Trek* episodes. Because of the popularity of such science fiction films as *Star Wars* and *Close Encounters of the Third Kind, Star Trek* was revived in 1979 by Paramount Pictures as an expensive ($40 million) feature film that starred members of the original cast including William Shatner and Leonard Nimoy. Even though it was only a moderate success at the box office, a second *Star Trek* feature film, also starring members of the original TV cast, called *Star Trek II: The Wrath of Khan,* proved to be more successful and encouraged the production of four additional feature films and the subsequent *Star Trek* series—*Star Trek: The Next Generation, Star Trek: Deep Space Nine,* and *Star Trek: Voyager. Star Trek* was the creation of Gene Roddenberry, who was also the executive producer of the TV series and the main force behind the continually growing success of the various television series and the *Star Trek* feature films. The series' first producer was Gene Coon, who was succeeded by John Meredyth

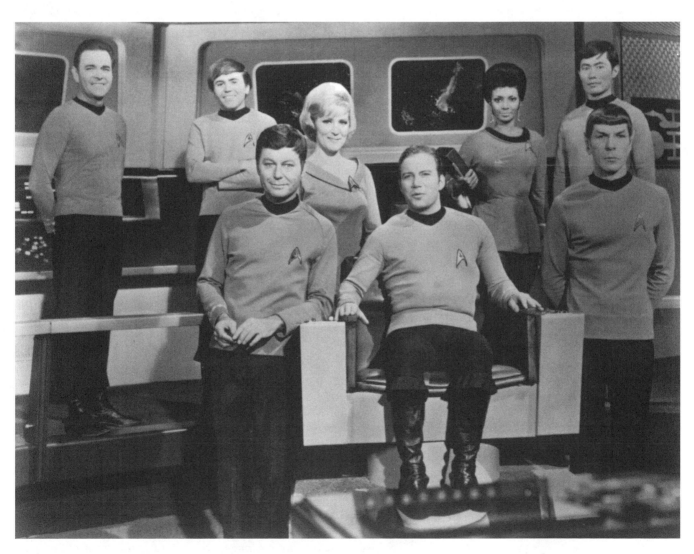

Star Trek: James Doohan, Walter Koenig, DeForest Kelly, Marjel Barrett, William Shatner, Nichelle Nichols, George Takei, and Leonard Nimoy (Author's collection)

Lucas and Fred Freiberger. The series' special effects were supplied by the Howard Anderson Company, Film Effects in Hollywood, Jim Rugg, and the Westeimer Company.

STAR TREK: DEEP SPACE NINE

1993–1999 Syndicated Various times and stations

This series was the second spin-off of the original *Star Trek* series, the first spin-off being STAR TREK: THE NEXT GENERATION. "Deep Space Nine" referred to a space station that orbited the planet Bajor after the hostile Cardassians's occupation of the planet ended. The commander of the station, which had been a mine that was located near a "wormhole" that was a shortcut to unexplored areas of the galaxy, was Benjamin Sinka, played by Avery Brooks, a widower whose teenage son, Jake, played by Cirroc Lofton, lived with him on the station. The station's chief operations officer was Miles O'Brien, played by Colm Meaney, who had been the transport officer on the previously produced *Star Trek: The Next Generation* series (see following entry). The alien Bajorian liaison officer on Deep Space Nine was Major Kira Nerys, played by Nana Visitor, who was a leading force behind the Bajorian fight for independence and who resented the Federation's replacing the Cardassians as administrators. Others on the station were Quark, a devious Ferengi alien who administered a gambling amusement facility on the station, played by Armin Shimerman; Constable Odo, played by René Auberjonois, who was the station's chief of security and an alien shape-shifter who had an adversarial relationship with Quark; a young medical officer, Dr. Julian Bashir, played by Alexander Siddig, who had just graduated from Starfleet Medical; and Dax, played by Terry Farnell, who was a joined species known as the Trills and who lived in various host bodies. Also appearing on the series regularly were Andrew J. Robinson as Elim Garak, Marc Alaimo as Gul Dukat, Max Grodenchik as Ram, Academy Award–winning actress Louise Fletcher as Kai Winn Adami, and for shorter periods of time Salome Jens, Rosalind Chao, Aron Eisenberg, Michael Dorn, Chase Masterson, J. G. Hertzler, Penny Johnson, Jeffrey Combs, Casey Biggs, Melanie Smith, James Darren, Nicole deBoer, and Barry Jenner. A total of 176 episodes of *Star Trek: Deep Space Nine* were filmed during the seven years the series was in production.

STAR TREK: THE NEXT GENERATION

1987–1994 Syndicated Various times and stations

The first spin-off series of *Star Trek* was *Star Trek: The Next Generation,* which surfaced as a syndicated series 18 years after the original series left the air and after several successful feature-length *Star Trek* feature films had been made. This series, which was produced by *Star Trek's* original creator, Gene Roddenberry, was set in the 24th century, 78 years after Captain Kirk and his crew patrolled space, and was set on a new *Enterprise* spaceship that had a new commander and crew, which numbered 2,000 beings, including Captain Jean-Luc Picard, played by Patrick Stewart, who was much older and a more fatherly, if formal, commander than Kirk had been; Picard's second in command on the *Enterprise* was Cdr. William Riker, who was more like Kirk, played by Jonathan Frakes; Counselor Deanna Troi, a half Betazoid–half human crew member, played by Marina Sirtis, who had an on-again off-again love affair with Riker and had the uncanny ability to sense the emotions of any living creature; Lt. Geordi La Forge, played by LeVar Burton, a blind helmsman who could see with the help of a high-tech visor that sent video signals directly to his brain; Lt. Worf, played by Michael Dorn, who was a Klingon officer (the Klingons were now members of the United Federation of Planets and not enemies) aboard the *Enterprise;* Lt. Tasha Yar, played by Denise Crosby, who was the spaceship's head of security; Lt. Cdr. Data, played by Brent Spiner, who was an android (mechanical being) who had total recall and wanted to be as human as possible; and Dr. Beverly Crusher, played by Gates McFadden, who was the ship's medical officer. Also appearing on the series were Wil Wheaton as Dr. Crusher's brilliant young son, Wesley; Colm Meaney as Transporter Chief Miles O'Brien; Diana Muldaur as Dr. Katherine "Kate" Pulaski; Whoopi Goldberg as Guinan, a mysterious and intuitive humanoid who was the bartender at the ship's "Ten Forward Bar"; Rosalind Chao as Keiko O'Brien; Brian Bonsall as Alexander Roshenko; Michele Forbes as Ens. Ro Laren; and Patti Yasutake as Dr. Elissa Ogawa. In all, 178 episodes of *Star Trek: The Next Generation* were produced during the seven years it was in production. In 1994, a feature film, also titled *Star Trek Generations,* was released that featured most of the television cast, and also starred William SHATNER in his original *Star Trek* role of Captain Kirk.

STAR TREK: VOYAGER

Jan. 1995–Aug. 1996	UPN	Mon. 8–9 P.M.
Aug. 1996–Oct. 1997	UPN	Wed. 9–10 P.M.
Nov. 1997–Apr. 1998	UPN	Wed. 8–9 P.M.
Apr. 1998–May 2001	UPN	Wed. 9–10 P.M.

The fourth of the *Star Trek* TV series, *Star Trek: Voyager,* was set during the same time period as STAR TREK: DEEP SPACE NINE but this series took place on a relatively small spacecraft called *Voyager,* which originally operated around the Deep Space Nine vicinity and chased a terrorist ship operated by the hostile Maquis. When the Maquis's ship was destroyed during a storm, the crew of the alien ship joined the staff on the *Voyager* in an uneasy alliance. *The Voyager's* captain, Kathryn Janeway, played by Kate Mulgrew (the role was originally played by Genevieve Bujold, who quit the show a few days after the series began filming), seemed to spend most of her time trying to get her original crew and the crew of the Maquis ship to get along with each other, while she tried to get her ship back to a more familiar area of the galaxy. Janeway appointed the captain of the Maquis ship, Chakotay, played by Robert Beltran, "First Officer" of the U.S.S. *Voyager*. Other members of Janeway's crew were Lt. Tom Paris, played by Robert Duncan McNeill, a former fighter pilot who was outgoing and had a talent for getting into trouble; a recent graduate of the Starfleet Academy, Ens. Harry Kim, played by Garret Wang, who was always questioning his own abilities; chief engineer B'Elanna Torres, played by Roxann Biggs-Dawson, a moody half-Klingon–half-human former crew member on the Maquis ship; security chief Tuvok, played by Tim Russ, an alien Vulcan who had been a spy for the federation and was previously stationed on the Maquis ship. Also seen on the series were Ethan Phillips as the alien Neelix; Robert Picardo as the holographic Doc Zimmerman; Jennifer Lien as the one-year-old Ocampan alien, Kes (Ocampans had only nine-year lifespans); the surgically altered Seska, played by Martha Hackett, who was a member of the Kazon warrior race of beings; and Robert Sbarge as Michael Jonas, Alexander Enberg as Ens. Vorick, Jeri Ryan as a character named Seven of Nine, and Scarlett Pumers as Naomi Wildman.

STERN, HOWARD (HOWARD ALLEN STERN 1954–)

Radio "shock jock" Howard Stern grew up in the predominantly African-American town of Roosevelt on Long Island in New York, which he claims often made him feel "different." Stern, who was only a fair student when he attended Roosevelt High School, attended Boston University and graduated from college magna cum laude. In 1974, Stern made his first appearance on television as a member of the audience on *The Uncle Floyd Show*. After graduating from Boston University, Stern, who had worked on the college radio station, decided to pursue a career as a radio disc jockey. He began his professional career at station WRNW in Briarcliff Manor, New York, in 1974, and he married his college sweetheart, Allison. His growing popularity led to an offer to host NBC's early morning radio show, but Stern was encouraged to leave NBC when the Federal Communications Commission objected to his "too shocking for radio" subject matter, which made officials at NBC nervous. In 1985, Stern found a permanent home at radio station WXRK (called "K-Rock") in New York City, and he began his climb to the top, becoming radio's most controversial and successful early morning show host. Stern claims that he "always resented the label 'shock jock' that the press came up with for [him]. I never intentionally set out to shock anybody," he has said in various interviews. Stern's early morning radio show became the most popular show in the New York metropolitan area and soon expanded its broadcasting arena, becoming a syndicated show that was heard in select cities throughout the United States. In 1992, Stern hosted *The Howard Stern Interviews* television show, which was not successful, but when the E! (Entertain-

ment) network began to videotape his morning radio talk show and edit episodes of the program that were then seen on an hour-long, late-evening TV offering, Stern soon became a TV, as well as radio, star. In 1998, because of the popularity of the E! show, CBS decided to produce a Saturday evening, hour-long late-night series, using segments from Stern's E! show that would compete with the NBC's popular SATURDAY NIGHT LIVE. Stern's program on CBS soon outrated *Saturday Night Live* in the audience polls. The new self-proclaimed "King of All Media," Stern became the best-selling author of a book about his life called *Private Parts,* and starred in a film adaptation of his book. In 2000, Stern became a TV producer with the syndicated *Son of the Beach* and *Doomsday* TV series. Stern is a frequent guest on both the Letterman and Leno programs and guest-starred on *The LARRY SANDERS SHOW* in 1993, as well as supplying the voice of Orinthal on his *Doomsday* series.

STEVE ALLEN SHOW, THE (ALSO *THE STEVE ALLEN COMEDY HOUR*)

The STEVE ALLEN SHOW:

Dec. 1950–Mar. 1951	CBS	Mon.–Fri. 7–7:30 P.M.
July 1952–Sept. 1952	CBS	Thurs. 8:30–9 P.M.
June 1956–Mar. 1959	NBC	Sun. 8–9 P.M.
Mar. 1959–June 1959	NBC	Sun. 7:30–8:30 P.M.
Apr. 1959–June 1959	NBC	Mon. 7:30–8:30 P.M.
Mar. 1959	NBC	Sun. 7:30–9 P.M.

(The STEVE ALLEN COMEDY HOUR)

June 1967–Aug. 1967	CBS	Wed. 10–11 P.M.
Oct. 1980	NBC	Sat. 10–11 P.M.
Dec. 1980	NBC	Tues. 10–11 P.M.
Jan. 1981	NBC	Sat. 10–11 P.M.

Although the television industry pays tribute to the master raconteur and interviewer Steve ALLEN as the original host of NBC'S TONIGHT SHOW, Allen also hosted several variety/comedy shows on TV from as early as 1950. Allen's first national television show, called *The Steve Allen Show,* was aired five days a week, Monday through Fridays, and was first seen on Christmas Day, 1950. Allen played the piano and had funny chats with guest stars and members of his studio audience. The show became an alternative nighttime show to CBS's *Amos 'n' Andy* situation comedy during the summer of 1952. Allen's most memorable variety program was seen on NBC from 1956 through 1961, and Allen's skills as a composer, pianist, comedian, singer, and writer were amply displayed on this series, with major emphasis on comedy routines and sketches. Among the performers who appeared with Allen regularly on this show were Louis Nye, Gene RAYBURN, Skitch Henderson, Tom Poston, Don KNOTTS, Pat Harrington, Jr., Bill Dana, Buck Henry, Jayne Meadows (Allen's wife), John Cameron Swayze, the Smothers Brothers, Tim Conway, Les Brown and His Band, Marilyn Jacobs, Gabe Dell, Dayton Allen, Cal Howard, Joey Forman, and Don Penny. Among the popular features regularly seen on the program were "Letters to the Editor," "The Allen Report to the Nation," "Mad-Libs," "Crazy Shots," "The Allen Bureau of Standards," "and "the Allen All Stars." Allen introduced many soon-to-be-famous guest stars on his program. On Allen's second telecast in this series, months before Ed Sullivan's TOAST OF THE TOWN introduced him to the national TV public, Allen's guest star was the new rock and roll sensation Elvis Presley.

The show originated in New York City, but Allen and his regular cast moved the program to Hollywood in the fall of 1959. After a six-year absence from hosting a regular TV series, Allen returned to regular television hosting in 1967 as the star of a summer replacement series for CBS called *The Steve Allen Comedy Hour*. The series, in addition to Allen's usual antics, also featured such segments as the "Man on the Street" interviews, during which comedian Louis Nye played the suave-but-silly Gordon Hathaway. Also seen on this series regularly were comedienne Ruth Buzzi, John Byner, and Jayne Meadows. A second *Steve Allen Comedy Hour* surfaced as an occasional program seen on NBC for four months in 1980 and 1981. The regular cast of the show, in addition to Allen and his former regular Joey Forman, were a group of relatively unknown performers that included Joe Baker, Tom Leopold, Bill Saluga, Bob Shaw, Helen Brooks, Carol Donelly, Fred Smoot, Nancy Steen, Catherine O'Hara, Kaye Ballard, Doris Hess, Tim Lund, Tim Gibbon, and Terry Gibbs and His Band.

STEVENS, CONNIE (CONCETTA ANN INGOLIA 1938–)

Singer/actress Connie Stevens, who was born in Brooklyn, New York, began her show business career as a member of a singing group called the Three Debs. In 1957, Connie decided she wanted to pursue a career as an actress, and before long she began getting small roles on such TV series as MAVERICK and in the feature films *Young and Dangerous* (1957), *Eighteen and Anxious* (1957), *Rock-a-Bye Baby* (1958), and *Dragstrip Riot* (1958). Connie's big break came, however, when she was cast as Cricket Blake on the HAWAIIAN EYE series, which became one of the 1959–60 TV season's biggest hits. After *Hawaiian Eye* left the air, Connie had featured roles in the films *Parrish* (1961), *Susan Slade* (1961), and *Palm Springs Weekend* (1963), before starring on her own TV situation comedy series, *Wendy and Me*, in 1964. The series was not a success, and Connie subsequently appeared in several less than memorable films, but her much-publicized marriage to singer Eddie Fisher kept Connie's name in the public's eye. In 1971, Stevens became a regular on *The Kraft Music Hall* which later became known as *The Des O'Connor Show*. Appearances in several TV films and in the popular 1980 TV miniseries *Scruples* followed. In the 1980s and 1990s, Stevens frequently performed in nightclubs around the country and had guest-starring roles on such TV series as *The MUPPET SHOW*, *The LOVE BOAT*, MURDER, SHE WROTE, *Tales of the Dark Side*, BURKE'S LAW, ELLEN, and BAYWATCH.

STEVENS, CRAIG (GAIL SHIKLES, JR. 1918–2000)

Perhaps best known as the star of the PETER GUNN television series from 1958 through 1961, Craig Stevens began his acting career in the classic film *Mr. Smith Goes to Washington* in 1939, playing the small role of a Senate reporter. Stevens, who was born in Liberty, Missouri, went on to become one of Hollywood's favorite second male leads in such 1940s and 1950s films as *Affectionately Yours* (1941), *Dive Bomber* (1941), *Spy Ship* (1942), *Since You Went Away* (1944), *God Is My Co-Pilot* (1945), *Humoresque* (1946), *Phone Call from a Stranger* (1952), and *The French Line* (1954). Although many filmgoers were familiar with his face, Stevens did not become a "name" star until he appeared on *Peter Gunn*, which became one of TV's most popular series in the late 1950s. After *Peter Gunn* left the airwaves, Stevens starred on the less successful *Man of the World* (1962) and *Mr. Broadway* (1964) TV series, and in such films as *The Limbo Line* (1968), and the TV film *Killer Bees* (1974), and in the popular TV miniseries *Rich Man, Poor Man* (1976). In 1981, Stevens appeared as a regular on DALLAS. Throughout the 1960s, 1970s, and 1980s, Stevens often appeared in various touring company productions of popular Broadway shows with his wife, film star Alexis Smith. In the late 1980s, Stevens had a featured role in the film *S.O.B.* as well as in the TV film *Marcus Welby, M.D.: A Holiday Affair* in 1988. Throughout the 1950s, 1960s, 1970s, and 1980s Stevens was also frequently a guest star on such TV series as *The LONE RANGER*, ALFRED HITCHCOCK PRESENTS, *Owen Marshall: Counselor at Law*, *The VIRGINIAN*, *Here's Lucy*, GUNSMOKE, *Harry-O*, STARSKY AND HUTCH, ELLERY QUEEN, HARDY BOYS/NANCY DREW MYSTERIES, *The INCREDIBLE HULK*, HAPPY DAYS, and MURDER, SHE WROTE.

STEVENS, INGER (INGER STENSLAND 1934–1970)

Although Inger Stevens's life was cut short at the age of 36, she enjoyed considerable success for the brief time she was in Hollywood in films and as the star of the popular FARMER'S DAUGHTER TV situation comedy series. Inger Stevens was born in Stockholm, Sweden, but immigrated to the United States with her parents when she was a young child. Stevens worked as a model after she finished high school, and before long she was playing increasingly larger roles on such TV series as ROBERT MONTGOMERY PRESENTS, *Armstrong Circle Theatre*, ALFRED HITCHCOCK PRESENTS, *The TWILIGHT ZONE*, ROUTE 66, ADVENTURES IN PARADISE, and *The Dick Powell Show*, as well as in such films as *Man on Fire* (1957), *Cry Terror!* (1958), *The Buccaneer* (1958) and *The World, the Flesh and the Devil* (1959). It was, however, as Katy Holstrum, the farm girl-turned-politician on *The Farmer's Daughter*, that Stevens actually became a star. After *The Farmer's Daughter* departed the airwaves, Stevens continued to star in such films as *The New Interns* (1964), *A Guide for the Married Man* (1967), *Madigan* (1968), *House of Cards* (1968), *The Mask of Sheba* (1970), and *Run, Simon, Run* (1970). Stevens died of a drug overdose in 1970.

STEWART, MARTHA (MARTHA HELEN KOSTYRA 1941–)

Lifestyle guru, TV personality, and extraordinary businesswoman, Martha Stewart, was born and grew up in Nutley, New Jersey, the second of six children born to working-class parents. When she was 13 years old, Stewart worked as a model in New York City and appeared in print ads, as well as in TV commercials. After she graduated from high school, Stewart went to Barnard College, from which she earned a degree in European and architectural history in 1962. In 1961, while she was a student at Barnard, Martha met and married a Yale law student named Andy Stewart. Six years later, she gave birth to her daughter, Alexis. Stewart worked for a boutique firm and then on Wall Street until 1972, when the Stewarts bought a 19th-century farmhouse in Westport, Connecticut. Martha decided to concentrate her energies on gourmet cooking and began a catering business. Within 10 years, Martha Stewart's company was earning a million dollars a year and she was writing best-selling books and making numerous TV guest appearances. In 1990, her husband filed for divorce after a bitter three-year separation. By 1991, Martha Stewart's company had become Martha Stewart Living Omnimedia and was producing household items, crafts projects, books, a successful magazine named *Martha Stewart Living,* and a daily TV show seen on CBS, as well as a series that featured reruns of former telecasts, shown on the Food Channel. All of this earned Stewart nearly a billion dollars in annual retail sales for her various products, publications, and TV shows. Capitalizing on her celebrity status, Stewart currently makes guest-starring appearances on many TV shows, and has even guest-starred on the legendary Julia Child's *Baking with Julia* program on the PBS network.

STOP THE MUSIC

May 1949–Apr. 1952	ABC	Thurs. 8–9 P.M.
Sept. 1954–May 1955	ABC	Tues. 10:30–11 P.M.
Sept. 1955–June 1956	ABC	Thurs. 8:30–9 P.M.

Before *Stop the Music* made its television debut in 1949, it was a popular show on radio in 1948. The radio and TV versions of the show both starred Bert PARKS as emcee and the Harry Salter Orchestra. Estelle Loring (1949–50) and Jimmy Blaine (1949–52), and Betty Ann Grove (1949–55), were the TV series' original vocalists, and subsequently featured on the show were singers Marion Morgan (1950–51), June Valli (1952), and Jaye P. Morgan (1954–55). Bert Parks and the featured singers performed parts of a song, leaving out the song's title if it was part of the lyric, and contestants chosen from the audience were asked to identify the tune for cash prizes. Viewers were asked to send in official entry blanks with their names and phone numbers, and they were telephoned during the show and asked to identify a song for a cash prize. One of TV's first big money game shows, *Stop the Music* gave the large, for its time, sum of $25,000 to viewers who identified the song correctly. Prizes for audience contestants consisted of cash, mink coats, and trips. Occasionally a "mystery melody" was played, and both a studio contestant and a home viewer (by telephone) tried to be the first to identify the tune. At times, guest singers also appeared on the series. Dennis James often substituted for Bert Parks. Also featured on the series were dancers Sonja and Courtney Van Horn and cartoonist Chuck Luchsinger. The series was produced by Louis McGowan, who was later responsible for the immensely popular *$64,000 QUESTION* game show.

STORCH, LARRY (1923–)

Larry Storch, known for playing Cpl. Randolph Agarn in the *F Troop* TV situation comedy in the 1960s, and as the voice of Koko the Clown, began his show business career as a stand-up comic. Storch, who was born in New York City, first appeared on television in 1949 on the CAVALCADE OF STARS. In 1953, he was the star of his own *Larry Storch Show,* a summer replacement in 1953, and was first heard as the voice of Koko the Clown on the *Out of the Inkwell* TV cartoon series. He continued to provide Koko's voice for numerous TV specials and TV cartoon films from 1961 through 1963. After appearing on the popular *F Troop* series, Storch continued to provide character voices for many animated films and TV series such as *The Pink Panther Show* (1969) *The Queen and I* (1969), *Scooby and Scrappy-Doo* (1979), and had a regular role in the original SABRINA, THE TEENAGE WITCH (1971), *The Brady Kids* (1972), *The Ghost Busters* (1975), and appeared in such films as *The Great Bank Robbery* (1969), *Airport 1975* (1974), *Without Warning* (1980), *S.O.B.* (1981), *Fake-Out* (1982), and *I Don't Buy Kisses Anymore* (1992). Storch was also a frequent guest star on such TV series as CHIPS, ALL IN THE FAMILY, EMERGENCY!, GOMER PYLE, U.S.M.C., The DORIS DAY SHOW, I DREAM OF JEANNIE, GILLIGAN'S ISLAND, CAR 54, WHERE ARE YOU?, and YOUR SHOW OF SHOWS.

STORM, GALE (JOSEPHINE OWAISSA COTTLE 1922–)

Gale Storm, who was born in Bloomington, Texas, was one of television's earliest stars and appeared on two TV shows of the 1950s–early 1960s, MY LITTLE MARGIE and *The GALE STORM SHOW.* Shortly after completing her schooling in Texas, the teenage Josephine Cottle became a singer in a band. When the band played an engagement in Hollywood, it didn't take long for movie scouts to sign her to a contract. Gale's first film appearance was in *Tom Brown's School Days,* when she was 18 years old, and she subsequently appeared in such Hollywood films as *Red River Valley* (1941), *Smart Alecks* (1942), *Lure of the Islands* (1942), *Rhythm Parade* (1942), *Revenge of the Zombies* (1943), *Sunbonnet Sue* (1945), *G.I. Honeymoon* (1945), *It Happened on 5th Avenue* (1947), *The Kid from Texas* (1950), *The Texas Rangers* (1951), and *Woman of the North Country* (1952), before starring on *My Little Margie* in 1952. When Storm's second TV series, *The Gale Storm Show,* which was originally called OH! SUSANNAH, left the airwaves in 1960, and except for two appearances on BURKE'S LAW 1963, Storm, who was married to Lee Bonnell, put her career on hold to raise her four children. In 1984, Storm came out of retirement to appear on an episode of MURDER, SHE WROTE, playing a character named Maisie Mayberry in "Something Borrowed, Something Blue."

STREETS OF SAN FRANCISCO, THE

Sept. 1972–Jan. 1973	ABC	Sat. 9–10 P.M.
Jan. 1973–Aug. 1974	ABC	Thurs. 10–11 P.M.
Sept. 1974–Sept. 1976	ABC	Thurs. 9–10 P.M.
Sept. 1976–June 1977	ABC	Thurs. 10–11 P.M.

A police procedural drama with a San Francisco setting, *The Streets of San Francisco* was one of television's most popular shows, rating in the top-30 Nielsen-rated rated shows for three of the five years it was on the air (1973–74, 1974–75 and 1975–76). Lt. Mike Stone of the San Francisco Police Department, played by veteran character actor Karl Malden, was the central character on the series. Stone and his staff, which included Inspector Steve Keller (1972–76), played by Michael Douglas, and then Inspector Dan Robbins (1976–77), played by Richard Hatch, and Lt. Lessing, played by Lee Harris, used modern police methods in their investigations. Stone was a 23-year veteran policeman, and Keller, his original partner, was a college-educated man who went from assistant inspector to full inspector. When he left to become a teacher, he was replaced by Dan Robbins. Also featured on the series from time to time was Darleen Carr as Mike's daughter, who was seen on the earlier episodes of the series. It was one of the first TV series to film on actual locations, and many people feel it was the actual streets of San Francisco that was the real "star" of the show. The series, based on characters introduced in Carolyn Weston's novel *Poor, Poor Ophelia*, was developed for television by Edward Hume and produced by Quinn Martin.

STRIKE IT RICH

| May 1951–Jan. 1958 | CBS | Mon.–Fri. Various daytime hours |
| July 1951–Jan. 1955 | CBS | Wed. 9–9:30 P.M. |

For four and a half seasons in the early 1950s, *Strike It Rich*, which was first heard on the radio in 1947, was one of the most popular prime-time game shows on television, as well as on radio. Hosted by Warren Hull, the show, which was first seen as a regular daytime TV program in 1951, gave "needy" people the chance to win prize money if they could tell the most heartbreaking tale of woe on the show. A quiz segment called "Heart Line" gave viewers a chance to call in by telephone with offers of aid for any of the contestants. In 1954, the program became the object of criticism from The New York City Welfare Department, which disclosed the fact that in 1953, 55

families had moved to New York City with the hope of becoming contestants on the show, had failed to get on the show but remained in New York and became welfare recipients. The series was produced for CBS by Walt Framer. In 1986, a lesser revival of the series, which bore little resemblance to the original show, was aired but soon canceled. This show, which was hosted by Joe Garagiola, had competing couples moving across the stage through a series of arches as they answered various questions correctly, hoping to be the first couple to make it to the finish line and win prizes.

STU ERWIN SHOW, THE (AKA LIFE WITH THE ERWINS, THE TROUBLE WITH FATHER)

Oct. 1950–Sept. 1951	ABC	Sat. 7:30–8 P.M.
Oct. 1951–Apr. 1952	ABC	Fri. 8:30–9 P.M.
May 1952–Oct. 1954	ABC	Fri. 7:30–8 P.M.
Oct. 1954–Apr. 1955	ABC	Wed. 8:30–9 P.M.

One of television's earliest successful situation comedy series, *The Stu Erwin Show* starred film funnyman Stu ERWIN playing himself. Erwin had played the same bumbling father in numerous short films, as well as on a popular radio series. A totally incompetent suburban middle-aged family man, but well-meaning and down-to-earth, Erwin was the principal of the fictitious Hamilton High School. Most of the show's action was in the Erwins' home. Stu's wife, June, played by June Collyer, was always coming to her bumbling husband's rescue. The Erwins' daughters, teenage Jackie, played by Shelia James, and tomboy Joyce, played by Ann Todd from 1950 until 1954, and then by Merry Anders in 1954–55, were constantly embarrassed by their father's ineptitude, but loved him anyway. Other regular characters on the series were Willie, the family's handyman, played by film actor Willie Best; Joyce's boyfriend, Jimmy Clark, played by Martin Milner; and Harry, played by Harry Hayden. For the series' final season, the title of the show was changed to *The New Stu Erwin Show*, but retained its subtitle, *The Trouble with Father*.

STUDIO ONE

Nov. 1948–Mar. 1949	CBS	Sun. 7:30–8 P.M.
Mar. 1949–May 1949	CBS	Sun. 7–8 P.M.
May 1949–Sept. 1949	CBS	Wed. 10–11 P.M.
Sept. 1949–Sept. 1958	CBS	Mon. 10–11 P.M.

One of television's first, and perhaps most famous, live-action dramatic anthology series, *Studio One* was first heard as a radio series that was produced and directed by Fletcher Markle in 1947. In 1949, CBS decided to present the series as a full-hour anthology, offering television adaptations of famous plays and novels. Worthington MINER was the program's executive producer and became the leading force behind the success of the series. Miner's emphasis in this series was the visual impact of the dramas being presented, without ever sacrificing the literary content of the original stories. The series in its later years was produced by Herbert Brodkin.

The first drama seen on this series was a mystery called "The Storm," which starred film actress Margaret Sullavan. During *Studio One*'s earliest years, three performers were featured on the show more than any others: Charlton Heston, Maria RIVA, and Mary SINCLAIR. During the series' run, Heston appeared in adaptations of such classics as *Julius Caesar, Of Human Bondage, Macbeth, Jane Eyre, The Taming of the Shrew, and Wuthering Heights,* to name just a few. Also seen on this series were live performances of *Mary Poppins,* with Mary Wickes and E. G. Marshall; *The Rockingham Tea Set* and *The Kill,* both with Grace Kelly; *The Laugh Maker,* with Jackie GLEASON; *Sentence of Death,* with James Dean in his first major role on TV; *A Handful of Diamonds,* with Lorne GREENE; *Sue Ellen,* with Inger STEVENS; Reginald ROSE's *Twelve Angry Men,* with Edward Arnold, Walter Abel, Robert CUMMINGS, and Franchot Tone; *A Picture in the Paper,* with Jason Robards, Jr.; *Dino,* with Sal Mineo; Reginald Rose's *The Defender,* with Ralph Bellamy, William SHATNER, and Steve MCQUEEN; *The Scarlet Letter,* with Mary SINCLAIR, *I Am Jonathan Scrivner,* with John FORSYTHE and Maria Riva; *Mrs. 'arris Goes to Paris,* with Gracie Fields; *The Mother Bit,* with Peter FALK; *The Night America Trembled* with Warren Beatty in one of his only TV appearances, and many, many others. Among the numerous directors who worked on *Studio One* were Franklin Shaffner, Paul Nickell, Yul Brynner, George Roy Hill, Sidney Lumet, and Robert Mulligan.

Many other actors appeared on *Studio One* during its 10-year run, including Elizabeth MONTGOMERY, Katherine Bard, Sheppard Strudwick, Barbara O'Neill, Edward Andrews, Stanley Ridges, Hildy Parks, Leslie Nielsen, Art CARNEY, James Daly, Everett Sloane, Betsy Palmer, Richard Kiley, Priscilla Gillette, Judson Laire, Harry Townes, Nina Foch, John FORSYTHE, Cliff Norton, and Felicia Montealegre. Over 500 dramas were presented on *Studio One* during its 10-year run.

SUDDENLY SUSAN

Sept. 1996–Jan. 1997	NBC	Thurs. 9:30–10 P.M.
Feb. 1997–May 1997	NBC	Thurs. 8:30–9 P.M.
June 1997–Aug. 1997	NBC	Thurs. 9:30–10 P.M.
June 1997–July 1997	NBC	Mon. 9:30–10 P.M.
July 1997–July 1998	NBC	Mon. 8–8:30 P.M.
July 1998–Aug. 1998	NBC	Thurs. 8:30–9 P.M.
Sept. 1998–Sept. 1999	NBC	Mon. 8–8:30 P.M.

Brooke Shields played a young copy editor named Susan Keane, who lived and worked in San Francisco on this situation comedy series. A woman who had always led a rather pampered life, Susan had decided to get some excitement into her life, and so she dumped her wealthy boyfriend and set out to make it on her own. Susan's boss, Jack Richmond, played by Judd Nelson, was the father of her ex-fiancé, but

he promoted her anyway and made her a columnist at his trendy local magazine *The Gate.* Susan's column was called "Suddenly Susan," and she wrote about being young and single and the odd and interesting people she met. Other characters who appeared regularly on the series were Vicki Groener, Susan's neurotic but spirited coworker, played by Kathy Griffin; Luis Rivera, a good-looking photographer who looked out for the bumbling Susan, played by Nestor Carbonell; Todd Stites, the magazine's randy music critic, played by David Strickland; Liz and Bill Keane, Susan's conservative parents, played by Ray Baker and Swoosie Kurtz; Helen Keane, Susan's understanding grandmother, played by Barbara Barrie; and Susan's high school nemesis, who continued to bother her, Maddy Piper, played by Andrea Bendewald. The series enjoyed a respectable three-year tenure on TV before being canceled.

SUGARFOOT

Sept. 1957–Sept. 1960	ABC	Tues. 7:30–8:30 P.M.
Oct. 1960–July 1961	ABC	Mon. 7:30–8:30 P.M.

In the late 1950s, series with western backgrounds became popular with viewers. *Sugarfoot,* an hour-long program was a series with a light, comedic touch that starred an engaging actor named Will HUTCHINS as Tom Brewster, aka "Sugarfoot," a young correspondence school law student from the East who went west in search of adventure in the late 1800s. An inept and awkward cowboy, Brewster was given the nickname "Sugarfoot," which was a step down from "Tenderfoot," by more experienced cowboys. A good-natured fellow, Tom accepted the nickname, but it didn't stop him from getting involved in some interesting adventures that often involved outlaws and shootouts, and lots of other western action. *Sugarfoot* was seen on an alternate-week basis with CHEYENNE from 1957 until 1959 and then with BRONCO from 1959 until 1960, and then became one of three alternating sections on *Cheyenne.* William T. Orr and Martin Cohan were the executive producers and Carroll Case was the producer of *Sugarfoot,* which was released by Warner Brothers.

SULLIVAN, ED (EDWARD VINCENT SULLIVAN 1902–1974)

The longtime emcee of the popular television variety program *TOAST OF THE TOWN* aka *The ED SULLIVAN SHOW,* Ed Sullivan was born in New York City. As a young man, Sullivan got a job as a reporter and then became a columnist for the New York *Daily News* from 1932 until 1974. His column, which concentrated on gossip about show business celebrities, socialites, and other New York City characters, made Sullivan New York City's best-known promoter, and from 1932 through 1946, he hosted a popular radio show on which he interviewed celebrities visiting New York. In 1948, Sullivan, who became known for his unique voice, began hosting a variety show that featured singers, acrobats, comedians, dancers, actors, etc. called *The Toast of the Town,* and later called *The Ed Sullivan*

Show, which became America's favorite Sunday evening TV program for the next 23 years. At the height of his TV career, Sullivan often played himself in various films and TV shows such as *Mr. Broadway* (1933), *Ed Sullivan's Headliners* (1934), *Senior Prom* (1958), *The Singing Nun* (1965), and *The Phynx* (1970).

SUPER CIRCUS

Jan. 1949–June 1955	ABC	Sat. 4–5 P.M.
June 1955–June 1956	ABC	Sat. 9–10 A.M.

One television children's show that anyone who owned a TV receiver in the early 1950s remembers well, *Super Circus* had begun as a Chicago-based radio show in the 1940s, and ruled its TV time slot from the entire time it was telecast from Chicago. The show's stars, the good-looking six foot-five inch Ringmaster, Claude Kirchner, and his assistant, the beautiful Mary Hartline, who, with her short-skirted majorette costume and long blond hair became one of TV's first sex symbols and a favorite with male viewers, became television legends. The show offered typical circus fare, and each week tightrope walkers, trapeze artists, clowns, animal acts, jugglers, and magicians were featured during the six seasons the show was aired. Produced by Jack Gibney, the show originated from Chicago the first five years it was on ABC, and for its sixth season, the production moved to New York, and was seen on Saturday mornings from 9 to 10 A.M. Claude Kirchner and Mary Hartline decided to leave the show and remain in Chicago to pursue other career interests. During the 1955–56 season, when the show originated in New York, former Bob HOPE radio show comedian Jerry Colonna took over Kirchner's ringmaster job, and Sandy Wirth was the show's baton twirler. Without Kirchner and Hartline, however, the show lost most of its loyal audience, and it was canceled after one season.

Other regulars on *Super Circus* were circus clowns Cliff Sobier, Sandy ("Scampy") Dobitch, and Nicky Francis. For most of the series' run, it had a single sponsor, Quaker Puff cereals, whose slogan was "the only cereal shot from a gun." Each episode of *Super Circus* ended with cereal being shot out of a cannon.

Before he appeared on *Super Circus,* Claude Kirchner had been one of radio's most recognizable voices and was the spokesman for Marx toys. After he left *Super Circus,* Kirchner hosted a short-lived Saturday morning show called *Magic Midway,* and then Kirchner faded from the national TV spotlight. When Mary Hartline left *Super Circus,* she briefly starred on a 15-minute, five-days-a-week series, *The Mary Hartline Show,* and then was seen on a local Chicago children's show called *Princess Mary's Castle.* Shortly after, like Kirchner, Mary Hartline faded from the television scene in the early 1960s.

Super Circus with Mary Hartline, Clyde Kirchner, and clowns (Photofest)

SUPERMAN, THE ADVENTURES OF

1952–1957   Syndicated   Various times and stations

America's favorite superhero, who first saw the light of day as an Action comic book character, was created by Jerry Siegel and Joe Shuster, and was subsequently featured on a radio series that starred Bud COLLYER in the 1930s and 1940, and in two 15-chapter movie serials that starred Kirk Allen, and then in a successful, long-running syndicated television series that starred George REEVES in the Superman/Clark Kent role. Although only 104 episodes of the television *Superman* series were filmed, it is the best-remembered of the various *Superman* productions, and George Reeves is the actor most closely identified with the role. Superman was a humanlike alien who had been sent to Earth as an infant by his parents when they discovered that their planet, Krypton, was about to be destroyed. The alien infant was found and raised by an elderly midwestern couple named the Kents, who named the baby Clark, and raised him as their own son. While he was growing up, Clark discovered that he had amazing strength and could even fly. When he became an adult, he decided to use his special physical abilities to fight a "never-ending battle for truth, justice, and the American way," while disguising himself as a mild-mannered reporter. In addition to George Reeves, who played Superman/Clark Kent, appearing on the series were Phyllis Coates (1951), and then, for the rest of the series run, Noel Neill (1951–57), as Clark's fellow reporter and on again–off again girlfriend, Lois Lane; Jack

Larsen as the youthful cub reporter and photographer Jimmy Olson, who often assisted Superman in his various missions; John Hamilton as Perry White, Clark Kent's managing editor at *The Daily Planet* newspaper in the city of Metropolis, where the series was set; and Robert Shayne as Police Inspector William Henderson, who often called upon Superman to help him with difficult cases. Robert Maxwell and Bernard Luber produced the *Superman* series in 1951, and then Whitney Ellsworth produced the series for the rest of its TV run.

Many actors had their first major TV exposure on *Superman,* including Claude Aikens, Hugh Beaumont, John Beradino, Paul Burke, Chuck CONNORS, and Joi Lansing, who all went on to star on various TV series. In 1966, an animated version of *Superman* was seen on television, and in 1988, a sequel TV cartoon series, *Superboy,* made its debut. In 1993, a new series called LOIS AND CLARK: THE NEW ADVENTURES OF SUPERMAN appeared on TV and became a moderate success. A subsequent big-budget feature-length *Superman* film that starred Christopher Reeve as Superman/Clark Kent and Margot Kidder as Lois Lane surfaced in 1978 and was one of the most successful films of the year. In addition to radio, films, and television, *Superman* has also been seen on Broadway as the title character of a musical comedy, and he also appeared as a major character in a novel. There is even a Superman museum in Metropolis, Illinois, which attests to the fact that Superman is unquestionably one of America's most beloved fictional characters.

SURVIVOR

Spring 2000–present	CBS	Thurs. 9–10 P.M. (in occasional 13-episode segments)

Although REALITY TV programs such as COPS and *America's Most Wanted* were firmly established on TV before the year 2000, the popularity of *Survivor*, which made its television debut that year, paved the way for many similar competition/game reality shows.

Survivor's premise was simple. In spring 2000, 16 ordinary Americans of varying ages, who were divided into two tribes called "Tagi" and "Pagong," and eventually merged into one team called "Rattana," were taken to the island of Palau in the South Pacific where they had to spend 39 days trying to survive with little more than the clothes on their backs, a huge sack of rice, and one "luxury item" each (a hair brush, shampoo, a notebook and pencil, etc.). They were accompanied by personnel (cameramen, segment directors, crew, makeup artists, art directors, producers, assistant producers, and associate producers) who observed and filmed everything individual tribe members did on the island, but had little, if any, interaction with them. The crew simply filmed and recorded conversations, competitions, and elimination gatherings, as well as any personal incidents that occurred, such as minor flirtations and attempts by individual team members to merge with other tribe members and thus strengthen their chance of remaining in the contest longer or place themselves in a more favorable position to win. Periodically, the two tribes competed against each other to win such luxuries as a phone call home, a barbeque, or such useful objects as matches, knives, and the like. They also competed against each other in physical and mental contests to win an "immunity reward," which meant that they could not be voted off the island until the next immunity challenge was waged. Every three days during the 13-episode series, a survivor was voted off the island by members of his or her team. The last survivor won a cash prize of $1 million dollars if he or she had outwitted, outplayed, and outlasted the others. When the two original teams had been reduced to 10 final contestants, the tribes merged into the team Ratanna, and it became a free-for-all. As the eight remaining survivors was voted off the island, they remained sequestered somewhere close by, only to reappear as observers in each following elimination session. These eight eventually voted for who they thought should be the final survivor.

The series' on-camera host is, as of 2002, Jeff Probst, who periodically appears on the island to conduct the challenges and the reward sessions and to preside over the elimination gatherings. The 16 original survivors included Sonja Christopher, who was the first person voted off the island, after three days; B. B. Anderson, banished second after six days; Stacey Stillman, third (nine days); Ramona Gray, fourth, (12 days); Dirk Breen, fifth (15 days); Joel Klug, sixth (18 days); Gretchen Cordy, 21 days; Greg Buis, 24 days; Jenna Lewis, 24 days; Gervase Peterson, 30 days; Colleen Haskell, 33 days; Sean Kenniff, 36 days; Susan Hawk, 37 days; and Rudy Moesch, 38 days. The last two survivors, whose fate was in the hands of the eight jurors who had remained nearby, were an athletic young woman named Kelly Wiglesworth, and Richard Hatch, an overweight gay man who enjoyed running around the island nude and was convinced that his ability to catch fish would make him an indispensable member of his tribe. When the jurors voted to award the million-dollar prize to Hatch, loyal viewers, who had made the show number one on the air in spring 2000, were disappointed. Hatch was not a favorite survivor with viewers; in audience polls, viewers had consistently voted him off the island.

The enormous success and high ratings of the original *Survivor* series resulted in three more 13-episode *Survivor* shows (as of 2002): *Survivor: The Australian Outback* in 2001, on which the million-dollar prize was won by an athletic woman named Tina Wesson who had not ruffled any feathers during her 39 days in the outback; *Survivor: Africa*, also in 2001, on which the top prize was awarded to a TV viewer favorite, a good-looking and compassionate young man named Ethan Zohn; and finally in *Survivor: Marquesas*, on which a young African-American woman named Vecepia Towery won the million-dollar prize. (Other team members thought she won by default.) The huge crew was headed by producers Maria Baltazzia, Jay Bienstock, and John Feist.

The distinctive original music for the series was composed by Russ Landau and David Vanacore.

SUSPENSE

Mar. 1949–June 1950	CBS	Tues. 9:30–10 P.M.
Aug. 1950–Aug. 1954	CBS	Tues. 9:30–10 P.M.
Mar. 1964–Sept. 1964	CBS	Wed. 8:30–9 P.M.

Radio's most honored mystery/crime series, which was heard on CBS from 1942 until 1962, *Suspense* became a weekly half-hour TV series on CBS television in 1949, but remained on the air for only four years. Although it was revived in 1964 for a few additional months, the *Suspense* TV series never garnered the honors bestowed upon the radio show, which included a special citation from the Mystery Writers of America and a Peabody Award. TV's first *Suspense* series was telecast live from New York City and the shows, like the radio series, featured well-known stars of Hollywood films, as well as famous radio and TV performers in roles that were usually departures from the usual type of parts they played. All the stories on both the radio and TV versions of *Suspense* dealt with characters who were in dangerous and threatening situations. Occasionally, adaptations of famous novels and short stories were presented, but the scripts were usually original works written especially for the series. Among the various well-known performers seen on this series were Grace Kelly, Basil Rathbone, William Prince, Ralph Bell, Ernest Truex, John FORSYTHE, Peter Lorre, Nina Foch, Mildred Natwick, Tom Drake, Barry Sullivan, Bela Lugosi, Boris Karloff, John Carradine, Henry Hull, Arlene FRANCIS, Eva Gabor, Jackie COOPER, Cloris LEACHMAN, novelist Jacqueline Susann, and newsman Mike WALLACE, among many others. For a brief time in 1964, *Suspense* was revived after a 10-year absence from TV (the radio show was on the air continuously until 1962), but the series, which was hosted by Sebastian Cabot and featured such performers as Basil Rathbone, E. G. Marshall, James Daly, and Skip Homeier, was canceled after a seven-month tenure. The 1949–58 *Suspense* series was directed and produced for television by Bob Stevens.

SUSSKIND, DAVID (1920–1987)

The prolific television, stage, and motion picture producer David Susskind was also one of the most recognized talk show hosts on television and hosted a popular two-hour, syndicated issues-oriented TV program, *Open End,* also called *The DAVID SUSSKIND SHOW,* from 1958 until 1987. Susskind, who was born in Brookline, Massachusetts, was 27 years old when, realizing television was the entertainment medium of the future, he launched his production company, Talent Associates. From 1947 until his death in 1987, Susskind produced a wide variety of quality television shows, feature films, and Broadway shows, including TV series such as *The Armstrong Circle Theater, Justice* (1954), *Way Out* (1961), *Mr. Broadway* (1964), and *ALICE;* TV drama specials such as *Medea* (1959), *Death of a Salesman* (1966), *Johnny Belinda* (1967), *The Glass Menagerie* (1973), *Eleanor and Franklin* (1976), *Eleanor and Franklin: The White House Years* (1977), *Norman Conquests* (1978), *The Family Man* (1979); films such as *Edge of the City* (1957), *A Raisin in the Sun* (1961), *Requiem for a Heavyweight* (1962), *Lovers and Other Strangers* (1970), *A Hatful of Rain* (1968), *Alice Doesn't Live Here Anymore* (1974), and *Fort Apache, the Bronx* (1981); and stage plays such as *Rashomon* (1959).

SWIT, LORETTA (1937–)

Before Loretta Swit became well known to TV viewers as Major Margaret "Hot Lips" Houlihan on the successful TV series *M*A*S*H,* the stage-trained actress guest-starred on such series as MANNIX, MISSION: IMPOSSIBLE, GUNSMOKE, *The* BOLD ONES, LOVE, AMERICAN STYLE, HAWAII FIVE-O, BONANZA, IRONSIDE, and had minor roles in the films *Stand Up and Be Counted* (1972) and *Deadhead Miles* (1972). After eight years on *M*A*S*H,* Swit wanted to leave the series in order to star on the TV series CAGNEY AND LACEY, but the producers of *M*A*S*H* refused to release her from her contract. While she was appearing on *M*A*S*H,* Swit was also a semiregular panelist on the popular game/panel show MATCH GAME, and she also appeared in such films as *Freebie and the Bean* (1974) and *Race with the Devil* (1975), as well as in the TV films *The Last Day* (1975), *Friendship, Secrets and Lies* (1979), *Cagney and Lacey* (1981), and others. After *M*A*S*H* left the air in 1983, Swit continued to appear as a guest star on such TV series as MURDER, SHE WROTE, BURKE'S LAW, and DIAGNOSIS MURDER, and in such TV films as *The Best Christmas Pageant Ever* (1983), *First Affair* (1983), *Beer* (1985), *Dreams of Gold: The Mel Fisher Story* (1986), *A Matter of Principle* (1990), *Hell Hath No Fury* (1991), *A Killer Among Friends* (1992), and *Forest Warrior* (1996).

T

TALES OF WELLS FARGO

Mar. 1957–July 1957	NBC	Mon. 8:30–9 P.M.
Sept. 1957–Sept. 1961	NBC	Mon. 8:30–9 P.M.
Sept. 1961–Sept. 1962	NBC	Sat. 7:30–8:30 P.M.

Film actor Dale Robertson played Wells Fargo agent Jim Hardie, a troubleshooter for the stagecoach company that served passengers and companies who were traveling west during the 19th century. Hardie's assignments for Wells Fargo dealt with everything from helping employees of the company with personal problems to acting as an unofficial lawman who fought outlaws who robbed Wells Fargo stagecoaches. During the 1961–62 season, Hardie not only worked for Wells Fargo, but he also had bought a ranch in the San Francisco area, and the weekly episodes featured stories that usually involved Hardie's Wells Fargo job or his ranch. Hardie's ranch-owning neighbor was a woman named Widow Ovie, played by Virginia Christine. Ovie had two daughters, Mary Gee and Tina, played by Mary Jane Saunders and Lory Patrick. Hardie had also acquired a young assistant named Beau McLoud, played by Jack Ging, and a gruff but lovable ranch foreman named Jeb Gaine, played by veteran film character actor William Demarest. The show was originally produced by Earle Lyon for Overland Productions and Universal Television, and then by Nat Holt for Juggernaut Productions and Universal. One of the many young actors who made one of his earliest television appearances on this series was Academy Award winner Jack Nicholson.

TARZAN (ALSO TARZAN: THE EPIC ADVENTURES)

Sept. 1966	NBC	Thurs. 7:30–8:30 P.M.
Sept. 1966– Sept. 1968	NBC	Fri. 7:30–8:30 P.M.
June 1969– Sept. 1969	CBS	Wed. 7:30–8:30 P.M.
1991–1994	Syndicated	Various times and stations

Tarzan: THE EPIC ADVENTURE:

1996–1997	Syndicated	Various times and stations

Edgar Rice Burroughs's celebrated tale of a boy who is found and raised by apes when his parents are killed in an airplane accident arrived on television for the first time in 1966 with Ron Ely playing the title role of Tarzan. Ely was actually the 14th actor to play the role, 13 other actors, including Elmo Lincoln in silent films and Buster Crabbe, Lex Barker, Johnny Weismuller, Gordon Scott, and others, having previously played the role in sound feature films. This adventure series, produced by Banner Productions, set in the jungles of Africa but actually filmed in Brazil and Mexico, involved the adventures of the Ape Man, Tarzan, who had been born the English earl of Greystoke, who after being found and taken to England to be educated, returned to the jungle where he had been raised by apes in order to protect the rights of the African natives and animal friends from poachers, renegade tribesmen, and other evil interlopers who visited the jungle.

On the original television series, Tarzan's closest friends were a small orphan boy named Jai, played by Manuel Padilla, Jr., whom he had taken under his wing and, of course, his pet chimpanzee, Cheetah, who, as in the films, was his constant companion. Also featured on the series were Alan Cailow as Jai's tutor, Jason Flood, and Rocke Tarkington as a veterinarian named Rao. Jane, who became Tarzan's wife in several of the *Tarzan* feature films, did not appear on the TV series. After a 22-year absence,

Tarzan (Author's collection)

Tarzan returned to television in 1991 in a syndicated series that starred Wolf Larsen as Tarzan, Lydie Denier as his resurrected female companion, Jane Porter, and Sean Roberge as Roger Taft, Jr., a boy who like Tarzan was lost in the jungle as a baby, and whom Tarzan and Jane adopt. The series also featured a chimp named Cheetah. In 1996, a third TV version of *Tarzan* appeared on American home screens that was titled *Tarzan: The Epic Adventure,* and 75 episodes of this series were filmed in Yucatán. This series starred Joe Lara as Tarzan, Aaron Seville as a character named Themba, Don McLeod as Bolgani, Nkhensani Mangahyi as Tasi, and Angela Harry as La. Unlike the previous *Tarzan* series, this program was actually filmed in Africa at Sun City Studios in South Africa. The series was canceled after 22 episodes were released.

TAXI

Sept. 1978–Oct. 1980	ABC	Tues. 9:30–10 P.M.
Nov. 1980–Jan. 1981	ABC	Wed. 9–9:30 P.M.
Feb. 1981–June 1982	ABC	Thurs. 9:30–10 P.M.
Sept. 1982–Dec. 1982	NBC	Thurs. 9:30–10 P.M.
Jan. 1983–Feb. 1983	NBC	Sat. 9:30–10 P.M.
Mar. 1983–May 1983	NBC	Wed. 9:30–10 P.M.
June 1983–July 1983	NBC	Wed. 10:30–11 P.M.

Taxi was a successful situation comedy series that had a large and loyal following. This series, which mainly took place in New York City's Sunshine Cab Company headquarters, where taxi drivers picked up their cabs, grabbed a bite to eat, and chatted before going to work, was an excellent example of ensemble acting. The cast of characters included a middle-aged career cabbie, Alex Rieger, played by Judd HIRSCH; a struggling actor, Bobby Wheeler, played by Jeff Conaway (1978–81); a young boxer who worked as a cabdriver while waiting for the big bout, Tony Banta, played by Tony DANZA; John Burns, played by Randall Carver (1978–79), an aspiring art dealer; Elaine Nardo, played by Marilu HENNER; a diminutive, sadistic taxi dispatcher, Louie De Palma, played by Danny DeVITO; and a befuddled immigrant, Latka Gravas, from a fictitious eastern European country, who worked as a mechanic, played

The cast of *Taxi*: (sitting, left to right) Christopher Lloyd (Reverend Jim), Marilu Henner (Elaine), Judd Hirsch (Alex), and Danny DeVito (Louie); (standing, left to right) Tony Danza (Tony), Andy Kaufman (Latka), and Carol Kane (Simka) (Author's collection)

Taylor concentrated on acting on stage, but in 1949 Taylor appeared on the live dramatic anthology television series The PHILCO TELEVISION PLAYHOUSE in a production of Shakespeare's *Twelfth Night,* and began what was surely the busiest acting career on television and in films. In the late 1940s to early 1950s, Taylor was seen in hundreds of live dramas on such celebrated series as STUDIO ONE, PLAYHOUSE 90, *Kraft Television Theatre,* as well as *The Philco Television Playhouse.* Over the years, Taylor also guest-starred in hundreds of TV series such as PERRY MASON, RICHARD DIAMOND, PRIVATE DETECTIVE, WAGON TRAIN, CHEYENNE, GUNSMOKE, WANTED: DEAD OR ALIVE, BRONCO, *Colt .45,* The UNTOUCHABLES, RAWHIDE, The TWILIGHT ZONE, NAKED CITY, The VIRGINIAN, The FUGITIVE, The OUTER LIMITS, MY FAVORITE MARTIAN, The WILD, WILD WEST, The ANDY GRIFFITH SHOW, The F.B.I., PETTICOAT JUNCTION, GOMER PYLE, U.S.M.C., BEWITCHED, *Family Affair,* MAUDE, and The STREETS OF SAN FRANCISCO. He also had a regular role on the TV series as *Johnny Jupiter* (1953), and had featured roles in the films *Francis Goes to the Races* (1951), *Meet Danny Wilson* (1952), *Jailhouse Rock* (1957), *The Young Lions* (1958), *Cat on a Hot Tin Roof* (1958), *Blue Denim* (1959), *Psycho* (1960), *The Carpetbaggers* (1964), *The Unsinkable Molly Brown* (1964), *The Russians Are Coming, The Russians Are Coming* (1966), *In Cold Blood* (1967), and many others. Taylor's last film appearance was in *The Gumball Rally* in 1976.

TED MACK'S ORIGINAL AMATEUR HOUR
(see *Original Amateur Hour, The*)

by Andy KAUFMAN. Joining the cast of regulars in the show's second season were Christopher LLOYD as a spaced-out product of the 1960s, "Reverend" Jim Ignatowski; J. Alan Thomas as assistant dispatcher Jeff Bennett, who was on the series from 1980 until 1983; and Carol Kane as Latka's wife, Simka, who came from Latka's native country. *Taxi* won three Emmys as Outstanding Comedy Series, but in spite of this, the show's ratings began to drop after its fourth season, and the series moved from ABC to NBC in 1982. The biggest blow that the popular series received, however, was the unexpected death of Andy Kaufman. In addition to the contributions of *Taxi*'s talented cast of regulars, the series' success was in no small part due to the fact that it was created by Ed Weinberger, David Davis, Stan Daniels, and James L. Brooks, who had previously been on the staff of The MARY TYLER MOORE SHOW.

TAYLOR, VAUGHN (1910–1983)
Although his name is not as well known as his face, character actor Vaughn Taylor was one of television's busiest performers. Born in Boston, Massachusetts, Vaughn Taylor made his film debut in 1933 playing a small role in *Picture Snatcher.* Throughout the 1930s and early 1940s,

TENNESSEE ERNIE FORD SHOW (AKA *THE FORD SHOW STARRING TENNESSEE ERNIE FORD*)
Jan. 1955–June 1957	NBC	Thurs. 9:30–10 P.M.
Oct. 1957–June 1961	NBC	Thurs. 9:30–10 P.M.
Apr. 1962–Mar. 1965	ABC	Mon.–Fri. 9–9:30 A.M.

After hosting the local Los Angeles TV program *Hometown Jamboree* and a revival of Kay Kyser's *Kollege of Musical Knowledge* in the early 1950s, country singer Tennessee Ernie FORD starred on a half-hour variety show that featured Ernie singing country, western, and gospel songs, as well as appearing in comedy sketches. For two years, *The Ford Show,* sponsored by the Ford Motor Company, was a popular program, mainly due to Ernie's relaxed, casual demeanor and the small-town atmosphere of the show. Several of Tennessee Ernie's catchphrases, such as "Bless your pea-pickin' heart," were quoted throughout the country. In addition to Ford, also featured on the series regularly were the Voices of Walter Schumann choral group, the more contemporary "Top Twenty" singing group, and the Henry Geller Orchestra. Ford also starred on a syndicated series that was similar to his network show. The third TV series that bore his name was a daytime show on ABC and, in addition to Ford, featured regulars singers Anita Gordon and Dick Noel. Ford's NBC show was produced by Bud Yorkin.

$10,000 PYRAMID (AKA THE $20,000 PYRAMID, THE $25,000 PYRAMID, THE $50,000 PYRAMID, AND THE $100,000 PYRAMID)

Mar. 1973–Mar. 1974	CBS	Various times
May 1974–June 1980	ABC	Various times
Sept. 1982–July 1989	CBS	Various days and times
(also)		
1974–1979	Syndicated	
1985–1989	Syndicated	
1991	Syndicated	

The amount of money contestants on this game show could win, as well as the name of this show, changed as the program's popularity grew. The show was originally hosted by Bill CULLEN. John Davidson became the show's host for the 1991 series, but Dick CLARK hosted most of the series. It was produced by Bob Stewart Productions. Two teams that consisted of a contestant and a celebrity competed with each other to identify a series of words in a given category by supplying definitions of these words. The team with the higher score after three rounds then progressed to a second round where the procedure was reversed. If they got all the words right, they won the top money prize.

TEXACO STAR THEATER, THE

(see *Milton Berle Show, The*)

THAT GIRL

Sept. 1966–Apr. 1967	ABC	Thurs. 9:30–10 P.M.
Apr. 1967–Jan. 1969	ABC	Thurs. 9–9:30 P.M.
Feb. 1969–Sept. 1970	ABC	Thus. 8–8:30 P.M.
Sept. 1970–Sept. 1971	ABC	Fri. 9–9:30 P.M.

Well-known comedian Danny THOMAS's daughter, Marlo, had a popular TV situation comedy series on the air in the late 1960s to early 1970s called *That Girl*, which centered on a "new independent woman" of the 1960s named Ann Marie. Ann was a high-spirited young woman who had left the luxury of her parents' comfortable suburban home in Brewster, New York, to move to the "Big Apple" in order to pursue a career as an actress. Although she did get work in TV commercials and occasional small parts in plays, stardom evaded her. On the first episode of the series, Ann met a young man, Donald Hollinger, played by Ted Bessell, who was the junior executive for *Newsview* magazine and the two began to date. On the September 1970 episode, they finally, after a long courtship, became engaged, much to the show's loyal fans' delight. Other characters who appeared on the series regularly were Ann's mother and father, Lou and Helen Marie, played by Lew Parker and Rosemary DeCamp; Ann's neighbors, Judy and Dr. Leon Bessemer, played by Bonnie Scott and Dabney Coleman; Ann's acting coach, Jules, played by Billy DeWolfe; Ann's friend, Marcy, played by Reva Rose; Donald's parents Bert and Mildred Hollinger, played by Frank Faylen and Mabel Albertson; her friends, Ruth and Jerry Bauman, played by Carolyn Daniels, and then Alice Borden, and Bernie Kopell; her agents, Sandy Stone, Harvey Peck, and George Lester, played by Morty Gunty, Ronnie Schell, and George Carlin; and Seymour and Margie Schwimmer, played by Don Penny and Ruth Buzzi. *That Girl* was created by Bill Persky and Sam Denoff.

3RD ROCK FROM THE SUN

Jan. 1996–Apr. 1996	NBC	Tues. 8:30–9 P.M.
Apr. 1996–July 1996	NBC	Tues. 8–8:30 P.M.
July 1996–Aug. 1996	NBC	Thurs. 9:30–10 P.M.
Aug. 1996–Sept. 1997	NBC	Sun. 8–8:30 P.M.
Aug. 1997–Sept. 1997	NBC	Thurs. 9:30–10 P.M.
Sept. 1997–May 1998	NBC	Wed. 9–9:30 P.M.
Dec. 1997–Feb. 1998	NBC	Wed. 8–8:30 P.M.
May 1998–June 1998	NBC	Wed. 9–9:30 P.M.
June 1998–Dec. 1998	NBC	Wed. 9–9:30 P.M.
Dec. 1998–July 1999	NBC	Tues. 8–8:30 P.M.
May 1999–June 1999	NBC	Tues. 9:30–10 P.M.
July 1999–present	NBC	Tues. 8:30–9 P.M.

A surprise hit of the 1996–97 season, *3rd Rock from the Sun* surprised most of the critics who had made sport of its improbable premise when it became an audience favorite and made it into the top-30 Nielsen-rated shows its first year. On this series, four aliens had arrived on the planet Earth to observe the behavior of the inhabitants of the planet they called "the 3rd rock." Pretending to be typical Earthlings, the aliens changed their unearthly appearances to look like a typical human family they called the Solomons. The alien High Commander, played by John Lithgow, assumed the identity of Dr. Dick Solomon, a professor of physics at Pendelton University, located in Rutherford, Ohio. The three other aliens, the High Commander's second in command, a male lieutenant, played by Kristen Johnston, assumed the identity of Sally Solomon, and the two other aliens, played by French Stewart and Joseph Gordon-Levitt, assumed the identities of the nerdy Harry Solomon and the young teenager Tommy. The alien who became Tommy was actually older than the High Commander, which made for amusing reactions from Tommy the teen. Much of the show's comedy stemmed from the fact that the four aliens knew nothing about how they were supposed to act as humans, causing people around them to think that they were oddballs. Also starring on the series were Dr. Solomon's friend at the university, the stuffy Dr. Albright, played by Jane Curtin, who was usually sarcastic and somewhat odd herself. The High Commander's boss, the Big Giant Head, discouraged him from pursuing a relationship with Dr. Albright, whom he had a crush on. Other regular characters were Nina Campbell, Drs. Solomon's

The cast of *3rd Rock from the Sun*: (left to right) Kirsten Johnston, John Lithgow, French Stewart, Joseph Gordon-Levitt, and Jane Curtin (Author's collection)

and Albright's spirited secretary, played by Simbi Khall; Alissa Strudwick, the daughter of a faculty member, played by Larissa Oleynik; Mrs. Mamie Dubcek, the Solomon's landlady, played by Elmarie Wendel; her daughter, Vicki, played by Jan Hooks; and during the 1997 season, Officer Don, Sally's boyfriend, played by Wayne Knight. During the first several years *3rd Rock from the Sun* was aired, its major actors consistently won Emmy Awards.

THIRTYSOMETHING

Sept. 1987–Sept. 1988	ABC	Tues. 10–11 P.M.
Dec. 1988–May 1991	ABC	Tues. 10–11 P.M.
July 1991–Sept. 1991	ABC	Tues. 10–11 P.M.

Thirtysomething was a comedy/drama series that kept returning, months after it had supposedly telecast its last show, due to audience appeal. The series centered on seven thirty-something yuppies. Created by Ed Zwick and Marshall Herskovitz, who were baby boomers themselves and had previously written the successful TV series *FAMILY*, the seven central characters were longtime friends. Four of the seven were married couples when the series began and three were single. They included wife and mother Hope Murdock (Mel Harris), who had taken time off from being a freelance writer to raise her children; Hope's husband, Michael Steadman, an advertising executive, played by Ken Olin; Elliot Weston, Mike's business partner, played by Timothy Busfield; Elliot's wife, Nancy, played by Patricia Wettig; Helen's best friend, Ellyn Warren, an administrator at City Hall, played by Polly Draper; Michael's cousin, Melissa Steadman, a photographer, played by Melanie Mayron; and Gary Shepherd, a college teacher, played by Peter Horton. Also appearing on the series regularly were Jade Mortimer (1987), and then Britany and Lacey Craven (1988–91), as Hope and Michael's young daughter, Jane; Luke Rossi as Elliot and Nancy's son, Ethan; and Jordana "Bink" Shapiro (1987–90), and then Lindsay Riddell (1990–91), as Elliot and Nancy's daughter, Hope. Well-reviewed by TV critics, *thirtysomething* won a Peabody Award in 1988, but in spite of this, the series failed to attract a large enough audience for ABC to keep it on the air.

THIS IS YOUR LIFE

Oct. 1952–	NBC	Wed. 10–10:30 P.M.
June 1953		
June 1953–	NBC	Tues. 9:30–10 P.M.
Aug. 1953		
July 1953–	NBC	Wed. 9:30–10 P.M.
June 1958		
Sept. 1958–	NBC	Wed. 10:00–10:30 P.M.
Sept. 1960		
Sept. 1960–	NBC	Sun. 10:30–11 P.M.
Sept. 1961		
1970–1972	Syndicated	Various times and stations
1983–1984	Syndicated	Various times and stations

For 10 seasons, *This Is Your Life*, which had made its debut as a radio show in 1948, was one of television viewers' favorite programs. Each week, for a half-hour, the show's host, Ralph EDWARDS, who created and produced the series, would surprise a guest celebrity who had been duped into appearing on camera on some false pretense and announced, "This is your life . . . " as he held a book that contained the details of the well-known person's life. The show was a winning combination of nostalgia, sentimentality, and tribute, and celebrated the life of the stunned and often tearful celebrity. People and events from their lives and careers were paraded before them with dizzying speed, aided by film clips and photos from the past. Film legends Stan Laurel and Oliver Hardy, Broadway star Eddie Cantor, educator Laurence C. Jones, news commentator Lowell Thomas, comedians Bob HOPE and Milton BERLE, film actresses Elizabeth Taylor and Ginger Rogers, and many, many others were among those who were honored on this show. One of the most memorable tributes was paid to singer Lillian Roth, who had survived many ups and downs during her life, including stage and film stardom and a bout with alcoholism; the program led to a brief revival of her career and a successful film about her life. The show was briefly revived in 1981 and 1983 with David FROST and then Joseph Campanella acting as show hosts. *This Is Your Life* also aired two TV specials, both hosted by Ralph Edwards, and both seen in 1987, that honored Dick VAN DYKE and Betty WHITE. Another *This Is Your Life* TV special was aired in 1993 and was hosted by Pat SAJAK. This special honored Kathie Lee GIFFORD and Roy Scheider.

THIS OLD HOUSE

1979–present PBS Various times (usually Saturdays)

The original host of this Public Broadcasting System series that featured old homes being restored to their former glory by expert carpenters, decorators, and gardeners was Bob Vila, whose name became synonymous with old-house restoration. All sorts of houses are shown, from Colonial homes to Victorian mansions, suburban ranch houses, and Greek revival farmhouses. As the show continued, the *Old House* team began to film renovation projects in such diverse places as London, New Orleans, and Hawaii. In 1983, *This Old House* even showed the construction of an entire house from start to finish. A regular member of the construction team was master carpenter Norm Abram, who, although he continued to contribute to this series, went on to star on his own woodworking PBS series *The New Yankee Workshop*. In the spring of 1989, Bob Vila was dropped as host of this series because of his promotion of several products on the show, which the producers of the program, the Morash Company, considered inappropriate. Vila was replaced by Steve Thomas, who continues to perform the hosting chores on the show as of this writing.

THOMAS, DANNY (AMOS MUZYAD JAHOUB 1914–1991)

Comedian, actor, and producer Danny Thomas, who was born to immigrant Lebanese parents in Deerfield, Michigan, began his career in show business as a stand-up nightclub comic and singer in the 1940s. Thomas first appeared in films in 1947 in *The Unfinished Dance,* and subsequently made his TV debut as one of the stars of the FOUR STAR REVUE in 1950. In the early 1950s, Thomas had major roles in such films as *I'll See You in My Dreams* (1951), *Call Me Mister* (1951), and *The Jazz Singer* (1952, which was a remake of the 1920s film that originally starred Al Jolson). In 1953, Thomas starred on a TV series that was an enormous success and made him one of the best-known performers in America, MAKE ROOM FOR DADDY, which was renamed *The DANNY THOMAS SHOW* in 1957, and remained on the air for eight seasons. In 1967, Thomas starred on the short-lived *Danny Thomas Hour* variety show, and then in 1970 on *Make Room for Granddaddy,* reviving his Danny Williams role. Thomas also became a regular on a series that, like a current series, was called *The Practice,* which was aired from 1976 through 1977. In addition to his TV appearances on such shows as *The Lucy-Desi Comedy Hour,* ZANE GREY THEATER, *The DICK VAN DYKE SHOW,* *The Joey Bishop Show,* MCCLOUD, HAPPY DAYS, KOJAK, and EMPTY NEST. Thomas, with his partner Sheldon Leonard, also became one of television's most successful producers and was mainly responsible for the success of such series as *The Dick Van Dyke Show, The ANDY GRIFFITH SHOW,* and *The MOD SQUAD.* In 1986, Thomas returned to the front of the cameras in *One Big Family,* which was less than well received by TV critics. Throughout his life, Thomas was active on behalf of various charities and was instrumental in the building of the St. Jude's Children's Research Hospital in Memphis, Tennessee. Thomas was once quoted as saying, "Success has nothing to do with what you gain in life or accomplish for yourself. It's what you do for others."

THOMAS, FRANKIE (FRANK M. THOMAS 1921–   )

Frankie Thomas's main claim to fame came from playing Space Cadet Tom Corbett on the TOM CORBETT, SPACE

CADET children's adventure series in the early 1950s. Thomas, who was the son of an actress named Mona Burns, was born in New York City and began his career as a child, appearing in such films as *Wednesday's Child* (1934), *A Dog of Flanders* (1935), *Tim Tyler's Luck* (1937), *Nancy Drew, Detective* (1938), *Boys Town* (1938), *Code of the Streets* 1939), *The Dead End Kids on Dress Parade* (1939), *The Major and the Minor* (1942), and others. After *Tom Corbett, Space Cadet* left the air, Thomas retired from show business and did not resurface as an actor until 1998, when he re-created his role of Tom Corbett as an elderly space traveler in the film *The Mercurian Invasion*.

THOMAS, MARLO (MARGARET JULIA THOMAS 1937–)

The daughter of well-known film and TV actor and producer Danny THOMAS, Marlo Thomas was born in Detroit, Michigan, and made her TV debut as an actress on *The MANY LOVES OF DOBIE GILLIS* in 1960. She subsequently appeared on such series as *The ZANE GREY THEATER, THRILLER*, and *MY FAVORITE MARTIAN*, and was a regular on *The Joey Bishop Show* from 1961 through 1962. In 1966, Thomas starred on her own TV series, *THAT GIRL*, playing an aspiring actress named Ann Marie. The series was a success and remained on the air for five seasons. In 1975, Thomas starred on *The Dream Factory*. She made guest appearances on such series as *ROSEANNE, FRIENDS*, and *FRASIER* from 1988 through 1993, and also starred in such specials and TV films as *The Human Body: Facts for Girls* (1980), *The Lost Honor of Kathryn Beck* (1984), *Consenting Adult* (1985), *Nobody's Child* (1986), *Held Hostage: The Sis and Jerry Levin Story* (1991), *Reunion* (1994), as well as in *Playing Mona Lisa* (2000). Thomas was one of the narrators, with her husband, talk show host Phil DONAHUE, of the TV miniseries *A Century of Women* (1994).

THOMAS, RICHARD (1951–)

The son of professional ballet dancers, Richard Thomas, who is best known for playing John Boy on the popular *WALTONS* TV series in the 1970s, was born in New York City. Thomas made his acting debut when he was eight years old playing the title character in a stage production of *Oliver Twist*. In 1961, Thomas was a regular on the *1,2,3, Go* TV series, and later joined the cast of the soap opera *AS THE WORLD TURNS* in 1966. After appearing in such films as *Winning* (1969), *Last Summer* (1969), *You'll Like My Mother* (1971), and *Red Sky at Morning* (1971), Thomas appeared in a TV film *The Homecoming: A Christmas Story* in 1971, the inspiration for *The Waltons*, which became one of television's most popular programs in the 1970s. While appearing on *The Waltons*, Thomas also starred in such TV films as *The Red Badge of Courage* (1974) and *The Silence* (1975), and after *The Waltons* left the air in 1981, he continued to be active in such films as *Getting Married* (1978), *No Other Love* (1979), as well as in such TV films as *Roots: The Next Generations* (1979),

All Quiet on the Western Front (1979), *Johnny Belinda* (1982), *Hobson's Choice* (1983), *It* (1990), *Yes Virginia, There Is a Santa Claus* (1991), *The Christmas Box* (1995), *Beyond the Prairie: The True Story of Laura Ingalls Wilder* (2000), and *Wonder Boys* (2000). Thomas also revived his John Boy Walton role on two television specials in 1993 and 1995, *A Walton Thanksgiving Reunion* and *A Walton Wedding*. Over the years, Thomas has guest-starred on such TV series as *BONANZA, The F.B.I., Night Gallery, The OUTER LIMITS, Promised Land*, and *The PRACTICE*.

THREE'S COMPANY

Mar. 1977–Apr. 1977	ABC	Thurs. 9:30–10 P.M.
Aug. 1977–Sept. 1977	ABC	Thurs. 9:30–10 P.M.
Sept. 1977–May 1984	ABC	Thurs. 9–9:30 P.M.
May 1984–Sept. 1984	ABC	Thurs. 8:30–9 P.M.

Few people in the television industry thought that a situation comedy about two women rooming in an apartment in Santa Monica, California, with a young man who went along with their landlord's belief that he was gay in order to make their living arrangement more acceptable to others, would be a hit. They were wrong, and *Three's Company* in its third season on the air became the second most

Three's Company: (clockwise from top) John Ritter (Jack Tripper), Suzanne Somers (Chrissy Snow), Joyce DeWitt (Janet Wood), Norman Fell (Stanley Roper), and Audra Lindley (Helen Roper) (Author's collection)

popular show on TV, according to the Nielsen ratings. The two female roommates, Janet Wood and Chrissy Snow, played by Joyce DEWITT and Suzanne SOMERS, were entirely different. Janet was a brunette, a serious, and intellectual florist, and Chrissy was a blonde, sensual, and flighty secretary, who was hired more for her looks than for her secretarial abilities. Their male roommate, Jack Tripper, played by John RITTER, was a secretary, who, when the series first went on the air, was a caterer. During the series he opened up his own restaurant, "The Little Bistro." Norman Fell played the group's befuddled landlord, Stanley Roper, and Audra Lindley played his sex-starved but patient wife, Helen. The Ropers became so popular with viewers that after two seasons they were given a series of their own, appropriately called The ROP-ERS. Richard Kline played Jack's best friend, Larry Dallas, from 1978 until the series left the air in 1984, and Don KNOTTS was added to the regular cast as the trio's even more befuddled landlord, Ralph Farley, when the Ropers went on to bigger and better things. Ann Wedgeworth was a regular on the series during the 1979–80 season, playing Jack, Janet and Chrissy's flighty neighbor, Lana Shields, who was a buyer for a department store. Before the 1980–81 season began, Suzanne Somers demanded a large salary increase, from $30,000 to $150,000 an episode, and a share of Three's Company's profits. The producers, Don Nicholl, Michael Ross, and Bernie West, refused her demands and held her to the final year of her contract, but she appeared only briefly talking on the telephone each week, and Jenilee Harrison was added to the cast in the fall of 1980 as Chrissy's cousin, Cindy Snow, who moved into the Santa Monica apartment with Jack and Janet. Priscilla Barnes joined the cast in the fall of 1981 as Jack and Janet's new roommate, Terri Alden, a nurse. Even though the series managed to remain on the air for three more seasons, without Somers, the public's interest in the show waned, and so a sequel called Three's a Crowd surfaced, with only John Ritter from the original cast retained. The series also starred Mary Cadorette as Jack's love interest, Vicky Bradford. This series was canceled after a short time on the air. Three's Company was based on a British series called Man About the House.

THRILLER

Sept. 1960–Sept. 1961	NBC	Tues. 9–10 P.M.
Sept. 1961–July 1962	NBC	Mon. 10–11 P.M.

Horror film star Boris Karloff was the host and sometimes leading player on this suspense-filled anthology series that presented stories of everyday people who found themselves trapped in terrifying situations. The series, which was on the air for two seasons, was originally produced by Fletcher Markle. Hubbell Robinson was the series' executive producer for Revue Studios. Robinson was replaced by Maxwell Shane. The series featured relatively unknown actors in major roles on most of the show's weekly, hour-long dramas.

TILLSTROM, BURR (FRANKLIN BURR TILLSTROM 1917–1985)

Burr Tillstrom was a pioneer puppeteer whose innovative KUKLA, FRAN & OLLIE is among the most beloved and most fondly remembered children's programs ever presented on TV. Tillstrom first became interested in puppets when he was a boy. A talented artist, Tillstrom, who was born in Chicago, created puppets for display at the 1930 Chicago World's Fair and made his television debut in 1947 on a local Chicago TV puppet show called Junior Jamboree. The show became so popular with viewers in the Chicago area that NBC gave Tillstrom a network show of his own, on which his puppets talked to a live actress, Fran ALLISON, as they did on his local show. Kukla, Fran & Ollie, became an instant hit and established Tillstrom as one of the world's most famous puppeteers, leading the way for later-to-be-famous puppeteers like Jim Henson, of Muppet fame, who acknowledged Tillstrom's contributions to puppetry. In addition to his regular, long-running Kukla, Fran & Ollie series, which was on the air from 1948 until 1971 and won two Peabody and three Emmy Awards, Tillstrom also produced and directed the TV series The Wizard of Oz in 1950 and was a frequent guest performer on such shows as NBC's YOUR SHOW OF SHOWS in 1952 and 1953. Throughout the 1960s, 70s, and early 80s, Tillstrom continued to appear as a guest star on numerous TV shows, was seen in several TV commercials, and was a frequent public service announcement spokesman until his death in 1985 at the age of 68.

TO TELL THE TRUTH

Dec. 1956–Sept. 1958	CBS	Tues. 9–9:30 P.M.
Sept. 1958–Sept. 1959	CBS	Tues. 8:30–9 P.M.
Oct. 1959–June 1960	CBS	Thurs. 7:30–8 P.M.
July 1960–Sept. 1960	CBS	Thurs. 10:30–11 P.M.
Sept. 1960–Sept. 1966	CBS	Mon. 7:30–8 P.M.
Dec. 1966–May 1967	CBS	Mon. 10–11 P.M.

Mark GOODSON and Bill TODMAN produced this long-running TV panel/game show that had three contestants all claiming to be one person who had done something unique. The show's panelists, by asking questions of the three contestants, only one of whom was who they said they were, tried to guess who was the person whose accomplishments had been described by the show's host. Bud COLLYER was To Tell the Truth's host for the entire 11 years it was aired on CBS. Celebrity panelists on the show included Polly Bergen (1956–61), Hy Gardner (1956–59), Hildy Parks (1956–57), Kitty Carlisle, Ralph Bellamy (1957–59), Tom Poston (1958–67), Orson Bean (1964–67), and Peggy Cass (1964–67). In 1990, NBC revived To Tell the Truth as a daytime offering with Gordon Elliott acting as the show's host, but the revival was short-lived and left the air six months after its debut.

TOAST OF THE TOWN, THE

(see Ed Sullivan Show, The)

TODAY

Jan. 1952–present   NBC   Mon.–Fri. Mornings

NBC's early morning news magazine show, *Today*, which was the first series of its kind on television, made its debut in 1952 and has been one of the most profitable shows for the NBC network. Created by Sylvester "Pat" Weaver, an executive at NBC, *Today* was a show designed for viewers who had to get ready to go to work or school and could watch only portions of the two-hour early morning telecast. The news of the day was given every half-hour, and other features, such as sports, the weather report, interviews with people in the news (politicians, actors, and citizens who had made the headlines), and special features were sandwiched in between the news breaks, which reported both national, and then local (from local network stations) news. The first host of the *Today* show was Dave GARROWAY, who had been a radio newscaster in Pittsburgh, and had a relaxed informal style that Weaver knew would appeal to early morning viewers. Assisting Garroway was Jack Lescoule, who gave the sports news and light features. Jim Fleming read the news of the day. The show was telecast live from the ground floor of the RCA Exhibition Hall on West 49th Street in New York City. In 1953, a lovable chimpanzee named J. Fred Muggs, who was usually dressed in human attire, joined the regular cast of the *Today* show and became one of the program's major attractions. In 1953, Jim Fleming was replaced by Frank Blair, who remained the *Today* shows newscaster for the next 22 years. Barbara WALTERS joined the cast as the first "Today Girl." Other "Today Girls" who appeared with Garroway over the next several years included actress Estelle Parsons, Lee Ann Merriweather, Helen O'Connell, Betsy Palmer, Florence Henderson, Robin Bain, Beryl Pinter, and Anita Colby. Dave Garroway left the show in 1961 and John CHANCELLOR became the *Today* show's new host. Appearing with Chancellor were Edwin Newman, who read the news, Louise King who was the new "Today Girl," and Frank Blair, who reluctantly remained on the show. Chancellor was succeeded by Hugh DOWNS in 1962. Frank Blair returned to the news desk and Jack Lescoule returned to the show for one year, and Barbara Walters began appearing on the show again as a news feature commentator and interviewer. In 1964, actress Maureen O'Sullivan joined the cast as the new "Today Girl," but left the show after a few months. Also in 1964, film and Broadway critics Judith Crist and Arline Saarinen became regulars on the show, and also joining the cast was former baseball catcher Joe Garagiola. In 1971, Downs left the show and was replaced by Frank McGee, who was subsequently replaced in 1974 by Jim Hartz. Film critic Gene Shalit joined the cast in 1974. Tom BROKAW became the show's host in 1976. Floyd Kalber read the news. Barbara Walters left the show in 1976, and succeeding her were Cassie Mackin, Betty Rolin, Linda Ellerbee, Kelly Lange, Betty Furness, and finally, Jane Pauley, who remained on the show longer than any of the others. Tony Guida replaced Floyd Kalber in 1977, and the jovial John Willard Scott, who succeeded Bob Ryan, became the show's new weatherman Tom Brokaw left the show in 1982 and was replaced by sportscaster Bryant Gumbel, and Deborah Norville read the news. In 1989, Jane Pauley left the show, and a memo from Bryant Gumbel criticizing popular fellow cast members Willard Scott and Gene Shalit was leaked to the press and the show's popularity began to decline. Katie Couric became the series' morning show coanchor in 1991. Al Roker eventually joined the show as its major weatherman and special features contributor and occasional cohost, although Willard Scott continued to be seen on occasion, and eventually, Gumbel was replaced by Matt Laurer.

TODMAN, BILL
(see Goodson, Mark)

TOM CORBETT, SPACE CADET

Oct. 1950–Dec. 1950	CBS	Mon./Wed./Fri. 6:45–7 P.M.
Jan. 1951–Sept. 1952	ABC	Mon./Wed./Fri. 6:30–6:45 P.M.
July 1951–Sept. 1951	NBC	Sat. 7–7:30 P.M.
Aug. 1953–May 1954	DuMont	Sat. A.M. hours
Dec. 1954–June 1955	NBC	Sat. A.M. hours

Even though it was aired on prime-time network television for only one year, *Tom Corbett, Space Cadet* remained on the air as a Saturday morning offering for another four years. One of the few TV shows to be seen

Tom Corbett, Space Cadet: Jan Merlin, Frankie Thomas, and Jack Grimes (Author's collection)

on all three major networks, *Tom Corbett, Space Cadet* was directed toward younger viewers. A science fiction adventure series that was set in the 2350s, this series took place at the Space Academy, a training school for "Solar Guards," who were being trained to patrol the universe. The series starred Frankie THOMAS as Tom Corbett, a young cadet at the academy, and Edward Bryce as Tom's mentor, Captain Steve Strong. Also appearing on the series were Jan Merlin and Jack Grimes as Tom's fellow cadets, Roger Manning and T. J. Thistle; Patricia Ferris, and then Margaret Garland, as Dr. Joan Dale; John Fiedler as Cadet Alfie Higgins; Frank Sutton as Cadet Attison; Denise Alexander as Tom's sister, Betty Corbett; Norma Clarke as Cadet Jo Spencer; and Al Markim as Astro, an alien Venusian crew member who served on the training spacecraft, *Polaris*. *Tom Corbett, Space Cadet* was one of the first television series to promote the sale of numerous products that used the show's title, including the best-selling academic educational aid, "The 20th Century Aid—The Study Machine." The series was based on a novel simply titled *Space Cadet*, which was written by the celebrated science fiction author Robert A. Heinlein.

TONIGHT SHOW, THE (AKA TONIGHT: AMERICA AFTER DARK, TONIGHT, THE JACK PAAR SHOW, AND THE TONIGHT SHOW STARRING JOHNNY CARSON)

Sept. 1954–Oct. 1956	NBC	Mon.–Fri. 11:30 P.M.–1 A.M.
Oct. 1956–Jan. 1957	NBC	Mon.–Fri. 11:30 P.M.–12:30 A.M.
Jan. 1957–Dec. 1964	NBC	Mon.–Fri. 11:15 P.M.–1 A.M.
Jan. 1965–Sept. 1966	NBC	Sun. 11:15 P.M.–1 A.M.
Sept. 1966–Sept. 1975	NBC	Sat. or Sun. 11:30 P.M.–1 A.M.
Jan. 1967–Sept. 1980	NBC	Fri. 11:30 P.M.–1 A.M.
Sept. 1980–Aug. 1991	NBC	Mon.–Fri. 11:30 P.M.–12:30 A.M.
Sept. 1991–present	NBC	Mon.–Fri. 11:35 P.M.–12:30 A.M.

The long-running NBC *Tonight Show*, which was a local offering on WNBT-TV in the New York City area, was originally hosted by Steve ALLEN, who remained with the show when it became an NBC late evening network program in 1957. When it was first aired on national TV, *Tonight* was an informal program that began each telecast with Allen sitting at a piano, chatting and playing some of his own songs (the most famous being "This Could Be the Start of Something Big"). Allen began what became a *Tonight Show* tradition, which was sitting at a desk and proceeding to chat with his announcer, Gene RAYBURN, and the show's orchestra leader, Skitch Henderson, and then LeRoy Holmes, and talking to and acting in sketches with show regulars that included singers Steve Lawrence, Eydie Gorme, and Andy WILLIAMS, and Pat Marshall (1954–55), Pat Kirby (1955–57), Hy Averback (1955),

Peter Hanley (1956–57), Maureen Arthur (1956–57), Bill Wendell (1956–57), and Barbara Loden (1956–57). Allen was also one of the first talk show hosts to talk directly to members of the studio audience, and to have remote broadcasts from outside the studio. A series of guest hosts, including comedian Ernie KOVACS, filled in for Allen when his busy schedule prohibited his appearing on the show. When Allen left the show in 1957, NBC tried a different format similar to NBC's popular early morning TODAY show, but it failed, and within six months was abandoned. Featured on this short-lived show at different times were Judy Johnson, the Lou Stein Trio, the Mort Lindsey Quartet, the Johnny Guanieri Quartet, columnists Hy Gardner, Bob Considine, Earl Wilson, and Irv Kupcinet, who went on to host a popular talk show that originated in Chicago, Vernon Scott, Paul Coates, and Lee Girous.

When the critics and public showed little interest in the new format, NBC returned to Steve Allen's concept and hired a young comedian named Jack PAAR to host the program. The show's name was later changed from *Tonight* to *The Jack Paar Show*, when Paar became a favorite of TV viewers. Paar, unlike Allen, concentrated on interviews and gathered a talented group of regulars around him that included announcer Hugh DOWNS, Jose Melis and His Orchestra, Tedi Thurman (1957), and comedienne Dody Goodman (1957–58). Within time, regular visits by such diverse performers as society partygiver Elsa Maxwell, Bill Baird's puppets, singer Betty Johnson, Gallic charmer Genevieve, actors Cliff Arquette as Charley Weaver and Pat Harrington, Jr., as Guido Panzini, talented radio and TV actor Hans CONRIED, comic actress Peggy Cass, Alexander King, comedian Joey Bishop, outrageous character actress/comedienne Hermione Gingold, Broadway and later TV star Florence HENDERSON, comedian Buddy Hackett, actress and writer Renee Taylor, and actress/TV personality Betty WHITE made *The Jack Paar Show* late night's most popular program. Among the features Paar introduced were his popular "It's All Relative" (a relative of a famous person would appear on the show and other guests would try to guess whom he or she was related to) and "What Is It?" (guests would try to guess what a strange-looking object was). Paar became well known for his emotional outbursts, as well as for his on-the-air feuds with such personalities as acerbic columnist Dorothy Kilgallen and columnist/TV show host ED SULLIVAN. In 1962, Paar decided that he had had enough of hosting the late evening show and made a surprise announcement that he would not be returning for the 1962–63 season. Paar's announcer, Hugh Downs, valiantly tried to keep the show going without Paar, and it was retitled *The Tonight Show*. Singer Jack Haskell and announcer Ed Herlihy gave Downs support, but in five months Downs left the show and was replaced by comedian Johnny CARSON, who enjoyed the longest run as the host of the late night show.

Carson's program, which became *The Tonight Show with Johnny Carson*, made its debut on October 1, 1962, and the comedian returned to the format established by

Steve Allen and continued by Jack Paar. Among Carson's regulars was announcer and sidekick Ed McMahon, whose nightly "Here's Johnny" heralded the entrance of the show's star, who began each show with a nightly stand-up comedy routine that usually centered on the news of the day. Skitch Henderson and His Orchestra was a holdover from previous *Tonight* shows, and then came Milton Delugg (1966–67), Doc Severinsen (1967–92), and on occasion Tommy Newman (1962–82). In addition to an impressive roster of celebrity guests, Carson also appeared in regular sketches such as "Carnac the Magnificent" (as a turban-wearing inept mind reader), "The Mighty Carson Art Players," "Aunt Blabby," "Stump the Band," "Carswell" (who predicted future events), "Faharishi" (with Carson as a yogi), "The Great Carsoni," "The Art Fern Tea Time Movie" (with Carol Wayne as the original "Matinee Lady"), and "Floyd R. Turbo," the superpatriot, to name just a few. One of the most publicized shows featured the on-the-air marriage of oddball singer Tiny Tim, whose rendition of the standard tune "Tip Toe Through the Tulips" briefly made him a "star," to a woman named "Miss Vicki." In 1992, after an impressive 20 years as the star of the *Tonight Show,* Carson, much to the dismay of his legion of fans, announced that it was to be his final season on the air. Johnny's final guest on his last show, which was seen on May 22, 1992, was singer/actress Bette Midler, who wistfully sang to a tearful Johnny about how "there [would] never be another quite like [him]."

Johnny Carson's replacement, after much speculation, (many felt it would be comedian David LETTERMAN), was to the surprise of many his oft-time substitute hosts, Jay LENO, who took over the show on May 25, 1992. Leno's new group of regulars included Branford Marsalis (1992–95), Kevin Eubanks (1995–) and his off-camera announcer, Edd Hall. Among Leno's regular skits that soon became popular were "Ask Jay Anything," "Police Blotter," "Iron Jay" (which had Leno dressed as a heavily padded muscle man), "Mr. Brain" (the smartest man in the universe, which showed Jay as a man whose head was bigger than the rest of him), "Jaywalking" (a man-in-the-street segment), and "Evil Jay," who depicted Leno's evil alter ego.

TONY ORLANDO AND DAWN (AKA *TONY ORLANDO AND DAWN RAINBOW HOUR,* THE)

July 1974	CBS	Wed. 8–9 P.M.
Dec. 1974–June 1976	CBS	Wed. 8–9 P.M.
Sept. 1976–Dec. 1976	CBS	Tues. 8–9 P.M.

For two seasons, the pop singing group Tony Orlando and Dawn, after several hit records that included "Tie a Yellow Ribbon 'Round the Old Oak Tree," became the hosts of a one-hour, weekly variety series on CBS. The show, which featured songs by Orlando and two female backup singers called "Dawn" (Telma Hopkins and Joyce Vincent Wilson), who also appeared in various comedy sketches with each other and various guest stars, filled a time slot that had been vacated by singers Sonny (Bono)

and CHER. In their first year on the air, the show proved very popular with viewers. During the show's second season, its title was changed to *The Tony Orlando and Dawn Rainbow Hour.* Comedian George Carlin became a regular on the show, and the emphasis was more on comedy than on music. The series was canceled before the end of its second season. Also appearing on the series regularly were Alice Nunn, Lonnie Schoer, the Jerry Jackson Singers, and the Bob Rozario Orchestra. Other performers were Adam Wade (1976), Nancy Stern (1976), Bob Holt (1976), Susan Lanier (1976), Jimmy Martinez (1976), and Edie McClurg (1976). Saul Ilson and Ernest Chambers produced the series.

TOO CLOSE FOR COMFORT/THE TED KNIGHT SHOW

Nov. 1980– Sept. 1982	ABC	Tues. 9:30–10 P.M.
Sept. 1982– June 1983	ABC	Thurs. 9–9:30 P.M.
Aug. 1983– Sept. 1983	ABC	Thurs. 8:30–9 P.M.
Sept. 1983	ABC	Thurs. 8–8:30 P.M.
Jan. 1984–1986	Syndicated	Various times and stations

After his success playing newscaster Ted Baxter on *The MARY TYLER MOORE SHOW,* Ted Knight starred on a situation comedy series called *Too Close for Comfort,* playing a character named Henry Rush, who was not unlike Ted Baxter. The series was based on a successful British TV show called *Keep It in the Family.* Rush was a cartoonist who had created a comic strip called "Cosmic Cow." Rush's wife, Muriel, played by Nancy Dussault, was a professional photographer. The couple lived in a two-family house in San Francisco. When their tenant, a transvestite, died, the Rushes turned over the other apartment in their building to their two grown daughters, Jackie and Sarah, played by Deborah Van Valkenburgh and Lydia Cornell. Jackie worked in a bank and Sarah attended San Francisco State College. Also appearing as regulars on the series were Hamilton Camp (1981) as Rush's publicist, Arthur Wainwright; Jim J. Bullock as Sarah's often confused friend, Munroe Ficus; Deena Freeman (1981–82) as Henry's niece, April; and Audrey Meadows (1982–83) as Muriel's mother, Iris Martin. Much of the show's comedy was based on the fact that Henry found it difficult to accept the lifestyles of his grown daughters, which were far different from the type of life with which he was comfortable. When the series was canceled after the 1983–84 season, *Too Close for Comfort* made TV history when it became one of the first shows to continue the production of new episodes that were syndicated across the country. Joining the cast were Joshua Goodwin, who took over the role of Andrew; Pat Carroll, as Rush's new partner, Hope Simon; and Lisa Antille as Lisa Flores, the Rushes' housekeeper. The series remained on the air using a new title, *The Ted Knight Show,* until 1986, when Ted Knight succumbed to cancer.

TOPPER

Oct. 1953–Sept. 1955	CBS	Fri. 8:30–9 P.M.
Dec. 1955–Mar. 1956	NBC	Mon. 7:30–8 P.M.
June 1956–Oct. 1956	NBC	Sun. 7–7:30 P.M.

Topper, an early popular TV situation comedy that was seen on all three major networks, was based on a successful novel by Thorne Smith and a 1937 film comedy adaptation of the same name. The TV series starred Leo G. Carroll as Cosmo Topper, a stuffy banker who discovers that the new house he moves into is occupied by the ghosts of its previous owners, Marion and George Kirby, played by Anne Jeffreys and Robert Sterling, whom only Cosmo is able to see. The Kirbys had been killed in a skiing accident while celebrating their fifth wedding anniversary, and as spirits they had returned to their former home with their pet St. Bernard dog, Neil, who had also died in the accident. Much to the distress of Cosmo Topper's dithery wife, Henrietta Topper, played by Lee Patrick, Cosmo would often become engaged in conversations with the Kirbys. Also appearing on the series were veteran film character actor Thurston Hall as Topper's boss, Mr. Schuyler; Edna Skinner (1953–54) as the Topper's spooked maid Maggie; and then Kathleen Freeman (1954–55) as their maid Katy. *Topper* was produced by John W. Loveton and Bernard L. Schubert.

TORKLESONS, THE

Sept. 1991–Nov. 1991	NBC	Sat. 8:30–9 P.M.
Nov. 1991–Mar. 1992	NBC	Sun. 7:30–8 P.M.
May 1992–June 1992	NBC	Sat. 8:30–9 P.M.
Feb. 1993–July 1993	NBC	Sat. 8–8:30 P.M.

This poignant situation comedy series about a sensitive teenager who was embarrassed by her working-class family's financial difficulties attracted a considerable following during its two years on the air. The teenager, Dorothy Jane Torkleson, age 14, played by Olivia Burnette, aspired to be a "normal" teen, like most of her less underprivileged young friends. Dorothy's hard-working mother, Millicent Torkleson, played by Connie Ray, took care of her family as best she could when her husband walked out on the family, and tried to put the best spin on their situation while doing everything she could to hold onto the family's rambling old house in Pyramid Corners. Besides Dorothy, Millicent's other children were Steven Floyd Torkleson, age 12, played by Aaron Methick; Ruth Ann Torkleson, age 10, played by Anna Slotky; Chuckie Lee Torkleson, age eight, played by Lee Norris; and Mary Sue Torkleson, age six, played by Rachel Duncan. In order to help make ends meet, Millicent took in an elderly boarder who rented a room in the Torkleson basement, a kind and benevolent widower named Wesley Hodges, played by William Schallert. Also appearing on the series as regulars were Paige Gosney as Kirby Scroggins, Michael Landes as Riley Roberts, and Perry King as Brian Morgan for whom Millicent worked as a nanny for his obnoxious children, Molly and Gregory Morgan, played by Brittany Murphy and Jason Marsden. Somewhere along the way, between the show's first and second seasons, Millicent "lost" her children Steven and Ruth Ann, who disappeared from the show without explanation.

TOUCHED BY AN ANGEL

Sept. 1994–Dec. 1994	CBS	Wed. 9–10 P.M.
Feb. 1995–Mar. 1995	CBS	Sat. 9–10 P.M.
June 1995–Sept. 1996	CBS	Sat. 9–10 P.M.
Aug. 1996–Present	CBS	Sun. 8–9 P.M.

Generally panned by TV critics who felt the series was too saccharine and sentimental, the less demanding viewing public took *Touched by an Angel* to their hearts and made it one of TV's most popular weekly series. An apprentice angel named Monica, played by Irish-born actress Roma Downey, had just been promoted to "caseworker" when the series began and was given search-and-rescue missions by the powers in heaven. Her superior, an angel named Tess, played by Della Reese, looked over her charge, giving her advice and counsel as they traveled around the country in a vintage Cadillac convertible. Each week, the team of angels encountered people who needed their help sorting out their lives. Also appearing on the series when it made its debut was a gentle Angel of Death named Andrew, played by John Dye; Special Agent Sam, played by Paul Winfield (1995–   ); and a streetwise angel named Rafael, played by Alexis Cruz, who showed up on occasion to help Monica and Tess. Among the mortals the angels came to assist were a female writer with a serious drinking problem, a baseball coach who feared his own mortality, a woman who wanted to commit suicide, and during one Christmas season, two orphaned brothers who needed help getting through a difficult holiday season without their parents. Seven years after critics dismissed *Touched by an Angel* as insignificant, the series was still popular.

TRACEY ULLMAN SHOW, THE

Apr. 1987–May 1987	FOX	Sun. 8:30–9 P.M.
May 1987–Sept. 1987	FOX	Sun. 9:30–10 P.M.
Sept. 1987–Feb. 1988	FOX	Sun. 9–10 P.M.
Mar. 1988–July 1988	FOX	Sun. 10–10:30 P.M.
July 1988–Aug. 1989	FOX	Sun. 9:30–10 P.M.
Aug. 1989–Mar. 1990	FOX	Sun. 10–10:30 P.M.
Apr. 1990–Sept. 1990	FOX	Sun. 9:30–10 P.M.
1996–1998	HBO	Various times

British comedienne Tracey ULLMAN brought her formidable talents as an actress, singer, dancer, and impersonator to American television in a half-hour variety show called *The Tracey Ullman Show.* Seen on the FOX network, the show usually contained three comedy playlets that featured Ullman and her regular cast of supporting players that included Julie Kavner, Dan Castellaneta, Joe Malone, Sam McMurray, and Anna Levine (1988–99). Among Ullman's comic characters, who were uniquely different from one another, both physically (thanks to expert makeup artists) and in behavior, were a South African golf pro named Kiki Howard-Smith; the materialistic yuppie Sara Downey; bucktoothed anthropologist Ceci Beckwith, who enjoyed living with monkeys; divorcée Ginny Tillman; Francesca, a teenager living with her gay father and his lover; an insecure spinster named Kay, who lived with her needy mother; and a postal worker named Tina. At the end of her shows, Ullman always appeared without her character makeup, lest her viewers had any doubt that it was she who had played all the diverse leading characters. Ullman won an Emmy Award for her work two weeks after the series left the air. In 1999, Ullman revised her show, with many new characters making appearances for the first time on a series of half-hour specials produced by Home Box Office; it was called *Tracey Takes On*, which met with equal critical and audience approval.

TRAPPER JOHN, M.D.

Sept. 1979–Jan. 1986	CBS	Sun. 10–11 P.M.
Feb. 1986–Mar. 1986	CBS	Tues. 8–9 P.M.
June 1986	CBS	Thurs. 9–10 P.M.
Aug. 1986–Sept. 1986	CBS	Thurs. 10–11 P.M.

The title character of this hour-long, weekly medical drama series, "Trapper John" McIntyre, who was played by Pernell ROBERTS, had originally been a character played by Wayne ROGERS on the very successful series M*A*S*H. *Trapper John, M.D.*, however, was set 28 years after Dr. Trapper John McIntyre had been discharged from the 4077th M*A*S*H unit that he served in during the Korean War. In those 28 years, Dr. John McIntyre had mellowed a great deal and no longer fought the system as he had during the war. As the chief of surgery at San Francisco Memorial Hospital, Dr. McIntyre's concern for his patients often tempted him to bend the rules at times, much to the chagrin of hospital administrator Arnold Slocum (1979–85), played by Simon Scott. Working alongside Dr. McIntyre was a brash young doctor who was not unlike Trapper John as a younger man. Gonzo Gates, played by Gregory Harrison, had an irreverent attitude toward authority and was somewhat of a hospital Casanova. Also working at the hospital with Dr. McIntyre and Dr. Gates were Nurse Clara Willoughly, nicknamed Starch, played by Mary McCarty (who was replaced by Nurse Ernestine Shoop, played by Madge Sinclair when McCarty died); Nurse Gloria Brancusi, nicknamed "Ripples," played by Christopher Norris; and Dr. Justin "Jackpot" Jackson, played by Brian Mitchell. As the series continued, other characters who were added to, or appeared only occasionally on the show, included Trapper John's ex-wife, Melanie, played by Jessica Walter; Dr. E. J. Riverside, played by Marcia Rodd, the hospital dentist who married Dr. Stanley Riverside II, played by Charles Siebert; Trapper John's son, J. T., who was also a doctor, played by Timothy Busfield; Nurse Libby Kegler, played by Lorna Luft; hospital administrator Catherine Hackett, played by Janis Paige; and surgeon

Andy Pagano, played by Beau Gravitte. At the end of the 1984–85 season, Gregory Harrison decided to leave the series. His character, Dr. Gates, after marrying Fran Brennan, a patient with multiple sclerosis, played by Andrea Marcovicci, was "killed off" by having the character suffer a stroke. *Trapper John, M.D.* was developed for television by Frank Glicksman and Don Brinkley, who also served as the show's executive producer and producer, respectively.

TRAVOLTA, JOHN (JOHN JOSEPH TRAVOLTA 1954–)

Before he became a film star, John Travolta, who was born in Englewood, New Jersey, was a dancer on Broadway and a teenage heartthrob, the swaggering Vinnie Barbarino on the hit TV situation comedy series WELCOME BACK, KOTTER. Soon after he finished high school, Travolta landed a featured role in the Broadway musical *Over There*, which starred Patty and Maxene Andrews, of the Andrews Sisters singing group. In 1975, Travolta made his screen debut in *The Devil's Rain*, and that same year he won the role of Vinnie in *Welcome Back, Kotter*. While he was appearing on that show, Travolta also appeared in important roles in the films *The Tenth Level* (1976), *The Boy in the Plastic Bubble* (1976), and *Carrie* (1976). In 1977, Travolta starred in a film called *Saturday Night Fever*, playing a disco-dancing Brooklyn boy, Tony Manero. He subsequently had leading roles in such films as *Grease* (1978), *Urban Cowboy* (1980), *Blow Out* (1981), *Staying Alive* (1983), and then a long string of less distinguished films, before making a comeback playing Vincent Vega in the very successful film *Pulp Fiction* in 1994. This role reestablished Travolta as one of Hollywood's major leading men. He subsequently starred in such popular films as *Get Shorty* (1995), *Phenomenon* (1996), *Michael* (1996), *Primary Colors* (1998), *The General's Daughter* (1999), and *Swordfish* (2001), to name just a few.

TREBEK, ALEX (1940–)

Since 1984 the host of the TV game show JEOPARDY!, Alex Trebek was born in Sudbury, Ontario, Canada. He first appeared on the American TV scene as the host of the *Wizard of Odds* series in 1973. He then hosted the more successful daytime quiz shows *High Rollers* from 1974 until 1980, *Double Dare* (1976–77), *The $128,000 Question* (1977–78), *Pitfall* (1981), and *Battlestars* (1981–83) before becoming host on *Jeopardy!*. In addition to his regular TV appearances, Trebek has also made guest-starring appearances playing himself on such series as MAMA'S FAMILY, CHEERS, *Rugrats*, GOLDEN GIRLS, The LARRY SANDERS SHOW, ELLEN, BLOSSOM, BEVERLY HILLS 90210, The NANNY, The X-FILES, The SIMPSONS (voice), and BAYWATCH.

TRUTH OR CONSEQUENCES

Sept. 1950–May 1951	CBS	Thurs. 10–10:30 P.M.
Jan. 1952–May 1952	NBC	Various daytime hours

May 1954–Sept. 1955	NBC	Tues. 10–10:30 P.M.	
Sept. 1955–Sept. 1956	NBC	Fri. 8–8:30 P.M.	
Dec. 1956–Sept. 1965	NBC	Various daytime hours	
1966–1974	Syndicated	Various times and stations	

Before and after it became a popular TV game show, *Truth or Consequences* was one of radio's most successful programs, completing a 16-year run (1940–56) before it finally left the air. Both the radio and TV versions of *Truth or Consequences* were hosted by veteran radio announcer and game show host Ralph EDWARDS, who created the show and was its producer. The show's premise was simple: Contestants would either correctly answer a question Edwards asked them, or they would have to "pay a consequence," which meant that they had to perform an outrageous, hilarious physical feat of some kind, such as jumping through hoops and landing in a tub of whipped cream or going out on the streets and asking passersby a ridiculous question, as the studio audience squealed with delight. When a contestant got a question wrong, or failed to answer it at all, which was usually within a second from when Edwards asked it in order to ensure that a "consequence" would follow, a buzzer called "Beulah" would bleat. On the 1954 prime-time version of the show, Jack Bailey acted as the show's new host. Bailey was succeeded by Bob BARKER in 1956. In 1958 the show was hosted by Steve Dunne. Barker continued to host the series during its eight-year run in syndication. In 1977, *Truth or Consequences* was revived as *The New Truth or Consequences*, and was hosted by Bob Hilton. Hilton was assisted by Murray "The Unknown Comic" Langston. The show disappeared from the airwaves after a short, unsuccessful run.

TUCKER, FORREST (1919–1986)

Although he had appeared in over 70 films and had been on the TV series *Crunch and Des* (1955) before he became the star of the television situation comedy *F TROOP* in 1965, Forrest Tucker is best remembered for the role he played on that series, Sergeant Morgan O'Rourke. Born in Woodland Hills, California, Forrest Tucker entered films in the late 1930s, playing a small role in *Weekend in Hollywood*. Tucker subsequently appeared in such films as *The Westerner* (1940), *Submarine Raider* (1942), *Canal Zone* (1942), *Boston Blackie Goes Hollywood* (1942), *Rage at Dawn* (1955), *The Abominable Snowman of the Himalayas* (1957), *The Deerslayer* (1957), *Auntie Mame* (1958), and *Fort Massacre* (1958), to name just a few, before fading from the spotlight for several years due to his alcoholism. In 1965, Tucker's career was revitalized when he was given the major role on *F Troop*, which became an audience favorite. After *F Troop* departed the airwaves, Tucker continued to appear in such films as *The Night They Raided Minsky's* (1968), *Chisum* (1970), *Cancel My Reservation* (1972), *The Wild McCullochs* (1975), *A Rare Breed* (1981), *Thunder Run*

(1985), among others, and had regular roles on the TV series *Dusty's Trail* (1973) and *Filthy Rich* (1982), and made guest-starring appearances on such TV series as *NIGHT GALLERY, LITTLE HOUSE ON THE PRAIRIE, The BIONIC WOMAN, KOJAK, ALICE, MURDER, SHE WROTE,* and *Ghostbusters* (1986).

TWENTY-ONE

Sept. 1956–Jan. 1957	NBC	Wed. 10:30–11 P.M.
June 1957–Sept. 1958	NBC	Mon. 9–9:30 P.M.
Sept. 1958–Oct. 1958	NBC	Thurs. 8:30–9 P.M.

The format of this popular evening quiz show hosted by Jack BARRY was loosely based upon the card game twenty-one (blackjack), in which players reach a point total of 21 to win the game. While contestants stood in two isolation booths, each was informed of the category of the group of questions and each could choose a question worth anywhere from one to 11 points, the difficulty increasing with the value of rising points. Each question was worth $300. If the contestants tied, the value of each question would rise to $500, and could continue to rise until there was a winner. In 1958, the future of big-money quiz shows was threatened when a former contestant on the *Dotto* show said he had been given the answers to questions on that show in order to assure that the game would continue and the prize money increase, thus keeping viewers interested. All the quiz shows on TV, including *Twenty-One*, fell victim to the TV game show scandal of the late 1950s. When former *Twenty-One* contestants Herb Stempel, and subsequently Charles Van Doren, who had secured a job at NBC as a result of his appearance on *Twenty-One*, admitted that the show had also been rigged, *Twenty-One* was canceled. Elfrida Von Nardroff, who it was proved had no prior answers, was the show's biggest money winner, earning a final total of $220,500.

TWILIGHT ZONE, THE

Oct. 1959–Sept. 1962	CBS	Fri. 10–10:30 P.M.
Jan. 1963–Sept. 1963	CBS	Thurs. 9–10 P.M.
Sept. 1963–Sept. 1964	CBS	Fri. 9:30–10 P.M.
May 1965–Sept. 1965	CBS	Sun. 9–10 P.M.
Sept. 1985–Apr. 1986	CBS	Fri. 8–9 P.M.
Sept. 1986–Oct. 1986	CBS	Sat. 10–11 P.M.
Dec. 1986	CBS	Thurs. 8–8:30 P.M.
July 1987	CBS	Fri. 10–11 P.M.
1987–1988	Syndicated	Various times and stations

One of early television's most successful dramatic anthology writers, Rod SERLING, who had won Emmy Awards for his TV plays *Requiem for a Heavyweight* and *Patterns* and had written scripts for such programs as *The KRAFT SUSPENSE THEATRE* and *PLAYHOUSE 90*, wrote 78 of the 151 scripts produced on the *The Twilight Zone*, and was the original narrator of the long-running, popular science fiction series. Each week, a different sci-fi tale, often with an ironic ending, was presented. Serling's introductions, the unique opening sequence, and the surprise endings of the weekly stories became the show's trademark. The original series was filmed in black and white, and although such well-known performers as Robert Redford, Burgess Meredith, Roddy McDowell, Inger STEVENS, Franchot Tone, Cliff Robertson, and Earl Holliman were often featured on the series, it was the stories that made the show most memorable. In addition to Serling, scripts were also written by Charles Beaumont, Richard Matheson, and Earl Hammer (who later created and wrote *The WALTONS* for television), and some of the best-remembered stories included "The Mighty Casey," "People Are Alike All Over," "Where Is Everybody?," "The Hitch-Hiker," "Nothing in the Dark," "The Silence," and "The Dummy," to name just a few. Serling, as the show's host and narrator, continued to introduce his viewers to "the twilight zone," where there was a "fifth dimension, beyond that which is known to man," from 1959 until 1964, when the series left the air after an impressive, for the time, five years. Thereafter, the series became one of the most-viewed syndicated shows, and it can still be seen on various cable and satellite channels. In 1994, CBS televised two episodes of *The Twilight Zone* written by Serling that had not been aired during the series' original run. The two stories, "The Theater" and "Where the Dead Are," were pre-sented on a CBS special called *Twilight Zone: Rod Serling's Lost Classics*. In 1985, *The Twilight Zone* was revived after 20 years off the air as a new series that was produced by Philip DeGuere. Science fiction writer Harlan Ellison served as the show's technical adviser. Two or three separate stories were seen on each week's presentation, and no on-air host appeared, although announcer Charles Aidman, who had been seen in two of the original series programs, was the show's off-screen narrator. The show remained on the air for one year. In 1988, another attempt to revive *The Twilight Zone* surfaced and 32 new stories were aired in syndication. Robin Ward was the series narrator. The previously produced *Twilight Zone* episodes were later added to the 30, and they all have remained in syndication ever since.

TWIN PEAKS

Apr. 1990	ABC	Sun. 9–10 P.M.
Apr. 1990–May 1990	ABC	Thurs. 9–10 P.M.
Aug. 1990–Feb. 1991	ABC	Sat. 10–11 P.M.
Mar. 1991–Apr. 1991	ABC	Thurs. 9–10 P.M.
June 1991	ABC	Mon. 9–11 P.M.

In spite of the fact that *Twin Peaks* was probably one of the most talked-about series ever presented on television, the series was able to remain on the air for just a little over one year. A quirky, surreal series that enfolded in episodes that were not unlike those of daytime TV soap operas, *Twin Peaks* was created by Mark Frost and the filmmaker David Lynch, who had previously been responsible for the equally surrealistic film *Blue Velvet,* among others. When the series was first aired, viewers became fascinated with the show's eerie atmosphere and were certainly curious about its odd events, but many found it difficult to follow the story line and tuned in to another channel, leaving *Twin Peaks* trailing in the ratings. The series, set in Twin Peaks, a picturesque town located in the Pacific Northwest, began with the murder of a 17-year-old homecoming queen named Laura Palmer and was about the investigation that followed the murder. Characters included a young F.B.I. agent named Dale Cooper, played by Kyle MacLachlan, who was called in to investigate the murder; Sheriff Harry S. Truman, played by Michael Ontkean, Twin Peaks' leading law enforcer; the victim's parents, Leland and Sarah Palmer, played by Ray Wise and Grace Zabriskie; the victim, Laura Palmer (who was seen in flashbacks and as a corpse), played by Sheryl Lee; Laura's biker-poet boyfriend, James Hurley, played by James Marshall; a strange psychiatrist who had treated Laura, Dr. Lawrence Jacoby, played by Russ Tamblyn; Laura's look-alike cousin Madeleine, also played by Sheryl Lee; the manipulative, wealthy Catherine Martell, played by Piper Laurie; her dead brother's widow, Jocelyn (aka Josie) Packard, played Joan Chen; and Benjamin Horne, played by Richard Beymer, a sinister character who lived at One Eyed Jacks, a whorehouse/casino where drugs and unusual sexual practices were commonplace. The complicated plot

Rod Serling of *The Twilight Zone* (Author's collection)

and numerous characters were apparently lost on most people who tuned in to see what all the talk was about, and as the series progressed it lost more and more viewers.

Among the many performers who were also seen were Jack Nance as Pete Martell, Don Davis as Major Garland Biggs, Dana Ashbrook as Bobby Briggs, Everett McGill as "Big Ed" Hurley, Sherilyn Fenn as Audrey Horne, David Patrick Kelly as Jerry Horne, Warren Frost as Dr. William Hayward, Mary Jo Deschanel as Eileen Hayard, Mädchen Amick as Shelly Johnson, Eric Da Re as Leo Johnson, Chris Mulkey as Hank Jennings, Peggy Lipton as Norma Jennings, Kimmy Robertson as Lucy Moran, Harry Goaz as Deputy Andy Brennan, Michael Horse as Deputy Danny "The Hawk" Hill, Gary Hershberger as Mike Nelson, Miguel Ferrer as Albert Rosenfeld, John Boylan as Mayor Dwayne Milford, Victoria Catlin as Blackie O'Reilly, David Lynch (the show's creator) as Gordon Cole, Ian Buchanan as Richard Tremayne, Catherine E. Coulson as Margaret the "Log Lady," Heather Graham as Annie Blackburne, and Kenneth Welsh as Windom Earle.

In 1990, the murder of Laura Palmer was solved by F.B.I. agent Dale Cooper, who stayed in Twin Peaks to investigate other murders, but by 1991 the series was canceled after little more than one year on the air.

U

ULLMAN, TRACEY (1959–)

Versatile comedienne/actress Tracey Ullman, who was born in Great Britain, received a scholarship to theatrical school when she was 12 years old. Dropping out of high school, Tracey went to work as a dancer and singer, touring England in various musical comedies. Eventually, Ullman made a name for herself on the stage and on British television. In 1981, Ullman was a regular on two TV series, *Three of a Kind* and *A Kick Up the Eighties*, and in

1984, she made her film debut opposite former Beatle Paul McCartney in *Give My Regards to Broad Street*. A starring role in the film *Plenty* (1985), and on the TV series *Girls on Top* (1985), and most notably, *The Tracey Ullman Show* (1987), which was produced in the United States, won Ullman praise from American TV critics. Film roles in *I Love You to Death* (1990), *Robin Hood: Men in Tights* (1993), *Household Saints* (1993), *Bullets Over Broadway* (1994), and *Small Time Crooks* (2000), and on HBO's *Tracey Takes On . . .* (1996), on which Ullman displayed her remarkable ability to become characters who were totally different from one another, established her as one of the entertainment industry's most talented performers. In 1997, Ullman became a semiregular on FOX's ALLY MCBEAL, playing Dr. Tracey Clark.

Tracey Ullman (Author's collection)

UNITED STATES STEEL HOUR, THE

Oct. 1953–June 1955	ABC	Tues. 9:30–10:30 P.M.
July 1955–June 1963	CBS	Wed. 10–11 P.M.

The United States Steel company sponsored one of television's earliest hour-long dramatic anthology series. *The United States Steel Hour,* was originally aired on radio as *The Theater Guild on the Air* in the 1940s. The series originated in New York City and originally presented live and then filmed plays. The first drama on this series was *P.O.W.,* which was seen on October 27, 1953, and featured Gary Merrill, Richard Kiley, and Sally Forrest. Subsequently, the show featured such stars and plays as Tallulah Bankhead in *Hedda Gabler,* Thomas Mitchell and Dorothy Gish in *The Rise and Fall of Silas Lapham,* Wendell Corey and Keenan Wynn in *The Rack,* and Andy GRIFFITH in *No Time for Sergeants,* prior to that show's being presented on Broadway and on film. When the series moved from NBC to CBS in July 1955, such performers as Paul Newman, Albert Salmi, Teresa Wright, Edward Mulhare. Dorothy Collins, Basil Rathbone, Jack Carson, Jimmy Boyd, Florence HENDERSON, Fred MAC-MURRAY, Carol BURNETT, Hans CONRIED, Johnny CARSON, Eddie ALBERT, Mary Astor, Patty DUKE, Faye EMERSON, Nina Foch, Mona Freeman, Farley Granger, Meg Mundy, Diana Lynn, June Lockhart, Jeff Donnell, Betsy Palmer, Cliff Robertson, and Franchot Tone, were featured in productions of *The Importance of Being Earnest, Huck Finn, Trap for a Stranger, The Two Worlds of Charlie Gordon, The American Cowboy, Queen of the Orange Bowl,* and many other plays.

UNSOLVED MYSTERIES

Sept. 1988–Sept. 1994	NBC	Wed. 8–9 P.M.
Sept. 1994	NBC	Sun. 7–9 P.M.
Oct. 1994–Sept. 1997	NBC	Fri. 8–9 P.M.
Apr. 1998–May 1998	CBS	Fri. 9–10 P.M.
July 1998–Aug. 1998	CBS	Fri. 9–10 P.M.
Apr. 1999–Aug. 1999	CBS	Fri. 9–10 P.M.

This public service series, which became one of the most popular programs on television in the late 1980s, starred Robert STACK, and in 1999, Virginia Madsen, and became the prototype for many shows subsequently seen in syndication. Initially, *Unsolved Mysteries,* which was created by John Cosgrove and Terry Dunn, began as a special on January 20, 1987, with Raymond BURR acting as the series host. Four real-life mysteries that remained unsolved were covered on this show. The special was so well received that a limited series of *Unsolved Mysteries* resulted. The first two shows in this limited series were hosted by Karl Malden, and Robert Stack took over for the third show and remained with the series when it went weekly in 1988. Various mysteries, such as reported UFO abductions and sightings, unclaimed fortunes, murders, disappearances, robberies, prison escapes, etc., were profiled on the series in minidramas on which actual participants or actors were used. Viewers were encouraged to call in any information they might have about the mystery they had just seen. By *Unsolved Mysteries'* eighth season, it claimed to be responsible for over 87 reunions, the apprehension of 140 fugitives from justice, and the solving of 250 cases. In 1992, a spin-off series called *Final Appeal: From the Files of Unsolved Mysteries* surfaced, but did not remain on the air longer than two months.

UNTOUCHABLES, THE

Oct. 1959–Oct. 1961	ABC	Thurs. 9:30–10:30 P.M.
Oct. 1961–Sept. 1962	ABC	Thurs. 10–11 P.M.
Sept. 1962–Sept. 1963	ABC	Tues. 9:30–10 P.M.

Few TV series attracted the attention or became as memorable as the police drama *The Untouchables,* which for four years was one of the most popular programs on TV. Nar-

The Untouchables' Robert Stack (Author's collection)

rated by fast-talking newspaper and radio personality Walter Winchell (who was never seen on the series), *The Untouchables* starred film actor Robert STACK as the legendary actual F.B.I. agent Eliot Ness, who tracked down organized gangsters and other criminals in the 1920s and 1930s. Also appearing regularly with Stack as F.B.I. agents were Jerry Paris as Agent Martin Flaherty (1959–60), Abel Fernandez as Agent William Youngfellow, Nick Georgiade as Agent Enrico Rossi, Anthony George as Agent Cam Allison (1960), Paul Picerni as Agent Lee Hobson (1960–63), and Steve London as Agent Rossman (1960–63). Ness and his fellow agents pursued and brought to justice such notorious mobsters as Al Capone, Jack "Greasy Thumb" Guzik, Frank "The Enforcer" Nitti, Bugs Moran, Ma Barker and her sons, and Dutch Schultz. Because so many of the criminals depicted on the show were of Italian-American extraction, protests about the way Italian-Americans were depicted on the series ensued, which caused the producers of *The Untouchables* to feature more Italian-American law enforcers and criminals of other ethnic groups. Produced by Lucille BALL and Desi ARNAZ's Desilu Productions, the series was supervised by a young producer named Quinn Martin, who went on to produce a string of TV crime shows. In 1987, after an absence of over 28 years, *The Untouchables* resurfaced as a motion picture starring Kevin Costner as Eliot Ness. In 1993, a new *Untouchables* TV series starred Tom Amandes as Ness and featured

Michael Horse, John Haymes, David James Elliott, John Rhys-Davies, Nancy Everhard, William Forsythe (as Al Capone), Paul Regina (as Frank Nitti), George Carson, Hynden Walch (as Capone's wife, Mae), Jack Thibeau (as Bugs Moran), and Bryne Piven. In all, 44 episodes of the series, which was syndicated, were produced.

URICH, ROBERT (1946–2002)

Robert Urich, who starred on such TV series as *Bob & Carol & Ted & Alice* (1973), *Tabitha* (1977), *S.W.A.T.* (1975), *SOAP* (1977), *American Dreamer* (1990), *Crossroads* (1992), *The Lazarus Man* (1996), *Boatworks* (1997), and *Invasion America* (1998), is perhaps best known as the star of the *VEGA$* and *SPENCER: FOR HIRE* series. Urich, who was born and grew up in Toronto, Ohio, displayed outstanding athletic abilities in high school and won a four-year scholarship to study and play football at Florida State University. Urich graduated with a degree in communications arts and went on to receive a master of arts degree from Michigan State University. After finishing his studies, Urich got a job at WGN in Chicago as a sales account executive and then briefly became a TV weatherman. In 1972, Urich auditioned for and won a role in a touring production of the play *The Rainmaker*, playing Burt Reynolds's younger brother. When the tour ended, Reynolds took Urich back to Hollywood and helped the young actor obtain auditions for various producers, which eventually led to Urich's being cast on such TV series as *KUNG FU* and *The F.B.I.*, and starring roles in a string of TV shows. In addition, Urich was also seen in such feature films as *Magnum Force* (1973), *Endangered Species* (1982), *The Ice Pirates* (1984), and in numerous TV films. While he was starring in the TV series *The Lazarus Man* in 1996, Urich discovered that he had cancer. After treatment, Urich's cancer went into remission and he resumed work on the TV series *Love Boat: The Next Wave*, playing ship's captain, Jim Kennedy III.

V

VAMPIRA (MAILA NURMI 1921–)

The original late-night TV horror film hostess, Vampira, who was born Maila Nurmi in Finland, migrated to the United States in the 1950s to pursue a career as a model and actress. While in Hollywood, Nurmi got a job hosting a local program that showed late-night horror films. Wearing a form-fitting black dress, long dark hair, and vampire makeup, Nurmi assumed the name "Vampira," and before long became a sensation with late-night viewers. Her fame as a TV hostess was, however, short-lived, and by the late 1950s she had already become somewhat of a has-been. In 1958, amateurish filmmaker Ed Wood cast Vampira in one of his low-budget films, *Plan 9 from Outer Space*, and she subsequently appeared in such second-feature films as *The Big Operator* (1959), *The Beat Generation* (1950), *Sex Kittens Go to College* (1960), and, as Maila Nurmi, *The Magic Sword* (1962). Thereafter, Vampira and Maila Nurmi disappeared from the spotlight until a film about the career of filmmaker Ed Wood, called *Ed Wood*, surfaced in 1994, and since her contribution in his *Plan 9 from Outer Space* was depicted in the film, there was interest in what had happened to Vampira. Before the film's release, Vampira was interviewed in the documentary *Flying Saucers Over Hollywood: The Plan 9 Companion* (1992) and was later seen in the documentary *The Haunted World of Edward D. Wood, Jr.* (1995), and played the "Mysterious Lady" in the film *I Woke Up Early the Day I Died* (1998). Maila Nurmi once sued actress Cassandra Peterson, who, in the 1980s, revived a vampire character named Elvira who was not unlike the Vampira character created by Maila Nurmi. Nurmi lost the case.

VAN DYKE, DICK (RICHARD WAYNE VAN DYKE 1925–)

Born in West Plains, Missouri, Dick Van Dyke went to New York City in the 1950s determined to become an actor on Broadway. The young Van Dyke's amiable personality and stage presence won him jobs as a TV host, and he was seen on such shows as *The Morning Show* (1954), *The CBS Cartoon Theater* (1956), *Mother's Day* (1958), *The Chevy Showroom Starring Andy Williams* (1958), and *Laugh Line* (1959). In 1960, he won the starring role in the Broadway musical *Bye-Bye Birdie*. In 1961, Van Dyke made his debut as the star of the situation comedy series *The DICK VAN DYKE SHOW*, which established him as one of Hollywood's favorite leading comedians, and he subsequently starred in the film version of *Bye-Bye Birdie* (1963), *Mary Poppins* (1964), *Lt. Robin Crusoe, U.S.N.* (1966), *Divorce American Style* (1967), *Chitty Chitty Bang Bang* (1968), and others. *The Dick Van Dyke Show* ended its successful TV run in 1966. In 1971, Van Dyke starred in the film *Cold Turkey* and a new TV series, *The New Dick Van Dyke Show*, but reports began to circulate concerning the actor's growing dependency on alcohol. In 1976, Dick starred in a short-lived TV series, *Van Dyke and Company*, and then, in 1977, appeared as a regular, performing various skit characters on *The CAROL BURNETT SHOW*. Although Van Dyke's alcoholism continued, he worked in such TV films as *The Country Girl* (1982), *Drop-Out Father* (1982), *Strong Medicine* (1986), among others, and a new TV series *The Dick Van Dyke Show*, playing a character named Dick Burgess. Eventually, Van Dyke was able to overcome his addiction to alcohol, and in 1993, he scored a comeback as the star of a new mystery series which as of this writing is still on the air, *DIAGNOSIS MURDER*, playing a crime-chasing doctor named Dr. Mark Sloan. Van Dyke continues to be active in films and over the years has made guest-starring appearances on such TV series as *The PHIL SILVERS SHOW*, *The UNITED STATES STEEL HOUR*, *The Danny Kaye Show* (1963), *The ANDY WILLIAMS SHOW*, *MATLOCK*, *COLUMBO*, *Highway to*

Heaven (1987), GOLDEN GIRLS, JAKE AND THE FATMAN, COACH, *Becker,* and SABRINA, THE TEENAGE WITCH.

VAN PATTEN, DICK (1928–)

Perhaps best known for playing Tom Bradford, the father of eight children in the hit TV series EIGHT IS ENOUGH, Dick Van Patten made his television debut playing a teenager, Nels Hansen, in the series MAMA. Born in New York City, Van Patten, before entering television, was a child actor on the stage and appeared with his sister, Joyce Van Patten, in *Reg'lar Fellers* on Broadway in 1941. After *Mama* left the air, Van Patten became a regular on the YOUNG DR. MALONE daytime drama series. He subsequently was seen on *The Partners* (1971–72), *The New Dick Van Dyke Show* (1973–74), and *When Things Were Rotten* (1975), as well as in the films *Zachariah* (1971), *Making It* (1971), *Beware! the Blob* (1972), *Westworld* (1973), *Gus* (1976), *High Anxiety* (1977), and *Freaky Friday* (1976), before starring on *Eight Is Enough*. Continually in demand as a character actor in films and on TV after *Eight Is Enough* left the air, Van Patten has been seen in such TV and feature films as *Diary of a Teenage Hitchhiker* (1979) *Picnic* (1986), *Spaceballs* (1987), several *Eight Is Enough* reunion films, *Robin Hood: Men in Tights* (1993), *Love Is All There Is* (1996), and as a guest star on such TV series as CHIPS, MURDER, SHE WROTE, *The* FACTS OF LIFE, BAYWATCH, BURKE'S LAW, LOIS AND CLARK, TOUCHED BY AN ANGEL, and BOY MEETS WORLD. Dick Van Patten is the father of actors Nels, James, and Vincent Van Patten.

VANCE, VIVIAN (VIVIAN ROBERTA JONES 1909–1979)

Although Vivian Vance, who was born Vivian Jones, played hundreds of roles in numerous stage plays throughout the 1930s and 1940s, she is best known for playing Lucy's friend and sidekick Ethel Mertz on the popular TV series I LOVE LUCY and Lucille BALL's subsequent *Lucy* shows. One of the six Jones children, Vivian was born in Cherryvale, Kansas. She decided early in life that she wanted to an actress, and she studied drama with Anna Ingleman in Albuquerque, New Mexico, which led to getting an acting job with the Albuquerque Little Theater. Jones saved her money and went to New York City to study acting with the famous actress and coach Eva Le Gallienne. After two years playing a small role in Jerome Kern and Oscar Hammerstein's musical *Music in the Air,* Jones got a job understudying Broadway star Ethel Merman in the musical *Anything Goes.* She changed her stage name to Vivian Vance and won a leading role replacing Kay Thompson in the Broadway musical *Hooray for What?* She subsequently appeared in Broadway shows opposite such stars as Eve ARDEN, Danny Kaye, and Ed WYNN. In 1945, while touring in a production of the play *The Voice of the Turtle,* Vance was seen by Desi ARNAZ, who was producing a new television series called *I Love Lucy.* Arnaz thought Vance was the perfect actress to play his wife, Lucille Ball's, sidekick in his new TV situation comedy. For the remainder of her career, although she made guest-staring appearances in such TV series as *The Westinghouse Desilu Playhouse, The* DEPUTY, LOVE, AMERICAN STYLE, and RHODA, to the American TV public Vivian Vance was Ethel Mertz. Vance's last appearance on TV was in the TV movie *The Great Houdini* (in 1976, playing a character named Minnie, the Nurse). Vance was the first actress to win an Emmy Award as Best Supporting Actress in a Regular TV Series in 1954.

VAUGHN, ROBERT (ROBERT FRANCIS VAUGHN 1932–)

Born in New York City to show business parents, Robert Vaughn made his acting debut as a child, but first came to the general public's attention when he was nominated for an Academy Award as Best Supporting Actor for his role in the film *The Young Philadelphians* in 1959. He subsequently appeared in the film *The Magnificent Seven* (1960), and made guest-starring appearances on over 200 TV series in the late 1950s–early 1960s. In 1964, Vaughn was given the role of Napoleon Solo on a TV series that became one of the 1960s' most popular programs, *The* MAN FROM U.N.C.L.E. The series made Vaughn world famous, and when the show left the air after a successful four year run, Vaughn became a sought-after character actor in films and on TV, appearing in such films as *Bullitt* (1968), *The Bridge at Remagen* (1969), *Julius Caesar* (1970), *The Towering Inferno* (1974), *Black Moon Rising* (1986), *Hour of the Assassin* (1987), *Buried Alive* (1990), *Joe's Apartment* (1996), and *McCinsey's Island* (1998), and on such TV series as *Emerald Point N.A.S.* (1983), *Danger Theatre* (host, 1993), and others. In 1995, Vaughn had a regular role on the daytime drama AS THE WORLD TURNS, and he has guest-starred on such popular TV series as *The* NANNY and LAW AND ORDER.

VEGA$

| Sept. 1978–June 1981 | ABC | Wed. 10–11 P.M. |
| Aug. 1981–Sept. 1981 | ABC | Wed. 9–10 P.M. |

Robert URICH starred as private detective Dan Tanna on this series that was set in glamorous Las Vegas. Dan was a contemporary P.I. who wore blue jeans and drove a vintage red Thunderbird sports car. Tanna's girl Friday on the show was a young woman named Beatrice Travis, played by Phyllis Davis, and his legman was Bobby Borso, nicknamed Binzer, played by Bart Braveman. Appearing regularly on the series were Naomi Stevens (1978–79) as Las Vegas Police Sgt. Bella Archer, Judy Landers as chorus girl Angie Turner, who often delivered messages to Tanna, and Greg Morris as Police Lt. Dave Nelson. Former film star Tony Curtis appeared on the show on occasion as hotel owner Philip Roth, who sometimes availed himself of Tanna's P.I. services. The executive producers of *Vega$* were Aaron SPELLING and Douglas S. Cramer.

VERDICT IS YOURS, THE

Sept. 1957–Sept. 1962	CBS	Mon.–Fri. Various daytime hours
July 1958–Sept. 1958	CBS	Thurs. 8:30–9:30 P.M.

This improvised daytime courtroom drama series used real lawyers and real judges as well as actors who played various witnesses. The actors were given an outline of the case being tried and the role they were to play before the show had begun, and they had to respond to the questions using their own answers (based upon the outline of the case they had been given). The jury members were selected from a studio audience. Some of the cases presented on this series included a trial of a young boy accused of shooting his best friend, a man accused of killing an older woman for her money, a couple fighting for custody of their two children, and the trial of an adopted son who was accused of killing his parents. Jim McKay, playing a court reporter, gave the background of each case before the show began. In 1960, McKay was replaced by Bill Stout, and for the last few months the series was aired, Jack Whitaker narrated the program. A popular five-days-a-week offering for five years, *The Verdict Is Yours* was seen during prime-time hours in the summer of 1958.

VERDUGO, ELENA (ELENA ANGELA VERDUGO 1926–)

Latin American actress Elena Verdugo played the title role in one of television's earliest situation comedy series, MEET MILLIE, which was on the air from 1952 until 1956. Prior to playing the leading role of Millie Bronson on *Meet Millie,* Verdugo, who was born in Hollywood, was seen in featured roles in such films as *Down Argentine Way* (1940), *The Moon and Sixpence* (1942), *House of Frankenstein* (1944), *The Big Sombrero* (1949), *Cyrano de Bergerac* (1950), *Gene Autry and The Mounties* (1951), and many others. After *Meet Millie* left the air, Verdugo had regular roles on the TV series *The New Phil Silvers Show* (1964) and *Mona McClusky* (1965), but played her second most memorable role on the popular MARCUS WELBY, M.D. series as Dr. Welby's office assistant, Consuelo Lopez. Over the years, Verdugo has made guest-starring appearances on such TV series as RAWHIDE, PETTICOAT JUNCTION, *The Iron Horse* (1967), and SCARECROW AND MRS. KING. In 1984, Verdugo revived her Consuelo Lopez role in the TV movie *The Return of Marcus Welby, M.D.*

VERONICA'S CLOSET

Sept. 1997–May 1998	NBC	Thurs. 9:30–10 P.M.
June 1998	NBC	Thurs. 8:30–9 P.M.
June 1998–July 1998	NBC	Mon. 9:30–10 P.M.
Sept. 1998–May 1999	NBC	Thurs. 9:30–10 P.M.
July 1999	NBC	Mon. 8:30–9 P.M.

Kirstie ALLEY played Veronica "Ronnie" Chase, a successful businesswoman who owns a trendy mail-order book and lingerie company called Veronica's Closet on this half-hour situation comedy. A successful businesswoman, Veronica's personal life was anything but perfect. Also appearing on the series were Kathy Najimy as Veronica's chubby, wisecracking executive, Olive Massery, who gave Veronica support in both her business and social lives; Wallace Langham as Veronica's assistant, Josh Blair; Dan Cortese as Veronica's Closet's publicist, Perry Rollins, who was a handsome former underwear model; Daryl "Chill" Mitchell as Veronica's insecure marketing manager, Leo Michaels; Robert Prosky as Veronica's father, Pat Chase, who worked for her as a chauffeur and was often inebriated; and, in the series' second season, Ron Silver as Alec Bilson, who, much to her horror, bought a controlling interest in Veronica's company.

VICTORY AT SEA

Oct. 1952–Apr. 1953	NBC	Various times

Seen in countless reruns over the years since it was first aired in 1952, the documentary series *Victory at Sea* presented 22 half-hour episodes of actual newsreel footage of World War II U.S. naval battles. Produced by Henry Salomon, *Victory at Sea* was narrated by Leonard Graves and featured an outstanding original score composed especially for the series by Richard Rodgers.

VICTORY GARDEN

1976–present	PBS	Various times

This popular half-hour garden show, which was first aired on Public Broadcasting System stations, was originally hosted by garden expert James Underwood Crockett and was called *Crockett's Victory Garden.* When Crockett died in 1979, Bob Thomas took over the role and hosted the program until 1990, when Jim Wilson, Bob Smaus, and Roger Swain hosted the show. Eventually, Swain became the *Victory Garden's* permanent host. The series, which is generally taped in Massachusetts, occasionally features segments that highlight gardens all around the world. The show also regularly features food prepared by chef Marion Morash, the wife of the show's producer.

VIGODA, ABE (1921–)

Abe Vigoda, who was born in New York City, was 45 years old when he first came to the attention of the TV-viewing public, playing Ezra Braithwaite/Otis on the daytime horror soap opera DARK SHADOWS in 1966. Before *Dark Shadows,* Vigoda was a stage actor. After appearing in the TV film *The Devil's Daughter* in 1972, Vigoda really made his mark playing mobster Sal Tessio (who eventually went to "sleep with the fishes") in Francis Ford Coppola's 1972 classic film *The Godfather.* In 1974, Vigoda appeared in Coppola's *The Godfather: Part II,* after playing featured roles in such films as *The Don Is Dead* (1973), *Toma* (1973), *The Story of Pretty Boy Floyd* (1974), and *Newman's Law* (1974). It was, however, as Det. Phil Fish on the

BARNEY MILLER TV situation comedy series that made its debut in 1975, that Vigoda had his most memorable role. The crusty old policeman he played proved so popular with viewers that Vigoda was given a TV series of his own, *FISH*, in 1977. *Fish* left the air after a two-year run, and Vigoda was seen in such films as *The Cheap Detective* (1978), *Cannonball Run II* (1984), *Look Who's Talking* (1989), *Sugar Hill* (1993), *Batman: Mask of the Phantasm* (1993, as the voice of Sal "the Wheezer" Valestra), *Home of Angels* (1994), *Love Is All There Is* (1996), *Witness to the Mob* (1998), and *Tea Cakes or Cannoli* (2000), among others. Vigoda has also been a guest star on such TV series as *B. L. Stryker* (1989), *MacGYVER, MURDER, SHE WROTE, DIAGNOSIS MURDER, LAW AND ORDER, TOUCHED BY AN ANGEL,* and *MAD ABOUT YOU.*

VILA, BOB (1946–)

Bob Vila has hosted several popular home improvement shows. Vila, who was born in Miami, served as a U.S. Peace Corps volunteer in Panama after graduating from Miami-Dade Junior College and the University of Florida with a degree in journalism. In 1979, Vila was the original host of the popular PBS home improvement series *THIS OLD HOUSE*. After leaving the show amidst controversy in 1989, Vila became a spokesman for various construction-based products, and in 1997, he resurfaced as the host of the *Home Again With Bob Vila* TV series. In addition to his *Home Again* cable show, Vila also became a correspondent on *The Early Show* in 1999. Not surprisingly, Vila also made several guest appearances on the popular TV situation comedy series *HOME IMPROVEMENT*, which starred Tim ALLEN.

VIRGINIAN, THE (MAN FROM SHILOH, THE)

Sept. 1962–Sept. 1970   NBC   Wed. 7:30–9 P.M.

As THE MAN FROM SHILOH:
Sept. 1970–Sept. 1971   NBC   Wed. 7:30–9 P.M.

For nine years, one and a half hours each Wednesday night, viewers were devoted to a popular TV western series called *The Virginian,* which was produced by Universal Television. The series starred James Drury as a laid-back, mysterious character who roamed the West seeking adventure and was known simply as "The Virginian." The Virginian "forced his idea of law and order on the Wyoming Territory community [of Medicine Bow] in the 1890s," according to the show's opening narrative. From 1962 until 1966, the series also prominently featured veteran character actor Lee J. Cobb as Judge Henry Garth. Appearing on the series with Drury for the series' full nine-year run were Doug McClure as a cowboy named Trampas, who worked on the Shiloh Ranch, which was owned successively by Judge Garth, and then by the elderly Grainger brothers, John and Clay, played by Charles Bickford and John McIntire, and finally by Col. Alan MacKenzie, played by English actor Stewart Granger. Also appearing on the series as regulars were Gary Clarke as Steve (1962–64), Pippa Scott as Molly Wood (1962–63), Roberta Shore as Betsy Garth (1962–65), Randy Boone as Randy Benton (1964–66), Clu Culager as Emmett Ryker (1964–66, 1967–68), L. Q. Jones as Belden (1964–67), Diane Roter as Jennifer Garth (1965–66), Don Quine as Stacey Grainger (1966–68), Sara Lane as Elizabeth Grainger (1966–70), Ross Elliott as Sheriff Mark Abbott (1966–70), Jeanette Nolan as Holly Grainger (1967–70), David Hartman as David Sutton (1968–69), Tim Matheson as Jim Horn (1969–70), Lee MAJORS as Roy Tate (1970–71), and John McLiam as Parker (1970–71).

VOICE OF FIRESTONE, THE

Sept. 1949–June 1954   NBC   Mon. 8:30–9 P.M.
June 1954–June 1957   ABC   Mon. 8:30–9 P.M.
Sept. 1957–June 1959   ABC   Mon. 9–9:30 P.M.
Sept. 1962–June 1963   ABC   Sun. 10–10:30 P.M.

A popular radio program, *The Voice of Firestone,* which was was first heard in 1928 on the NBC network, was one of television's earliest successes and made its debut on NBC-TV in 1949. The series' familiar theme music, "If I Could Tell You" and "In My Garden," heralded a half-hour program of well-known classical and pop music, and the series remained popular for 34 continuous years. Over the years, *The Voice of Firestone* barely changed its format, which was to present music in a straightforward, concert-style manner. During the show's later years, Broadway show tunes and occasionally pop music standards were featured, but for the most part, classical music remained in the forefront. For many years, most of the show's guest stars were recruited from the Metropolitan Opera House in New York City, and among the most prominent singers were opera stars Eleanor Steber, Risë Stevens, Thomas L. Thomas, Brian Sullivan, Robert Rounseville, and Jerome Hines. Also appearing on the series were musical comedy and radio stars Jane Froman and Gordon MacRae, and such popular music performers as singer Jo Stafford, Fred Waring and his Pennsylvanians, bandleader Xavier Cugat, and Carlos Montoya. Seen on the series on occasion were such diverse performers as tenor James McCracken, the Vienna Boys' Choir, and dancer Rudolph Nureyev, as well as members of the Ballet Russe of Monte Carlo. For most of the series' TV tenure, *The Voice of Firestone* orchestra was conducted by Howard Barlow, who had also conducted the series' radio program orchestra. After Barlow's departure from the series in 1962, the show's orchestra was conducted by such celebrated conductors as Arthur Fiedler, Wilfred Pelletier, and Harry John Brown. John DALY acted as the host when the show moved from NBC to ABC in 1954. The series' sponsor the entire time it was on both radio and TV was the Firestone Tire and Rubber Company. The program's announcer for many years was Hugh James. From 1959 until 1962, *The Voice of Firestone* was seen as a series of specials, but the show returned to regularly scheduled TV in autumn 1962 for one final season.

WAGNER, ROBERT (ROBERT JOHN WAGNER 1930–)

Best known to television viewers as the star of the TV series *IT TAKES A THIEF* and *HART TO HART*, Robert Wagner was born in Detroit, Michigan. Wagner decided he wanted to be an actor while he was attending college, and when he was 20 years old, he left school and went to Hollywood, determined to become a film star. His wholesome good looks soon landed him a contract with 20th Century Fox Studios, and he began to appear in small roles in such films as *The Happy Years* (his film debut, 1950), *The Halls of Montezuma* (1950), *What Price Glory* (1952), and most notably as a wounded veteran whom singer Jane Froman, played by Susan Hayward, serenades in the film *With a Song in My Heart* (1952). Filmgoers demanded to see more of the handsome young soldier, and 20th Century Fox, realizing that they had a potential film star under contract, began to cast Wagner in increasingly larger roles. He subsequently played the juvenile lead in such films as *Stars and Stripes Forever* (1952), *Titanic* (1953), *Beneath the 12-Mile Reef* (1953), *Prince Valiant* (1954, in the title role), *The Mountain* (1956, with Spencer Tracy), *Between Heaven and Hell* (1956), and *The Hunters* (1958). It wasn't until he played the leading role in *All the Fine Young Cannibals* in 1960, however, that Wagner became a full-fledged movie star. Major roles in such films as *The Longest Day* (1962), *The Pink Panther* (1963), *Harper* (1966), and *Banning* (1967), followed. In 1968, Wagner starred in his first TV series, *It Takes a Thief,* playing a former jewel thief turned government spy named Alexander Mundy. He followed his success on that series with leading roles on such series as the short-lived *Colditz* (1972), *Switch* (1975), *Pearl* (1978), and as a replacement on the more successful series, *The STREETS OF SAN FRANCISCO* (1972), while continuing to appear in such films as *Winning* (1969) and *The Towering Inferno* (1974), among

others. In 1979, Wagner was cast as a wealthy sleuth named Jonathan Hart, opposite Stefanie POWERS, who played his wife, Jennifer, on *Hart to Hart,* which became one of the 1979–80 TV season's biggest hits and remained on the air for five seasons. He also had roles in such films as *The Concorde: Airport '79, The Curse of the Pink Panther* (1983), and, again, on several unsuccessful TV series, including *To Catch a King* (1984), *Lime Street* (1985), *The Trials of Rosie O'Neill* (1990), and *Superstars of Action* (1993), as well as in several *Hart to Hart* TV films in 1993, 1994, 1995, and 1996. Wagner's last memorable film role to date was as "Number Two" in the film comedy *Austin Powers: The Spy Who Shagged Me* in 1999.

WAGON TRAIN

Sept. 1957–Sept. 1962	NBC	Wed.	7:30–8:30 P.M.
Sept. 1962–Sept. 1963	ABC	Wed.	7:30–8:30 P.M.
Sept. 1963–Sept. 1964	ABC	Mon.	8:30–10 P.M.
Sept. 1964–Sept. 1965	ABC	Sun.	7:30–8:30 P.M.

Wagon Train was one of TV viewers' favorite shows in the late 1950s to early 1960s. The series, which was set on a wagon train heading west to California from "St. Joe" (St. Joseph, Missouri) in the post–Civil War years, featured a cast that included veteran film character actor Ward BOND as wagon master Maj. Seth Adams (1957–62), Robert HORTON as frontier scout Flint McCullough, Terry Wilson as Bill Hawke, Frank McGrath as Charlie Wooster, Scott Miller as Duke Shannon (1961–64), John McIntire as Christopher Hale, who took over as wagon master upon Ward Bond's untimely death in 1961, Michael Burns as Barnaby West (1963–65), and Robert Fuller as the wagon train's final scout, Cooper Smith (1963–65). What made *Wagon Train* so popular with viewers, in addition to its regular players, were the interesting situations and the wide assortment of characters featured on the series. From 1963 through 1964, the series, usually seen for one full hour a week, became a weekly one-and-a-half-hour program. *Wagon Train* was produced for Revue Studios by Howard Christie.

WALKER, JIMMIE (1947–)

In 1974, *GOOD TIMES*, a spin-off of the popular TV series *MAUDE*, became a runaway hit, and one of the show's stars, actor Jimmie Walker, gained prominence. Walker, who was born in New York City, was 25 years old and had previously appeared in the film *Sing Sing Thanksgiving* when he was given the role of the teenage son of Maude's housekeeper, Florida, on *Good Times*. Walker's comic timing and amusing characterization of James "J. J." Evans won him legions of fans. J. J.'s expression, "Dy-no-mite," which he said whenever he was pleased with what was transpiring, became a catchphrase used by youngsters all across the United States and found its way onto millions of T-shirts. After *Good Times* left the air in 1979 after a five-year run, Walker was featured in such films as *The Concorde: Airport 79* (1979), *Airplane!* (1980), *Doin' Time* (1985), *Kidnapped* (1986), *Invasion of the Space Preachers* (1990), *Home Alone 2: Lost in New York* (1992), *Monster Mash: The Movie* (1995), *Open Season* (1996), and *Plump Fiction* (1997), as well as on the TV series *B.A.D. Cats* (1980), *At Ease* (1983), and *Bustin' Loose* (1987). Over the years, Walker has made guest-starring appearances on such TV series as *CAGNEY AND LACEY, BLOSSOM, The LARRY SANDERS SHOW,* and the *The JOHN LARROQUETTE SHOW*, among others.

WALKER, TEXAS RANGER (AKA *CHUCK NORRIS IS WALKER, TEXAS RANGER*)

Apr. 1993	CBS	Wed. 9–11 P.M.
Apr. 1993–May 1993	CBS	Sat. 10–11 P.M.
Sept. 1993–2001	CBS	Sat. 10–11 P.M.

Chuck Norris starred as a contemporary Texas Ranger named Cordell "Cord" Walker, who often used karate during his crime-fighting escapades. TV critics dismissed the show as "insignificant" when it made its debut in 1993 but the fast pace and action-packed weekly adventures made the series a favorite with younger viewers who helped place the series in Nielsen ratings top-30 list of shows in the 1996–97 season. In addition to Norris, also featured on the series were Clarence Gilyard as James "Jimmy" Trivette, Walker's Texas Ranger partner; Sheree J. Wilson as Asst. D. A. Alex Cahill, who was Walker's love interest, Noble Willingham as C. D. Parker, who owned the saloon/restaurant where Walker and his pals frequently hung out; Floyd "Red Crow" Westerman as Uncle Ray Firewalker (1993–94), a Native American who had raised Walker; Marco Sanchez as Det. Carlos Sandoval; and Jimmy Wleck as karate school manager Trent

Walker, Texas Ranger: (left to right) Sheree J. Wilson, Chuck Norris, and Clarence Gilyard Jr. (Author's collection)

Malloy. *Walker, Texas Ranger* was originally produced by Norris's own production company, Cannon Pictures, and then by CBS Entertainment, when it became apparent that there was indeed an audience for the series.

WALLACE, MIKE (MYRON LEON WALLACE 1918–)

Before he became a successful correspondent on the news magazine program *60 MINUTES* in 1968, Mike Wallace, who was born in Brookline, Massachusetts, had been one of television's earliest commercial spokesmen, actors, and game show hosts. Wallace starred on the TV series *Stand By for Crime* and *Majority Rules* in 1949, was a spokesman for Golden Fluffo Shortening, and hosted the game shows *Guess Again* (1951), *All Around the Town* (1951), *I'll Buy That* (1953), *Who's the Boss?* (1954), *What's in a Word* (1954), *The Name's the Same* (1951, as a panelist), *The Big Surprise* (1955), *Who Pays?* (1959), and *Biography* (1961). In 1988, Wallace made a memorable guest-starring appearance on *MURPHY BROWN* playing himself in an episode called "All the Life That's Fit to Print."

WALTERS, BARBARA (BARBARA ANN WALTERS 1931–)

Television newswoman/interviewer Barbara Walters, who was born in Boston, is the daughter of Lou Walters, who

Barbara Walters (Author's collection)

owned the famous Latin Quarter nightclubs in New York, Boston, and Florida. After graduating from Sarah Lawrence College with a B.A. in English, Walters got a job as a TV reporter on several local stations in the early 1960s. In 1963, Walters's big break came when she was hired to appear on the NBC News TODAY show, a job she held until 1976. In 1976, Walters, who claims that TV newsman Mike WALLACE was her mentor, became television's first major anchorwoman when she left NBC and went to ABC in a much-publicized move. At ABC, Walters appeared on ABC's *World News Tonight,* and in 1991, she became the substitute anchor on the ABC News *Nightline* program. Prior to that, in 1984, Walters had become the coanchor of ABC's *20/20* series with Hugh Downs, and in 1997, Walters produced and often cohosted with three other women the ABC daytime chat show *The View,* which is directed toward women. Walters is one of television's most honored newswomen, having been inducted into the Television Arts and Sciences Hall of Fame in 1990, honored by the American Museum of the Moving Image in 1992, the recipient of Lifetime Achievement Awards from International Women's Media Foundation in 1991 and the Women's Project and Productions in 1991, and she continues to interview internationally known celebrities on ABC specials. She has the distinction of having interviewed every American president since Richard Nixon.

WALTONS, THE

Sept. 1972–Aug. 1981   CBS   Thurs. 8–9 P.M.

For nine years, *The Waltons* was television's most popular award-winning family-oriented series. Created by Earl Hammer, Jr., who also narrated the series, *The Waltons,* which was first seen on TV as a Christmas special in 1991, became an hour-long drama series in 1992. The program, like the special, centered on a large family living in the rural South during the poverty-stricken depression years of the 1930s. The family, which consisted of John and Olivia Walton, who were in their forties, played by Ralph Waite and Michael Learned, and their seven children: John, Jr., called John Boy, played by Richard THOMAS (1972–77), and then by Robert Wrightman (1979–81), who was John and Olivia's eldest son, and when the series first aired was just about to graduate from high school; and, in decreasing age intervals of about a year or two, Mary Ellen, played by Judy Norton-Taylor; Jim-Bob, played by David W. Harper; Elizabeth, played by Kami Cotler; Jason, played by Jon Walmsley; Erin, played by Mary Elizabeth McDonough; and their youngest son, Ben, played by Eric Scott. Living with Olivia and John and their seven children were John, Sr.'s elderly parents, Zeb "Grandpa" and Esther "Grandma" Walton, played by veteran character actors Will Geer and Ellen Corby. The family made a meager living running a lumber mill in the rural Blue Ridge Mountains area of Jefferson County, Virginia. The series' episodes were told from John Boy Walton's viewpoint (narrated by Earl Hammer as the voice of a fully grown-up John Walton, Jr.). John Boy had succeeded in becoming a successful novelist, which had been his lifelong ambition.

During the 1977–78 season, the depression ended, and the Waltons moved into the turbulent World War II years. By this time, the children had all grown into young adulthood: John Boy had become a newspaper reporter, Mary Ellen had married and the following season become a widow, Grandma Walton had suffered a stoke (which had actually happened to the actress who played the role, Ellen Corby) and she was seen only occasionally on the series thereafter, Olivia had a tuberculosis scare, and Grandpa Walton died (when actor Will Geer died unexpectedly). Viewers remained loyal to the series until it finally departed, except for occasional special reunion shows, after nine years on the air. Also appearing on the series as regular residents of Jefferson County were Joe Conley as Ike Godsey; Ronnie Clair Edwards as Corabeth Godsey; John Crawford as Sheriff Ep Bridges; Helen Kleeb and Mary Jackson as the elderly Baldwin sisters, Mamie and Emily; Lynn Hamilton as Verdie Foster; John Ritter as Rev. Matthew Fordwick; Mariclare Costello as Rosemary Hunter Fordwick; Robert Donner as Yancy Tucker; Nora Marlowe as Flossie Brimmer; Merie Earle as Maude Gormsley; Tom Bower as Mary Ellen's husband, Dr. Curtis Willard; Peter Fox as Rev. Hank Buchanan; Lewis Arquette as J. D. Pickett; Marshall Reed, and then Michael Reed as John Curtis Willard, Mary Ellen's son;

Leslie Winston as Cindy Banson Walton; Peggy Rea as Rose Burton; Martha Nix as Serena Burton; Keith Mitchell as Jeffrey Burton; Lisa Harrison as Toni Hazelton; and Richard Gilliland as Arlington Wescott Jones.

The executive producers of *The Waltons* were Lee Rich and Earl Hammer. Hammer based the characters seen on the series and in the film *Spencer's Mountain,* which led to the TV series, on his own large family's experiences as he was growing up during the depression in Schuyler, Virginia.

WANTED: DEAD OR ALIVE

Sept. 1958–Sept. 1960	CBS	Sat. 8:30–9 P.M.
Sept. 1960–Mar. 1961	CBS	Wed. 8:30–9 P.M.

Wanted: Dead or Alive starred soon-to-be famous Steve MCQUEEN as Josh Randall, a bounty hunter who made a living tracking down wanted criminals in the Old West of the latter part of the 19th century. A man of few words, Randall was an expert with his sound-off carbine that was a combination handgun and rifle, which he called a "Mare's Leg." Although McQueen was the only regular character on this half-hour western adventure series when it was first aired in 1958, he was joined by a young sidekick named Jason Nichols, played by Wright King, in 1960. *Wanted: Dead or Alive,* which was first seen as an episode on the series *Trackdown* in March 1958, was produced by Vincent Fennelly for Four Star Films.

WATERMAN, WILLARD (WILLARD LEWIS WATERMAN 1914–1995)

Best known for playing Throckmorton P. Gildersleeve on *The GREAT GILDERSLEEVE* situation comedy on both radio and television, Willard Waterman was one of radio's busiest actors before he appeared on TV as Gildersleeve. Shortly after he graduated from the University of Wisconsin, Waterman was heard on such classic radio shows as *The Lux Radio Theater, The Whistler, Tom Mix, The Guiding Light, The Chicago Theater of the Air,* and many other shows. Waterman, who was born in Madison, Wisconsin, first played Throckmorton Gildersleeve when he replaced Hal Peary, who had originated the role on the popular radio program in the late 1940s. When *The Great Gildersleeve* became a syndicated series in 1955, Waterman continued playing the role on TV. In addition to playing Gildersleeve on TV, Waterman also appeared as a regular on the *DENNIS THE MENACE* show, playing Dennis's neighbor, Mr. Quigley. Among the memorable films Waterman appeared in over the years are *Father of the Bride* (1950), *Francis Goes to the Races* (1951), *Has Anybody Seen My Gal?* (1952), *It Happens Every Thursday* (1953), *Three Coins in the Fountain* (1954), *Auntie Mame* (1958), and *The Apartment* (1960), among others. Over the years, Waterman also had featured roles on such TV series as *The REAL MCCOYS, The ADVENTURES OF RIN TIN TIN, BAT MASTERSON, WAGON TRAIN, MAVERICK,* and *CHEYENNE.*

WEAVER, DENNIS (BILLY DENNIS WEAVER 1924–)

Dennis Weaver appeared in such films as *The Raiders* (1952), *War Arrow* (1953), *Law and Order* (1953), *The Lawless Breed* (1953), *Dragnet* (1954), and *Dangerous Mission* (1954), and was seen on such TV series as *DRAGNET* and *ALFRED HITCHCOCK PRESENTS,* but it wasn't until he played Chester Goode on the successful TV series *GUNSMOKE* in 1955 that he became really well known to the public. Born in Joplin, Missouri, Weaver, who was a talented athlete, placed sixth in the 1948 Olympic Trials in the decathlon. Shortly after, Weaver began to pursue a career as an actor, and credits actress Shelley Winters with giving him his first big break by helping him to get a part in a stage production of *Come Back, Little Sheba.* After his success on *Gunsmoke,* Weaver played the leading role on *Kentucky Jones* (1964) and *Gentle Ben* (1967), and played featured roles in such films as *Duel at Diablo* (1966), *Way . . . Way Out* at (1966), and *Gentle Giant* (1967). It wasn't until he starred on the TV series *MCCLOUD* in 1971, playing a contemporary lawman from the West who is on temporary assignment to the New York City police department, that he scored his second major TV success. When *McCloud* ended its regular run, it was revived several times as special TV movies. In addition, Weaver starred on the TV series *Centennial* (1978), *Stone* (1980), *Emerald Point N.A.S.* (1983), *Buck Jones* (1987), and *Lonesome Dove: The Series* (1992), as well as in several TV films, and in the feature films *Cry for Justice* (1977) and *Escape from Wildcat Canyon* (1998), to name a few, and was a guest star on such series as *The VIRGINIAN, The HARDY BOYS/NANCY DREW MYSTERIES* and *MAGNUM, P.I.*

WEBB, JACK (JOHN RANDOLPH WEBB 1920–1982)

Jack Webb became famous for saying, "Just the facts, ma'am," on the radio and TV series *DRAGNET.* Webb was a successful radio, film, and TV actor years before he began playing Sgt. Joe Friday of the Los Angeles Police Department on *Dragnet.* Webb, who was born in Santa Monica, California, was raised by his mother and maternal grandmother when his father left home in the early 1920s. Webb survived the difficult depression years and decided he would pursue a career in motion pictures as a director. Webb's first job in show business was as a disc jockey, and he subsequently entered network radio as the host of the *Pat Novack: Private Detective* series. Webb's first venture into motion pictures was a small role in *Hollow Triumph* in 1948. He continued to appear in such films as *He Walked by Night* (1948), *Halls of Montezuma* (1950), *Sunset Blvd.* (1950), *The Men* (1950), *Appointment with Danger* (1951), and *You're in the Navy Now* (1952), while continuing to work on radio. In 1949, Webb created, directed, and starred on a radio series called *Dragnet,* on which the actors used a unemotional delivery that seemed very natural to listeners and made the show one of the most popular programs on the air. *Dragnet* became an equally successful series on television in 1951. In 1955, Webb finally realized his boyhood dream of starring in and directing a feature film, *Pete Kelly's Blues*, which was a critical as well as a box office success. Webb continued to act in such films as a version of his popular *Dragnet* series, *The D.I.* (1957), *The Last Time I Saw Archie* (1961), and *The Commies Are Coming, the Commies Are Coming* (1962), but he became increasingly occupied with developing, producing, and directing TV projects such as ADAM-12, *The D.A.*, EMERGENCY! (which featured his wife at the time, singer Julie London), *Hec Ramsey* (1972), *Chase* (1973), and *Mobile One* (1975), among others. A heavy smoker most of his adult life, Webb died after suffering a massive heart attack in 1982, when he was 62 years old.

WEBSTER

Sept. 1983–Mar. 1985	ABC	Fri. 8:30–9 P.M.
Mar. 1985–Mar. 1987	ABC	Fri. 8–8:30 P.M.
Mar. 1987–Apr. 1987	ABC	Fri. 8:30–9 P.M.
May 1987	ABC	Fri. 8–8:30 P.M.
June 1987–Aug. 1987	ABC	Sat. 8–8:30 P.M.
Aug. 1987–Sept. 1987	ABC	Fri. 8–8:30 P.M.
1987–1988	Syndicated	Various times

Twelve-year-old, adorable 40-inch-tall African-American actor Emmanuel Lewis was the major attraction on the situation comedy *Webster*. Lewis played Webster Long, an orphaned boy who became the ward of ex-pro-football star George Papadapolis and his wife, Katherine Calder-Young Papadapolis, who was an ombudsperson for the city of Chicago. George and Katherine were played by real-life husband and wife Alex Karras and Susan Clark. George had promised Webster's father, a teammate who was a widower, that he would take care of his son when he learned that he was dying. Also appearing regularly on the series were Jerry Silver as Katherine's secretary, Henry Polic II; Eugene Roche and Cathryn Damon as Bill and Cassie Parker, who owned the Victorian house the Papadapolises moved to when they left the apartment they had lived in when the series began; Ben Vereen as Webster's uncle, Phillip Long, who tried to win custody of his nephew; and Corin "Corky" Nemec as George's nephew, Nicky, who moved in with George, Katherine, and Webster, for the series' final season. *Webster* was developed for television by ABC programming head Lew Erlicht, who had seen Emmanuel Lewis on a TV commercial, was impressed with his looks and comedic abilities, and decided to develop a series around the young actor.

WELCOME BACK, KOTTER

Sept. 1975–Jan. 1976	ABC	Tues. 8:30–9 P.M.
Jan. 1976–Aug. 1978	ABC	Thurs. 8–8:30 P.M.
Sept. 1978–Oct. 1978	ABC	Mon. 8–8:30 P.M.
Oct. 1978–Jan. 1979	ABC	Sat. 8–8:30 P.M.
Feb. 1979–Mar. 1979	ABC	Sat. 8:30–9 P.M.
May 1979–Aug. 1979	ABC	Fri. 8:30–9 P.M.

Comedian Gabe KAPLAN played the title character, Gabe Kotter, who is "welcomed back" to his former high school, James Buchanan in Brooklyn, New York, which he had attended 10 years earlier. Since Kotter had been academically challenged himself, as a student, he assumed it would be easy to handle his academically challenged students, but that was before he met the four students he was asked to teach. A newlywed, Kotter not only had to deal with his underachieving students, but he also had to adjust to married life with his wife, Julie, played by Marcia Strassman. The most frequently seen students in Kotter's class, who were called "sweathogs," included a good-looking but thick-headed Italian stud named Vinnie Barbarino, played by John TRAVOLTA; a half Latino-half Jewish fellow named Juan Luis Pedro Phillipo de Huevos Epstein, played by Robert Hegyes; a charming African-American young man who had more charm than brains but showed more promise than the other members of his class, Freddie "Boom Boom" Washington, played by Lawrence-Hilton Jacobs; and an undersized, sensitive, nervous, slightly effeminate fellow named Arnold Horshack, played by Ron Palillo. Horshack's favorite expression, "Up your nose with a rubber hose," became one of the show's more familiar catchphrases. The class, and Kotter, was the bane of the vice principal, Mr. Michael Woodman, played by John Sylvester White. Also appearing on the series as students were Debralee Scott as Roslie Totzie (1975–76), Vernee Watson as Verna Jean (1975–77), Helaine Lembeck as Judy Borden (1975–77), Dennis Bowen as Todd Ludlow (1975–77), Catherine Cellino as Maria (1975–76), Melanie Haller as Angie Globagoski (1976), Stephen Shortridge as Beau De Labarre (1978–79), Charles Fleischer as Carvelli (1978–79). Bob Harcum as Murray (1978–79), and Irene Arranga as Mary Johnson (1978–79), and James Wood as Kotter's fellow teacher, Alex Welles. The show enjoyed one of its highest ratings in fall 1975, when Kotter's wife, Julie, gave birth to twin girls, but the show began to lose viewers when John Travolta, one of the show's most popular performers, began to be seen less frequently because his contract gave him time off to appear in other projects such as feature films. The show's theme song, which became familiar to millions of viewers, was "Welcome Back," sung by John Sebastian. The executive producer of *Welcome Back, Kotter*, which enjoyed a successful four-year run, was James Komack.

WELK, LAWRENCE (1903–1992)

Bandleader Lawrence Welk had one of the longest-running and most successful weekly variety shows on television with his LAWRENCE WELK SHOW, which made its debut on the ABC-TV network in 1955 and remained on the air as a syndicated show until 1982. Welk was born to immigrant parents from Germany who settled in Strasberg, North Dakota. Shortly after finishing his schooling, Welk, who had studied the accordion, formed a band of

The cast of *Welcome Back, Kotter:* (standing) Gabe Kaplan (Gabe Kotter), (sitting, left to right) Robert Hegyes (Juan Luis Pedro Phillipo de Huevos Epstein), Lawrence Hilton Jacobs (Freddie Percy "Boom Boom" Washington), John Travolta (Vinnie Barbarino), and Ron Palillo (Arnold Dingfelder Horshack) (Author's collection)

his own and played local dance dates throughout the Midwest. The reputation and popularity of his band grew steadily, and Welk and his band became one of the most successful dance bands in the country by the late 1930s to 1940s. In 1955, Welk and his band made their TV debut on *The Lawrence Welk Show* (in 1958, *The Dodge Dancing Party*), which became part of millions of viewers' Saturday night television schedule until 1971, when it left network television, then continued for another 11 years as a weekly syndicated series. Welk's "a one and a two" before as he gave the band the downbeat, his bubble machine that blew bubbles into the air behind his band, and his dancing with the band's "Champagne Ladies," who were singers Alice Lon, and then Norma Zimmer, became Welk's trademarks. Even after Welk's death at the age of 89 in 1992, loyal fans had not had enough of Lawrence Welk and his music makers, and a weekly show that presented excerpts of programs from the past, which were hosted by former cast members, remained popular for several additional seasons.

WELLS FARGO
(see *Tales of Wells Fargo*)

WEST, ADAM (WILLIAM WEST ANDERSON 1928–)
Television's Batman, Adam West was born in Walla Walla, Washington. West made his professional film-acting debut playing a small role in *Voodoo Island* in 1957 and subsequently played increasingly larger roles in such films as *The Young Philadelphians* (1959), and eventually joined the regular cast of the TV series *The Detectives*, which starred Robert Taylor, in 1961. Roles in such films as *Geronimo* (1962), *Tammy and the Doctor* (1963), *Robinson Crusoe on Mars* (1964), *The Outlaw Is Coming* (1965), and on such TV series as NURSES followed. In 1966, West won the coveted role of Batman/Bruce Wayne on the comic strip–like, campy BATMAN TV series. It became one of the most popular shows on TV for several seasons. West starred in a *Batman* film in 1966, and after the series he played less stellar roles in such films as *The

Girl Who Knew Too Much (1969), *Partizani* (1974), *The Happy Hooker Goes to Washington* (1977), and revived his Batman/Bruce Wayne role as the voice of that character for the animated film series *The New Adventures of Batman* in 1977. Throughout the 1980s and 1990s, West continued to remain active, playing supporting roles in such films as *The Happy Hooker Goes Hollywood* (1980), *Young Lady Chatterley II* (1985), *Mad About You* (1988), *Maxim Xul* (1991), *The Best Movie Ever Made* (1994, playing himself), *Joyride* (1996), *Drop Dead Gorgeous* (1999), and as a regular voice-over performer on such TV series as *Legends of the Super-Heroes* (1977), *The Last Precinct* (1986), *Danger Theatre* (1993, as Capt. Mike Morgan), *The Adventures of Pete & Pete* (1993), *The Secret Files of the Spy Dogs* (1998), and on the *Black Scorpion* series (2001). West has also made many guest-starring appearances on such series as *Johnny Bravo*, DIAGNOSIS MURDER, and NEWSRADIO.

WHAT'S HAPPENING!! (ALSO WHAT'S HAPPENING NOW!!)

Aug. 1976	ABC	Thurs. 8:30–9 P.M.
Nov. 1976–Dec. 1976	ABC	Sat. 8:30–9 P.M.
Dec. 1976–Jan. 1978	ABC	Thurs. 8–8:30 P.M.
Jan. 1978–Apr. 1978	ABC	Sat. 8–8:30 P.M.
Apr. 1978–Jan. 1979	ABC	Thurs. 8:30–9 P.M.
Feb. 1979–Mar. 1979	ABC	Fri. 8:30–9 P.M.
Mar. 1979–Apr. 1979	ABC	Sat. 8–8:30 P.M.
Sept. 1985–Sept. 1988	Syndicated	Various times

As What's Happening Now!!:

1986–1988	Syndicated	Various times and stations

For three seasons, the situation comedy *What's Happening!!* was one of the most popular shows on the air among younger television viewers. The series revolved around three high school age African-American boys, Raj, Rerun, and Dwayne, whose real names were Roger Thomas, Freddie Stubbs, and Dwayne Clemens, who were engagingly played by Ernest Thomas, Fred Berry, and Haywood Nelson. Mabel King played Roger's mother, Mrs. Thomas, and Danielle Spencer played Roger's sassy pest of a younger sister, Dee, the bane of the boys' existence. Most of the action took place in the Thomas home, located in a large city. The boys were always getting into "typical" teenage scrapes, and various and sundry domestic squabbles also took place. The boys' favorite hangout was Rob's Diner, located near their school, where a gruff and hilarious waitress named Shirley, played by Shirley Hemphill, ruled the roost. In 1978, Raj and Rerun graduated from high school and moved to an apartment they shared that was located not far from the Thomas's house. New characters added to the series were Big Earl Babcock, a police detective, played by John Welsh, and "The Snake," a college basketball star, played by Leland Smith. Also featured on the series were Thalmus Rasulala as Bill Tomas (1978–79), Bryon O'Dell as Marvin (1976–77), and David

Hollander as Little Earl (1978–79). In 1979, Mabel King departed the series and at the end of the 1979 season, *What's Happening!!* left the air. Six years later, *What's Happening!!* returned to the airwaves as a syndicated show with a new title, *What's Happening Now!!* Raj was a newlywed and Anne-Marie Johnson played his wife, Nadine. Rerun was a used-car salesman, and Dwayne was a computer programmer. Shirley, the waitress from the original series, was also seen on this series, and she had become an owner of the boys' former hangout, Rob's Diner, with Roger. Raj and Nadine lived in the house he had grown up in, and the couple had a foster child named Carolyn, played by Reina King. Also seen on this series were Martin Lawrence as Maurice Warfield and Ken Sagoes as Darryl. First runs of the syndicated series were seen from 1986 through 1988. *What's Happening* was based on a popular film called *Cooley High*. The executive producers of the TV series were Bud Yorkin, Saul Turtletaub, and Bernie Orenstein.

WHAT'S MY LINE

Feb. 1950–Mar. 1950	CBS	Thurs. 8–8:30 P.M.
Apr. 1950–Sept. 1950	CBS	Wed. 9–9:30 P.M.
Oct. 1950–Sept. 1967	CBS	Sun. 10:30–11 P.M.
1968–1975	Syndicated	Various times and stations

For 17 years the *What's My Line* panel/game show owned the 10:30–11 P.M. time slot on Sunday evenings, although the series made its debut and was seen as an early evening offering in 1950. John DALY was the program's moderator/host and Arlene FRANCIS was one of the show's regular panelists. Other regular panelists included Dorothy Kilgallen (1950–65), Louis Untermeyer (1950–51), Hal Block (1950–53), Bennett Cerf (1951–67), Steve ALLEN (1953–54), and Fred Allen (1954–56). The premise of the show was simple. Four panelists would try to guess the occupation of a guest who sat next to moderator John Daly by asking the guest questions that were monitored by Daly. The panelists could continue to ask questions to determine the person's occupation as long as they received a "yes" answer. As soon as they got a "no" answer, the next panelist began to ask questions. Each "no" answer earned the guest $5, and when he or she had won $50, the game was over and the guest's occupation was revealed. The highlight of each week's show was the appearance of a celebrity guest, and the panelists, wearing blindfolds, had to try to guess who the celebrity was by asking him or her a series of questions. Familiar celebrity guests often tried to disguise their voices, which made for amusing exchanges between the guest and the panelists. Upon the death of popular regular panelist comedian Fred Allen in 1956, the fourth panelist seat on the show was left permanently open and various celebrity panelists occupied

What's My Line? featuring (l to r) Arlene Francis, Bennett Cerf, Dorothy Kilgallen, and moderator John Daly (Photofest)

Allen's chair until the series was canceled in 1967. One of the most memorable questions asked by a panelist, originated by Steve Allen, was "Is it bigger than a bread box?" was then to be asked thousands of times by various panelists during the program's long tenure on TV. *What's My Line* was produced by the prolific game show producers Mark GOODSON and Bill TODMAN. In 1968, a year after the original series was canceled, *What's My Line* resurfaced as a syndicated series. Long-time panelist Arlene Francis was the only member of the original cast who appeared on this series, and comedian Soupy SALES was also featured as one of the regular panelists. Wally Bruner was the show's moderator until 1972, when he was replaced by Larry Blyden, who hosted the show until it ceased production in 1975.

WHEEL OF FORTUNE

July 1953–Sept. 1953	CBS	Tues. 8:30–9 P.M.
Jan. 1975–June 1989	NBC	Various daytime hours
1983–present	Syndicated	Various times and stations

Television's longest-running and most popular game/quiz show, *Wheel of Fortune*, which was hosted by Todd Russell, was first seen as a prime-time network show in 1953, but the series lasted less than one year. In 1975, Chuck Woolery hosted a daytime version of the series on NBC. Woolery was eventually replaced by Pat SAJAK, and 30 years after the original series was aired, it became a syndicated show hosted by Sajak, assisted by Vanna WHITE, who turned the letters chosen by contestants. They had spun a large wheel that determined how much a contestant could win if he or she could supply a correct letter on the large game board.

When hosting both the daytime and early evening versions of *Wheel of Fortune* got to be too much for Pat Sajak, Rolf Benirschke, and then Bob Goen, took on the hosting assignment until the daytime series left the air. Sajak continued to host the evening version of the show, and Vanna White was seen on both the daytime and evening versions. The second *Wheel of Fortune* series was created by Merv GRIFFIN, who had been the host of a popular television talk show and later became one of TV's most successful producers and one of the wealthiest men in the United States.

WHEN THINGS WERE ROTTEN

Sept. 1975–Dec. 1975   ABC   Wed. 8–8:30 P.M.

On the air for only three months, *When Things Were Rotten* is a series remembered not for being a success, but because it was a such a disappointing failure. Created by humorist Mel Brooks, the series was a spoof that centered on the legendary hero of Sherwood Forest in medieval England, Robin Hood, played by Dick Gautier. Broadly played with numerous anachronistic references, *When Things Were Rotten* featured all the familiar characters from the original legend. There was Robin's Merry Men, Friar Tuck, played by Dick VAN PATTEN, Alan-a-Dale, played by Bernie Kopell, Little John, played by David Sabin, Maid Marian, played by Misty Rowe, and Robin's nemesis, the villainous sheriff of Nottingham, played by Henry Polic II, as well as new characters such as Bertram/Renaldo, played by Richard Dimitri, and Princess Isabelle, played by Jane A. Johnston. Although critics called the series one of the best shows of that TV season, the public did not take to it, and it was canceled. Brooks's idea of spoofing Robin Hood and his friends resurfaced in 1993, when he produced and directed the film *Robin Hood: Men in Tights*.

WHITE, BETTY (BETTY MARION WHITE 1922–)

Emmy Award–winning actress Betty White, who has been elected to the Television Hall of Fame, has probably appeared on more successful TV series than any other performer in television history. She is well known to viewers as Sue Ann Nivens on *The MARY TYLER MOORE SHOW*, Rose Nylund on *The GOLDEN GIRLS* and *The GOLDEN PALACE*, Ellen Harper Jackson on *MAMA'S FAMILY*, and starring on her own *Betty White Show* as early as 1954, as well as in 1958 and 1977, and for appearances as a regular panelist on *Make the Connection* (1955) and *MATCH GAME* (1973–79). White has been a familiar face to TV viewers ever since she starred on the 1953 situation comedy *Life With Elizabeth*, playing the title role, and when she was one of *The Jack Paar Show's* most popular regular guests. White, who was born in Oak Park, Illinois, made one of her first TV appearances on *The UNITED STATES STEEL HOUR* in 1953, and shortly after she won the leading role on the *Life With Elizabeth*. In addition to the major roles she played on series, White also made numerous guest-starring appearances on such series as *PETTICOAT JUNCTION*, *The SONNY AND CHER COMEDY HOUR*, *The ODD COUPLE*, *ELLERY QUEEN*, *FAME*, *WHO'S THE BOSS*, *ST. ELSEWHERE*, *MATLOCK*, *SANTA BARBARA*, *The DAYS OF OUR LIVES*, *EMPTY NEST*, *The JOHN LARROQUETTE SHOW*, *DIAGNOSIS, MURDER*, *SUDDENLY SUSAN*, *ALLY MCBEAL*, and also supplied voices for characters featured in the animated TV series *King of the Hill* and *The SIMPSONS*. White has also been featured in such films as *Advise and Consent* (1962), *Holy Man* (1998), and *The Story of Us* (1999). In addition to her successes, Betty White has also been seen on such TV shows as *Make the Connection* (1955), *The Liar's Club* (1976), *Maybe This Time* (1995), *Me & George* (1998), *The Lionhearts* (1998), and *Ladies Man* (1999). The actress also supplied the voice for the character Hestia in the animated film *Hercules* in 1998. Until his death in 1981, White was happily married to game show host Allen LUDDEN, and was often seen on his popular show *PASSWORD*.

WHITE, VANNA (VANNA MARIE ROSICH 1957–)

No one was more surprised than Vanna White when she became a television superstar for turning letters on a quiz show named *WHEEL OF FORTUNE*. White, who was born in North Myrtle Beach, South Carolina, was a cheerleader in high school and was encouraged to pursue a career as a model when she graduated from school because of her good looks and winning personality. White's first major assignment on TV came when she was hired to turn letters on *Wheel of Fortune* in 1982. Her popularity on the series continued to grow, and she eventually gained costarring billing with the show's host, Pat SAJAK. Before *Wheel of Fortune*, White played small roles in such films as *Gypsy Angels* (1980), *Graduation Day* (1980), and *Looker* (1981), and after her success on *Wheel of Fortune* she starred in the film *Goddess of Love* in 1988, which proved to be less than favorably reviewed by TV and film critics. Appearances as herself in the films *Double Dragon* (1993) and *Naked Gun 33 1/3* (1994) followed. White has also made guest-starring appearances on such television series as *The A-TEAM*, *SANTA BARBARA*, *L.A. LAW*, *MARRIED . . . WITH CHILDREN*, and *FULL HOUSE*.

WHITE SHADOW, THE

Nov. 1978–Jan. 1979	CBS	Mon. 8–9 P.M.
Jan. 1979–Feb. 1979	CBS	Sat. 8–9 P.M.
Mar. 1979–Dec. 1979	CBS	Mon. 8–9 P.M.
Dec. 1979–Sept. 1980	CBS	Tues. 8–9 P.M.
Dec. 1980–Jan. 1981	CBS	Tues. 8–9 P.M.
Feb. 1981–Mar. 1981	CBS	Mon. 8–9 P.M.
June 1981–Aug. 1981	CBS	Wed. 8–9 P.M.

A former forward on the Chicago Bulls, Ken Reeves, who was played by Ken Howard, was convinced by a college friend, Jim Willis, played by Jason Bernard, to coach basketball at the school where he was principal, Carver High School in Los Angeles, on the dramatic TV series *The White Shadow*. Carver High was located in a racially mixed, lower middle-class neighborhood, and Reeves soon learned his job would be a challenge. Ken's sister, Katie, played by Robin Rose, kept reminding Reeves that he could be making more money and gaining more satisfaction coaching at a more prestigious school, but he found that he enjoyed working at Carver High. Working with Reeves at Carver were the school's vice principal, Sybil Buchanon, played by Joan Pringle, who was one of his greatest supporters. Also appearing regularly as students on the series were Kevin Hooks as Morris Thorpe, Eric Kilpatrick as Curtis Jackson, Byron Stewart as Warren Coolidge, Thomas Carter as James Hayward, Nathan Cook as Milton Reese, Timothy Van Patten as Mario "Salami" Petrino, Ken Michelman as Abner Goldstein, Ira Angustain as Ricardo Gomez, and joining the cast in 1979, John Mengatti as Nick Vitaglia, Salami's cousin. The executive producer of *The White Shadow* was Bruce Paltrow, and the series was produced by Mark Tinker for MTM Enterprises.

WHO WANTS TO BE A MILLIONAIRE

Aug. 1999–present	ABC	Various times, several prime-time hours a week

Originally seen on British television, the American version of this hour-long quiz program, hosted by Regis PHILBIN, became an instant success when it made its American debut in 1999. Contestants on the show are selected by calling a phone number and answering a series of test questions correctly. In order to compete for the million-dollar prize offered on each show, several contestants who have passed the test travel to New York City, where the show is produced, and then must be the first to put a series of events, people, films, books, authors, geographical locations, etc., in correct order, according to the date on which they occurred, to their east to west or west to east locations, their chronological order, etc. Contestants who win this "fastest finger" bout gain a seat opposite Philbin and win the opportunity to answer the 15 multiple-choice questions correctly and win the top prize of $1 million. If a contestant sitting in the "hot seat" is not sure, or does not know, the answer to a question, he or she can use three "lifelines" to help determine the correct answer: 50/50 (two incorrect answers are eliminated); ask the studio audience to vote on what they think is the correct answer; or phone a friend and ask him or her to answer the question. Within a week or two after *Who Wants to Be a Millionaire* went on the air in the United States, it was one of the most watched programs on TV. Several special celebrity shows were aired with such guest stars as Rosie O'DONNELL, Florence HENDERSON, Chevy Chase, Ben Stiller, Alfre Woodard, Martin Short, and others, attempting to win money for their favorite charities.

As of 2002, the producer of *Who Wants to Be a Millionaire*, Michael Davies, has announced plans to drop *Who Wants to Be a Millionaire* as a regularly scheduled ABC network show. Instead, a new, half-hour syndicated show will make its debut in fall 2002, featuring *The View's* Meredith Vieira as host. Regis Philbin will continue to act as the host of occasional *Who Wants to Be a Millionaire* specials.

WHO'S THE BOSS?

Sept. 1984	ABC	Tues. 8:30–9 P.M.
Oct. 1984–Apr. 1985	ABC	Tues. 8:30–9 P.M.
Apr. 1985–Aug. 1985	ABC	Tues. 9–9:30 P.M.
Aug. 1985–Aug. 1991	ABC	Tues. 8–8:30 P.M.
Aug. 1991–Sept. 1991	ABC	Tues. 8:30–9 P.M.
Sept. 1991–Jan. 1992	ABC	Sat. 8–8:30 P.M.
Feb. 1992–Mar. 1992	ABC	Sat. 8:30–9 P.M.
Mar. 1992–June 1992	ABC	Sat. 8–8:30 P.M.
June 1992–July 1992	ABC	Wed. 9:30–10 P.M.
July 1992–Sept. 1992	ABC	Thurs. 8–8:30 P.M.

A former second baseman with the St. Louis Cardinals, a widower with a young daughter, quits the hustle and bustle of New York City to go to work as a domestic for a high-powered president of a successful advertising agency. She lives in a peaceful suburban Connecticut community with her young son and widowed mother, and there the baseball player finds more chaos than he had ever encountered playing baseball. *Who's the Boss?* remained on the air for eight seasons. Tony DANZA played the baseball player, Tony Micelli; Judith Light played his boss, Angela Bower; Katherine Helmond played Angela's mother, Mona Robinson; Alyssa Milano played Tony's daughter, Samantha; and Danny Pintauro played Angela's son, Jonathan. Angela and Tony become attracted to each other, but in the process there is a great deal of sexual innuendo and confused role reversals. Also appearing on the series were Jonathon Halyalkar, who played Billy, a five-year-old boy Tony takes in when his ailing grandmother becomes too sick to care for him, Nicole Eggert as Angela's best friend, Marci; and Curnal Aulisio as Samantha's boyfriend, Hank. The series ended, not with the expected marriage of Tony and Angela, but with Tony graduating from college.

WILCOX, LARRY (1947–)

Larry Wilcox, who played Officer Jon Baker on the successful police drama CHIPS from 1977 to 1982, was born in San Diego, California, but went to live in the state of Washington when he was a youngster and graduated from Rawlins High School in Rawlins, Washington. One of Wilcox's first major television appearances was as a regular on the LASSIE series from 1972 to 1974. Before assuming the role of Officer Baker on *Chips* in 1977, Wilcox had featured roles in the TV films *The Great American Beauty Contest* (1973), *The Girl Most Likely To . . .* (1973), *Death Stalk* (1974), *Sky Heist* (1975), and *Relentless* (1977), and appeared on such TV series as *The STREETS OF SAN FRANCISCO*, *The PARTRIDGE FAMILY*, *POLICE STORY*, *HAWAII FIVE-O*, and *M*A*S*H*. After *ChiPS* was canceled, although he guest-starred on such TV shows as MURDER, SHE WROTE, MATLOCK, MacGYVER, and PROFILER and played major roles in the TV films *Deadly Lessons* (1983), *The Dirty Dozen: The Next Mission* (1985), *Rich Men, Single Women* (1990), and *CHiPs '99*, Wilcox, who had made several wise investments during his acting career, became the owner of a successful pharmaceutical company in

Southern California, and acted on television only when he found a project he thought was worth his time and effort.

WILD BILL HICKOK (ADVENTURES OF WILD BILL HICKOK, THE)

1951–1958	Syndicated	Various times and stations

During the seven years this western adventure series was in production, 113 episodes were completed. Film actor Guy Madison starred as the western hero Wild Bill Hickok, a U.S. marshal. Gravelly voiced character actor Andy Devine played Hickok's sidekick, Jingles B. Jones, who was always calling out, "Wait for me, Wild Bill," as he tried to keep up with the the dashing and daring Wild Bill, who chased down outlaws and tried to right wrongs in the Wild West of the late 1800s.

WILD WILD WEST, THE

Sept. 1965–Sept. 1969	CBS	Fri. 7:30–8:30 P.M.
July 1970–Sept. 1970	CBS	Mon. 10–11 P.M.

The "West" in this hour-long western adventure series was not only the locale where the action took place, but also the show's major character, James T. West, who was played by Robert CONRAD. *The Wild Wild West*, which took place during the latter part of the 19th century, was a western that also employed humor and science fiction/fantasy. James T. West was an undercover Secret Service agent for President U. S. Grant. West was involved with exposing radical revolutionaries who sought to destroy the government of the United States. Working with West was his fellow Secret Service agent Artemus Gordon, played by Ross Martin, who had been an actor and was an expert at disguising himself and using various dialects to trap the bad guys. Like James Bond, West attracted his own fair share of beautiful women and bizarre equipment to help him in his work. Among the more ingenious villains who battled with West and Gordon was a dwarf named Dr. Miguelito Loveless, played by Michael Dunn. When Ross Martin had a heart attack in 1968, he was replaced by Charles Aidman, who played West's new assistant, Jeremy Pike. In 1979, Robert Conrad was reunited with Ross Martin, who had recovered from his heart attack, in a TV film, *The Wild Wild West Revisited*. *The Wild Wild West* series was created by Michael Garrison for Bruce Lansbury Productions.

WILL & GRACE

Sept. 1998–Nov. 1998	NBC	Mon. 9:30–10 P.M.
Dec. 1998–Mar. 1999	NBC	Tues. 9:30–10 P.M.
Apr. 1999–May 1999	NBC	Thurs. 8:30–9 P.M.
May 1999–July 1999	NBC	Thurs. 9:30–10 P.M.
June 1999	NBC	Tues. 9:30–10 P.M.
Aug. 1999–May 2000	NBC	Tues. 9–9:30 P.M.
Oct. 2000–present	NBC	Thurs. 9–9:30 P.M.

A handsome young gay lawyer, Will Truman, played by Eric McCormack, and a pretty, heterosexual interior designer, Grace Allen, played by Debra Messing, who was abandoned at the altar by her fiancé, decide to become roommates on this situation comedy series. The odd couple, who live in New York City and have been best friends for years, share a mutual interest in French films, playing poker with friends, and the home video version of *The $10,000 Pyramid* TV game show. The two friends support each other in all aspects of their single lives as if they were brother and sister. Unlike his flamboyant gay friend, Jack McFarland, played by Sean Hayes, who has a pet parrot named Guspo, Will is reserved. Unlike Grace's fluttery socialite assistant, Karen Walker, played by Megan Mullally, who is working only because she wants something to do, Grace is serious about her work. The show moved steadily higher in ratings over the years.

WILLIAMS, ANDY (HOWARD ANDREW WILLIAMS 1927–)

Singer Andy Williams, who was born in Wall Lake, Iowa, began his career in show business as a young boy performing with his brothers in a group called the Williams Brothers. The group's popularity steadily grew, and by the time Andy was a teenager the Williams Brothers were acting as a backup group for nightclub and stage performer Kay Thompson. By 1954, Andy was a regular singer on NBC'S TONIGHT SHOW. His popularity as a solo singer continued to grow, and in 1957 Williams starred with singer June Valli as the host of *The Andy Williams and June Valli Show*. The following year Andy had a variety show of his own, *The Chevy Showroom Starring Andy Williams*, and in 1959, and then in 1962 and 1969, he starred on three ANDY WILLIAMS SHOWs, which established him as one of television's most popular performers. In addition to his own TV series, Williams also made numerous guest-starring appearances on such shows as *The Big Record* (1957), *The Pat Boone–Chevy Showroom* (1958, 1959), *The PERRY COMO SHOW* (1960, 1961), *The Danny Kaye Show* (1964), *The Joey Bishop Show* (1964), *The JACK BENNY PROGRAM*, *The SMOTHERS BROTHERS COMEDY HOUR*, *The FLIP WILSON SHOW*, *The SONNY AND CHER COMEDY HOUR*, *The DINAH STORE SHOW*, *The MUPPET SHOW*, and *The LARRY SANDERS SHOW*.

WILLIAMS, CINDY (CYNTHIA JANE WILLIAMS 1947–)

Before playing Shirley Feeney on the LAVERNE & SHIRLEY situation comedy series that was on the air from 1976 through 1982, Cindy Williams, who was born and grew up in Van Nuys, California, played impressive supporting roles in such films as *Gas-s-s-s* (1970), *Travels with My Aunt* (1972), *Beware! The Blob* (1972), *American Graffiti* (1973), *The Migrants* (1974), *The Conversation* (1974) and *The First Nudie Musical* (1976), and had a regular role on the TV series *The Funny Side* (1971). While *Laverne & Shirley* was on the air, Williams continued to be active in such films as *Suddenly, Love* (1978), *More*

American Graffiti (1979), and *The Creature Wasn't Nice* (1981), and after her series left the air, she was seen in the TV films *When Dreams Come True* (1985), *Help Wanted: Kids* (1986), *Save the Dog!* (1988), and others, and in such feature films as *Rude Awakening* (1989) and *Big Man on Campus* (1989). In the 1990s, Williams concentrated on television and had regular roles on such series as *Normal Life* (1990), *Getting By* (1993), and several TV films. Among the many TV series Cindy Williams made guest-starring appearances on from 1971 through 1998 were CANNON, HAPPY DAYS, CHIPS, LOIS AND CLARK: *The* NEW ADVENTURES OF SUPERMAN, and TOUCHED BY AN ANGEL. She also appeared on *Instant Comedy with the Groundlings* in 1987, playing herself.

WILLIAMS, GUY (ARMAND CATALANO 1924–1989)
The actor who played the title role on the TV adventure series *The* MARK OF ZORRO, Guy Williams was born in New York City and made his first major acting appearance in the film *Bonzo Goes to College* in 1952. Williams's dark Latino good looks led to roles in such films as *Take Me to Town* (1953), *The Man from the Alamo* (1953), *The Mississippi Gambler* (1953), *Seven Angry Men* (1955), *Sincerely Yours* (1955), *I Was a Teenage Werewolf* (1957), and finally, to the leading role of Zorro on the TV series in 1957. Guest-starring appearances on such TV series as BONANZA in 1959, and starring roles roles in such films as *Zorro, the Avenger* (1960) and *The Sign of Zorro* (1960), as well as supporting roles in the films *The Prince and the Pauper* (1962), *Damon and Pythias* (1962), and *Captain Sinbad* (1963), and on the TV series LOST IN SPACE, playing Professor Will Robinson, followed. Unfortunately, by 1985, ill health and the fact that the public found it difficult to accept Williams in any role other than Zorro, forced Williams out of the show business spotlight, and in 1989, he died at the age of 65, all but forgotten by everyone but a few loyal fans.

WILLIAMS, ROBIN (ROBIN McLAURIM WILLIAMS 1952–)
Before he decided to embark upon a career as a comedian, Robin Williams, who first came to the public's attention as the zany alien from outer space Mork on the MORK & MINDY series, studied political science at Claremont McKenna College. Born in Chicago, Williams moved to San Francisco with his family when he was 16 years old, and after he graduated from college, he attended the famed Juilliard School in New York City, where he studied acting. Back in San Francisco, the energetic, if somewhat frenetic, young man developed a wildly improvisational comedic style and began performing a stand-up comedy act in comedy clubs in San Francisco, Chicago, and New York. His act soon won him legions of fans, and he was asked to audition for a role on the hit TV series HAPPY DAYS. When he auditioned for the role of Mork, an Orkan alien, for an episode of *Happy Days,* producer/director Garry Marshall told him to sit down, and when Williams proceeded to sit

on his head in a chair, Marshall hired him on the spot, saying that since Williams was "the only alien" who auditioned for the part, he should get it. His successful appearance as Mork on *Happy Days* led to a TV situation comedy of his own, *Mork & Mindy,* which he starred on from 1978 through 1982. In 1981, Williams made his film debut in the musical *Popeye,* and before long he had established himself as one of Hollywood's most popular leading men, appearing in such successful comedy and serious films as *The World According to Garp* (1982), *Moscow on the Hudson* (1984), *Good Morning, Vietnam* (1987), *Dead Poets Society* (1989), *The Fisher King* (1991), *Hook* (1991), *Mrs. Doubtfire* (1993), *Jumanji* (1995), *The Birdcage* (1996), *Hamlet* (1996, playing the small role of Osric), *Father's Day* (1997), *Flubber* (1997), *Good Will Hunting* (1997, winning an Academy Award as Best Supporting Actor), *Patch Adams* (1998), and *Bicentennial Man* (1999), to name just a few. Williams, in addition to his role on *Mork & Mindy* and his many film appearances, has also made guest-starring appearances on such TV series and specials as EIGHT IS ENOUGH, *Dame Edna's Hollywood* (1991), HOMICIDE: LIFE ON THE STREET, *The* LARRY SANDERS SHOW, FRIENDS, and *L.A. Doctors.*

WILLIS, BRUCE (WALTER BRUCE WILLIS 1955–)
Born in Idar-Oberstein, West Germany, where his father, a U.S. soldier, was stationed, Bruce Willis returned to the United States when he was a child and grew up in Penns Grove, New Jersey. After graduating from high school, Willis went to New York City, determined to become an actor. While he was tending bar in a New York restaurant, Willis was discovered by a casting director who liked his personality and was looking for a young actor to play a bartender. Small roles in several off-Broadway plays followed, and in 1985, he auditioned for and won the role of the wisecracking private detective David Addison opposite Cybill SHEPHERD on MOONLIGHTING. The series was a success, and in 1986, Willis was cast in his first major role in *Die Hard,* which made him a major movie star. Willis subsequently starred in such successful films as *Die Hard 2* (1990), *Pulp Fiction* (1994), *Nobody's Fool* (1994), *Die Hard: With a Vengeance* (1995), *Four Rooms* (1995), *Twelve Monkeys* (1995), *The Fifth Element* (1997), *The Jackal* (1997), *Mercury Rising* (1998), *Armageddon* (1998), *Apocalypse* (1998), *The Sixth Sense* (1999), *The Whole Nine Yards* (2000), and others, establishing himself as one of the "Top 100 Movie Stars of All Time," according to the English magazine *Empire.*

WILSON, FLIP (CLEROW WILSON 1933–1998)
Flip Wilson was one of the first post–World War II African-American comedians to became a major star. Born in Jersey City, New Jersey, Wilson was a funny boy who early in life discovered he had the ability to make people laugh. Shortly after he finished his schooling, Wilson began to work on a comedy act that he performed in

and around New York City. Immediately popular with black audiences, Wilson soon attracted the attention of big-time theatrical booking agents, and by 1948, he had made an impressive television debut as a guest comedian on Ed Sullivan's TOAST OF THE TOWN variety show. Subsequent guest-starring appearances on such shows as The TONIGHT SHOW starring Johnny CARSON in 1962, LOVE AMERICAN STYLE, and The ANDY WILLIAMS SHOW, and a regular spot on the popular ROWAN AND MARTIN'S LAUGH-IN, led to a TV comedy variety series of his own, The FLIP WILSON SHOW, in 1970. The show, and Wilson, became extremely popular with TV viewers, and a character he played on the show, a sassy black woman named Geraldine, became part of American comedy folklore. After his TV series left the air, Wilson appeared in such films as *Uptown Saturday Night* (1974) and *Skatetown, U.S.A.* (1979), as well as on the TV series HERE'S LUCY (1971), CHER, and The LOVE BOAT, and in the TV film *Pinocchio* (1976). In 1979, Wilson quit show business to raise his children, of whom he had gained custody after his divorce. In 1984, Wilson resumed his career as the host of a revival of the *People Are Funny* TV show. He subsequently starred on the less than successful TV series *Charlie & Co.* (1985), and then once again left the world of show business to concentrate on other business interests. Wilson came out of retirement briefly to appear on the TV series *Living Single* and The DREW CAREY SHOW in the mid-1990s.

WILSON, MARIE (KATHERINE ELIZABETH WILSON 1916–1972)

Marie Wilson, who made a career of playing dim-witted women, most notably Irma Peterson in the hit radio and TV series MY FRIEND IRMA, was born in Anaheim, California. Wilson began modeling as a teenager, and by 1934 she was given a small role in the film *Down to Their Last Yacht.* Filmmakers immediately recognized her photogenic attributes, and she was cast in a series of increasingly larger roles in such films as *Babes in Toyland* (1934), *Stars Over Broadway* (1935), *Miss Pacific Fleet* (1935), *Broadway Hostess* (1935), *Satan Met a Lady* (1936), *Melody for Two* (1937), *Swingtime in the Movies* (1938), *Boy Meets Girl* (1938), *She's in the Army* (1942), *Broadway* (1942), *Shine On, Harvest Moon* (1944), *Music for Millions* (1944), *No Leave, No Love* (1946) and *The Private Affairs of Bel Ami* (1947), continually improving her skills as a light comedienne. In 1947, Wilson played a starring role on a radio situation comedy series, *My Friend Irma,* which became an enormous success and led to such films as *My Friend Irma* (1949) and *My Friend Irma Goes West* (1950), and in 1952, a TV series *My Friend Irma.* Because of her success in the Irma Peterson role, Marie Wilson became inextricably associated with the character she played on the series, and other roles were only rarely offered to her after *My Friend Irma* left the air. She did appear in the films *Marry Me Again* (1953) and *Mr. Hobbs Takes a Vacation* (1962), but she died of cancer at the age of 56 in 1972.

WINFREY, OPRAH (OPRAH GAIL WINFREY 1954–)

Oprah Winfrey's climb from poverty to being a news anchorwoman and then the first woman in history to star in and produce her own phenomenally successful TV talk show is one of show business's most incredible stories. Oprah, who who was born in Kosciusko, Mississippi, attended East Nashville High School in Nashville, Tennessee, where she had moved as a girl. After attending and graduating from Tennessee State University with degrees in speech communication and performing arts, Oprah got a job as a news anchor at WJZ-TV 13 in Baltimore, Maryland, and hosted a local talk show on that station, *People Are Talking.* In 1985, Oprah was offered the part of Sofia in the Steven Spielberg film *The Color Purple,* and her performance in that film led to her being cast as Mrs. Thomas in the film *Native Son* (1986). That same year, The OPRAH WINFREY SHOW made its national debut, and its immediate popularity established Oprah as one of TV's major talk show hosts. Eventually, Oprah formed her own production company, Harpo Productions, and in addition to producing her own talk show, she also produced the *Brewster Place* and *The Wedding* TV series as well as the film *Beloved* (1998), and the TV film remake of *David and Lisa* (1998). In 1997, it was announced that Oprah would receive $130 million for continuing her talk show through the 1999–2000 season, making her one of the richest women in America. Among the awards and honors Oprah has received, in addition to many daytime Emmy Awards, are an honorary National Book Award and the 50th Anniversary medal by the National Book Foundation, for her promotion of reading on her TV show, her election to the National Women's Hall of Fame, being named one of *People* magazine's "50 Most Beautiful People in the World" in 1997, and a ranking of number one in *Entertainment Weekly's* 1998 list of the most powerful people in the entertainment industry and number six on its 1999 list. When asked about her fantastic show business success, Oprah Winfrey, is quoted as saying, "Luck is a matter of preparation meeting opportunity."

WINGS

Apr. 1990–May 1990	NBC	Thurs. 9:30–10 P.M.
Sept. 1990	NBC	Thurs. 9:30–10 P.M.
Sept. 1990–Dec. 1990	NBC	Fri. 9:30–10 P.M.
Jan. 1991–Mar. 1991	NBC	Thurs. 9:30–10 P.M.
June 1991–Jan. 1993	NBC	Thurs. 9:30–10 P.M.
Aug. 1992–Sept. 1992	NBC	Wed. 9:30–10 P.M.
Feb. 1993–Aug. 1994	NBC	Thurs. 8:30–9 P.M.
July 1994–Aug. 1994	NBC	Tues. 9:30–10 P.M.
Sept. 1994–Apr. 1996	NBC	Tues. 8–8:30 P.M.
Apr. 1996–June 1996	NBC	Tues. 8:30–9 P.M.
June 1996–July 1996	NBC	Tues. 9:30–10 P.M.
Aug. 1996–Feb. 1997	NBC	Wed. 8–8:30 P.M.
Mar. 1997–July 1997	NBC	Wed. 9–9:30 P.M.
July 1997	NBC	Wed. 9–10 P.M.
July 1997–Aug. 1997	NBC	Mon. 9:30–10 P.M.
Sept. 1997	NBC	Wed. 8–9 P.M.

In spite of not receiving the most favorable reviews from TV critics when it made its debut, *Wings* gradually became one of viewers' favorite programs and managed to remain on the air for seven seasons. *Wings* centered on two brothers, Joe and Brian Hackett, played by Timothy Daly and Steven Weber, who owned a one-plane airline company called Sandpiper Air that flew passengers from mainland Massachusetts to their tiny Nantucket Island–based airfield. Most of the show's action took place in the airplane terminal on Nantucket, where the Hackett brothers hung out with their cronies as they waited for their flights to take off. Among the characters who worked at the terminal were the Hackett brothers' lifelong friend, Helen Chappel, who later married Joe, played by Crystal Bernard, who ran the terminal's lunch counter and who was an aspiring concert cellist; the Hacketts' eccentric maintenance man and local philosopher, Lowell Mather, played by Thomas Haden Church; the spirited, middle-aged ticket clerk for Sandpiper, Faye Evelyn Cochran, played by Rebecca Schull; and the local taxi driver, Antonio Scarpacci, played by Tony Shalhoub. The group's nemesis, Roy Higgins, played by David Schramm, owned Nantucket's largest airplane service company, rival Aeromass, and was constantly trying to undermine the less successful Hackett brothers' efforts. Also appearing on the series were Farrah Forke and Amy Yasbeck as Alex Lambert (a daring helicopter pilot) and Casey Davenport (Helen's younger sister), who became two of the brothers' love interests. As the series continued, Brian and Casey had such a hot love affair that they accidentally burned Joe's house down (the following season Joe accidentally burned down Brian's house), and the brothers became so strapped for cash that they lost control of their company, and during the show's final episode, the brothers received an inheritance of $250,000, and decided to help Helen realize her dream of becoming a professional cellist.

WINKLER, HENRY (HENRY FRANKLIN WINKLER 1945–)

After graduating from Emerson College in Massachusetts with a degree in theater arts, New York City – born Henry Winkler almost immediately obtained a role in a film called *The Lords of Flatbush,* playing a streetwise young man named Butchey Weinstein. This led to his being cast in a new television situation comedy series called HAPPY DAYS in 1974, playing another streetwise kid named Arthur "Fonzie" Fonzarelli. *Happy Days* became one of the most successful and long-running TV series of all time and made Henry Winkler a household name and a major star. In addition to appearing on *Happy Days,* Winkler was also seen in such films as *Heroes* (1977) and *The One and Only* (1978). After *Happy Days* left the air, Winkler continued to appear in such films as *Night Shift* (1982), and the TV series *Monty* (1994), while producing and directing such films and TV shows as *Memories of Me* (1988), MacGYVER, and *Dead Man's Gun* (1999). Over the years, Winkler made guest-starring appearances on such TV series as *MacGyver,* JOANIE LOVES CHACHI, MORK & MINDY, LAVERNE & SHIRLEY, and *The* BOB NEWHART SHOW, and in the 1990s he returned to acting and was seen in the films *P.U.N.K.S.* (1998), *Ground Control* (1998), *The Waterboy* (1998), *Dill Scallion* (1999), and *Down to You* (2000). It is, however, as Arthur "the Fonz" Fonzarelli that Winkler is best remembered and that earned him a place in television's Hall of Fame.

WINKY-DINK AND YOU

Oct. 1953– May 1957	CBS	Sat. 11:30 a.m.–12 P.M.

Winky-Dink and You was co-created by and starred Jack BARRY. On this innovative children's instructional game series, Barry, who was live, talked to the cartoon characters Winky-Dink and his little dog, Woofer. Young viewers could actively participate in what was happening by drawing on a transparent screen, which was included in a "Winky-Dink Kit" that could be purchased and placed over their TV screens. After getting their instructions from Barry, children could trace letters with crayons that came in their "Winky-Dink Kits," and discover secret messages, play word games, and assist Winky and Woofer as they traveled to various locations. In addition to Barry, Winky-Dink, and Woofer as characters were sometimes seen on this series. Mr. Bungle, for one, who was played by Dayton Allen, was Jack Barry's incompetent assistant, an occasional reminder to children that it was important to carefully follow instructions.

WINTERS, JONATHAN (JONATHAN HARSHMAN WINTERS III 1925–)

Jonathan Winters was born in Dayton, Ohio. The son of a banker who lost all his money during the Great Depression and subsequently became an alcoholic, young Jonathan moved to Springfield, Ohio, with his mother when his parents were divorced. His mother remarried and became a personality on the radio in Springfield. When he was a senior in high school, Jonathan quit school and joined the U.S. Marine Corps. After his discharge, Winters entered Kenyon College and then attended Dayton Art Institute. After winning a talent contest, Winters became the host of a TV children's show in Dayton, and subsequently hosted the *And Here's the Show* program in 1955, where his unique extemporaneous comic style and ability to assume the identity of many funny characters first surfaced. In 1956, Winters was given a TV variety series of his own, *The* JONATHAN WINTERS SHOW, and in 1958, he became one of the regular panelists on the popular MASQUERADE PARTY program. As his popularity continued to grow, Winters was featured in several TV specials and won a role in the star-studded comedy film *It's a Mad, Mad, Mad, Mad, Mad World* in 1963. He became a regular performer on *The* ANDY WILLIAMS SHOW from 1965 to 1967, and starred in the films *The Loved One* (1965), *The Russians Are Coming, the Russians Are Coming* (1966), and on another Jonathan Winters TV show in 1967. After appearing in the film *Oh Dad, Poor Dad, Mama's Hung You in the Closet and I'm Feeling So Sad* in 1967, Winters began to have serious bouts with mental illness, but after treatment he was seen on the HEE HAW TV series (1969), and once again as a regular on the popular *Andy Williams Show* (1970–71). Winters starred on yet another TV series, *The Wacky World of Jonathan Winters* from 1972 to 1974, and then scored one of his greatest triumphs playing Mork's alien son, who looked older than his father, because Orkans aged differently from humans, on the MORK & MINDY situation comedy series in 1981. Winters continued to remain active throughout the 1980s and 1990s, and was featured in the *Alice in Wonderland* TV film in 1985, the films *Say Yes* (1986), *Moon Over Parador* (1988), and on several ill-fated TV series such as *Gravedale High* (1990), *Little Dracula (1991), Davis Rules* (1991), and *Fish Police* (1992). Winters has also had featured roles in the films as *The Flintstones* (1994), *The Shadow* (1994), and was the voice of the Thief and Santa in the animated films *The Arabian Knight* (1995) and *Santa vs. the Snowman* (1997). During his long and distinguished career, Jonathan Winters has also made 10 best-selling comedy recordings for which he was nominated for 10 Grammy Awards and won two, and he has made many guest-starring appearances on such TV series as *The* TWILIGHT ZONE, *Wait Till Your Father Gets Home*, and *The* MUPPET SHOW.

WISEGUY

Sept. 1987	CBS	Wed. 9–11 P.M.
Sept. 1987–Nov. 1987	CBS	Thurs. 9–10 P.M.
Jan. 1988–Mar. 1988	CBS	Mon. 10–11 P.M.
Jan. 1988–Apr. 1990	CBS	Wed. 10–11 P.M.
June 1990–July 1990	CBS	Thurs. 9–10 P.M.
Nov. 1990–Dec. 1990	CBS	Sat. 10–11 P.M.

Stephen J. Cannell Productions produced this one-hour-a-week police/crime drama series that attracted considerable favorable attention from viewers and TV critics when it made its debut in 1987. Ken Wahl starred as Vinnie Terranova, an undercover agent for the Federal Organized Crime Bureau who worked his way into a mob family as a "wiseguy" in order to gather information about organized crime activities. Terranova's major problem was how he could avoid carrying out some of the mob's more murderous activities while not giving away his true identity. Terranova's boss at the agency was Frank McPike, played by Jonathan Banks, and he depended heavily upon a character named Lifeguard, played by Jim Byrnes, who was his sole link to the Organized Crime Bureau (OCB) when he was on assignment. In order to establish his credibility as a mobster, Terranova actually had to serve 18 months in prison before infiltrating the mob. The various cases covered by Terranova were presented in "arcs"—stories that had from five to 10 episodes in each story line. Among the villains seen during the show's first season were Ray Sharkey as a mobster named Sonny Steelgrave, and a

nasty brother-and-sister team named Mel and Susan Profitt, played by Kevin Spacey and Joan Severence. The series, which was filmed in Vancouver, Canada, left the air midyear in 1990, when Wahl decided to leave the series. The show returned briefly during the 1990–91 season without Wahl, who had become the major reason for the show's continued success, which distressed viewers. Steven Bauer appeared as a new wiseguy/agent named Michael Santana. The villain during the final "arc" on the series was a character named Guzman, who was played by Academy Award–winning actor Maximillian Schell.

WKRP IN CINCINNATI

Sept. 1978–Nov. 1978	CBS	Mon. 8–8:30 P.M.
Jan. 1979–Dec. 1979	CBS	Mon. 9:30–10 P.M.
Dec. 1979–July 1980	CBS	Mon. 8–8:30 P.M.
July 1980–Aug. 1980	CBS	Mon. 8:30–9 P.M.
Aug. 1980–Sept. 1980	CBS	Sat. 8–8:30 P.M.
Sept. 1980–Oct. 1980	CBS	Mon. 9:30–10 P.M.
Nov. 1980–May 1981	CBS	Sat. 8–8:30 P.M.
June 1981–Sept. 1981	CBS	Mon. 8–8:30 P.M.
Oct. 1981–Jan. 1982	CBS	Wed. 8:30–9 P.M.
Jan. 1982–Feb. 1982	CBS	Wed. 8–8:30 P.M.
Mar. 1982–Apr. 1982	CBS	Wed. 9–9:30 P.M.
June 1982–Sept. 1982	CBS	Mon. 8:30–9 P.M.

A small radio station, WKRP, in Cincinnati, Ohio, was the setting for this situation comedy series that began with the arrival of a new station manager, Andy Travis, played by Gary Sandy, who had been hired to save the failing station from bankruptcy. The station, which had been playing only sedate music, upon Sandy's orders began to play upbeat top-40 rock and roll hits, and, although the station alienated its former elderly listeners and sponsors like the Shady Hill Rest Home and Barry's Fashions for the Short and Portly, it picked up a younger audience of listeners and many new sponsors. This pleased the station's owner, Lillian "Mama" Carlson, played by Sylvia Sydney, and then Carol Bruce, but it worried her son, the station's inept general manager, Arthur Carlson, played by Gordon Jump. On the staff at WKRP were such colorful characters as secretary Jennifer Marlowe, played by Loni Anderson; the newscaster, Les Nessman, played by Richard Sanders; the two WKRP disc jockeys, Gordon "Venus Flytrap" Sims, played by Tim Reid and Johnny "Dr. Johnny Fever" Caravella, played by Howard Hesseman; Andy Travis's enthusiastic young assistant, Bailey Quarters, played by Jan Smithers; and the station's fast-talking advertising salesman, Herb Tarlek, played by Frank Bonner. *WKRP in Cincinnati* was created by Hugh Wilson for MTM Enterprises. In 1991, after nine years off the air, the series was revived as a first-run syndicated show called *The New WKRP in Cincinnati* with only Gordon Jump, Frank Bonner, and Richards Sanders re-creating roles they had played on the original series. Edie McClurg played Herb Tarlek's wife, Lucille, who had only been talked about on the original series, on the new syndicated program.

WONDER WOMAN (NEW ADVENTURES OF WONDER WOMAN, THE)

Dec. 1976–Jan. 1977	ABC	Sat. 8–9 P.M.
May 1977–July 1977	ABC	Sat. 8–9 P.M.

As THE NEW ADVENTURES OF WONDER WOMAN:

Sept. 1977–Feb. 1979	CBS	Fri. 8–9 P.M.
Aug. 1979–Sept. 1979	CBS	Tues. 8–9 P.M.

The popular comic book character Wonder Woman, who was created by Charles Moulton in the 1940s, became the heroine of a weekly TV series in 1976. Wonder Woman, who was originally played on a TV pilot film by Cathy Lee Crosby, and then, when *Wonder Woman* became a TV series by Lynda Carter, was a superheroine who, like Superman, had super powers. Wonder Woman had been born on a "lost" island, where women with amazing strength and mystical powers had settled in the year 200 B.C., after they fled the male domination of the ancient Greek and Roman civilizations. On the island, which the Amazon women named Paradise, they discovered a magic substance called Feminum, and molded the substance into golden belts that gave them superhuman strength, and bracelets that deflected bullets. When Maj. Steve Trevor of the U.S. Army, played by Lyle Waggoner, was shot down over Paradise Island during World War II, when the TV series was set, he meets Wonder Woman. Trevor, who did not know about her special powers, and Wonder Woman fell in love and Wonder Woman returned

Lynda Carter as Wonder Woman (Author's collection)

to civilization with him, calling herself Diana Prince. Using her special powers she then helped fight the evil Axis during World War II, dressed in her Amazon costume and never revealing that she and Diana Prince were one and the same person. Also appearing on the series were Richard Eastham as Gen. Blankenship, Beatrice Colen as Cpl. Etta Candy, and, on occasion, Debra Winger as Wonder Woman's younger sister, Drusilla, or Wonder Girl. When *Wonder Woman* moved from ABC to CBS in 1977, the time of the story was updated from the 1940s to the present. Norman Burton joined Lynda Carter and Lyle Waggoner as a character named Joe Atkinson, who was Diana and Steve's boss at IADC (the Inter-Agency Defense Command). Like the original series, the revised *Wonder Woman* used strictly comic-book-style material and was very popular with younger viewers. Douglas S. Cramer was the executive producer of the series when it seen on CBS.

WONDER YEARS, THE

Mar. 1988–Apr. 1988	ABC	Tues. 8:30–9 P.M.
Oct. 1988–Feb. 1989	ABC	Wed. 9–9:30 P.M.
Feb. 1989–Aug. 1990	ABC	Tues. 8:30–9 P.M.
Aug. 1990–Aug. 1991	ABC	Wed. 8–8:30 P.M.
Aug. 1991–Feb. 1992	ABC	Wed. 8:30–9 P.M.
Mar. 1992–Sept. 1993	ABC	Wed. 8–8:30 P.M.

During *The Wonder Years'* five-year run, fans watched the protagonist grow from childhood to young manhood. The series was told from the point of view of high school student Kevin Arnold, engagingly played by Fred SAVAGE, and from Kevin's adult point of view, in voice-over by Daniel Stern. Set in the 1960s, it recalled many of that decade's major events, including the rise of rock and roll, the Vietnam War and stateside protests, and so on. Kevin, however, was more concerned with things and people that were closer to home, such as an older brother, Wayne, played by Jason Harvey, who seemed to exist only to torment him; an older sister, Karen, played by Olivia d'Abo, who barely acknowledged his existence; his parents, Norma and Jack Arnold, played by Alley Mills and Dan Lauria, who didn't have a clue as to the difficulties Kevin was having growing up; a best friend, Paul Pfeiffer, played by Josh Saviano, who was as confused about growing up as Kevin; and a girlfriend named Gwendolyn "Winnie" Cooper, played by Danica McKellar. Perhaps the most memorable of these characters were the rough-and-tough Coach Cutlip, played by Robert Picardo; one of Kevin's dates, Becky Slater, played by Crystal McKellar (Danica McKellar's sister); and Kevin's sister Karen's goofy boyfriend, Michael, played by David Schwimmer. *The Wonder Years,* which was created by Carol Black and Neal Marlens, became one of television's most acclaimed comedy/drama series, making it to the Nielsen top-10 list during the 1989–90 season, and winning several Emmys for the show, including a Best Comedy Series award.

WOOD, PEGGY (1892–1978)

Acclaimed stage actress Peggy Wood became most famous for playing the immigrant Norwegian wife and mother, Marta Hansen, on the successful early domestic comedy/drama TV series MAMA from 1949 through 1957. She was also often featured on such early TV dramatic anthology series as The PHILCO TELEVISION PLAYHOUSE, The ZANE GREY THEATER, and The UNITED STATES STEEL HOUR. In the 1930s, Wood, who was born in Brooklyn, New York, and became a professional actress when she was a toddler, was, in addition to her stage appearances, also featured in such silent films as Almost a Husband (1919), and the "talkies" Wonder of Women (1929), Handy Andy (1934), A Star Is Born (1937), The Bride Wore Boots (1946), and Dream Girl (1948), among others. After her successful TV series Mama left the air in 1957, Wood once again concentrated on her stage appearances, but in 1960, she resurfaced in the film The Story of Ruth, playing the major role of Naomi. In 1965, Wood made what was to be her last memorable appearance in the very successful film The Sound of Music, playing the Mother Abbess and singing "Climb Every Mountain," in a beautiful contralto voice few people knew she had.

WOPAT, TOM (1951–)

In 1979, a young actor with little professional experience, Tom Wopat, found himself cast as Luke Duke on The DUKES OF HAZZARD, which made him an instant star. Wopat was born in Lodi, Wisconsin, and studied acting in college, but originally hoped to become a professional singer. After his unexpected stardom on The Dukes of Hazzard, which remained on the air from 1979 through the 1981–82 season, Wopat continued to make guest-starring appearances on such TV series as MURDER, SHE WROTE and HOME IMPROVEMENT, and was a regular on the series The Dukes (1983), Blue Skies (1988), Peaceable Kingdom (1989), Cybill (1995), and Prime Time Country (1996), and also had major roles in such TV films as Burning Rage (1984), Just My Imagination (1992), Contagious (1997), and Meteorites! (1998). In 1997, Wopat realized a lifelong ambition when he starred in a revival of the musical comedy Annie Get Your Gun on Broadway with Bernadette Peters.

WRESTLING ON TELEVISION

When World War II ended and television began to replace radio as America's favorite home entertainment medium, viewers who were lucky enough to have one of the few TV receivers manufactured after the war watched anything that came on their TV screens. If it moved, people watched it, and if there was a great deal of movement, whatever was being telecast became an audience favorite. Two of the more active types of early programs that attracted attention were the ROLLER DERBY and wrestling. Professional wrestling was telecast live in prime-time hours from wrestling arenas around the country and was a major feature on both the DuMont and ABC-TV networks. Wrestlers like Antonino "Argentina" Rocca, Gorgeous George, the Mighty Atlas, the Swedish Angel, the Zebra Kid, and the Smith Brothers tag team were among television's earliest star attractions, and characters like "Hatpin Mary," who took delight in jabbing wrestlers she deemed deserving with her lethal-looking hatpin, and wrestling announcers such as DuMont's Jack Brickhouse, ABC's Wayne Griffith, CBS's Bill Johnstone, Jr., NBC's Bob Stanton, and most notably, DuMont's Dennis James, became household names. Two of TV's longest-running wrestling shows originated from Chicago's Marigold Garden on the DuMont network and from the Rainbow Arena on ABC. DuMont had other long-running wrestling shows that originated from New York City's Sunnyside Gardens and from the Columbia Park Arena. CBS's wrestling shows came from the Bronx Winter Garden Arena, and NBC's shows originated from the St. Nicholas Arena. Wrestling could be viewed by fans six days a week from Monday through Saturday. NBC and ABC began their wrestling telecasts in 1948; DuMont, which became the station most viewers seemed to prefer, also began their wrestling telecasts in 1948. CBS had a wrestling show on the air by 1950, and wrestling shows continued to remain popular until the mid-1950s, when new, more diverse programming began to take the viewers' fancy. In the 1980s, wrestling became popular again and was a popular feature on the USA and WTBS cable stations. New wrestler/celebrities emerged in the 1980s such as Ric Flair, Dusty Rhodes, Roddy Piper, Andre the Giant, Sergeant Slaughter, the Road Warriors, Larry Zbyszko, Hulk Hogan, and Jesse "the Body" Ventura (who in 1998 was elected governor of Minnesota). Wrestling's popularity continued to grow as the 20th century drew to a close, and the sport is currently one of cable TV's most popular attractions, enjoyed by millions of fans. Wrestlers such as "Stone Cold" Steve Austin, the Undertaker, the masked Mankind, and female wrestlers like Sable and Nichole Bass (a frequent guest on The HOWARD STERN RADIO SHOW and a member of his celebrated "Whack Pack"), have enjoyed the stardom and status that was given to the wrestling superstars of TV's earliest years.

The increased visibility of wrestling, especially on cable television stations since the 1990s, is mainly due to the promotional efforts of the World Wrestling Federation (WWF) and a competitive wrestling organization, World Championship Wrestling (WCW), run by television executive Ted Turner and his Turner Broadcasting System. The WCW was responsible for the emergence of such new wrestling stars as Ric Flasir, Lex Luger, and Diamon Dallas Page.

WYATT, JANE (JANE WADDINGTON WYATT 1911–)

Television's most celebrated mother of the 1950s, Jane Wyatt, who played Margaret Anderson on the popular FATHER KNOWS BEST series, was born into a socially prominent family in the New York suburb of Campgaw, New Jersey, but grew up in New York City. Jane's father was a Wall Street investment banker, and her mother was a theater critic for a New York newspaper. Wyatt attended the Chapin School and later Barnard College, but left college after two years to pursue her dream of becoming an actress. After serving as an acting apprentice at the famed Berkshire Playhouse in Stockbridge, Massachusetts, Jane got a job understudying Rose Hobart in a production of *Trade Winds* on Broadway, and soon after went to Hollywood as a contract player at Universal, where she made her film debut in *One More River* in 1934. She subsequently appeared in such films as *Great Expectations* (1934), *Lost Horizon* (1937), *None But the Lonely Heart* (1944), *Gentleman's Agreement* (1947), *Canadian Pacific* (1949), *My Blue Heaven* (1950), and *Criminal Lawyer* (1951), among many others, before joining the cast of *Father Knows Best* in 1954. After *Father Knows Best* ended its run in 1960, Wyatt continued to remain active in such TV films as *Weekend of Terror* (1970), *Tom Sawyer* (1973), *Amelia Earhart* (1976), *The Nativity* (1978), *Superdome* (1978), *Missing Children: A Mother's Story* (1982), *Amityville: The Evil Escapes* (1989), *Semisola* (1995), and others, and was seen in the feature film *Star Trek: The Voyage Home* (1986). During her long and distinguished career, Jane Wyatt has also made guest-starring appearances on such TV series as YOUR SHOW OF SHOWS, *The* UNITED STATES STEEL HOUR, *The Bell Telephone Hour*, WAGON TRAIN, STAR TREK, *The* VIRGINIAN, QUINCY, HAPPY DAYS, *The* YOUNG INDIANA JONES CHRONICLES, and ST. ELSEWHERE.

WYATT EARP (AKA *THE LIFE AND LEGEND OF WYATT EARP*)

Sept. 1955–Sept. 1961   ABC   Tues. 8:30–9 P.M.

Wyatt Earp was originally titled *The Life and Legend of Wyatt Earp* and starred Hugh O'BRIEN as Earp, a real-life, legendary western lawman. Although many of the actual Wyatt Earp's activities were questionable to say the least, the series showed Earp to be a heroic character who took on the bad guys in the Wild West of the late 1800s. Over the years, the series, which was on the air for six years, remained popular with viewers as it presented weekly episodes that involved such topics as politics and family values, as well as the apprehension of outlaws. The original scripts were written by author/playwright Frederick Hazlitt Brennan, and their contents were usually a step above most of the other western adventure series of the time. In addition to Hugh O'Brien as Earp, also seen as regulars on the series were Mason Alan Dinehart III, as Bat Masterson (1955–57), Denver Pyle as Ben Thompson (1955–56), Hal Baylor as Bill Thompson (1955–56), Gloria Talbot as Abbie Crandall (1955–56), Don Haggerty as Marsh Murdock (1955–56), Douglas Fowley as Doc Fabrique (1955–56), Lloyd Corrigan as Ned Buntline (1957–91), and occasionally, Myron Healy as Doc Holliday. Also featured were Paul Brinegar, Ralph Sanford, Selmer Jackson, William Tannen, Carol Stone, and Morgan Woodward. Dick London and John Anderson were on the series from 1959 to 1961 playing Wyatt's brothers, Morgan and Virgil. Randy Stuart played Nellie Cashman, who was a real-life western adventurer, and Trevor Bardette, Carol Thurston, Lash La Rue, Steve Brodie, William Phipps, Britt Lomond, Stacy Harris, and Damian O'Flynn were also regulars on the series at various times. The original series was produced by Robert S. Sisk. The Wyatt Earp character, re-created by Hugh O'Brien, returned to television after a 33-year absence, in a two-hour TV film called *Wyatt Earp: Return to Tombstone* in 1994. The film featured colorized clips from the original black-and-white series, as well as newly filmed sequences.

XENA: WARRIOR PRINCESS

1995–2001	Syndicated	Various times and stations

This 60-minute adventure series, which was produced with younger viewers in mind, starred Lucy Lawless as Xena, an evil warrior princess who originally battled the heroic Hercules on the *Hercules: The Legendary Journey* series. On her last regular appearances on the *Hercules* series, Xena vowed to amend her evil ways, and when she first appeared on her own series, *Xena: Warrior Princess,* with the help of her horse, Argo, she did indeed devote her time to tracking down and fighting bad guys and helping people in trouble. Xena was an expert with the sword and the chakran, a razor-sharp, discuslike weapon, and she was adept at acrobatics, karate, and a two-finger pinch at the neck of enemies that rendered them helpless and eager to give up any information Xena sought in her crusade against evil. Also appearing on the series regularly was Xena's friend and sometimes companion, Gabrielle, played by Renee O'Connor. One villain who frequently crossed Xena's path was a nasty lady named Callisto, played by Hudson Leick. Other characters who appeared regularly were a thief named Autolycus, played by Bruce Campbell, and the god of war, Ares, played by Kevin Smith, both of whom had originally been seen on the *Hercules* series. *Xena: Warrior Princess,* which is filmed in New Zealand, has remained one of most popular syndicated adventure programs on television.

X-FILES, THE

Sept. 1993–Oct. 1996 (also)	Fox	Fri. 9–10 P.M.
Nov. 1994	Fox	Sun. 7–8 P.M.
Oct. 1996–2002	Fox	Sun. 9–10 P.M.

F.B.I. agents Fox Mulder and Dana Scully, who were played by David DUCHOVNY and Gillian ANDERSON, were assigned to a special unit that investigated "X-Files"—cases that involved unusual phenomena of some kind, such as extraterrestrial abductions. Unidentified flying objects, alien sightings, genetically altered humans, cloning, telekinetic beings, odd human-killing parasites, and such were just a few of the strange cases Mulder and Scully tried to explain. Although Scully was usually skeptical about the cases they were investigating, Mulder was convinced the supernatural did indeed exist, because he believed his sister had been abducted by aliens when she was a child and he was determined to discover what had become of her. Mulder and Scully reported to Assistant Director Walter Skinner, played by Mitch Pileggi, who had a difficult time keeping his two agents in check. Strange people who seemed somehow to be involved in the unexplained activities Mulder and Scully were investigating frequently surfaced, such as "Deep Throat," played by Jerry Hardin (1993–94), and the Cigarette Smoking Man, played by William B. Davis, who seemed to know all about the alien events Scully and Mulder were involved with. Other unusual characters who appeared on the series at various times were a mystery man who was a "friend of the F.B.I.," Mr. X, played by Steven Williams (1994–96); a well-manicured man, played by John Neville, whom everyone, including Director Skinner, seemed to defer to; Special Agent Alex Krycek, played by Nicholas Lea, who when he first appeared on the series seemed to be assisting Scully and Mulder in their investigations, and then suddenly tried to kill Mulder; Agent Jeffrey Spender, played by Chris Owens, who was a double agent later revealed to be the Cigarette Smoking Man's son; three brilliant eccentric computer freaks, Byers, Langley, and Frohike, played by Bruce Harwood, Dean Haglund, and Tom Braidwood, who often assisted Mulder and Scully; and others like an alien bounty hunter, played by Brian Thompson, and Marita Covarrubias, played by Laurie Holden, who worked at the UN and helped Scully and Mulder on occasion. Other F.B.I. agents who appeared on the series were Assistant Director Alvin Kresh, played by James Pickens, Jr., Agent Pendrell, played by Brendan Beiser, and Special Agent Diana Fowley, played by Mimi Rogers.

Shortly after *The X-Files* made its debut in 1993, it became a hit show, attracting millions of loyal fans. David Duchovny and Gillian Anderson became TV stars and eventually began to appear in feature films. *The X-Files* was created by Chris Carter. The success of the show made the FOX-TV network a major prime-time player in the ratings wars that took place among the three major networks, CBS, NBC, and ABC, which until *The X-Files* came along, had the major share of viewers.

In 2000, David Duchovny left *The X-Files* to concentrate on his movie career. His character, Special Agent Mulder, was neatly disposed of in an alien abduction episode. Noted character actor Robert Patrick was brought in as Scully's new partner, Special Agent John Doggett. However, fans had apparently gotten attached to the Mulder-Scully team, and without Duchovny, ratings dropped sharply. In spring 2002, after a nine-year run, the show was canceled.

Y

YOU ARE THERE

Feb. 1953–June 1953	CBS	Sun. 6–6:30 P.M.
Sept. 1953–Oct. 1957	CBS	Sun. 6:30–7 P.M.
1971	Syndicated	Various times, Sunday afternoons

In 1947, a documentary drama series that was inspired by the "on-the-spot" news reporting style first heard on Orson Welles's classic Mercury Theater dramatization of H. G. Wells's *The War of the Worlds*, made its debut as a weekly dramatic anthology show on the CBS radio network. The radio series, which was called *You Are There* (later *CBS Is There*), presented major historical events such as the landing of the Pilgrims on Plymouth Rock, the signing of the Magna Carta, Lee's surrender at Appomattox, and the eruption of Mt. Vesuvius at Pompeii in A.D. 79 as if they were taking place at the moment the broadcast was being heard. The series was a hit, and in 1953, CBS decided to bring the series to television, using cameras instead of microphones to "report" the historical events being enacted. CBS News correspondent Walter CRONKITE served as the TV anchorman (James DALY had been the radio program's anchorman), and the initial telecast was "The Landing of the Hindenburg" in New Jersey in the 1930s. The final *CBS Is There* telecast was seen in 1957 and dramatized the scuttling of the *Graf Spee*. In between, the Salem witch trials, Lincoln's Gettysburg Address, and the fall of Troy, as well as all the above-mentioned events that had previously been heard on the radio program were dramatized on TV. Each episode ended with Cronkite saying, "What sort of a day was it? A day like all days, filled with those events that alter and illuminate our times . . . and you were there." In 1971, the program was revived for a brief time as a syndicated show aimed primarily at younger viewers and was seen on Saturday afternoons. Walter Cronkite repeated his role of chief correspondent on this syndicated series, which remained on the air for only a few months. The first event dramatized on the syndicated show was "The Mystery of Amelia Earhart," which starred Geraldine Brooks and Richard Dreyfuss.

YOU BET YOUR LIFE

Oct. 1950–June 1951	NBC	Thurs. 8–8:30 P.M.
Oct. 1951–Sept. 1958	NBC	Thurs. 8–8:30 P.M.
Sept. 1958–Sept. 1961	NBC	Thurs. 10–10:30P.M.

Radio and film comedian Groucho MARX brought his razor-sharp wit to television in 1951 as the master of ceremonies of a TV game show called *You Bet Your Life*. The show had originally made its debut as a radio show, which also starred Marx, in 1948, and for nine years, from 1950 until 1959, *You Bet Your Life* was broadcast simultaneously on both radio and television. George Fenneman was heard, and then seen, as the show's announcer and Groucho's straight man. Contestants were chosen to be on the show mainly because it was determined that they could easily become foils for Groucho's often insulting and suggestive barbs, which they never seemed to mind. At the beginning of each show, viewers, but not contestants, were informed what "secret word" (or "woid" as Groucho pronounced it) would be on that show, and if a contestant said the word during the course of the show, a stuffed duck would descend from above holding $100 in its beak that the contestant won for merely saying the word. The quiz part of the program consisted of question and answer rounds during which contestants could bet all or part of an initial amount of money they had been given to play with. The questions that Groucho asked were not very difficult, and if contestants wagered everything they had, they could win the top prize money available. On those rare occasions when a contestant failed to answer any of the questions correctly, Groucho always asked, "Who is buried in Grant's tomb?" and then added, "Nobody leaves here broke." The TV series remained extremely popular with viewers for 11 years, mainly due to Groucho's zany personality and acerbic wit. Occasionally, guest stars such as Broadway composer Richard Rodgers and lyricist Oscar Hammerstein II would make appearances, and several later-to-be-famous people such as Phyllis Diller, Candice Bergen, and William Blatty, the author of *The Exorcist*, made appearances as contestants on the show as well.

The original series with Groucho Marx was produced by John Guedel. In 1980, *You Bet Your Life* was unsuccessfully revived with comedian Buddy Hackett acting as the show's host and quiz master and Broadway's Ron Husmann as Hackett's announcer. In 1990, a second attempt to revive the series was launched with Bill Cosby acting as show's host and Robbi Chong appearing as his sidekick. It also failed to attract an audience. It seems that without Groucho Marx, the public just wasn't interested in watching *You Bet Your Life*.

YOU'LL NEVER GET RICH
(see *Phil Silvers Show, The*)

YOUNG, ALAN (ANGUS YOUNG 1919–)
British-born actor Alan Young, who was born in North Shields, Tyne-and-Wear, UK, immigrated to the United states with his parents when he was a youngster. In 1946, when he was 27 years old, Young, who had made a name for himself as a comic actor on the stage, made his film debut in *Margie*. He subsequently appeared in the popular films *Chicken Every Sunday* (1948) and *Mr. Belvedere Goes to College* (1949). In 1950, Young was given a comedy/variety television series of his own, which won him critical acclaim, but failed to attract a sizable enough audience to keep it on the air. Starring roles in the films *Aaron Slick From Punkin Crick* (1952), *Androcles and the Lion* (1953), *Gentlemen Marry Brunettes* (1955), *tom thumb* (1958), and *The Time Machine* (1960) followed. In 1961, Young was cast in the role of Wilbur Post on the TV series MISTER ED, for which he is perhaps best remembered. The series remained on the air for four years. In 1967, Young appeared on another less successful series, *Mr. Terrific*, and then, in 1978, in a series called *Battle of the Planets*. Supporting film roles in *Baker's Hawk* (1976), *The Cat from Outer Space* (1978), and on the series *The INCREDIBLE HULK*, among others, Kept the actor busy in front of the camera, but he became more active as the voice of several cartoons characters on such TV series as *Scooby and Scrappy-Doo* (1979), *Scruffy* (1980), *Spider-Man and His Amazing Friends* (1981), *Mickey's Christmas Carol* (1983, as the voice of Scrooge),

The SMURFS (as Miner Smurf), *Ducktales: Treasure of the Golden Sun* (1987), *Ducktales* (1987), *Super Ducktales* (1989), and *The Ren and Stimpy Show* (1991). In the 1990s, Young was also featured in the films *Beverly Hills Cop III* (1994), and as the voice of Haggis McMutton in the animated film *The Curse of Monkey Island* (1997). Over the years, Alan Young was also a guest star on such popular TV series as *The ANDY WILLIAMS SHOW, The LOVE BOAT, MURDER, SHE WROTE, ST. ELSEWHERE, COACH, PARTY OF FIVE, Batman: The Animated Series, Duckman, The Wayans brothers Show*, and SABRINA; THE TEENAGE WITCH.

YOUNG, LORETTA (GRETCHEN MICHAELA YOUNG 1913–2000)
Film and television star Loretta Young, who was born in Salt Lake City, Utah, made her professional acting debut when she was four years old with her elder sisters, Polly Ann and Elizabeth Jane. Loretta had moved to Hollywood with her mother, who ran a boardinghouse, when she was three years old, and her mother lost no time in trying to get work in films for her three pretty daughters. As early as 1917, Loretta had a small role in the silent films *The Primrose Ring* and *The Only Way*, but took leave from acting to attend a convent school. At 14, Loretta returned to the screen playing a small role in the Rudolph Valentino film *The Sheik*, and then was seen in a film that starred Colleen Moore, *Naughty but Nice*. Loretta's first major film role was in *The Magnificent Flirt* (1928), and she received second billing in *The Head Man* that same year. By the 1930s, Young had established herself as one of Hollywood's major leading ladies, and in the 1930s and 1940s she starred in such important films as *Call of the Wild* (1935), *The Story of Alexander Graham Bell* (1939), *And Now Tomorrow* (1944), *The Stranger* (1946), *The Bishop's Wife* (1947), *The Farmer's Daughter* (1947, for which she won a coveted Academy Award as Best Actress), *Rachel and the Stranger* (1948), *Mother Is a Freshman* (1949), *Come to the Stable* (1949), and *Key to the City* (1950). In 1953, with good film roles becoming more difficult to obtain, Loretta decided to devote her time to a career on television, and she starred on the very successful dramatic anthology show, *The LORETTA YOUNG SHOW*, on which she played different roles on each half-hour weekly drama presented on the series. Also called *a Letter to Loretta*, the show remained on the air for eight seasons, and won Loretta Emmy Awards as Best Actress in a Dramatic Series in 1954, 1956, and 1958. In 1962, Young appeared on a new anthology series, *The New Loretta Young Show*, which was not as successful as her first series, and Loretta quietly retired from show business, appearing only occasionally thereafter in the films *Christmas Eve* (1986) and *Lady in the Corner* (1989).

YOUNG, ROBERT (ROBERT GEORGE YOUNG 1907–1998)
Even though he was a veteran movie actor who was playing major roles in feature films as early as 1924, Robert

Young became best known for playing roles on two popular TV series: Jim Anderson, on the long-running TV situation comedy series *FATHER KNOWS BEST* from 1954 through 1963, and the lovable family doctor, Marcus Welby, on *MARCUS WELBY, M.D.*, from 1969 through 1976. Young, who was born in Chicago, first came to the public's attention in 1924, when he appeared in the silent film *It Is the Law*. He subsequently appeared in such talkies as *The Guilty Generation* (1931), *The Sin of Madelon Claudet* (1931), *Tugboat Annie* (1933), *The House of Rothschild* (1934), *Hollywood Party* (1934), *The Bride Comes Home* (1935), *Rich Man, Poor Girl* (1938), *Maisie* (1939), *Northwest Passage* (1940), *Lady Be Good* (1941), *Western Union* (1941), *The Enchanted Cottage* (1945), *Those Endearing Young Charms* (1945), and *That Forsyte Woman* (1949), to name just a few. After *Marcus Welby, M.D.* left the air, Young was seen on the short-lived TV series *Little Women* (1979). Young appeared only rarely on television, in such TV films as *Mercy or Murder?* (1987), *Conspiracy of Love* (1987), and *Marcus Welby, M.D.: A Holiday Affair* (1988). He suffered from periodic bouts with alcoholism and depression and attempted to commit suicide in 1991. He died of respiratory failure in 1998.

YOUNG AND THE RESTLESS, THE

Mar. 1973–present	CBS	Mon–Fri. Various daytime hours

When the CBS daytime drama *Where the Heart Is* failed to attract an audience, it was replaced by a series that CBS hoped would prove to be more appealing to younger soap opera viewers. The series was called *The Young and the Restless*, and it did indeed become immediately successful with the daytime audience. Created by William Bell and Lee Phillips Bell, the show's executive producer was John Conboy, and then William Bell and H. Wesley Kennedy, took over as executive producers in 1982. In 1989, Edward Scott became the show's executive producer. During its third season, *The Young and the Restless* won the first of its many subsequent "Best Daytime Drama" Emmy Awards.

The Young and the Restless is set in a town called Genoa City, and when it was first aired, the series centered on the Brooks and Foster families. By the early 1980s, both of these families had been written off the show, and the story lines thereafter mainly involved members of the Abbott, Newman, and Williams families. In its earliest days, Robert Colbert played Stuart, the patriarch of the Brooks clan, who owned Genoa City's newspaper, *The Chronicle*. Dorothy Green played Stuart's wife, Jennifer; Trish Stewart, and then Lynne Richter (aka Lynne Topping), played their daughter Chris; Janice Lynde, and then Victoria Mallory, played their daughter Leslie; Jaime Lyn Bauer played their daughter Lauralee; and Pamela Peters (aka Pamela Peters Solow), and then Patricia Everly, played their daughter Peggy. Other characters who

were regularly featured on the series during these years were Liz Foster, played by Julianna McCarthy; Greg Foster, played by James Houghton, Brian Kerwin, Wings Hauser, and Howard McGillan in turn; Bill "Snapper" Foster, played by William Gary Espy, and then David HASSELHOFF; and Jill Foster, played by Brenda Dickson, Bond Gideon, Deborah Adair, and finally Jess Walton, who played the role the longest and is still on the series as of this writing. Other popular characters introduced during these early years were Sally McGuire, played by Lee Crawford; Brad Elliot, played by Tom Hallick; Pierre Rouland, played by Robert Clary; and Kay Chancellor, a wealthy woman who had a preference for younger men and who had a face-lift during the course of the show, played by Jeanne Cooper, who had a real-life face-lift and remains one of the show's most popular regular characters to this day. Among the other actors who were featured on the series during its first decade were John Considine, Donnelly Rhodes, Robert Clarke, Paul Stevens, Steve Carlson, Beau Kazer (as Brock, Kay Chancellor's son), Anthony Herrera, John McCook, Dennis Cole, Deidre Hall, Jennifer Leak, Gwen Sherman, Charles Gray, Barry Cahill, Tom SELLECK, Jordeann Russo, Cathy Carricaburu, and Melody Thomas, who plays Nikki Reed, who evolved into one of the series' most visible presences and is a major character on the series to this day.

Eventually, in the 1980s, the Abbott, Newman, and Williams families replaced the Foster and Brooks families as, show's central characters. Brett Halsey, and finally Jerry Douglas, played John Abbott, who heads the Jabot Cosmetics company; Terry Lester, and finally Peter Bergman, played his son, Jack; Ellen Davidson and Brenda Epperson played Abbott's daughter Ashley; Beth Maitland played his daughter Tracy; Tammy Taylor, Lilibert Stern, and Andrea Evans-Massey played Jack's wife, Patty Williams Abbott; Doug Davidson, who is still a major actor on the series played Patty's brother, Paul Williams who became a private investigator: Carolyn Conwell played Patty and Paul's mother, Mary Williams; Eric Braeden played Victor Newman, the mighty mogul who headed Newman Enterprises, Genoa City's wealthiest and perhaps most romantic citizen (Newman married ex-stripper Nikki Reed and had two children who grew up in record time to become two of the series most important young adult characters, Victoria Newman, played by Heather Tom, and Nicholas Newman, played by John Nelson Alden, and finally by Joshua Morrow). Also prominently featured on the series in the 1980s and 90s were Michael Damian as rock singer Danny Romalotti; Marguerite Ray, and finally Veronica Redd-Forrest as Mamie Johnson; Patty Weaver as Gina Romalotti; Lauralee Bell as Christine "Crickett" Blair (who married Danny Romalotti and then married Paul Williams); Don Diamont as Brad Carlson, who married both of John Abbott's daughters; Scott Reeves as Ryan O'Neill; Devon Pierce as Diane Westin; Christian J. LeBlanc as crafty lawyer Michael Baldwin; Kimberlin Brown as the demented Shelia Carter Grainger; Heidi Marks, and then

Sharon Case, as Sharon Collins (who married Nicholas Newman); Tonya Lee Williams as Dr. Olivia Barber; Victoria Rowell as Olivia's sister, Drucilla; Kristoff St. John as Neil Winter (who married Drucilla), and Shemar Moore as Malcom Winters. Other popular actors and characters featured on *The Young and the Restless* during the show's last 20 years include Jerry Lacy (Jonas), Ellen Weston (Suzanne Lynch), Chris Holder (Kevin Bancroft), John Demos (Joe Blair), Tracey E. Bregman and Caryn Richman as Lauren Fenimore; Kate Linder as Esther (Kay Chancellor's maid); Quinn Reddeker (Rex Sterling, who married Kay Chancellor), Barbara Crampton (Leanna Randolph, aka Leanna Love), Peter Barton (Scott Granger), Laura Bryan Birn (Lynn Bassett, Paul's loyal secretary), Signy Coleman (Hope Adams, a blind girl who married Victor Newman), Tricia Cast (Nina Webster), John Castellanos (lawyer John Silva), Parley Baer (Miles Dugan), and Maxine Stuart (Margaret Anderson).

When *The Young and the Restless* first went on the air, it was a half-hour, five-day-a-week series, but in 1980, it was expanded to a full hour, five-day-a-week program. The show's theme music, which became known as "Nadia's Theme" after it was used as performance music for gymnast Nadia Comaneci during the 1976 Olympics, was composed by Barry DeVorzon and Perry Botkin, Jr. The theme is unquestionably the most recognized piece of soap opera music heard on television.

YOUNG DR. MALONE

Dec. 1958–Mar. 1963   NBC   Mon.–Fri. Various daytime hours

One of radio's most successful daytime drama series from 1939 until 1960, *Young Dr. Malone* was one of the first soap operas to transfer from radio to television, and for two years it was seen as well as heard. The series arrived on TV as a replacement for the less than successful soap series *Today Is Ours,* and six of the characters who were featured on that series were also seen on *Young Dr. Malone.* The series was mainly set in Valley Hospital, located in the fictional town of Three Oaks. The cast included William Prince and Virginia Dwyer, and then Augusta Dabney, as Dr. Jerry Malone, who was the chief of staff at Valley Hospital, and his wife, Tracey; John Connell as the Malone's adopted son, Dr. David Malone; Kathleen Widdoes, and then Freda Holloway and Sarah Hardy, as the Malone's daughter, Jill; Emily McLaughlin as Dr. Eileen Seaton, young doctor David Malone's love interest; Peter Brandon as Dr. Ted Powell; Lesley Woods as Clare Bannister; Martin Blaine as Lionel Steele; Zina Bethune, Michele Tuttle, Susan Hallaran, and Patty McCormack as Lisha Steele; and Diana Hyland as Gig Houseman.

YOUNG INDIANA JONES CHRONICLES, THE

Mar. 1992–Apr. 1992   ABC   Wed. 9–10 P.M.
Aug. 1992–Nov. 1992   ABC   Mon. 8–9 P.M.
Mar. 1993–Apr. 1993   ABC   Sat. 8–9 P.M.
June 1993–July 1993   ABC   Sat. 8–9 P.M.

After his success with his *Indiana Jones* films, which starred Harrison Ford, George Lucas brought the character of Indiana Jones as a young man to television in an expensively produced series that used elaborate sets and was filmed in exotic locations throughout the world with all the nonstop action for which the *Indiana Jones* films had become famous. Sean Patrick Flanery played Indiana at age 16, Corey Carrier played Indiana at the age of 10, and George Hall narrated as a 93-year-old Indiana recalling his days of past glory. During this short-lived series, the young explorer/archeologist Indiana ran across a wide variety of historical figures including the father of psychiatry, Sigmund Freud, Rough Rider and later President Theodore Roosevelt, Mexican patriot Pancho Villa, inventor Thomas Edison, adventurer Lawrence of Arabia, artist Norman Rockwell, war hero General George S. Patton, and others during the brief 16 months the series was on the air. In addition to Indiana, other regular characters included Ronny Coutteure as Indy's friend, Lloyd Owen as Indy's father, Professor Jones, and Ruth DeSosa as Anna Jones. The star of the *Indiana Jones* films, Harrison Ford, playing Jones at age 50, made a single appearance on the series in March 1993.

YOUNG RIDERS, THE

Sept. 1989   ABC   Wed. 8:30–9:30 P.M.
Sept. 1989–Apr. 1990   ABC   Thurs. 9–10 P.M.
May 1990   ABC   Mon. 8–9 P.M.
May 1990–Sept. 1990   ABC   Thus. 9–10 P.M.
Sept. 1990–Aug. 1991   ABC   Sat. 8–9 P.M.
Sept. 1991–Jan. 1992   ABC   Sat. 9–10 P.M.
May 1992–July 1992   ABC   Thurs. 8–9 P.M.

The Young Riders was an excellent western series that unfortunately surfaced at a time when TV series with western settings were not particularly popular. The hour-long adventure series centered on a group of young Pony Express riders who delivered the mail for a brief time in the Old West of the 1860s, and who also rescued runaway slaves, tracked down outlaws, protected innocents, and acted as liaisons between settlers and the Indians. The story lines involved both reality and fiction: "The Kid" apparently was supposed to be William Bonney, alias Billy the Kid, played by Ty Miller; Bill Cody (later Buffalo Bill Cody) was played by Stephen Baldwin; and Jimmy Hickok (Will Bill Hickok) was played by Josh Brolin. Other regular riders included Lou McCloud, played by Yvonne Suhor, a girl who disguised herself as a boy in order to become a Pony Express rider; Ike McSwain, played by Travis Fine (1989–91); and a young Native American, Little Buck Cross, played by Gregg Rainwater. Veteran character actor Anthony Zerbe played the riders' boss, Teaspoon Hunter; Melissa Leo (1989–90) played the riders' cook, Emma Shannon; and Brett Cullen (1989–90), played the local lawman, Marshall Sam Cain. Also appearing on the series as regulars were Clare Wren (1990–92) as Rachel Dunn, and Don Franklin (1990–92) as Noah Dixon. Originally, the Pony Express headquarters was located in Sweetwater, Wyoming, but in 1992, the series action shifted to Cross Creek, Nebraska. At that time, a new young rider named Jesse James, played by Christopher Pettiet, joined the group.

YOUR HIT PARADE

July 1950–Aug. 1950	NBC	Mon. 9–9:30 P.M.
Oct. 1950–June 1958	NBC	Sat. 10:30–11 P.M.
Oct. 1958–Apr. 1959	CBS	Fri. 7:30–8 P.M.
Aug. 1974	CBS	Fri. 8–8:30 P.M.

A popular radio show that was sponsored for many years by Lucky Strike cigarettes and was on the air from 1935 until 1956, *Your Hit Parade* presented the top seven songs in America sung by a regular cast of performers that included, at one time, Frank Sinatra. In 1950, running concurrently with the radio show, NBC decided to try out *Your Hit Parade* on television as a four-time-only summer replacement for the *ROBERT MONTGOMERY PRESENTS* dramatic anthology show. The public responded favorably to the TV version of one of their favorite radio programs, and it became a weekly feature on NBC that following October. The format of the TV show remained basically the same as it was for the radio show with one difference: since the TV show was visual, various settings had to be used for songs that remained on the Hit Parade for weeks on end, in order to give the show variety. Occasionally, the songs were presented as musical dance numbers, with only the music of the hit song being heard. Most of the time, however, singers, usually costumed appropriately, sang the hit songs for viewers. The hits were heard from the number-seven song to the number-one song for the week. Occasionally, popular songs from the past were featured as "extras." Several songs, such as "Too Young" and "Because of You" remained in the top seven for weeks on end. "Too Young" was featured 12 times and "Because of You" 11 weeks. Among the many singers who starred on the show were Eileen Wilson (1950–52), Snooky Lansen (1950–57), Dorothy Collins, who was also "The Lucky Strike Girl" during their sponsorship of the program (1950–57, 1958–59), Sue Bennett (1951–52), June Valli (1952–53), Russell Arms (1952–57), Gisele MacKenzie (1953–57), Tommy Leonetti (1957–58), Jill Corey (1957–58), Alan Copeland (1957–58), Virginia Gibson (1957–58), and Johnny Desmond (1958–59). Also featured during these years were the Hit Paraders (chorus and dancers, 1950–58), and the Peter Gennaro Dancers (1958–59). The show's orchestra was led by Raymond Scott (1950–57) and Harry Sosnik (1958–59). André Baruch was the show's announcer from 1950 to 1957, and Del Sharbutt from 1957 to 1958. Toward the end of the 1950s, rock-and-roll had begun to overtake the type of popular music that had been favored at the beginning of that decade, and it became increasingly difficult for the singers to sing the top seven songs, which, by 1958, were almost all rock and roll hits. The show began to lose favor with the public, and accordingly, it was canceled in 1959. In 1974, a revised version of *Your Hit Parade* surfaced that was more rock/and/roll oriented. The program featured singer Kelly Garrett, Chuck Woolery as show host, the Tom Hansen Dancers, and the orchestra of Milton Delugg. It failed to attract an audience and was canceled after less than one month on the air.

YOUR SHOW OF SHOWS

Feb. 1950–June 1954	NBC	Sat. 9–10:30 P.M.

One of early television's legendary programs, *Your Show of Shows* was a one-and-a-half-hour offering on NBC and featured hilarious comedy sketches, popular and classical music, and dance routines. The show, which starred comedians Sid CAESAR and Imogene COCA, was a successor to their *Admiral Broadway Revue*, a TV variety program that was first seen in 1949. *Your Show of Shows* began as the New York half of NBC's *Saturday Night Revue*, but its popularity soon surpassed the Jack Carter section of the show, which was telecast from Chicago. By the end of the 1950–51 season, Caesar and Coca became the sole

Sid Caesar and Imogene Coca in *Your Show of Shows* (Author's collection)

stars of the program, now called *Your Show of Shows.* Caesar and Coca appeared in such memorable comedy spoofs and sketches as "History as She Ain't," as well as in very funny spoofs of current popular films (such as their "From Here to Obscurity" spoof of the hit film *From Here to Eternity*), and well-known plays and novels. Caesar was also featured in numerous mime and monologue segments. Among the other performers who appeared on the series as regulars were Carl Reiner and Howard Morris (1951–54), who supported Caesar and Coca in numerous sketches, opera singer Robert Merrill (1950–53), singer Marguerite Piazza (1950–53), pop singer Bill Hayes (1950–53), Jerry Ross and Nellie Fisher (1950–52), Dancers Mata and Hari (1950–51), Tom Avera (1950), the Hamilton Dancers, singer Jack Russell, the Billy Williams Quartet, singer Judy Johnson (1950–53), musician Earl Redding (1950–51), Aariana Knowles (1951–52), Dick DeFreitas (1950–53), dancers Bambi Lynn and Rod Alexander (1952–54), James Starbuck, the Show of Shows Ballet Company, and the Charles Sanford Orchestra. The show, which was produced by Max Liebman, in no small way owed its success to the program's writers, who included such talented people as Mel Brooks, Neil Simon, Lucille Kallen, Larry Gelbart, Mel Tolkin, Woody Allen, Sam Denoff, and others. In 1954, Caesar and Coca decided to go their separate ways, and *Your Show of Shows* ended its successful run. The final telecast was a tearful, nostalgic program that featured the best of several of the most memorable comedy sketches from past shows. NBC President Pat Weaver made an appearance on the show, thanking everyone involved in the four successful seasons and wishing everyone in the cast success in all of their future endeavors. Sid Caesar and Imogene Coca were never able to recapture the magic of those four memorable years when *Your Show of Shows* reigned supreme.

Z

ZANE GREY THEATER (AKA DICK POWELL'S ZANE GREY THEATER)

Oct. 1956–July 1958	CBS	Fri. 8:30–9 P.M.
Oct. 1958–Sept. 1960	CBS	Thurs. 9–9:30 P.M.
Oct. 1960–July 1961	CBS	Thurs. 8:30–9 P.M.
Apr. 1962–Sept. 1962	CBS	Thurs. 9:30–10 P.M.

This dramatic anthology series dramatized the works of western adventure writer Zane Grey, and during the early years the show presented stories written only by Grey. As the series continued and Zane Grey material began to become scarce, the stories of other writers were featured on the series. The host was former film star Dick Powell, who frequently starred in one of the stories being dramatized. Also making appearances on the series at various times were such well-known performers as film stars Hedy Lamarr, Jack Lemmon, Ginger Rogers, Claudette Colbert, Esther Williams, and others. The series was produced by Hal Hudson for Dick Powell's Four Star Films, Zane Grey, and Pamric Productions.

ZIMBALIST, EFREM JR. (1918–)

The son of violinist Efrem Zimbalist and opera singer Alma Gluck, Efrem Zimablist, Jr. was born in New York City After finishing school, Efrem decided to enter show business, not as a musician, but as an actor. In 1953, he obtained a role in the film *House of Strangers* and in 1954 on *The UNITED STATES STEEL HOUR* and played a regular role on the *Concerning Miss Marlowe* TV series. He first came to the public's attention playing Dandy Jim Buckley on the popular western TV series MAVERICK in 1957. He also played roles in such films as *The Deep Six* (1957), *Band of Angels* (1957), *Home Before Dark* (1958), and *Girl on the Run* (1958). It wasn't until Zimbalist played Stuart Bailey on the successful TV series *77 SUNSET STRIP*, however, from 1958 through 1961, that he became a star. After *77 Sunset Strip* left the air, Zimbalist continued to be seen in such films as *Violent Road* (1958), *By Love Possessed* (1961), *Wait Until Dark* (1967), *Airport 1975*, as well as numerous TV films, and appeared on such TV series as *The F.B.I., Scruples* (1980), *Hotel* (1983), ZORRO (1990), *Prince Valiant* (1991), *Trade Winds* (1993), *Iron Man* (1994, voice of Justin Hammer), *Spider Man* (1995, voice of Otto Octavius/Dr. Octopus), and as the host of *A Year to Remember* (1999). Over the years, Efrem Zimbalist, Jr., has also made guest-starring appearances on such popular programs as ALFRED HITCHCOCK PRESENTS, MURDER, SHE WROTE, BURKE'S LAW, The NANNY, and PICKET FENCES. Zimbalist is the father of TV actress Stephanie Zimbalist.

ZOO PARADE

May 1950–Sept. 1957	NBC	Sunday afternoons

Zoo Parade was a very popular Sunday afternoon weekly series about animals and animal behavior that was seen on television in the 1950s and was cohosted by zookeeper Marlin PERKINS and Jim Hurlbut. The show was telecast from Chicago's Lincoln Park Zoo until 1955. During the show's final years, Perkins and Hurlbut traveled to various zoos around the world and filmed their telecasts.

ZORRO

(also Zorro and Son)

Oct. 1957–Sept. 1959	ABC	Thurs. 8–8:30 P.M.
Apr. 1983–June 1983	CBS	Wed. 8–8:30 P.M.
1990–1993	Family Channel	Various days and times

In addition to being the central character in successful feature films that starred Douglas Fairbanks, Sr., (1920) Tyrone Power (1940), Frank Langella (1974, as *The Mark of Zorro)*, Zorro (real name Don Diego de la Vega), a swashbuckling Spanish-American who fought for justice and decency in the developing southwestern United States during the early 1800s, was also the hero of a weekly television adventure series produced by William H. Anderson for the Walt Disney Studios. *Zorro* was the creation of author Johnston McCulley, who had written a series of adventure books with Zorro as the major character in the early 1900s. On the TV series, Guy Williams played Zorro, and also featured regularly in the cast were George J. Lewis as Don Alejandro, Gene Sheldon as Bernardo, and at various times, Britt Lemond (Capt. Monastario 1957–58), Henry Calvin (Sgt. Demetrio Lopez Garcia), Jan Arvan (Don Ignacio "Nacho" Torres 1957), Vinton Hayworth (Magistrate Carlos Gallindo), Romney Brent (Padre Felipe 1957), Charles Korvin (Jose Sebastian Varga 1958), Jolene Brand (Anna Maria Verdugo 1958–59), Eduard Franz (Senor Gregorio Verdugo 1959), and Don Diamond (Cpl. Reyes 1958–59). As in the *Zorro* films, Don Diego de la Vaga aka Zorro was the son of a wealthy family, returning home to the southwestern United States from Spain when his father summoned him back to California to help him deal with a ruthless army officer who was terrorizing local landowners and their workers. Don Diego pretended to be a lazy, shiftless playboy, but disguised as a hero who called himself Zorro he fought the army officer and numerous subsequent bad guys with the help of his trusted friend, Bernardo, who pretended to be deaf and mute and was the only person who knew his true identity. Zorro always left his trademark, a letter "Z" that he carved out with his sword to prove that he had been there. In 1983, a short-lived TV series called *Zorro and Son* was on the air for a few months and starred Henry Darrow as Don Diego/Zorro, and featured Paul Regina, Gregory Sierra, Richard Beauchamp, Bill Dana, Barney Martin, John Moschita, Catherine Parks, and Pete Leal. From 1989 through 1993, the Family Channel presented a 30-minute 88-episode series that starred Duncan Regehr as Don Diego/Zorro, Efrem Zimablist, Jr., and then Henry Darrow, as Don Alejandro, and Patrice Cahmi Martinez, James Victor, Michael Tylo, John Hertzler, and Ivan Diego Botto. Zorro returned to the big screen in *The Mask of Zorro* (1998), starring Antonio Banderas.

APPENDIXES

APPENDIX A:
Top-Rated Programs, 1952–1999

APPENDIX B:
The National Academy of Television Arts and Sciences's
Annual Emmy Awards, 1948–1999

APPENDIX A

TOP-RATED PROGRAMS, 1952–1999

OCTOBER 1952–APRIL 1953

Program	Network	Rating
I Love Lucy	CBS	67.3
Arthur Godfrey's Talent Scouts	CBS	54.7
Arthur Godfrey and His Friends	CBS	47.1
Dragnet	NBC	46.8
Texaco Star Theater	NBC	46.7
The Buick Circus Hour	NBC	46
The Colgate Comedy Hour	NBC	44.3
Gangbusters	NBC	42.4
You Bet Your Life	NBC	41.6
Fireside Theatre	NBC	40.6
The Red Buttons Show	CBS	40.2
The Jack Benny Program	CBS	39
Life with Luigi	CBS	38.5
Pabst Blue Ribbon Bouts	CBS	37.9
Goodyear TV Playhouse	NBC	37.8
The Life of Riley	NBC	37.4
Philco TV Playhouse	NBC	37.3
Mama	CBS	37
Your Show of Shows	NBC	36
What's My Line	CBS	35.3
Strike It Rich	CBS	35.3
Our Miss Brooks	CBS	35
The Big Story	NBC	35
Gillette Cavalcade of Sports	NBC	34.7
Amos 'n' Andy	CBS	34.4
All Star Revue	NBC	34.3
Treasury Men in Action	NBC	34.2
The Red Skelton Show	NBC	33.7
The Lone Ranger	ABC	33.7
Ford Theatre	NBC	33.6

OCTOBER 1953–APRIL 1954

Program	Network	Rating
I Love Lucy	CBS	58.8
Dragnet	NBC	53.2
Arthur Godfrey's Talent Scouts	CBS	43.6
You Bet Your Life	NBC	43.6
The Milton Berle Show	NBC	40.2
Arthur Godfrey and His Friends	CBS	38.9
Ford Theatre	NBC	38.8
The Jackie Gleason Show	CBS	38.1
Fireside Theatre	NBC	36.4
The Colgate Comedy Hour	NBC	36.2
This Is Your Life	NBC	36.2
The Red Buttons Show	CBS	35.3
The Life of Riley	NBC	35
Our Miss Brooks	CBS	34.2
Treasury Men in Action	NBC	33.9
The Jack Benny Program	CBS	33.3
The Toast of the Town	CBS	33
Gillette Cavalcade of Sports	NBC	32.7
Philco TV Playhouse	NBC	32.5
The George Burns and Gracie Allen Show	CBS	32.4
Kraft Television Theatre	NBC	31.3
Goodyear TV Playhouse	NBC	31
Pabst Blue Ribbon Bouts	CBS	30.9
Private Secretary	CBS	30.3
I Married Joan	NBC	30.2
Mama	CBS	30.2
General Electric Theater	NBC	29.9
What's My Line	CBS	29.6
The Big Story	NBC	29.5
Martin Kane, Private Eye	NBC	29.5
Your Hit Parade	NBC	29.5

OCTOBER 1954–APRIL 1955

Program	Network	Rating
I Love Lucy	CBS	49.3
The Jackie Gleason Show	CBS	42.4
Dragnet	NBC	42.1
You Bet Your Life	NBC	41
The Toast of the Town	CBS	39.6
Disneyland	ABC	39.1
The Jack Benny Program	CBS	38.3
The George Gobel Show	NBC	35.2
Ford Theatre	NBC	34.9
December Bride	CBS	34.7
Buick-Berle Show	NBC	34.6
This Is Your Life	NBC	34.5
I've Got a Secret	CBS	34
Two for the Money	CBS	33.9
Your Hit Parade	NBC	33.6
The Millionaire	CBS	33
General Electric Theater	CBS	32.6
Arthur Godfrey's Talent Scouts	CBS	32.5
Private Secretary	CBS	32.2
Fireside Theatre	NBC	31.1
The Life of Riley	NBC	30.9
Arthur Godfrey and His Friends	CBS	29.8
The Adventures of Rin Tin Tin	ABC	29.5
Topper	CBS	29.4
PabstBlue Ribbon Bouts	CBS	29.1
The George Burns and Gracie Allen Show	CBS	29
The Colgate Comedy Hour	NBC	28
The Loretta Young Show	NBC	27.7
My Little Margie	NBC	27.1
The Roy Rogers Show	NBC	26.9

OCTOBER 1955–APRIL 1956

Program	Network	Rating
The $64,000 Question	CBS	47.5
I Love Lucy	CBS	46.1
The Ed Sullivan Show	CBS	39.5
Disneyland	ABC	37.4
The Jack Benny Program	CBS	37.2
December Bride	CBS	37
You Bet Your Life	NBC	35.4
Dragnet	NBC	35
The Millionaire	CBS	33.8
I've Got a Secret	CBS	33.5
General Electric Theater	CBS	32.9
Private Secretary	CBS	32.4
Ford Theatre	NBC	32.4
The Red Skelton Show	CBS	32.3
The George Gobel Show	NBC	31.9
Arthur Godfrey's Talent Scouts	CBS	31.1
The Lineup	CBS	30.8
The Perry Como Show	NBC	30.3
The Honeymooners	CBS	30.2

Program	Network	Rating
The Adventures of Robin Hood	CBS	30.1
The Life of Riley	NBC	29.9
Climax	CBS	29.6
Your Hit Parade	NBC	29.1
Fireside Theatre	NBC	29
Lux Video Theatre	NBC	28.9
This is Your Life	NBC	28.8
People Are Funny	NBC	28.4
The George Burns and Gracie Allen Show	CBS	28.4
The Chevy Show	NBC	28.2
The Phil Silvers Show	CBS	28.1

OCTOBER 1956–APRIL 1957

Program	Network	Rating
I Love Lucy	CBS	43.7
The Ed Sullivan Show	CBS	38.4
General Electric Theater	CBS	36.9
The $64,000 Question	CBS	36.4
December Bride	CBS	35.2
Alfred Hitchcock Presents	CBS	33.9
I've Got a Secret	CBS	32.7
Gunsmoke	CBS	32.7
The Perry Como Show	NBC	32.6
The Jack Benny Program	CBS	32.3
Dragnet	NBC	32.1
Arthur Godfrey's Talent Scouts	CBS	31.9
The Millionaire	CBS	31.8
Disneyland	ABC	31.8
The Red Skelton Show	CBS	31.4
The Lineup	CBS	31.4
Your Bet Your Life	NBC	31.1
The Life & Legend of Wyatt Earp	ABC	31
The Ford Show	NBC	30.7
The Adventures of Robin Hood	CBS	30.3
People Are Funny	NBC	30.2
The $64,000 Challenge	CBS	29.7
The Phil Silvers Show	CBS	29.7
Lassie	CBS	29.5
Private Secretary	CBS	29
Climax	CBS	28.9
What's My Line	CBS	28.9
The George Burns and Gracie Allen Show	CBS	27.8
The Jackie Gleason Show	CBS	27.6
Name That Tune	CBS	27.2

OCTOBER 1957–APRIL 1958

Program	Network	Rating
Gunsmoke	CBS	43.1
The Danny Thomas Show	CBS	35.3
Tales of Wells Fargo	NBC	35.2
Have Gun Will Travel	CBS	33.7
I've Got a Secret	CBS	33.4
The Life and Legend of Wyatt Earp	ABC	32.6

General Electric Theater	CBS	31.5
The Restless Gun	NBC	31.4
December Bride	CBS	30.7
You Bet Your Life	NBC	30.6
The Perry Como Show	NBC	30.5
Alfred Hitchcock Presents	CBS	30.3
Cheyenne	ABC	30.3
The Ford Show	NBC	29.7
The Red Skelton Show	CBS	28.9
The Gale Storm Show	CBS	28.8
The Millionaire	CBS	28.5
The Lineup	CBS	28.4
This Is Your Life	NBC	28.1
The $64,000 Question	CBS	28.1
Zane Grey Theater	CBS	27.9
Lassie	CBS	27.8
Wagon Train	NBC	27.7
Sugarfoot	ABC	27.7
Father Knows Best	NBC	27.7
Twenty-One	NBC	27.6
The Ed Sullivan Show	CBS	27.3
The Jack Benny Program	CBS	27.1
People Are Funny	NBC	27
The Loretta Young Show	NBC	26.6
Zorro	ABC	26.6
The Real McCoys	ABC	26.6

OCTOBER 1958–APRIL 1959

Program	Network	Rating
Gunsmoke	CBS	39.6
Wagon Train	NBC	36.1
Have Gun Will Travel	CBS	34.3
The Rifleman	ABC	33.1
The Danny Thomas Show	CBS	32.8
Maverick	ABC	30.4
Tales of Wells Fargo	NBC	30.2
The Real McCoys	ABC	30.1
I've Got a Secret	CBS	29.8
The Life and Legend of Wyatt Earp	ABC	29.1
The Price Is Right	NBC	28.6
The Red Skelton Show	CBS	28.5
Zane Grey Theater	CBS	28.3
Father Knows Best	CBS	28.3
The Texan	CBS	28.2
Wanted: Dead or Alive	CBS	28
Peter Gunn	NBC	28
Cheyenne	ABC	27.9
Perry Mason	CBS	27.5
The Ford Show	NBC	27.2
Sugarfoot	ABC	27
The Ann Sothern Show	CBS	27
The Perry Como Show	NBC	27
Alfred Hitchcock Presents	CBS	26.8
Name That Tune	CBS	26.7
General Electric Theatre	CBS	26.7
The Lawman	ABC	26

Rawhide	CBS	25.9
This Is Your Life	NBC	25.8
The Millionaire	CBS	25.6

OCTOBER 1959–APRIL 1960

Program	Network	Rating
Gunsmoke	CBS	40.3
Wagon Train	NBC	38.4
Have Gun Will Travel	CBS	34.7
The Danny Thomas Show	CBS	31.1
The Red Skelton Show	CBS	30.8
Father Knows Best	CBS	29.7
7 Sunset Strip	ABC	29.7
The Price Is Right	NBC	29.2
Wanted: Dead or Alive	CBS	28.7
Perry Mason	CBS	28.3
The Real McCoys	ABC	28.2
The Ed Sullivan Show	CBS	28
The Rifleman	ABC	27.5
The Ford Show	NBC	27.4
The Lawman	ABC	26.2
Dennis the Menace	CBS	26
Cheyenne	ABC	25.9
Rawhide	CBS	25.8
Maverick	ABC	25.2
The Life and Legend of Wyatt Earp	ABC	25
Mr. Lucky	CBS	24.4
Zane Grey Theater	CBS	24.4
General Electric Theater	CBS	24.4
The Ann Sothern Show	CBS	24.2
Alfred Hitchcock Presents	CBS	24.1
You Bet Your Life	NBC	24
What's My Line	CBS	23.9
I've Got a Secret	CBS	23.5
The Perry Como Show	NBC	23.1
Lassie	CBS	23.1

OCTOBER 1960–APRIL 1961

Program	Network	Rating
Gunsmoke	CBS	37.3
Wagon Train	NBC	34.2
Have Gun Will Travel	CBS	30.9
The Andy Griffith Show	CBS	27.8
The Real McCoys	ABC	27.7
Rawhide	CBS	27.5
Candid Camera	CBS	27.3
The Untouchables	ABC	27
The Price Is Right	NBC	27
The Jack Benny Program	CBS	26.2
Dennis the Menace	CBS	26.1
The Danny Thomas Show	CBS	25.9
My Three Sons	ABC	25.8
77 Sunset Strip	ABC	25.8
The Ed Sullivan Show	CBS	25

Program	Network	Rating
Perry Mason	CBS	24.9
Bonanza	NBC	24.8
The Flintstones	ABC	24.3
The Red Skelton Show	CBS	24
General Electric Theater	CBS	23.4
Checkmate	CBS	23.2
What's My Line	CBS	23.1
The Many Loves of Dobie Gillis	CBS	23
The Ford Show	NBC	22.9
The Garry Moore Show	CBS	22.7
The Lawman	ABC	22.3
The Rifleman	ABC	22.1
Cheyenne	ABC	22
Peter Gunn	NBC	21.9
Route 66	CBS	21.7

OCTOBER 1961–APRIL 1962

Program	Network	Rating
Wagon Train	NBC	32.1
Bonanza	NBC	30
Gunsmoke	CBS	28.3
Hazel	NBC	27.7
Perry Mason	CBS	27.3
The Red Skelton Show	CBS	27.1
The Andy Griffith Show	CBS	27
The Danny Thomas Show	CBS	26.1
Dr. Kildare	NBC	25.6
Candid Camera	CBS	25.5
My Three Sons	ABC	24.7
The Garry Moore Show	CBS	24.6
Rawhide	CBS	24.5
The Real McCoys	ABC	24.2
Lassie	CBS	24
Sing Along with Mitch	NBC	24
Dennis the Menace	CBS	23.8
Ben Casey	ABC	23.7
The Ed Sullivan Show	CBS	23.5
Car 54, Where Are You?	NBC	23.2
The Flintstones	ABC	22.9
The Many Loves of Dobie Gillis	CBS	22.9
Walt Disney's Wonderful World of Color	NBC	22.7
The Joey Bishop Show	NBC	22.6
The Perry Como Show	NBC	22.5
The Defenders	CBS	22.4
The Price Is Right	NBC	22.3
The Rifleman	ABC	22.3
Have Gun, Will Travel	CBS	22.2
The Donna Reed Show	ABC	21.9
77 Sunset Strip	ABC	21.9

OCTOBER 1962–APRIL 1963

Program	Network	Rating
The Beverly Hillbillies	CBS	36.0
Candid Camera	CBS	31.1
The Red Skelton Show	CBS	31.1
Bonanza	NBC	29.8
The Lucy Show	CBS	29.8
The Andy Griffith Show	CBS	29.7
Ben Casey	ABC	28.7
The Danny Thomas Show	CBS	28.7
The Dick Van Dyke Show	CBS	27.1
Gunsmoke	CBS	27
Dr. Kildare	NBC	26.2
The Jack Benny Program	CBS	26.2
What's My Line	CBS	25.5
The Ed Sullivan Show	CBS	25.3
Hazel	NBC	25.1
I've Got a Secret	CBS	24.9
The Jackie Gleason Show	CBS	24.1
The Defenders	CBS	23.9
The Garry Moore Show	CBS	23.3
To Tell the Truth	CBS	23.3
Lassie	CBS	23.3
Rawhide	CBS	22.8
Perry Mason	CBS	22.4
Walt Disney's Wonderful World of Color	NBC	22.3
Wagon Train	ABC	22
The Virginian	NBC	21.7
Route 66	CBS	21.3
My Three Sons	ABC	21
Have Gun Will Travel	CBS	20.8
The Flintstones	ABC	20.5

OCTOBER 1963–APRIL 1964

Program	Network	Rating
The Beverly Hillbillies	CBS	39.1
Bonanza	NBC	36.9
The Dick Van Dyke Show	CBS	33.3
Petticoat Junction	CBS	30.3
The Andy Griffith Show	CBS	29.4
The Lucy Show	CBS	28.1
Candid Camera	CBS	27.7
The Ed Sullivan Show	CBS	27.5
The Danny Thomas Show	CBS	26.7
My Favorite Martian	CBS	26.3
The Red Skelton Show	CBS	25.7
I've Got A Secret	CBS	25
Lassie	CBS	25
The Jack Benny Program	CBS	25
The Jackie Gleason Show	CBS	24.6
The Donna Reed Show	ABC	24.5
The Virginian	NBC	24
The Patty Duke Show	ABC	23.9
Dr. Kildare	NBC	23.6
Gunsmoke	CBS	23.5
Walt Disney's Wonderful World of Color	NBC	23
Hazel	NBC	22.8

Program	Network	Rating
McHale's Navy	ABC	22.8
To Tell the Truth	CBS	22.6
What's My Line	CBS	22.6
Perry Mason	CBS	22.1
My Three Sons	ABC	21.9
The Fugitive	ABC	21.7
The Adventures of Ozzie and Harriet	ABC	21.6
The Danny Kaye Show	CBS	21.5
Bob Hope Presents the Chrysler Theatre	NBC	21.5

OCTOBER 1964–APRIL 1965

Program	Network	Rating
Bonanza	NBC	36.3
Bewitched	ABC	31
Gomer Pyle, U.S.M.C.	CBS	30.7
The Andy Griffith Show	CBS	28.3
The Fugitive	ABC	27.9
The Red Skelton Hour	CBS	27.4
The Dick Van Dyke Show	CBS	27.1
The Lucy Show	CBS	26.6
Peyton Place II	ABC	26.4
Combat	ABC	26.1
Walt Disney's Wonderful World of Color	NBC	25.7
The Beverly Hillbillies	CBS	25.6
My Three Sons	ABC	25.5
Branded	NBC	25.3
Petticoat Junction	CBS	25.2
The Ed Sullivan Show	CBS	25.2
Lassie	CBS	25.1
The Munsters	CBS	24.7
Gilligan's Island	CBS	24.7
Peyton Place I	ABC	24.6
The Jackie Gleason Show	CBS	24.4
The Virginian	NBC	24
The Addams Family	ABC	23.9
My Favorite Martian	CBS	23.7
Flipper	NBC	23.4
I've Got a Secret	CBS	23
Gunsmoke	CBS	22.6
The Patty Duke Show	ABC	22.4
McHale's Navy	ABC	22.3
The Lawrence Welk Show	ABC	22

OCTOBER 1965–APRIL 1966

Program	Network	Rating
Bonanza	NBC	31.8
Gomer Pyle, U.S.M.C.	CBS	27.8
The Lucy Show	CBS	27.7
The Red Skelton Hour	CBS	27.6
Batman (Thurs.)	ABC	27
The Andy Griffith Show	CBS	26.9
Bewitched	ABC	25.9
The Beverly Hillbillies	CBS	25.9
Hogan's Heroes	CBS	24.9
Batman (Wed.)	ABC	24.7
Green Acres	CBS	24.6
Get Smart	NBC	24.5
The Man from U.N.C.L.E.	NBC	24
Daktari	CBS	23.9
My Three Sons	CBS	23.8
The Dick Van Dyke Show	CBS	23.6
Walt Disney's Wonderful World of Color	NBC	23.2
The Ed Sullivan Show	CBS	23.2
The Lawrence Welk Show	ABC	22.4
I've Got a Secret	CBS	22.4
Petticoat Junction	CBS	22.3
Gilligan's Island	CBS	22.1
Wild, Wild West	CBS	22
The Jackie Gleason Show	CBS	22
The Virginian	NBC	22
Daniel Boone	NBC	21.9
Lassie	CBS	21.8
I Dream of Jeannie	NBC	21.8
Flipper	NBC	21.6
Gunsmoke	CBS	21.3

OCTOBER 1966–APRIL 1967

Program	Network	Rating
Bonanza	NBC	29.1
The Red Skelton Hour	CBS	28.2
The Andy Griffith Show	CBS	27.4
The Lucy Show	CBS	26.2
The Jackie Gleason Show	CBS	25.3
Green Acres	CBS	24.6
Daktari	CBS	23.4
Bewitched	ABC	23.4
The Beverly Hillbillies	CBS	23.4
Gomer Pyle, U.S.M.C.	CBS	22.8
The Virginian	NBC	22.8
The Lawrence Welk Show	ABC	22.8
The Ed Sullivan Show	CBS	22.8
The Dean Martin Show	NBC	22.6
Family Affair	CBS	22.6
The Smothers Brothers Comedy Hour	CBS	22.2
Friday Night Movies	CBS	21.8
Hogan's Heroes	CBS	21.8
Walt Disney's Wonderful World of Color	NBC	21.5
Saturday Night at the Movies	NBC	21.4
Dragnet	NBC	21.2
Get Smart	NBC	21
Petticoat Junction	CBS	20.9
Rat Patrol	ABC	20.9
Daniel Boone	NBC	20.8
Bob Hope Presents the Chrysler Theatre	NBC	20.7
Tarzan	NBC	20.5

Program	Network	Rating
ABC Sunday Night Movie	ABC	20.4
I Spy	NBC	20.2
CBS Thursday Movie	CBS	20.2
My Three Sons	CBS	20.2
The F.B.I.	ABC	20.2

OCTOBER 1967–APRIL 1968

Program	Network	Rating
The Andy Griffith Show	CBS	27.6
The Lucy Show	CBS	27
Gomer Pyle, U.S.M.C.	CBS	25.6
Gunsmoke	CBS	25.5
Family Affair	CBS	25.5
Bonanza	NBC	25.5
The Red Skelton Show	CBS	25.3
The Dean Martin Show	NBC	24.8
The Jackie Gleason Show	CBS	23.9
Saturday Night at the Movies	NBC	23.6
Bewitched	ABC	23.5
The Beverly Hillbillies	CBS	23.3
The Ed Sullivan Show	CBS	23.2
The Virginian	NBC	22.9
Friday Night Movie	CBS	22.8
Green Acres	CBS	22.8
The Lawrence Welk Show	ABC	21.9
The Smothers Brothers Comedy Hour	CBS	21.7
Gentle Ben	CBS	21.5
Tuesday Night at the Movies	NBC	21.4
Rowan & Martin's Laugh-In	NBC	21.3
The F.B.I.	ABC	21.2
Thursday Night Movie	CBS	21.1
My Three Sons	CBS	20.8
Walt Disney's Wonderful World of Color	NBC	20.7
Ironside	NBC	20.5
The Carol Burnett Show	CBS	20.1
Dragnet '67	NBC	20.1
Daniel Boone	NBC	20
Lassie	CBS	19.9
It Takes a Thief	ABC	19.9

OCTOBER 1968–APRIL 1969

Program	Network	Rating
Rowan & Martin's Laugh-In	NBC	31.8
Gomer Pyle, U.S.M.C.	CBS	27.2
Bonanza	NBC	26.6
Mayberry R.F.D.	CBS	25.4
Family Affair	CBS	25.2
Gunsmoke	CBS	24.9
Julia	NBC	24.6
The Dean Martin Show	NBC	24.1
Here's Lucy	CBS	23.8
The Beverly Hillbillies	CBS	23.5

Program	Network	Rating
Mission: Impossible	CBS	23.3
Bewitched	ABC	23.3
The Red Skelton Hour	CBS	23.3
My Three Sons	CBS	22.8
The Glen Campbell Goodtime Hour	CBS	22.5
Ironside	NBC	22.3
The Virginian	NBC	21.8
The F.B.I.	ABC	21.7
Green Acres	CBS	21.6
Dragnet	NBC	21.4
Daniel Boone	NBC	21.3
Walt Disney's Wonderful World of Color	NBC	21.3
The Ed Sullivan Show	CBS	21.2
The Carol Burnett Show	CBS	20.8
The Jackie Gleason Show	CBS	20.8
I Dream of Jeannie	NBC	20.7
The Smothers Brothers Comedy Hour	CBS	20.6
The Mod Squad	ABC	20.5
The Lawrence Welk Show	ABC	20.5
The Doris Day Show	CBS	20.4

OCTOBER 1969–APRIL 1970

Program	Network	Rating
Rowan & Martin's Laugh-In	NBC	26.3
Gunsmoke	CBS	25.9
Bonanza	NBC	24.8
Mayberry R.F.D.	CBS	24.4
Family Affair	CBS	24.2
Here's Lucy	CBS	23.9
The Red Skelton Hour	CBS	23.8
Marcus Welby, M.D.	ABC	23.7
Walt Disney's Wonderful World of Color	NBC	23.6
The Doris Day Show	CBS	22.8
The Bill Cosby Show	NBC	22.7
The Jim Nabors Hour	CBS	22.4
The Carol Burnett Show	CBS	22.1
The Dean Martin Show	NBC	21.9
My Three Sons	CBS	21.8
Ironside	NBC	21.8
The Johnny Cash Show	ABC	21.8
The Beverly Hillbillies	CBS	21.7
Hawaii Five-O	CBS	21.1
The Glen Campbell Goodtime Hour	CBS	21
Hee Haw	CBS	21
Movie of the Week	ABC	20.9
Mod Squad	ABC	20.8
Saturday Night Movie	NBC	20.6
Bewitched	ABC	20.6
The F.B.I.	ABC	20.6
The Ed Sullivan Show	CBS	20.3
Julia	NBC	20.1
CBS Thursday Movie	CBS	20
Mannix	CBS	19.9

OCTOBER 1970–APRIL 1971

Program	Network	Rating
Marcus Welby, M.D.	ABC	29.6
The Flip Wilson Show	NBC	27.9
Here's Lucy	CBS	26.1
Ironside	NBC	25.7
Gunsmoke	CBS	25.5
ABC Movie of the Week	ABC	25.1
Hawaii Five-O	CBS	25
Medical Center	CBS	24.5
Bonanza	NBC	23.9
The FBI	ABC	23
Mod Squad	ABC	22.7
Adam-12	NBC	22.6
Rowan & Martin's Laugh-In	NBC	22.4
The Wonderful World of Disney	NBC	22.4
Mayberry R.F.D.	CBS	22.3
Hee Haw	CBS	21.4
Mannix	CBS	21.3
The Men from Shiloh	NBC	21.2
My Three Sons	CBS	20.8
The Doris Day Show	CBS	20.7
The Smith Family	ABC	20.6
The Mary Tyler Moore Show	CBS	20.3
NBC Saturday Movie	NBC	20.1
The Dean Martin Show	NBC	20
The Carol Burnett Show	CBS	19.8
The Partridge Family	ABC	19.8
NBC Monday Movie	NBC	19.8
ABC Sunday Movie	ABC	19.7
The Jim Nabors Hour	CBS	19.5
CBS Thursday Movie	CBS	19.3

OCTOBER 1971–APRIL 1972

Program	Network	Rating
All in the Family	CBS	34
The Flip Wilson Show	NBC	28.2
Marcus Welby, M.D.	ABC	27.8
Gunsmoke	CBS	26
ABC Movie of the Week	ABC	25.5
Sanford and Son	NBC	25.2
Mannix	CBS	24.8
Funny Face	CBS	23.9
Adam-12	NBC	23.9
The Mary Tyler Moore Show	CBS	23.7
Here's Lucy	CBS	23.7
Hawaii Five-O	CBS	23.6
Medical Center	CBS	23.5
The NBC Mystery Movie	NBC	23.2
Ironside	NBC	23
The Partridge Family	ABC	22.6
The F.B.I.	ABC	22.4
The New Dick Van Dyke Show	CBS	22.2
The Wonderful World of Disney	NBC	22
Bonanza	NBC	21.9

Program	Network	Rating
Mod Squad	ABC	21.5
Rowan & Martin's Laugh-In	NBC	21.4
The Carol Burnett Show	CBS	21.2
The Doris Day Show	CBS	21.2
Monday Night Football	ABC	20.9
ABC Sunday Movie	ABC	20.8
The Sonny and Cher Comedy Hour	CBS	20.2
Room 222	ABC	19.8
Cannon	CBS	19.8
CBS Friday Movie	CBS	19.5

OCTOBER 1972–APRIL 1973

Program	Network	Rating
All in the Family	CBS	33.3
Sanford and Son	NBC	27.6
Hawaii Five-O	CBS	25.2
Maude	CBS	24.7
Bridget Loves Bernie	CBS	24.2
The NBC Sunday Mystery Movie	NBC	24.2
The Mary Tyler Moore Show	CBS	23.6
Gunsmoke	CBS	23.6
The Wonderful World of Disney	NBC	23.5
Ironside	NBC	23.4
Adam-12	NBC	23.3
The Flip Wilson Show	NBC	23.1
Marcus Welby, M.D.	ABC	22.9
Cannon	CBS	22.4
Here's Lucy	CBS	21.9
The Bob Newhart Show	CBS	21.8
Tuesday Movie of the Week	ABC	21.5
Monday Night Football	ABC	21
The Partridge Family	ABC	20.6
The Waltons	CBS	20.6
Medical Center	CBS	20.6
The Carol Burnett Show	CBS	20.3
ABC Sunday Movie	ABC	20
The Rookies	ABC	20
Barnaby Jones	CBS	19.9
The Little People	NBC	19.9
ABC Wednesday Movie of the Week	ABC	19.9
NBC Monday Movie	NBC	19.3
ABC Monday Movie	ABC	19.2
The F.B.I.	ABC	19.2
Kung Fu	ABC	19.2

SEPTEMBER 1973–APRIL 1974

Program	Network	Rating
All in the Family	CBS	31.2
The Waltons	CBS	28.1
Sanford and Son	NBC	27.5
M*A*S*H	CBS	25.7
Hawaii Five-O	CBS	24
Maude	CBS	23.5
Kojak	CBS	23.3

The Sonny and Cher Comedy Hour	CBS	23.3
The Mary Tyler Moore Show	CBS	23.1
Cannon	CBS	23.1
The Six Million Dollar Man	ABC	22.7
The Bob Newhart Show	CBS	22.3
The Wonderful World of Disney	NBC	22.3
The NBC Sunday Mystery Movie	NBC	22.2
Gunsmoke	CBS	22.1
Happy Days	ABC	21.5
Good Times	CBS	21.4
Barnaby Jones	CBS	21.4
Monday Night Football	ABC	21.2
CBS Friday Night Movie	CBS	21.2
Tuesday Movie of the Week	ABC	21
The Streets of San Francisco	ABC	20.8
Adam-12	NBC	20.7
ABC Sunday Night Movie	ABC	20.7
The Rookies	ABC	20.3
ABC Monday Movie	ABC	20.2
The Carol Burnett Show	CBS	20.1
Kung Fu	ABC	20.1
Here's Lucy	CBS	20
CBS Thursday Movie	CBS	19.9

SEPTEMBER 1974–APRIL 1975

Program	Network	Rating
All in the Family	CBS	30.2
Sanford and Son	NBC	29.6
Chico and The Man	NBC	28.5
The Jeffersons	CBS	27.6
*M*A*S*H*	CBS	27.4
Rhoda	CBS	26.3
Good Times	CBS	25.8
The Waltons	CBS	25.5
Maude	CBS	24.9
Hawaii Five-O	CBS	24.8
The Mary Tyler Moore Show	CBS	24
The Rockford Files	NBC	23.7
Little House on the Prairie	NBC	23.5
Kojak	CBS	23.3
Police Woman	NBC	22.8
S.W.A.T.	ABC	22.6
The Bob Newhart Show	CBS	22.4
The Wonderful World of Disney	NBC	22
The Rookies	ABC	22
Mannix	CBS	21.6
Cannon	CBS	21.6
Cher	CBS	21.3
The Streets of San Francisco	ABC	21.3
The NBC Sunday Mystery Movie	NBC	21.3
Paul Sand in Friends and Lovers	CBS	20.7
Tony Orlando & Dawn	CBS	20.7
Medical Center	CBS	20.6
Gunsmoke	CBS	20.5
The Carol Burnett Show	CBS	20.4
Emergency!	NBC	20

SEPTEMBER 1975–APRIL 1976

Program	Network	Rating
All in the Family	CBS	30.1
Rich Man, Poor Man	ABC	28
Laverne & Shirley	ABC	27.5
Maude	CBS	25
The Bionic Woman	ABC	24.9
Phyllis	CBS	24.5
Sanford and Son	NBC	24.4
Rhoda	CBS	24.4
The Six Million Dollar Man	ABC	24.3
ABC Monday Night Movie	ABC	24.2
Happy Days	ABC	23.9
One Day at a Time	CBS	23.1
ABC Sunday Night Movie	ABC	23
The Waltons	CBS	22.9
*M*A*S*H*	CBS	22.9
Starsky and Hutch	ABC	22.5
Good Heavens	ABC	22.5
Welcome Back, Kotter	ABC	22.1
The Mary Tyler Moore Show	CBS	21.9
Kojak	CBS	21.8
The Jeffersons	CBS	21.5
Baretta	ABC	21.3
The Sonny & Cher Show	CBS	21.2
Good Times	CBS	21
Chico and the Man	NBC	20.8
The Bob Newhart Show	CBS	20.7
Donny and Marie	ABC	20.7
The Streets of San Francisco	ABC	20.7
The Carol Burnett Show	CBS	20.3
Police Woman	NBC	20.2

SEPTEMBER 1976–APRIL 1977

Program	Network	Rating
Happy Days	ABC	31.5
Laverne & Shirley	ABC	30.9
ABC Monday Night Movie	ABC	26
*M*A*S*H*	CBS	25.9
Charlie's Angels	ABC	25.8
The Big Event	NBC	24.4
The Six Million Dollar Man	ABC	24.2
ABC Sunday Night Movie	ABC	23.4
Baretta	ABC	23.4
One Day at a Time	CBS	23.4
Three's Company	ABC	23.1
All in the Family	CBS	22.9
Welcome Back, Kotter	ABC	22.7
The Bionic Woman	ABC	22.4
The Waltons	CBS	22.3
Little House on the Prairie	NBC	22.3
Barney Miller	ABC	22.2
60 Minutes	CBS	21.9
Hawaii Five-O	CBS	21.9
NBC Monday Night Movie	NBC	21.8

Rich Man, Poor Man, Book II	ABC	21.6
Monday Night Football	ABC	21.2
Eight Is Enough	ABC	21.1
The Jeffersons	CBS	21
What's Happening!	ABC	20.9
Good Times	CBS	20.5
Sanford and Son	NBC	20.3
ABC Friday Night Movie	ABC	20.2
The Tony Randall Show	ABC	20.1
Alice	CBS	20

SEPTEMBER 1977–APRIL 1978

Program	Network	Rating
Laverne & Shirley	ABC	31.6
Happy Days	ABC	31.4
Three's Company	ABC	28.3
60 Minutes	CBS	24.4
Charlie's Angels	ABC	24.4
All in the Family	CBS	24.4
Little House on the Prairie	NBC	24.1
Alice	CBS	23.2
M*A*S*H	CBS	23.2
One Day at a Time	CBS	23
How the West Was Won	ABC	22.5
Eight Is Enough	ABC	22.2
Soap	ABC	22
The Love Boat	ABC	21.9
NBC Monday Night Movie	NBC	21.7
Monday Might Football	ABC	21.5
Fantasy Island	ABC	21.4
Barney Miller	ABC	21.4
Project U.F.O.	NBC	21.2
ABC Sunday Night Movie	ABC	20.8
The Waltons	CBS	20.8
Barnaby Jones	CBS	20.6
Hawaii Five-O	CBS	20.4
ABC Monday Night Movie	ABC	20.3
Rhoda	CBS	20.1
The Incredible Hulk	CBS	19.9
Family	ABC	19.9
Welcome Back, Kotter	ABC	19.9
On Our Own	CBS	19.6
The Big Event-Sunday	NBC	19.4

SEPTEMBER 1978–APRIL 1979

Program	Network	Rating
Laverne & Shirley	ABC	30.5
Three's Company	ABC	30.3
Mork & Mindy	ABC	28.6
Happy Days	ABC	28.6
Angie	ABC	26.7
60 Minutes	CBS	25.5
M*A*S*H	CBS	25.4

The Ropers	ABC	25.2
All in the Family	CBS	24.9
Taxi	ABC	24.9
Eight Is Enough	ABC	24.8
Charlie's Angels	ABC	24.4
Alice	CBS	23.2
Little House on the Prairie	NBC	23.1
ABC Sunday Night Movie	ABC	22.6
Barney Miller	ABC	22.6
The Love Boat	ABC	22.1
One Day at a Time	CBS	21.6
Soap	ABC	21.3
The Dukes of Hazzard	CBS	21
NBC Monday Night Movie	NBC	20.9
Fantasy Island	ABC	20.8
Vega$	ABC	20.5
Barnaby Jones	CBS	20.5
CHiPS	NBC	20.3
Stockard Channing in Just Friends	CBS	20.2
Different Strokes	NBC	19.9
Monday Night Football	ABC	19.8
What's Happening!	ABC	19.8
Lou Grant	CBS	19.7

SEPTEMBER 1979–APRIL 1980

Program	Network	Rating
60 Minutes	CBS	28.4
Three's Company	ABC	26.3
That's Incredible	ABC	25.8
Alice	CBS	25.3
M*A*S*H	CBS	25.3
Dallas	CBS	25
Flo	CBS	24.4
The Jeffersons	CBS	24.3
The Dukes of Hazzard	CBS	24.1
One Day at a Time	CBS	23
Archie Bunker's Place	CBS	22.9
Eight Is Enough	ABC	22.8
Taxi	ABC	22.4
House Calls	CBS	22.1
Real People	NBC	22.1
Little House on the Prairie	NBC	21.8
Happy Days	ABC	21.7
CHiPS	NBC	21.5
Trapper John, M.D.	CBS	21.2
Charlie's Angels	ABC	20.9
Barney Miller	ABC	20.9
WKRP in Cincinnati	CBS	20.7
Benson	ABC	20.6
The Love Boat	ABC	20.6
Soap	ABC	20.5
Diff'rent Strokes	NBC	20.3
Mork & Mindy	ABC	20.2
Fantasy Island	ABC	20.1
Tenspeed and Brown Shoe	ABC	20
ABC Sunday Night Movie	ABC	20

Vegas	ABC	20
Knots Landing	CBS	20

SEPTEMBER 1980–APRIL 1981

Program	Network	Rating
Dallas	CBS	34.5
The Dukes of Hazzard	CBS	27.3
60 Minutes	CBS	27
*M*A*S*H*	CBS	25.7
The Love Boat	ABC	24.3
The Jeffersons	CBS	23.5
Alice	CBS	22.9
House Calls	CBS	22.4
Three's Company	ABC	22.4
Little House on the Prairie	NBC	22.1
One Day at a Time	CBS	22
Real People	NBC	21.5
Archie Bunker's Place	CBS	21.4
Magnum, PI	CBS	21
Happy Days	ABC	20.8
Too Close for Comfort	ABC	20.8
Fantasy Island	ABC	20.7
Trapper John, M.D.	CBS	20.7
Diff'rent Strokes	NBC	20.7
Monday Night Football	ABC	20.6
Laverne & Shirley	ABC	20.6
That's Incredible	ABC	20.5
Hart to Hart	ABC	19.9
ABC Sunday Night Movie	ABC	19.4
CHiPS	NBC	19.4
The Facts of Life	NBC	19.3
Lou Grant	CBS	19.1
Knots Landing	CBS	19
NBC Monday Night Movie	NBC	18.8
The Waltons	CBS	18.6

SEPTEMBER 1981–APRIL 1982

Program	Network	Rating
Dallas	CBS	28.4
60 Minutes	CBS	27.7
The Jeffersons	CBS	23.4
Three's Company	ABC	23.3
Alice	CBS	22.7
The Dukes of Hazzard	CBS	22.6
Too Close for Comfort	ABC	22.6
ABC Monday Night Movie	ABC	22.5
*M*A*S*H*	CBS	22.3
One Day at a Time	CBS	22
Monday Night Football	ABC	21.8
Archie Bunker's Place	CBS	21.6
Falcon Crest	CBS	21.4
The Love Boat	ABC	21.2
Hart to Hart	ABC	21.1
Trapper John, M.D.	CBS	21.1

Magnum, PI	CBS	20.9
Happy Days	ABC	20.6
Dynasty	ABC	20.2
Laverne & Shirley	ABC	19.9
Real People	NBC	19.7
ABC Sunday Night Movie	ABC	19.5
House Calls	CBS	19.2
The Facts of Life	NBC	19.1
Little House on the Prairie	NBC	19.1
The Fall Guy	ABC	19
Hill Street Blues	NBC	18.6
That's Incredible	ABC	18.4
T.J. Hooker	ABC	18.4
Fantasy Island	ABC	18.3

SEPTEMBER 1982–APRIL 1983

Program	Network	Rating
60 Minutes	CBS	25.5
Dallas	CBS	24.6
*M*A*S*H*	CBS	22.6
Magnum, P.I.	CBS	22.6
Dynasty	ABC	22.4
Three's Company	ABC	21.2
Simon & Simon	CBS	21
Falcon Crest	CBS	20.7
The Love Boat	ABC	20.3
The A-Team	NBC	20.1
Monday Night Football	ABC	20.1
The Jeffersons	CBS	20
Newhart	CBS	20
The Fall Guy	ABC	19.4
9 to 5	ABC	19.3
One Day at a Time	CBS	19.1
Hart to Hart	ABC	18.9
Gloria	CBS	18.7
Trapper John, M.D.	CBS	18.7
Knots Landing	CBS	18.6
Hill Street Blues	NBC	18.4
That's Incredible	ABC	18.3
Archie Bunker's Place	CBS	18.3
ABC Monday Night Movie	ABC	18
Laverne & Shirley	ABC	17.8
ABC Sunday Night Movie	ABC	17.6
CBS Tuesday Night Movie	CBS	17.5
Happy Days	ABC	17.4
Little House: A New Beginning	NBC	17.4
Real People	NBC	17.2
The Dukes of Hazzard	CBS	17.2

SEPTEMBER 1983–APRIL 1984

Program	Network	Rating
Dallas	CBS	25.7
60 Minutes	CBS	24.2
Dynasty	NBC	24.1

The A-Team	NBC	24
Simon & Simon	CBS	23.8
Magnum, P.I.	CBS	22.4
Falcon Crest	CBS	22
Kate & Allie	CBS	21.9
Hotel	ABC	21.1
Cagney and Lacey	CBS	20.9
Knots Landing	CBS	20.8
ABC Sunday Night Movie	ABC	20.4
ABC Monday Night Movie	ABC	20.4
TV's Bloopers & Practical Jokes	NBC	20.3
After M*A*S*H	CBS	20.1
The Fall Guy	ABC	19.9
The Love Boat	ABC	19
Riptide	NBC	18.8
The Jeffersons	CBS	18.6
Scarecrow & Mrs. King	CBS	18.3
Monday Night Football	ABC	18.1
NBC Monday Night Movie	NBC	18.1
Newhart	CBS	18
The Facts of Life	NBC	17.3
CBS Tuesday Night Movie	CBS	17.2
Webster	ABC	17.2
Alice	CBS	17.2
Knight Rider	NBC	17.2
Hardcastle & McCormick	ABC	17.2
Trapper John, M.D.	CBS	17

SEPTEMBER 1984–APRIL 1985

Program	Network	Rating
Dynasty	ABC	25
Dallas	CBS	24.7
The Cosby Show	NBC	24.2
60 Minutes	CBS	22.2
Family Ties	NBC	22.1
The A-Team	NBC	21.9
Simon & Simon	CBS	21.8
Murder, She Wrote	CBS	20.1
Knots Landing	CBS	20
Falcon Crest	CBS	19.9
Crazy Like a Fox	CBS	19.9
Hotel	ABC	19.7
Cheers	NBC	19.7
Riptide	NBC	19.2
Magnum, P.I	CBS	19.1
Newhart	CBS	18.4
Kate & Allie	CBS	18.3
NBC Monday Night Movie	NBC	18.2
Highway to Heaven	NBC	17.7
Night Court	NBC	17.6
ABC Sunday Night Movie	ABC	17.5
Scarecrow & Mrs. King	CBS	17.1
TV's Bloopers & Practical Jokes	NBC	17.1
The Fall Guy	ABC	17.1
Monday Night Football	ABC	17
Remington Steele	NBC	17

Webster	ABC	17
Cagney & Lacey	CBS	16.9
Trapper John, M.D.	CBS	16.8
Hill Street Blues	NBC	16.6

SEPTEMBER 1985–APRIL 1986

Program	Network	Rating
The Cosby Show	NBC	33.7
Family Ties	NBC	30
Murder, She Wrote	CBS	25.3
60 Minutes	CBS	23.9
Cheers	NBC	23.7
Dallas	CBS	21.9
Dynasty	ABC	21.8
Golden Girls	NBC	21.8
Miami Vice	NBC	21.3
Who's the Boss?	ABC	21.1
Night Court	NBC	20.9
CBS Sunday Night Movie	CBS	20.5
Highway to Heaven	NBC	20.1
Kate & Allie	CBS	20
Monday Night Football	ABC	19.8
Newhart	CBS	19.6
Knots Landing	CBS	19.5
Growing Pains	ABC	19.5
You Again	NBC	19.2
227	NBC	18.8
NBC Sunday Night Movie	NBC	18.5
Hotel	ABC	18.3
NBC Monday Night Movie	NBC	18.3
Moonlighting	ABC	18.1
Falcon Crest	CBS	18.1
Valerie	NBC	18.1
The Facts of Life	NBC	17.7
Scarecrow and Mrs. King	CBS	17.4
Simon & Simon	CBS	17.2
The A-Team	NBC	16.9

SEPTEMBER 1986–APRIL 1987

Program	Network	Rating
The Cosby Show	NBC	34.9
Family Ties	NBC	32.7
Cheers	NBC	27.2
Murder, She Wrote	CBS	25.4
Golden Girls	NBC	24.5
60 Minutes	CBS	23.3
Night Court	NBC	23.2
Growing Pains	ABC	22.7
Moonlighting	ABC	22.4
Who's the Boss?	ABC	22
Dallas	CBS	21.3
Newhart	CBS	19.5
Amen	NBC	19.4
227	NBC	18.9

Matlock	NBC	18.6
CBS Sunday Night Movie	CBS	18.6
NBC Monday Night Movie	NBC	18.6
Monday Night Football	ABC	18.4
Kate & Allie	CBS	18.3
NBC Sunday Night Movie	NBC	18.2
L.A. Law	NBC	17.4
My Sister Sam	CBS	17.4
Falcon Crest	CBS	17.3
Highway to Heaven	NBC	17.2
Dynasty	ABC	17.2
Knots Landing	CBS	16.8
Miami Vice	NBC	16.8
Alf	NBC	16.5
Hunter	NBC	16.5
Head of the Class	ABC	16.4

SEPTEMBER 1987–APRIL 1988

Program	Network	Rating
The Cosby Show	NBC	27.8
A Different World	NBC	25
Cheers	NBC	23.4
Golden Girls	NBC	21.8
Growing Pains	ABC	21.3
Who's the Boss?	ABC	21.2
Night Court	NBC	20.8
60 Minutes	CBS	20.6
Murder, She Wrote	CBS	20.2
Alf	NBC	18.8
The Wonder Years	ABC	18.8
Moonlighting	ABC	18.3
L.A. Law	NBC	18.3
Matlock	NBC	17.8
Amen	NBC	17.5
Monday Night Football	ABC	17.4
Family Ties	NBC	17.3
CBS Sunday Night Movie	CBS	17.2
In the Heat of the Night	NBC	17
My Two Dads	NBC	16.9
Valerie's Family	NBC	16.9
Dallas	CBS	16.8
NBC Sunday Night Movie	NBC	16.7
Head of the Class	ABC	16.7
Newhart	CBS	16.5
NBC Monday Night Movie	NBC	16.4
227	NBC	16.3
Day by Day	NBC	16.2
Hunter	NBC	16.1
Aaron's Way	NBC	16

OCTOBER 1988–APRIL 1989

Program	Network	Rating
The Cosby Show	NBC	25.6
Roseanne	ABC	23.8

A Different World	NBC	23
Cheers	NBC	22.3
60 Minutes	CBS	21.7
Golden Girls	NBC	21.4
Who's the Boss?	ABC	20.8
Murder, She Wrote	CBS	19.9
Empty Nest	NBC	19.2
Anything But Love	ABC	19
Dear John	NBC	18.5
Matlock	NBC	17.7
L.A. Law	NBC	17.6
Growing Pains	ABC	17.6
Alf	NBC	17.5
Monday Night Football	ABC	17.5
Unsolved Mysteries	NBC	17.4
In the Heat of the Night	NBC	17.3
Hunter	NBC	17.2
Head of the Class	ABC	17.1
Night Court	NBC	16.9
The Hogan Family	NBC	16.3
NBC Sunday Night Movie	NBC	16.3
The Wonder Years	ABC	16.3
Amen	NBC	16.2
NBC Monday Night Movie	NBC	16.2
Knots Landing	CBS	16.1
CBS Sunday Movie	CBS	16.1
ABC Mystery Movie	ABC	15.4
Dallas	CBS	15.4

SEPTEMBER 1989–APRIL 1990

Program	Network	Rating
The Cosby Show	NBC	23.1
Roseanne	ABC	23.1
Cheers	NBC	22.7
A Different World	NBC	21.1
America's Funniest Home Videos	ABC	20.9
Golden Girls	NBC	20.1
60 Minutes	CBS	19.7
The Wonder Years	ABC	19.2
Empty Nest	NBC	18.9
Monday Night Football	ABC	18.1
Unsolved Mysteries	NBC	18
Who's the Boss?	ABC	17.9
Murder, She Wrote	CBS	17.7
Chicken Soup	ABC	17.7
Grand	NBC	17.6
L.A. Law	NBC	17.4
Dear John	NBC	17.1
Coach	ABC	17
In the Heat of the Night	NBC	16.9
Matlock	NBC	16.6
Growing Pains	ABC	15.4
Full House	ABC	15.3
Designing Women	CBS	15.3
CBS Sunday Movie	CBS	14.9
Hunter	NBC	14.9

Program	Network	Rating
Head of the Class	ABC	14.8
Murphy Brown	CBS	14.7
The Simpsons	FOX	14.5
Night Court	NBC	14.5
Doogie Howser, M.D.	ABC	14.5

SEPTEMBER 1990–APRIL 1991

Program	Network	Rating
Cheers	NBC	21.3
60 Minutes	CBS	20.6
Roseanne	ABC	18.1
A Different World	NBC	17.5
The Cosby Show	NBC	17.1
Murphy Brown	CBS	16.9
Empty Nest	NBC	16.7
America's Funniest Home Videos	ABC	16.7
Monday Night Football	ABC	16.6
Golden Girls	NBC	16.5
Designing Women	CBS	16.5
Murder, She Wrote	CBS	16.4
America's Funniest People	ABC	16.3
Full House	ABC	15.9
Family Matters	ABC	15.8
Unsolved Mysteries	NBC	15.7
Matlock	NBC	15.5
Coach	ABC	15.3
Who's the Boss?	ABC	15
CBS Sunday Movie	CBS	15
In the Heat of the Night	NBC	14.9
Major Dad	CBS	19.9
L.A. Law	NBC	14.8
Doogie Howser, M.D.	ABC	14.7
Grand	NBC	14.6
Head of the Class	ABC	14.5
Growing Pains	ABC	14.3
Baby Talk	ABC	14.3
Davis Rules	ABC	14.3
The Wonder Years	ABC	14.2

SEPTEMBER 1991–APRIL 1992

Program	Network	Rating
60 Minutes	CBS	21.9
Roseanne	ABC	19.9
Murphy Brown	CBS	18.6
Cheers	NBC	17.5
Home Improvement	ABC	17.5
Designing Women	CBS	17.3
Full House	ABC	17
Murder, She Wrote	CBS	16.9
Major Dad	CBS	16.8
Coach	ABC	16.7
Room for Two	ABC	16.7
Monday Night Football	ABC	16.6
Unsolved Mysteries	NBC	16.5
CBS Sunday Night Movie	CBS	15.9

Program	Network	Rating
Evening Shade	CBS	15.6
Northern Exposure	CBS	15.5
A Different World	NBC	15.2
The Cosby Show	NBC	15
Wings	NBC	14.6
Americas Funniest Home Videos	ABC	14.5
20/20	ABC	14.4
Fresh Prince of Bel Air	NBC	14.3
Empty Nest	NBC	14.3
NBC Monday Movie	NBC	13.9
America's Funniest People	ABC	13.8
ABC Monday Movie	ABC	13.8
Family Matters	ABC	13.5
L.A. Law	NBC	13.3
48 Hours	CBS	13.2
In the Heat of the Night	NBC	13.1
Golden Girls	NBC	13.1

SEPTEMBER 1992–APRIL 1993

Program	Network	Rating
60 Minutes	CBS	21.9
Roseanne	ABC	20.7
Home Improvement	ABC	19.4
Murphy Brown	CBS	17.9
Murder, She Wrote	CBS	17.7
Coach	ABC	17.5
Monday Night Football	ABC	16.7
CBS Sunday Movie	CBS	16.1
Cheers	NBC	16.1
Full House	ABC	15.8
Northern Exposure	CBS	15.2
20/20	ABC	15.1
Rescue: 911	CBS	15.1
CBS Tuesday Movie	CBS	14.8
Love & War	CBS	14.7
Fresh Prince of Bel Air	NBC	14.6
Hangin' with Mr. Cooper	ABC	14.6
The Jackie Thomas Show	ABC	14.6
Evening Shade	CBS	14.5
Hearts Afire	CBS	14.3
Unsolved Mysteries	NBC	14.2
Primetime Live	ABC	14.1
Dr. Quinn, Medicine Woman	CBS	14
NBC Monday Movie	NBC	13.9
Seinfeld	NBC	13.7
48 Hours	CBS	13.5
Blossom	NBC	13.5
ABC Sunday Night Movie	ABC	13.3
Matlock	ABC	13.3
Wings	NBC	13
The Simpsons	FOX	13

SEPTEMBER 1993–APRIL 1994

Program	Network	Rating
60 Minutes	CBS	20.9

Home Improvement	ABC	20.4
Seinfeld	NBC	19.4
Roseanne	ABC	19.1
Grace Under Fire	ABC	17.7
Coach	ABC	17.4
Frasier	NBC	16.8
Monday Night Football	ABC	16.5
Murphy Brown	CBS	16.3
CBS Sunday Movie	CBS	16.2
Murder, She Wrote	CBS	16
Thunder Alley	ABC	15.9
Love & War	CBS	14.5
Northern Exposure	CBS	14.4
20/20	ABC	14.3
Full House	ABC	14.2
Primetime Live	ABC	14
NYPD Blue	ABC	13.9
Wings	NBC	13.9
Turning Point	ABC	13.8
Dave's World	CBS	13.7
Fresh Prince of Bel Air	NBC	13.7
NBC Monday Movie	NBC	13.6
Homicide: Life on the Street	NBC	13.5
CBS Tuesday Movie	CBS	13.3
Dr. Quinn, Medicine Woman	CBS	13.3
Phenom	ABC	13.2
Evening Shade	CBS	13.2
Rescue: 911	CBS	13.2
ABC Sunday Night Movie	ABC	12.6
Family Matters	ABC	12.6

SEPTEMBER 1994–APRIL 1995

Program	Network	Rating
Seinfeld	NBC	20.6
ER	NBC	20
Home Improvement	ABC	19.5
Grace Under Fire	ABC	18.6
Monday Night Football	ABC	17.7
60 Minutes	CBS	17.2
NYPD Blue	ABC	16.5
Murder, She Wrote	CBS	15.6
Friends	NBC	15.6
Roseanne	ABC	15.5
Mad About You	NBC	15.2
Madman of the People	NBC	14.9
Ellen	ABC	14.8
Hope & Gloria	ABC	14.6
Frasier	ABC	14.5
Murphy Brown	CBS	14.1
20/20	ABC	14
CBS Sunday Movie	CBS	13.7
NBC Monday Movie	NBC	13.6
Me and the Boys	ABC	13.1
Dave's World	CBS	12.9
Cybill	CBS	12.8
ABC Sunday Movie	ABC	12.7

The Nanny	CBS	12.5
Full House	CBS	12.4
Wings	NBC	12.3
Law & Order	NBC	12.2
NBC Sunday Night Movie	NBC	12
Chicago Hope	CBS	11.7
ABC Monday Night Movie	ABC	11.7
The Martin Short Show	NBC	11.7
Primetime Live	ABC	11.7

SEPTEMBER 1995–MAY 1996

Program	Network	Rating
ER	NBC	22
Seinfeld	NBC	21.2
Friends	NBC	18.7
Caroline in the City	NBC	18
Monday Night Football	ABC	17.1
The Single Guy	NBC	16.7
Home Improvement	ABC	16.1
Boston Common	NBC	15.6
60 Minutes	CBS	14.2
NYPD Blue	ABC	14.1
20/20	ABC	13.6
Frasier	NBC	13.6
Grace Under Fire	ABC	13.2
NBC Monday Movie	NBC	12.9
Coach	ABC	12.9
The Nanny	CBS	12.5
Roseanne	ABC	12.5
Walker, Texas Ranger	CBS	12.3
Primetime Live	ABC	12.3
Murphy Brown	CBS	12.3
NBC Sunday Movie	NBC	12.2
3rd Rock from the Sun	NBC	12.1
Chicago Hope	CBS	11.9
Law & Order	NBC	11.4
CBS Sunday Movie	CBS	11.4
The Naked Truth	ABC	11.4
Can't Hurry Love	CBS	11.4
Dateline NBC-Tuesday	NBC	11.3
Dateline NBC-Wednesday	NBC	11.3
The Dana Carvey Show	ABC	11.2

SEPTEMBER 1996–MAY 1997

Program	Network	Rating
ER	NBC	21.2
Seinfeld	NBC	20.5
Suddenly Susan	NBC	17
Friends	NBC	16.8
The Naked Truth	NBC	16.8
Fired Up	NBC	16.5
Monday Night Football	ABC	16
The Single Guy	NBC	14.1
Home Improvement	ABC	14

Program	Network	Rating
Touched by an Angel	CBS	13.6
60 Minutes	CBS	13.3
20/20	ABC	12.8
NYPD Blue	ABC	12.5
CBS Sunday Movie	CBS	12.1
Primetime Live	ABC	11.9
Frasier	NBC	11.8
Spin City	ABC	11.7
NBC Sunday Movie	NBC	11.5
The Drew Carey Show	ABC	11.5
Dateline NBC-Tuesday	NBC	11.4
Cosby	CBS	11.2
The X-Files	FOX	11.2
Walker, Texas Ranger	CBS	11
Mad About You	NBC	11
Caroline in the City	NBC	11
NBC Monday Movie	NBC	11
Law & Order	NBC	10.8
3rd Rock from the Sun	NBC	10.8
Ellen	ABC	10.6
Chicago Hope	CBS	10.5
Dateline NBC-Friday	NBC	10.5
Cybill	CBS	10.5

SEPTEMBER 1997–MAY 1998

Program	Network	Rating
Seinfeld	NBC	21.7
ER	NBC	20.4
Veronica's Closet	NBC	16.6
Friends	NBC	16.1
Monday Night Football	ABC	15
Touched by an Angel	CBS	14.2
60 Minutes	CBS	13.8
Union Square	NBC	13.6
CBS Sunday Movie	CBS	13.1
Frasier	NBC	12
Home Improvement	ABC	12
Just Shoot Me	NBC	11.9
Dateline NBC-Tuesday	NBC	11.5
Dateline NBC-Monday	NBC	11.4
The Drew Carey Show	ABC	11.1
20/20-Friday	ABC	10.9
NYPD Blue	ABC	10.8
Primetime Live	ABC	10.8
The X-Files	FOX	10.6

Program	Network	Rating
Law & Order	NBC	10.2
20/20-Monday	ABC	10
Diagnosis Murder	CBS	9.8
King of the Hill	FOX	9.7
Mad About You	NBC	9.7
Cosby	CBS	9.5
Dharma & Greg	ABC	9.5
NBC Sunday Night Movie	NBC	9.4
Hiller and Diller	ABC	9.3
Walker, Texas Ranger	CBS	9.3
Everybody Loves Raymond	CBS	9.2
The Simpsons	FOX	9.2

SEPTEMBER 1998–MAY 1999

Program	Network	Rating
ER	NBC	17.8
Friends	NBC	15.7
Frasier	NBC	15.6
Monday Night Football	ABC	14
Veronica's Closet	NBC	13.7
Jesse	NBC	13.7
60 Minutes	CBS	13.2
Touched by an Angel	CBS	13.1
CBS Sunday Movie	CBS	12
Home Improvement	ABC	11
Everybody Loves Raymond	CBS	10.6
NYPD Blue	ABC	10.5
Law & Order	NBC	10.1
The Drew Carey Show	ABC	9.9
20/20-Friday	ABC	9.9
Providence	NBC	9.8
20/20-Wednesday	ABC	9.8
Jag	CBS	9.8
Dateline NBC-Tuesday	NBC	9.7
Dateline NBC-Monday	NBC	9.7
Becker	CBS	9.7
CBS Tuesday Movie	CBS	9.7
Ally McBeal	FOX	9.6
Dharma & Greg	ABC	9.3
Spin City	ABC	9.2
Walker, Texas Ranger	CBS	9.2
Dateline NBC-Friday	NBC	9.2
The X-Files	FOX	9.1
NBC Sunday Night Movie	NBC	9.1
60 Minutes II	CBS	9
Diagnosis Murder	CBS	9

APPENDIX B

The annual Emmys, which are awarded to various television programs, performers, directors, writers, technicians, etc., are unquestionably the most prestigious awards given to people who work in the television industry. The awards, which are presented in recognition of excellence in television performance and production, are determined by a vote of members of the National Academy of Television Arts and Sciences, people who work in the television industry. Performers, directors, writers, technicians, etc. vote for their fellow television professionals who they feel are most deserving of special attention because of their work in the previous season.

1948 (PRESENTED JANUARY 25, 1949)

BEST FILM MADE FOR TELEVISION: "The Necklace," *Your Show Time* (NBC)

1949 (PRESENTED JANUARY 27, 1950)

BEST LIVE SHOW: *The Ed Wynn Show* (CBS)
BEST KINESCOPE SHOW: *Texaco Star Theater* (NBC)
MOST OUTSTANDING LIVE PERSONALITY: Ed Wynn (CBS)
MOST OUTSTANDING KINESCOPE PERSONALITY: Milton Berle (NBC)
BEST FILM MADE FOR AND VIEWED ON TELEVISION: *The Life of Riley* (NBC)

1950 (PRESENTED JANUARY 23, 1951)

BEST ACTOR: Alan Young (CBS)
BEST ACTRESS: Gertrude Berg (CBS)
MOST OUTSTANDING PERSONALITY: Groucho Marx (NBC)

BEST VARIETY SHOW: *The Alan Young Show* (CBS)
BEST DRAMATIC SHOW: *Pulitzer Prize Playhouse* (ABC)
BEST GAME AND AUDIENCE PARTICIPATION SHOW: *Truth or Consequences* (CBS)

1951 (PRESENTED FEBRUARY 18, 1952)

BEST DRAMATIC SHOW: *Studio One* (CBS)
BEST COMEDY SHOW: *The Red Skelton Show* (CBS)
BEST VARIETY SHOW: *Your Show of Shows* (NBC)
BEST ACTOR: Sid Caesar (NBC)
BEST ACTRESS: Imogene Coca (NBC)
BEST COMEDIAN OR COMEDIENNE: Red Skelton (NBC)

1952 (PRESENTED FEBRUARY 5, 1953)

BEST DRAMATIC PROGRAM: *Robert Montgomery Presents* (NBC)
BEST VARIETY PROGRAM: *Your Show of Shows* (NBC)
BEST PUBLIC AFFAIRS PROGRAM: *See It Now* (CBS)
BEST MYSTERY, ACTION, OR ADVENTURE PROGRAM: *Dragnet* (NBC)
BEST SITUATION COMEDY: *I Love Lucy* (CBS)
BEST AUDIENCE PARTICIPATION, QUIZ, OR PANEL PROGRAM: *What's MyLine* (CBS)
BEST ACTOR: Thomas Mitchell
BEST ACTRESS: Helen Hayes
BEST COMEDIAN: Jimmy Durante (NBC)
BEST COMEDIENNE: Lucille Ball (CBS)
MOST OUTSTANDING PERSONALITY: Bishop Fulton J. Sheen (DUM)

1953 (PRESENTED FEBRUARY 11, 1954)

BEST DRAMATIC PROGRAM: *The United States Steel Hour* (ABC)

429

BEST SITUATION COMEDY: *I Love Lucy* (CBS)

BEST VARIETY PROGRAM: *Omnibus* (CBS)

BEST PROGRAM OF NEWS OR SPORTS: *See It Now* (CBS)

BEST PUBLIC AFFAIRS PROGRAM: *Victory at Sea* (NBC)

BEST CHILDREN'S PROGRAM: *Kukla, Fran & Oillie* (NBC)

BEST NEW PROGRAMS: *Make Room for Daddy* (ABC) and *The United States Steel Hour* (ABC)

BEST MALE STAR OF REGULAR SERIES: Donald O'-Connor, *Colgate ComedyHour* (NBC)

BEST FEMALE STAR OF REGULAR SERIES: Eve Arden, *Our Miss Brooks* (CBS)

BEST SERIES SUPPORTING ACTOR: Art Carney, *The Jackie Gleason Show* (CBS)

BEST SERIES SUPPORTING ACTRESS: Vivian Vance, *I Love Lucy* (CBS)

BEST MYSTERY, ACTION, OR ADVENTURE PROGRAM: *Dragnet* (NBC)

BEST AUDIENCE PARTICIPATION, QUIZ, OR PANEL PROGRAM: *This Is Your Life* (NBC) and *What's My Line* (CBS) MOST OUTSTANDING PERSONALITY: Edward R. Murrow (CBS)

1954 (PRESENTED MARCH 7, 1955)

MOST OUTSTANDING NEW PERSONALITY: George Gobel (NBC)

BEST CULTURAL, RELIGIOUS, OR EDUCATIONAL PROGRAM: *Omnibus* (CBS)

BEST SPORTS PROGRAM: *The Gillette Cavalacade of Sports* (NBC)

BEST CHILDREN'S PROGRAM: *Lassie* (CBS)

BEST WESTERN OR ADVENTURE SERIES: *Stories of the Century* (syndicated)

BEST NEWS REPORTER OR COMMENTATOR: John Daly (ABC)

BEST AUDIENCE, GUEST PARTICIPATION, OR PANEL PROGRAM: *This Is Your Life* (NBC)

BEST ACTOR IN A SINGLE PERFORMANCE: Robert Cummings, "Twelve Angry Men," *Studio One* (CBS)

BEST ACTRESS IN A SINGLE PERFORMANCE: Judith Anderson, "Macbeth," *Hallmark Hall of Fame* (NBC)

BEST MALE SINGER: Perry Como (CBS)

BEST FEMALE SINGER: Dinah Shore (NBC)

BEST SUPPORTING ACTOR IN A REGULAR SERIES: Art Carney, *The Jackie Gleason Show* (CBS)

BEST SUPPORTING ACTRESS IN A REGULAR SERIES: Audrey Meadows, *The Jackie Gleason Show* (CBS)

BEST ACTOR STARRING IN A REGULAR SERIES: Danny Thomas, *Make Room for Daddy* (ABC)

BEST ACTRESS IN A REGULAR SERIES: Loretta Young, *The Loretta Young Show*

BEST MYSTERY OR INTRIGUE SERIES: *Dragnet* (NBC)

BEST VARIETY SERIES INCLUDING MUSICAL VARIETIES: *Disneyland* (ABC)

BEST SITUATION COMEDY SERIES: *Make Room for Daddy* (ABC)

BEST DRAMATIC SERIES: *The United States Steel Hour* (ABC)

BEST INDIVIDUAL PROGRAM OF THE YEAR: "Operation Undersea," *Disneyland* (ABC)

BEST WRITTEN DRAMATIC MATERIAL: Reginald Rose, "Twelve Angry Men," *Studio One* (CBS)

BEST WRITTEN COMEDY MATERIAL: James Allardice, Jack Douglas, Hal Kanter, and Harry Winkler, *The George Gobel Show* (NBC)

BEST DIRECTION: Franklin Schaffner, "Twelve Angry Men," *Studio One* (CBS)

1955 (PRESENTED MARCH 17, 1956)

BEST CHILDREN'S SERIES: *Lassie* (CBS)

BEST DOCUMENTARY PROGRAM (RELIGIOUS, INFORMATIONAL, EDUCATIONAL, OR INTERVIEW): *Omnibus* (CBS)

BEST AUDIENCE PARTICIPATION SERIES (QUIZ, PANEL, ETC.): *The $64,000 Question* (CBS)

BEST ACTION OR ADVENTURE SERIES: *Disneyland* (ABC)

BEST COMEDY SERIES: *The Phil Silvers Show* (CBS)

BEST VARIETY SERIES: *The Ed Sullivan Show* (CBS)

BEST MUSIC SERIES: *Your Hit Parade* (NBC)

BEST DRAMATIC SERIES: *Producers' Showcase* (NBC)

BEST SINGLE PROGRAM OF THE YEAR: "Peter Pan," *Producers' Showcase* (NBC)

BEST ACTOR (SINGLE PERFORMANCE): Lloyd Nolan, "The Caine Mutiny Court-Martial," *Ford Star Jubilee* (CBS)

BEST ACTRESS (SINGLE PERFORMANCE): Mary Martin, "Peter Pan," *Producers' Showcase* (NBC)

BEST ACTOR (CONTINUING PERFORMANCE): Phil Silvers, *The Phil Silvers Show* (CBS)

BEST ACTRESS (CONTINUING PERFORMANCE): Lucille Ball, *I Love Lucy* (CBS)

BEST ACTOR IN A SUPPORTING ROLE: Art Carney, *The Jackie Gleason Show* (CBS)

BEST ACTRESS IN A SUPPORTING ROLE: Nanette Fabray, *Caesar's Hour* (NBC)

BEST COMEDIAN: Phil Silvers (CBS)

BEST COMEDIENNE: Nanette Fabray (NBC)

BEST MALE SINGER: Perry Como (NBC)

BEST FEMALE SINGER: Dinah Shore (NBC)

BEST MC OR PROGRAM HOST (MALE OR FEMALE): Perry Como (NBC)

BEST NEWS COMMENTATOR OR REPORTER: Edward R. Murrow (CBS)

BEST ORIGINAL TELEPLAY WRITING: Rod Serling, "Patterns," *Kraft Television Theatre*

BEST COMEDY WRITING: Nat Hiken, Barry Blitser, Arnold Auerbach, Harvey Orkin, Vincent Bogert, Arnold Rosen, Coleman Jacoby, Tony Webster, and Terry Ryan, *The Phil Silvers Show* (CBS)

BEST TELEVISION ADAPTATION: Paul Gregory and Franklin Schaffner, "The Caine Mutiny Court-Martial," *Ford Star Jubilee* (CBS)

BEST PRODUCER (LIVE SERIES): Fred Coe, *Producers' Showcase* (NBC)

BEST PRODUCER (FILM SERIES): Walt Disney, *Disneyland* (ABC)

BEST DIRECTOR (LIVE SERIES): Franklin Schaffner, "The Caine Mutiny Court-Martial," *Ford Star Jubilee* (CBS)

BEST DIRECTOR (FILM SERIES): Nat Hiken, *The Phil Silvers Show* (CBS)

1956 (PRESENTED MARCH 16, 1957)

BEST SINGLE PROGRAM OF THE YEAR: "Requiem for a Heavyweight," *Playhouse 90* (CBS)

BEST NEW PROGRAM SERIES: *Playhouse 90* (CBS)

BEST SERIES (HALF HOUR OR LESS): *The Phil Silvers Show* (CBS)

BEST SERIES (ONE HOUR OR MORE): *Caesar's Hour* (NBC)

BEST IN LIVE SERVICE SERIES: *See It Now* (CBS)

BEST CONTINUING PERFORMANCE BY AN ACTOR IN A DRAMATIC SERIES: Robert Young, *Father Knows Best* (NBC)

BEST CONTINUING PERFORMANCE BY AN ACTRESS IN A DRAMATIC SERIES: Loretta Young, *The Loretta Young Show* (NBC)

BEST CONTINUING PERFORMANCE BY A COMEDIAN IN A SERIES: Sid Caesar, *Caesar's Hour* (NBC)

BEST CONTINUING PERFORMANCE BY A COMEDIENNE IN A SERIES: Nanette Fabray, *Gaesar's Hour* (NBC)

BEST SINGLE PERFORMANCE BY AN ACTOR: Jack Palance, "Requiem for a Heavyweight," *Playhouse 90* (CBS)

BEST SINGLE PERFORMANCE BY AN ACTRESS: Claire Trevor, "Dodsworth," *Producers' Showcase* (NBC)

BEST SUPPORTING PERFORMANCE BY AN ACTOR: Carl Reiner, *Caesar's Hour* (NBC)

BEST SUPPORTING PERFORMANCE BY AN ACTRESS: Pat Carroll, *Caesar's Hour* (NBC)

BEST MALE PERSONALITY (CONTINUING PERFORMANCE): Perry Como (NBC)

BEST FEMALE PERSONALITY (CONTINUING PERFORMANCE): Dinah Shore (NBC)

BEST NEWS COMMENTATOR: Edward R. Murrow (CBS)

BEST TELEPLAY WRITING (HALF HOUR OR LESS): James P. Cavanagh, "Fog Closes In," *Alfred Hitchcock Presents* (CBS)

BEST TELEPLAY WRITING (ONE HOUR OR MORE): Rod Serling, "Requiem for a Heavyweight," *Playhouse 90* (CBS)

BEST COMEDY WRITING (VARIETY OR SITUATION COMEDY): Nat Hiken, Billy Friedberg, Tony Webster, Leonard Stern, Arnold Rosen, and Coleman Jacoby, *The Phil Silvers Show* (CBS)

BEST DIRECTION: (HALF HOUR OR LESS): Sheldon Leonard, "Danny's Comeback," *The Danny Thomas Show* (ABC)

BEST DIRECTION (ONE HOUR OR MORE): Ralph Nelson, "Requiem for a Heavyweight," *Playhouse 90* (CBS)

1957 (PRESENTED APRIL 15, 1958)

BEST SINGLE PROGRAM OF THE YEAR: "The Comedian," *Playhouse 90* (CBS)

BEST NEW PROGRAM SERIES OF THE YEAR: *The Seven LivelyArts* (CBS)

BEST DRAMATIC ANTHOLOGY SERIES: *Playhouse 90* (CBS)

BEST DRAMATIC SERIES WITH CONTINUING CHARACTERS: *Gunsmoke* (CBS)

BEST COMEDY SERIES: *The Phil Silvers Show* (CBS)

BEST MUSICAL, VARIETY, AUDIENCE PARTICIPATION, OR QUIZ SERIES: *The Dinah Shore Chevy Show* (NBC)

BEST PUBLIC SERVICE PROGRAM OR SERIES: *Omnibus* (ABC and NBC)

BEST CONTINUING PERFORMANCE BY AN ACTOR IN A LEADING ROLE IN A DRAMATIC OR COMEDY SERIES: Robert Young, *Father Knows Best* (NBC)

BEST CONTINUING PERFORMANCE BY AN ACTRESS IN A LEADING ROLE IN A DRAMATIC OR COMEDY SERIES: Jane Wyatt, *Father Knows Best* (NBC)

BEST CONTINUING PERFORMANCE (MALE) IN A SERIES BY A COMEDIAN, SINGER, HOST, DANCER, MC, ANNOUNCER, NARRATOR, PANELIST, OR ANY PERSON WHO ESSENTIALLY PLAYS HIMSELF: Jack Benny, *The Jack Benny Program* (CBS)

BEST CONTINUING PERFORMANCE (FEMALE) IN A SERIES BY A COMEDIENNE, SINGER, HOSTESS, DANCER, MC, ANNOUNCER, NARRATOR, PANELIST, OR ANY PERSON WHO ESSENTIALLY PLAYS HERSELF: Dinah Shore, *The Dinah Shore Chevy Show* (NBC)

ACTOR—BEST SINGLE PERFORMANCE (LEAD OR SUPPORT): Peter Ustinov, "The Life of Samuel Johnson," *Omnibus* (NBC)

ACTRESS—BEST SINGLE PERFORMANCE (LEAD OR SUPPORT): Polly Bergen, "The Helen Morgan Story," *Playhouse 90* (CBS)

BEST CONTINUING SUPPORTING PERFORMANCE BY AN ACTOR IN A DRAMATIC OR COMEDY SERIES: Carl Reiner, *Caesar's Hour* (NBC)

BEST CONTINUING SUPPORTING PERFORMANCE BY AN ACTRESS IN A DRAMATIC OR COMEDY

SERIES: Ann B. Davis, *The Bob Cummings Show* (CBS and NBC)

BEST NEWS COMMENTARY: Edward R. Murrow, *See It Now* (CBS)

BEST TELEPLAY WRITING (HALF HOUR OR LESS): Paul Moriash, "The Lonely Wizard," *Schlitz Playhouse of Stars* (CBS)

BEST TELEPLAY WRITING (ONE HOUR OR MORE): Rod Serling, "The Comedian," *Playhouse 90* (CBS)

BEST COMEDY WRITING: Nat Hiken, Billy Friedberg, Phil Sharp, Terry Ryan, Coleman Jacoby, Arnold Rosen, Sydney Zelinka, A. J. Russell, and Tony Webster, *The Phil Silvers Show* (CBS)

BEST DIRECTION (HALF HOUR OR LESS): Robert Stevens, "The Glass Eye," *Alfred Hitchcock Presents* (CBS) BEST DIRECTION (ONE HOUR OR MORE): Bob Banner, *Dinah Shore Chevy Show* (NBC)

1958–1959 (PRESENTED MAY 6, 1959)

MOST OUTSTANDING SINGLE PROGRAM OF THE YEAR: "An Evening with Fred Astaire" (NBC)

BEST DRAMATIC SERIES (ONE HOUR OR LONGER): *Playhouse 90* (CBS)

BEST DRAMATIC SERIES (LESS THAN ONE HOUR): *Alcoa-Goodyear Theatre* (NBC)

BEST COMEDY SERIES: *The Jack Benny Program* (CBS)

BEST MUSICAL OR VARIETY SERIES: *The Dinah Shore Chevy Show* (NBC)

BEST WESTERN SERIES: *Maverick* (ABC)

BEST PUBLIC SERVICE PROGRAM OR SERIES: *Omnibus* (NBC)

BEST NEWS REPORTING SERIES: *The Huntley-Brinkley Report* (NEC)

BEST PANEL, QUIZ, OR AUDIENCE PARTICIPATION SERIES: *What's My Line* (CBS)

BEST SPECIAL DRAMATIC PROGRAM (ONE HOUR OR LONGER): "Little Moon of Alban," *Hallmark Hall of Fame* (NBC)

BEST SPECIAL MUSICAL OR VARIETY PROGRAM (ONE HOUR OR LONGER): "An Evening with Fred Astaire" (NBC)

BEST ACTOR IN A LEADING ROLE (CONTINUING CHARACTER) IN A DRAMATIC SERIES: Raymond Burr, *Perry Mason* (CBS)

BEST ACTRESS IN A LEADING ROLE (CONTINUING CHARACTER) IN A DRAMATIC SERIES: Loretta Young, *The Loretta Young Show* (NBC)

BEST ACTOR IN A LEADING ROLE (CONTINUING CHARACTER) IN A COMEDY SERIES: Jack Benny, *The Jack Benny Program* (CBS)

BEST ACTRESS IN A LEADING ROLE (CONTINUING CHARACTER) IN A COMEDY SERIES: Jane Wyatt, *Father Knows Best* (CBS and NBC)

BEST SUPPORTING ACTOR (CONTINUING CHARACTER) IN A DRAMATIC SERIES: Dennis Weaver, *Gunsmoke* (CBS)

BEST SUPPORTING ACTRESS (CONTINUING CHARACTER) IN A DRAMATIC SERIES: Barbara Hale, *Perry Mason* (CBS)

BEST SUPPORTING ACTOR (CONTINUING CHARACTER) IN A COMEDY SERIES: Tom Poston, *The Steve Allen Show* (NBC)

BEST SUPPORTING ACTRESS (CONTINUING CHARACTER) IN A COMEDY SERIES: Ann B. Davis, *The Bob Cummings Show* (NBC)

BEST PERFORMANCE BY AN ACTOR (CONTINUING CHARACTER) IN A MUSICAL OR VARIETY SERIES: Perry Como, *The Perry Como Show* (NBC)

BEST PERFORMANCE BY AN ACTRESS (CONTINUING CHARACTER) IN A MUSICAL OR VARIETY SERIES: Dinah Shore, *The Dinah Shore Chevy Show* (NBC)

BEST SINGLE PERFORMANCE BY AN ACTOR: Fred Astaire, "An Evening with Fred Astaire" (NBC)

BEST SINGLE PERFORMANCE BY AN ACTRESS: Julie Harris, "Little Moon of Alban," *Hallmark Hall of Fame* (NBC)

BEST NEWS COMMENTATOR OR ANALYST: Edward R. Murrow (CBS)

BEST DIRECTION OF A SINGLE PROGRAM OF A DRAMATIC SERIES (LESS THAN ONE HOUR): Jack Smight, "Eddie," *Alcoa-Goodyear Theatre* (NBC)

BEST DIRECTION OF A SINGLE DRAMATIC PROGRAM (ONE HOUR OR LONGER): George Schaefer, "Little Moon of Alban," *Hallmark Hall of Fame* (NBC)

BEST DIRECTION OF A SINGLE PROGRAM OF A COMEDY SERIES: Peter Tewksbury, "Medal for Margaret," *Father Knows Best* (CBS)

BEST DIRECTION OF A SINGLE MUSICAL OR VARIETY PROGRAM: Bud Yorkin, "An Evening with Fred Astaire" (NBC)

BEST WRITING OF A SINGLE PROGRAM OF A DRAMATIC SERIES (LESS THAN ONE HOUR): Alfred Brenner and Ken Hughes, "Eddie," *Alcoa-Goodyear Theater* (NBC)

BEST WRITING OF A SINGLE DRAMATIC PROGRAM (ONE HOUR OR LONGER): James Costigan, "Little Moon of Alban," *Hallmark Hall of Fame* (NBC)

BEST WRITING OF A SINGLE PROGRAM OF A COMEDY SERIES: Sam Perrin, George Balzer, Hal Goldman, and Al Gordon, "Jack Benny Show with Ernie Kovacs," *The Jack Benny Program* (CBS)

BEST WRITING OF A SINGLE MUSICAL OR VARIETY PROGRAM: Bud Yorkin and Herbert Baker, "An Evening with Fred Astaire" (NBC)

1959–1960 (PRESENTED JUNE 20, 1960)

OUTSTANDING PROGRAM ACHIEVEMENT IN THE FIELD OF HUMOR: "The Art Carney Special" (NBC)

OUTSTANDING PROGRAM ACHIEVEMENT IN THE FIELD OF DRAMA: *Playhouse 90* (CBS)

OUTSTANDING PROGRAM ACHIEVEMENT IN THE FIELD OF VARIETY: "The Fabulous Fifties" (CBS)

OUTSTANDING PROGRAM ACHIEVEMENT IN THE FIELD OF NEWS: *The Huntley-Brinkley Report* (NBC)

OUTSTANDING PROGRAM ACHIEVEMENT IN THE FIELD OF PUBLIC AFFAIRS AND EDUCATION: *The Twentieth Century* (CBS)

OUTSTANDING SINGLE PERFORMANCE BY AN ACTOR (LEAD OR SUPPORT): Laurence Olivier, "The Moon and Sixpence" (NBC)

OUTSTANDING SINGLE PERFORMANCE BY AN ACTRESS (LEAD OR SUPPORT): Ingrid Bergman, "The Turn of the Screw," *Ford Startime* (NBC)

OUTSTANDING PERFORMANCE BY AN ACTOR IN A SERIES (LEAD OR SUPPORT): Robert Stack, *The Untouchables* (ABC)

OUTSTANDING PERFORMANCE BY AN ACTRESS IN A SERIES (LEAD OR SUPPORT): Jane Wyatt, *Father Knows Best* (CBS)

OUTSTANDING PERFORMANCE IN A VARIETY OR MUSICAL PROGRAM OR SERIES: Harry Belafonte, "Tonight with Belafonte," *The Revlon Revue* (CBS)

OUTSTANDING WRITING ACHIEVEMENT IN DRAMA: Rod Serling, *The Twilight Zone* (CBS)

OUTSTANDING WRITING ACHIEVEMENT IN COMEDY: Sam Perrin, George Balzer, Al Gordon, and Hal Goldman, *The Jack Benny Program* (CBS)

OUTSTANDING WRITING ACHIEVEMENT IN THE DOCUMENTARY FIELD: Howard K. Smith and Av Westin, "The Population Explosion" (CBS)

OUTSTANDING DIRECTORIAL ACHIEVEMENT IN DRAMA: Robert Mulligan, "The Moon and Sixpence" (NBC)

OUTSTANDING DIRECTORIAL ACHIEVEMENT IN COMEDY Bud Yorkin, *The Jack Benny Program*

1960–1961 (PRESENTED MAY 16, 1961)

THE PROGRAM OF THE YEAR: "Macbeth," *Hallmark Hall of Fame* (NBC)

OUTSTANDING PROGRAM ACHIEVEMENT IN THE FIELD OF HUMOR: *The Jack Benny Program* (CBS)

OUTSTANDING PROGRAM ACHIEVEMENT IN THE FIELD OF DRAMA: "Macbeth," *Hallmark Hall of Fame* (NBC)

OUTSTANDING PROGRAM ACHIEVEMENT IN THE FIELD OF VARIETY: "Astaire Time" (NBC)

OUTSTANDING PROGRAM ACHIEVEMENT IN THE FIELD OF NEWS: *The Huntley-Brinkley Report* (NBC)

OUTSTANDING PROGRAM ACHIEVEMENT IN THE FIELD OF PUBLIC AFFAIRS AND EDUCATION: *The Twentieth Century* (CBS)

OUTSTANDING SINGLE PERFORMANCE BY AN ACTOR IN A LEADING ROLE: Maurice Evans, "Macbeth," *Hallmark Hall of Fame* (NBC)

OUTSTANDING SINGLE PERFORMANCE BY AN ACTRESS IN A LEADING ROLE: Judith Anderson, "Macbeth," *Hallmark Hall of Fame* (NBC)

OUTSTANDING PERFORMANCE BY AN ACTOR IN A SERIES (LEAD): Raymond Burr, *Perry Mason* (CBS)

OUTSTANDING PERFORMANCE BY AN ACTRESS IN A SERIES (LEAD): Barbara Stanwyck, *The Barbara Stanwyck Show* (NBC)

OUTSTANDING PERFORMANCE IN A SUPPORTING ROLE BY AN ACTOR OR ACTRESS IN A SINGLE PROGRAM: Roddy McDowall, "Not Without Honor," *Equitable's* American Heritage (NBC)

OUTSTANDING PERFORMANCE IN A SUPPORTING ROLE BY AN ACTOR OR ACTRESS IN A SERIES: Don Knotts, *The Andy Griffith Show* (CBS)

OUTSTANDING PERFORMANCE IN A VARIETY OR MUSICAL PROGRAM OR SERIES: Fred Astaire, "Astaire Time" (NBC)

OUTSTANDING WRITING ACHIEVEMENT IN DRAMA: Rod Serling, *The Twilight Zone* (CBS)

OUTSTANDING WRITING ACHIEVEMENT IN COMEDY: Sherwood Schwartz, Dave O'Brien, Al Schwartz, Martin Ragaway and Red Skelton, *The Red Skelton Show* (CBS)

OUTSTANDING WRITING ACHIEVEMENT IN THE DOCUMENTARY FIELD: Victor Wolfson, *Winston Churchill—The Valiant Years* (ABC)

OUTSTANDING DIRECTORIAL ACHIEVEMENT IN DRAMA: George Schaefer, "Macbeth," *Hallmark Hall of Fame* (NBC)

OUTSTANDING DIRECTORIAL ACHIEVEMENT IN COMEDY: Sheldon Leonard, *The Danny Thomas Show* (CBS)

1961–1962 (PRESENTED MAY 22, 1962)

THE PROGRAM OF THE YEAR: "Victoria Regina," *Hallmark Hall of Fame* (NBC)

OUTSTANDING PROGRAM ACHIEVEMENT IN THE FIELD OF HUMOR: *The Bob Newhart Show* (NBC)

OUTSTANDING PROGRAM ACHIEVEMENT IN THE FIELD OF DRAMA: *The Defenders* (CBS)

OUTSTANDING PROGRAM ACHIEVEMENT IN THE FIELD OF VARIETY: *The Garry Moore Show* (CBS)

OUTSTANDING PROGRAM ACHIEVEMENT IN ThE FIELD OF NEWS: *The Huntley-Brinkley Report* (NBC)

OUTSTANDING PROGRAM ACHIEVEMENT IN THE FIELD OF EDUCATIONAL AND PUBLIC AFFAIRS PROGRAMMING: *David Brinkley's Journal* (NBC)

OUTSTANDING SINGLE PERFORMANCE BY AN ACTOR IN A LEADING ROLE: Peter Falk, "The Price of Tomatoes," *The Dick Powell Show* (NBC)

OUTSTANDING SINGLE PERFORMANCE BY AN ACTRESS IN A LEADING ROLE: Julie Harris, "Victoria Regina," *Hallmark Hall of Fame* (NBC)

OUTSTANDING CONTINUED PERFORMANCE BY AN ACTOR IN A SERIES (LEAD): E. G. Marshall, *The Defenders* (CBS)

OUTSTANDING CONTINUED PERFORMANCE BY AN ACTRESS IN A SERIES (LEAD): Shirley Booth, *Hazel* (NBC)

OUTSTANDING PERFORMANCE IN A SUPPORTING ROLE BYAN ACTOR: Don Knotts, *The Andy Griffith Show* (CBS)

OUTSTANDING PERFORMANCE IN A SUPPORTING ROLE BYAN ACTRESS: Pamela Brown, "Victoria Regina," *Hallmark Hall of Fame* (NBC)

OUTSTANDING PERFORMANCE IN A VARIETY OR MUSICAL PROGRAM OR SERIES: Carol Burnett, *The Garry Moore Show* (CBS)

OUTSTANDING WRITING ACHIEVEMENT IN DRAMA: Reginald Rose, *The Defenders* (CBS)

OUTSTANDING WRITING ACHIEVEMENT IN COMEDY: Carl Reiner, *The Dick Van Dyke Show* (CBS)

OUTSTANDING WRITING ACHIEVEMENT IN THE DOCUMENTARY FIELD: Lou Hazam, "Vincent Van Gogh: A Self-Portrait" (NBC)

OUTSTANDING DIRECTORIAL ACHIEVEMENT IN DRAMA: Franklin Schaffner, *The Defenders* (CBS)

OUTSTANDING DIRECTORIAL ACHIEVEMENT IN COMEDY: Nat Hiken, *Car 54, Where Are You?* (NBC)

1962–1963 (PRESENTED MAY 26,1963)

THE PROGRAM OF THE YEAR: "The Tunnel" (NBC)

OUTSTANDING PROGRAM ACHIEVEMENT IN THE FIELD OF HUMOR: *The Dick Van Dyke Show* (CBS)

OUTSTANDING PROGRAM ACHIEVEMENT IN THE FIELD OF DRAMA: *The Defenders* (CBS)

OUTSTANDING PROGRAM ACHIEVEMENT IN THE FIELD OF MUSIC: "Julie and Carol at Carnegie Hall" (CBS)

OUTSTANDING ACHIEVEMENT IN THE FIELD OF VARIETY: *The Andy Williams Show* (NBC)

OUTSTANDING PROGRAM ACHIEVEMENT IN THE FIELD OF PANEL, QUIZ, OR AUDIENCE PARTICIPATION: *The G. E. College Bowl* (CBS)

OUTSTANDING PROGRAM ACHIEVEMENT IN THE FIELD OF CHILDREN'S PROGRAMMING: *Walt Disney's Wonderful World of Color* (NBC)

OUTSTANDING ACHIEVEMENT IN THE FIELD OF DOCUMENTARY PROGRAMS: "The Tunnel," Reuven Frank (NBC)

OUTSTANDING ACHIEVEMENT IN THE FIELD OF NEWS: *The Huntley-Brinkley Report* (NBC)

OUTSTANDING PROGRAM ACHIEVEMENT IN THE FIELD OF NEWS COMMENTARY OR PUBLIC AFFAIRS: *David Brinkley's Journal* (NBC)

OUTSTANDING ACHIEVEMENT IN INTERNATIONAL REPORTING OR COMMENTARY: Piers Anderton, Berlin correspondent, "The Tunnel" (NBC)

OUTSTANDING SINGLE PERFORMANCE BY AN ACTOR IN A LEADING ROLE: Trevor Howard, "The Invincible Mr. Disraeli," *Hallmark Hall of Fame* (NBC)

OUTSTANDING SINGLE PERFORMANCE BY AN ACTRESS IN A LEADING ROLE: Kim Stanley, "A Cardinal Act of Mercy," *Ben Casey* (ABC)

OUTSTANDING CONTINUED PERFORMANCE BYAN ACTOR IN A SERIES (LEAD): E. G. Marshall, *The Defenders* (CBS)

OUTSTANDING CONTINUED PERFORMANCE BYAN ACTRESS IN A SERIES (LEAD): Shirley Booth, *Hazel* (NBC)

OUTSTANDING PERFORMANCE IN A SUPPORTING ROLE STAN ACTOR: Don Knotts, *The Andy Griffith Show* (CBS)

OUTSTANDING PERFORMANCE IN A SUPPORTING ROLE BY AN ACTRESS: Glenda Farrell, "A Cardinal Act of Mercy," *Ben Casey* (ABC)

OUTSTANDING PERFORMANCE IN A VARIETY OR MUSICAL PROGRAM OR SERIES: Carol Burnett, "Julie and Carol at Carnegie Hall" (CBS) and "Carol and Company" (CBS)

OUTSTANDING WRITING ACHIEVEMENT IN DRAMA: Robert Thom and Reginald Rose, "The Madman," *The Defenders* (CBS)

OUTSTANDING WRITING ACHIEVEMENT IN COMEDY: Carl Reiner, *The Dick Van Dyke Show* (CBS)

OUTSTANDING DIRECTORIAL ACHIEVEMENT IN DRAMA: Stuart Rosenberg, "The Madman," *The Defenders* (CBS)

OUTSTANDING DIRECTORIAL ACHIEVEMENT IN COMEDY: John Rich, *The Dick Van Dyke Show* (CBS)

1963–1964 (PRESENTED MAY 25, 1964)

THE PROGRAM OF THE YEAR: "The Making of the President 1960" (ABC)

OUTSTANDING PROGRAM ACHIEVEMENT IN THE FIELD OF COMEDY: *The Dick Van Dyke Show* (CBS)

OUTSTANDING PROGRAM ACHIEVEMENT IN THE FIELD OF DRAMA: *The Defenders* (CBS)

OUTSTANDING PROGRAM ACHIEVEMENT IN THE FIELD OF MUSIC: *The Bell Telephone Hour* (NBC)

OUTSTANDING PROGRAM ACHIEVEMENT IN THE FIELD OF VARIETY: *The Danny Kaye Show* (CBS)

OUTSTANDING ACHIEVEMENT IN THE FIELD OF DOCUMENTARY PROGRAMS: "The Making of the President 1960" (ABC)

OUTSTANDING PROGRAM ACHIEVEMENT IN THE FIELD OF NEWS REPORTS: *The Huntley-Brinkley Report* (NBC)

OUTSTANDING PROGRAM ACHIEVEMENT IN THE FIELD OF NEWS COMMENTARY OR PUBLIC AFFAIRS: "Cuba: Parts I and II—The Bay of Pigs and the Missile Crisis," *NBC White Paper* (NBC)

OUTSTANDING SINGLE PERFORMANCE BY AN ACTOR IN A LEADING ROLE: Jack Klugman, "Blacklist," *The Defenders* (CBS)

OUTSTANDING SINGLE PERFORMANCE BY AN ACTRESS IN A LEADING ROLE: Shelley Winters, "Two Is the Number," *Bob Hope Presents the Chrysler Theatre* (NBC)

OUTSTANDING CONTINUED PERFORMANCE BY AN ACTOR IN A SERIES (LEAD): Dick Van Dyke, *The Dick Van Dyke Show* (CBS)

OUTSTANDING CONTINUED PERFORMANCE BY AN ACTRESS IN A SERIES (LEAD): Mary Tyler Moore, *The Dick Van Dyke Show* (CBS)

OUTSTANDING PERFORMANCE IN A SUPPORTING ROLE BY AN ACTOR: Albert Paulsen, "One Day in the Life of Ivan Denisovich," *Bob Hope Presents the Chrysler Theatre* (NBC)

OUTSTANDING PERFORMANCE IN A SUPPORTING ROLE BY AN ACTRESS: Ruth White, "Little Moon of Alban," *Hallmark Hall of Fame* (NBC)

OUTSTANDING PERFORMANCE IN A VARIETY OR MUSICAL PROGRAM OR SERIES: Danny Kaye, *The Danny Kaye Show* (CBS)

OUTSTANDING WRITING ACHIEVEMENT IN DRAMA (ORIGINAL): Ernest Kinoy, "Blacklist," *The Defenders* (CBS)

OUTSTANDING WRITING ACHIEVEMENT IN DRAMA (ADAPTATION): Rod Serling, "It's Mental Work" (from the story by John O'Hara), *Bob Hope Presents the Chrysler Theatre* (NBC)

OUTSTANDING WRITING ACHIEVEMENT IN COMEDY OR VARIETY: Carl Reiner, Sam Denoff, and Bill Persky, *The Dick Van Dyke Show* (CBS)

OUTSTANDING DIRECTORIAL ACHIEVEMENT IN DRAMA: Tom Gries, "Who Do You Kill,"*East Side/West Side* (CBS)

OUTSTANDING DIRECTORIAL ACHIEVEMENT IN COMEDY: Jerry Paris, *The Dick Van Dyke Show* (CBS)

OUTSTANDING DIRECTORIAL ACHIEVEMENT IN VARIETY OR MUSIC: Robert Scheerer, *The Danny Kaye Show* (CBS)

1964–1965 (PRESENTED SEPTEMBER 12, 1965)

OUTSTANDING PROGRAM ACHIEVEMENTS IN ENTERTAINMENT: *The Dick Van Dyke Show,* Carl Reiner, producer (CBS); "The Magnificent Yankee," *Hallmark Hall of Fame,* George Schaefer, producer (NBC); "My Name Is Barbra," Richard Lewine, producer (CBS)

OUTSTANDING INDIVIDUAL ACHIEVEMENTS IN ENTERTAINMENT (ACTORS AND PERFORMERS): Lynn Fontanne, "The Magnificent Yankee," *Hallmark Hall of Fame* (NBC); Alfred Lunt, "The Magnificent Yankee," *Hallmark Hall of Fame* (NBC); Barbra Streisand, "My Name Is Barbra" (CBS); *Dick Van Dyke,* The Dick Van Dyke Show (CBS)

OUTSTANDING INDIVIDUAL ACHIEVEMENT IN ENTERTAINMENT (WRITER): David Karp, "The 700-Year-Old Gang," *The Defenders* (CBS)

OUTSTANDING INDIVIDUAL ACHIEVEMENT IN ENTERTAINMENT (DIRECTOR): Paul Bogart, "The 700-Year-Old Gang," *The Defenders* (CBS)

OUTSTANDING PROGRAM ACHIEVEMENTS IN NEWS, DOCUMENTARIES, INFORMATION, AND SPORTS: "I, Leonardo da Vinci," *The Saga of Western Man,* John H. Secondari and Helen Jean Rogers, producers (ABC); "The Louvre," Lucy Jarvis, producer, and Jolm J. Sughrue, coproducer (NBC)

OUTSTANDING INDIVIDUAL ACHIEVEMENT IN NEWS, DOCUMENTARIES, INFORMATION, AND SPORTS (DIRECTOR): John J. Sughrue, "The Louvre" (NBC)

OUTSTANDING INDIVIDUAL ACHIEVEMENT IN NEWS, DOCUMENTARIES, INFORMATION, AND SPORTS (WRITER): Sidney Carroll, "The Louvre" (NBC)

1965–1966 (PRESENTED MAY 22, 1966)

OUTSTANDING COMEDY SERIES: *The Dick Van Dyke Show,* Carl Reiner, producer (CBS)

OUTSTANDING VARIETY SERIES: *The Andy Williams Show,* Bob Finkel, producer (NBC)

OUTSTANDING VARIETY SPECIAL: "Chrysler Presents the Bob Hope Christmas Special," Bob Hope, executive producer (NBC)

OUTSTANDING DRAMATIC SERIES: *The Fugitive,* Alan Armer, producer (ABC)

OUTSTANDING DRAMATIC PROGRAM: "The Ages of Man," David Susskind, and Daniel Melnick, producers (CBS)

OUTSTANDING MUSICAL PROGRAM: "Frank Sinatra: A Man and His Music," Dwight Hemian, producer (NBC)

OUTSTANDING CHILDREN'S PROGRAM: "A Charlie Brown Christmas," Lee Mendelson and Bill Melendez, producers (CBS)

OUTSTANDING PERFORMANCE BY AN ACTOR IN A LEADING ROLE IN A DRAMA: Cliff Robertson, "The Game," *Bob Hope Presents the Chrysler Theatre* (NBC)

OUTSTANDING PERFORMANCE BY AN ACTRESS IN A LEADING ROLE IN A DRAMA: Simone Signoret, "A Small Rebellion," *Bob Hope Presents the Chrysler Theatre* (NBC)

OUTSTANDING CONTINUED PERFORMANCE BY AN ACTOR IN A LEADING ROLE IN A DRAMATIC SERIES: Bill Cosby, *I Spy* (NBC)

OUTSTANDING CONTINUED PERFORMANCE BY AN ACTRESS IN A LEADING ROLE IN A DRAMATIC SERIES: Barbara Stanwyck, *The Big Valley* (ABC)

OUTSTANDING CONTINUED PERFORMANCE BY AN ACTOR IN A LEADING ROLE IN A COMEDY SERIES: Dick Van Dyke, *The Dick Van Dyke Show* (CBS)

OUTSTANDING CONTINUED PERFORMANCE BY AN ACTRESS IN A LEADING ROLE IN A COMEDY SERIES: Mary Tyler Moore, *The Dick Van Dyke Show* (CBS)

OUTSTANDING PERFORMANCE BY AN ACTOR IN A SUPPORTING ROLE IN A DRAMA: James Daly, "Eagle in a Cage," *Hallmark Hall of Fame* (NBC)

OUTSTANDING PERFORMANCE BY AN ACTRESS IN A SUPPORTING ROLE IN A DRAMA: Lee Grant, *Peyton Place* (ABC)

OUTSTANDING PERFORMANCE BY AN ACTOR IN A SUPPORTING ROLE IN A COMEDY: Don Knotts, "The Return of Barney Fife," *The Andy Griffith Show* (CBS)

OUTSTANDING PERFORMANCE BY AN ACTRESS IN A SUPPORTING ROLE IN A COMEDY: Alice Pearce, *Bewitched* (ABC)

OUTSTANDING WRITING ACHIEVEMENT IN DRAMA: Millard Lampell, "Eagle in a Cage," *Hallmark Hall of Fame* (NBC)

OUTSTANDING WRITING ACHIEVEMENT IN COMEDY: Bill Persky and Sam Denoff, "Coast to Coast Big Mouth," *The Dick Van Dyke Show* (CBS)

OUTSTANDING WRITING ACHIEVEMENT IN VARIETY: Al Gordon, Hal Goldman, and Sheldon Keller, "An Evening with Carol Channing" (CBS)

OUTSTANDING DIRECTORIAL ACHIEVEMENT IN DRAMA: Sidney Pollack, "The Game," *Bob Hope Presents the Chrysler Theatre* (NBC)

OUTSTANDING DIRECTORIAL ACHIEVEMENT IN COMEDY: William Asher, *Bewitched* (ABC)

OUTSTANDING DIRECTORIAL ACHIEVEMENT IN VARIETY OR MUSIC: Alan Handley, "The Julie Andrews Show" (NBC)

ACHIEVEMENTS IN NEWS AND DOCUMENTARIES (PROGRAMS): "American White Paper: United States Foreign Policy," Fred Freed, producer (NBC); "KKK—The Invisible Empire," *CBS Reports,* David Lowe, producer (CBS); "Senate Hearings on Vietnam," Chet Hagen, producer (NBC)

SPECIAL CLASSIFICATIONS OF INDIVIDUAL ACHIEVEMENTS: Burr Tillstorm, "Berlin Wall" hand ballet, *That Was the Week That Was,* (NBC)

1966–1967 (PRESENTED JUNE 4, 1967)

OUTSTANDING COMEDY SERIES: *The Monkees,* Bert Schneider and Bob Rafelson, producers (NBC)

OUTSTANDING VARIETY SERIES: *The Andy Williams Show,* Edward Stephenson and Bob Finkel, producers (NBC)

OUTSTANDING VARIETY SPECIAL: "The Sid Caesar, Imogene Coca, Carl Reiner, Howard Morris Special," Jack Arnold, producer (CBS)

OUTSTANDING DRAMATIC SERIES: *Mission: Impossible,* Joseph Gahtnian and Bruce&Geller (Producers)

OUTSTANDING DRAMATIC PROGRAM: "Death of a Salesman," David Susskind and Daniel Melnick, producers (CBS)

OUTSTANDING MUSICAL PROGRAM: "Brigadoor," Fielder Cook, producer (ABC)

OUTSTANDING CHILDREN'S PROGRAM: "Jack and the Beanstalk," Gene Kelly producer (NBC)

OUTSTANDING SINGLE PERFORMANCE BY AN ACTOR IN A LEADING ROLE IN A DRAMA: Peter Ustinov, "Barefoot in Athens," *Hallmark Hall of Fame* (NBC)

OUTSTANDING SINGLE PERFORMANCE BY AN ACTRESS IN A LEADING ROLE IN A DRAMA: Geraldine Page, "A Christmas Memory," *ABC Stage 67* (ABC)

OUTSTANDING CONTINUED PERFORMANCE BY AN ACTOR IN A LEADING ROLE IN A DRAMATIC SERIES: Bill Cosby, *I Spy* (NBC)

OUTSTANDING CONTINUED PERFORMANCE BY AN ACTRESS IN A LEADING ROLE IN A DRAMATIC SERIES: Barbara Bain, *Mission: Impossible* (CBS)

OUTSTANDING CONTINUED PERFORMANCE BY AN ACTOR IN A LEADING ROLE IN A COMEDY SERIES: Don Adams, *Get Smart* (NBC)

OUTSTANDING CONTINUED PERFORMANCE BY AN ACTRESS IN A LEADING ROLE IN A COMEDY SERIES: Lucille Ball, *The Lucy Show* (CBS)

OUTSTANDING PERFORMANCE BY AN ACTOR IN A SUPPORTING ROLE IN A DRAMA: Eli Wallach, "The Poppy Is Also a Flower," *Xerox Special* (ABC)

OUTSTANDING PERFORMANCE BY AN ACTRESS IN A SUPPORTING ROLE IN A DRAMA: Agnes Moorehead, "Night of the Vicious Valentine," *The Wild Wild West* (CBS)

OUTSTANDING PERFORMANCE BY AN ACTOR IN A SUPPORTING ROLE IN A COMEDY: Don Knotts, "Barney Comes to Mayberry," *The Andy Griffith Show* (CBS)

OUTSTANDING PERFORMANCE BY AN ACTRESS IN A SUPPORTING ROLE IN A COMEDY: Frances Bavier, *The Andy Griffith Show* (CBS)

OUTSTANDING WRITING ACHIEVEMENT IN DRAMA: Bruce Geller, *Mission: Impossible* (CBS)

OUTSTANDING WRITING ACHIEVEMENT IN COMEDY: Buck Henry and Leonard Stern, "Ship of Spies," *Get Smart* (NBC)

OUTSTANDING WRITING ACHIEVEMENT IN VARIETY: Mel Brooks, Sam Denoff, Bill Persky, Carl Reiner, and Mel Tolkin, "The Sid Caesar, Imogene Coca, Carl Reiner, Howard Morris Special" (CBS)

OUTSTANDING DIRECTORIAL ACHIEVEMENT IN DRAMA: Alex Segal, "Death of a Salesman" (CBS)

OUTSTANDING DIRECTORIAL ACHIEVEMENT IN COMEDY: James Frawley, "Royal Flush," *The Monkees* (NBC)

OUTSTANDING DIRECTORIAL ACHIEVEMENT IN VARIETY OR MUSIC: Fielder Cook, "Brigadoon" (ABC)

ACHIEVEMENTS IN NEWS AND DOCUMENTARIES (PROGRAMS): "China: The Roots of Madness," Mel Stuart, producer (syndicated); "Hall of Kings," Harry Rasky, producer (ABC); "The Italians," Bernard Birnbaum, producer (CBS)

ACHIEVEMENTS IN NEWS AND DOCUMENTARIES (INDIVIDUAL): Theodore H. White, writer, "China: The Roots of Madness" (syndicated)

OUTSTANDING SINGLE PERFORMANCE BY AN ACTRESS IN A LEADING ROLE: Geraldine Page, "The Thanksgiving Visitor" (ABC)

OUTSTANDING CONTINUED PERFORMANCE BY AN ACTOR IN A LEADING ROLE IN A DRAMATIC SERIES: Carl Betz, *Judd for the Defense* (ABC)

OUTSTANDING CONTINUED PERFORMANCE BY AN ACTRESS IN A LEADING ROLE IN A DRAMATIC SERIES: Barbara Bain, *Mission: Impossible* (CBS)

OUTSTANDING CONTINUED PERFORMANCE BY AN ACTOR IN A LEADING ROLE IN A COMEDY SERIES: Don Adams, *Get Smart* (NBC)

OUTSTANDING CONTINUED PERFORMANCE BY AN ACTRESS IN A LEADING ROLE IN A COMEDY SERIES: Hope Lange, *The Ghost and Mrs. Muir* (NBC)

OUTSTANDING SINGLE PERFORMANCE BY AN ACTOR IN A SUPPORTING ROLE: no award given

OUTSTANDING SINGLE PERFORMANCE BY AN ACTRESS IN A SUPPORTING ROLE: Anna Calder-Marshall, "The Male of the Species," *Prudential's On Stage* (NBC)

OUTSTANDING CONTINUED PERFORMANCE BY AN ACTOR IN A SUPPORTING ROLE IN A SERIES: Werner Klemperer, *Hogan's Heroes* (CBS)

OUTSTANDING CONTINUED PERFORMANCE BY AN ACTRESS IN A SUPPORTING ROLE IN A SERIES: Susan Saint James, *The Name of the Game* (NBC)

OUTSTANDING WRITING ACHIEVEMENT IN DRAMA: J. P. Miller, "The People Next Door," *CBS Playhouse* (CBS)

OUTSTANDING WRITING ACHIEVEMENT IN COMEDY, VARIETY, OR MUSIC: Alan Blye, Bob Einstein, Murray Roman, Carl Gottlieb, Jerry Music, Steve Martin, Cecil Tuck, Paul Wayne, Cy Howard, and Mason Williams, *The Smothers Brothers Comedy Hour* (CBS)

OUTSTANDING DIRECTORIAL ACHIEVEMENT IN DRAMA: David Greene, "The People Next Door," *CBS Playhouse* (CBS)

OUTSTANDING PROGRAM ACHIEVEMENT (SPECIAL CLASSIFICATION): *Firing Line with William F. Buckley, Jr.,* Warren Steibel, producer (syndicated); *Wild Kingdom,* Don Meier, producer (NBC)

OUTSTANDING INDIVIDUAL ACHIEVEMENT (SPECIAL CLASSIFICATION): Arte Johnson, *Rowan & Martin's Laugh-In* (NBC); Harvey Korman, *The Carol Burnett Show* (CBS)

OUTSTANDING ACHIEVEMENT WITHIN REGULARLY SCHEDULED NEWS PROGRAMS: "Coverage of Hunger in the United States," *The Huntley-Brinkley Report,* Wallace Westfeldt, executive producer (NBC). "On the Road," *The CBS Evening News with Walter Cronkite,* Charles Kuralt, correspondent: James Wilson, cameraman; Robert Funk, soundman (CBS). "Police After Chicago," *The CBS Evening News with Walter Cronkite,* John Laurence, correspondent (CBS)

OUTSTANDING ACHIEVEMENT IN COVERAGE OF SPECIAL EVENTS: "Coverage of Martin Luther King Assassination and Aftermath," *CBS News Special Reports* and Broadcasts, Robert Wussler, Ernest Leiser, Don Hewitt, and Burton Benjamin, executive producers (CBS)

OUTSTANDING NEWS DOCUMENTARY PROGRAM ACHIEVEMENTS: "CBS Reports: Hunger in America," *CBS News Hour,* Martin Carr, producer (CBS); "Law and Order," *Public Broadcast Laboratory,* Frederick Wiseman, producer (NET)

OUTSTANDING NEWS DOCUMENTARY INDIVIDUAL ACHIEVEMENT: Perry Wolff and Andrew A. Rooney, writers, "Black History: Lost, Stolen or Strayed" [*Of Black America Series*], *CBS News Hour* (CBS)

OUTSTANDING CULTURAL DOCUMENTARY AND "MAGAZINE TYPE" PROGRAM OR SERIES ACHIEVEMENT (PROGRAMS): "Don't Count the Candles," *CBS News Hour,* William K. McClure, producer (CBS); "Justice Black and the Bill of Rights," *CBS News Special,* Burton Benjamin, producer (CBS); "Man Who Dances: Edward Viltela," *The Bell Telephone Hour,* Robert Drew and Mike Jackson, producers (NBC); "The Great American Novel," *CBS News Hour,* Arthur Barron, producer (CBS)

OUTSTANDING CULTURAL DOCUMENTARY AND "MAGAZINE TYPE" PROGRAM OR SERIES ACHIEVEMENT (INDIVIDUAL): Walter Dombrow and Jerry Sims, cinematographers, "The Great American Novel," *CBS News Hour* (CBS); Tom Pettit, producer, "CBW: The Secrets of Secrecy," *First Tuesday* (NBC); Lord Snowden, cinematographer, "Don't Count the Candles," *CBS News Hour* (CBS)

OUTSTANDING COMEDY SERIES: *My World and Welcome to It,* Sheldon Leonard, executive producer; Danny Arnold, producer (NBC)

OUTSTANDING DRAMATIC SERIES: *Marcus Welby, M.D.,* David Victor, executive producer; David J. O'Connell, producer (ABC)

OUTSTANDING DRAMATIC PROGRAM: "A Storm in Summer," *Hallmark Hall of Fame,* M. J. Rifkin, executive producer; Alan Landsburg, producer (NBC)

OUTSTANDING VARIETY OR MUSICAL SERIES: *The David Frost Show,* Peter, producer (Syndicated)

OUTSTANDING VARIETY OR MUSICAL PROGRAM (VARIETY AND POPULAR MUSIC): "Annie, the Women in the Life of a Man," Joseph Cates, executive producer; Martin Charnin, producer (CBS)

OUTSTANDING VARIETY OR MUSICAL PROGRAM (CLASSICAL MUSIC): "Cinderella," John Barnes and Curtis Davis, executive producers; Norman Campbell, producer (NET)

OUTSTANDING NEW SERIES: *Room 222,* Gene Reynolds, producer (ABC)

OUTSTANDING SINGLE PERFORMANCE BY AN ACTOR IN A LEADING ROLE: Peter Ustinov, "A Storm in Summer," *Hallmark Hall of Fame* (NBC)

OUTSTANDING SINGLE PERFORMANCE BY AN ACTRESS IN A LEADING ROLE: Patty Duke, "My Sweet Charlie," *NBC World Premiere Movie* (NBC)

OUTSTANDING CONTINUED PERFORMANCE BY AN ACTOR IN A LEADING ROLE IN A DRAMATIC SERIES: Robert Young, *Marcus Welby, M.D.* (ABC)

SPECIAL CLASSIFICATIONS OF INDIVIDUAL ACHIEVEMENTS: Art Carney, *The Jackie Gleason Show* (CBS); Truman Capote and Eleanor Perry, adaptation of "A Christmas Memory," *ABC Stage 67* (ABC); Arthur Miller, adaptation of "Death of a Salesman" (CBS)

1967–1968 (PRESENTED MAY 19, 1968)

OUTSTANDING ACHIEVEMENT WITHIN REGULARLY SCHEDULED NEWS PROGRAMS: "1st Cavalry, Con Thien," and other segments, *The CBS Evening News with Walter Cronkite,* CBS news correspondent John Laurence and CBS news cameraman Keith Kay (CBS); "Crisis in the Cities," *Public Broadcast Laboratory,* Av Wesfin, executive producer (NET)

OUTSTANDING ACHIEVEMENT IN NEWS DOCUMENTARIES: "Africa," James Fleming, executive producer (ABC); "Summer '67: What We Learned," Fred Freed, producer (NBC); "CBS Reports: What about Ronald Reagan?" *CBS News Hour,* Harry Reasoner, writer (CBS); "Same Mud, Same Blood," Vo Huynh, cameraman (NBC)

OUTSTANDING ACHIEVEMENT IN CULTURAL DOCUMENTARIES: "Eric Hoffer, the Passionate State of Mind," *CBS News Hour,* Jack Beck, producer (CBS); "Gauguin in Tahiti: The Search for Paradise," *CBS News Hour,* Martin Carr, producer (CBS); "John Steinbeck's America and the Americans," Lee Mendelson, producer (NBC); "Dylan Thomas: The World I Breathe," *NET Festival,* Perry Miller Adato, producer (NET); Nathaniel Dorsky, art photographer, "Gauguin in Tahiti: The Search for Paradise," *CBS News Hour* (CBS); Harry Morgan, writer, "The Wyeth Phenomenon," *Who, What, When, Where, Why* (CBS); Thomas A.Priestley, director of photography, and Robert Loweree, film editor, "John Steinbeck's America and the Americans" (NBC)

OUTSTANDING NEWS AND DOCUMENTARY ACHIEVEMENTS: *The Twenty-first Century,* Isaac Kleinerman, producer (CBS); "Science and Religion: Who Will Play God?" *CBS News Special,* Ben Flynn, producer (CBS); *Our World,* George Delerue, composer (NET)

OUTSTANDING COMEDY SERIES: *Get Smart,* Burt Nodella, producer (NBC)

OUTSTANDING DRAMATIC SERIES: *Mission: Impossible,* Joseph E. Gantinan, producer (CBS)

OUTSTANDING DRAMATIC PROGRAM: "Elizabeth the Queen," *Hallmark Hall of Fame,* George Schaefer, producer (NBC)

OUTSTANDING MUSICAL OR VARIETY SERIES: *Rowan & Martin's Laugh-In,* George Schlatter, producer (NBC)

OUTSTANDING MUSICAL OR VARIETY PROGRAM: "Rowan & Martin's Laugh-In Special," George Schlatter, producer (NBC)

OUTSTANDING SINGLE PERFORMANCE BY AN ACTOR IN A LEADING ROLE IN A DRAMA: Melvyn Douglas, "Do Not Go Gentle into That Good Night," *CBS Playhouse* (CBS)

OUTSTANDING SINGLE PERFORMANCE BY AN ACTRESS IN A LEADING ROLE IN A DRAMA: Maureen Stapleton, "Among the Paths to Eden," *Xerox Special Event* (ABC)

OUTSTANDING CONTINUED PERFORMANCE BY AN ACTOR IN A LEADING ROLE IN A DRAMATIC SERIES: Bill Cosby, *I Spy* (NBC)

OUTSTANDING CONTINUED PERFORMANCE BY AN ACTRESS IN A LEADING ROLE IN A DRAMATIC SERIES: Barbara Bain, *Mission: Impossible* (CBS)

OUTSTANDING CONTINUED PERFORMANCE BY AN ACTOR IN A LEADING ROLE IN A COMEDY SERIES: Don Adams, *Get Smart* (NBC)

OUTSTANDING CONTINUED PERFORMANCE BY AN ACTRESS IN A LEADING ROLE IN A COMEDY SERIES: Lucille Ball, *The Lucy Show* (CBS)

OUTSTANDING PERFORMANCE BY AN ACTOR IN A SUPPORTING ROLE IN A DRAMA: Milburn Stone, *Gunsmoke* (CBS)

OUTSTANDING PERFORMANCE BY AN ACTRESS IN A SUPPORTING ROLE IN A DRAMA: Barbara Anderson, *Ironside* (NBC)

OUTSTANDING PERFORMANCE BY AN ACTOR IN A SUPPORTING ROLE IN A COMEDY: Werner Klemperer, *Hogan's Heroes* (CBS)

OUTSTANDING PERFORMANCE BY AN ACTRESS IN A SUPPORTING ROLE IN A COMEDY: Marion Lorne, *Bewitched* (ABC)

OUTSTANDING WRITING ACHIEVEMENT IN DRAMA: Loring Mandel, "Do Not Go Gentle into That Good Night," *CBS Playhouse* (CBS)

OUTSTANDING WRITING ACHIEVEMENT IN COMEDY: Allan Burns and Chris Hayward, "The Coming-Out Party," *He & She* (CBS)

OUTSTANDING WRITING ACHIEVEMENT IN MUSIC OR VARIETY: Paul Keyes, Hugh Wedlock, Allan Manings, Chris Bearde, David Panich, Phil Hahn, Jack Hanrahan, Coslough Johnson, Marc London, and Digby Wolfe, *Rowan & Martin's Laugh-In* (NBC)

OUTSTANDING DIRECTORIAL ACHIEVEMENT IN DRAMA: Paul Bogart, "Dear Friends," *CBS Playhouse* (CBS)

OUTSTANDING DIRECTORIAL ACHIEVEMENT IN COMEDY: Bruce Bilson, "Maxwell Smart, Private Eye," *Get Smart* (NBC)

OUTSTANDING DIRECTORIAL ACHIEVEMENT IN MUSIC OR VARIETY: Jack Haley, Jr., "Movin' with Nancy" (NBC)

SPECIAL CLASSIFICATION OF OUTSTANDING INDIVIDUAL ACHIEVEMENT: Art Carney, *The Jackie Gleason Show* (CBS); Pat Paulsen, *The Smothers Brothers Comedy Hour*

1968–1969 (PRESENTED JUNE 8, 1969)

OUTSTANDING COMEDY SERIES: *Get Smart,* Arne Sultan, executive producer; Burt Nodella, producer (NBC)

OUTSTANDING DRAMATIC SERIES: *NET Playhouse,* Curtis Davis, executive producer (NET)

OUTSTANDING DRAMATIC PROGRAM: "Teacher, Teacher," Henry Jaffe, executive producer; George Lefferts, producer, *Hallmark Hall of Fame* (NBC)

OUTSTANDING MUSICAL OR VARIETY SERIES: *Rowan & Martin's Laugh-In,* George Schlatter, executive producer; Paul Keyes and Carolyn Raskin, producers (NBC)

OUTSTANDING VARIETY OR MUSICAL PROGRAM: "The Bill Cosby Special," Roy Silver, executive producer; Bill Hobin, Bill Persky, and Sam Denoff, producers (NBC)

OUTSTANDING SINGLE PERFORMANCE BY AN ACTOR IN A LEADING ROLE: Paul Scofield, "The Male of the Species," *Prudential's On Stage* (NBC)

OUTSTANDING CONTINUED PERFORMANCE BY AN ACTRESS IN A LEADING ROLE IN A DRAMATIC SERIES: Susan Hampshire, *The Forsyte Saga* (NET)

OUTSTANDING CONTINUED PERFORMANCE BY AN ACTOR IN A LEADING ROLE IN A COMEDY SERIES: William Windom, *My World and Welcome Tott* (NBC)

OUTSTANDING CONTINUED PERFORMANCE BY AN ACTRESS IN A LEADING ROLE IN A COMEDY SERIES: Hope Lange, *The Ghost and Mrs. Muir* (ABC)

OUTSTANDING PERFORMANCE BY AN ACTOR IN A SUPPORTING ROLE IN DRAMA: James Brolin, *Marcus Welby. M.D.* (ABC)

OUTSTANDING PERFORMANCE BY AN ACTRESS IN A SUPPORTING ROLE IN DRAMA: Gail Fisher, *Mannix* (CBS)

OUTSTANDING PERFORMANCE BY AN ACTOR IN A SUPPORTING ROLE IN COMEDY: Michael Constantine, *Room 222* (ABC)

OUTSTANDING PERFORMANCE BY AN ACTRESS IN A SUPPORTING ROLE IN COMEDY: Karen Valentine, *Room 222* (ABC)

OUTSTANDING WRITING ACHIEVEMENT IN DRAMA: Richard Levinson and William Link, "My Sweet Charlie," *NBC World Premiere Movie* (NBC)

OUTSTANDING WRITING ACHIEVEMENT IN COMEDY, VARIETY, OR MUSIC: Gary Belkin, Peter Bellwood, Herb Sargent, Thomas Meehan, and Judith Viorst, "Annie, the Women in the Life of a Man" (CBS)

OUTSTANDING DIRECTORIAL ACHIEVEMENT IN DRAMA: Paul Bogart, "Shadow Game," *CBS Playhouse* (CBS)

OUTSTANDING DIRECTORIAL ACHIEVEMENT IN COMEDY, VARIETY, OR MUSIC: Dwight Hemion, "The Sound of Burt Bacharach," *Kraft Music Hall* (NBC)

SPECIAL CLASSIFICATION OF OUTSTANDING PROGRAM AND INDIVIDUAL ACHIEVEMENT: *Wild Kingdom,* Don Meier, producer (NBC)

OUTSTANDING ACHIEVEMENT WITHIN REGULARLY SCHEDULED NEWS PROGRAMS: "An Investigation of Teenage Drug Addiction—Odyssey House," *The Huntley-Brinkley Report,* Wallace Westfeldt, executive producer; Les Crystal, producer (NBC). "Can the World Be Saved?," *The CBS Evening News with Walter Cronkite,* Ronald Bonn, producer (CBS)

OUTSTANDING ACHIEVEMENT IN MAGAZINE-TYPE PROGRAMMING: *Black Journal,* William Greaves, executive producer (NET); Tom Pettit, reporter-writer, "Some Footnotes to 25 Nuclear Years," *First Tuesday* (NBC)

OUTSTANDING ACHIEVEMENT IN NEWS DOCUMENTARY PROGRAMMING: "Hospital," *NET Journal,* Frederick Wiseman, producer (NET). "The Making of the President 1968," M. J. Rifkin, executive producer; Mel Stuart, producer (CBS)

OUTSTANDING ACHIEVEMENT IN CULTURAL DOCUMENTARY PROGRAMMING: "Artur Rubinstein," George A. Vicas, producer (NBC). Artur Rubinstein, commentator, "Artur Rubinstein" (NBC). "Fathers and Sons," *CBS News Hour,* Ernest Leiser, executive producer; Harry Morgan, producer (CBS). "The Japanese," *CBS News Hour,* Perry Wolff, executive producer; Igor Oganesoff, producer (CBS). Edwin 0. Reischauer, commentator, "The Japanese," *CBS News Hour* (CBS)

1970–1971 (PRESENTED MAY 9, 1971)

OUTSTANDING SERIES—COMEDY: *All in the Family,* Norman Lear, producer (CBS)

OUTSTANDING SERIES—DRAMA: *The Senator [The Bold Ones],* David Levinson, producer (NBC)

OUTSTANDING SINGLE PROGRAM—DRAMA OR COMEDY: "The Andersonville Trial," *Hollywood Television Theatre,* Lewis Freedman, producer (PBS)

OUTSTANDING VARIETY SERIES—MUSICAL: *The Flip Wilson Show,* Monte Kay, executive producer; Bob Henry, producer (NBC)

OUTSTANDING VARIETY SERIES—TALK: *The David Frost Show,* Peter Baker, producer (syndicated)

OUTSTANDING SINGLE PROGRAM—VARIETY OR MUSICAL (VARIETY AND POPULAR MUSIC): "Singer Presents Burt Bacharach," Gary Smith and Dwight Hemion, producers (CBS)

OUTSTANDING SINGLE PROGRAM—VARIETY OR MUSICAL (CLASSICAL MUSIC): "Leopold Stokowski," *NET Festival,* Curtis W. Davis, executive producer, Thomas Stevin, producer (PBS)

OUTSTANDING NEW SERIES: *All in the Family,* Norman Lear, producer (CBS)

OUTSTANDING SINGLE PERFORMANCE BY AN ACTOR IN A LEADING ROLE: George C. Scott, "The Price," *Hallmark Hall of Fame* (NBC)

OUTSTANDING SINGLE PERFORMANCE BY AN ACTRESS IN A LEADING ROLE: Lee Grant, "The Neon Ceiling," *World Premiere NBC Monday Night at the Movies* (NBC)

OUTSTANDING CONTINUED PERFORMANCE BY AN ACTOR IN A LEADING ROLE IN A DRAMATIC SERIES: Hal Holbrook, *The Senator [The Bold Ones]* (NBC)

OUTSTANDING CONTINUED PERFORMANCE BY AN ACTRESS IN A LEADING ROLE IN A DRAMATIC SERIES: Susan Hampshire, *The First Churchills [Masterpiece Theatre]* (PBS)

OUTSTANDING CONTINUED PERFORMANCE BY AN ACTOR IN A LEADING ROLE IN A COMEDY SERIES: Jack Klugman, *The Old Couple* (ABC)

OUTSTANDING CONTINUED PERFORMANCE BY AN ACTRESS IN A LEADING ROLE IN A COMEDY SERIES: Jean Stapleton, *All in the Family* (CBS)

OUTSTANDING PERFORMANCE BY AN ACTOR IN A SUPPORTING ROLE IN DRAMA: David Burns, "The Price," *Hallmark Hall of Fame* (NBC)

OUTSTANDING PERFORMANCE BY AN ACTRESS IN A SUPPORTING ROLE IN DRAMA: Margaret Leighten, "Hamlet," *Hallmark Hall of Fame* (NBC)

OUTSTANDING PERFORMANCE BY AN ACTOR IN A SUPPORTING ROLE IN COMEDY: Edward Asner, *The Mary Tyler Moore Show* (CBS)

OUTSTANDING PERFORMANCE BY AN ACTRESS IN A SUPPORTING ROLE IN COMEDY: Valerie Harper, *The Mary Tyler Moore Show* (CBS)

OUTSTANDING DIRECTORIAL ACHIEVEMENT IN DRAMA (SERIES): Daryl Duke, "The Day the Lion Died," *The Senator [The Bold Ones]* (NBC)

OUTSTANDING DIRECTORIAL ACHIEVEMENT IN DRAMA (SINGLE PROGRAM): Fielder Cook, "The Price," *Hallmark Hall of Fame* (NBC)

OUTSTANDING DIRECTORIAL ACHIEVEMENT IN COMEDY (SERIES): Jay Sandrich, "Toulouse-Lautrec Is One of My Favorite Artists," *The Mary Tyler Moore Show* (CBS)

OUTSTANDING DIRECTORIAL ACHIEVEMENT IN VARIETY OR MUSIC (SERIES): Mark Warren, *Rowan & Martin's Laugh-In,* 10/26/70 (NBC)

OUTSTANDING DIRECTORIAL ACHIEVEMENT IN VARIETY OR MUSIC (SPECIAL): Sterling Johnson, "Timex Presents Peggy Fleming at Sun Valley" (NBC)

OUTSTANDING WRITING ACHIEVEMENT IN DRAMA (SERIES): Joel Oliansky, "To Taste of Death but Once," *The Senator [The Bold Ones]* (NBC)

OUTSTANDING WRITING ACHIEVEMENT IN DRAMA, ORIGINAL TELEPLAY (SPECIAL): Tracy Kecnan Wynn and Marvin Schwartz, "Tribes," *Movie of the Week* (ABC)

OUTSTANDING WRITING ACHIEVEMENT IN DRAMA, ADAPTATION (SPECIAL): Saul Levitt, "The Andersonville Trial" (PBS)

OUTSTANDING WRITING ACHIEVEMENT IN COMEDY (SERIES): James L. Brooks and Allan Burns, "Support Your Local Mother," *The Mary Tyler Moore Show* (CBS)

OUTSTANDING WRITING ACHIEVEMENT IN VARIETY OR MUSIC (SERIES): Herbert Baker, Hal Goodman, Larry Klein, Bob Weiskopf, Bob Sculler, Norman Steinberg, and Flip Wilson, *The Flip Wilson Show,* with Lena Home and Tony Randall, 12/10/70 (NBC)

OUTSTANDING WRITING ACHIEVEMENT IN COMEDY, VARIETY, OR MUSIC (SPECIAL): Bob Ellison and Marty Farrel, "Singer Presents Burt Bacharach" (CBS)

OUTSTANDING ACHIEVEMENT WITHIN REGULARLY SCHEDULED NEWS PROGRAMS (PROGRAMS): "Five Part Investigation of Welfare," *The NBC Nightly News,* Wallace Westfeldt, executive producer; David Teitelbaum, producer (NBC)

OUTSTANDING ACHIEVEMENT WITHIN REGULARLY SCHEDULED NEWS PROGRAMS (INDIVIDUALS): Bruce Morton, correspondent, "Reports from the Lt. Calley Trial," *The CBS Evening News with Walter Cronkite* (CBS)

OUTSTANDING ACHIEVEMENT IN NEWS DOCUMENTARY PROGRAMMING (PROGRAMS): "The Selling of the Pentagon," Perry Wolff, executive producer; Peter Davis, producer (CBS). "The World of Charlie Company," Ernest Leiser, executive producer; Russ Bensley, producer (CBS); "NBC White Paper: Pollution Is a Matter of Choice," Fred Freed, producer (NBC)

OUTSTANDING ACHIEVEMENT IN NEWS DOCUMENTARY PROGRAMMING (INDIVIDUALS): John Laurence, correspondent, "The World of Charlie

Company" (CBS); Fred Freed, writer, "NBC News White Paper: Pollution Is a Matter of Choice" (NBC)

OUTSTANDING ACHIEVEMENT IN MAGAZINE-TYPE PROGRAMMING (PROGRAMS): "Gulf of Tonkin Segment," 60 Minutes, Joseph Wershba, producer; The Great American Dream Machine, A. H. Perlmutter and Jack Willis, executive producers (PBS)

OUTSTANDING ACHIEVEMENT IN MAGAZINE-TYPE PROGRAMMING (INDIVIDUALS): Mike Wallace, correspondent, 60 Minutes (CBS)

OUTSTANDING ACHIEVEMENT IN CULTURAL DOCUMENTARY PROGRAMMING (PROGRAMS): "The Everglades," Craig Fisher, producer (NBC); "The Making of Butch Cassidy & the Sundance Kid," Ronald Preissman, producer (NBC); "Arthur Penn, 1922 —: Themes and Variants," Robert Hughes, producer (PBS)

OUTSTANDING ACHIEVEMENT IN CULTURAL DOCUMENTARY PROGRAMMING (INDIVIDUALS): Nana Mahorno, narrator, "A Black View of South Africa" (CBS); Robert Guenette and Theodore I. Strauss, writers, "They've Killed President Lincoln" (NBC); Robert Young, director, "The Eskimo Fight for Life" (CBS)

SPECIAL CLASSIFICATION OF OUTSTANDING INDIVIDUAL ACHIEVEMENT: Harvey Korman, The Carol Burnett Show (CBS)

1971–1972 (PRESENTED MAY 6, 1972)

OUTSTANDING SERIES—COMEDY: All in the Family, Norman Lear, producer (CBS)

OUTSTANDING SERIES—DRAMA: Elizabeth B [Masterpiece Theatre], Christopher Sarson, executive producer; Roderick Graham, producer (PBS)

OUTSTANDING SINGLE PROGRAM—DRAMA OR COMEDY: "Brian's Song," Movie of the Week, Paul Junger Witt, producer (ABC)

OUTSTANDING VARIETY SERIES—MUSICAL: The Carol Burnett Show, Joe Hamilton, executive producer; Arnie Rosen, producer (CBS)

OUTSTANDING VARIETY SERIES—TALK: The Dick Cavett Show, John Gilroy, producer (ABC) OUTSTANDING SINGLE PROGRAM (VARIETY AND POPULAR MUSIC): "Jack Lemmon in 'S Wonderful, 'S Marvelous, 'S Gershwin," Bell System Family Theatre, Joseph Cates, executive producer; Martin Charnin, producer (NBC)

OUTSTANDING SINGLE PROGRAM (CLASSICAL MUSIC): "Beethoven's Birthday: A Celebration in Vienna with Leonard Bernstein," James Krayer, executive producer; Humphrey Burton, producer (CBS)

OUTSTANDING NEW SERIES: Elizabeth B [Masterpiece Theatre], Christopher Sarson, executive producer; Roderick Graham, producer (PBS)

OUTSTANDING SINGLE PERFORMANCE BY AN ACTOR IN A LEADING ROLE: Keith Michell, "Catherine Howard" The Six Wives of Henry VIII (CBS)

OUTSTANDING SINGLE PERFORMANCE BY AN ACTRESS IN A LEADING ROLE: Glenda Jackson, "Shadow in the Sun," Elizabeth R [Masterpiece Theatre] (PBS)

OUTSTANDING CONTINUED PERFORMANCE BY AN ACTOR IN A LEADING ROLE IN A DRAMATIC SERIES: Peter Falk, Columbo [NBC Mystery Movie] (NBC)

OUTSTANDING CONTINUED PERFORMANCE BY AN ACTRESS IN A LEADING ROLE IN A DRAMATIC SERIES: Glenda Jackson, Elizabeth B [Masterpiece Theatre] (PBS)

OUTSTANDING CONTINUED PERFORMANCE BY AN ACTOR IN A LEADING ROLE IN A COMEDY SERIES: Carroll O'Connor, All in the Family (CBS)

OUTSTANDING CONTINUED PERFORMANCE BY AN ACTRESS IN A LEADING ROLE IN A COMEDY SERIES: Jean Stapleton, All in the Family (CBS)

OUTSTANDING PERFORMANCE BY AN ACTOR IN A SUPPORTING ROLE IN DRAMA: Jack Warden, "Brian's Song," Movie of the Week (ABC)

OUTSTANDING PERFORMANCE BY AN ACTRESS IN A SUPPORTING ROLE IN DRAMA: Jenny Agutter, "The Snow Goose," Hallmark Hall of Fame (NBC)

OUTSTANDING PERFORMANCE BY AN ACTOR IN A SUPPORTING ROLE IN COMEDY: Edward Asner, The Mary Tyler Moore Show (CBS)

OUTSTANDING PERFORMANCE BY AN ACTRESS IN A SUPPORTING ROLE IN COMEDY: (TIE) Valerie Harper, The Mary Tyler Moore Show (CBS); Sally Struthers, All in the Family (CBS)

OUTSTANDING ACHIEVEMENT BY A PERFORMER IN MUSIC OR VARIETY: Harvey Korman, The Carol Burnett Show (CBS)

OUTSTANDING ACHIEVEMENT WITHIN REGULARLY SCHEDULED NEWS PROGRAMS (PROGRAMS): "Defeat of Dacca," The NBC Nightly News, Wallace Westfeldt, executive producer; Robert MuTholland and David Teitelbaum, producers (NBC)

OUTSTANDING ACHIEVEMENT WITHIN REGULARLY SCHEDULED NEWS PROGRAMS (INDIVIDUALS): Phil Brady, reporter, "Defeat of Dacca," The NBC Nightly News (NBC); Bob Schieffer, Phil Jones, Don Webster, and Bill Plante, correspondents, "The Air War," The CBS Evening News with Walter Cronkite (CBS)

OUTSTANDING ACHIEVEMENT FOR REGULARLY SCHEDULED MAGAZINE-TYPE PROGRAMS (PROGRAMS): The Great American Dream Machine, A. H. Perhnutter, executive producer (PBS); Chronolog, Eliot Frankel, executive producer (NBC)

OUTSTANDING ACHIEVEMENT FOR REGULARLY SCHEDULED MAGAZINE-TYPE PROGRAMS (INDIVIDUALS): Mike Wallace, correspondent, 60 Minutes (CBS)

OUTSTANDING DOCUMENTARY PROGRAM ACHIEVEMENT (PROGRAMS OF CURRENT SIG-

NIFICANCE): 'A Night in Jail, A Night in Court," *CBS Reports,* Burton Benjamin, executive producer; John Sharnik, producer (CBS). "This Child Is Rated X: An NBC News White Paper on Juvenile Justice," Martin Carr, producer (NBC)

OUTSTANDING DOCUMENTARY PROGRAM ACHIEVEMENT (CULTURAL PROGRAMS): "Hollywood: The Dream Factory," *The MondayNight Special,* Nicolas Noxon, executive producer; Irwin Rosten and Bud Friedman, producers (ABC). "A Sound of Dolphins," *The Undersea World of Jacques Cousteau,* Jacques Cousteau and Marshall Flaum, executive producers; Andy White, producer (ABC). "The Unsinkable Sea Otter," *The Undersea World of Jacques Cousteau,* Jacques Cousteau and Marshall Flaum, executive producers; Andy White, producer (ABC)

OUTSTANDING DOCUMENTARY PROGRAM ACHIEVEMENT (INDIVIDUALS): Louis J. Hazarn, writer, "Venice Be Damned" (NBC); Robert Northshield, writer, 'Suffer the Little Children—An NBC News White Paper on Northern Ireland" (NBC)

OUTSTANDING DIRECTORIAL ACHIEVEMENT IN DRAMA Alexander Singer, "The Invasion of Kevin Ireland," *The Lawyers [The Bold Ones]* (NBC)

OUTSTANDING DIRECTORIAL ACHIEVEMENT IN DRAMA (SINGLE PROGRAM): Tom Gries, "The Glass House," *The New CBS Friday Night Movies* (CBS)

OUTSTANDING DIRECTORIAL ACHIEVEMENT IN COMEDY (SERIES): John Rich, "Sammy's Visit," *All in the Family* (CBS)

OUTSTANDING DIRECTORIAL ACHIEVEMENT IN VARIETY OR MUSIC (SERIES): Art Fisher, *The Sonny and Cher Comedy Hour,* with Tony Randall, 1/31/72 (CBS)

OUTSTANDING DIRECTORIAL ACHIEVEMENT IN COMEDY, VARIETY, OR MUSIC (SPECIAL): Walter C. Miller and Martin Charnin, "Jack Lemmon in 'S Wonderful, 'S Marvelous, 'S Gershwin," *Bell System Family Theatre* (NBC)

OUTSTANDING WRITING ACHIEVEMENT IN DRAMA (SERIES): Richard L. Levinson and William Link, "Death Lends a Hand," *Columbo [NBC MysteryMovie]* (NBC)

OUTSTANDING WRITING ACHIEVEMENT IN DRAMA, ORIGINAL TELEPLAY: Allan Sloane, "To All My Friends on Shore" (CBS)

OUTSTANDING WRITING ACHIEVEMENT IN DRAMA, ADAPTATION: William Blinn, "Brian's Song," *Movie of the Week* (ABC)

OUTSTANDING WRITING ACHIEVEMENT IN COMEDY (SERIES): Burt Styler, "Edith's Problem," *All in the Family* (CBS)

OUTSTANDING WRiTING ACHIEVEMENT IN VARIETY OR MUSIC (SERIES): Don Hinldey, Stan Hart, Larry Siegel, Woody King, Roger Beatty, Art Baer, Ben Joelson, Stan Burns, Mike Mariner, and Arnie Rosen, *The Carol Burnett Show,* with Tim Conway and Ray Charles, 1/26/72 (CBS)

OUTSTANDING WRITING ACHIEVEMENT IN COMEDY, VARIETY, OR MUSIC (SPECIAL): Anne Howard Bailey, "The Trial of Mary Lincoln," *NET Opera Theatre* (PBS)

SPECIAL CLASSIFICATION OF OUTSTANDING PROGRAM AND INDIVIDUAL ACHIEVEMENT (GENERAL PROGRAMMING): "The Pentagon Papers," *PBS Special,* David Prowitt, executive producer; Martin Clancy, producer (PBS)

SPECIAL CLASSIFICATION OF OUTSTANDING PROGRAM AND INDIVIDUAL ACHIEVEMENT (DOCU-DRAMA): 'The Search for the Nile—Parts I—VI," Christopher Railing, producer (NBC)

SPECIAL CLASSIFICATION OF OUTSTANDING PROGRAM AND INDIVIDUAL ACHIEVEMENT (INDIVIDUALS): Michael Hastings et al, writers, "The Search for the Nile—Parts I—IV" (NBC)

1972–1973 (PRESENTED MAY 22, 1973)

OUTSTANDING COMEDY series: *All in the Family,* Norman Lear, executive producer; John Rich, producer (CBS)

OUTSTANDING DRAMA SERIES—CONTINUING: *The Waltons,* Lee Rich, executive producer; Robert L. Jacks, producer (CBS)

OUTSTANDING DRAMA/COMEDY—LIMITED EPISODES: *Tom Brown's Schooldays [Masterpiece Theatre],* John D. McRae, producer (PBS)

OUTSTANDING VARIETY MUSICAL SERIES: *The Julie Andrews Hour,* Nick Vanoff and William O. Harbach, producers (ABC)

OUTSTANDING SINGLE PROGRAM, DRAMA OR COMEDY: "A War of Children," *The New CBS Tuesday Night Movies,* Roger Gimbel, executive producer; George Schaefer, producer (CBS)

OUTSTANDING SINGLE PROGRAM VARIETY AND POPULAR MUSIC: "Singer Presents Liza with a 'Z,' "Bob Fosse and Fred Ebb, producers (NBC)

OUTSTANDING SINGLE PROGRAM-CLASSICAL MUSIC: "The Sleeping Beauty," J. W. Barnes and Robert Kotlowitz, executive producers; Norman Campbell, producer (PBS)

OUTSTANDING NEW SERIES: *America,* Michael Gill, producer (NBC)

OUTSTANDING SINGLE PERFORMANCE BY AN ACTOR IN A LEADING ROLE: Laurence Olivier, "Long Day's Journey into Night" (ABC)

OUTSTANDING SINGLE PERFORMANCE BY AN ACTRESS IN A LEADING ROLE: Cloris Leachman, "A Brand New Life," *Tuesday Movie of the Week* (ABC)

OUTSTANDING CONTINUED PERFORMANCE BY AN ACTOR IN A LEADING ROLE (DRAMA SERIES—CONTINUING): Richard Thomas, *The Waltons* (CBS)

OUTSTANDING CONTINUED PERFORMANCE BY AN ACTOR IN A LEADING ROLE (DRAMA/COMEDY—LIMITED EPISODES): Anthony Murphy, *Tom Brown's Schooldays [Masterpiece Theatre]* (PBS)

OUTSTANDING CONTINUED PERFORMANCE BY AN ACTRESS IN A LEADING ROLE (DRAMA SERIES—CONTINUING): Michael Learned, *The Waltons* (CBS)

OUTSTANDING CONTINUED PERFORMANCE BY AN ACTRESS IN A LEADING ROLE (DRAMA/COMEDY—LIMITED EPISODES): Susan Hampshire, *Vanity Fair [Masterpiece Theatre]* (PBS)

OUTSTANDING CONTINUED PERFORMANCE BY AN ACTOR IN A LEADING ROLE IN A COMEDY SERIES: Jack Klugman, *The Odd Couple* (ABC)

OUTSTANDING CONTINUED PERFORMANCE BY AN ACTRESS IN A LEADING ROLE IN A COMEDY SERIES: Mary Tyler Moore, *The Mary Tyler Moore* Show (CBS)

OUTSTANDING PERFORMANCE BY AN ACTOR IN A SUPPORTING ROLE IN DRAMA: Scott Jacoby, *That Certain Summer," Wednesday Movie of the Week* (ABC)

OUTSTANDING PERFORMANCE BY AN ACTRESS IN A SUPPORTING ROLE IN DRAMA: Ellen Corby, *The Waltons* (CBS)

OUTSTANDING PERFORMANCE BY AN ACTOR IN A SUPPORTING ROLE IN COMEDY: Ted Knight, *The Mary Tyler Moore Show* (CBS)

OUTSTANDING PERFORMANCE BY AN ACTRESS IN A SUPPORTING ROLE IN COMEDY: Valerie Harper, *The Mary Tyler Moore Show* (CBS)

OUTSTANDING ACHIEVEMENT BY A SUPPORTING PERFORMER IN MUSIC OR VARIETY: Tim Conway, *The Carol Burnett Show,* 2/17/73 (CBS)

OUTSTANDING DIRECTORIAL ACHIEVEMENT IN DRAMA (SERIES): Jerry Thorpe, "An Eye for an Eye," *Kung Fu* (ABC)

OUTSTANDING DIRECTORIAL ACHIEVEMENT IN DRAMA (SINGLE PROGRAM): Joseph Sargent, "The Marcus-Nelson Murders," *The CBS Thursday Night Movies* (CBS)

OUTSTANDING DIRECTORIAL ACHIEVEMENT IN COMEDY (SERIES): Jay Sandrich, "It's Whether You Win or Lose," *The Mary Tyler Moore Show* (CBS)

OUTSTANDING DIRECTORIAL ACHIEVEMENT IN VARIETY OR MUSIC (SERIES): Bill Davis, *The Julie Andrews Hour,* with "Liza Doolittle" and "Mary Poppins," 9/13/72 (ABC)

OUTSTANDING DIRECTORIAL ACHIEVEMENT IN VARIETY OR MUSIC (SPECIAL): Bob Fosse, "Singer Presents Liza with a 'Z'" (NBC)

OUTSTANDING WRITING ACHIEVEMENT IN DRAMA (SERIES): John McGreevey, "The Scholar," *The Waltons* (CBS)

OUTSTANDING WRITING ACHIEVEMENT IN DRAMA, ORIGINAL TELEPLAY (SINGLE PROGRAM): Abby Mann, "The Marcus-Nelson Murders," *The CBS Thursday Night Movies* (CBS)

OUTSTANDING WRITING ACHIEVEMENT IN DRAMA, ADAPTATION (SINGLE PROGRAM): Eleanor Perry, "The House without a Christmas Tree" (CBS)

OUTSTANDING WRITING ACHIEVEMENT IN COMEDY (SERIES): Michael Ross, Bernie West, and Lee Kalcheim, "The Bunkers and the Swingers," *All in the Family* (CBS)

OUTSTANDING WRITING ACHIEVEMENT IN VARIETY OR MUSIC (SERIES): Stan Hart, Larry Siegel, Gail Parent, Woody Kling, Roger Beatty, Tom Patchett, Jay Tarses, Robert Hilliard, Arnie Kogen, Bill Angelos, and Buz Kohan, *The Carol Burnett Show,* with Steve Lawrence and Lily Tomlin, 11/8/72 (CBS)

OUTSTANDING WRITING ACHIEVEMENT IN COMEDY, VARIETY, OR MUSIC (SPECIAL): Renee Taylor and Joseph Bologna, "Acts of Love—And Other Comedies" (ABC)

OUTSTANDING ACHIEVEMENT WITHIN REGULARLY SCHEDULED NEWS PROGRAMS (PROGRAM SEGMENTS): "The U.S./Soviet Wheat Deal: Is There a Scandal?" *The CBS Evening News with Walter Cronkite,* Paul Greenberg and Russ Bensley, executive producers; Stanhope Gould and Linda Mason, producers (CBS)

OUTSTANDING ACHIEVEMENT WITHIN REGULARLY SCHEDULED NEWS PROGRAMS (INDIVIDUALS): Walter Cronkite, Dan Rather, Daniel Schorr, and Joel Blocker, correspondents, "The Watergate Affair," *CBS Evening News with Walter Cronkite* (CBS); David Dick, Dan Rather, Roger Mudd, and Walter Cronkite, correspondents, "Coverage of the Shooting of Governor Wallace," *CBS Evening News with Walter Cronkite* (CBS); Eric Sevareid, correspondent, "LBJ—The Man and the President," *CBS Evening News with Walter Cronkite* (CBS)

OUTSTANDING ACHIEVEMENT FOR REGULARLY SCHEDULED MAGAZINE-TYPE PROGRAMS (PROGRAMS): "Poppy Fields of Turkey—The Heroin Labs of Marseilles—The New York Connection," *60 Minutes,* Don Hewitt, executive producer; William McClure, John Tiffln, and Philip Scheffler, producers (CBS). "The Selling of Colonel Herbert," *60 Minutes,* Don Hewitt, executive producer; Barry Lando, producer (CBS). *60 Minutes,* Don Hewitt, executive producer (CBS)

OUTSTANDING ACHIEVEMENT FOR REGULARLY SCHEDULED MAGAZINE-TYPE PROGRAMS (INDIVIDUALS): Mike Wallace, correspondent, "The Selling of Colonel Herbert," *60 Minutes* (CBS); Mike Wallace, correspondent, *60 Minutes* (CBS)

OUTSTANDING ACHIEVEMENT IN COVERAGE OF SPECIAL EVENTS (INDIVIDUALS): Jim McKay, commentator, "Coverage of the Munich Olympic Tragedy," *ABC Special* (ABC)

OUTSTANDING DOCUMENTARY PROGRAM ACHIEVEMENT (CURRENT EVENTS): "The Blue Collar Trap," *NBC News White Paper,* Fred Freed, producer (NBC). "The Mexican Connection," *CBS Reports,* Buxton Benjamin, executive producer; Jay McMullen, producer (CBS). "One Billion Dollar Weapon and Now the War Is Over—The American Military in the 1970's," *NBC Reports,* Fred Freed, executive producer; Al Davis, producer (NBC)

OUTSTANDING DOCUMENTARY PROGRAM ACHIEVEMENT (CULTURAL): *America,* Michael Gill, executive producer (NBC). "Jane Goodall and the World of Animal Behavior—The Wild Dogs of Africa," Marshall Fiaum, executive producer; Hugo Van Lawick, Bill Travers, and James Hill, producers (ABC)

OUTSTANDING DOCUMENTARY PROGRAM ACHIEVEMENT (INDIVIDUALS): Alistair Cooke, narrator, *America* (NBC); Alistair Cooke, writer, "A Fireball in the Night," *America* (NBC); Hugo Van Lawick, director, "Jane Goodall and the World of Animal Behavior—The Wild Dogs of Africa" (ABC)

SPECIAL CLASSIFICATION OF OUTSTANDING PROGRAM AND INDIVIDUAL ACHIEVEMENT: *The Advocates,* Greg Harney; executive producer; Tom Burrows, Russ Morash, and Peter McGhee, producers (PBS), "VD Blues," *The Special of the Week,* Don Fouser, producer (PBS)

1973–1974 (PRESENTED MAY 28, 1974)

OUTSTANDING COMEDY SERIES: *M*A*S*H,* Gene Reynolds and Larry Gelbart, producers (CBS)

OUTSTANDING DRAMA SERIES: *Upstairs, Downstairs [Masterpiece Theatre],* Rex Firkin, executive producer; John Hawkesworth, producer (PBS)

OUTSTANDING MUSIC-VARIETY SERIES: *The Carol Burnett Show,* Joe Hamilton, executive producer; Ed Simmons, producer (CBS)

OUTSTANDING LIMITED SERIES: *Columbo [NBC Sunday Mystery Movie],* Dean Hargrove and Roland Kibbee, executive producers; Douglas Benton, Robert F. O'Neill, and Edward K. Dodds, producers (NBC)

OUTSTANDING SPECIAL—COMEDY OR DRAMA (SINGLE SPECIAL PROGRAM): "The Autobiography of Miss Jane Pittman," Robert Christiansen and Rick Rosenberg, producers (CBS)

OUTSTANDING COMEDY-VARIETY, VARIETY, OR MUSIC SPECIAL (SINGLE SPECIAL PROGRAM): "Lily," Irene Pinn, executive producer; Herb Sargent and Jerry McPhie, producers (CBS)

OUTSTANDING CHILDREN'S SPECIAL (EVENING): "Marlo Thomas and Friends in Free to Be . . . You and Me," Marlo Thomas and Carole Hart, producers (ABC)

BEST LEAD ACTOR IN A COMEDY SERIES: Alan Alda, *M*A*S*H* (CBS)

BEST LEAD ACTOR IN A DRAMA SERIES: Tally Savalas, *Kojak* (CBS)

BEST LEAD ACTOR IN A LIMITED SERIES: William Holden, *The Blue Knight* (NBC)

BEST LEAD ACTOR IN A DRAMA (FOR A SPECIAL PROGRAM—COMEDY OR DRAMA; OR A SINGLE APPEARANCE IN A COMEDY OR DRAMA SERIES): Hal Holbrook, "Pueblo," *ABC Theatre* (ABC)

ACTOR OF THE YEAR—SERIES: Alan Alda, *M*A*S*H* (CBS)

ACTOR OF THE YEAR—SPECIAL: Hal Holbrook, "Pueblo," *ABC Theatre* (ABC)

BEST LEAD ACTRESS IN A COMEDY SERIES: Mary Tyler Moore, *The Mary Tyler Moore Show* (CBS)

BEST LEAD ACTRESS IN A DRAMA SERIES: Michael Learned, *The Waltons* (CBS)

BEST LEAD ACTRESS IN A LIMITED SERIES: Mildred Natwick, *The Snoop Sisters [NBC Tuesday Mystery Movie]* (NBC)

BEST LEAD ACTRESS IN A DRAMA (FOR A SPECIAL PROGRAM—COMEDY OR DRAMA; OR A SINGLE APPEARANCE IN A COMEDY OR DRAMA SERIES): Cicely Tyson, "The Autobiography of Miss Jane Pittman" (CBS)

ACTRESS OF THE YEAR—SERIES: Mary Tyler Moore, *The Mary Tyler Moore Show* (CBS)

ACTRESS OF THE YEAR—SPECIAL: Cicely Tyson, "The Autobiography of Miss Jane Pittman" (CBS)

BEST SUPPORTING ACTOR IN COMEDY (FOR SPECIAL PROGRAM; A ONE-TIME APPEARANCE IN A SERIES; OR A CONTINUING ROLE): Rob Reiner, *All in the Family* (CBS)

BEST SUPPORTING ACTOR IN DRAMA (FOR A SPECIAL PROGRAM; A ONE-TIME APPEARANCE IN A SERIES; OR CONTINUING ROLE): Michael Moriarty, "The Glass Menagerie" (ABC)

BEST SUPPORTING ACTOR IN COMEDY-VARIETY, VARIETY, OR MUSIC (FOR A SPECIAL PROGRAM; A ONE-TIME APPEARANCE IN A SERIES; OR A CONTINUING ROLE): Harvey Korman, *The Carol Burnett Show* (CBS)

SUPPORTING ACTOR OF THE YEAR: Michael Moriarty, "The Glass Menagerie" (ABC)

SUPPORTING ACTRESS IN COMEDY (FOR A SPECIAL PROGRAM; A ONE-TIME APPEARANCE IN A SERIES; OR A CONTINUING ROLE): Cloris Leachman, "The Lars Affair," *The Mary Tyler Moore Show,* 9/15/73 (CBS)

BEST SUPPORTING ACTRESS IN DRAMA (FOR A SPECIAL PROGRAM; A ONE-TIME APPEARANCE IN A SERIES; OR A CONTINUING ROLE): Joanna Miles, "The Glass Menagerie" (ABC)

BEST SUPPORTING ACTRESS IN COMEDY-VARIETY, VARIETY, OR MUSIC (FOR A SPECIAL PROGRAM; A ONE-TIME APPEARANCE IN A SERIES; OR A CONTINUING ROLE): Brenda Vaccaro, "The Shape of Things" (CBS)

SUPPORTING ACTRESS OF THE YEAR: Joanna Miles, "The Glass Menagerie" (ABC)

BEST DIRECTING IN DRAMA (A SINGLE PROGRAM OF A SERIES WITH CONTINUING CHARACTERS AND/OR THEME): Robert Butler, *The Blue Knight,* PART III, 11/15/73 (NBC)

BEST DIRECTING IN DRAMA (A SINGLE PROGRAM—COMEDY OR DRAMA): John Korty, "The Autobiography of Miss Jane Pittman" (CBS)

BEST DIRECTING IN COMEDY (A SINGLE PROGRAM OR A SERIES WITH CONTINUING CHARACTERS AND/OR THEME): Jackie Cooper, "Carry on Hawkeye," *M*A*S*H,* 11/24/73 (CBS)

BEST DIRECTING IN VARIETY OR MUSIC (A SINGLE PROGRAM OF A SERIES): Dave Powers, "The Australia Show," *The Carol Burnett Show,* 12/8/73 (CBS)

BEST DIRECTING IN COMEDY-VARIETY, VARIETY, OR MUSIC (A SPECIAL PROGRAM): Dwight Hemion, "Barbra Streisand . . . And Other Musical Instruments" (CBS)

DIRECTOR OF THE YEAR—SERIES: Robert Butler, *The Blue Knight,* Part III, 11/15/73 (NBC)

DIRECTOR OF THE YEAR—SPECIAL: Dwight Hemion, "Barbra Streisand . . . And Other Musical Instruments" (CBS)

BEST WRITING IN DRAMA (A SINGLE PROGRAM OF A SERIES WITH CONTINUING CHARACTERS AND/OR THEME): Joanna Lee, "The Thanksgiving Story," *The Waltons,* 11/15/73 (CBS)

BEST WRITING IN DRAMA, ORIGINAL TELEPLAY (A SINGLE PROGRAM~-COMEDY OR DRAMA): Fay Kanin, "Tell Me Where It Hurts," *G. E. Theater* (CBS)

BEST WRITING IN DRAMA, ADAPTATION (A SINGLE PROGRAM—COMEDY OR DRAMA): Tracy Keenan Wynn, "The Autobiography of Miss Jane Pittman" (CBS)

BEST WRITING IN COMEDY (A SINGLE PROGRAM OF A SERIES WITH CONTINUING CHARACTERS AND/OR THEME): Treva Silverman, "The Lou and Edie Story," *The Mary Tyler Moore Show,* 10/6/73 (CBS)

BEST WRITING IN VARIETY OR MUSIC (A SINGLE PROGRAM OF A SERIES): Ed Simmons, Gary Bellden, Roger Beatty, Arnie Kogen, Bill Richmond, Gene Perret, Rudy De Luca, Barry Levinson, Dick Clair, Jenna McMahon, and Barry Harman, *The Carol Burnett Show,* with Tim Conway and Bernadette Peters, 2/16/74 (CBS)

BEST WRITING IN COMEDY—VARIETY, VARIETY, OR MUSIC (A SPECIAL PROGRAM): Herb Sargent, Rosalyn Dre der, Lorne Michaels, Richard Pryor, Jim Rusk, James R. Stein, Robert Illes, Lily Tomlin, George Yanok, Jane Wagner, Rod Warren, Ann Elder, and Karyl Geld, "Lily" (CBS)

WRITER OF THE YEAR—SERIES: Treva Silverman, "The Lou and Edie Story," *The Mary Tyler Moore Show,* 10/6/73 (CBS)

WRITER OF THE YEAR—SPECIAL: Fay Kanin, "Tell Me Where It Hurts," *G. E. Theater* (CBS)

SPECIAL CLASSIFICATION OF OUTSTANDING PROGRAM AND INDIVIDUAL ACHIEVEMENT: *The Dick Cavett Show,* John Gilroy, producer (ABC); Tom Snyder, host, *Tomorrow* (NBC)

OUTSTANDING INDIVIDUAL ACHIEVEMENT IN CHILDREN'S PROGRAMMING: Charles M. Shultz, writer, "A Charlie Brown Thanksgiving" (CBS)

OUTSTANDING ACHIEVEMENT WITHIN REGULARLY SCHEDULED NEWS PROGRAMS: "Coverage of the October War from Israel's Northern Front," *CBS Evening News with Walter Cronkite,* John Laurence, correspondent. October 1973 (CBS). "The Agnew Resignation," Spiro Agnew *CBS Evening News with Walter Cronkite,* Paul Greenberg, executive producer; Ron Bonn, Ed Fouhy, John Lane, Don Bowers, John Armstrong, and Robert Mean, producers; Walter Cronkite, Robert Schakne, Fred Graham, Robert Pierpoint, Roger Mudd, Dan Rather, John Hart, and Eric Sevareid, correspondents, 10/10/73 (CBS). "The Key Biscayne Bank Charter Struggle," *CBS Evening News with Walter Cronkite,* Ed Fouhy, producer; Robert Pierpoint, correspondent, 10/15–10/17/73 (CBS). "Reports on World Hunger," *NBC Nightly News,* Lester M. Crystal, executive producer; Richard Fischer and Joseph Angotti, producer; Tom Streithorst, Phil Brady, John Palmer, and Liz Trotta, correspondents, March-June 1974 (NBC)

OUTSTANDING ACHIEVEMENT FOR REGULARLY SCHEDULED MAGAZINE-TYPE PROGRAMS: "America's Nerve Gas Arsenal," *First Tuesday,* Eliot Frankel, executive producer; William B. Hill and Anthony Potter, producers; Tom Peffit, correspondent, 6/5/73 (NBC), "The Adversaries," *Behind the Lines,* Carey Winfrey, executive producer; Peter Forbath, producer/reporter, Brendan Gill, host/moderator, 3/28/74 (PBS); "A Question of Impeachment," *Bil Moyers' Journal,* Jerome Toobin, executive producer; Martin Clancy, producer; Bill Moyers, broadcaster, 1/22/74 (PBS)

OUTSTANDING DOCUMENTARY PROGRAM ACHIEVEMENTS (CURRENT EVENTS): "Fire!," *ABC News Close Up,* Pamela Hill, producer; Jules Bergman, correspondent/narrator (ABC). "CBS News Special Report: The Senate and the Watergate Affair," Lesley Midgley, executive producer; Hal Haley, Bernard Birnbaum, and David Browning, producers; Dan Rather, Roger Mudd, Daniel Schorr, and Fred Graham correspondents (CBS)

OUTSTANDING DOCUMENTARY PROGRAM ACHIEVEMENTS (CULTURAL): "Journey to the Outer Limits," *National Geographic Specials,* Nicholas Clapp and Dennis Kane, executive producers; Alex Grasshoff, producer (ABC); *The World at War,* Jeremy Isaacs, producer (syndicated); CBS "Reports: The Rockefellers," Burton Benjamin, executive producer; Howard Stringer, producer; Walter Cronkite, correspondent (CBS)

OUTSTANDING INTERVIEW PROGRAM (FOR A SINGLE PROGRAM OF A SERIES): "Solzhenitsyn," *CBS News Special,* Burton Benjamin, producer; Walter Cronkite, correspondent, 6/24/74 (CBS). "Henry Steele Commager," *Bill Moyers' Journal,* Jerome Toobin, executive producer; Martin Clancy, producer; Bill Moyers, broadcaster, 3/26/74 (PBS)

OUTSTANDING TELEVISION NEWS BROADCASTER: Harry Reasoner, *ABC* News (ABC); Bill Moyers, "Essay on Watergate," *Bill Moyers' Journal,* 10/31/73 (PBS)

1974–1975 (PRESENTED MAY 19, 1975)

OUTSTANDING COMEDY SERIES: *The Mary Tyler Moore Show,* James L. Brooks and Allan Burns, executive producers; Ed Weinberger and San Daniels, producers (CBS)

OUTSTANDING DRAMA SERIES: *Upstairs, Downstairs [Masterpiece Theatre],* Rex Firkin, executive producer; John Hawkesworth, producer (PBS)

OUTSTANDING COMEDY-VARIETY OR MUSIC SERIES: *The Carol Burnett Show,* Joe Hamilton, executive producer; Ed Simmons, producer (CBS)

OUTSTANDING LIMITED SERIES: *Benjamin Franklin,* Lewis Freedman, executive producer; George Lefferts and Glenn Jordan, producers (CBS)

OUTSTANDING SPECIAL—DRAMA OR COMEDY: "The Law," *NBC World Premiere Movie,* William Sackheim, producer, 10/22/74 (NBC)

OUTSTANDING SPECIAL—COMEDY' OR VARIETY OR MUSIC: "An Evening with John Denver," Jerry Weintaub, executive producer; Al Rogers and Rich Eustis, producers (ABC)

OUTSTANDING CLASSICAL MUSIC PROGRAM (FOR A SPECIAL PROGRAM OR FOR A SERIES): "Profile in Music: Beverly Sills," *Festival '75,* Patricia Foy, producer, 3/10/75 (PBS)

OUTSTANDING LEAD ACTOR IN A COMEDY SERIES: Tony Randall, *The Odd Couple* (ABC)

OUTSTANDING LEAD ACTOR IN A DRAMA SERIES: Robert Blake, *Baretta* (ABC)

OUTSTANDING LEAD ACTOR IN A LIMITED SERIES: Peter Falk, *Columbo [NBC Sunday Mystery Movie]* (NBC)

OUTSTANDING LEAD ACTOR IN A SPECIAL PROGRAM—DRAMA OR COMEDY (FOR A SPECIAL PROGRAM; OR A SINGLE APPEARANCE IN A DRAMA OR COMEDY SERIES): Laurence Olivier, "Love Among the Ruins," *ABC Theatre* (ABC)

OUTSTANDING LEAD ACTRESS IN A COMEDY SERIES: Valerie Harper, *Rhoda* (CBS)

OUTSTANDING LEAD ACTRESS IN A DRAMA SERIES: Jean Marsh, *Upstairs, Downstairs [Masterpiece Theatre]* (PBS)

OUTSTANDING LEAD ACTRESS IN A LIMITED SERIES: Jessica Walter, *Amy Prentiss [NBC Sunday MysteryMovie]* (NBC)

OUTSTANDING LEAD ACTRESS IN A SPECIAL PROGRAM—DRAMA OR COMEDY (FOR A SPECIAL PROGRAM; OR A SINGLE APPEARANCE IN A DRAMA OR COMEDY SERIES): Katharine Hepburn, "Love Among the Ruins," *ABC Theatre* (ABC)

OUTSTANDING CONTINUING PERFORMANCE BY A SUPPORTING ACTOR IN A COMEDY SERIES: Ed Asner, *The Mary Tyler Moore Show* (CBS)

OUTSTANDING CONTINUING PERFORMANCE BY A SUPPORTING ACTOR IN A DRAMA SERIES: Will Geer, *The Waltons* (CBS)

OUTSTANDING CONTINUING OR SINGLE PERFORMANCE BY A SUPPORTING ACTOR IN VARIETY OR MUSIC (FOR A CONTINUING ROLE IN A REGULAR OR LIMITED SERIES; OR A ONE-TIME APPEARANCE IN A SERIES; OR A SPECIAL): Jack Albertson, *Char,* 3/2/75 (CBS)

OUTSTANDING SINGLE PERFORMANCE BY A SUPPORTING ACTOR IN A COMEDY OR DRAMA SPECIAL: Anthony Quayle, "QB VII," Parts 1 & 2, *ABC Movie Special* (ABC)

OUTSTANDING SINGLE PERFORMANCE BY A SUPPORTING ACTOR IN A COMEDY OR DRAMA SERIES (FOR A ONE-TIME APPEARANCE IN A REGULAR OR LIMITED SERIES): Patrick McGoohan, "By Dawn's Early Light," *Columbo [NBC Sunday Mystery Movie],* 10/27/74 (NBC)

OUTSTANDING CONTINUING PERFORMANCE BY A SUPPORTING ACTRESS IN A COMEDY SERIES: Betty White, *The Mary Tyler Moore Show* (CBS)

OUTSTANDING CONTINUING PERFORMANCE BY A SUPPORTING ACTRESS IN A DRAMA SERIES: Ellen Corby, *The Waltons* (CBS)

OUTSTANDING CONTINUING OR SINGLE PERFORMANCE BY A SUPPORTING ACTRESS IN VARIETY OR MUSIC (FOR CONTINUING ROLE IN A REGULAR OR LIMITED SERIES; OR A ONE-TIME APPEARANCE IN A SERIES; OR A SPECIAL): Cloris Leachman, *Char,* 3/2/75 (CBS)

OUTSTANDING SINGLE PERFORMANCE BY A SUPPORTING ACTRESS IN A COMEDY OR DRAMA SPECIAL: Juliet Mills, "QB VU," Parts 1 & 2, *ABC Movie Special* (ABC)

OUTSTANDING SINGLE PERFORMANCE BY A SUPPORTING ACTRESS IN A COMEDY OR DRAMA SERIES (FOR A ONE-TIME APPEARANCE IN A REGULAR OR LIMITED SERIES): (TIE) Cloris Leachmnan, "Phyllis Whips Inflation," *The Mary Tyler Moore Show,* 1/18/75 (CBS); Zohra Lampert, "Queen of the Gypsies," *Kojak,* 1/19/75 (CBS)

OUTSTANDING DIRECTING IN A DRAMA SERIES (A SINGLE EPISODE OF A REGULAR OR LIMITED SERIES WITH CONTINUING CHARACTERS

AND [OR THEME): Bill Bain, "A Sudden Storm," *Upstairs, Downstairs [Masterpiece Theatre]*, 12/22/74 (PBS)

OUTSTANDING DIRECTING IN A COMEDY SERIES (A SINGLE EPISODE OF A REGULAR OR LIMITED SERIES WITH CONTINUING CHARACTERS AND/OR THEME): Gene Reynolds, "O.R.," *M*A*S*H*, 10/8/74 (CBS)

OUTSTANDING DIRECTING IN A COMEDY-VARIETY OR MUSIC SERIES (A SINGLE EPISODE OF A REGULAR OR LIMITED SERIES): Dave Powers, *The Carol Burnett Show*, with Alan Alda, 12/21/74 (CBS)

OUTSTANDING DIRECTING IN A COMEDY-VARIETY OR MUSICAL SPECIAL: Bill Davis, "An Evening with John Denver" (ABC)

OUTSTANDING DIRECTING IN A SPECIAL PROGRAM—DRAMA OR COMEDY: George Cukor, "Love Among the Ruins," *ABC Theatre* (ABC)

OUTSTANDING WRITING IN A DRAMA SERIES (A SINGLE EPISODE OF A REGULAR OR LIMITED SERIES WITH CONTINUING CHARACTERS AND/OR THEME): Howard Fast, "The Ambassador," *Benjamin Franklin*, 11/21/74 (CBS)

OUTSTANDING WRITING IN A COMEDY SERIES (A SINGLE EPISODE OF A REGULAR OR LIMITED SERIES WITH CONTINUING CHARACTERS AND/OR THEME): Ed Weinberger and Stan Daniels, "Mary Richards Goes to Jail," *The Mary Tyler Moore Show*, 9/14/74 (CBS)

OUTSTANDING WRITING IN A COMEDY-VARIETY OR MUSIC SERIES (A SINGLE EPISODE OF A REGULAR OR LIMITED SERIES): Ed Simmons, Gary Belkin, Roger Beatty, Arnie Kogen, Bill Richmond, Gene Perret, Rudy De Luca, Barry Levinson, Dick Clair, and Jenna McMahon, *The Carol Burnett Show*, with Alan Alda, 12/21/74 (CBS)

OUTSTANDING WRITING IN A COMEDY-VARIETY OR MUSIC SPECIAL: Bob Wells, John Bradford, and Cy Coleman, "Shirley MacLaine: If They Could See Me Now" (CBS)

OUTSTANDING WRITING IN A SPECIAL PROGRAM—DRAMA OR COMEDY—ORIGINAL TELEPLAY: James Costigan, "Love Among the Ruins," *ABC Theatre* (ABC)

OUTSTANDING WRITING IN A SPECIAL PROGRAM—DRAMA OR COMEDY ADAPTATION: David W. Rintels, "IBM Presents Clarence Darrow" (NBC)

OUTSTANDING CHILDREN'S SPECIAL (EVENING): "Yes Virginia, There Is a Santa Claus," Burt Rosen, executive producer; Bill Melendez and Mort Greene, producers (ABC)

SPECIAL CLASSIFICATION OF OUTSTANDING PROGRAM ACHIEVEMENT: "The American Film Institute Salute to James Cagney," George Stevens, Jr., executive producer; Paul W. Keyes, producer (CBS)

SPECIAL CLASSIFICATION OF OUTSTANDING INDIVIDUAL ACHIEVEMENT: Alistair Cooke, host, *Masterpiece Theatre* (PBS)

1975–1976 (PRESENTED MAY 17, 1976)

OUTSTANDING COMEDY SERIES; *The Mary Tyler Moore Show*, James L. Brooks and Allan Burns, executive producers; Ed Weinberger and Stan Daniels, producers (CBS)

OUTSTANDING DRAMA SERIES: *Police Story*, David Gerber and Stanley Kallis, executive producers; Liam O'Brien and Carl Pingitore, producers (NBC)

OUTSTANDING COMEDY-VARIETY OR MUSIC SERIES: *NBC's Saturday Night Live*, Lorne Michaels, producer (NBC)

OUTSTANDING LIMITED SERIES: *Upstairs, Downstairs [Masterpiece Theatre]*, Rex Firkin, executive producer; John Hawkesworth, producer (PBS)

OUTSTANDING SPECIAL—DRAMA OR COMEDY: "Eleanor and Franklin," *ABC Theatre*, David Susskind, executive producer; Harry Sherman and Audrey Mass, producers (ABC)

OUTSTANDING SPECIAL COMEDY-VARIETY OR MUSIC: "Gypsy in My Soul," William O. Harbach, executive producer; Cy Coleman and Fred Ebb, producers (CBS)

OUTSTANDING CLASSICAL MUSIC PROGRAM: "Bernstein and the New York Philharmonic," *Great Performances*, Klaus Hallig and Harry Kraut, executive producers; David Griffiths, producer, 11/26/75 (PBS)

OUTSTANDING LEAD ACTOR IN A COMEDY SERIES: Jack Albertson, *Chico and the Man* (NBC)

OUTSTANDING LEAD ACTOR IN A DRAMA SERIES: Peter Falk, *Columbo [NBC Sunday Mystery Movie]* (NBC)

OUTSTANDING LEAD ACTOR IN A LIMITED SERIES: Hal Holbrook, "Sandburg's Lincoln" (NBC)

OUTSTANDING LEAD ACTOR IN A DRAMA OR COMEDY SPECIAL: Anthony Hopkins, "The Lindbergh Kidnapping Case," *NBC World Premiere Movie* (NBC)

OUTSTANDING LEAD ACTOR FOR A SINGLE APPEARANCE IN A DRAMA OR COMEDY SERIES: Edward Asner, *Rich Man, Poor Man*, 2/1/76 (ABC)

OUTSTANDING LEAD ACTRESS IN A COMEDY SERIES: Mary Tyler Moore, *The Mary Tyler Moore Show* (CBS)

OUTSTANDING LEAD ACTRESS IN A DRAMA SERIES Michael Learned, *The Waltons* (CBS)

OUTSTANDING LEAD ACTRESS IN A LIMITED SERIES: Rosemary Harris, *Notorious Woman [Masterpiece Theatre]* (PBS)

OUTSTANDING LEAD ACTRESS IN A DRAMA OR COMEDY SPECIAL: Susan Clark, "Babe" (CBS)

OUTSTANDING LEAD ACTRESS FOR A SINGLE APPEARANCE IN A DRAMA OR COMEDY SERIES:

Kathryn Walker, "John Adams, Lawyer," *The Adams Chronicles*, 1/20/76 (PBS)

OUTSTANDING CONTINUING PERFORMANCE BY A SUPPORTING ACTOR IN A COMEDY SERIES: Ted Knight, *The Mary Tyler Moore Show* (CBS)

OUTSTANDING CONTINUING PERFORMANCE BY A SUPPORTING ACTOR IN A DRAMA SERIES: Anthony Zerbe, *Harry-O* (ABC)

OUTSTANDING CONTINUING OR SINGLE PERFORMANCE BY A SUPPORTING ACTOR IN VARIETY OR MUSIC: Chevy Chase, *NBC's Saturday Night Live*, 1/17/76 (NBC)

OUTSTANDING SINGLE PERFORMANCE BY A SUPPORTING ACTOR IN A COMEDY OR DRAMA SPECIAL: Ed Flanders, "A Moon for the Misbegotten," *ABC Theatre* (ABC)

OUTSTANDING SINGLE PERFORMANCE BY A SUPPORTING ACTOR IN A COMEDY OR DRAMA SERIES: Gordon Jackson, "The Beastly Hun," *Upstairs, Downstairs [Masterpiece Theatre]*, 1/18/76 (PBS)

OUTSTANDING CONTINUING PERFORMANCE BY A SUPPORTING ACTRESS IN A COMEDY SERIES: Betty White, *The Mary Tyler Moore Show* (CBS)

OUTSTANDING CONTINUING PERFORMANCE BY A SUPPORTING ACTRESS IN A DRAMA SERIES: Ellen Corby, *The Waltons* (CBS)

OUTSTANDING CONTINUING OR SINGLE PERFORMANCE BY A SUPPORTING ACTRESS IN VARIETY OR MUSIC: Vicki Lawrence, *The Carol Burnett Show,* 2/7/76 (CBS)

OUTSTANDING SINGLE PERFORMANCE BY A SUPPORTING ACTRESS IN A COMEDY OR DRAMA SPECIAL: Rosemary Murphy, "Eleanor and Franklin," *ABC Theatre* (ABC)

OUTSTANDING SINGLE PERFORMANCE BY A SUPPORTING ACTRESS IN A COMEDY OR DRAMA SERIES: Fionnula Flanagan, *Rich Man, Poor Man,* 2/2/76 (ABC)

OUTSTANDING DIRECTING IN A DRAMA SERIES (A SINGLE EPISODE OF A REGULAR OR LIMITED SERIES WITH CONTINUING CHARACTERS AND/OR THEME): David Greene, "Episode 8," *Rich Man, Poor Man,* 3/15/76 (ABC)

OUTSTANDING DIRECTING IN A COMEDY SERIES (A SINGLE EPISODE OF A REGULAR OR LIMITED SERIES WITH CONTINUING CHARACTERS AND/OR THEME): Gene Reynolds, "Welcome to Korea," *M*A*S*H* 9/12/75 (CBS)

OUTSTANDING DIRECTING IN A COMEDY-VARIETY OR MUSIC SERIES (A SINGLE EPISODE OF A REGULAR OR LIMITED SERIES): Dave Wilson, *NBC's Saturday Night Live*, with host Paul Simon, 10/18/75 (NBC)

OUTSTANDING DIRECTING IN A COMEDY-VARIETY OR MUSIC SPECIAL: Dwight Hemion, "Steve and Eydie: 'Our Love Is Here to Stay'" (CBS)

OUTSTANDING DIRECTING IN A SPECIAL PROGRAM—DRAMA OR COMEDY: Daniel Petrie, "Eleanor and Franklin," *ABC Theatre* (ABC)

OUTSTANDING WRITING IN A DRAMA SERIES (A SINGLE EPISODE OF A REGULAR OR LIMITED SERIES WITH CONTINUING CHARACTERS AND/OR THEME): Sherman Yellen, "John Adams, Lawyer," *The Adams Chronicles,* 1/20/76 (PBS)

OUTSTANDING WRITING IN A COMEDY SERIES (A SINGLE EPISODE OF A REGULAR OR LIMITED SERIES WITH CONTINUING CHARACTERS AND/OR THEME): David Lloyd, "Chuckles Bites the Dust," *The Mary Tyler Moore Show,* 10/25/75 (CBS)

OUTSTANDING WRITING IN A COMEDY-VARIETY OR MUSIC SERIES (A SINGLE EPISODE OF A REGULAR OR LIMITED SERIES): Anne Beatts, Chevy Chase, Al Franken, Tom Davis, Lorne Michaels, Marilyn Suzanne Miller, Michael O'Donoghue, Herb Sargent, Tom Schiller, Rosie Schuster, and Alan Zweibel, *NBC's Saturday Night Live*, with host Elliott Gould, 1/10/76 (NBC)

OUTSTANDING WRITING IN A COMEDY-VARIETY OR MUSIC SPECIAL: Jane Wagner, Lorne Michaels, Ann Elder, Christopher Guest, Earl Pomerantz, Jim Rusk, Lily Tomlin, Rod Warren, and George Yanok, "Lily Tomlin" (ABC)

OUTSTANDING WRITING IN A SPECIAL PROGRAM—DRAMA OR COMEDY-ORIGINAL TELEPLAY: James Costigan, "Eleanor and Franklin," *ABC Theatre* (ABC)

OUTSTANDING WRITING IN A SPECIAL PROGRAM—DRAMA OR COMEDY—ADAPTATION: David XV. Rintels, "Fear on Trial" (CBS)

OUTSTANDING EVENING CHILDREN'S SPECIAL: "You're a Good Sport, Charlie Brown," Lee Mendelson, executive producer; Bill Melendez, producer (CBS). "Huckleberry Finn," Steven North, producer (ABC)

SPECIAL CLASSIFICATION OF OUTSTANDING PROGRAM AND INDIVIDUAL ACHIEVEMENT: *Bicentennial Minutes,* Bob Markel I. executive producer; Gareth Davies and Paul Walgner, producers (CBS); *The Tonight Show Starring Johnny Carson,* Fred De Cordova, producer (NBC); Ann Marcus, Jerry Adelman, and Daniel Gregory Browne, writers, *Mary Hartman, Mary Hartman* (syndicated)

1976–1977 (PRESENTED SEPTEMBER 12, 1977)

OUTSTANDING COMEDY SERIES: *The Mary Tyler Moore Show,* Allan Burns and James L. Brooks, executive producers; Ed Weinberger and Stan Daniels, producers (CBS)

OUTSTANDING DRAMA SERIES: *Upstairs, Downstairs [Masterpiece Theatre],* John Hawkesworth and Joan Sullivan, producers (PBS)

OUTSTANDING COMEDY-VARIETY OR MUSIC SERIES: *Van Dyke and Company,* Bryan Paul, executive producer; Alan Blye and Bob Einstein, producers (NBC)

OUTSTANDING LIMITED SERIES: *Roots ABC Novel for Television]*, David L. Wolper, executive producer; Stan Margulies, producer (ABC)

OUTSTANDING SPECIAL—DRAMA OR COMEDY: "Eleanor and Franklin: The White House Years," *ABC Theatre*, David Susskind, executive producer; Harry R. Sherman, producer (ABC). "Sybil," *The Big Event/NBC World Premiere Movie*, Peter Dunne and Philip Capice, executive producers; Jacqueline Babbin, producer (NBC)

OUTSTANDING SPECIAL—COMEDY-VARIETY OR MUSIC: "The Barry Manilow Special," Miles Lourie, executive producer; Steve Binder, producer (ABC)

OUTSTANDING CLASSICAL PROGRAM IN THE PERFORMING ARTS: "American Ballet Theatre: Swan Lake Live from Lincoln Center," *Great Performances*, John Goberman, producer, 6/30/76 (PBS)

OUTSTANDING LEAD ACTOR IN A COMEDY SERIES: Carroll O'Connor, *All in the Family* (CBS)

OUTSTANDING LEAD ACTOR IN A DRAMA SERIES: James Garner, *The Rockford Files* (NBC)

OUTSTANDING LEAD ACTOR IN A LIMITED SERIES: Christopher Plummer, "The Moneychangers," *The Big Event/NBC World Premiere Movie* (NBC)

OUTSTANDING LEAD ACTOR IN A DRAMA OR COMEDY SPECIAL: Ed Flanders, "Harry S Truman: Plain Speaking" (PBS)

OUTSTANDING LEAD ACTOR FOR A SINGLE APPEARANCE IN A DRAMA OR COMEDY SERIES: Louis Gossett, Jr., *Roots—Part Two*, 1/24/77 (ABC)

OUTSTANDING LEAD ACTRESS IN A COMEDY SERIES: Beatrice Arthur, *Maude* (CBS)

OUTSTANDING LEAD ACTRESS IN A DRAMA SERIES: Lindsay Wagner, *The Bionic Woman* (ABC)

OUTSTANDING LEAD ACTRESS IN A LIMITED SERIES: Patty Duke Astin, *Captains and the Kings, NBC's Best Sellers* (NBC)

OUTSTANDING LEAD ACTRESS IN A DRAMA OR COMEDY SPECIAL: Sally Field, "Sybil," *The Big Event/NBC World Premiere Movie* (NBC)

OUTSTANDING LEAD ACTRESS FOR A SINGLE APPEARANCE IN A DRAMA OR COMEDY SERIES: Beulah Bondi, "The Pony Cart," *The Waltons*, 12/2/76 (CBS)

OUTSTANDING CONTINUING PERFORMANCE BY A SUPPORTING ACTOR IN A COMEDY SERIES: Gary Burghoff, *M*A*S*H* (CBS)

OUTSTANDING CONTINUING PERFORMANCE BY A SUPPORTING ACTOR IN A DRAMA SERIES: Gary Frank, *Family* (ABC)

OUTSTANDING CONTINUING OR SINGLE PERFORMANCE BY A SUPPORTING ACTOR IN *A* VARIETY OR MUSIC: Tim Conway, *The Carol Burnett Show* (CBS)

OUTSTANDING PERFORMANCE BY A SUPPORTING ACTOR IN A COMEDY OR DRAMA SPECIAL: Burgess Meredith, "Tailgunner Joe," *The Big Event,* 2/6/77 (NBC)

OUTSTANDING SINGLE PERFORMANCE BY A SUPPORTING ACTOR IN A COMEDY OR DRAMA SERIES: Edward Asner, *Roots—Part One*, 1/23/77 (ABC)

OUTSTANDING CONTINUING PERFORMANCE BY A SUPPORTING ACTRESS IN A COMEDY SERIES: Mary Kay Place, *Mary Hartman, Mary Hartman* (syndicated)

OUTSTANDING CONTINUING PERFORMANCE BY A SUPPORTING ACTRESS IN A DRAMA SERIES: Kristy McNichol, *Family* (ABC)

OUTSTANDING CONTINUING OR SINGLE PERFORMANCE BY A SUPPORTING ACTRESS IN VARIETY OR MUSIC: Rita Moreno, *The Muppet Show* (syndicated)

OUTSTANDING PERFORMANCE BY A SUPPORTING ACTRESS IN A COMEDY OR DRAMA SPECIAL: Diana Hyland, "The Boy in the Plastic Bubble," *The ABC Friday Night Movie*, 11/12/76 (ABC)

OUTSTANDING SINGLE PERFORMANCE BY A SUPPORTING ACTRESS IN A COMEDY OR DRAMA SERIES: Olivia Cole, *Roots—Part Eight*, 1/30/77 (ABC)

OUTSTANDING DIRECTING IN A DRAMA SERIES (A SINGLE EPISODE OF A REGULAR OR LIMITED SERIES WITH CONTINUING CHARACTERS AND/OR THEME): David Greene, *Roots—Part One*, 1/23/77 (ABC)

OUTSTANDING DIRECTING IN A COMEDY SERIES (A SINGLE EPISODE OF A REGULAR OR LIMITED SERIES WITH CONTINUING CHARACTERS AND/OR THEME): Alan Alda, "Dear Sigmund," *M*A*S*H* 11/9/76 (CBS)

OUTSTANDING DIRECTING IN A COMEDY-VARIETY OR MUSIC SERIES (A SINGLE EPISODE OF A REGULAR OR LIMITED SERIES): Dave Powers, The *Carol Burnett Show*, with Eydie Gorme, 2/12/77 (CBS)

OUTSTANDING DIRECTING IN A COMEDY-VARIETY OR MUSIC SPECIAL: Dwight Hemion, "America Salutes Richard Rodgers: The Sound of His Music" (CBS)

OUTSTANDING DIRECTING IN A SPECIAL PROGRAM—DRAMA OR COMEDY: Daniel Petrie, "Eleanor and Franklin: The White House Years," *ABC Theatre* (ABC)

OUTSTANDING WRITING IN A DRAMA SERIES (A SINGLE EPISODE OF A REGULAR OR LIMITED SERIES WITH CONTINUING CHARACTERS AND/OR THEME): William Blinn, *Roots-Part Two*, 1/24/77 (ABC)

OUTSTANDING WRITING IN A COMEDY SERIES (A SINGLE EPISODE OF A REGULAR OR LIMITED SERIES WITH CONTINUING CHARACTERS AND/OR THEME): Allan Burns, James L. Brooks, Ed Weinberger, Stan Daniels, David Lloyd, and Bob

Eflison, "The Final Show," *The Mary Tyler Moore Show,* 3/19/77 (CBS)

OUTSTANDING WRITING IN A COMEDY-VARIETY OR MUSIC SERIES (A SINGLE EPISODE OF A REGULAR OR LIMITED SERIES): Anne Beatts, Dan Aykroyd, Al Franken, Tom Davis, James Downey, Lame Michaels, Marilyn Suzanne Miller, Michael O'Donoghue, Herb Sargent, Tom Schiller, Rosie Schuster, Alan Zweibel, John Belushi, and Bill Murray, *NBC's Saturday Night Live,* with host Sissy Spacek, 3/12/77 (NBC)

OUTSTANDING WRITING IN A COMEDY-VARIETY OR MUSIC SPECIAL: Alan Buz Kohan and Ted Strauss, "America Salutes Richard Rodgers: The Sound of His Music" (CBS)

OUTSTANDING WRITING IN A SPECIAL PRO-GRAM—DRAMA OR COMEDY—ORIGINAL TELEPLAY: Lane Slate, "Tailgunner Joe," *The Big Event,* 2/6/77 (NBC)

OUTSTANDING WRITING IN A SPECIAL PROGRAM-DRAMA OR COMEDY—ADAPTATION: Stewart Stern, "Sybil," *The Big Event/NBC World Premiere Movie* (NBC)

OUTSTANDING EVENING CHILDREN'S SPECIAL: "Ballet Shoes, Parts 1 & 2," *Piccadilly Circus,* 12/27 & 12/28/76 (PBS)

SPECIAL CLASSIFICATION OF OUTSTANDING PRO-GRAM ACHIEVEMENT: *The Tonight Show Starring Johnny Carson,* Fred DeCordova, producer (NBC)

1977–1978 (PRESENTED SEPTEMBER 17, 1978)

OUTSTANDING COMEDY SERIES: *All in the Family,* Mort Lachman, executive producer; Milt Josefsberg, producer (CBS)

OUTSTANDING DRAMA SERIES: *The Rockford Files,* Meta Rosenberg, executive producer; Stephen J. Cannell, supervising producer; David Chase and Charles F. Johnson, producers (NBC)

OUTSTANDING COMEDY-VARIETY OR MUSIC SE-RIES: *The Muppet Show,* David Lazer, executive producer; Jim Henson, producer; The Muppets—Frank Oz, Jerry Nelson, Richard Hunt, Dave Goelz, and Jim Hanson, stars (syndicated)

OUTSTANDING LIMITED SERIES: *Holocaust,* Herbert Brodkln, executive producer; Robert Berger, producer (NBC)

OUTSTANDING INFORMATION SERIES: *The Body Human,* Thomas W. Moore, executive producer; Alfred R. Kelman, producer (CBS)

OUTSTANDING SPECIAL—DRAMA OR COMEDY: "The Gathering," Joseph Barbera, executive producer; Harry R. Sherman, producer (ABC)

OUTSTANDING SPECIAL—COMEDY-VARIETY OR MUSIC: "Bette Midler—Old Red Hair Is Back," Aaron Russo, executive producer; Gary Smith and Dwight Hemion, producers; Bette Midler, star (NBC)

OUTSTANDING INFORMATION SPECIAL: "The Great Whales: National Geographic," Thomas Skinner and Dennis B. Kane, executive producers; Nicolas Noxon, producer (PBS)

OUTSTANDING CLASSICAL PROGRAM IN THE PER-FORMING ARTS: "American Ballet Theatre; 'Giselle' Live from Lincoln Center," John Goberman, producer, 6/2/77 (PBS)

OUTSTANDING LEAD ACTOR IN A COMEDY SE-RIES: Carroll O'Connor, *All in the Family* (CBS)

OUTSTANDING LEAD ACTOR IN A DRAMA SERIES: Ed Asner, *Lou Grant* (CBS)

OUTSTANDING LEAD ACTOR IN A LIMITED SE-RIES: Michael Moriarty, *Holocaust* (NBC)

OUTSTANDING LEAD ACTOR IN A DRAMA OR COMEDY SPECIAL: Fred Astaire, "A Family Upside Down" (NBC)

OUTSTANDING LEAD ACTOR FOR A SINGLE AP-PEARANCE IN A DRAMA OR COMEDY SERIES: Barnard Hughes, "Judge," *Lou Grant,* 11/15/77 (CBS)

OUTSTANDING LEAD ACTRESS IN A COMEDY SE-RIES: Jean Stapleton, *All in the Family* (CBS)

OUTSTANDING LEAD ACTRESS IN A DRAMA SE-RIES: Sada Thompson, *Family* (ABC)

OUTSTANDING LEAD ACTRESS IN A LIMITED SE-RIES: Meryl Streep, *Holocaust* (NBC)

OUTSTANDING LEAD ACTRESS IN A DRAMA OR COMEDY SPECIAL: Joanne Woodward, "See How She Runs," *General Electric Theater* (CBS)

OUTSTANDING LEAD ACTRESS FOR A SINGLE AP-PEARANCE IN A DRAMA OR COMEDY SERIES: Rita Moreno, "The Paper Palace," *The Rockford Files,* 1/20/78 (NBC)

OUTSTANDING CONTINUING PERFORMANCE BY A SUPPORTING ACTOR IN A COMEDY SERIES: Rob Reiner, *All in the Family* (CBS)

OUTSTANDING CONTINUING PERFORMANCE BY A SUPPORTING ACTOR IN A DRAMA SERIES: Robert Vaughn, *Washington: Behind Closed Doors* (ABC)

OUTSTANDING CONTINUING OR SINGLE PERFOR-MANCE BY A SUPPORTING ACTOR IN VARIETY OR MUSIC: Tim Conway, *The Carol Burnett Show* (CBS)

OUTSTANDING PERFORMANCE BY A SUPPORTING ACTOR IN A COMEDY OR DRAMA SPECIAL: Howard Da Silva, "Verna: USC Girl," *Great Performances,* 1/25/78 (PBS)

OUTSTANDING SINGLE PERFORMANCE BY A SUP-PORTING ACTOR IN A COMEDY OR DRAMA SERIES: Ricardo Montalban, *How the West Was Won—Part II,* 2/19/78 (ABC)

OUTSTANDING CONTINUING PERFORMANCE IN A SUPPORTING ACTRESS IN A COMEDY SE-RIES: Julie Kavner, *Rhoda* (CBS)

OUTSTANDING CONTINUING PERFORMANCE BY A SUPPORTING ACTRESS IN A DRAMA SERIES: Nancy Marchand, *Lou Grant* (CBS)

OUTSTANDING CONTINUING OR SINGLE PERFORMANCE BY A SUPPORTING ACTRESS IN VARIETY OR MUSIC: Gilda Radner, *NBC's Saturday Night Live* (NBC)

OUTSTANDING PERFORMANCE BY A SUPPORTING ACTRESS IN A COMEDY OR DRAMA SPECIAL: Eva La Gallienne, "The Royal Family," 11/9/77 (PBS)

OUTSTANDING SINGLE PERFORMANCE BY A SUPPORTING ACTRESS IN A COMEDY OR DRAMA SERIES: Blanche Baker, *Holocaust—Part 1,* 4/16/78 (NBC)

OUTSTANDING DIRECTING IN A DRAMA SERIES (A SINGLE EPISODE OF A REGULAR OR LIMITED SERIES WITH CONTINUING CHARACTERS AND/OR THEME): Marvin J. Chomsky, *Holocaust,* entire series (NBC)

OUTSTANDING DIRECTING IN A COMEDY SERIES (A SINGLE EPISODE OF A REGULAR OR LIMITED SERIES WITH CONTINUING CHARACTERS AND/OR THEME): Paul Bogart, "Edith's 50th Birthday," *All in the Family,* 10/16/77 (CBS)

OUTSTANDING DIRECTING IN A COMEDY-VARIETY OR MUSIC SERIES (A SINGLE EPISODE OF A REGULAR OR LIMITED SERIES): Dave Powers, *The Carol Burnett Show,* with Steve Martin and Betty White, 3/5/78 (CBS)

OUTSTANDING DIRECTING IN A COMEDY-VARIETY OR MUSIC SPECIAL: Dwight Hemion, "The Sentry Collection Presents Ben Vereen—His Roots," 3/2/78 (ABC)

OUTSTANDING DIRECTING IN A SPECIAL PROGRAM—DRAMA OR COMEDY: David Lowell Rich, "The Defection of Simas Kudirka," 1/23/78 (CBS)

OUTSTANDING WRITING IN A DRAMA SERIES (A SINGLE EPISODE OF A REGULAR OR LIMITED SERIES WITH CONTINUING CHARACTERS AND/OR THEME): Gerald Green, *Holocaust,* entire series (NBC)

OUTSTANDING WRITING IN A COMEDY SERIES (A SINGLE EPISODE OF A REGULAR OR LIMITED SERIES WITH CONTINUING CHARACTERS AND/OR THEME): Bob Weiskopf, Bob Schiller, Barry Harman, and Harve Broston, "Cousin Liz," *All in the Family,* 10/9/77 (CBS)

OUTSTANDING WRITING IN A COMEDY-VARIETY OR MUSIC SERIES (A SINGLE EPISODE OF A REGULAR OR LIMITED SERIES): Ed Simmons, Roger Beatty, Rich Hawkins, Liz Sage, Robert Illes, James Stein, Franelle Silver, Larry Siegel, Tim Conway, Bill Richmond, Gene Perret, Dick Clair, and Jenna McMahon, *The Carol Burnett Show,* with Steve Martin and Betty White, 3/5/78 (CBS)

OUTSTANDING WRITING IN A COMEDY-VARIETY OR MUSIC SPECIAL: Chevy Chase, Tom Davis, Al Franken, Charles Grodin, Lorne Michaels, Paul Simon, Lily Tomlin, and Alan Zweibel, "The Paul Simon Special," 12/8/77 (NBC)

OUTSTANDING WRITING IN A SPECIAL PROGRAM DRAMA OR COMEDY—ORIGINAL TELEPLAY: George Rubino, "The Last Tenant," 6/25/78 (ABC)

OUTSTANDING WRITING IN A SPECIAL PROGRAM—DRAMA OR COMEDY—ADAPTATION: Caryl Ledner, "Mary White," 11/18/77 (ABC)

OUTSTANDING EVENING CHILDREN'S SPECIAL: "Halloween Is Grinch Night," David H. DePatie and Friz Freleng, executive producers; Ted Geisel, producer, 10/29/77 (CBS)

SPECIAL CLASSIFICATION OF OUTSTANDING PROGRAM ACHIEVEMENT: *The Tonight Show Starring Johnny Carson,* Fred De Cordova, producer; Johnny Carson, star (NBC)

FIRST ANNUAL ATAS GOVERNOR'S AWARD: William S. Paley, Chairman of the Board (CBS)

1978–1979 (PRESENTED SEPTEMBER 9, 1979)

OUTSTANDING COMEDY SERIES: *Taxi,* James L. Brooks, Stan Daniels, David Davis, and Ed Weinberger, executive producers; Glen Charles and Les Charles, producers (ABC)

OUTSTANDING DRAMA SERIES: *Lou Grant,* Gene Reynolds, executive producer; Seth Freeman and Gary David Goldberg, producers (CBS)

OUTSTANDING LIMITED SERIES: *Roots: The Next Generations,* David L. Wolper, executive producer; Stan Margulies, producer (ABC)

OUTSTANDING SPECIAL—DRAMA OR COMEDY: "Friendly Fire," Martin Starger, executive producer; Philip Barry and Fay Kanin, producers (ABC)

OUTSTANDING COMEDY-VARIETY OR MUSIC PROGRAM (SPECIAL OR SERIES): "Steve and Eydie Celebrate Irving Berlin," Steve Lawrence and Gary Smith, executive producers; Gary Smith and Dwight Hemion, producers; Steve Lawrence and Eydie Gorme, stars, 8/22/78 (NBC)

OUTSTANDING INFORMATION PROGRAM (SPECIAL OR SERIES): "Scared Straight," Arnold Shapiro, producer (syndicated)

OUTSTANDING CLASSICAL PROGRAM IN THE PERFORMING ARTS: "Balanchine IV Dance in America," *Great Performances,* Jac Venza, executive producer; Merrill Brockway, series producer; Emile Ardolino, series coordinating producer; Judy Kunberg, producer, 3/7/79 (PBS)

OUTSTANDING ANIMATED PROGRAM (SPECIAL OR SERIES): "The Lion, the Witch, and the Wardrobe," David Connell, executive producer; Steve Melendez, producer (CBS)

OUTSTANDING CHILDREN'S PROGRAM (SPECIAL OR SERIES): "Christmas Eve on Sesame Street," Jon Stone, executive producer; Dulcy Singer, producer, 12/3/78 (PBS)

OUTSTANDING PROGRAM ACHIEVEMENT—SPECIAL EVENTS: "51st Annual Awards Presentation of the Academy of Motion Picture Arts and Sciences," Jack Haley, Jr., producer, 4/9/79 (ABC)

OUTSTANDING LEAD ACTOR IN A COMEDY SERIES (FOR A CONTINUING OR SINGLE PERFORMANCE IN A REGULAR SERIES): Carroll O'Connor, *All in the Family* (CBS)

OUTSTANDING LEAD ACTOR IN A DRAMA SERIES (FOR A CONTINUING OR SINGLE PERFORMANCE IN A REGULAR SERIES): Ron Leibman, *Kaz* (CBS)

OUTSTANDING LEAD ACTOR IN A LIMITED SERIES OR A SPECIAL: Peter Strauss, "The Jericho Mile," 3/18/79 (ABC)

OUTSTANDING LEAD ACTRESS IN A COMEDY SERIES (FOR A CONTINUING OR SINGLE PERFORMANCE IN A REGULAR SERIES): Ruth Gordon, "Sugar Mama," *Taxi*, 1/16/79 (ABC)

OUTSTANDING LEAD ACTRESS IN A DRAMA SERIES (FOR A CONTINUING OR SINGLE PERFORMANCE IN A REGULAR SERIES): Mariette Hartley, "Married," *The Incredible Hulk,* 9/23/78 (CBS)

OUTSTANDING LEAD ACTRESS IN A LIMITED SERIES OR A SPECIAL: Belle Davis, "Strangers: The Story of a Mother and Daughter," 5/13/79 (CBS)

OUTSTANDING SUPPORTING ACTOR IN A COMEDY OR COMEDY-VARIETY OR MUSIC SERIES (FOR A CONTINUING OR SINGLE PERFORMANCE IN A REGULAR SERIES): Robert Guillaume, *Soap* (ABC)

OUTSTANDING SUPPORTING ACTOR IN A DRAMA SERIES (FOR A CONTINUING OR SINGLE PERFORMANCE IN A REGULAR SERIES): Stuart Margolin, *The Rockford Files* (NBC)

OUTSTANDING SUPPORTING ACTOR IN A LIMITED SERIES OR A SPECIAL: Marlon Brando, *Roots: The Next Generations*—Episode Seven, 2/25/79 (ABC)

OUTSTANDING SUPPORTING ACTRESS IN A COMEDY OR COMEDY-VARIETY OR MUSIC SERIES (FOR A CONTINUING OR SINGLE PERFORMANCE IN A REGULAR SERIES): Sally Struthers, "California Here We Are," *All in the Family,* 12/17/78 (CBS)

OUTSTANDING SUPPORTING ACTRESS IN A DRAMA SERIES (FOR A CONTINUING OR SINGLE PERFORMANCE IN A REGULAR SERIES): Kristy McNichol, *Family* (ABC)

OUTSTANDING SUPPORTING ACTRESS IN A LIMITED SERIES OR A SPECIAL: Esther Rolle, "Summer of My German Soldier," 10/30/78 (NBC)

OUTSTANDING INDIVIDUAL ACHIEVEMENT-INFORMATIONAL PROGRAM: John Korty, director; "Who Are the Debolts—And Where Did They Get 19 Kids?," 12/17/78 (ABC)

OUTSTANDING INDIVIDUAL ACHIEVEMENT—SPECIAL EVENTS: Mikhail Baryshnikov, star; "Baryshnikov at the White House," 4/15/79 (PBS)

OUTSTANDING DIRECTING IN A COMEDY OR COMEDY-VARIETY OR MUSIC SERIES (A SINGLE EPISODE OF A REGULAR SERIES): Noam Pitlik, "The Harris Incident," *Barney Miller,* 11/30/78 (ABC)

OUTSTANDING DIRECTING IN A DRAMA SERIES (A SINGLE EPISODE OF A REGULAR SERIES): Jackie Cooper, "Pilot," The *White Shadow,* 11/27/78 (CBS)

OUTSTANDING DIRECTING IN A LIMITED SERIES OR A SPECIAL: David Greene, "Friendly Fire," 4/22/79 (ABC)

OUTSTANDING WRITING IN A COMEDY OR COMEDY-VARIETY OR MUSIC SERIES (A SINGLE EPISODE OF A REGULAR SERIES): Alan Alda, "Inga," *M*A*S*H,* 1/8/79 (CBS)

OUTSTANDING WRITING IN A DRAMA SERIES (A SINGLE EPISODE OF A REGULAR SERIES): Michele Gallery, "Dying," *Lou Grant,* 11/6/78 (CBS)

OUTSTANDING WRITING IN A LIMITED SERIES OR A SPECIAL: Patrick Nolan and Michael Mann, "The Jericho Mile," 3/18/79 (ABC)

SPECIAL CLASSIFICATION OF OUTSTANDING PROGRAM ACHIEVEMENT: *The Tonight Show Starring Johnny Carson,* Fred De Cordova, producer; Johnny Carson, star. *Lifeline;* Thomas W. Moore and Robert E. Fuisz, M.D., executive producers; Alfred Keiman and Geof Bartz, producers (NBC)

SECOND ANNUAL ATAS GOVERNOR'S AWARD: Walter Cronkite

1979–1980 (PRESENTED SEPTEMBER 7, 1980)

OUTSTANDING COMEDY SERIES: *Taxi,* James L. Brooks, Stan Daniels, and Ed Weinberger, executive producers; Glen Charles and Las Charles, producers (ABC)

OUTSTANDING DRAMA SERIES: *Lou Grant,* Gene Reynolds, executive producer; Seth Freeman, producer (CBS)

OUTSTANDING LIMITED SERIES: *Edward & Mrs. Simpson,* Andrew Brown, producer (syndicated)

OUTSTANDING SPECIAL—DRAMA OR COMEDY: "The Miracle Worker," Raymond Katz and Sandy Gallin, executive producers; Fred Coe, producer, 10/14/79 (NBC)

OUTSTANDING VARIETY OR MUSIC PROGRAM (SPECIAL OR SERIES): "IBM Presents Baryshnikov on Broadway," Herman Krawitz, executive producer; Gary Smith and Dwight Hemion, producers; Mikhail Baryshnikov, star, 4/24/80 (ABC)

OUTSTANDING INFORMATION PROGRAM (SPECIAL OR SERIES): "The Body Human: The Magic Sense," Thomas W. Moore, executive producer; Alfred R. Kelman, Robert E. Fuisz, M.D., Charles A. Bangert, and Vivian R. Moss, producers, 9/6/79 (CBS)

OUTSTANDING CLASSICAL PROGRAM IN THE PERFORMING ARTS: "Live from Studio 8H: A Tribute to Toscanini," Alvin Cooperman and Judith De Paul, producers, 1/9/80 (NBC)

OUTSTANDING ANIMATED PROGRAM (SPECIAL OR SERIES): "Canton, Your Doorman," Lorenzo Music and Barton Dean, producers, 5/21/80 (CBS)

OUTSTANDING PROGRAM ACHIEVEMENT—SPECIAL EVENTS: "The 34th Annual Tony Awards," Alexander H. Cohen, executive producer; Hildy Parks and Roy A. Somlyo, producers, 6/8/80 (CBS)

OUTSTANDING LEAD ACTOR IN A COMEDY SERIES (FOR A CONTINUING OR SINGLE PERFORMANCE IN A REGULAR SERIES): Richard Mulligan, *Soap* (ABC)

OUTSTANDING LEAD ACTOR IN A DRAMA SERIES (FOR A CONTINUING OR SINGLE PERFORMANCE IN A REGULAR SERIES): Ed Asner, *Lou Grant* (CBS)

OUTSTANDING LEAD ACTOR IN A LIMITED SERIES OR A SPECIAL: Powers Boothe, "Guyana Tragedy," 4/15—16/80 (CBS)

OUTSTANDING LEAD ACTRESS IN A COMEDY SERIES (FOR A CONTINUING OR SINGLE PERFORMANCE IN A REGULAR SERIES): Cathryn Damon, *Soap* (ABC)

OUTSTANDING LEAD ACTRESS IN A DRAMA SERIES (FOR A CONTINUING OR SINGLE PERFORMANCE IN A REGULAR SERIES): Barbara Bel Geddes, *Dallas* (CBS)

OUTSTANDING LEAD ACTRESS IN A LIMITED SERIES OR A SPECIAL: Patty Duke Astin, "The Miracle Worker," 10/14/79 (NBC)

OUTSTANDING SUPPORTING ACTOR IN A COMEDY OR COMEDY-VARIETY OR MUSIC SERIES (FOR A CONTINUING OR SINGLE PERFORMANCE IN A REGULAR SERIES): Harry Morgan, *M*A*S*H* (CBS)

OUTSTANDING SUPPORTING ACTOR IN A DRAMA SERIES (FOR A CONTINUING OR SINGLE PERFORMANCE IN A REGULAR SERIES): Stuart Margolin, *The Rockford Files* (NBC)

OUTSTANDING SUPPORTING ACTOR IN A LIMITED SERIES OR A SPECIAL: George Grizzard, "The Oldest Living Graduate," 4/7/80 (NBC)

OUTSTANDING SUPPORTING ACTRESS IN A COMEDY OR COMEDY-VARIETY OR MUSIC SERIES (FOR A CONTINUING OR SINGLE PERFORMANCE IN A REGULAR SERIES): Loretta Swit, *M*A*S*H* (CBS)

OUTSTANDING SUPPORTING ACTRESS IN A DRAMA SERIES (FOR A CONTINUING OR SINGLE PERFORMANCE IN A REGULAR SERIES): Nancy Marchand, *Lou Grant* (CBS)

OUTSTANDING SUPPORTING ACTRESS IN A LIMITED SERIES OR A SPECIAL: Mare Winningham, "Amber Waves," 3/9/80 (ABC)

OUTSTANDING INDIVIDUAL ACHIEVEMENT-SPECIAL CLASS: "Operation: Lifeline," Dr. James "Red" Duke, 8/13/79 (NBC)

OUTSTANDING DIRECTING IN A COMEDY SERIES (A SINGLE EPISODE OF A REGULAR SERIES): James Burrows, *Taxi,* 9/11/79 (ABC)

OUTSTANDING DIRECTING IN A DRAMA SERIES (A SINGLE EPISODE OF A REGULAR SERIES): Roger Young, "Cop," *Lou Grant,* 9/17/79 (CBS)

OUTSTANDING DIRECTING IN A LIMITED SERIES OR A SPECIAL: Marvin J. Chomsky, "Attica," 3/2/80 (ABC)

OUTSTANDING DIRECTING IN A VARIETY OR MUSIC PROGRAM (A SINGLE EPISODE OF A REGULAR OR LIMITED SERIES, OR FOR A SPECIAL): Dwight Hemion, "Baryshnikov on Broadway," 4/24/80 (ABC)

OUTSTANDING WRITING IN A COMEDY SERIES (A SINGLE EPISODE OF A REGULAR SERIES): Bob Colleary, "Photographer," *Barney Miller,* 9/20/79 (ABC)

OUTSTANDING WRITING IN A DRAMA SERIES (A SINGLE EPISODE OF A REGULAR SERIES): Seth Freeman, "Cop," *Lou Grant,* 9/17/79 (CBS)

OUTSTANDING WRITING IN A LIMITED SERIES OR A SPECIAL: David Chase, "Off the Minnesota Strip," 5/5/80 (ABC)

OUTSTANDING WRITING IN A VARIETY OR MUSIC PROGRAM (A SINGLE EPISODE OF A REGULAR OR LIMITED SERIES, OR FOR A SPECIAL: Buz Kohan and Shirley MacLaine, "Every Little Movement," 5/22/80 (CBS)

SPECIAL CLASSIFICATION OF OUTSTANDING PROGRAM ACHIEVEMENT: "Fred Astaire, Change Partners and Dance," David Heeley, producer, 3/14/80 (PBS)

THIRD ANNUAL ATAS GOVERNOR'S AWARD: Johnny Carson

1980–1981 (PRESENTED SEPTEMBER 13, 1981)

OUTSTANDING COMEDY SERIES: *Taxi,* James L. Brooks, Stan Daniels, and Ed Weinberger, executive producers; Glen Charles and Las Charles, producers (ABC)

OUTSTANDING DRAMA SERIES: *Hill Street Blues,* Steven Bochco and Michael Kozoll, executive producers; Gregory Hoblit, producer (NBC)

OUTSTANDING LIMITED SERIES: *Shogun,* James Clavell, executive producer; Eric Bercovici, producer (NBC)

OUTSTANDING VARIETY, MUSIC, OR COMEDY PROGRAM: "Lily: Sold Out," Lily Tomlin and Jane Wagner, executive producers; Rocco Urbisci, producer (CBS)

OUTSTANDING DRAMA SPECIAL: "Playing for Time," Linda Yellen, executive producer; John E. Quill, coproducer (CBS)

OUTSTANDING INFORMATIONAL SERIES: *Steve Allen's Meeting of Minds,* Loring d'Usseau, producer (PBS)

OUTSTANDING INFORMATIONAL SPECIAL: "The Body Human: The Bionic Breakthrough," Thomas W. Moore, executive producer; Alfred R. Kelman and Robert E. Fuisz, M.D., producers; Charles A. Bangert and Nancy Smith, coproducers (CBS)

OUTSTANDING CLASSICAL PROGRAM IN THE PERFORMING ARTS: "Live from Studio 8H: An Evening of Jerome Robbins' Ballets with Members of the New York City Ballet," Alvin Cooperman and Judith De Paul, producers (NBC)

OUTSTANDING CHILDREN'S PROGRAM: "Donahue and Kids. Project Peacock," Walter Bartlett, executive producer; Don Mischer, producer; Jan Cornell, coproducer (NBC)

OUTSTANDING ANIMATED PROGRAM: "Life Is a Circus, Charlie Brown," Lee Mendelson, executive producer; Bill Melendez, producer (CBS)

OUTSTANDING LEAD ACTOR IN A DRAMA SERIES: Daniel J. Travanti, *Hill Street Blues* (NBC)

OUTSTANDING LEAD ACTOR IN A COMEDY SERIES: Judd Hirsch, *Taxi* (ABC)

OUTSTANDING LEAD ACTOR IN A LIMITED SERIES OR A SPECIAL: Anthony Hopkins, "The Bunker" (CBS)

OUTSTANDING LEAD ACTRESS IN A DRAMA SERIES: Barbara Babcock, *Hill Street Blues* (NBC)

OUTSTANDING LEAD ACTRESS IN A COMEDY SERIES: Isabel Sanford, *The Jeffersons* (CBS)

OUTSTANDING LEAD ACTRESS IN A LIMITED SERIES OR A SPECIAL: Vanessa Redgrave, "Playing for Time" (CBS)

OUTSTANDING SUPPORTING ACTOR IN A DRAMA SERIES: Michael Conrad, *Hill Street Blues* (NBC)

OUTSTANDING SUPPORTING ACTOR IN A COMEDY OR VARIETY OR MUSIC SERIES: Danny DeVito, *Taxi* (ABC)

OUTSTANDING SUPPORTING ACTOR IN A LIMITED SERIES OR A SPECIAL: David Warner, *Masada* (ABC)

OUTSTANDING SUPPORTING ACTRESS IN A DRAMA SERIES: Nancy Marchand, *Lou Grant* (CBS)

OUTSTANDING SUPPORTING ACTRESS IN A COMEDY OR VARIETY OR MUSIC SERIES: Eileen Brennan, *Private Benjamin* (CBS)

OUTSTANDING SUPPORTING ACTRESS IN A LIMITED SERIES OR A SPECIAL: Jane Alexander, "Playing for Time" (CBS)

OUTSTANDING INDIVIDUAL ACHIEVEMENT—SPECIAL CLASS: Sarah Vaughan, performer, "Rhapsody and Song—A Tribute to George Gershwin" (PBS)

OUTSTANDING DIRECTING IN A DRAMA SERIES (SINGLE EPISODE): Robert Butler, "Hill Street Station," *Hill Street Blues* (NBC)

OUTSTANDING DIRECTING IN A COMEDY SERIES (SINGLE EPISODE): James Burrows, "Elaine's Strange Triangle," *Taxi* (ABC)

OUTSTANDING DIRECTING IN A LIMITED SERIES OR A SPECIAL: James Goldstone, "Kent State" (NBC)

OUTSTANDING DIRECTING IN A VARIETY, MUSIC, OR COMEDY PROGRAM: Don Mischer, "The Kennedy Center Honors: A National Celebration of the Performing Arts" (CBS)

OUTSTANDING WRITING IN A DRAMA SERIES (SINGLE EPISODE): Michael Kozoll and Steven Bochco, "Hill Street Station," *Hill Street Blues* (NBC)

OUTSTANDING WRITING IN A COMEDY SERIES (SINGLE EPISODE): Michael Leeson, "Tony's Sister and Jim," *Taxi* (ABC)

OUTSTANDING WRITING IN A LIMITED SERIES OR A SPECIAL: Arthur Miller, "Playing for Time" (CBS)

OUTSTANDING WRITING IN A VARIETY, MUSIC, OR COMEDY PROGRAM: Jerry Juhl, David O'Dell, Chris Langham, Jim Henson, and Don Hinkley; "The Muppet Show with Carol Burnett" (syndicated)

FOURTH ANNUAL ATAS GOVERNOR'S AWARD: Elton H. Rule, President, American Broadcasting Company

1981–1982 (PRESENTED SEPTEMBER 19, 1982)

OUTSTANDING COMEDY SERIES: *Barney Miller,* Danny Arnold and Roland Kibbee, executive producers; Frank Dungaii and Jeff Stein, producers; Gary Shaw, coproducer (ABC)

OUTSTANDING DRAMA SERIES: *Hill Street Blues,* Steven Bochco, executive producer; Gregory Hoblit, supervising producer; David Anspaugh and Anthony Yerkovich, producers (NBC)

OUTSTANDING LIMITED SERIES: *Marco Polo,* Vincenzo Labella, producer (NBC)

OUTSTANDING VARIETY, MUSIC, OR COMEDY PROGRAM: "Night of 100 Stars," Alexander H. Cohen, executive producer; Hildy Parks, producer; Roy A. Somlyo, coproducer (ABC)

OUTSTANDING DRAMA SPECIAL: "A Woman Called Golda," Have Bennett, executive producer; Gene Corman, producer (syndicated)

OUTSTANDING INFORMATIONAL SERIES: *Creativity with Bill Moyers,* Merton Koplin and Charles Grinker, executive producers; Betsy McCarthy, coordinating producer (PBS)

OUTSTANDING INFORMATIONAL SPECIAL: "*Making of Raiders of the Lost Ark,*" Sidney Ganis, executive producer; Howard Kazanjian, producer (PBS)

OUTSTANDING CLASSICAL PROGRAM IN THE PERFORMING ARTS: '*La Bohème,* Live from the Met," Michael Bronson, executive producer; Clement d'Alessio, producer (PBS)

OUTSTANDING CHILDREN'S PROGRAM: "The Wave," Virginia L. Cater, executive producer; Fern Field, producer (ABC)

OUTSTANDING ANIMATED PROGRAM: "Grinch Grinches the Cat in the Hat," David H. DePatie, executive producer; Ted Geisel and Friz Freleng, producers (ABC)

OUTSTANDING LEAD ACTOR IN A DRAMA SERIES: Daniel J. Travanti, *Hill Street Blues* (NBC)

OUTSTANDING LEAD ACTOR IN A COMEDY SERIES: Alan Alda, *M*A*S*H* (CBS)

OUTSTANDING LEAD ACTOR IN A LIMITED SERIES OR A SPECIAL: Mickey Rooney, "Bill" (CBS)

OUTSTANDING LEAD ACTRESS IN A DRAMA SERIES: Michael Learned, *Nurse* (CBS)

OUTSTANDING LEAD ACTRESS IN A COMEDY SERIES: Carol Kane, "Simka Returns," *Taxi* (ABC)

OUTSTANDING LEAD ACTRESS IN A LIMITED SERIES OR A SPECIAL: Ingrid Bergman, "A Woman Called Golda" (syndicated)

OUTSTANDING SUPPORTING ACTOR IN A DRAMA SERIES: Michael Conrad, *Hill Street Blues* (NBC)

OUTSTANDING SUPPORTING ACTOR IN A COMEDY OR VARIETY OR MUSIC SERIES: Christopher Lloyd, *Taxi* (ABC)

OUTSTANDING SUPPORTING ACTOR IN A LIMITED SERIES OR A SPECIAL: Laurence Olivier, *Brideshead Revisited* (PBS)

OUTSTANDING SUPPORTING ACTRESS IN A DRAMA SERIES: Nancy Marchand, *Lou Grant* (CBS)

OUTSTANDING SUPPORTING ACTRESS IN A COMEDY OR VARIETY OR MUSIC SERIES: Loretta Swit, *M*A*S*H* (CBS)

OUTSTANDING SUPPORTING ACTRESS IN A LIMITED SERIES OR A SPECIAL: Penny Fuller, "The Elephant Man" (ABC)

OUTSTANDING INDIVIDUAL ACHIEVEMENT-SPECIAL CLASS: Nell Carter, performer, "Ain't Misbehavin'" (NBC); Andre De Shields, performer, "Ain't Misbehavin'" (NBC)

OUTSTANDING DIRECTING IN A DRAMA SERIES (SINGLE EPISODE): Harry Harris, "To Soar and Never Falter," *Fame* (NBC)

OUTSTANDING DIRECTING IN A COMEDY SERIES (SINGLE EPISODE): Alan Rafkin, "Barbara's Crisis," *One Day at a Time* (CBS)

OUTSTANDING DIRECTING IN A LIMITED SERIES OR A SPECIAL: Marvin J. Chomsky, "Inside the Third Reich" (ABC)

OUTSTANDING WRITING IN A DRAMA SERIES (SINGLE EPISODE): Steve Bochco, Anthony Yerkovich, Jeffrey Lewis, and Michael Wagner, teleplay; Michael Kozoll and Steven Bochco, story; "Freedom's Last Stand," *Hill Street Blues* (NBC)

OUTSTANDING WRITING IN A COMEDY SERIES (SINGLE EPISODE): Ken Estin, "Elegant Iggy," *Taxi* (ABC)

OUTSTANDING WRITING IN A LIMITED SERIES OR A SPECIAL: Corey Blechman, teleplay; Barry Morrow, story; "Bill" (CBS)

FIFTH ANNUAL ATAS GOVERNOR'S AWARD: *The Hallmark Hall of Fame*

1982–1983 (PRESENTED SEPTEMBER 25, 1983)

OUTSTANDING COMEDY SERIES: *Cheers,* James Burrows, Glen Charles, and Les Charles, producers; Ken Levine and David lsaacs, coproducers (NBC)

OUTSTANDING DRAMA SERIES: *Hill Street Blues,* Steven Bochco, executive producer; Gregory Hoblit, coexecutive producer; Anthony Yerkovich, supervising producer; David Anspaugh and Scott Brazil, producers (NBC)

OUTSTANDING LIMITED SERIES: *Nicholas Nickleby,* Cohn Callender, producer (syndicated)

OUTSTANDING VARIETY, MUSIC, OR COMEDY PROGRAM: "Motown 25: Yesterday, Today, Forever," Suzanne de Passe, executive producer; Don Mischer and Buz Kohan, producers; Suzanne Coston, producer for Motown (NBC)

OUTSTANDING DRAMA SPECIAL: "Special Bulletin," Don Ohlmeyer, executive producer; Marshall Herskovitz and Edward Zwick, producers (NBC)

OUTSTANDING INFORMATIONAL SERIES: *The Barbara Walters Specials,* Beth Poison, producer; Barbara Walters, host (ABC)

OUTSTANDING INFORMATIONAL SPECIAL: "The Body Human: The Living Code," Thomas W. Moore, executive producer; Robert E. Fuisz, M.D., and Alfred R. Kelman, M.D., producers; Charles A. Bangert, Franklin Getchell, and Nancy Smith, coproducers (CBS)

OUTSTANDING CLASSICAL PROGRAM IN THE PERFORMING ARTS: "Pavarotti in Philadelphia: *La Bohème,*" Margaret Anne Everitt, executive producer; Clement D'Alessio, producer; Luciano Pavarotti, star (PBS)

OUTSTANDING CHILDREN'S PROGRAM: "Big Bird in China," Jon Stone, executive producer; David Liu, Kuo BaoXiang, and Xu Ja-Cha, producers (NBC)

OUTSTANDING ANIMATED PROGRAM: "Ziggy's Gift," Lena Tabori, executive producer; Richard Williams, Tom Wilson, and Lena Tabori, producers (ABC)

OUTSTANDING LEAD ACTOR IN A DRAMA SERIES: Ed Flanders, *St. Elsewhere* (NBC)

OUTSTANDING LEAD ACTOR IN A COMEDY SERIES: Judd Hirsch, *Taxi* (NBC)

OUTSTANDING LEAD ACTOR IN A LIMITED SERIES OR A SPECIAL: Tommy Lee Jones, "The Executioner's Song" (NBC)

OUTSTANDING LEAD ACTRESS IN A DRAMA SERIES: Tyne Daly, *Cagney & Lacey* (CBS)

OUTSTANDING LEAD ACTRESS IN A COMEDY SERIES: Shelley Long, *Cheers* (NBC)

OUTSTANDING LEAD ACTRESS IN A LIMITED SERIES OR A SPECIAL: Barbara Stanwyck, *The Thorn Birds-Part I* (ABC)

OUTSTANDING SUPPORTING ACTOR IN A DRAMA SERIES: James Coco, "Cora and Arnie," *St. Elsewhere* (NBC)

OUTSTANDING SUPPORTING ACTOR IN A COMEDY, VARIETY, OR MUSIC SERIES: Christopher Lloyd, *Taxi* (NBC)

OUTSTANDING SUPPORTING ACTOR IN A LIMITED SERIES OR A SPECIAL: Richard Kiley, *The Thorn Birds-Part 1* (ABC)

OUTSTANDING SUPPORTING ACTRESS IN A DRAMA SERIES: Doris Roberts, "Cora and Arnie," *St. Elsewhere* (NBC)

OUTSTANDING SUPPORTING ACTRESS IN A COMEDY, VARIETY, OR MUSIC SERIES: Carol Kane, *Taxi* (NBC)

OUTSTANDING SUPPORTING ACTRESS IN A LIMITED SERIES OR A SPECIAL: Jean Simmons, *The Thorn Birds* (ABC)

OUTSTANDING INDIVIDUAL PERFORMANCE IN A VARIETY OR MUSIC PROGRAM: Leontyne Price, "Live from Lincoln Center: Leontyne Price, Zubin Mehta, and the New York Philharmonic" (PBS)

OUTSTANDING INDIVIDUAL ACHIEVEMENT—INFORMATIONAL PROGRAMMING: Alfred R. Kelman, M.D., and Charles Bangert, directors, "The Body Human: The Living Code"; Louis H. Gorfain and Robert E. Fuisz, M.D., writers, "The Body Human: The Living Code" (CBS)

OUTSTANDING DIRECTING IN A DRAMA SERIES (SINGLE EPISODE): Jeff Bheckner, "Life in the Minors," *Hill Street Blues* (NBC)

OUTSTANDING DIRECTING IN A COMEDY SERIES (SINGLE EPISODE): James Burrows, "Showdown, Part 2," *Cheers* (NBC)

OUTSTANDING DIRECTING IN A LIMITED SERIES OR A SPECIAL: John Erman, "Who Will Love My Children?" (ABC)

OUTSTANDING DIRECTING IN A VARIETY OR MUSICAL PROGRAM: Dwight Hemion, "Sheena Easton, Act I" (NBC)

OUTSTANDING WRITING IN A DRAMA SERIES (SINGLE EPISODE): David Milch, "Trial by Fury," *Hill Street Blues* (NBC)

OUTSTANDING WRITING IN A COMEDY SERIES (SINGLE EPISODE): Glen Charles and Les Charles, "Give Me a Ring Sometime," *Cheers* (NBC)

OUTSTANDING WRITING IN A LIMITED SERIES OR A SPECIAL: Marshall Herskovitz, teleplay; Edward Zwick and Marshall Herskovitz, story; "Special Bulletin" (NBC)

OUTSTANDING WRITING IN A VARIETY OR MUSICAL PROGRAM: John Candy, Joe Flaherty, Eugene Levy, Andrea Martin, Martin Short, Dick Blasucci, Paul Flaherty, John McAndrew, Doug Steckler, Bob Dolman, Michael Short, and Mary Charlotte Wilcox; "The Energy Ball/Sweeps Week," *SCTV Network* (NBC)

SIXTH ANNUAL ATAS GOVERNOR'S AWARD: Sylvester L. "Pat" Weaver, Jr., former president of the National Broadcasting Company

1983–1984 (PRESENTED SEPTEMBER 23, 1984)

OUTSTANDING COMEDY SERIES: *Cheers,* James Burrows, Glen Charles, and Les Charles, producers (NBC)

OUTSTANDING DRAMA SERIES: *Hill Street Blues,* Steven Bochco, executive producer; Gregory Hobhit, coexecutive producer; Scott Brazil, supervising producer; Jeff Lewis and Sascha Schneider, producers; David Latt, coproducer (NBC)

OUTSTANDING LIMITED SERIES: "Concealed Enemies," *American Playhouse,* Lindsay Law and David Elstein, executive producers; Peter Cook, producer (PBS)

OUTSTANDING VARIETY, MUSIC, OR COMEDY PROGRAM: Nick Vanoff and George Stevens, Jr., producers; "The 6th Annual Kennedy Center Honors: A Celebration of the Performing Arts" (CBS)

OUTSTANDING DRAMA SPECIAL "Something About Amelia," Leonard Goldberg, executive producer; Michele Rappaport, producer (ABC)

OUTSTANDING INFORMATIONAL SERIES: *A Walk Through the 20th Century,* Merton Y. Kophin, senior executive producer; Charles Grinker and Sanford H. Fisher, producers; Betsy McCarthy, coordinating producer; David Grubin and Ronald Blumer, producers; Bill Moyers, host (PBS)

OUTSTANDING INFORMATIONAL SPECIAL: "America Remembers John F. Kennedy," Thomas F. Horton, producer (syndicated)

OUTSTANDING CLASSICAL PROGRAM IN THE PERFORMING ARTS: "Placido Domingo Celebrates Seville," *Great Performances,* Horant H. Holfeid, executive producer; David Griffiths, producer; Placido Domingo, host (PBS)

OUTSTANDING CHILDREN'S PROGRAM: "He Makes Me Feel Like Dancin'," Edgar J. Scherick and Scott Rudin, executive producers; Emile/Ardolino and Judy Kinberg, producers (NBC)

OUTSTANDING ANIMATED PROGRAM: "Garfield on the Town," Jay Poynor, executive producer; Lee Mendelson and Bill Mehendez, producers (CBS)

OUTSTANDING LEAD ACTOR IN A DRAMA SERIES: Tom Selleck, *Magnum, P.I.* (CBS)

OUTSTANDING LEAD ACTOR IN A COMEDY SERIES: John Ritter, *Three's Company* (ABC)

OUTSTANDING LEAD ACTOR IN A LIMITED SERIES OR A SPECIAL: Sir Laurence Olivier, King Lear (syndicated)

OUTSTANDING LEAD ACTRESS IN A DRAMA SERIES: Tyne Daly, *Cagney & Lacey* (CBS)

OUTSTANDING LEAD ACTRESS IN A COMEDY SERIES: Jane Curtin, *Kate & Allie* (CBS)

OUTSTANDING LEAD ACTRESS IN A LIMITED SE-
RIES OR A SPECIAL: Jane Fonda, *The Dollmaker*
(ABC)

OUTSTANDING SUPPORTING ACTOR IN A DRAMA
SERIES: Bruce Weitz, *Hill Street Blues* (CBS)

OUTSTANDING SUPPORTING ACTOR IN A COM-
EDY, VARIETY, OR MUSIC SERIES: Pat Harrington, Jr., *One Day at a Time* (CBS)

OUTSTANDING SUPPORTING ACTOR IN A LIM-
ITED SERIES OR A SPECIAL: Art Carney, "Terrible
Joe Moran" (CBS)

OUTSTANDING SUPPORTING ACTRESS IN A
DRAMA SERIES: Alfre Woodard, "Doris in Wonderland," *Hill Street Blues* (NBC)

OUTSTANDING SUPPORTING ACTRESS IN A COM-
EDY, VARIETY, OR MUSIC SERIES: Rhea Perlman,
Cheers (NBC)

OUTSTANDING SUPPORTING ACTRESS IN A LIM-
ITED SERIES OR A SPECIAL: Roxana Zal, "Something About Amelia" (ABC)

OUTSTANDING INDIVIDUAL PERFORMANCE IN A
VARIETY OR MUSIC PROGRAM: Cloris Leachman, "Screen Actors Guild 50th Anniversary Celebration" (CBS)

OUTSTANDING INDIVIDUAL ACHIEVEMENT-IN-
FORMATIONAL PROGRAMMING: Emile Ar-
dolino, director; "He Makes Me Feel Like Dancin'"
(NBC) and Bill Moyers, writer; "Marshall, Texas—
Marshall, Texas" (PBS)

OUTSTANDING DIRECTING IN A DRAMA SERIES
(SINGLE EPISODE): Corey Allen, "Goodbye Mr.
Scripps," *Hill Street Blues* (NBC)

OUTSTANDING DIRECTING IN A COMEDY SERIES
(SINGLE EPISODE): Bill Persky, "Very Loud Family," *Kate & Allie* (CBS)

OUTSTANDING DIRECTING IN A LIMITED SERIES
OR A SPECIAL: Jeff Bleckner, "Concealed Enemies,"
American Playhouse (PBS)

OUTSTANDING DIRECTING IN A VARIETY, MUSIC,
OR COMEDY PROGRAM: Dwight Hemion,
"Here's Television Entertainment" (PBS)

OUTSTANDING WRITING IN A DRAMA SERIES
(SINGLE EPISODE): John Ford Noonan, teleplay;
John Masius and Tom Fontana, story; "The Women,"
St. Elsewhere (NBC)

OUTSTANDING WRITING IN A COMEDY SERIES
(SINGLE EPISODE): David Angell, "Old Flames,"
Cheers (NBC)

OUTSTANDING WRITING IN A LIMITED SERIES OR
SPECIAL: William Hanley, "Something About
Amelia" (ABC)

OUTSTANDING WRITING IN A VARIETY, MUSIC,
OR COMEDY PROGRAM: Steve O'Donnell, Gerard
Mulligan, Sandy Frank, Joe Toplyn, Chris Elliott,
Matt Wickline, Jeff Martin, Todd Greenberg, David
Yazbek, Merrill Markoe, and David Letterman; *Late
Night with David Letterman*, with Dr. Ruth West-
heimer and Teri Garr, 11/15/83 (NBC)

SEVENTH ANNUAL ATAS GOVERNOR'S AWARD:
Bob Hope

1984–1985 (PRESENTED SEPTEMBER 22, 1985)

OUTSTANDING COMEDY SERIES: *The Cosby Show*,
Marcy Carsey and Tom Werner, executive producers;
Earl Pomerantz and Elliot Schoenman, coexecutive
producers; John Markus, supervising producer; Caryn
Sneider, producer; Earle Hyman, Jerry Ross, and
Michael Loman, coproducers (NBC)

OUTSTANDING DRAMA SERIES: *Cagney & Lacey*,
Barney Rosenzweig, executive producer; Steven
Brown, Terry Louise Fisher, and Peter Lefcourt, pro-
ducers (CBS)

OUTSTANDING LIMITED SERIES: "The Jewel in the
Crown," *Masterpiece Theatre*, Denis Forman, executive producer; Christopher Morahan, producer (PBS)

OUTSTANDING VARIETY, MUSIC, OR COMEDY
PROGRAM: "Motown Returns to the Apollo,"
Suzanne de Passe, executive producer; Don Mischer,
producer; Suzanne Coston and Michael Weisbarth,
coproducers (NBC)

OUTSTANDING DRAMA/COMEDY SPECIAL: "Do
You Remember Love?," Dave Bell, executive pro-
ducer; Marilyn Hall, coexecutive producer; Wayne
Threm and James E. Thompson, producers; Walter
Halsey Davis, coproducer (CBS)

OUTSTANDING INFORMATIONAL SERIES: *The Living Planet: A Portrait of Earth*, Richard Brock, executive producer; Adrian Warren, Ned Kelly, Andrew
Neal, and Richard Brock, producers (PBS)

OUTSTANDING INFORMATIONAL SPECIAL:
"Cousteau: Mississippi," Jacques-Yves Cousteau and
Jean-Michel Cousteau, executive producers; Andrew
Solt, producer; Jacques-Yves Cousteau, host (SYN)

OUTSTANDING CLASSICAL PROGRAM IN THE PER-
FORMING ARTS: "*Tosca*, Live from the Met,"
Michael Bronson, executive producer; Samuel J. Paul,
producer (PBS)

OUTSTANDING CHILDREN'S PROGRAM: "Displaced
Person," *American Playhouse*, Allison Maher, Barry
Solomon, Rick Traum, and Patrick Lynch, executive
producers; Patrick Dromgoole, supervising executive
producer; Barry Levinson, producer (PBS)

OUTSTANDING ANIMATED PROGRAM: "Garfield in
the Rough," Jay Poynor, executive producer; Phil
Roman, producer; Jim Davis, writer; Phil Roman, director (CBS)

OUTSTANDING LEAD ACTOR IN A DRAMA SERIES:
William Daniels, *St. Elsewhere* (NBC)

OUTSTANDING LEAD ACTOR IN A COMEDY SE-
RIES: Robert Guillaume, *Benson* (ABC)

OUTSTANDING LEAD ACTOR IN A LIMITED SERIES
OR A SPECIAL: Richard Crenna, "The Rape of
Richard Beck," *ABC Theatre* (ABC)

OUTSTANDING LEAD ACTRESS IN A DRAMA SE-
RIES: Tyne Daly, *Cagney & Lacey* (CBS)

OUTSTANDING LEAD ACTRESS IN A COMEDY SERIES: Jane Curtin, *Kate & Allie* (CBS)

OUTSTANDING LEAD ACTRESS IN A LIMITED SERIES OR A SPECIAL: Joanne Woodward, "Do You Remember Love?" (CBS)

OUTSTANDING SUPPORTING ACTOR IN A DRAMA SERIES: Edward James Olmos, *Miami Vice* (NBC)

OUTSTANDING SUPPORTING ACTOR IN A COMEDY SERIES: John Larroquette, *Night Court* (NBC)

OUTSTANDING SUPPORTING ACTOR IN A LIMITED SERIES OR A SPECIAL: Karl Maiden, "Fatal Vision" (NBC)

OUTSTANDING SUPPORTING ACTRESS IN A DRAMA SERIES: Betty Thomas, *Hill Street Blues* (NBC)

OUTSTANDING SUPPORTING ACTRESS IN A COMEDY SERIES: Rhea Perlman, *Cheers* (NBC)

OUTSTANDING SUPPORTING ACTRESS IN A LIMITED SERIES OR A SPECIAL: Kim Stanley, "Cat on a Hot Tin Roof," *American Playhouse* (PBS)

OUTSTANDING INDIVIDUAL PERFORMANCE IN A VARIETY OR MUSIC PROGRAM: George Hearn, "Sweeney Todd," *Great Performances* (PBS)

OUTSTANDING INDIVIDUAL ACHIEVEMENT-INFORMATIONAL PROGRAMMING—WRITING: Howard Enders, John G. Fox, Michael Joseloff, and Marc Siegel; "The Crucible of Europe," *Heritage: Civilization and the Jews* (PBS) and Brian Wilson, "Out of the Ashes," *Heritage: Civilization and the Jews* (PBS)

OUTSTANDING DIRECTING IN A DRAMA SERIES (SINGLE EPISODE): Arthur Karen, "Heat," *Cagney & Lacey* (CBS)

OUTSTANDING DIRECTING IN A COMEDY SERIES (SINGLE EPISODE): Jay Sandrich, "The Younger Woman," *The Cosby Show* (NBC)

OUTSTANDING DIRECTING IN A LIMITED SERIES OR A SPECIAL: Lamont Johnson, "Wallenberg: A Hero's Story" (NBC)

OUTSTANDING DIRECTING IN A VARIETY OR MUSIC PROGRAM: Terry Hughes, "Sweeney Todd," *Great Performances* (PBS)

OUTSTANDING WRITING IN A DRAMA SERIES (SINGLE EPISODE): Patricia M. Green, "Who Said It's Fair—Part II," *Cagney & Lacey* (CBS)

OUTSTANDING WRITING IN A COMEDY SERIES (SINGLE EPISODE): Ed Weinbergen and Michael Leeson, premiere episode, *The Cosby Show* (NBC)

OUTSTANDING WRITING IN A LIMITED SERIES OR A SPECIAL: Vickie Patik, "Do You Remember Love?" (CBS)

OUTSTANDING WRITING IN A VARIETY OR MUSIC PROGRAM: Gerard Mulligan, Sandy Frank, Joe Toplyn, Chris Elliott; Matt Wickline, Jeff Martin, Eddie Gorodetsky, Randy Cohen, Larry Jacobson, Kevin Curran, Fred Graver. Merrill Markoe, and David Letterman; "Christmas with the Lettermans," show #491, *Late Night with David Letterman* (NBC)

EIGHTH ANNUAL ATAS GOVERNOR'S AWARD: Alistair Cooke

1985–1986 (PRESENTED SEPTEMBER 20, 1986)

OUTSTANDING COMEDY SERIES: *Golden Girls*, Paul Junger Witt and Tony Thomas executive producers; Paul Bogart, supervising producer; Paul Junger Witt, Tony Thomas, Kathy Speer, and Terry Grossman producers; Marsha Posner Williams coproducer (NBC)

OUTSTANDING DRAMA SERIES: *Cagney & Lacey*, Barney Rosenzweig, executive producer; Liz Coe, supervising producer; Ralph Singleton, Patricia Green, and Steve Brown, producers; P. K. Knelman, coproducer (CBS)

OUTSTANDING MINI-SERIES: "Peter the Great," Marvin J. Chomsky, producer; Konstantin Theoren, line producer (NBC)

OUTSTANDING VARIETY, MUSIC, OR COMEDY PROGRAM: "The Kennedy Center Honors: A Celebration of the Performing Arts," Nick Vanoff and George Stevens, Jr., producers (CBS)

OUTSTANDING DRAMA/COMEDY SPECIAL: "Love Is Never Silent," Marian Rees, executive producer; Juliana Field, Ca-executive producer (NBC)

OUTSTANDING INFORMATIONAL SERIES: *Laurence Olivier-A Life*, Nick Evans and Nick Elliott, executive producers, Bob Bee, producer (PBS); *Planet Earth*, Thomas Skinner, executive producer; Gregory Andorfer, series producer; Georgann Kane, coordinating producer (PBS)

OUTSTANDING INFORMATIONAL SPECIAL: "W.C. Fields Straight Up," Robert B. Weide, executive producer; Ronald J. Fields, coproducer (PBS)

OUTSTANDING CLASSICAL PROGRAM IN THE PERFORMING ARTS: "Walftrap Presents the Kirov: Swan Lake," Michael B. Styer, executive producer; Phillip Byrd, senior producer; John T. Pottliast, producer (PBS)

OUTSTANDING CHILDREN'S PROGRAM: *Anne of Green Gables-Wonderworks*, Kevin Sullivan and Lee Polk executive producers; Kevin Sullivan and Ian McDougall producers (PBS)

OUTSTANDING ANIMATED PROGRAM: "Garfield's Halloween Adventure," Jay Poynon, executive producer (CBS)

OUTSTANDING LEAD ACTOR IN A DRAMA SERIES: William Daniels, *St. Elsewhere* (NBC)

OUTSTANDING LEAD ACTOR IN A COMEDY SERIES: Michael J. Fox, *Family Ties* (NBC)

OUTSTANDING LEAD ACTOR IN A MINI-SERIES OR A SPECIAL: Dustin Hoffman, "Death of a Salesman" (CBS)

OUTSTANDING LEAD ACTRESS IN A DRAMA SERIES: Sharon Gless, *Cagney & Lacey* (CBS)

OUTSTANDING LEAD ACTRESS IN A COMEDY SERIES: Betty White, *Golden Girls* (NBC)

OUTSTANDING LEAD ACTRESS IN A MINI-SERIES OR A SPECIAL: Marlo Thomas, "Nobody's Child" (NBC)

OUTSTANDING SUPPORTING ACTOR IN A DRAMA SERIES: John Karlen, *Cagney & Lacey* (CBS)

OUTSTANDING SUPPORTING ACTOR IN A COMEDY SERIES: John Larroquette, *Night Court* (NBC)

OUTSTANDING SUPPORTING ACTOR IN A MINI-SERIES OR A SPECIAL: John Malkovich, "Death of a Salesman" (CBS)

OUTSTANDING SUPPORTING ACTRESS IN A DRAMA SERIES: Bonnie Bartlett, *St. Elsewhere* (NBC)

OUTSTANDING SUPPORTING ACTRESS IN A COMEDY SERIES: Rhea Perlman, *Cheers* (NBC)

OUTSTANDING SUPPORTING ACTRESS IN A MINI-SERIES OR A SPECIAL: Colleen Dewhurst, "Between Two Women" (ABC)

OUTSTANDING INDIVIDUAL PERFORMANCE IN A VARIETY OR MUSIC PROGRAM: Whitney Houston, "The 28th Annual Grammy Awards" (CBS)

OUTSTANDING GUEST PERFORMER IN A DRAMA SERIES: John Lithgow, *Amazing Stories* (NBC)

OUTSTANDING GUEST PERFORMER IN A COMEDY SERIES: Roscoe Lee Browne, *The Cosby Show* (NBC)

OUTSTANDING INDIVIDUAL ACHIEVEMENT IN CLASSICAL MUSIC/DANCE PROGRAMMING-PERFORMING: Placido Domingo, "Cavalleria Rusticana," *Great Performances* (PBS)

OUTSTANDING INDIVIDUAL ACHIEVEMENT—INFORMATIONAL PROGRAMMING—WRITING: John L. Miller, "The Spencer Tracy Legacy: A Tribute by Katharine Hepburn" (PBS)

OUTSTANDING DIRECTING IN A DRAMA SERIES (SINGLE EPISODE): Georg Stanford Brown, "Parting Shots," *Cagney & Lacey* (CBS)

OUTSTANDING DIRECTING IN A COMEDY SERIES (SINGLE EPISODE): Jay Sandrich, "Denise's Friend," *The Cosby Show* (NBC)

OUTSTANDING DIRECTING IN A MINI-SERIES OR A SPECIAL: Joseph Sargent, "Love Is Never Silent," *Hallmark Hall of Fame* (NBC)

OUTSTANDING DIRECTING IN A VARIETY OR MUSIC PROGRAM: Warns Hussein, "Copacabana," (CBS)

OUTSTANDING WRITING IN A DRAMA SERIES (SINGLE EPISODE): Tom Fontana, John Tinker, and John Masius, "Time Heals," *St. Elsewhere* (NBC)

OUTSTANDING WRITING IN A COMEDY SERIES (SINGLE EPISODE): Barry Fanaro and Mont Nathan, "A Little Romance," *Golden Girls* (NBC)

OUTSTANDING WRITING IN A MINI-SERIES OR A SPECIAL: Ron Cowen and Daniel Lipman, teleplay; Sherman Yellen, story; "An Early Frost" (NBC)

OUTSTANDING WRITING IN A VARIETY OR MUSIC PROGRAM: David Letterman, Joe O'Donnell, Sandy Frank, Joe Toplyn, Chris Elliott, Matt Wickline, Jeff Martin, Gerard Mulligan, Randy Cohen, Larry Jacboson, Kevin Curran, Fred Graver, and Merrill Markoe; Fourth Anniversary Show, *Late Night with David Letterman* (NBC)

OUTSTANDING INDIVIDUAL ACHIEVEMENT IN CLASSICAL MUSIC/DANCE PROGRAMMING-WRITING: John Ardion, "Gala of Stars 1985" (PBS)

NINTH ANNUAL ATAS GOVERNOR'S AWARD: Red Skelton

1986–1987 (PRESENTED SEPTEMBER 20, 1987)

OUTSTANDING COMEDY SERIES: *Golden Girls,* Paul Junger Witt, Tony Thomas, and Susan Harris, executive producers; Kathy Speer and Terry Grossman, producers; Mont Nathan, Barry Fanaro, Winifred Hervey, and Marsha Posner Williams, coproducers (NBC)

OUTSTANDING DRAMA SERIES: *L.A. Law,* Steven Bochco, executive producer; Gregory Hoblit, coexecutive producer; Terry Louise Fisher, supervising producer; Ellen S. Pressman and Scott Goldstein, producers; Phillip M. Goldfarb, coordinating producer (NBC)

OUTSTANDING MINI-SERIES: "A Year in the Life," Joshua Brand and John Falsey, executive producers; Stephen Cnagg, producer (NBC)

OUTSTANDING VARIETY, MUSIC, OR COMEDY PROGRAM: "The 1987 Tony Awards," Don Mischer, executive producer; David J. Goldberg, producer (CBS)

OUTSTANDING DRAMA/COMEDY SPECIAL: "Promise," *Hallmark Hall of Fame,* Peter K. Duchow and James Garner, executive producers; Glenn Jordan, producer; Richard Friedenberg, coproducer (CBS)

OUTSTANDING INFORMATIONAL SERIES: *Smithsonian World,* Adrian Malone, executive producer; David Grubin, producer (PBS); "Unknown Chaplin," *American Masters,* Kevin Brownlow and David Gill, producers (PBS)

OUTSTANDING INFORMATIONAL SPECIAL: "Dance in America: Agnes, The Indomitable De Mille," *Great Performances,* Jac Venza, executive producer; Judy Kinberg, producer (PBS)

OUTSTANDING CLASSICAL PROGRAM IN THE PERFORMING ARTS: "Vladimir Horowitz: The Last Romantic," Peter Gelb, executive producer; Susan Froemke, producer; Vladimir Horowitz, star (PBS)

OUTSTANDING CHILDREN'S PROGRAM: *Jim Henson the Storyteller,* "Hans My Hedgehog," Jim Henson, executive producer; Mark Shivas, producer (NBC)

OUTSTANDING ANIMATED PROGRAM: "Cathy," Lee Mendelson, executive producer; Bill Melendez, producer; Cathy Guisewite, writer (CBS)

OUTSTANDING LEAD ACTOR IN A DRAMA SERIES: Bruce Willis, *Moonlighting* (ABC)

OUTSTANDING LEAD ACTOR IN A COMEDY SERIES: Michael J. Fox, *Family Ties* (NBC)

OUTSTANDING LEAD ACTOR IN A MINI-SERIES OR A SPECIAL: James Woods, "Promise," *Hallmark Hall of Fame* (CBS)

OUTSTANDING LEAD ACTRESS IN A DRAMA SERIES: Sharon Gless, *Cagney & Lacey* (CBS)

OUTSTANDING LEAD ACTRESS IN A COMEDY SERIES: Rue McClanahan, *Golden Girls* (NBC)

OUTSTANDING LEAD ACTRESS IN A MINI-SERIES OR A SPECIAL: Gena Rowlands, "The Betty Ford Story" (ABC)

OUTSTANDING SUPPORTING ACTOR IN A DRAMA SERIES: John Hilenman, *Magnum, P.I.* (CBS)

OUTSTANDING SUPPORTING ACTOR IN A COMEDY SERIES: John Larroquette, *Night Court* (NBC)

OUTSTANDING SUPPORTING ACTOR IN A MINI-SERIES OR A SPECIAL: Dabney Coleman, "Sworn to Silence" (ABC)

OUTSTANDING SUPPORTING ACTRESS IN A DRAMA SERIES: Bonnie Bartlett, *St. Elsewhere* (NBC)

OUTSTANDING SUPPORTING ACTRESS IN A COMEDY SERIES: Jackee Harry, *227* (NBC)

OUTSTANDING SUPPORTING ACTRESS IN A MINI-SERIES OR A SPECIAL: Piper Laurie, "Promise," *Hallmark Hall of Fame* (CBS)

OUTSTANDING INDIVIDUAL PERFORMANCE IN A VARIETY OR MUSIC PROGRAM: Robin Williams, "A Carol Burnett Special: Carol, Carl, Whoopi & Robin" (ABC)

OUTSTANDING GUEST PERFORMER IN A DRAMA SERIES: Alfre Woodard, *L.A. Law* (NBC)

OUTSTANDING GUEST PERFORMER IN A COMEDY SERIES: John Cleese, *Cheers* (NBC)

OUTSTANDING INDIVIDUAL ACHIEVEMENT IN CLASSICAL MUSIC/DANCE PROGRAMMING: Albert Maysles and David Maysles, directors; "Vladimir Horowitz: The Last Romantic" (PBS)

OUTSTANDING INDIVIDUAL ACHIEVEMENT IN INFORMATIONAL PROGRAMMING: Robert McCrum and Robert MacNeil, writers; *The Story of English*, "A Muse of Fire" (PBS)

OUTSTANDING DIRECTING IN A DRAMA SERIES (SINGLE EPISODE): Gregory Hoblit, "Pilot," *L.A. Law* (NBC)

OUTSTANDING DIRECTING IN A COMEDY SERIES (SINGLE EPISODE): Terry Hughes, "Isn't It Romantic?," *Golden Girls* (NBC)

OUTSTANDING DIRECTING IN A MINI-SERIES OR A SPECIAL: Glenn Jordan, "Promise," *Hallmark Hall of Fame* (CBS)

OUTSTANDING DIRECTING IN A VARIETY OR MUSIC PROGRAM: Don Mischer, "The Kennedy Center Honors: A Celebration of the Performing Arts" (CBS)

OUTSTANDING WRITING IN A DRAMA SERIES (SINGLE EPISODE): Terry Louise Fisher, "Venus Butterfly," *L.A. Law* (NBC)

OUTSTANDING WRITING IN A COMEDY SERIES (SINGLE EPISODE): Gary David Goldberg and Alan Uger, " 'A,' My Name Is Alex," *Family Ties* (NBC)

OUTSTANDING WRITING IN A MINI-SERIES OR A SPECIAL: Richard Friedenberg, teleplay; Kenneth Blackwell, Tennyson Flowers, and Richard Friedenberg, story; "Promise," *Hallmark Hall of Fame* (CBS)

OUTSTANDING WRITING IN A VARIETY OR MUSIC PROGRAM: Steve O'Donnell, Sandy Frank, Joe Toplyn, Chris Elliott, Matt Wickline, Jeff Martin, Gerard Mulligan, Randy Cohen, Larry Jacobson, Kevin Curran, Fred Graver, Adam Resnick, and David Letterman; Fifth Anniversary Special, *Late Night with David Letterman* (NBC)

TENTH ANNUAL ATAS GOVERNOR'S AWARD: Grant Tinker

1987–1988 (PRESENTED AUGUST 28, 1988)

OUTSTANDING COMEDY SERIES: *The Wonder Years,* Carol Black and Neil Manlens, executive producers; Jeff Silver, producer (ABC)

OUTSTANDING DRAMA SERIES: *thirtysomething,* Edward Zwick and Marshall Herskovitz, executive producers; Paul Haggis, supervising producer; Edward Zwick and Scott Winant, producers (ABC)

OUTSTANDING MINI-SERIES: "The Murder of Mary Phagan," George Stevens, Jr., producer (NBC)

OUTSTANDING VARIETY, MUSIC, OR COMEDY PROGRAM: "Irving Berlin's 100th Birthday Celebration," Don Mischer, executive producer; Jan Cornell and David J. Goldberg, producers; Sara Lakinson, co-producer (CBS)

OUTSTANDING DRAMA/COMEDY SPECIAL: "Inherit the Wind," Peter Douglas, executive producer; Robert A. Papazian, producer (NBC)

OUTSTANDING CLASSICAL PROGRAM IN THE PERFORMING ARTS: "Nixon in China," *Great Performances,* Jac Venza, executive producer; David Horn, series producer; Michael Bronson, producer; John Walker, coordinating producer (PBS)

OUTSTANDING INFORMATIONAL SERIES: *Buster Keaton: A Hard Act To Follow: American Masters,* Kevin Brownlow and David Gill, producers (PBS). *Nature,* David Heeley, executive producer; Fred Kaifman, series producer (PBS)

OUTSTANDING INFORMATIONAL SPECIAL: "Dear America: Letters Home from Vietnam," Bill Couturie and Thomas Bird, producers (HBO)

OUTSTANDING CHILDREN'S PROGRAM: "The Secret Garden," *Hallmark Hall of Fame,* Norman Rosemont, executive producer; Steven Lanning, producer (CBS)

OUTSTANDING ANIMATED PROGRAM: "A Claymation Christmas Celebration," Will Vinton, executive producer; David Altschul, producer; Will Vinton, director; Ralph Liddle, writer (CBS)

OUTSTANDING VARIETY/MUSIC EVENTS PROGRAMMING: "The 60th Annual Academy Awards," Samuel Goldwyn, Jr., producer (ABC)

OUTSTANDING LEAD ACTOR IN A DRAMA SERIES: Richard Kiley, *A Year in the Life* (NBC)

OUTSTANDING LEAD ACTOR IN A COMEDY SERIES: Michael J. Fox, *Family Ties* (NBC)

OUTSTANDING LEAD ACTOR IN A MINI-SERIES OR SPECIAL: Jason Robards, "Inherit the Wind" (NBC)

OUTSTANDING LEAD ACTRESS IN A DRAMA SERIES: Tyne Daly, *Cagney & Lacey* (CBS)

OUTSTANDING LEAD ACTRESS IN A COMEDY SERIES: Beatrice Arthur, *Golden Girls* (NBC)

OUTSTANDING LEAD ACTRESS IN A MINI-SERIES OR SPECIAL: Jessica Tandy, "Foxfire," *Hallmark Hall of Fame* (CBS)

OUTSTANDING SUPPORTING ACTOR IN A DRAMA SERIES: Larry Drake, *L.A. Law* (NBC)

OUTSTANDING SUPPORTING ACTOR IN A COMEDY SERIES: John Larroquette, *Night Court* (NBC)

OUTSTANDING SUPPORTING ACTOR IN A MINI-SERIES OR SPECIAL: John Shea, "Baby M" (ABC)

OUTSTANDING SUPPORTING ACTRESS IN A DRAMA SERIES: Patricia Wettig, *thirtysomething* (ABC)

OUTSTANDING SUPPORTING ACTRESS IN A COMEDY SERIES: Estelle Getty, *Golden Girls* (NBC)

OUTSTANDING SUPPORTING ACTRESS IN A MINI-SERIES OR SPECIAL: Jane Seymour, "Onassis: The Richest Man in the World" (ABC)

OUTSTANDING INDIVIDUAL PERFORMANCE IN A VARIETY OR MUSIC PROGRAM: Robin Williams, "ABC Presents a Royal Gala" (ABC)

OUTSTANDING GUEST PERFORMER IN A DRAMA SERIES: Shirley Knight, *thirtysomething* (ABC)

OUTSTANDING GUEST PERFORMER IN A COMEDY SERIES: Beairi Richards, *Frank's Place* (CBS)

OUTSTANDING DIRECTING IN A DRAMA SERIES (SINGLE EPISODE): Mark Tinker, "Weigh In, Weigh Out," *St. Elsewhere* (NBC)

OUTSTANDING DIRECTING IN A COMEDY SERIES (SINGLE EPISODE): Gregory Hoblit, "Pilot," *Hooperman* (ABC)

OUTSTANDING DIRECTING IN A MINI-SERIES OR A SPECIAL: Lamont Johnson, "Gore Vidal's Lincoln" (CBS)

OUTSTANDING DIRECTING IN A VARIETY OR MUSIC PROGRAM: Patricia Birch and Humphrey Burton, "Celebrating Gershwin," *Great Performances* (PBS)

OUTSTANDING WRITING IN A DRAMA SERIES (SINGLE EPISODE): Paul Haggis and Marshall Herskovitz, "Business As Usual, aka Michael's Father's Death," *thirtysomething* (ABC)

OUTSTANDING WRITING IN A COMEDY SERIES (SINGLE EPISODE): Hugh Wilson, "The Bridge," *Frank's Place* (CBS)

OUTSTANDING WRITING IN A MINI-SERIES OR A SPECIAL: William Hanley, "The Attic: The Hiding of Anne Frank," *General Foods Golden Showcase* (CBS)

OUTSTANDING WRITING IN A VARIETY OR MUSIC PROGRAM: Jackie Mason, "Jackie Mason on Broadway" (HBO)

OUTSTANDING INDIVIDUAL ACHIEVEMENT IN INFORMATIONAL PROGRAMMING—PERFORMING: Hal Holbrook, "New York City," *Portrait of America* (TBS)

OUTSTANDING INDIVIDUAL ACHIEVEMENT IN INFORMATIONAL PROGRAMMING—DIRECTING: Kevin Brownlow and David Gill, *Buster Keaton: A Hard Act to Follow, Part 1, American Masters* (PBS)

OUTSTANDING INDIVIDUAL ACHIEVEMENT IN INFORMATIONAL PROGRAMMING-WRITING: Kevin Brownlow and David Gill, *Buster Keaton: A Hard Act to Follow, Part 1, American Masters* (PBS); Bill Couturie and Richard Dewhurst, "Dear America: Letters Home from Vietnam" (HBO)

OUTSTANDING INDIVIDUAL ACHIEVEMENT IN CLASSICAL MUSIC/DANCE PROGRAMMING—DIRECTING: Kirk Browning, "The Metropolitan Opera Presents: *Turandot*" (PBS)

OUTSTANDING INDIVIDUAL ACHIEVEMENT IN CLASSICAL MUSIC/DANCE PROGRAMMING—WRITING: David Gordon "Dance in America: David Gordon's Made in U.S.A.," *Great Performances* (PBS)

OUTSTANDING INDIVIDUAL ACHIEVEMENT IN SPECIAL EVENTS PROGRAMMING—PERFORMER: Billy Crystal, "The 30th Annual Grammy Awards" (CBS)

OUTSTANDING INDIVIDUAL ACHIEVEMENT IN SPECIAL EVENTS PROGRAMMING-DIRECTING: Marty Pasetta, "The 60th Annual Academy Awards" (ABC)

ELEVENTH ANNUAL ATAS GOVERNOR'S AWARD: William Hanna and Joseph Barbera

1988–1989 (PRESENTED SEPTEMBER 17, 1989)

OUTSTANDING COMEDY SERIES: *Cheers*, James Burrows, Glen Charles, and Les Charles, executive producers; Cheri Eichen and Bill Steinkellner, producers; Tim Berry and Phil Sutton, coproducers (NBC)

OUTSTANDING DRAMA SERIES: *L.A. Law*, Steven Bochco, executive producer; Rick Wallace, coexecutive producer; David E. Kelley, supervising producer; Scott Goldstein and Michele Gallery, producers; William M. Finkelstein and Judith Parker, coproducers; Phillip M. Goldfarb and Alice West, coordinating producers (NBC)

OUTSTANDING MINI-SERIES: "War and Remembrance," Dan Curtis, executive producer; Barbara Steele, producer (ABC)

OUTSTANDING VARIETY, MUSIC, OR COMEDY PROGRAM: *The Tracey Ullman Show*, James L. Brooks, Heide Penman, Jerry Belson, Ken Estin, and

Sam Simon, executive producers; Richard Sakai and Ted Bessel, producers; Marc Flanagan, coproducer; Tracey Ullman, host (FOX)

OUTSTANDING DRAMA/COMEDY SPECIAL: "Day One," *AT&T Presents*, Aaron Spelling and E. Duke Vincent, executive producers; David W. Rintels, producer (CBS); "Roe vs. Wade," Michael Manheim, executive producer; Gregory Hoblit, producer; Alison Cross, coproducer (NBC)

OUTSTANDING CLASSICAL PROGRAM IN THE PERFORMING ARTS: "Bernstein at 70!," *Great Performances*, Harry Kraut and Klaus Hallig, executive producers; Michael Bronson and Thomas Skinner, producers (PBS)

OUTSTANDING INFORMATIONAL SERIES: *Nature*, David Heeley, executive producer; Fred Kaifman, series producer (PBS)

OUTSTANDING INFORMATIONAL SPECIAL: "Lillian Gish: The Actor's Life for Me," *American Masters*, Freida Lee Mock and Susan Lacy, executive producers; Terry Sanders, producer; William T. Cartwright, coproducer (PBS)

OUTSTANDING CHILDREN'S PROGRAM: "Free to Be . . . a Family," Marlo Thomas and Christopher Cerf, executive producers, U.S.; Robert Dalrymple, producer, U.S.; Leonid Zolotarevsky, executive producer, USSR; Igor Menzelintsev, producer, USSR; Vern T. Calhoun, coproducer (ABC)

OUTSTANDING ANIMATED PROGRAM: "Garfield: Babes and Bullets," Phil Roman, producer; Jim Davis, writer; Phil Roman, director; John Sparey and Bob Nesler; codirectors (CBS)

OUTSTANDING SPECIAL EVENTS PROGRAMMING: "Cirque de Soleil" (The Magic Circus), Helene Dufresne, producer (HBO); "The 11th Annual Kennedy Center Honors: A Celebration of the Performing Arts," George Stevens, Jr., and Nick Vanoff, producers (CBS); "The 42nd Annual Tony Awards," Don Mischer, executive producer; David J. Goldberg, producer; Jeffrey Lane, coproducer (CBS); "The 17th Annual American Film Institute Life Achievement Award: A Salute to Gregory Peck," George Stevens, Jr., producer, Jeffrey Lane, coproducer (NBC)

OUTSTANDING LEAD ACTOR IN A DRAMA SERIES: Carroll O'Connor, *In the Heat of the Night* (NBC)

OUTSTANDING LEAD ACTOR IN A COMEDY SERIES: Richard Mulligan, *Empty Nest* (NBC)

OUTSTANDING LEAD ACTOR IN A MINI-SERIES OR SPECIAL: James Woods, "My Name is Bill W.," *Hallmark Hall of Fame* (ABC)

OUTSTANDING LEAD ACTRESS IN A DRAMA SERIES: Dana Delany, *China Beach* (ABC)

OUTSTANDING LEAD ACTRESS IN A COMEDY SERIES: Candice Bergen, *Murphy Brown* (CBS)

OUTSTANDING LEAD ACTRESS IN A MINI-SERIES OR SPECIAL: Holly Hunter, "Roe vs. Wade" (NBC)

OUTSTANDING SUPPORTING ACTOR IN A DRAMA SERIES: Larry Drake, *L.A. Law* (NBC)

OUTSTANDING SUPPORTING ACTOR IN A COMEDY SERIES: Woody Harrelson, *Cheers* (NBC)

OUTSTANDING SUPPORTING ACTOR IN A MINI-SERIES OR SPECIAL: Derek Jacobi, "The Tenth Man," *Hallmark Hall of Fame* (CBS)

OUTSTANDING SUPPORTING ACTRESS IN A DRAMA SERIES: Melanie Mayron, *thirtysomething* (ABC)

OUTSTANDING SUPPORTING ACTRESS IN A COMEDY: Rhea Perlman, *Cheers* (NBC)

OUTSTANDING SUPPORTING ACTRESS IN A MINI-SERIES OR SPECIAL: Colleen Dewhurst, "Those She Left Behind" (NBC)

OUTSTANDING INDIVIDUAL PERFORMANCE IN A VARIETY OR MUSIC PROGRAM: Linda Ronstadt, "Canciones de Mi Padre," *Great Performances* (PBS)

OUTSTANDING GUEST ACTOR IN A DRAMA SERIES: Joe Spano, "The Execution of John Saringo," *Midnight Caller* (NBC)

OUTSTANDING GUEST ACTOR IN A COMEDY SERIES: Cleavon Little, "Stand By Your Man," *Dear John* (NBC)

OUTSTANDING GUEST ACTRESS IN A DRAMA SERIES: Kay Lenz, "After It Happened . . . ," *Midnight Caller* (NBC)

OUTSTANDING GUEST ACTRESS IN A COMEDY SERIES: Colleen Dewhurst, "Mama Said," *Murphy Brown* (CBS)

OUTSTANDING DIRECTING IN A DRAMA SERIES (SINGLE EPISODE): Robert Altman, "The Boiler Room," *Tanner 88* (HB0)

OUTSTANDING DIRECTING IN A COMEDY SERIES (SINGLE EPISODE): Peter Baldwin, "Our Miss White," *The Wonder Years* (ABC)

OUTSTANDING DIRECTING IN A MINI-SERIES OR A SPECIAL: Simon Wincer, "Lonesome Dove" (CBS)

OUTSTANDING DIRECTING IN A VARIETY OR MUSIC PROGRAM: Jim Henson, "Dog City," *The Jim Henson Hour* (NBC)

OUTSTANDING WRITING IN A DRAMA SERIES (single episode): Joseph Dougherty, "First Day/Last Day," *thirtysomething* (ABC)

OUTSTANDING WRITING IN A COMEDY SERIES (SINGLE EPISODE): Diane English, "Respect," *Murphy Brown* (CBS)

OUTSTANDING WRITING IN A MINI-SERIES OR A SPECIAL: Abby Mann, Rubin Vote, and Ron Hutchinson, "Murderers Among Us: The Simon Wiesenthal Story" (HBO)

OUTSTANDING WRITING IN A VARIETY OR MUSIC PROGRAM: James Downey, head writer; John Bowman, A. Whitney Brown, Gregory Daniels, Tom Davis, Al Franken, Shannon Gaughan, Jack Handy, Phil Hartman, Lorne Michaels, Mike Myers, Conan O'Brien, Bob Odenkirk, Herb Sargent, Tom Schiller, Robert Smigel, Bonnie Turner, Terry Turner, and Christine Zander, writers; George Meyer, additional sketches, *Saturday Night Live* (NBC)

OUTSTANDING INDIVIDUAL ACHIEVEMENT IN INFORMATIONAL PROGRAMMING—PERFORMING: Hal Holbrook, "Alaska," *Portrait of America* (TBS)

OUTSTANDING INDIVIDUAL ACHIEVEMENT IN INFORMATIONAL PROGRAMMING—WRITING: John Hemingway, "Search for Mind," *The Mind* (PBS)

OUTSTANDING INDIVIDUAL ACHIEVEMENT IN CLASSICAL MUSIC/DANCE PROGRAMMING—PERFORMING: Mikhail Baryshnikov, "Dance in America: Baryshnikov Dances Balanchine," *Great Performances* (PBS)

OUTSTANDING INDIVIDUAL ACHIEVEMENT IN SPECIAL EVENTS PROGRAMMING—PERFORMER: Billy Crystal, "The 31st Annual Grammy Awards" (CBS)

OUTSTANDING INDIVIDUAL ACHIEVEMENT IN SPECIAL EVENTS PROGRAMMING—DIRECTING: Dwight Hemion, "The 11th Annual Kennedy Center Honors: A Celebration of the Performing Arts" (CBS)

OUTSTANDING INDIVIDUAL ACHIEVEMENT IN SPECIAL EVENTS PROGRAMMING—WRITING: Jeffrey Lane, "The 42nd Annual Tony Awards" (CBS)

TWELFTH ANNUAL ATAS GOVERNOR'S AWARD: Lucille Ball

1989–1990 (PRESENTED SEPTEMBER 16, 1990)

OUTSTANDING COMEDY SERIES: *Murphy Brown,* Diane English and Joel Shukovsky, executive producers; Korby Siamis, consulting producer; Tom Seeley, Norm Gunzenliauser, Russ Woody, Gary Dontzig, Steven Peter-man, and Barnet Kellman, producers; Deborah Smith, coproducer (CBS)

OUTSTANDING DRAMA SERIES: *L.A. Law,* David E. Kelley, executive producer; Rick Wallace, coexecutive producer; William M. Finkelstein, supervising producer; Elodie Keene and Michael M. Robin, producers; Alice West, coordinating producer; Robert M. Breech, coproducer (NBC)

OUTSTANDING MINI-SERIES: "Drug Wars: The Camarena Story," Michael Mann, executive producer; Richard Abrams, coexecutive producer; Christopher Calahan, Rose Schacht, and Ann Powell, supervising producers; Branko Lustig, producer; Mark Allan, coproducer (NBC)

OUTSTANDING VARIETY, MUSIC, OR COMEDY PROGRAM: *In Living Color,* Keenen Ivory Wayans, executive producer; Kevin S. Bright, supervising producer; Tamara Rawitt, producer; Michael Petok, coproducer (FOX)

OUTSTANDING DRAMA/COMEDY SPECIAL: "Caroline?," *Hallmark Hall of Fame,* Dan Enright and Les Alexander, executive producers; Barbara Hiser and Joseph Broido, coexecutive producers; Dorothea G. Petrie, producer (CBS); "The Incident," *AT&T Presents,* Robert Halmi, executive producer; Bill Brademan and Ed Self, producers (CBS)

OUTSTANDING VARIETY, MUSIC, OR COMEDY SPECIAL: "Sammy Davis, Jr.'s 60th Anniversary Celebration," George Schlatter, producer; Buz Kohan, Jeff Margolis, and Gary Necessary, coproducers (ABC)

OUTSTANDING CLASSICAL PROGRAM IN THE PERFORMING ARTS: "Aida," *The Metropolitan Opera Presents,* Peter Gelb, executive producer (PBS)

OUTSTANDING INFORMATIONAL SERIES: *Smithsonian World,* Adrian Malone, executive producer; Sandra W. Bradley, producer (PBS)

OUTSTANDING INFORMATIONAL SPECIAL: "Dance in America: Bob Fosse Steam Heat," *Great Performances,* Jac Venza, executive producer; Judy Kinberg, producer (PBS); "Broadway's Dreamers: The Legacy of The Group Theater," *American Masters,* Jac Venza and Susan Lacy, executive producers; Joan Kramer and David Heeley, producers; Joanne Woodward, host/producer (PBS)

OUTSTANDING CHILDREN'S PROGRAM: "A Mother's Courage: The Mary Thomas Story," *The Magical World of Disney,* Ted Field and Robert W. Cart, executive producers; Patricia Clifford and Kate Wright, coexecutive producers; Richard L. O'Connor, producer; Chet Walker, coproducer (NBC)

OUTSTANDING ANIMATED PROGRAM: *The Simpsons* (series), James L. Brooks, Matt Groening, and Sam Simon, executive producers; Richard Sakai, producer; Al Jean, Mike Reiss, and Larina Jean Adamson, coproducers; Magot Pipkin, animation producer; Gabor Csupo, supervising animation director; David Silverman, director; John Swartzwelder, writer (FOX)

OUTSTANDING LEAD ACTOR IN A DRAMA SERIES: Peter Falk, *Columbo* (ABC)

OUTSTANDING LEAD ACTOR IN A COMEDY SERIES: Ted Danson, *Cheers* (NBC)

OUTSTANDING LEAD ACTOR IN A MINI-SERIES OR SPECIAL: Hume Cronyn, "Age-Old Friends" (HBO)

OUTSTANDING LEAD ACTRESS IN A DRAMA SERIES: Patricia Wettig, *thirtysomething* (ABC)

OUTSTANDING LEAD ACTRESS IN A COMEDY SERIES: Candice Bergen, *Murphy Brown* (CBS)

OUTSTANDING LEAD ACTRESS IN A MINI-SERIES OR SPECIAL: Barbara Hershey, "A Killing in a Small Town" (CBS)

OUTSTANDING SUPPORTING ACTOR IN A DRAMA SERIES: Jimmy Smits, *L.A. Law* (NBC)

OUTSTANDING SUPPORTING ACTOR IN A COMEDY SERIES: Alex Rocco, *The Famous Teddy Z* (CBS)

OUTSTANDING SUPPORTING ACTOR IN A MINI-SERIES OR SPECIAL: Vincent Gardenia, "Age-Old Friends" (HBO)

OUTSTANDING SUPPORTING ACTRESS IN A DRAMA SERIES: Marg Helgenberger, *China Beach* (ABC)

OUTSTANDING SUPPORTING ACTRESS IN A COMEDY SERIES: Bebe Neuwirth, *Cheers* (NBC)

OUTSTANDING SUPPORTING ACTRESS IN A MINI-SERIES OR SPECIAL: Eva Marie Saint, "People Like Us" (NBC)

OUTSTANDING INDIVIDUAL PERFORMANCE IN A VARIETY OR MUSIC PROGRAM: Tracey Ullman, "The Best of The Tracey Ullman Show" (FOX)

OUTSTANDING GUEST ACTOR IN A DRAMA SERIES: Patrick McGoohan, "Agenda for Murder," *Columbo* (ABC)

OUTSTANDING GUEST ACTOR IN A COMEDY SERIES: Darren McGavin, "Brown Like Me," *Murphy Brown* (CBS)

OUTSTANDING GUEST ACTRESS IN A DRAMA SERIES: Viveca Lindfors, "Save the Last Dance for Me," *Life Goes On* (ABC)

OUTSTANDING GUEST ACTRESS IN A COMEDY SERIES: Swoosie Kurtz, "Reunion," *Carol & Company* (NBC)

OUTSTANDING DIRECTING IN A DRAMA SERIES (SINGLE EPISODE): Thomas Carter, "Promises to Keep," *Equal Justice* (ABC)

OUTSTANDING DIRECTING IN A COMEDY SERIES (SINGLE EPISODE): Michael Dinner, "Good-Bye," *The Wonder Years* (ABC)

OUTSTANDING DIRECTING IN A MINI-SERIES OR A SPECIAL: Joseph Sargent, "Caroline?," *Hallmark Hall of Fame* (CBS)

OUTSTANDING DIRECTING IN A VARIETY OR MUSIC PROGRAM: Dwight Hemion, "The Kennedy Center Honors: A Celebration of the Performing Arts" (CBS)

OUTSTANDING WRITING IN A DRAMA SERIES (SINGLE EPISODE): David E. Kelley, "Blood, Sweat & Fears," *L.A. Law* (NBC)

OUTSTANDING WRITING IN A COMEDY SERIES (SINGLE EPISODE): Bob Brush, "Good-Bye," *The Wonder Years* (ABC)

OUTSTANDING WRITING IN A MINI-SERIES OR A SPECIAL: Terrence McNally, "Andre's Mother," *American Playhouse* (PBS)

OUTSTANDING WRITING IN A VARIETY OR MUSIC PROGRAM: Billy Crystal, "Billy Crystal: Midnight Train to Moscow" (HBO); James L. Brooks, Heide Perlman, Sam Simon, Jerry Belson, Marc Flanagan, Dinah Kirgo, Jay Kogen, Wallace Wolodarsky, Ian Praiser, Marilyn Suzanne Miller, and Tracey Ullman, *The Tracey Ullman Show* (FOX)

OUTSTANDING INDIVIDUAL ACHIEVEMENT IN INFORMATIONAL PROGRAMMING—PERFORMING: George Burns, *A Conversation With . . .* (DIS)

OUTSTANDING INDIVIDUAL ACHIEVEMENT IN INFORMATIONAL PROGRAMMING—DIRECTING: Gene Lasko, "W. Eugene Smith—Photography Made Difficult," *American Masters* (PBS)

OUTSTANDING INDIVIDUAL ACHIEVEMENT IN CLASSICAL MUSIC/DANCE PROGRAMMING—PERFORMING: Katarina Witt, Brian Orser, and Brian Boitano, "Carmen on Ice" (HBO)

OUTSTANDING INDIVIDUAL ACHIEVEMENT IN CLASSICAL MUSIC/DANCE PROGRAMMING—DIRECTING: Peter Rosen, director; Alan Skog, director of concert performances, "The Eighth Van Cliburn International Piano Competition: How to Make Music" (PBS)

THIRTEENTH ANNUAL ATAS GOVERNOR'S AWARD: Leonard Goldenson

1990–1991 (PRESENTED AUGUST 25, 1991)

OUTSTANDING COMEDY SERIES: *Cheers,* James Burrows, Glen Charles, Les Charles, Cheri Eichen, Bill Steinkellner, and Phoef Sutton, executive producers; Tim Berry, producer; Andy Ackerman, Brian Poilack, Mert Rich, Dan O'Shannon, Tom Anderson, and Larry Balmagia, coproducers (NBC)

OUTSTANDING DRAMA SERIES: *L.A. Law,* David E. Kelley and Rick Wallace, executive producers; Patricia M. Green, supervising producer; Elodie Keene, James C. Hart, Alan Brennert, Robert M. Breech, and John Hill, producers; Alice West, coordinating producer (NBC)

OUTSTANDING VARIETY, MUSIC, OR COMEDY PROGRAM: "The 63rd Annual Academy Awards," Gilbert Gates, producer (ABC)

OUTSTANDING DRAMA/COMEDY SPECIAL OR MINI-SERIES: "Separate but Equal," George Stevens, Jr., and Stan Margulies, executive producers (ABC)

OUTSTANDING CLASSICAL PROGRAM IN THE PERFORMING ARTS: "The Tchaikovsky 150th Birthday Gala from Leningrad," Peter Gelb, executive producer; Helmut Rost, producer; Anne Cauvin and Laura Mitgang, coordination producers (PBS)

OUTSTANDING INFORMATIONAL SERIES: *The Civil War* (A General Motors Mark of Excellence Presentation). Ken Burns and Ric Burns, producers; Stephen Ives, Julie Dunfey, and Mike Hill, coproducers; Catherine Eisele, coordinating producer (PBS)

OUTSTANDING INFORMATIONAL SPECIAL: Edward R. Murrow: This Reporter," *American Masters,* Susan Lacy, executive producer; Susan Steinberg, producer; Elizabeth Kreutz and Harlene Freezer, coproducers (PBS)

OUTSTANDING CHILDREN'S PROGRAM: "You Can't Go Home Again: a 3-2-1 Contact Extra," Anne MacLead, executive producer; Tom Cammisa, producer (PBS)

OUTSTANDING ANIMATED PROGRAM: *The Simpsons* (series), James L. Brooks, Matt Groening, and Sam Simon, executive producers; Al Jean and Mike Reiss, supervising producers; Jay Kogen, Wallace Wolodarsky, Richard Sakai, and Larina Jean Adamson, producers; George Meyer, coproducer; Gabor Csupo, executive animation producer; Sherry Gunther, animation producer; Steve Pepoon, writer; Rich Moore, director (FOX)

OUTSTANDING LEAD ACTOR IN A DRAMA SERIES: James Earl Jones, *Gabriel's Fire* (ABC)

OUTSTANDING LEAD ACTOR IN A COMEDY SERIES: Burt Reynolds, *Evening Shade* (CBS)

OUSTANDING LEAD ACTOR IN A MINI-SERIES OR SPECIAL: John Gielgud, "Summer's Lease," *Masterpiece Theatre* (PBS)

OUTSTANDING LEAD ACTRESS IN A DRAMA SERIES: Patricia Wettig, *thirtysomething* (ABC)

OUTSTANDING LEAD ACTRESS IN A COMEDY SERIES: Kirstie Alley, *Cheers* (NBC)

OUTSTANDING LEAD ACTRESS IN A MINI-SERIES OR SPECIAL: Lynn Whitfield, "The Josephine Baker Story" (HBO)

OUTSTANDING SUPPORTING ACTOR IN A DRAMA SERIES: Timothy Busfleld, *thirtysomething* (ABC)

OUTSTANDING SUPPORTING ACTOR IN A COMEDY SERIES: Jonathan Winters, *Davis Rules* (ABC)

OUTSTANDING ACTOR IN A MINI-SERIES OR SPECIAL: James Earl Jones, "Heat Wave" (TNT)

OUTSTANDING SUPPORTING ACTRESS IN A DRAMA SERIES: Madge Sinclair, *Gabriel's Fire* (ABC)

OUTSTANDING SUPPORTING ACTRESS IN A COMEDY SERIES: Bebe Neuwirth, *Cheers* (NBC)

OUTSTANDING SUPPORTING ACTRESS IN A MINI-SERIES OR SPECIAL: Ruby Dee, "Decoration Day," *Hallmark Hall of Fame* (CBS)

OUTSTANDING INDIVIDUAL PERFORMANCE IN A VARIETY OR MUSIC PROGRAM: Billy Crystal "The 63rd Annual Academy Awards" (ABC)

OUTSTANDING GUEST ACTOR IN A DRAMA SERIES: David Opatoshu, "A Prayer for the Goldsteins," *Gabriel's Fire* (ABC)

OUTSTANDING GUEST ACTOR IN A COMEDY SERIES: Jay Thomas, "Gold Rush," *Murphy Brown* (CBS)

OUTSTANDING GUEST ACTRESS IN A DRAMA SERIES: Peggy McCay, "State of Mind," *The Trials of Rosie O'Neill* (CBS)

OUTSTANDING GUEST ACTRESS IN A COMEDY SERIES: Colleen Dewhurst, "Bob and Murphy and Ted and Avery," *Murphy Brown* (CBS)

OUTSTANDING DIRECTING IN A DRAMA SERIES (SINGLE EPISODE): Thomas Carter, "in Confidence," *Equal Justice* (ABC)

OUTSTANDING DIRECTING IN A COMEDY SERIES (SINGLE EPISODE): James Burrows, "Woody Interruptus," *Cheers* (NBC)

OUTSTANDING DIRECTING IN A MINI-SERIES OR A SPECIAL: Brian Gibson, "The Josephine Baker Story" (HBO)

OUTSTANDING DIRECTING IN A VARIETY OR MUSIC PROGRAM: Hal Gurnee, Show 1425, *Late Night with David Letterman,* (NBC)

OUTSTANDING WRITING IN A DRAMA SERIES (SINGLE EPISODE): David E. Kelley, "On the Road Again," *L.A. Law* (NBC)

OUTSTANDING WRITING IN A COMEDY SERIES (SINGLE EPISODE): Gary Dontzig and Steven Peterman, "Jingle Hell, Jingle Hell, Jingle All the Way," *Murphy Brown* (CBS)

OUTSTANDING WRITING IN A MINI-SERIES OR A SPECIAL: Andrew Davies, "House of Cards," *Masterpiece Theatre* (PBS)

OUTSTANDING WRITING IN A VARIETY OR MUSIC PROGRAM: Hal Kanter, Buz Kohan, Billy Crystal, David Steinberg. Bruce Vilanch, and Robert Wuhl, "The 63rd Annual Academy Awards" (ABC)

OUTSTANDING INDIVIDUAL ACHIEVEMENT IN INFORMATIONAL PROGRAMMING—WRITING: Geoffrey C. Wand, Ric Burns, and Ken Burns, "The Better Angels of Our Nature," *The Civil War* (PBS); Todd McCarthy, "Preston Sturges: The Rise and Fall of an American Dreamer," *American Masters* (PBS)

OUTSTANDING INDIVIDUAL ACHIEVEMENT IN INFORMATIONAL PROGRAMMING—DIRECTING: Peter Gelb, Susan Froernke, Albert Maysles, and Bob Eisenhardt, "Soldiers of Music: Rostropovich Returns to Russia" (PBS)

OUTSTANDING INDIVIDUAL ACHIEVEMENT IN CLASSICAL MUSIC/DANCE PROGRAMMING—PERFORMING: Kurt Mall, "The Rine of the Nibelungs," *The Metropolitan Opera Presents* (PBS); Yo-Yo Ma, "Tchaikovsky 150th Birthday Gala from Leningrad" (PBS)

FOURTEENTH ANNUAL ATAS GOVERNOR'S AWARD: *Masterpiece Theatre* (PBS)

1991–1992 (PRESENTED AUGUST 30, 1992)

OUTSTANDING COMEDY SERIES: *Murphy Brown,* Diane English and Joel Shukovsky, executive producers; Steven Peterrnan and Gary Dontzig; supervising producers; Tom Palmer, cosupervising producer; Korby Siarnis, consulting producer; Deborah Smith, producer; Peter Tolan, coproducer (CBS)

OUTSTANDING DRAMA SERIES: *Northern Exposure,* Joshua Brand and John Falsey, executive producers; Andrew Schneider, coexecutive producer; Diane Frolov, Jeff Melvoin, Cheryl Bloch, and Robin Green, supervising producers; Matthew Nodella and Rob Thompson, producers (CBS)

OUTSTANDING VARIETY, MUSIC, OR COMEDY PROGRAM: *The Tonight Show Starring Johnny Carson,* Fred De Cordova and Peter Lassally, executive producers; Jeff Sotzing, producer; Jim McCawley, coproducer; Johnny Carson, host (NBC)

OUTSTANDING MINI-SERIES: "A Woman Named Jackie," Lester Persky, executive producer; Lorin Bennett Salob. producer, Tomlinson Dean, coproducer (NBC)

OUTSTANDING MADE-FOR-TELEVISION MOVIE: "Miss Rose White," *Hallmark Hall of Fame,* Marian Rees, executive producer; Andrea Baynes and Francine LeFrak, coexecutive producers; Anne Hopkins, producer (NBC)

OUTSTANDING CLASSICAL PROGRAM IN THE PERFORMING ARTS: "Perlman in Russia," Robert Dakymple, producer; Itzhak Perlman, performer (PBS)

OUTSTANDING INFORMATIONAL SERIES: *MGM: When the Lion Roars,* Joni Levin, producer (TNT)

OUTSTANDING INFORMATIONAL SPECIAL: "Abortion: Desperate Choices," Susan Froemke, executive producer (HBO)

OUTSTANDING CHILDREN'S PROGRAM: "Mark Twain and Me," Geoffrey Cowan and Julian Fowles, executive producers; Daniel Petnie, producer (The Disney Channel)

OUTSTANDING ANIMATED PROGRAM: "A Claymation Easter," Will Vinton, executive producer; Paul Diener, producer; Mark Gustafson, director-writer; Barry Bruce and Ryan Holznagel, writers (CBS)

OUTSTANDING LEAD ACTOR IN A DRAMA SERIES: Christopher Lloyd, *Avonlea* (The Disney Channel)

OUTSTANDING LEAD ACTOR IN A COMEDY SERIES: Craig T. Nelson, *Coach* (ABC)

OUTSTANDING LEAD ACTOR IN A MINI-SERIES OR SPECIAL: Beau Bridges, "Without Warning: The James Brady Story" (HBO)

OUTSTANDING LEAD ACTRESS IN A DRAMA SERIES: Dana Delany, *China Beach* (ABC)

OUTSTANDING LEAD ACTRESS IN A COMEDY SERIES: Candice Bergen, *Murphy Brown* (CBS)

OUTSTANDING LEAD ACTRESS IN A MINI-SERIES OR SPECIAL: Gena Rowlands, "Faces of a Stranger" (CBS)

OUTSTANDING SUPPORTING ACTOR IN A DRAMA SERIES: Richard Dysart, *L.A. Law* (NBC)

OUTSTANDING SUPPORTING ACTOR IN A COMEDY SERIES: Michael Jeeter, *Evening Shade* (CBS)

OUTSTANDING SUPPORTING ACTOR IN A MINI-SERIES OR SPECIAL: Hume Cronyn, "Broadway Bound" (ABC)

OUTSTANDING SUPPORTING ACTRESS IN A DRAMA SERIES: Valerie Malhiaffey, *Northern Exposure* (CBS)

OUTSTANDING SUPPORTING ACTRESS IN A COMEDY SERIES: Laurie Metcalf, *Roseanne* (ABC)

OUTSTANDING SUPPORTING ACTRESS IN A MINI-SERIES OR SPECIAL: Amanda Plummer, "Miss Rose White," *Hallmark Hall of Fame* (NBC)

OUTSTANDING INDIVIDUAL PERFORMANCE IN A VARIETY OR MUSIC PROGRAM: Bette Midler, performer, *The Tonight Show Starring Johnny Carson* (NBC)

OUTSTANDING VOICEOVER PERFORMANCE: Nancy Cartwright, Jackie Mason, Julie Kavner, Yeardley Smith, Marcia Wallace, and Dan Castellaneta, *The Simpsons* (FOX)

OUTSTANDING DIRECTING IN A DRAMA SERIES (SINGLE EPISODE): Eric Laneuville, "All God's Children," *I'll Fly Away* (NBC)

OUTSTANDING DIRECTING IN A COMEDY SERIES (SINGLE EPISODE): Barnet Kellman, "Birth 101," *Murphy Brown* (CBS)

OUTSTANDING DIRECTING IN A MINI-SERIES OR A SPECIAL: Joseph Sargent, "Miss Rose White," *Hallmark Hall of Fame* (NBC)

OUTSTANDING DIRECTING IN A VARIETY OR MUSIC PROGRAM: Patricia Birch, "Unforgettable, with Love: Natalie Cole Sings the Songs of Nat King Cole," *Great Performances* (PBS)

OUTSTANDING WRITING IN A DRAMA SERIES (SINGLE EPISODE): Andrew Schneider and Diane Frolov, "Seoul Mates," *Northern Exposure* (CBS)

OUTSTANDING WRITING IN A COMEDY SERIES (SINGLE EPISODE): Elaine Pope and Larry Charles, "The Fix Up," *Seinfeld* (NBC)

OUTSTANDING WRITING IN A MINI-SERIES OR A SPECIAL: Joshua Brand and John Falsey, pilot, *I'll Fly Away* (NBC)

OUTSTANDING WRITING IN A VARIETY OR MUSIC PROGRAM: Hal Kanter, Buz Kohan, Billy Crystal, Mark Shairnan, David Steinberg, Bruce Vilanch, and Robert Wuhl, "The 64th Annual Academy Awards" (ABC)

OUTSTANDING INDIVIDUAL ACHIEVEMENT IN INFORMATIONAL PROGRAMMING—DIRECTING: George Hickenlooper, Fax Balm, and Eleanor Coppola, "Hearts of Darkness: A Filmmaker's Apocalypse" (Showtime)

OUTSTANDING INDIVIDUAL ACHIEVEMENT IN CLASSICAL MUSIC/DANCE PROGRAMMING—PERFORMING: Placido Domingo and Kathleen Battle, "The Metropolitan Opera Silver Anniversary Gala" (PBS)

OUTSTANDING INDIVIDUAL ACHIEVEMENT IN CLASSICAL MUSIC/DANCE PROGRAMMING—DIRECTING: Brian Large, "The Metropolitan Opera Silver Anniversary Gala" (PBS)

FIFTEENTH ANNUAL ATAS GOVERNOR'S AWARD: R. E. "Ted" Turner

1992–1993 (PRESENTED SEPTEMBER 19, 1993)

OUTSTANDING COMEDY SERIES: *Seinfeld,* Larry David, Andrew Sheinman, George Shapiro, and Howard West, executive producers; Larry Charles and Tom Cherones, supervising producers; Jerry Seinfeld, producer; Joan Van Horn, line producer; Tim Kaiser, coordinating producer (NBC)

OUTSTANDING DRAMA SERIES: *Picket Fences,* David E. Kelley, executive producer; Michael Pressman, coexecutive producer; Alice West, senior producer; Robert Breech and Mark B. Perry, producers; Jonathan Pontell, coproducer (CBS)

OUTSTANDING VARIETY, MUSIC, OR COMEDY SE-RIES: *Saturday Night Live,* Lorne Michaels, executive producer; James Downey and Al Franken, producers (NBC)

OUTSTANDING VARIETY, MUSIC, OR COMEDY SPECIAL: "Bob Hope: The First 90 Years," Linda Hope, executive producer; Nancy Malone, supervising producer; Don Mischen, producer (NBC)

OUTSTANDING MINI-SERIES: "Prime Suspect 2," *Mystery!,* Sally Head, executive producer; Paul Marcus, producer (PBS)

OUTSTANDING MADE-FOR-TELEVISION MOVIE: "Barbarians at the Gate," Thomas M. Hammel and Glenn Jordan, executive producers; Ray Stark, producer; Marykay Powell, coproducer (HBO); "Stalin," Mark Calmer, producer; Don West, line producer; Ilene Kahn, coproducer (HBO)

OUTSTANDING CLASSICAL PROGRAM IN THE PER-FORMING ARTS: "Tosca in the Settings and at the Times of Tosca," Ronda Rassimov, executive producer; Andrea Andermann, producer; Zubin Mehta, conductor (PBS)

OUTSTANDING INFORMATIONAL SERIES: *Healing and the Mind with Bill Moyers,* David Grubin, executive producer; Alice Markowitz, producer; Bill Moyers, editorial producer/host; Judith Davidson Moyers, editorial producer (PBS)

OUTSTANDING INFORMATIONAL SPECIAL: "Lucy and Desi: A Home Movie," Lucie Arnaz and Laurence Luckinbile, executive producers; Don Buford, producer (NBC)

OUTSTANDING CHILDREN'S PROGRAM: *Avonlea,* Kevin Sullivan and Trudy Grant, executive producers; Brian Leslie Parker, line producer (The Disney Channel); "Beethoven Lives Upstairs," Terence E. Robinson, executive producer; David Devine and Richard Moser, producers (HBO)

OUTSTANDING ANIMATED PROGRAM: *Batman: The Series,* Jean H. MacCurdy and Tom Ruegger, executive producers; Alan Burnett, Eric Radomski, and Bruce W. Timm, producers; Randy Rogel, writer; Dick Sebast, director (FOX)

OUTSTANDING LEAD ACTOR IN A DRAMA SERIES: Tom Skerritt, *Picket Fences* (CBS)

OUTSTANDING LEAD ACTOR IN A COMEDY SE-RIES: Ted Danson, *Cheers* (NBC)

OUTSTANDING LEAD ACTOR IN A MINI-SERIES OR SPECIAL: Robert Morse, "Tru," *American Playhouse* (PBS)

OUTSTANDING LEAD ACTRESS IN A DRAMA SE-RIES: Kathy Baker, *Picket Fences* (CBS)

OUTSTANDING LEAD ACTRESS IN A COMEDY SE-RIES: Roseanne Arnold, *Roseanne* (ABC)

OUTSTANDING LEAD ACTRESS IN A MINI-SERIES OR SPECIAL: Holly Hunter, "The Positively True Adventures of the Alleged Texas Cheerleader-Murdering Mom" (HBO)

OUTSTANDING SUPPORTING ACTOR IN A DRAMA SERIES: Chad Lowe, *Life Goes On* (ABC)

OUTSTANDING SUPPORTING ACTOR IN A COM-EDY SERIES: Michael Richards, *Seinfeld* (NBC)

OUTSTANDING SUPPORTING ACTOR IN A MINI-SERIES OR SPECIAL: Beau Bridges, "The Positively True Adventures of the Alleged Texas Cheerleader-Murdering Mom" (HBO)

OUTSTANDING SUPPORTING ACTRESS IN A DRAMA SERIES: Mary Alice, *I'll Fly Away* (NBC)

OUTSTANDING SUPPORTING ACTRESS IN A COM-EDY SERIES: Laurie Metcalf, *Roseanne* (ABC)

OUTSTANDING SUPPORTING ACTRESS IN A MINI-SERIES OR SPECIAL: Mary Tyler Moore, "Stolen Babies" (Lifetime)

OUTSTANDING INDIVIDUAL PERFORMANCE IN A VARIETY OR MUSIC PROGRAM: Dana Carvey, "Saturday Night Live's Presidential Bash," *Saturday Night Live* (NBC)

OUTSTANDING GUEST ACTOR IN A DRAMA SERIES: Laurence Fishburne, "The Box," *Tribeca* (FOX)

OUTSTANDING GUEST ACTOR IN A COMEDY SE-RIES: David Clennon, "For Peter's Sake," *Dream On* (HBO)

OUTSTANDING GUEST ACTRESS IN A DRAMA SE-RIES: Elaine Stritch, "Point of View" *Law & Order* (NBC)

OUTSTANDING GUEST ACTRESS IN A COMEDY SE-RIES: Tracey Ullman, "The Prima Dava," *Love & War* (CBS)

OUTSTANDING VOICEOVER PERFORMANCE: Dan Castellaneta, *The Simpsons* (FOX)

OUTSTANDING DIRECTING IN A DRAMA SERIES (SINGLE EPISODE): Barry Levinson, "Gone for Goode," *Homicide—Life on the Street* (NBC)

OUTSTANDING DIRECTING IN A COMEDY SERIES (SINGLE EPISODE): Betty Thomas, "For Peter's Sake," *Dream On* (HBO)

OUTSTANDING DIRECTING IN A MINI-SERIES OR A SPECIAL: James Sadwith, "Sinatra" (CBS)

OUTSTANDING DIRECTING IN A VARIETY OR MUSIC PROGRAM: Walter C. Miller, "The 1992 Tony Awards" (CBS)

OUTSTANDING WRITING IN A DRAMA SERIES (SINGLE EPISODE): Tom Fontana, "Three Men and Adena," *Homicide—Life on the Street* (NBC)

OUTSTANDING WRITING IN A COMEDY SERIES (SINGLE EPISODE): Larry David, "The Contest," *Seinfeld* (NBC)

OUTSTANDING WRITING IN A MINI-SERIES OR A SPECIAL: Jane Anderson, "The Positively True Adventures of the Alleged Texas Cheerleader-Murdering Mom" (HBO)

OUTSTANDING WRITING IN A VARIETY OR MUSIC PROGRAM: Judd Apatow, Robert Cohen, David Cross, Brent Forrester. Jeff Kahn, Bruce Kirshbaum, Bob Odenkirk, Sultan Pepper, D. Stamatopoulos, and Ben Stiller, *The Ben Stiller Show* (FOX)

OUTSTANDING INDIVIDUAL ACHIEVEMENT IN INFORMATIONAL PROGRAMMING—HOST: Audrey Hepburn, "Flower Gardens," *Gardens of the World* (PBS)

OUTSTANDING INDIVIDUAL ACHIEVEMENT IN INFORMATIONAL PROGRAMMING—DIRECTING: Lee Stanley, "Gridiron Gano" (syndicated)

OUTSTANDING INDIVIDUAL ACHIEVEMENT IN CLASSICAL MUSIC/DANCE PROGRAMMING—PERFORMING: Catherine Malfitano "Tosca in the Settings and at the Times of Tosca" (PBS)

OUTSTANDING INDIVIDUAL ACHIEVEMENT IN CLASSICAL MUSIC/DANCE PROGRAMMING—DIRECTING: Guiseppe Patroni Griffi and Brian Large, "Tosca in the Settings and at the Times of Tosca" (PBS)

1993–1994 (PRESENTED SEPTEMBER 11, 1994)

OUTSTANDING COMEDY SERIES: *Frasier,* Peter Casey, David Angell, and David Lee, executive producers; Christopher Lloyd, coexecutive producer; Denise Moss and Sy Dukane, supervising producers; Maggie Randell, producer; Linda Morris and Vic Rauseo, consulting producers (NBC)

OUTSTANDING DRAMA SERIES: *Picket Fences,* David E. Kelley, executive producer; Michael Pressman, coexecutive producer; Alice West, senior producer; Robert Breech and Aria Donahue, producers; Jonathan Pontell and Geoffrey Neigher, coproducers; Jack Phulbrick, coordinating producer (CBS)

OUTSTANDING VARIETY, MUSIC, OR COMEDY SERIES: *Late Show with David Letterman,* Peter Lassally and Robert Morton, executive producers; Hal Gurnee, supervising producer; Jude Brennan, producer; David Letterman, host (CBS)

OUTSTANDING VARIETY, MUSIC, OR COMEDY SPECIAL: "The Kennedy Center Honors," George Stevens, Jr., and Don Mischer, producers (CBS)

OUTSTANDING MINI-SERIES: "Prime Suspect 3," *Mystery!,* Sally Head, executive producer; Paul Marcus, producer (PBS)

OUTSTANDING MADE-FOR-TELEVISION MOVIE: "And the Band Played On," Aaron Spelling and E. Duke Vincent, executive producers; Midge Sanford and Sarah Pillsbury, producers (HBO)

OUTSTANDING CULTURAL PROGRAM: "Vladimir Horowitz: A Reminiscence," Peter Gelb, executive producer; Pat Jaffe, producer (PBS)

OUTSTANDING INFORMATIONAL SERIES: *Later with Bob Costas,* Lou Del Prete and Matthew McArthy, executive producers; Fred Rothenberg and Bruce Cornblatt, senior producers; Michael L. Weinberg, producer; Bob Costas. host (NBC)

OUTSTANDING INFORMATIONAL SPECIAL: "I Am a Promise: The Children of Stanton Street Elementary School," Alan Raymond and Susan Raymond, producers (HBO)

OUTSTANDING CHILDREN'S PROGRAM: "Kids Killing Kids/Kids Saving Kids," Arnold Shapiro, executive producer: David J. Eagle and Kerry Neal, producers; Norman Macus and Michael Killen, coproducers (CBS and FOX)

OUTSTANDING ANIMATED PROGRAM: "The Roman City," Bob Kurtz, producer-director-writer; Mark Olshaker, writer (PBS)

OUTSTANDING LEAD ACTOR IN A DRAMA SERIES: Dennis Franz, *NYPD Blue* (ABC)

OUTSTANDING LEAD ACTOR IN A COMEDY SERIES: Kelsey Grammer, *Frasier* (NBC)

OUTSTANDING LEAD ACTOR IN A MINI-SERIES OR SPECIAL: Hume Cronyn, "To Dance with the White Dog," *Hallmark Hall of Fame* (CBS)

OUTSTANDING LEAD ACTRESS IN A DRAMA SERIES: Sela Ward, *Sisters* (NBC)

OUTSTANDING LEAD ACTRESS IN A COMEDY SERIES: Candice Bergen, *Murphy Brown* (CBS)

OUTSTANDING LEAD ACTRESS IN A MINI-SERIES OR SPECIAL: Kirstie Alley, "David's Mother" (CBS)

OUTSTANDING SUPPORTING ACTOR IN A DRAMA SERIES: Fyvush Finkel, *Picket Fences* (CBS)

OUTSTANDING SUPPORTING ACTOR IN A COMEDY SERIES: Michael Richards, *Seinfeld* (NBC)

OUTSTANDING SUPPORTING ACTOR IN A MINI-SERIES OR SPECIAL: Michael Goorjian, "David's Mother" (CBS)

OUTSTANDING SUPPORTING ACTRESS IN A DRAMA SERIES: Leigh Taylor-Young *Picket Fences* (CBS)

OUTSTANDING SUPPORTING ACTRESS IN A COMEDY SERIES: Laurie Metcalf, *Roseanne* (ABC)

OUTSTANDING SUPPORTING ACTRESS IN A MINI-SERIES OR SPECIAL: Cicely Tyson, "Oldest Living Confederate Widow Tells All" (CBS)

OUTSTANDING INDIVIDUAL PERFORMANCE IN A VARIETY OR MUSIC PROGRAM: Tracey Ullman, "Tracey Ullman Takes on New York" (HBO)

OUTSTANDING GUEST ACTOR IN A DRAMA SERIES: Richard Kiley, "Buried Alive," *Picket Fences* (CBS)

OUTSTANDING GUEST ACTOR IN A COMEDY SERIES: Martin Sheen, "Angst for the Memories," *Murphy Brown* (CBS)

OUTSTANDING GUEST ACTRESS IN A DRAMA SERIES: Faye Dunaway, "It's All in the Game," *Columbo* (ABC)

OUTSTANDING GUEST ACTRESS IN A COMEDY SERIES: Eileen Heckart, "You Make Me Feel So Young," *Love & War* (CBS)

OUTSTANDING VOICEOVER PERFORMANCE: Christopher Plummer, narrator, *Madeline* (The Family Channel)

OUTSTANDING DIRECTING IN A DRAMA SERIES (SINGLE EPISODE): Daniel Sackheim, "Tempest in a C-Cup," *NYPD Blue* (ABC)

OUTSTANDING DIRECTING IN A COMEDY SERIES (SINGLE EPISODE): James Burrows, "The Good Son," *Frasier* (NBC)

OUTSTANDING DIRECTING IN A MINI-SERIES OR SPECIAL: John Frankenheimer, "Against the Wall" (HBO)

OUTSTANDING DIRECTING IN A VARIETY OR MUSIC PROGRAM: Walter C. Miller, "The 1993 Tony Awards" (CBS)

OUTSTANDING WRITING IN A DRAMA SERIES (SINGLE EPISODE): Ann Biderman, "Steroid Roy," *NYPD Blue* (ABC)

OUTSTANDING WRITING IN A COMEDY SERIES (SINGLE EPISODE): David Angell, Peter Casey, and David Lee, "The Good Son," *Frasier* (NBC)

OUTSTANDING WRITING IN A MINI-SERIES OR SPECIAL: Bob Randall, "David's Mother" (CBS)

OUTSTANDING WRITING IN A VARIETY OR MUSIC PROGRAM: Jeff Cesario, Mike Dugan, Eddie Feldmann, Gregory Greenberg, Dennis Miller, and Kevin Rooney, *Dennis Miller Live* (HBO)

OUTSTANDING INDIVIDUAL ACHIEVEMENT IN INFORMATIONAL PROGRAMMING—NARRATOR: George Stevens, Jr., "George Stevens: D-Day to Berlin" (The Disney Channel)

OUTSTANDING INDIVIDUAL ACHIEVEMENT IN INFORMATIONAL PROGRAMMING—DIRECTING: Robin Leahman, "Cats & Dogs, Dogs Segment" (TBS)

OUTSTANDING INDIVIDUAL ACHIEVEMENT IN INFORMATIONAL PROGRAMMING—WRITING: George Stevens, Jr., "George Stevens: D-Day to Berlin" (The Disney Channel); Todd Robinson, "The Legend of Billy the Kid" (The Disney Channel); Dereck Joubert, "Reflections on Elephants" (PBS); Dennis Watlington, "The Untold West" and "The Black West" (TBS)

OUTSTANDING INDIVIDUAL ACHIEVEMENT IN CULTURAL PROGRAMMING—PERFORMING: Itzhak Perlman, violinist, "The Dvořák Concert from Prague: A Celebration" (PBS); Seiji Ozawa, conductor, "The Dvořák Concert from Prague: A Celebration" (PBS)

OUTSTANDING INDIVIDUAL ACHIEVEMENT IN CULTURAL PROGRAMMING—WRITING: Nuala O'Conner, "Irish Music and America . . . A Musical Migration" (The Disney Channel)

1994–1995 (PRESENTED SEPTEMBER 10, 1995)

OUTSTANDING COMEDY SERIES: *Frasier,* Peter Casey, David Angell, David Lee, and Christopher Lloyd, executive producers; Vic Rauseo and Linda Morris, coexecutive producers; Maggie Randell, Elias Davis, and David Pollock, producers; Chuck Ranberg, Anne Flett-Giordano, and Joe Keenan, coproducers (NBC)

OUTSTANDING DRAMA SERIES: *NYPD Blue,* Steven Bochco, David Much, Gregory Hoblit, and Mark Tinker, executive producers; Michael E. Robin, Walon Green, Charles H. Eglee, and Channing Gibson, coexecutive producers; Ted Mann, producer; Burton Armus, Gardner Stern, and Steven DePaul, coproducers; Robert Doherty, coordinating producer; Bill Clark, consulting producer (ABC)

OUTSTANDING VARIETY, MUSIC, OR COMEDY SERIES: *The Tonight Show with Jay Leno,* Debbie Vickers, executive producer; Larry Goita, line producer; Bill Royce, coproducer; Jay Leno, host (NBC)

OUTSTANDING VARIETY, MUSIC, OR COMEDY SPECIAL: "Barbra Streisand: The Concert," Martin Enlichman and Gay Smith, executive producers; Barbra Streisand and Dwight Hemion, producers (HBO)

OUTSTANDING MINI-SERIES: "Joseph," Gerald Rafshoon, executive producer; Lorenzo Minoli, producer; Laura Fattori, line producer (TNT)

OUTSTANDING MADE-FOR-TELEVISION MOVIE: "Indictment: The McMartin Trial," Oliver Stone, Janet Yang, and Abby Mann, executive producers; Diana Pokorny, producer (HBO)

OUTSTANDING CULTURAL PROGRAM: "Verdi's *La Traviata* with the New York City Opera," *Live from Lincoln Center,* John Goberman, producer; Marc Bauman, coordinating producer (PBS)

OUTSTANDING INFORMATIONAL SERIES: *Baseball: A General Motors Mark of Excellence Production,* Ken Burns, producer-director; Lynn Novick, producer; Geoffrey C. Ward and Ken Bums, writers; John Chancellor, narrator (PBS); *TV Nation,* Michael Moore, executive producer-director-writer-host; Kathleen Glynn, producer; Jerry Kupfer, supervising producer; Eric Zicklin, Stephen Sherrill, Chris Kelly, and Randy Cohen, writers (NBC)

OUTSTANDING INFORMATIONAL SPECIAL: "Taxicab Confessions," Sheila Nevins, executive producer; Joe Gantz and Harry Gantz, producer-directors (HBO); "The United States Holocaust Memorial Museum Presents: One Survivor Remembers," Kay Antholis, producer; Sheila Nevins, senior producer; Michael Berenbaum and Raye Far, coproducers (HBO)

OUTSTANDING CHILDREN'S PROGRAM: "The World Wildlife Fund Presents 'Going, Going, Almost Gone! Animals in Danger,'" Sheila Nevins, executive producer; Ellen Goosenberg Kent, producer; Carole Rosen, senior producer; Amy Schatz, coproducer (HBO)

OUTSTANDING ANIMATED PROGRAM: *The Simpsons,* David Mirkin, James L. Brooks, Mali Groening, and Sam Simon, executive producers; lace Richdale, George Meyer, J. Michael Mendel, Greg Daniels, Bill Oakley, David Sacks, Josh Weinstein, Jonathan Collier, Richard Raynis, Richard Sakai, Mike Scully, and David Silverman, producers; Al Jean and Mike Reiss, consulting producers; Phil Roman, animation executive producer; Bill Schultz and Michael Wolf, animation producers; Greg Daniels, writing; Jim Reardon, director (FOX)

OUTSTANDING LEAD ACTOR IN A DRAMA SERIES: Mandy Patinken, *Chicago Hope* (CBS)

OUTSTANDING LEAD ACTOR IN A COMEDY SERIES: Kelsey Grammer, *Frasier* (NBC)

OUTSTANDING LEAD ACTOR IN A MINI-SERIES OR SPECIAL: Raul Julia, "The Burning Season" (HBO)

OUTSTANDING LEAD ACTRESS IN A DRAMA SERIES: Kathy Baker, *Picket Fences* (CBS)

OUTSTANDING LEAD ACTRESS IN A COMEDY SERIES: Candice Bergen, *Murphy Brown* (CBS)

OUTSTANDING LEAD ACTRESS IN A MINI-SERIES OR SPECIAL: Glenn Close, "Serving in Silence: The Margarethe Cammermeyer Story" (NBC)

OUTSTANDING SUPPORTING ACTOR IN A DRAMA SERIES: Ray Walston, *Picket Fences* (CBS)

OUTSTANDING SUPPORTING ACTOR IN A COMEDY SERIES: David Hyde Pierce, *Frasier* (NBC)

OUTSTANDING SUPPORTING ACTOR IN A MINI-SERIES OR SPECIAL: Donald Sutherland, "Citizen X" (HBO)

OUTSTANDING SUPPORTING ACTRESS IN A DRAMA SERIES: Julianna Margulies, *ER* (NBC)

OUTSTANDING SUPPORTING ACTRESS IN A COMEDY SERIES: Christine Baranski, *Cybill* (CBS)

OUTSTANDING SUPPORTING ACTRESS IN A MINI-SERIES OR SPECIAL: Judy Davis, "Serving in Silence: The Margarethe Cammermeyer Story" (NBC); Shirley Knight, "Indictment: The McMartin Trial" (HBO)

OUTSTANDING INDIVIDUAL PERFORMANCE IN A VARIETY OR MUSIC PROGRAM: Barbra Streisand, "Barbra Streisand: The Concert" (HBO)

OUTSTANDING GUEST ACTOR IN A DRAMA SERIES: Paul Winfield, "Enemy Lines," *Picket Fences* (CBS)

OUTSTANDING GUEST ACTOR IN A COMEDY SERIES: Carl Reiner, "The Alan Brady Show," *Mad About You* (NBC)

OUTSTANDING GUEST ACTRESS IN A DRAMA SERIES: Shirley Knight, "Large Mouth Bass," *NYPD Blue* (ABC)

OUTSTANDING GUEST ACTRESS IN A COMEDY SERIES: Cyndi Lauper, "Money Changes Everything," *Mad About You* (NBC)

OUTSTANDING VOICE-OVER PERFORMANCE: Jonathan Katz, "Dr. Katz Professional Therapist," (Comedy Central)

OUTSTANDING DIRECTING IN A DRAMA SERIES (SINGLE EPISODE): Mimi Leder, "Love's Labor Lost," *ER* (NBC)

OUTSTANDING DIRECTING IN A COMEDY SERIES (SINGLE EPISODE): David Lee, "The Matchmaker," *Frasier* (NBC)

OUTSTANDING DIRECTING IN A MINI-SERIES OR A SPECIAL: John Frankenheimer, "The Burning Season" (HBO)

OUTSTANDING DIRECTING IN A VARIETY OR MUSIC PROGRAM: Jeff Margolis, "The 67th Annual Academy Awards" (ABC)

OUTSTANDING WRITING IN A DRAMA SERIES (SINGLE EPISODE): Lance A. Gentile, "Love's Labor Lost," *ER* (NBC)

OUTSTANDING WRITING IN A COMEDY SERIES (SINGLE EPISODE): Chuck Ranberg and Anne Flett-Giordano, "An Affair to Forget," *Frasier* (NBC)

OUTSTANDING WRITING IN A MINI-SERIES OR A SPECIAL: Alison Cross, "Serving in Silence: The Margarethe Cammermeyer Story" (NBC)

OUTSTANDING WRITING IN A VARIETY OR MUSIC PROGRAM: Eddie Feldmann, writing supervisor; Jeff Cesario, Ed Driscoll, David Feldman, Gregory Greenberg, Dennis Miller, and Kevin Rooney, writers, *Dennis Miller Live* (HBO)

OUTSTANDING INDIVIDUAL ACHIEVEMENT IN CULTURAL PROGRAMMING—DIRECTING: David Hinton, "Two By Dove," *Great Performances, Dance in America* (PBS)

1995–1996 (PRESENTED SEPTEMBER 8, 1996)

OUTSTANDING COMEDY SERIES: *Frasier,* Peter Casey, David Angell, David Lee, Christopher Lloyd, Vic Rauseo, and Linda Morris, executive producers; Steven Levitan, coexecutive producer; Maggie Randell, Chuck Ranberg and Anne Flett-Giordano, producers; Joe Keenan, Jack Burditt, and Mary Fukuto, coproducers (NBC)

OUTSTANDING DRAMA SERIES: *ER,* John Wells and Michael Crichton, executive producers; Carol Flint, Mimi Leder. and Lydia Woodward, coexecutive producers; Chris Chulack, producer; Paul Manning, supervising producer; Wendy Spence, coproducer (NBC)

OUTSTANDING VARIETY, MUSIC, OR COMEDY SERIES: *Dennis Miller Live,* Dennis Miller, executive producer/host Kevin C. Slattery, executive producer; Eddie Feldmann, producer (HBO)

OUTSTANDING VARIETY, MUSIC, OR COMEDY SPECIAL: "The Kennedy Center Honors," George Stevens, Jr., and Don Mischer, producers (CBS)

OUTSTANDING MINI-SERIES: "Gulliver's Travels," Robert Halmi, Sr., and Brian Henson, executive producers; Duncan Kenworthy, producer (NBC)

OUTSTANDING MADE-FOR-TELEVISION MOVIE: "Truman," Paula Weinstein and Anthea Sylbert, executive producers: Doro Bachrach, producer (HBO)

OUTSTANDING CULTURAL MUSIC-DANCE PROGRAM: "Itzhak Perlman: In the Fiddler's House," *Great Performances,* Jac Venza, executive producer; Glenn DuBose, executive producer/codirector; James Arntz, producer/writer: Bill Murphy, coordinating producer; Sara Lukinson, producer/writer; Don Lenzer, codirector; Itzhak Perlman, performer (PBS)

OUTSTANDING INFORMATIONAL SERIES: *Time Life's Lost Civilizations,* Joel Westbrook, executive producer; Jason Williams, producer; Robert Gardner; producer/director/writer; William Morgan, coordinating producer; Ed Fields, writer; Sam Waterston, host (NBC)

OUTSTANDING INFORMATIONAL SPECIAL: "Survivors of the Holocaust," Pat Mitchell, executive producer; Vivian Schiller, senior producer; June Beallor and James Moll, producers; Jacoba Atlas, supervising producer; Allan Holzman, director (TBS)

OUTSTANDING CHILDREN'S PROGRAM: "Peter and the Wolf," George Daugherty, executive producer; David Wong, coexecutive producer; Linda Jones Clough and Adrian Workman, producers; Christine Losecast, coproducer (ABC)

OUTSTANDING ANIMATED PROGRAM: "A Pinky & the Brain Christmas Special," Steven Spielberg, executive producen Tom Ruegger, senior producer; Peter Hastings, producer/writer; Rusty Mills, producer/director (WB)

OUTSTANDING LEAD ACTOR IN A DRAMA SERIES: Dennis Franz, *NYPD Blue* (ABC)

OUTSTANDING LEAD ACTOR IN A COMEDY SERIES: John Lithgow, *3rd Rock from the Sun* (NBC)

OUTSTANDING LEAD ACTOR IN A MINISERIES OR SPECIAL: Alan Rickman, "Rasputin" (HBO)

OUTSTANDING LEAD ACTRESS IN A DRAMA SERIES: Kathy Baker, *Picket Fences* (CBS)

OUTSTANDING LEAD ACTRESS IN A COMEDY SERIES: Helen Hunt, *Mad About You* (NBC)

OUTSTANDING LEAD ACTRESS IN A MINI-SERIES OR SPECIAL: Helen Mirren, "Prime Suspect: Scent of Darkness" (PBS)

OUTSTANDING SUPPORTING ACTOR IN A DRAMA SERIES: Ray Walston, *Picket Fences* (CBS)

OUTSTANDING SUPPORTING ACTOR IN A COMEDY SERIES: Rip Torn, *The Larry Sanders Show* (NBC)

OUTSTANDING SUPPORTING ACTOR IN A MINI-SERIES OR SPECIAL: Tom Hulce, "The Heidi Chronicles" (TNT)

OUTSTANDING SUPPORTING ACTRESS IN A DRAMA SERIES: Tyne Daly, *Christy* (CBS)

OUTSTANDING SUPPORTING ACTRESS IN A COMEDY SERIES: Julia Louis-Dreyfus, *Seinfeld* (NBC)

OUTSTANDING SUPPORTING ACTRESS IN A MINI-SERIES OR SPECIAL: Greta Scacchi "Rasputin" (HBO)

OUTSTANDING INDIVIDUAL PERFORMANCE IN A VARIETY OR MUSIC PROGRAM: Tony Bennett, "Tony Bennett Live by Request: A Valentine Special" (A&E)

OUTSTANDING GUEST ACTOR IN A DRAMA SERIES: Peter Boyle, "Clyde Bruckman's Final Repose," *The X-Files* (FOX)

OUTSTANDING GUEST ACTOR IN A COMEDY SERIES: Tim Conway, "The Gardener," *Coach* (ABC)

OUTSTANDING GUEST ACTRESS IN A DRAMA SERIES: Amanda Plummer, "A Stitch in Time," *The Outer Limits* (Showtime)

OUTSTANDING GUEST ACTRESS IN A COMEDY SERIES: Betty White, "Here We Go Again," *The John Larroquette Show* (NBC)

OUTSTANDING DIRECTING IN A DRAMA SERIES (SINGLE EPISODE): Jeremy Kagan, "Leave of Absence," *Chicago Hope* (CBS)

OUTSTANDING DIRECTING IN A COMEDY SERIES (SINGLE EPISODE): Michael Lembeck, "The One After the Super Bowl," *Friends* (NBC)

OUTSTANDING DIRECTING IN A MINI-SERIES OR A SPECIAL: John Frankenheimer, *Andersonville* (TNT)

OUTSTANDING DIRECTING IN A VARIETY OR MUSIC PROGRAM: Louis I. Horvitz, "The Kennedy Center Honors" (CBS)

OUTSTANDING WRITING IN A DRAMA SERIES (SINGLE EPISODE): Darin Morgan, "Clyde Bruckman's Final Repose," *The X-Files* (FOX)

OUTSTANDING WRITING IN A COMEDY SERIES (SINGLE EPISODE): Joe Keenan, Christopher Lloyd, Rob Greenberg, Jack Burditt, Chuck Ranberg, Anne Flett-Giordano, Linda Morris, and Vic Rauseo, "Moon Dance," *Frasier* (NBC)

OUTSTANDING WRITING IN A MINI-SERIES OR A SPECIAL: Simon Moore, "Gulliver's Travels" (NBC)

OUTSTANDING WRITING IN A VARIETY OR MUSIC PROGRAM: Dennis Miller, Eddie Feldmann, David Feldman, Mike Candolfl, Tom Hertz, Leah Krinsky, and Rick Overton, *Dennis Miller Live* (HBO)

ATAS GOVERNORS AWARD "The Native American: Beyond the Legends, Beyond the Myths" (TBS); Erase the Hate Campaign (USA)

PRESIDENT'S AWARD: "Blacklist: Hollywood on Trial" (American Movie Classics)

1996–1997 (PRESENTED SEPTEMBER 14, 1997)

OUTSTANDING COMEDY SERIES: *Frasier*, Peter Casey, David Angell, David Lee, and Christopher Lloyd, executive producers; Chuck Ranberg, Anne Flett-Giordano, Joe Keenan, and Michael B. Kaplan, supervising producers; Maggie Randell, William Lucas Walker, and Suzanne Martin, producers; Rob Greenberg and Mary Fukuto, coproducers (NBC)

OUTSTANDING DRAMA SERIES: *Law & Order*, Dick Wolf, Rene Balcer, and Ed Sherin, executive producers; Ed Zuckerman, coexecutive producer; Arthur Forney and Gardner Stern, supervising producers; Jeffrey Hayes, Lewis H. Gould, and Billy Fox, producers; Jeremy R. Littman, coproducer (NBC)

OUTSTANDING VARIETY, MUSIC, OR COMEDY SERIES: *Tracey Takes On...*, Allan McKeown and Tracey Ullman, executive producers; Dick Clement and Ian La Frenais, supervising producers; Carey Dietrich, Thomas Schlamme, Robert Klane, Jenji Kohan, Molly Newman, and Gail Parent, producers; Allen J. Zipper, coordinating producer; Stephanie

Cone, associate producer; Jerry Belson, consulting producer (HBO)

OUTSTANDING VARIETY, MUSIC, OR COMEDY SPECIAL: "Chris Rock: Bring the Pain," Chris Rock, Michael Rotenberg, and Sandy Chanley, executive producers; Tom Bull, producer (HBO)

OUTSTANDING MINI-SERIES: "Prime Suspect 5: Errors of Judgment," Gub Neal and Rebecca Eaton, executive producers; Lynn Horsford, producer (PBS)

OUTSTANDING MADE-FOR-TELEVISION MOVIE: "Miss Evers' Boys," Robert Benedetti and Laurence Fishburne, executive producers; Kip Konwiser and Derek Kavanagh, producers; Peter Stelzer and Kern Konwiser coproducers (HBO)

OUTSTANDING CULTURAL MUSIC-DANCE PROGRAM: "*La Bohéme* with the New York City Opera," *Live from Lincoln Center,* John Goberman, producer; Marc Baumarn, coordinating producer (PBS)

OUTSTANDING INFORMATIONAL SERIES: *A&E Biography,* Michael Cascio, executive producer; Carol Ann Dolan, supervising producer; Diane Ferenczi, coordinating producer; Peter Graves and Jack Perkins, hosts (A&E); *The Great War and the Shaping of the 20th Century,* Elaine Baggett, executive producer-writer; Jay Winter, coproducer-writer; Carl Byker, producer-director-writer (PBS)

OUTSTANDING INFORMATIONAL SPECIAL: "Without Pity: A Film About Abilities," Sheila Nevins, executive producer; Michael Mierendorf, producer-director-writer; Jonathan Moss, coordinating producer; Christopher Reeve, narrator (HBO)

OUTSTANDING CHILDREN'S PROGRAM: "How Do You Spell God?" Sheila Nevins, executive producer; Carole Rosen, senior producer; Ellen Greenberg Kent and Amy Schatz, producers (HBO)

OUTSTANDING ANIMATED PROGRAM: "Homer's Phobia," *The Simpsons,* Bill Oakley, Josh Weinstein, Matt Groening, James L. Brooks, Sam Simon, Mike Scully, George Meyer, and Steve Tompkins, executive producers; Phil Roman, animation executive producer; Jonathan Collier, Ken Keeler, David S. Cohen, Richard Appel, J. Michael Mendel, Richard Raynis, David Silverman, Richard Sakai, Denise Sirkot, Cohn A.B.V. Lewis, David Mirkin, Ian Maxtonè-Graham, and Dan McGrath, producers; Bill Schultz and Michael Wolf, animation producers; Mike B. Anderson, director; Ron Hauge, writer (FOX)

OUTSTANDING LEAD ACTOR IN A DRAMA SERIES: Dennis Franz, *NYPD Blue* (ABC)

OUTSTANDING LEAD ACTOR IN A COMEDY SERIES: John Lithgow, *3rd Rock from the Sun* (NBC)

OUTSTANDING LEAD ACTOR IN A MINI-SERIES OR SPECIAL: Armand Assante, "Gotti" (HBO)

OUTSTANDING LEAD ACTRESS IN A DRAMA SERIES: Gillian Anderson, *The X-Files* (FOX)

OUTSTANDING LEAD ACTRESS IN A COMEDY SERIES: Helen Hunt, *Mad About You* (NBC)

OUTSTANDING LEAD ACTRESS IN A MINI-SERIES OR SPECIAL: Alfre Woodard, "Miss Evers' Boys" (HBO)

OUTSTANDING SUPPORTING ACTOR IN A DRAMA SERIES: Hector Elizondo, *Chicago Hope* (CBS)

OUTSTANDING SUPPORTING ACTOR IN A COMEDY SERIES: Michael Richards, *Seinfeld* (NBC)

OUTSTANDING SUPPORTING ACTOR IN A MINI-SERIES OR SPECIAL: Beau Bridges, "The Second Civil War" (HBO)

OUTSTANDING SUPPORTING ACTRESS IN A DRAMA SERIES: Kim Delaney, *NYPD Blue* (ABC)

OUTSTANDING SUPPORTING ACTRESS IN A COMEDY SERIES: Kristen Johnston, *3rd Rock from the Sun* (NBC)

OUTSTANDING SUPPORTING ACTRESS IN A MINI-SERIES OR SPECIAL Diana Rigg, "Rebecca" (PBS)

OUTSTANDING INDIVIDUAL PERFORMANCE IN A VARIETY OR MUSIC PROGRAM: Bette Midler, "Bette Midler: Diva Las Vegas" (HBO)

OUTSTANDING GUEST ACTOR IN A DRAMA SERIES: Pruitt Taylor Vince, *Murder One* (ABC)

OUTSTANDING GUEST ACTOR IN A COMEDY SERIES: Mel Brooks, *Mad About You* (NBC)

OUTSTANDING GUEST ACTRESS IN A DRAMA SERIES: Dianne Wiest, *Avonlea* (Disney Channel)

OUTSTANDING GUEST ACTRESS IN A COMEDY SERIES: Carol Burnett, *Mad About You* (NBC)

OUTSTANDING VOICE-OVER PERFORMANCE: Jeremy Irons as the voice of Siegfried Sassoon, "The Great War and the Shaping of the 20th Century" (PBS); Rik Mayall as the voice of the Toad, "The Willows in Winter" (The Family Channel)

OUTSTANDING DIRECTING IN A DRAMA SERIES (SINGLE EPISODE): Mark Tinker, "Where's Swaldo," *NYPD Blue* (ABC)

OUTSTANDING DIRECTING IN A COMEDY SERIES (SINGLE EPISODE): David Lee, "To Kill a Talking Bird," *Frasier* (NBC)

OUTSTANDING DIRECTING IN A MINI-SERIES OR A SPECIAL: Andrei Konochalovsky, *The Odyssey* Part I and Part II (NBC)

OUTSTANDING DIRECTING IN A VARIETY OR MUSIC PROGRAM: Don Mischer, "Centennial Olympic Games: Opening Ceremonies" (NBC)

OUTSTANDING WRITING IN A DRAMA SERIES (SINGLE EPISODE): David Milch, Stephen Gaghan, and Michael R. Perry, "Where's Swaldo," *NYPD Blue* (ABC)

OUTSTANDING WRITING IN A COMEDY SERIES (SINGLE EPISODE): Ellen DeGeneres, story; Mark Driscoll, Dava Savel, Tracy Newman, and Jonathan Stark, teleplay, "The Puppy Episode," *Ellen* (ABC)

OUTSTANDING WRITING IN A MINI-SERIES OR A SPECIAL: Horton Foote, teleplay, "William Faulkner's Old Man," *Hallmark Hall of Fame* (CBS)

OUTSTANDING WRITING IN A VARIETY OR MUSIC PROGRAM: Chris Rock, writer, "Chris Rock: Bring the Pain" (HBO)

OUTSTANDING INDIVIDUAL ACHIEVEMENT IN CULTURAL PROGRAMMING—PERFORMANCE: Pilobolus Dance Theatre Performers, "John F. Kennedy Center 25th Anniversary Celebration" (PBS)

THE PRESIDENT'S AWARD: "Miss Evers' Boys" (HBO)

1997–1998 (PRESENTED SEPTEMBER 13, 1998)

OUTSTANDING COMEDY SERIES: *Frasier*, Peter Casey, David Angell, David Lee, and Christopher Lloyd, executive producers; Joe Keenan, coexecutive producer; Jay Kogen and Jeffrey Richman, supervising producers; Maggie Randell, Suzanne Martin, Rob Greenberg, and David Lloyd, producers; Mary Fukuto and Lori Kirkland, coproducers (NBC)

OUTSTANDING DRAMA SERIES: *The Practice*, David E. Kelley, executive producer; Jeffrey Kramer, coexecutive producer; Robert Breech, supervising producer; Ed Redlich, Gary Strangis, Jonathan Pontell, and Alice West, producers; Pam Wisne and Christina Musrey, coproducers (ABC)

OUTSTANDING VARIETY, MUSIC, OR COMEDY SERIES: *Late Show with David Letterman*, Rob Burnett, executive producer; Barbara Gaines and Maria Pope, producers; Jon Beckerman, supervising producer (CBS)

OUTSTANDING VARIETY, MUSIC, OR COMEDY SPECIAL: "The 1997 Tony Awards," Gary Smith, executive producer; Walter C. Miller, producer; Roy A. Somlyo, supervising producer (CBS)

OUTSTANDING MINI-SERIES: "From the Earth to the Moon," Tom Hanks, executive producer; Brian Grazer, Ron Howard, and Michael Bostick, producers; Tony To, coexecutive producer; John Melft and Graham Yost, supervising producers; Janace Tashjian, Bruce Richmond, and Erik Bork, coproducers (HBO)

OUTSTANDING MADE-FOR-TELEVISION MOVIE: "Don King: Only in America," Thomas Carter, executive producer; David Blocker, producer (HBO)

OUTSTANDING CLASSICAL MUSIC DANCE PROGRAM: "Yo-Yo Ma Inspired By Bach," Niv Fishman, producer; Patricia Rozema, director-writer (PBS)

OUTSTANDING NONFICTION SERIES: *(Truman) The American Experience*, Margaret Drain, executive producer; David Grubin, producer-writer; Mark Samuels, senior producer; Judy Crichton, consulting executive producer; Allyson Luchak, senior producer (PBS)

OUTSTANDING NONFICTION SPECIAL: "Vietnam POWs: Stories of Survival," *Discovery Sunday*, Bob Reid, executive producer; Jacinda A. Davis, coordinating producer; Brian Leonard, producer-director-writer (Discovery Channel)

OUTSTANDING CHILDREN'S PROGRAM: *Muppets Tonight*, Brian Henson and Dick Blasucci, executive producers; Paul Flaherty and Kirk R. Thatcher, supervising producers; Patric M. Verrone, Martin G. Baker, and Chris Plourde, producers (Disney Channel); "Nick News Special Edition: What Axe You Staring At?" Linda Ellerbee and Rolfe Tessem, executive producers; Mark Lyons, senior producer; Anne-Marie Cunniffe, producer (Nickelodeon)

OUTSTANDING ANIMATED PROGRAM: "Trash of the Titans," *The Simpsons*, Mike Skully, Matt Groening, James L. Brooks, and Sam Simon, executive producers; George Meyer, David S. Cohen, and Richard Appel, coexecutive producers; Dan Greaney, Ron Hauge, Donick Carey, Cohn A.B, V. Lewis, Bonita Pietela, J. Michael Mendel, Richard Raynis, Richard Sakai, and Denise Sirkot, producers; Ian Maxtone-Graham consulting producer-writer; David Mirkin, Jace Richdale, Bill Oakley, and Josh Weinstein, consulting producers; Phil Roman, animation executive producer; Lolee Aries and Michael Wolf, animation producers; Brian Scully and Julie Thacker, coproducers; Jim Reardon, director (FOX)

OUTSTANDING LEAD ACTOR IN A DRAMA SERIES Andre Braugher, *Homicide: Life on the Street* (NBC)

OUTSTANDING LEAD ACTOR IN A COMEDY SERIES: Kelsey Grammer, *Frasier* (NBC)

OUTSTANDING LEAD ACTOR IN A MINI-SERIES OR MOVIE: Gary Sinise, "George Wallace" (TNT)

OUTSTANDING LEAD ACTRESS IN A DRAMA SERIES: Christine Lahti, *Chicago Hope* (CBS)

OUTSTANDING LEAD ACTRESS IN A COMEDY SERIES: Helen Hunt, *Mad About You* (NBC)

OUTSTANDING LEAD ACTRESS IN A MINI-SERIES OR MOVIE: Ellen Barkin, "Before Women Had Wings" (ABC)

OUTSTANDING SUPPORTING ACTOR IN A DRAMA SERIES: Gordon Clapp, *NYPD Blue* (ABC)

OUTSTANDING SUPPORTING ACTOR IN A COMEDY SERIES: David Hyde Pierce, *Frasier* (NBC)

OUTSTANDING SUPPORTING ACTOR IN A MINI-SERIES OR MOVIE: George C. Scott, "12 Angry Men" (Showtime)

OUTSTANDING SUPPORTING ACTRESS IN A DRAMA SERIES: Camryn Manheim, *The Practice* (ABC)

OUTSTANDING SUPPORTING ACTRESS IN A COMEDY SERIES: Lisa Kudrow, *Friends* (NBC)

OUTSTANDING SUPPORTING ACTRESS IN A MINI-SERIES OR MOVIE: Mare Winningham, "George Wallace" (TNT)

OUTSTANDING INDIVIDUAL PERFORMANCE IN A VARIETY OR MUSIC PROGRAM: Billy Crystal, host, "The 70th Annual Academy Awards" (ABC)

OUTSTANDING GUEST ACTOR IN A DRAMA SERIES: John Larroquette, *The Practice* (ABC)

OUTSTANDING GUEST ACTOR IN A COMEDY SERIES: Mel Brooks, *Mad About You* (NBC)

OUTSTANDING GUEST ACTRESS IN A DRAMA SERIES: Cloris Leachman, *Promised Land* (CBS)

OUTSTANDING GUEST ACTRESS IN A COMEDY SERIES: Emma Thompson, *Ellen* (ABC)

OUTSTANDING VOICE-OVER PERFORMANCE: Hank Azaria, various voices, *The Simpsons* (FOX)

OUTSTANDING DIRECTING IN A DRAMA SERIES (SINGLE EPISODE): Mark Tinker, pilot, *Brooklyn South* (CBS)

OUTSTANDING DIRECTING IN A COMEDY SERIES (SINGLE EPISODE): Todd Holland, "Flip," *The Larry Sanders Show* (HBO)

OUTSTANDING DIRECTING IN A MINI-SERIES OR A MOVIE: John Frankenlheimer, "George Wallace" (TNT)

OUTSTANDING DIRECTING IN A VARIETY OR MUSIC PROGRAM: Louis J. Horvitz, "The 70th Annual Academy Awards" (ABC)

OUTSTANDING WRITING IN A DRAMA SERIES (SINGLE EPISODE): David Much, Nicholas Wootton, and Bill Clark, "Lost Israel, part II," *NYPD Blue* (ABC)

OUTSTANDING WRITING IN A COMEDY SERIES (SINGLE EPISODE): Peter Tolan and Garry Shandling, "Flip," *The Larry Sanders Show* (HBO)

OUTSTANDING WRITING IN A MINI-SERIES OR A SPECIAL: Kario Salem, "Don King: Only in America" (HBO)

OUTSTANDING WRITING IN A VARIETY OR MUSIC PROGRAM: Eddie Feldmann, head writer; Dennis Miller, David Feldman, Leah Krinsky, Jim Hanna, David Weiss, and Jose Arroyo, writers, *Dennis Miller Live* (HBO)

THE GOVERNORS AWARD: The Learning Channel

BIBLIOGRAPHY

Barabas, Gabriel & Barabas, Suzanne. *Gunsmoke: A Complete History*. North Carolina: McFarland, 1990.

Bobbitt, David G. *World Radio TV Handbook*. Watson-Guptill, 2000.

Brooks, Tim & Marsh, Earl. *The Complete Directory to Prime Time Network and Cable TV Shows 1946–Present,* Seventh Edition. New York: Ballantine Books, 1999.

Buxton, Frank & Owen, Bill. *The Big Broadcast: 1920–1950*. New York: Viking Press, 1972.

Chernow, Barbara A & Vallasi, George A. ed. *Columbia Encyclopedia Fifth Edition*. New York: Columbia University, 1993.

Cusic, Don. *Cowboys and the Wild West*. New York: Facts On File, 1994.

Davis, Jeffrey. *Children's Television, 1947–1990*. North Carolina: McFarland, 1995.

Garner, Joe. *We Interrupt This Broadcast: The Events That Shaped Our Lives . . . from the Hindenberg to the Death of John F. Kennedy, Jr.* New York: Sourcebooks, 2000.

Halliwell, Leslie. *The Filmgoers Companion*. New York: Hill and Wang, 1967.

Jennings, Peter & Brewster, Todd. *The Century*. New York: Doubleday, 1998.

Lackmann, Ronald. *The Encyclopedia of American Radio: An A-Z Guide to Radio from Jack Benny to Howard Stern*. New York: Facts On File, 1996.

Lamparski, Richard. *Whatever Became Of . . .* series. New York: Crown: 1967–1989.

Lenberg, Jeff. *The Encyclopedia of Animated Cartoons, Second edition*. New York: Facts On File, Inc., 1999.

Maltin, Leonard. ed. *TV Movies*. New York: New American Library, 1983–1984.

McNeil, Alex. *Total Television: The Comprehensive Guide to Programming From 1948 to the Present, Fourth Edition*. New York: Penguin Books, 1996.

Michael, Paul. *The American Movies Reference Book: The Sound Era*. New Jersey: Prentice-Hall, 1970.

Okuda, Michael & Mirek, Debbie. *The Star Trek Encyclopedia*. New York: Simon and Shuster, 1999.

Schemering, Christopher. The Soap Opera Almanac (TV). New York: Ballantine Books, 1987.

Shulman, Arthir & Youman, Roger. *How Sweet It Was: Television: A pictorial commentary with 1435 photographs*. New York: Bonanza Books, 1976.

Skretvedt, Randy & Young, Jordan R. *The Nostalgia Entertainment Sourcebook: The Complete Guide of Classic Movies, Vintage Music, Old Time Radio and Theater*. Beverly Hills Calif.: Moonstone Press, 1991.

Smith, Ronald L. *Who's Who In Comedy: Comedians, Comics and Clowns from Vaudeville to Today's Stand-Ups*. New York: Facts On File, 1992.

Terrace, Vincent. *Television Specials: 3,201 Entertainment Spectaculars, 1939–1993*. North Carolina: McFarland, 1995.

TV GUIDE magazine, 1953–present.

TV Radio/TV Mirror magazine, 1947–1970.

WEBSITES

http://www.biography.com (Personalities)

http://www.imdb.com (Personalities, TV Series, and Feature Films)

INDEX

Note: Page numbers in **bold** indicate main entries. Page numbers followed by *f* indicate illustrations.